MEDALLION EDITION · AMERICA READS

UNITED STATES in Literature

MEDALLION EDITION • AMERICA READS

PURPOSE in Literature
Edmund J. Farrell
Ruth S. Cohen
L. Jane Christensen
H. Keith Wright

LITERATURE and LIFE
Helen McDonnell
Ruth S. Cohen
Thomas Gage
Alan L. Madsen

ARRANGEMENT in Literature
Edmund J. Farrell
Ouida H. Clapp
James L. Pierce
Raymond J. Rodrigues

QUESTION and FORM in Literature
James E. Miller, Jr.
Roseann Dueñas Gonzalez
Nancy C. Millett

UNITED STATES in Literature
James E. Miller, Jr.
Carlota Cárdenas de Dwyer
Robert Hayden
Russell J. Hogan
Kerry M. Wood

ENGLAND in Literature
Helen McDonnell
Neil E. Nakadate
John Pfordresher
Thomas E. Shoemate

MEDALLION EDITION • AMERICA READS

UNITED STATES in Literature

James E. Miller, Jr.

Carlota Cárdenas de Dwyer

Robert Hayden

Russell J. Hogan

Kerry M. Wood

Scott, Foresman and Company

Editorial Offices: Glenview, Illinois

Regional Offices: Palo Alto, California •
Tucker, Georgia • Glenview, Illinois •
Oakland, New Jersey • Dallas, Texas

JAMES E. MILLER, JR. Department Chairman and Professor of English, University of Chicago. Fulbright Lecturer in Naples and Rome, 1958–1959, and in Kyoto, 1968. Guggenheim Fellow, 1969–1970. Chairman, Commission on Literature, National Council of Teachers of English, 1967–1969. President of NCTE, 1970. Recipient of the Distinguished Service Award, NCTE, 1975. Publications include *Theory of Fiction: Henry James* and *T. S. Eliot's Personal Wasteland*.

CARLOTA CÁRDENAS DE DWYER English teacher at Thomas C. Clark High School, San Antonio. Formerly Assistant Professor of English, University of Texas at Austin. Formerly Member of the Executive Committee of the Conference on College Composition and Communication and of the Task Force on Racism and Bias of the National Council of Teachers of English.

ROBERT HAYDEN (1913–1980) Formerly Poetry Consultant to the Library of Congress and Professor of English, University of Michigan. Fellow of the Academy of American Poets. Recipient of the Russell Loines Award from the National Institute of Arts and Letters. Awarded the Grand Prize for Poetry at the First World Festival of Negro Arts, Dakar, Senegal. Volumes of poetry include *A Ballad of Remembrance* and *Angle of Ascent*.

RUSSELL J. HOGAN Chairman of the English Department, Clayton High School, Missouri. Associate Chairman of the Committee on Comparative and World Literature of the National Council of Teachers of English. Contributor of an article on the poetry of Francois Villon to *Teachers' Guide to World Literature* (NCTE).

KERRY M. WOOD English teacher at Woodside High School, California. Member of the University of California Bay Area Writing Project. Formerly coordinator of the Advanced Placement English program, Sequoia Union High School District, California.

ISBN: 0-673-12934-9 *(The Glass Menagerie)*
ISBN: 0-673-12935-7 *(I Never Sang for My Father)*

Copyright © 1982, 1979
Scott, Foresman and Company, Glenview Illinois.
All Rights Reserved. Printed in the United States of America.

This publication is protected by Copyright and permission should be obtained from the publisher prior to any prohibited reproduction, storage in a retrieval system, or transmission in any form or by any means, electronic, mechanical, photocopying, recording, or otherwise. For information regarding permission, write to: Scott, Foresman and Company, 1900 East Lake Avenue, Glenview, Illinois 60025.

345678910-RRW-A-908988878685848382
345678910-RRW-B-908988878685848382

Contents

Unit **1**

American Mosaic

Unit **2**

The New Land

1500-1800

Unit 3

Literary Nationalism

1800-1840

Unit **4**

American Classic

1840-1870

Unit 5

Variations and Departures

1870-1915

Unit **6**

The Modern Temper

1915-1945

Unit 7

A Modern Drama*

*The MEDALLION EDI-TION of *United States in Literature* is available in two versions, one con-taining *I Never Sang for My Father*, the other pre-senting *The Glass Me-nagerie*. Thus two listings appear in the Table of Contents above and in the index although only one of the two plays will be found in this book.

Unit 8

New Frontiers

1945-

*Items in *Definitions of Literary Terms* when introduced in the editorial material accompanying selections are printed in **bold face.**

1

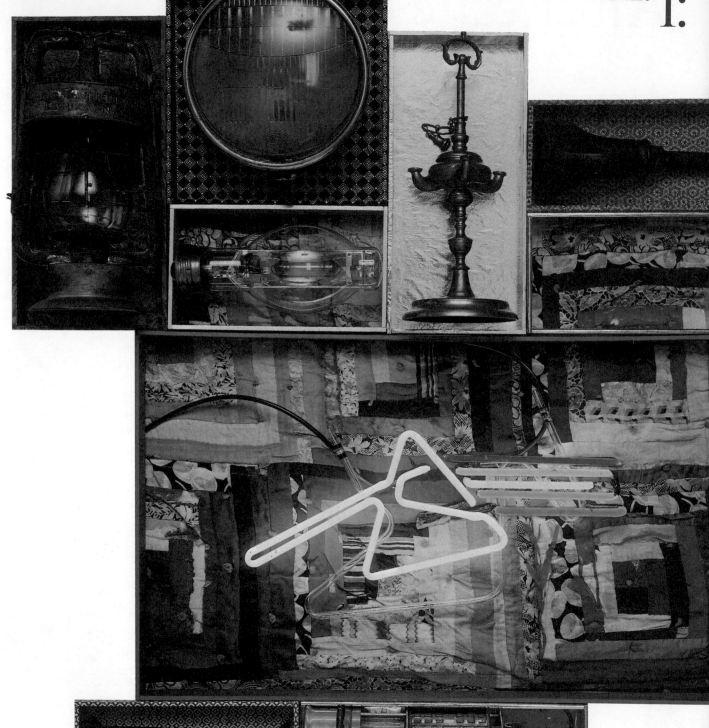

American Mosaic

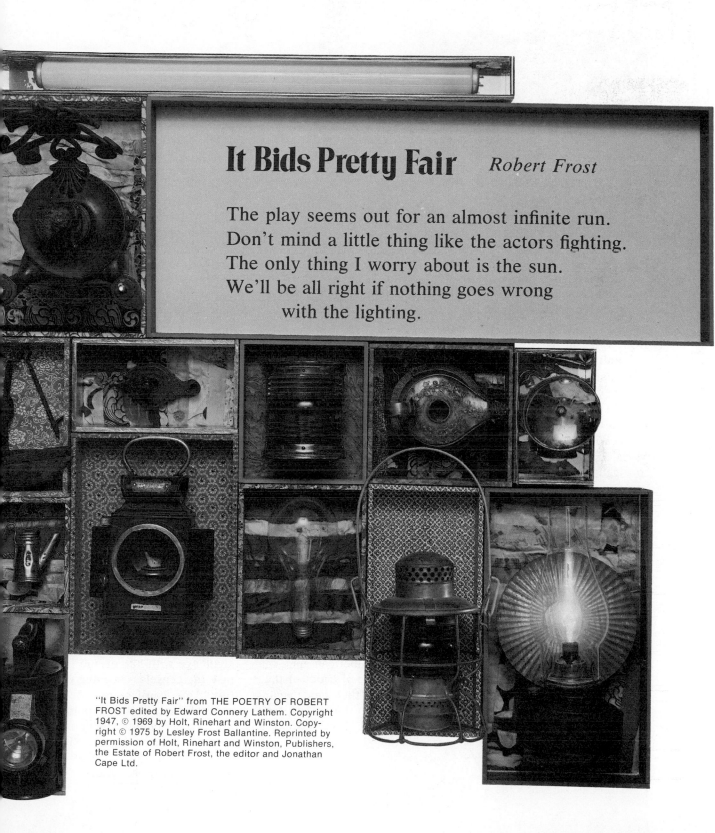

It Bids Pretty Fair   *Robert Frost*

The play seems out for an almost infinite run.
Don't mind a little thing like the actors fighting.
The only thing I worry about is the sun.
We'll be all right if nothing goes wrong
        with the lighting.

Background: American Mosaic

United States in Literature surveys American literature from the speeches and oral poetry of native Americans to the rich cultural diversity of contemporary writing. "American Mosaic" introduces that survey by sampling a variety of works by twentieth-century authors from different parts of the nation and different ethnic backgrounds. A mosaic is more than a mere collection of bits and pieces: its various parts must form a harmonious whole. The "pieces" in this "American Mosaic" have been organized to suggest, not a formula, but some useful approaches to a wide-ranging literature.

Many observers, both foreign and American, have suggested that America is a land of practical dreamers. We optimistically trust in a future we cannot know, and we are eager to seek it, to grasp it, to mold it to fit our often conflicting dreams.

The theme of discovery runs throughout this unit—discovery of self, exploration of the meaning of being human, discovery or rediscovery of ties with a past, an ethnic identity, a cultural heritage. All of these are needed to build a future.

Optimism is, however, not always easily seen, probably because events of the past century forbid easy optimism. Yet, the traditional optimism endures, expressed in the cautious and wryly humorous tone of Robert Frost's poem, "It Bids Pretty Fair," on the title page of this unit.

In "My Mother Pieced Quilts," by Teresa Palomo Acosta, the quilts become much more than quilts—they become family tradition, history, art, life, singing, love. Acosta is exploring her heritage, and in choosing the symbol of a quilt—itself a mosaic—she builds on a folk art once practiced by women throughout a growing, developing America.

The selections by Steinbeck and Momaday also portray people seeking personal identity from and within their respective traditions. But these traditions represent the rival sides of an American epic: the bitter struggle of tribes of the West to hold their lands against pioneers from the eastern United States and Mexico. Steinbeck's old "Leader" of the wagon trains laments the clos-

ing of the frontier, the end of the "westering," the death of the pioneer spirit; while Momaday celebrates the vitality of his Kiowa "centaur culture."

Other works explore different problems of being human in our society. E. B. White insists that the spirit of our language transcends mechanical readability formulas which seem to be a mania of this computer age. Lorraine Hansberry recounts youthful experiences of the pain, pride, toughness, and final triumph of being black in a predominantly white society. Bernard Malamud depicts the struggle of a European Jewish immigrant and his daughter, caught between the marriage customs of the Old World and the New. In a magical plant from Puerto Rico, Jesús Papoleto Meléndez finds a power to prevail over the grimness of the ghetto. William Saroyan creates "O.K.-by-the-Sea," a mythical California town whose people challenge with humor and fantasy the ceaseless striving of the "American Dream." Resourcefulness and determination are the qualities which enable the father in Tomás Rivera's "The Portrait" to "recover" a cherished family possession. These selections present basic values—of family or community solidarity, of the support of living cultures—from which any of us can draw strength.

In other selections in "American Mosaic," authors turn their vision inward. May Sarton with serenity, and Sylvia Plath with anxiety, reflect on the growing self-knowledge that comes as we age. Behind the grime and shabbiness of a family's gas-station home, Elizabeth Bishop senses some guardian spirit that transforms this dreary urban landscape. In Willa Cather's quiet tale of a rural midwestern family of eighty years ago, a chance recollection brings husband and wife to a mutual understanding they had lost in the surface practicalities of rearing their children.

In her essay and poem on the execution of Sacco and Vanzetti in 1927, Edna St. Vincent Millay asks readers to examine the sincerity of their commitment to the American ideals of "liberty and justice for all." Robert Hayden takes up these central values of the American experiment when he portrays Frederick Douglass (Unit 4) not only as a giant in the history of the black struggle, but even more as a symbol of the human yearning for freedom, "the beautiful, needful thing."

These journeys of discovery, whether outward or inward, reveal the vigorous, searching spirit of our literature. Among the authors here, Faulkner, Steinbeck, and Bellow received the Nobel Prize for Literature. Winners of Pulitzer Prizes include those three as well as Frost, Cather, Millay, Saroyan, Malamud, and Momaday. Hansberry's play, *A Raisin in the Sun,* was honored with the New York Drama Critics Circle Award, while E. B. White's contribution to the entire field of American letters was recognized by a National Medal for Literature. Hayden, the first black poet to be named Poetry Consultant to the Library of Congress, was internationally acclaimed at the First World Festival of Negro Arts, where he received the *Grand Prix de la Poesie.* Many other awards are given to recognize and encourage distinguished achievement in particular fields of writing. Among these are Hayden's Loines Award for Poetry; Rivera's *Premio Quinto Sol,* an annual award given to the best Chicano work of the year; and Sarton's Guggenheim Fellowship for poetry.

Yet it is usually not the award that gives prestige to the work, but rather the excellent work that gives prestige to the award.

Faulkner and Bellow's Nobel speeches and Thurber's "The Last Flower" echo Frost's wryly hopeful poem. These writers do not hide from the fears and griefs of our modern age; they confront them. They admit, and lament, that many writers have surrendered to a superficially justifiable, yet futile cynicism. In an era of H-bombs and environmental crises, they know that survival will not be easy and that mere physical survival is not enough. But they all hold to the faith that, through the creations of the human mind and spirit, we will not merely survive, but will preserve the qualities which define us as human beings.

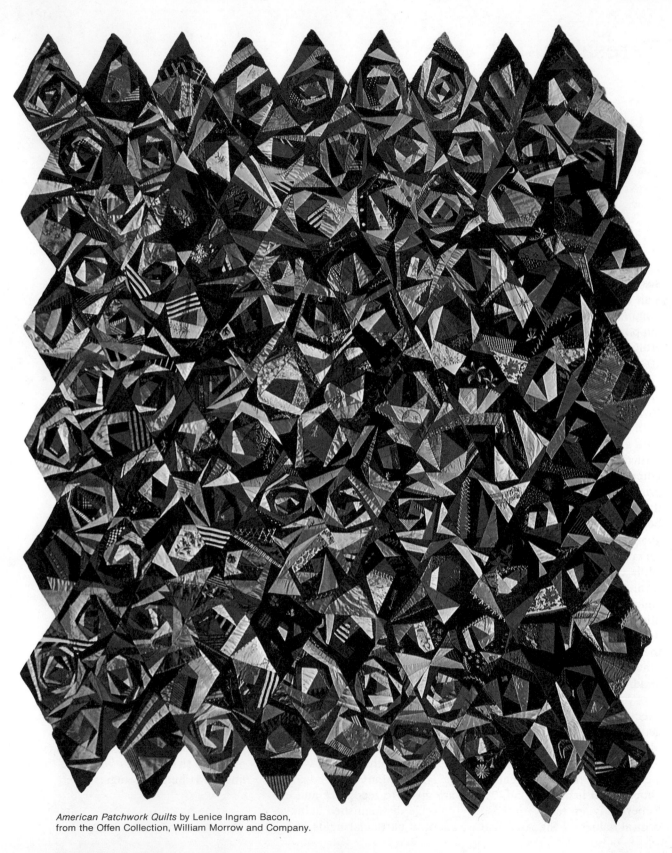

American Patchwork Quilts by Lenice Ingram Bacon,
from the Offen Collection, William Morrow and Company.

Teresa Palomo Acosta

My Mother Pieced Quilts

they were just meant as covers
in winters
as weapons
against pounding january winds

5 but it was just that every morning I awoke to these
october ripened canvases
passed my hand across their cloth faces
and began to wonder how you pieced
all these together

10 these strips of gentle communion cotton and flannel nightgowns
wedding organdies
dime store velvets

how you shaped patterns square and oblong and round
positioned
15 balanced
then cemented them
with your thread
a steel needle
a thimble

20 how the thread darted in and out
galloping along the frayed edges, tucking them in
as you did us at night
oh how you stretched and turned and re-arranged
your michigan spring[1] faded curtain pieces
25 my father's sante fe work shirt[2]
the summer denims, the tweeds of fall

in the evening you sat at your canvas
—our cracked linoleum floor the drawing board
me lounging on your arm
30 and you staking out the plan:

Teresa Palomo Acosta (te reˈsä pä lôˈmô ä kôsˈtä).
Copyright © 1975 by Teresa Palomo Acosta. From FESTIVAL DE FLOR Y CANTO, AN ANTHOLOGY OF CHICANO LITERATURE, published by the University of Southern California Press, 1976. Reprinted by permission of the author.
1. *michigan spring.* In spring migrant workers go to Michigan to pick crops.
2. *santa fe work shirt,* the work clothes of the Santa Fe Railroad.

Discussion

1. (a) In the Background essay for this unit, it is suggested that the quilt remembered by the speaker in this poem is in itself a kind of mosaic. Re-read lines 5–19 and select words and phrases that are appropriate to the meaning of *mosaic.* (b) Of what materials were parts of the mosaic composed? (c) What emotional significance did these materials have for the speaker?

2. Throughout this poem the speaker compares the quilt to a painting. (a) What did the Mother use for a drawing board? (b) What were some of the decisions the artist had to make?

3. (a) What do you learn about the speaker's family from the various pieces of cloth that went into the quilt? (b) What feelings toward her family does the speaker express? Cite specific lines that indicate these feelings. (c) Which member of the family do you think played the most important role? Cite lines that support your answer.

Extension • Writing

In your home are there any quilts, afghans, embroidered shirts, or other objects crafted by a relative? If so, describe the article in a paragraph, explaining the materials used and their history. If your family has no such article, you might de-

whether to put the lilac purple of easter against the red
        plaid of winter-going-
into-spring
whether to mix a yellow with blue and white and paint the
corpus christi[3] noon when my father held your hand
35 whether to shape a five-point star from the
somber black silk you wore to grandmother's funeral

you were the river current
carrying the roaring notes
forming them into pictures of a little boy reclining
40 a swallow flying
you were the caravan master at the reins
driving your threaded needle artillery across the mosaic
        cloth bridges
delivering yourself in separate testimonies.

oh mother you plunged me sobbing and laughing
45 into our past
into the river crossing at five
into the spinach fields
into the plainview[4] cotton rows
into tuberculosis wards
50 into braids and muslin dresses
sewn hard and taut to withstand the thrashings of
        twenty-five years

stretched out they lay
armed/ready/shouting/celebrating

knotted with love
55 the quilts sing on

---

3. *corpus christi* (kôr′pəs krisʹtē), a southern Texas city.
4. *plainview,* a Texas town surrounded by cotton fields.

sign one based on important
family memories. Draw a
sketch for a quilt, list and describe the pieces you would
use, and explain why you chose
these particular pieces.

Teresa Palomo Acosta 1949 •

In the Texas town where
Acosta grew up, her grandfather, Maximino Palomo, would
spend summer evenings on the
porch, entertaining the neighborhood children with tales of
his childhood in Mexico and his
exploits as a cowboy. These
stories formed Acosta's interest
in literature.

After studying at the University of Texas and Columbia
University, she became a journalist. In 1973, "My Mother
Pieced Quilts" was read at the
University of Southern California, during the first national
festival of Chicano literature
and art. Poems by Acosta have
appeared in *Festival de Flor y
Canto: An Anthology of
Chicano Literature.*

John Steinbeck

The Leader of the People

On Saturday afternoon Billy Buck, the ranch-hand, raked together the last of the old year's haystack and pitched small forkfuls over the wire fence to a few mildly interested cattle. High in the air small clouds like puffs of cannon smoke were driven eastward by the March wind. The wind could be heard whishing in the brush on the ridge crests, but no breath of it penetrated down into the ranch-cup.

The little boy, Jody, emerged from the house eating a thick piece of buttered bread. He saw Billy working on the last of the haystack. Jody tramped down scuffling his shoes in a way he had been told was destructive to good shoe-leather. A flock of white pigeons flew out of the black cypress tree as Jody passed, and circled the tree and landed again. A half-grown tortoise-shell cat leaped from the bunkhouse porch, galloped on stiff legs across the road, whirled and galloped back again. Jody picked up a stone to help the game along, but he was too late, for the cat was under the porch before the stone could be discharged. He threw the stone into the cypress tree and started the white pigeons on another whirling flight.

Arriving at the used-up haystack, the boy leaned against the barbed-wire fence. "Will that be all of it, do you think?" he asked.

The middle-aged ranch-hand stopped his careful raking and stuck his fork into the ground. He took off his black hat and smoothed down his hair. "Nothing left of it that isn't soggy from ground moisture," he said. He replaced his hat and rubbed his dry leathery hands together.

"Ought to be plenty mice," Jody suggested.

"Lousy with them," said Billy. "Just crawling with mice."

"Well, maybe, when you get all through, I could call the dogs and hunt the mice."

"Sure, I guess you could," said Billy Buck. He lifted a forkful of the damp ground-hay and threw it into the air. Instantly three mice leaped out and burrowed frantically under the hay again.

Jody sighed with satisfaction. Those plump, sleek, arrogant mice were doomed. For eight months they had lived and multiplied in the haystack. They had been immune from cats, from traps, from poison and from Jody. They had grown smug in their security, overbearing and fat. Now the time of disaster had come; they would not survive another day.

Billy looked up at the top of the hills that surrounded the ranch. "Maybe you better ask your father before you do it," he suggested.

"Well, where is he? I'll ask him now."

"He rode up to the ridge ranch after dinner. He'll be back pretty soon."

Jody slumped against the fence post. "I don't think he'd care."

As Billy went back to his work he said ominously, "You'd better ask him anyway. You know how he is."

Jody did know. His father, Carl Tiflin, insisted upon giving permission for anything that was done on the ranch, whether it was important or not. Jody sagged farther against the post until he was sitting on the ground. He looked up at the little puffs of wind-driven cloud. "Is it like to rain, Billy?"

"It might. The wind's good for it, but not strong enough."

"Well, I hope it don't rain until after I kill those damn mice." He looked over his shoulder to see whether Billy had noticed the mature profanity. Billy worked on without comment.

Jody turned back and looked at the side-hill where the road from the outside world came down. The hill was washed with lean March sunshine. Silver thistles, blue lupins and a few poppies bloomed among the sagebushes. Half-way up the hill Jody could see Doubletree Mutt, the black dog, digging in a squirrel hole. He paddled for a while and then paused to kick bursts of dirt out between his hind legs, and he dug with an earnestness which belied the knowledge he must have had that no dog had ever caught a squirrel by digging in a hole.

Suddenly, while Jody watched, the black dog stiffened, and backed out of the hole and looked up the hill toward the cleft in the ridge where the road came through. Jody looked up too. For a moment Carl Tiflin on horseback stood out against the pale sky and then he moved down the road toward the house. He carried something white in his hand.

The boy started to his feet. "He's got a letter," Jody cried. He trotted away toward the ranch house, for the letter would probably be read aloud and he wanted to be there. He reached the house before his father did, and ran in. He heard Carl dismount from his creaking saddle and slap the horse on the side to send it to the barn where Billy would unsaddle it and turn it out.

Jody ran into the kitchen. "We got a letter!" he cried.

His mother looked up from a pan of beans. "Who has?"

"Father has. I saw it in his hand."

Carl strode into the kitchen then, and Jody's mother asked, "Who's the letter from, Carl?"

He frowned quickly. "How did you know there was a letter?"

She nodded her head in the boy's direction. "Big-Britches Jody told me."

Jody was embarrassed.

His father looked down at him contemptuously. "He *is* getting to be a Big-Britches," Carl said. "He's minding everybody's business but his own. Got his big nose into everything."

Mrs. Tiflin relented a little. "Well, he hasn't enough to keep him busy. Who's the letter from?"

Carl still frowned on Jody. "I'll keep him busy if he isn't careful." He held out a sealed letter. "I guess it's from your father."

Mrs. Tiflin took a hairpin from her head and slit open the flap. Her lips pursed judiciously. Jody saw her eyes snap back and forth over the lines. "He says," she translated, "he says he's going to drive out Saturday to stay for a little while. Why, this is Saturday. The letter must have been delayed." She looked at the postmark. "This was mailed day before yesterday. It should have been here yesterday." She looked up questioningly at her husband, and then her face darkened angrily. "Now what have you got that look on you for? He doesn't come often."

Carl turned his eyes away from her anger. He could be stern with her most of the time, but when occasionally her temper arose, he could not combat it.

"What's the matter with you?" she demanded again.

In his explanation there was a tone of apology Jody himself might have used. "It's just that he talks," Carl said lamely. "Just talks."

"Well, what of it? You talk yourself."

"Sure I do. But your father only talks about one thing."

"Indians!" Jody broke in excitedly. "Indians and crossing the plains!"

Carl turned fiercely on him. "You get out, Mr. Big-Britches! Go on, now! Get out!"

Jody went miserably out the back door and closed the screen with elaborate quietness. Under the kitchen window his shamed, downcast eyes fell upon a curiously shaped stone, a stone of such fascination that he squatted down and picked it up and turned it over in his hands.

The voices came clearly to him through the open kitchen window. "Jody's damn well right," he heard his father say. "Just Indians and crossing the plains. I've heard that story about how the horses got driven off about a thousand times. He just goes on and on, and he never changes a word in the things he tells."

When Mrs. Tiflin answered her tone was so changed that Jody, outside the window, looked up from his study of the stone. Her voice had become soft and explanatory. Jody knew how her face would have changed to match the tone. She said quietly, "Look at it this way, Carl. That was the big thing in my father's life. He led a wagon train clear across the plains to the coast, and when it was finished, his life was done. It was a big thing to do, but it didn't last long enough. Look!" she continued, "it's as though he was born to do that, and after he finished it, there wasn't anything more for him to do but think about it and talk about it. If there'd been any farther west to go, he'd have gone. He's told me so himself. But at last there was the ocean. He lives right by the ocean where he had to stop."

She had caught Carl, caught him and entangled him in her soft tone.

"I've seen him," he agreed quietly. "He goes down and stares off west over the ocean." His voice sharpened a little. "And then he goes up to the Horseshoe Club in Pacific Grove, and he tells people how the Indians drove off the horses."

She tried to catch him again. "Well, it's everything to him. You might be patient with him and pretend to listen."

Carl turned impatiently away. "Well, if it gets too bad, I can always go down to the bunkhouse and sit with Billy," he said irritably. He walked through the house and slammed the front door after him.

Jody ran to his chores. He dumped the grain to the chickens without chasing any of them. He gathered the eggs from the nests. He trotted into the house with the wood and interlaced it so carefully in the wood-box that two armloads seemed to fill it to overflowing.

His mother had finished the beans by now. She stirred up the fire and brushed off the stove-top with a turkey wing. Jody peered cautiously at her to see whether any rancor toward him remained. "Is he coming today?" Jody asked.

"That's what his letter said."

"Maybe I better walk up the road to meet him."

Mrs. Tiflin clanged the stove-lid shut. "That would be nice," she said. "He'd probably like to be met."

"I guess I'll just do it then."

Outside, Jody whistled shrilly to the dogs. "Come on up the hill," he commanded. The two dogs waved their tails and ran ahead. Along the roadside the sage had tender new tips. Jody tore off some pieces and rubbed them on his hands until the air was filled with the sharp wild smell. With a rush the dogs leaped from the road and yapped into the brush after a rabbit. That was the last Jody saw of them, for when they failed to catch the rabbit, they went back home.

Jody plodded on up the hill toward the ridge top. When he reached the little cleft where the road came through, the afternoon wind struck him and blew up his hair and ruffled his shirt. He looked down on the little hills and ridges below and then out at the huge green Salinas Valley.[1] He could see the white town of Salinas far out in the flat and the flash of its windows under the waning sun. Directly below him, in an oak tree, a crow congress had convened. The tree was black with crows all cawing at once. Then Jody's eyes followed the wagon road down from the ridge where he stood, and lost it behind a hill, and picked it up again on the other side. On that distant stretch he saw a cart slowly pulled by a bay horse. It disappeared behind the hill. Jody sat down on the ground and watched the place where the cart would reappear again. The wind sang on the hilltops and the puffball clouds hurried eastward.

Then the cart came into sight and stopped. A man dressed in black dismounted from the seat and walked to the horse's head. Although it was so far away, Jody knew he had unhooked the check-rein, for the horse's head dropped forward. The horse moved on, and the man walked slowly up the hill beside it. Jody gave a glad cry and ran down the road toward them. The squirrels bumped along off the road, and a roadrunner flirted its tail and raced over the edge of the hill and sailed out like a glider.

Jody tried to leap into the middle of his shadow at every step. A stone rolled under his foot and he went down. Around a little bend he raced, and there, a short distance ahead, were his grandfather and the cart. The boy dropped from his unseemly running and approached at a dignified walk.

The horse plodded stumble-footedly up the hill and the old man walked beside it. In the lowering sun their giant shadows flickered darkly behind them. The grandfather was dressed in a black broadcloth suit and he wore kid congress gaiters and a black tie on a short, hard collar. He carried his black slouch hat in his hand. His white beard was cropped close and his white

---

1. *Salinas Valley* (sə lēʹnəs), an agriculturally rich valley of California, about a hundred miles south of San Francisco.

eyebrows overhung his eyes like mustaches. The blue eyes were sternly merry. About the whole face and figure there was a granite dignity, so that every motion seemed an impossible thing. Once at rest, it seemed the old man would be stone, would never move again. His steps were slow and certain. Once made, no step could ever be retraced; once headed in a direction, the path would never bend nor the pace increase nor slow.

When Jody appeared around the bend, Grandfather waved his hat slowly in welcome, and he called, "Why, Jody! Come down to meet me, have you?"

Jody sidled near and turned and matched his step to the old man's step and stiffened his body and dragged his heels a little. "Yes, sir," he said. "We got your letter only today."

"Should have been here yesterday," said Grandfather. "It certainly should. How are all the folks?"

"They're fine, sir." He hesitated and then suggested shyly, "Would you like to come on a mouse hunt tomorrow, sir?"

"Mouse hunt, Jody?" Grandfather chuckled. "Have the people of this generation come down to hunting mice? They aren't very strong, the new people, but I hardly thought mice would be game for them."

"No, sir. It's just play. The haystack's gone. I'm going to drive out the mice to the dogs. And you can watch, or even beat the hay a little."

The stern, merry eyes turned down on him. "I see. You don't eat them, then. You haven't come to that yet."

Jody explained, "The dogs eat them, sir. It wouldn't be much like hunting Indians, I guess."

"No, not much—but then later, when the troops were hunting Indians and shooting children and burning teepees, it wasn't much different from your mouse hunt."

They topped the rise and started down into the ranch-cup, and they lost the sun from their shoulders. "You've grown," Grandfather said. "Nearly an inch, I should say."

"More," Jody boasted. "Where they mark me on the door, I'm up more than an inch since Thanksgiving even."

Grandfather's rich throaty voice said, "Maybe you're getting too much water and turning to pith and stalk. Wait until you head out, and then we'll see."

Jody looked quickly into the old man's face to see whether his feelings should be hurt, but there was no will to injure, no punishing nor putting-in-your-place light in the keen blue eyes. "We might kill a pig," Jody suggested.

"Oh, no! I couldn't let you do that. You're just humoring me. It isn't the time and you know it."

"You know Riley, the big boar, sir?"

"Yes. I remember Riley well."

"Well, Riley ate a hole into that same haystack, and it fell down on him and smothered him."

"Pigs do that when they can," said Grandfather.

"Riley was a nice pig, for a boar, sir. I rode him sometimes, and he didn't mind."

A door slammed at the house below them, and they saw Jody's mother standing on the porch waving her apron in welcome. And they saw Carl Tiflin walking up from the barn to be at the house for the arrival.

The sun had disappeared from the hills by now. The blue smoke from the house chimney hung in flat layers in the purpling ranch-cup. The puffball clouds, dropped by the falling wind, hung listlessly in the sky.

Billy Buck came out of the bunkhouse and flung a wash-basin of soapy water on the ground. He had been shaving in midweek, for Billy held Grandfather in reverence, and Grandfather said that Billy was one of the few men of the new generation who had not gone soft. Although Billy was in middle age, Grandfather considered him a boy. Now Billy was hurrying toward the house too.

When Jody and Grandfather arrived, the three were waiting for them in front of the yard gate.

Carl said, "Hello, sir. We've been looking for you."

Mrs. Tiflin kissed Grandfather on the side of his beard, and stood still while his big hand patted her shoulder. Billy shook hands solemnly, grinning under his straw mustache. "I'll put up your horse," said Billy, and he led the rig away.

Grandfather watched him go, and then, turning back to the group, he said as he had said a

hundred times before, "There's a good boy. I knew his father, old Mule-tail Buck. I never knew why they called him Mule-tail except he packed mules."

Mrs. Tiflin turned and led the way into the house. "How long are you going to stay, Father? Your letter didn't say."

"Well, I don't know. I thought I'd stay about two weeks. But I never stay as long as I think I'm going to."

In a short while they were sitting at the white oilcloth table eating their supper. The lamp with the tin reflector hung over the table. Outside the dining room windows the big moths battered softly against the glass.

Grandfather cut his steak into tiny pieces and chewed slowly. "I'm hungry," he said. "Driving out here got my appetite up. It's like when we were crossing. We all got so hungry every night we could hardly wait to let the meat get done. I could eat about five pounds of buffalo meat every night."

"It's moving around does it," said Billy. "My father was a government packer. I helped him when I was a kid. Just the two of us could about clean up a deer's ham."

"I knew your father, Billy," said Grandfather. "A fine man he was. They called him Mule-tail Buck. I don't know why except he packed mules."

"That was it," Billy agreed. "He packed mules."

Grandfather put down his knife and fork and looked around the table. "I remember one time we ran out of meat—" His voice dropped to a curious low sing-song, dropped into a tonal groove the story had worn for itself. "There was no buffalo, no antelope, not even rabbits. The hunters couldn't even shoot a coyote. That was the time for the leader to be on the watch. I was the leader, and I kept my eyes open. Know why? Well, just the minute the people began to get hungry they'd start slaughtering the team oxen. Do you believe that? I've heard of parties that just ate up their draft cattle. Started from the middle and worked toward the ends. Finally they'd eat the lead pair, and then the wheelers. The leader of a party had to keep them from doing that."

In some manner a big moth got into the room and circled the hanging kerosene lamp. Billy got up and tried to clap it between his hands. Carl struck with a cupped palm and caught the moth and broke it. He walked to the window and dropped it out.

"As I was saying," Grandfather began again, but Carl interrupted him. "You'd better eat some more meat. All the rest of us are ready for our pudding."

Jody saw a flash of anger in his mother's eyes. Grandfather picked up his knife and fork. "I'm pretty hungry, all right," he said. "I'll tell you about that later."

When supper was over, when the family and Billy Buck sat in front of the fireplace in the other room, Jody anxiously watched Grandfather. He saw the signs he knew. The bearded head leaned forward; the eyes lost their sternness and looked wonderingly into the fire; the big lean fingers laced themselves on the black knees.

"I wonder," he began, "I just wonder whether I ever told you how those thieving Piutes drove off thirty-five of our horses."

"I think you did," Carl interrupted. "Wasn't it just before you went up into the Tahoe country?"

Grandfather turned quickly toward his son-in-law. "That's right. I guess I must have told you that story."

"Lots of times," Carl said cruelly, and he avoided his wife's eyes. But he felt the angry eyes on him, and he said, "'Course I'd like to hear it again."

Grandfather looked back at the fire. His fingers unlaced and laced again. Jody knew how he felt, how his insides were collapsed and empty. Hadn't Jody been called a Big-Britches that very afternoon? He arose to heroism and opened himself to the term Big-Britches again. "Tell about Indians," he said softly.

Grandfather's eyes grew stern again. "Boys always want to hear about Indians. It was a job for men, but boys want to hear about it. Well, let's see. Did I ever tell you how I wanted each wagon to carry a long iron plate?"

Everyone but Jody remained silent. Jody said, "No. You didn't."

"Well, when the Indians attacked, we always put the wagons in a circle and fought from between the wheels. I thought that if every wagon carried a long plate with rifle holes, the men could stand the plates on the outside of the wheels when the wagons were in the circle and they would be protected. It would save lives and that would make up for the extra weight of the iron. But of course the party wouldn't do it. No party had done it before and they couldn't see why they should go to the expense. They lived to regret it, too."

Jody looked at his mother, and knew from her expression that she was not listening at all. Carl picked at a callus on his thumb and Billy Buck watched a spider crawling up the wall.

Grandfather's tone dropped into its narrative groove again. Jody knew in advance exactly what words would fall. The story droned on, speeded up for the attack, grew sad over the wounds, struck a dirge at the burials on the great plains. Jody sat quietly watching Grandfather. The stern blue eyes were detached. He looked as though he were not very interested in the story himself.

When it was finished, when the pause had been politely respected as the frontier of the story, Billy Buck stood up and stretched and hitched his trousers. "I guess I'll turn in," he said. Then he faced Grandfather. "I've got an old powder horn and a cap and ball pistol down to the bunkhouse. Did I ever show them to you?"

Grandfather nodded slowly. "Yes, I think you did, Billy. Reminds me of a pistol I had when I was leading the people across." Billy stood politely until the little story was done, and then he said, "Good night," and went out of the house.

Carl Tiflin tried to turn the conversation then. "How's the country between here and Monterey? I've heard it's pretty dry."

"It is dry," said Grandfather. "There's not a drop of water in the Laguna Seca. But it's a long pull from '87. The whole country was powder then, and in '61 I believe all the coyotes starved to death. We had fifteen inches of rain this year."

"Yes, but it all came too early. We could do with some now." Carl's eye fell on Jody. "Hadn't you better be getting to bed?"

Jody stood up obediently. "Can I kill the mice in the old haystack, sir?"

"Mice? Oh! Sure, kill them all off. Billy said there isn't any good hay left."

Jody exchanged a secret and satisfying look with Grandfather. "I'll kill every one tomorrow," he promised.

Jody lay in his bed and thought of the impossible world of Indians and buffaloes, a world that had ceased to be forever. He wished he could have been living in the heroic time, but he knew he was not of heroic timber. No one living now, save possibly Billy Buck, was worthy to do the things that had been done. A race of giants had lived then, fearless men, men of a staunchness unknown in this day. Jody thought of the wide plains and of the wagons moving across like centipedes. He thought of Grandfather on a huge white horse, marshaling the people. Across his mind marched the great phantoms, and they marched off the earth and they were gone.

He came back to the ranch for a moment, then. He heard the dull rushing sound that space and silence make. He heard one of the dogs, out in the doghouse, scratching a flea and bumping his elbow against the floor with every stroke. Then the wind arose again and the black cypress groaned and Jody went to sleep.

He was up half an hour before the triangle sounded for breakfast. His mother was rattling the stove to make the flames roar when Jody went through the kitchen. "You're up early," she said. "Where are you going?"

"Out to get a good stick. We're going to kill the mice today."

"Who is 'we'?"

"Why, Grandfather and I."

"So you've got him in it. You always like to have some one in with you in case there's blame to share."

"I'll be right back," said Jody. "I just want to have a good stick ready for after breakfast."

He closed the screen door after him and went out into the cool blue morning. The birds were noisy in the dawn and the ranch cats came down from the hill like blunt snakes. They had been hunting gophers in the dark, and although the four cats were full of gopher meat, they sat in a semicircle at the back door and mewed piteously for milk. Doubletree Mutt and Smasher moved sniffing along the edge of the brush, performing the duty with rigid ceremony, but when Jody whistled, their heads jerked up and their tails waved. They plunged down to him, wriggling their skins and yawning. Jody patted their heads seriously, and moved on to the weathered scrap pile. He selected an old broom handle and a short piece of inch-square scrap wood. From his pocket he took a shoelace and tied the ends of the sticks loosely together to make a flail. He whistled his new weapon through the air and struck the ground experimentally, while the dogs leaped aside and whined with apprehension.

Jody turned and started down past the house toward the old haystack ground to look over the field of slaughter, but Billy Buck, sitting patiently on the back steps, called to him, "You better come back. It's only a couple of minutes till breakfast."

Jody changed his course and moved toward the house. He leaned his flail against the steps. "That's to drive the mice out," he said. "I'll bet they're fat. I'll bet they don't know what's going to happen to them today."

"No, nor you either," Billy remarked philosophically, "nor me, nor anyone."

Jody was staggered by this thought. He knew it was true. His imagination twitched away from the mouse hunt. Then his mother came out on the back porch and struck the triangle, and all thoughts fell in a heap.

Grandfather hadn't appeared at the table when they sat down. Billy nodded at his empty chair. "He's all right? He isn't sick?"

"He takes a long time to dress," said Mrs.

Tiflin. "He combs his whiskers and rubs up his shoes and brushes his clothes."

Carl scattered sugar on his mush. "A man that's led a wagon train across the plains has got to be pretty careful how he dresses."

Mrs. Tiflin turned on him. "Don't do that, Carl! Please don't!" There was more of threat than of request in her tone. And the threat irritated Carl.

"Well, how many times do I have to listen to the story of the iron plates, and the thirty-five horses? That time's done. Why can't he forget it, now it's done?" He grew angrier while he talked, and his voice rose. "Why does he have to tell them over and over? He came across the plains. All right! Now it's finished. Nobody wants to hear about it over and over."

The door into the kitchen closed softly. The four at the table sat frozen. Carl laid his mush spoon on the table and touched his chin with his fingers.

Then the kitchen door opened and Grandfather walked in. His mouth smiled tightly and his eyes were squinted. "Good morning," he said, and he sat down and looked at his mush dish.

Carl could not leave it there. "Did—did you hear what I said?"

Grandfather jerked a little nod.

"I don't know what got into me, sir. I didn't mean it. I was just being funny."

Jody glanced in shame at his mother, and he saw that she was looking at Carl, and that she wasn't breathing. It was an awful thing that he was doing. He was tearing himself to pieces to talk like that. It was a terrible thing to him to retract a word, but to retract it in shame was infinitely worse.

Grandfather looked sidewise. "I'm trying to get right side up," he said gently. "I'm not being mad. I don't mind what you said, but it might be true, and I would mind that."

"It isn't true," said Carl. "I'm not feeling well this morning. I'm sorry I said it."

"Don't be sorry, Carl. An old man doesn't see things sometimes. Maybe you're right. The crossing is finished. Maybe it should be forgotten, now it's done."

Carl got up from the table. "I've had enough to eat. I'm going to work. Take your time, Billy!" He walked quickly out of the dining room. Billy gulped the rest of his food and followed soon after. But Jody could not leave his chair.

"Won't you tell any more stories?" Jody asked.

"Why, sure I'll tell them, but only when—I'm sure people want to hear them."

"I like to hear them, sir."

"Oh! Of course you do, but you're a little boy. It was a job for men, but only little boys like to hear about it."

Jody got up from his place. "I'll wait outside for you, sir. I've got a good stick for those mice."

He waited by the gate until the old man came out on the porch. "Let's go down and kill the mice now," Jody called.

"I think I'll just sit in the sun, Jody. You go kill the mice."

"You can use my stick if you like."

"No, I'll just sit here a while."

Jody turned disconsolately away, and walked down toward the old haystack. He tried to whip up his enthusiasm with thoughts of the fat juicy mice. He beat the ground with his flail. The dogs coaxed and whined about him, but he could not go. Back at the house he could see Grandfather sitting on the porch, looking small and thin and black.

Jody gave up and went to sit on the steps at the old man's feet.

"Back already? Did you kill the mice?"

"No, sir. I'll kill them some other day."

The morning flies buzzed close to the ground and the ants dashed about in front of the steps. The heavy smell of sage slipped down the hill. The porch boards grew warm in the sunshine.

Jody hardly knew when Grandfather started to talk. "I shouldn't stay here, feeling the way I do." He examined his strong old hands. "I feel as though the crossing wasn't worth doing." His eyes moved up the side-hill and stopped on a motionless hawk perched on a dead limb. "I tell those old stories, but they're not what I want to tell. I only know how I want people to feel when I tell them.

"It wasn't Indians that were important, nor adventures, nor even getting out here. It was a whole bunch of people made into one big crawling beast. And I was the head. It was westering and westering. Every man wanted something for himself, but the big beast that was all of them

wanted only westering. I was the leader, but if I hadn't been there, someone else would have been the head. The thing had to have a head.

"Under the little bushes the shadows were black at white noonday. When we saw the mountains at last, we cried—all of us. But it wasn't getting here that mattered, it was movement and westering.

"We carried life out here and set it down the way those ants carry eggs. And I was the leader. The westering was as big as God, and the slow steps that made the movement piled up and piled up until the continent was crossed.

"Then we came down to the sea, and it was done." He stopped and wiped his eyes until the rims were red. "That's what I should be telling instead of stories."

When Jody spoke, Grandfather stared and looked down at him. "Maybe I could lead the people some day," Jody said.

The old man smiled. "There's no place to go. There's the ocean to stop you. There's a line of old men along the shore hating the ocean because it stopped them."

"In boats I might, sir."

"No place to go, Jody. Every place is taken. But that's not the worst—no, not the worst. Westering has died out of the people. Westering isn't a hunger any more. It's all done. Your father is right. It is finished." He laced his fingers on his knee and looked at them.

Jody felt very sad. "If you'd like a glass of lemonade I could make it for you."

Grandfather was about to refuse, and then he saw Jody's face. "That would be nice," he said. "Yes, it would be nice to drink a lemonade."

Jody ran into the kitchen where his mother was wiping the last of the breakfast dishes. "Can I have a lemon to make a lemonade for Grandfather?"

His mother mimicked—"And another lemon to make a lemonade for you."

"No, ma'am. I don't want one."

"Jody! You're sick!" Then she stopped suddenly. "Take a lemon out of the cooler," she said softly. "Here, I'll reach the squeezer down to you." □ □

JOHN STEINBECK 17

Discussion

1. **(a)** Find several examples of Jody's sensitivity to the feelings and opinions of the adults around him. **(b)** Do you think he acts less or more mature than ten-year-olds you know? Explain. **(c)** How might Jody's life on the ranch make him more mature? Less mature?

2. Jody's grandfather explains that it wasn't getting *to* the West that mattered to the pioneers, ". . . it was movement and westering." Can you think of any recent cause or goal that has captured the spirit of "westering" in a similar way? Explain.

3. Jody's father becomes impatient with the old man's repetitious storytelling. How do you explain Jody's willingness to listen to the stories? For what reasons does Jody's mother listen to them? Billy Buck?

4. **(a)** How does Jody's attitude toward killing mice change between the beginning and the end of the story? **(b)** What, in your opinion, has brought about this change?

5. At the beginning of the story Jody sees his grandfather as a "giant shadow." Near the end of the story, Jody sees his grandfather looking "small and thin and black." **(a)** Explain what has brought about this change in Jody's attitude toward his grandfather. **(b)** How does this change relate to his change in attitude toward the mice?

Extension • Writing

1. "The Leader of the People" is from Steinbeck's collection of stories, *The Red Pony.* Read another story in that collection and write a brief review of Steinbeck's depiction of another aspect of Jody's life.

2. Toward which character do you feel the most sympathy? The least? Write a paragraph for each alternative and be prepared to read or explain to the class your position on each character.

Vocabulary • Context

You can often figure out the meaning of an unfamiliar word by looking at the *context* (the surrounding words or paragraphs) in which the word appears. Context can also alert you to which meaning of a word is intended. Analyzing the *structure* or the parts of words can also be useful in figuring out the meaning of words.

Using context clues in the following sentences, write definitions of the italicized words.

1. Always a *judicious* person, Sarah read several college catalogues before making her final decision on which college to attend.

2. The prophet warned the empress not to act so *arrogantly* toward her subjects, because people resent an overly proud leader.

John Steinbeck 1902 • 1968

John Steinbeck grew up in a rich but strike-tormented valley around Salinas, California, where the plight of agricultural and factory workers made a deep impression on him. Between 1919 and 1925 he intermittently attended Stanford University, taking whatever courses attracted him. After leaving Stanford, he worked for a while as a newspaper reporter in New York City. His first three books were financial failures. However, his literary popularity began in 1935 with a book that is said to have been rejected by nine publishers: this was *Tortilla Flat,* a series of stories about Mexican Americans on the Monterey Peninsula. His short novel, *Of Mice and Men,* became a best seller in 1937. Two years later, *The Grapes of Wrath,* his novel dealing with the plight of migratory workers, earned the Pulitzer Prize in letters. In 1962, when he was awarded the Nobel Prize, Steinbeck published *Travels with Charley,* the account of a journey he and his dog, Charley, made through the United States.

N. Scott Momaday

from The Names

The first word gives origin to the second, the first and second to the third, the first, second, and third to the fourth, and so on. You cannot begin with the second word and tell the story, for the telling of the story is a cumulative process, a chain of becoming, at last of being.

Oh, it is summer in New Mexico, in the bright legend of my youth. I want you to see the very many deep colors of the distance. I want you to live, to be for an hour or a day more completely alive in me than you have ever been. There are moments in that time when I live so intensely in myself that I wonder how it is possible to keep from flying apart. I want you to feel that, too, the vibrant ecstasy of so much being—to know beyond any doubt that it is only the merest happy accident that you can hold together at all in the exhilaration of such wonder. The wonder: I want to tell you of it; I want to speak and to write it all out for you.

I sometimes think of what it means that in their heyday—in 1830, say—the Kiowas owned more horses *per capita* than any other tribe on the Great Plains, that the Plains Indian culture, the last culture to evolve in North America, is also known as "the horse culture" and "the centaur culture,"[1] that the Kiowas tell the story of a horse that died of shame after its owner committed an act of cowardice, that I am a Kiowa, that therefore there is in me, as there is in the Tartars,[2] an old, sacred notion of the horse. I believe that at some point in my racial life, this notion must needs be expressed in order that I may be true to my nature.

It happened so: I was thirteen years old, and my parents gave me a horse. It was a small nine-year-old gelding of that rare, soft color that is called strawberry roan. This my horse and I came to be, in the course of our life together, in good understanding, of one mind, a true story

From pp. 154–160 in THE NAMES: A MEMOIR by N. Scott Momaday. Copyright © 1976 by N. Scott Momaday. By permission of Harper & Row, Publishers, Inc.
1. *centaur culture* (sen′tôr), a society of horsemen. In Greek myth, the centaur had the head of a man and body of a horse.
2. *Tartars* (tär′tər), Mongolian and Turkish tribes famed as horsemen.

and history of that large landscape in which we made the one entity of whole motion, one and the same center of an intricate, pastoral composition, evanescent, ever changing. And to this my horse I gave the name Pecos.

On the back of my horse I had a different view of the world. I could see more of it, how it reached away beyond all the horizons I had ever seen; and yet it was more concentrated in its appearance, too, and more accessible to my mind, my imagination. My mind loomed upon the farthest edges of the earth, where I could feel the full force of the planet whirling into space. There was nothing of the air and light that was not pure exhilaration, and nothing of time and eternity. Oh, Pecos, *un poquito mas!*[3] Oh, my hunting horse! Bear me away, bear me away!

It was appropriate that I should make a long journey. Accordingly I set out one early morning, traveling light. Such a journey must begin in the nick of time, on the spur of the moment, and one must say to himself at the outset: Let there be wonderful things along the way; let me hold to the way and be thoughtful in my going; let this journey be made in beauty and belief.

I sang in the sunshine and heard the birds call out on either side. Bits of down from the cottonwoods drifted across the air, and butterflies fluttered in the sage. I could feel my horse under me, rocking at my legs, the bobbing of the reins to my hand; I could feel the sun on my face and the stirring of a little wind at my hair. And through the hard hooves, the slender limbs, the supple shoulders, the fluent back of my horse I felt the earth under me. Everything was under me, buoying me up; I rode across the top of the world. My mind soared; time and again I saw the fleeting shadow of my mind moving about me as it went winding upon the sun.

When the song, which was a song of riding, was finished, I had Pecos pick up the pace. Far down on the road to San Ysidro I overtook my friend Pasqual Fragua.[4] He was riding a rangy, stiff-legged black and white stallion, half wild, which horse he was breaking for the rancher Cass Goodner. The horse skittered and blew as I drew up beside him. Pecos began to prance, as he did always in the company of another horse. "Where are you going?" I asked in the Jemez[5] language. And he replied, "I am going down the

road." The stallion was hard to manage, and Pasqual had to keep his mind upon it; I saw that I had taken him by surprise. "You know," he said after a moment, "when you rode up just now I did not know who you were." We rode on for a time in silence, and our horses got used to each other, but still they wanted their heads. The longer I looked at the stallion the more I admired it, and I suppose that Pasqual knew this, for he began to say good things about it: that it was a thing of good blood, that it was very strong and fast, that it felt very good to ride it. The thing was this: that the stallion was half wild, and I came to wonder about the wild half of it; I wanted to know what its wildness was worth in the riding. "Let us trade horses for a while," I said, and, well, all right, he agreed. At first it was exciting to ride the stallion, for every once in a while it pitched and bucked and wanted to run. But it was heavy and raw-boned and full of resistance, and every step was a jolt that I could feel deep down in my bones. I saw soon enough that I had made a bad bargain, and I wanted my horse back, but I was ashamed to admit it. There came a time in the late afternoon, in the vast plain far south of San Ysidro, after thirty miles, perhaps, when I no longer knew whether it was I who was riding the stallion or the stallion who was riding me. "Well, let us go back now," said Pasqual at last. "No. I am going on; and I will have my horse back, please," I said, and he was surprised and sorry to hear it, and we said goodbye. "If you are going south or east," he said, "look out for the sun, and keep your face in the shadow of your hat. *Vaya con Dios.*"[6] And I went on my way alone then, wiser and better mounted, and thereafter I held on to my horse. I saw no one for a long time, but I saw four falling stars and any number of jackrabbits, roadrunners, and coyotes, and once, across a distance, I saw a bear, small and black, lumbering in a ravine. The mountains drew close and withdrew and drew close again, and after several days I swung east.

Now and then I came upon settlements. For

---

3. *un poquito mas!* (ùn pô kē′tô mäs), "a little more," used by Momaday to urge on his horse. [*Spanish*]
4. *Pasqual Fragua* (päs kwäl′ frä′gwä).
5. *the Jemez language* (hā′mās), the language of the Tanoan tribe near Santa Fe, New Mexico.
6. *Vaya con Dios* (vī′yä con dē′ôs), "go with God," a Spanish farewell.

the most part they were dry, burnt places with Spanish names: Arroyo Seco, Las Piedras, Tres Casas.[7] In one of these I found myself in a narrow street between high adobe walls. Just ahead, on my left, was a door in the wall. As I approached the door was flung open, and a small boy came running out, rolling a hoop. This happened so suddenly that Pecos shied very sharply, and I fell to the ground, jamming the thumb of my left hand. The little boy looked very worried and said that he was sorry to have caused such an accident. I waved the matter off, as if it were nothing; but as a matter of fact my hand hurt so much that tears welled up in my eyes. And the pain lasted for many days. I have fallen many times from a horse, both before and after that, and a few times I fell from a running horse on dangerous ground, but that was the most painful of them all.

In another settlement there were some boys who were interested in racing. They had good horses, some of them, but their horses were not so good as mine, and I won easily. After that, I began to think of ways in which I might even the odds a little, might give some advantage to my competitors. Once or twice I gave them a head start, a reasonable head start of, say, five or ten yards to the hundred, but that was too simple, and I won anyway. Then it came to me that I might try this: we should all line up in the usual way, side by side, but my competitors should be mounted and I should not. When the signal was given I should then have to get up on my horse while the others were breaking away; I should have to mount my horse during the race. This idea appealed to me greatly, for it was both imaginative and difficult, not to mention dangerous; Pecos and I should have to work very closely together. The first few times we tried this I had little success, and over a course of a hundred yards I lost four races out of five. The principal problem was that Pecos simply could not hold still among the other horses. Even before they broke away he was hard to manage, and when they were set running nothing could hold him back, even for an instant. I could not get my foot in the stirrup, but I had to throw myself up across the saddle on my stomach, hold on as best I could, and twist myself into position, and all this while racing at full speed. I could ride

well enough to accomplish this feat, but it was a very awkward and inefficient business. I had to find some way to use the whole energy of my horse, to get it all into the race. Thus far I had managed only to break his motion, to divert him from his purpose and mine. To correct this I took Pecos away and worked with him through the better part of a long afternoon on a broad reach of level ground beside an irrigation ditch. And it was hot, hard work. I began by teaching him to run straight away while I ran beside him a few steps, holding on to the saddle horn, with no pressure on the reins. Then, when we had mastered this trick, we proceeded to the next one, which was this: I placed my weight on my arms, hanging from the saddle horn, threw my feet out in front of me, struck them to the ground, and sprang up against the saddle. This I did again and again, until Pecos came to expect it and did not flinch or lose his stride. I sprang a little higher each time. It was in all a slow process of trial and error, and after two or three hours both Pecos and I were covered with bruises and soaked through with perspiration. But we had much to show for our efforts, and at last the moment came when we must put the whole performance together. I had not yet leaped into the saddle, but I was quite confident that I could now do so; only I must be sure to get high enough. We began this dress rehearsal then from a standing position. At my signal Pecos lurched and was running at once, straight away and smoothly. And at the same time I sprinted forward two steps and gathered myself up, placing my weight precisely at my wrists, throwing my feet out and together, perfectly. I brought my feet down sharply to the ground and sprang up hard, as hard as I could, bringing my legs astraddle of my horse—and everything was just right, except that I sprang too high. I vaulted all the way over my horse, clearing the saddle by a considerable margin, and came down into the irrigation ditch. It was a good trick, but it was not the one I had in mind, and I wonder what Pecos thought of it after all. Anyway, after a while I could mount my horse in this way and so well that there was no challenge in it, and I went on winning race after race.

---

7. *Arroyo Seco, Las Piedras, Tres Casas* (ä rôʹyô seʹkô, läs pē edʹräs, tres käʹsäs), names meaning, in order, "dry stream," "the stones," and "three houses." [*Spanish*]

I went on, farther and farther into the wide world. Many things happened. And in all this I knew one thing: I knew where the journey was begun, that it was itself a learning of the beginning, that the beginning was infinitely worth the learning. The journey was well undertaken, and somewhere in it I sold my horse to an old Spanish man of Vallecitos.[8] I do not know how long Pecos lived. I had used him hard and well, and it may be that in his last days an image of me like thought shimmered in his brain. □ □

---

8. **Vallecitos** (vĭ′ye sē′tôs), New Mexico town north of Santa Fe.

Discussion

1. In journeying away from the security of his home, Momaday has experiences that help him learn about himself. What do you think he learns about himself in the incident with Pasqual Fragua?

2. **(a)** For what reasons is his first horse important to young Momaday? **(b)** By the time he sells Pecos, how have his feelings for the horse changed?

3. There are two distinct writing styles in this selection. Parts of the selection are poetic and almost mystical in tone. Other parts are clear, concrete narrative prose. Find passages that exemplify each of these contrasting styles. What do you think Momaday accomplishes by combining them?

4. What aspects of the author's culture have found expression in his writing?

Extension • Writing

1. Consider what you have learned about the narrator's personality. Write a sketch of his character, based on his specific actions, such as leaving home or refusing to reveal the pain of his injured thumb.

2. Early in this selection Momaday draws our attention to his unusual concern for the reader's ability to visualize the setting of his experiences. He says, "I want you to see the very many deep colors of the distance." Write a short composition on why the landscape is important to Momaday. Or, if you prefer, paint a scene or assemble a collage of magazine photos that illustrates Momaday's descriptions.

notes and comments

From the Author

I chose *The Names* as the title of my book because names fascinate me. I believe that an essential part of my reality, my being, consists in my name. If I had a name other than my own, I would be someone else. This equation of names and being is very old, and it is very important in American Indian tradition. I am a writer, and therefore words are especially important to me. And what are words but the names of things? In a play or a story that I sometimes dream of writing, I have one of the characters say to another: "You must be true to your word, for your word is truly the name of yourself; your word, your name, is finally all that you have, all that you are." I tried to write *The Names* in this spirit, and I dedicated it: "In devotion, to those whose names I bear, and to those who bear my names."

In The Names *(1976), Momaday explored his Kiowa heritage through a chronicle of his ancestors. His father, the distinguished painter, Alfred Morris Momaday, illustrated this selection. For a biography of N. Scott Momaday, see page 607.*

E. B. White

The Calculating Machine

A publisher in Chicago has sent us a pocket calculating machine by which we may test our writing to see whether it is intelligible. The calculator was developed by General Motors, who, not satisfied with giving the world a Cadillac, now dream of bringing perfect understanding to men. The machine (it is simply a celluloid card with a dial) is called the Reading-Ease Calculator and shows four grades of "reading-ease"—Very Easy, Easy, Hard, and Very Hard. You count your words and syllables, set the dial, and an indicator lets you know whether anybody is going to understand what you have written. An instruction book came with it, and after mastering the simple rules we lost no time in running a test on the instruction book itself, to see how *that* writer was doing. The poor fellow! His leading essay, the one on the front cover, tested Very Hard.

Our next step was to study the first phrase on the face of the calculator: "How to test Reading-Ease of written matter." There is, of course, no such thing as reading ease of written matter. There is the ease with which matter can be read, but that is a condition of the reader, not of the matter. Thus the inventors and distributors of this calculator get off to a poor start, with a Very Hard instruction book and a slovenly phrase. Already they have one foot caught in the brier patch of English usage.

Not only did the author of the instruction book score badly on the front cover, but inside the book he used the word "personalize" in an essay on how to improve one's writing. A man who likes the word "personalize" is entitled to his choice, but we wonder whether he should be in the business of giving advice to writers. "Whenever possible," he wrote, "personalize your writing by directing it to the reader." As for us, we would as lief Simonize our grandmother as personalize our writing.

In the same envelope with the calculator, we received another training aid for writers—a booklet called "How to Write Better," by Rudolf Flesch. This, too, we studied, and it quickly demonstrated the broncolike ability of the English language to throw whoever leaps cocksurely into the saddle. The language not only can toss a rider but knows a thousand tricks for tossing him, each more gay than the last. Dr. Flesch stayed in the saddle only a moment or two. Under the heading "Think Before You Write," he wrote, "The main thing to consider is your *purpose* in writing. Why are you sitting down to write?" And echo answered: Because, sir, it is more comfortable than standing up.

Communication by the written word is a subtler (and more beautiful) thing than Dr. Flesch and General Motors imagine. They contend that the "average reader" is capable of reading only what tests Easy, and that the writer should write at or below this level. This is a presumptuous and degrading idea. There is no average reader, and to reach down toward this mythical character is to deny that each of us is on the way up, is ascending. ("Ascending," by the way, is a word Dr. Flesch advises writers to stay away from. Too unusual.)

It is our belief that no writer can improve his work until he discards the dulcet notion that the reader is feeble-minded, for writing is an act of faith, not a trick of grammar. Ascent is at the heart of the matter. A country whose writers are following a calculating machine downstairs is not ascending—if you will pardon the expression—and a writer who questions the capacity of the person at the other end of the line is not a writer at all, merely a schemer. The movies long ago decided that a wider communication could be achieved by a deliberate descent to a lower level, and they walked proudly down until they reached the cellar. Now they are groping for the light switch, hoping to find the way out.

We have studied Dr. Flesch's instructions diligently, but we return for guidance in these matters to an earlier American, who wrote with more patience, more confidence. "I fear chiefly," he wrote, "lest my expression may not be *extravagant* enough, may not wander far enough beyond the narrow limits of my daily experience, so as to be adequate to the truth of which I have been convinced. . . . Why level downward to our dullest perception always, and praise that as common sense? The commonest sense is the sense of men asleep, which they express by snoring."[1]

Run that through your calculator! It may come out Hard, it may come out Easy. But it will come out whole, and it will last forever. □ □

---

1. *earlier American* . . . *"snoring,"* a quotation from the conclusion of *Walden* by Henry David Thoreau (see Unit 4).

Discussion

1. (a) What standards do the makers of the Calculator use to judge the quality of written material? **(b)** What factors does White think they have left out?

2. Give examples of White's use of humor in criticizing those who want to calculate "reading ease."

3. (a) At what point do you think White is most serious? **(b)** What qualities in writing does he value most highly? **(c)** Give examples from his essay that reflect the qualities he values.

4. (a) What tendencies in modern society are symbolized by the Calculator? **(b)** Name some other symbols of these tendencies. **(c)** Do you agree with White's criticism of these tendencies? Discuss.

Extension • Writing

Examine several recent issues of *The New Yorker* and *Time* magazine and compare them in style, tone, and content. Write two short accounts of any current event as it might appear in each magazine.

E. B. White 1899 •

After he graduated from Cornell University, E. B. White adventured for a while in the West, but returned to his native state to work for two unsatisfying years as a production assistant and copywriter for an advertising agency in New York. He began sending contributions to *The New Yorker* and eventually earned an editorial post in "The Talk of the Town" department where he wrote "Notes and Comment" for many years. Since it is this department that really sets the tone for the entire magazine, the style of *The New Yorker* became identified with that of E. B. White.

Many people believe that White is the best of modern essayists, and some have tried to describe his unique gift. *Time* magazine has said that his style is "a sort of precocious offhand humming." This seemingly offhand grace serves to heighten the brilliant precision of his insights.

Ray Bradbury

April 2005: Usher II

During the whole of a dull, dark, and soundless day in the autumn of the year, when the clouds hung oppressively low in the heavens, I had been passing alone, on horseback, through a singularly dreary tract of country, and at length found myself, as the shades of evening drew on, within view of the melancholy House of Usher. . . .'"

Mr. William Stendahl paused in his quotation. There, upon a low black hill, stood the House, its cornerstone bearing the inscription 2005 A.D.

Mr. Bigelow, the architect, said, "It's completed. Here's the key, Mr. Stendahl."

The two men stood together silently in the quiet autumn afternoon. Blueprints rustled on the raven grass at their feet.

"The House of Usher," said Mr. Stendahl with pleasure. "Planned, built, bought, paid for. Wouldn't Mr. Poe[1] be *delighted?*"

Mr. Bigelow squinted. "Is it everything you wanted, sir?"

"Yes!"

"Is the color right? Is it *'desolate'* and *'terrible'?*"

"*Very* desolate, *very* terrible!"

"The walls are— *'bleak'?*"

"Amazingly so!"

"The tarn,[2] is it 'black and lurid' enough?"

"Most incredibly black and lurid."

"And the sedge—we've dyed it, you know— is it the proper gray and ebon?"

"Hideous!"

Mr. Bigelow consulted his architectural plans. From these he quoted in part: "Does the whole structure cause an 'iciness, a sickening of the heart, a dreariness of thought'? The House, the lake, the land, Mr. Stendahl?"

"Mr. Bigelow, it's worth every penny! Good Lord, it's beautiful!"

"Thank you. I had to work in total ignorance. Thank the Lord you had your own private rockets or we'd never have been allowed to bring most of the equipment through. You notice, it's always twilight here, this land, always October, barren, sterile, dead. It took a bit of doing. We killed everything. Ten thousand tons of DDT. Not a snake, frog, or Martian fly left! Twilight always, Mr. Stendahl; I'm proud of that. There are machines, hidden, which blot out the sun. It's always properly 'dreary.'"

Stendahl drank it in, the dreariness, the oppression, the fetid vapors, the whole "atmosphere," so delicately contrived and fitted. And that House! That crumbling horror, that evil lake, the fungi, the extensive decay! Plastic or otherwise, who could guess?

He looked at the autumn sky. Somewhere above, beyond, far off, was the sun. Somewhere it was the month of April on the planet Mars, a yellow month with a blue sky. Somewhere above, the rockets burned down to civilize a beautifully dead planet. The sound of their screaming passage was muffled by this dim, soundproofed world, this ancient autumn world.

"Now that my job's done," said Mr. Bigelow uneasily, "I feel free to ask what you're going to do with all this."

"With Usher? Haven't you guessed?"

"No."

"Does the name Usher mean nothing to you?"

"Nothing."

"Well, what about *this* name: Edgar Allan Poe?"

Mr. Bigelow shook his head.

"Of course." Stendahl snorted delicately, a combination of dismay and contempt. "How

Adaptation of "April 2005: Usher II" from THE MARTIAN CHRONICLES by Ray Bradbury. © 1950 by Ray Bradbury. Renewal © 1977 by Ray Bradbury. Reprinted by permission of Harold Matson Co., Inc.

1. *Mr. Poe,* Edgar Allan Poe (see Unit 3).
2. *tarn,* a small lake or pool in the mountains.

could I expect you to know blessed Mr. Poe? He died a long while ago, before Lincoln. All of his books were burned in the Great Fire. That's thirty years ago—1975."

"Ah," said Mr. Bigelow wisely. "One of *those!*"

"Yes, one of those, Bigelow. He and Lovecraft and Hawthorne and Ambrose Bierce[3] and all the tales of terror and fantasy and horror and, for that matter, tales of the future were burned. Heartlessly. They passed a law. Oh, it started very small. In 1950 and '60 it was a grain of sand. They began by controlling books of cartoons and then detective books and, of course, films, one way or another, one group or another, political bias, religious prejudice, union pressures; there was always a minority afraid of something, and a great majority afraid of the dark, afraid of the future, afraid of the past, afraid of the present, afraid of themselves and shadows of themselves."

"I see."

"Afraid of the word 'politics' (which eventually became a synonym for Communism among the more reactionary elements, so I hear, and it was worth your life to use the word!), and with a screw tightened here, a bolt fastened there, a push, a pull, a yank, art and literature were soon like a great twine of taffy strung about, being twisted in braids and tied in knots and thrown in all directions, until there was no more resiliency and no more savor to it. Then the film cameras chopped short and the theaters turned dark, and the print presses trickled down from a great Niagara of reading matter to a mere innocuous dripping of 'pure' material. Oh, the word 'escape' was radical, too, I tell you!"

"Was it?"

"It was! Every man, they said, must face reality. Must face the Here and Now! Everything that was 'not so' must go. All the beautiful literary lies and flights of fancy must be shot in midair! So they lined them up against a library wall one Sunday morning thirty years ago, in 1975; they lined them up, St. Nicholas and the Headless Horseman and Snow White and Rumpelstiltskin and Mother Goose—oh, what a wailing!—and shot them down, and burned the paper castles and the fairy frogs and old kings and the people who lived happily ever after (for of course it was a fact that *nobody* lived happily ever after!), and Once Upon A Time became No More! And they spread the ashes of the Phantom Rickshaw with the rubble of the Land of Oz; they filleted the bones of Glinda the Good and Ozma and shattered Polychrome in a spectroscope and served Jack Pumpkinhead with meringue at the Biologists' Ball! The Beanstalk died in a bramble of red tape! Sleeping Beauty awoke at the kiss of a scientist and expired at the fatal puncture of his syringe. And they made Alice drink something from a bottle which reduced her to a size where she could no longer cry 'Curiouser and curiouser,' and they gave the Looking Glass one hammer blow to smash it and every Red King and Oyster away!"

He clenched his fists. Lord, how immediate it was! His face was red and he was gasping for breath.

As for Mr. Bigelow, he was astounded at this long explosion. He blinked and at last said, "Sorry. Don't know what you're talking about. Just names to me. From what I hear, the Burning was a good thing."

"Get out!" screamed Stendahl. "You've done your job, now let me alone, you idiot!"

Mr. Bigelow summoned his carpenters and went away.

Mr. Stendahl stood alone before his House.

"Listen here," he said to the unseen rockets. "I came to Mars to get away from you Clean-Minded people, but you're flocking in thicker every day, like flies to offal. So I'm going to show you. I'm going to teach you a fine lesson for what you did to Mr. Poe on Earth. As of this day, beware. The House of Usher is open for business!"

He pushed a fist at the sky.

The rocket landed. A man stepped out jauntily. He glanced at the House, and his gray eyes were displeased and vexed. He strode across the moat to confront the small man there.

"Your name Stendahl?"

"Yes."

"I'm Garrett, Investigator of Moral Climates."

---

3. *Lovecraft . . . Hawthorne . . . Bierce.* H. P. Lovecraft (1890–1937), Nathaniel Hawthorne (Unit 4) and Ambrose Bierce (Unit 5) were noted as writers of tales of fantasy.

"So you finally got to Mars, you Moral Climate people? I wondered when you'd appear."

"We arrived last week. We'll soon have things as neat and tidy as Earth." The man waved an identification card irritably toward the House. "Suppose you tell me about that place, Stendahl?"

"It's a haunted castle, if you like."

"I don't like, Stendahl, I *don't* like. The sound of that word 'haunted.'"

"Simple enough. In this year of our Lord 2005 I have built a mechanical sanctuary. In it copper bats fly on electronic beams, brass rats scuttle in plastic cellars, robot skeletons dance; robot vampires, harlequins, wolves, and white phantoms, compounded of chemical and ingenuity, live here."

"That's what I was afraid of," said Garrett, smiling quietly. "I'm afraid we're going to have to tear your place down."

"I knew you'd come out as soon as you discovered what went on."

"I'd have come sooner, but we at Moral Climates wanted to be sure of your intentions before we moved in. We can have the Dismantlers and Burning Crew here by supper. By midnight your place will be razed to the cellar. Mr. Stendahl, I consider you somewhat of a fool, sir. Spending hard-earned money on a folly. Why, it must have cost you three million dollars—"

"Four million! But, Mr. Garrett, I inherited twenty-five million when very young. I can afford to throw it about. Seems a dreadful shame, though, to have the House finished only an hour and have you race out with your Dismantlers. Couldn't you possibly let me play with my Toy for just, well, twenty-four hours?"

"You know the law. Strict to the letter. No books, no houses, nothing to be produced which in any way suggests ghosts, vampires, fairies, or any creature of the imagination."

"You'll be burning Babbitts[4] next!"

"You've caused us a lot of trouble, Mr. Stendahl. It's in the record. Twenty years ago. On Earth. You and your library."

"Yes, me and my library. And a few others like me. Oh, Poe's been forgotten for many years now, and Oz and the other creatures. But I had my little cache. We had our libraries, a few

private citizens, until you sent your men around with torches and incinerators and tore my fifty thousand books up and burned them. Just as you put a stake through the heart of Halloween and told your film producers that if they made anything at all they would have to make and remake Ernest Hemingway. Good grief, how many times have I seen *For Whom the Bell Tolls*[5] done! Thirty different versions. All realistic. Oh, realism! Oh, blistering blazes!"

"It doesn't pay to be bitter!"

"Mr. Garrett, you must turn in a full report, mustn't you?"

"Yes."

"Then, for curiosity's sake, you'd better come in and look around. It'll take only a minute."

"All right. Lead the way. And no tricks. I've a gun with me."

The door to the House of Usher creaked wide. A moist wind issued forth. There was an immense sighing and moaning, like a subterranean bellows breathing in the lost catacombs.

A rat pranced across the floor stones. Garrett, crying out, gave it a kick. It fell over, the rat did, and from its nylon fur streamed an incredible horde of metal fleas.

"Amazing!" Garrett bent to see.

An old witch sat in a niche, quivering her wax hands over some orange-and-blue tarot cards.[6] She jerked her head and hissed through her toothless mouth at Garrett, tapping her greasy cards.

"Death!" she cried.

"Now *that's* the sort of thing I mean," said Garrett. "Deplorable!"

"I'll let you burn her personally."

"Will you, really?" Garrett was pleased. Then he frowned. "I must say you're taking this all so well."

"It was enough just to be able to create this place. To be able to say I did it. To say I nurtured a medieval atmosphere in a modern, incredulous world."

"I've a somewhat reluctant admiration for your genius myself, sir." Garrett watched a mist

---

4. **Babbitts.** George Babbitt, a stereotype of a salesman, is the main character of Sinclair Lewis's satirical novel, *Babbitt* (1922).
5. **For Whom the Bell Tolls,** a novel by Ernest Hemingway (Unit 6). who is noted for realistic fiction.
6. **tarot** (tar′ō) **cards.** cards used to tell fortunes.

drift by, whispering and whispering, shaped like a beautiful and nebulous woman. Down a moist corridor a machine whirled. Like the stuff from a cotton-candy centrifuge, mists sprang up and floated, murmuring, in the silent halls.

An ape appeared out of nowhere.

"Hold on!" cried Garrett.

"Don't be afraid." Stendahl tapped the animal's black chest. "A robot. Copper skeleton and all, like the witch. See?" He stroked the fur, and under it metal tubing came to light.

"Yes." Garrett put out a timid hand to pet the thing. "But why, Mr. Stendahl, why all *this?* What obsessed you?"

"Bureaucracy, Mr. Garrett. But I haven't time to explain. The government will discover soon enough." He nodded to the ape. "All right. *Now.*"

The ape killed Mr. Garrett.

"Are we almost ready, Pikes?"

Pikes looked up from the table. "Yes, sir."

"You've done a splendid job."

"Well, I'm paid for it, Mr. Stendahl," said Pikes softly as he lifted the plastic eyelid of the robot and inserted the glass eyeball to fasten the rubberoid muscles neatly. "There."

"The spitting image of Mr. Garrett."

"What do we do with him, sir?" Pikes nodded at the slab where the real Mr. Garrett lay dead.

"Better burn him, Pikes. We wouldn't want two Mr. Garretts, would we?"

Pikes wheeled Mr. Garrett to the brick incinerator. "Good-by." He pushed Mr. Garrett in and slammed the door.

Stendahl confronted the robot Garrett. "You have your orders, Garrett?"

"Yes, sir." The robot sat up. "I'm to return to Moral Climates. I'll file a complementary report. Delay action for at least forty-eight hours. Say I'm investigating more fully."

"Right, Garrett. Good-by."

The robot hurried out to Garrett's rocket, got in, and flew away.

Stendahl turned. "Now, Pikes, we send the remainder of the invitations for tonight. I think we'll have a jolly time, don't you?"

"Considering we waited twenty years, quite jolly!"

They winked at each other.

Seven o'clock. Stendahl studied his watch. Almost time. He twirled the sherry glass in his hand. He sat quietly. Above him, among the oaken beams, the bats, their delicate copper bodies hidden under rubber flesh, blinked at him and shrieked. He raised his glass to them. "To our success." Then he leaned back, closed his eyes, and considered the entire affair. How he would savor this in his old age. This paying back of the antiseptic government for its literary terrors and conflagrations. Oh, how the anger and hatred had grown in him through the years. Oh, how the plan had taken a slow shape in his numbed mind, until that day three years ago when he had met Pikes.

Ah yes, Pikes. Pikes with the bitterness in him as deep as a black, charred well of green acid. Who was Pikes? Only the greatest of them all! Pikes, the man of ten thousand faces, a fury, a smoke, a blue fog, a white rain, a bat, a gargoyle, a monster, that was Pikes! Better than Lon Chaney,[7] the father? Stendahl ruminated. Night after night he had watched Chaney in the old, old films. Yes, better than Chaney. Better than that other ancient mummer? What was his name? Karloff? Far better! Lugosi?[8] The comparison was odious! No, there was only one Pikes, and he was a man stripped of his fantasies now, no place on Earth to go, no one to show off to. Forbidden even to perform for himself before a mirror!

Poor impossible, defeated Pikes! How must it have felt, Pikes, the night they seized your films, like entrails yanked from the camera, out of your guts, clutching them in rolls and wads to stuff them up a stove to burn away? Did it feel as bad as having some fifty thousand books annihilated with no recompense? Yes. Yes. Stendahl felt his hands grow cold with the senseless anger. So what more natural than they would one day talk over endless coffeepots into innumerable midnights, and out of all the talk and the bitter brewings would come—the House of Usher.

A great church bell rang. The guests were arriving.

Smiling, he went to greet them.

---

7. *Lon Chaney,* an actor who wore many eerie disguises in horror films of the 1920s.
8. *Karloff . . . Lugosi.* Boris Karloff and Bela Lugosi starred in horror films of the 1930s and '40s.

Full grown without memory, the robots waited. In green silks the color of forest pools, in silks the color of frog and fern, they waited. In yellow hair the color of the sun and sand, the robots waited. Oiled, with tube bones cut from bronze and sunk in gelatin, the robots lay. In coffins for the not dead and not alive, in planked boxes, the metronomes[9] waited to be set in motion. There was a smell of lubrication and lathed brass. There was a silence of the tomb yard. Sexed but sexless, the robots. Named but unnamed, and borrowing from humans everything but humanity, the robots stared at the nailed lids of their labeled F.O.B.[10] boxes, in a death that was not even a death, for there had never been a life. And now there was a vast screaming of yanked nails. Now there was a lifting of lids. Now there were shadows on the boxes and the pressure of a hand squirting oil from a can. Now one clock was set in motion, a faint ticking. Now another and another, until this was an immense clock shop, purring. The marble eyes rolled wide their rubber lids. The nostrils winked. The robots, clothed in hair of ape and white of rabbit, arose: Tweedledum following Tweedledee, Mock-Turtle, Dormouse,[11] drowned bodies from the sea compounded of salt and whiteweed, swaying; hanging blue-throated men with turned-up, clam-flesh eyes, and creatures of ice and burning tinsel, loam-dwarfs and pepper-elves, Tik-Tok, Ruggedo, St. Nicholas with a self-made snow flurry blowing on before him, Bluebeard with whiskers like acetylene flame, and sulphur clouds from which green fire snouts protruded, and, in scaly and gigantic serpentine, a dragon with a furnace in its belly reeled out the door with a scream, a tick, a bellow, a silence, a rush, a wind. Ten thousand lids fell back. The clock shop moved out into Usher. The night was enchanted.

A warm breeze came over the land. The guest rockets, burning the sky and turning the weather from autumn to spring, arrived.

The men stepped out in evening clothes and the women stepped out after them, their hair coiffed up in elaborate detail.

"So *that's* Usher!"

"But where's the door?"

At this moment Stendahl appeared. The women laughed and chattered. Mr. Stendahl raised a hand to quiet them. Turning, he looked up to a high castle window and called:

"Rapunzel, Rapunzel,[12] let down your hair."

And from above, a beautiful maiden leaned out upon the night wind and let down her golden hair. And the hair twined and blew and became a ladder upon which the guests might ascend, laughing, into the House.

What eminent sociologists! What clever psychologists! What tremendously important politicians, bacteriologists, and neurologists! There they stood, within the dank walls.

"Welcome, all of you!"

Mr. Tryon, Mr. Owen, Mr. Dunne, Mr. Lang, Mr. Steffens, Mr. Fletcher, and a double-dozen more.

"Come in, come in!"

Miss Gibbs, Miss Pope, Miss Churchil, Miss Blunt, Miss Drummond, and a score of other women, glittering.

Eminent, eminent people, one and all, members of the Society for the Prevention of Fantasy, advocators of the banishment of Halloween and Guy Fawkes,[13] killers of bats, burners of books, bearers of torches; good clean citizens, every one, who had waited until the rough men had come up and buried the Martians and cleansed the cities and built the towns and repaired the highways and made everything safe. And then, with everything well on its way to Safety, the Spoil-Funs, the people with mercurochrome for blood and iodine-colored eyes, came now to set up their Moral Climates and dole out goodness to everyone. And they were his friends! Yes, carefully, carefully, he had met and befriended each of them on Earth in the last year!

"Welcome to the vasty halls of Death!" he cried.

"Hello, Stendahl, what *is* all this?"

"You'll see. Everyone off with their clothes. You'll find booths to one side there. Change into costumes you find there. Men on this side, women on that."

---

9. **metronome.** This device ticks to mark musical beats.
10. **F.O.B.,** free on board.
11. **Tweedledum . . . Dormouse,** characters in *Alice in Wonderland* by Lewis Carroll (1832–1898).
12. **Rapunzel,** a fairy tale princess with long golden hair.
13. **Guy Fawkes** tried to blow up the British Parliament on November 5, 1605, an event still commemorated in England.

The people stood uneasily about.

"I don't know if we should stay," said Miss Pope. "I don't like the looks of this. It verges on—blasphemy."

"Nonsense, a *costume* ball!"

"Seems quite illegal." Mr. Steffens sniffed about.

"Come off it." Stendahl laughed. "Enjoy yourselves. Tomorrow it'll be a ruin. Get in the booths!"

The House blazed with life and color; harlequins rang by with belled caps and white mice danced miniature quadrilles to the music of dwarfs who tickled tiny fiddles with tiny bows, and flags rippled from scorched beams while bats flew in clouds about gargoyle mouths which spouted down wine, cool, wild, and foaming. A creek wandered through the seven rooms of the masked ball. Guests sipped and found it to be sherry. Guests poured from the booths, transformed from one age into another, their faces covered with dominoes, the very act of putting on a mask revoking all their licenses to pick a quarrel with fantasy and horror. The women swept about in red gowns, laughing. The men danced them attendance. And on the walls were shadows with no people to throw them, and here or there were mirrors in which no image showed. "All of us vampires!" laughed Mr. Fletcher. "Dead!"

There were seven rooms, each a different color, one blue, one purple, one green, one orange, another white, the sixth violet, and the seventh shrouded in black velvet. And in the black room was an ebony clock which struck the hour loud. And through these rooms the guests ran, drunk at last, among the robot fantasies, amid the Dormice and Mad Hatters, the Trolls and Giants, the Black Cats and White Queens, and under their dancing feet the floor gave off the massive pumping beat of a hidden and telltale heart.

"Mr. Stendahl!"

A whisper.

"Mr. Stendahl!"

A monster with the face of Death stood at his elbow. It was Pikes. "I must see you alone."

"What is it?"

"Here." Pikes held out a skeleton hand. In it

were a few half-melted, charred wheels, nuts, cogs, bolts.

Stendahl looked at them for a long moment. Then he drew Pikes into a corridor. "Garrett?" he whispered.

Pikes nodded. "He sent a robot in his place. Cleaning out the incinerator a moment ago, I found these."

They both stared at the fateful cogs for a time.

"This means the police will be here any minute," said Pikes. "Our plan will be ruined."

"I don't know." Stendahl glanced in at the whirling yellow and blue and orange people. The music swept through the misting halls. "I should have guessed Garrett wouldn't be fool enough to come in person. But wait!"

"What's the matter?"

"Nothing. There's nothing the matter. Garrett sent a robot to us. Well, we sent one back. Unless he checks closely, he won't notice the switch."

"Of course!"

"Next time he'll come *himself.* Now that he thinks it's safe. Why, he might be at the door any minute, in *person!* More wine, Pikes!"

The great bell rang.

"There he is now, I'll bet you. Go let Mr. Garrett in."

Rapunzel let down her golden hair.

"Mr. Stendahl?"

"Mr. Garrett. The *real* Mr. Garrett?"

"The same." Garrett eyed the dank walls and the whirling people. "I thought I'd better come see for myself. You can't depend on robots. Other people's robots, especially. I also took the precaution of summoning the Dismantlers. They'll be here in one hour to knock the props out from under this horrible place."

Stendahl bowed. "Thanks for telling me." He waved his hand. "In the meantime, you might as well enjoy this. A little wine?"

"No, thank you. What's going on? How low can a man sink?"

"See for yourself, Mr. Garrett."

"Murder," said Garrett.

"Murder most foul," said Stendahl.

A woman screamed. Miss Pope ran up, her face the color of a cheese. "The most horrid thing just happened! I saw Miss Blunt strangled by an ape and stuffed up a chimney!"

They looked and saw the long yellow hair trailing down from the flue. Garrett cried out.

"Horrid!" sobbed Miss Pope, and then ceased crying. She blinked and turned. "Miss Blunt!"

"Yes," said Miss Blunt, standing there.

"But I just saw you crammed up the flue!"

"No," laughed Miss Blunt. "A robot of myself. A clever facsimile!"

"But, but . . ."

"Don't cry, darling. I'm quite all right. Let me look at myself. Well, so there I *am!* Up the chimney. Like you said. Isn't that funny?"

Miss Blunt walked away, laughing.

"Have a drink, Garrett?"

"I believe I will. That unnerved me. Bless my soul, what a place. This *does* deserve tearing down. For a moment there . . ."

Garrett drank.

Another scream. Mr. Steffens, borne upon the shoulders of four white rabbits, was carried down a flight of stairs which magically appeared in the floor. Into a pit went Mr. Steffens, where, bound and tied, he was left to face the advancing razor steel of a great pendulum which now whirled down, down, closer and closer to his outraged body.

"Is that me down there?" said Mr. Steffens, appearing at Garrett's elbow. He bent over the pit. "How strange, how odd, to see yourself die."

The pendulum made a final stroke.

"How realistic," said Mr. Steffens, turning away.

"Another drink, Mr. Garrett?"

"Yes, please."

"It won't be long. The Dismantlers will be here."

"Thank God!"

And for a third time, a scream.

"What now?" said Garrett apprehensively.

"It's my turn," said Miss Drummond. "Look."

And a second Miss Drummond, shrieking, was nailed into a coffin and thrust into the raw earth under the floor.

"Why, I remember *that,*" gasped the Investigator of Moral Climates. "From the old forbid-den books. The Premature Burial. And the others. The Pit, the Pendulum, and the ape, the chimney, the Murders in the Rue Morgue. In a book I burned, yes!"

"Another drink, Garrett. Here, hold your glass steady."

"Dear me, you *have* an imagination, haven't you?"

They stood and watched five others die, one in the mouth of a dragon, the others thrown off into the black tarn, sinking and vanishing.

"Would you like to see what we have planned for you?" asked Stendahl.

"Certainly," said Garrett. "What's the difference? We'll blow the whole blasted thing up, anyway. You're nasty."

"Come along then. This way."

And he led Garrett down into the floor, through numerous passages and down again upon spiral stairs into the earth, into the catacombs.

"What do you want to show me down here?" said Garrett.

"Yourself killed."

"A duplicate?"

"Yes. And also something else."

"What?"

"The Amontillado," said Stendahl, going ahead with a blazing lantern which he held high. Skeletons froze half out of coffin lids. Garrett held his hand to his nose, his face disgusted.

"The what?"

"Haven't you ever heard of the Amontillado?"

"No!"

"Don't you recognize this?" Stendahl pointed to a cell.

"Should I?"

"Or this?" Stendahl produced a trowel from under his cape, smiling.

"What's that thing?"

"Come," said Stendahl.

They stepped into the cell. In the dark, Stendahl affixed the chains to the half-drunken man.

"For God's sake, what are you doing?" shouted Garrett, rattling about.

"I'm being ironic. Don't interrupt a man in the midst of being ironic, it's not polite. There!"

"You've locked me in chains!"

"So I have."

"What are you going to do?"

"Leave you here."

"You're joking."

"A very good joke."

"Where's my duplicate? Don't we see him killed?"

"There is no duplicate."

"But the *others!*"

"The others are dead. The ones you saw killed were the real people. The duplicates, the robots, stood by and watched."

Garrett said nothing.

"Now you're supposed to say, 'For the love of God, Montresor!'" said Stendahl. "And I will reply, 'Yes, for the love of God.' Won't you say it? Come on. *Say* it."

"You fool."

"Must I coax you? Say it. Say 'For the love of God, Montresor!'"

"I won't, you idiot. Get me out of here." He was sober now.

"Here. Put this on." Stendahl tossed in something that belled and rang.

"What is it?"

"A cap and bells. Put it on and I might let you out."

"Stendahl!"

"Put it on, I said!"

Garrett obeyed. The bells tinkled.

"Don't you have a feeling that this has all happened before?" inquired Stendahl, setting to work with trowel and mortar and brick now.

"What're you doing?"

"Walling you in. Here's one row. Here's another."

"You're insane!"

"I won't argue that point."

"You'll be prosecuted for this!"

He tapped a brick and placed it on the wet mortar, humming.

Now there was a thrashing and pounding and a crying out from within the darkening place. The bricks rose higher. "More thrashing, please," said Stendahl. "Let's make it a good show."

"Let me out, let me out!"

There was one last brick to shove into place. The screaming was continuous.

"Garrett?" called Stendahl softly. Garrett silenced himself. "Garrett," said Stendahl, "do you know why I've done this to you? Because you burned Mr. Poe's books without really reading them. You took other people's advice that they needed burning. Otherwise you'd have realized what I was going to do to you when we came down here a moment ago. Ignorance is fatal, Mr. Garrett."

Garrett was silent.

"I want this to be perfect," said Stendahl, holding his lantern up so its light penetrated in upon the slumped figure. "Jingle your bells softly." The bells rustled. "Now, if you'll please say, 'For the love of God, Montresor,' I might let you free."

The man's face came up in the light. There was a hesitation. Then grotesquely the man said, "For the love of God, Montresor."

"Ah," said Stendahl, eyes closed. He shoved the last brick into place and mortared it tight. *"Requiescat in pace.*[14] dear friend."

He hastened from the catacomb.

In the seven rooms the sound of a midnight clock brought everything to a halt.

The Red Death appeared.

Stendahl turned for a moment at the door to watch. And then he ran out of the great House, across the moat, to where a helicopter waited.

"Ready, Pikes?"

"Ready."

"There it goes!"

They looked at the great House, smiling. It began to crack down the middle, as with an earthquake, and as Stendahl watched the magnificent sight he heard Pikes reciting behind him in a low, cadenced voice:

"'. . . my brain reeled as I saw the mighty walls rushing asunder—there was a long tumultous shouting sound like the voice of a thousand waters—and the deep and dank tarn at my feet closed sullenly and silently over the fragments of the House of Usher.'"

The helicopter rose over the steaming lake and flew into the west. □□

---

14. *Requiescat in pace* (re′kwē es′kat in pä′ke), rest in peace. [*Latin*]

Discussion

1. (a) Describe the personality of Stendahl. For instance, what characteristics and attitudes are revealed by what he says as well as his manner of speaking? (b) In characterizing him, Bradbury uses a device termed the **foil**. In what way is Garrett a foil to Stendahl?

2. Stendahl thinks of his guests as "the people with mercurochrome for blood and iodine-colored eyes." What does this description imply about their outlook on life?

3. (a) Explain the **motivation** for the plan of Stendahl and Pikes. (b) For what reason are their victims unable to guess the scheme? (c) How have the guests contributed to their own destruction?

4. This story is full of **ironies.** In what way is each of the following situations ironic? (a) Stendahl's use of machines to create his House; (b) the guests' pleasure at the costume ball; (c) Garrett's belief that Stendahl fears to lose his House.

5. Bradbury is noted for his vivid, lyrical prose style. Reread the scene of the robots' awaking and point out phrases that you find especially poetic.

6. (a) Describe the two contrasting **moods** suggested by the description of the costume ball. What details help create each mood? (b) How is suspense built in this scene?

7. (a) Describe the society ruled by the Moral Climates agency. (b) What does the story imply would be the harmful effects of banning art, literature, fantasy, and imagination? (c) In what way is Garrett's attitude toward literature like that of the designers of "The Calculating Machine"?

Extension • Writing

1. This story relies heavily on **allusions.** As well as alluding to fairy tales and works by various authors, "April 2005" echoes many stories by Poe (Unit 3). Read two of the following stories by Poe and explain to a friend who has not read the stories how knowing them would increase the enjoyment and suspense of reading "April 2005."

a) "The Fall of the House of Usher";

b) "The Masque of the Red Death";

c) "The Pit and the Pendulum";

d) "The Cask of Amontillado" (see Unit 3).

2. Bradbury's dramatic style lends itself to filming. Working in groups, choose any vivid scene from this story and create a film script for that scene.

Vocabulary • Dictionary

Use the Glossary to answer each question about the italicized words from "April 2005: Usher II."

1. The House is surrounded by "*fetid* vapors." What does this mean?

2. Explain this comparison: ". . . you're flocking in thicker every day, like flies to *offal.*"

3. Which meaning of *nebulous* (29a, li. 2) fits the context of the story?

4. Write the Latin prefix and root of *conflagration* and tell what each means.

Ray Bradbury 1920 •

Despite his life-long devotion to science fiction, Bradbury has never learned to drive, does not fly, and often rides a bicycle to business appointments.

In high school, he founded *Futuria Fantasia,* a mimeographed quarterly of science fantasy. In 1941, while selling newspapers to finance his writing, he sold his first story. Since then he has published more than a thousand short stories as well as novels and plays for stage, screen, radio, and TV. He advises young authors to write daily to overcome the nervous self-criticism that paralyzes creativity.

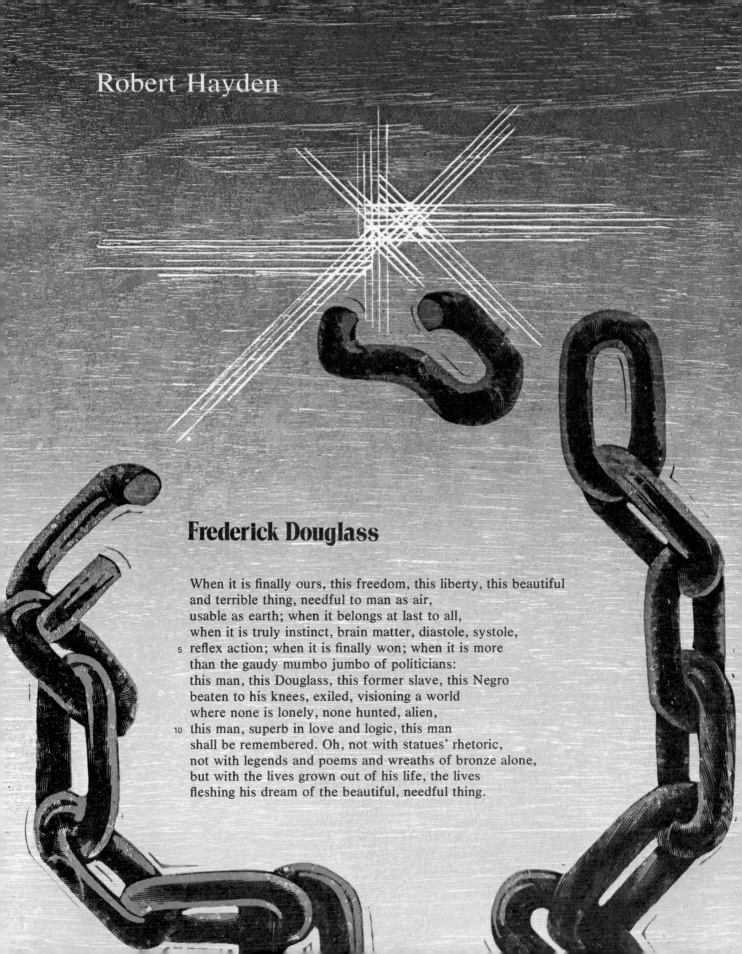

Robert Hayden

Frederick Douglass

When it is finally ours, this freedom, this liberty, this beautiful
and terrible thing, needful to man as air,
usable as earth; when it belongs at last to all,
when it is truly instinct, brain matter, diastole, systole,
5 reflex action; when it is finally won; when it is more
than the gaudy mumbo jumbo of politicians:
this man, this Douglass, this former slave, this Negro
beaten to his knees, exiled, visioning a world
where none is lonely, none hunted, alien,
10 this man, superb in love and logic, this man
shall be remembered. Oh, not with statues' rhetoric,
not with legends and poems and wreaths of bronze alone,
but with the lives grown out of his life, the lives
fleshing his dream of the beautiful, needful thing.

Discussion

1. (a) To what things is freedom compared in this poem? (b) In what sense do these comparisons make freedom an "ordinary" rather than a "special" human state? (c) What false symbols of freedom are mentioned?

2. (a) What experiences and qualities of Frederick Douglass make him representative of freedom? (b) How will his example realize itself?

3. Describe the **tone** of the poem.

notes and comments

From the Author

"Frederick Douglass" was written as part of a sonnet sequence on heroic men and women of the antislavery struggle. . . . I thought of the tribute to Douglass as the climactic poem in the series, but it is now the only one of these sonnets I kept, scrapping the others because I felt they were facile and poorly constructed.

I had intended the sonnets to be one of two sequences in a long poem—an epic of sorts—on slavery and the Civil War, entitled *The Black Spear.* . . . I worked on *The Black Spear* intermittently from about 1941 to 1946, reading biographies, memoirs, histories of slavery and the war, poring over Matthew Brady's photographs. . . .

Well, *The Black Spear* did not emerge as the great poem I

had struggled to achieve. After tinkering with the manuscript, following its several rejections, I abandoned *The Black Spear*, and it distresses me to realize that at present I don't know where the manuscript is. However, it is not a complete loss, for certain parts of it have proved viable over the years. And among them "Frederick Douglass" seems to be one of the hardiest survivors. . . .

Since I wished to express my feeling that the achievements of Douglass were of fundamental value to the entire human race, I tried to use words and images evoking some sense of the elemental, the organic, the universal. Hence, "earth," "air," "diastole," "systole," "reflex action," etc. . . .

If I were writing "Douglass"

at this stage in my life, it would be quite different. Or would it? I would still want to honor Douglass not only as a hero in the struggle for the freedom of his people but also as a man whose vision of humanity was all-embracing. This is my vision too. People of all races and creeds respond warmly to this poem. I am indeed grateful for that.

Hayden had been publishing his poetry since 1940, but not until 1966 did he receive the attention his work merits. Since then, however, his work has been recognized throughout the world. For his biography, see page 616.

A speech by Frederick Douglass himself is in Unit 4.

Edna St. Vincent Millay

In 1920, Nicola Sacco (1891–1927) and Bartolomeo Vanzetti (1888–1927) were charged with robbery and murder. Although the prosecution's case was weak, they faced much hostility because they were draft resisters, anarchists, and labor-union advocates. After many appeals, and in spite of a condemned criminal's admission that he knew others were guilty, Sacco and Vanzetti were executed in 1927. The case inspired many literary protests, such as the following essay and poem. In 1977, Governor Dukakis of Massachusetts proclaimed Sacco and Vanzetti innocent and declared a Memorial Day for them.

Ben. Shahn, *Bartolomeo Vanzetti and Nicola Sacco* (1931–32), tempera on paper over composition board, 10 ½″ x 14 ½″, Collection, The Museum of Modern Art, New York. Gift of Abby Aldrich Rockefeller.

Fear

There are two names you would not have me mention, for you are sick of the sound of them. All men must die, you say, and these men have died, and would that their names might die with them; would that their names were as names written in the sand, you say, to be dissipated by the next incoming tide! For you long to return to your gracious world of a year ago, where people had pretty manners and did not raise their voices; where people whom you knew, whom you had entertained in your houses, did not shout and weep and walk the streets vulgarly carrying banners, because two quite inconsequential people, two men who could not even speak good English, were about to be put forever out of mischief's way. *Do* let us forget, you say; after all, what *does* it matter?

You are right; it does not matter very much. In a world more beautiful than this it would have mattered more. On the surface of a Christianity already so spotted and defaced by the crimes of the Church this stain does not show very dark. In a freedom already so riddled and gashed by the crimes of the state this ugly rent is with difficulty to be distinguished at all.

And you are right; it is well to forget that men die. So far we have devised no way to defeat death, or to outwit him, or to buy him over. At any moment the cloud may split above us and the golden spear of death leap at the heart; at any moment the earth crack and the hand of death reach up from the abyss to grasp our ankles; at any moment the wind rise and sweep the roofs from our houses, making one dust of our ceilings and ourselves. And if not, we shall die soon, anyhow. It is well to forget that this is so.

But that man before his time, wantonly and without sorrow, is thrust from the light of the sun into the darkness of the grave by his brother's blindness or fear it is well to remember, at least until it has been shown to the satisfaction of all that this too is beyond our power to change.

Two months ago, in Massachusetts, these men whom I do not name were efficiently despatched out of the sunlight into the darkness of the grave. The executions of the death sentence upon them went forward without interference; there were no violent demonstrations. Whatever of agitation there was has steadily decreased since that night. Today things are very quiet. From time to time some small newspaper remarks editorially that the hysteria which swept the country has abated, and congratulates its readers upon having escaped disintegration. Aside from this there is little comment. The general opinion is that the affair has pretty well blown over. And the world sleeps easy on this pillow.

Yet if all is quiet today, it is more for this reason than for any other; that though you sit in the same room with a man you cannot hear his thoughts. And the tumult is in the mind; the shouting and rioting are in the thinking mind. Nothing has abated; nothing has changed; nothing is forgotten. It is as if the two months which have elapsed were but the drawing of a breath. In very truth, for those who sat in silence on that night of the 22d of August, waiting for news from the prison, and in silence when the news came, it is still the night of the 22d of August, for there has been no dawn.

I do not call these men by name, for I know how nervous and irritable you become at the sight of these names on the printed page; how your cheek flushes and you cluck with exasperation; how you turn to your family with words on your tongue which in former days you would not have used at all—"vipers, vermin, filth." This is because you were just dozing off nicely again after the shocking uproar of two months ago, and do not wish to be disturbed. You are as cross as an old dog asleep on the hearth if I shake you and try to get you out into the rainy wind. This is because what you most want out of life is not to be disturbed. You wish to lie peacefully asleep for a few years yet, and then to lie peacefully dead.

If you should rouse yourself for a moment and look about you at the world, you would be troubled, I think, and feel less peaceful and secure, seeing how it is possible for a man as innocent as yourself of any crime to be cast into prison and be killed. For whether or not these men whom I do not name were guilty of the crime of murder, it was not for murder that they died. The crime for which they died was the crime of breathing upon the frosty window and looking out.

"These Anarchists!" you say; "shall I never hear the last of them?"

Indeed, I fear it will be some time before you hear the last of them. I do not mean by this what you think I mean. I do not mean that plotting mischief is afoot, that thousands of people hitherto gentle and retired are now grimly engaged in fashioning engines of death to plant beneath the State House floor. This is not what I mean, although you will say it is what I meant.

It is of your children I was thinking, your young sons and daughters, your grandsons and granddaughters, these young people with whom you have already so much difficulty, because, as you say, they have so few illusions. How often already have they not stood looking at you coldly while with warm cheek and faltering accent you presented your pretty concepts: duty, honor, courage, purity, sacrifice—those fragile dolls of yours, that are always dressed for summer, no matter what the sky?

Your children heard you discussing the case in question. "Anarchists, murderers, Anarchists, Anarchists." This was your discussion of the case. They looked at you, yawned, and left the room.

Their minds are dark to you. But they are busy. Out of your sight they read, they ponder, they work things out. In your presence they often sit in a not too respectful silence, interrupting suddenly your placid remarks by their brisk utterance of some untidy truth never mentioned in your house before.

They are frankly occupied chiefly with the real business of life, which, as everybody knows, is having your own way, and getting as much as possible for as little as possible. It is you who have taught them this angular truth; you have failed only in that you have not been able to impart to them as well the ruffles and passementerie with which you are accustomed to adorn it. They were just beginning to look about them at life when war broke out and surrounded them with death. They know how important it is to have a good time while you can; in the next war it is they who will be taken.

As for their illusions, well, they have seen you at war, and they are beginning to understand why you went to war; they have seen you engaged in many another dubious and embarrassing activity; and now they have seen this. They who have been chidden time and again for having so little softness in them see now their parents, for all their gentle voices and courteous ways, more hard, more unscrupulous, more relentless, than themselves in their most iron moods. It is from these children, I fear, that you are likely to hear again on the subject, though not in so many words.

But, you say, what we did was done for the good of the country, to protect its honor, its institutions, the glory of its flag.

What is this honor, that a breath can tarnish? This glory, that a whisper can bring it low? What are these noble institutions, that a wind from any quarter can set to trembling like towers of jelly?

You do not know exactly what they are. For you do not live with them. They are not trees to shade you, water to quench your thirst. They are golden coins, hidden under the mattress in a very soiled wallet. The only pleasure they afford you is the rapturous dread lest some one may be taking them away. And some one is taking them away. But not the one you think.

Unkindness, hypocrisy, and greed—these are the forces that shall bring us low and enslave our children. Yet we quarter their troops in our houses without a murmur. We show them where the treasure is hid. But they know it already.

This is the way you look at it: These men were Anarchists, and they are well out of the way; you are fortunate to have escaped destruction at their hands; they were probably murderers; but, in any case, they are well out of the way. It was that word Anarchist which brought them to the chair; that word, and your ignorance of its meaning.

For you do not at all know what an Anarchist is. And all through this trial in which the word Anarchist has played such an important part you have not even looked up the word in the dictionary, your position being that, in the first place, you know quite well enough, and, in the second place, you would think shame to know.

An Anarchist, you insist, is a man who makes bombs and puts them under the State House, and that is that. On the contrary, that is by no means that. The person you have in mind is not an Anarchist, he is a bomber. You will find him everywhere—among Anarchists, among Fascists, among dry-law enforcers, among Modernists, among Fundamentalists, and freely distributed throughout the Ku Klux Klan. He is that person who, when he does not like a thing, lynches it, tars and feathers it, lays a curse upon it, or puts a bomb under it. His name is legion, and you will find him in every party.

An Anarchist, according to the dictionary, is a person who believes that human beings are naturally good, and that if left to themselves they would, by mutual agreement, govern themselves much better and much more peaceably than they are being governed now by a government based on violence. An interesting theory. Nonsense, of course, because man is not naturally good; man is naturally cruel, selfish, and vain, and what he would be if left to his own devices it is horrible to contemplate. Still, it is an interesting concept, very idealistic, very pretty.

Of those who hold with the theory of Anarchism, the dictionary further tells us, there is one group whose members "occasionally resort to an act of violence against representatives of oppression to express a protest against, or to draw public attention to, existing social wrongs." (It is in this group that your bombers are happy and at home.) But "generally speaking," says the dictionary, "Anarchism repudiates violent methods, and hopes for a gradual evolution towards its goal."

Ah, you will say, but these men belonged to the violent group!

Their history would indicate otherwise. Up to the time of their detention for the crime for which they were later sentenced to die no slightest act of violence had ever been attributed to either of them. There are those who would have given much to be able to bring to light against them such an act of violence, and were unable to do so; it is to the counsel for the prosecution that I refer. "Throughout the entire trial" (I quote the uncontested statement of one who was in a position to know the facts)—"not one word of testimony was introduced against their character for honesty, peace, and good order."

I am going into this in some detail because I find it interesting. You, I fear, find it not only uninteresting, but vaguely and uncomfortably obscene. Yet, after all, you have very plentifully had your say on the subject—that action of yours, you know, that spoke so much louder than any words.

These men were castaways upon our shore, and we, an ignorant and savage tribe, have put them to death because their speech and their manners were different from our own, and because to the untutored mind that which is strange is in its infancy ludicrous, but in its prime evil, dangerous, and to be done away with.

These men were put to death because they made you nervous; and your children know it. The minds of your children are like clear pools, reflecting faithfully whatever passes on the bank; whereas in the pool of your own mind, whenever an alien image bends above, a fish of terror leaps to meet it, shattering its reflection.

I am free to say these things because I am not an Anarchist, although you will say that I am. It is unreasonable to you that a person should go to any trouble in behalf of another person unless the two are members of the same family, or of the same fraternity, or, at the remotest, of the same political party. As regards yourself and the man who lives next door to you, you wish him well, but not so very well. Even if he is a member of the same church as yourself, you do not wish him so inordinately well. Whereas if he does not belong to the same church as yourself, and if, in addition, he does things a little out of the ordinary, such as walk in the street without a hat, you do not wish him well at all. In any case, as regards your neighbor and yourself, although you have no desire to see his house burn down or his children killed in a motor accident, a most modest worldly success will do very well for him, as far as you are concerned. For these and other reasons sufficiently naïve and and self-revealing, you take it as a matter of course that, of the many persons involved in the recent agitation in Boston, those who were not in the thing for what they could get out of it were revolutionists of the most flagrant dye. It is impossible for you to conceive that men could weep in public and women permit themselves to be thrown in jail because (as it seemed to them) the blue hem of Justice was being dragged in the mire. In the world in which you live Justice is a woman of stone above a court-house door.

As I said before, I am not sufficiently idealistic to share the political opinions of these men with whose fate I am concerned. It is impossible for me to be an Anarchist, for I do not believe in the essential goodness of man; man is quite patently, to my sight, the worm of the Moody and Sankey[1] hymns. Except for this fact, I should of course think twice before writing as I do. For, although I was born in this country, and am possessed of that simple right of the citizen to hold any opinions he may choose and to express any opinions he may hold, yet to avail one's self of this right and express opinions contrary to the opinions of the majority may become, as we have lately seen, a folly punishable by the extreme correction. For surely you are not still insisting that these two poor wretches were put to death solely for the crime of murder? You and I both know that we must be careful, not only what we do, but also what we say, and even what

---

1. *Moody and Sankey.* Evangelist Dwight L. Moody and composer Ira D. Sankey wrote gospel hymns and conducted several evangelical crusades together.

we think, if we would not have one day our sleep brutally broken in upon and ourselves rudely forced to enter a place where we do not at all wish to go. And surely you will not deny that, if you would remain undisturbed, it is more important to be on the side of the established order of things than to be innocent of even the grossest crime?

As I said before, I dare say these things because I am not an Anarchist; but I dare say them for another reason, too: because my personal physical freedom, my power to go in and out when I choose, my personal life even, is no longer quite as important to me as it once was. Death even, that outrageous intrusion, appears to me at moments, and more especially when I think of what happened in Boston two months ago, death appears to me somewhat as a dark-ened room, in which one might rest one's battered temples out of the world's way, leaving the sweeping of the crossings to those who still think it important that the crossings be swept. As if indeed it mattered the least bit in the world whether the crossings be clean or foul, when of all the people passing to and fro there in the course of an eight-hour day not one out of ten thousand has a spark of true courage in his heart, or any love at all, beyond the love of a cat for the fire, for any earthly creature other than himself. The world, the physical world, and that once was all in all to me, has at moments such as these no road through a wood, no stretch of shore, that can bring me comfort. The beauty of these things can no longer at such moments make up to me at all for the ugliness of man, his cruelty, his greed, his lying face. □ □

Discussion

1. (a) In what ways does the title of this essay reflect its content? (b) Does the essay gain or lose force because it glosses over details of the case to which it refers? Explain.

2. (a) To what audience is this essay addressed? (b) What is Millay's attitude toward them? (c) What type of person might be expected to be most sympathetic to its point of view?

3. Millay argues that the word *anarchist* was widely misused, its meaning completely distorted. Can you think of any words, likewise misapplied and emotionally loaded, in use today?

4. (a) What is the **tone** of the last sentence? (b) Giving examples, describe the dominant tone of the essay.

5. "Mankind cannot bear too much reality." Discuss the essay in terms of this statement.

Extension • Speaking

Millay's essay responded to a social and human issue over which there had been bitter debate, and of which many people had grown tired. Pick an issue you think has been neglected by the public, and plan a discussion about it with an imaginary opponent. What counterarguments should you anticipate? How would you handle the response? Consider whether you want to argue in highly emotional language or whether calm reason would be more effective. Which approach has Millay used?

Edna St. Vincent Millay
1892 • 1950

Even before Millay entered Vassar College, she had been publishing poetry. At nineteen she wrote "Renascence," a long lyric whose quiet melodic beginning is followed by an ecstatic affirmation of life.

Born in Maine, she moved to Greenwich Village in New York City and became the poetic voice of "flaming youth" of the 1920s. The hopefulness voiced in "Renascence" was submerged in the cynicism and disillusionment that followed World War I. In 1923 she was awarded the Pulitzer Prize for *The Harp-Weaver and Other Poems.*

Millay spent most of her last twenty-five years at Steepletop Farm in northern New York. The lyrics and sonnets of this period are more subdued and less self-conscious than her earlier work. Showing genuine poetic power, they bear the mark of a striking and intense personality.

Justice Denied in Massachusetts

Discussion

1. Compare the **tone** of the poem with that of "Fear."

2. In what ways does nature seem to be affected by human evil?

3. **(a)** What might the broken hoe symbolize? **(b)** How is it related to what we have inherited from the "splendid dead"?

Extension • Reading

In what ways might an artistic protest such as this poem be more forceful than direct action? Find other protest writing in this unit and in Units 6 and 8. You can also consider other works of protest that you know, including songs, films, etc. By sampling such works, try to develop guidelines for distinguishing between successful and unsuccessful propaganda. These questions may help your study.

(a) Which are more effective—direct protest messages, or indirect ones?

(b) Is it more persuasive to denounce an evil with strongly emotional language, or merely to present it concretely and objectively?

(c) Should protest art demand action from the reader?

(d) Would you consider other media more powerful forms of protest than writing? Explain why or why not.

Let us abandon then our gardens and go home
And sit in the sitting-room.
Shall the larkspur blossom or the corn grow under this cloud?
Sour to the fruitful seed
5 Is the cold earth under this cloud,
Fostering quack and weed, we have marched upon but
       cannot conquer;
We have bent the blades of our hoes against the stalks of them.

Let us go home, and sit in the sitting-room.
Not in our day
10 Shall the cloud go over and the sun rise as before,
Beneficent upon us
Out of the glittering bay,
And the warm winds be blown inward from the sea
Moving the blades of corn
15 With a peaceful sound.
Forlorn, forlorn,
Stands the blue hay-rack by the empty mow.
And the petals drop to the ground,
Leaving the tree unfruited.
20 The sun that warmed our stooping backs and withered the
       weed uprooted—
We shall not feel it again.
We shall die in darkness, and be buried in the rain.

What from the splendid dead
We have inherited—
25 Furrows sweet to the grain, and the weed subdued—
See now the slug and the mildew plunder.
Evil does overwhelm
The larkspur and the corn;
We have seen them go under.

30 Let us sit here, sit still,
Here in the sitting-room until we die;
At the step of Death on the walk, rise and go;
Leaving to our children's children this beautiful doorway,
And this elm,
35 And a blighted earth to till
With a broken hoe.

From COLLECTED POEMS, Harper & Row. Copyright 1928, 1955 by Edna St. Vincent Millay and Norma Millay Ellis.

May Sarton

These facing poems are parallel in theme. Consider their contrasting attitudes toward the aging process.

Now I Become Myself

Now I become myself. It's taken
Time, many years and places;
I have been dissolved and shaken,
Worn other people's faces,
5 Run madly, as if Time were there,
Terribly old, crying a warning,
"Hurry, you will be dead before—"
(What? Before you reach the morning?
Or the end of the poem is clear?
10 Or love safe in the walled city?)
Now to stand still, to be here,
Feel my own weight and density!
The black shadow on the paper
Is my hand; the shadow of a word
15 As thought shapes the shaper
Falls heavy on the page, is heard.
All fuses now, falls into place
From wish to action, word to silence,
My work, my love, my time, my face
20 Gathered into one intense

Gesture of growing like a plant.
As slowly as the ripening fruit
Fertile, detached, and always spent,
Falls but does not exhaust the root,
25 So all the poem is, can give,
Grows in me to become the song,
Made so and rooted so by love.
Now there is time and Time is young.
O, in this single hour I live
30 All of myself and do not move.
I, the pursued, who madly ran,
Stand still, stand still, and stop the sun!

Reprinted from COLLECTED POEMS (1930–1973) by May Sarton, with the permission of W. W. Norton & Company, Inc. and Russell & Volkening, Inc., Copyright © 1974 by May Sarton.

Discussion

1. In what state or condition does the poet think she was before "becoming" herself?

2. **(a)** Contrast her outlook in youth and after maturing. **(b)** What qualities of youth has she preserved into age?

3. In what sense has the poet "found herself" as a writer? A human being?

Extension • Writing

1. "Worn other people's faces" is a vivid image. What meanings does the phrase suggest to you? Explain your ideas in a paragraph.

2. In a form of poetic "free writing," try creating a series of images that express your feelings about growing older. Or you might create a photo collage or other artwork on this theme.

May Sarton 1912 •

Sarton was born in Belgium, but her family eventually moved to America. While in her teens she was attracted to the theater. During the Depression, however, her acting career came to a standstill. Since her first book of poems, *Encounter in April* (1937), Sarton has written over twenty-five books of fiction and poetry. As shown by "Now I Become Myself," she is interested in attitudes toward maturity.

Robert Amft.

Sylvia Plath

Mirror

I am silver and exact. I have no preconceptions.
Whatever I see I swallow immediately
Just as it is, unmisted by love or dislike.
I am not cruel, only truthful—
5 The eye of a little god, four-cornered.
Most of the time I meditate on the opposite wall.
It is pink, with speckles. I have looked at it so long
I think it is a part of my heart. But it flickers.
Faces and darkness separate us over and over.

10 Now I am a lake. A woman bends over me,
Searching my reaches for what she really is.
Then she turns to those liars, the candles or the moon.
I see her back, and reflect it faithfully.
She rewards me with tears and an agitation of hands.
15 I am important to her. She comes and goes.
Each morning it is her face that replaces the darkness.
In me she has drowned a young girl, and in me an old woman
Rises toward her day after day, like a terrible fish.

Discussion

1. (a) In what sense is the mirror "a little god" to the woman? (b) What three stages of life does she imagine seeing in the mirror/lake?

2. (a) Who has drowned? (b) What does the "terrible fish" represent?

3. Compare this poem with Sarton's in **tone** and meaning.

Extension • Speaking

Imagine you are any object other than a mirror. Describe a scene or situation from the **point of view** of this object, but without revealing what object you are. Can your audience determine your identity?

Sylvia Plath 1932 • 1963

In a short career, Plath published several volumes of poetry, including *Colossus, Ariel,* and *Winter Trees.* Her only novel, *The Bell Jar,* appeared under the pseudonym Victoria Lucas in 1963, the year of her suicide. It was republished in 1966 under her real name, and has enjoyed enormous success in the United States.

Plath's explorations of the inner being are often illustrated in terms of exciting and fantastic leaps of the imagination, as here with the transformation of mirror into lake and the appearance of the "terrible fish."

Jesús Papoleto Meléndez

A bruja [brü✓hä] *is a very thick and strong plant native to the jungle of Puerto Rico. A* bruja *can be regrown from a single leaf because there are seeds on the leaves. Another meaning of* bruja *is "witch."*

Bruja

a plastic Bruja
fell
from a 4th floor windowsill
against the cold concrete
5 of sidewalks
that describe this metal city.
it did not break.
but it will not grow
this plastic flower that is store-bought
10 impersonating Spirits
that are real.
no it will not grow.
it is not real in that way
in that respect.

15 now had it been a Bruja from Puerto Rico
broken-away from the join of its family
beneath trees & rocks
in jungles
of birds that sing
20 & animals
that crawl within the dirt
& eat the fruits that grow from trees/
had that Bruja that fell
come from where the Sun sinks close enough
25 to touch the trees
& be blessed as a Natural God
(unlike airplanes)
had that Bruja that fell against the concrete
been one of those
30 the same that grow
on Doña Juana's[1] windowsill
the ones that she brought back
from her last trip to the Island
the one about her father's death   there

35 her plants grow
in all colors of the Sun & Moon
& in all seasons of this Earth & stretch
to enter onto the walls
that make her home/
40 had that fallen Bruja been one of those
it would have dug its hole
in through that concrete that is man-made
& found itself a home
deep
45 where the Earth is warm again
& soon
it would have grown between the cracks
the Sun makes when it's hot
& it would have joined the flowers
50 of colors that are different
& that have come to meet
on this battlefield of concrete
& then
that same Bruja that once felt
55 the cold of steel & asphalt
it would have raised its hand
to throw its brick
too.

Jesús Papoleto Meléndez (he süs✓ pä pô le✓tô me len✓des).
Copyright © 1975 by Jesús Papoleto Meléndez. Published in NUYORICAN POETRY Edited by Miguel Algarín and Miguel Piñero. Reprinted by permission.

1. ***Doña Juana*** (dô✓nyä hwä✓nä). *Doña* is a term of respect for a woman. [*Spanish*]

STEVE BERMAN

Discussion

1. In what physical characteristic does the "Bruja" in the first line of the poem differ from the "Bruja" described in the first line of the headnote?

2. (a) What words in the first six lines of the poem convey the **atmosphere** of the city? (b) Compare this with the environment of the living and growing Bruja, as described in lines 15–39.

3. To which meaning of "Bruja" does line 10 refer?

4. Had the "Bruja" that fell from the windowsill been real, what would have happened to it?

5. What do you learn from the poem about Doña Juana?

6. Explain in your own words the last three lines of the poem.

Jesús Papoleto Meléndez
1948 •

Meléndez says, "Any work of art comes from inside a certain culture, is a part of that culture, but shouldn't be restricted by a cultural label. A poem is a cosmic happening that should transcend the walls of its culture." Among the poems which he feels match this ideal are "In Memory of W. B. Yeats" by W. H. Auden; "The Love Song of J. Alfred Prufrock" by T. S. Eliot (see page 454); and, above all, the poems of Dylan Thomas. In Meléndez's own career, "Bruja" represents a transition from his political poetry of the early 1970s toward a more universal, romantic vision.

He belongs to the Latin Insomniacs Motorcycle Club, a group of New York poets, playwrights, and filmmakers including Pedro Juan Pietri, Willie Pietri, and Juan Valenzuela. The Insomniacs practice *surrealism*, a philosophy of painting and literature in which dreamlike image patterns reflect the sudden shifts of the unconscious mind, as in Plath's "The Mirror." Meléndez believes that in surrealism, symbols can have as much emotional as intellectual power.

Meléndez was born in San Francisco but brought to New York as a baby. At the age of about seven, he began writing poems and stories "of my own accord." At twenty-two, he published *Casting Long Shadows*, his first volume of verse. He has since published *Have You Seen Liberation?* (1971) and *Street Poetry and Other Poems* (1972).

Elizabeth Bishop

Filling Station

Oh, but it is dirty!
—this little filling station,
oil-soaked, oil-permeated
to a disturbing, over-all
5 black translucency.
Be careful with that match!

Father wears a dirty,
oil-soaked monkey suit
that cuts him under the arms,
10 and several quick and saucy
and greasy sons assist him
(it's a family filling station),
all quite thoroughly dirty.

Do they live in the station?
15 It has a cement porch
behind the pumps, and on it
a set of crushed and grease-
impregnated wickerwork;
on the wicker sofa
20 a dirty dog, quite comfy.

Some comic books provide
the only note of color—
of certain color. They lie
upon a big dim doily
25 draping a taboret[1]
(part of the set), beside
a big hirsute begonia.

Why the extraneous plant?
Why the taboret?
30 Why, oh why, the doily?
(Embroidered in daisy stitch
with marguerites, I think,
and heavy with gray crochet.)

Somebody embroidered the doily.
35 Somebody waters the plant,
or oils it, maybe. Somebody
arranges the rows of cans
so that they softly say:
ESSO—SO—SO—SO
40 to high-strung automobiles.
Somebody loves us all.

Reprinted with the permission of Farrar, Straus & Giroux, Inc. from THE COMPLETE POEMS by Elizabeth Bishop, Copyright © 1955 by Elizabeth Bishop.
1. *taboret* (tab′er it), a low, round stool or table.

Garage Lights by Stuart Davis.
(Memorial Art Gallery of the University of Rochester,
Marion Stratton Gould Fund.)

Discussion

1. The speaker says several times that the filling station is dirty. How do the owner and his sons seem to regard their surroundings?

2. (a) What "homey" or colorful items are scattered around the station? **(b)** Why do you think the speaker asks so many questions about these items?

3. (a) Who might be the "somebody" of the last stanza? Discuss several possible interpretations. **(b)** What **tone** does this ending give to the poem?

4. In what ways are the **setting** and **theme** of this poem similar to those of "Bruja"?

Elizabeth Bishop 1911 • 1979

Elizabeth Bishop's poems are distinguished for their clarity and accessibility. Yet, when considering poets who rewrite repeatedly, she said "All that revision never interested me."

Bishop's poetry is stimulated by her far-ranging travels. Two award-winning collections of such poems are *Poems, North and South* and *Geography II*.

Bernard Malamud

The First Seven Years

Feld, the shoemaker, was annoyed that his helper, Sobel, was so insensitive to his reverie that he wouldn't for a minute cease his fanatic pounding at the other bench. He gave him a look, but Sobel's bald head was bent over the last as he worked and he didn't notice. The shoemaker shrugged and continued to peer through the partly frosted window at the near-sighted haze of falling February snow. Neither the shifting white blur outside, nor the sudden deep remembrance of the snowy Polish village where he had wasted his youth could turn his thoughts from Max the college boy, (a constant visitor in the mind since early that morning when Feld saw him trudging through the snowdrifts on his way to school) whom he so much respected because of the sacrifices he had made throughout the years—in winter or direst heat—to further his education. An old wish returned to haunt the shoemaker: that he had had a son instead of a daughter, but this blew away in the snow for Feld, if anything, was a practical man. Yet he could not help but contrast the diligence of the boy, who was a peddler's son, with Miriam's unconcern for an education. True, she was always with a book in her hand, yet when the opportunity arose for a college education, she had said no she would rather find a job. He had begged her to go, pointing out how many fathers could not afford to send their children to college, but she said she wanted to be independent. As for education, what was it, she asked, but books, which Sobel, who diligently read the classics, would as usual advise her on. Her answer greatly grieved her father.

A figure emerged from the snow and the door opened. At the counter the man withdrew from a wet paper bag a pair of battered shoes for repair. Who he was the shoemaker for a moment had no idea, then his heart trembled as he realized, before he had thoroughly discerned the face, that Max himself was standing there, embarrassedly explaining what he wanted done to his old shoes. Though Feld listened eagerly, he couldn't hear a word, for the opportunity that had burst upon him was deafening.

He couldn't exactly recall when the thought had occurred to him, because it was clear he had more than once considered suggesting to the boy that he go out with Miriam. But he had not dared speak, for if Max said no, how would he face him again? Or suppose Miriam, who harped so often on independence, blew up in anger and shouted at him for his meddling? Still, the chance was too good to let by: all it meant was an introduction. They might long ago have become friends had they happened to meet somewhere, therefore was it not his duty—an obligation—to bring them together, nothing more, a harmless connivance to replace an accidental encounter in the subway, let's say, or a mutual friend's introduction in the street? Just let him once see and talk to her and he would for sure be interested. As for Miriam, what possible harm for a working girl in an office, who met only loud-mouthed salesmen and illiterate shipping clerks, to make the acquaintance of a fine scholarly boy? Maybe he would awaken in her a desire to go to college; if not—the shoemaker's mind at last came to grips with the truth—let her marry an educated man and live a better life.

When Max finished describing what he wanted done to his shoes, Feld marked them, both with enormous holes in the soles which he pretended not to notice, with large white-chalk x's, and the rubber heels, thinned to the nails, he marked with o's, though it troubled him he might have mixed up the letters. Max inquired the price, and the shoemaker cleared his throat and asked the boy, above Sobel's insistent hammering, would he please step through the side door there into the hall. Though surprised, Max did as the shoemaker requested, and Feld went in after him. For a minute they were both silent, because Sobel had stopped banging, and it seemed they understood neither was to say anything until the noise began again. When it did, loudly, the shoemaker quickly told Max why he had asked to talk to him.

"Ever since you went to high school," he said, in the dimly-lit hallway, "I watched you in the morning go to the subway to school, and I said always to myself, this is a fine boy that he wants so much an education."

"Thanks," Max said, nervously alert. He was tall and grotesquely thin, with sharply cut features, particularly a beak-like nose. He was wearing a loose, long slushy overcoat that hung down to his ankles, looking like a rug draped over his bony shoulders, and a soggy, old brown hat, as battered as the shoes he had brought in.

"I am a business man," the shoemaker abruptly said to conceal his embarrassment, "so I will explain you right away why I talk to you. I have a girl, my daughter Miriam—she is nineteen—a very nice girl and also so pretty that everybody looks on her when she passes by in the street. She is smart, always with a book, and I thought to myself that a boy like you, an educated boy—I thought maybe you will be interested sometime to meet a girl like this." He laughed a bit when he had finished and was tempted to say more but had the good sense not to.

Max stared down like a hawk. For an uncomfortable second he was silent, then he asked, "Did you say nineteen?"

"Yes."

"Would it be all right to inquire if you have a picture of her?"

"Just a minute." The shoemaker went into the store and hastily returned with a snapshot that Max held up to the light.

"She's all right," he said.

Feld waited.

"And is she sensible—not the flighty kind?"

"She is very sensible."

After another short pause, Max said it was okay with him if he met her.

"Here is my telephone," said the shoemaker, hurriedly handing him a slip of paper. "Call her up. She comes home from work six o'clock."

Max folded the paper and tucked it away into his worn leather wallet.

"About the shoes," he said. "How much did you say they will cost me?"

"Don't worry about the price."

"I just like to have an idea."

"A dollar—dollar fifty. A dollar fifty," the shoemaker said.

At once he felt bad, for he usually charged two twenty-five for this kind of job. Either he should have asked the regular price or done the work for nothing.

Later, as he entered the store, he was startled by a violent clanging and looked up to see Sobel pounding with all his might upon the naked last. It broke, the iron striking the floor and jumping with a thump against the wall, but before the enraged shoemaker could cry out, the assistant had torn his hat and coat from the hook and rushed out into the snow.

So Feld, who had looked forward to anticipating how it would go with his daughter and Max, instead had a great worry on his mind. Without his temperamental helper he was a lost man, especially since it was years now that he had carried the store alone. The shoemaker had for an age suffered from a heart condition that threatened collapse if he dared exert himself. Five years ago, after an attack, it had appeared as though he would have either to sacrifice his business upon the auction block and live on a pittance thereafter, or put himself at the mercy of some unscrupulous employee who would in the end probably ruin him. But just at the moment of his darkest despair, this Polish refugee, Sobel, appeared one night from the street and begged for work. He was a stocky man, poorly dressed, with a bald head that had once been blond, a severely plain face and soft blue eyes prone to tears over the sad books he read, a young man but old—no one would have guessed thirty. Though he confessed he knew nothing of shoemaking, he said he was apt and would work for a very little if Feld taught him the trade. Thinking that with, after all, a landsman,[1] he would have less to fear than from a complete stranger, Feld took him on and within six weeks the refugee rebuilt as good a shoe as he, and not long thereafter expertly ran the business for the thoroughly relieved shoemaker.

Feld could trust him with anything and did, frequently going home after an hour or two at the store, leaving all the money in the till, knowing Sobel would guard every cent of it. The amazing thing was that he demanded so little. His wants were few; in money he wasn't interested—in nothing but books, it seemed—which he one by one lent to Miriam, together with his profuse, queer written comments, manufactured during his lonely rooming house evenings, thick pads of commentary which the shoemaker peered at and twitched his shoulders over as his daughter, from her fourteenth year, read page by sanctified page, as if the word of God were inscribed on them. To protect Sobel, Feld himself had to see that he received more than he asked for. Yet his conscience bothered him for not insisting that the assistant accept a better wage than he was getting, though Feld had honestly told him he could earn a handsome salary if he worked elsewhere,

or maybe opened a place of his own. But the assistant answered, somewhat ungraciously, that he was not interested in going elsewhere, and though Feld frequently asked himself what keeps him here? why does he stay? he finally answered it that the man, no doubt because of his terrible experiences as a refugee, was afraid of the world.

After the incident with the broken last, angered by Sobel's behavior, the shoemaker decided to let him stew for a week in the rooming house, although his own strength was taxed dangerously and the business suffered. However, after several sharp nagging warnings from both his wife and daughter, he went finally in search of Sobel, as he had once before, quite recently, when over some fancied slight—Feld had merely asked him not to give Miriam so many books to read because her eyes were strained and red—the assistant had left the place in a huff, an incident which, as usual, came to nothing for he had returned after the shoemaker had talked to him, and taken his seat at the bench. But this time, after Feld had plodded through the snow to Sobel's house—he had thought of sending Miriam but the idea became repugnant to him—the burly landlady at the door informed him in a nasal voice that Sobel was not at home, and though Feld knew this was a nasty lie, for where had the refugee to go? still for some reason he was not completely sure of—it may have been the cold and his fatigue—he decided not to insist on seeing him. Instead he went home and hired a new helper.

Having settled the matter, though not entirely to his satisfaction, for he had much more to do than before, and so, for example, could no longer lie late in bed mornings because he had to get up to open the store for the new assistant, a speechless, dark man with an irritating rasp as he worked, whom he would not trust with the key as he had Sobel. Furthermore, this one, though able to do a fair repair job, knew nothing of grades of leather or prices, so Feld had to make his own purchases; and every night at closing time it was necessary to count the money in the till and lock up. However, he was not dissatisfied, for he lived

---

1. *landsman,* a fellow countryman.

much in his thoughts of Max and Miriam. The college boy had called her, and they had arranged a meeting for this coming Friday night. The shoemaker would personally have preferred Saturday, which he felt would make it a date of the first magnitude, but he learned Friday was Miriam's choice, so he said nothing. The day of the week did not matter. What mattered was the aftermath. Would they like each other and want to be friends? He sighed at all the time that would have to go by before he knew for sure. Often he was tempted to talk to Miriam about the boy, to ask whether she thought she would like his type—he had told her only that he considered Max a nice boy and had suggested he call her— but the one time he tried she snapped at him— justly—how should she know?

At last Friday came. Feld was not feeling particularly well so he stayed in bed, and Mrs. Feld thought it better to remain in the bedroom with him when Max called. Miriam received the boy, and her parents could hear their voices, his throaty one, as they talked. Just before leaving, Miriam brought Max to the bedroom door and he stood there a minute, a tall, slightly hunched figure wearing a thick, droopy suit, and apparently at ease as he greeted the shoemaker and his wife, which was surely a good sign. And Miriam, although she had worked all day, looked fresh and pretty. She was a large-framed girl with a well-shaped body, and she had a fine open face and soft hair. They made, Feld thought, a first-class couple.

Miriam returned after 11:30. Her mother was already asleep, but the shoemaker got out of bed and after locating his bathrobe went into the kitchen, where Miriam, to his surprise, sat at the table, reading.

"So where did you go?" Feld asked pleasantly.

"For a walk," she said, not looking up.

"I advised him," Feld said, clearing his throat, "he shouldn't spend so much money."

"I didn't care."

The shoemaker boiled up some water for tea and sat down at the table with a cupful and a thick slice of lemon.

"So how," he sighed after a sip, "did you enjoy?"

"It was all right."

He was silent. She must have sensed his disappointment, for she added, "You can't really tell much the first time."

"You will see him again?"

Turning a page, she said that Max had asked for another date.

"For when?"

"Saturday."

"So what did you say?"

"What did I say?" she asked, delaying for a moment—"I said yes."

Afterwards she inquired about Sobel, and Feld, without exactly knowing why, said the assistant had got another job. Miriam said nothing more and began to read. The shoemaker's conscience did not trouble him; he was satisfied with the Saturday date.

During the week, by placing here and there a deft question, he managed to get from Miriam some information about Max. It surprised him to learn that the boy was not studying to be either a doctor or lawyer but was taking a business course leading to a degree in accountancy. Feld was a little disappointed because he thought of accountants as bookkeepers and would have preferred "a higher profession." However, it was not long before he had investigated the subject and discovered that Certified Public Accountants were highly respected people, so he was thoroughly content as Saturday approached. But because Saturday was a busy day, he was much in the store and therefore did not see Max when he came to call for Miriam. From his wife he learned there had been nothing especially revealing about their meeting. Max had rung the bell and Miriam had got her coat and left with him—nothing more. Feld did not probe, for his wife was not particularly observant. Instead, he waited up for Miriam with a newspaper on his lap, which he scarcely looked at so lost was he in thinking of the future. He awoke to find her in the room with him, tiredly removing her hat. Greeting her, he was suddenly inexplicably afraid to ask anything about the evening. But since she volunteered nothing he was at last forced to inquire how she had enjoyed herself. Miriam began something non-committal but apparently changed her mind, for she said after a minute, "I was bored."

When Feld had sufficiently recovered from

his anguished disappointment to ask why, she answered without hesitation, "Because he's nothing more than a materialist."

"What means this word?"

"He has no soul. He's only interested in things."

He considered her statement for a long time but then asked, "Will you see him again?"

"He didn't ask."

"Suppose he will ask you?"

"I won't see him."

He did not argue; however, as the days went by he hoped increasingly she would change her mind. He wished the boy would telephone, because he was sure there was more to him than Miriam, with her inexperienced eye, could discern. But Max didn't call. As a matter of fact he took a different route to school, no longer passing the shoemaker's store, and Feld was deeply hurt.

Then one afternoon Max came in and asked for his shoes. The shoemaker took them down from the shelf where he had placed them, apart from the other pairs. He had done the work himself and the soles and heels were well built and firm. The shoes had been highly polished and somehow looked better than new. Max's Adam's apple went up once when he saw them, and his eyes had little lights in them.

"How much?" he asked, without directly looking at the shoemaker.

"Like I told you before," Feld answered sadly. "One dollar fifty cents."

Max handed him two crumpled bills and received in return a newly-minted silver half dollar.

He left. Miriam had not been mentioned. That night the shoemaker discovered that his new assistant had been all the while stealing from him, and he suffered a heart attack.

Though the attack was very mild, he lay in bed for three weeks. Miriam spoke of going for Sobel, but sick as he was Feld rose in wrath against the idea. Yet in his heart he knew there was no other way, and the first weary day back in the shop thoroughly convinced him, so that night after supper he dragged himself to Sobel's rooming house.

He toiled up the stairs, though he knew it was bad for him, and at the top knocked at the door.

Sobel opened it and the shoemaker entered. The room was a small, poor one, with a single window facing the street. It contained a narrow cot, a low table and several stacks of books piled haphazardly around on the floor along the wall, which made him think how queer Sobel was, to be uneducated and read so much. He had once asked him, Sobel, why you read so much? and the assistant could not answer him. Did you ever study in a college someplace? he had asked, but Sobel shook his head. He read, he said, to know. But to know what, the shoemaker demanded, and to know, why? Sobel never explained, which proved he read much because he was queer.

Feld sat down to recover his breath. The assistant was resting on his bed with his heavy back to the wall. His shirt and trousers were clean, and his stubby fingers, away from the shoemaker's bench, were strangely pallid. His face was thin and pale, as if he had been shut in this room since the day he had bolted from the store.

"So when you will come back to work?" Feld asked him.

To his surprise, Sobel burst out, "Never."

Jumping up, he strode over to the window that looked out upon the miserable street. "Why should I come back?" he cried.

"I will raise your wages."

"Who cares for your wages!"

The shoemaker, knowing he didn't care, was at a loss what else to say.

"What do you want from me, Sobel?"

"Nothing."

"I always treated you like you was my son."

Sobel vehemently denied it. "So why you look for strange boys in the street they should go out with Miriam? Why you don't think of me?"

The shoemaker's hands and feet turned freezing cold. His voice became so hoarse he couldn't speak. At last he cleared his throat and croaked, "So what has my daughter got to do with a shoemaker thirty-five years old who works for me?"

"Why do you think I worked so long for you?" Sobel cried out. "For the stingy wages I sacrificed five years of my life so you could have to eat and drink and where to sleep?"

"Then for what?" shouted the shoemaker.

"For Miriam," he blurted—"for her."

The shoemaker, after a time, managed to say, "I pay wages in cash, Sobel," and lapsed into silence. Though he was seething with excitement, his mind was coldly clear, and he had to admit to himself he had sensed all along that Sobel felt this way. He had never so much as thought it consciously, but he had felt it and was afraid.

"Miriam knows?" he muttered hoarsely.

"She knows."

"You told her?"

"No."

"Then how does she know?"

"How does she know?" Sobel said, "because she knows. She knows who I am and what is in my heart."

Feld had a sudden insight. In some devious way, with his books and commentary, Sobel had given Miriam to understand that he loved her. The shoemaker felt a terrible anger at him for his deceit.

"Sobel, you are crazy," he said bitterly. "She will never marry a man so old and ugly like you."

Sobel turned black with rage. He cursed the shoemaker, but then, though he trembled to hold it in, his eyes filled with tears and he broke into deep sobs. With his back to Feld, he stood at the window, fists clenched, and his shoulders shook with his choked sobbing.

Watching him, the shoemaker's anger diminished. His teeth were on edge with pity for the man, and his eyes grew moist. How strange and sad that a refugee, a grown man, bald and old with his miseries, who had by the skin of his teeth escaped Hitler's incinerators,[2] should fall in love, when he had got to America, with a girl less than half his age. Day after day, for five years he had sat at his bench, cutting and hammering away, waiting for the girl to become a woman, unable to ease his heart with speech, knowing no protest but desperation.

"Ugly I didn't mean," he said half aloud.

Then he realized that what he had called ugly was not Sobel but Miriam's life if she married him. He felt for his daughter a strange and gripping sorrow, as if she were already Sobel's bride, the wife, after all, of a shoemaker, and had in her life no more than her mother had had. And all his dreams for her—why he had slaved and destroyed his heart with anxiety and labor—all these dreams of a better life were dead.

The room was quiet. Sobel was standing by the window reading, and it was curious that when he read he looked young.

"She is only nineteen," Feld said brokenly. "This is too young yet to get married. Don't ask her for two years more, till she is twenty-one, then you can talk to her."

Sobel didn't answer. Feld rose and left. He went slowly down the stairs but once outside, though it was an icy night and the crisp falling snow whitened the street, he walked with a stronger stride.

But the next morning, when the shoemaker arrived, heavy-hearted, to open the store, he saw he needn't have come, for his assistant was already seated at the last, pounding leather for his love. ☐ ☐

---

2. **Hitler's incinerators,** the ovens used by the Nazis for the mass-disposal of their victims' bodies.

Discussion

1. Of Feld, Sobel, Miriam, and Max, which do you feel is the central character—who most nearly comes to life? Whom can you most easily visualize?

2. Malamud's characters retain traces of Eastern European culture in some of their mannerisms, speech, and attitudes. Cite examples of their original cultural background.

3. The hope for success in the future that many immigrants to the United States wanted to attain is often called "the American Dream."
(a) How does each character seem to interpret this dream?
(b) Compare their aspirations.

BERNARD MALAMUD 55

4. What lesson about life does Feld learn from the events he seeks to control?

Extension • Reading

Malamud's title is an **allusion** to the Biblical story of Jacob, who worked two seven-year periods to earn the right to marry Rachel. Read the Biblical version (Genesis 29:13–31) and compare it with Malamud's. For instance, how do characters differ in role or personality from their Biblical counterparts? In what ways has Malamud adapted the Biblical plot to modern life? Note especially that Malamud's story deals with the *first* seven years. What might this imply about Feld's final agreement with Sobel?

Vocabulary •
Dictionary and Structure

Follow the directions about each italicized word below.

1. The narrator describes Sobel as "*grotesquely* thin" and says that the thought of sending Miriam to Sobel's apartment was "*repugnant*" to Feld.

(a) Which definition of each word fits the context given?

(b) Though similar in connotation, the words are not synonyms. Explain the difference in meaning between them.

2. After Feld has his heart attack, he is afraid he will be at the mercy of some "*unscrupulous* employee."

(a) What is the root word and its meaning?

(b) Using your knowledge of *un-* and *-ous*, what does *unscrupulous* mean?

3. Miriam does not like Max because she thinks he is a *materialist.*

(a) What is the root word and its meaning?

(b) Using your knowledge of *-ist*, what is a *materialist*?

(c) Using your knowledge of *-ism*, what is *materialism*?

4. Sobel "*vehemently*" denies that Feld always treated him as a son.

(a) What does *vehement* mean?

(b) Use the word in a sentence that shows you understand the definition.

Bernard Malamud 1914 •

Malamud rewrites painstakingly and has said, "I know it's finished when I can no longer stand working on it." In much of his fiction, he enters a world where life is hard and people must struggle for money, happiness, and dignity. Yet Malamud finds humor and a resilient love of life in his characters. This literature comes from the American ghetto of the era of great immigrations.

Malamud's fictional world can be further explored in *The Magic Barrel,* a volume of stories which includes "The First Seven Years." *The Assistant,* an acknowledged masterpiece, is also set in the old Jewish ghetto of New York and tells the story of a poor shopkeeper and his helper.

Born and raised in Brooklyn, Malamud is the son of Russian Jewish immigrants. He graduated from City College of New York and then in 1940, while earning his M.A. at Columbia University, began teaching evening English classes at his old high school. He has continued to teach while writing and is a professor of English at Bennington College, Vermont.

Willa Cather

The Sentimentality of William Tavener

It takes a strong woman to make any sort of success of living in the West, and Hester undoubtedly was that. When people spoke of William Tavener as the most prosperous farmer in McPherson County, they usually added that his wife was a "good manager." She was an executive woman, quick of tongue and something of an imperatrix.[1] The only reason her husband did not consult her about his business was that she did not wait to be consulted.

It would have been quite impossible for one man, within the limited sphere of human action, to follow all Hester's advice, but in the end William usually acted upon some of her suggestions. When she incessantly denounced the "shiftlessness" of letting a new threshing machine stand unprotected in the open, he eventually built a shed for it. When she sniffed contemptuously at his notion of fencing a hog corral with sod walls, he made a spiritless beginning on the structure—merely to "show his temper," as she put it—but in the end he went off quietly to town and bought enough barbed wire to complete the fence. When the first heavy rains came on, and the pigs rooted down the sod wall and made little paths all over it to facilitate their ascent, he heard his wife relate with relish the story of the little pig that built a mud house, to the minister at the dinner table, and William's gravity never relaxed for an instant. Silence, indeed, was William's refuge and his strength.

William set his boys a wholesome example to respect their mother. People who knew him very well suspected that he even admired her. He was a hard man towards his neighbors, and even towards his sons: grasping, determined and ambitious.

There was an occasional blue day about the house when William went over the store bills, but he never objected to items relating to his wife's gowns or bonnets. So it came about that many of the foolish, unnecessary little things that Hester bought for her boys, she had charged to her personal account.

One spring night Hester sat in a rocking chair by the sitting room window, darning socks. She rocked violently and sent her long needle vigorously back and forth over her gourd, and it took only a very casual glance to see that she was wrought up over something. William sat on the other side of the table reading his farm paper. If he had noticed his wife's agitation, his calm, clean-shaven face betrayed no sign of concern. He must have noticed the sarcastic turn of her remarks at the supper table, and he must have noticed the moody silence of the older boys as they ate. When supper was but half over little Billy, the youngest, had suddenly pushed back his plate and slipped away from the table, manfully trying to swallow a sob. But William Tavener never heeded ominous forecasts in the domestic horizon, and he never looked for a storm until it broke.

After supper the boys had gone to the pond under the willows in the big cattle corral, to get rid of the dust of plowing. Hester could hear an occasional splash and a laugh ringing clear through the stillness of the night, as she sat by the open window. She sat silent for almost an hour reviewing in her mind many plans of attack. But she was too vigorous a woman to be much of a strategist, and she usually came to her point with directness. At last she cut her thread and suddenly put her darning down, saying emphatically:

"William, I don't think it would hurt you to let the boys go to that circus in town tomorrow."

William continued to read his farm paper, but it was not Hester's custom to wait for an answer.

Reprinted from WILLA CATHER'S COLLECTED SHORT FICTION, 1892–1912, edited by Virginia Faulkner, by permission of University of Nebraska Press. Copyright © 1970 by the University of Nebraska Press.

1. *imperatrix* (im′pə rā′trix), an empress or a woman who rules.

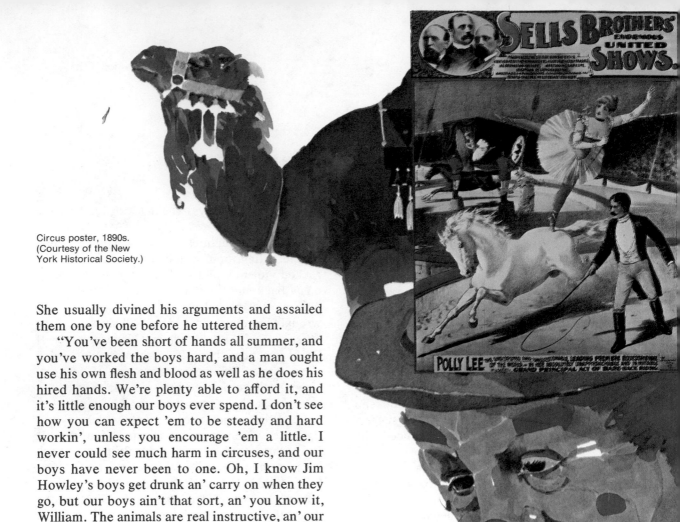

Circus poster, 1890s.
(Courtesy of the New
York Historical Society.)

She usually divined his arguments and assailed them one by one before he uttered them.

"You've been short of hands all summer, and you've worked the boys hard, and a man ought use his own flesh and blood as well as he does his hired hands. We're plenty able to afford it, and it's little enough our boys ever spend. I don't see how you can expect 'em to be steady and hard workin', unless you encourage 'em a little. I never could see much harm in circuses, and our boys have never been to one. Oh, I know Jim Howley's boys get drunk an' carry on when they go, but our boys ain't that sort, an' you know it, William. The animals are real instructive, an' our boys don't get to see much out here on the prairie. It was different where we were raised, but the boys have got no advantages here, an' if you don't take care, they'll grow up to be green-horns."

Hester paused a moment, and William folded up his paper, but vouchsafed no remark. His sisters in Virginia had often said that only a quiet man like William could ever have lived with Hester Perkins. Secretly, William was rather proud of his wife's "gift of speech," and of the fact that she could talk in prayer meeting as fluently as a man. He confined his own efforts in that line to a brief prayer at Covenant meetings.

Hester shook out another sock and went on.

"Nobody was ever hurt by goin' to a circus. Why, law me! I remember I went to one myself once, when I was little. I had most forgot about it. It was over at Pewtown, an' I remember how I had set my heart on going. I don't think I'd ever forgiven my father if he hadn't taken me, though that red clay road was in a frightful way after the rain. I mind they had an elephant and six poll parrots, an' a Rocky Mountain lion, an' a cage of monkeys, an' two camels. My! but they were a sight to me then!"

Hester dropped the black sock and shook her head and smiled at the recollection. She was not expecting anything from William yet, and she was fairly startled when he said gravely, in much the same tone in which he announced the hymns in prayer meeting:

"No, there was only one camel. The other was a dromedary."

She peered around the lamp and looked at him keenly.

"Why, William, how come you to know?"

William folded his paper and answered with some hesitation, "I was there, too."

Hester's interest flashed up. "Well, I never, William! To think of my finding it out after all these years! Why, you couldn't have been much bigger'n our Billy then. It seems queer I never saw you when you was little, to remember about you. But then you Back Creek folks never have anything to do with us Gap people. But how come you to go? Your father was stricter with you than you are with your boys."

"I reckon I shouldn't 'a gone," he said slowly, "but boys will do foolish things. I had done a good deal of fox hunting the winter before, and father let me keep the bounty money. I hired Tom Smith's Tap to weed the corn for me, an' I slipped off unbeknownst to father an' went to the show."

Hester spoke up warmly: "Nonsense, William! It didn't do you no harm, I guess. You was always worked hard enough. It must have been a big sight for a little fellow. That clown must have just tickled you to death."

William crossed his knees and leaned back in his chair.

"I reckon I could tell all that fool's jokes now. Sometimes I can't help thinkin' about 'em in meetin' when the sermon's long. I mind I had on a pair of new boots that hurt me like the mischief, but I forgot all about 'em when that fellow rode the donkey. I recall I had to take them boots off as soon as I got out of sight o' town, and walked home in the mud barefoot."

"O poor little fellow!" Hester ejaculated, drawing her chair nearer and leaning her elbows on the table. "What cruel shoes they did use to make for children. I remember I went up to Back Creek to see the circus wagons go by. They came down from Romney, you know. The circus men stopped at the creek to water the animals, an' the elephant got stubborn an' broke a big limb off the yellow willow tree that grew there by the toll house porch, an' the Scribners were 'fraid as death he'd pull the house down. But this much I saw him do; he waded in the creek an' filled his trunk with water and squirted it in at the window and nearly ruined Ellen Scribner's pink lawn dress that she had just ironed an' laid out on the bed ready to wear to the circus."

"I reckon that must have been a trial to Ellen," chuckled William, "for she was mighty prim in them days."

Hester drew her chair still nearer William's. Since the children had begun growing up, her conversation with her husband had been almost wholly confined to questions of economy and expense. Their relationship had become purely a business one, like that between landlord and tenant. In her desire to indulge her boys she had unconsciously assumed a defensive and almost hostile attitude towards her husband. No debtor ever haggled with his usurer more doggedly than did Hester with her husband in behalf of her sons. The strategic contest had gone on so long that it had almost crowded out the memory of a closer relationship. This exchange of confidences tonight, when common recollections took them unawares and opened their hearts, had all the miracle of romance. They talked on and on; of old neighbors, of old familiar faces in the valley where they had grown up, of long forgotten incidents of their youth—weddings, picnics, sleighing parties and baptizings. For years they had talked of nothing else but butter and eggs and the prices of things, and now they had as much to say to each other as people who meet after a long separation.

When the clock struck ten, William rose and went over to his walnut secretary and unlocked it. From his red leather wallet he took out a ten-dollar bill and laid it on the table beside Hester.

"Tell the boys not to stay late, an' not to drive the horses hard," he said quietly, and went off to bed.

Hester blew out the lamp and sat still in the dark a long time. She left the bill lying on the table where William had placed it. She had a painful sense of having missed something, or lost something; she felt that somehow the years had cheated her.

The little locust trees that grew by the fence were white with blossoms. Their heavy odor floated in to her on the night wind and recalled a night long ago, when the first whippoorwill of the spring was heard, and the rough, buxom girls of Hawkins Gap had held her laughing and struggling under the locust trees, and searched in her bosom for a lock of her sweetheart's hair, which is supposed to be on every girl's breast when the first whippoorwill sings. Two of those same girls had been her bridesmaids. Hester had been a very happy bride. She rose and went softly into the room where William lay. He was sleeping heavily, but occasionally moved his hand before his face to ward off the flies. Hester went into the parlor and took the piece of mosquito net from the basket of wax apples and pears that her sister had made before she died. One of the boys had brought it all the way from Virginia, packed in a tin pail, since Hester would not risk shipping so precious an ornament by freight. She went back to the bedroom and spread the net over William's head. Then she sat down by the bed and listened to his deep, regular breathing until she heard the boys returning. She went out to meet them and warn them not to waken their father.

"I'll be up early to get your breakfast, boys. Your father says you can go to the show." As she handed the money to the eldest, she felt a sudden throb of allegiance to her husband and said sharply, "And you be careful of that, an' don't waste it. Your father works hard for his money."

The boys looked at each other in astonishment and felt that they had lost a powerful ally. ▢ ▢

Discussion

1. (a) In what ways does Hester display the qualities of an "imperatrix"? **(b)** How do you think her husband would describe her?

2. William and Hester seem to be serious and stern. **(a)** What are some signs of their "softer" nature that appear early in the story? **(b)** When and how does William show his "sentimentality"?

3. (a) Why do Hester's feelings toward William change? **(b)** Name some clues to her new attitude. **(c)** In what ways will their sons be affected?

4. Considering their actions as well as their words, name qualities or goals that both Hester and William regard highly.

Extension
Writing and Speaking

The dialogue between William and Hester is very convincing because Cather has captured the rhythms and flavor of her characters' speech. Working in pairs or small groups, create a short conversation between two characters in which their contrasting speech patterns reflect their individual social background, level of education, regional dialect, and personality (for instance, a nervous person might speak very rapidly or in brief, incomplete sentences). Before writing any dialogue, you should clearly describe each character's background and personality. Then act out and revise your dialogue until it sounds convincing when finally performed.

Vocabulary • Dictionary

Look up the definitions of the two italicized words in the sentence below. Then use each in a sentence that shows you understand the meaning of the word.

"No debtor ever *haggled* with his *usurer* more doggedly than did Hester with her husband in behalf of her sons" (60a, 3).

Willa Cather 1873 • 1947

Some critics have characterized Cather's work as being aloof. Others regard the dignity of her writing as timeless. She herself said she reached her objective when she stopped trying to write and began to remember.

Though born in Virginia, Cather grew up on a ranch in rural Nebraska. Since there were no schools nearby, she was taught the English classics and Latin at home by her grandmothers. Her neighbors were pioneers, most of them foreign-born or second-generation Americans. It was these people and the Midwest landscape which would dominate much of her writing.

While studying at the University of Nebraska, Cather edited a literary magazine and wrote acidic play reviews for the Lincoln *State Journal*. In 1896, she moved to Pittsburgh. There, though busy as a journalist, Cather continued to create poetry and stories.

Her already-growing literary reputation was firmly established by *O Pioneers!* (1913) and *My Ántonia* (1918), novels which grew from her memories of Nebraska. *Death Comes for the Archbishop* (1927), which chronicles the spiritual pioneering of the Catholic Church in New Mexico, is considered her masterpiece.

William Saroyan

The Oyster and the Pearl

Characters

HARRY VAN DUSEN, *a barber*

CLAY LARRABEE, *a boy on Saturday*

VIVIAN MCCUTCHEON, *a new schoolteacher*

CLARK LARRABEE, CLAY'*s father*

MAN, *a writer*

ROXANNA LARRABEE, CLAY'*s sister*

GREELEY, CLAY'*s pal*

JUDGE APPLEGARTH, *a beachcomber*

WOZZECK, *a watch repairer*

ATTENDANT, *a man from the gasoline station*

Scene: HARRY VAN DUSEN'*s barbershop in O.K.-by-the-Sea, California, population 909. The sign on the window says:* Harry Van Dusen, Barber. *It's an old-fashioned shop, crowded with stuff not usually found in barbershops . . .* HARRY *himself, for instance. He has never been known to put on a barber's white jacket or to work without a hat of some sort on his head: a stovepipe, a derby, a western, a homburg, a skullcap, a beret, or a straw, as if putting on these various hats somewhat expressed the quality of his soul, or suggested the range of it.*

On the walls, on shelves, are many odds and ends, some apparently washed up by the sea, which is a block down the street: abalone and other shells, rocks, pieces of driftwood, a life jacket, rope, sea plants. There is one old-fashioned chair.

When the play begins, HARRY *is seated in the chair. A boy of nine or ten named* CLAY LARRABEE *is giving him a haircut.* HARRY *is reading a book, one of many in the shop.*

CLAY. Well, I did what you told me, Mr. Van Dusen. I hope it's all right. I'm no barber, though. *(He begins to comb the hair.)*

HARRY. You just gave me a haircut, didn't you?

CLAY. I don't know *what* you'd call it. You want to look at it in the mirror? *(He holds out a small mirror.)*

HARRY. No thanks. I remember the last one.

CLAY. I guess I'll never be a barber.

HARRY. Maybe not. On the other hand, you may turn out to be the one man hidden away in the junk of the world who will bring merriment to the tired old human heart.

CLAY. Who? Me?

HARRY. Why not?

CLAY. Merriment to the tired old human heart? How do you do that?

HARRY. Compose a symphony, paint a picture, write a book, invent a philosophy.

CLAY. Not me! Did you ever do stuff like that?

HARRY. I did.

CLAY. What did you do?

HARRY. Invented a philosophy.

CLAY. What's that?

HARRY. A way to live.

CLAY. What way did you invent?

HARRY. The *Take-it-easy way.*

CLAY. That sounds pretty good.

HARRY. All philosophies *sound* good. The trouble with mine was, I kept forgetting to take it easy. Until one day. The day I came off the highway into this barbershop. The barber told me the shop was for sale. I told him all I had to my name was eighty dollars. He sold me the shop for seventy-five, and threw in the haircut. I've been here ever since. That was twenty-four years ago.

CLAY. Before I was born.

HARRY. Fifteen or sixteen years before you were born.

CLAY. How old were you then?

HARRY. Old enough to know a good thing when I saw it.

CLAY. What did you see?

HARRY. O.K.-by-the-Sea, and this shop—the proper place for me to stop. That's a couplet. Shakespeare had them at the end of a scene, so I guess that's the end of this haircut. *(He gets*

Reprinted from PERSPECTIVES 4, Summer 1953, by permission of the author. Copyright 1953 by William Saroyan. This play was first presented on February 4, 1953, on the TV–Radio Workshop's television program, "Omnibus."

out of the chair, goes to the hat tree, and puts on a derby.)

CLAY. I guess I'd never get a haircut if you weren't in town, Mr. Van Dusen.

HARRY. Nobody would, since I'm the only barber.

CLAY. I mean, free of charge.

HARRY. I give you a haircut free of charge, you give me a haircut free of charge. That's fair and square.

CLAY. Yes, but you're a barber. You get a dollar a haircut.

HARRY. Now and then I do. Now and then I don't.

CLAY. Well, anyhow, thanks a lot. I guess I'll go down to the beach now and look for stuff.

HARRY. I'd go with you but I'm expecting a little Saturday business.

CLAY. This time I'm going to find something *real good,* I think.

HARRY. The sea washes up some pretty good things at that, doesn't it?

CLAY. It sure does, except money.

HARRY. What do you want with money?

CLAY. Things I need.

HARRY. What do you need?

CLAY. I want to get my father to come home again. I want to buy Mother a present. . .

HARRY. Now, wait a minute, Clay, let me get this straight. Where *is* your father?

CLAY. I don't know. He went off the day after I got my last haircut, about a month ago.

HARRY. What do you mean, he went off?

CLAY. He just picked up and went off.

HARRY. Did he say when he was coming back?

CLAY. No. All he said was, "Enough's enough." He wrote it on the kitchen wall.

HARRY. Enough's enough?

CLAY. Yeah. We all thought he'd be back in a day or two, but now we know we've got to *find* him and *bring* him back.

HARRY. How do you expect to do that?

CLAY. Well, we put an ad in the *The O.K.-by-the-Sea Gull* . . . that comes out every Saturday.

HARRY *(opening the paper).* This paper? But your father's not in town. How will he see an ad in this paper?

CLAY. He *might* see it. Anyhow, we don't know what else to do. We're living off the money we

saved from the summer we worked, but there ain't much left.

HARRY. The summer you worked?

CLAY. Yeah. Summer before last, just before we moved here, we picked cotton in Kern County. My father, my mother, and me.

HARRY *(indicating the paper).* What do you say in your ad?

CLAY *(looking at it).* Well, I say. . . Clark Larrabee. Come home. Your fishing tackle's in the closet safe and sound. The fishing's good, plenty of cabezon, perch, and bass. Let bygones be bygones. We miss you. Mama, Clay, Roxanna, Rufus, Clara.

HARRY. That's a good ad.

CLAY. Do you think if my father reads it, he'll come home?

HARRY. I don't know, Clay. I hope so.

CLAY. Yeah. Thanks a lot for the haircut, Mr. Van Dusen.

(CLAY goes out. HARRY takes off the derby, lathers his face, and begins to shave with a straightedge razor. A pretty girl in a swimming suit comes into the shop, closing a colorful parasol. She has long blond hair.)

HARRY. Miss America, I presume.

THE GIRL. Miss McCutcheon.

HARRY. Harry Van Dusen.

THE GIRL. How do you do.

HARRY *(bowing).* Miss McCutcheon.

THE GIRL. I'm new here.

HARRY. You'd be new anywhere—brand-new, I might say. Surely you don't live here?

THE GIRL. As a matter of fact, I do. At any rate, I've been here since last Sunday. You see, I'm the new teacher at the school.

HARRY. You are?

THE GIRL. Yes, I am.

HARRY. How do you like it?

THE GIRL. One week at this school has knocked me for a loop. As a matter of fact, I want to quit and go home to San Francisco. At the same time I have a feeling I ought to stay. What do you think?

HARRY. Are you serious? I mean, in asking me?

THE GIRL. Of course I'm serious. You've been here a long time. You know everybody in town. Shall I go, or shall I stay?

HARRY. Depends on what you're looking for. I stopped here twenty-four years ago because I decided I wasn't looking for anything any more. Well, I was mistaken. I *was* looking, and I've found exactly what I was looking for.

THE GIRL. What's that?

HARRY. A chance to take my time. That's why I'm still here. What are *you* looking for, Miss McCutcheon?

THE GIRL. Well. . .

HARRY. I mean, besides a husband. . .

THE GIRL. I'm not looking for a husband. I expect a husband to look for me.

HARRY. That's fair.

THE GIRL. I'm looking for a chance to teach.

HARRY. That's fair too.

THE GIRL. But this town! . . . The children just don't seem to care about anything—whether they get good grades or bad, whether they pass or fail, or anything else. On top of that, almost all of them are unruly. The only thing they seem to be interested in is games, and the sea. That's why I'm on my way to the beach now. I thought if I could watch them on a Saturday I might understand them better.

HARRY. Yes, that's a thought.

THE GIRL. Nobody seems to have any sensible ambition. It's all fun and play. How can I teach children like that? What can I teach them?

HARRY. English.

THE GIRL. Of course.

HARRY (drying his face). Singing, dancing, cooking. . .

THE GIRL. Cooking?. . . I must say I expected to see a much older man.

HARRY. Well! Thank you!

THE GIRL. Not at all.

HARRY. The question is, Shall you stay, or shall you go back to San Francisco?

THE GIRL. Yes.

HARRY. The answer is, Go back while the going's good.

THE GIRL. Why? I mean, a moment ago I believed you were going to point out why I ought to stay, and then suddenly you say I ought to go back. Why?

HARRY (after a pause). You're too good for a town like this.

THE GIRL. I am not!

HARRY. Too young and too intelligent. Youth and intelligence need excitement.

THE GIRL. There are *kinds* of excitement.

HARRY. Yes, there are. You need the big-city kind. There isn't an eligible bachelor in town.

THE GIRL. You seem to think all I want is to find a husband.

HARRY. But only to teach. You want to teach him to become a father, so you can have a lot of children of your own—to teach.

THE GIRL. (She sits almost angrily in the chair and speaks very softly.) I'd like a poodle haircut if you don't mind, Mr. Van Dusen.

HARRY. You'll have to get that in San Francisco, I'm afraid.

THE GIRL. Why? Aren't you a barber?

HARRY. I am.

THE GIRL. Well, this is your shop. It's open for business. I'm a customer. I've got money. I want a poodle haircut.

HARRY. I don't know how to give a poodle haircut, but even if I knew how, I wouldn't do it.

THE GIRL. Why not?

HARRY. I don't give women haircuts. The only women who visit this shop bring their small children for haircuts.

THE GIRL. I want a poodle haircut, Mr. Van Dusen.

HARRY. I'm sorry, Miss McCutcheon. In my sleep, in a nightmare, I would *not* cut your hair.

(The sound of a truck stopping is heard from across the street.)

THE GIRL (softly, patiently, but firmly). Mr. Van Dusen, I've decided to stay, and the first thing I've got to do is change my appearance. I don't fit into the scenery around here.

HARRY. Oh, I don't know—if I were a small boy going to school, I'd say you look just right.

THE GIRL. You're just like the children. They don't take me seriously, either. They think I'm nothing more than a pretty girl who is going to give up in despair and go home. If you give me a poodle haircut I'll look more—well, plain and simple. I plan to dress differently, too. I'm determined to teach here. You've got to help me. Now, Mr. Van Dusen, the shears, please.

HARRY. I'm sorry, Miss McCutcheon. There's no need to change your *appearance* at all.

(CLARK LARRABEE comes into the shop.)

HARRY. You're next, Clark. (HARRY helps MISS McCUTCHEON out of the chair. She gives him an angry glance.)

THE GIRL *(whispering).* I won't forget this rudeness, Mr. Van Dusen.

HARRY *(also whispering).* Never whisper in O.K.-by-the-Sea. People misunderstand. *(Loudly.)* Good day, Miss.

(MISS MCCUTCHEON opens her parasol with anger and leaves the shop. CLARK LARRABEE has scarcely noticed her. He stands looking at HARRY's junk on the shelves.)

HARRY. Well, Clark, I haven't seen you in a long time.

CLARK. I'm just passing through, Harry. Thought I might run into Clay here.

HARRY. He was here a little while ago.

CLARK. How is he?

HARRY. He's fine, Clark.

CLARK. I been working in Salinas. Got a ride down in a truck. It's across the street now at the gasoline station.

HARRY. You've been home, of course?

CLARK. No, I haven't.

HARRY. Oh?

CLARK *(after a slight pause).* I've left Fay, Harry.

HARRY. You got time for a haircut, Clark?

CLARK. No thanks, Harry. I've got to go back to Salinas on that truck across the street.

HARRY. Clay's somewhere on the beach.

CLARK *(handing HARRY three ten-dollar bills).* Give him this, will you? Thirty dollars. Don't tell him I gave it to you.

HARRY. Why not?

CLARK. I'd rather he didn't know I was around. Is he all right?

HARRY. Sure, Clark. They're *all* O.K. I mean. . .

CLARK. Tell him to take the money home to his mother. *(He picks up the newspaper, The Gull.)*

HARRY. Sure, Clark. It came out this morning. Take it along.

CLARK. Thanks. *(He puts the paper in his pocket.)* How've things been going with *you,* Harry?

HARRY. Oh, I can't kick. Two or three haircuts a day. A lot of time to read. A few laughs. A few surprises. The sea. The fishing. It's a good life.

CLARK. Keep an eye on Clay, will you? I mean—well, I *had* to do it.

HARRY. Sure.

CLARK. Yeah, well. . . That's the first money I've been able to save. When I make some more, I'd like to send it here, so you can hand it to Clay, to take home.

HARRY. Anything you say, Clark.

(There is the sound of the truck's horn blowing.)

CLARK. Well. . . *(He goes to the door.)* Thanks, Harry, thanks a lot.

HARRY. Good seeing you, Clark.

(CLARK LARRABEE goes out. HARRY watches him. A truck shifting gears is heard, and then the sound of the truck driving off. HARRY picks up a book, changes hats, sits down in the chair and begins to read. A MAN of forty or so, well dressed, rather swift, comes in.)

THE MAN. Where's the barber?

HARRY. I'm the barber.

THE MAN. Can I get a haircut, real quick?

HARRY *(getting out of the chair).* Depends on what you mean by real quick.

THE MAN *(sitting down).* Well, just a haircut, then.

HARRY *(putting an apron around the MAN).* O.K. I don't believe I've seen you before.

THE MAN. No. They're changing the oil in my car across the street. Thought I'd step in here and get a haircut. Get it out of the way before I get to Hollywood. How many miles is it?

HARRY. About two hundred straight down the highway. You can't miss it.

THE MAN. What town is *this?*

HARRY. O.K.-by-the-Sea.

THE MAN. What do the people do here?

HARRY. Well, I cut hair. Friend of mine named Wozzeck repairs watches, radios, alarm clocks, and sells jewelry.

THE MAN. Who does he sell it to?

HARRY. The people here. It's imitation stuff mainly.

THE MAN. Factory here? Farms? Fishing?

HARRY. No. Just the few stores on the highway, the houses further back in the hills, the church, and the school. You a salesman?

THE MAN. No, I'm a writer.

HARRY. What do you write?

THE MAN. A little bit of everything. How about the haircut?

HARRY. You got to be in Hollywood tonight?

THE MAN. I don't have to be anywhere tonight, but that was the idea. Why?

HARRY. Well, I've always said a writer could step into a place like this, watch things a little while, and get a whole book out of it, or a play.

THE MAN. Or if he was a poet, a sonnet.

HARRY. Do you like Shakespeare's?

THE MAN. They're just about the best in English.

HARRY. It's not often I get a writer in here. As a matter of fact you're the only writer I've had in here in twenty years, not counting Fenton.

THE MAN. Who's he?

HARRY. Fenton Lockhart.

THE MAN. What's he write?

HARRY. He gets out the weekly paper. Writes the whole thing himself.

THE MAN. Yeah. Well. . . How about the haircut?

HARRY. O.K.

(HARRY *puts a hot towel around the man's head.* MISS MCCUTCHEON, *carrying a cane chair without one leg and without a seat, comes in. With her is* CLAY *with something in his hand, a smaller boy named* GREELEY *with a bottle of sea water, and* ROXANNA *with an assortment of shells.*)

CLAY. I got an oyster here, Mr. Van Dusen.

GREELEY. Miss McCutcheon claims there *ain't* a big pearl in it.

HARRY (*looking at* MISS MCCUTCHEON). Is she willing to admit there's a *little* one in it?

GREELEY. I don't know. I know I got sea water in this bottle.

MISS McCUTCHEON. Mr. Van Dusen, Clay Larrabee seems to believe there's a pearl in this oyster he happens to have found on the beach.

CLAY. I didn't *happen* to find it. I went looking for it. You know Black Rock, Mr. Van Dusen? Well, the tide hardly ever gets low enough for a fellow to get around to the ocean side of Black Rock, but a little while ago it did, so I went around there to that side. I got to poking around and I found this oyster.

HARRY. I've been here twenty-four years, Clay, and this is the first time I've ever heard of anybody finding an oyster on our beach—at Black Rock, or anywhere else.

CLAY. Well, *I* did, Mr. Van Dusen. It's shut tight, it's alive, and there's a pearl in it, worth at least three hundred dollars.

GREELEY. A *big* pearl.

MISS McCUTCHEON. Now, you children listen to me. It's never too soon for any of us to face the truth, which is supposed to set us free, not imprison us. The truth is, Clay, you want money because you need money. The truth is also that you have found an oyster. The truth is also that there is no pearl in the oyster.

GREELEY. How do you know? Did you look?

MISS McCUTCHEON. No, but neither did Clay, and inasmuch as only one oyster in a million has a pearl in it, truth favors the probability that this is not the millionth oyster. . . the oyster with the pearl in it.

CLAY. There's a *big* pearl in the oyster.

MISS McCUTCHEON. Mr. Van Dusen, shall we open the oyster and show Clay and his sister Roxanna and their friend Greeley that there is no pearl in it?

HARRY. In a moment, Miss McCutcheon. And what's that *you* have?

MISS McCUTCHEON. A chair, as you see.

HARRY. How many legs does it have?

MISS McCUTCHEON. Three of course. I can count to three, I hope.

HARRY. What do you want with a chair with only three legs?

MISS McCUTCHEON. I'm going to bring things from the sea the same as everybody else in town.

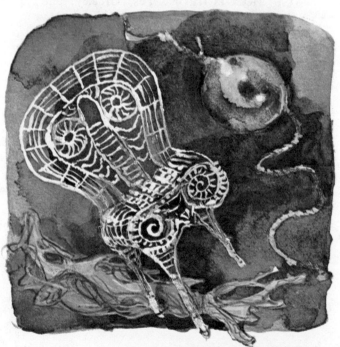

HARRY. But everybody else in town *doesn't* bring things from the sea—just the children, Judge Applegarth, Fenton Lockhart, and myself.

MISS McCUTCHEON. In any case, the same as the children, Judge Applegarth, Fenton Lockhart, and you. Judge Applegarth? Who's he?

HARRY. He judged swine at a county fair one time, so we call him judge.

MISS McCUTCHEON. Pigs?

HARRY. Swine's a little old-fashioned but I prefer it to pigs, and since both words mean the same thing——Well, I wouldn't care to call a man like Arthur Applegarth a pig judge.

MISS McCUTCHEON. Did he actually judge swine, as you prefer to put it, at a county fair, one time? Did he even do *that*?

HARRY. Nobody checked up. He *said* he did.

MISS McCUTCHEON. So that entitled him to be called Judge Applegarth?

HARRY. It certainly did.

MISS McCUTCHEON. On that basis, Clay's oyster has a big pearl in it because he *says* so, is that it?

HARRY. I didn't say that.

MISS McCUTCHEON. Are we living in the Middle Ages, Mr. Van Dusen?

GREELEY. No, this is 1953, Miss McCutcheon.

MISS McCUTCHEON. Yes, Greeley, and to illustrate what I mean, that's water you have in that bottle. Nothing else.

GREELEY. *Sea* water.

MISS McCUTCHEON. Yes, but there's nothing else in the bottle.

GREELEY. No, but there's little things in the water. You can't see them now, but they'll show up later. The water of the sea is full of things.

MISS McCUTCHEON. Salt, perhaps.

GREELEY. No. *Living* things. If I look hard I can see some of them now.

MISS McCUTCHEON. You can *imagine* seeing them. Mr. Van Dusen, are you going to help me or not?

HARRY. What do you want me to do?

MISS McCUTCHEON. Open the oyster of course, so Clay will see for himself that there's no pearl in it. So he'll begin to face reality, as he should, as each of us should.

HARRY. Clay, do you mind if I look at the oyster a minute?

CLAY (*handing the oyster to* HARRY). There's a big pearl in it, Mr. Van Dusen.

HARRY (*examining the oyster*). Clay . . . Roxanna . . . Greeley . . . I wonder if you'd go down the street to Wozzeck's. Tell him to come here the first chance he gets. I'd rather he opened this oyster. I might damage the pearl.

CLAY, GREELEY, *and* ROXANNA. O.K., Mr. Van Dusen.

(*They go out.*)

MISS McCUTCHEON. What pearl? What in the world do you think you're trying to do to the minds of these children? How am I ever going to teach them the principles of truth with an influence like yours to fight against?

HARRY. Miss McCutcheon. The people of O.K.-by-the-Sea are all poor. Most of them can't afford to pay for the haircuts I give them. There's no excuse for this town at all, but the sea is here, and so are the hills. A few people find jobs a couple of months every year North or South, come back half dead of homesickness, and live on next to nothing the rest of the year. A few get pensions. Every family has a garden and a few chickens, and they make a few dollars selling vegetables and eggs. In a town of almost a thousand people there isn't one rich man. Not even one who is well-off. And yet these people are the richest I have ever known. Clay doesn't really want money, as you seem to think. He wants his father to come home, and he thinks money will help get his father home. As a matter of fact his father is the man who stepped in here just as you were leaving. He left thirty dollars for me to give to Clay, to take home. His father and his mother haven't been getting along. Clark Larrabee's a fine man. He's not the town drunk or anything like that but having four kids to provide for he gets to feeling ashamed of the showing he's making, and he starts drinking. He wants his kids to live in a good house of their own, wear good clothes, and all the other things fathers have always wanted for their kids. His wife wants these things for the kids, too. They don't have these things, so they fight. They had one too many fights about a month ago, so Clark went off—he's working in

Salinas. He's either going to keep moving away from his family, or he's going to come back. It all depends on—well, I don't know what. This oyster maybe. Clay maybe. (*Softly.*) You and me maybe.

(*There is a pause. He looks at the oyster.* MISS MCCUTCHEON *looks at it, too.*)

HARRY. Clay believes there's a pearl in this oyster for the same reason you and I believe whatever *we* believe to keep *us* going.

MISS McCUTCHEON. Are you suggesting we play a trick on Clay, in order to carry out your mumbo-jumbo ideas?

HARRY. Well, maybe it *is* a trick. I know Wozzeck's got a few pretty good-sized culti-vated pearls.

MISS McCUTCHEON. You plan to have Woz-zeck pretend he has found a pearl in the oyster when he opens it, is that it?

HARRY. I plan to get three hundred dollars to Clay.

MISS McCUTCHEON. Do you *have* three hun-dred dollars?

HARRY. Not quite.

MISS McCUTCHEON. What about the other children who need money? Do you plan to put pearls in oysters for them, too? Not just here in O.K.-by-the-Sea. Everywhere. This isn't the only town in the world where people are poor, where fathers and mothers fight, where fami-lies break up.

HARRY. No, it isn't, but it's the only town where I live.

MISS McCUTCHEON. I give up. What do you want me to do?

HARRY. Well, could you find it in your heart to

be just a little less sure about things when you talk to the kids—I mean, the troubled ones? You can get Clay around to the truth easy enough just as soon as he gets his father home.

(ARTHUR APPLEGARTH *comes in.*)

HARRY. Judge Applegarth, may I present Miss McCutcheon?

THE JUDGE (*removing his hat and bowing low*). An honor, Miss.

MISS McCUTCHEON. How do you do, Judge.

HARRY. Miss McCutcheon's the new teacher at the school.

THE JUDGE. We are honored to have you. The children, the parents, and—the rest of us.

MISS McCUTCHEON. Thank you, Judge. (*To* HARRY, *whispering.*) I'll be back as soon as I change my clothes.

HARRY (*whispering*). I told you not to whisper.

MISS McCUTCHEON (*whispering*). I shall ex-pect you to give me a poodle haircut.

HARRY (*whispering*). Are you out of your mind?

MISS McCUTCHEON (*aloud*). Good day, Judge.

THE JUDGE (*bowing*). Good day, Miss.

(*While he is bent over he takes a good look at her knees, calves, ankles, and bow-tied sandals.*)

(MISS McCUTCHEON *goes out.* JUDGE APPLE-GARTH *looks from the door to* HARRY.)

THE JUDGE. She won't last a month.

HARRY. Why not?

THE JUDGE. Too pretty. Our school needs an old battle-ax, like the teachers we had when we went to school, not a bathing beauty. Well, Harry, what's new?

HARRY. Just the teacher, I guess.

THE JUDGE. You know, Harry, the beach isn't what it used to be—not at all. I don't mind the competition we're getting from the kids. It's just that the quality of the stuff the sea's wash-ing up isn't good any more. (*Goes to door.*)

HARRY. I don't know. Clay Larrabee found an oyster this morning.

THE JUDGE. He did? Well, one oyster don't make a stew, Harry. On my way home I'll drop in and let you see what I find.

HARRY. O.K., Judge.

(*The* JUDGE *goes out.* HARRY *comes to life sud-denly and becomes businesslike.*)

HARRY. Now, for the haircut! (*He removes the towel he had wrapped around the* WRITER'*s head.*)

THE WRITER. Take your time.

HARRY (*He examines the shears, clippers, and combs.*) Let's see now.

(*The* WRITER *turns and watches. A gasoline station* ATTENDANT *comes to the door.*)

THE ATTENDANT (*to the* WRITER). Just wanted to say your car's ready now.

THE WRITER. Thanks.

(*The* ATTENDANT *goes out.*)

THE WRITER. Look. I'll tell you what. How much is a haircut?

HARRY. Well, the regular price is a dollar. It's too much for a haircut, though, so I generally take a half or a quarter.

THE WRITER (*getting out of the chair*). I've changed my mind. I don't want a haircut after all, but here's a dollar just the same.

(*He hands* HARRY *a dollar, and he himself removes the apron.*)

HARRY. It won't take a minute.

THE WRITER. I know.

HARRY. You don't have to pay me a dollar for a hot towel. My compliments.

THE WRITER. That's O.K. (*He goes to the door.*)

HARRY. Well, take it easy now.

THE WRITER. Thanks. (*He stands a moment, thinking, then turns.*) Do you mind if I have a look at that oyster?

HARRY. Not at all.

(*The* WRITER *goes to the shelf where* HARRY *has placed the oyster, picks it up, looks at it thoughtfully, puts it back without comment, but instead of leaving the shop he looks around at the stuff in it. He then sits down on a wicker chair in the corner, and lights a cigarette.*)

THE WRITER. You know, they've got a gadget in New York now like a safety razor that anybody can give anybody else a haircut with.

HARRY. They have?

THE WRITER. Yeah, there was a full-page ad about it in last Sunday's *Times*.

HARRY. Is that where you were last Sunday?

THE WRITER. Yeah.

HARRY. You been doing a lot of driving.

THE WRITER. I like to drive. I don't know, though—those gadgets don't always work. They're asking two-ninety-five for it. You take a big family. The father could save a lot of money giving his kids a haircut.

HARRY. Sounds like a great idea.

THE WRITER. Question of effectiveness. If the father gives the boy a haircut the boy's ashamed of, well, that's not so good.

HARRY. No, a boy likes to get a professional-looking haircut all right.

THE WRITER. I thought I'd buy one, but I don't know.

HARRY. You got a big family?

THE WRITER. I mean for myself. But I don't know—there's something to be said for going to a barbershop once in a while. No use putting the barbers out of business.

HARRY. Sounds like a pretty good article, though.

THE WRITER (*getting up lazily*). Well, it's been nice talking to you.

(WOZZECK, *carrying a satchel, comes in, followed by* CLAY, ROXANNA, *and* GREELEY.)

WOZZECK. What's this all about, Harry?

HARRY. I've got an oyster I want you to open.

WOZZECK. That's what the kids have been telling me.

ROXANNA. *He* doesn't believe there's a pearl in the oyster, either.

WOZZECK. Of course not! What foolishness!

CLAY. There's a *big* pearl in it.

WOZZECK. O.K., give me the oyster. I'll open it. Expert watch repairer, to open an oyster!

HARRY. How much is a big pearl worth, Louie?

WOZZECK. Oh, a hundred. Two hundred, maybe.

HARRY. A very big one?

WOZZECK. Three, maybe.

THE WRITER. I've looked at that oyster, and I'd like to buy it. (*To* CLAY.) How much do you want for it?

CLAY. I don't know.

THE WRITER. How about three hundred?

GREELEY. Three hundred dollars?

CLAY. Is it all right, Mr. Van Dusen?

HARRY. (*He looks at the* WRITER, *who nods.*) Sure it's all right.

(*The* WRITER *hands* CLAY *the money.*)

CLAY (*looking at the money and then at the* WRITER). But suppose there ain't a pearl in it?

THE WRITER. There *is,* though.

WOZZECK. Don't you want to open it first?

THE WRITER. No, I want the whole thing. I don't think the pearl's stopped growing.

CLAY. He says there *is* a pearl in the oyster, Mr. Van Dusen.

HARRY. I think there is, too, Clay; so why don't you just go on home and give the money to your mother?

CLAY. Well . . . I *knew* I was going to find something good today!

(*The children go out.* WOZZECK *is bewildered.*)

WOZZECK. Three hundred dollars! How do you know there's a pearl in it?

THE WRITER. As far as I'm concerned, the whole thing's a pearl.

WOZZECK (*a little confused*). Well, I got to get back to the shop, Harry.

HARRY. Thanks for coming by.

(WOZZECK *goes out. The* WRITER *holds the oyster in front of him as if it were an egg, and looks at it carefully, turning it in his fingers. As he is doing so,* CLARK LARRABEE *comes into the shop. He is holding the copy of the newspaper that* HARRY *gave him.*)

CLARK. We were ten miles up the highway when I happened to see this classified ad in the paper. (*He hands the paper to* HARRY *and sits down in the chair.*) I'm going out to the house, after all. Just for the weekend of course, then back to work in Salinas again. Two or three months, I think I'll have enough to come back for a long time. Clay come by?

HARRY. No. I've got the money here.

CLARK. O.K., I'll take it out myself, but first let me have the works—shave, haircut, shampoo, massage.

HARRY (*putting an apron on* CLARK). Sure thing, Clark. (*He bends the chair back, and begins to lather* CLARK*'s face.*)

(MISS MCCUTCHEON, *dressed neatly, looking like another person almost, comes in.*)

MISS McCUTCHEON. Well?

HARRY. You look fine, Miss McCutcheon.

MISS McCUTCHEON. I don't mean that. I mean the oyster.

HARRY. Oh, that! There *was* a pearl in it.

MISS McCUTCHEON. I don't believe it.

HARRY. A *big* pearl.

MISS McCUTCHEON. You might have done me the courtesy of waiting until I had come back before opening it.

HARRY. Couldn't wait.

MISS McCUTCHEON. Well, I don't believe you, but I've come for my haircut. I'll sit down and wait my turn.

HARRY. Mr. Larrabee wants the works. You'll have to wait a long time.

MISS McCUTCHEON. Mr. Larrabee? Clay's father? Roxanna's father?

(CLARK *sits up.*)

HARRY. Clark, I'd like you to meet our new teacher, Miss McCutcheon.

CLARK. How do you do.

MISS McCUTCHEON. How do you do, Mr. Larrabee. (*She looks bewildered.*) Well, perhaps some other time, then, Mr. Van Dusen.

(*She goes out.* CLARK *sits back.* JUDGE APPLEGARTH *stops at the doorway of the shop.*)

THE JUDGE. Not one thing on the beach, Harry. Not a blessed thing worth picking up and taking home.

(JUDGE APPLEGARTH *goes on. The* WRITER *looks at* HARRY.)

HARRY. See what I mean?

THE WRITER. Yeah. Well . . . so long. (*He puts the oyster in his coat pocket.*)

HARRY. Drop in again any time you're driving to Hollywood.

THE WRITER. Or away.

(*He goes out.*)

CLARK (*after a moment*). You know, Harry, that boy of mine, Clay . . . well, a fellow like that, you can't just go off and leave him.

HARRY. Of course you can't, Clark.

CLARK. I'm taking him fishing tomorrow morning. How about going along, Harry?

HARRY. Sure, Clark. Be like old times again. (*There is a pause.*)

CLARK. What's all this about an oyster and a pearl?

HARRY. Oh, just having a little fun with the new teacher. You know, she came in here and asked me to give her a poodle haircut? A poodle haircut! I don't believe I remember what a poodle *dog* looks like, even.

The End

Discussion

1. In the opening scene Harry Van Dusen tells Clay that he "may turn out to be the one man hidden away in the junk of the world who will bring merriment to the tired old human heart." Explain how this description characterizes Van Dusen himself.

2. (a) Contrast Miss McCutcheon's and Mr. Van Dusen's attitudes toward life, pointing out specific speeches which express their philosophies. **(b)** How does the oyster bring these two philosophies into focus?

3. Miss McCutcheon complains that Harry Van Dusen doesn't take her seriously. **(a)** What remarks of his lead her to think this? **(b)** Is she a serious or a frivolous person? Explain. **(c)** What characters arc **stereotypes** in this play? Explain. **(d)** Is there ever a valid reason for stereotyping? Discuss.

4. (a) What do you think the writer means when he says of the oyster, "As far as I'm concerned, the whole thing's a pearl"? **(b)** Why do you suppose Saroyan never reveals whether or not there is a pearl in the oyster?

Extension • Writing

Suppose Saroyan had elected to have the pearl opened. Rewrite the final scene.

notes and comments

From the Author

But what we really want to know is how I happened to write the play: well, you must surely know there is no real answer. . . . A writer writes, period. The rest is mystery. . . . Among your students may be one or two who are writers: they will write. And you may report to them if you like that I don't even know grammar, since it is the truth. . . .

I happened to write the play because I had a program of writing short plays at that time. It happened to be about a small town by the sea because that's where I was living. I frequently saw kids on the beach excited about stuff they had found, and that may have given me the idea of a kid finding an oyster. . . . I once found an oyster myself, and that may have figured in the play, for any oyster can mean the *hope* of a pearl, since pearls come only from oysters. The barber shop in the play is there because I like barber shops, and barbers, and they figure in quite a few of my stories. The barber is a kind of poet, and frequently slightly eccentric, certainly free and independent when he owns and operates his own shop. The rest is the consequence of the way I write in any case: the consequence of myself.

The play took its own course, pretty much as all of my writing does: . . . a small boy, an oyster, a barber, and soon a little of the whole world and all of the human race is involved in the thing, somehow. I never knew while I was writing precisely how the play was going to develop and how it was going to end. . . .

I do not think it is astonishing that a writer writes. That's his work. The astonishing thing is that he doesn't write better, most likely. . . . It's a good trade, in some ways almost as good as being a barber.

Saroyan (1908–1981) won fame for his short stories, novels, and plays. The Time of Your Life *earned him a Pulitzer Prize for drama in 1940. Born in Fresno, California, he left school at thirteen and worked in many jobs. These experiences, his ceaseless reading, and his recollections of Fresno's Armenian community lie behind his many works. (See Michael Arlen's description of his encounter with Saroyan, on page 561.)*

Tomás Rivera

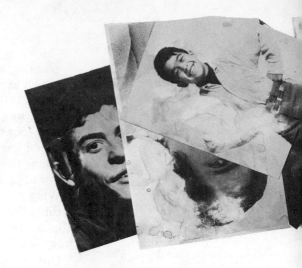

The Portrait

The portrait salesmen were just waiting for the people to return from up north before coming from San Antonio.[1] They came down to water. They knew that the people had money, and that was the reason why, as Father used to say, they came down in droves. Their suitcases were full of samples. They always wore white shirts and ties, that way they looked more important and the people believed everything they said and welcomed them into their homes without a second thought. I think that secretly they wished that their children would someday grow up to be like that. Anyway, they came and walked along the dusty streets loaded down with their suitcases full of samples.

I remember once I was at the house of one of my father's friends when one of these salesmen arrived. I also remember that that particular one seemed a little frightened and timid. Don Mateo[2] asked him to come in because he wanted to do business.

"Good afternoon, sir; look, I would like to explain something new that we have this year."

"Let's see, let's see."

"Well, look, give us a picture, any picture you have, and we will not only enlarge it, but also frame it in wood, with wood inlays, one might say three-dimensional."

"Yes, but what's the reason for that?"

"So he'll look as though he were alive. Like this, look. Let me show you this one. What do you think? Doesn't he look lifelike, as though he were alive?"

"Yes, you're right. Look, *vieja*.[3] This one looks great. You know, we wanted to enlarge some pictures. But that must cost a lot, right?"

"Not at all; you know, it costs about the same. Of course it takes more time."

"Well, alright, let's see. How much does it cost?"

"For just thirty dollars we'll have it inlaid for you. One this size."

"Damn, it's expensive. Didn't you say it didn't cost too much more? Can one take it on payments?"

"You know, we have another manager and he wants everything in cash. The thing is that it's excellent workmanship. We'll make him look like real. Inlaid, like this. Look, what do you think? Beautiful job, isn't it? We'll bring it back to you all finished within a month. You just tell us the color of his clothes, and we'll be back with it before you know it, all finished, frame and all. You wouldn't believe it, but not much more than a month. But, as I told you, this man who is the manager now wants cash. He's very demanding, even with us."

"But it's much too expensive."

"Well, yes. But it's excellent work. Don't tell me you've seen pictures inlaid with wood before?"

"No. You're right. What do you say, *vieja?*"

"Well, I like it very much. Why don't we have one made? And if it turns out all right . . .

Tomás Rivera (tô mäs′ rē ve′rä).
From Y NO SE LO TRAGO LA TIERRA/AND THE EARTH DID NOT PART, published by Quinto Sol Publications, Inc., 1971. Copyright © 1971 by Tomás Rivera. Reprinted by permission of the author.
1. *San Antonio* (sän än tô′nē ô), a city in southern Texas.
2. *Don Mateo* (dôn mä te′ô). *Don* is a term of respect for a man. [*Spanish*]
3. *vieja* (vē e′hä), "old woman," a term of endearment for a wife. [*Spanish*]

Chuy's[4] picture. May his soul rest in peace. It's the only one we have of him. We took it before he went to Korea. My poor son; we never saw him again. Look, here is his picture. Do you think you can have it inlaid to make him look lifelike?"

"And why not? You know, we've made many dressed in soldier's uniform. Inlaid they're more than pictures. Yes, why not? You just tell me what size you want it, and if you want a square or a round frame. What do you say? How shall I write it up?"

"What do you say, *vieja?* Shall we have it made like this?"

"I told you what I want. I'd like to have my son's picture inlaid like this and in color."

"Alright, write it down. But take good care of the picture for us because it's the only one we have of our son grown up. He promised to send us one all dressed up as a soldier, with the American and Mexican flags crossed above his head. But as soon as he arrived over there we received a letter telling us that he was missing in action. So take good care of it."

"Don't worry. We're responsible people. We know very well what a sacrifice it is for everyone. Don't worry. You'll see how pretty it'll look when we bring it back. What do you say, shall we give him a navy blue suit?"

"But he's not wearing a uniform in the picture."

"Yes, however, it's just a matter of fixing it up with a little wood. Look at this one. He didn't have a uniform, but we gave him one. So, what do you say? Shall we give him a navy blue uniform?"

"Alright."

"And don't worry about the picture."

All that day the portrait salesmen traveled from one street to another filling their suitcases with pictures. At the end, a great number of people had ordered that kind of enlargement.

"It's about time to get our portraits, don't you think?"

"I think so, but the workmanship is excellent. That takes longer. Those people do excellent work. Did you notice how lifelike the pictures were?"

"Yes, you're right. They do excellent work. No one can deny that. But remember, it's been more than a month since they came through here."

"Yes, but they were picking up pictures all day along the little towns from here to San Antonio, that's for sure. So they probably took a little longer."

"That's right, that's right."

Two more weeks went by before the whole matter became clear, when some very heavy rains came down and some children who were playing in one of the tunnels that led to the dump found a sack full of wet, dissolving pictures. What identified them as pictures was the fact that there were many of them, all the same size, and the faces could almost be made out. Everyone understood immediately. Don Mateo became so angry that he left for San Antonio in search of the man who had tricked them.

"Well, you know, I stayed at Esteban's[5]

---

4. *Chuy* (chü/ē), nickname for Don Mateo's son.
5. *Esteban* (es te/bän).

house. And every day I went out with him to sell vegetables at the market. I helped him in everything. I hoped to meet up with that particular man one fine day. After being there for a few days, I started going out to the different barrios[6] and I learned many things that way. I didn't care so much about the money, what concerned me was my wife's crying, since it was the only picture of Chuy that we had. And even though we found it in the sack along with the other pictures, it was completely destroyed, as you can imagine."

"Yes, but how did you find him?"

"Well, you see, to make a long story short, he turned up at the vegetable stand one day. He stood right there in front of us and bought some vegetables. He seemed to recognize me. Of course I recognized him, because when one is harboring anger one doesn't forget faces. And right there and then I grabbed him. The poor man couldn't even say anything. He was really scared. All I said was that I wanted my son's picture, inlaid, and that he'd better do it or he'd get it. I went with him to where he lived. And right there I made him get to work. The poor man didn't even know where to begin. He had to do it all from memory."

"And how did he do it?"

"I don't know. But I think that a person is capable of doing anything out of fear. Three days later he brought me the finished portrait, just as you see it there close to the Virgin on the table. What do you think? How does my son look?"

"Well, quite frankly I don't remember what Chuy looked like anymore. But more and more he was beginning to resemble you, right?"

"Yes, I think so. That's what everyone tells me now. That Chuy resembled me more and more, and that he was beginning to look like me. There's the portrait. One might say we're one and the same." ☐ ☐

---

6. **barrio** (bär′ryô). In the United States, a section of a city where Latinos, in this case, Mexican Americans, live. [*Spanish*]

From the Author

During the Second World War . . . these portraits were especially popular with families who had young men in the service. . . . Somehow, families thought that this type of representation was closer to the living being. . . . As a child, I became aware that the same three or four colors were used in all the portraits, that the eyes were almost all alike, that the same profile was used in all the pictures . . . There was not really much resemblance except what one's mind put into the picture. . . .

One man had gone to San Antonio . . . because the salesman had (never) returned. This man returned with the inlaid picture of his son who had been killed in the war. . . . It didn't look like him at all. Everyone said it did and of course the parents were sure it did.

(In writing) "The Portrait" I deliberately wanted to be ambiguous. I wanted to convey the feeling I had as a child—the person was as real as the portrait. I wanted to convey the power of suggestion and the power of imagination, but, most of all, the sense of relationships that comes through objects.

Author, scholar, and university administrator, Rivera did migrant farm work before he became an educator. His award-winning book of fiction,

". . . y no se lo tragó la tierra"/". . . and the earth did not part" *(1971), contains "The Portrait."*

Discussion

1. (a) What clues in the first scene suggest that the portrait offer may be a fraud? (b) By what remarks does Don Mateo show he is suspicious of the salesman?

2. (a) Why do Don Mateo and his wife decide to accept the offer? (b) Why are her remarks about the photograph important to the story?

3. In what ways does the **theme** of this story represent more than just one family's experience?

Lorraine Hansberry

from To Be Young, Gifted and Black

Chicago: Southside Summers

1.

For some time now—I think since I was a child—I have been possessed of the desire to put down the stuff of my life. That is a commonplace impulse, apparently, among persons of massive self-interest; sooner or later we all do it. And, I am quite certain, there is only one internal quarrel: how much of the truth to tell? How much, how much, how much! It *is* brutal, in sober uncompromising moments, to reflect on the comedy of concern we all enact when it comes to our precious images!

Even so, when such vanity as propels the writing of such memoirs is examined, certainly one would wish at least to have some boast of social serviceability on one's side. I shall set down in these pages what shall seem to me to be the truth of my life and essences . . . which are to be found, first of all, on the Southside of Chicago, where I was born. . . .

2.

All travelers to my city should ride the elevated trains that race along the back ways of Chicago. The lives you can look into!

I think you could find the tempo of my people on their back porches. The honesty of their living is there in the shabbiness. Scrubbed porches that sag and look their danger. Dirty gray wood steps. And always a line of white and pink clothes scrubbed so well, waving in the dirty wind of the city.

My people are poor. And they are tired. And they are determined to live.

Our Southside is a place apart: each piece of our living is a protest.

3.

I was born May 19, 1930, the last of four children.

Of love and my parents there is little to be written: their relationship to their children was utilitarian. We were fed and housed and dressed and outfitted with more cash than our associates and that was all. We were also vaguely taught certain vague absolutes: that we were better than no one but infinitely superior to everyone; that we were the products of the proudest and most mistreated of the races of man; that there was nothing enormously difficult about life; that one *succeeded* as a matter of course.

Life was not a struggle—it was something that one *did*. One won an argument because, if facts gave out, one invented them—with color! The only sinful people in the world were dull people. And, above all, there were two things which were never to be betrayed: the family and the race. But of love, there was nothing ever said.

If we were sick, we were sternly, impersonally and carefully nursed and doctored back to health. Fevers, toothaches were attended to with urgency and importance; one always felt *important* in my family. Mother came with a tray to your room with the soup and Vick's salve or gave the enemas in a steaming bathroom. But we were not fondled, any of us—head held to breast, fingers about that head—until we were grown, all of us, and my father died.

From the book TO BE YOUNG, GIFTED AND BLACK; Lorraine Hansberry in Her Own Words, adapted by Robert Nemiroff. Copyright © 1969 by Robert Nemiroff and Robert Nemiroff as Executor of the Estate of Lorraine Hansberry. Reprinted by permission of Prentice-Hall, Inc., Englewood Cliffs, New Jersey and William Morris Agency, Inc.

At his funeral I at last, in my memory, saw my mother hold her sons that way, and for the first time in her life my sister held me in her arms I think. We were not a loving people: we were passionate in our hostilities and affinities, but the caress embarrassed us.

We have changed little. . . .

4.

Seven years separated the nearest of my brothers and sisters and myself; I wear, I am sure, the earmarks of that familial station to this day. Little has been written or thought to my knowledge about children who occupy that place: the last born separated by an uncommon length of time from the next youngest. I suspect we are probably a race apart.

The last born is an object toy which comes in years when brothers and sisters who are seven, ten, twelve years older are old enough to appreciate it rather than poke out its eyes. They do not mind diapering you the first two years, but by the time you are five you are a pest that has to be attended to in the washroom, taken to the movies and "sat with" at night. You are not a person—you are a nuisance who is not particular fun any more. Consequently, you swiftly learn to play alone. . . .

5.

My childhood Southside summers were the ordinary city kind, full of the street games which other rememberers have turned into fine ballets these days, and rhymes that anticipated what some people insist on calling modern poetry:

Oh, Mary Mack, Mack, Mack
With the silver buttons, buttons, buttons
All down her back, back, back.
She asked her mother, mother, mother
For fifteen cents, cents, cents
To see the elephant, elephant, elephant
Jump the fence, fence, fence.
Well, he jumped so high, high, high
'Til he touched the sky, sky, sky
And he didn't come back, back, back
'Til the Fourth of Ju—ly, ly, ly!

I remember skinny little Southside bodies by the fives and tens of us panting the delicious hours away:
"May I?"
And the voice of authority: "Yes, you may—you may take one giant step."
One drew in all one's breath and tightened one's fist and pulled the small body against the heavens, stretching, straining all the muscles in the legs to make—one giant step.

It is a long time. One forgets the reason for the game. (For children's games are always explicit in their reasons for being. To play is to win something. Or not to be "it." Or to be high pointer, or outdoer or, sometimes—just *the winner.* But after a time one forgets.)

Why was it important to take a small step, a teeny step, or the most desired of all—one GIANT step?

A giant step *to where?*

6.

Evenings were spent mainly on the back porches where screen doors slammed in the darkness with those really very special summertime sounds. And, sometimes, when Chicago nights got too steamy, the whole family got into the car and went to the park and slept out in the open on blankets. Those were, of course, the best times of all because the grownups were invariably reminded of having been children in the South and told the best stories then. And it was also cool and sweet to be on the grass and there was usually the scent of freshly cut lemons or melons in the air. Daddy would lie on his back, as fathers must, and explain about how men thought the stars above us came to be and how far away they were.

I never did learn to believe that anything could be as far away as *that.* Especially the stars. . . .

7.

The man that I remember was an educated soul, though I think now, looking back, that it was as much a matter of the physical bearing of my father as his command of information and of thought that left that impression upon me. I know nothing of the "assurance of kings" and will not use that metaphor on account of it. Suffice it to say that my father's enduring image in my mind is that of a man whom kings might have imitated and properly created their own flattering descriptions of. A man who always seemed to be doing something brilliant and/or unusual to such an extent that to be doing something brilliant and/or unusual was the way I assumed fathers behaved.

He digested the laws of the State of Illinois and put them into little booklets. He invented complicated pumps and railroad devices. He could talk at length on American history and private enterprise (to which he utterly subscribed). And he carried his head in such a way that I was quite certain that there was nothing he was afraid of. Even writing this, how profoundly it shocks my inner senses to realize suddenly that *my father,* like all men, must have known *fear. . . .*

8.

April 23, 1964

To the Editor,
The New York Times:

With reference to civil disobedience and the Congress of Racial Equality stall-in:
. . . My father was typical of a generation of Negroes who believed that the "American way" could successfully be made to work to democratize the United States. Thus, twenty-five years ago, he spent a small personal fortune, his considerable talents, and many years of his life fighting, in association with NAACP[1] attorneys, Chicago's "restrictive covenants" in one of this nation's ugliest ghettoes.

That fight also required that our family occupy the disputed property in a hellishly hostile "white neighborhood" in which, literally, howling mobs surrounded our house. One of their missiles almost took the life of the then eight-year-old signer of this letter. My memories of this "correct" way of fighting white supremacy in America include being spat at, cursed and pummeled in the daily trek to and from school. And I also remember my desperate and coura-geous mother, patrolling our house all night with a loaded German luger, doggedly guarding her four children, while my father fought the respectable part of the battle in the Washington court.

The fact that my father and the NAACP "won" a Supreme Court decision, in a now famous case which bears his name in the lawbooks, is—ironically—the sort of "progress" our satisfied friends allude to when they presume to deride the more radical means of struggle. The cost, in emotional turmoil, time and money, which led to my father's early death as a permanently embittered exile in a foreign country when he saw that after such sacrificial efforts the Negroes of Chicago were as ghetto-locked as ever, does not seem to figure in their calculations.

That is the reality that I am faced with when I now read that some Negroes my own age and younger say that we must now lie down in the streets, tie up traffic, do whatever we can—take to the hills with guns if necessary—and fight back. Fatuous people remark these days on our "bitterness." Why, of course we are bitter. The entire situation suggests that the nation be reminded of the too little noted final lines of Langston Hughes' mighty poem.[2]

What happens to a dream deferred?
Does it dry up
Like a raisin in the sun?
Or fester like a sore—
And then run?
Does it stink like rotten meat?
Or crust and sugar over—
Like a syrupy sweet?
Maybe it just sags
Like a heavy load.

Or does it explode?

Sincerely, ☐☐

1. *NAACP,* National Association for the Advancement of Colored People.
2. *Langston Hughes' mighty poem,* "Harlem," later published under the title "Dream Deferred."

Discussion

1. Giving examples from the text, describe Hansberry's varied feelings (a) about growing up on Chicago's South Side; (b) toward her family in general; (c) toward her father.

2. (a) What ideals and attitudes did Hansberry's parents instill in their children? (b) In what way does she relate childhood games to these attitudes?

3. (a) What was the effect on Hansberry of being by far the youngest child in her family? (b) How may this position have influenced her to become a writer?

4. (a) What details of the Hansberry family's experiences support the concluding letter of protest? (b) In what way do these experiences illustrate the meaning of Langston Hughes's poem? (c) Compare the **tone** of the poem with that of the letter.

5. Lorraine Hansberry states that in her family "nothing was ever said of love." Do the relationships between her and the other members of her family, as described in this selection, indicate that they were unloving? Giving examples from the text, describe their attitude toward each other in your own words.

Vocabulary
Structure and Dictionary

A. Hansberry describes her relationship with her parents as *utilitarian.*

1. After reading the definition of *utilitarian*, explain this relationship.

Utilitarian has been formed by adding to the root word *utility* two suffixes, *-ar* and *-ian.* Answer the following questions about other suffixes that can be added to *utility.*

2. Considering the meaning of *-ize*, what does *utilize* mean?

3. Considering the meaning of *-ism*, what does *utilitarianism* mean?

B. Hansberry says of her father that ". . . he spent a small personal fortune, his considerable talents, and many years of his life fighting . . . Chicago's *'restrictive covenants'* in one of this nation's ugliest ghettoes" (79a,4).

Find the Glossary definitions of the two italicized words. Then explain what Hansberry's father was fighting in Chicago.

Lorraine Hansberry
1930 • 1965

Lorraine Hansberry was twenty-one when she wrote the following note: "And so the sun will pass away—die away. Tones of blue—of deep quiet—lovely blue—float down and all the people's voices seem to grow quiet—quiet.

"And I remember all the twilights I have ever known—they float across my eyes.

"I think of forests and picnics—of being very warm in something cotton. Of smelling the earth—and loving life.

"Long live good life! And beauty . . . and love!"

When Hansberry was twenty-eight, her first play, *A Raisin in the Sun,* opened on Broadway. Two months later she became the youngest American playwright, the fifth woman, and the first black writer to win the New York Drama Critics Circle Award for the Best Play of the Year.

Six years later, at the age of thirty-four, she died of cancer.

The Sign in Sidney Brustein's Window is the only other of her plays performed while she lived. But she left behind three file cabinets of manuscripts of all kinds. Her husband, Robert Nemiroff, and others have been editing the papers. They include the autobiographical pieces which formed the basis for the play and novel of *To Be Young, Gifted and Black.*

One of her last notes read, "If anything should happen—before 'tis done—may I trust that all commas and periods will be placed and someone will complete my thoughts—

"This last should be the least difficult—since there are so many who think as I do—"

Saul Bellow and William Faulkner: On the Writer's Responsibility

The following works allow you to compare the viewpoints of major authors on the challenges of our era. Thurber's "The Last Flower" (page 84) was published on the eve of World War II. Faulkner's Nobel Address (1950), a classic of eloquence, came at a peak of global tension. The excerpt from Bellow's Nobel Lecture (1976) reflects his faith in the "human enterprise."

Nobel Prize Medallion.
(Nobel Foundation.)

Saul Bellow:

We stand open to all anxieties. The decline and fall of everything is our daily dread.

And art and literature—what of them? Well, there is a violent uproar but we are not absolutely dominated by it. We are still able to think, to discriminate, and to feel. Books continue to be written and read. It may be more difficult to reach the whirling mind of a modern reader but it is possible to cut through the noise and reach the quiet zone. In the quiet zone we may find that he is devoutly waiting for us. The unending cycle of crises that began with the First World War has formed a kind of person, one who has lived through terrible, strange things, and in whom there is an observable shrinkage of prejudices, a casting off of disappointing ideologies, an ability to live with many kinds of madness, and immense desire for certain durable human goods—truth, for instance, or freedom, or wisdom. But for a long time art has not been connected, as it was in the past, with the main human enterprise. Ingenuity, daring exploration, freshness of invention have replaced the art of "direct relevance."

There were European writers in the nineteenth century who would not give up the connection of literature with the main human enterprise. But a separation between great artists and the general public took place. They developed a marked contempt for the average reader and the bourgeois mass. The historian Erich Auerbach tells us that some of these writers produced "strange and vaguely terrifying works, or shocked the public by paradoxical and extreme opinions. Many of them took no trouble to facilitate the understanding of what they wrote."

What would writers do today if it would occur to them that literature might once again engage the "central energies" of man, if they were to recognize that an immense desire had arisen for a return from the periphery, for what was simple and true? One can't tell writers what to do. The imagination must find its own path. But one can fervently wish that they—that we—would come back from the periphery. We do not, we writers, represent mankind adequately. What account do Americans give of themselves? In a kind of contractual daylight they see themselves in the ways with which we are all so desperately familiar. We put into our books the consumer, civil servant, football fan, lover, television viewer. And in the contractual daylight version their life is a kind of death. There is another life, coming from an insistent sense of what we are, that denies these daylight formulations and the false life—the death in life—they make for us. For it is false, and we know it, and our secret and incoherent resistance to it cannot stop, for that resistance

Excerpts from "The Nobel Lecture" by Saul Bellow in *The American Scholar* (Summer 1977). © the Nobel Foundation 1976. Reprinted by permission.

arises from persistent intuitions.

I am drawing attention to the fact that there is in the intellectual community a sizable inventory of attitudes that have become respectable. Few writers, even among the best, have taken the trouble to reexamine these attitudes or orthodoxies. Essay after essay, book after book, confirm the most serious thoughts—all the usual things about mass society, dehumanization, and the rest. How weary we are of them. How poorly they represent us. The pictures they offer no more resemble us than we resemble the reconstructed reptiles and other monsters in a museum of paleontology. We are much more limber, versatile, better articulated; there is much more to us; we all feel it.

Writers are greatly respected. The intelligent public is wonderfully patient with them, continues to read them, and endures disappointment after disappointment, waiting to hear from art what it does not hear from theology, philosophy, social theory, and what it cannot hear from pure science. Out of the struggle at the center has come an immense, painful longing for a broader, more flexible, fuller, more coherent, more comprehensive account of what we human beings are, who we are, and what this life is for. At the center, humankind struggles with collective powers for its freedom; the individual struggles with dehumanization for the possession of his soul. If writers do not come again into the center it will not be because the center is preempted. It is not. They are free to enter. If they so wish.

William Faulkner:

I feel that this award was not made to me as a man, but to my work—a life's work in the agony and sweat of the human spirit, not for glory and least of all for profit, but to create out of the materials of the human spirit something which did not exist before. So this award is only mine in trust. It will not be difficult to find a dedication for the money part of it commensurate with the purpose and significance of its origin. But I would like to do the same with the acclaim too, by using this moment as a pinnacle from which I might be listened to by the young men and women already dedicated to the same anguish and travail, among whom is already that one who will some day stand here where I am standing.

Our tragedy today is a general and universal physical fear so long sustained by now that we can even bear it. There are no longer problems of the spirit. There is only the question: When will I be blown up? Because of this, the young man or woman writing today has forgotten the problems of the human heart in conflict with itself which alone can make good writing because only that is worth writing about, worth the agony and the sweat.

He must learn them again. He must teach himself that the basest of all things is to be afraid; and, teaching himself that, forget it forever, leaving no room in his workshop for anything but the old verities and truths of the heart, the old universal truths lacking which any story is ephemeral and doomed—love and honor and pity and pride and compassion and sacrifice. Until he does so, he labors under a curse. He writes not of love but of lust, of defeats in which nobody loses anything of value, of victories without hope and, worst of all, without pity or compassion. His griefs grieve on no universal bones, leaving no scars. He writes not of the heart but of the glands.

Until he relearns these things, he will write as though he stood among and watched the end of man. I decline to accept the end of man. It is easy enough to say that man is immortal simply because he will endure: that when the last dingdong of doom has clanged and faded from the last worthless rock hanging tideless in the last red and dying evening, that even then there will still be one more sound: that of his puny inexhaustible voice, still talk-

Nobel Prize Speech from THE FAULKNER READER by William Faulkner, published by Random House, Inc., 1954.

ing. I refuse to accept this. I believe that man will not merely endure: he will prevail. He is immortal, not because he alone among creatures has an inexhaustible voice, but because he has a soul, a spirit capable of compassion and sacrifice and endurance. The poet's, the writer's, duty is to write about these things. It is his privilege to help man endure by lifting his heart, by reminding him of the courage and honor and hope and pride and compassion and pity and sacrifice which have been the glory of his past. The poet's voice need not merely be the record of man, it can be one of the props, the pillars to help him endure and prevail.

Discussion

1. **(a)** What major faults do both Bellow and Faulkner criticize in the outlook of contemporary writers? **(b)** Based on your reading in this unit and elsewhere, do you agree or disagree with their criticisms of modern literature? Discuss.

2. Discuss the various comments made by Bellow, Faulkner, and Thurber on the strength of the human spirit. **(a)** On what points do they all generally agree? Where do they differ? **(b)** Which author seems to you the most hopeful? And the least? Explain.

3. Does Thurber's picture story communicate more or less effectively than the speeches? Explain.

Saul Bellow 1915 •

Bellow defies the pessimism of modern literature by demonstrating in his novels that the individual is important and that goodness is possible despite the absurdities and anxieties of the twentieth century.

Though born in Canada, he has spent most of his life in Chicago, where he is a professor at the University of Chicago. He began developing his art with novels like *Dangling Man* and *The Adventures of Augie March*. Though the latter book won the 1953 National Book Award, popularity eluded Bellow until 1964, when he published *Herzog*. Besides gaining him another National Book Award, this novel was immediately recognized as one of the pivotal works of contemporary American literature.

William Faulkner 1897 • 1962

Faulkner's fiction draws inspiration from the traditions, myths, and historical conflicts of the South. But his work surpasses regional limits, for Faulkner is a poet of the human condition, portraying the strivings of individuals against alienation and loss of values. (See his story, "The Bear," in Unit 6.)

The Last Flower

A parable in pictures by James Thurber

FOR ROSEMARY

IN THE WISTFUL HOPE THAT HER WORLD
WILL BE BETTER THAN MINE

James Thurber 1894 • 1961

The 1930s and '40s had no more popular humorist than James Thurber, whose stories, essays, and cartoons for *The New Yorker* created a style of humor that will never be duplicated.

Born in Columbus, Ohio, Thurber experienced a childhood that had its share of strange incidents, which he later chronicled in *My Life and Hard Times.*

After graduating from Ohio State University and working as a journalist, Thurber became a regular contributor to *The New Yorker,* where his stories and pencil-line cartoons helped establish the style of that magazine. In 1940 he branched out into the theater by collaborating with Elliott Nugent on *The Male Animal,* which was a great success on Broadway.

A moody, absent-minded man, Thurber wrote with a casual style that disguised the amount of work that went into all his writing. Indeed, it was not unusual for him to revise a piece ten times. *A Thurber Carnival* remains the most representative compendium of his work.

WORLD WAR XII, AS EVERYBODY KNOWS,

1.

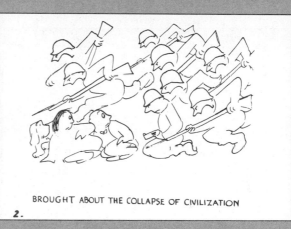

BROUGHT ABOUT THE COLLAPSE OF CIVILIZATION

2.

TOWNS, CITIES, AND VILLAGES DISAPPEARED
FROM THE EARTH

3.

ALL THE GROVES AND FORESTS WERE
DESTROYED

4.

AND ALL THE GARDENS

5.

AND ALL THE WORKS OF ART

6.

MEN, WOMEN, AND CHILDREN BECAME LOWER
THAN THE LOWER ANIMALS

7.

DISCOURAGED AND DISILLUSIONED, DOGS DESERTED
THEIR FALLEN MASTERS

8.

EMBOLDENED BY THE PITIFUL CONDITION
OF THE FORMER LORDS OF THE EARTH,
RABBITS DESCENDED UPON THEM

9.

BOOKS, PAINTINGS, AND MUSIC DISAPPEARED
FROM THE EARTH, AND HUMAN BEINGS
JUST SAT AROUND, DOING NOTHING

10.

YEARS AND YEARS WENT BY

11.

EVEN THE FEW GENERALS WHO WERE LEFT
FORGOT WHAT THE LAST WAR HAD DECIDED

12.

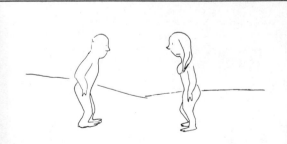

BOYS AND GIRLS GREW UP TO STARE AT EACH OTHER
BLANKLY, FOR LOVE HAD PASSED FROM THE EARTH

13.

ONE DAY A YOUNG GIRL WHO HAD NEVER
SEEN A FLOWER CHANCED TO COME
UPON THE LAST ONE IN THE WORLD

14.

SHE TOLD THE OTHER HUMAN BEINGS
THAT THE LAST FLOWER WAS DYING

15.

THE ONLY ONE WHO PAID ANY ATTENTION
TO HER WAS A YOUNG MAN SHE
FOUND WANDERING ABOUT

16.

TOGETHER THE YOUNG MAN AND THE GIRL
NURTURED THE FLOWER AND IT BEGAN
TO LIVE AGAIN

17.

ONE DAY A BEE VISITED THE FLOWER,
AND A HUMMINGBIRD

18.

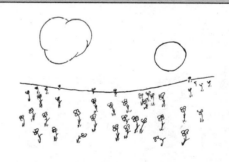

BEFORE LONG THERE WERE TWO FLOWERS, AND
THEN FOUR, AND THEN A GREAT MANY

19.

GROVES AND FORESTS FLOURISHED AGAIN

20.

JAMES THURBER   87

THE YOUNG GIRL BEGAN TO TAKE
AN INTEREST IN HOW SHE LOOKED

21.

THE YOUNG MAN DISCOVERED THAT
TOUCHING THE GIRL WAS PLEASURABLE

22.

LOVE WAS REBORN INTO THE WORLD

23.

THEIR CHILDREN GREW UP STRONG AND HEALTHY
AND LEARNED TO RUN AND LAUGH

24.

DOGS CAME OUT OF THEIR EXILE

25.

THE YOUNG MAN DISCOVERED, BY PUTTING ONE
STONE UPON ANOTHER, HOW TO BUILD A SHELTER

26.

PRETTY SOON EVERYBODY WAS BUILDING SHELTERS

27.

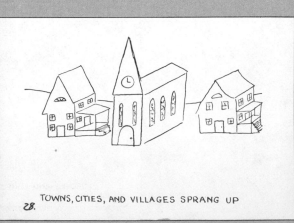

TOWNS, CITIES, AND VILLAGES SPRANG UP

28.

SONG CAME BACK INTO THE WORLD

28.

AND TROUBADOURS AND JUGGLERS

30.

AND TAILORS AND COBBLERS

31.

AND PAINTERS AND POETS

32.

AND SCULPTORS AND WHEELWRIGHTS

33.

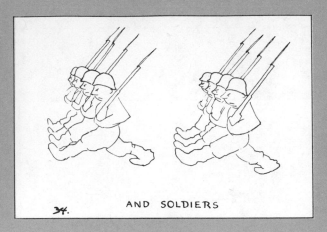

34. AND SOLDIERS

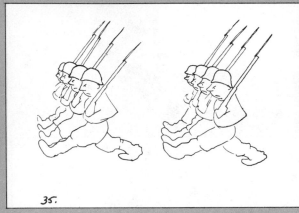

35.

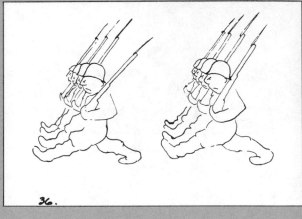

36.

37. AND LIEUTENANTS AND CAPTAINS

38. AND GENERALS AND MAJOR-GENERALS

39. AND LIBERATORS

SOME PEOPLE WENT ONE PLACE TO LIVE,
AND SOME ANOTHER

40.

BEFORE LONG, THOSE WHO WENT TO LIVE IN THE VALLEYS
WISHED THEY HAD GONE TO LIVE IN THE HILLS

41.

AND THOSE WHO HAD GONE TO LIVE IN THE HILLS
WISHED THEY HAD GONE TO LIVE IN THE VALLEYS

42.

THE LIBERATORS, UNDER THE GUIDANCE OF GOD,
SET FIRE TO THE DISCONTENT

43.

SO PRESENTLY THE WORLD WAS AT WAR AGAIN

44.

45.

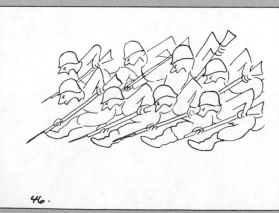

46.

THIS TIME THE DESTRUCTION WAS SO COMPLETE...

47.

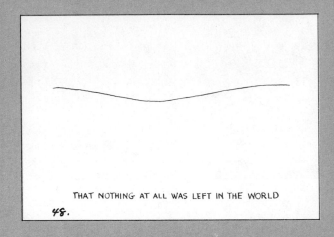

THAT NOTHING AT ALL WAS LEFT IN THE WORLD

48.

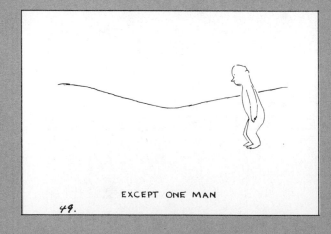

EXCEPT ONE MAN

49.

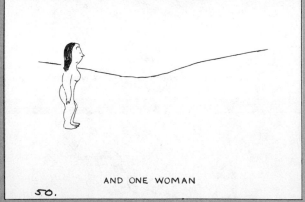

AND ONE WOMAN

50.

AND ONE FLOWER

1: American Mosaic

1. Pick three selections in this unit and explain how either their authors or a major character in each displays an urge to challenge an existing situation or to explore his or her personal limits.

2. What various criticisms of technological society are implied by "The Calculating Machine," "April 2005: Usher II," and "Bruja"?

3. Compare the characters of Miriam ("The First Seven Years"), Hester ("The Sentimentality of William Tavener"), and Miss McCutcheon ("The Oyster and the Pearl").

4. What aspect of family life seems most important in each of the following works? "My Mother Pieced Quilts"; "The Leader of the People"; "The Oyster and the Pearl"; "The Portrait"; and "To Be Young, Gifted and Black."

5. Comparing the poems in this unit, try to define some common characteristics of both style and subject matter in modern poetry. What differences do you notice between "Justice Denied in Massachusetts" and the more recent poems?

The Use of Force

William Carlos Williams

Though best known as a poet and short-story writer, William Carlos Williams spent much of his life as a practicing physician. Read the following story by him, and answer the questions that follow.

They were new patients to me, all I had was the name, Olson. Please come down as soon as you can, my daughter is very sick.

When I arrived I was met by the mother, a big startled looking woman, very clean and apologetic who merely said, Is this the doctor? and let me in. In the back, she added, You must excuse us, doctor, we have her in the kitchen where it is warm. It is very damp here sometimes.

The child was fully dressed and sitting on her father's lap near the kitchen table. He tried to get up, but I motioned for him not to bother, took off my overcoat and started to look things over. I could see that they were all very nervous, eyeing me up and down distrustfully. As often, in such cases, they weren't telling me more than they had to, it was up to me to tell them; that's why they were spending three dollars on me.

The child was fairly eating me up with her cold, steady eyes, and no expression to her face whatever. She did not move and seemed, inwardly, quiet; an unusually attractive little thing, and as strong as a heifer in appearance. But her face was flushed, she was breathing rapidly, and I realized that she had a high fever. She had magnificent blonde hair, in profusion. One of those picture children often reproduced in advertising leaflets and the photogravure sections of the Sunday papers.

She's had a fever for three days, began the father and we don't know what it comes from. My wife has given her things, you know, like people do, but it don't do no good. And there's been a lot of sickness around. So we tho't you'd better look her over and tell us what is the matter.

As doctors often do I took a trial shot at it as a point of departure. Had she had a sore throat?

Both parents answered me together, No . . . No, she says her throat don't hurt her.

Does your throat hurt you? added the mother to the child. But the little girl's expression didn't change nor did she move her eyes from my face.

Have you looked?

I tried to, said the mother, but I couldn't see.

As it happens we had been having a number of cases of diphtheria[1] in the school to which this child went during that month and we were all, quite apparently, thinking of that, though no one had as yet spoken of the thing.

Well, I said, suppose we take a look at the throat first. I smiled in my best professional manner and asking for the child's first name I said, come on, Mathilda, open your mouth and let's take a look at your throat.

Nothing doing.

Aw, come on, I coaxed, just open your mouth wide and let me take a look. Look, I said opening both hands wide, I haven't anything in my hands. Just open up and let me see.

Such a nice man, put in the mother. Look how kind he is to you. Come on, do what he tells you to. He won't hurt you.

At that I ground my teeth in disgust. If only they wouldn't use the word "hurt" I might be able to get somewhere. But I did not allow myself to be hurried or disturbed but speaking quietly and slowly I approached the child again.

As I moved my chair a little nearer suddenly with one cat-like movement both her hands clawed instinctively for my eyes and she almost reached them too. In fact she knocked my glasses flying and they fell, though unbroken, several feet away from me on the kitchen floor.

Both the mother and father almost turned themselves inside out in embarrassment and apology. You bad girl, said the mother, taking her and shaking her by one arm. Look what you've done. The nice man . . . .

For heaven's sake, I broke in. Don't call me a nice man to her. I'm here to look at her throat on the chance that she might have diphtheria and possibly die of it. But that's nothing to her. Look here, I said to the child, we're going to look at your throat. You're old enough to understand what I'm saying. Will you open it now by yourself or shall we have to open it for you?

Not a move. Even her expression hadn't changed. Her breaths however were coming faster and faster. Then the battle began. I had to do it. I had to have a throat culture for her own protection. But first I told the parents that it was entirely up to them. I explained the danger but said that I would not insist on a throat examination so long as they would take the responsibility.

1. *diphtheria* (dif thir/ē ə *or* dip thir/ē ə), a serious throat disease accompanied by formation of a membrane, or thin layer of tissue.

If you don't do what the doctor says you'll have to go to the hospital, the mother admonished her severely.

Oh yeah? I had to smile to myself. After all, I had already fallen in love with the savage brat, the parents were contemptible[2] to me. In the ensuing struggle they grew more and more abject, crushed, exhausted while she surely rose to magnificent heights of insane fury of effort bred of her terror of me.

The father tried his best, and he was a big man but the fact that she was his daughter, his shame at her behavior and his dread of hurting her made him release her just at the critical moment several times when I had almost achieved success, till I wanted to kill him. But his dread also that she might have diphtheria made him tell me to go on, go on though he himself was almost fainting, while the mother moved back and forth behind us raising and lowering her hands in an agony of apprehension.

Put her in front of you on your lap, I ordered, and hold both her wrists.

But as soon as he did the child let out a scream. Don't, you're hurting me. Let go of my hands. Let them go I tell you. Then she shrieked terrifyingly, hysterically. Stop it! Stop it! You're killing me!

Do you think she can stand it, doctor! said the mother.

You get out, said the husband to his wife. Do you want her to die of diphtheria?

Come on now, hold her, I said.

Then I grasped the child's head with my left hand and tried to get the wooden tongue depressor between her teeth. She fought, with clenched teeth, desperately! But now I also had grown furious—at a child. I tried to hold myself down but I couldn't. I know how to expose a throat for inspection. And I did my best. When finally I got the wooden spatula behind the last teeth and just the point of it into the mouth cavity, she opened up for an

1. The author indicates dialogue in the story through the use of **(a)** quotation marks; **(b)** colons and semicolons; **(c)** italics; **(d)** words like *said* plus commas.

2. Which word does *not* apply to Mathilda? **(a)** attractive; **(b)** suspicious; **(c)** generous; **(d)** feverish.

3. Mathilda is characterized through all of the following means *except* **(a)** the narrator's reactions to her; **(b)** her actions; **(c)** her thoughts; **(d)** her appearance.

4. Mathilda's refusal to open her mouth is foreshadowed when **(a)** the doctor sees her face is flushed; **(b)** her parents eye the doctor suspiciously; **(c)** her mother says that she tried to look down the throat but could see nothing; **(d)** her mother says that the daughter is sick.

5. Through the comparison in paragraph 12, page 95, the narrator makes Mathilda appear **(a)** machinelike; **(b)** animalistic; **(c)** human; **(d)** dead.

6. In paragraph 14, page 95, the narrator's rising anger is indicated by his **(a)** description of his tone of voice; **(b)** explanation of his feelings; **(c)** remarks to the mother and child; **(d)** actions.

7. What emotion does the narrator feel toward the parents? **(a)** admiration; **(b)** fear; **(c)** love; **(d)** scorn.

8. Judging from her reaction when the father tries to get hold of her wrists, we can infer that Mathilda will not open her mouth because of **(a)** fear; **(b)** disbelief in medicine; **(c)** vani-

instant but before I could see anything she came down again and gripping the wooden blade between her molars she reduced it to splinters before I could get it out again.

Aren't you ashamed, the mother yelled at her. Aren't you ashamed to act like that in front of the doctor?

Get me a smooth-handled spoon of some sort, I told the mother. We're going through with this. The child's mouth was already bleeding. Her tongue was cut and she was screaming in wild hysterical shrieks. Perhaps I should have desisted and come back in an hour or more. No doubt it would have been better. But I have seen at least two children lying dead in bed of neglect in such cases, and feeling that I must get a diagnosis now or never I went at it again. But the worst of it was that I too had got beyond reason. I could have torn the child apart in my own fury and enjoyed it. It was a pleasure to attack her. My face was burning with it.

The damned little brat must be protected against her own idiocy, one says to one's self at such times. Others must be protected against her. It is a social necessity. And all these things are true. But a blind fury, a feeling of adult shame, bred of a longing for muscular release are the operatives. One goes on to the end.

In a final unreasoning assault I overpowered the child's neck and jaws. I forced the heavy silver spoon back of her teeth and down her throat till she gagged. And there it was—both tonsils covered with membrane. She had fought valiantly to keep me from knowing her secret. She had been hiding that sore throat for three days at least and lying to her parents in order to escape just such an outcome as this.

Now truly she *was* furious. She had been on the defensive before but now she attacked. Tried to get off her father's lap and fly at me while tears of defeat blinded her eyes.

ty; (d) insanity.

9. The doctor forces the heavy silver spoon down Mathilda's throat out of (a) jealousy and fear; (b) rage and necessity; (c) pride and ignorance; (d) anger and jealousy.

10. In this story the doctor is *not* in conflict with (a) the daughter; (b) the parents; (c) the school; (d) himself.

11. This story is told from the point of view of (a) Mathilda; (b) the mother; (c) a narrator outside the story; (d) the doctor.

12. The theme is best summarized as an exploration of (a) the lack of good medical care in rural areas; (b) mistrust of medical science; (c) society's intrusion into the privacy of its citizens; (d) how fear and frustration can lead to violence.

13. In a paragraph tell which character in the story you most sympathize with, and give at least three reasons for your sympathy.

Choose one topic:

1. Define your concept of "The American Dream." Write an essay or a speech in which you clarify and support your ideas with examples from various selections in this unit.

2. Pick three selections from this unit that you would strongly recommend to next year's American literature students. Write two or three paragraphs on each selection, explaining what you learned from reading that selection and what aspects of it you think the new students would enjoy.

3. The following pairs of characters hold conflicting views on important values:

Jody's father and grandfather in "The Leader of the People."

Stendahl and Garrett in "April 2005: Usher II."

Miriam and Feld in "The First Seven Years."

Hester and William in "The Sentimentality of William Tavener."

Imagine you are one of these characters and write a letter to the other member of the pair, trying either to settle your dispute, or to explain and justify your position.

Unit 2:

- Columbus's New World Letter

Spaniards found St. Augustine •

Drake maps Pacific coast •

British "Lost Colony," Roanoke •

Bradford: *The History of Plymouth Plantation* •

Massachusetts law requiring public schools •

Bradstreet: *The Tenth Muse*

- New World named after Amerigo Vespucci

• Spaniards colonize New Mexico

• British found Jamestown

• Dutch settle on Hudson River

African slaves imported to Jamestown •

• Pilgrims land

• Smith: *A True Relation*

Harvard College founded •

Bay Psalm Book •

Early French and Spanish expeditions   Explorers' narratives

Plains tribes acquire horses

Iroquois Confederation formed

The New Land 1500 to 1800

1700   1750   1800

- Knight begins her *Journal*
- Franklin's kite experiment
- First colonial newspapers
- Edwards: *Freedom of the Will*
- King Philip's War
- Father Serra founds California missions
- French promote Mississippi Bubble land boom
- Franklin: *Autobiography*
- Bacon's Rebellion against English governor
- First Emancipation Society
- Byrd: *A History of the Dividing Line*
- Battle of Lexington
- Pueblos of New Mexico revolt against Spaniards
- Declaration of Independence
- Paine: *Common Sense*
- First *Poor Richard's Almanack*
- Salem witch trials
- The Great Awakening
- Constitutional Convention •
- Cotton Mather: *Wonders of the Invisible World*
- Paine: *Rights of Man* •

Religious tracts, sermons   Political protest pamphlets

Journals, almanacs

European rivalry for land, Indian wars   Early westward migration

Background: The New Land 1500–1800

From the beginning, the European discovery and settlement of the Western Hemisphere was an enterprise of many nations. The fifteenth century saw the stability of Medieval Europe giving way to the ferment of the Renaissance. Turkish invasions of eastern Europe cut off the ancient trade routes to the wealth of Asia. At the same time, there was a surge of creative energy, seen in such technological accomplishments as the cannon and the printing press. Many Europeans were gazing toward new horizons, in art, religion, and politics, as well as in geography. The Portuguese and other nations facing the Atlantic became especially venturesome seafarers. According to much fable and some solid fact—such as those half-forgotten reports of Leif Ericson's voyage to "Vinland"—lands of rich soil and mild winters lay across the Western Sea.

Columbus, a Genoese navigator, combined facts and rumors from Arabic, Jewish, Portuguese, Irish, and even ancient Greek maps and writings, and convinced Ferdinand and Isabella of Spain to fund a quest for the western route to Asia. When he found the "new" land, he thought it to be the coast of India, and so its varied inhabitants received the misleading name of "Indians."

Although Columbus died believing he had reached India, Amerigo Vespucci, a Florentine merchant-adventurer, realized a continent had been found and the *Mundus Novus* or "New World," was named "America" in his honor. Medieval Europe was dwarfed by the new lands—by their tropical paradises, their menacing forests, their endless plains, their vast mountain ranges, their wealth of exotic plants and animals, and by the fabulous cities of the Aztec, Maya, and Inca Empires. This was truly a New World of marvels for Europeans.

A continuous stream of immigrants—Spanish explorers, French trappers, Dutch traders, English buccaneers, and others—began to flow toward the ancient American civilizations already on the continent. The original Americans and the Europeans-becoming-Americans changed each other, and what began as simple practical changes eventually overturned whole ways of life. For instance, the "gold of the Indies," by starting economic revolutions such as inflation and large-scale banking, also gave birth to our modern middle-class civilization, with values totally different from those of either feudal Europe or America before Columbus.

After more than two centuries of the shaping of new societies on both continents of America, the French immigrant Hector de Crèvecoeur would ask: "What, then, is the American, this new man?" Crèvecoeur, examining British North America, went on to give his answer, presented at the end of this unit. But then, as now, no definition could contain the complexity of people from all continents mingling and clashing in the formation of a New Land. The selections in this unit are chosen to give some idea of that diversity, yet also to suggest some common elements of the North American experience. Such shared characteristics include a fascination with the wilderness, which was potent to the imagination of original Americans and settlers alike; a devotion to fair government, seen equally in the Iroquois Constitution and the Declaration of Independence; and an abiding concern with practical affairs, which was essential in the times of exploration, colonization, and revolution.

Every American grows up learning the myths of our country's past. At Thanksgiving, a popular illustration shows starched and sober Pilgrims breaking bread peacefully with romantically stalwart and friendly Indians. Generations of schoolchildren have reenacted the rescue of John Smith by the beautiful princess Pocahontas. In the Southwest, the deeds of Spanish conquistadores and missionaries are similarly recalled. These images form an American heritage of myth and legend; but the realities, though they are as dramatic as the myths, are not so simple.

The earliest display of American diversity appears in the distinct cultures of native Americans. The concerns and values of the mounted buffalo hunters of the Plains, for instance, contrast markedly with those of the farmers, such as the Pueblo communities of the Southwest. The individualistic tendencies of the Plains tribes are underscored by the fact that a youth passed to adulthood when he experienced his own, private medicine dream. Though bound by clan loyalties, these societies prized most highly the coups of the lone hunter or warrior. But Pueblo communities cherished stability and communal solidarity, as evidenced by the anonymous collective authorship of their poems, like "Song Addressed to a New Chief," and by that song's concern with the welfare of the whole group. The Iroquois Constitution, like our own, embodies a fundamental sense of a divine order that serves to inspire a stable political order and to emphasize the duties, rather than the privileges, of leadership.

However, even before permanent European settlement began, native American societies were affected by European exploration and trade. For example, in the sixteenth century, the Plains tribes adopted from the Spaniards the use of the horse, which profoundly changed their culture and made them an American legend. On the other hand, Canassatego, speaking for the Iroquois in 1744, declined an invitation to allow young Iroquois to be educated in English fashion at the College of William and Mary. But, from the perspective of the newly arrived Europeans, the colonization and Christianization of the "new" continent was one of the most heroic endeavors in world history.

The sixteenth century was the golden age of the explorer. The earliest penetrations of North America, like the journeys of Cabeza de Vaca and Coronado recorded here, were accomplished by a few intrepid French and Spanish soldiers and Catholic missionaries who followed wilderness trails from the St. Lawrence River to the mouth of the Mississippi and from Florida to California. Cabeza de Vaca's ordeal is one of the greatest adventures in American exploration. His record, despite the perils and hardships described, lured Coronado and others to seek in vain the fabled Seven Golden Cities of Cibola—which were actually cliff-towns of Pueblo farmers.

John Smith

The chronicles of Cabeza de Vaca and Pedro de Castañeda also stimulated the imagination and the ambition of Englishmen like Sir Walter Raleigh and John Smith. Smith's own *True Relation* (1608) is the earliest firsthand narrative of the English settlement of the New World. His various books were composed to attract future settlers, to furnish economic reports for investors in colonial ventures, and to provide news and information for the curious back in England. And, as such, they succeeded. Before their journey to America, the Puritans carefully studied Smith's *Description of New England* (1616).

The Spaniards had long settled at St. Augustine (1565) and were moving into New Mexico when John Smith founded the first permanent English settlement at Jamestown (1607). There were two distinct types of English colonists, a division

which was to prove crucial in American history. To the Southeast came landed aristocrats, who established large plantations requiring endless shiploads of white bond servants and African slaves. To the North came the Pilgrims and Puritans, drawn from various Protestant groups seeking religious freedom. They developed a society of small farmers, craftsmen, shopkeepers, and merchants. Just as the seeds of the Mexican-American War of 1848 were sown in the parallel settlement by the Spanish in the West and the English in the East, the seeds of the American Civil War were sown in that contrast between the first settlers of Massachusetts and of Virginia.

The Puritans were called by that name because they had attempted to "purify" or reform the Church of England by reducing its ritual to the simplest Biblical terms. In the Calvinistic tradition, they believed that each person was fated from birth to be among the elect and saved, or among the damned and doomed. Such religious convictions dominated New England, as the earliest English settlers attempted to establish a theocracy with the clergy as God's governors and the Bible as the law of the land.

The leading force in early New England was William Bradford, author of *The History of Plymouth Plantation* and governor of Plymouth, Massachusetts, for thirty-one successive terms. Bradford's grave, dignified style expresses the Puritans' sense that their divine mission permeated all

aspects of life. This powerful feeling lay beneath the variety of journals, histories, and sermons that comprised most New England prose. Puritans generally shunned imaginative literature because art, to them, did not contribute to the glory of God and was therefore a foolish—even devilish—waste of valuable time. But exuberant prayers and sermons incorporated much of the creativity we now associate with drama, fiction, and poetry.

The few New England poets, notably Anne Bradstreet and Edward Taylor, were "private poets." Their works are nonetheless moving and illustrate depth and sensitivity not usually associated with the Puritans. They do, however, reflect the inward and upward direction of the Puritan vision, converging on a divine originator, the "mighty Architect" who "in this bowling alley bowled the sun."

The greatest of the Puritan theologians was Jonathan Ed-

Anne Bradstreet

wards. His sermon, "Sinners in the Hands of an Angry God," is considered the most passionate and terrifying sermon of the time. He was at first a leader, then a dubious critic of the religious revival known as "The Great Awakening" (1739–40). By the time of this movement, religious fervor was already yielding to the political ferment which led to the Revolution.

The Puritan virtues of practical wisdom and self-discipline survived the decline of their power. Sarah Kemble Knight's *Journal* of 1704 reveals these qualities of staunch independence and shrewdness, but accompanied by a lively wit that Puritans, when they had it, generally suppressed.

William Byrd, a sharp observer like Knight, was a typical Virginia aristocrat, as much at home in the literary salons of London as in the Virginia backwoods that he helped survey. His polished, witty style, his learned allusions, and, above all, his fascination with human and natural curiosities rather than with divine order represent the contrast between New England and Southern writers, a contrast which outlasted this era.

Yet, even in New England, the latter eighteenth century saw the dawn of imaginative literature. The scarcity of printing presses—not until 1763 was there one in every colony—had largely confined production to utilitarian materials. In fact, most of the works in this unit were published either in Europe or not until after the Revolution. But with more presses came more newspapers (see page 137), then the publication of poetry, and, by the 1790s, of novels. Philip Freneau and Phillis Wheatley were among the pioneers of this literature. Their verse—as shown by Wheatley's poem on page 141—was modeled both in form and theme on English poetry of their day. Nonetheless, although their standards were borrowed from Europe, Wheatley and other American writers, both white and black, reflected an impulse to create an American literature to accompany the growing impulse toward independence.

The chief symbol of both these aspirations, literary and political, was Benjamin Franklin. The excerpt from his *Autobiography* on how to attain "Moral Perfection" is based on the rationalist's confidence in self and certainty of progress. Franklin's optimism, shrewd common sense, plain speaking, and down-to-earth humor are considered by some critics to be the keynotes of American literature.

But the single most significant literary, as well as political, work of the eighteenth century is Thomas Jefferson's Declaration of Independence. In it is the core of American identity and expression.

As demonstrated by the selections in "The New Land," the conditions of colonial life demanded an almost exclusively pragmatic literature. The Revolution intensified the need for practical political writing and so, although it created a nation, it provided only the potential for a national literature.

Phillis Wheatley

Yet the very fact of nationhood posed the question asked by Crèvecoeur: "What, then, is the American, this new man?" His emphasis was on newness, yet the legacies of the "Old Worlds" of Europe, of Africa, and of pre-Columbian America would remain vital. Each selection in this unit casts light on this riddle of identity, which would become a central theme for most American writers to come, and a mystery yet to be unraveled.

Benjamin Franklin

Dekanawidah

from The Iroquois Constitution

Dekanawidah (de′kä nä wē′dä) *is considered the founding father of the Iroquois Confederation. This union of native American peoples comprised, by 1720, six nations of the northeastern woodlands. Like many stories, poems, and songs of native American peoples, the Iroquois Constitution embodies concepts of personal and political conduct and recognizes the supremacy of a divine power.*

I am Dekanawidah, and with the Five Nations confederate lords I plant the Tree of the Great Peace. . . . I name the tree the Tree of the Great Long Leaves. Under the shade of this Tree of the Great Peace we spread the soft white feather down of the globe thistle as seats for you, Atotarho and your cousin lords. There shall you sit and watch the council fire of the confederacy of the Five Nations. Roots have spread out from the Tree, and the name of these roots is the Great White Roots of Peace. If any man of any nation shall show a desire to obey the laws of the Great Peace, they shall trace the roots to their source, and they shall be welcomed to take shelter beneath the Tree of the Long Leaves. The smoke of the confederate council fire shall pierce the sky so that all nations may discover the central council fire of the Great Peace. I, Dekanawidah, and the confederate lords now uproot the tallest pine tree and into the cavity thereby made we cast all weapons of war. Into the depth of the earth, down into the deep underearth currents of water flowing into unknown regions; we cast all weapons of war. We bury them from sight forever and plant again the Tree.

We do now crown you with the sacred emblem of the antlers, the sign of your lordship. You shall now become a mentor of the people of the Five Nations. The thickness of your skin will be seven spans, for you will be proof against

A council of the Onondaga, an Iroquois nation. (The Bettmann Archive, Inc.)

anger, offensive action, and criticism. With endless patience you shall carry out your duty, and your firmness shall be tempered with compassion for your people. Neither anger nor fear shall find lodgment in your mind, and all your words and actions shall be tempered with calm deliberation. In all your official acts, self-interest shall be cast aside. You shall look and listen to the welfare of the whole people, and have always in view, not only the present but the coming generations—the unborn of the future Nation.

The Onondaga lords shall open each council by expressing their gratitude to their cousin lords, and greeting them, and they shall make an address and offer thanks to the earth where men dwell, to the streams of water, the pools, the springs, the lakes, to the maize and the fruits, to the medicinal herbs and the trees, to the forest

William N. Fenton, ed., PARKER ON THE IROQUOIS, Book III, 30–31, 49, 38–39, 32.

trees for their usefulness, to the animals that serve as food and who offer their pelts as clothing, to the great winds and the lesser winds, to the Thunderers, and the Sun, the mighty warrior, to the moon, to the messengers of the Great Spirit who dwells in the skies above, who gives all things useful to men, who is the source and the ruler of health and life.

Then shall the Onondaga lords declare the council open. □□

notes and comments

Benjamin Franklin on The Iroquois Constitution

Thomas Jefferson is said to have studied the Constitution of the Iroquois when it came time to frame the United States Constitution. Earlier, in 1754, when Benjamin Franklin was pleading the cause of political union of the American colonies at Albany, New York, Franklin referred to the Iroquois Confederation:

It would be a strange thing if Six Nations of ignorant savages should be capable of forming a scheme for such a union, and be able to execute it in such a manner as that it has subsisted for ages and appears indissoluble; and yet that a like union should be impracticable for ten or a dozen English colonies, to whom it is more necessary and must be more advantageous, and who cannot be supposed to want an equal understanding of their interests.

Albert Henry Smyth, ed., THE WRITINGS OF BENJAMIN FRANKLIN, Vol. IV, 182.

Discussion

1. When referring to the Iroquois Constitution that unites the separate nations of the Iroquois Confederation, Dekanawidah speaks of planting a tree. (a) What are some of the specific terms he uses to develop the comparison? (b) How appropriate is the metaphor of the tree?
2. (a) What personal qualities are necessary for the new rulers? (b) What kinds of greetings should comprise an opening ceremony?
3. What ideas regarding personal conduct and belief in a supreme being are reflected in the speech?

Extension • Writing

1. Almost every modern population center in the United States was inhabited at one time by native Americans. Determine if you can what groups lived in your area or in an area near you. Check your local library for reference works on the early history of your chosen area, and write a report on one of these groups, explaining any signs of their society that exist today.
2. When the first Europeans arrived on the shores of this continent they discovered a "new world" of experience. Enlist the class in creating a display of the fruits, vegetables, animals, implements, clothing, and musical instruments native to the American continent. Use index cards to label each item, showing the etymology of names. Chocolate, tomatoes, squash, corn, coyotes, and turkeys are a few of the things that might be included. Pictures, drawings, or models might be used in addition to actual samples. Write a report on this exhibit for your school newspaper.

Acoma Pueblo, New Mexico.
(Elliott Erwitt/Magnum Photos, Inc.)

Keres Acoma Pueblo

Song Addressed to a New Chief

I wonder if somewhere in an eastern village a new chief has
     arisen for the year,
This is what I said,
I wonder if somewhere in an eastern village a new chief has
     arisen for the year,
This is what I said.
5 From the north direction it has rained,
From the west direction the water comes in streams,
In front of the streams of water.
Down toward the east the lightnings come down and strike
     the earth.
All of us receive life.
10 Now, chief, for this life-giving rain, you must love the earth
     and the sky.
We all receive the benefit from the rain,
It is the duty of the chief to look after his people,
This is what I ask you to do.
From the south it is raining,
15 From the east the water is coming in streams,
In front of the streams of water toward the west,
From there westward the lightning strikes the earth,
All of us receive crops.
Now here, chief, are crops. With this you may love your
     people.
20 This I ask of you.

Keres Acoma (ke′res ä′kō mä).
From MUSIC OF ACOMA, ISLETA, COCHITI AND ZUNI PUEBLOS by Frances
Densmore, published by Da Capo Press, Inc. Reprinted by permission.

Discussion

1. Throughout this ritual song numerous references are made to rain. **(a)** What is the importance of the rain? **(b)** What can you tell from the poem about the society and environment of the Acoma people?

2. What are the primary responsibilities of the new chief?

Extension • Writing

1. Some Southwestern Pueblo cultures, like the Keresan people of the village of Acoma, have an interesting folk tradition involving ancestral spirits—the kachina doll. Find information on the kachina doll in a text on native American cultures. Then draw, paint, or make your own version of a kachina doll, accompanying your illustration with a brief explanatory paragraph.

2. Modern life features many forms of ritual songs and chants: group prayers, the song of "Happy Birthday," and "fight" songs at a pep rally. Compile a list of the oral traditions in modern American culture. After each entry, record its type, purpose, and origin.

Alvar Núñez Cabeza de Vaca

The first people from the Old World to cross North America were Cabeza de Vaca (kä be′sä de vä′kä) and a Moor called Esteban (es te′bän). Shipwrecked in Florida in 1528, they wandered for eight years before reaching northwest Mexico.

from The Narrative of His Journey

The Indians bring us food.

At sunrise the next day, the time the Indians appointed, they came according to their promise, and brought us a large quantity of fish with certain roots, some a little larger than walnuts, others a trifle smaller, the greater part got from under the water and with much labor. In the evening they returned and brought us more fish and roots. They sent their women and children to look at us, who went back rich with the hawk-bells and beads given them, and they came afterwards on other days, returning as before. Finding that we had provision, fish, roots, water, and other things we asked for, we determined to embark again and pursue our course. Having dug out our boat from the sand in which it was buried, it became necessary that we should strip, and go through great exertion to launch her, we being in such a state that things very much lighter sufficed to make us great labor.

Thus embarked, at the distance of two cross-bow shots in the sea we shipped a wave that entirely wet us. As we were naked, and the cold was very great, the oars loosened in our hands, and the next blow the sea struck us, capsized the boat. The assessor[1] and two others held fast to her for preservation, but it happened to be far otherwise; the boat carried them over, and they were drowned under her. As the surf near the shore was very high, a single roll of the sea threw the rest into the waves and half-drowned upon the shore of the island, without our losing any more than those the boat took down. The survivors escaped naked as they were born, with the loss of all they had; and although the whole was of little value, at that time it was worth much, as we were then in November, the cold was severe, and our bodies were so emaciated the bones might be counted with little difficulty, having become the perfect figures of death. For myself I can say that from the month of May past, I had eaten no other thing than maize, and sometimes I found myself obliged to eat it unparched; for although the beasts[2] were slaughtered while the boats were building, I could never eat their flesh, and I did not eat fish ten times. I state this to avoid giving excuses, and that every one may judge in what condition we were. Besides all these misfortunes, came a north wind upon us, from which we were nearer to death than life. Thanks be to our Lord that, looking among the brands we had used there, we found sparks from which we made great fires. And thus were we asking mercy of Him and pardon for our transgressions, shedding many tears, and each regretting not his own fate alone, but that of his comrades about him.

At sunset, the Indians thinking that we had not gone, came to seek us and bring us food; but when they saw us thus, in a plight so different from what it was before, and so extraordinary, they were alarmed and turned back. I went toward them and called, when they returned much frightened. I gave them to understand by signs that our boat had sunk and three of our

---

Excerpts from pp. 45–48, Chapter 12 "The Indians Bring Us Food" and excerpt from pp. 52–54, Chapter 15 "What Befell Us Among the People of Malhado" from THE NARRATIVES OF ALVAR NUÑEZ CABEÇA DE VACA edited by Frederick W. Hodge, Copyright 1907 by Harper & Row, Publishers, Inc. Reprinted by permission of Barnes & Noble Books (Div. of Harper & Row, Publishers, Inc.).

1. **assessor,** the expedition's legal advisor.
2. **beasts,** horses.

to their idols. But seeing no better course, and that any other led to a nearer and more certain death, I disregarded what was said, and besought the Indians to take us to their dwellings. They signified that it would give them delight, and that we should tarry a little, that they might do what we asked. Presently thirty men loaded themselves with wood and started for their houses, which were far off, and we remained with the others until near night, when, holding us up, they carried us with all haste. Because of the extreme coldness of the weather, lest any one should die or fail by the way, they caused four or five very large fires to be placed at intervals, and at each they warmed us; and when they saw that we had regained some heat and strength, they took us to the next so swiftly that they hardly let us touch our feet to the ground. In this manner we went as far as their habitations, where we found that they had made a house for us with many fires in it. An hour after our arrival, they began to dance and hold great rejoicing, which lasted all night, although for us there was no joy, festivity nor sleep, awaiting the hour they should make us victims. In the morning they again gave us fish and roots, showing us such hospitality that we were reassured, and lost somewhat the fear of sacrifice.

What befell us among the people of Malhado.[5]

On an island of which I have spoken, they wished to make us physicians without examination or inquiring for diplomas. They cure by blowing upon the sick, and with that breath and the imposing of hands they cast out infirmity. They ordered that we also should do this, and be of use to them in some way. We laughed at what they did, telling them it was folly, that we knew not how to heal. In consequence, they withheld food from us until we should practise what they required. Seeing our persistence, an Indian told me I knew not what I uttered, in saying that what he knew availed nothing; for stones and other matters growing about in the fields have virtue, and that passing a pebble along the stomach would take away pain and restore health, and certainly then we who were extraordinary men

number had been drowned. There, before them, they saw two of the departed, and we who remained were near joining them. The Indians, at sight of what had befallen us, and our state of suffering and melancholy destitution, sat down among us, and from the sorrow and pity they felt, they all began to lament so earnestly that they might have been heard at a distance, and continued so doing more than half an hour. It was strange to see these men, wild and untaught, howling like brutes over our misfortunes. It caused in me as in others, an increase of feeling and a livelier sense of our calamity.

The cries having ceased, I talked with the Christians,[3] and said that if it appeared well to them, I would beg these Indians to take us to their houses. Some, who had been in New Spain,[4] replied that we ought not to think of it; for if they should do so, they would sacrifice us

---

3. **Christians,** other Spaniards stranded on the island.
4. **New Spain,** Spanish name for colonial Mexico.
5. **Malhado** (mäl häd′ô), Bad Luck Island. [*Spanish*]

must possess power and efficacy over all other things. At last, finding ourselves in great want we were constrained to obey; but without fear lest we should be blamed for any failure or success.

Their custom is, on finding themselves sick to send for a physician, and after he has applied the cure, they give him not only all they have, but seek among their relatives for more to give. The practitioner scarifies over the seat of pain, and then sucks about the wound. They make cauteries with fire, a remedy among them in high repute, which I have tried on myself and found benefit from it. They afterwards blow on the spot, and having finished, the patient considers that he is relieved.

Our method was to bless the sick, breathing upon them, and recite a Pater-noster and an Ave-Maria,[6] praying with all earnestness to God our Lord that he would give health and influence them to make us some good return. In his clemency he willed that all those for whom we supplicated, should tell the others that they were sound and in health, directly after we made the sign of the blessed cross over them. For this the Indians treated us kindly; they deprived themselves of food that they might give to us, and presented us with skins and some trifles.

So protracted was the hunger we there experienced, that many times I was three days without eating. The natives also endured as much; and it appeared to me a thing impossible that life could be so prolonged, although afterwards I found myself in greater hunger and necessity. . . . □□

---

6. **Pater-noster** (päʹter näsʹtər) . . . **Ave-Maria** (äʹvä mə räʹə), the Lord's Prayer and the Hail Mary. [*Latin*]

Pedro de Castañeda

In 1540, stimulated by de Vaca's report, Francisco Vazquez de Coronado (kô rô näʹdô) led a small army north of the Rio Grande and eventually reached the Colorado River. Pedro de Castañeda (pedʹrô de käs tä nyeʹdä) was the chief chronicler of this journey.

Europeans See Buffalo
from The Journey of Coronado

From an early European sketch of a buffalo, about 1550. (Historical Pictures Service, Inc.)

My silence was not without mystery and dissimulation when, in chapter 7 of the second part of this book, I spoke of the plains and of the things of which I will give a detailed account in this chapter, where all these things may be found together; for these things were remarkable and something not seen in other parts. I dare to write of them because I am writing at a time when many men are still living who saw them and who will vouch for my account. Who could believe that a thousand horses and five hundred of our cows and more than five thousand rams and ewes and more than fifteen hundred friendly Indians and servants, in traveling over those plains, would leave no more trace where they had passed than if nothing had been there— nothing—so that it was necessary to make piles of bones and cow dung now and then, so that the

---

From THE JOURNEY OF CORONADO 1540–1542, Translated and Edited with an Introduction by George Parker Winship. New York: Allerton Book Co., 1904.

rear guard could follow the army. The grass never failed to become erect after it had been trodden down, and, although it was short, it was as fresh and straight as before.

Another thing was a heap of cow bones, a crossbow shot long, or a very little less, almost twice a man's height in places, and some eighteen feet or more wide, which was found on the edge of a salt lake in the southern part, and this in a region where there are no people who could have made it. The only explanation of this which could be suggested was that the waves which the north winds must make in the lake had piled up the bones of the cattle which had died in the lake, when the old and weak ones who went into the water were unable to get out. The noticeable thing is the number of cattle that would be necessary to make such a pile of bones.

Now that I wish to describe the appearance of the bulls, it is to be noticed first that there was not one of the horses that did not take flight when he saw them first, for they have a narrow, short face, the brow two palms across from eye to eye, the eyes sticking out at the side, so that, when they are running, they can see who is following them. They have very long beards, like goats, and when they are running they throw their heads back with the beard dragging on the ground. There is a sort of girdle round the middle of the body. The hair is very woolly, like a sheep's, very fine, and in front of the girdle the hair is very long and rough like a lion's. They have a great hump, larger than a camel's. The horns are short and thick, so that they are not seen much above the hair. In May they change the hair in the middle of the body for a down, which makes perfect lions of them. They rub against the small trees in the little ravines to shed their hair, and they continue this until only the down is left, as a snake changes his skin. They have a short tail, with a bunch of hair at the end. When they run, they carry it erect like a scorpion. It is worth noticing that the little calves are red and just like ours, but they change their color and appearance with time and age.

Another strange thing was that all the bulls that were killed had their left ears slit, although these were whole when young. The reason for this was a puzzle that could not be guessed. The wool ought to make good cloth on account of its fineness, although the color is not good, because it is the color of buriel.[1]

Another thing worth noticing is that the bulls traveled without cows in such large numbers that nobody could have counted them, and so far away from the cows that it was more than forty leagues from where we began to see the bulls to the place where we began to see the cows. The country they traveled over was so level and smooth that if one looked at them the sky could be seen between their legs, so that if some of them were at a distance they looked like smooth-trunked pines whose tops joined, and if there was only one bull it looked as if there were four pines. When one was near them, it was impossible to see the ground on the other side of them. The reason for all this was that the country seemed as round as if a man should imagine himself in a three-pint measure, and could see the sky at the edge of it, about a crossbow shot from him, and even if a man only lay down on his back he lost sight of the ground.

I have not written about other things which were seen nor made any mention of them, because they were not of so much importance, although it does not seem right for me to remain silent concerning the fact that they venerate the sign of the cross in the region where the settlements have high houses.[2] For at a spring which was in the plain near Acuco they had a cross two palms high and as thick as a finger, made of wood with a square twig for its crosspiece, and many little sticks decorated with feathers around it, and numerous withered flowers, which were the offerings. In a graveyard outside the village at Tutahaco there appeared to have been a recent burial. Near the head there was another cross made of two little sticks tied with cotton thread, and dry withered flowers. It certainly seems to me that in some way they must have received some light from the cross of Our Redeemer, Christ, and it may have come by way of India, from whence they proceeded.[3] □□

---

1. **buriel** (bü rē el⁄), coarse, gray-brown wool. [*Spanish*]
2. **high houses,** the multi-storied or terraced homes of the Pueblo communities of the American Southwest.
3. **India . . . proceeded,** Europeans believed that native Americans had originally migrated from India.

1. (a) How do the Indians treat the surviving members of de Vaca's expedition? **(b)** What kind of food do they bring them?

2. What is the general condition of the Spanish explorers? Describe some of their greatest difficulties.

3. Why are the Spanish afraid of the Indians at first?

4. (a) What do de Vaca and his companions do to heal the sick? **(b)** What is their response to the Indians' belief in their healing power?

5. Cabeza de Vaca seems to be a careful observer of his rescuers' society. What specific aspects of their life does he record?

6. De Vaca's account reveals something of his personality. What qualities enable him to survive? Where in his narrative do you note evidence of these qualities?

Extension • Writing

If possible, plan a trip to an area you have never visited—another section of town, a nearby city, or another school. Compose a journal account of your experiences, noting anything new or different.

Alvar Núñez Cabeza de Vaca
c. 1490 • c. 1560

During a battle in the thirteenth century, an ancestor of Cabeza de Vaca's, named Alhaja, helped the Spanish forces by marking a crucial mountain pass with the head of a cow. In gratitude, the king ennobled the family, and they changed their name to Cabeza de Vaca (head of a cow).

After returning from Mexico to Spain, de Vaca was appointed governor of Paraguay. In 1540, he led another epic journey through the Amazonian jungles to Paraguay, but the Paraguayan colonists revolted and de Vaca was shipped back to Spain in chains. He was tried and exiled to Africa, but was later pardoned and lived out his retirement in Spain, writing the accounts of his various journeys.

Discussion

1. Castañeda gives the most detailed early description of buffalo. Name some of the features he mentions.

2. What quality or atmosphere does the landscape have that impresses Castañeda most strongly at the beginning?

3. What signs of European civilization does Castañeda observe? Where does he think they originate?

Extension • Reading

Following the European discovery of America in 1492, the sixteenth and early seventeenth centuries saw a variety of Spanish, French, English, and Dutch expeditions whose main purposes were to explore and settle the new continent. Consult a reference work and construct a chronological outline of the major dates of importance. Note specific individuals and places of interest. For example:

1492 Columbus, sailing for India, arrives at the American continent.

1528 Ill-fated Narváez expedition lands in Florida.

Pedro de Castañeda

Little is known of this early chronicler of American history. A soldier in the Coronado expedition, he came from Najera, Spain, and later settled in Mexico. His account of the Coronado expedition was written twenty years after his return and is considered the most important document of the expedition.

John Smith

Like earlier European explorers, Captain Smith was adventurous yet shrewd. A natural leader, he organized the first successful English colony in North America. In England, his books sparked interest in "the new land." This selection is a partly modernized excerpt from his Description of New England *(1616).*

The New Land

Who can desire more content, that hath small means, or but only his merit to advance his fortunes, than to tread and plant that ground he hath purchased by the hazard of his life? If he have but the taste of virtue and magnanimity, what to such a mind can be more pleasant, than planting and building a foundation for his Posterity, got from the rude earth, by God's blessing and his own industry without prejudice to any? If he have any grain of faith or zeal in Religion, what can he do less hurtful to any, or more agreeable to God, than to seek to convert those poor Savages to know Christ, and humanity, whose labours with discretion will triple requite thy charge and pains? What so truly suits with honor and honesty, as the discovering things unknown, erecting Towns, peopling Countries, informing the ignorant, reforming things unjust, teaching virtue? and gain to our native Mother-Country, a kingdom to attend her; find employment for those that are idle because they know not what to do: so far from wronging any, as to cause posterity to remember thee; and remembering thee, ever honour that remembrance with praise? . . .

Here nature and liberty affords us that freely, which in England we want, or it costeth us dearly. What pleasure can be more, than (being tired with any occasion ashore, in planting Vines, Fruits, or Herbs, in contriving their own grounds to the pleasure of their own minds, their Fields, Gardens, Orchards, Buildings, Ships, and other works, etc.) to recreate themselves before their own doors in their own boats upon the Sea; where man, woman and child, with a small hook and line, by angling, may take divers sorts of excellent fish, at their pleasures? And is it not pretty sport, to pull up two pence, six pence, and twelve pence,[1] as fast as you can haul and veer a line? He is a very bad Fisher [that] cannot kill in one day with his hook and line, one, two, or three hundred Cods: which dressed and dried, if they be sold there for ten shillings a hundred, though in England they will give more than twenty, may not both the servant, the master, and merchant, be well content with his gain? If a man work but three days in seven, he may get more than he can spend unless he will be excessive.[2] Now that Carpenter, Mason, Gardener, Tailor, Smith, Sailor, Forgers, or what other, may they not make this a pretty recreation though they fish but an hour in a day, to take more than they can eat in a week? Or if they will not eat it, because there is so much better choice, yet sell it, or change it, with the fishermen or merchants for any thing they want. And what sport doth yield a more pleasing content, and less hurt and charge than angling with a hook; and crossing the sweet air from Isle to Isle, over the silent streams of a calm Sea? Wherein the most curious may find pleasure, profit, and content.

Thus, though all men be not fishers, yet all men, whatsoever, may in other matters do as well. For necessity doth in these cases so rule a Commonwealth, and each in their several functions, as their labours in their qualities may be as profitable, because there is a necessary mutual use of all.

For Gentlemen, what exercise should more

From A DESCRIPTION OF NEW ENGLAND (1616) in Captain John Smith, WORKS, 1608–1613, edited by Edward Arber. Birmingham: The English Scholar's Library, No. 16, 1884.
1. **pence** (pents), pennies, the basic coins of the old British currency.
2. **excessive** (ek ses′iv), wasteful.

delight them, than ranging daily these unknown parts, using fowling and fishing, for hunting and hawking?[3] And yet you shall see the wild hawks give you some pleasure, in seeing them stoop[4] (six or seven times after one another) an hour or two together, at the schools of fish in the fair harbours, as those ashore at a fowl; and never trouble nor torment yourselves, with watching, mewing,[5] feeding and attending them; nor kill horse and man with running and crying, "See you not a hawk?" For hunting also, the woods, lakes and rivers afford not only chase sufficient, for any that delights in that kind of toil or pleasure; but such beasts to hunt, that besides the delicacy of their bodies for food, their skins are so rich, as they will recompense thy daily labour with a Captain's pay.

For labourers, if those that sow hemp, rape, turnips, parsnips, carrots, cabbage, and such like, give twenty, thirty, forty, fifty shillings yearly for an acre of ground, and meat, drink, and wages to use it, and yet grow rich; when better, or at least as good ground may be had and cost nothing but labour; it seems strange to me, any such should there grow poor.

My purpose is not to persuade children from their parents; men from their wives; nor servants from their masters; only such as with free con-sent may be spared: But that each parish, or village, in City, or Country, that will but apparel their fatherless children of thirteen or fourteen years of age, or young married people that have small wealth to live on, here by their labour may live exceeding well: provided always, that first there be a sufficient power to command them, houses to receive them, means to defend them, and meet provisions necessary for them; for any place may be over-lain[6] and it is most necessary to have a fortress (ere this grow to practice[7]) and sufficient masters, (as, Carpenters, Masons, Fishers, Fowlers, Gardeners, Husbandmen, Sawyers, Smiths, Spinsters,[8] Tailors, Weavers, and such like) to take ten, twelve, or twenty, or as there is occasion, for Apprentices. The Masters by this may quickly grow rich; these may learn their trades themselves, to do the like, to a general and an incredible benefit, for King and Country, Master and Servant. ☐☐

---

3. *using fowling . . . hawking.* Smith suggests hunting wild fowl and fishing can substitute for the English gentlemen's usual sports of hunting game and catching birds with trained hawks.
4. *stoop,* swoop of a hawk toward its prey.
5. *mewing,* putting hawks in cages when they are shedding their feathers.
6. *over-lain,* probably "besieged."
7. *ere . . . practice,* before an attack occurs.
8. *Spinsters,* spinners of wool.

William Bradford

William Bradford's strong religious beliefs led him to seek religious freedom as a leader of the Pilgrims who sailed to Massachusetts on the Mayflower. His chronicle, written between 1620 and 1647, was probably not intended for publication. It was not published until 1856, when the manuscript was found in the library of the Bishop of London. Bradford's writing is characterized by a Biblical style, as his life was marked by unwavering faith in divine providence.

from The History of Plymouth Plantation

OF THEIR VOYAGE, AND HOW THEY PASSED THE SEA; AND OF THEIR SAFE ARRIVAL AT CAPE COD

September 6. These troubles being blown over, and now all being compact together in one ship, they put to sea again with a prosperous wind, which continued divers days together, which was some encouragement unto them; yet according to the usual manner, many were afflicted with seasickness. And I may not omit here a special work of God's providence. There was a proud and very profane young man, one of the seamen, of a lusty, able body, which made him the more haughty; he would alway be contemning the poor people in their sickness and cursing them daily with grievous execrations; and did not let to tell them that he hoped to help to cast half of them overboard before they came to their journey's end, and to make merry with what they had; and if he were by any gently reproved, he would curse and swear most bitterly. But it pleased God before they came half seas over, to smite this young man with a grievous disease, of which he died in a desperate manner, and so was himself the first that was thrown overboard. Thus his curses light on his own head, and it was an astonishment to all his fellows for they noted it to be the just hand of God upon him.

After they had enjoyed fair winds and weather for a season, they were encountered many times with cross winds and met with many fierce storms with which the ship was shroudly[1] shaken, and her upper works made very leaky; and one of the main beams in the midships was bowed and cracked, which put them in some fear that the ship could not be able to perform the voyage. So some of the chief of the company, perceiving the mariners to fear the sufficiency of the ship as appeared by their mutterings, they entered into serious consultation with the master and other officers of the ship, to consider in time of the danger, and rather to return than to cast themselves into a desperate and inevitable peril. And truly there was great distraction and difference of opinion amongst the mariners themselves; fain would they do what could be done for their wages' sake (being now near half the seas over) and on the other hand they were loath to hazard their lives too desperately. But in examining of all opinions, the master and others affirmed they knew the ship to be strong and firm under water; and for the buckling of the main beam, there was a great iron screw the passengers brought out of Holland, which would raise the beam into his place; the which being done, the carpenter and master affirmed that with a post put under it, set firm in the lower deck and otherways bound, he would make it sufficient. And as for the decks and upper works, they would caulk them as well as they could, and though with the working of the ship they would not long keep staunch, yet there would otherwise be no great danger, if they did not overpress her with sails. So they committed themselves to the will of God and resolved to proceed.

In sundry of these storms the winds were so fierce and the seas so high, as they could not bear a knot of sail, but were forced to hull[2] for divers days together. And in one of them, as they thus lay at hull in a mighty storm, a lusty young man called John Howland,[3] coming upon some occasion above the gratings was, with a seele[4] of the ship, thrown into sea; but it pleased God that he caught hold of the topsail halyards which hung overboard and ran out at length. Yet he held his hold (though he was sundry fathoms under water) till he was hauled up by the same rope to the brim of the water, and then with a boat hook and other means got into the ship again and his life saved. And though he was something ill with it, yet he lived many years after and became a profitable member both in church and commonwealth. In all this voyage there died but one of the passengers, which was William Butten, a youth, servant to Samuel Fuller, when they drew near the coast.

But to omit other things (that I may be brief) after long beating at sea they fell with that land which is called Cape Cod, the which being made and certainly known to be it, they were not a little joyful. After some deliberation had amongst themselves and with the master of the ship, they tacked about and resolved to stand for the southward (the wind and weather being fair) to find some place about Hudson's River for their habitation. But after they had sailed that course about half the day, they fell amongst dangerous shoals and roaring breakers, and they were so far entangled therewith as they conceived themselves in great danger; and the wind shrinking upon them withal, they resolved to bear up again for the Cape and thought themselves happy to get out of those dangers before night overtook them, as by God's good providence they did. And the next day they got into the Cape Harbor[5] where they rid in safety. . . .

. . . Being thus arrived in a good harbor, and brought safe to land, they fell upon their knees and blessed the God of Heaven who had brought them over the vast and furious ocean, and delivered them from all the perils and miseries thereof, again to set their feet on the firm and stable earth, their proper element. And no marvel if they were thus joyful, seeing wise Seneca[6] was so affected with sailing a few miles on the coast of his own Italy, as he affirmed, that he had rather remain twenty years on his way by land than pass by sea to any place in a short time, so tedious and dreadful was the same unto him.

But here I cannot but stay and make a pause, and stand half amazed at this poor people's

---

1. **shroudly,** an old form of *shrewdly* that means "harshly."
2. **to hull,** to drift with the wind using very little sail.
3. **John Howland.** Howland became an influential member of the Massachusetts Bay Colony.
4. **seele,** the pitch or roll of a ship.
5. **Cape Harbor,** Provincetown Harbor at the tip of Cape Cod.
6. **Seneca,** a famous Roman poet and tragedian.

A nineteenth-century engraving of the Pilgrims' landing. (The Bettmann Archive, Inc.)

Besides, what could they see but a hideous and desolate wilderness, full of wild beasts and wild men—and what multitudes there might be of them they knew not. Neither could they, as it were, go up to the top of Pisgah[8] to view from this wilderness a more goodly country to feed their hopes; for which way soever they turned their eyes (save upward to the heavens) they could have little solace or content in respect of any outward objects. For summer being done, all things stand upon them with a weather-beaten face, and the whole country, full of woods and thickets, represented a wild and savage hue. If they looked behind them, there was the mighty ocean which they had passed and was now as a main bar and gulf to separate them from all the civil parts of the world. If it be said they had a ship to succour them, it is true; but what heard they daily from the master and company? But that with speed they should look out a place (with their shallop) where they would be, at some near distance; for the season was such as he would not stir from thence till a safe harbor was discovered by them, where they would be, and he might go without danger; and that victuals consumed apace but he must and would keep sufficient for themselves and their return. Yea, it was muttered by some that if they got not a place in time, they would turn them and their goods ashore and leave them. Let it also be considered what weak hopes of supply and succour they left behind them, that might bear up their minds in this sad condition and trials they were under; and they could not but be very small. It is true, indeed, the affections and love of their brethen at Leyden was cordial and entire towards them, but they had little power to help them or themselves; and how the case stood between them and the merchants at their coming away hath already been declared.

What could now sustain them but the Spirit of God and His grace? May not and ought not the children of these fathers rightly say: "Our fathers were Englishmen which came over this great ocean, and were ready to perish in this wilderness; but they cried unto the Lord, and He

present condition; and so I think will the reader, too, when he well considers the same. Being thus passed the vast ocean, and a sea of troubles before in their preparation (as may be remembered by that which went before), they had now no friends to welcome them nor inns to entertain or refresh their weather-beaten bodies; no houses or much less towns to repair to, to seek for succour. It is recorded in Scripture as a mercy to the Apostle[7] and his shipwrecked company, that the barbarians showed them no small kindness in refreshing them, but these savage barbarians, when they met with them (as after will appear) were readier to fill their sides full of arrows than otherwise. And for the season it was winter, and they that know the winters of that country know them to be sharp and violent, and subject to cruel and fierce storms, dangerous to travel to known places, much more to search an unknown coast.

---

7. *a mercy to the Apostle.* The allusion is to Paul's shipwreck on Malta (see Acts 28:2).
8. *Pisgah.* Moses led the Hebrews up Mt. Pisgah near the Dead Sea to view the Promised Land (Numbers 21:18–20).

heard their voice and looked on their adversity,"[9] etc. "Let them therefore praise the Lord, because He is good: and His mercies endure forever," "Yea, let them which have been redeemed of the Lord, shew[10] how He hath delivered them from the hand of the oppressor. When they wandered in the desert wilderness out of the way, and found no city to dwell in, both hungry and thirsty, their soul was overwhelmed in them. Let them confess before the Lord His loving-kindness and His wonderful works before the sons of men."[11] □□

---

9. **He . . . adversity,** Deut. 26:5, 7.
10. **shew** (shō), variant of *show.*
11. **"Yea, let them . . . before the sons of men,** Ps. 107:1–5, 8.

Discussion

1. In an attempt to stimulate an interest in America, Smith begins by asking a series of questions. Each seems to appeal to a slightly different concern of the readers. What are some of the particular desires to which Smith appeals?

2. How does Smith contrast opportunity in America with that in England?

3. Smith addresses certain remarks to individual groups of workers. What does Smith seem to promise each?

Extension • Writing

Land development was among the first colonial enterprises. Assume that Captain Smith's "advertisement" appeared in an English newspaper and that you are an American visiting England. Compose a letter to the editor of an English newspaper in which you discuss some of the conditions of colonial life that have been omitted or misrepresented by Smith.

John Smith 1579 • 1631

John Smith led the expedition that in 1607 established Jamestown, Virginia, the first British colony in America. Smith remained in Virginia until 1609, and during that period wrote *A True Relation* (1607), the first English book written in America. Later explorations in the new country were described in other accounts, which he wrote partly to encourage colonization. Among these accounts was *The Generall Historie of Virginia, New England, and the Summer Isles* (1624).

Discussion

1. Does the new world as described by Bradford impress you as a friendly or unfriendly place to settle? Support your answer.

2. Today we tend to idealize nature and natural beauty. What is Bradford's view of nature?

3. Bradford makes use of a number of Biblical **allusions,** three of which are footnoted in the text. Read these footnotes and explain how the allusions are related to Bradford's account.

4. If you were going to explore an unknown region, such as another planet, you also might want to keep a diary of your adventures. Disregarding some of the more obvious differences, how would your chronicle differ from Bradford's in the topics covered? Explain.

William Bradford 1590 • 1657

While a boy in England, William Bradford joined a religious group who believed in separation from the Church of England. He went with this group for an eleven-year stay in Holland. He was still with the group when it sailed on the historic *Mayflower* and landed at Plymouth, Massachusetts, in December, 1620. Bradford assumed the position of principal leader of the colony and was chosen governor thirty times.

Anne Bradstreet

Upon the Burning of Our House
July 10th, 1666

In silent night when rest I took,
For sorrow near I did not look,
I waken'd was with thund'ring noise
And piteous shrieks of dreadful voice.
5 That fearful sound of fire and fire,
Let no man know is my desire.

I, starting up, the light did spy,
And to my God my heart did cry
To strengthen me in my distress
10 And not to leave me succorless.
Then coming out beheld a space,
The flame consume my dwelling place.

And, when I could no longer look,
I blest his Name that gave and took,
15 That laid my goods now in the dust:
Yea so it was, and so 'twas just.
It was his own: it was not mine;
Far be it that I should repine.

He might of all justly bereft,
20 But yet sufficient for us left.
When by the ruins oft I past,
My sorrowing eyes aside did cast,
And here and there the places spy
Where oft I sat, and long did lie.

25 Here stood that trunk, and there that chest;
There lay that store I counted best:
My pleasant things in ashes lie,
And them behold no more shall I.
Under thy roof no guest shall sit,
30 Nor at they table eat a bit.

No pleasant tale shall e'er be told,
Nor things recounted done of old.
No candle e'er shall shine in thee,
Nor bridegroom's voice ere heard shall be.
35 In silence ever shalt thou lie;
Adieu, adieu; all's vanity.

Then straight I gin my heart to chide,
And did thy wealth on earth abide?
Didst fix thy hope on mould'ring dust,
40 The arm of flesh didst make thy trust?
Raise up thy thoughts above the sky
That dunghill mists away may fly.

Thou hast an house on high erect,
Fram'd by that mighty Architect,
45 With glory richly furnished,
Stands permanent tho' this be fled.
It's purchased, and paid for too
By him who hath enough to do.

A prize so vast as is unknown,
50 Yet, by his gift, is made thine own.
There's wealth enough, I need no more;
Farewell my pelf, farewell my store.
The world no longer let me love,
My hope and treasure lies above.

The "keeping room" or family sitting room in a seventeenth-century Massachusetts house. (Historical Pictures Service, Inc.)

Discussion

1. Today, we try to find logical explanations for unfortunate disasters of this nature. What attitude toward her loss does the speaker express?

2. (a) Cite lines from the text which show the affection the speaker feels for objects that were in her home. (b) In the sixth stanza, Bradstreet's attitude toward her home changes. Identify the line of that stanza that best summarizes her feelings.

3. Bradstreet speaks of *two* homes in the poem. (a) Identify the literal owner of each home. (b) In the philosophical sense of the poem, identify the *true* owner of both homes. Explain.

4. In line 52 the poet uses the word *pelf*. Find the meaning of this word and explain its use in the poem. Does the poet use the word connotatively or denotatively?

At the age of eighteen, Anne Bradstreet came to America with her husband, settling in the Massachusetts Bay Colony. In spite of the demands made on her as a housewife and mother of eight children, she found time to write poetry. Her first volume of poems was published in London, entitled *The Tenth Muse Lately Sprung Up in America* (1650). Some of her best, less bookish, and more personal poems were published after her death.

Edward Taylor

Upon What Base?

Upon what base was fixed the lathe wherein
He turned this globe and rigolled it[1] so trim?
Who blew the bellows of His furnace vast?
Or held the mold wherein the world was cast?
5 Who laid its cornerstone? Or whose command?
Where stand the pillars upon which it stands?
Who laced and filleted[2] the earth so fine
With rivers like green ribbons smaragdine?[3]
Who made the seas its selvage,[4] and its locks
10 Like a quilt ball within a silver box?[5]
Who spread its canopy? Or curtains spun?
Who in this bowling alley bowled the sun?

From THE POETICAL WORKS OF EDWARD TAYLOR, ed. Thomas H. Johnson (Princeton Paperback, 1966). Copyright Rockland 1939; Princeton University Press, 1943. Reprinted by permission of Princeton University Press.

1. *rigolled* (rig′əld) *it*, shaped and grooved it so that its various parts fitted snugly together.
2. *filleted*, edged.
3. *smaragdine* (smä rag′din), having the deep green color of emeralds.
4. *Who made . . . selvage* (sel′vij), "Who made the seas the edges or border of the land?"
5. *locks . . . box,* landlocked lakes that look like balls of quilting materials in a silver-colored sewing box.

The Ancient of Days by William Blake (1757–1827). (Whitworth Art Gallery, University of Manchester.)

Discussion

1. Edward Taylor is known for his simple **metaphors** drawn from personal experience. **(a)** State the central image in "Upon What Base?" **(b)** To what kinds of earthly craftsmen does Taylor refer in reinforcing his central image?

2. **(a)** What particular aspects of the beauty of the earth does Taylor select for comment in lines 7–11? **(b)** What line in this poem might surprise the modern reader?

3. In what ways does reading Taylor's poetry increase your understanding of everyday life in colonial New England?

Edward Taylor c. 1645 • 1729

The most talented American poet of the early period, Edward Taylor was born in England and came to America in his early twenties. He attended Harvard and later became pastor of a church in Massachusetts. Taylor did not publish his poems during his lifetime. They were generally forgotten until the twentieth century, when a few were printed in 1939. His genius was then recognized, and his complete poems were published in 1960. He is the only American poet of the metaphysical school, a group of seventeenth-century British poets, such as John Donne, who were fond of using complex metaphors, called "conceits."

Sarah Kemble Knight

When Sarah Kemble Knight traveled from Boston to New York in 1704 to settle an estate, she went on horseback because stagecoaches were not yet common. The following excerpt from her journal of the five-month journey has been partly modernized, though some archaic spellings have been retained to give the flavor of the original.

Traveling in the New Land

When we had Ridd about an how'r, we come into a thick Swamp, which, by Reason of a great fog, very much startled me, it being now very Dark. But nothing dismay'd John: He had encountered a thousand and a thousand such Swamps, having a Universal Knowledge in the woods; and readily answered all my inquiries, which were not a few.

In about an how'r, or something more, after we left the Swamp, we come to Billinges,[1] where I was to lodge. My Guide dismounted and very complaisantly help't me down and showed the door, signing to me with his hand to go in; which I gladly did—But had not gone many steps into the Room, ere I was interrogated by a young lady I understood afterwards was the Eldest daughter of the family, with these, or words to this purpose *(viz.):* "Law for me—what in the world brings You here at this time a night?—I never see a woman on the Road so dreadful late, in all the days of my versall[2] life. Who are You? Where are You going? I'm scar'd out of my wits"—with much now of the same kind. I stood aghast, preparing to reply, when in comes my Guide—to him Madam turn'd Roaring out: "Lawful heart, John, is it You?—how de do! Where in the world are you going with this woman? Who is she?" John made no Answer but sat down in the corner, fumbled out his black Junk,[3] and saluted that instead of Debb; she then turned agen to me and fell anew into her silly questions, without asking me to sit down.

I told her she treated me very rudely, and I did not think it my duty to answer her unmannerly Questions. But to get rid of them, I told her I come there to have the Post's[4] company with me to-morrow on my Journey, etc. Miss star'd awhile, drew a chair, bid me sit, and then run upstairs and puts on two or three Rings (or else I had not seen them before), and returning, set herself just before me, showing the way to Reding,[5] that I might see her Ornaments, perhaps to gain the more respect. But her Granam's new-rung sow,[6] had it appeared, would [have] affected me as much.

I paid honest John with money and dram[7] according to contract, and dismissed him, and pray'd Miss to shew me where I must Lodge. She conducted me to a parlour in a little back Lean-to, which was almost filled with the bedsted, which was so high I was forced to climb on a chair to git up to the wretched bed that lay on it; on which having Stretch't my tired Limbs, and lay'd my head on a Sad-colour'd pillow, I began to think on the transactions of the past day.

Tuesday, October the third, about 8 in the morning, I with the Post proceeded forward without observing any thing remarkable; and about two, afternoon, Arrived at the Post's stage, where the western Post met him and exchanged Letters. Here, having called for something to eat,

From THE JOURNAL OF MADAM KNIGHT by Sarah Kemble Knight. Albany: Frank Little, 1865.

1. *Billinges,* probably a colonial village south of Boston.
2. *versall* (vėr/səl), an archaic word meaning "individual."
3. *black Junk,* tobacco.
4. *Post,* messenger carrying the mail.
5. *showing . . . Reding,* an idiom meaning "to make a display of oneself."
6. *Granam's new-rung sow,* Grandmother's sow with a ring through its snout.
7. *dram,* small drink of whiskey.

the woman brought in a twisted thing like a cable, but something whiter; and laying it on the board, tugg'd for life to bring it into a capacity to spread; which having with great pains accomplished, she serv'd in a dish of Pork and Cabbage, I suppose the remains of Dinner. The sause was of a deep Purple, which I thought was boil'd in her dye Kettle; the bread was Indian,[8] and every thing on the Table service agreeable to these. I, being hungry, got a little down; but my stomach was soon cloy'd, and what cabage I swallowed serv'd me for a Cud the whole day after.

Having here discharged the Ordinary[9] for self and Guide (as I understood was the custom), about three, afternoon, went on with my third Guide, who Rode very hard: and having crossed Providence Ferry, we come to a River which they generally Ride thro'. But I dare not venture; so the Post got a Lad and Cannoo to carry me to t'other side, and he rid thro' and Led my hors. The Cannoo was very small and shallow, so that when we were in, she seem'd ready to take in water, which greatly terrified me, and caused me to be very circumspect, sitting with my hands fast on each side, my eyes steady, not daring so much as to lodge my tongue a hair's breadth more on one side of my mouth than t'other, nor so much as think on Lot's wife,[10] for a wry thought would have overset our wherry. But was soon put out of this pain, by feeling the Cannoo on shore, which I as soon almost saluted with my feet; and Rewarding my sculler, again mounted and made the best of our way forwards. The Road here was very even and the day pleasant, it being now near Sunset. But the Post told me we had near 14 miles to Ride to the next Stage (where we were to Lodge). I ask't him of the rest of the Road, foreseeing we must travel in the night. He told me there was a bad River we were to Ride thro', which was so very fierce a hors could sometimes hardly stem it: But it was but narrow, and we should soon be over. I cannot express the concern of mind this relation set me in: no thoughts but those of the dangerous River could entertain my Imagination; and they were as formidable as various, still Tormenting me with blackset Ideas of my Approaching fate— Sometimes seeing myself drowning, otherwhiles drowned, and at the best like a Holy Sister just come out of a Spiritual Bath in dripping Garments.

Now was the Glorious Luminary with his swift Coursers arrived at his Stage,[11] leaving poor me with the rest of this part of the lower world in darkness, with which we were soon Surrounded. The only Glimmering we now had was from the spangled Skies, whose Imperfect Reflections rendered every Object formidable. Each lifeless Trunk, with its shatter'd Limbs, appear'd an Armed Enemy; and every little stump like a Ravenous Devourer. Nor could I so much as discern my Guide, when at any distance, which added to the terror.

Thus, absolutely lost in Thought, and dying with the very thoughts of drowning, I come up with the Post, who I did not see till even with his hors: he told me he stop't for me; and we Rode on very deliberately a few paces, when he entered a Thicket of Trees and Shrubs, and I perceived by the hors's going we were on the descent of a Hill, which, as we come nearer the bottom, 'twas totally dark with the Trees that surrounded it. But I knew by the going of the hors we had entered the water, which my Guide told me was the hazardous River he had told me of; and he, Riding up close to my side, Bid me not fear—we should be over immediately. I now rallied all the Courage I was mistress of, knowing that I must either Venture my fate of drowning, or be left like the Children in the wood.[12] So, as the Post bid me, I gave reins to my Nag; and sitting as Steady as just before in the Cannoo, in a few minutes got safe to the other side, which he told me was the Narragansett country.[13]

Here we found great difficulty in Traveling, the way being very narrow, and on each side the Trees and bushes gave us very unpleasant welcome with their branches and boughs, which we could not avoid, it being so exceeding dark. My Guide, as before so now, put on harder than I, with my weary bones, could follow; so left me

---

8. **bread was Indian,** bread made from Indian corn.
9. **discharged the Ordinary,** paid the bill.
10. **Lot's wife.** In the Bible, Lot's wife was turned into a pillar of salt when she looked back at Sodom (Genesis 19:26).
11. **Glorious Luminary** (lü′mə ner′ē) . . . **Stage.** The sun went down.
12. **Children in the wood,** a fairy tale, in which two young children die in the forest where they have been left by their greedy uncle.
13. **Narragansett** (nar ə gan′sət) **country,** area around the town of Narragansett in southern Rhode Island.

Twilight in the Wilderness by Fredric Edwin Church (1826–1900). (The Cleveland Museum of Art, Mr. and Mrs. William H. Marlatt Fund.)

and the way behind him. Now returned my distressed apprehensions of the place where I was: the dolesome woods, my Company next to none, going I knew not whither, and encompassed with terrifying darkness; the least of which was enough to startle a more Masculine courage. Added to which the Reflections, as in the afternoon of the day, that my Call was very questionable, which till then I had not so Prudently as I ought considered. Now, coming to the foot of a hill, I found great difficulty in ascending; but being got to the Top, was there amply recompenced with the friendly Appearance of the Kind Conductress of the night, just then advancing above the Horisontal Line. The Raptures which the Sight of that fair Planet produced in me, caus'd me, for the moment, to forget my present wearyness and past toils; and Inspir'd me for most of the remaining way with very diverting thoughts, some of which, with the other occurrences of the day, I reserved to note down when I should come to my Stage. My thoughts on the sight of the moon were to this purpose:

Fair Cynthia,[14] all the Homage that I may
Unto a Creature, unto thee I pay;
In Lonesome woods to meet so kind a guide,
To me's more worth than all the world beside.
Some Joy I felt just now, when safe got o'er
Yon Surly River to this Rugged shore,
Deeming Rough welcomes from these
     clownish Trees,
Better than Lodgings with Nereidees.[15]
Yet swelling fears surprise; all dark appears—
Nothing but Light can dissipate those fears.

---

14. *Fair Cynthia,* Greek goddess of the hunt.
15. *Nereidees* (nir′ē əd ēz), Greek sea nymphs.

My fainting vitals can't lend strength to say,
But softly whisper, O I wish 'twere day.
The murmur hardly warm'd the Ambient air,
Ere thy Bright Aspect rescues from despair:
Makes the old Hag[16] her sable mantle loose,
And a Bright Joy do's through my Soul diffuse.
The Boistero's Trees now Lend a Passage Free,
And pleasant prospects thou giv'st light to see.

From hence we kept on, with more ease than before: the way being smooth and even, the night warm and serene, and the tall and thick Trees at a distance, especially when the moon glar'd light through the branches, fill'd my Imagination with the pleasant delusion of a Sumptuous city, fill'd with famous Buildings and Churches, with their spiring Steeples, Balconies, Galleries and I know not what: Grandeurs which I had heard of and which the stories of foreign countries had given me the Idea of.

Here stood a Lofty church—there is a steeple
And there the Grand Parade—O see the people!
That Famous Castle there, were I but nigh,
To see the moat and Bridge and walls so high—
They're very fine! says my deluded eye.

Being thus agreeably entertain'd without a thought of anything but thoughts themselves, I on a sudden was Rous'd from these pleasing Imaginations, by the Post's sounding his horn, which assured me he was arrived at the Stage, where we were to Lodge: and that musick was then most musickal and agreeable to me. □□

---

16. *the old Hag,* evil female spirit, here the night.

Discussion

1. Although some of her spelling and vocabulary are outdated, Knight's journal has a lively and engaging quality. (a) What elements of the diary contribute to this quality? (b) Cite examples of humor, **irony,** and **satire.**

2. What personal qualities does the author reveal when she speaks with the woman at Billinges? When she is in the small boat crossing the river?

3. (a) What effect on her does seeing the moon have? (b) How would you contrast the style of the poem beginning "Fair Cynthia" with the poem in the later portion of the journal?

Extension · Reading

The selections given here from the journal of Sarah Kemble Knight cover the first few days of her journey. Using your local or school library, try to locate other extracts from the diary. Compare entries on later days to determine how Knight's spirit or style changed.

Vocabulary
Pronunciation and Dictionary

(a) Divide the following words into syllables and underline the syllable that has the primary accent.

(b) Write a word that rhymes with each syllable that has a primary accent.

As you do this exercise, be sure you know the definition of each word.

1. supplicate
2. transgression
3. requite
4. recompense
5. execration
6. bereft
7. adieu
8. ambient

Sarah Kemble Knight
1666 • 1727

Knight was a person of unusual accomplishments. In Boston, where she spent most of her life, she taught school and managed a shop and a boarding house. According to tradition, the young Ben Franklin was one of her pupils. Knight gained considerable knowledge of law by preparing court records and other legal documents. When a cousin in New Haven died and left an unsettled estate, she did not hesitate to travel to New York to settle it. She later moved to Connecticut, where she continued to engage successfully in business.

William Byrd II

William Byrd II, a member of the Virginia plantation aristocracy, belonged to the commission that surveyed the dividing line between North Carolina and Virginia. The notes he made during this expedition were not meant for publication, but were printed almost a century after his death.

Bears
from The History of the Dividing Line

"The Grizzly Bear" before 1857, steel and wood engraving by George Catlin from "Letters and Notes on the Manners, Customs, and Conditions of the North American Indians," vol. 2 by George Catlin, 1857.

The grapes we commonly met with were black, tho' there be two or three kinds of white grapes that grow wild. The black are very sweet, but small, because the strength of the vine spends itself in wood; tho' without question a proper culture would make the same grapes both larger and sweeter. But, with all these disadvantages, I have drunk tolerably good wine prest from them, tho' made without skill. There is then good Reason to believe it might admit of great improvement, if rightly managed.

Our Indian kill'd a Bear, of two years old, that was feasting on these grapes. He was very fat, as they generally are in that season of the year. In the fall, the flesh of this animal has a high relish, different from that of the other creatures, tho' inclining nearest to that of Pork, or rather of Wild Boar.

A true Woodsman prefers this sort of meat to that of the fattest Venison, not only for the *Hautgout*[1] but also because the fat of it is well tasted, and never rises in the stomach. Another proof of the goodness of this meat is, that it is less apt to corrupt than any other we are acquainted with. As agreeable as such rich diet was to the men, yet we who were not accustom'd to it, tasted it at first with some sort of squeamishness, that animal being of the Dog-kind; tho' a little use soon reconcil'd us to this American Venison. And that its being of the Dog kind might give us the less disgust, we had the example of that ancient and polite People, the Chinese, who reckon Dog's flesh too good for any under the quality of a mandarin.[2]

This Beast is in truth a very clean feeder, living, while the season lasts, upon acorns, chestnuts and chinkapins,[3] wild honey and wild grapes. They are naturally not carnivorous, unless hunger constrains them to it, after the mast is all gone, and the products of the woods quite exhausted.

They are not provident enough to lay up any hoard, like the Squirrels, nor can they, after all, live very long upon licking their paws, as Sir John Mandevil[4] and some Travellers tell us, but are forced in the winter months to quit the mountains, and visit the inhabitants.

Their errand is then to surprise a poor Hog at a pinch to keep them from starving. And to shew that they are not flesh-eaters by trade, they devour their prey very awkwardly.

From WILLIAM BYRD'S HISTORIES OF THE DIVIDING LINE BE-TWIXT VIRGINIA AND NORTH CAROLINA. Originally published by the North Carolina Historical Commission. Published 1967 by Dover Publications.
1. *Hautgout* (ō gü⁄), highly seasoned flavor. [*French*]
2. *mandarin* (man⁄dər ən), a high-ranking public official in the Chinese Empire.
3. *chinkapin* (chink⁄ə pin), a dwarf chestnut.
4. *Sir John Mandevil* (man⁄də vil⁄), the pen name of an author of a fourteenth-century travel book.

They don't kill it right out, and feast upon its blood and entrails, like other ravenous Beasts, but having, after a fair pursuit, seiz'd it with their paws, they begin first upon the rump, and so devour one collop after another, till they come to the vitals, the poor Animal crying all the while, for several minutes together. However, in so doing, Bruin acts a little imprudently, because the dismal outcry of the Hog alarms the neighbourhood, and 'tis odds but he pays the forfeit with his Life,[5] before he can secure his retreat.

But Bears soon grow weary of this unnatural diet, and about January, when there is nothing to be got in the woods, they retire into some cave or hollow tree, where they sleep away two or three months very comfortably. But then they quit their holes in March, when the Fish begin to run up the rivers, on which they are forced to keep Lent,[6] till some fruit or berry comes in season.

But Bears are fondest of chestnuts, which grow plentifully towards the mountains, upon very large trees, where the soil happens to be rich. We were curious to know how it happen'd that many of the outward branches of those trees came to be broke off in that solitary place, and were inform'd that the Bears are so discreet as not to trust their unwieldy bodies on the smaller limbs of the tree, that would not bear their weight; but after venturing as far as is safe, which they can judge to an inch, they bite off the end of the branch, which falling down, they are content to finish their repast upon the ground. In the same cautious manner they secure the acorns that grow on the weaker limbs of the oak. And it must be allow'd that, in these instances, a Bear carries Instinct a great way, and acts more reasonably than many of his betters, who indiscreetly venture upon frail projects that won't bear them. ☐☐

---

5. **forfeit . . . Life,** pay the penalty with a loss of life.
6. **Lent,** the Christian season of penance.

Discussion

1. (a) How would you characterize Byrd's attitude toward the bears? Do you think it is more objective or subjective? Explain. (b) In which of their actions does Byrd feel that the bears are cautious and even calculating?

2. (a) In what ways does Byrd **personify** or humanize the bears? (b) Is there any point in the story where you feel sympathy for the bears? If so, describe.

Extension
Reading and Writing

1. Byrd's *History of the Dividing Line* is a long and varied chronicle. Locate a copy and read samples of it to gain a fuller understanding of the work. Explain your findings to the class.

2. Write a children's story about an incident in the life of a bear. Incorporate as many details from Byrd's account as possible.

William Byrd 1674 • 1744

William Byrd, although born in Virginia Colony, spent almost half his life in England. His father left him a large Virginia estate, near Williamsburg, and there Byrd set himself up as a member of the landed gentry devoted to civilized and gracious pursuits. His earlier education in England had given him a knowledge of Latin, Greek, and Hebrew, and he continued to read these languages daily to retain his fluency. His fame rests on a series of histories and diaries that give vivid and sometimes embarrassingly intimate glimpses into the personal, social, and public life of the time.

Canassatego: An Offer of Help

*At treaty talks in 1744, the Iroquois leader Canassatego
(kä′näs sä tä′gō) made the following reply to an offer from the
Virginia government to educate some Iroquois youths at the
College of William and Mary. What is the* **tone** *of his speech?*

We know you highly esteem the kind of Learning taught in these Colleges, and the maintenance of our young Men, while with you, would be very expensive to you. We are convinced, therefore, that you mean to do us Good by your Proposal; and we thank you heartily. But you who are so wise must know that different Nations have different Conceptions of things; and you will not therefore take it amiss, if our Ideas of this kind of Education happens not to be the same with yours. We have had some experience of it. Several of our young People were formerly brought up in the Colleges of the Northern Provinces;[1] they were instructed in all your Sciences; but, when they came back to us, they were bad Runners, ignorant of every means of living in the Woods, unable to bear either Cold or Hunger, knew neither how to build a Cabin, take a deer, or kill an enemy, spoke our language imperfectly, were therefore neither fit for Hunters, Warriors, nor Counsellors, they were totally good for nothing. We are however not the less obliged for your kind Offer, tho' we decline accepting it; and to show our grateful Sense of it, if the Gentlemen of Virginia shall send us a Dozen of their Sons, we will take great care of their Education, instruct them in all we know, and make Men of them.

Albert Henry Smyth, ed., THE WRITINGS OF BENJAMIN FRANKLIN, Vol. X, 98–99.
1. ***Northern Provinces,*** New Hampshire and Massachusetts, which were ruled by officers appointed by the King.

Jonathan Edwards

from Sinners in the Hands of an Angry God

The wrath of God is like great waters that are dammed for the present; they increase more and more and rise higher and higher, till an outlet is given; and the longer the stream is stopped, the more rapid and mighty is its course when once it is let loose. 'Tis true that judgment against your evil work has not been executed hitherto; the floods of God's vengeance have been withheld; but your guilt in the meantime is constantly increasing, and you are every day treasuring up more wrath; the waters are continually rising and waxing more and more mighty; and there is nothing but the mere pleasure of God that holds the waters back, that are unwilling to be stopped, and press hard to go forward. If God should only withdraw his hand from the floodgate it would immediately fly open, and the fiery floods of the fierceness and wrath of God would rush forth with inconceivable fury, and would come upon you with omnipotent power; and if your strength were ten thousand times greater than it is, yea, ten thousand times greater than the strength of the stoutest, sturdiest devil in hell, it would be nothing to withstand or endure it.

The bow of God's wrath is bent, and the arrow made ready on the string, and justice bends the arrow at your heart and strains the bow, and it is nothing but the mere pleasure of God, and that of an angry God, without any promise or obligation at all, that keeps the arrow one moment from being made drunk with your blood.

Thus are all you that never passed under a great change of heart by the mighty power of the Spirit of God upon your souls; all that were never born again and made new creatures, and raised from being dead in sin to a state of new and before altogether unexperienced light and life (however you may have reformed your life in many things, and may have had religious affections, and may keep up a form of religion in your families and closets and in the house of God, and may be strict in it), you are thus in the hands of an angry God; 'tis nothing but his mere pleasure that keeps you from being this moment swallowed up in everlasting destruction.

However unconvinced you may now be of the truth of what you hear, by and by you will be fully convinced of it. Those that are gone from being in the like circumstances with you, see that it was so with them; for destruction came suddenly upon most of them; when they expected nothing of it, and while they were saying, Peace and Safety. Now they see that those things that they depended on for peace and safety were nothing but thin air and empty shadows.

The God that holds you over the pit of hell much as one holds a spider or some loathsome insect over the fire, abhors you, and is dreadfully provoked; his wrath toward you burns like fire; he looks upon you as worthy of nothing else but to be cast into the fire; he is of purer eyes than to bear to have you in his sight; you are ten thousand times so abominable in his eyes as the most hateful and venomous serpent is in ours. You have offended him infinitely more than ever a stubborn rebel did his prince; and yet it is nothing but his hand that holds you from falling into the fire every moment. 'Tis ascribed to nothing else, that you did not go to hell the last night; that you were suffered to awake again in this world after you closed your eyes to sleep and there is no other reason to be given why you have not dropped into hell since you arose in the morning, but that God's hand has held you up. There is no other reason to be given why you have not gone to hell since you have sat here in the house of God, provoking his pure eyes by your sinful wicked manner of attending his solemn worship. Yea, there is nothing else that is to be given as a reason why you don't this very moment drop down into hell.

O sinner! Consider the fearful danger you are in. 'Tis a great furnace of wrath, a wide and bottomless pit, full of the fire of wrath, that you are held over in the hand of that God whose wrath is provoked and incensed as much against you as against many of the damned in hell. You hang by a slender thread, with the flames of divine wrath flashing about it, and ready every moment to singe it and burn it asunder; and you have no interest in any Mediator, and nothing to lay hold of to save yourself, nothing to keep off the flames of wrath, nothing of your own, nothing that you ever have done, nothing that you can do, to induce God to spare you one moment. . . . □□

Discussion

1. Edwards develops three **extended metaphors** to create the image of an angry God condemning sinners to suffer forever. Identify the extended metaphors in the selection, as well as the individual figures of speech that develop them.

2. Edwards's sermons were powerful to the congregations and readers of his time. **(a)** What can you deduce about the religious convictions of the average member of his congregation? **(b)** How effective do you think his sermons would be today? Explain your answer.

3. **(a)** Why do you think Edwards chose to portray a God of wrath instead of a loving God? **(b)** Which image lends itself to a more vivid sermon, and why?

Extension • Reading

Read the definitions of **simile** and **metaphor** in the Definitions of Literary Terms. Then read another famous sermon such as the Sermon on the Mount or Martin Luther King's "I Have a Dream." In a paragraph discuss the similarities and differences in the use of figurative language between that sermon and "Sinners in the Hands of an Angry God."

Vocabulary • Dictionary

Use your Glossary to answer the questions about each italicized word below. The words are taken from the selections by William Bradford, Anne Bradstreet, and Jonathan Edwards.

1. In Bradford's "The History of Plymouth Plantation," the man who cursed and swore at the other passengers on the ship became ill and died. How was this an example of God's *providence*?

2. During the fire in "Upon the Burning of Our House," Bradstreet says that she was awakened by "*piteous* shrieks." What other words could describe these shrieks?

The rest of the questions deal with words in Edwards's "Sinners in the Hands of an Angry God."

3. Edwards characterizes God as *omnipotent*. What does he mean?

4. Man is compared to a "*loathsome* insect." What kind of insect is this?

5. What characteristics of humanity does Edwards find *abominable*?

6. Edwards says his listeners are hanging by a thread over the fires of eternal punishment. What will happen when this thread comes *asunder*?

Jonathan Edwards 1703 • 1758

Edwards is probably the most eminent theologian that America has yet produced. He was born in Connecticut and educated at Yale. During his early career as minister in the church at Northampton, Massachusetts, he encouraged the Great Awakening, the first of a series of religious revivals in America. His congregation became uneasy when he began to place emphasis on public accounts of religious experiences, and dismissed him in 1750. He went then to Stockbridge, Massachusetts, where he served as minister from 1751 to 1757. Among the important religious works by Edwards are *A Divine and Supernatural Light* (1734) and *Freedom of the Will* (1754).

Benjamin Franklin

Moral Perfection
from The Autobiography

It was about this time I conceiv'd the bold and arduous project of arriving at moral perfection. I wish'd to live without committing any fault at any time; I would conquer all that either natural inclination, custom, or company might lead me into. As I knew, or thought I knew, what was right and wrong, I did not see why I might not always do the one and avoid the other. But I soon found I had undertaken a task of more difficulty than I had imagined. While my care was employ'd in guarding against one fault, I was often surprised by another; habit took the advantage of inattention; inclination was sometimes too strong for reason. I concluded, at length, that the mere speculative conviction that it was our interest to be completely virtuous, was not sufficient to prevent our slipping; and that the contrary habits must be broken, and good ones acquired and established, before we can have any dependence on a steady, uniform rectitude of conduct. For this purpose I therefore contrived the following method.

In the various enumerations of the moral virtues I had met with in my reading, I found the catalogue more or less numerous, as different writers included more or fewer ideas under the same name. Temperance, for example, was by some confined to eating and drinking, while by others it was extended to mean the moderating every other pleasure, appetite, inclination, or passion, bodily or mental, even to our avarice and ambition. I propos'd to myself, for the sake of clearness, to use rather more names, with fewer ideas annex'd to each, than a few names with more ideas; and I included under thirteen names of virtues all that at that time occurr'd to me as necessary or desirable, and annexed to each a short precept, which fully express'd the extent I gave to its meaning.

These names of virtues, with their precepts, were:

1. Temperance

Eat not to dullness; drink not to elevation.

2. Silence

Speak not but what may benefit others or yourself; avoid trifling conversation.

3. Order

Let all your things have their places; let each part of your business have its time.

4. Resolution

Resolve to perform what you ought; perform without fail what you resolve.

5. Frugality

Make no expense but to do good to others or yourself; *i.e.,* waste nothing.

6. Industry

Lose no time; be always employ'd in something useful; cut off all unnecessary actions.

7. Sincerity

Use no hurtful deceit; think innocently and justly, and, if you speak, speak accordingly.

8. Justice

Wrong none by doing injuries, or omitting the benefits that are your duty.

9. Moderation

Avoid extreams; forbear resenting injuries so much as you think they deserve.

10. Cleanliness

Tolerate no uncleanliness in body, cloaths, or habitation.

From THE WRITINGS OF BENJAMIN FRANKLIN, edited by Albert Henry Smyth (1905–1907).

11. Tranquillity

Be not disturbed at trifles, or at accidents common or unavoidable.

12. Chastity

Rarely use venery but for health or offspring, never to dullness, weakness, or the injury of your own or another's peace or reputation.

13. Humility

Imitate Jesus and Socrates.[1]

My intention being to acquire the *habitude* of all these virtues, I judg'd it would be well not to distract my attention by attempting the whole at once, but to fix it on one of them at a time; and, when I should be master of that, then to proceed to another, and so on, till I should have gone thro' the thirteen; and, as the previous acquisition of some might facilitate the acquisition of certain others, I arrang'd them with that view, as they stand above. *Temperance* first, as it tends to procure that coolness and clearness of head, which is so necessary where constant vigilance was to be kept up, and guard maintained against the unremitting attraction of ancient habits, and the force of perpetual temptations. This being acquir'd and establish'd, *Silence* would be more easy; and my desire being to gain knowledge at the same time that I improv'd in virtue, and considering that in conversation it was obtain'd rather by the use of the ears than of the tongue, and therefore wishing to break a habit I was getting into of prattling, punning, and joking, which only made me acceptable to trifling company, I gave *Silence* the second place. This and the next, *Order,* I expected would allow me more time for attending to my project and my studies. *Resolution,* once become habitual, would keep me firm in my endeavours to obtain all the subsequent virtues; *Frugality* and *Industry* freeing me from my remaining debt, and producing affluence and independence, would make more easy the practice of *Sincerity* and *Justice,* etc., etc. Conceiving then, that, agreeably to the advice of Pythagoras in his *Golden Verses,*[2] daily examination would be necessary, I contrived the following method for conducting that examination.

I made a little book, in which I allotted a page for each of the virtues. I rul'd each page with red ink, so as to have seven columns, one for each day of the week, marking each column with a letter for the day. I cross'd these columns with thirteen red lines, marking the beginning of each line with the first letter of one of the virtues, on which line, and in its proper column, I might mark, by a little black spot, every fault I found upon examination to have been committed respecting that virtue upon that day.

Form of the Pages

TEMPERANCE. EAT NOT TO DULNESS. DRINK NOT TO ELEVATION.	S.	M.	T.	W.	T.	F.	S.
T.							
S.	*	*		*		*	
O.	* *	*	*		*	*	*
R.			*			*	
F.		*			*		
I.			*				
S.							
J.							
M.							
C.							
T.							
C.							
H.							

I determined to give a week's strict attention to each of the virtues successively. Thus, in the first week, my great guard was to avoid every the least offence against *Temperance,* leaving the other virtues to their ordinary chance, only marking every evening the faults of the day.

1. *Socrates* (sok′rə tēz′), c. 469–399 B.C., Greek philosopher who lived humbly.
2. *Pythagoras* (pə thag′ər əs) . . . *Golden Verses,* a Greek philosopher (c. 582–c. 500 B.C.), whose practical sayings are known as the Golden Verses.

Benjamin Franklin: "As Poor Richard Says . . ."

Never leave that till tomorrow, which you can do today.

He that riseth late must trot all day, and shall scarce overtake his business at night; while Laziness travels so slowly, that Poverty soon overtakes him.

Sloth, like rust, consumes faster than labor wears; while the used key is always bright.

The sleeping fox catches no poultry, and there will be sleeping enough in the grave.

It would be thought a hard government that should tax its people one-tenth part of their time, to be employed in its service. But idleness taxes many of us much more.

From *Colonial Living* by Edwin Tunis. Copyright © 1957 by Edwin Tunis. By permission of Thomas Y. Crowell.

Help, hands, for I have no lands; or, if I have, they are smartly taxed.

At the workingman's house hunger looks in, but dares not enter.

Then plough deep while sluggards sleep, and you shall have corn to sell and to keep.

Early to bed, and early to rise, makes a man healthy, wealthy, and wise.

Thus, if in the first week I could keep my first line, marked *T*, clear of spots, I suppos'd the habit of that virtue so much strengthen'd, and its opposite weaken'd, that I might venture extending my attention to include the next, and for the following week keep both lines clear of spots. Proceeding thus to the last, I could go thro' a course compleat in thirteen weeks, and four courses in a year. And like him who, having a garden to weed, does not attempt to eradicate all the bad herbs at once, which would exceed his reach and his strength, but works on one of the beds at a time, and, having accomplish'd the first, proceeds to a second; so I should have, I hoped, the encouraging pleasure of seeing on my pages the progress I made in virtue, by clearing successively my lines of their spots, till in the end, by a number of courses, I should be happy in viewing a clean book, after a thirteen weeks' daily examination.

The precept of *Order* requiring that *every part of my business should have its allotted time*, one page in my little book contain'd the following scheme of employment for the twenty-four hours of a natural day.

The Morning.

Question. What good shall I do this day?

5, 6, 7 — Rise, wash, and address *Powerful Goodness!*[3] Contrive day's business, and take the resolution of the day; prosecute the present study, and breakfast.

8, 9, 10, 11 — Work.

Noon.

12, 1 — Read, or overlook my accounts, and dine.

2, 3, 4, 5 — Work.

---

3. *Powerful Goodness,* God.

Handle your tools without mittens; remember, that the cat in gloves catches no mice.

It is true there is much to be done, and perhaps you are weak-handed; but stick to it steadily, and you will see great effects; for constant dropping wears away stones.

Methinks I hear some of you say, "Must a man afford himself no leisure?" I will tell thee, my friend, what Poor Richard says, "Employ thy time well, if thou meanest to gain leisure."

Leisure is time for doing something useful; this leisure the diligent man will obtain, but the lazy man never.

Fly pleasures, and they will follow you.

Now I have a sheep and a cow, everybody bids me good morrow.

Evening.		
Question. What good have I done today?	$\begin{cases} 6 \\ 7 \\ 8 \\ 9 \end{cases}$	Put things in their places. Supper. Music or diversion, or conversation. Examination of the day.
Night.	$\begin{cases} 10 \\ 11 \\ 12 \\ 1 \\ 2 \\ 3 \\ 4 \end{cases}$	Sleep.

I enter'd upon the execution of this plan for self-examination, and continu'd it with occasional intermissions for some time. I was surpris'd to find myself so much fuller of faults than I had imagined; but I had the satisfaction of seeing them diminish. To avoid the trouble of renewing now and then my little book, which, by scraping out the marks on the paper of old faults to make room for new ones in a new course, became full of holes; I transferr'd my tables and precepts to the ivory leaves of a memorandum book, on which the lines were drawn with red ink, that made a durable stain, and on those lines I mark'd my faults with a black-lead pencil, which marks I could easily wipe out with a wet sponge. After a while I went thro' one course only in a year, and afterward only one in several years, till at length I omitted them entirely, being employ'd in voyages and business abroad, with a multiplicity of affairs that interfered; but I always carried my little book with me.

My scheme of *Order* gave me the most trouble; and I found that, tho' it might be practicable where a man's business was such as to leave him the disposition of his time, that of a journeyman printer, for instance, it was not possible to be exactly observed by a master, who must mix with the world, and often receive people of business at their own hours. *Order,* too, with regard to places for things, papers, etc., I found extreamly difficult to acquire. I had not been early accustomed to it, and, having an exceeding good memory, I was not so sensible of the inconvenience attending want of method. This article, therefore, cost me so much painful attention, and my faults in it vexed me so much, and I made so little progress in amendment, and had such frequent relapses, that I was almost ready to give up the attempt, and content myself with a faulty character in that respect; like the man who, in buying an ax of a smith, my neighbour, desired to have the whole of its surface as bright as the edge. The smith consented to grind it bright for him if he would turn the wheel; he turn'd, while the smith press'd the broad face of the ax hard and heavily on the stone, which made the turning of it very fatiguing. The man came every now and then from the wheel to see how

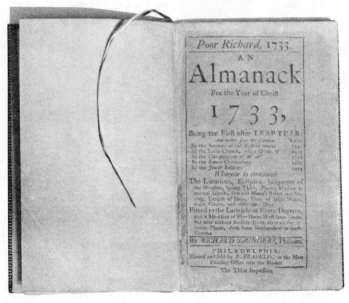

the work went on, and at length would take his ax as it was, without farther grinding. "No," said the smith, "turn on, turn on; we shall have it bright by-and-by; as yet, it is only speckled." "Yes," says the man, *"but I think I like a speckled ax best."* And I believe this may have been the case with many, who, having, for want of some such means as I employ'd, found the difficulty of obtaining good and breaking bad habits in other points of vice and virtue, have given up the struggle, and concluded that *"a speckled ax was best";* for something, that pretended to be reason, was every now and then suggesting to me that such extream nicety as I exacted of myself might be a kind of foppery in morals, which, if it were known, would make me ridiculous; that a perfect character might be attended with the inconvenience of being envied and hated; and that a benevolent man should allow a few faults in himself, to keep his friends in countenance.

In truth, I found myself incorrigible with respect to *Order;* and now I am grown old, and my memory bad, I feel very sensibly the want of it. But, on the whole, tho' I never arrived at the perfection I had been so ambitious of obtaining, but fell far short of it, yet I was, by the endeavour, a better and a happier man than I otherwise should have been if I had not attempted it; as those who aim at perfect writing by imitating the engraved copies, tho' they never reach the wish'd-for excellence of those copies, their hand is mended by the endeavour, and is tolerable while it continues fair and legible.

It may be well my posterity should be informed that to this little artifice, with the blessing of God, their ancestor ow'd the constant felicity of his life, down to his seventy-ninth year in which this is written. What reverses may attend the remainder is in the hand of Providence; but, if they arrive, the reflection on past happiness enjoy'd ought to help his bearing them with more resignation. To *Temperance* he ascribes his long-continued health, and what is still left to him of a good constitution; to *Industry* and *Frugality,* the early easiness of his circumstances and acquisition of his fortune, with all that knowledge that enabled him to be a useful citizen, and obtained for him some degree of reputation among the learned; to *Sincerity* and *Justice,* the confidence of his country, and the honorable employs it conferred upon him; and to the joint influence of the whole mass of the virtues, even in the imperfect state he was able to acquire them, all that evenness of temper, and that cheerfulness in conversation, which makes his company still sought for, and agreeable even to his younger acquaintance. I hope, therefore, that some of my descendants may follow the example and reap the benefit. ☐☐

1. Franklin is considered the embodiment of "the American Way" of thinking. **(a)** How is his faith in the individual's ability to achieve moral or practical goals unaided illustrated in his chart of moral perfection? **(b)** Would Jonathan Edwards find Franklin's system equally useful? What might Edwards feel was lacking in Franklin's notions of morality?

Extension • Writing

Franklin presents a fairly detailed explanation of the logic behind the order in which he arranges his practical virtues. Compose a list of the virtues you most admire in the order that makes most sense to you. Explain the reasoning behind your arrangement.

Vocabulary
Structure and Dictionary

Use your Glossary to answer the questions about each italicized word below.

1. (a) What is *rectitude*?

(b) The Latin root *rectus* means "right" or "straight." Combine the letters *rect* with the following prefixes and suffixes.

cor-　　　-ify
　　-angle

2. (a) What is an *enumeration*?

(b) The Latin root *numerus* means "number." Combine the letters *numer* with both the prefix and suffix to form one word.

super-　　-ary

(c) What does this word mean?

3. (a) What is an *artifice*?

(b) The Latin root *artum* means "art." Combine the letters *arti* with the following suffixes.

-fact　　-ficial

A Witch Trial at Mount Holly

Saturday last, at Mount-Holly, about eight miles from this place (Burlington, N.J.) near three hundred People were gathered together to see an Experiment or two tried on some Persons accused of Witchcraft. It seems the Accused had been charged with making their Neighbours' Sheep dance in an uncommon manner, and with causing Hogs to speak and sing Psalms, etc., to the great Terror and Amazement of the king's good and peaceable Subjects in this Province; and the Accusers, being very positive that if the Accused were weighed in scales against a Bible, the Bible would prove too heavy for them; or that, if they were bound and put into the river they would swim;[1] the said Accused, desirous to make Innocence appear, voluntarily offered to undergo the said Trials if two of the most violent of their Accusers would be tried with them. Accordingly the time and place was agreed on and advertised about the Country. The Accusers were one Man and one Woman; and the Accused the same. The Parties being met and the People got together, a grand Consultation was held, before they proceeded to Trial, in which it was agreed to use the scales first; and a Committee of Men were appointed to search the Men, and a Committee of Women to search the Women, to see if they had any thing of weight about them, particularly pins. After the scrutiny was over a huge great Bible belonging to the Justice of the Place was provided, and a lane through the Populace was made from the Justice's house to the scales, which were fixed on a Gallows erected for that Purpose opposite to the house, that the Justice's wife and the rest of the Ladies might see the Trial without coming amongst the Mob, and after the manner of Moorfields[2] a large ring was also made. Then came out of the house a grave, tall Man carrying the Holy Writ before the supposed Wizard etc., (as solemnly as the Sword-bearer of London before the Lord May-

---

From the *Pennsylvania Gazette*, Oct. 22, 1730.
1. swim, float.
2. Moorfields, an English resort near London that has a walk for promenades.

or[3]) the Wizard was first put in the scale, and over him was read a Chapter out of the Books of Moses,[4] and then the Bible was put in the other scale, (which, being kept down before, was immediately let go); but, to the great surprize of the spectators, flesh and bones came down plump, and outweighed that great good Book by abundance. After the same manner the others were served, and their Lumps of Mortality severally were too heavy for Moses and all the Prophets and Apostles. This being over, the Accusers and the rest of the Mob, not satisfied with this Experiment, would have the Trial by Water. Accordingly a most solemn Procession was made to the Millpond, where both Accused and Accusers being stripped (saving only to the Women their shifts), were bound hand and foot and severally placed in the water, lengthways, from the side of a barge or flat, having for security only a rope about the middle of each, which was held by some in the flat. The accused man being thin and spare with some difficulty began to sink at last; but the rest, every one of them, swam very light upon the water. A Sailor in the flat jump'd out upon the back of the Man accused thinking to drive him down to the bottom; but the Person bound, without any help, came up some time before the other. The Woman Accuser being told that she did not sink, would be duck'd a second time; when she swam again as light as before. Upon which she declared, that she believed the Accused had bewitched her to make her so light, and that she would be duck'd again a Hundred Times but she would duck the Devil out of her. The Accused Man, being surpriz'd at his own swimming, was not so confident of his Innocence as before, but said, "If I am a Witch, it is more than I know." The more thinking part of the spectators were of opinion that any Person so bound and placed in the water (unless they were mere skin and bones) would swim, till their breath was gone, and their lungs fill'd with water. But it being the general Belief of the Populace that the Women's shifts and the garters with which they were bound help'd to support them, it is said they are to be tried again the next warm weather, naked. ☐☐

---

3. **Sword-bearer . . . Lord Mayor,** an official who, in processions, carries the sword of state before the mayor of London.
4. **Books of Moses.** The first five books of the Bible: Genesis, Exodus, Leviticus, Numbers, and Deuteronomy.

Early American Journalism

The modern American newspaper shows almost no sign of its descent from such pioneers as the handwritten newsletter which John Campbell, the Boston postmaster, circulated around 1703. The growth of the American press coincided with the early development of news reporting in Europe. The short-lived Boston newspapers at the end of the seventeenth century were among the earliest in the world.

In 1538, less than a century after Gutenberg introduced movable type to Europe, the Spanish set up a printing press in Mexico City. In 1638, the English brought a printing press to Massachusetts. Almanacs, law books, and religious pamphlets were the main publications for about fifty years, until the first Boston newspaper, *Publick Occurrences*, was founded in 1690. It was suppressed by the government, the fate of many colonial periodicals.

The New England Courant, founded by Benjamin Franklin's older brother James, was among the first papers to protest English colonial rule. The younger Franklin wrote for it and for his own *Pennsylvania Gazette*, in which he drew the first American political cartoon, and where "A Witch Trial" appeared in 1730.

Franklin was the most renowned of the many politician-journalists whose pursuit of human rights and freedom of the press helped bring independence to the New World.

Discussion

1. What two tests for witchcraft are described in the selection? On what assumptions are they based?
2. This selection appeared originally as a news article. At what points does the story inform the reader of the "five W's" of news reporting: who, what, where, when, why?
3. Where do you see traces of Franklin's opinion revealed in this news story? On the basis of this account, do you think he believed in witches? Did he believe in the witch tests?

Extension · Writing

Some writers have abandoned attempts at objective journalism in favor of advocacy journalism, in which the author's opinion is clearly evident. Choose a controversial event and write two news stories, one illustrating objective reporting, the other exemplifying advocacy journalism.

Benjamin Franklin 1706 · 1790

The circumstances of Ben Franklin's childhood gave no indication that he would eventually become world famous as a symbol of American ingenuity and practicality. Born the son of a Boston tallow maker, he became a printer's apprentice. Eventually he acquired his own printing shop in Philadelphia and by 1730 was publishing *Poor Richard's Almanack*.

In subsequent years Franklin became deeply involved in community affairs and started his famous scientific experiments. By 1757, however, tensions between the American colonies and England caused the Pennsylvania legislature to send Franklin to England as a spokesman. For several years he pleaded the colonial cause, but by 1775 he gave up hope for reconciliation and returned to America.

Later in that year he sailed to France to obtain military assistance for the colonies. His quick wit and worldly wisdom made him extremely popular, and he secured the support of both France and Spain.

Franklin's aim as a writer was to be clear and persuasive; these two skills made him the finest pamphleteer of his day. The *Autobiography*, which was written over a period of several years, set a standard for realism and clarity which autobiographers have attempted to match ever since.

Thomas Jefferson

The Declaration of Independence

When, in the course of human events, it becomes necessary for one people to dissolve the political bands which have connected them with another, and to assume, among the Powers of the earth, the separate and equal station to which the Laws of Nature and of Nature's God entitle them, a decent respect to the opinions of mankind requires that they should declare the causes which impel them to the separation.

Library of Congress. Jim Ballard.

We hold these truths to be self-evident: that all men are created equal; that they are endowed by their Creator with certain inalienable Rights; that among these are Life, Liberty, and the pursuit of Happiness. That, to secure these Rights, Governments are instituted among Men, deriving their just powers from the consent of the governed—That, whenever any Form of Government becomes destructive of these ends, it is the Right of the People to alter or abolish it, and to institute new Government, laying its foundation on such Principles, and organizing its Powers in such form, as to them shall seem most likely to effect their Safety and Happiness. Prudence, indeed, will dictate that Governments long established should not be changed for light and transient causes; and, accordingly, all experience hath shown that mankind are more disposed to suffer, while evils are sufferable, than to right themselves by abolishing the forms to which they are accustomed. But, when a long train of abuses and usurpations, pursuing invariably the same Object, evinces a design to reduce them under absolute Despotism, it is their right, it is their duty, to throw off such Government, and to provide new Guards for their future security. Such has been the patient sufferance of these Colonies, and such is now the necessity which constrains them to alter their former Systems of Government. The history of the present King of Great Britain is a history of repeated injuries and usurpations, all having in direct object the establishment of an absolute Tyranny over these States. To prove this, let Facts be submitted to a candid world:

He has refused his Assent to Laws the most wholesome and necessary for the public good.

He has forbidden his Governors to pass Laws of immediate and pressing importance, unless suspended in their operation till his Assent should be obtained; and, when so suspended, he has utterly neglected to attend to them.

He has refused to pass other Laws for the

accommodation of large districts of people, unless those people would relinquish the rights of Representation in the Legislature; a right inestimable to them, and formidable to tyrants only.

He has called together legislative bodies at places unusual, uncomfortable, and distant from the depository of their Public Records, for the sole purpose of fatiguing them into compliance with his measures.

He has dissolved Representative Houses repeatedly for opposing, with manly firmness, his invasions on the rights of the people.

He has refused for a long time after such dissolutions to cause others to be elected; whereby the Legislative Powers, incapable of Annihilation, have returned to the People at large for their exercise; the State remaining, in the meantime, exposed to all the dangers of invasions from without, and convulsions within.

He has endeavored to prevent the Population of these States; for that purpose obstructing the Laws for Naturalization of Foreigners; refusing to pass others to encourage their migrations hither, and raising the conditions of new Appropriations of Lands.

He has obstructed the Administration of Justice by refusing his Assent to Laws for establishing Judiciary Powers.

He has made Judges dependent on his Will alone for the tenure of their offices, and the amount and Payment of their salaries.

He has erected a multitude of New Offices, and sent hither swarms of Officers to harass our People and eat out their substance.

He has kept among us, in times of Peace, Standing Armies, without the Consent of our legislatures.

He has affected to render the Military independent of and superior to the Civil Power.

He has combined with others to subject us to a jurisdiction foreign to our constitution, and unacknowledged by our laws: giving his Assent to their Acts of pretended Legislation:

For quartering large bodies of armed troops among us;

For protecting them, by a mock Trial, from Punishment for any Murders which they should commit on the Inhabitants of these States;

For cutting off our Trade with all parts of the world;

For imposing Taxes on us without our Consent;

For depriving us, in many cases, of the benefits of Trial by Jury;

For transporting us beyond Seas to be tried for pretended offences;

For abolishing the free System of English Laws in a neighboring Province,[1] establishing therein an Arbitrary government, and enlarging its Boundaries, so as to render it at once an example and fit instrument for introducing the same absolute rule into these Colonies;

For taking away our Charters, abolishing our most valuable Laws, and altering, fundamentally, the Forms of our Governments;

For suspending our own Legislatures, and declaring themselves invested with Power to legislate for us in all cases whatsoever.

He has abdicated Government here by declaring us out of his Protection, and waging War against us.

He has plundered our seas, ravaged our Coasts, burnt our towns, and destroyed the Lives of our People.

He is, at this time, transporting large Armies of foreign Mercenaries to complete the works of death, desolation, and tyranny, already begun with circumstances of Cruelty and Perfidy scarcely paralleled in the most barbarous ages, and totally unworthy the Head of a civilized nation.

He has constrained our fellow Citizens, taken Captive on the high Seas, to bear Arms against their Country, to become the executioners of their friends and Brethren, or to fall themselves by their Hands.

He has excited domestic insurrections amongst us, and has endeavored to bring on the inhabitants of our frontiers the merciless Indian Savages, whose known rule of warfare is an undistinguished destruction of all ages, sexes, and conditions.

In every stage of these Oppressions, We have Petitioned for Redress, in the most humble

---

1. *a neighboring Province.* After capturing Quebec, the English in 1774 imposed its rigid French laws on British colonists living in former French domains.

terms: Our repeated Petitions have been answered only by repeated injury. A Prince, whose character is thus marked by every act which may define a Tyrant, is unfit to be the ruler of a free People.

Nor have We been wanting in attentions to our British brethren. We have warned them, from time to time, of attempts by their legislature to extend an unwarrantable jurisdiction over us. We have reminded them of the circumstances of our emigration and settlement here. We have appealed to their native justice and magnanimity, and we have conjured them, by the ties of our common kindred, to disavow these usurpations, which would inevitably interrupt our connections and correspondence. They, too, have been deaf to the voice of justice and of consanguinity. We must, therefore, acquiesce in the necessity which denounces our Separation, and hold them, as we hold the rest of mankind—Enemies in War—in Peace, Friends.

WE, THEREFORE, the REPRESENTATIVES of the UNITED STATES OF AMERICA, in GENERAL CONGRESS Assembled, appealing to the Supreme Judge of the world for the rectitude of our intentions, Do, in the Name and by the Authority of the good People of these Colonies, solemnly PUBLISH and DECLARE, That these United Colonies are, and of Right ought to be, FREE AND INDEPENDENT STATES; that they are Absolved from all Allegiance to the British Crown, and that all political connection between them and the State of Great Britain is, and ought to be, totally dissolved; and that, as FREE AND INDEPENDENT STATES, they have full Power to levy War, conclude Peace, contract Alliances, establish Commerce, and to do all other Acts and Things which INDEPENDENT STATES may of right do. And, for the support of this Declaration, with a firm reliance on the Protection of Divine Providence, we mutually pledge to each other our Lives, our Fortunes, and our Sacred Honor. □□

Discussion

1. What is the purpose of the first paragraph?

2. Reread the first sentence of paragraph 2. In listing what he believes to be man's "inalienable Rights," why does Jefferson say "the pursuit of Happiness" rather than merely "Happiness"?

3. According to paragraph 2, what is the purpose of government? Where does government get its power?

4. Under what circumstances may a government be changed or abolished? Whose job is it to do the changing or abolishing? Why?

5. What is the purpose of the last half of paragraph 2?

6. After listing the colonists' grievances (paragraphs 3–29), Jefferson makes clear the fact that they have tried using peaceful means to draw the king's attention to their plight. What is the purpose of this statement?

7. (a) What is the purpose of the last paragraph? (b) Is its tone in keeping with that of the body of the Declaration? Why or why not?

8. What particular words, by both their sounds and meanings, contribute to the creation of the emotional effect in the last line?

Thomas Jefferson 1743 • 1826

When speaking at a dinner for Nobel prizewinners, John Kennedy described the assembly as "the most extraordinary collection of talent, of human knowledge, that has ever been gathered together at the White House, with the possible exception of when Thomas Jefferson dined alone."

A Virginia planter and aristocrat, a graduate of William and Mary College, and a lawyer by profession, Jefferson served first in the Virginia House of Burgesses and was one of the Virginia representatives to the Second Continental Congress. At the Congress Jefferson reluctantly agreed to attempt a draft of a document declaring colonial independence. The resulting Declaration of Independence remains his masterpiece.

He subsequently served as governor of Virginia, minister to France, secretary of state, Vice-President, and finally President from 1801 to 1809. When he died he was buried at his home at Monticello.

Phillis Wheatley

To S.M.,[1] A Young African Painter on Seeing His Works

To show the lab'ring bosom's deep intent,
And thought in living characters to paint,
When first thy pencil did those beauties give,
And breathing figures learnt from thee to live,
5 How did those prospects give my soul delight,
A new creation rushing on my sight!
Still, wondrous youth! each noble path pursue;
On deathless glories fix thine ardent view:
Still may the painter's and the poet's fire,
10 To aid thy pencil and thy verse conspire!
And may the charms of each seraphic theme
Conduct thy footsteps to immortal fame!
High to the blissful wonders of the skies
Elate thy soul, and raise thy wishful eyes.
15 Thrice happy, when exalted to survey
That splendid city, crowned with endless day,
Whose twice six gates on radiant hinges ring:
Celestial Salem blooms in endless spring.
Calm and serene thy moments glide along,
20 And may the muse inspire each future song!
Still, with the sweets of contemplation blessed,
May peace with balmy wings your soul invest!
But when these shades of time are chased away,
And darkness ends in everlasting day,
25 On what seraphic pinions shall we move,
And view the landscapes in the realms above!
There shall thy tongue in heavenly murmurs flow,
And there my muse with heavenly transport glow;
No more to tell of Damon's[2] tender sighs,
30 Or rising radiance of Aurora's[3] eyes;
For nobler themes demand a nobler strain,
And purer language on the ethereal plain.
Cease, gentle Muse![4] the solemn gloom of night
Now seals the fair creation from my sight.

From EARLY NEGRO AMERICAN WRITERS, edited by Benjamin Brawley. Published by The University of North Carolina Press.
1. *S. M.,* Scipio Moorhead, a black slave who lived and painted in colonial Boston.
2. *Damon,* a man in Roman legend who became a hostage and nearly lost his life for his friend Pythias.
3. *Aurora,* Roman goddess of dawn.
4. *Muse,* the spirit believed to inspire a poet in the act of creating a poem.

Discussion

1. (a) What has S.M. been able to do that makes the poet admire him? **(b)** What hopes does she have for his future?

2. Of what is the poet speaking when referring to "shades of time," "darkness," and "everlasting day"?

3. What fate does Wheatley envision for both herself and the painter? How is this role to differ from their present, earthly one?

Phillis Wheatley c. 1753 • 1784

Phillis Wheatley was born in Africa and at the age of eight was brought by slave ship to Boston. She was bought by John Wheatley, a prosperous tailor, who encouraged her studies. She quickly taught herself English and Latin, grew fond of classical literature, and modeled her poetry after such contemporary English poets as Pope and Gray. Wheatley was formally given her freedom when she was twenty.

After the Wheatleys died she married, but the marriage proved an unhappy one. Isolated and poor, she took on menial work despite her frail condition. She died alone and in poverty at the age of thirty-one.

Robert Hayden:
A Letter from Phillis Wheatley (London, 1773)

The following poem by Robert Hayden (see Units 1 and 8) is meant as an imaginary letter written by Wheatley from London to a friend in Boston. In such a work, the actual author (here, Hayden) gives us his impression of the personality and outlook of the supposed author (Wheatley). What are the opinions, beliefs, and personality traits of the imaginary Wheatley as presented in Hayden's poem? For instance, how observant is she about the attitude of the English aristocrats toward her? To get the tone and flavor of her remarks, the poem should be read aloud. After doing so, compare Hayden's portrait of Wheatley with the impression you get from reading her own poem, "To S.M."

Dear Obour,
    Our crossing was without
event. I could not help, at times,
reflecting on that first—my Destined—
voyage[1] long ago (I yet
5 have some remembrance of its Horrors)
and marvelling at God's Ways.
   Last evening, her Ladyship presented me
to her illustrious Friends.
I scarce could tell them anything
10 of Africa, though much of Boston
and my hope of Heaven. I read
my latest Elegies to them.
"O Sable Muse!" the Countess cried,
embracing me, when I had done.
15 I held back tears, as is my wont,[2]
and there were tears in Dear
Nathaniel's eyes.
   At supper—I dined apart
like captive Royalty—
20 the Countess and her Guests promised
signatures affirming me
True Poetess, albeit once a slave.
Indeed, they were most kind, and spoke,
moreover, of presenting me
25 at Court (I thought of Pochahontas[3])—
an Honor, to be sure, but one,
I should, no doubt, as Patriot[4] decline.
   My health is much improved;
I feel I may, if God so Wills,
30 entirely recover here.
Idyllic England! Alas, there is
no Eden without its Serpent. Under

the chiming Complaisance[5] I hear him Hiss;
I see his flickering tongue
35 when foppish would-be Wits
murmur of the Yankee Pedlar
and his Cannibal Mockingbird.
   Sister, forgive th'intrusion of
my Sombreness—Nocturnal Mood
40 I would not share with any save
your trusted Self. Let me disperse
in closing, such unseemly Gloom
by mention of an Incident
you may, as I, consider Droll:
45 Today, a little Chimney Sweep,
his face and hands with soot quite Black,
staring hard at me, politely asked:
"Does you, M'lady, sweep chimneys too?"
I was amused, but dear Nathaniel
50 (ever Solicitous) was not.
   I pray the Blessings of our Lord
and Saviour Jesus Christ be yours
Abundantly. In His Name,
       Phillis

"A Letter from Phillis Wheatley" by Robert Hayden. Reprinted by permission.
1. *my Destined—voyage.* Wheatley was brought to America from Africa in 1761 on a slave-trading ship.
2. *wont* (wunt), custom.
3. *Pochahontas* (pō/kə hon/təs). Pocahontas, a native American princess (c. 1595–1617), was taken to England and presented at the king's court.
4. *Patriot,* one loyal to the colonial cause.
5. *Complaisance* (kəm plā/zns), agreeableness.

Hector St. John de Crèvecoeur

What Is an American?

What, then, is the American, this new man? He is neither an European nor the descendant of an European; hence that strange mixture of blood, which you will find in no other country. I could point out to you a family whose grandfather was an Englishman, whose wife was Dutch, whose son married a French woman, and whose present four sons have now four wives of different nations. He is an American, who, leaving behind him all his ancient prejudices and manners, receives new ones from the new mode of life he has embraced, the new government he obeys, and the new rank he holds. He becomes an American by being received in the broad lap of our great Alma Mater. Here individuals of all nations are melted into a new race of men, whose labours and posterity will one day cause great changes in the world. Americans are the western pilgrims who are carrying along with them that great mass of arts, sciences, vigour, and industry which began long since in the East; they will finish the great circle. The Americans were once scattered all over Europe; here they are incorporated into one of the finest systems of population which has ever appeared, and which will hereafter become distinct by the power of the different climates they inhabit. The American ought therefore to love this country much better than that wherein either he or his forefathers were born. Here the rewards of his industry follow with equal steps the progress of his labour; his labour is founded on the basis of nature, self-interest; can it want a stronger allurement? Wives and children, who before in vain demanded of him a morsel of bread, now, fat and frolicsome, gladly help their father to clear those fields whence exuberant crops are to arise to feed and to clothe them all, without any part being claimed, either by a despotic prince, a rich abbot, or a mighty lord. Here religion demands but little of him: a small voluntary salary to the minister and gratitude to God; can he refuse these? The American is a new man, who acts upon new principles; he must therefore entertain new ideas and form new opinions. From involuntary idleness, servile dependence, penury, and useless labour, he has passed to toils of a very different nature, rewarded by ample subsistence. This is an American.

British America is divided into many provinces, forming a large association scattered along a coast of 1,500 miles extent and about 200 wide. This society I would fain examine, at least such as it appears in the middle provinces; if it does not afford that variety of tinges and gradations which may be observed in Europe, we have colours peculiar to ourselves. For instance, it is natural to conceive that those who live near the sea must be very different from those who live in the woods; the intermediate space will afford a separate and distinct class.

Men are like plants; the goodness and flavour of the fruit proceeds from the peculiar soil and exposition in which they grow. We are nothing but what we derive from the air we breathe, the climate we inhabit, the government we obey, the system of religion we profess, and the nature of our employment. Here you will find but few crimes; these have acquired as yet no root among us. I wish I were able to trace all my ideas; if my ignorance prevents me from describing them properly, I hope I shall be able to delineate a few of the outlines; which is all I propose.

Those who live near the sea feed more on fish

Crèvecoeur (krev/kėr).

From LETTERS FROM AN AMERICAN FARMER. The New American Library of World Literature, Inc.

than on flesh and often encounter that boisterous element. This renders them more bold and enterprising; this leads them to neglect the confined occupations of the land. They see and converse with a variety of people; their intercourse with mankind becomes extensive. The sea inspires them with a love of traffic, a desire of transporting produce from one place to another, and leads them to a variety of resources which supply the place of labour. Those who inhabit the middle settlements, by far the most numerous, must be very different; the simple cultivation of the earth purifies them, but the indulgences of the government, the soft remonstrances of religion, the rank of independent freeholders, must necessarily inspire them with sentiments, very little known in Europe among a people of the same class. What do I say? Europe has no such class of men; the early knowledge they acquire, the early bargains they make, give them a great degree of sagacity. As freemen, they will be litigious; pride and obstinacy are often the cause of lawsuits; the nature of our laws and governments may be another. As citizens, it is easy to imagine that they will carefully read the newspapers, enter into every political disquisition, freely blame or censure governors and others. As farmers, they will be careful and anxious to get as much as they can, because what they get is their own. As northern men, they will love the cheerful cup. As Christians, religion curbs them not in their opinions; the general indulgence leaves every one to think for themselves in spiritual matters; the law inspects our actions; our thoughts are left to God. Industry, good living, selfishness, litigiousness, country politics, the pride of freemen, religious indifference, are their characteristics. If you recede still farther from the sea, you will come into more modern settlements; they exhibit the same strong lineaments, in a ruder appearance. Religion seems to have still less influence, and their manners are less improved.

Now we arrive near the great woods, near the last inhabited districts; there men seem to be placed still farther beyond the reach of government, which in some measure leaves them to themselves. How can it pervade every corner, as they were driven there by misfortunes, necessity of beginnings, desire of acquiring large tracks of

The Bettmann Archive, Inc.

land, idleness, frequent want of economy, ancient debts; the reunion of such people does not afford a very pleasing spectacle. When discord, want of unity and friendship, when either drunkenness or idleness prevail in such remote districts, contention, inactivity, and wretchedness must ensue. There are not the same remedies to these evils as in a long-established community. The few magistrates they have are in general little better than the rest; they are often in a perfect state of war; that of man against man, sometimes decided by blows, sometimes by means of the law; that of man against every wild inhabitant of these venerable woods, of which they are come to dispossess them. There men appear to be no better than carnivorous animals of a superior rank, living on the flesh of wild animals when they can catch them, and when they are not able, they subsist on grain. He who would wish to see America in its proper light and have a true idea of its feeble beginnings and barbarous rudiments must visit our extended line of frontiers, where the last settlers dwell and where he may see the first labours of settlement, the mode of clearing the earth, in all their different appearances, where men are wholly left dependent on their native tempers and on the spur of uncertain industry, which often fails when not sanctified by the efficacy of a few moral rules. There, remote from the power of example and check of shame, many families exhibit the most hideous parts of our society. They are a kind of forlorn hope, preceding by ten or twelve years the most respectable army of veterans which come after them. In that space, prosperity will polish some, vice and the law will drive off the rest, who, uniting again with others like themselves, will recede still farther, making room for more industrious people, who will finish their improvements, convert the log-house into a convenient habitation, and rejoicing that the first heavy labours are finished, will change in a few years that hitherto barbarous country into a fine, fertile, well-regulated district. Such is our progress; such is the march of the Europeans toward the interior parts of this continent. In all societies there are off-casts; this impure part serves as our precursors or pioneers; my father himself was one of that class, but he came upon honest principles and was therefore one of the few who held fast; by good conduct and temper-

ance, he transmitted to me his fair inheritance, when not above one in fourteen of his contemporaries had the same good fortune.

Forty years ago, this smiling country was thus inhabited; it is now purged, a general decency of manners prevails throughout, and such has been the fate of our best countries.

Exclusive of those general characteristics, each province has its own, founded on the government, climate, mode of husbandry, customs, and peculiarity of circumstances. Europeans submit insensibly to these great powers and become, in the course of a few generations, not only Americans in general, but either Pennsylvanians, Virginians, or provincials under some other name. Whoever traverses the continent must easily observe those strong differences, which will grow more evident in time. The inhabitants of Canada, Massachusetts, the middle provinces, the southern ones, will be as different as their climates; their only points of unity will be those of religion and language. □□

Discussion

1. What ways of life described in the essay are no longer part of present-day America?

2. Crèvecoeur's best-known theory is that of America's being a melting pot. Reread the first half of his opening paragraph. Has history proven the theory true or false? Give examples from contemporary life to prove your point.

3. In elaborating on the melting-pot idea, Crèvecoeur states that the American should love America more than he does the country of his forefathers. (a) With what reasons does he support his statement? (b) Do you think the majority of American colonists accepted

these reasons? Would the majority of Americans today accept them? Discuss.

4. What adjectives might describe the author's attitude toward the frontiersman?

5. What happens to the frontiersman when the "more respectable army of veterans" takes over the frontier?

6. In Crèvecoeur's time the possibility for westward expansion seemed limitless. What attitudes toward the land itself might be bred by such a belief?

7. At present, with most of the United States land settled, many consider the frontier a thing of the past; others see new, nongeographic frontiers yet to be conquered. What are some frontiers still open to exploration?

Hector St. John de Crèvecoeur
1735 • 1813

Born in France, Crèvecoeur was educated in England. At nineteen he sailed for Canada to become a mapmaker with the French army. Eventually he settled on a frontier farm in New York. Despite his fondness for the American way of life, he favored English rule of the colonies, so, when the colonists revolted, he left for France to await the end of the war. Crèvecoeur returned to America only to discover his home had been burned and his wife killed during an Indian raid. After spending seven years as French consul, he took a leave of absence in 1790, sailed for Europe, and never returned.

2: The New Land

CONTENT REVIEW

1. Compare and contrast the Iroquois Constitution with the Declaration of Independence. What does each reveal about the ideals of the people who created it?

2. Compare the following individuals by observing differences and similarities in their personalities and their writings.

  a) Cabeza de Vaca and John Smith;

  b) Anne Bradstreet and Sarah Kemble Knight;

  c) William Bradford and William Byrd;

  d) Edward Taylor and Phillis Wheatley.

3. List the different genres or types of literature represented in this collection of early American literature. Which genre do you think described the newly colonized land most vividly? Which of these genres would probably be found only in the New World? In what ways are these types uniquely "American"?

4. Some people believe that the quality of American literature has improved with time. Of the works collected here, which two or three do you consider to be the best? Why? Could they be "improved

upon" by modern writers? How?

5. The native Americans, the Spanish explorers, the English Puritans, and the Southern aristocrats display a variety of cultural identities. Yet, each selection manages to convey something about our collective national character and literary tradition. Choose a few works that represent one aspect of our heritage that has survived to the present. Discuss how each work treats that one aspect.

The Valley Forge Campground.
(Werner Wolff/Black Star.)

from The American Crisis
Thomas Paine

The American Crisis is the title given to sixteen pamphlets that Paine wrote from December, 1776, to December, 1783, to boost the sagging spirits of colonists during the Revolution. This excerpt from the first pamphlet, published on December 19, 1776, remains the most famous. After reading it, choose the correct answer for each question that follows.

These are the times that try men's souls: The summer soldier and the sunshine patriot will in this crisis, shrink from the service of his country; but he that stands it NOW, deserves the love and thanks of man and woman. Tyranny,[1] like hell, is not easily conquered; yet we have this consolation with us, that the harder the conflict, the more glorious the triumph. What we obtain too cheap, we esteem[2] too lightly:—'Tis dearness only that gives everything its value. Heaven knows how to put a proper price upon its goods; and it would be strange indeed, if so celestial[3] an article as FREEDOM should not be highly rated. Britain, with an army to enforce her tyranny, has declared that she has a right *(not only to)* TAX but "to BIND *us in* ALL CASES WHATSOEVER," and if being *bound in that manner,* is not slavery, then is there not such a thing as slavery upon earth. Even the expression is impious,[4] for so unlimited a power can belong only to GOD. . . .

I have as little superstition in me as any man living, but my secret opinion has ever been, and still is, that God Almighty will not give up a people to military destruction, or leave them unsupportedly to perish, who have so earnestly and so repeatedly sought to avoid the calamities of war, by every decent method which wisdom could invent. Neither have I so much of the infidel[5] in me, as to suppose that he has relinquished[6] the government of the world, and given us up to the care of devils; and as I do not, I cannot see on what grounds the king of Britain can look up to Heaven for help against us: a common murderer, a highwayman, or a house-breaker, has as good a pretence[7] as he. . . .

I once felt all that kind of anger, which a man ought to feel against the mean principles that are held by the tories:[8] A noted one, who kept a tavern at Amboy, was standing at his door, with as pretty a child in his hand, about eight or nine years old, as I ever saw, and after speaking his mind as freely as he thought was prudent,[9] finished with this unfatherly expression, *"Well! give me peace in my day."* Not a man lives on the continent but fully believes that a separation must some time or other finally take place, and a generous parent should have said, *"If there must be*

1. *tyranny,* unjust use of power.

2. *esteem,* value.

3. *celestial* (sə les′chəl), heavenly.

4. *impious* (im′pe əs), disrespectful of God.

5. *infidel* (in′fə dəl), person who does not believe in religion.
6. *relinquish* (ri ling′kwish), give up.

7. *pretence* (pri tens′), claim to justice.

8. *tory,* an American who favored British rule of the colonies.

9. *prudent,* showing good judgment.

trouble, let it be in my day, that my child may have peace," and this single reflection, well applied, is sufficient to awaken every man to duty. Not a place upon earth might be so happy as America. Her situation is remote from all the wrangling world, and she has nothing to do but to trade with them. A man can distinguish himself between temper and principle, and I am as confident, as I am that GOD governs the world, that America will never be happy till she gets clear of foreign dominion.[10] Wars, without ceasing, will break out till that period arrives, and the continent must in the end be conqueror; for though the flame of liberty may sometimes cease to shine, the coal can never expire. . . .

The heart that feels not now is dead; the blood of his children will curse his cowardice, who shrinks back at a time when a little might have saved the whole, and made *them* happy. I love the man that can smile in trouble, that can gather strength from distress, and grow brave by reflection. 'Tis the business of little minds to shrink; but he whose heart is firm, and whose conscience approves his conduct, will pursue his principles unto death. My own line of reasoning is to myself as straight and clear as a ray of light. Not all the treasures of the world, so far as I believe, could have induced me to support an offensive war, for I think it murder; but if a thief breaks into my house, burns and destroys my property, and kills or threatens to kill me, or those that are in it, and to *"bind me in all cases whatsoever"* to his absolute will, am I to suffer it? What signifies it to me, whether he who does it is a king or a common man; my countryman or not my countryman; whether it be done by an individual villain, or an army of them? If we reason to the root of things we shall find no difference; neither can any just cause be assigned why we should punish in the one case and pardon in the other. . . .

1. Paine begins his appeal with the stirring statement that "These are the times that try men's souls," and continues with the observation that people value most the possessions they **(a)** obtain cheaply; **(b)** pay for dearly; **(c)** win through war; **(d)** inherit.

2. The expressions "summer soldier" and "sunshine patriot" refer to **(a)** people of honor; **(b)** people who are not able to fight in the winter; **(c)** villains; **(d)** people who support the cause only when it suits them.

3. Which of the following words is *not* used for its connotative effect in the opening paragraph? **(a)** *tyranny;* **(b)** *freedom;* **(c)** *hell;* **(d)** *everything.*

4. Paine compares the struggle for liberty to **(a)** the purchase of goods; **(b)** winter; **(c)** going to heaven; **(d)** fighting a war.

5. Paine implies that King George is **(a)** a fool; **(b)** a criminal; **(c)** an infidel; **(d)** a martyr.

6. Paine says that God will support the colonies because they **(a)** tried to avoid the war;

(b) are kinder parents than the British; (c) have been treated unjustly by the British; (d) all of the above; (e) a and b; (f) a and c.

7. The main idea of the anecdote of the tavern owner at Amboy is that (a) those who really care about their children will support the Revolution; (b) the Revolution is inevitable; (c) those with children are rightfully desirous of peace; (d) Tories are not very good fathers.

8. A concept Paine supports in paragraph 3 is that of (a) sectionalism; (b) inalienable rights; (c) isolation from foreign conflicts; (d) unanimity.

9. The last sentence of the third paragraph ("Wars, without ceasing . . .") contains an example of (a) personification; (b) allusion; (c) metaphor; (d) a and c; (e) all of the above.

10. In the first sentence of paragraph 4, the heart represents a (a) child; (b) person who does not support the Revolution; (c) person who does not weep for the dead; (d) person who can smile in the midst of great difficulty.

11. Paine implies that the colonies are justified in fighting this war (a) to prove themselves; (b) to gain economic autonomy; (c) out of self-defense; (d) for religious freedom.

12. Choose the best summary of this sentence: "'Tis the business of little minds to shrink; but he whose heart is firm, and whose conscience approves his conduct, will pursue his principles unto death." (a) The brave will ignore to the end what their consciences tell them; (b) Unused minds shrink away and die; (c) The courageous will die for their beliefs; (d) Stupidity can mean an early death.

13. To convince the people of the justice of the Revolution, Paine, throughout the entire excerpt, appeals to all *but* their (a) feelings for their children's future security; (b) religious convictions; (c) sense of injustice; (d) desire to become wealthy.

14. The "crisis" in the title of the excerpt refers to (a) lack of strong American leadership; (b) lack of support for the Revolution; (c) the threat of economic depression; (d) American cowardice on the battlefield.

Unit 2, Test II
COMPOSITION

Choose one of the following topics for a composition.

1. "What is the right thing to do?" This is a question that has concerned writers of all ages, including the Puritan and Revolutionary. In an essay that will help your classmates understand this unit, contrast the concepts of morality in the Puritan and the Revolutionary era. What were considered virtues? What were considered sins? How were sinners dealt with?

2. As a writer for an eighteenth-century newspaper, you are to write an article that will give prospective European travelers an accurate answer to the question, "what is an American?" In reaching an answer, draw on the writings of two or three writers from this unit for both ideas and specific examples.

3. Writers of early American literature used a much different writing style from the one we are accustomed to. Their sentences were more complicated and their vocabularies more formal.

Choose either the first three paragraphs of "Sinners in the Hands of an Angry God" or the first two paragraphs of the Declaration of Independence and translate the selection into a modern style. You are not to change the ideas or the order of the ideas.

4. One of the most creative tensions in American culture has been between freedom and authority. As a historian writing an article for the general reader on this topic, you want to compare and contrast Puritan and Revolutionary-era assumptions about freedom and authority. Explore the attitudes in each period toward the strength of authority required in religion, government, education, work, moral behavior, and other areas.

1800   1805   1810   1815   182

• Louisiana Purchase   "The Star-Spangled Banner" composed •   Missouri Compromise on slavery •

Lewis and Clark expedition •   *North American Review,* a major early magazine •

Importation of slaves outlawed •   First free public school, Boston

Irving: *Knickerbocker's History of New York* •   Bryant: "Thanatopsis" •

First river steamboats •   Irving: *The Sketch Book* •

Academy of Natural Sciences founded •   Iron plow introduced •

• War of 1812

First textile factory, Lowell, Massachusetts •

Noah Webster developing schoolbooks   Industrial Revolution   Great westward migrations

Latin-American Wars of Independence

Literary Nationalism 1800 to 1840

1825	1830	1835	1840

- Cooper: *The Last of the Mohicans*
- Poe: *Tamerlane and Other Poems*
- *Freedom's Journal,* first black newspaper
- Noah Webster: *American Dictionary of the English Language*
- Indian Removal Act
- Nat Turner's slave revolt in Virginia
- "Trail of Tears," forced migration of Cherokees
- First clipper ship
- First Atlantic crossing by steamship
- Slavery abolished in British Empire
- Poe: *Tales of the Grotesque and Arabesque*
- Rise of North/South rivalry
- U.S. abolition movement grows
- Canal system constructed

- Samuel Morse develops telegraph
- Holmes: *Poems*
- Emerson: *The American Scholar*
- Hawthorne: *Twice-Told Tales*
- Mt. Holyoke, first women's college
- Baseball invented
- Cooper: *The Pathfinder*

Background: Literary Nationalism 1800-1840

The period of literary nationalism in the new nation saw the country expand both culturally and physically. President Thomas Jefferson increased the area of the nation by about 140 percent with the Louisiana Purchase of 1803. The famed Lewis and Clark expedition to the Pacific Northwest pointed the way to the nation's growth, both physical and psychological. The knowledge that there was always some virgin land lying out West to explore and settle, especially if the going got too rough in the East, shaped the lives and dreams of generations of Americans. To be able to "light out" for the "territory" (as Huckleberry Finn suggests at the end of his *Adventures)* was to be able always to begin anew.

As the nation grew in size and ambition, many observers worried about its spirit, especially as revealed by its arts. Each nation in Europe had begun to seek the expression of its individual character, and Americans joined in this desire. An English critic, Sydney Smith, wrote in *The Edinburgh Review* in 1819: "In the four quarters of the globe, who reads an American book? or goes to an American play? or looks at an American picture?" The question stung the national pride. Ironically, within two years of Smith's challenge, three distinctively American works appeared. These works were *The Sketch Book,* 1819–20, by Washington Irving; *The Spy,* 1821, by James Fenimore Cooper; and the *Poems,* 1821, of William Cullen Bryant.

Despite his view that literature was not to be taken too seriously by a gentleman, Washington Irving spent long, pleasant hours reading renowned English authors like Fielding, Sterne, Goldsmith, and Scott. Despite their influence on him, much of his writing is uniquely American in its themes, good-humored presentation of American eccentricities, and special feeling for setting and local custom. Irving, during his seventeen years in Europe, was accepted by the European establishment. He gave to the United States what it had long desired: a man of letters admired by the Old World.

Cooper also was influenced by Old World models, notably the adventure novels of Sir Walter Scott. After his novel *The Spy,* Cooper created *The Leatherstocking Tales (The Deerslayer* is one of these novels), which depict his romantic vision of the "noble savage," the heroic frontiersman, and the unsurpassed beauty of the American wilderness.

Poems by William Cullen Bryant included "Thanatopsis," written when Bryant was just seventeen. In his verse is apparent the struggle to find a compromise between conflicting ideas of the eighteenth and nineteenth centuries: between deism (a religion substituting reason for faith) and Christianity; between social progress and unchangeable moral law.

Many of the best known poets of this period are sometimes referred to as the "Fireside Poets." Perhaps they are so named because of the seeming ease and gentle persuasiveness of their best verse. All of them celebrated the Common Man and Jacksonian Democracy. Henry Wadsworth Longfellow celebrated the village blacksmith, and John Greenleaf Whittier celebrated the barefoot boy. Longfellow's poems are written in rather simple words and in sometimes memorable rhythms.

John Greenleaf Whittier, like so many of the poets of his time, was a public rather than a private poet—an orator for the public interest, not a quiet voice speaking to the private self. His greatest efforts were spent in the fight against slavery. Whittier's poetry is marked by clarity of subject matter and intensity of conviction.

In both verse and prose, Oliver Wendell Holmes is best when he is most informal. He wrote numerous occasional verses, frequently employing the mock-heroic form, ballad stanzas, and heroic couplets. "I hold it to be a gift of a certain value," he wrote to James Russell Lowell, "to give that slight passing spasm of pleasure which a few ringing couplets often cause, read at the right moment."

James Russell Lowell was a man of wit, imagination, and science. His poetry was similar

Henry Wadsworth Longfellow

in material, arrangement, and form to Holmes's and Longfellow's. Lowell showed considerable freedom from well-established verse patterns and often used the regional idioms of New England. Like the other Fireside Poets, Lowell

Washington Irving

William Cullen Bryant

championed many humanitarian causes, especially the abolition of slavery.

Slavery was the greatest national issue of this era. North and South became increasingly divided while, inspired by slave revolts, the abolition movement grew strong in the 1830s. This controversy produced a flood of writing, much of it by black writers, slave and free. *Freedom's Journal,* the first black newspaper, was founded in 1827, and in 1829 David Walker issued his *Appeal* for a black war of independence. Some of the finest creations of this movement are represented here by the spirituals and by Pennington's slave narrative. While eloquently expressing the yearning for freedom, many

spirituals were also sung to pass coded messages among slaves.

One of the ironies of American literary history is that at least two of the writers of this period have had greater critical acclaim abroad than at home. Edgar Allan Poe was early translated into French, many important French poets praised and imitated him, and his critical reputation is still higher in France than in America. Cooper, too, has been highly praised abroad, not so much by critics as by European youths whose ideas of America have been shaped by Cooper's novels about American frontiersmen and Indians.

Perhaps the myth of the frontiersman symbolizes the essence of this period; for the ever expanding frontier gave an optimistic sense of destiny which largely shaped the people and the literature of a youthful America. And the writers of this era remain the pioneers of our literature.

Washington Irving

Wouter Van Twiller

The renowned Wouter (or Walter) Van Twiller was descended from a long line of Dutch burgomasters, who had successively dozed away their lives, and grown fat upon the bench of magistracy in Rotterdam; and who had comported themselves with such singular wisdom and propriety, that they were never either heard or talked of—which, next to being universally applauded, should be the object of ambition of all magistrates and rulers. There are two opposite ways by which some men make a figure in the world: one, by talking faster than they think, and the other, by holding their tongues and not thinking at all. By the first, many a smatterer acquires the reputation of a man of quick parts; by the other, many a dunderpate, like the owl, the stupidest of birds, comes to be considered the very type of wisdom. This, by the way, is a casual remark, which I would not, for the universe, have it thought I apply to Governor Van Twiller. It is true he was a man shut up within himself, like an oyster, and rarely spoke, except in monosyllables; but then it was allowed he seldom said a foolish thing. So invincible was his gravity that he was never known to laugh or even to smile through the whole course of a long and prosperous life. Nay, if a joke were uttered in his presence, that set lightminded hearers in a roar, it was observed to throw him into a state of perplexity. Sometimes he would deign to inquire into the matter, and when, after much explanation, the joke was made as plain as a pikestaff, he would continue to smoke his pipe in silence, and at length, knocking out the ashes, would exclaim, "Well! I see nothing in all that to laugh about."

With all his reflective habits, he never made up his mind on a subject. His adherents accounted for this by the astonishing magnitude of his ideas. He conceived every subject on so grand a scale that he had not room in his head to turn it over and examine both sides of it. Certain it is, that, if any matter were propounded to him on which ordinary mortals would rashly determine at first glance, he would put on a vague, mysterious look, shake his capacious head, smoke some time in profound silence, and at length observe, that "he had his doubts about the matter"; which gained him the reputation of a man slow of belief and not easily imposed upon. What is more, it gained him a lasting name; for to this habit of the mind has been attributed his surname of Twiller; which is said to be a corruption of the original Twijfler, or, in plain English, *Doubter.*

The person of this illustrious old gentleman was formed and proportioned, as though it had been moulded by the hands of some cunning Dutch statuary, as a model of majesty and lordly grandeur. He was exactly five feet six inches in height, and six feet five inches in circumference. His head was a perfect sphere, and of such stupendous dimensions, that Dame Nature, with all her sex's ingenuity, would have been puzzled to construct a neck capable of supporting it; wherefore she wisely declined the attempt, and settled it firmly on the top of his backbone, just between the shoulders. His body was oblong and particularly capacious at bottom; which was wisely ordered by Providence, seeing that he was a man of sedentary habits, and very averse to the idle labor of walking. His legs were short, but sturdy in proportion to the weight they had to sustain; so that when erect he had not a little the appearance of a beer barrel on skids. His face, that infallible index of the mind, presented a vast expanse, unfurrowed by any of those lines and angles which disfigure the human countenance with what is termed expression. Two small gray eyes twinkled feebly in the midst, like two stars

"Wouter Van Twiller" from SELECTED WRITINGS OF WASHINGTON IRVING, edited by Saxe Commins, published by Random House, Inc., 1945.

of lesser magnitude in a hazy firmament, and his full-fed cheeks, which seemed to have taken toll of everything that went into his mouth, were curiously mottled and streaked with dusky red, like a spitzenberg apple.

His habits were as regular as his person. He daily took his four stated meals, appropriating exactly an hour to each; he smoked and doubted eight hours, and he slept the remaining twelve of the four-and-twenty. Such was the renowned Wouter Van Twiller—a true philosopher, for his mind was either elevated above, or tranquilly settled below, the cares and perplexities of this world. He had lived in it for years, without feeling the least curiosity to know whether the sun revolved round it, or it round the sun; and he had watched, for at least half a century, the smoke curling from his pipe to the ceiling, without once troubling his head with any of those numerous theories by which a philosopher would have perplexed his brain, in accounting for its rising above the surrounding atmosphere.

In his council he presided with great state and solemnity. He sat in a huge chair of solid oak, hewn in the celebrated forest of the Hague, fabricated by an experienced timmerman[1] of Amsterdam, and curiously carved about the arms and feet, into exact imitations of gigantic eagle's claws. Instead of a sceptre, he swayed a long Turkish pipe, wrought with jasmin and amber, which had been presented to a stadtholder[2] of Holland at the conclusion of a treaty with one of the petty Barbary powers.[3] In this stately chair would he sit, and this magnificent pipe would he smoke, shaking his right knee with a constant motion, and fixing his eye for hours together upon a little print of Amsterdam, which hung in a black frame against the opposite wall of the council-chamber. Nay, it has even been said, that when any deliberation of extraordinary length and intricacy was on the carpet, the renowned Wouter would shut his eyes for full two hours at a time, that he might not be disturbed by external objects; and at such times the internal commotion of his mind was evinced by certain regular guttural sounds, which his admirers declared were merely the noise of conflict, made by his contending doubts and opinions. □□

---

1. *timmerman,* a carpenter.
2. *stadtholder* (stät'hōl dər), a provincial governor.
3. *Barbary powers,* North African coastal countries that pirated trading ships until the nineteenth century.

Discussion

1. Irving achieves humor in this selection by treating his subject with mock dignity. For example, the opening lines tell the reader that Van Twiller is "renowned." Irving then mocks this suggested dignity by contradicting the word's conventional meaning when he adds that such men "successfully dozed away their lives." List several other such examples of mockery.

2. (a) What character traits are suggested by Van Twiller's physical appearance? (b) By his surroundings?

3. (a) What faults of society does Irving satirize through its representative, Wouter Van Twiller? (b) Is the **tone** of this **satire** bitter or gentle? Explain.

Vocabulary • Dictionary

Use your Glossary to find the meaning of the italicized word in each sentence below. Then explain why the word is or is not used properly in the sentence. Your explanation must show that you understand the meaning of the word.

1. He sat in the easy chair in such great *comport* that he fell asleep.

2. As he made the witty reply, there was a *capacious* twinkle in his eye.

3. People who act with *propriety* may find themselves in jail if they are caught.

4. That child is simply too *sedentary*, the way he runs around all the time. Can't you calm him down?

5. Surprise! I guess we fooled you when we *fabricated* that story about going off on vacation so that we couldn't be here for your birthday.

6. Most people will admit they are *infallible* and do make mistakes once in a while.

The Devil and Tom Walker

A few miles from Boston in Massachusetts, there is a deep inlet, winding several miles into the interior of the country from Charles Bay, and terminating in a thickly wooded swamp or morass. On one side of this inlet is a beautiful dark grove; on the opposite side the land rises abruptly from the water's edge into a high ridge, on which grow a few scattered oaks of great age and immense size.

Under one of these gigantic trees, according to old stories, there was a great amount of treasure buried by Kidd the pirate. The inlet allowed a facility to bring the money in a boat secretly and at night to the very foot of the hill; the elevation of the place permitted a good lookout to be kept that no one was at hand; while the remarkable trees formed good landmarks by which the place might easily be found again. The old stories add, moreover, that the devil presided at the hiding of the money, and took it under his guardianship; but this, it is well known, he always does with buried treasure, particularly when it has been ill-gotten. Be that as it may, Kidd never returned to recover his wealth, being shortly after seized at Boston, sent out to England, and there hanged for a pirate.

About the year 1727, just at the time that earthquakes were prevalent in New England, and shook many tall sinners down upon their knees, there lived near this place a meager, miserly fellow, of the name of Tom Walker. He had a wife as miserly as himself; they were so miserly that they even conspired to cheat each other. Whatever the woman could lay hands on, she hid away; a hen could not cackle but she was on the alert to secure the new-laid egg. Her husband was continually prying about to detect her secret hoards, and many and fierce were the conflicts that took place about what ought to have been common property.

They lived in a forlorn-looking house that stood alone, and had an air of starvation. A few straggling savin trees, emblems of sterility, grew near it; no smoke ever curled from its chimney; no traveler stopped at its door. A miserable horse, whose ribs were as articulate as the bars of a gridiron, stalked about a field, where a thin carpet of moss, scarcely covering the ragged beds of pudding stone, tantalized and balked his hunger; and sometimes he would lean his head over the fence, look piteously at the passer-by, and seem to petition deliverance from this land of famine.

The house and its inmates had altogether a bad name. Tom's wife was a tall termagant, fierce of temper, loud of tongue, and strong of arm. Her voice was often heard in wordy warfare with her husband; and his face sometimes showed signs that their conflicts were not confined to words. No one ventured, however, to interfere between them. The lonely wayfarer shrunk within himself at the horrid clamor and clapper-clawing,[1] eyed the den of discord askance; and hurried on his way, rejoicing, if a bachelor, in his celibacy.

One day that Tom Walker had been to a distant part of the neighborhood, he took what he considered a short cut homeward, through the swamp. Like most short cuts, it was an ill-chosen route. The swamp was thickly grown with great gloomy pines and hemlocks, some of them ninety feet high, which made it dark at noonday and a retreat for all the owls of the neighborhood. It was full of pits and quagmires, partly covered with weeds and mosses, where the green surface often betrayed the traveler into a gulf of black, smothering mud; there were also dark and stag-

---

1. *clapper-clawing,* an argument accompanied by scratching and slapping.

nant pools, the abodes of the tadpole, the bull-frog, and the water snake, where the trunks of pines and hemlocks lay half-drowned, half-rotting, looking like alligators sleeping in the mire.

Tom had long been picking his way cautiously through this treacherous forest, stepping from tuft to tuft of rushes and roots, which afforded precarious footholds among deep sloughs; or pacing carefully, like a cat, along the prostrate trunks of trees, startled now and then by the sudden screaming of the bittern, or the quacking of wild duck rising on the wing from some solitary pool. At length he arrived at a firm piece of ground, which ran out like a peninsula into the deep bosom of the swamp. It had been one of the strongholds of the Indians during their wars with the first colonists. Here they had thrown up a kind of fort, which they had looked upon as almost impregnable, and had used as a place of refuge for their squaws and children. Nothing remained of the old Indian fort but a few embankments, gradually sinking to the level of the surrounding earth and already overgrown in part by oaks and other forest trees, the foliage of which formed a contrast to the dark pines and hemlocks of the swamp.

It was late in the dusk of evening when Tom Walker reached the old fort, and he paused there awhile to rest himself. Anyone but he would have felt unwilling to linger in this lonely, melancholy place, for the common people had a bad opinion of it, from the stories handed down from the time of the Indian wars, when it was asserted that the savages held incantations here and made sacrifices to the evil spirit.

Tom Walker, however, was not a man to be troubled with any fears of the kind. He reposed himself for some time on the trunk of a fallen hemlock, listening to the boding cry of the tree toad, and delving with his walking staff into a mound of black mold at his feet. As he turned up the soil unconsciously, his staff struck against something hard. He raked it out of the vegetable mold, and lo! a cloven skull, with an Indian tomahawk buried deep in it, lay before him. The rust on the weapon showed the time that had elapsed since this deathblow had been given. It was a dreary memento of the fierce struggle that had taken place in this last foothold of the Indian

warriors. "Humph!" said Tom Walker as he gave it a kick to shake the dirt from it.

"Let that skull alone!" said a gruff voice. Tom lifted up his eyes and beheld a great black man seated directly opposite him, on the stump of a tree. He was exceedingly surprised, having neither heard nor seen anyone approach; and he was still more perplexed on observing, as well as the gathering gloom would permit, that the stranger was neither Negro nor Indian. It is true he was dressed in a rude half-Indian garb, and had a red belt or sash swathed round his body; but his face was neither black nor copper color, but swarthy and dingy, and begrimed with soot, as if he had been accustomed to toil among fires and forges. He had a shock of coarse black hair that stood out from his head in all directions, and bore an ax on his shoulder.

He scowled for a moment at Tom with a pair of great red eyes.

"What are you doing on my grounds?" said the black man, with a hoarse, growling voice.

"Your grounds!" said Tom, with a sneer, "no more your grounds than mine; they belong to Deacon Peabody."

"Deacon Peabody be damned," said the stranger, "as I flatter myself he will be, if he does not look more to his own sins and less to those of his neighbors. Look yonder, and see how Deacon Peabody is faring."

Tom looked in the direction that the stranger pointed and beheld one of the great trees, fair and flourishing without, but rotten at the core, and saw that it had been nearly hewn through, so that the first high wind was likely to blow it down. On the bark of the tree was scored the name of Deacon Peabody, an eminent man who had waxed wealthy by driving shrewd bargains with the Indians. He now looked around, and found most of the tall trees marked with the name of some great man of the colony, and all more or less scored by the ax. The one on which he had been seated, and which had evidently just been hewn down, bore the name of Crowninshield; and he recollected a mighty rich man of that name, who made a vulgar display of wealth, which it was whispered he had acquired by buccaneering.

"He's just ready for burning!" said the black man, with a growl of triumph. "You see I am

"The Devil and Tom Walker," one of seventeen scenes from tales by Irving, painted by John Quidor (1801–1881). (The Cleveland Museum of Art, Mr. and Mrs. William H. Marlatt Fund.)

likely to have a good stock of firewood for winter."

"But what right have you," said Tom, "to cut down Deacon Peabody's timber?"

"The right of a prior claim," said the other. "This woodland belonged to me long before one of your white-faced race put foot upon the soil."

"And pray, who are you, if I may be so bold?" said Tom.

"Oh, I go by various names. I am the wild huntsman in some countries; the black miner in others. In this neighborhood I am known by the name of the black woodsman. I am he to whom the red men consecrated this spot, and in honor of whom they now and then roasted a white man, by way of sweet-smelling sacrifice. Since the red men have been exterminated by you white savages, I amuse myself by presiding at the persecutions of Quakers and Anabaptists;[2] I am the great patron and prompter of slave dealers, and the grand master of the Salem witches."[3]

"The upshot of all which is, that, if I mistake not," said Tom sturdily, "you are he commonly called Old Scratch."

"The same, at your service!" replied the black man, with a half-civil nod.

Such was the opening of this interview, according to the old story; though it has almost too familiar an air to be credited. One would think that to meet with such a singular personage, in this wild, lonely place, would have shaken any man's nerves; but Tom was a hard-minded fellow, not easily daunted, and he had lived so long with a termagant wife that he did not even fear the devil.

It is said that after this commencement they had a long and earnest conversation together, as Tom returned homeward. The black man told him of great sums of money buried by Kidd the pirate, under the oak trees on the high ridge, not

2. **Anabaptists** (an′ə bap′tists), members of a Protestant sect which originated in the 1500s. Quakers and Anabaptists were persecuted in the Massachusetts colony.
3. **Salem witches,** defendants in the Salem witch trials of 1692.

far from the morass. All these were under his command, and protected by his power, so that none could find them but such as propitiated his favor. These he offered to place within Tom Walker's reach, having conceived an especial kindness for him; but they were to be had only on certain conditions. What these conditions were may be easily surmised, though Tom never disclosed them publicly. They must have been very hard, for he required time to think of them, and he was not a man to stick at trifles when money was in view.

When they had reached the edge of the swamp, the stranger paused. "What proof have I that all you have been telling me is true?" said Tom. "There's my signature," said the black man, pressing his finger on Tom's forehead. So saying, he turned off among the thickest of the swamp, and seemed, as Tom said, to go down, down, down, into the earth, until he totally disappeared.

When Tom reached home, he found the black print of a finger burned, as it were, into his forehead, which nothing could obliterate.

The first news his wife had to tell him was the sudden death of Absalom Crowninshield, the rich buccaneer. It was announced in the papers with the usual flourish that "A great man had fallen in Israel."[4]

Tom recollected the tree which his black friend had just hewn down and which was ready for burning. "Let the freebooter roast," said Tom; "who cares!" He now felt convinced that all he had heard and seen was no illusion.

He was not prone to let his wife into his confidence; but as this was an uneasy secret, he willingly shared it with her. All her avarice was awakened at the mention of hidden gold, and she urged her husband to comply with the black man's terms, and secure what would make them wealthy for life. However Tom might have felt disposed to sell himself to the devil, he was determined not to do so to oblige his wife; so he flatly refused, out of the mere spirit of contradiction. Many were the quarrels they had on the subject; but the more she talked, the more resolute was Tom not to be damned to please her.

At length she determined to drive the bargain on her own account, and if she succeeded, to keep all the gain to herself. Being of the same fearless temper as her husband, she set off for the old Indian fort toward the close of a summer's day. She was many hours absent. When she came back, she was reserved and sullen in her replies. She spoke something of a black man, whom she met about twilight hewing at the root of a tall tree. He was sulky, however, and would not come to terms; she was to go again with a propitiatory offering, but what it was she forbore to say.

The next evening she set off again for the swamp, with her apron heavily laden. Tom waited and waited for her, but in vain; midnight came, but she did not make her appearance; morning, noon, night returned, but still she did not come. Tom now grew uneasy for her safety, especially as he found she had carried off in her apron the silver tea pot and spoons, and every portable article of value. Another night elapsed, another morning came; but no wife. In a word, she was never heard of more.

What was her real fate nobody knows, in consequence of so many pretending to know. It is one of those facts which have become confounded by a variety of historians. Some asserted that she lost her way among the tangled mazes of the swamp, and sank into some pit or slough; others, more uncharitable, hinted that she had eloped with the household booty, and made off to some other province; while others surmised that the tempter had decoyed her into a dismal quagmire, on the top of which her hat was found lying. In confirmation of this, it was said a great black man, with an ax on his shoulder, was seen late that very evening coming out of the swamp, carrying a bundle tied in a check apron, with an air of surly triumph.

The most current and probable story, however, observes that Tom Walker grew so anxious about the fate of his wife and his property that he set out at length to seek them both at the Indian fort. During a long summer's afternoon he searched about the gloomy place, but no wife was to be seen. He called her name repeatedly, but she was nowhere to be heard. The bittern alone responded to his voice, as he flew screaming by; or the bullfrog croaked dolefully from a

---

4. **Israel,** Massachusetts. The Puritans of Massachusetts regarded their colony as the Promised Land (Israel).

neighboring pool. At length, it is said, just in the brown hour of twilight, when the owls began to hoot, and the bats to flit about, his attention was attracted by the clamor of carrion crows hovering about a cypress tree. He looked up and beheld a bundle tied in a check apron and hanging in the branches of the tree, with a great vulture perched hard by, as if keeping watch upon it. He leaped with joy; for he recognized his wife's apron and supposed it to contain the household valuables.

"Let us get hold of the property," said he consolingly to himself, "and we will endeavor to do without the woman."

As he scrambled up the tree, the vulture spread its wide wings and sailed off screaming into the deep shadows of the forest. Tom seized the checked apron, but, woeful sight! found nothing but a heart and liver tied up in it!

Such, according to this most authentic old story, was all that was to be found of Tom's wife. She had probably attempted to deal with the black man as she had been accustomed to deal with her husband; but though a female scold is generally considered a match for the devil, yet in this instance she appears to have had the worst of it. She must have died game, however; for it is said Tom noticed many prints of cloven feet deeply stamped upon the tree, and found handfuls of hair that looked as if they had been plucked from the coarse black shock of the woodsman. Tom knew his wife's prowess by experience. He shrugged his shoulders as he looked at the signs of a fierce clapper-clawing. "Egad," said he to himself, "Old Scratch must have had a tough time of it!"

Tom consoled himself for the loss of his property with the loss of his wife, for he was a man of fortitude. He even felt something like gratitude toward the black woodsman, who, he considered, had done him a kindness. He sought, therefore, to cultivate a further acquaintance with him, but for some time without success; the old blacklegs played shy, for whatever people may think, he is not always to be had for calling for; he knows how to play his cards when pretty sure of his game.

At length, it is said, when delay had whetted Tom's eagerness to the quick, and prepared him to agree to anything rather than not gain the promised treasure, he met the black man one evening in his usual woodsman's dress, with his ax on his shoulder, sauntering along the swamp and humming a tune. He affected to receive Tom's advances with great indifference, made brief replies, and went on humming his tune.

By degrees, however, Tom brought him to business, and they began to haggle about the terms on which the former was to have the pirate's treasure. There was one condition which need not be mentioned, being generally understood in all cases where the devil grants favors; but there were others about which, though of less importance, he was inflexibly obstinate. He insisted that the money found through his means should be employed in his service. He proposed, therefore, that Tom should employ it in the black traffic; that is to say, that he should fit out a slave ship. This, however, Tom resolutely refused; he was bad enough in all conscience, but the devil himself could not tempt him to turn slave trader.

Finding Tom so squeamish on this point, he did not insist upon it, but proposed, instead, that he should turn usurer, the devil being extremely anxious for the increase of usurers, looking upon them as his peculiar people.

To this no objections were made, for it was just to Tom's taste.

"You shall open a broker's shop in Boston next month," said the black man.

"I'll do it tomorrow, if you wish," said Tom Walker.

"You shall lend money at two per cent a month."

"Egad, I'll charge four!" replied Tom Walker.

"You shall extort bonds, foreclose mortgages, drive the merchants to bankruptcy—"

"I'll drive them to the devil," cried Tom Walker.

"You are the usurer for my money!" said blacklegs with delight. "When will you want the rhino?"[5]

"This very night."

"Done!" said the devil.

"Done!" said Tom Walker. So they shook hands and struck a bargain.

A few days' time saw Tom Walker seated behind his desk in a counting house in Boston.

___

5. **rhino** (rī′nō), money. [*Slang*]

His reputation for a ready-moneyed man, who would lend money out for a good consideration, soon spread abroad. Everybody remembers the time of Governor Belcher,[6] when money was particularly scarce. It was a time of paper credit.[7] The country had been deluged with government bills, the famous Land Bank[8] had been established; there had been a rage for speculating; the people had run mad with schemes for new settlements, for building cities in the wilderness; land jobbers[9] went about with maps of grants, and townships, and El Dorados,[10] lying nobody knew where, but which everybody was ready to purchase. In a word, the great speculating fever which breaks out every now and then in the country had raged to an alarming degree, and everybody was dreaming of making sudden fortunes from nothing. As usual the fever had subsided; the dream had gone off, and the imaginary fortunes with it; the patients were left in doleful plight, and the whole country resounded with the consequent cry of "hard times."

At this propitious time of public distress did Tom Walker set up as usurer in Boston. His door was soon thronged by customers. The needy and adventurous, the gambling speculator, the dreaming land jobber, the thriftless tradesman, the merchant with cracked credit—in short, everyone driven to raise money by desperate means and desperate sacrifices hurried to Tom Walker.

Thus Tom was the universal friend of the needy, and acted like a "friend in need"; that is to say, he always exacted good pay and good security. In proportion to the distress of the applicant was the hardness of his terms. He accumulated bonds and mortgages; gradually squeezed his customers closer and closer; and sent them at length, dry as a sponge, from his door.

In this way he made money hand over hand; became a rich and mighty man, and exalted his cocked hat upon 'Change.[11] He built himself, as usual, a vast house, out of ostentation; but left the greater part of it unfinished and unfurnished, out of parsimony. He even set up a carriage in the fullness of his vain-glory, though he nearly starved the horses which drew it; and as the ungreased wheels groaned and screeched on the axletrees, you would have thought you heard the souls of the poor debtors he was squeezing.

As Tom waxed old, however, he grew thoughtful. Having secured the good things of this world, he began to feel anxious about those of the next. He thought with regret on the bargain he had made with his black friend, and set his wits to work to cheat him out of the conditions. He became, therefore, all of a sudden, a violent churchgoer. He prayed loudly and strenuously, as if heaven were to be taken by force of lungs. Indeed, one might always tell when he had sinned most during the week by the clamor of his Sunday devotion. The quiet Christians who had been modestly and steadfastly traveling Zionward,[12] were struck with self-reproach at seeing themselves so suddenly outstripped in their career by this new-made convert. Tom was as rigid in religious as in money matters; he was a stern supervisor and censurer of his neighbors, and seemed to think every sin entered up to their account became a credit on his own side of the page. He even talked of the expediency of reviving the persecution of Quakers and Anabaptists. In a word, Tom's zeal became as notorious as his riches.

Still, in spite of all this strenuous attention to forms, Tom had a lurking dread that the devil, after all, would have his due. That he might not be taken unawares, therefore, it is said he always carried a small Bible in his coat pocket. He had also a great folio Bible on his counting-house desk, and would frequently be found reading it when people called on business; on such occasions he would lay his green spectacles in the book, to mark the place, while he turned round to drive some usurious bargain.

Some say that Tom grew a little crack-

---

6. **Governor Belcher,** Jonathan Belcher, who governed Massachusetts from 1730 to 1741.
7. **paper credit,** assets that existed on paper but were actually of no value.
8. **Land Bank,** a scheme to relieve the shortage of gold in Massachusetts by establishing a bank whose resources rested on real-estate mortgages.
9. **land jobbers,** men who bought tracts of undeveloped land as a speculation and sold them to others.
10. **El Dorado,** imaginary country abounding in gold searched for by Spaniards in the sixteenth century. The name now applies to any place where riches can be had easily and quickly.
11. **'Change,** the Exchange, or the financial center of Boston, where merchants, traders, and brokers do business.
12. **Zionward,** toward heaven. Zion, originally the hill in Jerusalem on which the temple stood, is often used to typify heaven.

brained in his old days, and that, fancying his end approaching, he had his horse new shod, saddled and bridled, and buried with his feet uppermost; because he supposed that at the last day the world would be turned upside down in which case he should find his horse standing ready for mounting, and he was determined at the worst to give his old friend a run for it. This, however, is probably a mere old wives' fable. If he really did take such a precaution, it was totally superfluous; at least so says the authentic old legend, which closes his story in the following manner.

One hot summer afternoon in the dog days, just as a terrible black thundergust was coming up, Tom sat in his counting house in his white cap and India silk morning gown. He was on the point of foreclosing a mortgage, by which he would complete the ruin of an unlucky land speculator for whom he had professed the greatest friendship. The poor land jobber begged him to grant a few months' indulgence. Tom had grown testy and irritated, and refused another day.

"My family will be ruined and brought upon the parish,"[13] said the land jobber.

"Charity begins at home," replied Tom; "I must take care of myself in these hard times."

"You have made so much money out of me," said the speculator.

Tom lost his patience and his piety. "The devil take me," said he, "if I have made a farthing!"

Just then there were three loud knocks at the street door. He stepped out to see who was there. A black man was holding a black horse, which neighed and stamped with impatience.

"Tom, you're come for," said the black fellow, gruffly. Tom shrank back, but too late. He had left his little Bible at the bottom of his coat pocket, and his big Bible on the desk buried under the mortgage he was about to foreclose; never was sinner taken more unawares. The black man whisked him like a child into the saddle, gave the horse the lash, and away he galloped, with Tom on his back, in the midst of the thunderstorm. The clerks stuck their pens behind their ears, and stared after him from the windows. Away went Tom Walker, dashing down the streets, his white cap bobbing up and down, his morning gown fluttering in the wind,

and his steed striking fire out of the pavement at every bound. When the clerks turned to look for the black man, he had disappeared.

Tom Walker never returned to foreclose the mortgage. A countryman, who lived on the border of the swamp, reported that in the height of the thundergust he had heard a great clattering of hoofs and a howling along the road, and running to the window caught sight of a figure, such as I have described, on a horse that galloped like mad across the fields, over the hills, and down into the black hemlock swamp toward the old Indian fort; and that shortly after, a thunderbolt falling in that direction seemed to set the whole forest in a blaze.

The good people of Boston shook their heads and shrugged their shoulders, but had been so much accustomed to witches and goblins and tricks of the devil in all kinds of shapes, from the first settlement of the colony, that they were not so much horror-struck as might have been expected. Trustees were appointed to take charge of Tom's effects. There was nothing, however, to administer upon. On searching his coffers, all his bonds and mortgages were found reduced to cinders. In place of gold and silver, his iron chest was filled with chips and shavings; two skeletons lay in his stable instead of his half-starved horses, and the very next day his great house took fire and burned to the ground.

Such was the end of Tom Walker and his ill-gotten wealth. Let all griping money brokers lay this story to heart. The truth of it is not to be doubted. The very hole under the oak trees whence he dug Kidd's money is to be seen to this day; and the neighboring swamp and old Indian fort are often haunted on stormy nights by a figure on horseback, in morning gown and white cap, which is doubtless the troubled spirit of the usurer. In fact, the story has resolved itself into a proverb, and is the origin of that popular saying, so prevalent throughout New England, of "The Devil and Tom Walker." □□

---

13. **brought upon the parish,** forced to depend upon public charity for support.

1. (a) What is the meaning of the Woodsman's scoring of trees? (b) What do the trees **symbolize**?

2. Tom strongly objects to the Woodsman's suggestion that he become a slave trader but readily agrees to engage in usury. Do you think Irving is implying that there are degrees of morality and sinfulness? Explain.

3. Irving describes land speculation as a "fever" and the speculators as "patients." What do you think he is saying through these metaphors about love of money?

4. As Tom ages he becomes "a violent churchgoer." Is Tom's conversion genuine? Explain.

5. (a) Is Irving satirizing an individual, society, or the whole of humankind? (b) At what foibles does he level his attack?

6. **Dramatic irony** is a literary device whereby a character inadvertently speaks the truth, foreshadowing tragic events of which he is unaware. Find the sentence in the conclusion of the tale where Tom makes this kind of ironic statement.

7. Some tales about pacts with the devil end tragically for their heroes, illustrating the moral that one should never sell one's soul. Is "The Devil and Tom Walker" a tragedy? Explain. What, if any, is the moral of the tale?

Vocabulary
Dictionary and Structure

Propitiated and *propitious* both appear in this story. Another word that comes from the same root is *propitiatory*. Look all three words up in the Glossary. On your paper write the word next to the number of the sentence that it correctly completes. Be sure you can pronounce each word.

1. The man made a _____ move toward his mortal enemy and shook his hand.

2. "All these were under his command, and protected by his power, so that none could find them but such as _____ his favor."

3. "At this _____ time of public distress did Tom Walker set up as usurer in Boston."

4. Three o'clock in the morning is not a _____ time to run screaming down the middle of the street.

Washington Irving 1783 • 1859

Washington Irving is called the "Father of American literature." Coming at a time when Europe doubted that anything of real literary merit could spring from such an uncultured wilderness, Irving provided America with a much longed-for measure of self-esteem.

At the age of nineteen he began writing satirical society sketches which appeared first in a four-page daily paper put out by one of his brothers and then later in *Salmagundi*, a magazine published by Irving and an assortment of friends.

Though his first full-length book, *Knickerbocker's History of New York,* was immensely successful, Irving was still not committed to writing. He spent six years dabbling in Washington society, editing a magazine, and acting as an aide-de-camp in the War of 1812. Finally he left New York for Liverpool, England, having been asked to put in order a business owned by the five Irving brothers. Within a few years the business had collapsed and Irving was left with little alternative but to support himself through his writing. The stories and articles he wrote appeared in installments between 1819 and 1820 and were subsequently published as *The Sketch Book.* The book was proclaimed a masterpiece and Irving became famous.

With success and fortune Irving once again neglected his work. He published *Tales of a Traveller* in 1824, a collection of second-hand, poorly finished stories.

His solution was an escape to Spain where he immersed himself in Spanish history and legend. He spent four diligent years writing the *History of the Life and Voyages of Christopher Columbus, Chronicle of the Conquest of Granada,* and *The Alhambra.*

On his return to New York he was honored and eulogized as the symbol of American literature, but his prime was past. With the exception of four successful years as minister to Spain, Irving lived the rest of his life at "Sunnyside," an estate along the Hudson. He died at the age of seventy-six, completing in his last year the fifth and final volume of a biography of Washington, the man for whom he had been named.

James Fenimore Cooper

The events of The Deerslayer *take place between 1740 and 1745. Natty Bumppo, the young "Deerslayer," has been reared as a hunter and warrior by the Delaware tribe. His closest friend is a young Delaware chief, Chingachgook, whose beloved, Hist, has been stolen by the Hurons. In attempting her rescue, Deerslayer has himself been captured.*

A Rescue: from The Deerslayer

It was one of the common expedients of the savages, on such occasions, to put the nerves of their victims to the severest proofs. On the other hand, it was a matter of Indian pride to betray no yielding to terror or pain, but for the prisoner to provoke his enemies to such acts of violence as would soonest produce death. Many a warrior had been known to bring his own sufferings to a more speedy termination, by taunting reproaches and reviling language . . . . This happy expedient of taking refuge from the ferocity of his foes in their passions was denied Deerslayer, however, by his peculiar notions of the duty of a white man; and he had stoutly made up his mind to endure everything in preference to disgracing his color.

No sooner did the young men understand that they were at liberty to commence than some of the boldest and most forward among them sprang into the arena, tomahawk in hand. Here they prepared to throw that dangerous weapon, the object being to strike the tree as near as possible to the victim's head without absolutely hitting him. This was so hazardous an experiment that none but those who were known to be exceedingly expert with the weapon were allowed to enter the lists[1] at all, lest an early death might interfere with the expected entertainment. In the truest hands, it was seldom that the captive escaped injury in these trials; and it often happened that death followed even when the blow was not premeditated. In the particular case of our hero, Rivenoak[2] and the older warriors were apprehensive that the example of the Panther's fate[3] might prove a motive with some fiery spirit . . . . This circumstance, of itself, rendered the ordeal of the tomahawk doubly critical for the Deerslayer. . . .

The first youth who presented himself for the trial was called the Raven, having as yet had no opportunity of obtaining a more warlike sobriquet. He was remarkable for high pretension rather than for skill or exploits, and those who knew his character thought the captive in imminent danger when he took his stand and poised the tomahawk. Nevertheless, the young man was good-natured, and no thought was uppermost in his mind other than the desire to make a better cast than any of his fellows. . . . Still, our hero maintained an appearance of self-possession. He had made up his mind that his hour was come, and it would have been a mercy, instead of a calamity, to fall by the unsteadiness of the first hand that was raised against him.

After a suitable number of flourishes and gesticulations that promised much more than he could perform, the Raven let the tomahawk quit his hand. The weapon whirled through the air with the usual evolutions, cut a chip from the sapling to which the prisoner was bound, within a few inches of his cheek, and stuck in a large oak that grew several yards behind him. This was decidedly a bad effort, and a common sneer proclaimed as much, to the great mortification of the young man. On the other hand, there was a

---

1. *enter the lists,* join in the contest. This is a phrase borrowed from the jousting tournaments of the Middle Ages.
2. *Rivenoak* (riv′ən ōk′), a Huron chief who wanted Deerslayer to join his tribe.
3. *the Panther's fate.* Deerslayer had killed the Panther, a Huron warrior, with his tomahawk.

general but suppressed murmur of admiration at the steadiness with which the captive stood the trial. The head was the only part he could move, and this had been purposely left free, that the tormentors might have the amusement, and the tormented endure the shame, of dodging and otherwise attempting to avoid the blows. Deerslayer disappointed these hopes by a command of nerve that rendered his whole body as immovable as the tree to which he was bound. Nor did he even adopt the natural and usual expedient of shutting his eyes . . . .

The Raven had no sooner made his unsuccessful and puerile effort than he was succeeded by Le Daim-Mose,[4] or the Moose, a middle-aged warrior, who was particularly skillful in the use of the tomahawk, and from whose attempt the spectators confidently looked for gratification. This man had none of the good nature of the Raven, but he would gladly have sacrificed the captive to his hatred of the palefaces generally, were it not for the greater interest he felt in his own success as one particularly skillful in the use of this weapon. He took his stand quietly but with an air of confidence, poised his little ax but a single instant, advanced a foot with a quick motion, and threw. Deerslayer saw the keen instrument whirling toward him, and believed all was over; still he was not touched. The tomahawk had actually bound the head of the captive to the tree by carrying before it some of his hair, having buried itself deep beneath the soft bark. A general yell expressed the delight of the spectators, and the Moose felt his heart soften a little toward the prisoner, whose steadiness of nerve alone enabled him to give this evidence of his consummate skill.

Le Daim-Mose was succeeded by the Bounding Boy, or Le Garçon qui Bondi,[5] who came leaping into the circle like a hound or a goat at play. . . . Nevertheless he was both brave and skillful, and had gained the respect of his people by deeds in war as well as success in the hunts. . . . The Bounding Boy skipped about in front of the captive, menacing him with his tomahawk, now on one side and now on another and then again in front, in the vain hope of being able to extort some sign of fear by this parade of danger. At length Deerslayer's patience became exhausted by all this mummery, and he spoke for the first time since the trial had actually commenced.

"Throw away, Huron!" he cried, "or your tomahawk will forget its arr'nd.[6] Why do you keep loping about like a fa'an[7] that's showing its dam how well it can skip, when you're a warrior grown, yourself, and a warrior grown defies you and all your silly antics? Throw, or the Huron gals will laugh in your face."

The last words aroused the "Bounding" warrior to fury. The same nervous excitability which rendered him so active in his person made it difficult to repress his feelings, and the words were scarcely past the lips of the speaker than the tomahawk left the hand of the Indian. Nor was it cast without good will, and a fierce determination to slay. Had the intention been less deadly, the danger might have been greater. The aim was uncertain, and the weapon glanced near the cheek of the captive, slightly cutting the shoulder in its evolutions. This was the first instance in which any other object than that of terrifying the prisoner and of displaying skill had been manifested; and the Bounding Boy was immediately led from the arena and was warmly rebuked for his intemperate haste, which had come so near defeating all the hopes of the band.

To this irritable person succeeded several other young warriors, who not only hurled the tomahawk but who cast the knife . . . . Several times Deerslayer was grazed, but in no instance did he receive what might be termed a wound. The unflinching firmness with which he faced his assailants . . . excited a profound respect in the spectators . . . .

Rivenoak now told his people that the paleface had proved himself to be a man. He might live with the Delawares, but he had not been made woman with that tribe. He wished to know whether it was the desire of the Hurons to proceed any further. Even the gentlest of the females, however, had received too much satisfaction in the late trials to forego their expectations of a gratifying exhibition; and there was but

---

4. *Le Daim-Mose* (lə da′mōz′), "the moose deer." Many Hurons were called by names the French had given them.
5. *Le Garçon qui Bondi* (lə gär sōn′ kē bôn di′), "the boy who bounds." [*French*]
6. *arr'nd,* errand.
7. *fa'an,* fawn.

one voice[8] in the request to proceed. The politic chief, who had some such desire to receive so celebrated a hunter into his tribe as a European minister had to devise a new and available means of taxation, sought every plausible means of arresting the trial in season; for he well knew if permitted to go far enough to arouse the more ferocious passions of the tormentors, it would be as easy to dam the waters of the great lakes of his own region as to attempt to arrest them in their bloody career. He therefore called four or five of the best marksmen to him and bid them put the captive to the proof of the rifle, while, at the same time, he cautioned them touching the necessity of their maintaining their own credit by the closest attention to the manner of exhibiting their skill.

When Deerslayer saw the chosen warriors step into the circle with their arms prepared for service, he felt some such relief as the miserable sufferer who had long endured the agonies of disease feels at the certain approach of death. . . .

The warriors prepared to exhibit their skill, as there was a double object in view: that of putting the constancy of the captive to the proof, and that of showing how steady were the hands of the marksmen under circumstances of excitement. The distance was small, and, in one sense, safe. But in diminishing the distance taken by the tormentors, the trial to the nerves of the captive was essentially increased. The face of Deerslayer, indeed, was just removed sufficiently from the ends of the guns to escape the effects of the flash, and his steady eye was enabled to look directly into their muzzles . . . .

Shot after shot was made, all the bullets coming in close proximity to the Deerslayer's head, without touching it. Still, no one could detect even the twitching of a muscle on the part of the captive, or the slightest winking of an eye. . . . When five or six had discharged their bullets into the trees, he could not refrain from expressing his contempt.

"You may call this shooting, Mingos,"[9] he exclaimed, "but we've squaws among the Delawares, and I have known Dutch gals on the Mohawk, that could outdo your greatest indivors. Ondo these arms of mine; put a rifle into my hands; and I'll pin the thinnest war lock in your party to any tree you can show me, and this at a hundred yards—aye, or at two hundred, if the object can be seen—nineteen shots in twenty—or, for that matter, twenty in twenty, if the piece is creditable and trusty!"

A low, menacing murmur followed this cool taunt; the ire of the warriors kindled at listening to such a reproach from one who so far disdained their efforts as to refuse even to wink when a rifle was discharged as near his face as could be done without burning it. Rivenoak perceived that the moment was critical; and, still retaining his hope of adopting so noted a hunter into his tribe, the politic old chief interposed in time, probably, to prevent an immediate resort to that portion of the torture which must necessarily have produced death . . . .

"I see how it is," he said. "We have been like the palefaces when they fasten their doors at night, out of fear of the red man. They use so many bars that the fire comes and burns them before they can get out. We have bound the Deerslayer too tight; the thongs keep his limbs from shaking, and his eyes from shutting. Loosen him; let us see what his own body is really made of."

The proposal of the chief found instant favor; and several hands were immediately at work cutting and tearing the ropes of bark from the body of our hero. In half a minute Deerslayer stood free from bonds. . . . Deerslayer, by rubbing his limbs, stamping his feet, and moving about, soon regained the circulation, recovering all his physical powers as if nothing had occurred to disturb them.

It is seldom men think of death in the pride of their health and strength. So it was with Deerslayer. Having been helplessly bound, and, as he had every reason to suppose, so lately on the very verge of the other world, to find himself so unexpectedly liberated, in possession of his strength, and with a full command of limb, acted on him like a sudden restoration to life, reanimating hopes that he had once absolutely abandoned. . . . The change was so great that his mind resumed its elasticity; and, no longer

---

8. **there was but one voice.** All of the Hurons spoke together in agreement.
9. **Mingos** (min′gōz), a name scornfully applied by the Delawares to their enemies.

A rescue by Pathfinder (another alias of Natty Bumppo), disguised as a bear. This is an early illustration from Cooper's *The Last of the Mohicans.* (Historical Pictures Service, Inc.)

thinking of submission, it dwelt only on the devices of the sort of warfare in which he was engaged. . . .

The honor of the band was now involved in the issue; and even the female sex lost all its sympathy with suffering, in the desire to save the reputation of the tribe. The voices of the girls, soft and melodious as nature had made them, were heard mingling with the menaces of the men; and the wrongs of Sumach[10] suddenly assumed the character of injuries inflicted on every Huron female. Yielding to this rising tumult the men drew back a little, signifying to the females that they left the captive, for a time, in their hands, it being a common practice on such occasions for the women to endeavor to throw the victim into a rage by their taunts and revilings, and then to turn him suddenly over to the men in a state of mind that was little favorable to resisting the agony of bodily suffering. . . .

But Deerslayer's mind was too much occupied to permit him to be disturbed by the abuse of excited hags; and their rage necessarily increasing with his indifference, as his indifference increased with their rage, the furies soon rendered themselves impotent by their own excesses. Perceiving that the attempt was a complete failure, the warriors interfered to put a stop to this scene . . . . Fragments of dried wood were

---

10. **Sumach** (sü′mak *or* shü′mak), the sister of the Panther.

rapidly collected near the sapling; the splinters which it was intended to thrust into the flesh of the victim, previously to lighting, were all collected; and the thongs were already produced to bind him to the tree. . . .

Suddenly a young Indian came bounding through the Huron ranks, leaping into the very center of the circle in a way to denote the utmost confidence or a temerity bordering on foolhardiness. Five or six sentinels were still watching the lake at different and distant points; and it was the first impression of Rivenoak that one of these had come in with tidings of import. Still, the movements of the stranger were so rapid, and his war dress, which scarcely left him more drapery than an antique statue, had so little distinguishing about it, that, at the first moment, it was impossible to ascertain whether he were friend or foe. Three leaps carried this warrior to the side of Deerslayer. . . . Then he turned and showed the astonished Hurons the noble brow, fine person, and eagle eye of a young warrior in the paint and panoply of a Delaware. He had a rifle in each hand, the butts of both resting on the earth, while from one dangled its proper pouch and horn. This was Killdeer,[11] which even as he looked boldly and in defiance on the crowd around him, he suffered to fall back into the hands of the proper owner. The presence of two armed men, though it was in their midst, startled the Hurons. Their rifles were scattered about against the different trees and their only weapons were their knives and tomahawks. Still, they had too much self-possession to betray fear. . . .

"Hurons," the stranger said, "this earth is very big. The great lakes are big, too; there is room beyond them for the Iroquois; there is room for the Delawares on this side. I am Chingachgook, the son of Uncas, the kinsman of Tamenund. That paleface is my friend. My heart was heavy when I missed him. Come, let us say farewell, and go on our path."

"Hurons, this is your mortal enemy, the Great Serpent of them you hate!" cried Briarthorn.[12] "If he escape, blood will be in your moccasin prints from this spot to the Canadas. . . ."

As the last words were uttered, the traitor cast his knife at the naked breast of the Delaware. With a quick movement Chingachgook avoided the blow, the dangerous weapon burying its point in a pine. At the next instant a similar weapon glanced from the hand of the Serpent, and quivered in the recreant's heart. . . . Briarthorn fell, like a dog, dead in his tracks. . . . A common exclamation followed, and the whole party was in motion. At this instant a sound unusual to the woods was heard, and every Huron, male and female, paused to listen . . . . The sound was regular and heavy, as if the earth were struck with beetles. Objects became visible among the trees of the background, and a body of troops was seen advancing with measured tread. They came upon the charge, the scarlet of the King's livery shining among the bright green foliage of the forest. . . .

A general yell burst from the enclosed Hurons; it was succeeded by the hearty cheers of England. Still, not a musket or rifle was fired, though that steady, measured tramp continued, and the bayonet was seen gleaming in advance of a line that counted nearly sixty men. The Hurons were taken at a fearful disadvantage. On three sides was the water, while their formidable and trained foes cut them off from flight on the fourth. Each warrior rushed for his arms, and then all on the point, man, woman, and child, eagerly sought cover. In this scene of confusion and dismay, however, nothing could surpass the discretion and coolness of Deerslayer. He threw himself on a flank of the retiring Hurons . . . . Deerslayer watched his opportunity, and finding two of his recent tormentors in range, his rifle first broke the silence of the terrific scene. The bullet brought down both at one discharge. This drew a general fire from the Hurons, and the rifle and war cry of the Serpent were heard in the clamor. Still the trained men returned no answering volley . . . . Presently, however, the shrieks, groans, and denunciations that usually accompany the use of the bayonet followed. That terrible and deadly weapon was glutted in vengeance. The scene that succeeded was one of those of which so many have occurred in our own times, in which neither age nor sex forms an exemption to the lot of a savage warfare. ☐☐

---

11. *Killdeer,* Deerslayer's rifle.
12. *the Great Serpent . . . Briarthorn.* The Great Serpent is Chingachgook, and Briarthorn is a Delaware traitor who had joined the Hurons.

Bret Harte: Muck-a-Muck
A Modern Indian Novel After Cooper

"Muck-a-Muck" is from Bret Harte's Condensed Novels and Other Papers, *a book of* **parodies** *making fun of famous novels by Cooper, Irving, and others.*

Chapter I

It was toward the close of a bright October day. The last rays of the setting sun were reflected from one of those sylvan lakes peculiar to the Sierras of California. On the right the curling smoke of an Indian village rose between the columns of the lofty pines, while to the left the log cottage of Judge Tompkins, embowered in buckeyes, completed the enchanting picture.

Although the exterior of the cottage was humble and unpretentious, and in keeping with the wildness of the landscape, its interior gave evidence of the cultivation and refinement of its inmates. An aquarium, containing goldfishes, stood on a marble center-table at one end of the apartment, while a magnificent grand piano occupied the other. The floor was covered with a yielding tapestry carpet, and the walls were adorned with paintings from the pencils of Van Dyke, Rubens, Tintoretto, Michael Angelo,[1] and the productions of the more modern Turner, Kensett, Church, and Bierstadt.[2] Although Judge Tompkins had chosen the frontiers of civilization as his home, it was impossible for him to entirely forego the habits and tastes of his former life. He

was seated in a luxurious armchair, writing at a mahogany *éscritoire*, while his daughter, a lovely young girl of seventeen summers, plied her crochet needle on an ottoman beside him. A bright fire of pine logs flickered and flamed on the ample hearth.

Genevra Octavia Tompkins was Judge Tompkins's only child. Her mother had long since died on the Plains. Reared in affluence, no pains had been spared with the daughter's education. She was a graduate of one of the principal seminaries, and spoke French with a perfect Benicia accent.[3] Peerlessly beautiful, she was dressed in a white *moire antique* robe trimmed with *tulle*.[4] That simple rosebud, with which most heroines exclusively decorate their hair, was all she wore in her raven locks.

The Judge was the first to break the silence.

"Genevra, the logs which compose yonder fire seem to have been incautiously chosen. The sibilation produced by the sap, which exudes copiously therefrom, is not conducive to composition."

"True, father, but I thought it would be preferable to the con-

stant crepitation which is apt to attend the combustion of more seasoned ligneous fragments."

The Judge looked admiringly at the intellectual features of the graceful girl, and half forgot the slight annoyances of the green wood in the musical accents of his daughter. He was smoothing her hair tenderly, when the shadow of a tall figure, which suddenly darkened the doorway, caused him to look up.

Chapter II

It needed but a glance at the newcomer to detect at once the form and features of the haughty aborigine—the untaught and untrammelled son of the forest. Over one shoulder a blanket, negligently but gracefully thrown, disclosed a bare and powerful breast, decorated with a quantity of three-cent postage stamps which he had

From NINETEENTH-CENTURY AMERICAN SHORT FICTION, edited by William Holmes and Edward Mitchell.

1. **Van Dyke, Rubens, Tintoretto** (tin′tō ret′tō), **Michael Angelo,** painters of the sixteenth and seventeenth centuries.
2. **Turner, Kensett, Church, and Bierstadt** (bēr′stat), nineteenth-century painters.
3. **Benicia** (bə nē′shə) **accent.** Benicia is a town in California. The phrase implies that Genevra spoke French with a strong American accent.
4. **moire antique** (mwär′ än tēk′) . . . **tulle** (tül), a robe of watered silk, trimmed with netting.

despoiled from an Overland Mail stage a few weeks previously. A castoff beaver[5] of Judge Tompkins's, adorned by a simple feather, covered his erect head, from beneath which his straight locks descended. His right hand hung lightly by his side, while his left was engaged in holding on a pair of pantaloons, which the lawless grace and freedom of his lower limbs evidently could not brook.

"Why," said the Indian, in a low sweet tone,—"why does the Pale Face still follow the track of the Red Man? Why does he pursue him, even as *O-kee-chow,* the wildcat, chases *Ka-ka,* the skunk? Why are the feet of *Sorreltop,* the white chief, among the acorns of *Muck-a-Muck,* the mountain forest? Why," he repeated, quietly but firmly abstracting a silver spoon from the table,—"why do you seek to drive him from the wigwams of his fathers? His brothers are already gone to the happy hunting grounds. Will the Pale Face seek him there?" And, averting his face from the Judge, he hastily slipped a silver cake-basket beneath his blanket, to conceal his emotion.

"Muck-a-Muck has spoken," said Genevra, softly. "Let him now listen. Are the acorns of the mountain sweeter than the esculent and nutritious bean of the Pale Face miner? Does my brother prize the edible qualities of the snail above that of the crisp and oleaginous bacon? Delicious are the grasshoppers that sport on the hillside,—are they better than the dried apples of the Pale Faces? Pleas-

ant is the gurgle of the torrent, *Kish-Kish,* but is it better than the cluck-cluck of old Bourbon from the old stone bottle?"

"Ugh!" said the Indian,— "ugh! good. The White Rabbit is wise. Her words fall as the snow on *Tootoonolo,* and the rocky heart of Muck-a-Muck is hidden. What says my brother the Gray Gopher of Dutch Flat?"

"She has spoken, Muck-a-Muck," said the Judge, gazing fondly on his daughter. "It is well. Our treaty is concluded. No, thank you,—you need *not* dance the Dance of Snow Shoes, or the Moccasin Dance, the Dance of Green Corn, or the Treaty Dance. I would be alone. A strange sadness overpowers me."

"I go," said the Indian. "Tell your great chief in Washington, the Sachem Andy,[6] that the Red Man is retiring before the footsteps of the adventurous Pioneer. Inform him, if you please, that westward the star of empire takes its way, that the chiefs of the Pi-Ute nation are for Reconstruction[7] to a man, and that Klamath will poll a heavy Republican vote in the fall."

And folding his blanket more tightly around him, Muck-a-Muck withdrew.

Chapter III

Genevra Tompkins stood at the door of the log cabin, looking after the retreating Overland Mail stage which conveyed her father to Virginia City. "He may never return again," sighed the young girl as she glanced at the frightfully rolling vehicle and wildly ca-

reering horses,—"at least, with unbroken bones. Should he meet with an accident! I mind me now a fearful legend, familiar to my childhood. Can it be that the drivers on this line are privately instructed to despatch all passengers maimed by accident, to prevent tedious litigation? No, no. But why this weight upon my heart?"

She seated herself at the piano and lightly passed her hand over the keys. Then, in a clear mezzo-soprano voice, she sang the first verse of one of the most popular Irish ballads:—

"O Arrah, my dheelish, the distant dudheen
Lies soft in the moonlight, ma bouchal vourneen:
The springing gossoons on the heather are still,
And the caubeens and colleens are heard on the hills."

But as the ravishing notes of her sweet voice died upon the air, her hands sank listlessly to her side. Music could not chase away the mysterious shadow from her heart. Again she rose. Putting on a white crape bonnet, and carefully drawing a pair of lemon-colored gloves over her taper fingers, she seized her parasol and plunged into the depths of the pine forest.

Chapter IV

Genevra had not proceeded many miles before a weariness

---

5. *beaver,* a hat made of beaver fur.
6. *Sachem Andy,* Andrew Johnson (1808-1875), President after the Civil War.
7. *Pi-Ute . . . Reconstruction.* The Paiutes are native Americans of the Southwest. Reconstruction was the Republican Party's policy to reunite the nation after the Civil War.

seized upon her fragile limbs, and she would fain seat herself upon the trunk of a prostrate pine, which she previously dusted with her handkerchief. The sun was just sinking below the horizon, and the scene was one of gorgeous and sylvan beauty. "How beautiful is Nature!" murmured the innocent girl, as, reclining gracefully against the root of the tree, she gathered up her skirts and tied a handkerchief around her throat. But a low growl interrupted her meditation. Starting to her feet, her eyes met a sight which froze her blood with terror. The only outlet to the forest was the narrow path, barely wide enough for a single person, hemmed in by trees and rocks, which she had just traversed. Down this path, in Indian file, came a monstrous grizzly, followed by a California lion, a wildcat, and a buffalo, the rear being brought up by a

wild Spanish bull. The mouths of the first three animals were distended with frightful significance; the horns of the last were lowered as ominously. As Genevra was preparing to faint, she heard a low voice behind her.

"Eternally dog-gone my skin ef this ain't the puttiest chance yet."

At the same moment, a long, shining barrel dropped lightly from behind her, and rested over her shoulder.

Genevra shuddered.

"Dern ye—don't move!"

Genevra became motionless.

The crack of a rifle rang through the woods. Three frightful yells were heard, and two sullen roars. Five animals bounded into the air and five lifeless bodies lay upon the plain. The well-aimed bullet had done its work. Entering the open throat of the grizzly, it had traversed his body only to enter the throat of the California lion, and in like manner the catamount, until it passed through into the respective foreheads of the bull and the buffalo, and finally fell flattened from the rocky hillside.

Genevra turned quickly. "My preserver!" she shrieked, and fell into the arms of Natty Bumppo, the celebrated Pike Ranger of Donner Lake.

Chapter V

The moon rose cheerfully above Donner Lake. On its placid bosom a dugout canoe glided rapidly, containing Natty Bumppo and Genevra Tompkins.

Both were silent. The same thought possessed each, and perhaps there was sweet companionship even in the unbroken quiet. Genevra bit the handle of her parasol and blushed. Natty Bumppo took a fresh chew of tobacco. At length Genevra said, as if in half-spoken revery:—

"The soft shining of the moon and the peaceful ripple of the waves seem to say to us various things of an instructive and moral tendency."

"You may bet yer pile on that, Miss," said her companion, gravely. "It's all the preachin' and psalm-singin' I've heern since I was a boy."

"Noble being!" said Miss Tompkins to herself, glancing at the stately Pike as he bent over his paddle to conceal his emotion. "Reared in this wild seclusion, yet he has become penetrated with visible consciousness of a Great First Cause." Then, collecting herself, she said aloud: "Methinks

't were pleasant to glide ever thus down the stream of life, hand in hand with the one being whom the soul claims as its affinity. But what am I saying?"—and the delicate-minded girl hid her face in her hands.

A long silence ensued, which was at length broken by her companion.

"Ef you mean you're on the marry," he said, thoughtfully, "I ain't in no wise partikler!"[8]

"My husband," faltered the blushing girl; and she fell into his arms. In ten minutes more the loving couple had landed at Judge Tompkins's.

Chapter VI

A year has passed away. Natty Bumppo was returning from Gold Hill, where he had been to purchase provisions. On his way to Donner Lake, rumors of an Indian uprising met his ears. "Dern their pesky skins, ef they dare to touch my Jenny," he muttered between his clenched teeth.

It was dark when he reached the borders of the lake. Around a glittering fire he dimly discerned dusky figures dancing. They were in war paint. Conspicuous among them was the renowned Muck-a-Muck. But why did the fingers of Natty Bumppo tighten convulsively around his rifle?

The chief held in his hand long tufts of raven hair. The heart of the pioneer sickened as he recognized the clustering curls of Genevra. In a moment his rifle was at his shoulder,

and with a sharp "ping," Muck-a-Muck leaped into the air a corpse. To knock out the brains of the remaining savages, tear the tresses from the stiffening hand of Muck-a-Muck, and dash rapidly forward to the cottage of Judge Tompkins, was the work of a moment.

He burst open the door. Why did he stand transfixed with open mouth and distended eyeballs? Was the sight too horrible to be borne? On the contrary, before him, in her peerless beauty, stood Genevra Tompkins, leaning on her father's arm.

"Ye'r not scalped, then!" gasped her lover.

"No. I have no hesitation in saying that I am not; but why this abruptness?" responded Genevra.

Bumppo could not speak, but frantically produced the silken tresses. Genevra turned her face aside.

"Why, that's her waterfall!"[9] said the Judge.

Bumppo sank fainting to the floor.

The famous Pike chieftain never recovered from the deceit, and refused to marry Genevra, who died, twenty years afterwards, of a broken heart. Judge Tompkins lost his fortune in Wild Cat. The stage passes twice a week the deserted cottage at Donner Lake. Thus was the death of Muck-a-Muck avenged.

---

8. *"I . . . partikler!"* "I don't care one way or the other."
9. *waterfall,* artificial hair worn on the back of the head by women.

Discussion

1. (a) What virtues do the Deerslayer and the Hurons share? (b) What faults? (c) Describe their attitude toward each other.

2. Explain how the character traits of the Deerslayer and the Hurons determine the events of the story.

3. (a) By what means does the order of events create suspense? (b) Describe both the convincing and the contrived aspects of the ending.

4. Cooper in his novels was fond of moralizing. Cite an example.

5. "Muck-a-Muck" is a literary **parody** achieved through an exaggerated imitation of the elements of Cooper's style. Give examples from "Muck-a-Muck" which ridiculously exaggerate the following elements of "A Rescue": (a) characterization; (b) dialogue; (c) heroic action; (d) contrived plot; (e) moralizing.

Vocabulary • Dictionary

Answer the questions that follow this passage:

"The first youth who presented himself for the trial was called the Raven, having as yet had no opportunity of obtaining a more warlike *sobriquet.*"

1. What is a *sobriquet*?

2. Does the word rhyme with *coquette* or *croquet*?

3. List some of the sobriquets that Cooper employs.

4. What does each of the following sobriquets refer to?

paleface	Old Glory
redcoat	Bard of Avon
John Bull	Jolly Roger

James Fenimore Cooper
1789 • 1851

The Deerslayer, from which "A Rescue" is taken, was the last and perhaps finest novel in Cooper's five-part adventure saga, *The Leatherstocking Tales.* As our first famous novelist, Cooper developed not only the adventure tale, a new literary mode for America, but also one of the most memorable and often imitated heroes in our fiction: Natty Bumppo, frontiersman.

Many elements typical of Cooper's fiction can be found in "A Rescue." These include: the brave, faultless hero; the loyal Indian companion; the encounter with physical danger; physical danger as a test of prowess; and, of course, the hair-breadth rescue. Because they have been imitated so often, these elements may seem today to be almost cliché. One must remember that in Cooper's day they were indeed novel.

Cooper was a thirty-year-old gentleman-farmer who disliked even writing a letter. While reading out loud to his wife from a boring English novel, Cooper insisted he could write a better book himself. Within the year he had completed his first novel, but with genteel English characters and English settings of which he knew next to nothing, it would be difficult to find many duller novels. Cooper quickly turned to more familiar subjects. He began to write about the Revolutionary War (*The Spy*); about the New York frontier he had known as a child (*The Leatherstocking Tales*); and about the sea, where he had been an officer in the Navy (*The Pilot*). Despite the romantic excesses, the melodrama, the sometimes stilted dialogue, the occasional indifference to craft and detail, there was a vitality and energy to his narratives which made him a magnificent storyteller. Within a few years he was famous even in Europe and by the end of his career had completed thirty-three novels as well as volumes of social comment, naval history, and travel description.

Bret Harte 1836 • 1902

Harte was a journalist and prolific short story writer who became famous for his "reportorial" fiction of the West in the Gold Rush days. These stories are filled with **local color,** dramatic though artificial plotting, and endearing characters which have become Western stereotypes. His work is characterized by humor and sentimental portraits of gamblers and other unrespectable types.

William Cullen Bryant

Thanatopsis

Thanatopsis, in Greek, means "a view of death."

To him who in the love of Nature holds
Communion with her visible forms, she speaks
A various language; for his gayer hours
She has a voice of gladness, and a smile
5 And eloquence of beauty, and she glides
Into his darker musings with a mild
And healing sympathy that steals away
Their sharpness ere he is aware. When thoughts
Of the last bitter hour come like a blight
10 Over thy spirit, and sad images
Of the stern agony, and shroud, and pall,
And breathless darkness, and the narrow house[1]
Make thee to shudder and grow sick at heart—
Go forth, under the open sky, and list
15 To Nature's teachings, while from all around—
Earth and her waters, and the depths of air—
Comes a still voice—
          Yet a few days, and thee
The all-beholding sun shall see no more
In all his course; nor yet in the cold ground,
20 Where thy pale form was laid with many tears,
Nor in the embrace of ocean shall exist
Thy image. Earth, that nourished thee, shall claim
Thy growth, to be resolved to earth again,
And, lost each human trace, surrendering up
25 Thine individual being, shalt thou go
To mix forever with the elements,
To be a brother to the insensible rock
And to the sluggish clod which the rude swain
Turns with his share and treads upon. The oak
30 Shall send his roots abroad and pierce thy mold.
Yet not to thine eternal resting place
Shalt thou retire alone; nor couldst thou wish
Couch more magnificent. Thou shalt lie down
With patriarchs of the infant world—with kings,
35 The powerful of the earth—the wise, the good,
Fair forms, and hoary seers of ages past,
All in one mighty sepulcher. The hills
Rock-ribbed and ancient as the sun; the vales
Stretching in pensive quietness between;
40 The venerable woods; rivers that move
In majesty; and the complaining brooks
That make the meadows green; and,
          poured round all

Old Ocean's gray and melancholy waste—
Are but the solemn decorations all
45 Of the great tomb of man. The golden sun,
The planets, all the infinite host of heaven,
Are shining on the sad abodes of death
Through the still lapse of ages. All that tread
The globe are but a handful to the tribes
50 That slumber in its bosom. Take the wings
Of morning, pierce the Barcan wilderness,[2]
Or lose thyself in the continuous woods
Where rolls the Oregon,[3] and hears no sound
Save his own dashings—yet the dead are there;
55 And millions in those solitudes, since first
The flight of years began, have laid them down
In their last sleep—the dead reign there alone.
So shalt thou rest, and what if thou withdraw
In silence from the living, and no friend
60 Take note of thy departure? All that breathe
Will share thy destiny. The gay will laugh
When thou art gone, the solemn brood of care
Plod on, and each one as before will chase
His favorite phantom; yet all these shall leave
65 Their mirth and their employments, and shall come
And make their bed with thee. As the long train
Of ages glides away, the sons of men,
The youth in life's green spring, and he who goes
In the full strength of years, matron and maid,
70 The speechless babe, and the gray-headed man—
Shall one by one be gathered to thy side,
By those who in their turn shall follow them.
So live, that when thy summons comes to join
The innumerable caravan which moves
75 To that mysterious realm, where each shall take
His chamber in the silent halls of death,
Thou go not, like the quarry slave at night,
Scourged to his dungeon, but, sustained
          and soothed
By an unfaltering trust, approach thy grave
80 Like one who wraps the drapery of his couch
About him, and lies down to pleasant dreams.

---

1. **the narrow house,** the grave.
2. **Barcan wilderness,** the desert land of Cyrenaica (sir′ə nā′ə kə) in northern Africa.
3. **the Oregon,** the old name for the Columbia River.

1. The best way to grasp the meaning of "Thanatopsis" is to consider first its various parts. (a) *Lines 1–17:* What does the poet suggest that someone do when oppressed by thoughts of death? (b) *Lines 17–57:* What comfort does Nature offer a person facing death? (c) *Lines 58–72:* Why is dying unmourned not important? (d) *Lines 73–81:* What is important?

2. In the last two lines, to what does Bryant compare death?

3. Do you find the ideas expressed in "Thanatopsis" consoling or disturbing? Explain your answer.

William Cullen Bryant
1794 • 1878

Bryant wrote "Thanatopsis," his finest poem, when he was only seventeen years old. Perhaps fearing that the strictly religious members of his family would object to it, he hid it in his desk.

Bryant was apprenticed to the law and continued to deposit his poems in his desk. His father eventually discovered the cache and secretly took the poems to the *North American Review,* the editors of which initially assumed the verses to be a hoax since they felt there was no author on this side of the Atlantic capable of such quality. Recognition came very slowly, but at last Bryant was made managing editor of the *Evening Post* when he was thirty-four. During his forty-nine years in control of the paper, Bryant was a vigorous advocate of the abolitionist movement.

notes and comments

Bryant and Romanticism

Though writers during this period displayed a more remarkable degree of independence from the main currents of European and English literature than did their predecessors, the influences of the Old World were nevertheless felt throughout a large portion of the nineteenth century. Such was the case in the poetry of Bryant; the major influence upon his technique and ideology was **romanticism.**

Briefly, some ideological concepts of romanticism that are reflected in Bryant's poetry are a belief in the mutability of the physical world, that it is subject to decline and decay; the belief that while everything changes and dies, God, the Absolute, remains immortal; and lastly, that this immutable Spirit reveals Himself through His greatest—though mutable—work, Nature.

Stylistically, Bryant also borrowed from the poets of the romantic movement. One finds in his poetry the same use of artificially lofty diction and syntax. Like other romantic poets, Bryant was fond of using archaic syntax in order to convey a serious, philosophical tone. Thus, Bryant used in his poetry such words as "thou," "thy," "shalt," "couldst," and "list" (for "listen"). Another interesting stylistic technique which is found again and again in his poetry, is **inversion.** Inversion, or **anastrophe,** is the displacement of a word, phrase, or clause from its normal position in a sentence, either for emphasis or poetic effect. It is frequently used in poetry so as to maintain meter and/or rhyme. An example of the simple inversion of a word, in this case the adjective, from Henry Wadsworth Longfellow's "Prelude to Evangeline" is, ". . . the forest primeval." Perhaps a more familiar example is one from Samuel Francis Smith's poem "America": ". . . Of thee I sing. . . ." Here, the prepositional phrase has been placed before the noun clause. A more complex example of inversion involving word, phrase, and clause displacements is found in Samuel Taylor Coleridge's poem "Kubla Khan":

"In Xanadu did Kubla Khan
A stately pleasure-dome
    decree . . ."

Henry Wadsworth Longfellow

Mezzo Cammin[1]

Half of my life is gone, and I have let
  The years slip from me and have not fulfilled
  The aspiration of my youth, to build
  Some tower of song with lofty parapet.
5 Not indolence, nor pleasure, nor the fret
  Of restless passions that would not be stilled,
  But sorrow, and a care that almost killed,
  Kept me from what I may accomplish yet;
Though, half-way up the hill, I see the Past
10   Lying beneath me with its sounds and sights,—
  A city in the twilight dim and vast,
With smoking roofs, soft bells, and gleaming lights,—
  And hear above me on the autumnal blast
  The cataract of Death far thundering from the heights.

---

1. *Mezzo Cammin,* halfway up the road. [*Italian*] Dante uses this phrase in *Divina Commedia* to signify the middle of his life, a period of lost ideals, moral disillusionment, and wasted efforts.

Jean Roubier.

Discussion

Mezzo Cammin

1. (a) What was the speaker's youthful aspiration? (b) Why has he been unable to fulfill it? (c) Has he completely abandoned his efforts to do so? Support your answer with lines from the poem.

2. What effect does the word *though* in line 9 have on the tone of the poem?

3. Reread the description of the past as the speaker sees it from his vantage point "half-way up the hill" (lines 9–12). What temptation might be inherent in viewing one's past in such a way?

4. Contrast the last two lines of the poem with lines 9–12. What particular words in the final lines create the contrast between the speaker's past and his future?

Divina Commedia I

1. (a) What situation do the first eight lines describe? (b) What is the **tone** of this description? (c) What particular words and phrases contribute to this tone?

2. (a) What is the purpose of the word *so* at the beginning of line 9? (b) In what way is the speaker like the workman?

3. Read the last three lines aloud. With what emotion do they leave the listener?

Divina Commedia II

1. What **irony** do you find in the contrasts presented in the first eight lines?

2. (a) What is the cause of

the "agonies of heart and brain" in line 9? **(b)** What is the result of these agonies?

3. Note that the last six lines are an outpouring of wonder and awe. What has aroused this feeling in the speaker?

Henry Wadsworth Longfellow
1807 • 1882

Longfellow was born in Portland, Maine, and educated at Bowdoin College. He remained at Bowdoin for six years, dividing his time between teaching and writing. On the strength of his work there he was offered a professorship at Harvard where he taught for nearly twenty years, years of great creative activity. His first book of original poems, *Voices of the Night* (1839), gained him a national reputation. He finally resigned his professorship in 1855 in favor of James Russell Lowell in order to devote his attention exclusively to writing.

In January 1840, he wrote his ballad, "The Wreck of the Hesperus," in which he naturalized a form which had long flourished abroad. Longfellow's chief literary achievement was the introduction of foreign themes and poetic forms into American literature. *Evangeline* (1847), *The Song of Hiawatha* (1855), and *The Courtship of Miles Standish* (1858), were long narrative poems in the manner of similar European poems but treating American legends. *Tales of a Wayside Inn* (1863) collected a series of stories, most of them of American origin, in a poem constructed in the manner of Chaucer's *Canterbury Tales*.

In 1861, to master his grief at his wife's accidental death, Longfellow began to translate the Divina Commedia *(di vē/nä kôm mā/dyä), or* Divine Comedy, *by the Italian poet Dante (dän/tā; 1265–1321). This epic describes Dante's imaginary journey to Hell, Purgatory, and Paradise. Longfellow prefaced each section with two* **sonnets,** *of which the following are the first pair. The cathedral represents Dante's epic, a majestic "temple" of poetry.*

Divina Commedia I and II

Oft have I seen at some cathedral door
    A laborer, pausing in the dust and heat,
    Lay down his burden, and with reverent feet
    Enter, and cross himself, and on the floor
5 Kneel to repeat his paternoster[1] o'er;
    Far off the noises of the world retreat;
    The loud vociferations of the street
    Become an undistinguishable roar.
So, as I enter here from day to day,
10   And leave my burden at this minster gate,[2]
    Kneeling in prayer, and not ashamed to pray,
The tumult of the time disconsolate
    To inarticulate murmurs dies away,
    While the eternal ages watch and wait.

How strange the sculptures that adorn these towers!
    This crowd of statues, in whose folded sleeves
    Birds build their nests; while canopied with leaves
    Parvis[3] and portal bloom like trellised bowers,
5 And the vast minster seems a cross of flowers![4]
    But fiends and dragons on the gargoyled eaves
    Watch the dead Christ between the living thieves,
    And, underneath, the traitor Judas lowers!
Ah! from what agonies of heart and brain,
10   What exultations trampling on despair,
    What tenderness, what tears, what hate of wrong,
What passionate outcry of a soul in pain,
    Uprose this poem of the earth and air,
    This medieval miracle of song!

---

1. *paternoster* (pat/ər nos/tər), the Lord's Prayer, so called because the opening words are "Pater Noster" in Latin.
2. *minster gate,* the cathedral door.
3. *Parvis,* church porch.
4. *the vast minster . . . cross of flowers.* Most European cathedrals were built in the shape of a cross. To the poet, the carved and ornamental cathedral seen from above suggests a cross of flowers.

Oliver Wendell Holmes

The Chambered Nautilus

This is the ship of pearl, which, poets feign,
    Sails the unshadowed main—
    The venturous bark that flings
On the sweet summer wind its purpled wings
5 In gulfs enchanted, where the Siren sings,[1]
    And coral reefs lie bare,
Where the cold sea-maids[2] rise to sun their streaming hair.

Its webs of living gauze[3] no more unfurl;
    Wrecked is the ship of pearl!
10   And every chambered cell,
Where its dim dreaming life was wont to dwell,
As the frail tenant shaped his growing shell,
    Before thee lies revealed—
Its irised[4] ceiling rent, its sunless crypt unsealed!

15 Year after year beheld the silent toil
    That spread his lustrous coil;
    Still, as the spiral grew,
He left the past year's dwelling for the new,
Stole with soft step its shining archway through,
20   Built up its idle door,
Stretched in his last-found home, and knew the old no more.

Thanks for the heavenly message brought by thee,
    Child of the wandering sea,
    Cast from her lap, forlorn!
25 From thy dead lips a clearer note is born
Than ever Triton[5] blew from wreathèd horn!
    While on mine ear it rings,
Through the deep caves of thought I hear a voice that sings:

---

1. **the Siren sings.** In Greek mythology, the sirens were nymphs who by their sweet singing lured sailors to destruction.
2. **sea-maids,** mermaids.
3. **webs of living gauze,** tentacles.
4. **irised,** containing the colors of the rainbow.
5. **Triton,** in Greek mythology, the son of Poseidon, god of the sea. His conch shell horn makes the roaring of the ocean.

Discussion

1. From the illustration on page 179, you can recognize that the "ship of pearl" in the first line of the poem is a sea-shell. Reread the first three stanzas and explain what has happened to the creature in the shell.

2. In stanza 4, line 1, who is the "thee"?

3. (a) Who is addressed in the last stanza? (b) In your own words, express the philosophy of the speaker.

4. What lesson might a writer with a less optimistic outlook have derived from viewing the broken shell?

Oliver Wendell Holmes
1809 • 1894

Holmes was born in Cambridge and educated at Harvard. He began to study law, but abandoned this for medicine after a year. Holmes studied in Edinburgh, then Paris, before returning home to receive his M.D. from the Harvard Medical School in 1836, the same year in which he published *Poems,* his first volume. After practicing a very short time he taught medicine at Dartmouth for two years. He returned to practice in Boston after his marriage in 1840, but again abandoned it in favor of a professorship of anatomy and physiology at Harvard, where he remained until his retirement in 1882.

In both his poetry and prose Holmes strove for the light informal tone. Many of his vers-

Build thee more stately mansions, O my soul,
30   As the swift seasons roll!
        Leave thy low-vaulted past!
Let each new temple, nobler than the last,
Shut thee from heaven with a dome more vast,
        Till thou at length art free,
35 Leaving thine outgrown shell by life's unresting sea!

es were "occasional"; that is, they were composed for reading aloud on certain festive occasions and are some of the most graceful and witty examples of this type of writing ever composed.

Holmes's essays began appearing serially in the *Atlantic Monthly* after it was founded by Holmes and a group of friends in 1857. The first collection of these essays, which are in the form of conversations among a group of people gathered around a boardinghouse table, appeared in 1858 as *The Autocrat of the Breakfast-Table.* It was followed by three similar volumes, the last in 1891.

A chambered nautilus.
(William Franklin McMahon.)

John Greenleaf Whittier

This poem, written in 1858, is based upon a superstition which Whittier explained: "A remarkable custom, brought from the Old Country, formerly prevailed in the rural districts of New England. On the death of a member of the family, the bees were at once informed of the event, and their hives dressed in mourning. This ceremonial was supposed to prevent the swarms from leaving their hives and seeking a new home." This use of folk tradition is typical of Whittier's best work.

Telling the Bees

Here is the place; right over the hill
   Runs the path I took;
You can see the gap in the old wall still,
   And the stepping-stones in the shallow brook.

5 There is the house, with the gate red-barred,
   And the poplars tall;
And the barn's brown length, and the
      cattle-yard,
   And the white horns tossing above the wall.

There are the beehives ranged in the sun;
10   And down by the brink
Of the brook are her poor flowers, weed-o'errun,
   Pansy and daffodil, rose and pink.

A year has gone, as the tortoise goes,
   Heavy and slow;
15 And the same rose blows, and the same
      sun glows,
   And the same brook sings of a year ago.

There's the same sweet clover-smell in the breeze;
    And the June sun warm
Tangles his wings of fire in the trees,
20   Setting, as then, over Fernside farm.

I mind me how with a lover's care
    From my Sunday coat
I brushed off the burs, and smoothed my hair,
    And cooled at the brookside my brow
        and throat.

25 Since we parted, a month had passed—
    To love, a year;
Down through the beeches I looked at last
    On the little red gate and the well-sweep near.

I can see it all now—the slantwise rain
30   Of light through the leaves,
The sundown's blaze on her windowpane,
    The bloom of her roses under the eaves.

Just the same as a month before—
    The house and the trees,
35 The barn's brown gable, the vine by the door—
    Nothing changed but the hives of bees.

Before them, under the garden wall,
    Forward and back,
Went drearily singing the chore-girl small,
40   Draping each hive with a shred of black.

Trembling, I listened: the summer sun
    Had the chill of snow;
For I knew she was telling the bees of one
    Gone on the journey we all must go!

45 Then I said to myself, "My Mary weeps
    For the dead today:
Haply her blind old grandsire sleeps
    The fret and the pain of his age away."

But her dog whined low; on the doorway sill,
50   With his cane to his chin,
The old man sat; and the chore-girl still
    Sung to the bees stealing out and in.

And the song she was singing ever since
    In my ear sounds on:—
55 "Stay at home, pretty bees, fly not hence!
    Mistress Mary is dead and gone!"

Discussion

1. Reread the first three stanzas, paying particular attention to the imagery. What change in tone is created by the last two lines of stanza three? What particular words bring about this change?

2. (a) How much time has elapsed since the speaker last saw the farm? (b) From his point of view, what irony is contained in the fact that ". . . the same rose blows, and the same sun glows, / and the same brook sings . . ."?

3. (a) Reread the entire poem. Choose lines that are particularly effective in making you able to see, feel, and smell the place being described. (b) In which stanzas do you most share the speaker's emotions? Explain.

John Greenleaf Whittier
1807 • 1892

Whittier was born and reared on a farm in the township of Haverhill, Massachusetts. He had almost no formal education and even his reading was limited to the few devotional books that his Quaker parents had in their home. However, at an early age he did encounter the works of the Scottish rural poet, Robert Burns, (1759–1796), which exerted a great influence over him.

When he was nineteen, one of Whittier's poems was published by the abolitionist William Lloyd Garrison in a paper which he edited. This was the beginning of a lifelong association between the two men and marked the start of Whittier's career both as a writer and as a reformer. Under Garrison's influence, Whittier returned to school, spending two terms at the Haverhill Academy. After this he taught school and held various types of editorial positions while continuing to write poems and articles in support of the abolitionist cause.

During these years he matured as a poet, but it was not until the publication of his masterpiece, *Snow-Bound*, which appeared in 1866, that he achieved a national reputation as a poet.

James Russell Lowell

Stanzas on Freedom

Men! whose boast it is that ye
Come of fathers brave and free,
If there breathe on earth a slave,
Are ye truly free and brave?
5 If ye do not feel the chain,
When it works a brother's pain,
Are ye not base slaves indeed,
Slaves unworthy to be freed?

Women! who shall one day bear
10 Sons to breathe New England air,
If ye hear, without a blush,
Deeds to make the roused blood rush
Like red lava through your veins,
For your sisters now in chains,—
15 Answer! are ye fit to be
Mothers of the brave and free?

Is true Freedom but to break
Fetters for our own dear sake,
And, with leathern hearts, forget
20 That we owe mankind a debt?
No! true freedom is to share
All the chains our brothers wear,
And, with heart and hand, to be
Earnest to make others free!

25 They are slaves who fear to speak
For the fallen and the weak;
They are slaves who will not choose
Hatred, scoffing, and abuse,
Rather than in silence shrink
30 From the truth they needs must think;
They are slaves who dare not be
In the right with two or three.

Discussion

1. The poem progresses from particular examples to a general concept of slavery. Explain.

2. (a) Which lines of the poem best summarize the nature of slavery? (b) The nature of freedom?

3. Can you think of any applications this poem has to life today? Explain.

James Russell Lowell
1819 • 1891

Lowell, born in Cambridge, Massachusetts, received a gentleman's education—at home, the dame's school, and then Harvard, graduating from the College in 1838 and the Law School in 1840. However, with-in two years he had abandoned the practice of law for literature. During the next few years he contributed fervent essays and poems that dealt with current issues to magazines which took sides on current affairs.

In 1855, when Longfellow retired from his professorship at Harvard, Lowell succeeded him, teaching there until 1876. In 1857 Lowell helped found the *Atlantic Monthly*. He was the first editor and continued in this role until 1861. Lowell was appointed to diplomatic posts, serving as ambassador to Spain and later to England. Queen Victoria said of Lowell, "During my reign no ambassador or minister has created so much

interest or won so much regard."

During the last six years of his life, Lowell lived quietly in Cambridge, and died in the home in which he was born.

James W. C. Pennington

Escape: A Slave Narrative

It was in the month of November, somewhat past the middle of the month. It was a bright day, and all was quiet. Most of the slaves were resting about their quarters; others had leave to visit their friends on other plantations, and were absent. The evening previous I had arranged my little bundle of clothing, and had secreted it at some distance from the house.

It is impossible for me now to recollect all the perplexing thoughts that passed through my mind during that forenoon; it was a day of heartaching to me. But I distinctly remember the two great difficulties that stood in the way of my flight: I had a father and mother whom I dearly loved,—I had also six sisters and four brothers on the plantation. The question was, shall I hide my purpose from them? Moreover, how will my flight affect them when I am gone? Will they not be suspected? Will not the whole family be sold off as a disaffected family, as is generally the case when one of its members flies? But a still more trying question was, how can I expect to succeed, I have no knowledge of distance or direction—I know that Pennsylvania is a free state, but I know not where its soil begins, or where that of Maryland ends? . . .

One of my perplexing questions I had settled—I had resolved to let no one into my secret; but the other difficulty was now to be met. Within my recollection no one had attempted to escape from my master; but I had many cases in my mind's eye, of slaves of other planters who had failed, and who had been made examples of the most cruel treatment, by flogging and selling to the far South, where they were never to see their friends more. I was not without serious apprehension that such would be my fate. The bare possibility was impressively solemn; but the hour was now come, and the man must act and be free, or remain a slave for ever. How the impression came to be upon my mind I cannot tell; but there was a strange and horrifying belief, that if I did not meet the crisis that day, I should be self-doomed. Hope, fear, dread, terror, love, sorrow, and deep melancholy were mingled in my mind together; my mental state was one of most painful distraction. When I looked at my numerous family—a beloved father and mother, eleven brothers and sisters, etc.; but when I looked at slavery as such; when I looked at it in its mildest form, with all its annoyances; and above all, when I remembered that one of the chief annoyances of slavery, in the most mild form, is the liability of being at any moment sold into the worst form, it seemed that no consideration, not even that of life itself, could tempt me to give up the thought of flight. . . .

It was now two o'clock. . . . I sallied forth thoughtfully and melancholy, and after crossing the barn-yard, a few moments' walk brought me to a small cave, near the mouth of which lay a pile of stones, and into which I had deposited my clothes. From this, my course lay through thick and heavy woods and back lands to——town, where my brother lived. . . .

I entered the town about dark, resolved, all things in view, *not* to shew myself to my brother. Having passed through the town without being recognised, I now found myself under cover of night, a solitary wanderer from home and friends; my only guide was the *north star;* by this I knew my general course northward, but at what point I should strike Penn., or when and where I should find a friend I knew not. . . . Only now and then I was cheered by the *wild* hope, that I should somewhere and at some time be free. . . .

The day dawned upon me, in the midst of an open extent of country, where the only shelter I could find, without risking my travel by daylight, was a corn shock, but a few hundred yards from the road, and here I must pass my first day out. The day was an unhappy one; my hiding-place was extremely precarious. I had to sit in a squatting position the whole day, without the least chance to rest. Night came again to my relief, and I sallied forth to pursue my journey.

As I travelled I felt my strength failing and my spirits wavered; my mind was in a deep and melancholy dream. It was cloudy; I could not see my star, and had serious misgivings about my course.

In this way the night passed away, and just at the dawn of day I found a few sour apples, and took my shelter under the arch of a small bridge that crossed the road. Here I passed the second day in ambush.

The day passed away again without any further incident, and as I set out at nightfall I felt quite satisfied that I could not pass another twenty-four hours without nourishment. I made but little progress during the night, and often sat down, and slept frequently fifteen or twenty minutes. At the dawn of the third day I continued my travel. As I had found my way to a public turnpike road during the night, I came very early in the morning to a toll-gate, where the only person I saw, was a lad about twelve years of age. I inquired of him where the road led to. He informed me it led to Baltimore. I asked him the distance, he said it was eighteen miles.

This intelligence was perfectly astounding to me. My master lived eighty miles from Baltimore. I was now sixty-two miles from home. That distance in the right direction, would have placed me several miles across Mason and Dixon's line,[1] but I was evidently yet in the state of Maryland.

I ventured to ask the lad at the gate another question—Which is the best way to Philadelphia? Said he, you can take a road which turns off about half-a-mile below this, and goes to Getsburgh, or you can go on to Baltimore and take the packet.[2] . . .

When I had walked a mile on this road, and when it had now gotten to be about nine o'clock, I met a young man with a load of hay. He drew up his horses, and addressed me in a very kind tone.

"Are you travelling any distance, my friend?"

"I am on my way to Philadelphia."

"Are you free?"

"Yes, sir."

"I suppose, then, you are provided with free papers?"

"No, sir. I have no papers."

"Well, my friend, you should not travel on this road: you will be taken up before you have gone three miles."

He then very kindly gave me advice where to turn off the road at a certain point, and how to find my way to a certain house, where I would meet with an old gentleman who would further advise me whether I had better remain till night, or go on.

I left this interesting young man; and such was my surprise and chagrin at the thought of having so widely missed my way, and my alarm at being in such a dangerous position, that in ten minutes I had so far forgotten his directions as to deem it unwise to attempt to follow them, lest I should miss my way, and get into evil hands. . . .

I went about a mile, making in all two miles from the spot where I met my young friend, and about five miles from the toll-gate to which I have referred, and I found myself at the twenty-four miles' stone from Baltimore. It was now about ten o'clock in the forenoon; my strength was greatly exhausted by reason of the want of suitable food. Under ordinary circumstances as a traveller, I should have been glad to see the "Tavern," which was near the mile-stone; but as the case stood with me, I deemed it a dangerous place to pass, much less to stop at. I was therefore passing it as quietly and as rapidly as possible, when from the lot just opposite the house, or sign-post, I heard a coarse stern voice cry, "Halloo!"

I turned my face to the left, the direction from which the voice came, and observed that it proceeded from a man who was digging potatoes. I answered him politely; when the following occurred:——

"Who do *you* belong to?"

"I am free, sir."

"Have you got papers?"

"No, sir."

"Well, you must stop here."

---

1. *Mason and Dixon's line,* the southern border of Pennsylvania, surveyed by Charles Mason and Jeremiah Dixon, British astronomers. The line became part of the boundary between the free and slave states.
2. *Getsburgh . . . packet.* Gettysburg (Getsburg) is in southern Pennsylvania. A packet is a scheduled passenger ship.

"My business is onward, sir, and I do not wish to stop."

"I will see then if you don't stop, you black rascal."

He was now in the middle of the road, making after me in a brisk walk.

I saw that a crisis was at hand; I had no weapons of any kind, not even a pocket-knife; but I asked myself, shall I surrender without a struggle. The instinctive answer was, No. What will you do? continue to walk; if he runs after you, run; get him as far from the house as you can, then turn suddenly and smite him on the knee with a stone; that will render him, at least, unable to pursue you.

He began to breathe short. He was evidently vexed because I did not halt, and I felt more and more provoked at the idea of being thus pursued by a man to whom I had not done the least injury. At this moment he yelled out "Jake Shouster!" and at the next moment the door of a small house standing to the left was opened, and out jumped a shoemaker girded up in his leather apron, with his knife in hand. He sprang forward and seized me by the collar, while the other seized my arms behind.

Standing in the door of the shoemaker's shop, was a third man; and in the potato lot I had passed, was still a fourth man. Thus surrounded by superior physical force, the fortune of the day it seemed to me was gone.

A few moments after I was taken into the bar-room, the news having gone as by electricity, the house and yard were crowded with gossipers. But among the whole, there stood one whose name I have never known. Said he, "That fellow is a runaway I know; put him in jail a few days, and you will soon hear where he came from." And then fixing a fiend-like gaze upon me, he continued, "if I lived on this road, *you* fellows would not find such clear running as you do, I'd trap more of you."

But now comes the pinch of the case, the case of conscience to me even at this moment. Emboldened by the cruel speech just recited, my captors enclosed me, and said, "Come now, this matter may easily be settled without you going to jail; who do you belong to, and where did you come from?"

I knew according to the law of slavery, who I belonged to and where I came from, and I must now do one of three things—I must refuse to speak at all, or I must communicate the fact, or I must tell an untruth. The first point decided was, the facts in this case are my private property. These men have no more right to them than a highway robber has to my purse. . . .

I resolved, therefore, to insist that I was free. This not being satisfactory without other evidence, they tied my hands and set out, and went to a magistrate who lived about half a mile distant. It so happened, that when we arrived at his house he was not at home. But I soon learned by their conversation, that there was still another magistrate in the neighbourhood, and that they would go to him. In about twenty minutes, and after climbing fences and jumping ditches, we, captors and captive, stood before his door, but it was after the same manner as before—he was not at home. By this time the day had worn away to one or two o'clock, and my captors evidently began to feel somewhat impatient of the loss of time. We were about a mile and a quarter from the tavern. As we set out on our return, they began to parley. Finding it was difficult for me to get over fences with my hands tied, they untied me . . . .

We got to the tavern at three o'clock. Here they again cooled down, and made an appeal to me to make a disclosure. I said to them, "If you will not put me in jail, I will now tell you where I am from." They promised. "Well," said I, "a few weeks ago, I was sold from the eastern shore to a slave-trader, who had a large gang, and set out for Georgia, but when he got to a town in Virginia, he was taken sick, and died with the small-pox. Several of his gang also died with it, so that the people in the town became alarmed, and did not wish the gang to remain among them. No one claimed us, or wished to have anything to do with us; I left the rest, and thought I would go somewhere and get work."

When I said this, it was evidently believed by those who were present, and notwithstanding the unkind feeling that had existed, there was a murmur of approbation. At the same time I perceived that a panic began to seize some, at the idea that I was one of a small-pox gang. Several who had clustered near me, moved off to a respectful distance. . . .

I was now left alone with the man who first called to me in the morning. In a sober manner, he made this proposal to me: "John, I have a brother living in Risterstown, four miles off, who keeps a tavern; I think you had better go and live with him, till we see what will turn up. He wants an ostler."[3] I at once assented to this. "Well," said he, "take something to eat, and I will go with you." . . .

I sat down to eat; it was Wednesday, four o'clock, and this was the first regular meal I had since Sunday morning. This over, we set out, and to my surprise, he proposed to walk. We had gone about a mile and a half, and we were approaching a wood through which the road passed with a bend. I fixed upon that as the spot where I would either free myself from this man, or die in his arms. I had resolved upon a plan of operation—it was this: to stop short, face about, and commence action; and neither ask or give quarters, until I was free or dead!

We had got within six rods of the spot, when a gentleman turned the corner, meeting us on horseback. He came up, and entered into conversation with my captor. After a few moments, this gentleman addressed himself to me and I then learned that he was one of the magistrates on whom we had called in the morning. . . . I re-peated carefully all I had said; at the close, he said, "Well, you had better stay among us a few months, until we see what is to be done with you." It was then agreed that we should go back to the tavern, and there settle upon some further plan. He seemed quite satisfied of the correctness of my statement, and made the following proposition: that I should go and live with him for a short time, stating that he had a few acres of corn and potatoes to get in, and that he would give me twenty-five cents per day. I most cheerfully assented to this proposal. It was also agreed that I should remain at the tavern with my captor that night, and that he would accompany me in the morning. . . .

My captor had left his hired man most of the day to dig potatoes alone; but the waggon being now loaded, it being time to convey the potatoes into the barn, and the horses being all ready for that purpose, he was obliged to go into the potato field and give assistance. . . . This left no one in the house, but a boy, about nine years of age.

The potato lot was across the public road, directly in front of the house; at the back of the house, and about three hundred yards distant, there was a thick wood. The circumstances of

---

3. **ostler**, someone who takes care of horses.

the case would not allow me to think for one moment of remaining there for the night—the time had come for another effort—but there were two serious difficulties. One was, that I must either deceive or dispatch this boy who is watching me with intense vigilance. I am glad to say, that the latter did not for a moment seriously enter my mind. To deceive him effectually, I left my coat and went to the back door, from which my course would be direct to the wood. When I got to the door, I found that the barn, to which the waggon must soon come, lay just to the right, and overlooking the path I must take to the wood. But on looking through the gate, I saw that my captor, being with the team, would see me if I attempted to start before he moved from the position he then occupied. To add to my difficulty the horses had baulked; while waiting for the decisive moment, the boy came to the door and asked me why I did not come in. I told him I felt unwell, and wished him to be so kind as to hand me a glass of water; he came with the water and I quickly used it up by gargling my throat and by drinking a part. I asked him to serve me by giving me another glass: he gave me a look of close scrutiny, but went in for the water. I heard him fill the glass, and start to return with it; when the hind end of the waggon cleared the corner of the house. As I passed out the gate, I cast a last glance over my right shoulder, and saw the boy just perch his head above the garden picket to look after me. I felt some assurance that although the boy might give the alarm, my captor could not leave the team until it was in the barn. I heard the horses' feet on the barn-floor, just as I leaped the fence, and darted into the wood. . . .

The reader may well imagine how the events of the past day affected my mind. You have seen what was done to me; you have heard what was said to me—you have also seen what I have done, and heard what I have said. If you ask me whether I had expected before I left home, to gain my liberty by shedding men's blood, or breaking their limbs? I answer, No! and as evidence of this, I had provided no weapon whatever; not so much as a penknife—it never once entered my mind. I cannot say that I expected to have the ill fortune of meeting with any human being who would attempt to impede my flight.

If you ask me if I expected when I left home to gain my liberty by fabrications and untruths? I answer, No! my parents, slaves as they were, had always taught me, when they could, that "truth may be blamed but cannot be ashamed"; so far as their example was concerned, I had no habits of untruth. I was arrested, and the demand made upon me, "Who do you belong to?" Knowing the fatal use these men would make of *my* truth, I at once concluded that they had no more right to it than a highwayman has to a traveller's purse. . . .

Whatever my readers may think, therefore, of the history of events of the day, do not admire in it the fabrications; but *see* in it the impediments that often fall into the pathway of the flying bondman. *See* how when he would do good, evil is thrust upon him. . . .

I penetrated through the wood, thick and thin, and more or less wet, to the distance I should think of three miles. By this time my clothes were all thoroughly soaked through, and I felt once more a gloom and wretchedness; the recollection of which makes me shudder at this distant day. . . .

I was now out of the hands of those who had so cruelly teased me during the day; but a number of fearful thoughts rushed into my mind to alarm me. It was dark and cloudy, so that I could not see the *north star.* How shall I regain the road? How shall I know when I am on the right road again?

At a venture I struck an angle northward in search of the road. After several hours of zigzag and laborious travel, dragging through briars, thorns and running vines, I emerged from the wood and found myself wading marshy ground and over ditches.

I can form no correct idea of the distance I travelled, but I came to a road, I should think about three o'clock in the morning. It so happened that I came out near where there was a fork in the road of three prongs.

Now arose a serious query—Which is the right prong for me? After a few moments parley with myself, I took the central prong of the road and pushed on with all my speed. . . .

The day dawned upon me when I was near a small house and barn, situated close to the road-side. The barn was too near the road, and too small to afford secure shelter for the day; but as I cast my eye around by the dim light, I could see no wood, and no larger barn. It seemed to be an open country to a wide extent. I therefore took to the mow[4] of the little barn at a great risk, as the events of the day will shew. Besides inflicting upon my own excited imagination the belief that I made noise enough to be heard by the inmates of the house who were likely to be rising at the time, I had the misfortune to attract the notice of a little house-dog. This little creature commenced a fierce barking. I had at once great fears that the mischievous little thing would betray me. It now being entirely daylight, it was too late to retreat from this shelter, even if I could have found another.

It was Thursday morning. It was not until about an hour after the sun rose that I heard any out-door movements about the house. As soon as I heard those movements, I was satisfied there was but one man about the house, and that he was preparing to go some distance to work for the day. This was fortunate for me; the busy movements about the yard, and especially the active preparations in the house for breakfast, silenced my unwelcome little annoyer until after the man had gone, when he commenced afresh, and continued with occasional intermissions through the day. . . .

In this way I passed the day till about the middle of the afternoon, when there seemed to be an unusual stir about the public road, which passed close by the barn. Men seemed to be passing in parties on horseback, and talking anxiously. From a word which I now and then overheard, I had not a shadow of doubt that they were in search of me. . . . I listened and trembled.

Just before the setting of the sun, the labouring man of the house returned, and commenced his evening duties about the house and barn; chopping wood, getting up his cow, feeding his pigs, etc., attended by the little brute, who continued barking at short intervals. He came several times into the barn below. While matters were passing thus, I heard the approach of horses again, and as they came up nearer, I was led to believe that all I had heard pass were returning in one party. They passed the barn and halted at the house, when I recognized the voice of my old captor; addressing the labourer . . . .

To my great relief, however, the party rode off, and the labourer after finishing his work went into the house. Hope seemed now to dawn for me once more. About eight o'clock I ventured to descend from the mow of the barn into the road. The little dog the while began a furious fit of barking, so much so, that I was sure that with what his master had learned about me, he could not fail to believe I was about his premises. I quickly crossed the road, and got into an open field opposite. After stepping lightly about two hundred yards, I halted, and on listening, I heard the door open. Feeling about on the ground, I picked up two stones, and one in each hand I made off as fast as I could, but I heard nothing more that indicated pursuit, and after going some distance I discharged my encumbrance . . . .

All I could do was to keep my legs in motion, and this I continued to do with the utmost difficulty. The latter part of the night I suffered extremely from cold. There came a heavy frost; I expected at every moment to fall on the road and perish. I came to a corn-field covered with heavy shocks of Indian corn that had been cut; I went into this and got an ear, and then crept into one of the shocks; ate as much of it as I could, and I sunk to sleep.

When I awoke, the sun was shining around; I started with alarm, but it was too late to think of seeking any other shelter. After recovering a little from my fright, I commenced again eating my whole corn. Grain by grain I worked away at it; when my jaws grew tired, as they often did, I would rest, and then begin afresh. Thus, although I began an early breakfast, I was nearly the whole of the forenoon before I had done. . . .

Friday night came without any other incident worth naming. As I sallied out, I felt evident benefit from the ear of corn I had nibbled away. Thus encouraged, I set out with better speed than I had made since Sunday and Monday night. I had a presentiment, too, that I must be near free soil. I had not yet the least idea where I should find a home or a friend, still my spirits were so highly elated, that I took the whole of the road to myself; I ran, hopped, skipped, jumped,

---

4. *mow,* a loft for storing hay.

clapped my hands, and talked to myself. But to the old slaveholder I had left, I said, "Ah! ah! old fellow, I told you I'd fix you." . . .

Saturday morning dawned upon me; and although my strength seemed yet considerably fresh, I began to feel a hunger somewhat more destructive and pinching, if possible, than I had before. I resolved, at all risk, to continue my travel by day-light, and to ask information of the first person I met. . . .

I continued my flight on the public road; and a little after the sun rose, I came in sight of a toll-gate again. . . . I found it attended by an elderly woman, whom I afterwards learned was a widow, and an excellent Christian woman. I asked her if I was in Pennsylvania. On being informed that I was, I asked her if she knew where I could get employ? She said she did not; but advised me to go to W. W., a Quaker, who lived about three miles from her, whom I would find to take an interest in me.

In about half an hour I stood trembling at the door of W. W. After knocking, the door opened upon a comfortably spread table; the sight of which seemed at once to increase my hunger sevenfold. Not daring to enter, I said I had been sent to him in search of employ. "Well," said he, "Come in and take thy breakfast, and get warm, and we will talk about it; thee must be cold without any coat." . . .

From that day to this, whenever I discover the least disposition in my heart to disregard the wretched condition of any poor or distressed persons with whom I meet, I call to mind these words—*"Come in and take thy breakfast, and get warm."* . . . ⊓⊓

Discussion

1. (a) What mental conflicts did Pennington have to resolve before he could make a definite and final decision to run away? How did he resolve these conflicts?

2. (a) What particular aspect of Pennington's philosophy allowed him to view his owner, his pursuers, and his captors with the degree of charity that he did? (b) What irony is contained in this situation?

Extension · Reading

The Pennington narrative is only one of a number of writings by those who experienced slavery. Collections with contents ranging from accounts of the passage from Africa to the escape and subsequent activities of former slaves are now available. Interested students may want to check school and public libraries for such works and present reports and bibliographies to the class.

James W. C. Pennington
1809 • 1870

Pennington was born a slave in Maryland. He was trained as a blacksmith and continued in that trade until, at twenty-one, he escaped from his master and fled to Pennsylvania where he was taken in by a Quaker family. He spent six months there and received his first education. He then moved to Long Island, found work, and continued his education, attending school at

night. He became a teacher and a minister and was active in the antislavery movement. After the passage of the Fugitive Slave Law in 1850, fearing recapture, he went abroad until friends had successfully negotiated with his former master to secure his freedom. His account of his early life, *The Fugitive Blacksmith,* was published in 1850.

Frances Wright

A Fourth-of-July Oration (1828)

The custom which commemorates in rejoicing the anniversary of the national independence of these states has its origin in a human feeling, amiable in its nature and beneficial, under proper direction, in its indulgence.

From the era which dates the national existence of the American people dates also a mighty step in the march of human knowledge. And it is consistent with that principle in our conformation which leads us to rejoice in the good which befalls our species, and to sorrow for the evil, that our hearts should expand on this day. On this day, which calls to memory the conquest achieved by knowledge over ignorance, willing cooperation over blind obedience, opinion over prejudice, new ways over old ways—when,

"The Fourth of July in Center Square, Philadelphia," about 1810, by John Lewis Krimmel (?1789–1821). (The Pennsylvania Academy of Fine Arts.)

fifty-two years ago, America declared her national independence, and associated it with her republic federation. Reasonable is it to rejoice on this day, and useful to reflect thereon; so that we rejoice for the real, and not any imaginary, good; and reflect on the positive advantages obtained, and on those which it is ours farther to acquire.

Dating, as we justly may, a new era in the history of man from the Fourth of July, 1776, it would be well—that is, it would be useful—if on each anniversary we examined the progress made by our species in just knowledge and just practice. Each Fourth of July would then stand as a tidemark in the flood of time by which to ascertain the advance of the human intellect, by which to note the rise and fall of each successive error, the discovery of each important truth, the gradual melioration[1] in our public institutions, social arrangements, and, above all, in our moral feelings and mental views. . . .

In continental Europe, of late years, the words patriotism and patriot have been used in a more enlarged sense than it is usual here to attribute to them, or than is attached to them in Great Britain. Since the political struggles of France, Italy, Spain, and Greece,[2] the word patriotism has been employed, throughout continental Europe, to express a love of the public good; a preference for the interests of the many to those of the few; a desire for the emancipation of the human race from the thrall of despotism, religious and civil: in short, patriotism there is used rather to express the interest felt in the human race in general than that felt for any country, or inhabitants of a country, in particular. And patriot, in like manner, is employed to signify a lover of human liberty and human improvement rather than a mere lover of the country in which he lives, or the tribe to which he belongs. Used in this sense, patriotism is a virtue, and a patriot a virtuous man. With such an interpretation, a patriot is a useful member of society, capable of enlarging all minds and bettering all hearts with which he comes in contact; a useful member of the human family, capable of establishing fundamental principles and of merging his own interests, those of his associates, and those of his nation in the interests of the human race. Laurels and statues are vain things, and mischievous as they are childish; but could we

imagine them of use, on *such* a patriot alone could they be with any reason bestowed. . . .

If such a patriotism as we have last considered should seem likely to obtain in any country, it should be certainly in this. In this which is truly the home of all nations and in the veins of whose citizens flows the blood of every people on the globe. Patriotism, in the exclusive meaning, is surely not made for America. Mischievous everywhere, it were here both mischievous and absurd. The very origin of the people is opposed to it. The institutions, in their principle, militate against it. The day we are celebrating protests against it. It is for Americans, more especially, to nourish a nobler sentiment; one more consistent with their origin, and more conducive to their future improvement. It is for them more especially to know why they love their country; and to *feel* that they love it, not because it *is* their country, but because it is the palladium[3] of human liberty—the favored scene of human improvement. It is for them, more especially, to examine their institutions; and to *feel* that they honor them because they are based on just principles. It is for them, more especially, to examine their institutions, because they have the means of improving them; to examine their laws, because at will they can alter them. It is for them to lay aside luxury whose wealth is in industry; idle parade whose strength is in knowledge; ambitious distinctions whose principle is equality. It is for them not to rest satisfied with words, who can seize upon things; and to remember that equality means, not the mere equality of political rights, however valuable, but equality of instruction and equality in virtue; and that liberty means, not the mere voting at elections, but the free and fearless exercise of the mental faculties and that self-possession which springs out of well-reasoned opinions and consistent practice. It is for them to honor principles rather than men—to commemorate events rather than days; when they rejoice, to know for what they rejoice, and to rejoice only for what has brought and what brings peace and happiness to men. The

---

1. *melioration* (mē′lyə rā′shən), improvement.
2. *political struggles . . . Greece.* The French Revolution of 1789 touched off more than three decades of wars for national independence in these and other European lands.
3. *palladium* (pə lā′dē əm), safeguard.

event we commemorate this day has procured much of both, and shall procure in the onward course of human improvement more than we can now conceive of. For this—for the good obtained and yet in store for our race—let us rejoice! But let us rejoice as men, not as children—as human beings rather than as Americans—as reasoning beings, not as ignorants. So shall we rejoice to good purpose and in good feeling; so shall we improve the victory once on this day achieved, until all mankind hold with us the Jubilee of Independence. □□

Discussion

1. An orator must take account of all the available means of persuasion. These approaches include logical proof, emotional appeal, a call to action, and a concern for the public welfare. **(a)** Illustrate the use of any of these approaches in this oration. **(b)** Which type of argument is less evident than the others? **(c)** What might the avoidance of this approach suggest about the speaker's character?

2. Oratory is not often concerned with permanence nor beauty, but with effect. Identify several effects sought by the orator.

Vocabulary • Dictionary

Like countries and people, words have histories, and it often helps us to understand and remember a word if we are familiar with its history. You will find also that many words have interesting origins. For these reasons, several word studies in *The United States in Literature* ask you to use the Glossary to learn about words that have had interesting origins.

For the three words below you should write:

(a) the language from which the word comes.

(b) the root of the word.

(c) the English meaning of the word.

The words are:

1. ascertain
2. melioration
3. conducive

Frances Wright 1795 • 1852

Frances Wright was born in Dundee, Scotland, into a family of independent means. Orphaned at two, she was raised in England by an aunt but returned later to study at Glasgow College where she was fascinated by her studies of the American Revolution. Excited by the American ideal of freedom, she turned to an atlas to convince herself that such a country really existed. At twenty-three she made the first of many voyages to America. The result of her first journey was the publication in 1821 of *Views of Society and Manners in America,* an enthusiastic and flattering view of the New World.

From 1821 to 1824, Frances Wright lived in Paris where she formed a lasting friendship with Lafayette and other liberal leaders. She returned to America to further her visionary schemes to improve the lot of the slaves. The plan was a failure, and she settled in New Harmony, Indiana, the setting of "A Fourth-of-July Oration." Back in Paris in 1831, Frances Wright married W. d'Arusmont. The marriage did not last long.

Returning to the United States, Miss Wright became notorious with her crusading lectures and writings against established institutions and beliefs. The years prior to the Civil War marked a time of great influence for American orators.

Taken by his father to hear her lecture on free inquiry, Walt Whitman was later to describe Frances Wright as "one of the few characters to excite in me a wholesale respect and love." Although she began as an idealist, Frances Wright moved toward a view of society as "a complicated system of errors." She died in Cincinnati in 1852.

Spirituals

Spirituals can be grouped into plantation songs, songs about current events, work songs, and sorrow songs. The work songs helped ease labor by their steady rhythms and by the communal feeling evoked by group chanting. The sorrow songs clearly reveal the longing to escape bondage, a strong religious faith, a passionate hope for a better life, and unyielding defiance of slavery. Many spirituals of all types could be used by slaves to send secret messages safely from plantation to plantation. Some critics have speculated that modern black poets owe much to the skill with which the apparently simple language of spirituals conveys complex, multiple meanings. "Follow the Drinking Gourd" is one "coded" spiritual, indicating a northward route to freedom. As you read these spirituals, look for other examples of possible double meanings.

Swing Low, Sweet Chariot

    Swing low, sweet chariot,
    Comin' for to carry me home.

I looked over Jordan and what did I see,
Comin' for to carry me home?
A band of angels comin' aftah me,
Comin' for to carry me home.

5 If you git there before I do,
Comin' for to carry me home,
Tell all my frien's I'm a-comin', too,
Comin' for to carry me home.

The brightes' day that ever I saw,
10 Comin' for to carry me home,
When Jesus washed my sins away,
Comin' for to carry me home.

I'm sometimes up an' sometimes down,
Comin' for to carry me home,
15 But still my soul feel heavenly-boun',
Comin' for to carry me home.

You May Bury Me in de Eas'

You may bury me in de Eas'
You may bury me in de Wes'
But I'll hear de trumpet soun'
    in dat mornin'
    in dat mornin'
5 My Lord, How I long to go
For to hear de trumpet soun'
In dat mornin'.

Good ole Christians in dat day
10 Dey'll take wings an' fly away
For to hear de trumpet soun'
    in dat mornin'
    in dat mornin'
My Lord, How I long to go
15 For to hear de trumpet soun'
In dat mornin'.

"You May Bury Me in de Eas'" from STORY OF THE JUBILEE SINGERS. Boston: Houghton Mifflin Company, 1881.

James R. Holland/Stock, Boston, Inc.

Go Down, Moses

When Israel was in Egypt's land,
   Let my people go!
Oppress'd so hard dey could not stand,
   Let my people go!

Chorus
5 Go down, Moses,
   Way down in Egypt's land.
Tell ole Pha-raoh,
   Let my people go!

Thus say de Lord, bold Moses said,
10   Let my people go!
If not I'll smite your first-born dead,
   Let my people go!

Chorus
Go down, Moses,
   Way down in Egypt's land.

15 Tell ole Pha-raoh,
   Let my people go!

No more shall dey in bondage toil,
   Let my people go!
Let dem come out wid Egypt's spoil,
20   Let my people go!

Chorus
Go down, Moses,
   Way down in Egypt's land.
Tell ole Pha-raoh,
   Let my people go!

Deep River

Deep river, my home is over Jordan.
Deep river, Lord, I want to cross over into Campground.
Oh, chillun, oh, don't you want to go
To that gospel feast, that promised land,
5 That land where all is peace?
Walk into heaven and take my seat
And cast my crown at Jesus' feet. Lord,
Deep river, my home is over Jordan.
Deep river, Lord, I want to cross over into Campground.

Lyn Gardiner/
Stock, Boston, Inc.

Follow the Drinking Gourd

When the sun comes back and the first quail calls,
   Follow the drinking gourd,
For the old man is a-waiting for to carry you to freedom
   If you follow the drinking gourd.

5 Follow the drinking gourd,
   Follow the drinking gourd,
For the old man is a-waiting for to carry you to freedom
   If you follow the drinking gourd.

The river bank will make a very good road,
10   The dead trees show you the way,
Left foot, peg foot traveling on
   Follow the drinking gourd.

The river ends between two hills
   Follow the drinking gourd.
15 There's another river on the other side,
   Follow the drinking gourd.

Where the little river meets the great big river,
   Follow the drinking gourd.
The old man is a-waiting for to carry you to freedom,
20   If you follow the drinking gourd.

"Follow the Drinking Gourd." Taken from A TREASURY OF SOUTHERN FOLK-LORE by B. A. Botkin. Copyright, 1949, by B. A. Botkin. Copyright renewed, 1977, by Gertrude Botkin. Used by permission of Crown Publishers, Inc.

W. E. B. Du Bois: Of the Sorrow Songs

Little of beauty has America given the world save the rude grandeur God himself stamped on her bosom; the human spirit in this new world has expressed itself in vigor and ingenuity rather than in beauty. And so by fateful chance the Negro folk song—the rhythmic cry of the slave—stands today not simply as the sole American music, but as the most beautiful expression of human experience born this side the seas. It has been neglected, it has been, and is, half despised, and above all it has been persistently mistaken and misunderstood; but notwithstanding, it still remains as the singular spiritual heritage of the nation and the greatest gift of the Negro people. . . .

Through all the sorrow of the Sorrow Songs there breathes a hope—a faith in the ultimate justice of things. The minor cadences of despair change often to triumph and calm confidence. Sometimes it is faith in life, sometimes a faith in death, sometimes assurance of boundless justice in some fair world beyond.

Du Bois (dü bois′).
From "Of the Sorrow Songs," THE SOULS OF BLACK FOLK by W. E. B. Du Bois. Chicago: A. C. McClurg & Co., 1903.

James Weldon Johnson: On the Spirituals

"Singing Johnson" . . . was a small, dark-brown, one-eyed man, with a clear, strong, high-pitched voice, a leader of singing, a maker of songs, a man who could improvise at the moment lines to fit the occasion. . . . It is indispensable to the success of the singing, when the congregation is a large one made up of people from different communities, to have someone with a strong voice who knows just what hymn to sing and when to sing it, who can pitch it in the right key, and who has all the leading lines committed to memory. Sometimes it devolves upon the leader to "sing down" a long-winded or uninteresting speaker. Committing to memory the leading lines of all the Negro spiritual songs is no easy task, for they run up into the hundreds. But the accomplished leader must know them all, because the congregation sings only the refrains and repeats; every ear in the church is fixed upon him, and if he becomes mixed in his lines or forgets them, the responsibility falls directly on his shoulders.

For example, most of these hymns are constructed to be sung in the following manner:

Leader: Swing low, sweet chariot.
Congregation: Coming for to carry me home.

Leader: Swing low, sweet chariot.
Congregation: Coming for to carry me home.
Leader: I look over yonder, what do I see?
Congregation: Coming for to carry me home.
Leader: Two little angels coming after me.
Congregation: Coming for to carry me home. . . .

The solitary and plaintive voice of the leader is answered by a sound like the roll of the sea, producing a most curious effect.

In only a few of these songs do the leader and the congregation start off together. Such a song is the well-known "Steal away to Jesus."

From THE AUTOBIOGRAPHY OF AN EX-COLORED MAN, by James Weldon Johnson. Copyright 1927 by Alfred A. Knopf, Inc. renewal copyright 1955 by Carl Van Vechten. Reprinted by permission of Alfred A. Knopf, Inc.

The leader and the congregation begin with part-singing:

Steal away, steal away,
Steal away to Jesus;
Steal away, steal away home,
I ain't got long to stay here.

Then the leader alone or the congregation in unison:

My Lord he calls me,
He calls me by the thunder,
The trumpet sounds within-a my
    soul.

Then all together:

I ain't got long to stay here.

The leader and the congregation again take up the opening refrain; then the leader sings three more leading lines alone, and so on almost *ad infinitum.* It will be seen that even here most of the work falls upon the leader, for the congregation sings the same lines over and over, while his memory and ingenuity are taxed to keep the songs going.

Generally the parts taken up by the congregation are sung in a three-part harmony, the women singing the soprano and a transposed tenor, the men with high voices singing the melody, and those with low voices a thundering bass. In a few of these songs, however, the leading part is sung in unison by the whole congregation, down to the last line, which is harmonized. The effect of this is intensely thrilling. Such a hymn is "Go Down, Moses." It stirs the heart like a trumpet call.

"Singing Johnson" was an ideal leader, and his services were in great demand. He spent his time going about the country from one church to another. He received his support in much the same way as the preachers—part of a collection, food and lodging. All of his leisure time he devoted to originating new words and melodies and new lines for old songs. He always sang with his eyes—or, to be more exact, his eye—closed, indicating the tempo by swinging his head to and fro. He was a great judge of the proper hymn to sing at a particular moment; and I noticed several times, when the preacher reached a certain climax, or expressed a certain sentiment, that Johnson broke in with a line or two of some appropriate hymn. The speaker understood and would pause until the singing ceased.

As I listened to the singing of these songs, the wonder of their production grew upon me more and more. How did the men who originated them manage to do it? The sentiments are easily accounted for; they are mostly taken from the Bible; but the melodies, where did they come from? Some of them so weirdly sweet, and others so wonderfully strong. Take for instance, "Go down, Moses." I doubt that there is a stronger theme in the whole musical literature of the world. And so many of these songs contain more than mere melody; there is sounded in them that elusive undertone, the note in music which is not heard with the ears. I sat often with the tears rolling down my cheeks and my heart melted within me. Any musical person who has never heard a Negro congregation under the spell of religious fervor sing these old songs has missed one of the most thrilling emotions which the human heart may experience. Anyone who without shedding tears can listen to Negroes sing "Nobody knows de trouble I see, Nobody knows but Jesus" must indeed have a heart of stone.

As yet, the Negroes themselves do not fully appreciate these old slave songs. The educated classes are rather ashamed of them and prefer to sing hymns from books. This feeling is natural; they are still too close to the conditions under which the songs were produced; but the day will come when this slave music will be the most treasured heritage of the American Negro.

Edgar Allan Poe

The Cask of Amontillado

The thousand injuries of Fortunato I had borne as I best could; but when he ventured upon insult, I vowed revenge. You, who so well know the nature of my soul, will not suppose, however, that I gave utterance to a threat. *At length* I would be avenged; this was a point definitively settled—but the very definitiveness with which it was resolved, precluded the idea of risk. I must not only punish, but punish with impunity. A wrong is unredressed when retribution overtakes its redresser. It is equally unredressed when the avenger fails to make himself felt as such to him who has done the wrong.

It must be understood, that neither by word nor deed had I given Fortunato cause to doubt my good-will. I continued, as was my wont, to smile in his face, and he did not perceive that my smile *now* was at the thought of his immolation.

He had a weak point—this Fortunato—although in other regards he was a man to be respected and even feared. He prided himself on his connoisseurship in wine. Few Italians have the true virtuoso spirit. For the most part their enthusiasm is adopted to suit the time and opportunity—to practise imposture upon the British and Austrian millionnaires. In painting and gemmary Fortunato, like his countrymen, was a quack—but in the matter of old wines he was sincere. In this respect I did not differ from him materially: I was skilful in the Italian vintages myself, and bought largely whenever I could.

It was about dusk, one evening during the supreme madness of the carnival season, that I encountered my friend. He accosted me with excessive warmth, for he had been drinking much. The man wore motley.[1] He had on a tight-fitting parti-striped dress, and his head was surmounted by the conical cap and bells. I was so pleased to see him, that I thought I should never have done wringing his hand.

I said to him: "My dear Fortunato, you are luckily met. How remarkably well you are looking to-day! But I have received a pipe of what passes for Amontillado,[2] and I have my doubts."

"How?" said he. "Amontillado? A pipe? Impossible! And in the middle of the carnival!"

"I have my doubts," I replied; "and I was silly enough to pay the full Amontillado price without consulting you in the matter. You were not to be found, and I was fearful of losing a bargain."

"Amontillado!"

"I have my doubts."

"Amontillado!"

"And I must satisfy them."

"Amontillado!"

"As you are engaged, I am on my way to Luchesi. If any one has a critical turn, it is he. He will tell me——"

"Luchesi cannot tell Amontillado from Sherry."

"And yet some fools will have it that his taste is a match for your own."

"Come, let us go."

"Whither?"

"To your vaults."

"My friend, no; I will not impose upon your good nature. I perceive you have an engagement. Luchesi——"

"I have no engagement;—come."

"My friend, no. It is not the engagement, but the severe cold with which I perceive you are afflicted. The vaults are insufferably damp. They are encrusted with nitre."[3]

"Let us go, nevertheless. The cold is merely nothing. Amontillado! You have been imposed upon. And as for Luchesi, he cannot distinguish Sherry from Amontillado."

Thus speaking, Fortunato possessed himself of my arm. Putting on a mask of black silk, and

---

1. *motley* (mot'lē), the multi-colored costume characteristic of the professional jester.
2. *Amontillado* (ə mon'tə lä'dō), a dry, pale sherry wine.
3. *nitre* (nī'tər), potassium nitrate. Also spelled *niter*.

drawing a *roquelaire*[4] closely about my person, I suffered him to hurry me to my palazzo.

There were no attendants at home; they had absconded to make merry in honor of the time. I had told them that I should not return until the morning, and had given them explicit orders not to stir from the house. These orders were sufficient, I well knew, to insure their immediate disappearance, one and all, as soon as my back was turned.

I took from their sconces two flambeaux,[5] and giving one to Fortunato, bowed him through several suites of rooms to the archway that led into the vaults. I passed down a long and winding staircase, requesting him to be cautious as he followed. We came at length to the foot of the descent, and stood together on the damp ground of the catacombs of the Montresors.

The gait of my friend was unsteady, and the bells upon his cap jingled as he strode.

"The pipe?" said he.

"It is farther on," said I; "but observe the white web-work which gleams from these cavern walls."

He turned toward me, and looked into my eyes with two filmy orbs that distilled the rheum of intoxication.

"Nitre?" he asked, at length.

"Nitre," I replied. "How long have you had that cough?"

"Ugh! ugh! ugh!—ugh! ugh! ugh!—ugh! ugh! ugh!—ugh! ugh! ugh!—ugh! ugh! ugh!"

My poor friend found it impossible to reply for many minutes.

"It is nothing," he said, at last.

"Come," I said, with decision, "we will go back; your health is precious. You are rich, respected, admired, beloved; you are happy, as once I was. You are a man to be missed. For me it is no matter. We will go back; you will be ill, and I cannot be responsible. Besides, there is Luchesi——"

"Enough," he said; "the cough is a mere nothing; it will not kill me. I shall not die of a cough."

"True—true," I replied; "and, indeed, I had no intention of alarming you unnecessarily; but you should use all proper caution. A draught of this Medoc will defend us from the damps."

Here I knocked off the neck of a bottle which I drew from a long row of its fellows that lay upon the mould.

"Drink," I said, presenting him the wine.

He raised it to his lips with a leer. He paused and nodded to me familiarly, while his bells jingled.

"I drink," he said, "to the buried that repose around us."

"And I to your long life."

He again took my arm, and we proceeded.

"These vaults," he said, "are extensive."

"The Montresors," I replied, "were a great and numerous family."

"I forget your arms."

"A huge human foot d'or, in a field azure; the foot crushes a serpent rampant[6] whose fangs are imbedded in the heel."

"And the motto?"

"Nemo me impune lacessit."[7]

"Good!" he said.

The wine sparkled in his eyes and the bells jingled. My own fancy grew warm with the Medoc. We had passed through walls of piled bones, with casks and puncheons intermingling, into the inmost recesses of the catacombs. I paused again, and this time I made bold to seize Fortunato by an arm above the elbow.

"The nitre!" I said; "see, it increases. It hangs like moss upon the vaults. We are below the river's bed. The drops of moisture trickle among the bones. Come, we will go back ere it is too late. Your cough——"

"It is nothing," he said; "let us go on. But first, another draught of the Medoc."

I broke and reached him a flagon of De Grâve. He emptied it at a breath. His eyes flashed with a fierce light. He laughed and threw the bottle upward with a gesticulation I did not understand.

I looked at him in surprise. He repeated the movement—a grotesque one.

"You do not comprehend?" he said.

"Not I," I replied.

---

4. *roquelaire* (rō′kə lār′), a knee-length cloak buttoned in front.
5. *sconces . . . two flambeaux.* A sconce (skons) is a candlestick projecting from a wall bracket. Flambeaux (flam bōs′) are flaming torches.
6. *arms . . . rampant.* The Montresor coat-of-arms (a shield) shows, on a blue (azure) background, a golden foot crushing a snake reared up to strike.
7. *Nemo me impune lacessit* (nā′mō mā im pü′nā la kes′sit). "No one can harm me unpunished." [*Latin*]

"Then you are not of the brotherhood."

"How?"

"You are not of the masons."[8]

"Yes, yes," I said; "yes, yes."

"You? Impossible! A mason?"

"A mason," I replied.

"A sign," he said.

"It is this," I answered, producing a trowel from beneath the folds of my *roquelaire.*

"You jest," he exclaimed, recoiling a few paces. "But let us proceed to the Amontillado."

"Be it so," I said, replacing the tool beneath the cloak, and again offering him my arm. He leaned upon it heavily. We continued our route in search of the Amontillado. We passed through a range of low arches, descended, passed on, and descending again, arrived at a deep crypt, in which the foulness of the air caused our flambeaux rather to glow than flame.

At the most remote end of the crypt there appeared another less spacious. Its walls had been lined with human remains, piled to the vault overhead, in the fashion of the great catacombs of Paris. Three sides of this interior crypt were still ornamented in this manner. From the fourth the bones had been thrown down, and lay promiscuously upon the earth, forming at one point a mound of some size. Within the wall thus exposed by the displacing of the bones, we perceived a still interior recess, in depth about four feet, in width three, in height six or seven. It seemed to have been constructed for no especial use within itself, but formed merely the interval between two of the colossal supports of the roof of the catacombs, and was backed by one of their circumscribing walls of solid granite.

It was in vain that Fortunato, uplifting his dull torch, endeavored to pry into the depth of the recess. Its termination the feeble light did not enable us to see.

"Proceed," I said; "herein is the Amontillado. As for Luchesi——"

"He is an ignoramus," interrupted my friend, as he stepped unsteadily forward, while I followed immediately at his heels. In an instant he had reached the extremity of the niche, and finding his progress arrested by the rock, stood stupidly bewildered. A moment more and I had fettered him to the granite. In its surface were two iron staples, distant from each other about

two feet, horizontally. From one of these depended a short chain, from the other a padlock. Throwing the links about his waist, it was but the work of a few seconds to secure it. He was too much astounded to resist. Withdrawing the key I stepped back from the recess.

"Pass your hand," I said, "over the wall; you cannot help feeling the nitre. Indeed it is *very* damp. Once more let me *implore* you to return. No? Then I must positively leave you. But I must first render you all the little attentions in my power."

"The Amontillado!" ejaculated my friend, not yet recovered from his astonishment.

"True," I replied; "the Amontillado."

As I said these words I busied myself among the pile of bones of which I have before spoken. Throwing them aside, I soon uncovered a quantity of building stone and mortar. With these materials and with the aid of my trowel, I began vigorously to wall up the entrance of the niche.

I had scarcely laid the first tier of the masonry when I discovered that the intoxication of Fortunato had in a great measure worn off. The earliest indication I had of this was a low moaning cry from the depth of the recess. It was *not* the cry of a drunken man. There was then a long and obstinate silence. I laid the second tier, and the third, and the fourth; and then I heard the furious vibrations of the chain. The noise lasted for several minutes, during which, that I might hearken to it with the more satisfaction, I ceased my labors and sat down upon the bones. When at last the clanking subsided, I resumed the trowel, and finished without interruption the fifth, the sixth, and the seventh tier. The wall was now nearly upon a level with my breast. I again paused, and holding the flambeaux over the mason-work, threw a few feeble rays upon the figure within.

A succession of loud and shrill screams, bursting suddenly from the throat of the chained form, seemed to thrust me violently back. For a brief moment I hesitated—I trembled. Unsheathing my rapier, I began to grope with it about the recess; but the thought of an instant reassured

---

8. masons, a play on words. Fortunato refers to a member of a fraternal society. Montresor implies one who builds with stone or brick.

me. I placed my hand upon the solid fabric of the catacombs, and felt satisfied. I reapproached the wall. I replied to the yells of him who clamored. I re-echoed—I aided—I surpassed them in volume and in strength. I did this, and the clamorer grew still.

It was now midnight, and my task was drawing to a close. I had completed the eighth, the ninth, and the tenth tier. I had finished a portion of the last and the eleventh; there remained but a single stone to be fitted and plastered in. I struggled with its weight; I placed it partially in its destined position. But now there came from out the niche a low laugh that erected the hairs upon my head. It was succeeded by a sad voice, which I had difficulty in recognizing as that of the noble Fortunato. The voice said——

"Ha! ha! ha!—he! he!—a very good joke indeed—an excellent jest. We will have many a rich laugh about it at the palazzo—he! he! he!—over our wine —he! he! he!"

"The Amontillado!" I said.

"He! he! he!—he! he! he!—yes, the Amontillado. But is it not getting late? Will not they be awaiting us at the palazzo, the Lady Fortunato and the rest? Let us be gone."

"Yes," I said, "let us be gone."

"For the love of God, Montresor!"

"Yes," I said, "for the love of God!"

But to these words I hearkened in vain for a reply. I grew impatient. I called aloud:

"Fortunato!"

No answer. I called again:

"Fortunato!"

No answer still. I thrust a torch through the remaining aperture and let it fall within. There came forth in return only a jingling of the bells. My heart grew sick—on account of the dampness of the catacombs. I hastened to make an end of my labor. I forced the last stone into its position; I plastered it up. Against the new masonry I re-erected the old rampart of bones. For the half of a century no mortal has disturbed them. *In pace requiescat!*[9] □□

---

9. *In pace requiescat* (in pa′kā re′kwi es′kat). "Rest in peace." [*Latin*]

Discussion

1. What two conditions does Montresor say must be fulfilled for a satisfactory revenge? Does he succeed in fulfilling these conditions?

2. Point out the contrast between Montresor's revenge and "the supreme madness of the carnival season."

3. (a) Are the evils which we are told were committed by Fortunato ever explained? (b) Do you feel that Fortunato is a wicked man? (c) For which character do you have more sympathy? Why?

4. What is particularly appropriate about the coat of arms of the Montresor family?

5. (a) At what point does Montresor indicate a brief feeling of remorse for his actions? (b) How does he explain his feeling?

6. Irony plays an important role in this tale. (a) Explain the irony of Fortunato's name. (b) Who is the greater victim, Fortunato or Montresor? Explain your answer.

Vocabulary • Dictionary

Poe tells the reader that "A wrong is *unredressed* when *retribution* overtakes its *redresser*."

Use your Glossary to answer the following questions about the italicized words above.

1. What is the root word of *unredressed* and *redresser*?

2. What does *unredressed* mean?

3. What does *redresser* mean?

4. What does *retribution* mean?

5. Explain in your own words what the narrator is saying in the quoted sentence.

Edward Rowe Snow:
The Facts Behind
"The Cask of Amontillado"

Edgar Allan Poe became a private in the army in 1827, and was sent out to Fort Independence on Castle Island in Boston Harbor. Actually, were it not for Poe's serving at Castle Island, "The Cask of Amontillado" would never have been written.

While at Fort Independence Poe became fascinated with the inscriptions on a gravestone on a small monument outside the walls of the fort. . . .

One Sunday morning he arose early and . . . copied with great care the entire wording on the marble monument. The following inscription was recorded from the western side of the monument:

The officers of the U.S. Regiment of Lt. Art'y erected this monument as a testimony of their respect & friendship for an amiable man & gallant officer.

Then he moved to the eastern panel, where he inscribed in his notebook the famous lines from Collins' ode:[1]

"Here honour comes, a Pilgrim gray, To deck the turf, that wraps his clay."

After resting briefly, he attacked the northern side of the edifice, and then copied the fourth panel facing South Boston:

Beneath this stone are deposited the remains of Lieut. ROBERT F. MASSIE, of the U.S. Regt. of Light Artillery.
Near this spot on the 25th, Decr, 1817, fell Lieut. Robert F. Massie, Aged 21 years.

Extremely interested in the wording of the fourth panel, which said "Near this spot fell" Lieutenant Massie, he decided to find out all he could about the duel. Interviewing every officer at the fort, he soon learned the unusual tale of the two officers and their fatal combat.

During the summer of 1817, Poe learned, twenty-year-old Lieutenant Robert F. Massie of Virginia had arrived at Fort Independence as a newly appointed officer. Most of the men at the post came to enjoy Massie's friendship, but one officer, Captain Green, took a violent dislike to him. Green was known at the fort as a bully and a dangerous swordsman.

When Christmas vacations were allotted, few of the officers were allowed to leave the fort, and Christmas Eve found them up in the old barracks hall, playing cards. Just before midnight, at the height of the card game, Captain Green sprang to his feet, reached across the table and slapped Lieutenant Massie squarely in the face. "You're a cheat," he roared, "and I demand immediate satisfaction!"

Massie quietly accepted the bully's challenge, naming swords as the weapons for the contest. Seconds[2] arranged for the duel to take place the next morning at dawn.

Christmas morning was clear but bitter. The two contestants and their seconds left the inner walls of the fort at daybreak for Dearborn Bastion. Here the seconds made a vain attempt at reconciliation. The duel began.

From MYSTERIOUS NEW ENGLAND. Copyright © 1971, YANKEE, INC. Reprinted by permission.

1. *Collins' ode,* "Ode Written in the Year 1746" by William Collins (1721–1759), a British poet.
2. *Seconds,* supporters who arranged combats for duelists, saw to the observance of fair play, and secured the help of a doctor on the scene.

Captain Green, an expert swordsman, soon had Massie at a disadvantage and ran him through. Fatally wounded, the young Virginian was carried back to the fort, where he died that afternoon. His many friends mourned the passing of a gallant officer.

A few weeks later a fine marble monument was erected to Massie's memory. Placed over his grave at the scene of the encounter, the monument reminded all who saw it that an overbearing bully had killed the young Virginian.

Feeling against Captain Green ran high for many weeks, and then suddenly he completely vanished. Years went by without a sign of him, and Green was written off the army records as a deserter.

According to the story which Poe finally gathered together, Captain Green had been so detested by his fellow officers at the fort that they decided to take a terrible revenge on him for Massie's death. . . .

Visiting Captain Green one moonless night, they pretended to be friendly and plied him with wine until he was helplessly intoxicated. Then, carrying the captain down to one of the ancient dungeons, the officers forced his body through a tiny opening which led into the subterranean casemate. . . .[3]

By this time Green had awakened from his drunken stupor and demanded to know what was taking place. Without answering, his captors began to shackle him to the floor, using the heavy iron handcuffs and footcuffs fastened into the stone. Then they all left the dungeon and proceeded to seal the captain up alive inside the windowless casemate, using bricks and mortar which they had hidden close at hand.

Captain Green shrieked in terror and begged for mercy, but his cries fell on deaf ears. The last brick was finally inserted, mortar applied and the room sealed up, the officers believed, forever. Captain Green undoubtedly died a horrible death within a few days. . . .

As Edgar Allan Poe heard this story, he took many notes. . . . Poe was soon asked to report to the post commander, and the following conversation is said to have taken place:

"I understand," began the officer, "that you've been asking questions about Massie's monument and the duel which he fought?"

"I have, sir," replied Poe meekly.

"And I understand that you've learned all about the subsequent events connected with the duel?"

"I have, sir."

"Well, you are never to tell that story outside the walls of this fort."

Poe agreed that he would never *tell* the story, but years afterwards he did *write* the tale based on this incident, transferring the scene across the ocean to Europe and changing both the characters and the story itself. He named the tale "The Cask of Amontillado."

In 1905, eighty-eight years after the duel, when the workmen were repairing a part of the old fort, they came across a section of the ancient cellar marked on the plans as a small dungeon. They were surprised to find only a blank wall where the dungeon was supposed to be. . . . Several lanterns were brought down and a workman was set to chipping out the old mortar. . . . Eventually it was possible for the smallest man in the group to squeeze through the aperture.

"It's a skeleton!" they heard him cry a moment later, and he rushed for the opening, leaving the lantern behind him.

Several of the others then pulled down the entire brick barrier and went into the dungeon where they saw a skeleton shackled to the floor with a few fragments of an 1812 army uniform clinging to the bones.

The remains could not be identified but they were given a military funeral and placed in the Castle Island cemetery in a grave marked UNKNOWN.

---

3. *casemate,* a vault with openings for the firing of cannon.

Hop-Frog

I never knew any one so keenly alive to a joke as the king was. He seemed to live only for joking. To tell a good story of the joke kind, and to tell it well, was the surest road to his favor. Thus it happened that his seven ministers were all noted for their accomplishments as jokers. They all took after the king, too, in being large, corpulent, oily men, as well as inimitable jokers. Whether people grow fat by joking, or whether there is something in fat itself which predisposes to a joke, I have never been quite able to determine; but certain it is that a lean joker is a *rara avis in terris*.[1]

About the refinements, or, as he called them, the "ghosts" of wit, the king troubled himself very little. He had an especial admiration for *breadth* in a jest, and would often put up with *length*, for the sake of it. Overniceties wearied him. He would have preferred Rabelais' *Gargantua* to the *Zadig* of Voltaire:[2] and, upon the whole, practical jokes suited his taste far better than verbal ones.

At the date of my narrative, professing jesters had not altogether gone out of fashion at court. Several of the great continental "powers" still retained their "fools," who wore motley, with caps and bells, and who were expected to be always ready with sharp witticisms, at a moment's notice, in consideration of the crumbs that fell from the royal table.

Our king, as a matter of course, retained his "fool." The fact is, he *required* something in the way of folly—if only to counterbalance the heavy wisdom of the seven wise men who were his ministers—not to mention himself.

His fool, or professional jester, was not *only* a fool, however. His value was trebled in the eyes of the king, by the fact of his being also a dwarf and a cripple. Dwarfs were as common at court, in those days, as fools; and many monarchs would have found it difficult to get through their days (days are rather longer at court than elsewhere) without both a jester to laugh *with*, and a dwarf to laugh *at*. But, as I have already observed, your jesters, in ninety-nine cases out of a hundred, are fat, round, and unwieldy—so that it was no small source of self-gratulation with our king that, in Hop-Frog (this was the fool's name), he possessed a triplicate treasure in one person.

I believe the name "Hop-Frog" was *not* that given to the dwarf by his sponsors at baptism, but it was conferred upon him, by general consent of the seven ministers, on account of his inability to walk as other men do. In fact, Hop-Frog could only get along by a sort of interjectional gait—something between a leap and a wriggle,—a movement that afforded illimitable amusement, and of course consolation, to the king, for (notwithstanding the protuberance of his stomach and a constitutional swelling of the head) the king, by his whole court, was accounted a capital figure.

But although Hop-Frog, through the distortion of his legs, could move only with great pain and difficulty along a road or floor, the prodigious muscular power which nature seemed to have bestowed upon his arms, by way of compensation for deficiency in the lower limbs, enabled him to perform many feats of wonderful dexterity, where trees or ropes were in question, or anything else to climb. At such exercises he certainly much more resembled a squirrel, or a small monkey, than a frog.

I am not able to say, with precision, from what country Hop-Frog originally came. It was from some barbarous region, however, that no person ever heard of—a vast distance from the court of our king. Hop-Frog, and a young girl very little less dwarfish than himself (although of exquisite proportions, and a marvelous dancer), had been forcibly carried off from their respective homes in adjoining provinces, and sent as presents to the king, by one of his ever-victorious generals.

---

1. *rara avis in terris* (rä′rä ä′vēs in ter′rēs), "a rare bird on earth." [*Latin*]
2 *Rabelais' Gargantua . . . Zadig of Voltaire* (räb′ə lā′; gär gan′chü ə; zä dēg′; vōl ter′). Gargantua, a creation of the French author Rabelais (?1494–1553), had an enormous appetite for eating and drinking and a love of practical jokes. In contrast, Zadig, hero of a novel of the same name by the French satirist Voltaire (1694–1778), was a "sensible young man," extremely prudent and virtuous.

Under these circumstances, it is not to be wondered at that a close intimacy arose between the two little captives. Indeed, they soon became sworn friends. Hop-Frog, who, although he made a great deal of sport, was by no means popular, had it not in his power to render Trippetta many services; but *she*, on account of her grace and exquisite beauty (although a dwarf), was universally admired and petted; so she possessed much influence; and never failed to use it, whenever she could, for the benefit of Hop-Frog.

On some grand state occasion—I forget what—the king determined to have a masquerade; and whenever a masquerade, or any thing of that kind, occurred at our court, then the talents both of Hop-Frog and Trippetta were sure to be called into play. Hop-Frog, in especial, was so inventive in the way of getting up pageants, suggesting novel characters, and arranging costume, for masked balls, that nothing could be done, it seems, without his assistance.

The night appointed for the *fête* had arrived. A gorgeous hall had been fitted up, under Trippetta's eye, with every kind of device which could feasibly give *éclat*[3] to a masquerade. The whole court was in a fever of expectation. As for costumes and characters, it might well be supposed that everybody had come to a decision on such points. Many had made up their minds (as to what *rôles* they should assume) a week, or even a month, in advance; and, in fact, there was not a particle of indecision anywhere—except in the case of the king and his seven ministers. Why they hesitated I never could tell, unless they did it by way of a joke. More probably, they found it difficult, on account of being so fat, to make up their minds. At all events, time flew; and, as a last resort, they sent for Trippetta and Hop-Frog.

When the two little friends obeyed the summons of the king, they found him sitting at his wine with the seven members of his cabinet council; but the monarch appeared to be in a very ill humor. He knew that Hop-Frog was not fond of wine; for it excited the poor cripple almost to madness; and madness is no comfortable feeling. But the king loved his practical jokes, and took pleasure in forcing Hop-Frog to drink and (as the king called it) "to be merry."

"Come here, Hop-Frog," said he, as the jester and his friend entered the room; "swallow this bumper to the health of your absent friends (here Hop-Frog sighed) and then let us have the benefit of your invention. We want characters—*characters*, man,—something novel—out of the way. We are wearied with this everlasting sameness. Come, drink! the wine will brighten your wits."

Hop-Frog endeavored, as usual, to get up a jest in reply to these advances from the king; but the effort was too much. It happened to be the poor dwarf's birthday, and the command to drink to his "absent friends" forced the tears to his eyes. Many large, bitter drops fell into the goblet as he took it, humbly, from the hand of the tyrant.

"Ah! ha! ha! ha!" roared the latter, as the dwarf reluctantly drained the beaker. "See what a glass of good wine can do! Why, your eyes are shining already!"

Poor fellow! his large eyes *gleamed,* rather than shone; for the effect of wine on his excitable brain was not more powerful than instantaneous. He placed the goblet nervously on the table, and looked round upon the company with a half-insane stare. They all seemed highly amused at the success of the king's *"joke."*

"And now to business," said the prime minister, a *very* fat man.

"Yes," said the king. "Come, Hop-Frog, lend us your assistance. Characters, my fine fellow; we stand in need of characters[4]—all of us— ha! ha! ha!" and as this was seriously meant for a joke, his laugh was chorused by the seven.

Hop-Frog also laughed, although feebly and somewhat vacantly.

"Come, come," said the king, impatiently, "have you nothing to suggest?"

"I am endeavoring to think of something *novel,*" replied the dwarf, abstractedly, for he was quite bewildered by the wine.

"Endeavoring!" cried the tyrant, fiercely; "what do you mean by *that?* Ah, I perceive. You are sulky, and want more wine. Here, drink this!" and he poured out another goblet full and offered it to the cripple, who merely gazed at it, gasping for breath.

---

3. *éclat* (ā klä′), brilliant spirit.
4. *characters,* a pun, meaning both imaginary roles and good character references.

Poe and the Horror Tale

In 1840 Poe divided twenty-five of his tales into two categories and published them under the title *Tales of the Grotesque and Arabesque.*

The *grotesque* is characterized by macabre gothicism. A **gothic tale** is a story of the ghastly and horrible, filled with old, decaying castles, rattling chains, ghosts, zombies, mutilations, premature entombments, and other elements that we associate with the supernatural.

In contrast, the *arabesque* deals with the "terror of the soul" where Poe distorts the mental, emotional, and spiritual nature of the person. In the *grotesque,* the emphasis is on physical suffering; in the *arabesque,* on spiritual agony. Most of Poe's tales, including "The Cask of Amontillado" and "Hop-Frog," have elements of both.

Montresor and Hop-Frog suffer from an extraordinary sense of injured pride. Both of these characters can be seen as reflections of Poe's own paranoid state of mind. Recent literary criticism links Poe's tales to pre-Freudian studies in abnormal psychology. His poetry as well as his prose reveals truths about his own life. Poe's feeling for his childlike wife, Virginia Clemm, whom he married when she was fourteen, is revealed in his poem "Annabel Lee." His poem "To Helen" reveals Poe's vision of beauty as the essence of being.

The haunting musical quality of Poe's poetry is intended to heighten a carefully designed effect: pleasure, remote beauty, mortal sadness, and spiritual ideals.

"Drink, I say!" shouted the monster, "or by the fiends——"

The dwarf hesitated. The king grew purple with rage. The courtiers smirked. Trippetta, pale as a corpse, advanced to the monarch's seat, and, falling on her knees before him, implored him to spare her friend.

The tyrant regarded her, for some moments, in evident wonder at her audacity. He seemed quite at a loss what to do or say—how most becomingly to express his indignation. At last, without uttering a syllable, he pushed her violently from him, and threw the contents of the brimming goblet in her face.

The poor girl got up as best she could, and, not daring even to sigh, resumed her position at the foot of the table.

There was a dead silence for about half a minute, during which the falling of a leaf, or of a feather, might have been heard. It was interrupted by a low, but harsh and protracted *grating* sound which seemed to come at once from every corner of the room.

"What—what—*what* are you making that noise for?" demanded the king, turning furiously to the dwarf.

The latter seemed to have recovered, in great measure, from his intoxication, and looking fixedly but quietly into the tyrant's face, merely ejaculated:

"I—I? How could it have been me?"

"The sound appeared to come from without," observed one of the courtiers. "I fancy it was the parrot at the window, whetting his bill upon his cage-wires."

"True," replied the monarch, as if much relieved by the suggestion; "but, on the honor of a knight, I could have sworn that it was the gritting of this vagabond's teeth."

Hereupon the dwarf laughed (the king was too confirmed a joker to object to any one's laughing), and displayed a set of large, powerful, and very repulsive teeth. Moreover, he avowed his perfect willingness to swallow as much wine as desired. The monarch was pacified; and having drained another bumper with no very perceptible ill effect, Hop-Frog entered at once, and with spirit, into the plans for the masquerade.

"I cannot tell what was the association of idea," observed he, very tranquilly, and as if he had never tasted wine in his life, "but *just after* your majesty had struck the girl and thrown the wine in her face—*just after* your majesty had done this, and while the parrot was making that odd noise outside the window, there came into my mind a capital diversion—one of my own country frolics—often enacted among us, at our masquerades: but here it will be new altogether. Unfortunately, however, it requires a company of eight persons, and——"

"Here we *are!*" cried the king, laughing at his acute discovery of the coincidence; "eight to a fraction—I and my seven ministers. Come! what is the diversion?"

"We call it," replied the cripple, "the Eight Chained Ourang-Outangs, and it really is excellent sport if well enacted."

"*We* will enact it," remarked the king, drawing himself up, and lowering his eyelids.

"The beauty of the game," continued Hop-Frog, "lies in the fright it occasions among the women."

"Capital!" roared in chorus the monarch and his ministry.

"I will equip you as ourang-outangs," proceeded the dwarf; "leave all that to me. The resemblance shall be so striking, that the company of masqueraders will take you for real beasts—and of course, they will be as much terrified as astonished."

"Oh, this is exquisite!" exclaimed the king. "Hop-Frog! I will make a man of you."

"The chains are for the purpose of increasing the confusion by their jangling. You are supposed to have escaped, *en masse,* from your keepers. Your majesty cannot conceive the *effect* produced, at a masquerade, by eight chained ourang-outangs, imagined to be real ones by most of the company; and rushing in with savage cries, among the crowd of delicately and gorgeously habited men and women. The *contrast* is inimitable."

"It *must* be," said the king: and the council arose hurriedly (as it was growing late), to put in execution the scheme of Hop-Frog.

His mode of equipping the party as ourang-outangs was very simple, but effective enough for his purposes. The animals in question had, at the epoch of my story, very rarely been seen in any part of the civilized world; and as the imitations made by the dwarf were sufficiently beast-like and more than sufficiently hideous, their truthfulness to nature was thus thought to be secured.

The king and his ministers were first encased in tight-fitting stockinet shirts and drawers. They were then saturated with tar. At this stage of the process, some one of the party suggested feathers; but the suggestion was at once overruled by the dwarf, who soon convinced the eight, by ocular demonstration, that the hair of such a brute as the ourang-outang was much more efficiently represented by *flax*. A thick coating of the latter was accordingly plastered upon the coating of tar. A long chain was now procured. First, it was passed about the waist of the king, *and tied;* then about another of the party, and also tied; then about all successively, in the same manner. When this chaining arrangement was complete, and the party stood as far apart from each other as possible, they formed a circle; and to make all things appear natural, Hop-Frog passed the residue of the chain, in two diameters, at right angles, across the circle, after the fashion adopted, at the present day, by those who capture chimpanzees, or other large apes, in Borneo.

The grand saloon in which the masquerade was to take place, was a circular room, very lofty, and receiving the light of the sun only through a single window at top. At night (the season for which the apartment was especially designed) it was illuminated principally by a large chandelier, depending by a chain from the centre of the sky-light, and lowered, or elevated, by means of a counterbalance as usual; but (in order not to look unsightly) this latter passed outside the cupola and over the roof.

The arrangements of the room had been left to Trippetta's superintendence; but, in some particulars, it seems, she had been guided by the calmer judgment of her friend the dwarf. At his suggestion it was that, on this occasion, the chandelier was removed. Its waxen drippings (which, in weather so warm, it was quite impossible to prevent) would have been seriously detrimental to the rich dresses of the guests, who, on account of the crowded state of the saloon, could not *all* be expected to keep from out its centre—

that is to say, from under the chandelier. Additional sconces were set in various parts of the hall, out of the way; and a flambeau, emitting sweet odor, was placed in the right hand of each of the Caryatides[5] that stood against the wall—some fifty or sixty all together.

The eight ourang-outangs, taking Hop-Frog's advice, waited patiently until midnight (when the room was thoroughly filled with masqueraders) before making their appearance. No sooner had the clock ceased striking, however, than they rushed, or rather rolled in, all together—for the impediments of their chains caused most of the party to fall, and all to stumble as they entered.

The excitement among the masqueraders was prodigious, and filled the heart of the king with glee. As had been anticipated, there were not a few of the guests who supposed the ferocious-looking creatures to be beasts of *some* kind in reality, if not precisely ourang-outangs. Many of the women swooned with affright; and had not the king taken the precaution to exclude all weapons from the saloon, his party might soon have expiated their frolic in their blood. As it was, a general rush was made for the doors; but the king had ordered them to be locked immediately upon his entrance; and, at the dwarf's suggestion, the keys had been deposited with *him.*

While the tumult was at its height, and each masquerader attentive only to his own safety (for, in fact, there was much *real* danger from the pressure of the excited crowd), the chain by which the chandelier ordinarily hung, and which had been drawn up on its removal, might have been seen very gradually to descend, until its hooked extremity came within three feet of the floor.

Soon after this, the king and his seven friends having reeled about the hall in all directions, found themselves, at length, in its centre, and, of course, in immediate contact with the chain. While they were thus situated, the dwarf, who had followed noiselessly at their heels, inciting them to keep up the commotion, took hold of their own chain at the intersection of the two portions which crossed the circle diametrically and at right angles. Here, with the rapidity of thought, he inserted the hook from which the chandelier had been wont to depend; and, in an instant, by some unseen agency, the chandelier-chain was drawn so far upward as to take the hook out of reach, and, as an inevitable consequence, to drag the ourang-outangs together in close connection, and face to face.

The masqueraders, by this time, had recovered, in some measure, from their alarm; and, beginning to regard the whole matter as a well-contrived pleasantry, set up a loud shout of laughter at the predicament of the apes.

"Leave them to *me!*" now screamed Hop-Frog, his shrill voice making itself easily heard through all the din. "Leave them to *me.* I fancy *I* know them. If I can only get a good look at them, *I* can soon tell who they are."

Here, scrambling over the heads of the crowd, he managed to get to the wall; when, seizing a flambeau from one of the Caryatides, he returned, as he went, to the centre of the room—leaped, with the agility of a monkey, upon the king's head—and thence clambered a few feet up the chain—holding down the torch to examine the group of ourang-outangs, and still screaming: "*I* shall soon find out who they are!"

And now, while the whole assembly (the apes included) were convulsed with laughter, the jester suddenly uttered a shrill whistle; when the chain flew violently up for about thirty feet—dragging with it the dismayed and struggling ourang-outangs, and leaving them suspended in mid-air between the sky-light and the floor. Hop-Frog, clinging to the chain as it rose, still maintained his relative position in respect to the eight maskers, and still (as if nothing were the matter) continued to thrust his torch down toward them, as though endeavoring to discover who they were.

So thoroughly astonished was the whole company at this ascent, that a dead silence, of about a minute's duration, ensued. It was broken by just such a low, harsh, *grating* sound, as had before attracted the attention of the king and his councillors when the former threw the wine in the face of Trippetta. But, on the present occasion, there could be no question as to *whence* the sound issued. It came from the fang-like teeth of the dwarf, who ground them and gnashed them

---

5. **Caryatides** (kar′ē at′id ēz), statues of women used as columns.

as he foamed at the mouth, and glared, with an expression of maniacal rage, into the upturned countenances of the king and his seven companions.

"Ah, ha!" said at length the infuriated jester. "Ah, ha! I begin to see who these people *are*, now!" Here, pretending to scrutinize the king more closely, he held the flambeau to the flaxen coat which enveloped him, and which instantly burst into a sheet of vivid flame. In less than half a minute the whole eight ourang-outangs were blazing fiercely, amid the shrieks of the multitude who gazed at them from below, horror-stricken, and without the power to render them the slightest assistance.

At length the flames, suddenly increasing in virulence, forced the jester to climb higher up the chain, to be out of their reach; and, as he made this movement, the crowd again sank, for a brief instant, into silence. The dwarf seized his opportunity, and once more spoke:

"I now see *distinctly*," he said, "what manner of people these maskers are. They are a great king and his seven privy-councillors,—a king who does not scruple to strike a defenceless girl, and his seven councillors who abet him in the outrage. As for myself, I am simply Hop-Frog, the jester—and *this is my last jest*."

Owing to the high combustibility of both the flax and the tar to which it adhered, the dwarf had scarcely made an end of his brief speech before the work of vengeance was complete. The eight corpses swung in their chains, a fetid, blackened, hideous, and indistinguishable mass. The cripple hurled his torch at them, clambered leisurely to the ceiling, and disappeared through the sky-light.

It is supposed that Trippetta, stationed on the roof of the saloon, had been the accomplice of her friend in his fiery revenge, and that, together, they effected their escape to their own country; for neither was seen again. ☐☐

Discussion

1. Hop-Frog, like Montresor, plots a horrible revenge. The motives for Hop-Frog's vengeance are readily seen. Can his revenge be morally justified? Support your opinion with specific details from the tale.

2. What effect, *grotesque* or *arabesque*, or both, does Poe seek in this tale? Support your opinion with specific details from the tale.

3. (a) In what ways is Hop-Frog crippled in spirit? (b) Is he as crippled in spirit as he is in body? Explain. (c) In what respect are the king and his seven ministers more crippled than Hop-Frog?

4. Contrast your emotional reaction to this tale with your emotional reaction to "The Cask of Amontillado." Which particular details of each story help to create your reaction?

Vocabulary • Context

Use context clues to determine the meaning of each italicized word below. Then write the correct choice of definition on your paper.

1. The doctor warned Ivan that he was too *corpulent* and should lose weight, or he would have trouble with his blood pressure. (a) good-looking; (b) heavy; (c) light; (d) depressed.

2. "Trippetta, pale as a corpse, advanced to the monarch's seat, and, falling on her knees before him, *implored* him to spare her friend." (a) ig- nored; (b) laughed at; (c) ordered; (d) begged.

3. "He seemed quite at a loss what to do or say . . . to express his *indignation*. At last, without uttering a syllable, he pushed her violently from him, and threw the contents of the brimming goblet in her face." (a) anger; (b) happiness; (c) boredom; (d) love.

4. She has such a *prodigious* appetite that we just kept bringing her food until the pantry was empty. (a) great; (b) tiny; (c) organized; (d) boring.

5. There have been repeated warnings that smoking is *detrimental* to one's health, so try not to start. (a) harmful; (b) helpful; (c) unrelated; (d) immature.

Annabel Lee

It was many and many a year ago,
  In a kingdom by the sea,
That a maiden there lived whom you may know
  By the name of Annabel Lee;
5 And this maiden she lived with no other thought
  Than to love and be loved by me.

I was a child and *she* was a child,
  In this kingdom by the sea,
But we loved with a love that was more than love—
10   I and my Annabel Lee;
With a love that the wingèd seraphs of heaven
  Coveted her and me.

And this was the reason that, long ago,
  In this kingdom by the sea,
15 A wind blew out of a cloud, chilling
  My beautiful Annabel Lee;
So that her highborn kinsmen came
  And bore her away from me,
To shut her up in a sepulcher
20   In this kingdom by the sea.

The angels, not half so happy in heaven,
  Went envying her and me—
Yes! that was the reason (as all men know,
  In this kingdom by the sea)
25 That the wind came out of the cloud by night,
  Chilling and killing my Annabel Lee.

But our love it was stronger by far than the love
  Of those who were older than we,
  Of many far wiser than we;
30 And neither the angels in heaven above,
  Nor the demons down under the sea,
Can ever dissever my soul from the soul
  Of the beautiful Annabel Lee;

For the moon never beams, without bringing me dreams
35   Of the beautiful Annabel Lee;
And the stars never rise, but I feel the bright eyes
  Of the beautiful Annabel Lee;
And so, all the night-tide, I lie down by the side
Of my darling—my darling—my life and my bride,
40   In the sepulcher there by the sea,
  In her tomb by the sounding sea.

Poe's wife, Virginia Clemm Poe (see biography).
(The Bettmann Archive, Inc.)

Discussion

1. This poem is an account of Poe's wife, Virginia Clemm. Cite lines which indicate an extreme idealism.

2. Poe's poetry is loved for its sound and mood. Point out examples of **rhyme, alliteration, assonance,** and repetition that contribute to both the sound and mood of this poem.

To Helen

Helen, thy beauty is to me
Like those Nicean barks of yore,
That gently, o'er a perfumed sea,
The weary, wayworn wanderer bore
5 To his own native shore.

On desperate seas long wont to roam,
Thy hyacinth hair, thy classic face,
Thy Naiad[1] airs, have brought me home
  To the Glory that was Greece
10 And the grandeur that was Rome.

Lo! in yon brilliant window niche
How statuelike I see thee stand,
The agate lamp within thy hand!
Ah, Psyche,[2] from the regions which
15 Are Holy Land!

---

1. Naiad, a nymph believed to live in and give life to lakes, rivers, springs, and fountains.
2. Psyche, in Greek mythology, the personification of the soul. Cupid fell in love with her and visited her at night. He forbade her to seek to learn who he was, but because her sisters told her he was a monster, she brought a lamp to the bedside one night when he was asleep.

Discussion

1. This poem is addressed to a boyhood idol of Poe's and its meaning depends upon classical imagery. **(a)** In the first stanza, what likeness does Poe draw between Helen and the "Nicean barks"? **(b)** What does this simile reveal about the speaker?

2. (a) What meaning or "glory" does the speaker associate with Greece? **(b)** To "the grandeur that was Rome"? **(c)** What meaning does Poe give to "Holy Land"?

Edgar Allan Poe 1809 • 1849

The persisting picture of Edgar Allan Poe is one of a romantic eccentric. In reality, he was more insecure than haunted, his life more poverty-stricken than mad.

Orphaned before he was three, Poe was taken into the home of John Allan, a wealthy Richmond, Virginia, merchant. When Poe declined an offer to become a merchant and spoke of a literary career, Mr. Allan was contemptuous. After many violent quarrels Poe left home resolved to live off his writing. In 1830, with the influence of John Allan, Poe received an appointment to West Point. He remained only one year.

Meeting only limited success with his stories and poetry, Poe took on the editorship of a series of magazines. He worked diligently, vastly increasing circulation, yet he was not paid well. His editorial positions were interrupted by unstable periods of the deepest despair.

As a critic, he was an important force in the literary world and argued that American literature should not imitate European literature. He was also concerned that it was becoming "merely" nationalistic as opposed to universal in nature.

In 1845 Poe's poem, "The Raven," brought fame but did little to alleviate his poverty. Poe probably received five or ten dollars for this poem. Ironically, in 1929 the manuscript sold for $100,000.

Two winters later Poe was ill, unable to work. His wife, Virginia, died of tuberculosis

and with her death the instability which haunted Poe intensified. Though his last years were not without periods of achievement, his paranoid sense of persecution increased. He disappeared one day to be found later, battered and drunk. After four days of delirium he died.

His contemporaries abroad and at home differed widely in their appraisals. Alfred, Lord Tennyson, the foremost English poet of the time, saw Poe as "the most American genius," while Ralph Waldo Emerson thought Poe a mere "jingle man." Poe's literary reputation remains controversial.

3: Literary Nationalism

CONTENT REVIEW

1. During the period of Literary Nationalism, American authors were seeking to develop a literature distinct from European literature. However, their work shared with Europe the spirit of romanticism with its philosophy of idealism and optimism. Discuss the idealism found in the selections by Irving, Cooper, and Poe.

2. Much of the literature of the period reveals a concern with social improvement and is propagandistic in intention. Discuss the characteristic methods of propaganda used by Lowell in "Stanzas on Freedom" and by Wright in "A Fourth-of-July Oration."

3. Discuss the ways in which Poe's work is universal in its themes, rather than being nationalistic.

4. Some distinctly American themes explored by the authors of the period are **(a)** frontier character, **(b)** heroic action, **(c)** the beauty of nature, **(d)** the celebration of the common man, and **(e)** the humanitarian spirit. Show where these themes appear in the work of several authors.

5. In many ways the spirituals best achieved the distinctive literary qualities so eagerly sought by American authors. Discuss the validity of this statement.

Unit 3, Test I
INTERPRETATION: NEW MATERIAL

A Republic of Prairie Dogs
Washington Irving

In 1832 Irving travelled in the West and jotted down his observations in journals which he used later to write *Tour on the Prairies.* Read the following account of one of his experiences, and write on your paper the best answer to each question that follows. Do not write in your book.

In returning from our expedition . . . I learned that a burrow, or village, as it is termed, of prairie-dogs had been discovered on the level summit of a hill, about a mile from the camp. Having heard much of the habits and peculiarities of these little animals, I determined to pay a visit to the community. The prairie-dog is, in fact, one of the curiosities of the Far West, about which travellers delight to tell marvelous tales, endowing[1] him at times with something of the politic and social habits of a rational being, and giving

1. *endowing* (en dou′ing), providing with certain qualities.

him systems of civil government and domestic economy almost equal to what they used to bestow upon the beaver.

The prairie-dog is an animal of the coney[2] kind, and about the size of a rabbit. He is of a sprightly, mercurial[3] nature; quick, sensitive, and somewhat petulant.[4] He is very gregarious,[5] living in large communities, sometimes of several acres in extent, where innumerable little heaps of earth show the entrances to the subterranean cells of the inhabitants, and the well beaten tracks, like lanes and streets, show their mobility and restlessness. According to the accounts given of them, they would seem to be continually full of sport, business, and public affairs; whisking about hither and thither, as if on gossiping visits to each other's houses, or congregating in the cool of the evening, or after a shower, and gambolling[6] together in the open air. . . . While in the height of their playfulness and clamor, however, should there be the least alarm, they all vanish into their cells in an instant, and the village remains blank and silent. . . .

The prairie-dogs are not permitted to remain sole and undisturbed inhabitants of their own homes. Owls and rattlesnakes are said to take up their abodes with them; but whether as invited guests or unwelcome intruders, is a matter of controversy. . . .

Fanciful speculators represent the owl as a kind of housekeeper to the prairie-dog; and, from having a note very similar, insinuate[7] that it acts, in a manner, as family preceptor,[8] and teaches the young litter to bark.

As to the rattlesnake, nothing satisfactory has been ascertained[9] of the part he plays in this most interesting household, though he is considered as little better than a sycophant[10] and sharper,[11] that winds himself into the concerns of the honest, credulous little dog, and takes him in most sadly. Certain it is, if he acts as toad-eater, he occasionally solaces himself with more than the usual perquisites[12] of his order, as he is now and then detected with one of the younger members of the family in his maw.[13] . . .

It was towards evening that I set out with a companion, to visit the village in question. Unluckily, it had been invaded in the course of the day by some of the rangers, who had shot two or three of its inhabitants, and thrown the whole sensitive community in confusion. As we approached, we could perceive numbers of the inhabitants seated at the entrances of their cells, while sentinels seemed to have been posted on the outskirts, to keep a look-out. At sight of us, the picket guards scampered in and gave the alarm; whereupon every inhabitant gave a short yelp, or bark, and dived into his hole, his heels twinkling in the air as if he had thrown a somerset.[14]

We traversed the whole village, or republic, which covered an area of about thirty acres; but not a whisker of an inhabitant was to be seen. . . . By-and-by a cautious old burgher would slowly put forth the end of his nose, but instantly draw it in again. . . . At length, some who resided on the opposite side of the village,

2. *coney,* rabbit-like mammal.
3. *mercurial* (mər kyur′ ē əl), changeable.
4. *petulant* (pech′əl ənt), having fits of bad temper.
5. *gregarious* (grə ger′ē əs), fond of being with others.

6. *gambolling,* running and jumping about in play.

7. *insinuate* (in sin′yü āt), hint.
8. *preceptor* (pri sep′tər), teacher.

9. *ascertained* (as′ər tān′d), learned certainly.
10. *sycophant* (sik′ə fənt), self-seeking flatterer.
11. *sharper,* cheater.

12. *perquisites* (pėr′kwə zits), any rewards received for work, beyond the regular pay.
13. *maw,* mouth.

14. *somerset,* somersault.

taking courage from the continued stillness, would steal forth, and hurry off to a distant hole, the residence possibly of some family connection, or gossiping friend, about whose safety they were solicitous, or with whom they wished to compare notes about the late occurrences.

Others, still more bold, assembled in little knots, in the streets and public places, as if to discuss the recent outrages offered to the commonwealth, and the atrocious murders of their fellow-burghers.

We rose from the ground and moved forward, to take a nearer view of these public proceedings, when, yelp! yelp! yelp!—there was a shrill alarm passed from mouth to mouth; the meetings suddenly dispersed; feet twinkled in the air in every direction; and in an instant all had vanished into the earth. . . .

Late in the night, as I lay awake after all the camp was asleep, and heard, in the stillness of the hour, a faint clamor of shrill voices from the distant village, I could not help picturing to myself the inhabitants gathered together in noisy assemblage, and windy debate, to devise plans for the public safety, and to vindicate[15] the invaded rights and insulted dignity of the republic.

15. *vindicate* (vin′də kāt), defend successfully against opposition.

1. In the first paragraph Irving compares the organization of prairie dogs to that of (a) people; (b) regular dogs; (c) beavers; (d) a and c.

2. In paragraph two Irving does *not* say that prairie dogs are (a) vicious; (b) outgoing; (c) fun-loving; (d) fearful.

3. Which phrase implies that Irving does not entirely believe the theory stated in paragraph four that the owl teaches the prairie dog young? (a) "it [the owl] acts, in a manner, as family preceptor"; (b) the owl "teaches the young litter to bark"; (c) "Other fanciful speculators represent the owl as a kind of housekeeper"; (d) all of the above.

4. Reread the second sentence of paragraph five (Certain it is . . ."). The tone here is best described as (a) emotional; (b) disrespectful; (c) understated; (d) admiring.

5. The overall characteriza-tion of the rattlesnake in paragraph five is that he is (a) to be trusted; (b) hungry; (c) to be distrusted; (d) interesting to the household.

6. "As we approached, we could perceive numbers of the inhabitants seated at the entrances of their cells, while sentinels seemed to have been posted on the outskirts, to keep a look-out." The device used in this sentence is (a) simile; (b) hyperbole; (c) personification; (d) analogy.

7. The main idea of paragraph seven ("We traversed the whole village") is best stated by which sentence? (a) The prairie dogs liked to play games; (b) The prairie dogs were characterized by fearful curiosity; (c) The prairie dogs gathered in groups; (d) The men entered the village of prairie dogs.

8. In the last sentence of the excerpt, to which human

activity is Irving alluding? **(a)** a meeting for worship; **(b)** a town meeting; **(c)** a riot; **(d)** a party.

9. Which of the following quotations does *not* help to create the comparison between dogs and people? **(a)** "Having heard much of the habits and peculiarities of these little animals, I determined to pay a visit"; **(b)** "He is very gregarious, living in large communities, sometimes of several acres in extent"; **(c)** "We traversed the whole village, or republic, which covered an area of about thirty acres; but not a whisker of an inhabitant was to be seen"; **(d)** "By-and-by a cautious old burgher would slowly put forth the end of his nose, but instantly draw it in again."

10. The tone of this entire selection is best described as **(a)** critical; **(b)** sarcastic; **(c)** envious; **(d)** light.

11. The style in this entire selection is best described as **(a)** scientific; **(b)** reportorial; **(c)** poetic; **(d)** dramatic.

12. What is the best brief outline of this selection?

First

   I. Author is in the West

   II. Two kinds of owl are different from each other

   III. Prairie dogs have sentinels to keep guard

   IV. Author can't stop thinking about dogs

Second

   I. Description of society created by prairie dogs

   II. Relationship of dogs to owls and rattlesnakes

   III. Cautious reaction of dogs to approach of the unknown

   IV. Cooperation of dogs to protect themselves

Third

   I. Prairie dogs like to run in open air

   II. Rattlesnakes are threat to dogs

   III. Hunters appreciate the prairie dogs

   IV. Dogs can disappear quickly on approach of danger

Unit 3, Test II
COMPOSITION

Choose one of the following topics for writing. Unless otherwise indicated, assume you are writing for your class.

1. As an American newspaper writer of the early nineteenth century, you are writing an article for the *London Times* to inform the British of the movement in America toward a literature that is increasingly independent from Europe for both its subject matter and its style. In the article you will show why that movement can be termed "literary nationalism." Focus on three or four representative selections, each by a different author.

2. The tradition of the American hero has its roots in the Literary Nationalism period. Discuss heroism as it is portrayed in two or three selections in this unit. Is being a hero a matter of thought, action, or both? Do the heroes plan out their actions or act spontaneously? Are they realistic or superhuman? You might compare and contrast nineteenth and twentieth-century concepts of heroism.

3. Critics describe a satirist as one who uses humor to try to make the world a better place in which to live. For a more detailed definition of satire, look in the Definitions of Literary Terms (page 682). Then discuss Harte's "Muck-a-Muck" and either Irving's "Wouter van Twiller" or "The Devil and Tom Walker" as satires. What is the target of satire in each selection? How is the satire developed? Is one author more successful in his satire than the other? How?

4. Many of Poe's stories employ the theme of revenge, and the two in this textbook are no exception. Suppose you are Poe writing his autobiography. In the segment you are now working on, you want to explain your point in making revenge the focus of so many stories. Do so by comparing and contrasting the treatment of revenge in "The Cask of Amontillado" with that in "Hop-Frog." As a conclusion, explain to the reader the picture of humanity that you were trying to create in both stories.

5. Choose two or three poems from this unit and compare and contrast the uses of nature in them. What qualities are associated with nature? What natural images dominate? What thoughts are being expressed with those images?

- *The Lowell Offering* founded

- *The Dial* founded

  - Emerson: *Essays*

  - Experimental commune movement

    - Longfellow: *Poems on Slavery*

    - Oregon and California wagon trails opened

    - Douglass: *Narrative of the Life of an American Slave*

- First Women's Rights convention

- Treaty of Guadalupe Hidalgo, U.S. takes Southwest

  - Thoreau: *Civil Disobedience*

    - Hawthorne: *The Scarlet Letter*

Hawthorne: *The House of the Seven Gables* •

Melville: *Moby Dick* •

Harriet Beecher Stowe: *Uncle Tom's Cabin* •

Thoreau: *Walden* •

Treaty with Japan •

Whitman: *Leaves of Grass*

Longfellow: *Hiawatha*

Teaching of Spanish outlawed in California

- Mexican-American War

  - *The North Star* founded by Douglass

Lowell: *Biglow Papers* •

Transcendental movement

1200 cotton mills in U.S.

Era of "Manifest Destiny":
U.S. expands to Rio Grande and Pacific

Mass immigration from Europe

New England's "Golden Day"

American Classic 1840 to 1870

1860   1865   1870

- *The Atlantic Monthly* founded
  - Lincoln-Douglas debates
  - Holmes: *The Autocrat of the Breakfast-Table*
    - John Brown's raid on Harper's Ferry
    - Oil found in Pennsylvania
    - Juan Cortina's revolt in Texas
      - Lincoln elected
        - Transcontinental telegraph
          - Homestead Act: cheap land for pioneers
          - Black soldiers join Union Army
            - Emancipation Proclamation
            - Lincoln: *Gettysburg Address*

- Slavery abolished
- Confederate surrender at Appomattox
- Lincoln shot
- Whitman: *Drum-Taps*

Alcott: *Little Women* •
Transcontinental railroad •
National Women's Suffrage convention •

exican-Anglo conflict in Southwest 3000 newspapers in U.S.   Reconstruction era   Steel industry started

Wars against Plains tribes   Civil War   Labor unions founded

Background: American Classic 1840–1870

Ralph Waldo Emerson wrote in 1837: "We have listened too long to the courtly muses of Europe. We will walk on our own feet; we will work with our own hands; and we will speak our own minds."

Emerson's call for independence turned out to be prophetic. A few years after Emerson spoke, some of the greatest classics of American literature began to appear. Indeed, so many of them crowded into the first half of the 1850s that the period has been variously called America's Golden Day, the Flowering of New England, and the American Renaissance. Whatever the title of the period, it clearly was the era of the American Classic.

During a brief five-year period, 1850–1855, many of the most enduring of American books appeared: 1850: Emerson's *Representative Men,* Hawthorne's *The Scarlet Letter;* 1851: Melville's *Moby Dick,* Hawthorne's *The House of the Seven Gables;* 1852: Harriet Beecher Stowe's *Uncle Tom's Cabin,* Hawthorne's *The Blithedale Romance,* Melville's *Pierre;* 1854: Thoreau's *Walden;* 1855: Walt Whitman's *Leaves of Grass.*

Why was it that a country that had produced some very fine, but no indisputably classic literature, should suddenly produce a number of authors who would ultimately be read and acclaimed around the world? Emerson, Thoreau, Hawthorne, Melville, and Whitman were writers of this stature.

Obviously no single answer can be given to such a complex question. There was, first of all, a native relish for intellectual discussion and combat. Religious debates had been carried on from the moment of the first settlement in the 1600s down into the nineteenth century.

What began as argument over minor points of Puritan dogma had become by the eighteenth century (sometimes called the Age of Enlightenment) an outright challenge to the dominance of Puritanism. The Quakers, unlike the Puritans, held that individuals did not need a minister to mediate between them and God but could know the Deity directly through an Inner Light. The

Deists affirmed that Nature, not the Bible, was the principal Revelation of God.

These and other beliefs lay behind the gradual displacement of Puritanism by Unitarianism. Unitarianism derived its name from its rejection of a belief in the Trinity (or a Tripartite God) in favor of a belief in a Unitary God; and it rejected the Calvinistic notions of Original Sin and Determinism in favor of beliefs in the basic goodness and innate free will of the individual.

By the time that Emerson went to Harvard Divinity School, it was Unitarian, and the Boston church in which he became a minister was Unitarian. But even Unitarianism was too restrictive for Emerson, and he resigned his ministry in 1832 because he could not in good conscience administer the sacrament of the Lord's Supper. Carrying with him many of the Unitarian beliefs, Emerson began his search for a philosophy in which he could place his faith. Transcendentalism was partly his discovery and partly his invention.

Transcendentalism is, as the

name implies, a belief that the *transcendent* (or spiritual) reality, rather than the material world, is the ultimate reality. This transcendental reality can be known not by the rational faculty or logic, but only by intuition or mystical insight. But

Henry David Thoreau

Ralph Waldo Emerson

Nathaniel Hawthorne

Herman Melville

all people are open to this higher knowledge, and thus Transcendentalism is a philosophy of individualism and self-reliance, traits that had always been treasured in the American frontier society.

Thoreau, Emerson's friend (and his one-time live-in handyman), expressed his independence characteristically: "I would rather sit on a pumpkin and have it all to myself, than be crowded on a velvet cushion." No writer of the period of the American Classic escaped the influence of Transcendentalism. Even those who attacked Transcendentalist thought, like Hawthorne and Melville, were affected by it.

The period saw the establish-

ment of a number of Utopian communities which experimented with new ideas in cooperative living. The most famous was Brook Farm, established in 1841 by the Transcendental Club. Brook Farm attracted many of the leading writers of the day including Nathaniel Hawthorne and Margaret Fuller. All members of the community shared in the work on the farm, drew similar pay, and participated in the cultural and intellectual life.

Hawthorne was quickly disillusioned with Brook Farm, left after a few months, and later wrote *The Blithedale Romance* based on his experience: "No sagacious man will long retain his sagacity, if he live exclusively among reformers and progressive people, without periodically returning into the settled system of things."

There were other debates during this period. There were women like Elizabeth Cady Stanton who spoke up courageously in what has been iden-

tified as the first women's rights convention, held in Seneca Falls, New York, in 1848. And there were courageous Indians like Chief Seattle, who spoke out forthrightly to a government that often seemed indifferent to rights of native Americans. But there is no doubt that the issue that aroused the fiercest emotions was the issue of slavery in the "land of the free."

Throughout the first half of the nineteenth century, tension on the issue grew as the Abolitionists of the North confronted the slaveholders of the South. The Mexican War of 1846–1848, though brought about by a number of causes, was viewed by Abolitionists as an attempt by slavery-advocates to extend slaveholding territory. And the war's treaty ceded two-fifths of Mexico, including California, to the United States. One of the most unpopular wars in American history, the Mexican War inspired indignation and resistance especially among Abolitionists. It was one of the causes for which Thoreau refused to pay his poll tax, resulting in his brief imprisonment. In his essay on the experience, "Civil Disobedience," Thoreau ringingly declares: "There will never be a really free and enlightened State, until the State comes to recognize the individual as a higher and independent power, from which its own power and authority are derived."

Congressional acts frequently inflamed the controversy over slavery, and often inspired outright defiance. The Fugitive Slave Law of 1850 compelled the return of runaway slaves to their owners. Many Northerners, including Emerson and Thoreau, swore that they would not uphold it. Indeed, Abolitionists and others in the North participated in setting up stations along an "underground railroad" to assist the slaves to escape from the South to the North and up into Canada. The escape of slaves to Canada provided the climax for Harriet Beecher Stowe's *Uncle Tom's Cabin* (1852), the novel that Abraham Lincoln once credited with bringing on the Civil War.

The story of the Civil War is as familiar to Americans as the story of the Revolutionary War. In the latter the nation was born, and in the Civil War the country survived its severest test and came of age. The events of the period and their dates have been lifted from history and mythologized: in 1861, the Southern states seceded and the firing on Fort Sumter began the conflict; in 1863 the "Emancipation Proclamation" freed the slaves; and also in 1863, the Union Army won the crucial battle at Gettysburg and Lincoln delivered his "Gettysburg Address"; in 1864, Sherman made his March to the sea; Lee surrendered to Grant at Appomattox on April 9, 1865, and on April 14, Abraham Lincoln was assassinated.

The Civil War has proved an almost inexhaustible subject for the American imagination; it has been sung in poetry, memorialized in fiction, and endlessly reenacted on stage, screen, and television.

The selections on the following pages offer a rich sampling of the American Classic writers. Emerson and Thoreau have been paired because, in fact, there was a biographical relationship between them. Thoreau was only twenty-four years old when Emerson, fourteen years his senior, invited Thoreau to join the Emerson household, earning his board and room by doing odd jobs. Thoreau read deeply in Emerson's works, and it was Emerson's ideas in large part that inspired Thoreau to retreat to Walden Pond for his experiment in simple living.

Although Emerson has justly been called the fountainhead of American literature, and although Thoreau looked up to Emerson as a disciple to a master, Thoreau's work has had a greater influence than Emerson's on the actual behavior of human beings in the twentieth century. The major example is Mahatma Gandhi, who read Thoreau before developing his techniques of passive resistance to win India's independence.

Emerson's essays, though studded with brilliant sentences that sparkle like gems in the memory, tend on the whole to be elusively abstract and difficult to follow. Thoreau's style, on the other hand, is concrete even as it conveys complex ideas: "I long ago lost a hound, a bay horse, and a turtledove, and am still on their trail." Readers must decide for themselves what these items symbolize, but there is no problem conjuring a vivid image from the sentence.

In their essays included here, Emerson and Thoreau exhibit many of the elements of the Transcendentalists, and they also show the fierce independence and individualism that characterized the time. The excerpts from Emerson's "Self-Reliance" may be seen as the kind of Emersonian theory that inspired Thoreau to concrete action, as in his refusal to pay his taxes to a government whose policies he disapproved.

The excerpts from *Walden* and "Civil Disobedience" may be seen as an account of Thoreau's acting out of Emerson's theory. But the works of Emerson and Thoreau included here may show how similar or closely related ideas may be clothed in radically different styles, and how the styles can make a

Abraham Lincoln

major difference in the impact of the ideas on the reader.

As with Emerson and Thoreau, the names of Hawthorne and Melville are linked in literary history, Hawthorne filling the role of master, Melville that of disciple. Melville was thirty-one, Hawthorne forty-six when, in 1850, Melville discovered that he and Hawthorne lived in neighboring towns in the Berkshire Hills of Massachusetts. A friendship quickly developed and they exchanged ideas and books.

In 1851, Melville dedicated his masterpiece, *Moby Dick,* to Hawthorne. Though the novel was little noted at the time, it

has gained in the twentieth century a worldwide reputation that overshadows Nathiel Hawthorne's masterpiece, *The Scarlet Letter* (1850). As in the case

Frederick Douglass

of Thoreau and Emerson, the disciple unwittingly excelled the master.

Hawthorne wrote in his journal: [Melville] "can neither believe, nor be comfortable in his unbelief; and he is too honest and courageous not to try to do one or the other. If he were a religious man, he would be one of the most truly religious and reverential; he has a very high and noble nature, and better worth immortality than most of us."

Hawthorne and Melville are represented here by stories which show that the Puritan strain in the American imagination had not entirely faded from the scene; though neither author could be justly labeled Puritan, they both embody in their fiction what might be called a Puritanically dark view of human nature and fate. This dark view is obscurely sym-

bolized by the mysterious veil worn by the minister in Hawthorne's "The Minister's Black Veil." The youthful protagonists in both Hawthorne's story, "My Kinsman, Major Molineux," and Melville's tale, "What Redburn Saw in Launcelott's-Hey," discover the universality of every human heart.

Other selections in this unit convey a sense of the times. Lincoln's "Gettysburg Address" offers a glimpse into the deep passion evoked by the tragedy of the Civil War. A number of other pieces capture some of the flavor of life at the time. Harriet Robinson gives a picture of women factory-workers in Lowell, Mass., while Louisa May Alcott reveals in her dairy what it was like growing up in a Transcendental household, and Mollie Sanford tells in her journal something of the hard life homesteading in Nebraska. All of these women reveal remarkable self-reliance in the face of hardship and adversity. Two speeches, one by a black and the other by a native American, round out the section: Frederick Douglass presents an eloquent case for independence (and the vote) for the black man, and Chief Seattle speaks forcefully (and poetically) for his tribe. All of these writers demonstrate that independence, individualism, and self-reliance were not ideas confined to the American Classic authors but were ideals deeply embedded in the American consciousness.

Ralph Waldo Emerson

Maxims of Emerson

Speak your latent conviction, and it shall be the universal sense.

Society everywhere is in conspiracy against the manhood of every one of its members.

Nothing is at last sacred but the integrity of your own mind.

My life is for itself and not for a spectacle.

A foolish consistency is the hobgoblin of little minds,
Adored by little statesmen and philosophers and divines.

An institution is the lengthened shadow of one man.

Life only avails, not the having lived.

Insist on yourself; never imitate.

The civilized man has built a coach, but has lost the use of his feet.

Fable

The mountain and the squirrel
Had a quarrel,
And the former called the latter "Little Prig";
Bun replied,
5 "You are doubtless very big;
But all sorts of things and weather
Must be taken in together,
To make up a year
And a sphere.
10 And I think it no disgrace
To occupy my place.
If I'm not so large as you,
You are not so small as I,
And not half so spry.
15 I'll not deny you make
A very pretty squirrel track;
Talents differ; all is well and wisely put;
If I cannot carry forests on my back,
Neither can you crack a nut."

Discussion

1. (a) Which lines in the poem state the moral of this **fable? (b)** What attitude toward both other people and the surrounding world is implied by this moral? **(c)** If you followed this philosophy, what practices and institutions might conflict with your ideals?

2. What characteristics does the fable form have in common with the **aphorisms** and **epigrams** of Franklin's "As Poor Richard Says"?

from Nature
I Become a Transparent Eyeball

Crossing a bare common, in snow puddles, at twilight, under a clouded sky, without having in my
     thoughts any occurrence of special good fortune, I have enjoyed a perfect exhilaration.
I am glad to the brink of fear.
In the woods, too, a man casts off his years, as the snake his slough, and at what period soever of
     life is always a child.
In the woods is perpetual youth.
Within these plantations of God, a decorum and sanctity reign, a perennial festival is dressed, and
     the guest sees not how he should tire of them in a thousand years.
In the wood, we return to reason and faith.
There I feel that nothing can befall me in life,—no disgrace, no calamity (leaving me my eyes),
     which nature cannot repair.
Standing on the bare ground,—my head bathed by the blithe air and uplifted into infinite space,—all
     mean egotism vanishes.

I become a transparent eyeball;
  I am nothing;
    I see all;
      the currents of the Universal Being circulate through me;
        I am part or parcel of God.

The name of the nearest friend sounds then foreign and accidental: to be brothers, to be
     acquaintances, master or servant, is then a trifle and a disturbance.
I am the lover of uncontained and immortal beauty.
In the wilderness, I find something more dear and connate than in streets or villages.
In the tranquil landscape, and especially in the distant line of the horizon, man beholds somewhat as
     beautiful as his own nature.

notes and comments

Emerson's Notebooks

Throughout his life Emerson recorded his daily thoughts and experiences in a series of notebooks. He referred to these journals when preparing a lecture or writing a poem or essay, often incorporating whole passages from them into the new text. The above selection, though part of the essay "Nature," was originally a journal entry. The other selections also contain many ideas first recorded in the notebooks.

Discussion

1. The first sentence in the selection gives the background or the circumstances under which the author becomes "glad to the brink of fear." What are the sources of this "perfect exhilaration"?

2. According to Emerson, where is one most likely to have the experience being described? Why?

3. What human quality must one give up before becoming a "transparent eyeball"? What helps a person reach this state?

from Self-Reliance

A Nonconformist

Whoso would be a man, must be a nonconformist. He who would gather immortal palms must not be hindered by the name of goodness, but must explore if it be goodness. Nothing is at last sacred but the integrity of your own mind. Absolve you to yourself, and you shall have the suffrage of the world. I remember an answer which when quite young I was prompted to make to a valued adviser who was wont to importune me with the dear old doctrines of the church. On my saying, "What have I to do with the sacredness of traditions, if I live wholly from within?" my friend suggested,—"But these impulses may be from below, not from above." I replied, "They do not seem to me to be such; but if I am the Devil's child, I will live then from the Devil." No law can be sacred to me but that of my nature. Good and bad are but names very readily transferable to that or this; the only right is what is after my constitution; the only wrong what is against it. A man is to carry himself in the presence of all opposition as if every thing were titular and ephemeral but he. I am ashamed to think how easily we capitulate to badges and names, to large societies and dead institutions. Every decent and well-spoken individual affects and sways me more than is right. I ought to go upright and vital, and speak the rude truth in all ways. If malice and vanity wear the coat of philanthropy, shall that pass? If an angry bigot assumes this bountiful cause of Abolition, and comes to me with his last news from Barbadoes,[1] why should I not say to him, "Go love thy infant; love thy wood-chopper; be good-natured and modest; have that grace; and never varnish your hard, uncharitable ambition with this incredible tenderness for black folk a thousand miles off. Thy love afar is spite at home." Rough and graceless would be such greeting, but truth is handsomer than the affectation of love. Your goodness must have some edge to it,—else it is none. The doctrine of hatred must be preached, as the counteraction of the doctrine of love, when that pules and whines. I shun father and mother and wife and brother when my genius calls me. I would write on the lintels of the door-post, *Whim.* I hope it is somewhat better than whim at last, but we cannot spend the day in explanation. Expect me not to show cause why I seek or why I exclude company. Then again, do not tell me, as a good man did today, of my obligation to put all poor men in good situations. Are they *my* poor? I tell thee, thou foolish philanthropist, that I grudge the dollar, the dime, the cent I give to such men as do not belong to me and to whom I do not belong. There is a class of persons to whom by all spiritual affinity I am bought and sold; for them I will go to prison if need be; but your miscellaneous popular charities; the education at college of fools; the building of meeting-houses to the vain end to which many now stand; alms to sots, and the thousand-fold Relief Societies;—though I confess with shame I sometimes succumb and give the dollar, it is a wicked dollar, which by and by I shall have the manhood to withhold. □□

Traveling

It is for want of self-culture that the superstition of Traveling, whose idols are Italy, England, Egypt, retains its fascination for all educated Americans. They who made England, Italy, or Greece venerable in the imagination, did so by sticking fast where they were, like an axis of the earth. In manly hours we feel that duty is our place. The soul is no traveler; the wise man stays at home, and when his necessities, his duties, on any occasion call him from his house, or into foreign lands, he is at home still and shall make men sensible by the expression of his counte-

---

1. *Barbadoes.* Slaves had arrived in America from Barbados in the West Indies where they had been brought from Africa. The British abolished slavery in the West Indies in 1833.

Sightseers at Cologne Cathedral.
(The Bettmann Archive, Inc.)

A properly dressed tourist,
mid-1800s. (Culver Pictures, Inc.)

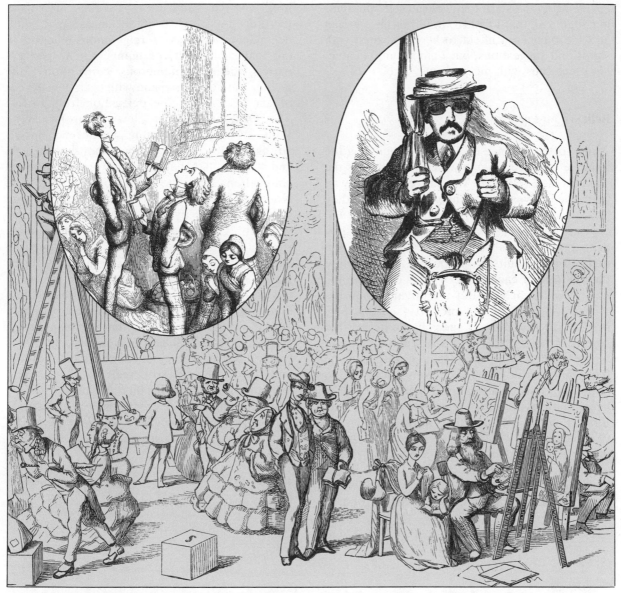

Art lovers at the *Accademia,* Venice, Italy. (The Bettmann Archive, Inc.)

nance that he goes, the missionary of wisdom and virtue, and visits cities and men like a sovereign and not like an interloper or a valet.

I have no churlish objection to the circumnavigation of the globe for the purposes of art, of study, and benevolence, so that the man is first domesticated, or does not go abroad with the hope of finding somewhat greater than he knows. He who travels to be amused, or to get somewhat which he does not carry, travels away from himself, and grows old even in youth among old things. In Thebes, in Palmyra,[2] his will and mind have become old and dilapidated as they. He carries ruins to ruins.

Traveling is a fool's paradise. Our first journeys discover to us the indifference of places. At home I dream that at Naples, at Rome, I can be intoxicated with beauty and lose my sadness. I pack my trunk, embrace my friends, embark on the sea and at last wake up in Naples, and there

---

2. *Thebes . . . Palmyra,* ancient cities. Thebes was the capital of ancient Egypt. Palmyra, in Syria, was known as the city of Tadmor in the Bible and was said to have been founded by Solomon.

beside me is the stern fact, the sad self, unrelenting, identical, that I fled from. I seek the Vatican and the palaces. I affect to be intoxicated with sights and suggestions, but I am not intoxicated. My giant goes with me wherever I go. ☐☐

Reliance on Property

And so the reliance on Property, including the reliance on governments which protect it, is the want of self-reliance. Men have looked away from themselves and at things so long that they have come to esteem the religious, learned and civil institutions as guards of property, and they deprecate assaults on these, because they feel them to be assaults on property. They measure their esteem of each other by what each has, and not by what each is. But a cultivated man becomes ashamed of his property, out of new respect for his nature. Especially he hates what he has if he see that it is accidental,—came to him by inheritance, or gift, or crime; then he feels that it is not having; it does not belong to him, has no root in him and merely lies there because no revolution or no robber takes it away. But that which a man is, does always by necessity acquire; and what the man acquires, is living property, which does not wait the beck of rulers, or mobs, or revolutions, or fire, or storm, or bankruptcies, but perpetually renews itself wherever the man breathes. "Thy lot or portion of life," said the Caliph Ali,[3] "is seeking after thee; therefore be at rest from seeking after it." Our dependence on these foreign goods leads us to our slavish respect for numbers. The political parties meet in numerous conventions; the greater the concourse and with each new uproar of announcement, The delegation from Essex! The Democrats from New Hampshire! The Whigs of Maine! the young patriot feels himself stronger than before by a new thousand of eyes and arms. In like manner the reformers summon conventions and vote and resolve in multitude. Not so, O friends! will the God deign to enter and inhabit you, but by a method precisely the reverse. It is only as a man puts off all foreign support and stands alone that I see him to be strong and to prevail. He is weaker by every recruit to his banner. Is not a man better than a town? Ask nothing of men, and, in the endless mutation, thou only firm column must presently appear the upholder of all that surrounds thee. He who knows that power is inborn, that he is weak because he has looked for good out of him and elsewhere, and, so perceiving, throws himself unhesitatingly on his thought, instantly rights himself, stands in the erect position, commands his limbs, works miracles; just as a man who stands on his feet is stronger than a man who stands on his head. ☐☐

---

3. **Caliph Ali**, the fourth successor of Mohammed as civil and spiritual leader of the Moslems. A collection of his sayings had been translated into English in 1832.

===

Discussion

1. (a) In "A Nonconformist," against what established ideas and customs does Emerson rebel? What are his reasons for refusing to conform to each? (b) In each case, do you agree or disagree with Emerson? Why? (c) How can his ideas be applied to your own life?

2. Emerson objects to a person's traveling " . . . to get somewhat which he does not carry." To what is Emerson referring? Support your answer.

3. (a) What is the "giant" of the last line? (b) Why does traveling not rid the traveler of it? (c) How could the traveler rid himself of the giant?

4. (a) According to Emerson, man's interest in amassing property is done at the expense of what? Support your answer with lines from the selection.

(b) Do you agree with Emerson? Does his idea hold true today? Give reasons for your answer.

5. Speaking figuratively, what is the "man who stands on his feet" doing differently from the "man who stands on his head"?

from The American Scholar

Man Thinking

It is one of those fables which out of an unknown antiquity convey an unlooked-for wisdom, that the gods, in the beginning, divided Man into men, that he might be more helpful to himself; just as the hand was divided into fingers, the better to answer its end.

The old fable covers a doctrine ever new and sublime; that there is One Man,—present to all particular men only partially, or through one faculty; and that you must take the whole society to find the whole man. Man is not a farmer, or a professor, or an engineer, but he is all. Man is priest, and scholar, and statesman, and producer, and soldier. In the *divided* or social state these functions are parcelled out to individuals, each of whom aims to do his stint of the joint work, whilst each other performs his. The fable implies that the individual, to possess himself, must sometimes return from his own labor to embrace all the other laborers. But, unfortunately, this original unit, this fountain of power, has been so distributed to multitudes, has been so minutely subdivided and peddled out, that it is spilled into drops, and cannot be gathered. The state of society is one in which the members have suffered amputation from the trunk, and strut about so many walking monsters,—a good finger, a neck, a stomach, an elbow, but never a man.

Man is thus metamorphosed into a thing, into many things. The planter, who is Man sent out into the field to gather food, is seldom cheered by any idea of the true dignity of his ministry. He sees his bushel and his cart, and nothing beyond, and sinks into the farmer, instead of Man on the farm. The tradesman scarcely ever gives an ideal worth to his work, but is ridden by the routine of his craft, and the soul is subject to dollars. The priest becomes a form; the attorney a statute-book; the mechanic a machine; the sailor a rope of the ship.

In this distribution of functions the scholar is the delegated intellect. In the right state he is *Man Thinking*. In the degenerate state, when the victim of society, he tends to become a mere thinker, or still worse, the parrot of other men's thinking.

In this view of him, as Man Thinking, the theory of his office is contained. Him Nature solicits with all her placid, all her monitory pictures; him the past instructs; him the future invites. Is not indeed every man a student, and do not all things exist for the student's behoof? And, finally, is not the true scholar the only true master? □□

A Phi Beta Kappa key, badge of America's oldest college honor society. "The American Scholar," which Oliver Wendell Holmes called America's "intellectual declaration of independence," was Emerson's speech to Phi Beta Kappa members at Harvard in 1837.

Discussion

1. What truth about man is the fable, discussed in the first two paragraphs, designed to illustrate?

2. According to Emerson, how has the fable's original idea been perverted?

3. What is the difference between "a mere thinker" and "Man Thinking"?

Brahma[1]

If the red slayer think he slays,
   Or if the slain think he is slain,
They know not well the subtle ways
   I keep, and pass, and turn again.

5 Far or forgot to me is near;
   Shadow and sunlight are the same;
The vanished gods to me appear;
   And one to me are shame and fame.

They reckon ill who leave me out;
10   When me they fly, I am the wings;
I am the doubter and the doubt,
   And I the hymn the Brahmin[2] sings.

The strong gods pine for my abode,
   And pine in vain the sacred Seven;[3]
15 But thou, meek lover of the good!
   Find me, and turn thy back on heaven.

---

1. **Brahma,** according to Hindu belief, the supreme soul of the universe. Brahma is illimitable, timeless, formless.
2. **Brahmin,** a member of the highest, priestly caste in the Hindu religion.
3. **sacred Seven,** the seven most revered saints in the Brahmin's religion.

Days

Daughters of Time, the hypocritic Days,
Muffled and dumb like barefoot dervishes,
And marching single in an endless file,
Bring diadems and fagots in their hands.
5 To each they offer gifts after his will,
Bread, kingdoms, stars, and sky that holds them all.

I, in my pleached garden, watched the pomp,
Forgot my morning wishes, hastily
Took a few herbs and apples, and the Day
10 Turned and departed silent. I, too late,
Under her solemn fillet saw the scorn.

Discussion

In discussing Emerson's poetry, pay special attention to the speaker in each poem. In some cases, the poet may choose to speak in his own voice. At other times he may create a character and describe events from that character's point of view.

1. Who is the speaker, the *I* in "Brahma"?

2. What image does the term "red slayer" evoke?

3. A number of apparent contradictions can be found in the poem; name several of these.

4. Explain logically the paradox in line 6: "Shadow and sunlight are the same."

5. In what sense might one slay and yet not slay? Be slain and yet not be slain? (In answering this question, consider the lines from the New Testament: "He who loses his life for my sake shall find it.")

Discussion

1. Is the speaker in "Days" the same as that in "Brahma"? How do you know?

2. What examples of **personification** occur in the poem? Cite specific lines.

3. What images are created through the use of the following: "muffled and dumb," "barefoot dervishes," "pomp," and "solemn fillet"?

4. The speaker calls the Days "hypocritic" and later describes their marching in a single, "endless file." From the speaker's viewpoint, in what sense might Days be called hypocritic?

5. According to line 4, what do the Days carry? What relationship, if any, exists between the two things?

6. What "gifts" do the Days offer? Can you see any sort of progression in the list of gifts?

7. Where in the list of gifts would "a few herbs and apples" fall? What might the speaker's "morning wishes" have been?

8. Why is the Day scornful? At whom is the scorn directed?

Interested students might report in class on any of the following Transcendentalists and their activities:

(a) Bronson Alcott and free schools;

(b) the Brook Farm experiment in communal living;

(c) *The Dial;*

(d) Margaret Fuller, Elizabeth Peabody, and feminism in the Transcendentalist movement.

Vocabulary
Dictionary and Structure

Follow the directions after each explanation below.

A. Verbs that end in *-ate* can often be changed into nouns by droping *e* and adding the suffix *-ion,* which means "in the state or condition of." For example, *dilapidation* means "in the state of falling apart."

For each word below do the following:

(a) Change each word into a noun by adding the suffix *-ion.*

(b) Using your Glossary if necessary, use either the noun or verb form of each word in a sentence that shows you understand the meaning of that word.

The words are:
1. circumnavigate
2. delegate
3. deprecate
4. mutate
5. capitulate
6. domesticate

B. In "A Nonconformist" Emerson indicates that he is against the concept of *philanthropy.* In the poem "Nature" he longs for an end to *egotism.* Use your Glossary to find definitions of both these words. Then write on your paper whether each sentence below is a description of philanthropy or of egotism.

1. After the play, Marilyn allowed no one but herself to be interviewed by the press.

2. Andrew Carnegie was famous for using part of his money to start libraries.

3. Many hospitals would run short of money if it weren't for large contributors.

4. The boy was always looking in the mirror and admiring himself.

Ralph Waldo Emerson
1803 • 1882

In one of his essays ("Fate"), Emerson reduced his topic to its simplest terms: it was "a practical question of the conduct of life. How shall I live?" This elemental question might well be taken as the central theme of Emerson's life as well as his work.

After graduating from Harvard and teaching for several years, Emerson entered Harvard Divinity School. When in 1829 he married and was assigned the pastorate of the Second Church of Boston, he appeared settled and contented. But in 1831 his wife died; a year later he resigned his ministry because he did not hold with some forms of the worship. He went abroad and was exposed to transcendental thought.

When he returned to America and settled in Concord, he began to lecture on his transcendentalist philosophy. Though in most ways a private, introspective man, he enjoyed the response of a live audience. "In all my lectures," Emerson wrote, "I have taught one doctrine, namely, the infinitude of the private man."

Henry David Thoreau

My life has been the poem I would have writ,
But I could not both live and utter it. (1849)

from Walden

Why I Went to the Woods

I went to the woods because I wished to live deliberately, to front only the essential facts of life, and see if I could not learn what it had to teach, and not, when I came to die, discover that I had not lived. I did not wish to live what was not life, living is so dear; nor did I wish to practice resignation, unless it was quite neces-sary. I wanted to live deep and suck out all the marrow of life, to live so sturdily and Spartan-like as to put to rout all that was not life, to cut a broad swath and shave close, to drive life into a corner, and reduce it to its lowest terms, and, if it proved to be mean, why then to get the whole and genuine meanness of it, and publish its meanness to the world; or if it were sublime, to know it by experience, and be able to give a true account of it in my next excursion.[1] For most men, it appears to me, are in a strange uncertainty about it, whether it is of the devil or of God, and have *somewhat hastily* concluded that it is the chief end of man here to "glorify God and enjoy Him forever."[2]

Still we live meanly, like ants, though the fable tells us that we were long ago changed into men;[3] like pygmies we fight with cranes;[4] it is error upon error, and clout upon clout, and our best virtue has for its occasion a superfluous and evitable wretchedness. Our life is frittered away by detail. An honest man has hardly need to count more than his ten fingers or in extreme cases he may add his ten toes, and lump the rest.

Simplicity, simplicity, simplicity! I say, let your affairs be as two or three, and not a hundred or a thousand; instead of a million count half a dozen, and keep your accounts on your thumbnail. In the midst of this chopping sea of civilized life, such are the clouds and storms and quicksands and thousand-and-one items to be allowed for, that a man has to live, if he would not founder and go to the bottom and not make his port at all, by dead reckoning,[5] and he must be a great calculator indeed who succeeds. Simplify, simplify. Instead of three meals a day, if it be necessary eat but one; instead of a hundred dishes, five; and reduce other things in proportion. Our life is like a German Confederacy, made up of petty states,[6] with its boundary forever fluctuating, so that even a German cannot tell you how it is bounded at any moment. The nation itself, with all its so-called internal improvements, which, by the way, are all external and superficial, is just such an unwieldy and overgrown establishment, cluttered with furniture and tripped up by its own traps, ruined by luxury and heedless expense, by want of calculation and a worthy aim, as the million households in the land; and the only cure for it as for them is in a rigid economy, a stern and more than Spartan simplicity of life and elevation of purpose. It lives too fast. Men think that it is essential that the *Nation* have commerce, and export ice, and talk through a telegraph, and ride thirty miles an hour, without a doubt, whether *they* do or not; but whether we should live like baboons or like men is a little uncertain. If we do not get out sleepers, and forge rails, and devote days and nights to the work, but go to tinkering upon our *lives* to improve them, who will build railroads? And if railroads are not built, how shall we get to heaven in season? But if we stay at home and mind our business, who will want railroads? We do not ride on the railroad; it rides upon us. □□

The Battle of the Ants

One day when I went out to my woodpile, or rather my pile of stumps, I observed two large ants, the one red, the other much larger, nearly half an inch long, and black, fiercely contending with one another. Having once got hold, they never let go, but struggled and wrestled and rolled on the chips incessantly. Looking farther, I was surprised to find the chips were covered with such combatants—that it was not a *duellum*, but a *bellum*,[7] a war between two races of ants, the red always pitted against the black, and frequently two red ones to one black. The legions of these Myrmidons[8] covered all the hills and vales in my woodyard, and the ground was

---

1. *my next excursion,* my next or future life.
2. *"glorify God and enjoy Him forever,"* the answer in the Westminster Catechism of the Presbyterian Church to the question, "What is the chief end of man?"
3. *ants . . . men.* According to Greek legend, the Myrmidons, the followers of Achilles, were ants changed into men.
4. *like pygmies we fight with cranes.* Homer and other ancient writers believed that the pygmies, dwarf inhabitants of Africa, carried on warfare with the cranes.
5. *dead reckoning,* calculation of a ship's position by using a compass and studying the record of the voyage, and without using observations of the sun and stars.
6. *a German Confederacy, made up of petty states.* At the time Thoreau wrote *Walden,* Germany as a nation did not exist. Until the rise of Napoleon at the end of the eighteenth century, there had been a German emperor, but he was a mere figurehead; in each of the several hundred German states the real ruler was its prince or duke. At the Congress of Vienna (1814–1815), which met to reorganize Europe after Napoleon's defeat at the Battle of Waterloo, the German states were reduced in number from several hundred to thirty-eight and a loose German Confederation was formed. However, the real power remained with the heads of the states rather than in the confederation. In 1871 Bismarck, a statesman from Prussia, the strongest of the German states, welded Germany into an empire.
7. *not a* duellum (dü el′əm) *but a* bellum (bel′əm), not merely a duel between two contestants but a war between two armies.
8. *Myrmidons* (mèr′mi donz), warriors of ancient Thessaly, according to Greek legend.

already strewn with the dead and dying, both red and black.

It was the only battle which I have ever witnessed, the only battlefield I ever trod while the battle was raging; internecine war; the red republicans on the one hand, and the black imperialists[9] on the other. On every side they were engaged in deadly combat, yet without any noise that I could hear, and human soldiers never fought so resolutely.

I watched a couple that were fast locked in each other's embraces, in a little sunny valley amid the chips, now at noonday prepared to fight till the sun went down, or life went out. The smaller red champion had fastened himself like a vise to his adversary's front, and through all the tumblings on that field never for an instant ceased to gnaw at one of his feelers near the root, having already caused the other to go by the board; while the stronger black one dashed him from side to side, and, as I saw on looking nearer, had already divested him of several of his members. They fought with more pertinacity than bulldogs. Neither manifested the least disposition to retreat. It was evident that their battle cry was "Conquer or die."

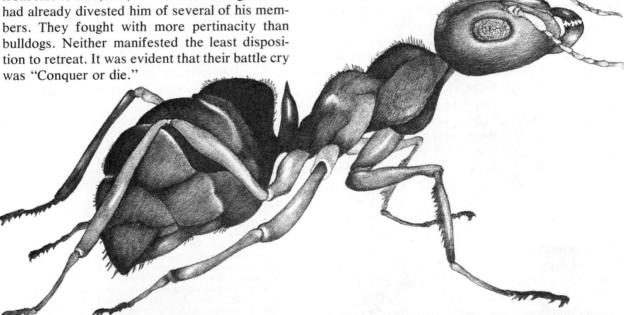

In the meanwhile there came along a single red ant on the hillside of this valley, evidently full of excitement, who either had dispatched his foe or had not yet taken part in the battle (probably the latter, for he had lost none of his limbs); whose mother had charged him to return with his shield or upon it.[10] Or perchance he was some Achilles, who had nourished his wrath apart, and had now come to avenge or rescue his Patroclus.[11] He saw this unequal combat from afar. He drew near with rapid pace till he stood on his guard within half an inch of the combatants; then, watching his opportunity, he sprang upon the black warrior, and commenced his operations near the root of his right foreleg, leaving the foe to select among his own members.

And so there were three united for life, as if a new kind of attraction had been invented which put all other locks and cements to shame. I should not have wondered by this time to find that they had their respective musical bands stationed on some eminent chip, and playing their national airs the while, to excite the slow and cheer the dying combatants. I was myself excited somewhat even as if they had been men.

9. *red republicans . . . black imperialists.* At the time this selection was published in 1854, Europe had recently undergone several revolutions in which the people of a number of countries had rebelled against their rulers.
10. *whose mother . . . with his shield or upon it.* According to tales of ancient Greece this was the command given by Spartan mothers to their sons when the sons went off to war. It means: Die rather than surrender.
11. *Achilles* (ə kilʹēz) . . . *Patroclus* (pə trōʹkləs). Because of a quarrel with Agamemnon (agʹə memʹnon), the Greek commander in chief in the Trojan War, Achilles sulked in his tent. But when he heard that his friend Patroclus had been killed, he hurried into the battle to avenge him.

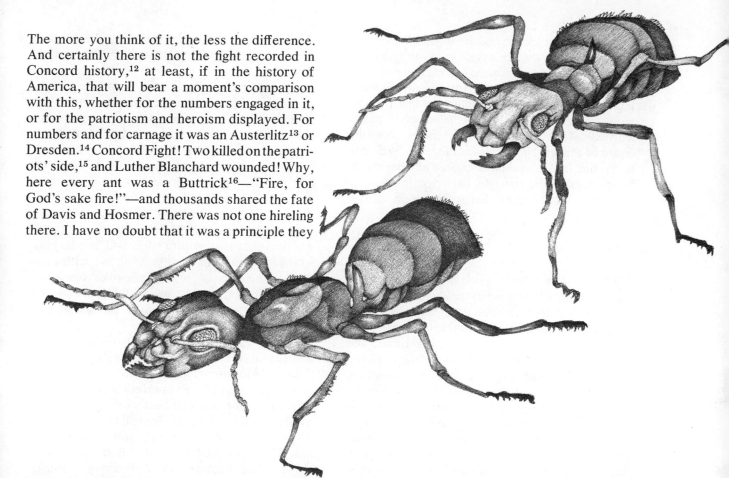

The more you think of it, the less the difference. And certainly there is not the fight recorded in Concord history,[12] at least, if in the history of America, that will bear a moment's comparison with this, whether for the numbers engaged in it, or for the patriotism and heroism displayed. For numbers and for carnage it was an Austerlitz[13] or Dresden.[14] Concord Fight! Two killed on the patriots' side,[15] and Luther Blanchard wounded! Why, here every ant was a Buttrick[16]—"Fire, for God's sake fire!"—and thousands shared the fate of Davis and Hosmer. There was not one hireling there. I have no doubt that it was a principle they fought for, as much as our ancestors, and not to avoid a threepenny tax on their tea,[17] and the results of this battle will be as important and memorable to those whom it concerns as those of the battle of Bunker Hill, at least.

I took up the chip on which the three I have particularly described were struggling, carried it into my house, and placed it under a tumbler on my window sill, in order to see the issue. Holding a microscope to the first-mentioned red ant, I saw that, though he was assiduously gnawing at the near foreleg of his enemy, having severed his remaining feeler, his own breast was all torn away, exposing what vitals he had there to the jaws of the black warrior, whose breastplate was apparently too thick for him to pierce; and the dark carbuncles of the sufferer's eyes shone with ferocity such as war only could excite. They struggled half an hour longer under the tumbler, and when I looked again the black soldier had severed the heads of his foes from their bodies, and the still living heads were hanging on either side of him like ghastly trophies at his saddlebow, still apparently as firmly fastened as ever, and he was endeavoring with feeble struggles, being without feelers and with only the remnant of a leg, and I know not how many other wounds, to divest himself of them; which after half an hour more he accomplished.

12. *the fight recorded in Concord history,* the second battle of the Revolutionary War, on April 19, 1775.
13. *Austerlitz* (ôs′tər lïts), battle fought in old Austria (now Czechoslovakia) during the Napoleonic Wars. Here in 1805 Napoleon defeated the Russians and Austrians. Many thousands were killed.
14. *Dresden,* the last of Napoleon's great victories, in which he defeated the Russian, Austrian, and Prussian forces in 1813. Dresden is in Germany.
15. *Two killed on the patriots' side.* Thoreau is writing of the mid-morning fight at the North Bridge when the militia advanced and attacked the British on guard there. Two Americans, Captain Isaac Davis and a man named Hosmer (both mentioned below), were killed.
16. *Buttrick,* the major in command of the Concord militia in the fight at the North Bridge.
17. *a threepenny tax on their tea,* a reference to the Boston Tea Party and the colonists' objections to taxation without representation.

I raised the glass, and he went off over the window sill in that crippled state. Whether he finally survived that combat, and spent the remainder of his days in some Hôtel des Invalides,[18] I do not know; but I thought that his industry would not be worth much thereafter. I never learned which party was victorious, nor the cause of the war; but I felt for the rest of that day as if I had had my feelings excited and harrowed by witnessing the struggle, the ferocity and carnage, of a human battle before my door. □□

Why I Left the Woods

I left the woods for as good a reason as I went there. Perhaps it seemed to me that I had several more lives to live, and could not spare any more time for that one. It is remarkable how easily and insensibly we fall into a particular route, and make a beaten track for ourselves. I had not lived there a week before my feet wore a path from my door to the pondside; and though it is five or six years since I trod it, it is still quite distinct. It is true, I fear, that others may have fallen into it, and so helped to keep it open. The surface of the earth is soft and impressible by the feet of men; and so with the paths which the mind travels. How worn and dusty, then, must be the highways of the world, how deep the ruts of tradition and conformity! I did not wish to take a cabin passage, but rather to go before the mast and on the deck of the world, for there I could best see the moonlight amid the mountains. I do not wish to go below now.

I learned this, at least, by my experiment: that if one advances confidently in the direction of his dreams, and endeavors to live the life which he has imagined, he will meet with a success unexpected in common hours. He will put some things behind, will pass an invisible boundary; new, universal, and more liberal laws will begin to establish themselves around and within him; or the old laws be expanded, and interpreted in his favor in a more liberal sense, and he will live with the license of a higher order of beings. In proportion as he simplifies his life, the laws of the universe will appear less complex, and solitude will not be solitude, nor poverty poverty, nor weakness weakness. If you have built castles in

the air, your work need not be lost; that is where they should be. Now put the foundations under them. . . .

Why should we be in such desperate haste to succeed and in such desperate enterprises? If a man does not keep pace with his companions, perhaps it is because he hears a different drummer. Let him step to the music which he hears, however measured or far away. It is not important that he should mature as soon as an apple tree or an oak. Shall he turn his spring into summer? If the condition of things which we were made for is not yet, what were any reality which we can substitute? We will not be shipwrecked on a vain reality. Shall we with pains erect a heaven of blue glass over ourselves, though when it is done we shall be sure to gaze still at the true ethereal heaven far above, as if the former were not?

There was an artist in the city of Kouroo who was disposed to strive after perfection. One day it came into his mind to make a staff. Having considered that in an imperfect work time is an ingredient, but into a perfect work time does not enter, he said to himself, It shall be perfect in all respects, though I should do nothing else in my life. He proceeded instantly to the forest for wood, being resolved that it should not be made of unsuitable material; and as he searched for and rejected stick after stick, his friends gradually deserted him, for they grew old in their works and died, but he grew not older by a moment. His singleness of purpose and resolution, and his elevated piety, endowed him, without his knowledge, with perennial youth. As he made no compromise with Time, Time kept out of his way, and only sighed at a distance because he could not overcome him. Before he had found a stick in all respects suitable the city of Kouroo was a hoary ruin, and he sat on one of its mounds to peel the stick. Before he had given it the proper shape the dynasty of the Candahars[19] was at an end, and with the point of the stick he wrote the name of the last of that race in the sand, and

---

18. Hôtel des Invalides (ō tel′ dā zän vä lēd′), a beautiful monument in Paris founded by Louis XIV as a residence for old and wounded veterans of the French armies.
19. Candahars, Kandahar, an Afghanistan city long ruled by Darius I, king of the Achaemenid dynasty of Persia, and taken by Alexander in 329 B.C.

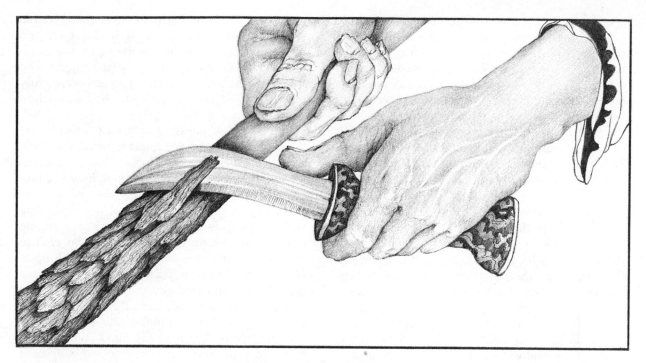

then resumed his work. By the time he had smoothed and polished the staff Kalpa was no longer the pole-star; and ere he had put on the ferule and the head adorned with precious stones, Brahma had awoke and slumbered many times.[20] But why do I stay to mention these things? When the finishing stroke was put to his work, it suddenly expanded before the eyes of the astonished artist into the fairest of all the creations of Brahma. He had made a new system in making a staff, a world with full and fair proportions; in which, though the old cities and dynasties had passed away, fairer and more glorious ones had taken their places. And now he saw by the heap of shavings still fresh at his feet, that, for him and his work, the former lapse of time had been an illusion, and that no more time had elapsed than is required for a single scintillation from the brain of Brahma to fall on and inflame the tinder of a mortal brain. The material was pure, and his art was pure; how could the result be other than wonderful?

No face which we can give to a matter will stead us so well at last as the truth. This alone wears well. For the most part, we are not where we are, but in a false position. Through an infirmity of our natures, we suppose a case, and put ourselves into it, and hence are in two cases at the same time, and it is doubly difficult to get out. In sane moments we regard only the facts, the case that is. Say what you have to say, not what you ought. Any truth is better than make-believe. Tom Hyde, the tinker, standing on the gallows, was asked if he had anything to say. "Tell the tailors," said he, "to remember to make a knot in their thread before they take the first stitch." His companion's prayer is forgotten.

However mean your life is, meet it and live it; do not shun it and call it hard names. It is not so bad as you are. It looks poorest when you are richest. The fault-finder will find faults even in paradise. Love your life, poor as it is. You may perhaps have some pleasant, thrilling, glorious hours, even in a poor-house. The setting sun is reflected from the windows of the alms-house as brightly as from the rich man's abode; the snow melts before its door as early in the spring. I do not see but a quiet mind may live as contentedly there, and have as cheering thoughts, as in a palace. The town's poor seem to me often to live the most independent lives of any. Maybe they

---

20. Kalpa . . . many times. According to Hindu belief, Brahma is the creator of the world which endures for 2,160,000,000 years and then is destroyed, only to be recreated by him after a like duration. Each 4,320,000,000-year period of this sort constitutes a day and a night of Brahma, or a Kalpa.

are simply great enough to receive without misgiving. Most think that they are above being supported by the town; but it oftener happens that they are not above supporting themselves by dishonest means, which should be more disreputable. Cultivate poverty like a garden herb, like sage. Do not trouble yourself much to get new things, whether clothes or friends. Turn the old; return to them. Things do not change; we change. Sell your clothes and keep your thoughts. God will see that you do not want society. If I were confined to a corner of a garret all my days, like a spider, the world would be just as large to me while I had my thoughts about me. The philosopher said: "From an army of three divisions one can take away its general, and put it in disorder; from the man the most abject and vulgar one cannot take away his thought." Do not seek so anxiously to be developed, to subject yourself to many influences to be played on; it is all dissipation. Humility like darkness reveals the heavenly lights. The shadows of poverty and meanness gather around us, "and lo! creation widens to our view."[21] We are often reminded that if there were bestowed on us the wealth of Croesus,[22] our aims must still be the same, and our means essentially the same. Moreover, if you are restricted in your range by poverty, if you cannot buy books and newspapers, for instance, you are but confined to the most significant and vital experiences; you are compelled to deal with the material which yields the most sugar and the most starch. It is life near the bone where it is sweetest. You are defended from being a trifler. No man loses ever on a lower level by magnanimity on a higher. Superfluous wealth can buy superfluities only. Money is not required to buy one necessary of the soul. . . .

Rather than love, than money, than fame, give me truth: I sat at a table where were rich food and wine in abundance, an obsequious attendance, but sincerity and truth were not; and I went away hungry from the inhospitable board. The hospitality was as cold as the ices. I thought that there was no need of ice to freeze them. They talked to me of the age of the wine and the fame of the vintage; but I thought of an older, a newer, and purer wine, of a more glorious vintage, which they had not got, and could not buy. The style, the house and grounds and "entertain-

ment" pass for nothing with me. I called on the king, but he made me wait in his hall, and conducted like a man incapacitated for hospitality. There was a man in my neighborhood who lived in a hollow tree. His manners were truly regal. I should have done better had I called on him. . . .

There is an incessant influx of novelty into the world, and yet we tolerate incredible dullness. I need only suggest what kind of sermons are still listened to in the most enlightened countries. There are such words as joy and sorrow, but they are only the burden of a psalm, sung with a nasal twang, while we believe in the ordinary and mean. We think that we can change our clothes only. It is said that the British Empire is very large and respectable, and that the United States are a first-rate power. We do not believe that a tide rises and falls behind every man which can float the British Empire like a chip, if he should ever harbor it in his mind. Who knows what sort of seventeen-year locust will next come out of the ground? The government of the world I live in was not framed, like that of Britain, in after-dinner conversations over the wine.

The life in us is like the water in the river. It may rise this year higher than man has ever known it, and flood the parched uplands; even this may be the eventful year, which will drown out all our muskrats. It was not always dry land where we dwell. I see far inland the banks which the stream anciently washed, before science began to record its freshets. Everyone has heard the story which has gone the rounds of New England, of a strong and beautiful bug which came out of the dry leaf of an old table of apple-tree wood, which had stood in a farmer's kitchen for sixty years, first in Connecticut, and afterward in Massachusetts,—from an egg deposited in the living tree many years earlier still, as appeared by counting the annual layers beyond it; which was heard gnawing out for several weeks, hatched perchance by the heat of an urn. Who does not feel his faith in a resurrection and

---

21. *"and lo . . . view,"* a slight misquotation from "Night," a sonnet by Joseph Blanco White (1775–1841).
22. *Croesus* (krē′səs), a king of Lydia in the 6th century B.C. renowned for his vast wealth.

immortality strengthened by hearing of this? Who knows what beautiful and winged life, whose egg has been buried for ages under many concentric layers of woodenness in the dead dry life of society, deposited at first in the alburnum of the green and living tree, which has been gradually converted into the semblance of its well-seasoned tomb,—heard perchance gnawing out now for years by the astonished family of man, as they sat round the festive board,—may unexpectedly come forth from amidst society's most trivial and handselled furniture, to enjoy its perfect summer life at last!

I do not say that John or Jonathan will realize all this; but such is the character of that morrow which mere lapse of time can never make to dawn. The light which puts out our eyes is darkness to us. Only that day dawns to which we are awake. There is more day to dawn. The sun is but a morning star. □□

Discussion

1. How might a person "live what was not life"?

2. Reread the paragraph beginning "Simplicity, simplicity, simplicity . . ." (233a, 2). (a) Are the ideas in it applicable to contemporary life? Discuss. (b) Do you think it possible or desirable today to "keep your accounts on your thumbnail"? Why or why not?

3. What is the **tone** of "The Battle of the Ants"? How does this tone differ from that of the other two selections from *Walden?* Support your answer.

4. Compare and contrast Thoreau's reason for going to the woods and his reason for leaving them. Give lines from the text to support your answer.

5. According to Emerson's philosophy, is Thoreau standing on his head or on his feet? Explain.

6. (a) If somebody today wanted to imitate Thoreau's Walden experiment, what difficulties might such an individual encounter? (b) What would you suggest might be done to overcome these difficulties?

Vocabulary • Context

Use clues within each sentence to determine the meaning of the italicized words. The questions will direct you to the right clues.

A. "Our life is like a German Confederacy, made up of petty states, with its boundary forever *fluctuating*, so that even a German cannot tell you how it is bounded at any moment."

1. Why wouldn't somebody be able to tell where the borders of our life are?

2. *Fluctuate* probably means (a) stay the same; (b) fenced-in; (c) change; (d) measure.

B. ". . . *internecine* war; the red republicans on the one hand, and the black imperialists on the other. On every side they were engaged in deadly combat. . . ."

1. Thoreau implies here that both sides will fight until what happens?

2. *Internecine* probably means (a) between families; (b) humane; (c) nuclear; (d) deadly.

C. "They fought with more *pertinacity* than bulldogs."

1. What are bulldogs traditionally known for?

2. *Pertinacity* probably means (a) persistence; (b) apathy; (c) vengeance; (d) cleverness.

from Civil Disobedience

I heartily accept the motto,—"That government is best which governs least"; and I should like to see it acted up to more rapidly and systematically. Carried out, it finally amounts to this, which also I believe,—"That government is best which governs not at all" and when men are prepared for it, that will be the kind of government which they will have. Government is at best but an expedient; but most governments are usually, and all governments are sometimes, inexpedient. The objections which have been brought against a standing army, and they are many and weighty, and deserve to prevail, may also at last be brought against a standing government. The standing army is only an arm of the standing government. The government itself, which is only the mode which the people have chosen to execute their will, is equally liable to be abused and perverted before the people can act through it. Witness the present Mexican war, the work of comparatively a few individuals using the standing government as their tool;[1] for, in the outset, the people would not have consented to this measure.

This American government,—what is it but a tradition, though a recent one, endeavoring to transmit itself unimpaired to posterity, but each instant losing some of its integrity? It has not the vitality and force of a single living man; for a single man can bend it to his will. It is a sort of wooden gun to the people themselves. But it is not the less necessary for this; for the people must have some complicated machinery or other, and hear its din, to satisfy that idea of government which they have. Governments show thus how successfully men can be imposed on, even impose on themselves, for their own advantage. It is excellent, we must all allow. Yet this government never of itself furthered any enterprise, but by the alacrity with which it got out of its way. *It* does not keep the country free. *It* does not settle the West. *It* does not educate. The character inherent in the American people has done all that has been accomplished; and it would have done somewhat more, if the government had not sometimes got in its way. For government is an expedient by which men would fain succeed in letting one another alone; and, as has been said, when it is most expedient, the governed are most let alone by it. Trade and commerce, if they were not made of India-rubber, would never manage to bounce over the obstacles which legislators are continually putting in their way; and, if one were to judge these men wholly by the effects of their actions and not partly by their intentions, they would deserve to be classed and punished with those mischievous persons who put obstructions on the railroads.

But, to speak practically and as a citizen, unlike those who call themselves no-government men, I ask for, not at once no government, but *at once* a better government. Let every man make known what kind of government would command his respect, and that will be one step toward obtaining it.

After all, the practical reason why, when the power is once in the hands of the people, a majority are permitted, and for a long period continue, to rule is not because they are most likely to be in the right, nor because this seems fairest to the minority, but because they are physically the strongest. But a government in which the majority rule in all cases cannot be based on justice, even as far as men understand it. Can there not be a government in which majorities do not virtually decide right and wrong, but conscience?—in which majorities decide only those questions to which the rule of expediency is applicable? Must the citizen ever for a moment, or in the least degree, resign his conscience to the legislator? Why has every man a conscience, then? I think that we should be men first, and subjects afterward. It is not desirable to cultivate a respect for the law, so much as for the right. The only obligation which I have a right to assume is to do at any time what I think right. . . .

It is not a man's duty, as a matter of course,

1. *Mexican war . . . tool.* The Mexican War (1846–1848) ended with the United States taking half of Mexico, which became the Southwestern states. Northern abolitionists blamed the war on the desire of Southern planters and Northern merchants to enlarge slave territory.

to devote himself to the eradication of any, even the most enormous wrong; he may still properly have other concerns to engage him; but it is his duty, at least, to wash his hands of it, and, if he gives it no thought longer, not to give it practically his support. If I devote myself to other pursuits and contemplations, I must first see, at least, that I do not pursue them sitting upon another man's shoulders. I must get off him first, that he may pursue his contemplations too. See what gross inconsistency is tolerated. I have heard some of my townsmen say, "I should like to have them order me out to help put down an insurrection of the slaves, or to march to Mexico;—see if I would go"; and yet these very men have each, directly by their allegiance, and so indirectly, at least, by their money, furnished a substitute. The soldier is applauded who refuses to serve in an unjust war by those who do not refuse to sustain the unjust government which makes the war; is applauded by those whose own act and authority he disregards and sets at naught; as if the state were penitent to that degree that it hired one to scourge it while it sinned, but not to that degree that it left off sinning for a moment. Thus, under the name of Order and Civil Government, we are all made at last to pay homage to and support our own meanness. After the first blush of sin comes its indifference; and from immoral it becomes, as it were, *unmoral,* and not quite unnecessary to that life which we have made. . . .

If the injustice is part of the necessary friction of the machine of government, let it go, let it go: perchance it will wear smooth,—certainly the machine will wear out. If the injustice has a spring, or a pulley, or a rope, or a crank, exclusively for itself, then perhaps you may consider whether the remedy will not be worse than the evil; but if it is of such a nature that it requires you to be the agent of injustice to another, then, I say, break the law. Let your life be a counter friction to stop the machine. What I have to do is to see, at any rate, that I do not lend myself to the wrong which I condemn.

As for adopting the ways which the state has provided for remedying the evil, I know not of such ways. They take too much time, and a man's life will be gone. I have other affairs to attend to. I came into this world, not chiefly to make this a good place to live in, but to live in it, be it good or bad. A man has not everything to do, but something; and because he cannot do *everything,* it is not necessary that he should do *something* wrong. It is not my business to be petitioning the Governor or the Legislature any more than it is theirs to petition me; and if they should not hear my petition, what should I do then? But in this case the state has provided no way: its very Constitution is the evil. This may seem to be harsh and stubborn and unconciliatory; but it is to treat with the utmost kindness and consideration the only spirit that can appreciate or deserves it. So is all change for the better, like birth and death, which convulse the body.

I do not hesitate to say, that those who call themselves Abolitionists should at once effectually withdraw their support, both in person and property, from the government of Massachusetts, and not wait till they constitute a majority of one, before they suffer the right to prevail through them. I think that it is enough if they have God on their side, without waiting for that other one. Moreover, any man more right than his neighbors constitutes a majority of one already.

I meet this American government, or its representative, the state government, directly, and face to face, once a year—no more—in the person of its tax-gatherer; this is the only mode in which a man situated as I am necessarily meets it; and it then says distinctly, Recognize me; and the simplest, the most effectual, and, in the present posture of affairs, the indispensablest mode of treating with it on this head, of expressing your little satisfaction with and love for it is to deny it then. My civil neighbor, the tax-gatherer, is the very man I have to deal with, —for it is, after all, with men and not with parchment that I quarrel,—and he has voluntarily chosen to be an agent of the government. How shall he ever know well what he is and does as an officer of the government, or as a man, until he is obliged to consider whether he shall treat me, his neighbor, for whom he has respect, as a neighbor and well-disposed man, or as a maniac and disturber of the peace, and see if he can get over this obstruction to his neighborliness without a ruder and more impetuous thought or speech

corresponding with his action. I know this well, that if one thousand, if one hundred, if ten men whom I could name,—if ten *honest* men only, —ay, if *one* HONEST man, in this State of Massachusetts, *ceasing to hold slaves,* were actually to withdraw from this copartnership, and be locked up in the county jail therefore, it would be the abolition of slavery in America. For it matters not how small the beginning may seem to be: what is once well done is done forever. . . .

I have paid no poll-tax for six years. I was put into a jail once on this account, for one night; and, as I stood considering the walls of solid stone, two or three feet thick, the door of wood and iron, a foot thick, and the iron grating which strained the light, I could not help being struck with the foolishness of that institution which treated me as if I were mere flesh and blood and bones, to be locked up. I wondered that it should have concluded at length that this was the best use it could put me to, and had never thought to avail itself of my services in some way. I saw that, if there was a wall of stone between me and

my townsmen, there was a still more difficult one to climb or break through before they could get to be as free as I was. I did not for a moment feel confined, and the walls seemed a great waste of stone and mortar. I felt as if I alone of all my townsmen had paid my tax. They plainly did not know how to treat me, but behaved like persons who are underbred. In every threat and in every compliment there was a blunder; for they thought that my chief desire was to stand the other side of that stone wall. I could not but smile to see how industriously they locked the door on my meditations, which followed them out again without let or hindrance, and *they* were really all that was dangerous. As they could not reach me, they had resolved to punish my body; just as boys, if they cannot come at some person against whom they have a spite, will abuse his dog. I saw that the State was half-witted, that it was timid as a lone woman with her silver spoons, and that it did not know its friends from its foes, and I lost all my remaining respect for it, and pitied it. . . .

When I came out of prison,—for some one

interfered, and paid that tax,[2] —I did not perceive that great changes had taken place on the common, such as he observed who went in a youth and emerged a tottering and gray-headed man; and yet a change had to my eyes come over the scene,—the town, and State, and country, —greater than any that mere time could effect. I saw yet more distinctly the State in which I lived. I saw to what extent the people among whom I lived could be trusted as good neighbors and friends; that their friendship was for summer weather only; that they did not greatly propose to do right; that they were a distinct race from me by their prejudices and superstitions, as the Chinamen and Malays are; that in their sacrifices to humanity they ran no risks, not even to their property; that after all they were not so noble but they treated the thief as he had treated them, and hoped, by a certain outward observance and a few prayers, and by walking in a particular straight though useless path from time to time, to save their souls. This may be to judge my neighbors harshly; for I believe that many of them are not aware that they have such an institution as the jail in their village. . . .

If others pay the tax which is demanded of me, from a sympathy with the State, they do but what they have already done in their own case, or rather they abet injustice to a greater extent than the State requires. If they pay the tax from a mistaken interest in the individual taxed, to save his property, or prevent his going to jail, it is because they have not considered wisely how far they let their private feelings interfere with the public good. . . .

The authority of government, even such as I am willing to submit to,—for I will cheerfully obey those who know and can do better than I, and in many things even those who neither know nor can do so well,—is still an impure one: to be strictly just, it must have the sanction and consent of the governed. It can have no pure right over my person and property but what I conceded to it. The progress from an absolute to a limited monarchy, from a limited monarchy to a democracy, is a progress toward a true respect for the individual. Even the Chinese philosopher[3] was wise enough to regard the individual as the basis of the empire. Is a democracy, such as we know it, the last improvement possible in government? Is it not possible to take a step further towards recognizing and organizing the rights of man? There will never be a really free and enlightened State until the State comes to recognize the individual as a higher and independent power, from which all its own power and authority are derived, and treats him accordingly. I please myself with imagining a State at last which can afford to be just to all men, and to treat the individual with respect as a neighbor; which even would not think it inconsistent with its own repose if a few were to live aloof from it, not meddling with it, nor embraced by it, who fulfilled all the duties of neighbors and fellowmen. A State which bore this kind of fruit, and suffered it to drop off as fast as it ripened, would prepare the way for a still more perfect and glorious State, which also I have imagined, but not yet anywhere seen. □□

2. *some one . . . tax.* According to legend, Ralph Waldo Emerson paid the tax, but according to Thoreau family reminiscence, it was paid by Thoreau's Aunt Maria.
3. *Chinese philospher,* Confucius (?551–478 B.C.), whose ethical teachings emphasize dutiful obedience by individuals to their parents, elders, and the state.

Discussion

1. What similarities, if any, exist between Thoreau's attitude toward government and Emerson's philosophy in "A Nonconformist" (p. 226)? Support your answer with lines from both essays.

2. Thoreau presents his reader with two major justifications for civil disobedience. What are these justifications? Support your answer with lines from the text.

3. (a) Do you think any of Thoreau's points apply to current situations? Explain. (b) Do you think that the attitude of most people toward law and government has changed since Thoreau's time? If so, give examples.

Choose any one of the quotations below as the topic for a personal essay. In writing your essay, keep in mind Thoreau's technique of using concrete examples to make abstract philosophical points both clear and interesting.

1. "Rather than love, than money, than fame, give me truth."

2. "Our life is frittered away by detail."

3. "We do not ride on the railroad; it rides upon us."

4. "If a man does not keep pace with his companions, perhaps it is because he hears a different drummer."

5. "There is an incessant influx of novelty into the world, and yet we tolerate incredible dullness."

6. "Under a government which imprisons any unjustly the true place for a just man is also a prison."

Thoreau presents a tightly constructed argument in his essay on civil disobedience. To follow the argument closely, the reader must know the vocabulary Thoreau is using in order to understand the meaning of each sentence.

Check the Glossary for the definitions of the italicized words in the sentences below. Then, using your own words entirely, write a paraphrase of each passage. Be sure you can spell all the italicized words.

1. "Government is at best but an *expedient;* but most governments are usually, and all governments are sometimes, *inexpedient.*"

2. "Yet this government never of itself furthered any enterprise, but by the *alacrity* with which it got out of its way. . . . The character *inherent* in the American people has done all that has been accomplished; and it would have done somewhat more, if the government had not sometimes got in its way."

3. "It is not a man's duty, as a matter of course, to devote himself to the *eradication* of any, even the most enormous wrong. . . ."

4. "The soldier is applauded who refuses to serve in an unjust war by those who do not refuse to sustain the unjust government which makes the war . . . as if the state were *penitent* to that degree that it hired one to *scourge* it while it sinned, but not to that degree that it left off sinning for a moment."

Henry David Thoreau
1817 • 1862

Though generally liked by most of the Concord townspeople, Thoreau was considered something of an eccentric. A Harvard graduate, he nonetheless spent his life walking the woods, making pencils in the family business, working occasionally as a handyman, and seeming to cherish idleness. In the eyes of his contemporaries, Henry David Thoreau had not amounted to much.

But Thoreau acted out the dictates of his conscience with a determination unsettling to more cautious lives. While Emerson and most others were holding themselves aloof from the slavery problem, Thoreau was helping runaway slaves escape to Canada. When others advised caution, Thoreau became the first American to speak in defense of John Brown. It is said when Emerson visited Thoreau on his day in jail and asked, "Henry, why are you here?" Thoreau answered, "Waldo, why are you not here?"

Thoreau was raised in Concord and lived most of his life there, extolling its virtues and proclaiming it a microcosm of the world. He was strongly influenced by Emerson, but as the years passed, the friendship between them waned because of differing values and expectations.

At the age of twenty-eight, in 1845, Thoreau began his stay at Walden Pond. His retreat there allowed him the time for introspection, nature study, and writing. The journals he wrote would result in *Walden.* In addition, he completed the rough draft of his first book: *A Week on the Concord and Merrimack Rivers.*

Thoreau died from tuberculosis at the age of forty-four. A few hours before his death an aunt asked if he had "made his peace with God." Thoreau replied, "I have never quarreled with Him."

Harriet Robinson: from Loom and Spindle

Although the mid-nineteenth century saw the flowering of American literature, it also saw the development of industries with factories in which the workers labored long hours for low pay at demanding jobs. In her autobiographical work, Loom and Spindle, or Life Among the Early Mill Girls, *Harriet Robinson has provided a vivid account of the women working in the Lowell, Massachusetts, cotton mills.*

At the time the Lowell cotton-mills were started, the factory girl was the lowest among women. In England, and in France particularly, great injustice had been done to her real character; she was represented as subjected to influences that could not fail to destroy her purity and self-respect. In the eyes of her overseer she was but a brute, a slave, to be beaten, pinched, and pushed about. It was to overcome this prejudice that such high wages had been offered to women that they might be induced to become mill-girls, in spite of the opprobrium that still clung to this "degrading occupation." At first only a few came; for, though tempted by the high wages to be regularly paid in "cash," there were many who still preferred to go on working at some more *genteel* employment at seventy-five cents a week and their board.

But in a short time the prejudice against factory labor wore away, and the Lowell mills became filled with blooming and energetic New England women.

One of the first strikes of cotton-factory operatives that ever took place in this country was that in Lowell, in October, 1836. When it was announced that the wages were to be cut down, great indignation was felt, and it was decided to strike, *en masse.*[1] This was done. The mills were shut down, and the girls went in procession from their several corporations to the "grove" on Chapel Hill, and listened to "incendiary" speeches from early labor reformers.

One of the girls stood on a pump, and gave vent to the feelings of her companions in a neat speech, declaring that it was their duty to resist all attempts at cutting down the wages. This was the first time a woman had spoken in public in Lowell, and the event caused surprise and consternation among her audience.

Cutting down the wages was not their only grievance, nor the only cause of the strike. Hitherto the corporations had paid twenty-five cents a week towards the board of each operative, and now it was their purpose to have the girls pay the sum; and this, in addition to the cut in wages, would make a difference of at least one dollar a week. It was estimated that as many as twelve or fifteen hundred girls turned out, and walked in procession through the streets. They had neither flags nor music, but sang songs, a favorite (but rather inappropriate) one being a parody on "I won't be a nun."

"Oh! isn't it a pity, such a pretty
    girl as I—
Should be sent to the factory to
    pine away and die?
Oh! I cannot be a slave,
I will not be a slave.
For I'm so fond of liberty
That I cannot be a slave."

My own recollection of this first strike (or "turn out" as it was called) is very vivid. I worked in a lower room, where I had heard the proposed strike fully, if not vehemently, discussed; I had been an ardent listener to what was said against this attempt at "oppression" on the part of the corporation, and naturally I took sides with the strikers. When the day came on which the girls were to turn out, those in the upper rooms started first, and so many of them left that our

Portions of LOOM AND SPINDLE, Revised Edition, Copyright © 1976 by Press Pacifica, are reprinted by permission of Press Pacifica, Kailua, Hawaii.
1. *en masse* (en mas′), all together. [*French*]

mill was at once shut down. Then, when the girls in my room stood irresolute, uncertain what to do, asking each other, "Would you?" or "Shall we turn out?" and not one of them having the courage to lead off, I, who began to think they would not go out, after all their talk, became impatient, and started on ahead, saying, with childish bravado, "I don't care what you do, *I* am going to turn out, whether any one else does or not;" and I marched out, and was followed by the others.

As I looked back at the long line that followed me, I was more proud than I have ever been since at any success I may have achieved, and more proud than I shall ever be again until my own beloved State gives to its women citizens the right of suffrage.

The agent of the corporation where I then worked took some small revenges on the supposed ringleaders; on the principle of sending the weaker to the wall, my mother was turned away from her boarding-house, that functionary saying, "Mrs. Hanson, you could not prevent the older girls from turning out, but your daughter is a child, and *her* you could control."

It is hardly necessary to say that so far as results were concerned this strike did no good. The dissatisfaction of the operatives subsided, or burned itself out, and though the authorities did not accede to their demands, the majority returned to their work, and the corporation went on cutting down the wages.

One of the most curious

The Bettmann Archive, Inc.

phases in the life of New England, and one that must always puzzle the historian of its literature, is its sudden intellectual blossoming half a century ago.

Emerson says, "The children of New England between 1820 and 1840 were born with knives in their brains;" and this would seem to be true, since during or very near that time, were born the majority of those writers and thinkers whose lives have been so recently and so nobly rounded out,—Emerson, Bryant, Longfellow, Lowell, Whittier, John Pierpont,—they whose influence cannot be overestimated in bringing an ideal element into our hitherto prosaic New England life.

And the "literary" girls among us would often be seen writing on scraps of paper which we hid "between whiles" in the waste-boxes upon which we sat while waiting for the looms or frames to need attention. Some of these studious ones kept note-books, with abstracts of their reading and studies, or jotted down what they were pleased to call their "thoughts." It was natural that such a thoughtful life should bear fruit, and this leads me to speak of *The Lowell Offering*, a publication which was the natural outgrowth of the mental habit of the early mill-girls, for many of the pieces that were printed there were thought out amid the hum of the wheels, while the skilful fingers and well-trained eyes of the writers tended the loom or the frame.

The Lowell Offering was a small, thin magazine of about thirty pages, with one column to the page. The price of the first number was six and a quarter cents. Its title-page was plain, with a motto from Gray;[2] the verse beginning:—

"Full many a gem of purest ray serene."

This motto was used for two years, when another was adopted:—

"Is Saul also among the prophets?"[3]

---

2. *Gray,* Thomas Gray (1716–1771), an English poet best known for his odes and elegies.
3. *"Is Saul also among the prophets?"* a Biblical allusion to the first king of Israel, who was called to leadership by the prophet Samuel. (I Samuel 10:11).

In January, 1845, the magazine had on its outside cover a vignette, a young girl simply dressed, with feet visible and sleeves rolled up. She had a book in one hand, and her shawl and bonnet were thrown over her arm. She was represented as standing in a very sentimental attitude, contemplating a beehive at her right hand. This vignette was adopted, as the editor said, "To represent the New England school-girl, of which our factories are made up, standing near a beehive, emblem of industry and intelligence, and in the background the Yankee schoolhouse, church, and factory." The motto was:—

"The worm on the earth
May look up to the star."

This rather abject sentiment was not suited to the independent spirit of most of the contributors, who did not feel a bit like worms; and in the February number it was changed to one from Bunyan:—[4]

"And do you think the words of your book are certainly true?"
"Yea, verily."

The magazine finally died, however, under its favorite motto:—

"Is Saul also among the prophets?"

The contributions to *The Offering* were on a great variety of subjects. There were allegories, poems, conversations on physiology, astronomy, and other scientific subjects, dissertations on poetry, and on the beauties of nature, didactic pieces on highly moral and religious subjects, translations from French and Latin, stories of factory and other life, sketches of local New England history, and sometimes the chapters of a novel. Miss Curtis, in 1840, wrote an article on "Woman's Rights," in which were so many familiar arguments in favor of the equality of the sexes, that it might have been the production of the pen of almost any modern advocate of woman's rights; but there was this difference, that the writer, though she felt sure of her ground, was too timid to

maintain it against the world, and towards the end throws out the query, "whether public life is, after all, woman's most appropriate and congenial sphere?"

These authors represent what may be called the poetic element of factory-life. They were the ideal mill-girls, full of hopes, desires, aspirations; poets of the loom, spinners of verse, artists of factory-life.

The Lowell Offering did a good work, not only among the operatives themselves, but among the rural population from which they had been drawn. It was almost the only magazine that reached their secluded homes, where it was lent from house to house, read and re-read, and thus set the women to thinking, and added its little leaven of progressive thought to the times in which it lived.

---

4. **Bunyan,** John Bunyan (1628–1688), an English writer whose most famous work, *The Pilgrim's Progress,* is an allegorical account of the attainment of heaven.

Discussion

1. From her actions during the strike, what particular qualities did the author demonstrate?

2. Based on the author's description of *The Lowell Offering,* what was the intellectual level of the women who worked at the Lowell Mills? Give examples to support your answer.

Harriet Hanson Robinson
1825 • 1911

A leader of the women's movement of the nineteenth century, Harriet Robinson began to work in the Lowell Mills after finishing school. She contributed to *The Lowell Offering,* a periodical edited by and for women working in the mills. She and her husband, a journalist, campaigned against

slavery and for women's rights and reform of factory working conditions. Her writing in support of these causes was very influential and included the plays, *Captain Mary Miller* (1887), and *The New Pandora* (1889). Her most notable work is *Loom and Spindle, or Life Among the Early Mill Girls* (1898).

Louisa May Alcott

Louisa May Alcott's father, Bronson Alcott, established Fruitlands at Harvard, Massachusetts, in 1842, as a cooperative family community. Although the experiment soon failed, the young Louisa May described in this diary many of Fruitlands' aspirations as well as her own exuberant experiences.

from Early Diary Kept at Fruitlands

Ten Years Old

September 1*st.*—I rose at five and had my bath. I love cold water! Then we had our singing-lesson with Mr. Lane. After breakfast I washed dishes, and ran on the hill till nine, and had some thoughts,—it was so beautiful up there. Did my lessons,—wrote and spelt and did sums; and Mr. Lane read a story, "The Judicious Father": How a rich girl told a poor girl not to look over the fence at the flowers, and was cross to her because she was unhappy. The father heard her do it, and made the girls change clothes. The poor one was glad to do it, and he told her to keep them. But the rich one was very sad; for she had to wear the old ones a week, and after that she was good to shabby girls. I liked it very much, and I shall be kind to poor people.

Father asked us what was God's noblest work. Anna said *men,* but I said *babies.* Men are often bad; babies never are. We had a long talk, and I felt better after it, and *cleared up.*

We had bread and fruit for dinner. I read and walked and played till supper-time. We sung in the evening. As I went to bed the moon came up very brightly and looked at me. I felt sad because I have been cross today, and did not mind Mother. I cried, and then I felt better, and said that piece from Mrs. Sigourney,[1] "I must not tease my mother." I get to sleep saying poetry,—I know a great deal.

Thursday, 11*th.*—Mr. Parker Pillsbury[2] came, and we talked about the poor slaves. I had a music lesson with Miss P. I hate her, she is so fussy. I ran in the wind and played be a horse, and had a lovely time in the woods with Anna and Lizzie. We were fairies, and made gowns and paper wings. I "flied" the highest of all. In the evening they talked about travelling. I thought about Father going to England, and said this piece of poetry I found in Byron's[3] poems:—

"When I left thy shores, O Naxos,
  Not a tear in sorrow fell;
Not a sigh or faltered accent
  Told my bosom's struggling swell."

It rained when I went to bed, and made a pretty noise on the roof.

Sunday, 21*st.*—Father and Mr. Lane have gone to N. H. to preach. It was very lovely. . . . Anna and I got supper. In the eve I read "Vicar of Wakefield."[4] I was cross to-day, and I cried when I went to bed. I made good resolutions, and felt better in my heart. If I only *kept* all I make, I should be the best girl in the world. But I don't, and so am very bad.

From EARLY DIARY KEPT AT FRUITLANDS, 1843–46 by Louisa May Alcott in LOUISA MAY ALCOTT: HER LIFE, LETTERS AND JOURNALS, edited by Ednah D. Cheney. Boston: Roberts Brothers, 1889.

1. *Mrs. Sigourney* (sig′ėr nə). Lydia Howard Sigourney (1791-1865) was a popular writer.
2. *Mr. Parker Pillsbury,* (1809-1898), a leading abolitionist and supporter of women's suffrage.
3. *Byron's,* George Gordon, Lord Byron (1788-1824), English Romantic poet.
4. *"Vicar of Wakefield,"* a novel by Oliver Goldsmith, published in 1766.

The Alcott home, Concord, Mass.
(Milton Feinberg/Stock, Boston, Inc.)

October 8th.—When I woke up, the first thought I got was, "It's Mother's birthday: I must be very good." I ran and wished her a happy birthday, and gave her my kiss. After breakfast we gave her our presents. I had a moss cross and a piece of poetry for her.

We did not have any school, and played in the woods and got red leaves. In the evening we danced and sung, and I read a story about "Contentment." I wish I was rich, I was good, and we were all a happy family this day.

Tuesday, 12th.—After lessons I ironed. We all went to the barn and husked corn. It was good fun. We worked till eight o'clock and had lamps. Mr. Russell[5] came. Mother and Lizzie are going to Boston. I shall be very lonely without dear little Betty, and no one will be as good to me as Mother. I read in Plutarch.[6] I made a verse about sunset:—

Softly doth the sun descend
    To his couch behind the hill,
Then, oh, then, I love to sit
    On mossy banks beside the rill.

Anna thought it was very fine; but I didn't like it very well.

Friday, Nov. 2nd.—Anna and I did the work. In the evening Mr. Lane asked us, "What is man?" These were our answers: A human being; an animal with a mind; a creature; a body; a soul and a mind. After a long talk we went to bed very tired.

A sample of the vegetarian wafers[7] we used at Fruitlands:—

Vegetable diet
and sweet repose.
Animal food and
nightmare.

Pluck your body
from the orchard;
do not snatch it
from the shamble.

Without flesh diet
there could be no
blood-shedding war.

Apollo[8] eats no
flesh and has no
beard; his voice is
melody itself.

Snuff is no less snuff
though accepted from
a gold box.

Tuesday, 20th.—I rose at five, and after breakfast washed the dishes, and then helped Mother work. Miss P. is gone, and Anna in Boston with Cousin Louisa. I took care of Abby (May) in the afternoon. In the evening I made some pretty things for my dolly. Father and Mr. L. had a talk, and Father asked us if *we* saw any reason for us to separate. Mother wanted to, she is so tired. I like it, but not the school part or Mr. L.

Eleven Years Old

Thursday, 29th.—It was Father's and my birthday. We had some nice presents. We played in the snow before school. Mother read "Rosamond"[9] when we sewed. Father asked us in the eve what fault troubled us most. I said my bad temper.

I told Mother I liked to have her write in my book. She said she would put in more, and she wrote this to help me:—

DEAR LOUY,—Your handwriting improves very fast. Take pains and do not be in a hurry. I like to have you make observations about our conversations and your own thoughts. It helps you to express them and to understand your little self. Remember, dear girl, that a diary should be an epitome of your life. May it be a record of pure thought and good actions, then you will indeed be the precious child of your loving mother.

[*January,* 1845], *Wednesday.*—I am so cross I wish I had never been born.

---

5. *Mr. Russell,* William Russell (1798–1873), a prominent teacher and educational writer and reformer.
6. *Plutarch* (plü′tärk), a famous Greek biographer (?46–120?).
7. *vegetarian wafers,* thin adhesive disks used to seal envelopes. Mottoes advocating vegetarian diet were printed on the Fruitlands stickers.
8. *Apollo* (ə pol′ō), in Greek mythology, the son of Zeus and god of light, music, and poetry.
9. *"Rosamond"* (roz′ə mənd), heroine of a popular English legend.

Thursday.—Read the "Heart of Mid-Lothian,"[10] and had a very happy day. Miss Ford gave us a botany lesson in the woods. I am always good there. In the evening Miss Ford told us about the bones in our bodies, and how they get out of order. I must be careful of mine, I climb and jump and run so much.

I found this note from dear Mother in my journal:—

My Dearest Louy,—I often peep into your diary, hoping to see some record of more happy days. "Hope, and keep busy," dear daughter, and in all perplexity or trouble come freely to your
                                                        Mother.

Dear Mother,—You *shall* see more happy days, and I *will* come to you with my worries, for you are the best woman in the world.
                                                        L. M. A.

A Sample of our Lessons.

"What virtues do you wish more of?" asks Mr. L.
I answer:—

Patience,
Obedience,
Industry,

     Love,
     Generosity,
     Respect,

          Silence,
          Perseverance,
          Self-denial.

"What vices less of?"

Idleness,
Impatience,
Selfishness,

     Wilfulness,
     Impudence,
     Activity,

          Vanity,
          Pride,
          Love of cats.

MR. LANE (SOCRATES): How can you get what you need?
LOUISA (ALCIBIADES[11]): By trying.
MR. L: How do you try?
L: By resolution and perseverance.
MR. L: How gain love?
L: By gentleness.
MR. L: What is gentleness?
L: Kindness, patience, and care for other people's feelings.
MR. L: Who has it?
L: Father and Anna.
MR. L: Who means to have it?
L: Louisa, if she can.
MR. L: Write a sentence about anything.
L: "I hope it will rain; the garden needs it."
MR. L: What are the elements of *hope?*
L: Expectation, desire, faith.
MR. L: What are the elements in *wish?*
L: Desire.
MR. L: What is the difference between faith and hope?
L: "Faith can believe without seeing; hope is not sure, but tries to have faith when it desires."
MR. L: What are the most valuable kinds of self-denial?
L: Appetite, temper.
MR. L: How is self-denial of temper known?
L: If I control my temper, I am respectful and gentle, and every one sees it.
MR. L: What is the result of this self-denial?
L: Every one loves me, and I am happy.
MR. L: Why use self-denial?
L: For the good of myself and others.
MR. L: How shall we learn this self-denial?
L: By resolving, and then trying *hard.*
MR. L: What then do you mean to do?
L: To resolve and try.

---

10. *"Heart of Midlothian"* (mid lō′thē ən), a novel by the Scottish writer Sir Walter Scott (1771–1832).
11. *Socrates* (sok′rə tēz′). . . . *Alcibiades* (al′sə bi′ə dēz′). Socrates (c. 469–399 B.C.) was a Greek philosopher and Alcibiades (c. 450–404 B.C.) an Athenian nobleman. In Socrates' dialogues, one of which was with Alcibiades, the philosopher would teach by questioning his student, as Mr. Lane here questions Louisa.

Thirteen Years Old

FRUITLANDS.

March, 1846,—I have at last got the little room I have wanted so long, and am very happy about it. It does me good to be alone, and Mother has made it very pretty and neat for me. My work-basket and desk are by the window, and my closet is full of dried herbs that smell very nice. The door that opens into the garden will be very pretty in summer, and I can run off to the woods when I like.

I have made a plan for my life, as I am in my teens, and no more a child. I am old for my age, and don't care much for girl's things. People think I'm wild and queer; but Mother understands and helps me. I have not told any one about my plan; but I'm going to *be* good. I've made so many resolutions, and written sad notes, and cried over my sins, and it doesn't seem to do any good! Now I'm going to *work really,* for I feel a true desire to improve, and be a help and comfort, not a care and sorrow, to my dear mother. ▢▢

Discussion

1. Judging solely from her diary, what kind of personality do you imagine Louisa May Alcott had as a young girl? Support your answers by citing specific passages.

2. The diary presents a sample of the school lessons Louisa May had. How did her education at her age differ from yours at the same age?

Extension • Writing

Note the thrill expressed by Louisa May Alcott in having her own room (entry of March, 1846). Reread her account, and then write a short essay expressing your ideas on everyone's need for occasional solitude and ways in which this need might be met.

Louisa May Alcott
1832 • 1888

When Louisa May Alcott published her most popular novel, *Little Women,* in 1868–1869, her characters Amy, Jo, Beth, and Meg (based mainly on personal experience) became familiar in most American households and admired by most young readers. Whatever the novel did for others, it did more for Louisa May and her family: it provided them with the financial security that had eluded Louisa's father, Bronson Alcott.

Louisa May was educated by her father (who was a great experimentalist in modern education) and by her father's friends, including Emerson, Thoreau, and other thinkers of the time. She wrote her first book at the age of sixteen. After serving as a nurse during the Civil War, she began to write and publish a series of books that became ever more popular. *Little Women* was followed by *An Old-Fashioned Girl* (1870) and *Little Men* (1871).

In spite of her success as a writer, Louisa May Alcott never lost her interest in moral and social reform. She supported various movements, including that for women's right to vote. Many of her books, like *Jo's Boys* (1886), were written especially for children, and she provided an account of her father's idealistic experiment in community living in "Transcendental Wild Oats." Probably no other writer of the time has been read as widely as Louisa May Alcott.

Nathaniel Hawthorne

The Minister's Black Veil

A Parable

The sexton stood in the porch of Milford meeting-house, pulling busily on the bell-rope. The old people of the village came stooping along the street. Children, with bright faces, tripped merrily beside their parents, or mimicked a graver gait, in the conscious dignity of their Sunday clothes. Spruce bachelors looked sidelong at the pretty maidens, and fancied that the Sabbath sunshine made them prettier than on week days. When the throng had mostly streamed into the porch, the sexton began to toll the bell, keeping his eye on the Reverend Mr. Hooper's door. The first glimpse of the clergyman's figure was the signal for the bell to cease its summons.

"But what has good Parson Hooper got upon his face?" cried the sexton in astonishment.

All within hearing immediately turned about, and beheld the semblance of Mr. Hooper, pacing slowly his meditative way towards the meeting-house. With one accord they started, expressing more wonder than if some strange minister were coming to dust the cushions of Mr. Hooper's pulpit.

"Are you sure it is our parson?" inquired Goodman Gray of the sexton.

"Of a certainty it is good Mr. Hooper," replied the sexton. "He was to have exchanged pulpits with Parson Shute, of Westbury; but Parson Shute sent to excuse himself yesterday, being to preach a funeral sermon."

The cause of so much amazement may appear sufficiently slight. Mr. Hooper, a gentlemanly person, of about thirty, though still a bachelor, was dressed with due clerical neatness, as if a careful wife had starched his band, and brushed the weekly dust from his Sunday's garb. There was but one thing remarkable in his appearance. Swathed about his forehead, and hanging down over his face, so low as to be shaken by his breath, Mr. Hooper had on a black veil. On a nearer view it seemed to consist of two folds of crape, which entirely concealed his features, except the mouth and chin, but probably did not intercept his sight, further than to give a darkened aspect to all living and inanimate things. With this gloomy shade before him, good Mr. Hooper walked onward, at a slow and quiet pace, stooping somewhat, and looking on the ground, as is customary with abstracted men, yet nodding kindly to those of his parishioners who still waited on the meeting-house steps. But so wonder-struck were they that his greeting hardly met with a return.

"I can't really feel as if good Mr. Hooper's face was behind that piece of crape," said the sexton.

"I don't like it," muttered an old woman, as she hobbled into the meeting-house. "He has changed himself into something awful, only by hiding his face."

"Our parson has gone mad!" cried Goodman Gray, following him across the threshold.

A rumor of some unaccountable phenomenon had preceded Mr. Hooper into the meeting-house, and set all the congregation astir. Few could refrain from twisting their heads towards the door; many stood upright, and turned directly about; while several little boys clambered upon the seats, and came down again with a terrible racket. There was a general bustle, a rustling of the women's gowns and shuffling of the men's feet, greatly at variance with that hushed repose which should attend the entrance of the minister. But Mr. Hooper appeared not to notice the perturbation of his people. He entered with an almost noiseless step, bent his head mildly to the pews on each side, and bowed as he passed his oldest parishioner, a white-haired great-grandsire, who occupied an armchair in the centre of the aisle. It was strange to observe how slowly this venerable man became conscious of something singular in the appearance of his pastor. He seemed not fully to partake of the prevailing wonder, till Mr. Hooper had ascended the stairs, and showed himself in the pulpit, face to face with his congregation, except for the black veil. That mysterious emblem was never once withdrawn. It shook with his measured breath, as he gave out the psalm; it threw its obscurity between him and the holy page, as he read the Scriptures; and while he prayed, the veil lay heavily on his uplifted countenance. Did he seek to hide it from the dread Being whom he was addressing?

Such was the effect of this simple piece of crape, that more than one woman of delicate nerves was forced to leave the meeting-house. Yet perhaps the pale-faced congregation was almost as fearful a sight to the minister, as his black veil to them.

Mr. Hooper had the reputation of a good preacher, but not an energetic one: he strove to win his people heavenward by mild, persuasive influences, rather than to drive them thither by the thunders of the Word. The sermon which he now delivered was marked by the same characteristics of style and manner as the general series of his pulpit oratory. But there was something, either in the sentiment of the discourse itself, or in the imagination of the auditors, which made it greatly the most powerful effort that they had ever heard from their pastor's lips. It was tinged, rather more darkly than usual, with the gentle gloom of Mr. Hooper's temperament. The subject had reference to secret sin, and those sad mysteries which we hide from our nearest and dearest, and would fain conceal from our own consciousness, even forgetting that the Omniscient can detect them. A subtle power was breathed into his words. Each member of the congregation, the most innocent girl, and the man of hardened breast, felt as if the preacher had crept upon them, behind his awful veil, and discovered their hoarded iniquity of deed or thought. Many spread their clasped hands on their bosoms. There was nothing terrible in what Mr. Hooper said, at least, no violence; and yet, with every tremor of his melancholy voice, the hearers quaked. An unsought pathos came hand in hand with awe. So sensible were the audience of some unwonted attribute in their minister, that they longed for a breath of wind to blow aside the veil, almost believing that a stranger's visage would be discovered, though the form, gesture, and voice were those of Mr. Hooper.

At the close of the services, the people hurried out with indecorous confusion, eager to communicate their pent-up amazement, and conscious of lighter spirits the moment they lost sight of the black veil. Some gathered in little circles, huddled closely together, with their mouths all whispering in the centre; some went homeward alone, wrapt in silent meditation; some talked loudly, and profaned the Sabbath day with ostentatious laughter. A few shook their sagacious heads, intimating that they could penetrate the mystery; while one or two affirmed that there was no mystery at all, but only that Mr. Hooper's eyes were so weakened by the midnight lamp, as to require a shade. After a brief interval, forth came good Mr. Hooper also, in the rear of his flock. Turning his veiled face from one group to another, he paid due reverence to the hoary heads, saluted the middle aged with kind dignity as their friend and spiritual guide, greeted the young with mingled authority and love, and laid his hands on the little children's heads to bless them. Such was always his custom on the Sabbath day. Strange and bewildered looks repaid him for his courtesy. None, as on former occasions, aspired to the honor of walking by their pastor's side. Old Squire Saunders, doubtless by an accidental lapse of memory, neglected to invite Mr. Hooper to his table, where the good clergyman had been wont to bless the food, almost every Sunday since his settlement. He returned, therefore, to the parsonage, and, at the moment of closing the door, was observed to look back upon the people, all of whom had their eyes fixed upon the minister. A sad smile gleamed faintly from beneath the black veil, and flickered about his mouth, glimmering as he disappeared.

"How strange," said a lady, "that a simple black veil, such as any woman might wear on her bonnet, should become such a terrible thing on Mr. Hooper's face!"

"Something must surely be amiss with Mr. Hooper's intellects," observed her husband, the physician of the village. "But the strangest part of the affair is the effect of this vagary, even on a sober-minded man like myself. The black veil, though it covers only our pastor's face, throws its influence over his whole person, and makes him ghost-like from head to foot. Do you not feel it so?"

"Truly do I," replied the lady; "and I would not be alone with him for the world. I wonder he is not afraid to be alone with himself!"

"Men sometimes are so," said her husband.

The afternoon service was attended with similar circumstances. At its conclusion, the bell tolled for the funeral of a young lady. The relatives and friends were assembled in the house, and the more distant acquaintances stood about the door, speaking of the good qualities of the deceased, when their talk was interrupted by the appearance of Mr. Hooper, still covered with his black veil. It was now an appropriate emblem. The clergyman stepped into the room where the corpse was laid, and bent over the coffin, to take a last farewell of his deceased parishioner. As he stooped, the veil hung straight down from his forehead, so that, if her eyelids had not been closed forever, the dead maiden might have seen his face. Could Mr. Hooper be fearful of her glance, that he so hastily caught back the black veil? A person who watched the interview between the dead and living, scrupled not to affirm, that, at the instant when the clergyman's features were disclosed, the corpse had slightly shuddered, rustling the shroud and muslin cap, though the countenance retained the composure of death. A superstitious old woman was the only witness of this prodigy. From the coffin Mr. Hooper passed into the chamber of the mourners, and thence to the head of the staircase, to make the funeral prayer. It was a tender and heart-dissolving prayer, full of sorrow, yet so imbued with celestial hopes, that the music of a heavenly harp, swept by the fingers of the dead, seemed faintly to be heard among the saddest accents of the minister. The people trembled, though they but darkly understood him when he prayed that they, and himself, and all of mortal race, might be ready, as he trusted this young maiden had been, for the dreadful hour that should snatch the veil from their faces. The bearers went heavily forth, and the mourners followed, saddening all the street, with the dead before them, and Mr. Hooper in his black veil behind.

"Why do you look back?" said one in the procession to his partner.

"I had a fancy," replied she, "that the minister and the maiden's spirit were walking hand in hand."

"And so had I, at the same moment," said the other.

That night, the handsomest couple in Milford village were to be joined in wedlock. Though reckoned a melancholy man, Mr. Hooper had a placid cheerfulness for such occasions, which often excited a sympathetic smile where livelier merriment would have been thrown away. There was no quality of his disposition which made him more beloved than this. The company at the wedding awaited his arrival with impatience, trusting that the strange awe, which had gathered over him throughout the day, would now be dispelled. But such was not the result. When Mr. Hooper came, the first thing that their eyes rested on was the same horrible black veil, which had added deeper gloom to the funeral, and could portend nothing but evil to the wedding. Such was its immediate effect on the guests that a cloud seemed to have rolled duskily from beneath the black crape, and dimmed the light of the candles. The bridal pair stood up before the minister. But the bride's cold fingers quivered in the tremulous hand of the bridegroom, and her deathlike paleness caused a whisper that the maiden who had been buried a few hours before was come from her grave to be married. If ever another wedding were so dismal, it was that famous one where they tolled the wedding knell. After performing the ceremony, Mr. Hooper raised a glass of wine to his lips, wishing happiness to the new-married couple in a strain of mild pleasantry that ought to have brightened the features of the guests, like a cheerful gleam from the hearth. At that instant, catching a glimpse of his figure in the looking-glass, the black veil involved his own spirit in the horror with which it overwhelmed all others. His frame shuddered, his lips grew white, he spilt the untasted wine upon the carpet, and rushed forth into the darkness. For the Earth, too, had on her Black Veil.

The next day, the whole village of Milford talked of little else than Parson Hooper's black veil. That, and the mystery concealed behind it, supplied a topic for discussion between ac-

quaintances meeting in the street, and good women gossiping at their open windows. It was the first item of news that the tavernkeeper told to his guests. The children babbled of it on their way to school. One imitative little imp covered his face with an old black handkerchief, thereby so affrighting his playmates that the panic seized himself, and he well-nigh lost his wits by his own waggery.

It was remarkable that of all the busybodies and impertinent people in the parish, not one ventured to put the plain question to Mr. Hooper, wherefore he did this thing. Hitherto, whenever there appeared the slightest call for such interference, he had never lacked advisers, nor shown himself averse to be guided by their judgment. If he erred at all, it was by so painful a degree of self-distrust, that even the mildest censure would lead him to consider an indifferent action as a crime. Yet, though so well acquainted with this amiable weakness, no individual among his parishioners chose to make the black veil a subject of friendly remonstrance. There was a feeling of dread, neither plainly confessed nor carefully concealed, which caused each to shift the responsibility upon another, till at length it was found expedient to send a deputation of the church, in order to deal with Mr. Hooper about the mystery, before it should grow into a scandal. Never did an embassy so ill discharge its duties. The minister received them with friendly courtesy, but became silent, after they were seated, leaving to his visitors the whole burden of introducing their important business. The topic, it might be supposed, was obvious enough. There was the black veil swathed round Mr. Hooper's forehead, and concealing every feature above his placid mouth, on which, at times, they could perceive the glimmering of a melancholy smile. But that piece of crape, to their imagination, seemed to hang down before his heart, the symbol of a fearful secret between him and them. Were the veil but cast aside, they might speak freely of it, but not till then. Thus they sat a considerable time, speechless, confused, and shrinking uneasily from Mr. Hooper's eye, which they felt to be fixed upon them with an invisible glance. Finally, the deputies returned abashed to their constituents, pronouncing the matter too weighty to be handled, except by a council of the churches, if, indeed, it might not require a general synod.

But there was one person in the village unappalled by the awe with which the black veil had impressed all beside herself. When the deputies returned without an explanation, or even venturing to demand one, she with the calm energy of her character, determined to chase away the strange cloud that appeared to be settling round Mr. Hooper, every moment more darkly than before. As his plighted wife, it should be her privilege to know what the black veil concealed. At the minister's first visit, therefore, she entered upon the subject with a direct simplicity, which made the task easier both for him and her. After he had seated himself, she fixed her eyes steadfastly upon the veil, but could discern nothing of the dreadful gloom that had so overawed the multitude: it was but a double fold of crape, hanging down from his forehead to his mouth, and slightly stirring with his breath.

"No," said she aloud, and smiling, "there is nothing terrible in this piece of crape, except that it hides a face which I am always glad to look upon. Come, good sir, let the sun shine from behind the cloud. First lay aside your black veil: then tell me why you put it on."

Mr. Hooper's smile glimmered faintly.

"There is an hour to come," said he, "when all of us shall cast aside our veils. Take it not amiss, beloved friend, if I wear this piece of crape till then."

"Your words are a mystery, too," returned the young lady. "Take away the veil from them, at least."

"Elizabeth, I will," said he, "so far as my vow may suffer me. Know, then, this veil is a type and a symbol, and I am bound to wear it ever, both in light and darkness, in solitude and before the gaze of multitudes, and as with strangers, so with my familiar friends. No mortal eye will see it withdrawn. This dismal shade must separate me from the world: even you, Elizabeth, can never come behind it!"

"What grievous affliction hath befallen you," she earnestly inquired, "that you should thus darken your eyes forever?"

"If it be a sign of mourning," replied Mr. Hooper, "I, perhaps, like most other mortals, have sorrows dark enough to be typified by a black veil."

"But what if the world will not believe that it is the type of an innocent sorrow?" urged Elizabeth. "Beloved and respected as you are, there may be whispers that you hide your face under the consciousness of secret sin. For the sake of your holy office, do away this scandal!"

The color rose into her cheeks as she intimated the nature of the rumors that were already abroad in the village. But Mr. Hooper's mildness did not forsake him. He even smiled again—the same sad smile, which always appeared like a faint glimmering of light, proceeding from the obscurity beneath the veil.

"If I hide my face for sorrow, there is cause enough," he merely replied; "and if I cover it for secret sin, what mortal might not do the same?"

And with this gentle, but unconquerable obstinacy did he resist all her entreaties. At length Elizabeth sat silent. For a few moments she appeared lost in thought, considering, probably, what new methods might be tried to withdraw her lover from so dark a fantasy, which, if it had no other meaning, was perhaps a symptom of mental disease. Though of a firmer character than his own, the tears rolled down her cheeks. But, in an instant, as it were, a new feeling took the place of sorrow: her eyes were fixed insensibly on the black veil, when, like a sudden twilight in the air, its terrors fell around her. She arose, and stood trembling before him.

"And do you feel it then, at last?" said he mournfully.

She made no reply, but covered her eyes with her hand, and turned to leave the room. He rushed forward and caught her arm.

"Have patience with me, Elizabeth!" cried he, passionately. "Do not desert me, though this veil must be between us here on earth. Be mine, and hereafter there shall be no veil over my face, no darkness between our souls! It is but a mortal veil—it is not for eternity! O! you know not how lonely I am, and how frightened, to be alone behind my black veil. Do not leave me in this miserable obscurity forever!"

"Lift the veil but once, and look me in the face," said she.

"Never! It cannot be!" replied Mr. Hooper.

"Then farewell!" said Elizabeth.

She withdrew her arm from his grasp, and slowly departed, pausing at the door, to give one long shuddering gaze, that seemed almost to penetrate the mystery of the black veil. But, even amid his grief, Mr. Hooper smiled to think that only a material emblem had separated him from happiness, though the horrors, which it shadowed forth, must be drawn darkly between the fondest of lovers.

From that time no attempts were made to remove Mr. Hooper's black veil, or, by a direct appeal, to discover the secret which it was supposed to hide. By persons who claimed a superiority to popular prejudice, it was reckoned merely an eccentric whim, such as often mingles with the sober actions of men otherwise rational, and tinges them all with its own semblance of insanity. But with the multitude, good Mr. Hooper was irreparably a bugbear. He could not walk the street with any peace of mind, so conscious was he that the gentle and timid would turn aside to avoid him, and that others would make it a point of hardihood to throw themselves in his way. The impertinence of the latter class compelled him to give up his customary walk at sunset to the burial ground; for when he leaned pensively over the gate, there would always be faces behind the gravestones, peeping at his black veil. A fable went the rounds that the stare of the dead people drove him thence. It grieved him, to the very depth of his kind heart, to observe how the children fled from his approach, breaking up their merriest sports, while his melancholy figure was yet afar off. Their instinctive dread caused him to feel more strongly than aught else, that a preternatural horror was interwoven with the threads of the black crape. In truth, his own antipathy to the veil was known to be so great, that he never willingly passed before a mirror, nor stooped to drink at a still fountain, lest, in its peaceful bosom, he should be affrighted by himself. This was what gave plausibility to the whispers, that Mr. Hooper's conscience tortured him for some great crime too horrible to be entirely concealed, or otherwise than so obscurely intimated. Thus, from beneath the black veil, there rolled a cloud into the sunshine, an ambiguity of sin or sorrow, which enveloped the poor minister, so that love or sympathy could never reach him. It was said that ghost and fiend consorted with him there. With self-shudderings and outward terrors, he walked continually in its shadow, groping darkly within his own soul, or gazing through a medium that saddened the whole world. Even the lawless wind, it was believed, respected his dreadful secret, and never blew aside the veil. But still good Mr. Hooper sadly smiled at the pale visages of the worldly throng as he passed by.

Among all its bad influences, the black veil had the one desirable effect, of making its wearer a very efficient clergyman. By the aid of his mysterious emblem—for there was no other apparent cause—he became a man of awful power over souls that were in agony for sin. His converts always regarded him with a dread peculiar to themselves, affirming, though but figuratively, that, before he brought them to celestial light, they had been with him behind the black veil. Its gloom, indeed, enabled him to sympathize with all dark affections. Dying sinners cried aloud for Mr. Hooper, and would not yield their breath till he appeared; though ever, as he stooped to whisper consolation, they shuddered at the veiled face so near their own. Such were the terrors of the black veil, even when Death had bared his visage! Strangers came long distances to attend service at his church, with the mere idle purpose of gazing at his figure, because it was forbidden them to behold his face. But many were made to quake ere they departed! Once, during Governor Belcher's administration, Mr. Hooper was appointed to preach the election sermon. Covered with his black veil, he stood before the chief magistrate, the council, and the representatives, and wrought so deep an impression, that the legislative measures of that year were characterized by all the gloom and piety of our earliest ancestral sway.

In this manner Mr. Hooper spent a long life, irreproachable in outward act, yet shrouded in dismal suspicions; kind and loving, though unloved, and dimly feared; a man apart from men, shunned in their health and joy, but ever summoned to their aid in mortal anguish. As years wore on, shedding their snows above his sable veil, he acquired a name throughout the New England churches, and they called him Father Hooper. Nearly all his parishioners, who were of mature age when he was settled, had been borne away by many a funeral: he had one congregation in the church, and a more crowded one in the churchyard; and having wrought so late into the evening, and done his work so well, it was now good Father Hooper's turn to rest.

Several persons were visible by the shaded candle-light, in the death chamber of the old clergyman. Natural connections he had none. But there was the decorously grave, though unmoved physician, seeking only to mitigate the last pangs of the patient whom he could not save. There were the deacons, and other eminently pious members of his church. There, also, was the Reverend Mr. Clark, of Westbury, a young and zealous divine, who had ridden in haste to pray by the bedside of the expiring minister. There was the nurse, no hired handmaiden of death, but one whose calm affection had endured thus long in secrecy, in solitude, amid the chill of age, and would not perish, even at the dying hour. Who, but Elizabeth! And there lay the hoary head of good Father Hooper upon the death pillow, with the black veil still swathed about his brow, and reaching down over his face, so that each more difficult gasp of his faint breath caused it to stir. All through life that piece of crape had hung between him and the world: it had separated him from cheerful brotherhood and woman's love, and kept him in that saddest of all prisons, his own heart; and still it lay upon his face, as if to deepen the gloom of his darksome chamber, and shade him from the sunshine of eternity.

For some time previous, his mind had been confused, wavering doubtfully between the past and the present, and hovering forward, as it were, at intervals, into the indistinctness of the world to come. There had been feverish turns, which tossed him from side to side, and wore away what little strength he had. But in his most convulsive struggles, and in the wildest vagaries of his intellect, when no other thought retained its sober influence, he still showed an awful solicitude lest the black veil should slip aside. Even if his bewildered soul could have forgotten, there was a faithful woman at his pillow, who, with averted eyes, would have covered that aged face, which she had last beheld in the comeliness of manhood. At length the death-stricken old man lay quietly in the torpor of mental and bodily exhaustion, with an imperceptible pulse, and breath that grew fainter and fainter, except when a long, deep, and irregular inspiration seemed to prelude the flight of his spirit.

The minister of Westbury approached the bedside.

"Venerable Father Hooper," said he, "the moment of your release is at hand. Are you ready for the lifting of the veil that shuts in time from eternity?"

Father Hooper at first replied merely by a feeble motion of his head; then, apprehensive, perhaps, that his meaning might be doubtful, he exerted himself to speak.

"Yes," said he, in faint accents, "my soul hath a patient weariness until that veil be lifted."

"And is it fitting," resumed the Reverend Mr. Clark, "that a man so given to prayer, of such a blameless example, holy in deed and thought, so far as mortal judgment may pronounce; is it fitting that a father in the church should leave a shadow on his memory, that may seem to blacken a life so pure? I pray you, my venerable brother, let not this thing be! Suffer us to be gladdened by your triumphant aspect as you go to your reward. Before the veil of eternity be lifted, let me cast aside this black veil from your face!"

And thus speaking, the Reverend Mr. Clark bent forward to reveal the mystery of so many years. But, exerting a sudden energy, that made all the beholders stand aghast, Father Hooper snatched both his hands from beneath the bedclothes, and pressed them strongly on the black veil, resolute to struggle, if the minister of Westbury would contend with a dying man.

"Never!" cried the veiled clergyman. "On earth, never!"

"Dark old man!" exclaimed the affrighted minister, "with what horrible crime upon your soul are you now passing to the judgment?"

Father Hooper's breath heaved; it rattled in his throat; but, with a mighty effort, grasping forward with his hands, he caught hold of life, and held it back till he should speak. He even raised himself in bed; and there he sat, shivering with the arms of death around him, while the black veil hung down, awful, at that last moment, in the gathered terrors of a lifetime. And yet the faint, sad smile, so often there, now seemed to glimmer from its obscurity, and linger on Father Hooper's lips.

"Why do you tremble at me alone?" cried he, turning his veiled face round the circle of pale spectators. "Tremble also at each other. Have men avoided me, and women shown no pity, and children screamed and fled, only for my black veil? What, but the mystery which it obscurely typifies, has made this piece of crape so awful? When the friend shows his inmost heart to his friend; the lover to his best beloved; when man does not vainly shrink from the eye of his Creator, loathsomely treasuring up the secret of his sin; then deem me a monster, for the symbol beneath which I have lived, and die! I look around me, and, lo! on every visage a Black Veil!"

While his auditors shrank from one another, in mutual affright, Father Hooper fell back upon his pillow, a veiled corpse, with a faint smile, lingering on the lips. Still veiled, they laid him in his coffin, and a veiled corpse they bore him to the grave. The grass of many years has sprung up and withered on that grave, the burial stone is moss-grown, and good Mr. Hooper's face is dust; but awful is still the thought that it mouldered beneath the Black Veil! ☐☐

Discussion

1. (a) How does the black veil, when he first begins to wear it, affect the minister's parishioners? (b) How does it affect the minister's sermons?

2. At the funeral of the young lady, the minister leans over the coffin, and a "person who watched . . . scrupled not to affirm, that, at the instant when the clergyman's features were disclosed, the corpse had slightly shuddered." From the details in this passage, what can the reader infer about the features hidden behind the black veil?

3. (a) When the minister presides at the wedding, what happens to the wedding party? To

him? **(b)** Explain: "For the Earth, too, had on her Black Veil."

4. Even with his "plighted wife" Elizabeth, the minister refuses to remove the veil. Elizabeth thinks that the veil might well be a "symptom of mental disease." What is the specific nature of the disease? What evidence is there that she might be right?

5. "Among all its bad influences, the black veil had . . . one desirable effect." Explain.

6. Hawthorne writes: "All through life that piece of crape had hung between him and the world; it had separated him from cheerful brotherhood and woman's love, and kept him in that saddest of all prisons, his own heart." What does the veil symbolize?

7. As the minister dies, he says: "I look around me, and, lo! on every visage a Black Veil!" Explain.

Extension • Writing

Note that "The Minister's Black Veil" is subtitled "A Parable"—a short, simple story that conveys a moral or lesson. The moral of the story may be presented in the minister's dying words—that an individual should not "loathsomely [treasure] up the secret of his sin" but reveal it to his friend, his lover, his Creator. Or the moral may be revealed in the portrayal of the minister as cutting himself off from the "magnetic chain of humanity."

Write a brief essay explaining whether you believe the minister was right or wrong—or both—in wearing the black veil.

Vocabulary • Dictionary

On your paper write each of the words listed below next to the number of the description that it matches. Use your Glossary for the definitions of the words. Be sure you can spell and pronounce all the words in the list.

swathe   omniscient
pathos   torpor   mitigate

1. Has a Latin prefix meaning "all"

2. Has a Latin origin meaning "make gentle"

3. Has an Old English origin

4. Comes from a Latin root meaning "numb"

5. Comes from a Greek word meaning "suffering"

My Kinsman, Major Molineux

After the kings of Great Britain had assumed the right of appointing the colonial governors, the measures of the latter seldom met with the ready and generous approbation which had been paid to those of their predecessors, under the original charters. The people looked with most jealous scrutiny to the exercise of power which did not emanate from themselves, and they usually rewarded their leaders with slender gratitude for the compliances by which, in softening their instructions from beyond the sea, they had incurred the reprehension of those who gave them. The annals of Massachusetts Bay will inform us, that of six governors in the space of about forty years from the surrender of the old charter, under James II,[1] two were imprisoned by a popular insurrection; a third, as Hutchinson inclines to believe, was driven from the province by the whizzing of a musket-ball; a fourth, in the opinion of the same historian, was hastened to his grave by continual bickerings with the House of Representatives, and the remaining two, as well as their successors, till the Revolution, were favored with few and brief intervals of peaceful sway. The inferior members of the court party, in times of high political excitement, led scarcely a more desirable life. These remarks may serve as a preface to the following adventures, which chanced upon a summer night, not far from a hundred years ago. The reader, in order to avoid

---

1. **James II,** (1633–1701), King of England from 1685–1688. He was driven from his throne by a rebellion against his tyrannical rule.

a long and dry detail of colonial affairs, is requested to dispense with an account of the train of circumstances that had caused much temporary inflammation of the popular mind.

It was near nine o'clock of a moonlight evening, when a boat crossed the ferry with a single passenger, who had obtained his conveyance at that unusual hour by the promise of an extra fare. While he stood on the landing-place, searching in either pocket for the means of fulfilling his agreement, the ferryman lifted a lantern, by the aid of which, and the newly risen moon, he took a very accurate survey of the stranger's figure. He was a youth of barely eighteen years, evidently country-bred, and now, as it should seem, upon his first visit to town. He was clad in a coarse gray coat, well worn, but in excellent repair; his under garments were durably constructed of leather, and fitted tight to a pair of serviceable and well-shaped limbs; his stockings of blue yarn were the incontrovertible work of a mother or a sister; and on his head was a three-cornered hat, which in its better days had perhaps sheltered the graver brow of the lad's father. Under his left arm was a heavy cudgel formed of an oak sapling, and retaining a part of the hardened root; and his equipment was completed by a wallet, not so abundantly stocked as to incommode the vigorous shoulders on which it hung. Brown, curly hair, well-shaped features, and bright, cheerful eyes were nature's gifts, and worth all that art could have done for his adornment.

The youth, one of whose names was Robin, finally drew from his pocket the half of a little province bill of five shillings, which, in the depreciation in that sort of currency, did but satisfy the ferryman's demand, with the surplus of a sexangular piece of parchment, valued at three pence. He then walked forward into the town, with as light a step as if his day's journey had not already exceeded thirty miles, and with as eager an eye as if he were entering London city, instead of the little metropolis of a New England colony. Before Robin had proceeded far, however, it occurred to him that he knew not whither to direct his steps; so he paused, and looked up and down the narrow street, scrutinizing the small and mean wooden buildings that were scattered on either side.

"This low hovel cannot be my kinsman's dwelling," thought he, "nor yonder old house, where the moonlight enters at the broken casement; and truly I see none hereabouts that might be worthy of him. It would have been wise to inquire my way of the ferryman, and doubtless he would have gone with me, and earned a shilling from the Major for his pains. But the next man I meet will do as well."

He resumed his walk, and was glad to perceive that the street now became wider, and the houses more respectable in their appearance. He soon discerned a figure moving on moderately in advance, and hastened his steps to overtake it. As Robin drew nigh, he saw that the passenger was a man in years, with a full periwig of gray hair, a wide-skirted coat of dark cloth, and silk stockings rolled above his knees. He carried a long and polished cane, which he struck down perpendicularly before him at every step; and at regular intervals he uttered two successive hems, of a peculiarly solemn and sepulchral intonation. Having made these observations, Robin laid hold of the skirt of the old man's coat, just when the light from the open door and windows of a barber's shop fell upon both their figures.

"Good evening to you, honored sir," said he, making a low bow, and still retaining his hold of the skirt. "I pray you tell me whereabouts is the dwelling of my kinsman, Major Molineux."

The youth's question was uttered very loudly; and one of the barbers, whose razor was descending on a well-soaped chin, and another who was dressing a Ramillies wig, left their occupations, and came to the door. The citizen, in the mean time, turned a long-favored countenance upon Robin, and answered him in a tone of excessive anger and annoyance. His two sepulchral hems, however, broke into the very center of his rebuke, with most singular effect, like a thought of the cold grave obtruding among wrathful passions.

"Let go my garment, fellow! I tell you, I know not the man you speak of. What! I have authority, I have—hem, hem—authority; and if this be the respect you show for your betters, your feet shall be brought acquainted with the stocks by daylight, tomorrow morning!"

Robin released the old man's skirt, and hastened away, pursued by an ill-mannered roar of laughter from the barber's shop. He was at first considerably surprised by the result of his question, but, being a shrewd youth, soon thought himself able to account for the mystery.

"This is some country representative," was his conclusion, "who has never seen the inside of my kinsman's door, and lacks the breeding to answer a stranger civilly. The man is old, or verily—I might be tempted to turn back and smite him on the nose. Ah, Robin, Robin! even the barber's boys laugh at you for choosing such a guide! You will be wiser in time, friend Robin."

He now became entangled in a succession of crooked and narrow streets, which crossed each other, and meandered at no great distance from the water-side. The smell of tar was obvious to his nostrils, the masts of vessels pierced the moonlight above the tops of the buildings, and the numerous signs, which Robin paused to read, informed him that he was near the center of business. But the streets were empty, the shops were closed, and lights were visible only in the second stories of a few dwelling-houses. At length, on the corner of a narrow lane, through which he was passing, he beheld the broad countenance of a British hero swinging before the door of an inn, whence proceeded the voices of many guests. The casement of one of the lower windows was thrown back, and a very thin curtain permitted Robin to distinguish a party at supper, round a well-furnished table. The fragrance of the good cheer steamed forth into the outer air, and the youth could not fail to recollect that the last remnant of his travelling stock of provision had yielded to his morning appetite, and that noon had found and left him dinnerless.

"Oh, that a parchment three-penny might give me a right to sit down at yonder table!" said Robin, with a sigh. "But the Major will make me welcome to the best of his victuals; so I will even step boldly in, and inquire my way to his dwelling."

He entered the tavern, and was guided by the murmur of voices and the fumes of tobacco to the public-room. It was a long and low apartment, with oaken walls, grown dark in the continual smoke, and a floor which was thickly sanded, but of no immaculate purity. A number of persons—the larger part of whom appeared to be mariners, or in some way connected with the

sea—occupied the wooden benches, or leather-bottomed chairs, conversing on various matters, and occasionally lending their attention to some topic of general interest. Three or four little groups were draining as many bowls of punch, which the West India trade had long since made a familiar drink in the colony. Others, who had the appearance of men who lived by regular and laborious handicraft, preferred the insulated bliss of an unshared potation, and became more taciturn under its influence. Nearly all, in short, evinced a predilection for the Good Creature in some of its various shapes, for this is a vice to which, as Fast Day sermons of a hundred years ago will testify, we have a long hereditary claim. The only guests to whom Robin's sympathies inclined him were two or three sheepish countrymen, who were using the inn somewhat after the fashion of a Turkish caravansary; they had gotten themselves into the darkest corner of the room, and heedless of the Nicotian[2] atmosphere,

---

2. **Nicotian** (ni kō′shən), filled with the smoke of tobacco. From Jean Nicot, who introduced tobacco into France.

were supping on the bread of their own ovens, and the bacon cured in their own chimney-smoke. But though Robin felt a sort of brotherhood with these strangers, his eyes were attracted from them to a person who stood near the door, holding whispered conversation with a group of ill-dressed associates. His features were separately striking almost to grotesqueness, and the whole face left a deep impression on the memory. The forehead bulged out into a double prominence, with a vale between; the nose came boldly forth in an irregular curve, and its bridge was of more than a finger's breadth; the eyebrows were deep and shaggy, and the eyes glowed beneath them like fire in a cave.

While Robin deliberated of whom to inquire respecting his kinsman's dwelling, he was accosted by the innkeeper, a little man in a stained white apron, who had come to pay his professional welcome to the stranger. Being in the second generation from a French Protestant, he seemed to have inherited the courtesy of his parent nation; but no variety of circumstances was ever known to change his voice from the one shrill note in which he now addressed Robin.

"From the country, I presume, sir?" said he, with a profound bow. "Beg leave to congratulate you on your arrival, and trust you intend a long stay with us. Fine town here, sir, beautiful buildings, and much that may interest a stranger. May I hope for the honor of your commands in respect to supper?"

"The man sees a family likeness! the rogue has guessed that I am related to the Major!" thought Robin, who had hitherto experienced little superfluous civility.

All eyes were now turned on the country lad, standing at the door, in his worn three-cornered hat, gray coat, leather breeches, and blue yarn stockings, leaning on an oaken cudgel, and bearing a wallet on his back.

Robin replied to the courteous innkeeper, with such an assumption of confidence as befitted the Major's relative. "My honest friend," he said, "I shall make it a point to patronize your house on some occasion, when"—here he could not help lowering his voice—"when I may have more than a parchment three-pence in my pocket. My present business," continued he, speaking with lofty confidence, "is merely to inquire my

way to the dwelling of my kinsman, Major Molineux."

There was a sudden and general movement in the room, which Robin interpreted as expressing the eagerness of each individual to become his guide. But the innkeeper turned his eyes to a written paper on the wall, which he read, or seemed to read, with occasional recurrences to the young man's figure.

"What have we here?" said he, breaking his speech into little dry fragments. "'Left the house of the subscriber, bounden servant, Hezekiah Mudge,—had on, when he went away, gray coat, leather breeches, master's third-best hat. One pound currency reward to whosoever shall lodge him in any jail of the province.' Better trudge, boy, better trudge!"

Robin had begun to draw his hand towards the lighter end of the oak cudgel, but a strange hostility in every countenance induced him to relinquish his purpose of breaking the courteous innkeeper's head. As he turned to leave the room, he encountered a sneering glance from the bold-featured personage whom he had before noticed; and no sooner was he beyond the door, than he heard a general laugh, in which the innkeeper's voice might be distinguished, like the dropping of small stones into a kettle.

"Now, is it not strange," thought Robin, with his usual shrewdness,—"is it not strange that the confession of an empty pocket should outweigh the name of my kinsman, Major Molineux? Oh, if I had one of those grinning rascals in the woods, where I and my oak sapling grew up together, I would teach him that my arm is heavy though my purse be light!"

On turning the corner of the narrow lane, Robin found himself in a spacious street, with an unbroken line of lofty houses on each side, and a steepled building at the upper end, whence the ringing of a bell announced the hour of nine. The light of the moon, and the lamps from the numerous shop-windows, discovered people promenading on the pavement, and amongst them Robin had hoped to recognize his hitherto inscrutable relative. The result of his former inquiries made him unwilling to hazard another, in a scene of such publicity, and he determined to walk slowly and silently up the street, thrusting his face close to that of every elderly gentleman, in search of the Major's lineaments. In his progress, Robin encountered many gay and gallant figures. Embroidered garments of showy colors, enormous periwigs, gold-laced hats, and silver-hilted swords glided past him and dazzled his optics. Travelled youths, imitators of the European fine gentlemen of the period, trod jauntily along, half dancing to the fashionable tunes which they hummed, and making poor Robin ashamed of his quiet and natural gait. At length, after many pauses to examine the gorgeous display of goods in the shop-windows, and after suffering some rebukes for the impertinence of his scrutiny into people's faces, the Major's kinsman found himself near the steepled building, still unsuccessful in his search. As yet, however, he had seen only one side of the thronged street; so Robin crossed, and continued the same sort of inquisition down the opposite pavement, with stronger hopes than the philosopher seeking an honest man, but with no better fortune. He had arrived about midway towards the lower end, from which his course began, when he overheard the approach of some one who struck down a cane on the flag-stones at every step, uttering at regular intervals, two sepulchral hems.

"Mercy on us!" quoth Robin, recognizing the sound.

Turning a corner, which chanced to be close at his right hand, he hastened to pursue his researches in some other part of the town. His patience was now wearing low, and he seemed to feel more fatigue from his rambles since he crossed the ferry, than from his journey of several days on the other side. Hunger also pleaded loudly within him, and Robin began to balance the propriety of demanding, violently, and with lifted cudgel, the necessary guidance from the first solitary passenger whom he should meet. While a resolution to this effect was gaining strength, he entered a street of mean appearance, on either side of which a row of ill-built houses was straggling towards the harbor. The moonlight fell upon no passenger along the whole extent, but in the third domicile which Robin passed there was a half-open door, and his keen glance detected a woman's garment within.

"My luck may be better here," said he to himself.

Accordingly, he approached the door, and beheld it shut closer as he did so; yet an open space remained, sufficing for the fair occupant to observe the stranger, without a corresponding displaying on her part. All that Robin could discern was a strip of scarlet petticoat, and the occasional sparkle of an eye, as if the moonbeams were trembling on some bright thing.

"Pretty mistress," for I may call her so with a good conscience, thought the shrewd youth, since I know nothing to the contrary,—"my sweet pretty mistress, will you be kind enough to tell me whereabouts I must seek the dwelling of my kinsman, Major Molineux?"

Robin's voice was plaintive and winning, and the female, seeing nothing to be shunned in the handsome country youth, thrust open the door, and came forth into the moonlight. She was a dainty little figure, with a white neck, round arms, and a slender waist, at the extremity of which her scarlet petticoat jutted out over a hoop, as if she were standing in a balloon. Moreover, her face was oval and pretty, her hair dark beneath the little cap, and her bright eyes possessed a sly freedom, which triumphed over those of Robin.

"Major Molineux dwells here," said this fair woman.

Now, her voice was the sweetest Robin had heard that night, yet he could not help doubting whether that sweet voice spoke Gospel truth. He looked up and down the mean street, and then surveyed the house before which they stood. It was a small, dark edifice of two stories, the second of which projected over the lower floor, and the front apartment had the aspect of a shop for petty commodities.

"Now, truly, I am in luck," replied Robin, cunningly, "and so indeed is my kinsman, the Major, in having so pretty a housekeeper. But I prithee trouble him to step to the door; I will deliver him a message from his friends in the country, and then go back to my lodgings at the inn."

"Nay, the Major has been abed this hour or more," said the lady of the scarlet petticoat; "and it would be to little purpose to disturb him to-night, seeing his evening draught was of the strongest. But he is a kind-hearted man, and it would be as much as my life's worth to let a kinsman of his turn away from the door. You are the good old gentleman's very picture, and I could swear that was his rainy-weather hat. Also he has garments very much resembling those leather small-clothes. But come in, I pray, for I bid you hearty welcome in his name."

So saying, the fair and hospitable dame took our hero by the hand; and the touch was light, and the force was gentleness, and though Robin read in her eyes what he did not hear in her words, yet the slender-waisted woman in the scarlet petticoat proved stronger than the athletic country youth. She had drawn his half-willing footsteps nearly to the threshold, when the opening of a door in the neighborhood startled the Major's housekeeper, and, leaving the Major's kinsman, she vanished speedily into her own domicile. A heavy yawn preceded the appearance of a man, who, like the Moonshine of Pyramus and Thisbe,[3] carried a lantern, needlessly aiding his sister luminary in the heavens. As he walked sleepily up the street, he turned his broad, dull face on Robin, and displayed a long staff, spiked at the end.

"Home, vagabond, home!" said the watchman, in accents that seemed to fall asleep as soon as they were uttered. "Home, or we'll set you in the stocks by peep of day!"

"This is the second hint of the kind," thought Robin. "I wish they would end my difficulties, by setting me there to-night."

Nevertheless, the youth felt an instinctive antipathy towards the guardian of midnight order, which at first prevented him from asking his usual question. But just when the man was about to vanish behind the corner, Robin resolved not to lose the opportunity, and shouted lustily after him,—

"I say, friend! will you guide me to the house of my kinsman, Major Molineux?"

The watchman made no reply, but turned the corner and was gone; yet Robin seemed to hear the sound of drowsy laughter stealing along the solitary street. At that moment, also, a pleasant titter saluted him from the open window above his head; he looked up, and caught the sparkle of a saucy eye; a round arm beckoned to him, and next he heard light footsteps descending the staircase within. But Robin, being of the household of a New England clergyman, was a good youth, as well as a shrewd one; so he resisted temptation, and fled away.

He now roamed desperately, and at random, through the town, almost ready to believe that a spell was on him, like that by which a wizard of his country had once kept three pursuers wandering, a whole winter night, within twenty paces of the cottage which they sought. The streets lay before him, strange and desolate, and the lights were extinguished in almost every house. Twice, however, little parties of men, among whom Robin distinguished individuals in outlandish attire, came hurrying along; but, though on both occasions, they paused to address him, such intercourse did not at all enlighten his perplexity. They did but utter a few words in some language of which Robin knew nothing, and perceiving his inability to answer, bestowed a curse upon him in plain English and hastened away. Finally, the lad determined to knock at the door of every mansion that might appear worthy to be occupied by his kinsman, trusting that perseverance would overcome the fatality that had hitherto thwarted him. Firm in this resolve, he was passing beneath the walls of a church, which formed the corner of two streets, when, as he turned into the shade of its steeple, he encountered a bulky stranger, muffled in a cloak. The man was proceeding with the speed of earnest business, but Robin planted himself full before him, holding the oak cudgel with both hands across his body as a bar to further passage.

"Halt, honest man, and answer me a question," said he, very resolutely. "Tell me, this instant, whereabouts is the dwelling of my kinsman, Major Molineux!"

"Keep your tongue between your teeth, fool, and let me pass!" said a deep, gruff voice, which Robin partly remembered. "Let me pass, or I'll strike you to the earth!"

"No, no, neighbor!" cried Robin, flourishing his cudgel, and then thrusting its larger end close to the man's muffled face. "No, no, I'm not the fool you take me for, nor do you pass till I have an answer to my question. Whereabouts is the dwelling of my kinsman, Major Molineux?"

---

3. **Moonshine of Pyramus** (pir′ə məs) **and Thisbe** (thiz′bē). Pyramus and Thisbe were Babylonian lovers who planned a moonlight rendezvous that ended in tragedy.

The stranger, instead of attempting to force his passage, stepped back into the moonlight, unmuffled his face, and stared full into that of Robin.

"Watch here an hour, and Major Molineux will pass by," said he.

Robin gazed with dismay and astonishment on the unprecedented physiognomy of the speaker. The forehead with its double prominence, the broad hooked nose, the shaggy eyebrows, and fiery eyes were those which he had noticed at the inn, but the man's complexion had undergone a singular, or, more properly, a twofold change. One side of the face blazed in intense red, while the other was black as midnight, the division line being in the broad bridge of the nose; and a mouth which seemed to extend from ear to ear was black or red, in contrast to the color of the cheek. The effect was as if two individual devils, a fiend of fire and a fiend of darkness, had united themselves to form this infernal visage. The stranger grinned in Robin's face, muffled his party-colored features, and was out of sight in a moment.

"Strange things we travellers see!" ejaculated Robin.

He seated himself, however, upon the steps of the church-door, resolving to wait the appointed time for his kinsman. A few moments were consumed in philosophical speculations upon the species of man who had just left him; but having settled this point shrewdly, rationally, and satisfactorily, he was compelled to look elsewhere for his amusement. And first he threw his eyes along the street. It was of more respectable appearance than most of those into which he had wandered; and the moon, creating, like the imaginative power, a beautiful strangeness in familiar objects, gave something of romance to a scene that might not have possessed it in the light of day. The irregular and often quaint architecture of the houses, some of whose roofs were broken into numerous little peaks, while others ascended, steep and narrow, into a single point, and others again were square; the pure snow-white of some of their complexions, the aged darkness of others, and the thousand sparklings, reflected from bright substances in the walls of many; these matters engaged Robin's attention for a while, and then began to grow wearisome. Next he

endeavored to define the forms of distant objects, starting away, with almost ghostly indistinctness, just as his eye appeared to grasp them; and finally he took a minute survey of an edifice which stood on the opposite side of the street, directly in front of the church-door, where he was stationed. It was a large, square mansion, distinguished from its neighbors by a balcony, which rested on tall pillars, and by an elaborate Gothic window, communicating therewith.

"Perhaps this is the very house I have been seeking," thought Robin.

Then he strove to speed away the time, by listening to a murmur which swept continually along the street, yet was scarcely audible, except to an unaccustomed ear like his; it was a low, dull, dreamy sound, compounded of many noises, each of which was at too great a distance to be separately heard. Robin marvelled at this snore of a sleeping town, and marvelled more whenever its continuity was broken by now and then a distant shout, apparently loud where it originated. But altogether it was a sleep-inspiring sound, and, to shake off its drowsy influence, Robin arose, and climbed a window-frame, that he might view the interior of the church. There the moonbeams came trembling in, and fell down upon the deserted pews, and extended along the quiet aisles. A fainter yet more awful radiance was hovering around the pulpit, and one solitary ray had dared to rest upon the open page of the great Bible. Had nature, in that deep hour, become a worshipper in the house which man had builded? Or was that heavenly light the visible sanctity of the place,—visible because no earthly and impure feet were within the walls? The scene made Robin's heart shiver with a sensation of loneliness stronger than he had ever felt in the remotest depths of his native woods; so he turned away and sat down again before the door. There were graves around the church, and now an uneasy thought obtruded into Robin's breast. What if the object of his search, which had been so often and so strangely thwarted, were all the time mouldering in his shroud? What if his kinsman should glide through yonder gate, and nod and smile to him in dimly passing by?

"Oh, that any breathing thing were here with me!" said Robin.

Recalling his thoughts from this uncomfortable track, he sent them over forest, hill, and stream, and attempted to imagine how that evening of ambiguity and weariness had been spent by his father's household. He pictured them assembled at the door, beneath the tree, the great old tree, which had been spared for its huge twisted trunk and venerable shade, when a thousand leafy brethren fell. There, at the going down of the summer sun, it was his father's custom to perform domestic worship, that the neighbors might come and join with him like brothers of the family, and that the wayfaring man might pause to drink at that fountain, and keep his heart pure by freshening the memory of home. Robin distinguished the seat of every individual of the little audience; he saw the good man in the midst, holding the Scriptures in the golden light that fell from the western clouds; he beheld him close the book and all rise up to pray. He heard the old thanksgivings for daily mercies, the old applications for their continuance, to which he had so often listened in weariness, but which were now among his dear remembrances. He perceived the slight inequality of his father's voice when he came to speak of the absent one; he noted how his mother turned her face to the broad and knotted trunk; how his elder brother scorned, because the beard was rough upon his upper lip, to permit his features to be moved; how the younger sister drew down a low hanging branch before her eyes; and how the little one of all, whose sports had hitherto broken the decorum of the scene, understood the prayer for her playmate, and burst into clamorous grief. Then he saw them go in at the door; and when Robin would have entered also, the latch tinkled into its place, and he was excluded from his home.

"Am I here, or there?" cried Robin, starting; for all at once, when his thoughts had become visible and audible in a dream, the long, wide, solitary street shone out before him.

He aroused himself, and endeavored to fix his attention steadily upon the large edifice which he had surveyed before. But still his mind kept vibrating between fancy and reality; by turns, the pillars of the balcony lengthened into the tall, bare stems of pines, dwindled down to human figures, settled again into their true shape and size, and then commenced a new succession of changes. For a single moment, when he deemed himself awake, he could have sworn that a visage—one which he seemed to remember, yet could not absolutely name as his kinsman's—was looking towards him from the Gothic window. A deeper sleep wrestled with and nearly overcame him, but fled at the sound of footsteps along the opposite pavement. Robin rubbed his eyes, discerned a man passing at the foot of the balcony, and addressed him in a loud, peevish, and lamentable cry.

"Hallo, friend! must I wait here all night for my kinsman, Major Molineux?"

The sleeping echoes awoke, and answered the voice; and the passenger, barely able to discern a figure sitting in the oblique shade of the steeple, traversed the street to obtain a nearer view. He was himself a gentleman in his prime, of open, intelligent, cheerful, and altogether prepossessing countenance. Perceiving a country youth, apparently homeless and without friends, he accosted him in a tone of real kindness, which had become strange to Robin's ears.

"Well, my good lad, why are you sitting here?" inquired he. "Can I be of service to you in any way?"

"I am afraid not, sir," replied Robin, despondently; "yet I shall take it kindly, if you'll answer me a single question. I've been searching half the night, for one Major Molineux; now, sir, is there really such a person in these parts, or am I dreaming?"

"Major Molineux! The name is not altogether strange to me," said the gentleman, smiling. "Have you any objection to telling me the nature of your business with him?"

Then Robin briefly related that his father was a clergyman, settled on a small salary, at a long distance back in the country, and that he and Major Molineux were brothers' children. The Major, having inherited riches, and acquired civil and military rank, had visited his cousin, in great pomp, a year or two before; had manifested much interest in Robin and an elder brother, and, being childless himself, had thrown out hints respecting the future establishment of one of them in life. The elder brother was destined to succeed to the farm which his father cultivated in the interval of sacred duties; it was therefore determined that Robin should profit by his kinsman's generous intentions, especially as he seemed to be rather the favorite, and was thought to possess other necessary endowments.

"For I have the name of being a shrewd youth," observed Robin, in this part of his story.

"I doubt not you deserve it," replied his new friend, good-naturedly; "but pray proceed."

"Well, sir, being nearly eighteen years old, and well grown, as you see," continued Robin, drawing himself up to his full height, "I thought it high time to begin in the world. So my mother and sister put me in handsome trim, and my father gave me half the remnant of his last year's salary, and five days ago I started for this place, to pay the Major a visit. But, would you believe it, sir! I crossed the ferry a little after dark, and have yet found nobody that would show me the way to his dwelling; only, an hour or two since, I was told to wait here, and Major Molineux would pass by."

"Can you describe the man who told you this?" inquired the gentleman.

"Oh, he was a very ill-favored fellow, sir," replied Robin, "with two great bumps on his forehead, a hook nose, fiery eyes; and, what struck me as the strangest, his face was of two different colors. Do you happen to know such a man, sir?"

"Not intimately," answered the stranger, "but I chanced to meet him a little time previous to your stopping me. I believe you may trust his word, and that the Major will very shortly pass through this street. In the mean time, as I have a singular curiosity to witness your meeting, I will sit down here upon the steps and bear you company."

He seated himself accordingly, and soon engaged his companion in animated discourse. It was but of brief continuance, however, for a noise of shouting, which had long been remotely audible, drew so much nearer that Robin inquired its cause.

"What may be the meaning of this uproar?" asked he. "Truly, if your town be always as noisy, I shall find little sleep while I am an inhabitant."

"Why, indeed, friend Robin, there do appear to be three or four riotous fellows abroad tonight," replied the gentleman. "You must not expect all the stillness of your native woods here

in our streets. But the watch will shortly be at the heels of these lads and"—

"Ay, and set them in the stocks by peep of day," interrupted Robin, recollecting his own encounter with the drowsy lantern-bearer. "But, dear sir, if I may trust my ears, an army of watchmen would never make head against such a multitude of rioters. There were at least a thousand voices went up to make that one shout."

"May not a man have several voices, Robin, as well as two complexions?" said his friend.

"Perhaps a man may; but Heaven forbid that a woman should!" responded the shrewd youth, thinking of the seductive tones of the Major's housekeeper.

The sounds of a trumpet in some neighboring street now became so evident and continual, that Robin's curiosity was strongly excited. In addition to the shouts, he heard frequent bursts from many instruments of discord, and a wild and confused laughter filled up the intervals. Robin rose from the steps, and looked wistfully towards a point whither people seemed to be hastening.

"Surely some prodigious merry-making is going on," exclaimed he. "I have laughed very little since I left home, sir, and should be sorry to lose an opportunity. Shall we step round the corner by that darkish house, and take our share of the fun?"

"Sit down again, sit down, good Robin," replied the gentleman, laying his hand on the skirt of the gray coat. "You forget that we must wait here for your kinsman; and there is reason to believe that he will pass by, in the course of a very few moments."

The near approach of the uproar had now disturbed the neighborhood; windows flew open on all sides; and many heads, in the attire of the pillow, and confused by sleep suddenly broken, were protruded to the gaze of whoever had leisure to observe them. Eager voices hailed each other from house to house, all demanding the explanation, which not a soul could give. Half-dressed men hurried towards the unknown commotion, stumbling as they went over the stone steps that thrust themselves into the narrow footwalk. The shouts, the laughter, and the tuneless bray, the antipodes of music, came onwards with increasing din, till scattered individuals, and then denser bodies, began to appear round a corner at the distance of a hundred yards.

"Will you recognize your kinsman, if he passes in this crowd?" inquired the gentleman.

"Indeed, I can't warrant it, sir; but I'll take my stand here, and keep a bright lookout," answered Robin, descending to the outer edge of the pavement.

A mighty stream of people now emptied into the street, and came rolling slowly towards the church. A single horseman wheeled the corner in the midst of them, and close behind him came a band of fearful wind-instruments, sending forth a fresher discord now that no intervening buildings kept it from the ear. Then a redder light disturbed the moonbeams, and a dense multitude of torches shone along the street, concealing, by their glare, whatever object they illuminated. The single horseman, clad in a military dress, and bearing a drawn sword, rode onward as the leader, and, by his fierce and variegated countenance, appeared like war personified; the red of one cheek was an emblem of fire and sword; the blackness of the other betokened the mourning that attends them. In his train were wild figures in the Indian dress, and many fantastic shapes without a model, giving the whole march a visionary air, as if a dream had broken forth from some feverish brain, and were sweeping visibly through the midnight streets. A mass of people, inactive, except as applauding spectators, hemmed the procession in; and several women ran along the sidewalk, piercing the confusion of heavier sounds with their shrill voices of mirth or terror.

"The double-faced fellow has his eye upon me," muttered Robin, with an indefinite but an uncomfortable idea that he was himself to bear a part in the pageantry.

The leader turned himself in the saddle, and fixed his glance full upon the country youth, as the steed went slowly by. When Robin had freed his eyes from those fiery ones, the musicians were passing before him, and the torches were close at hand; but the unsteady brightness of the latter formed a veil which he could not penetrate. The rattling of wheels over the stones sometimes found its way to his ear, and confused traces of a human form appeared at intervals, and then melted into the vivid light. A moment more, and the leader thundered a command to halt: the trumpets vomited a horrid breath, and then held their peace; the shouts and laughter of the people died away, and there remained only a universal hum, allied to silence. Right before Robin's eyes was an uncovered cart. There the torches blazed the brightest, there the moon shone out like day, and there, in tar-and-feathery dignity, sat his kinsman, Major Molineux!

He was an elderly man, of large and majestic person, and strong, square features, betokening a steady soul; but steady as it was, his enemies had found means to shake it. His face was pale as death, and far more ghastly; the broad forehead was contracted in his agony, so that his eyebrows formed one grizzled line; his eyes were red and wild, and the foam hung white upon his quivering lip. His whole frame was agitated by a quick and continual tremor, which his pride strove to quell,

even in those circumstances of overwhelming
humiliation. But perhaps the bitterest pang of all
was when his eyes met those of Robin; for he
evidently knew him on the instant, as the youth
stood witnessing the foul disgrace of a head
grown gray in honor. They stared at each other in
silence, and Robin's knees shook, and his hair
bristled, with a mixture of pity and terror. Soon,
however, a bewildering excitement began to
seize upon his mind; the preceding adventures of
the night, the unexpected appearance of the
crowd, the torches, the confused din and the
hush that followed, the spectre of his kinsman
reviled by that great multitude,—and this, and,
more than all, a perception of tremendous ridicule in the whole scene, affected him with a sort
of mental inebriety. At that moment a voice of
sluggish merriment saluted Robin's ears; he
turned instinctively, and just behind the corner
of the church stood the lantern-bearer, rubbing

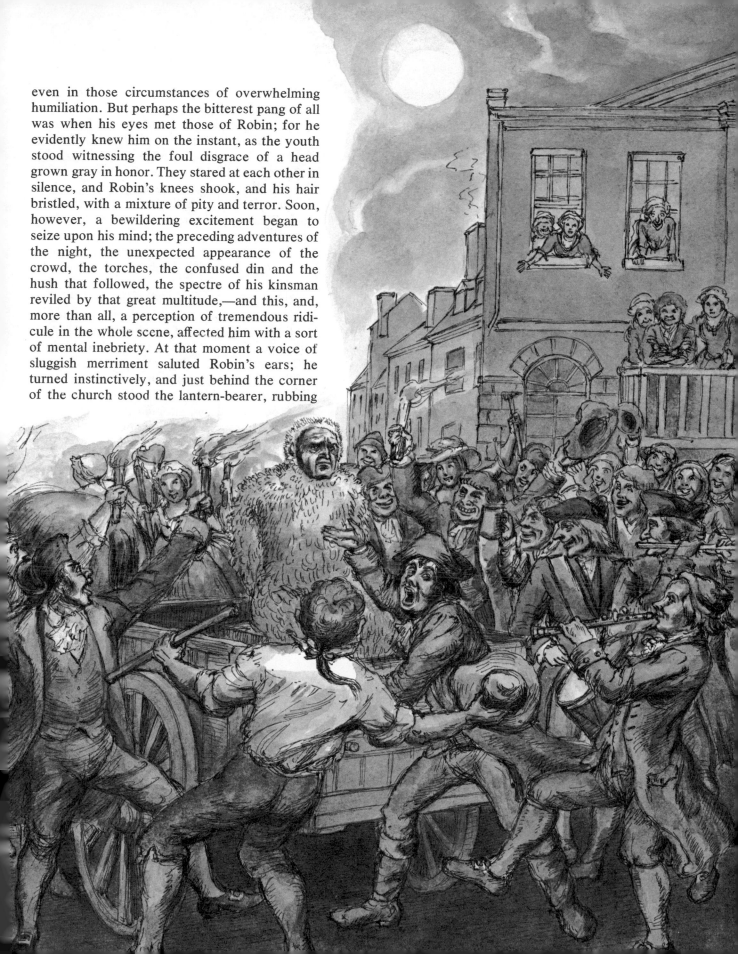

his eyes, and drowsily enjoying the lad's amazement. Then he heard a peal of laughter like the ringing of silvery bells; a woman twitched his arm, a saucy eye met his, and he saw the lady of the scarlet petticoat. A sharp, dry cachinnation appealed to his memory, and standing on tiptoe in the crowd, with his white apron over his head, he beheld the courteous little innkeeper. And lastly, there sailed over the heads of the multitude a great, broad laugh, broken in the midst by two sepulchral hems; thus, "Haw, haw, haw,—hem, hem,—haw, haw, haw, haw!"

The sound proceeded from the balcony of the opposite edifice, and thither Robin turned his eyes. In front of the Gothic windows stood the old citizen, wrapped in a wide gown, his gray periwig exchanged for a nightcap, which was thrust back from his forehead, and his silk stockings hanging about his legs. He supported himself on his polished cane in a fit of convulsive merriment, which manifested itself on his solemn old features like a funny inscription on a tombstone. Then Robin seemed to hear the voices of the barbers, of the guests of the inn, and of all who had made sport of him that night. The contagion was spreading among the multitude, when all at once, it seized upon Robin, and he sent forth a shout of laughter that echoed through the street—every man shook his sides, every man emptied his lungs, but Robin's shout was the loudest there. The cloud-spirits peeped from their silvery islands, as the congregated mirth went roaring up the sky! The Man in the Moon heard the far bellow. "Oho," quoth he, "the old earth is frolicsome tonight!"

When there was a momentary calm in that tempestuous sea of sound, the leader gave the sign, the procession resumed its march. On they went, like fiends that throng in mockery around some dead potentate, mighty no more, but majestic still in his agony. On they went, in counterfeited pomp, in senseless uproar, in frenzied merriment, trampling all on an old man's heart. On swept the tumult, and left a silent street behind.

"Well, Robin, are you dreaming?" inquired the gentleman, laying his hand on the youth's shoulder.

Robin started, and withdrew his arm from the stone post to which he had instinctively clung, as the living stream rolled by him. His cheek was somewhat pale, and his eye not quite as lively as in the earlier part of the evening.

"Will you be kind enough to show me the way to the ferry?" said he, after a moment's pause.

"You have, then, adopted a new subject of inquiry?" observed his companion, with a smile.

"Why, yes, sir," replied Robin, rather dryly. "Thanks to you, and to my other friends, I have at last met my kinsman, and he will scarce desire to see my face again. I begin to grow weary of a town life, sir. Will you show me the way to the ferry?"

"No, my good friend Robin,—not tonight, at least," said the gentleman. "Some few days hence, if you wish it, I will speed you on your journey. Or, if you prefer to remain with us, perhaps, as you are a shrewd youth, you may rise in the world without the help of your kinsman, Major Molineux." ▢▢

Discussion

1. The first paragraph of "My Kinsman, Major Molineux" describes the local unpopularity of the royally appointed Colonial governors in the American Colonies during the seventeenth century. How does this information serve as a "preface" to the story?

2. The first scene of the story shows Robin crossing a river on a ferry boat. What details do we learn in this scene about his situation and character?

3. Robin's town adventures teach him something about life and the world. Discuss the experiences that he has in three successive scenes and what he learns from each of them: in the barber shop; at the tavern; and at the house with the "pretty mistress."

4. Robin finds himself near a church and catches a glimpse of its interior, and then he has a reverie and imaginatively recreates an evening at his father's home. (a) How does the view of the church's interior affect Robin? (b) What happens in his imaginative re-creation of the evening in his father's house?

5. Shortly after these scenes, Robin has his first friendly encounter, a man who joins him in his wait and listens to him talk about his adventures. What does Robin learn from him?

6. As the procession appears, Robin sees that it is led by the brusque, strange-looking man whom he had first encountered at the tavern and later by the church. What is the man's appearance and what does he seem to symbolize?

7. As the motley and merry-making crowd comes into view, there is a momentary lessening of noise. Then there is a peal of laughter. Why does Robin eventually join in this laughter?

Extension • Writing

In the closing of the story, Robin's kind friend urges him to postpone going back home, but rather to stay around for a few days, for he might rise in the world without the help of his kinsman. Write an ending for the story in which you reveal what happened to Robin.

Vocabulary
Dictionary and Structure

Use your Glossary to do the following exercises.

A. All the words below have prefixes and Latin roots. On your paper make three columns. Write the prefix in the first column, the Latin root in the second, and the meaning of the word in the third.

For the word *reprehension* your paper would look like this:

re—*prehendere*—blame

The words are:

1. superfluous **2.** inscrutable
3. antipathy

B. The words below have been formed by adding suffixes to their root forms. On your paper write each root.

1. perseverance **2.** clamorous
3. tempestuous **4.** depreciation

Now write the word from the list above that fits correctly into each sentence below. You will use only the root-plus-suffix form of the word.

5. To do a job right requires patience and _____.

6. When Bob tried to sell his car, he was surprised at the amount of _____ in its value.

7. The telephones were so _____ that the city editor lost his temper.

8. The relationship of the brothers was so _____ that they were always fighting.

Nathaniel Hawthorne
1804 • 1864

One of Hawthorne's ancestors was involved in persecution of the "witches" in Salem, Massachusetts, in the 1690s, and Hawthorne, born in Salem, was haunted by this ancestral guilt. In the introductory essay to his most widely acclaimed work, *The Scarlet Letter,* Hawthorne proclaimed that he took their shame upon himself, and hoped thereby to dispel the curse on them.

Hawthorne was the son of a shipmaster who died when the boy was four. Brought up in a disciplined household where his mother took all her meals in her room, he acquired what he called the "cursed habits" of solitude. After attending Bowdoin College in Maine, he returned home and devoted himself to writing (and destroying) stories, learning his craft while living in isolation. He later romanticized this period as the "twelve dark years."

Gradually Hawthorne's tales began to appear in magazines, and in 1837 he gathered a number of these already published pieces into a volume which he appropriately entitled *Twice-Told Tales* (including "The Minister's Black Veil"). Other volumes of stories appeared: *Mosses from an Old Manse,* 1846 (the Old Manse was the house Hawthorne occupied in the 1840s); and *The Snow Image,* 1851 (containing "My Kinsman, Major Molineux").

In addition to his masterpiece, *The Scarlet Letter* (1850), Hawthorne wrote three notable novels: *The House of the Seven Gables,* an account of an ancestral curse; *The Blithedale Romance,* based on Hawthorne's experiences in the ill-fated experiment in communal living at Brook Farm in the early 1840s; and *The Marble Faun,* a tale of "innocent" Americans in "decadent and treacherous" Italy.

However much Hawthorne criticized his Puritan heritage in his work, he never fully emerged from its shadow. Herman Melville, a close friend and kindred spirit, wrote of him: " . . . in spite of all the Indian-summer sunlight on the hither side of Hawthorne's soul, the other side—like the dark half of the physical sphere—is shrouded in a blackness, ten times black."

Herman Melville

*With the "scent and savor of poverty" upon him, young
Wellingborough Redburn sailed as a "ship's boy" on a
merchant vessel bound for Liverpool, England. On the
voyage over from New York, he learned much from his
fellow seamen about hoisting sails and surviving in a wicked
world. He learned even more about humanity during his
weeks in Liverpool as he roamed the port city's swarming,
dirty streets.*

Culver Pictures, Inc.

What Redburn Saw in Launcelott's-Hey

In going to our boarding-house, the sign of the
Baltimore Clipper, I generally passed through a
narrow street called "Launcelott's-Hey," lined
with dingy, prison-like cotton warehouses. In
this street, or rather alley, you seldom see any
one but a truck-man, or some solitary old
warehouse-keeper, haunting his smoky den like a
ghost.

Once, passing through this place, I heard a
feeble wail, which seemed to come out of the
earth. It was but a strip of crooked side-walk
where I stood; the dingy wall was on every side,
converting the mid-day into twilight; and not a
soul was in sight. I started, and could almost
have run, when I heard that dismal sound. It
seemed the low, hopeless, endless wail of some
one forever lost. At last I advanced to an opening
which communicated downward with deep tiers
of cellars beneath a crumbling old warehouse;
and there, some fifteen feet below the walk,
crouching in nameless squalor, with her head
bowed over, was the figure of what had been a
woman. Her blue arms folded to her livid bosom
two shrunken things like children, that leaned
toward her, one on each side. At first, I knew not
whether they were alive or dead. They made no
sign; they did not move or stir; but from the vault
came that soul-sickening wail.

I made a noise with my foot, which, in the
silence, echoed far and near; but there was no
response. Louder still; when one of the children
lifted its head, and cast upward a faint glance;
then closed its eyes, and lay motionless. The
woman also, now gazed up, and perceived me;

but let fall her eye again. They were dumb and next to dead with want. How they had crawled into that den, I could not tell; but there they had crawled to die. At that moment I never thought of relieving them; for death was so stamped in their glazed and unimploring eyes, that I almost regarded them as already no more. I stood looking down on them, while my whole soul swelled within me; and I asked myself, What right had any body in the wide world to smile and be glad, when sights like this were to be seen? It was enough to turn the heart to gall; and make a man-hater of a Howard. For who were these ghosts that I saw? Were they not human beings? A woman and two girls? With eyes, and lips, and ears like any queen? with hearts which, though they did not bound with blood, yet beat with a dull, dead ache that was their life.

At last, I walked on toward an open lot in the alley hoping to meet there some ragged old women, whom I had daily noticed groping amid foul rubbish for little particles of dirty cotton, which they washed out and sold for a trifle.

I found them; and accosting one, I asked if she knew of the persons I had just left. She replied, that she did not; nor did she want to. I then asked another, a miserable, toothless old woman, with a tattered strip of coarse baling stuff round her body. Looking at me for an instant, she resumed her raking in the rubbish, and said that she knew who it was that I spoke of; but that she had no time to attend to beggars and their brats. Accosting still another, who seemed to know my errand, I asked if there was no place to which the woman could be taken. "Yes," she replied, "to the churchyard." I said she was alive, and not dead.

"Then she'll never die," was the rejoinder. "She's been down there these three days, with nothing to eat;—that I know myself."

"She desarves it," said an old hag, who was just placing on her crooked shoulders her bag of pickings, and who was turning to totter off, "that Betsey Jennings desarves it—was she ever married? tell me that."

Leaving Launcelott's-Hey, I turned into a more frequented street; and soon meeting a policeman, told him of the condition of the woman and the girls.

"It's none of my business, Jack," said he. "I don't belong to that street."

"Who does then?"

"I don't know. But what business is it of yours? Are you not a Yankee?"

"Yes," said I, "but come, I will help you remove that woman, if you say so."

"There, now, Jack, go on board your ship, and stick to it; and leave these matters to the town."

I accosted two more policemen, but with no better success; they would not even go with me to the place. The truth was, it was out of the way, in a silent, secluded spot; and the misery of the three outcasts, hiding away in the ground, did not obtrude upon any one.

Returning to them, I again stamped to attract their attention; but this time, none of the three looked up, or even stirred. While I yet stood irresolute, a voice called to me from a high, iron-shuttered window in a loft over the way; and asked what I was about. I beckoned to the man, a sort of porter, to come down, which he did; when I pointed down into the vault.

"Well," said he, "what of it?"

"Can't we get them out?" said I, "haven't you some place in your warehouse where you can put them? have you nothing for them to eat?"

"You're crazy, boy," said he; "do you suppose, that Parkins and Wood want their warehouse turned into a hospital?"

I then went to my boarding-house, and told Handsome Mary of what I had seen; asking her if she could not do something to get the woman and girls removed; or if she could not do that, let me have some food for them. But though a kind person in the main, Mary replied that she gave away enough to beggars in her own street (which was true enough) without looking after the whole neighborhood.

Going into the kitchen, I accosted the cook, a little shriveled-up old Welshwoman, with a saucy tongue, whom the sailors called *Brandy-Nan*; and begged her to give me some cold victuals, if she had nothing better, to take to the vault. But she broke out in a storm of swearing at the miserable occupants of the vault, and refused. I then stepped into the room where our dinner was being spread; and waiting till the girl had gone out, I snatched some bread and cheese from a stand, and thrusting it into the bosom of my frock, left the house. Hurrying to the lane, I dropped the food down into the vault. One of the girls caught at it convulsively, but fell back, apparently fainting; the sister pushed the other's arm aside, and took the bread in her hand; but with a weak uncertain grasp like an infant's. She placed it to her mouth; but letting it fall again, murmured faintly something like "water." The woman did not stir; her head was bowed over, just as I had first seen her.

Seeing how it was, I ran down toward the docks to a mean little sailor tavern, and begged for a pitcher; but the cross old man who kept it refused, unless I would pay for it. But I had no money. So as my boardinghouse was some way off, and it would be lost time to run to the ship for my big iron pot; under the impulse of the moment, I hurried to one of the Boodle Hydrants, which I remembered having seen running near the scene of a still smoldering fire in an old rag house; and taking off a new tarpaulin hat, which had been loaned me that day, filled it with water.

With this, I returned to Launcelott's-Hey; and with considerable difficulty, like getting down into a well, I contrived to descend with it into the vault; where there was hardly space enough left to let me stand. The two girls drank out of the hat together; looking up at me with an unalterable, idiotic expression, that almost made me faint. The woman spoke not a word, and did not stir. While the girls were breaking and eating the bread, I tried to lift the woman's head; but, feeble as she was, she seemed bent upon holding it down. Observing her arms still clasped upon her bosom, and that something seemed hidden under the rags there, a thought crossed my mind, which impelled me forcibly to withdraw her hands for a moment; when I caught a glimpse of a meager little babe, the lower part of its body thrust into an old bonnet. Its face was dazzlingly white, even in its squalor; but the closed eyes looked like balls of indigo. It must have been dead some hours.

The woman refusing to speak, eat, or drink, I asked one of the girls who they were, and where they lived; but she only stared vacantly, muttering something that could not be understood.

The air of the place was now getting too much for me; but I stood deliberating a moment, whether it was possible for me to drag them out of the vault. But if I did, what then? They would only perish in the street, and here they were at least protected from the rain; and more than that, might die in seclusion.

I crawled up into the street, and looking down upon them again, almost repented that I had brought them any food; for it would only tend to prolong their misery, without hope of any permanent relief: for die they must very soon; they were too far gone for any medicine to help them. I hardly know whether I ought to confess another thing that occurred to me as I stood there; but it was this—I felt an almost irresistible impulse to do them the last mercy, of in some way putting an end to their horrible lives; and I should almost have done so, I think, had I not been deterred by thoughts of the law. For I well knew that the law, which would let them perish of themselves without giving them one cup of water, would spend a thousand pounds, if necessary, in convicting him who should so much as offer to relieve them from their miserable existence.

The next day, and the next, I passed the vault three times, and still met the same sight. The girls leaning up against the woman on each side, and the woman with her arms still folding the babe, and her head bowed. The first evening I did not see the bread that I had dropped down in the morning; but the second evening, the bread I had dropped that morning remained untouched. On the third morning the smell that came from the vault was such, that I accosted the same policeman I had accosted before, who was patrolling the same street, and told him that the persons I had spoken to him about were dead, and he had better have them removed. He looked as if he did not believe me, and added, that it was not his street.

When I arrived at the docks on my way to the ship, I entered the guard-house within the walls, and asked for one of the captains, to whom I told the story; but, from what he said, was led to infer that the Dock Police was distinct from that of the town, and this was not the right place to lodge my information.

I could do no more that morning, being obliged to repair to the ship; but at twelve o'clock, when I went to dinner, I hurried into Launcelott's-Hey, when I found that the vault was empty. In place of the woman and children, a heap of quick-lime was glistening.

I could not learn who had taken them away, or whither they had gone; but my prayer was answered—they were dead, departed, and at peace.

But again I looked down into the vault, and in fancy beheld the pale, shrunken forms still crouching there. Ah! what are our creeds, and how do we hope to be saved? Tell me, oh Bible, that story of Lazarus[1] again, that I may find comfort in my heart for the poor and forlorn. Surrounded as we are by the wants and woes of our fellow-men, and yet given to follow our own pleasures, regardless of their pains, are we not like people sitting up with a corpse, and making merry in the house of the dead? □□

---

1. *Lazarus* (laz′ə rəs), an allusion to Jesus' parable of the beggar Lazarus and the rich man who did not help him. Lazarus is comforted in Heaven (Luke 16:19–31).

Discussion

1. (a) What was the nature of the sound that attracted Redburn's attention to the opening in the street called Launcelott's-Hey? **(b)** Describe Redburn's reaction to what he saw.

2. Redburn exerts great effort in an attempt to get someone to do something about what he has seen. **(a)** What is the reaction of the "ragged old woman"? The policeman? The "sort of porter"? Handsome Mary? Brandy-Nan? The owner of the "mean little sailor tavern"? **(b)** What does Redburn learn about human nature from his attempt to get help for the destitute woman and her children?

3. What is the thought that Redburn hesitantly confesses after he has brought water and food to the dying woman and children? Discuss.

Herman Melville
1819 • 1891

Herman Melville was born into a distinguished but financially unstable New York family. When his father died in 1832 Melville left school to take on a series of jobs, finally shipping as cabin boy to Liverpool. This voyage, to be described in *Redburn* (1849), was the beginning of many remarkable experiences which would become the foundation for his novels. He next sailed for the South Seas on a whaler, the voyage which would later provide the background for *Moby Dick* (1851). He jumped ship at the Marquesas Islands, and as related in *Typee* (1846), took refuge among the cannibalistic Typees. He lived with them a short while and then left on a passing Australian whaler which dropped him off in Tahiti. His stay in Tahiti resulted in *Omoo* (1847). He then enlisted as an ordinary seaman on the frigate *United States* until the ship's eventual return to Boston. His account of cruelty and tyranny in *White Jacket* (1850) added fuel to a movement which would shortly result in the abolition of flogging on ships of the U.S. Navy.

The colorful descriptions of Melville's experiences in *Typee* and *Omoo* won the interest of a curious and fascinated public. He was widely read and became known as the man who had lived amongst cannibals. But with succeeding works Melville's craft became deeper and more demanding. A public which preferred simple adventure had little use for symbolism and allegory. As the brilliance of his writing increased, his popularity diminished. His criticism of missionaries in *Omoo* had further set segments of the public against him. Thus when his masterpiece *Moby Dick* was published just five years after his initial success, it was ignored, and remained largely unread for over seventy years.

After the exhaustive effort of *Moby Dick* and the disappointment of its reception, Melville's productivity decreased sharply. He supported himself in his later years as a customs inspector and died forgotten at the age of seventy-two.

Some of the subsequent histories of American literature did not even mention his name, for it was widely felt he had failed to fulfill his early promise. However, Robert Louis Stevenson is said to have stated that Melville's books about the South Pacific were the best ever written. Melville was finally rediscovered in the 1920s and today *Moby Dick* is considered by many the greatest American novel ever written.

Frederick Douglass

from What the Black Man Wants

*(Delivered at the Annual Meeting of the Massachusetts
Anti-Slavery Society in Boston, 1865)*

. . . I have had but one idea for the last three years to present to the American people, and the phraseology in which I clothe it is the old abolition phraseology. I am for the "immediate, unconditional, and universal" enfranchisement of the black man, in every state in the Union. Without this, his liberty is a mockery; without this, you might as well almost retain the old name of slavery for his condition; for, in fact, if he is not the slave of the individual master, he is the slave of society, and holds his liberty as a privilege, not as a right. He is at the mercy of the mob, and has no means of protecting himself.

It may be objected, however, that this pressing of the Negro's right to suffrage is premature. Let us have slavery abolished, it may be said, let us have labor organized, and then, in the natural course of events, the right of suffrage will be extended to the Negro. I do not agree with this. The constitution of the human mind is such, that if it once disregards the conviction forced upon it by a revelation of truth, it requires the exercise of a higher power to produce the same conviction afterward. The American people are now in tears. The Shenandoah has run blood,[1] the best blood of the North. All around Richmond, the blood of New England and of the North has been shed, of your sons, your brothers, and your fathers. We all feel, in the existence of this rebellion, that judgments terrible, widespread, far-reaching, overwhelming, are abroad in the land; and we feel, in view of these judgments, just now, a disposition to learn righteousness. This is the hour. Our streets are in mourning, tears are falling at every fireside, and under the chastisement of this rebellion we have almost come up to the point of conceding this great, this all-important right of suffrage. I fear that if we fail to do it now, if Abolitionists fail to press it now, we may not see, for centuries to come, the same disposition that exists at this moment. Hence, I say, now is the time to press this right.

It may be asked, "Why do you want it? Some men have got along very well without it. Women have not this right." Shall we justify one wrong by another? That is a sufficient answer. Shall we at this moment justify the deprivation of the Negro of the right to vote, because some one else is deprived of that privilege? I hold that women, as well as men, have the right to vote, and my heart and my voice go with the movement to extend suffrage to woman; but that question rests upon another basis than that on which our right rests. We may be asked, I say, why we want it. I will tell you why we want it. We want it because it is our right, first of all. No class of men can, without insulting their own nature, be content with any deprivations of their rights. We want it, again, as a means for educating our race. Men are so constituted that they derive their conviction of their own possibilities largely from the estimate formed of them by others. If nothing is expected of a people, that people will find it difficult to contradict that expectation. By depriving us of suffrage, you affirm our incapacity to form an intelligent judgment respecting public men and public measures; you declare before the world that we are unfit to exercise the elective franchise, and by this means lead us to undervalue ourselves, to put a low estimate upon ourselves, and to feel that we have no possibilities like other men. Again, I want the elective franchise, for one, as a colored man, because ours is a peculiar government, based upon a peculiar idea, and that idea is universal suffrage. If I were in a monarchical government, or an autocratic or

---

1. **Shenandoah . . . blood.** The valley of the Shenandoah River in Virginia was the scene of some of the bloodiest campaigns in the Civil War.

aristocratic government, where the few bore rule and the many were subject, there would be no special stigma resting upon me, because I did not exercise the elective franchise. It would do me no great violence. Mingling with the mass, I should partake of the strength of the mass, and I should have the same incentives to endeavor with the mass of my fellow men; it would be no particular burden, no particular deprivation; but here, where universal suffrage is the rule, where that is the fundamental idea of the government, to rule us out is to make us an exception, to brand us with the stigma of inferiority, and to invite to our heads the missiles of those about us; therefore, I want the franchise for the black man. . . .

I ask my friends who are apologizing for not insisting upon this right, where can the black man look in this country for the assertion of this right, if he may not look to the Massachusetts Anti-Slavery Society? Where under the whole heavens can he look for sympathy in asserting this right, if he may not look to this platform? Have you lifted us up to a certain height to see that we are men, and then are any disposed to leave us there, without seeing that we are put in possession of all our rights? We look naturally to this platform for the assertion of all our rights, and for this one especially. I understand the anti-slavery societies of this country to be based on two principles—first, the freedom of the blacks of this country; and, second, the elevation of them. Let me not be misunderstood here. I am not asking for sympathy at the hands of Abolitionists, sympathy at the hands of any. I think the American people are disposed often to be generous rather than just. I look over this country at the present time, and I see educational societies, sanitary commissions, freedmen's associations and the like,—all very good: but in regard to the colored people there is always more that is benevolent, I perceive, than just, manifested towards us. What I ask for the Negro is not benevolence, not pity, not sympathy, but simple justice. The American people have always been anxious to know what they shall do with us. . . .

Everybody has asked the question, and they learned to ask it early of the Abolitionists, "What shall we do with the Negro?" I have had but one answer from the beginning. Do nothing with us!

Your doing with us has already played the mischief with us. Do nothing with us! If the apples will not remain on the tree of their own strength, if they are worm-eaten at the core, if they are early ripe and disposed to fall, let them fall! I am not for tying or fastening them on the tree in any way, except by nature's plan, and if they will not stay there, let them fall. And if the Negro can not

Black voters at the polls in 1867, early in the Reconstruction Era, when the South was occupied by Federal troops. (The Bettmann Archive, Inc.)

JOURNAL OF CIVILIZATION.

Vol. XI.—No. 568.]   NEW YORK, SATURDAY, NOVEMBER 16, 1867.

"THE FIRST VOTE."—Drawn by A. R. Waud.—[See Next Page.]

stand on his own legs, let him fall also. All I ask is, give him a chance to stand on his own legs! Let him alone! If you see him on his way to school, let him alone,—don't disturb him. If you see him going to the dinner table at a hotel, let him go! If you see him going to the ballot-box, let him alone,—don't disturb him! If you see him going into a workshop, just let him alone,—your interference is doing him a positive injury. . . . Let him fall if he can not stand alone! If the Negro can not live by the line of eternal justice, . . . the fault will not be yours; it will be his who made the Negro, and established that line for his government. Let him live or die by that. If you will only untie his hands, and give him a chance, I think he will live. . . . ▢▢

Discussion

1. (a) What is Douglass's purpose in speaking to his audience as he does? **(b)** Of what does he hope to convince them?

2. Notice the date of the address. Why is Douglass afraid that the society will not sustain its zeal in working for black suffrage? Support your answer with passages from the text.

3. One rhetorical technique often used by those who hope to convince is that of anticipating and stating the arguments that one's opponent is likely to give, and answering these arguments even before the opponent has had a chance to voice them. Douglass makes use of this technique at least three times in his address. **(a)** What are these arguments? **(b)** How does Douglass refute them? Support your answers with passages from the text.

4. Douglass states that the " . . . American people are disposed often to be generous rather than just." What is the difference between generosity and justice? Which quality do you find more admirable? Why?

5. Reread the last two paragraphs of the address; contrast their tone with that of Pennington's narrative (p. 185). Support any points you make.

Frederick Douglass
1817 • 1895

Douglass was born a slave in Maryland. During his childhood he spent some time in a Baltimore home as a house servant, where he was taught to read and write. After one attempt to escape failed, he made another try, got away, and went to New York City.

Upon reading William Lloyd Garrison's abolitionist newspaper, *The Liberator,* Douglass became active in the antislavery movement. In 1845 he published *Narrative of the Life of Frederick Douglass.* The next two years found him traveling to Ireland and England, where his experiences made him see emancipation as only a first step in the struggle of blacks for complete independence.

When Douglass returned to the United States he purchased his freedom and established an independent black newspaper, the *North Star.* During the Civil War, he helped organize regiments of black soldiers for the Union Army, and after the war he continued his activities by working for black suffrage and civil rights. After holding a number of official government positions in his later years, he was finally appointed Minister to Haiti.

Abraham Lincoln

Gettysburg Address

Four score and seven years ago our fathers brought forth on this continent a new nation, conceived in liberty and dedicated to the proposition that all men are created equal.

Now we are engaged in a great civil war, testing whether that nation or any nation so conceived and so dedicated can long endure. We are met on a great battlefield of that war. We have come to dedicate a portion of that field as a final resting place for those who here gave their lives that that nation might live. It is altogether fitting and proper that we should do this.

But, in a larger sense, we cannot dedicate— we cannot consecrate— we cannot hallow—this ground. The brave men, living and dead, who struggled here have consecrated it far above our poor power to add or detract. The world will little note nor long remember what we say here, but it can never forget what they did here. It is for us, the living, rather, to be dedicated here to the unfinished work which they who fought here have thus far so nobly advanced.

It is rather for us to be here dedicated to the great task remaining before us—that from these honored dead we take increased devotion to that cause for which they gave the last full measure of devotion; that we here highly resolve that these dead shall not have died in vain; that this nation, under God, shall have a new birth of freedom; and that government of the people, by the people, for the people shall not perish from the earth. □□

Discussion

1. The Gettysburg Address has been much admired for its eloquence. (a) What emotional effect on the audience is Lincoln trying to create? (b) With what means does he achieve this effect? (c) What is the climactic point of the speech? Explain.

2. What do you think is meant by each of the three following phrases: "a government of the people, by the people, and for the people"?

Abraham Lincoln
1809 • 1865

James Russell Lowell once described Lincoln as "the first American." A hundred years later he remains the foremost figure in our national mythology. Homely, largely self-educated, faced with the greatest crisis that his country had yet faced, Lincoln was hated as well as loved. He suffered patiently through setback after setback before the Union he loved was finally saved. Then he died at the hands of an assassin, calling forth national mourning.

Chief Seattle

Before signing a treaty yielding his tribe's lands to white settlers, Chief Seattle of the Dwamish people made the following speech to Isaac Stevens, Governor of Washington Territory, in 1854.

This Sacred Soil

Yonder sky that has wept tears of compassion upon my people for centuries untold, and which to us appears changeless and eternal, may change. Today is fair. Tomorrow it may be overcast with clouds. My words are like the stars that never change. Whatever Seattle says the great chief at Washington can rely upon with as much certainty as he can upon the return of the sun or the seasons. The White Chief says that Big Chief at Washington sends us greetings of friendship and goodwill. That is kind of him for we know he has little need of our friendship in return. His people are many. They are like the grass that covers vast prairies. My people are few. They resemble the scattering trees of a storm-swept plain. . . . I will not dwell on, nor mourn over, our untimely decay, nor reproach our paleface brothers with hastening it, as we too may have been somewhat to blame. . . .

Your God is not our God. Your God loves your people and hates mine. He folds his strong and protecting arms lovingly about the paleface and leads him by the hand as a father leads his infant son—but He has forsaken His red children—if they really are his. Our God, the Great Spirit, seems also to have forsaken us. Your God makes your people strong every day. Soon they will fill the land. Our people are ebbing away like a rapidly receding tide that will never return. The white man's God cannot love our

From NORTHWEST GATEWAY: THE STORY OF THE PORT OF SEATTLE by Archie Binns, Copyright 1941, pp. 100–104. Reprinted by permission of Ellen F. Binns.

Scotts Bluff on the Oregon Trail (1837), by Alfred Jacob Miller. (Walters Art Gallery, Baltimore.)

people or He would protect them. They seem to be orphans who can look nowhere for help. How then can we be brothers? . . . We are two distinct races with separate origins and separate destinies. There is little in common between us.

To us the ashes of our ancestors are sacred and their resting place is hallowed ground. You wander far from the graves of your ancestors and seemingly without regret. Your religion was written upon tables of stone by the iron finger of your God so that you could not forget. The Red Man could never comprehend nor remember it. Our religion is the traditions of our ancestors— the dreams of our old men, given them in solemn hours of night by the Great Spirit; and the visions of our sachems; and it is written in the hearts of our people.

Your dead cease to love you and the land of their nativity as soon as they pass the portals of the tomb and wander way beyond the stars. They are soon forgotten and never return. Our dead never forget the beautiful world that gave them being.

Day and night cannot dwell together. The Red Man has ever fled the approach of the White Man, as the morning mist flees before the morning sun. However, your proposition seems fair and I think that my people will accept it and will retire to the reservation you offer them. Then we will dwell apart in peace. . . . It matters little where we pass the remnant of our days. They will not be many. A few more moons; a few more winters—and not one of the descendants of the mighty hosts that once moved over this broad

CHIEF SEATTLE 283

land or lived in happy homes, protected by the Great Spirit, will remain to mourn over the graves of a people once more powerful and hopeful than yours. But why should I mourn at the untimely fate of my people? Tribe follows tribe, and nation follows nation, like the waves of the sea. It is the order of nature, and regret is useless. Your time of decay may be distant, but it will surely come, for even the White Man whose God walked and talked with him as friend with friend, cannot be exempt from the common destiny. We may be brothers after all. We will see. . . .

Every part of this soil is sacred in the estimation of my people. Every hillside, every valley, every plain and grove, has been hallowed by some sad or happy event in days long vanished. The very dust upon which you now stand responds more lovingly to their footsteps than to yours, because it is rich with the blood of our ancestors and our bare feet are conscious of the sympathetic touch. Even the little children who lived here and rejoiced here for a brief season will love these somber solitudes and at eventide they greet shadowy returning spirits. And when the last Red Man shall have perished, and the memory of my tribe shall have become a myth among the White Men, these shores will swarm with the invisible dead of my tribe, and when your children's children think themselves alone in the field, the store, the shop, upon the highway, or in the silence of the pathless woods, they will not be alone. At night when the streets of your cities and villages are silent and you think them deserted, they will throng with the returning hosts that once filled and still love this beautiful land. The White Man will never be alone.

Let him be just and deal kindly with my people, for the dead are not powerless. Dead, did I say? There is no death, only a change of worlds. □□

Discussion

1. (a) Identify the following figures of speech and explain what element they have in common: "yonder sky that *has wept tears* of compassion"; "my words are *like the stars* that never change"; "they [the white people] are *like the grass* that covers vast prairies"; "they [the Indians] *resemble the scattering trees* of a storm-swept plain." (b) What can you infer about the speaker from his use of these particular images?

2. The Chief says: " . . . when the last Red Man shall have perished, and the memory of my tribe shall have become a myth among the White Men, these shores will swarm with the invisible dead of my tribe. . . . they will throng with the returning hosts that once filled and still love this beautiful land." In what ways has Seattle's prophecy come true in contemporary attitudes toward (a) native American cultures—past and present—and (b) America's natural environment?

3. (a) Compare Seattle's speech in **tone** with those of Douglass and Lincoln. (b) Discuss how the historical setting and audience of each speech apparently influenced each speaker's tone and purpose.

Chief Seattle
?1786 • 1866

Seattle was a chief of the Dwamish, Squamish, and allied Indian tribes of the Northwest. He befriended the first white settlers and signed a treaty ceding land in 1855. After becoming a Roman Catholic, he incorporated some of the Catholic rituals in Indian ceremonies. Seattle, Washington, was built in the area of his birth, but he did not want the city named after him because legend said that, after his death, his spirit would be troubled each time his name was spoken.

Mollie Dorsey Sanford

Mollie Dorsey was only eighteen years old when she traveled with her mother, father, and seven brothers and sisters into Nebraska Territory to settle the new frontier.

Homesteading on the Little Nemaha (1857)

"Little Nemaha"—June 5th

By sunrise on Wednesday morning, the wagons were packed, and we had started upon the road. Father, Mother, and the smaller children rode with Mr. Hemphill, a towheaded delegate from the settlement (and if he is a specimen of the fellows out there, oh! deliver us, sweet fate, deliver us!) We girls rode with Mr. Henry Brown, a Neb. City gent and a nice travelling companion!

It was cool and cloudy all day. The prairies were soft and green as velvet carpets, the atmosphere laden with the perfume of a thousand flowers.

We travelled 14 miles before stopping, over a road sometimes level as a floor, then up and down, through gullies and ruts, through tangled grass and muddy sloughs, until we reached the cabin of Mr. McWilliams and the only one to be seen. On the trip, here and there as we came along we could see small claim shanties, where people had taken up land, but not a tree or shrub in sight until we reached the first branch of the Nemaha.

We borrowed a table and had our dinners in the "bachelors hall." During the two hours nooning rambled through the woods. It is refreshing to come to these patches of timber, after travelling for hours over a treeless plain.

Leaving the Nemaha, we were again on the prairie, on, on, with no travelled road, and apparently no object in view.

We had planned to make the trip to our home that day, and whose line of timber was visible in the twilight only several miles away. One of the horses gave out and we lost our track in the grass. Father lost his bearings, and we were compelled to stop for the night. We were near a slough of brackish water, warm and muddy, and had to use the dry weeds for fuel to boil our kettle for tea. It tasted deliciously, the hot steaming beverage, but when we came to use the rest of the water for our dishes, we found the dishrag had been boiled up in it, and that accounted for the rich flavor of the tea. "Campers" must expect such things, the men say. Mother tried to get rid of her supper by retching herself almost to death,

Reprinted from MOLLIE: THE JOURNAL OF MOLLIE DORSEY SANFORD IN NEBRASKA AND COLORADO TERRITORIES by Mollie Dorsey Sanford, with an introduction and notes by Donald F. Danker, by permission of University of Nebraska Press. Copyright © 1959 by the University of Nebraska Press.

but I held on determinedly to mine, after having so hard a time to get it.

By the light of dried weeds we made our beds on the ground beneath the wagons. The teamsters laid on the grass with nothing to shelter them.

The sensation of sleeping out of doors was queer enough, *out* under the twinkling stars, in the bosom of the broad prairie, *sounds* romantic enough but we did not speculate about it and were glad to close our weary eyes in sleep, and dreams.

About one o'clock, the wind came up, the horses were uneasy, and Father thought we had better be travelling on, as a storm was coming, and the rain is something dreadful on the plains with no place of shelter.

Hitching up in a hurry, they piled us into the wagons again, and we took up our line of march.

But where were we going? Darkness was over all, no light, no road! Father made a torch and finally found the track but so faint he had to *keep* hunting it. We sometimes stopped entirely, until the voice of our guide would hallo for us to "come ahead."

As morning approached, the clouds passed away and our fears were allayed, the storm spirit no doubt pitying our helpless condition.

Soon the bright face of morning peeped o'er the eastern horizon, when we again came in view of the timber surrounding our home. It gave new hope to us, and new speed to the horses; and we soon reached the woods. I never felt more relieved and thankful, now that we had come through safely and were coming to a home of our own once more.

The sunrise was glorious! the trees full of singing birds, ringing out a welcome. Soft zephyrs floated o'er us, bright flowers gave out their perfume, and all nature was glad. Father had named the place "Hazel Dell," and we christened it by singing that sweet song. And such a chorus as went up from those lumbering wagons! Birds stopped their carols to listen, and festive chipmunks flew from their hiding places, bewildered with the noise. And when we reached the cabin joyful hurrahs! resounded long and loud.

It was not long before the cook stove was set out and a bounteous breakfast was served, delicious coffee made from the clear, sparkling water of the Nemaha, with no taint of stewed dishrags to spoil the effect. Even Father and Mother were as gleeful as the children, for a while.

The "Nemaha" here is about 20 ft. wide, a clear, sparkling stream where myriads of tiny fish sport, and whose banks are overhung with creeping vines and flowers.

Great elm trees grow on its margin, their branches intertwining, forming an arch overhead. The foliage is dense, and such an air of quiet seclusion as surrounds the place! is restful at least.

The little boys have been chasing squirrels and finding all sorts of curiosities in the woods, and are wild with delight.

Our cabin is of hewn logs, a good-sized room of 20 ft. square, two windows and one door, and a clapboard roof. We are quite settled and look cozy, and if there is not room enough inside there is plenty out of doors, yes! plenty!!

Mother hardly enters into extacies. She no doubt realizes what it is to bring a young rising family away from the advantages of the world. To *me*, it seems a glorious holiday, a freedom from restraint, and I believe it will be a blessing to we girls. We were getting too fond of style, too unhappy not to have the necessary things to carry it out.

Uncle George and Mr. Daily are keeping bachelors hall across the creek. They say, no more quiet for them, no more morning snoozes. It seems when Father left we were handed over to their tender care. I informed them I could care for myself.

Wednesday, 12th

A week in our new home already. One would suppose time would hang heavily upon our hands, but no. We all work in the garden. With the help of Mr. Daily and George we have quite a patch. The soil is light and loamy and easily prepared. I never made garden before, but then, I'm prepared to do anything.

Father returned to the city with Mr. Brown the day after we got here. He will come home occasionally. He has work, and needs to keep employed, and I often feel guilty to think he is working hard and we are almost idle. With our increased health and appetites it will take hard work to keep the "wolf from the door." That

Photograph from Mollie Sanford/Museum of New Mexico.

reminds me that we may have to *fight* to keep the wolf from the door ourselves, for the woods are full of them, or the *prairies* are. The family are horrified because I sleep with my head outside the door. The nights are suffocating, and I lie on the floor, with the door half open and my head on the threshold. I suppose it is hardly wise, for there are rattle snakes around here, altho we have not seen any yet.

June 20th

Had another call today, a black-eyed lawyer from Neb. City, Mr. Mann. He had walked, and was very tired, besides having an encounter with a rattle snake, and had the rattles as a trophy of his bravery.

I said, "O! Mr. Mann, describe a rattle snake. I never saw one." He began by saying, "It is as long as a common stick, dark in color, and has a bunch of rattles on the end of its—" then a blank—filled by his taking his handkerchief and wiping the perspiration from his "man-ly" brow. I meekly suggested, "On the end of its tail, Mr. Mann." "Yes! Yes!" he gasped, "on the end of its t-a-i-l."

I might have said "narrative," since he was too modest to use the more vulgar expression. He brought a bundle of letters and some messages from Father.

After Mr. Mann left we went to the creek to bathe. We have a lovely bathing hole, and some improvised bathing suits, a secluded place, where we have grand sport splashing in the water. The boys have a swimming hole, and I have almost learned to float.

We were called to the house to meet Mr. Will Hemphill, our "tow-headed" teamster, who, with his brother, has a claim nearby. He was rigged in a white cotton suit with "yaller" necktie and huge straw hat and looked "blonder" and *blander* than ever and, but for the twirling of the hat, I don't know what he would have done with his hands. He stayed, and lingered, until I exhausted my powers of entertainment, and finally said "guessed he'd go but would come again soon." No sooner had he left than Daily and Uncle George came in, full of fun, with "O! ho! had a beau!" and come to find out they had persuaded him to come and ask for my company, telling him that I had fallen in love with him on

the trip from town. He was goose enough to believe it.

Then I understood why all the folks had left the room, and we alone. I suppose I must have *awed* him—I certainly tried to. I'll be even with those boys yet, if it takes me all summer!

Sabbath eve, June 27th (?)

The hands of the clock, even now, point to bedtime, but I generally take time to write, when all are asleep, and by the dim light of my candle scribble my conflicting thoughts, for they are sometimes sad, and sometimes gay. Life is full of smiles and tears.

I do try to feel that it is all for the best to be away off here. I can see and feel that it chafes Mother's spirit. It worries her to think that we are in such straitened circumstances, but my father had to make a change. His idea is to secure this land for the benefit of his boys, who will soon be able to care for it. If the country would only fill up, if there were only schools or churches, or even some society. We do not see a woman at all. All men, single, or bachelors, and one gets tired of them. Then it is unpleasant for Father to be gone from home. *That* seems to discourage Mother. He will be home now in a few days to make us a visit. We will make home happy for him.

June 29th

Father came home last night with Mr. Hochstetter's family. Mr. H. is to take a piece of land a mile above us. They were brought out by my hero of the "coffee scrape," Mr. Byron N. Sanford. They are with us until their cabin can be fixed up some. They came to live on the place long enough to secure it. We are delighted to have a family near us, to see a live woman again.

I have become a little acquainted with "By," as they call him. I have made it all right about shutting the door in his face. Today while mixing up my bread he came and planted himself directly before me. I felt embarrassed and asked him to leave, but he would not and kept on watching me. I think I never made such a mess in my life, with a batch of dough. I felt like daubing it into his whiskers (which, by the way, are splendid), and I find he has pleasant blue eyes.

It is refreshing to meet a fellow like him after

seeing so many flattering fops. It is wonderful how free and easy people become in this country.

I would once have thought it too presuming for a gent to make himself so much at home on so short an acquaintance. Our floor is piled full of beds tonight. The menfolks have gone to Daily's cabin to sleep.

June 30th

I killed a rattle snake today, a huge one, with eleven rattles. But for its timely warning I might not be here to tell the tale. I was in my bare feet going down the path to the creek, and almost stepped upon it. The "rattles" are preserved as a trophy and his defunct snakeship hung on the limb of a tree, a warning to all of its kind. Only to think of being out here among wild cats, wolves, and snakes!!

July 2nd

"My" Mr. Sanford came out today, bringing that load of provision. We find plenty of wild berries through the woods and will have quanti-ties of fruit later. I don't know *why* I should call Mr. Sanford "mine" unless because the folks have assigned him to me, and because I like him. He is the cutest fellow I ever met. Father has come back to spend the Fourth. The weather is intensely hot. We almost live out of doors, gypsies that we are.

July 5th

The heat is intense. The glorious "Fourth" has passed. The little brothers tried to make it seem like "Fourth of July back home" by marching to the tune of "Yankee Doodle," with tin pans as drum accompaniment, with flags and banners of red flannel. Will was disgusted because we did not all join in the procession, and only comforted to know that we were preparing dinner, and by Mr. Daily firing his revolver. So "Hazel Dell" can boast of a *demonstration.* Mr. Daily had sent for a box of lemons and some confectionery. We had baked up some good things and with Mr. Hochstetter and Sanford as guests, had our dinner under the trees. We sang the national songs, and had a nice time. □□

Discussion

1. There are many descriptions and accounts presented in Sanford's diary that were written soon after the places were seen or the events experienced. How might the effect be changed if she had waited until several years later and written from memory? Choose a passage you particularly like and explain in what ways that passage might have changed.

2. In the accounts of the episodes with Will Hemphill and Byron Sanford, what details suggest that Mollie Dorsey might become Mollie Dorsey Sanford and not Mollie Dorsey Hemphill?

3. What qualities in the writing suggest that Mollie can endure frontier life—and even prevail? Discuss.

Mollie Dorsey Sanford
1839 • 1915

Sanford's adventures did not end with the homesteading in Nebraska. She married the man mentioned in the excerpts from her *Diary,* Byron N. Sanford. The young couple caught "Pikes Peak Fever" and joined the gold rush to Colorado in 1860. Mollie kept her diary dur-ing the seven-week trip across the Great Plains to Denver, then continued it for several years after. It records hazards and hardships, as well as triumphs and achievements. She willed her diary to her grandson, saying: "I desire that it shall be kept in the family and treasured as a relic of bygone days, not from any especial merit it possesses, but because I do not want to be forgotten."

Tests 4: American Classic

CONTENT REVIEW

1. It has been said that Thoreau put Emerson's theory into practice. What ideas do you find in the excerpts from *Walden* that parallel or relate in some way to those found in the excerpts from "Self-Reliance"?

2. Melville's Redburn learned something about human nature (in "What Redburn Saw in Launcelott's-Hey") when he tried to get people to help the dying woman in Liverpool. Compare what he learned with the portrayal of human nature in Hawthorne's two stories, "The Minister's Black Veil" and "My Kinsman, Major Molineux."

3. Emerson and Thoreau have often been called the party of hope (optimists) in American literature, and Hawthorne and Melville have been called the party of despair (pessimists). Or it is sometimes said that Emerson and Thoreau emphasize the bright side of life, while Hawthorne and Melville emphasize the dark side. From your knowledge of their work discuss the applicability or suitability of these labels or categories.

4. In the diaries of Louisa May Alcott and Mollie Sanford, do you detect any of the traits that Emerson and Thoreau called for in "Self-Reliance" or *Walden?* Discuss.

5. The speeches by Frederick Douglass and Chief Seattle embody protests (directly or by implication) against the way blacks and native Americans have been treated in America. **(a)** What do you suppose the Thoreau of "Civil Disobedience" might have advised them to do? **(b)** In what way are these protests relevant today?

Unit 4, Test I
INTERPRETATION: NEW MATERIAL

Speech to the First Women's Rights Convention

Elizabeth Cady Stanton

On July 19, 1848, Elizabeth Cady Stanton was the principal speaker at the first convention of the women's rights movement. Stanton first became aware that women were denied political and economic rights when she heard the stories of women who came to her father, an attorney, for legal aid. As she grew older, she became increasingly convinced of the need for women to organize to attain those rights.

Her ambitions culminated in the first women's rights convention in Seneca Falls, New York. Stanton's keynote address to the small but enthusiastic audience got the movement off to a rousing start.

Read the selection. Then on your paper write the letter of the correct answer for each item. Do not write in the book.

We have met here today to discuss our rights and wrongs, civil and political, and not, as some have supposed, to go into the detail of social life alone. We do not propose to petition the legislature to make our husbands just, generous, and courteous, to seat every man at the head of a cradle, and to clothe every woman in male attire. None of these points, however important they may be considered by leading men, will be touched in this convention. As to their costume, the gentlemen need feel no fear of our imitating that, for we think it in violation of every principle of taste, beauty, and dignity; notwithstanding all the contempt cast upon our loose, flowing garments, we still admire the graceful folds, and consider our costume far more artistic than theirs. Many of the nobler sex seem to agree with us in this opinion, for the bishops, priests, judges, barristers, and lord mayors of the first nation on the globe, and the pope of Rome, with his cardinals, too, all wear the loose flowing robes, thus tacitly acknowledging that the male attire is neither dignified nor imposing. No, we shall not molest you in your philosophical experiments with stocks, pants, high-heeled boots, and Russian belts. . . .

But we are assembled to protest against a form of government existing without the consent of the governed—to declare our right to be free as man is free, to be represented in the government which we are taxed to support, to have [abolished] such disgraceful laws as give man the power to chastise and imprison his wife, to take the wages which she earns, the property which she inherits, and, in case of separation, the children of her love; laws which make her the mere dependent on his bounty. It is to protest against such unjust laws as these that we are assembled today, and to have them, if possible, forever erased from our statute books, deeming them a shame and a disgrace to a Christian republic in the nineteenth century. We have met

> *To uplift woman's fallen divinity*
> *Upon an even pedestal with man's.*

And, strange as it may seem to many, we now demand our right to vote according to the declaration of the government under which we live. This right no one pretends to deny. We need not prove ourselves equal to Daniel Webster to enjoy this privilege, for the ignorant Irishman in the ditch has all the civil rights he has. We need not prove our muscular power equal to this same Irishman to enjoy this privilege, for the most tiny, weak, ill-shaped stripling of twenty-one has all the civil rights of the Irishman. We have no objection to discuss the question of equality, for we feel that the weight of argument lies wholly with us, but we wish the question of equality kept distinct from the question of rights, for the proof of the one does not determine the truth of the other. All white men in this country have the same rights, however they may differ in mind, body, or estate.

The right is ours. The question now is: how shall we get possession of what rightfully belongs to us? We should not feel so sorely grieved if no man who had not attained the full stature of a Webster, Clay, Van Buren, or Gerrit Smith could claim the right of the elective franchise. But to have drunkards, idiots, horse-racing, rum-selling rowdies, ignorant foreigners, and silly boys fully recognized, while we ourselves are thrust out from all the rights that belong to citizens, it is too grossly insulting to the dignity of woman to be longer quietly submitted to. The right is ours. Have it, we must. Use it, we will. The pens, the tongues, the fortunes, the indomitable wills of many women are already pledged to secure this right. The great truth that no just government can be formed without the consent of the governed we shall echo and re-echo in the ears of the unjust judge, until by continual coming we shall weary him. . . .

There seems now to be a kind of moral stagnation in our midst. Philanthropists have done their utmost to rouse the nation to a sense of its sins. War, slavery, drunkenness, licentiousness, gluttony, have been dragged naked before the people, and all their abominations and deformities fully brought to light, yet with idiotic laugh we hug those monsters to our breasts and rush on to destruction. Our churches are multiplying on all sides, our missionary societies, Sunday schools, and prayer meetings and innumerable charitable and reform organizations are all in operation, but still the tide of vice is swelling, and threatens the destruction of everything, and the battlements of righteousness are weak against the raging elements of sin and death. Verily, the world waits the coming of some new element, some purifying power, some spirit of mercy and love. The voice of woman has been silenced in the state, the church, and the home, but man cannot fulfill his destiny alone, he cannot redeem his race unaided. There are deep and tender chords of sympathy and love in the hearts of the downfallen and oppressed that woman can touch more skillfully than man.

The world has never yet seen a truly great and virtuous nation, because in the degradation of woman the very fountains of life are poisoned at their source. It is vain to look for silver and gold from mines of copper and lead. It is the wise mother that has the wise son. So long as your women are slaves you may throw your colleges and churches to the winds. You can't have scholars and saints so long as your mothers are ground to powder between the upper and nether millstone of tyranny and lust. How seldom, now, is a father's pride gratified, his fond hopes realized, in the budding genius of his son! The wife is degraded, made the mere creature of caprice, and the foolish son is heaviness to his heart. Truly are the sins of the fathers visited upon the children to the third and fourth generation. God, in His wisdom, has so linked the whole human family together that any violence done at one end of the chain is felt throughout its length, and here, too, is the law of restoration, as in woman all have fallen, so in her elevation shall the race be recreated. . . .

We do not expect our path will be strewn with the flowers of popular applause, but over the thorns of bigotry and prejudice will be our way, and on our banners will beat the dark storm clouds of opposition from those who have entrenched themselves behind the stormy bulwarks of custom and authority, and who have fortified their position by every means, holy and unholy. But we will steadfastly abide the result. Unmoved we will bear it aloft. Undauntedly we will unfurl it to the gale, for we know that the storm cannot rend from it a shred, that the electric flash will but more clearly show to us the glorious words inscribed upon it, "Equality of Rights." . . .

1. In the second sentence of the first paragraph ("We do not propose . . .), Stanton is expressing what main idea about the women's movement? **(a)** It will not cause husbands to do more babysitting; **(b)** it will not result in women dressing like men; **(c)** it will not make men more courteous; **(d)** it will not cause the roles of men and women to be entirely reversed.

2. Reread the passage beginning with the fourth sentence of the first paragraph ("As to their costume . . . ") and continuing to the end of the paragraph. Which sentence below best summarizes Stanton's thoughts? **(a)** The pope supports women's right to vote; **(b)** women's attire is more dignified and graceful than men's; **(c)** women's attire is similar to that of the clergy; **(d)** men should also wear gowns.

3. When Stanton refers to "the nobler sex," her tone is probably **(a)** respectful; **(b)** fearful; **(c)** bitter; **(d)** ironic.

4. Which device has Stanton used in the first paragraph to interest the audience in her address? **(a)** a call for action to rouse the audience; **(b)** a question to stimulate the audience's thoughts; **(c)** a humorous introduction to warm up the audience; **(d)** a list of injustices to anger the audience.

5. Reread the first sentence of the second paragraph. Which sentence below best summarizes the purpose of the women's assembly? **(a)** to protest against laws that allow men to take the wages of their wives; **(b)** to protest against the growing power of the American government; **(c)** to protest against laws that deprive women of their rights; **(d)** to ask men for a place in government.

6. Which word best describes the tone of the second paragraph?

(a) determined; (b) ironic; (c) hateful; (d) whining.

7. In the sixth sentence of the second paragraph, Stanton talks about the "Irishman in the ditch." With this example she is saying that the right to vote should not be refused women because of (a) sinfulness; (b) a foreign birth; (c) apathy; (d) ignorance.

8. Which sentence below best summarizes Stanton's meaning when she says, "we wish the question of equality kept distinct from the question of rights, for the proof of the one does not determine the truth of the other." (a) Equality of the sexes must be established if women are to get the right to vote; (b) women should be given the right to vote because they are just as intelligent as men; (c) the question of equality is irrelevant to the question of rights; (d) women can never be equal to men in intelligence or strength.

9. In the fourth sentence of the third paragraph ("But to have drunkards . . ."), the author says that it is especially insulting that women do not have the right to vote because (a) most men are irresponsible; (b) men believe that women will become immoral and irresponsible; (c) women are blamed for making men immoral and irresponsible; (d) even the most immoral and irresponsible men may vote.

10. In the final sentence of the third paragraph ("The great truth . . ."), Stanton is implying the use of what method to gain the right to vote? (a) outlasting the enemy; (b) insulting the enemy; (c) raising a deafening

shout against the enemy; (d) pleading with the enemy.

11. The main idea of the fourth paragraph is that (a) women are more religious than men; (b) society is more immoral than it was previously; (c) society is growing more corrupt because women have been denied a role in running it; (d) organized religion has been ineffective in dealing with sinfulness and poverty.

12. In the first sentence of the fifth paragraph Stanton says that "in the degradation of woman the very fountains of life are poisoned at their source." Which sentence below best states the idea she is expressing with this comparison? (a) The denial of rights to women keeps nations from achieving their full potential; (b) when denied their rights, women do not give birth to healthy babies; (c) many women have died because they did not have full rights; (d) those who deny rights to women will die.

13. In the next sentence she says, "It is vain to look for silver and gold from mines of copper and lead." What kind of figure of speech is contained in this sentence? (a) simile; (b) hyperbole; (c) personification; (d) metaphor.

14. Which object is *not* used in a metaphor in the fifth paragraph? (a) a mine; (b) a chain; (c) a mill; (d) a ladder.

15. The main idea of the fifth paragraph is that (a) fathers only care about the achievements of their sons; (b) to deprive women of their rights is to go against the law of God; (c) the continued denial

of women's rights will prevent society from achieving its highest potential; (d) wisdom is passed from one generation to the next.

16. In the first sentence of the sixth paragraph ("We do not expect . . ."), Stanton warns that the opponent will hide behind (a) tradition and law; (b) religion and prejudice; (c) prejudice and bigotry; (d) applause and laughter.

17. What is the best brief outline of Stanton's address?

First
I. Reasons why women should not dress like men
II. Reasons why women are as good as the Irish
III. Sinfulness of society as result of lost influence of religion
IV. Necessity for women to lead society back to God
V. Call for courage in battle for rights;

Second
I. Purpose of the assembly
II. Reasons why women should have rights
III. Methods of attaining rights
IV. How women's rights will improve society
V. Call for courage in battle for rights;

Third
I. Purpose of assembly
II. Methods of attaining rights
III. How women's rights will improve society
IV. Reasons why women should have rights
V. Call for courage in battle for rights.

Choose one of the topics below for a composition.

1. Legend has it that when Thoreau was in jail for not paying his poll tax, Emerson visited him and asked, "Henry, what are you doing in there?"

Supposedly Thoreau answered, "Waldo, what are you doing out there?" In this answer Thoreau was implying to his friend that one should not conform to a value of society when it conflicts with one's own values.

Write a letter to Thoreau in which you either compliment him on his actions or attempt to convince him he was wrong. Explain thoroughly the reasons for the point of view you take.

2. Understanding symbolism can greatly increase one's understanding of a story. Symbolism plays an important part in three stories in this unit, "The Minister's Black Veil," "My Kinsman, Major Molineux," and "What Redburn Saw in Launcelott's-Hey."

In an essay explain to your class what symbolism is. Then pick the most important symbol from each of the three stories and explain how each one contributes to the meaning of that story.

3. The selections by Robinson, Alcott, Thoreau, and Chief Seattle are first-person accounts in which the writers reveal their personalities through tone. In *Walden* one can see that Thoreau was thoughtful and independent. Robinson's *Loom and Spindle* reveals her as a self-assured and observant woman. Alcott was eager to please and conscientious. Chief Seattle's proud patience is revealed throughout "This Sacred Soil."

Think of an incident that has been very important to you. Write a first-person, informal (though correctly written) narrative to a friend in which you control the tone of your writing so that two or three of your important personality characteristics are revealed. This incident should be described in some detail.

4. Both Alcott's *Diary Kept at Fruitlands* and Robinson's *Loom and Spindle* present accurate but differing pictures of women's roles in American society in the mid-1800s. Write an article that examines these similarities and differences. Be sure to make specific references to the writings of each author. This is to be an article that might appear in a magazine of our own time.

Unit 5: Variations and

Departures 1870 to 1915

1895	1900	1905	1910	1915

Edison develops movies

Railroad strikes

"Coxey's Army" of unemployed marches on Washington

● Marconi invents trans-Atlantic wireless

● U.S. Steel becomes first billion-dollar corporation

Panama Canal opened ●

World War I ●

Masters: *Spoon River Anthology* ●

● Wright brothers' flight

● Crane: *The Red Badge of Courage*

● Du Bois: *The Souls of Black Folk*

● James: *The Ambassadors*

● Dunbar: *Lyrics of Lowly Life*

● Robinson: *Children of the Night*

● Niagara movement for racial equality founded

● Wharton: *The House of Mirth*

● Spanish-American War

● Restriction of Japanese immigration

● Peary at North Pole

● *The Crisis* founded by Du Bois

● Wharton: *Ethan Frome*

Poetry magazine founded by Harriet Monroe ●

Alaska Gold Rush

Muckraking journalism

Auto assembly lines

Greatest migrations: Europeans, Mexicans, Asians

Black migration to North

Background: Variations and Departures 1870–1915

The North's victory in the Civil War preserved the Union, freed the slaves, and left the South in bitterness and poverty which would take a century to overcome. But, in the searing experience of war, the nation had gained a lasting, though disillusioned, maturity.

Lincoln had indicated that he would be conciliatory to the defeated South. His assassination therefore heightened tension and strengthened those factions on both sides which wanted revenge rather than reconciliation. The resulting exploitation of the South during the Reconstruction Era did not end until 1877, when federal troops were withdrawn and the area reverted to local rule.

By this time the nation's energies were focused on the explosive growth of business and industry. The chief symbol of this growth was the development of the railroads. In 1869 the Union Pacific Railroad at last linked the Atlantic and Pacific coasts and opened vast stretches of wilderness. Celebrating this event in "Passage to India," Walt Whitman called for a spiritual achievement to match the amazing engineering feats of the age. Spiritual reform was urgently needed, for this period of industrial growth was also a time of plunder and exploitation, of greedy materialism and political corruption, of financial piracy and labor strife. Great fortunes were accumulated while many people went hungry in the swelling cities. Immigrants from Europe poured into the United States in search of fortune, but most found themselves laboring on railroads or in sweatshop factories for low wages.

The Civil War, the industrial boom that it helped set off, and the flood of immigrants lured by this prosperity—these factors laid the foundations of modern American society and literature. During the war, people from various regions of the country mingled more freely than ever before, and so came to know each other's folk ballads and tall tales. The nation's traditional fascination with the frontier was further enhanced. And the problems of materialism and poverty aroused many writers to social satire and protest.

This period also saw the final stage of the centuries-long displacement of native Americans, as the army pushed the hunters of the Plains onto reservations to make way for railroads and land-hungry settlers. The buffalo herds, on which the diet and even the culture of the Plains tribes largely depended, were slaughtered to feed railroad workers. Most white Americans at the time saw only one-sided reports denouncing the "savage Indians," or admired romanticized paintings of the "Vanishing Indian" by such artists as Frederic Remington. The contrasting native American view of these bitter wars is represented in this unit by the speeches of Satanta, the Kiowa "Orator of the Plains," and of Chief Joseph, the great Nez Percé leader, respected even by his enemies.

Magazine and book publishing flourished with the growth of a prosperous, literate middle class, who especially thirsted for practical information and fiction representing "real life." Such writers as Walt Whitman, Samuel Clemens, Emily Dickinson, Stephen Crane, W. E. B.

Du Bois, and Edith Wharton no longer had to look to Europe for literary inspiration, because America teemed with subjects—and audiences—for writers. These authors were largely concerned with finding new points of departure in theme, in content, in form, and in the use of language. The major departures were *free verse* and related technical experiments, *local color* or regional fiction, *realism,* and *naturalism.*

Sidney Lanier made limited experiments with verse forms. Although he largely followed conventions of rhyme, meter, and "poetic" language, he considerably extended Poe's experiments with sound effects by developing a theory of poetic composition based on music. His poetry thus foreshadows some future developments in technique. Nonetheless, he was horrified by Whitman's defiance of old forms.

Whitman's great departure from the past was his development of the possibilities of free verse. This self-proclaimed "poet of America" was convinced that he had something

new to say and that only a natural poetic form and language could convey his buoyant vision of the great democracy. He used bold images, colloquial speech, and symbols drawn

Walt Whitman

from workaday life to capture a truth greater than the individual—the truth of the American experience.

Dickinson, rather than following set poetic forms, used rhyme, rhythm, and sentence patterns according to the demands of her ideas. She seldom

left her home in Amherst, Massachusetts, but she drew on the small events of household life for her perceptive comments on the inner self, on the self facing death, and on conflicts between doubt and religious faith. Her language is simple and direct and her ability to capture experience through im-

Emily Dickinson

agery of the commonplace is extraordinary.

These tendencies toward greater naturalness of style in

prose and poetry ran parallel with the increased recognition of American folk traditions. Frontier humor, popular even before the Civil War, was shaped into literature by Clemens and others, while the wartime ballads aroused interest in the folk songs of all regions. Tales and ballads of the Far West, such as "Shenandoah" and the legend of Gregorio Cortez, became especially popular. Eastern publishers began to produce a spate of cowboy song books and of tawdry dime novels romanticizing outlaws like Jesse James and the Sundance Kid.

But serious writers from New England to California were also now using folk tales and ballads in local-color writing. Paul Laurence Dunbar's poems in black dialect are an example of the imaginative conversion of folk material into literature. Regional writing, with its accurate portrayal of local customs and dialect, was even more important in fiction. In "A New England Nun," for example, Freeman concentrated on representing faithfully New England customs and speech. This story also illustrates the realistic tendencies of local-color writing. For instance, Freeman presented ordinary people in ordinary situations. And, although the story affirmed conventional notions of romance and morality, "rightness" was not imposed on the characters—or readers—by the author; instead, the characters were realistically motivated to behave according to their personal code of morality.

Realism began with Clem-

ens's writing in the 1860s and dominated most fiction written up through the 1930s. During the Civil War, readers hungered for detailed accounts of the cataclysm. Accuracy of detail had always been characteristic of most American writing, but Civil War journalism greatly reinforced public taste for truthful representation of daily life.

Realism was partly a reaction against romanticism, for the proponents of realism felt that romantic fiction was too idealized, too neatly patterned, too grandly tragic and heroic to reflect real life. The realists were concerned with the immediate ethical consequences of everyday actions. To help readers "experience" real life, they allowed a story to tell itself, for

Samuel Clemens

they believed the truth of experience was to be found in events described accurately and objectively, not in the writer's imagination.

Clemens also brought to the novel an easygoing style and a

folksy humor that it had not embraced before. He frequently borrowed material from folklore, as in "The Celebrated Jumping Frog." In his longer works, such as *Huckleberry Finn,* he used the *vignette*—another element of realism. Huck's speech is salty, his mind uncluttered by romantic notions, and his emotions are clear when he elects to "go to Hell" rather than betray a friend. The honesty of Huck's choice is the believable result of his experiences, detailed through a series of vignettes.

Du Bois and Wharton were among the later developers of realism. Very different in background, they nevertheless shared the view that social circumstance can destroy individual character and potential. Du Bois explored the identity and situation of black Americans—

Edith Wharton

barely a generation away from slavery—in essays, sociological studies, and in fiction. He dealt with the realities of segregation: opportunities lost and talents destroyed. In capturing this bleak reality he became one of the major leaders in the struggle of blacks for freedoms and opportunities enjoyed by other Americans. Wharton detailed the realities of her world of New York high society and satirized its snobbery in *The Age of Innocence.* To Du Bois ignorance was the destroyer of the human soul; to Wharton, idleness and genteel social convention were equally menacing.

Growing concern with social injustice and the gradual acceptance of realistic subject matter and techniques opened the way for naturalistic fiction. The new theories of Darwin, Freud, and Marx were suggesting that biology, psychology, and economics determine each individual's destiny. Naturalistic novelists applied these theories to their presentation and interpretation of human experience. Writers like Stephen Crane and Ambrose Bierce tended to depict life as a grim futility, the universe as cold and spiritless, and the individual as a hapless victim of heredity, society, and natural forces. Naturalism was therefore in direct opposition to romanticism and Transcendentalism, which had maintained a holy and mystical presence in nature. Crane, Frank Norris, and Theodore Dreiser pessimistically exposed poverty, cruelty, the futility of war, and corruption.

In method, naturalism closely resembled realism. But where the realists sought to arrange their material so as to permit ideals to reveal themselves, the

Stephen Crane

naturalists selected details to provide a scientifically precise, usually grim view of the human condition. Life—to the naturalistic writer—was meaningless.

The poetry of Dunbar, Robinson, and Edgar Lee Masters, while not so innovative as the poetry of Whitman and Dickinson, revealed both realistic and naturalistic tendencies. These poets all used commonplace images and everyday language to convey their view of the darker side of existence. They depicted human weaknesses, foibles, and vanities. But they also shared a deep sympathy for the plight of ordinary people in the real world. However, instead of denouncing injustice, Dunbar symbolized its effects by accurately detailing the behavior of a caged bird. The selection and arrangement of material in "Miniver Cheevy" readily conveyed—without comment from Robinson—the reality of the embittered dreamer. *Spoon River Anthology* by Masters was realistic both in subject and in technique. The subjects were small-town Midwesterners who,

speaking from the grave, recalled their lives with quiet contentment or angry disappointment. The realistic technique Masters employed was to reveal the attitudes and circumstances of his characters directly through their own language.

The writers of this period captured the new America which was emerging in its headlong pursuit of world power and of the "American Dream." The spiritual values and social manners of a stable rural society were being challenged by a nation rushing into an urban, industrial future. New values, new attitudes, new goals were sought to match the new spirit of America, and the writers tested both the old and the new. They gave the nation the opportunity to examine its philosophy and to judge what should yield and what still held merit.

Sidney Lanier

As mentioned in the Unit Background, Lanier (lə nir′) used musical principles in composing poetry. Try reading this poem aloud to hear its musical effects.

Song of the Chattahoochee

Out of the hills of Habersham,
Down the valleys of Hall,[1]
I hurry amain to reach the plain,
Run the rapid and leap the fall,
5 Split at the rock and together again,
Accept my bed, or narrow or wide,
And flee from folly on every side
With a lover's pain to attain the plain
Far from the hills of Habersham,
10 Far from the valleys of Hall.

All down the hills of Habersham,
All through the valleys of Hall,

The rushes cried *Abide, abide,*
The willful waterweeds held me thrall,
15 The laving laurel turned my tide,
The ferns and the fondling grass said *Stay,*
The dewberry dipped for to work delay,
And the little reeds sighed *Abide, abide,*
Here in the hills of Habersham,
20 Here in the valleys of Hall.

From Vol. I of CENTENNIAL EDITION OF THE WORKS OF SIDNEY LANIER, edited by Charles R. Anderson. Copyright 1945, The Johns Hopkins University Press. Reprinted by permission.

1. Habersham (hab′ẽr sham) . . . **Hall,** two counties of Georgia through which the Chattahoochee River flows.

High o'er the hills of Habersham,
  Veiling the valleys of Hall,
The hickory told me manifold
Fair tales of shade, the poplar tall
25 Wrought me her shadowy self to hold,
The chestnut, the oak, the walnut, the pine,
Overleaning, with flickering meaning and sign,
Said, *Pass not, so cold, these manifold*
  Deep shades of the hills of Habersham,
30   *These glades in the valleys of Hall.*

  And oft in the hills of Habersham,
  And oft in the valleys of Hall,
The white quartz shone, and the smooth
  brook-stone
Did bar me of passage with friendly brawl,
35 And many a luminous jewel lone
—Crystals clear or a-cloud with mist,

Ruby, garnet and amethyst—
Made lures with the lights of streaming stone
  In the clefts of the hills of Habersham,
40   In the beds of the valleys of Hall.

  But oh, not the hills of Habersham,
  And oh, not the valleys of Hall
Avail: I am fain for to water the plain.
Downward the voices of Duty call—
45 Downward, to toil and be mixed with the main,[2]
The dry fields burn, and the mills are to turn,
And a myriad flowers mortally yearn,
And the lordly main from beyond the plain
  Calls o'er the hills of Habersham,
50   Calls through the valleys of Hall.

---

2. the main, the sea.

Discussion

1. Trace the development of **personification** throughout the poem, giving examples of its use.

2. (a) Compare the **mood** of the first four stanzas with that of the last stanza. (b) How does Lanier's choice of verbs contribute to this change of moods?

3. The poem can be read as an expression of conflicting desires of the human spirit. (a) What are these desires? (b) Which desire wins? Explain.

4. In another of his poems, Lanier states that "Music is Love in search of a word." In the poem you have just read, what things does Lanier seem to love?

Sidney Lanier 1842 • 1881

Lanier rebelled against what he called the "prim smugness and cleanshaven propriety" of conventional verse. He was a gifted flutist and, in *The Science of English Verse* (1880), he declared that the principles of music and poetry are the same. His emphasis on sound over meaning resembles the ideas of Poe. He used musical notations to analyze verse rhythms and wrote his most characteristic poems as if he were composing music. Although Whitman's poetry shocked Lanier, the technical innovations of these poets and Emily Dickinson run parallel in many ways.

Lanier graduated from Oglethorpe University, then joined the Confederate Army. He spent five months in a Federal prison camp, where his health was permanently ruined by exposure. After the war, he worked hard to perfect his po-

etry, but his volume *Poems* (1877) was poorly received and his hope of a professorship at Johns Hopkins University was disappointed. His last years were spent in lecturing on poetry and writing some of his finest poems.

Walt Whitman

I Hear America Singing

I hear America singing, the varied carols I hear,
Those of mechanics, each one singing his as it should be blithe and strong,
The carpenter singing his as he measures his plank or beam,
The mason singing his as he makes ready for work, or leaves off work,
5 The boatman singing what belongs to him in his boat, the deckhand singing on the steamboat deck,
The shoemaker singing as he sits on his bench, the hatter singing as he stands,
The wood-cutter's song, the ploughboy's on his way in the morning, or at noon
       intermission or at sundown,
The delicious singing of the mother, or of the young wife at work, or of the girl sewing or washing,
Each singing what belongs to him or her and to none else,
10 The day what belongs to the day—at night the party of young fellows, robust, friendly,
Singing with open mouths their strong melodious songs.

There Was a Child Went Forth

There was a child went forth every day,
And the first object he look'd upon, that object he became,
And that object became part of him for the day or a certain part of the day,
Or for many years or stretching cycles of years.

5 The early lilacs became part of this child,
And grass and white and red morning-glories, and white and red clover, and the song of the
       phoebe-bird,
And the Third-month lambs and the sow's pink-faint litter, and the mare's foal and the cow's calf,
And the noisy brood of the barnyard or by the mire of the pond-side,
And the fish suspending themselves so curiously below there, and the beautiful curious liquid,
10 And the water-plants with their graceful flat heads, all became part of him.

The field-sprouts of Fourth-month and Fifth-month became part of him,
Winter-grain sprouts and those of the light-yellow corn, and the esculent roots of the garden,
And the apple-trees cover'd with blossoms and the fruit afterward, and woodberries, and the
       commonest weeds by the road,
And the old drunkard staggering home from the outhouse of the tavern whence he had lately risen,
15 And the schoolmistress that pass'd on her way to the school,
And the friendly boys that pass'd, and the quarrelsome boys,
And the tidy and fresh-cheek'd girls, and the barefoot Negro boy and girl,
And all the changes of city and country wherever he went.

His own parents, he that had father'd him and she that had conceiv'd him in
      her womb and birth'd him
20 They gave this child more of themselves than that,
They gave him afterward every day, they became part of him.

The mother at home quietly placing the dishes on the supper-table,
The mother with mild words, clean her cap and gown, a wholesome odor falling off her person and
      clothes as she walks by,
The father, strong, self-sufficient, manly, mean, anger'd, unjust,
25 The blow, the quick loud word, the tight bargain, the crafty lure,
The family usages, the language, the company, the furniture, the yearning and swelling heart,
Affection that will not be gainsay'd, the sense of what is real, the thought if after all it
      should prove unreal,
The doubts of day-time and the doubts of night-time, the curious whether and how,
Whether that which appears so is so, or is it all flashes and specks?
30 Men and women crowding fast in the streets, if they are not flashes and specks what are they?
The streets themselves and the facades of houses, and goods in the windows,
Vehicles, teams, the heavy-plank'd wharves, the huge crossing at the ferries,
The village on the highland seen from afar at sunset, the river between,
Shadows, aureola and mist, the light falling on roofs and gables of white or brown two miles off,
35 The schooner near by sleepily dropping down the tide, the little boat slack-tow'd astern,
The hurrying tumbling waves, quick-broken crests, slapping,
The strata of color'd clouds, the long bar of maroon-tint away solitary by itself, the spread of purity
      it lies motionless in,
The horizon's edge, the flying sea-crow, the fragrance of salt marsh and shore mud,
These became part of that child who went forth every day, and who now goes, and will always go
      forth every day.

Discussion

I Hear America Singing

1. In general, most poetry written prior to Whitman's day dealt with idealized characters or extraordinary heroes. What class of people did Whitman choose to portray?

2. Why is "each [person] singing what belongs to him or her and to none else" (line 9)? Explain.

There Was a Child Went Forth

In this poem, Whitman has taken a seemingly simple sub-ject, the commonplaces of daily life, and used them as the start-ing point for a lyrical medita-tion on the diversity, continu-ity, and unity of all time, all life, and all objects.

1. Each of the following groups of lines presents an **image** pattern: lines 1–13; 14–17; 19–26; 30–34; and 35–38. (a) Classify the imagery in each by subject matter. (b) Do the "pictures" form a progressive pattern? If so, how? (c) Does the imagery unify the poem? Explain.

2. Explicate lines 19–21.

How did the child's parents be-come "part of him"?

3. What natural phenomenon is the poet describing through the use of imagery in line 37?

4. How long a period of time does the poem encompass?

Extension • Writing

After rereading the poem write a short essay of two or three paragraphs discussing the significance of the ideas pre-sented in lines 2–4. Include, if you wish, examples from your own experience in support of your views.

Cavalry Crossing a Ford

A line in long array where they wind betwixt green islands,
They take a serpentine course, their arms flash in the sun—hark to the musical clank,
Behold the silvery river, in it the splashing horses loitering stop to drink,
Behold the brown-faced men, each group, each person a picture, the negligent rest on the saddles,
5 Some emerge on the opposite bank, others are just entering the ford—while,
Scarlet and blue and snowy white,
The guidon flags flutter gaily in the wind.

Bivouac on a Mountain Side

I see before me now a traveling army halting,
Below a fertile valley spread, with barns and the orchards of summer,
Behind, the terraced sides of a mountain, abrupt, in places rising high,
Broken, with rocks, with clinging cedars, with tall shapes dingily seen,
5 The numerous camp-fires scatter'd near and far, some away up on the mountain,
The shadowy forms of men and horses, looming, large-sized, flickering,
And over all the sky—the sky! far, far out of reach, studded, breaking out, the eternal stars.

Discussion

Cavalry Crossing a Ford

1. At one time during his life Whitman was a journalist. **(a)** What journalistic elements do you find in this poem? **(b)** What skills needed for writing poetry might be strengthened by experience in news reporting?

2. Give examples of words or phrases which create the pictorial impression of a realistic military experience.

Bivouac on a Mountain Side

1. What relationships—both of similarity and contrast—can you see between the "camp-fires" of war and "the eternal stars" of nature?

2. Many of Whitman's poems are **vignettes**. **(a)** Explain how the arrangement or composition of images in each of the above poems forms a unified vignette. **(b)** In what way do the titles of both poems reflect the purpose of titles of paintings? **(c)** Compare the images of war in these poems with the facing photograph.

A Union Army field hospital.
(Association of American Railroads.)

Crossing Brooklyn Ferry

1

Flood-tide below me! I see you face to face!
Clouds of the west—sun there half an hour high—I see you also face to face.

Crowds of men and women attired in the usual costumes, how curious you are to me!
On the ferry-boats the hundreds and hundreds that cross, returning home, are more curious to me than you suppose,
And you that shall cross from shore to shore years hence are more to me, and more in my meditations, than you might suppose.

2

The impalpable sustenance of me from all things at all hours of the day,
The simple, compact, well-join'd scheme, myself disintegrated, every one disintegrated yet part of the scheme,
The similitudes of the past and those of the future,
The glories strung like beads on my smallest sights and hearings, on the walk in the street and the passage over the river,
10 The current rushing so swiftly and swimming with me far away,
The others that are to follow me, the ties between me and them,
The certainty of others, the life, love, sight, hearing of others.

Others will enter the gates of the ferry and cross from shore to shore,
Others will watch the run of the flood-tide,
Others will see the shipping of Manhattan north and west, and the heights of Brooklyn to the south and east,
Others will see the islands large and small;
Fifty years hence, others will see them as they cross, the sun half an hour high,
A hundred years hence, or ever so many hundred years hence, others will see them,
Will enjoy the sunset, the pouring-in of the flood-tide, the falling-back to the sea of the ebb-tide.

3

20 It avails not, time nor place—distance avails not,
I am with you, you men and women of a generation, or ever so many generations hence,
Just as you feel when you look on the river and sky, so I felt,
Just as any of you is one of a living crowd, I was one of a crowd,
Just as you are refresh'd by the gladness of the river and the bright flow, I was refresh'd,
Just as you stand and lean on the rail, yet hurry with the swift current, I stood yet was hurried,
Just as you look on the numberless masts of ships and the thick-stemm'd pipes of steamboats, I look'd.

I too many and many a time cross'd the river of old,
Watched the Twelfth-month sea-gulls, saw them high in the air floating with motionless wings, oscillating their bodies,
Saw how the glistening yellow lit up parts of their bodies and left the rest in strong shadow,
30 Saw the slow-wheeling circles and the gradual edging toward the south,
Saw the reflection of the summer sky in the water,
Had my eyes dazzled by the shimmering track of beams,

Look'd at the fine centrifugal spokes of light round the shape of my head in the sunlit water,
Look'd on the haze on the hills southward and south—westward,
Look'd on the vapor as it flew in fleeces tinged with violet,
Look'd toward the lower bay to notice the vessels arriving,
Saw their approach, saw aboard those that were near me,
Saw the white sails of schooners and sloops, saw the ships at anchor,
The sailors at work in the rigging or out astride the spars,
40 The round masts, the swinging motion of the hulls, the slender serpentine pennants,
The large and small steamers in motion, the pilots in their pilot-houses,
The white wake left by the passage, the quick tremulous whirl of the wheels,
The flags of all nations, the falling of them at sunset,
The scallop-edged waves in the twilight, the ladled cups, the frolicsome crests and glistening,
The stretch afar growing dimmer and dimmer, the gray walls of the granite
    storehouses by the docks,
On the river the shadowy group, the big steam-tug closely flank'd on each side by the barges, the
    hay-boat, the belated lighter,
On the neighboring shore the fires from the foundry chimneys burning high and glaringly
    into the night,
Casting their flicker of black contrasted with wild red and yellow light over the tops of houses, and
    down into the clefts of streets.

4

These and all else were to me the same as they are to you,
50 I loved well those cities, loved well the stately and rapid river,
The men and women I saw were all near to me,
Others the same—others who look back on me because I look'd forward to them,
(The time will come, though I stop here to-day and to-night.)

5

What is it then between us?
What is the count of the scores or hundreds of years between us?

Whatever it is, it avails not—distance avails not, and place avails not,
I too lived, Brooklyn of ample hills was mine,
I too walk'd the streets of Manhattan island, and bathed in the waters around it,
I too felt the curious abrupt questionings stir within me,
60 In the day among crowds of people sometimes they came upon me,
In my walks home late at night or as I lay in my bed they came upon me,
I too had been struck from the float forever held in solution,
I too had receiv'd identity by my body,
That I was I knew was of my body, and what I should be I knew I should be of my body.

6

It is not upon you alone the dark patches fall,
The dark threw its patches down upon me also,
The best I had done seem'd to me blank and suspicious,

My great thoughts as I supposed them, were they not in reality meagre?
Nor is it you alone who know what it is to be evil,
70 I am he who knew what it was to be evil,
I too knitted the old knot of contrariety,
Blabb'd, blush'd, resented, lied, stole, grudg'd,
Had guile, anger, lust, hot wishes I dared not speak,
Was wayward, vain, greedy, shallow, sly, cowardly, malignant,
The wolf, the snake, the hog, not wanting in me,
The cheating look, the frivolous word, the adulterous wish, not wanting,
Refusals, hates, postponements, meanness, laziness, none of these wanting,
Was one with the rest, the days and haps of the rest,
Was call'd by my nighest name by clear loud voices of young men as they saw me
      approaching or passing,
80 Felt their arms on my neck as I stood, or the negligent leaning of their flesh against me as I sat,
Saw many I loved in the street or ferry-boat or public assembly, yet never told them a word,
Lived the same life with the rest, the same old laughing, gnawing, sleeping,
Play'd the part that still looks back on the actor or actress,
The same old role, the role that is what we make it, as great as we like,
Or as small as we like, or both great and small.

7

Closer yet I approach you,
What thought you have of me now, I had as much of you—I laid in my stores in advance,
I consider'd long and seriously of you before you were born.

Who was to know what should come home to me?
90 Who knows but I am enjoying this?
Who knows, for all the distance, but I am as good as looking at you now, for all
      you cannot see me?

8

Ah, what can ever be more stately and admirable to me than mast-hemm'd Manhattan?
River and sunset and scallop-edg'd waves of flood-tide?
The sea-gulls oscillating their bodies, the hay-boat in the twilight, and the belated lighter?
What gods can exceed these that clasp me by the hand, and with voices I love call me promptly
      and loudly by my nighest name as I approach?
What is more subtle than this which ties me to the woman or man that looks in my face?
Which fuses me into you now, and pours my meaning into you?
We understand then do we not?
What I promis'd without mentioning it, have you not accepted?
100 What the study could not teach—what the preaching could not accomplish is
      accomplish'd, is it not?

9

Flow on, river! flow with the flood-tide, and ebb with the ebb-tide!
Frolic on, crested and scallop-edg'd waves!
Gorgeous clouds of the sunset! drench with your splendor me, or the men and women generations
      after me!
Cross from shore to shore, countless crowds of passengers!
Stand up, tall masts of Mannahatta! stand up, beautiful hills of Brooklyn!

Throb, baffled and curious brain! throw out questions and answers!
Suspend here and everywhere, eternal float of solution!
Gaze, loving and thirsting eyes, in the house or street or public assembly!
Sound out, voices of young men! loudly and musically call me by my nighest name!
110 Live, old life! play the part that looks back on the actor or actress!
Play the old role, the role that is great or small according as one makes it!
Consider, you who peruse me, whether I may not in unknown ways be looking upon you;
Be firm, rail over the river, to support those who lean idly, yet haste with the hasting current;
Fly on, sea-birds! Fly sideways, or wheel in large circles high in the air;
Receive the summer sky, you water, and faithfully hold it till all downcast eyes have time to take
        it from you!
Diverge, fine spokes of light, from the shape of my head, or any one's head, in the sunlit water!
Come on, ships from the lower bay! pass up or down, white-sail'd schooners, sloops, lighters!
Flaunt away, flags of all nations! be duly lower'd at sunset!
Burn high your fires, foundry chimneys! cast black shadows at nightfall! cast red and yellow light
        over the tops of the houses!
120 Appearances, now or henceforth, indicate what you are,
You necessary film, continue to envelop the soul,
About my body for me, and your body for you, be hung our divinest aromas,
Thrive, cities—bring your freight, bring your shows, ample and sufficient rivers,
Expand, being than which none else is perhaps more spiritual,
Keep your places, objects than which none else is more lasting.

You have waited, you always wait, you dumb, beautiful ministers,
We receive you with free sense at last, and are insatiate henceforward,
Not you any more shall be able to foil us, or withhold yourselves from us,
We use you, and do not cast you aside—we plant you permanently within us,
130 We fathom you not—we love you—there is perfection in you also,
You furnish your parts toward eternity,
Great or small, you furnish your parts toward the soul.

Discussion

1. (a) Whom is the poet addressing in line 5 of the first section? **(b)** Whom is he addressing throughout the poem?

2. (a) Explicate line 20: "It avails not, time nor place—distance avails not." **(b)** When this line is echoed later in the poem it is in answer to what question? **(c)** Does this statement remind you of any other philosophy that you have studied? If so, which one?

3. What does the poet mean in line 52 when he says:

". . . others . . . look back on me because I look'd forward to them"? What is meant by "back" and "forward"? Who are the "others"?

4. (a) What is meant by "dark patches" (line 65, section 6)? **(b)** What is "the same old role" (line 84, section 6)? Why is it as great or small as we make it (lines 84–5, section 6)?

5. Who are the "gods" the poet refers to in line 95, section 8? Why does the poet call them gods? Are they "real" gods?

6. (a) What is Whitman doing

with imagery in section 9? **(b)** What impact does this technique have on the reader?

7. What are the "dumb, beautiful ministers" (line 126, section 9)? How do we "use" them (line 129)?

8. Gay Wilson Allen, a noted Whitman critic and biographer, has said that, by analogy, the poem itself becomes a ferry between the poet and the reader. What does the poem cross, if not an actual river? Do you agree or disagree with this statement? Explain.

When I Heard the Learn'd Astronomer

When I heard the learn'd astronomer,
When the proofs, the figures, were ranged in columns before me,
When I was shown the charts and diagrams, to add, divide, and measure them,
When I sitting heard the astronomer where he lectured with much applause in the lecture-room,
5 How soon unaccountable I became tired and sick,
Till rising and gliding out I wander'd off by myself,
In the mystical moist night-air, and from time to time,
Look'd up in perfect silence at the stars.

Sparkles from the Wheel

Where the city's ceaseless crowd moves on the livelong day,
Withdrawn I join a group of children watching, I pause aside with them.

By the curb toward the edge of the flagging,
A knife-grinder works at his wheel sharpening a great knife,
5 Bending over he carefully holds it to the stone, by foot and knee,
With measur'd tread he turns rapidly, as he presses with light but firm hand,
Forth issue then in copious golden jets,
Sparkles from the wheel.

The scene and all its belongings, how they seize and affect me,
10 The sad sharp-chinn'd old man with worn clothes and broad shoulder-band of leather,
Myself effusing and fluid, a phantom curiously floating, now here absorb'd and arrested,
The group, (an unminded point set in a vast surrounding),
The attentive, quiet children, the loud, proud, restive base of the streets,
The low hoarse purr of the whirling stone, the light-press'd blade,
15 Diffusing, dropping, sideways-darting, in tiny showers of gold,
Sparkles from the wheel.

Discussion

When I Heard the Learn'd Astronomer

1. (a) What is the astronomer trying to do? (b) What line summarizes the speaker's response to the astronomer's lecture? (c) What feelings does the speaker get from looking at the stars? Point out words that reflect this mood.

2. What attitudes does this poem express toward science and toward nature?

Sparkles from the Wheel

1. The poem is a detailed "snapshot" of a common street scene. (a) Explain in your own words the image which catches the speaker's attention. (b) With whom does the speaker identify in the poem? (c) What does this identification suggest about the speaker?

2. Give an example of **ono-matopoeia** from the last stanza and explain how it contributes to the "picture" the poet wished to present.

1. Using examples from the preceding poems (or others by Whitman), summarize his views on one of the following topics:

(a) The individual's relationship to the group or society.

(b) The individual's relationship to the physical world.

(c) The importance of experience in developing the individual's consciousness.

2. Recalling that **vignettes** are composed of carefully selected images, write a sketch of your own based on some scene that you have observed. Whether you decide to write in prose or poetry, remember that the best descriptions use concise, concrete language to conjure clear "pictures" in the reader's mind.

Vocabulary • Dictionary

Use your Glossary to answer the questions about each italicized word from Whitman's poems. Write the answers on your paper, and be sure you can spell and pronounce each word.

1. *strata*

(a) What is the singular form of this word? (b) What is the meaning of the Latin root *sternere?*

2. *copious*

(a) From what Latin root does this word come? (b) What is the meaning of the root?

3. *diffuse, effuse*

(a) What is the common Latin root of these two words? (b) Explain the difference in meaning between *diffuse* and *effuse.*

4. *restive*

(a) From what language does this word come? (b) What is its definition?

Walt Whitman 1819 • 1892

Although Whitman was a contemporary of Bryant, Poe, Emerson, Thoreau, Whittier, Lowell, and Longfellow, there is sufficient reason for considering him our first modern poet. He embraced the ideal of working-class democracy more fully than any of these writers, and his experiments with free-verse rhythms and realistic imagery inspired many twentieth-century poets.

Whitman's family was poor and his education ceased early in his teens. When Whitman was four, his father moved the family to the growing village of Brooklyn. Whitman, much later in life, once remarked that his early friendships with the merchants, sailors, farmers, and fishermen of Brooklyn were ". . . my best experiences and deepest lessons in human nature."

Between 1839 and 1848 he worked on Manhattan and Brooklyn newspapers as an editor-reporter. Unconsciously, he was developing much of the material and the crisp, objective reporter's style that would later appear in his poetry.

Whitman's journey to New Orleans in 1848 fired his imagination by showing him the diversity of the young nation. Sometime during 1854 Whitman underwent a great internal turmoil, perhaps brought on by his father's paralysis and subsequent death. By early July of 1855, he published a thin volume of twelve long, untitled poems. This was the first of many editions of *Leaves of Grass.*

Many who read his poetry rejected it as crude or gross. Whittier reportedly threw his copy into a fire. Bryant broke off his friendship with the younger poet. Though the book was a financial failure, some influential readers admired Whitman's revolutionary verse, among them Emerson, Thoreau, and Abe Lincoln. However, Whitman returned to newspaper work to support himself, while writing his greatest poetry in his spare hours.

Whitman was too old to enlist when the Civil War broke out, but he went to care for his brother George, who had been wounded at Fredericksburg. Poems based on his observations of war appeared in later editions of *Leaves of Grass.* After the war, he worked in veterans' hospitals and minor government jobs until 1873, when he suffered a paralytic stroke.

He continued to revise and expand *Leaves of Grass* and approved the last edition from his deathbed. But his later work lacked the vigor and force of his earlier poems. It is for these works that he is now considered one of the greatest American poets.

In the later nineteenth century, the folk songs of the West began to be hailed by many as a truly American poetry of the sort Whitman was proclaiming. Two of the major folk traditions from many cultures are represented here. "Shenandoah," named after a river in Virginia, hauntingly echoes the nostalgia of pioneers for the East they were leaving behind. "El Corrido de Gregorio Cortez," from the Rio Grande frontier, belongs to a time-honored, worldwide tradition of border ballads. Similar ballads stem from the border of Scotland and England where, as along the Rio Grande long ago, officials of both countries were annoying "outsiders," borderers settled their own feuds according to a strict code of honor, and the hero was the lone underdog "defending his right" against all odds.

Shenandoah

Oh, Missouri, she's a mighty river,
  Away you rolling river.
The Red-skins' camp lies on its borders,
  Ah-ha, I'm bound away 'cross the wide Missouri.

5 The white man loved the Indian maiden,
  Away you rolling river.
With notions sweet his canoe was laden.
  Ah-ha, I'm bound away 'cross the wide Missouri.

"O Shenandoah, I love your daughter,
10 Away you rolling river.
I'll take her 'cross yon rolling water."
  Ah-ha, I'm bound away 'cross the wide Missouri.

The chief disdained the trader's dollars:
  Away you rolling river.
15 "My daughter never you shall follow."
  Ah-ha, I'm bound away 'cross the wide Missouri.

At last there came a Yankee skipper,
  Away you rolling river.
He winked his eye, and he tipped his flipper.
20 Ah-ha, I'm bound away 'cross the wide Missouri.

He sold the chief that fire-water,
  Away you rolling river.
And 'cross the river he stole his daughter,
  Ah-ha, I'm bound away 'cross the wide Missouri.

25 "O Shenandoah, I long to hear you,
  Away you rolling river.
Across that wide and rolling river."
  Ah-ha, I'm bound away 'cross the wide Missouri.

Discussion

1. There seem to be several "voices" in this song. **(a)** Identify the various speakers. **(b)** Identify the lines spoken by these voices.

2. (a) What new meaning is suggested by the word *bound* in the final refrain if the speaker is the Indian maid? **(b)** What different meanings does *bound* have if the various refrains are delivered by the different characters in the story?

"Shenandoah" by W. B. Whall from SEA SONGS AND SHANTIES. Reprinted by permission of Brown Son & Ferguson Ltd.

El Corrido de Gregorio Cortez

In the county of El Carmen
A great misfortune befell;
The Major Sheriff is dead;
Who killed him no one can tell.

5 At two in the afternoon,
In half an hour or less,
They knew that the man who killed him
Had been Gregorio Cortez.

They let loose the bloodhound dogs;
10 They followed him from afar.
But trying to catch Cortez
Was like following a star.

All the rangers of the county
Were flying, they rode so hard;
15 What they wanted was to get
The thousand-dollar reward.

And in the county of Kiansis
They cornered him after all;
Though they were more than three hundred
20 He leaped out of their corral.

Then the Major Sheriff[1] said,
As if he was going to cry,
"Cortez, hand over your weapons;
We want to take you alive."

25 Then said Gregorio Cortez,
And his voice was like a bell,
"You will never get my weapons
Till you put me in a cell."

Then said Gregorio Cortez,
30 With his pistol in his hand,
"Ah, so many mounted Rangers
Just to take one Mexican!"

El Corrido de Gregorio Cortez (el kôr rē′dô de gre gô′ryô kôr tes′). A *corrido* is a form of heroic **ballad** popular in Mexico and along the Rio Grande border.

From WITH HIS PISTOL IN HIS HAND by Américo Paredes. Copyright © 1958 The University of Texas Press. Reprinted by permission of The University of Texas Press and the author.

1. Major Sheriff. This refers to the second county sheriff to pursue Cortez, not to the sheriff he shot.

notes and comments

Américo Paredes: from With His Pistol in His Hand

They still sing of him—in the *cantinas*[1] and the country stores, in the ranches when men gather at night to talk in the cool dark, sitting in a circle, smoking and listening to the old songs and the tales of other days. Then the *guitarreros*[2] sing of the border raids and the skirmishes, of the men who lived by the phrase, "I will break before I bend."

They sing with deadly serious faces, throwing out the words of the song like a challenge, tearing savagely with their stiff, callused fingers at the strings of the guitars.

And that is how, in the dark quiet of the ranches, in the lighted noise of the saloons, they sing of Gregorio Cortez. . . .

He was a man, a Border man. What did he look like? Well, that is hard to tell. Some say he was short and some say he was tall; some say he was Indian brown and some say he was blond like a newborn cockroach. But I'd say he was not too dark and not too fair, not too thin and not too fat, not too short and not too tall; and he looked just a little bit like me.

Américo Paredes (ä me′rē kô pä re′des).

1. *cantinas* (kän tē′näs), saloons. [*Spanish*]
2. *guitarreros* (gē tär re′rôs), guitar players.

But does it matter so much what he looked like? He was a man, very much of a man; and he was a Border man. . . .

He was a *vaquero*,[3] and a better one there has not ever been from Laredo to the mouth.[4] He could talk to horses, and they would understand. They would follow him around, like dogs, and no man knew a good horse better than Gregorio Cortez. As for cattle, he could set up school for your best *caporal*.[5] And if an animal was lost, and nobody could pick up a trail, they would send for Gregorio Cortez. He could always find a trail. There was no better tracker in all the Border country, nor a man who could hide his tracks better if he wanted to. That was Gregorio Cortez, the best *vaquero* and range man that there ever was.

But that is not all. You farmers, do you think that Gregorio Cortez did not know your business too? You could have told him nothing about cotton or beans or corn. He knew it all. He could look into the sky of a morning and smell it, sniff it the way a dog sniffs, and tell you what kind of weather there was going to be. And he would take a piece of dirt in his hands and rub it back and forth between his fingers—to see if the land had reached its point—and you would say he was looking into it. And perhaps he was, for Gregorio Cortez was the seventh son of a seventh son. . . . [6]

The legend tells how Cortez and his younger brother, Román, left Mexico to work as ranch hands in Texas. After

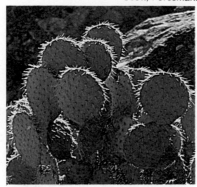

some years there, Román, as a reckless practical joke, tricked an American in a horse trade. The next day, the American came to the Cortez ranch to accuse Román of theft, bringing with him the first Major Sheriff of the corrido. *During the dispute, the Sheriff shot Román fatally and Gregorio Cortez then killed the Sheriff. After leaving his dying brother at their mother's home, Cortez rode out for the Mexican Border.*

But by then the whole wasp's nest was beginning to buzz. The President of the United States offered a thousand dollars for him, and many men went out to get Gregorio Cortez. The Major Sheriffs of the counties and all their sheriffs were out. There were Rangers from the counties, armed to the teeth, and the King Ranch Rangers from the Capital,[7] the meanest of them all, all armed and looking for Cortez. Every road was blocked and every bridge guarded. There were trackers out with those dogs they call hounds, that can follow a track better than the best tracker. . . . And Gregorio Cortez rode out for the Border, through brush and fields and

barbed wire fences, on his little sorrel mare. . . .

"So many mounted Rangers," said Gregorio Cortez, "to catch just one Mexican."

It was from the big bunches that he ran. Now and again he would run into little ones of ten or a dozen men, and they were so scared of him that they would let him pass. Then, when he was out of range they would shoot at him, and he would shoot back at them once or twice, so they could go back and say, "We met up with Gregorio Cortez, and we traded shots with him." But from the big ones he had to run. And it was the little sorrel mare that took him safe away, over the open spaces and into the brush, and once in the brush, they might as well have been following a star.

So it went for a day, and when night fell Cortez arrived at a place named Los Fresnos and called at a Mexican house. When the man of the house came out, Cortez told him, "I am Gregorio Cortez."

That was all he had to say. He was given to eat and drink, and the man of the house offered Gregorio Cortez his own horse and his rifle and his saddle. But Cortez would not take them. He thanked the man, but he would not give up his little sorrel mare. Cortez was sitting there, drinking a cup of coffee,

---

3. vaquero (va keʹrô), cowboy.
4. Laredo . . . mouth, from the Texas town of Laredo to the mouth of the Rio Grande.
5. caporal (kä pô rälʹ), ranch foreman.
6. seventh . . . son. In many folk traditions, this is a sign of great good luck.
7. King Ranch . . . Capital. This expresses a misconception that deputies from the huge King Ranch actually were Rangers from Austin, the state capital.

when the Major Sheriff of Los Fresnos came up with his three hundred men. All the other people ran out of the house and hid, and no one was left in the house, only Gregorio Cortez, with his pistol in his hand.

Then the Major Sheriff called out, in a weepy voice, as the *corrido* says. He sounded as if he wanted to cry, but it was all done to deceive Gregorio Cortez.

"Cortez," the Major Sheriff said, "hand over your weapons. I did not come to kill you. I am your friend."

"If you come as my friend," said Gregorio Cortez, "why did you bring three hundred men? Why have you made me a corral?"

The Major Sheriff knew that he had been caught in a lie, and the fighting began. He killed the Major Sheriff and the second sheriff under him, and he killed many sheriffs more. Some of the sheriffs got weak in the knees, and many ran away.

"Don't go away," said Gregorio Cortez. "I am the man you are looking for. I am Gregorio Cortez."

They were more than three hundred, but he jumped their corral, and he rode away again, and those three hundred did not chase him any more. . . .

After many more days and miles of daring feats and clever escapes, Cortez reached the Border and prepared to cross the Rio Grande. But then he learned that the frustrated Rangers had jailed his mother, wife, and sons, and were punishing everyone who had helped him.

And he decided to turn back, and to give himself up to the Governor of the State so that his own people would not suffer because of him.

He turned and walked back until he came to a place called Goliad, where he met eleven Mexicans, and among them there was one that called himself his friend. This man was a *vaquero* named El Teco,[8] but Judas should have been his name. Gregorio Cortez was thirsty, and he came up to the eleven Mexicans to ask for water, and when El Teco saw Gregorio Cortez he thought how good it would be if he could get the thousand-dollar reward. So he walked up to Cortez and shook his hand and told the others, "Get some water for my friend Gregorio Cortez."

Then El Teco asked Gregorio Cortez to let him see the pistols he had, and that he would get him some ammunition. Gregorio Cortez smiled, because he knew. But he handed over the guns to El Teco, and El Teco looked at them and put them in his own *morral*.[9] Then El Teco called the sheriffs to come and get Gregorio Cortez.

When Gregorio Cortez saw what El Teco had done, he smiled again and said to him, "Teco, a man can only be what God made him. May you enjoy your reward."

But El Teco did not enjoy the reward, though the sheriffs gave him the money, one thousand dollars in silver, more than a *morral* could hold. He did not enjoy it because he could not spend it anywhere. If he went to buy a taco at the market place, the taco vender would tell him that tacos were worth two thousand dollars gold that day. People cursed him in the streets and wished that he would be killed or die. So El Teco became very much afraid. He buried the money and never spent it, and he never knew peace until he died.

---

8. *El Teco* (el te′kô), perhaps a nickname from *el tecol*, a kind of worm.
9. *morral* (môr räl′), saddlebag.

Discussion

1. Compare the **ballad** and the prose versions of the **legend** of Gregorio Cortez. **(a)** Are the details left out of the ballad essential to meaning? Why or why not? **(b)** What different aspects of the story does each version emphasize?

2. **(a)** What elements of the tall tale do you find in the prose legend? **(b)** How is this account like and unlike the legend of Robin Hood?

Extension • Writing

Now that you have compared the ballad and prose versions of the legend of Gregorio Cortez, write a story based on "Shenandoah."

Samuel Clemens

The Celebrated Jumping Frog of Calaveras County

In compliance with the request of a friend of mine, who wrote me from the East, I called on good-natured, garrulous old Simon Wheeler, and inquired after my friend's friend, Leonidas W. Smiley, as requested to do, and I hereunto append the result. I have a lurking suspicion that *Leonidas W.* Smiley is a myth; that my friend never knew such a personage; and that he only conjectured that if I asked old Wheeler about him, it would remind him of his infamous *Jim* Smiley, and he would go to work and bore me to death with some exasperating reminiscence of him as long and as tedious as it should be useless to me. If that was the design, it succeeded.

I found Simon Wheeler dozing comfortably by the barroom stove of the dilapidated tavern in the decayed mining camp of Angel's, and I noticed that he was fat and baldheaded, and had an expression of winning gentleness and simplicity upon his tranquil countenance. He roused up, and gave me good day. I told him a friend of mine had commissioned me to make some inquiries about a cherished companion of his boyhood named *Leonidas W.* Smiley—*Rev. Leonidas W.* Smiley, a young minister of the Gospel, who he had heard was at one time a resident of Angel's Camp. I added that if Mr. Wheeler could tell me anything about this Rev. Leonidas W. Smiley, I would feel under many obligations to him.

Simon Wheeler backed me into a corner and blockaded me there with his chair, and then sat down and reeled off the monotonous narrative which follows this paragraph. He never smiled, he never frowned, he never changed his voice from the gentle-flowing key to which he tuned his initial sentence, he never betrayed the slightest suspicion of enthusiasm; but all through the interminable narrative there ran a vein of impressive earnestness and sincerity which showed me plainly that, so far from his imagining that there was anything ridiculous or funny about his story, he regarded it as a really important matter, and admired its two heroes as men of transcendent genius in finesse. I let him go on in his own way, and never interrupted him once.

"Rev. Leonidas W. H'm, Reverend Le—well, there was a feller here once by the name of *Jim Smiley*, in the winter of '49—or maybe it was the spring of '50—I don't recollect exactly, somehow, though what makes me think it was one or the other is because I remember the big flume wasn't finished when he first came to the camp. But anyway, he was the curiousest man about always betting on anything that turned up you ever see, if he could get anybody to bet on the other side; and if he couldn't, he'd change sides. Any way that suited the other man would suit *him*—any way just so's he got a bet, *he* was satisfied. But still he was lucky, uncommon lucky; he most always come out winner. He was always ready and laying for a chance; there couldn't be no solit'ry thing mentioned but that feller'd offer to bet on it, and take any side you please, as I was just telling you. If there was a horse race, you'd find him flush or you'd find him busted at the end of it; if there was a dog fight, he'd bet on it; if there was a cat fight, he'd bet on it; if there was a chicken fight, he'd bet on it. Why, if there was two birds setting on a fence, he would bet you which one would fly first; or if there was a camp meeting, he would be there reg'lar to bet on Parson Walker, which he judged to be the best exhorter about there, and so he was too, and a good man. If he even see a straddlebug start to go anywheres, he would bet you how long it would take him to get wherever he was going to, and if you took him up, he would foller that straddlebug to Mexico but what he would find out where he was bound for and how long he was on the road.

"Lots of the boys here has seen Smiley, and can tell you about him. Why, it never made no difference to *him*—he'd bet on *any*thing—the dangdest feller. Parson Walker's wife laid very sick once, for a good while, and it seemed as if they warn't going to save her; but one morning he come in, and Smiley asked how she was, and he said she was considerable better—thank the Lord for His inf'nite mercy—and coming on so smart that with the blessing of Prov'dence she'd get well yet; and Smiley, before he thought, says, 'Well, I'll resk two-and-a-half that she don't anyway.'

"Thish-yer Smiley had a mare—the boys called her the fifteen-minute nag, but that was only in fun, you know, because of course she was faster than that—and he used to win money on that horse, for all she was so slow and always had the asthma, or the distemper, or the consumption, or something of that kind. They used to give her two or three hundred yards' start, and then pass her under way; but always at the fag end of the race she'd get excited and desperate-like, and come cavorting and straddling up, and scattering her legs around limber, sometimes in the air, and sometimes out to one side among the fences, and kicking up m-o-r-e dust and raising m-o-r-e racket with her coughing and sneezing and blowing her nose—and *always* fetch up at the stand just about a neck ahead, as near as you could cipher it down.

"And he had a little small bull pup, that to look at him you'd think he wan't worth a cent but to set around and look ornery and lay for a chance to steal something. But as soon as money was up on him he was a different dog; his under jaw'd begin to stick out like the fo'castle of a steamboat, and his teeth would uncover and shine like the furnaces. And a dog might tackle him and bullyrag him, and bite him, and throw him over his shoulder two or three times, and Andrew Jackson—which was the name of the pup—Andrew Jackson would never let on but what *he* was satisfied, and hadn't expected nothing else—and the bets being doubled and doubled on the other side all the time, till the money was all up; and then all of a sudden he would grab that other dog jest by the j'int of his hind leg and freeze to it—not chaw, you understand, but only just grip and hang on till they throwed up the sponge, if it was a year.

"Smiley always come out winner on that pup, till he harnessed a dog once that didn't have no hind legs, because they'd been sawed off by a circular saw, and when the thing had gone along far enough, and the money was all up, and he come to make a snatch for his pet holt, he saw in a minute how he'd been imposed on, and how the other dog had him in the door,[1] so to speak, and he 'peared surprised, and then he looked sorter discouraged-like, and didn't try no more to win the fight, and so he got shucked out[2] bad. He give Smiley a look, as much as to say his heart was broke, and it was *his* fault, for putting up a dog that hadn't no hind legs for him to take holt of, which was his main dependence in a fight, and then he limped off a piece and laid down and died. It was a good pup, was that Andrew Jackson, and would have made a name for hisself if he'd lived, for the stuff was in him and he had genius—I know it, because he hadn't had no opportunities to speak of, and it don't stand to reason that a dog could make such a fight as he could under them circumstances if he hadn't no talent. It always makes me feel sorry when I think of that last fight of his'n, and the way it turned out.

"Well, thish-yer Smiley had rat terriers, and chicken cocks, and tomcats and all them kind of things, till you couldn't rest, and you couldn't fetch nothing for him to bet on but he'd match you. He ketched a frog one day, and took him home, and said he calk'lated to edercate him; and so he never done nothing for three months but set in his back yard and learn that frog to jump. And you bet he *did* learn him, too. He'd give him a little punch behind, and the next minute you'd see that frog whirling in the air like a doughnut—see him turn one summer-set, or maybe a couple, if he got a good start, and come down flat-footed and all right, like a cat. He got him up so in the matter of catching flies, and kep' him in practice so constant, that he'd nail a fly every time as far as he could see him.

"Smiley said all a frog wanted was education, and he could do 'most anything—and I believe him. Why, I've seen him set Dan'l Webster down here on this floor—Dan'l Webster was the name of the frog—and sing out, 'Flies, Dan'l, flies!' and quicker'n you could wink he'd spring straight up and snake a fly off'n the counter there, and flop down on the floor ag'in as solid as a gob of mud, and fall to scratching the side of his head with his hind foot as indifferent as if he hadn't no idea

he'd been doin' any more'n any frog might do. You never see a frog so modest and straightfor-'ard as he was, for all he was so gifted. And when it come to fair and square jumping on a dead level, he could get over more ground at one straddle than any animal of his breed you ever see. Jumping on a dead level was his strong suit, you understand; and when it come to that, Smiley would ante up money on him as long as he had a red.[3] Smiley was monstrous proud of his frog, and well he might be, for fellers that had traveled and been everywheres all said he laid over any frog that ever *they* see.

"Well, Smiley kept the beast in a little lattice box, and he used to fetch him downtown sometimes and lay for a bet. One day a feller—a stranger in the camp, he was—come across him with his box, and says:

"'What might it be that you've got in the box?'

"And Smiley says, sorter indifferent-like, 'It might be a parrot, or it might be a canary, maybe, but it ain't—it's only just a frog.'

"And the feller took it, and looked at it careful, and turned it round this way and that, and says, 'H'm—so 'tis. Well, what's *he* good for?'

"'Well,' Smiley says, easy and careless, 'he's good enough for *one* thing, I should judge—he can out-jump ary frog in Calaveras County.'

"The feller took the box again, and took another long, particular look, and give it back to Smiley, and says, very deliberate, 'Well, I don't see no p'ints about that frog that's any better'n any other frog.'

"'Maybe you don't,' Smiley says. 'Maybe you understand frogs and maybe you don't understand 'em; maybe you've had experience, and maybe you ain't only a amature, as it were. Anyways, I've got *my* opinion, and I'll resk forty dollars that he can outjump any frog in Calaveras County.'

"And the feller studied a minute, and then says, kinder sad-like, 'Well, I'm only a stranger here, and I ain't got no frog; but if I had a frog, I'd bet you.'

---

1. *had him in the door,* had him at a disadvantage.
2. *shucked out,* beaten.
3. *a red,* a red cent, or any money at all.

"And then Smiley says, 'That's all right—that's all right—if you'll hold my box a minute, I'll go and get you a frog.' And so the feller took the box, and put up his forty dollars along with Smiley's, and set down to wait.

"So he set there a good while thinking and thinking to himself, and then he got the frog out and prized his mouth open and took a teaspoon and filled him full of quail shot—filled him pretty near up to his chin—and set him on the floor.

"Smiley he went to the swamp and slopped around in the mud for a long time, and finally he ketched a frog, and fetched him in, and give him to this feller, and says:

"'Now, if you're ready, set him alongside of Dan'l, with his forepaws just even with Dan'l's, and I'll give the word.' Then he says, 'One—two—three—jump!' and him and the feller touched up the frogs from behind, and the new frog hopped off, but Dan'l give a heave and hysted up his shoulders —so—like a Frenchman, but it wan't no use—he couldn't budge; he was planted as solid as an anvil, and he couldn't no more stir than if he was anchored out. Smiley was a good deal surprised, and he was disgusted too, but he didn't have no idea what the matter was, of course.

"The feller took the money and started away; and when he was going out at the door, he sorter jerked his thumb over his shoulder—this way—at Dan'l, and says again, very deliberate, 'Well, I don't see no p'ints about that frog that's any better'n any other frog.'

"Smiley he stood scratching his head and looking down at Dan'l a long time, and at last he says, 'I do wonder what in the nation that frog throw'd off for—I wonder if there ain't something the matter with him—he 'pears to look mighty baggy, somehow.' And he ketched Dan'l by the nap of the neck, and lifted him up, and says, 'Why blame my cats if he don't weigh five pound!' and turned him upside down, and he belched out a double handful of shot. And then Smiley see how it was, and he was the maddest man—he set the frog down and took out after that feller, but he never ketched him. And—"

[Here Simon Wheeler heard his name called from the front yard, and got up to see what was wanted.] And turning to me as he moved away, he said: "Just set where you are, stranger, and rest easy—I ain't going to be gone a second."

But, by your leave, I did not think that a continuation of the history of the enterprising vagabond *Jim* Smiley would be likely to afford me much information concerning the Rev. *Leonidas W.* Smiley, and so I started away.

At the door I met the sociable Wheeler returning, and he buttonholed me and recommenced:

"Well, thish-yer Smiley had a yaller one-eyed cow that didn't have no tail, only just a short stump like a bannanner, and—"

However, lacking both time and inclination, I did not wait to hear about the afflicted cow, but took my leave. □ □

Discussion

"The Celebrated Jumping Frog" is an example of a truly native genre, the **tall tale**. Originally an oral tradition that included tales of such American folk heroes as Paul Bunyan, John Henry, and Mike Fink (the Missisippi Riverman), the tall tale eventually found its way into the American literary tradition after the Civil War. It is said that the tales originated as mutual entertainment during the long, lonely, frontier nights.

1. To capture the flavor of the oral yarn in writing, it is necessary for an author to help readers see the **narrator** as well as hear him speak. **(a)** What parts of this story are devoted to acquainting the reader with Simon Wheeler? **(b)** What kinds of information does Clemens give about Wheeler? **(c)** How does this information add to the humor of the story. **(d)** Discuss why Clemens uses peculiar sentence patterns, intentional misspellings, and grammatical errors in the yarn itself. **(e)** Why does he italicize certain words?

2. (a) Cite two particularly comic passages in Wheeler's **monologue** and explain why they are humorous. **(b)** Do you think the story is still funny today? Why or why not?

3. An old tradition of literature involves the classic situation of "the trickster tricked." Relate Smiley to this convention.

from Life on the Mississippi

When I was a boy, there was but one permanent ambition among my comrades in our village on the west bank of the Mississippi River. That was, to be a steamboatman. We had transient ambitions of other sorts, but they were only transient. When a circus came and went, it left us all burning to become clowns; the first Negro minstrel show that ever came to our section left us all suffering to try that kind of life; now and then we had a hope that if we lived and were good, God would permit us to be pirates. These ambitions faded out, each in its turn; but the ambition to be a steamboatman always remained.

Once a day a cheap, gaudy packet arrived upward from St. Louis, and another downward from Keokuk.[1] Before these events, the day was glorious with expectancy; after them, the day was a dead and empty thing. Not only the boys, but the whole village, felt this. After all these years I can picture that old time to myself now, just as it was then: the white town drowsing in the sunshine of a summer's morning; the streets empty, or pretty nearly so; one or two clerks sitting in front of the Water Street stores, with their splint-bottomed chairs[2] tilted back against the walls, chins on breasts, hats slouched over their faces, asleep—with shingle–shavings enough around to show what broke them down; a sow, and a litter of pigs loafing along the sidewalk, doing a good business in watermelon rinds and seeds; two or three lonely little freight piles scattered about the levee; a pile of skids on the slope of the stone-paved wharf, and the fragrant town drunkard asleep in the shadow of them; two or three wood flats[3] at the head of the wharf, but nobody to listen to the peaceful lapping of the wavelets against them; the great Mississippi, the majestic, the magnificent Mississippi, rolling its mile-wide tide along, shining in the sun; the dense forest away on the other side; the point above the town, and the point below, bounding the river-glimpse and turning it into a sort of sea, and withal a very still and brilliant and lonely one. Presently a film of dark smoke appears above one of those remote points: instantly a Negro drayman, famous for his quick eye and prodigious voice, lifts up the cry, "S-t-e-a-m-boat a-comin'!" and the scene changes! The town drunkard stirs, the clerks wake up, a furious clatter of drays follows, every house and store pours out a human contribution, and all in a twinkling the dead town is alive and moving. Drays, carts, men, boys, all go hurrying from many quarters to a common center, the wharf. Assembled there, the people fasten their eyes upon the coming boat as upon a wonder they are seeing for the first time. And the boat *is* rather a handsome sight, too. She is long and sharp and trim and pretty; she has two tall, fancy-topped chimneys, with a gilded device of some kind swung between them; a fanciful pilot house, all glass and gingerbread, perched on top of the texas deck[4] behind them; the paddle boxes[5] are gorgeous with a picture or with gilded rays above the boat's name; the boiler deck, the hurricane deck,[6] and the texas deck are fenced and ornamented with clean white railings; there is a flag gallantly flying from the jack staff;[7] the furnace doors are open and the fires glaring bravely; the upper decks are black with passengers; the captain stands by the big bell, calm, imposing, the envy of all; great volumes of the blackest smoke are rolling and tumbling out of the chimneys—a husbanded grandeur created with a bit of pitch pine just before arriving at a town; the crew are grouped on the forecastle; the broad stage[8] is run

---

1. Keokuk (kē′ə kuk), a Mississippi River town in the southeastern corner of Iowa, about fifty miles above Hannibal.
2. splint-bottomed chairs, chairs with seats woven of thin strips (splints) of wood.
3. wood flats, small flat-bottomed boats.
4. texas deck. The texas is a range of staterooms adjacent to the pilot house reserved for officers. The texas deck adjoins these living quarters.
5. paddle boxes, the wooden coverings built over the upper part of the paddle wheels which propelled the steamer.
6. the boiler deck, the hurricane deck. The boiler deck is that part of the upper deck immediately over the boilers; the hurricane deck is the topmost deck.
7. jack staff, a short pole erected at the front of the vessel.
8. forecastle . . . stage. The forecastle is an upper deck at the forward part of the ship; the stage is a stage-plank or gangplank.

far out over the port bow, and a deck hand stands picturesquely on the end of it with a coil of rope in his hand; the pent steam is screaming through the gauge cocks; the captain lifts his hand, a bell rings, the wheels stop; then they turn back, churning the water to foam, and the steamer is at rest. Then such a scramble as there is to get aboard, and to get ashore, and to take in freight and to discharge freight, all at one and the same time; and such a yelling and cursing as the mates facilitate it all with! Ten minutes later the steamer is under way again, with no flag on the jack staff and no black smoke issuing from the chimneys. After ten more minutes the town is dead again, and the town drunkard asleep by the skids once more.

My father was a justice of the peace, and I supposed he possessed the power of life and death over all men, and could hang anybody that offended him. This was distinction enough for

Low Water in the Mississippi by Currier and Ives.
(Museum of the City of New York.)

me as a general thing; but the desire to be a steamboatman kept intruding, nevertheless. I first wanted to be a cabin boy, so that I could come out with a white apron on and shake a tablecloth over the side, where all my old comrades could see me; later I thought I would rather be the deck hand who stood on the end of the stage-plank with the coil of rope in his hand, because he was particularly conspicuous. But these were only daydreams—they were too heavenly to be contemplated as real possibilities.

By and by one of our boys went away. He was not heard of for a long time. At last he turned up as apprentice engineer or "striker" on a steamboat. This thing shook the bottom out of all my Sunday-school teachings. That boy had been notoriously worldly, and I just the reverse; yet he was exalted to this eminence, and I left in obscurity and misery. There was nothing generous about this fellow in his greatness. He would always manage to have a rusty bolt to scrub while his boat tarried at our town, and he would sit on the inside guard[9] and scrub it, where we all could see him and envy him and loathe him. And whenever his boat was laid up he would come home and swell around the town in his blackest and greasiest clothes, so that nobody could help remembering that he was a steamboatman; and he used all sorts of steamboat technicalities in his talk, as if he were so used to them that he forgot common people could not understand them. He would speak of the "lab-board"[10] side of a horse in an easy, natural way that would make one wish he was dead. And he was always talking about "St. Looy" like an old citizen; he would refer casually to occasions when he was "coming down Fourth Street," or when he was "passing by the Planter's House," or when there was a fire and he took a turn on the brakes of "the old Big Missouri"; and then he would go on and lie about how many towns the size of ours were burned down there that day. Two or three of the boys had long been persons of consideration among us because they had been to St. Louis once and had a vague general knowledge of its wonders, but the day of their glory was over now. They lapsed into a humble silence, and learned to disappear when the ruthless cub engineer approached. This fellow had money, too, and hair oil. Also an ignorant silver watch and a showy brass watch

chain. He wore a leather belt and used no suspenders. If ever a youth was cordially admired and hated by his comrades, this one was. No girl could withstand his charms. He "cut out" every boy in the village. When his boat blew up at last, it diffused a tranquil contentment among us such as we had not known for months. But when he came home the next week, alive, renowned, and appeared in church all battered up and bandaged, a shining hero, stared at and wondered over by everybody, it seemed to us that the partiality of Providence for an undeserving reptile had reached a point where it was open to criticism.

This creature's career could produce but one result, and it speedily followed. Boy after boy managed to get on the river. The minister's son became an engineer. The doctor's and the postmaster's sons became mud clerks;[11] the wholesale liquor dealer's son became a barkeeper on a boat; four sons of the chief merchant, and two sons of the county judge, became pilots. Pilot was the grandest position of all. The pilot, even in those days of trivial wages, had a princely salary—from a hundred and fifty to two hundred and fifty dollars a month, and no board to pay. Two months of his wages would pay a preacher's salary for a year. Now some of us were left disconsolate. We could not get on the river—at least our parents would not let us.

So, by and by, I ran away. I said I would never come home again till I was a pilot and could come in glory. But somehow I could not manage it. I went meekly aboard a few of the boats that lay packed together like sardines at the long St. Louis wharf, and humbly inquired for the pilots, but got only a cold shoulder and short words from mates and clerks. I had to make the best of this sort of treatment for the time being, but I had comforting daydreams of a future when I should be a great and honored pilot, with plenty of money, and could kill some of these mates and clerks and pay for them. □ □

---

9. *inside guard,* part of the steamboat's deck which curves out over the paddle wheel.
10. *"labboard,"* larboard, the left or port side of a ship.
11. *mud clerks,* second clerks, so called because it was their duty to go ashore at unimportant stops, often mere mudbanks, to receive or check off freight.

Discussion

1. In the selection from *Life on the Mississippi,* Clemens mentions three passing ambitions of the boys of Hannibal. **(a)** What were these ambitions? **(b)** What is Clemens's purpose in mentioning them?

2. The second paragraph is very long, but it is not difficult to follow if you notice Clemens's careful arrangement of his materials. **(a)** What simple fact does he state in the first sentence? **(b)** In the second sentence what contrast does he suggest that he will illustrate? **(c)** Where does he begin and end the "before" picture? **(d)** the "after" picture? **(e)** What does he place between these contrasting pictures? **(f)** Cite some of the details that are most helpful to you in sensing the mood of each section of the paragraph.

3. In what ways does Clemens introduce humor into the story of the local boy who became an apprentice engineer?

4. How does one go about choosing a career for life? Do you think Clemens's description of the process is accurate? Explain.

Samuel Langhorne Clemens
1835 • 1910

Clemens was reared in the Mississippi River town of Hannibal, Missouri; many of the adventures of Tom Sawyer can be traced back to his own childhood. His father died when Sam was twelve and Clemens left school to help support the family. He was apprenticed as a printer's devil and for a number of years worked on his brother's paper. In his early twenties Clemens was able to apprentice himself to a steamboat pilot on the Mississippi. After a year and a half he graduated to licensed pilot and the next few years were perhaps the happiest of his life. They ended when the Civil War put a stop to traffic on the Mississippi.

Torn between regional loyalties and his opposition to slavery, Clemens eventually left with his brother for Nevada. After unsuccessfully trying his hand at prospecting, Clemens became a journalist under the pseudonym of Mark Twain, a depth measurement in river navigation. He was a reporter and correspondent in Virginia City and then in California, where in 1865 he wrote "The Celebrated Jumping Frog of Calaveras County." It appeared in a New York magazine and was quickly picked up and printed by newspapers across the nation.

Capitalizing on the success of the story, Clemens sailed to New York and in 1867 a collection of sketches headed by the "Jumping Frog" story was published. That same year he joined a group of tourists sailing for the Mediterranean and the Holy Land. His humorous accounts of the Americans taking in the wonders of the Old World were collected and released as *The Innocents Abroad.* It sold prodigiously and Clemens was very quickly becoming both renowned and rich.

At thirty-five Clemens married Olivia Langdon, with whom he settled in Hartford, Connecticut. In the following seventeen years he produced his finest writing: *The Adventures of Tom Sawyer* (1876), *A Tramp Abroad* (1880), *The Prince and the Pauper* (1882), *Life on the Mississippi* (1883), *The Adventures of Huckleberry Finn* (1884), and *A Connecticut Yankee at King Arthur's Court* (1889). He spent his royalty money carelessly, living sumptuously and investing in schemes which all failed. Clemens invested in his own publishing firm which eventually collapsed. He finally faced bankruptcy, but instead of filing such papers, he insisted he would pay all his creditors in full and set off on an around-the-world lecture tour to raise the money.

Life was especially hard on him in the final years; his wife and two of his three daughters died. Clemens seems to have experienced a combination of despair, pity, and resignation. He once said, "Everything human is pathetic. The secret source of humor itself is not joy but sorrow. There is no humor in heaven."

Satanta

My Heart Feels Like Bursting

Satanta's speech was given in 1867 to the United States commissioners at the great council at Medicine Lodge Creek, Kansas, where chiefs of some Plains tribes, including Satanta, accepted a treaty limiting where their people could live and hunt. Chief Joseph's famous speech on the facing page was made when he surrendered with his people to General Nelson Miles in 1877.

Smithsonian Institution.

I love the land and the buffalo and will not part with it. I want you to understand well what I say. Write it on paper. . . . I hear a great deal of good talk from the gentlemen whom the Great Father[1] sends us, but they never do what they say. I don't want any of the medicine lodges[2] within the country. I want the children raised as I was. . . .

I have heard that you intend to settle us on a reservation near the mountains. I don't want to settle. I love to roam over the prairies. There I feel free and happy, but when we settle down we grow pale and die. I have laid aside my lance, bow, and shield, and yet I feel safe in your presence. I have told you the truth. I have no little lies hid about me, but I don't know how it is with the commissioners. Are they as clear as I am? A long time ago this land belonged to our fathers; but when I go up to the river I see camps of soldiers on its banks. These soldiers cut down my timber; they kill my buffalo; and when I see that, my heart feels like bursting; I feel sorry. I have spoken. □□

James Mooney, "Calendar History of the Kiowa Indians," U.S. Bureau of American Ethnology, 17th Annual Report, 1895–96, pt. 1, 207–08.

1. **Great Father,** President Andrew Johnson.
2. **medicine lodges,** schools and churches like those of the whites.

Discussion

1. **(a)** What are Satanta's ideals of good conduct and the good life? **(b)** Explain how each of the developments he mentions threatens his way of life.

2. What emotional responses is his speech designed to evoke from the government commissioners?

Satanta   ?1830 • 1878

After the Civil War, a new surge of homesteaders and repeated violations of U.S. government treaties infuriated the Plains tribes. As second chief of the Kiowas, Satanta led attacks on settlers. Chiefs of some nations, including Satanta, the "Orator of the Plains," agreed to the Medicine Lodge treaty. But hostilities soon resumed and Satanta was imprisoned. He killed himself in the Texas state prison, perhaps attempting by his death to inspire the Kiowas to resist total subjugation.

Chief Joseph

I Will Fight No More Forever

The Museum of the American Indian, Heye Foundation.

Tell General Howard I know his heart. What he told me before, I have in my heart. I am tired of fighting. Our chiefs are killed. Looking Glass is dead. Toohoolhoolzote[1] is dead. The old men are all dead. It is the young men who say yes and no. He who led on the young men is dead. It is cold and we have no blankets. The little children are freezing to death. My people, some of them, have run away to the hills and have no blankets, no food; no one knows where they are—perhaps freezing to death. I want to have time to look for my children and see how many I can find. Maybe I shall find them among the dead. Hear me, my chiefs. I am tired; my heart is sick and sad. From where the sun now stands I will fight no more forever. □□

From INDIAN ORATORY: FAMOUS SPEECHES BY NOTED INDI-AN CHIEFTAINS, compiled by W. C. Vanderwerth. Copyright 1971 by the University of Oklahoma Press. Reprinted by permission.

1. **Toohoolhoolzote** (tü hül′hül′zōt), a prophet who once served as Chief Joseph's spokesman.

Discussion

1. What characteristics of a great leader are revealed in this speech?

2. What phrases suggest that Chief Joseph experienced opposition from his own people?

Chief Joseph ?1832 • 1904

At the age of only thirty, Chief Joseph, or Hinmatonya-laktit, became council leader of the Shahaptians (Nez Percé), a tribe of the Pacific Northwest. In 1876, the government ordered the tribe to yield its already restricted lands. Chief Joseph's legal arguments failed and he left for Canada with 750 followers, few of them warriors. For two months and over 1600 miles of mountains, his war chiefs brilliantly outfought veteran troops. The exhausted survivors were trapped barely thirty miles from Canada.

Exiled first to Oklahoma, then to a reservation in Washington, Chief Joseph visited Washington, D.C. and the East in 1903.

Emily Dickinson

Life

This is my letter to the world,
  That never wrote to me,—
The simple news that Nature told,
  With tender majesty.

5 Her message is committed
  To hands I cannot see;
For love of her, sweet countrymen,
  Judge tenderly of me!

Much madness is divinest sense
To a discerning eye;
Much sense the starkest madness.
'Tis the majority
5 In this, as all, prevails.
Assent, and you are sane;
Demur,—you're straightway dangerous,
And handled with a chain.

Emily Dickinson. POEMS (1890–1896) edited by H. R. Warfel.
(Gainesville, Florida: Scholars' Facsimilies and Reprints), 1967.

Discussion

This Is My Letter to the World

1. What two interpretations can be given to "Her message" in line 5?

2. What does this introductory poem suggest about Dickinson and her poetry?

Much Madness Is Divinest Sense

1. How can "madness" ever be "divinest sense"?

2. What view of society does this poem imply?

I Taste a Liquor Never Brewed

1. (a) Explain the **extended metaphor** of the poem. **(b)** What feelings does the speaker express through this metaphor?

A Narrow Fellow in the Grass

1. Identify some **images** drawn from everyday experience.

2. Contrast the speaker's responses to the "narrow fellow" and to others "of nature's people."

3. Explore the different attitudes toward nature expressed in this poem and in "I Taste a Liquor Never Brewed."

To Make a Prairie . . .

1. In what sense could "revery alone" make a prairie?

Nature

I taste a liquor never brewed,
From tankards scooped in pearl;
Not all the vats upon the Rhine
Yield such an alcohol!

5 Inebriate of air am I,
And debauchee of dew,
Reeling, through endless summer days,
From inns of molten blue.

When landlords turn the drunken bee
10 Out of the foxglove's door,
When butterflies renounce their drams,
I shall but drink the more!

Till seraphs swing their snowy hats,
And saints to windows run,
15 To see the little tippler
Leaning against the sun!

A narrow fellow in the grass
Occasionally rides;
You may have met him,—did you not,
His notice sudden is.

5 The grass divides as with a comb,
A spotted shaft is seen;
And then it closes at your feet
And opens further on.

He likes a boggy acre,
10 A floor too cool for corn.
Yet when a child, and barefoot,
I more than once, at morn,

Have passed, I thought, a whip-lash
Unbraiding in the sun,—
15 When, stooping to secure it,
It wrinkled, and was gone.

Several of nature's people
I know, and they know me;
I feel for them a transport
20 Of cordiality;

But never met this fellow,
Attended or alone,
Without a tighter breathing,
And zero at the bone.

Dr. E. R. Degginger.

To make a prairie it takes a clover
        and one bee,—
One clover, and a bee,
And revery.
The revery alone will do
If bees are few.

Love

If you were coming in the fall,
I'd brush the summer by
With half a smile and half a spurn,
As housewives do a fly.

5 If I could see you in a year,
I'd wind the months in balls,
And put them each in separate drawers,
Until their time befalls.

If only centuries delayed,
10 I'd count them on my hand,
Subtracting till my fingers dropped
Into Van Diemen's land.[1]

If certain, when this life was out,
That yours and mine should be,
15 I'd toss it yonder like a rind,
And taste eternity.

But now, all ignorant of the length
Of time's uncertain wing,
It goads me, like the goblin bee,
20 That will not state its sting.

---

1. *Van Diemen's* (dē′mənz) *Land,* Tasmania, a large island south of Australia. It was discovered in 1642 by the Dutch explorer Tasman, who originally named it for Antony van Diemen, a Dutch colonial governor.

Of all the souls that stand create
I have elected one.
When sense from spirit files away,
And subterfuge is done;

5 When that which is and that which was
Apart, intrinsic, stand,
And this brief tragedy of flesh
Is shifted like a sand;

When figures show their royal front
10 And mists are carved away,—
Behold the atom I preferred
To all the lists of clay!

Discussion

If You Were Coming in the Fall

1. Contrast the metaphor used for time in the final stanza with those that suggest the speaker's attitude toward the passing of time in the first four stanzas.

Of All the Souls That Stand Create

1. (a) What is the "subterfuge" referred to in line 4? **(b)** When would "mists" be "carved away"? And what would then remain?
2. What contrast is suggested by calling the chosen soul an "atom" and the others "lists of clay"?

Anguish

I felt a funeral in my brain,
   And mourners, to and fro,
Kept treading, treading, till it seemed
   That sense was breaking through.

5 And when they all were seated,
   A service like a drum
Kept beating, beating, till I thought
   My mind was going numb.

And then I heard them lift a box,
10   And creak across my soul
With those same boots of lead, again.
   Then space began to toll

As all the heavens were a bell,
   And Being but an ear,
15 And I and silence some strange race,
   Wrecked, solitary, here.

I years had been from home,
   And now, before the door,
I dared not open, lest a face
   I never saw before

5 Stare vacant into mine
   And ask my business there.
My business,—just a life I left,
   Was such still dwelling there?

I fumbled at my nerve,
10 I scanned the windows near;
   The silence like an ocean rolled,
   And broke against my ear.

I laughed a wooden laugh
   That I could fear a door,
15 Who danger and the dead had faced,
   But never quaked before.

I fitted to the latch
   My hand, with trembling care,
Lest back the awful door should spring,
20 And leave me standing there.

I moved my fingers off
   As cautiously as glass,
And held my ears, and like a thief
   Fled gasping from the house.

I Felt a Funeral in My Brain

1. (a) To what sense do the **images** in this poem appeal? **(b)** What is their effect on the speaker?

2. What state of mind does the speaker describe in the last two lines?

I Years Had Been from Home

1. (a) What experience is the speaker describing? **(b)** What is she afraid of?

Elliott Erwitt/Magnum Photos, Inc.

Death

I heard a fly buzz when I died;
　The stillness round my form
Was like the stillness in the air
　Between the heaves of storm.

5 The eyes beside had wrung them dry,
　And breaths were gathering sure
For that last onset, when the king
　Be witnessed in his power.

I willed my keepsakes, signed away
10 　What portion of me I
Could make assignable,—and then
　There interposed a fly,

With blue, uncertain, stumbling buzz,
　Between the light and me;
15 And then the windows failed, and then
　I could not see to see.

Because I could not stop for Death,
He kindly stopped for me;
The carriage held but just ourselves
And Immortality.

5 We slowly drove, he knew no haste,
And I had put away
My labor, and my leisure too,
For his civility.

We passed the school where children played,
10 Their lessons scarcely done;
We passed the fields of gazing grain,
We passed the setting sun.

We paused before a house that seemed
A swelling of the ground;
15 The roof was scarcely visible.
The cornice but a mound.

Since then 't is centuries; but each
Feels shorter than the day
I first surmised the horses' heads
20 Were toward eternity.

I Heard a Fly Buzz . . .

1. Contrast the attitude of the deathbed watchers to that of the person dying.

2. How does the fly's buzz affect the speaker?

Because I Could Not Stop for Death

1. (a) What metaphorical meaning does line 12 suggest to you? **(b)** What is meant by the "house," line 13?

2. How is the speaker's outlook in the last stanza different from her initial response to Death?

3. By what means does this poem make death—both the experience and the character "Death"—seem pleasant rather than terrifying?

Emily Dickinson 1830 • 1886

Dickinson once described her concept of poetry: "If I read a book and it makes my body so cold no fire can ever warm me, I know that is poetry. If I feel physically as if the top of my head were taken off, I know that is poetry." During her life, she published only a handful of the 1,775 poems that she wrote and her complete poetic works were not finally published until 1955. She and her poetry never fully belonged to their own time. Neither conformed to popular expectations, and each was unique.

Dickinson lived all her life in Amherst, Massachusetts. In her youth she was vivacious and fun loving. But the society in which she grew up was very strict, with precise specifica-tions as to the proper manners and beliefs for young women. It was a world where fun itself was officially frowned upon, where intellectual curiosity and agility were deemed most unladylike. Though religious, Dickinson did not accept the Calvinist views of the New England church; and her attendance at Mount Holyoke Female Seminary, which she had excitedly anticipated, was marred by daily sessions with the school's headmistress who worked tirelessly for her conversion. But while apparently shy, Dickinson had an unrelenting firmness and after a year's struggle she was removed from the school.

In her mid-twenties Dickinson gradually withdrew from public life and lived thereafter in almost total seclusion from all but the immediate members of her family.

Her poetry writing began in earnest in the late fall of 1861. The most direct influence on her style seems to have come from some of Emerson's poetry. Dickinson also took to heart Emerson's admonition for self-reliance, a prerequisite to her unconventional life and poetry. Nevertheless, she at times wished for critical appraisal. Reading an article of advice to beginning writers by Thomas Wentworth Higginson, Dickinson mailed four of her poems to this abolitionist editor and asked, "Are you too deeply occupied to say if my verse is alive?" Though he never realized the true importance of her work, he found himself intrigued and went on to encourage her.

There are indications that Dickinson realized the quality and possible importance of her work. Yet she had no wish for recognition in her own time and despite the urging of friends declined to publish, saying her "barefoot rank" was better. She lived out her life in seclusion, her privacy a complex preference which had stiffened into habit. She seemed contented with the company of her family, with her large Newfoundland dog, with nature, and with her poetry.

Mary Wilkins Freeman

A New England Nun

It was late in the afternoon, and the light was waning. There was a difference in the look of the tree shadows out in the yard. Somewhere in the distance, cows were lowing and a little bell was tinkling; now and then a farm wagon tilted by, and the dust flew; some blue-shirted laborers with shovels over their shoulders plodded past; little swarms of flies were dancing up and down before the people's faces in the soft air. There seemed to be a gentle stir arising over everything for the mere sake of subsidence—a very premonition of rest and hush and night.

This soft diurnal commotion was over Louisa Ellis also. She had been peacefully sewing at her sitting-room window all the afternoon. Now she quilted her needle carefully into her work, which she folded precisely, and laid in a basket with her thimble and thread and scissors. Louisa Ellis could not remember that ever in her life she had mislaid one of these little feminine appurtenances, which had become, from long use and constant association, a very part of her personality.

Louisa tied a green apron round her waist,

From A NEW ENGLAND NUN AND OTHER STORIES by Mary E. Wilkins, published by Harper and Brothers, 1891.

and got out a flat straw hat with a green ribbon. Then she went into the garden with a little blue crockery bowl, to pick some currants for her tea. After the currants were picked she sat on the back doorstep and stemmed them, collecting the stems carefully in her apron and afterward throwing them into the hencoop. She looked sharply at the grass beside the step to see if any had fallen there.

Louisa was slow and still in her movements; it took her a long time to prepare her tea; but when ready it was set forth with as much grace as if she had been a veritable guest to her own self. The little square table stood exactly in the center of the kitchen, and was covered with a starched linen cloth whose border pattern of flowers glistened. Louisa had a damask napkin on her tea tray, where were arranged a cut-glass tumbler full of teaspoons, a silver cream pitcher, a china sugar bowl, and one pink china cup and saucer. Louisa used china every day—something which none of her neighbors did. They whispered about it among themselves. Their daily tables were laid with common crockery, their sets of best china stayed in the parlor closet, and Louisa Ellis was no richer nor better bred than they. Still she would use the china. She had for her supper a glass dish full of sugared currants, a plate of little cakes, and one of light white biscuits. Also a leaf or two of lettuce, which she cut up daintily. Louisa was very fond of lettuce, which she raised to perfection in her little garden. She ate quite heartily, though in a delicate, pecking way; it seemed almost surprising that any considerable bulk of the food should vanish.

After tea she filled a plate with nicely baked thin corn cakes, and carried them out into the back yard.

"Caesar!" she called. "Caesar! Caesar!"

There was a little rush, and the clank of a chain, and a large yellow-and-white dog appeared at the door of his tiny hut, which was half hidden among the tall grasses and flowers. Louisa patted him and gave him the corn cakes. Then she returned to the house and washed the tea things, polishing the china carefully. The twilight had deepened; the chorus of the frogs floated in at the open window wonderfully loud and shrill, and once in a while a long sharp drone from a tree toad pierced it. Louisa took off her green gingham apron, disclosing a shorter one of pink-and-white print. She lighted her lamp, and sat down again with her sewing.

In about half an hour Joe Dagget came. She heard his heavy step on the walk, and rose and took off her pink-and-white apron. Under that was still another—white linen with a little cambric edging on the bottom; that was Louisa's company apron. She never wore it without her calico sewing apron over it unless she had a guest. She had barely folded the pink-and-white one with methodical haste and laid it in a table drawer when the door opened and Joe Dagget entered.

He seemed to fill up the whole room. A little yellow canary that had been asleep in his green cage at the south window woke up and fluttered wildly, beating his little yellow wings against the wires. He always did so when Joe Dagget came into the room.

"Good evening," said Louisa. She extended her hand with a kind of solemn cordiality.

"Good evening, Louisa," returned the man, in a loud voice.

She placed a chair for him, and they sat facing each other, with the table between them. He sat bolt upright, toeing out his heavy feet squarely, glancing with a good-humored uneasiness around the room. She sat gently erect, folding her slender hands in her white-linen lap.

"Been a pleasant day," remarked Dagget.

"Real pleasant," Louisa assented, softly. "Have you been haying?" she asked, after a little while.

"Yes, I've been haying all day, down in the ten-acre lot. Pretty hot work."

"It must be."

"Yes, it's pretty hot work in the sun."

"Is your mother well today?"

"Yes, Mother's pretty well."

"I suppose Lily Dyer's with her now?"

Dagget colored. "Yes, she's with her," he answered, slowly.

He was not very young, but there was a boyish look about his large face. Louisa was not quite so old as he, her face was fairer and smoother, but she gave people the impression of being older.

"I suppose she's a good deal of help to your mother," she said, further.

"I guess she is; I don't know how Mother'd get along without her," said Dagget, with a sort of embarrassed warmth.

"She looks like a real capable girl. She's pretty-looking too," remarked Louisa.

"Yes, she is pretty fair-looking."

Presently Dagget began fingering the books on the table. There was a square red autograph album, and a Young Lady's Gift Book which had belonged to Louisa's mother. He took them up one after the other and opened them; then laid them down again, the album on the Gift Book.

Louisa kept eyeing them with mild uneasiness. Finally she rose and changed the position of the books, putting the album underneath. That was the way they had been arranged in the first place.

Dagget gave an awkward little laugh. "Now what difference did it make which book was on top?" said he.

Louisa looked at him with a deprecating smile. "I always keep them that way," murmured she.

"You do beat everything," said Dagget, trying to laugh again. His large face was flushed.

He remained about an hour longer, then rose to take leave. Going out, he stumbled over a rug, and trying to recover himself, hit Louisa's work basket on the table, and knocked it on the floor.

He looked at Louisa, then at the rolling spools; he ducked himself awkwardly toward them, but she stopped him. "Never mind," said she; "I'll pick them up after you're gone."

She spoke with a mild stiffness. Either she was a little disturbed, or his nervousness affected her and made her seem constrained in her effort to reassure him.

When Joe Dagget was outside he drew in the sweet evening air with a sigh, and felt much as an innocent and perfectly well-intentioned bear might after his exit from a china shop.

Louisa, on her part, felt much as the kind-hearted, long-suffering owner of the china shop might have done after the exit of the bear.

She tied on the pink, then the green apron, picked up all the scattered treasures and replaced them in her work basket, and straightened the rug. Then she set the lamp on the floor and began sharply examining the carpet. She even rubbed her fingers over it, and looked at them.

"He's tracked in a good deal of dust," she murmured. "I thought he must have."

Louisa got a dustpan and brush, and swept Joe Dagget's track carefully.

If he could have known it, it would have increased his perplexity and uneasiness, although it would not have disturbed his loyalty in the least. He came twice a week to see Louisa Ellis, and every time, sitting there in her delicately sweet room, he felt as if surrounded by a hedge of lace. He was afraid to stir lest he should put a clumsy foot or hand through the fairy web, and he had always the consciousness that Louisa was watching fearfully lest he should.

Still the lace and Louisa commanded perforce his perfect respect and patience and loyalty. They were to be married in a month, after a singular courtship which had lasted for a matter of fifteen years. For fourteen out of the fifteen years the two had not once seen each other, and they had seldom exchanged letters. Joe had been all those years in Australia, where he had gone to make his fortune, and where he had stayed until he made it. He would have stayed fifty years if it had taken so long, and come home feeble and tottering, or never come home at all, to marry Louisa.

But the fortune had been made in the fourteen years, and he had come home now to marry the woman who had been patiently and unquestioningly waiting for him all that time.

Shortly after they were engaged he had announced to Louisa his determination to strike out into new fields and secure a competency[1] before they should be married. She had listened and assented with the sweet serenity which never failed her, not even when her lover set forth on that long and uncertain journey. Joe, buoyed up as he was by his steady determination, broke down a little at the last, but Louisa kissed him with a mild blush, and said goodbye.

"It won't be for long," poor Joe had said, huskily; but it was for fourteen years.

In that length of time much had happened. Louisa's mother and brother had died, and she was all alone in the world. But greatest happening of all—a subtle happening which both were

---

1. *a competency* (kom′pə tən sē), a sufficient income on which to live.

too simple to understand—Louisa's feet had turned into a path, smooth maybe under a calm, serene sky, but so straight and unswerving that it could only meet a check at her grave, and so narrow that there was no room for anyone at her side.

Louisa's first emotion when Joe Dagget came home (he had not apprised her of his coming) was consternation, although she would not admit it to herself, and he never dreamed of it. Fifteen years ago she had been in love with him—at least she considered herself to be. Just at that time, gently acquiescing with and falling into the natural drift of girlhood, she had seen marriage ahead as a reasonable feature and a probable desirability of life. She had listened with calm docility to her mother's views upon the subject. Her mother was remarkable for her cool sense and sweet, even temperament. She talked wisely to her daughter when Joe Dagget presented himself, and Louisa accepted him with no hesitation. He was the first lover she had ever had.

She had been faithful to him all these years. She had never dreamed of the possibility of marrying anyone else. Her life, especially for the last seven years, had been full of a pleasant peace; she had never felt discontented nor impatient over her lover's absence; still, she had always looked forward to his return and their marriage as the inevitable conclusion of things. However, she had fallen into a way of placing it so far in the future that it was almost equal to placing it over the boundaries of another life.

When Joe came she had been expecting him, and expecting to be married for fourteen years, but she was as much surprised and taken aback as if she had never thought of it.

Joe's consternation came later. He eyed Louisa with an instant confirmation of his old admiration. She had changed but little. She still kept her pretty manner and soft grace, and was, he considered, every whit as attractive as ever. As for himself, his stent was done; he had turned his face away from fortune seeking, and the old winds of romance whistled as loud and sweet as ever through his ears. All the song which he had been wont to hear in them was Louisa; he had for a long time a loyal belief that he heard it still, but finally it seemed to him that although the winds sang always that one song, it had another name.

But for Louisa the wind had never more than murmured; now it had gone down, and everything was still. She listened for a little while with half-wistful attention; then she turned quietly away and went to work on her wedding clothes.

Joe had made some extensive and quite magnificent alterations in his house. It was the old homestead; the newly married couple would live there, for Joe could not desert his mother, who refused to leave her old home. So Louisa must leave hers. Every morning, rising and going about among her neat maidenly possessions, she felt as one looking her last upon the faces of dear friends. It was true that in a measure she could take them with her, but, robbed of their old environments, they would appear in such new guises that they would almost cease to be themselves.

Then there were some peculiar features of her happy solitary life which she would probably be obliged to relinquish altogether. Sterner tasks than these graceful but half-needless ones would probably devolve upon her. There would be a large house to care for; there would be company to entertain; there would be Joe's rigorous and feeble old mother to wait upon; and it would be contrary to all thrifty village traditions for her to keep more than one servant.

Louisa had a little still, and she used to occupy herself pleasantly in summer weather with distilling the sweet and aromatic essences from roses and peppermint and spearmint. By-and-by her still must be laid away. Her store of essences was already considerable, and there would be no time for her to distill for the mere pleasure of it. Then Joe's mother would think it foolishness; she had already hinted her opinion in the matter.

Louisa dearly loved to sew a linen seam, not always for use, but for the simple, mild pleasure which she took in it. She would have been loath to confess how more than once she had ripped a seam for the mere delight of sewing it together again. Sitting at her window during long sweet afternoons, drawing her needle gently through the dainty fabric, she was peace itself. But there was small chance of such foolish comfort in the future. Joe's mother, domineering, shrewd old matron that she was even in her old age, and very likely even Joe himself, with his honest masculine rudeness, would laugh and frown down all these pretty but senseless old maiden ways.

Louisa had almost the enthusiasm of an artist over the mere order and cleanliness of her solitary home. She had throbs of genuine triumph at the sight of the windowpanes which she had polished until they shone like jewels. She gloated gently over her orderly bureau drawers, with their exquisitely folded contents redolent with lavender and sweet clover and very purity. Could she be sure of the endurance of even this? She had visions, so startling that she half repudiated them as indelicate, of coarse masculine belongings strewn about in endless litter; of dust and disorder arising necessarily from a coarse masculine presence in the midst of all this delicate harmony.

Among her forebodings of disturbance, not the least was with regard to Caesar. Caesar was a veritable hermit of a dog. For the greater part of his life he had dwelt in his secluded hut, shut out from the society of his kind and all innocent canine joys. Never had Caesar since his early youth watched at a woodchuck's hole; never had he known the delights of a stray bone at a neighbor's kitchen door. And it was all on account of a sin committed when hardly out of his puppyhood. No one knew the possible depth of remorse of which this mild-visaged, although innocent-looking old dog might be capable; but whether or not he had encountered remorse, he had encountered a full measure of righteous retribution. Old Caesar seldom lifted up his voice in a growl or a bark; he was fat and sleepy; there were yellow rings which looked like spectacles around his dim old eyes; but there was a neighbor who bore on his hand the imprint of several of Caesar's sharp white youthful teeth, and for that he had lived at the end of a chain, all alone in a little hut, for fourteen years. The neighbor, who was choleric and smarting with the pain of his wound, had demanded either Caesar's death or complete ostracism. So Louisa's brother, to whom the dog had belonged, had built him his little kennel and tied him up. It was now fourteen years since, in a flood of youthful spirits, he had inflicted that memorable bite, and with the exception of short excursions, always at the end of the chain, under the strict guardianship of his master or Louisa, the old dog had remained a close prisoner. It is doubtful if, with his limited ambition, he took much pride in the fact, but it is certain that he was possessed of considerable cheap fame. He was regarded by all the children in the village and by many adults as a very monster of ferocity. St. George's dragon[2] could hardly have surpassed in evil repute Louisa Ellis's old yellow dog. Mothers charged their children with solemn emphasis not to go too near to him, and the children listened and believed greedily, with a fascinated appetite for terror, and ran by Louisa's house stealthily, with many sidelong and backward glances at the terrible dog. If perchance he sounded a hoarse bark, there was a panic. Wayfarers chancing into Louisa's yard eyed him with respect, and inquired if the chain were stout. Caesar at large might have seemed a very ordinary dog and excited no comment whatever; chained, his reputation overshadowed him, so that he lost his own proper outlines and looked darkly vague and enormous. Joe Dagget, however, with his good-humored sense and shrewdness, saw him as he was. He strode valiantly up to him and patted him on the head, in spite of Louisa's soft clamor of warning, and even attempted to set him loose. Louisa grew so alarmed that he desisted, but kept announcing his opinion in the matter quite forcibly at intervals. "There ain't a better-natured dog in town," he would say, "and it's downright cruel to keep him tied up there. Some day I'm going to take him out."

Louisa had very little hope that he would not, one of these days, when their interests and possessions should be more completely fused in one. She pictured to herself Caesar on the rampage through the quiet and unguarded village. She saw innocent children bleeding in his path. She was herself very fond of the old dog, because he had belonged to her dead brother, and he was always very gentle with her; still she had great faith in his ferocity. She always warned people not to go too near him. She fed him on ascetic fare of corn mush and cakes, and never fired his dangerous temper with heating and sanguinary diet of flesh and bones. Louisa looked at the old dog munching his simple fare,

---

2. *St. George's dragon.* In legend, St. George, patron saint of England, killed a dragon.

and thought of her approaching marriage and trembled. Still no anticipation of disorder and confusion in lieu of sweet peace and harmony, no forebodings of Caesar on the rampage, no wild fluttering of her little yellow canary, were sufficient to turn her a hair's-breadth. Joe Dagget had been fond of her and working for her all these years. It was not for her, whatever came to pass, to prove untrue and break his heart. She put the exquisite little stitches into her wedding garments, and the time went on until it was only a week before her wedding day. It was a Tuesday evening, and the wedding was to be a week from Wednesday.

There was a full moon that night. About nine o'clock Louisa strolled down the road a little way. There were harvest fields on either hand, bordered by low stone walls. Luxuriant clumps of bushes grew beside the wall, and trees—wild cherry and old apple trees—at intervals. Presently Louisa sat down on the wall and looked about her with mildly sorrowful reflectiveness. Tall shrubs of blueberry and meadowsweet, all woven together and tangled with blackberry vines and horsebriers, shut her in on either side. She had a little clear space between them. Opposite her, on the other side of the road, was a spreading tree; the moon shone between its boughs, and the leaves twinkled like silver. The road was bespread with a beautiful shifting dapple of silver and shadow; the air was full of a mysterious sweetness. "I wonder if it's wild grapes?" murmured Louisa. She sat there some time. She was just thinking of rising, when she heard footsteps and low voices, and remained quiet. It was a lonely place, and she felt a little timid. She thought she would keep still in the shadow and let the persons, whoever they might be, pass her.

But just before they reached her the voices ceased, and the footsteps. She understood that their owners had also found seats upon the stone wall. She was wondering if she could not steal away unobserved, when the voice broke the stillness. It was Joe Dagget's. She sat still and listened.

The voice was announced by a loud sigh, which was as familiar as itself. "Well," said Dagget, "you've made up your mind, then, I suppose?"

"Yes," returned another voice. "I'm going day after tomorrow."

"That's Lily Dyer," thought Louisa to herself. The voice embodied itself in her mind. She saw a girl tall and full-figured, with a firm, fair face, looking fairer and firmer in the moonlight, her strong yellow hair braided in a close knot. A girl full of a calm rustic strength and bloom, with a masterful way which might have beseemed a princess. Lily Dyer was a favorite with the village folk; she had just the qualities to arouse the admiration. She was good and handsome and smart. Louisa had often heard her praises sounded.

"Well," said Joe Dagget, "I ain't got a word to say."

"I don't know what you could say," returned Lily Dyer.

"Not a word to say," repeated Joe, drawing out the words heavily. Then there was a silence. "I ain't sorry," he began at last, "that that happened yesterday—that we kind of let on how we felt to each other. I guess it's just as well we knew. Of course I can't do anything any different. I'm going right on an' get married next week. I ain't going back on a woman that's waited for me fourteen years, an' break her heart."

"If you should jilt her tomorrow, I wouldn't have you," spoke up the girl, with sudden vehemence.

"Well, I ain't going to give you the chance," said he; "but I don't believe you would, either."

"You'd see I wouldn't. Honor's honor, an' right's right. An' I'd never think anything of any man that went against 'em for me or any other girl; you'd find that out, Joe Dagget."

"Well, you'll find out fast enough that I ain't going against 'em for you or any other girl," returned he. Their voices sounded almost as if they were angry with each other. Louisa was listening eagerly.

"I'm sorry you feel as if you must go away," said Joe, "but I don't know but it's best."

"Of course it's best. I hope you and I have got common sense."

"Well, I suppose you're right." Suddenly Joe's voice got an undertone of tenderness. "Say, Lily," said he, "I'll get along well enough myself, but I can't bear to think—You don't suppose you're going to fret much over it?"

"I guess you'll find out I shan't fret much over a married man."

"Well, I hope you won't—I hope you won't, Lily. God knows I do. And—I hope—one of these days—you'll—come across somebody else——"

"I don't see any reason why I shouldn't." Suddenly her tone changed. She spoke in a sweet, clear voice, so loud that she could have been heard across the street. "No, Joe Dagget," said she, "I'll never marry any other man as long as I live. I've got good sense, an' I ain't going to break my heart nor make a fool of myself; but I'm never going to be married, you can be sure of that. I ain't that sort of a girl to feel this way twice."

Louisa heard an exclamation and a soft commotion behind the bushes; then Lily spoke again—the voice sounded as if she had risen. "This must be put a stop to," said she. "We've stayed here long enough. I'm going home."

Louisa sat there in a daze, listening to their retreating steps. After a while she got up and slunk softly home herself. The next day she did her housework methodically; that was as much a matter of course as breathing; but she did not sew on her wedding clothes. She sat at her window and meditated. In the evening Joe came. Louisa Ellis had never known that she had any diplomacy in her, but when she came to look for it that night she found it, although meek of its kind, among her little feminine weapons. Even now she could hardly believe that she had heard right, and that she would not do Joe a terrible injury should she break her troth plight. She wanted to sound him out without betraying too soon her own inclinations in the matter. She did it successfully, and they finally came to an understanding; but it was a difficult thing, for he was as afraid of betraying himself as she.

She never mentioned Lily Dyer. She simply said that while she had no cause of complaint against him, she had lived so long in one way that she shrank from making a change.

"Well, I never shrank, Louisa," said Dagget. "I'm going to be honest enough to say that I think maybe it's better this way; but if you'd wanted to keep on, I'd have stuck to you till my dying day. I hope you know that."

"Yes, I do," said she.

That night she and Joe parted more tenderly than they had done for a long time. Standing in the door, holding each other's hands, a last great wave of regretful memory swept over them.

"Well, this ain't the way we've thought it was all going to end, is it, Louisa?" said Joe.

She shook her head. There was a little quiver on her placid face.

"You let me know if there's ever anything I can do for you," said he. "I ain't ever going to forget you, Louisa." Then he kissed her, and went down the path.

Louisa, all alone by herself that night, wept a little, she hardly knew why; but the next morning, on waking, she felt like a queen who, after fearing lest her domain be wrested away from her, sees it firmly insured in her possession.

Now the tall weeds and grasses might cluster around Caesar's little hermit hut, the snow might fall on its roof year in and year out, but he never would go on a rampage through the unguarded village. Now the little canary might turn itself into a peaceful yellow ball night after night, and have no need to wake and flutter with wild terror against its bars. Louisa could sew linen seams, and distill roses, and dust and polish and fold away in lavender, as long as she listed. That afternoon she sat with her needlework at the window, and felt fairly steeped in peace. Lily Dyer, tall and erect and blooming, went past; but she felt no qualm. If Louisa Ellis had sold her birthright she did not know it; the taste of the pottage[3] was so delicious, and had been her sole satisfaction for so long. Serenity and placid narrowness had become to her as the birthright itself. She gazed ahead through a long reach of future days strung together like pearls in a rosary, every one like the others, and all smooth and flawless and innocent, and her heart went up in thankfulness. Outside was the fervid summer afternoon; the air was filled with the sounds of the busy harvest of men and birds and bees; there were halloos, metallic clatterings, sweet calls, and long hummings. Louisa sat, prayerfully numbering her days, like an uncloistered nun.

□□

---

3. **pottage** (pot′ij), a thick soup.

Discussion

1. (a) What clues early in the story indicate that both Louisa Ellis and Joe Dagget are uncomfortable in their relationship with each other? **(b)** What aspects of Louisa's life and personality are **symbolized** by her canary and by Caesar?

2. (a) In what ways do Lily Dyer's character and situation make her a **foil** to Louisa? **(b)** What qualities do they have in common?

3. (a) How does Louisa's reaction at Joe's departure fourteen years earlier **foreshadow** the end of the story? **(b)** Explain how the resolution of the story depends both on chance and on the characters of Louisa, Joe, and Lily. **(c)** In the last paragraph, what does Freeman mean by the "birthright" Louisa has sold?

4. Would you call the ending "happy" or "unhappy"? Explain.

5. Point out and explain examples of **realism** in **plot** and in **characterization** in this story. (See the discussion of Realism in the Unit Background.)

Vocabulary • Dictionary

In your Glossary look up the definition of each word below from "A New England Nun." On your paper write the word next to the number of the sentence that it correctly completes. Be sure you can spell and pronounce all the words.

redolence   docile
methodical   ostracize
premonition   consternation

1. From the moment Carrie got up that morning, she had a feeling that something was going to go wrong, and the _____ grew as she drove to work.

2. The class is so _____ and obedient that the teacher almost never has to quiet them down.

3. As Carmen walked into the florist's, a sweet _____ drifted into her nostrils. Never before had she experienced a fragrance this pleasant.

4. Raymond was warned that if he kept being a bully, the rest of the class would _____ him for the year.

5. The oxen pulled the plow with the _____ motion of a machine that does its task a thousand times a day.

Mary E. Wilkins Freeman
1852 • 1930

Freeman spent her first fifty years in Massachusetts and Vermont, and so knew as an insider the people and ways of rural New England. Eastern Massachusetts is the locale of her best work. Publication in *Harper's Magazine* in 1884 brought immediate public recognition and enthusiasm for her tales of local color. In short stories of country life she was a skilled artist, writing with unsentimental objectivity uncharacteristic of many writers of the time. Her major theme is people whose lives are limited by circumstance or by chains of their own creation. However, moral correctness gives dignity to their painful adherence to the "right."

Ambrose Bierce

An Occurrence at Owl Creek Bridge

I

A man stood upon a railroad bridge in northern Alabama, looking down into the swift water twenty feet below. The man's hands were behind his back, the wrists bound with a cord. A rope closely encircled his neck. It was attached to a stout cross-timber above his head and the slack fell to the level of his knees. Some loose boards laid upon the sleepers supporting the metals of the railway supplied a footing for him and his executioners—two private soldiers of the Federal army, directed by a sergeant who in civil life may have been a deputy sheriff. At a short remove upon the same temporary platform was an officer in the uniform of his rank, armed. He

From GHOST AND HORROR STORIES OF AMBROSE BIERCE. Published by the Neale Publishing Co., 1909, 1912.

was a captain. A sentinel at each end of the bridge stood with his rifle in the position known as "support," that is to say, vertical in front of the left shoulder, the hammer resting on the forearm thrown straight across the chest—a formal and unnatural position, enforcing an erect carriage of the body. It did not appear to be the duty of these two men to know what was occurring at the centre of the bridge; they merely blockaded the two ends of the foot planking that traversed it.

Beyond one of the sentinels nobody was in sight; the railroad ran straight away into a forest for a hundred yards, then, curving, was lost to view. Doubtless there was an outpost farther along. The other bank of the stream was open ground—a gentle acclivity topped with a stockade of vertical tree trunks, loop-holed for rifles, with a single embrasure through which protruded the muzzle of a brass cannon commanding the bridge. Midway of the slope between bridge and fort were the spectators—a single company of infantry in line, at "parade rest," the butts of the rifles on the ground, the barrels inclining slightly backward against the right shoulder, the hands crossed upon the stock. A lieutenant stood at the right of the line, the point of his sword upon the ground, his left hand resting upon his right. Excepting the group of four at the centre of the bridge, not a man moved. The company faced the bridge, staring stonily, motionless. The sentinels, facing the banks of the stream, might have been statues to adorn the bridge. The captain stood with folded arms, silent, observing the work of his subordinates, but making no sign. Death is a dignitary who when he comes announced is to be received with formal manifestations of respect, even by those most familiar with him. In the code of military etiquette silence and fixity are forms of deference.

The man who was engaged in being hanged was apparently about thirty-five years of age. He was a civilian, if one might judge from his habit, which was that of a planter. His features were good—a straight nose, firm mouth, broad forehead, from which his long, dark hair was combed straight back, falling behind his ears to the collar of his well-fitting frock coat. He wore a mustache and pointed beard, but no whiskers; his eyes were large and dark gray, and had a kindly expression which one would hardly have expected in one whose neck was in the hemp. Evidently this was no vulgar assassin. The liberal military code makes provision for hanging many kinds of persons, and gentlemen are not excluded.

The preparations being complete, the two private soldiers stepped aside and each drew away the plank upon which he had been standing. The sergeant turned to the captain, saluted and placed himself immediately behind that officer, who in turn moved apart one pace. These movements left the condemned man and the sergeant standing on the two ends of the same plank, which spanned three of the cross-ties of the bridge. The end upon which the civilian stood almost, but not quite, reached a fourth. This plank had been held in place by the weight of the captain; it was now held by that of the sergeant. At a signal from the former the latter would step aside, the plank would tilt and the condemned man go down between two ties. The arrangement commended itself to his judgment as simple and effective. His face had not been covered nor his eyes bandaged. He looked a moment at his "unsteadfast footing," then let his gaze wander to the swirling water of the stream racing madly beneath his feet. A piece of dancing driftwood caught his attention and his eyes followed it down the current. How slowly it appeared to move! What a sluggish stream!

He closed his eyes in order to fix his last thoughts upon his wife and children. The water, touched to gold by the early sun, the brooding mists under the banks at some distance down the stream, the fort, the soldiers, the piece of drift—all had distracted him. And now he became conscious of a new disturbance. Striking through the thought of his dear ones was a sound which he could neither ignore nor understand, a sharp, distinct, metallic percussion like the stroke of a blacksmith's hammer upon the anvil; it had the same ringing quality. He wondered what it was, and whether immeasurably distant or nearby—it seemed both. Its recurrence was regular, but as slow as the tolling of a death knell. He awaited each stroke with impatience and—he knew not why—apprehension. The intervals of silence grew progressively longer; the delays became maddening. With their greater infrequency the sounds increased in strength and sharpness.

They hurt his ear like the thrust of a knife; he feared he would shriek. What he heard was the ticking of his watch.

He unclosed his eyes and saw again the water below him. "If I could free my hands," he thought, "I might throw off the noose and spring into the stream. By diving I could evade the bullets and swimming vigorously, reach the bank, take to the woods and get away home. My home, thank God, is as yet outside their lines; my wife and little ones are still beyond the invader's farthest advance."

As these thoughts, which have here to be set down in words, were flashed into the doomed man's brain rather than evolved from it the captain nodded to the sergeant. The sergeant stepped aside.

II

Peyton Farquhar was a well-to-do planter, of an old and highly respected Alabama family. Being a slave owner and like other slave owners a politician he was naturally an original secessionist and ardently devoted to the Southern cause. Circumstances of an imperious nature, which it is unnecessary to relate here, had prevented him from taking service with the gallant army that had fought the disastrous campaigns ending with the fall of Corinth, and he chafed under the inglorious restraint, longing for the release of his energies, the larger life of the soldier, the opportunity for distinction. That opportunity, he felt, would come, as it comes to all in war time. Meanwhile he did what he could. No service was too humble for him to perform in aid of the South, no adventure too perilous for him to undertake if consistent with the character of a civilian who was at heart a soldier, and who in good faith and without too much qualification assented to at least a part of the frankly villainous dictum that all is fair in love and war.

One evening while Farquhar and his wife were sitting on a rustic bench near the entrance to his grounds, a gray-clad soldier[1] rode up to the gate and asked for a drink of water. Mrs. Farquhar was only too happy to serve him with her own white hands. While she was fetching the water her husband approached the dusty horseman and inquired eagerly for news from the front.

"The Yanks are repairing the railroads," said the man, "and are getting ready for another advance. They have reached the Owl Creek bridge, put it in order and built a stockade on the north bank. The commandant has issued an order, which is posted everywhere, declaring that any civilian caught interfering with the railroad, its bridges, tunnels or trains will be summarily hanged. I saw the order."

"How far is it to the Owl Creek bridge?" Farquhar asked.

"About thirty miles."

"Is there no force on this side of the creek?"

"Only a picket post half a mile out, on the railroad, and a single sentinel at this end of the bridge."

"Suppose a man—a civilian and student of hanging—should elude the picket post and perhaps get the better of the sentinel," said Farquhar, smiling, "what could he accomplish?"

The soldier reflected. "I was there a month ago," he replied. "I observed that the flood of last winter had lodged a great quantity of driftwood against the wooden pier at this end of the bridge. It is now dry and would burn like tow."

The lady had now brought the water, which the soldier drank. He thanked her ceremoniously, bowed to her husband and rode away. An hour later, after nightfall, he repassed the plantation, going northward in the direction from which he had come. He was a Federal scout.

III

As Peyton Farquhar fell straight downward through the bridge he lost consciousness and was as one already dead. From this state he was awakened—ages later, it seemed to him—by the pain of a sharp pressure upon his throat, followed by a sense of suffocation. Keen, poignant agonies seemed to shoot from his neck downward through every fibre of his body and limbs. These pains appeared to flash along well-defined

---

1. *a gray-clad soldier.* Confederate soldiers wore gray uniforms.

lines of ramification and to beat with an inconceivably rapid periodicity. They seemed like streams of pulsating fire heating him to an intolerable temperature. As to his head, he was conscious of nothing but a feeling of fulness—of congestion. These sensations were unaccompanied by thought. The intellectual part of his nature was already effaced; he had power only to feel, and feeling was torment. He was conscious of motion. Encompassed in a luminous cloud, of which he was now merely the fiery heart, without material substance, he swung through unthinkable arcs of oscillation, like a vast pendulum. Then all at once, with terrible suddenness, the light about him shot upward with the noise of a loud plash; a frightful roaring was in his ears, and all was cold and dark. The power of thought was restored; he knew that the rope had broken and he had fallen into the stream. There was no additional strangulation; the noose about his neck was already suffocating him and kept the water from his lungs. To die of hanging at the bottom of a river!—the idea seemed to him ludicrous. He opened his eyes in the darkness and saw above him a gleam of light, but how distant, how inaccessible! He was still sinking for the light became fainter and fainter until it was a mere glimmer. Then it began to grow and brighten, and he knew that he was rising toward the surface—knew it with reluctance, for he was now very comfortable. "To be hanged and drowned," he thought, "that is not so bad; but I do not wish to be shot. No; I will not be shot; that is not fair."

He was not conscious of an effort, but a sharp pain in his wrist apprised him that he was trying to free his hands. He gave the struggle his attention, as an idler might observe the feat of a juggler, without interest in the outcome. What splendid effort!—what magnificent, what superhuman strength! Ah, that was a fine endeavor! Bravo! The cord fell away; his arms parted and floated upward, the hands dimly seen on each side in the growing light. He watched them with a new interest as first one and then the other pounced upon the noose at his neck. They tore it away and thrust it fiercely aside, its undulations resembling those of a water-snake. "Put it back, put it back!" He thought he shouted these words to his hands, for the undoing of the noose had

been succeeded by the direst pang that he had yet experienced. His neck ached horribly; his brain was on fire; his heart, which had been fluttering faintly, gave a great leap, trying to force itself out at his mouth. His whole body was racked and wrenched with an insupportable anguish! But his disobedient hands gave no heed to the command. They beat the water vigorously with quick, downward strokes, forcing him to the surface. He felt his head emerge; his eyes were blinded by the sunlight; his chest expanded convulsively, and with a supreme and crowning agony his lungs engulfed a great draught of air, which instantly he expelled in a shriek!

He was now in full possession of his physical senses. They were, indeed, preternaturally keen and alert. Something in the awful disturbance of his organic system had so exalted and refined them that they made record of things never before perceived. He felt the ripples upon his face and heard their separate sounds as they struck. He looked at the forest on the bank of the stream, saw the individual trees, the leaves and the veining of each leaf—saw the very insects upon them: the locusts, the brilliant-bodied flies, the gray spiders stretching their webs from twig to twig. He noted the prismatic colors in all the dewdrops upon a million blades of grass. The humming of the gnats that danced above the eddies of the stream, the beating of the dragon-flies' wings, the strokes of the water-spiders' legs, like oars which had lifted their boat—all these made audible music. A fish slid along beneath his eyes and he heard the rush of its body parting the water.

He had come to the surface facing down the stream; in a moment the visible world seemed to wheel slowly round, himself the pivotal point, and he saw the bridge, the fort, the soldiers upon the bridge, the captain, the sergeant, the two privates, his executioners. They were in silhouette against the blue sky. They shouted and gesticulated, pointing at him. The captain had drawn his pistol, but did not fire; the others were unarmed. Their movements were grotesque and horrible, their forms gigantic.

Suddenly he heard a sharp report and something struck the water smartly within a few inches of his head, spattering his face with spray. He heard a second report, and saw one of the sentinels with his rifle at his shoulder, a light cloud of blue smoke rising from the muzzle. The man in the water saw the eye of the man on the bridge gazing into his own through the sights of the rifle. He observed that it was a gray eye and remembered having read that gray eyes were keenest, and that all famous marksmen had them. Nevertheless, this one had missed.

A counter-swirl had caught Farquhar and turned him half round; he was again looking into the forest on the bank opposite the fort. The sound of a clear, high voice in a monotonous singsong now rang out behind him and came across the water with a distinctness that pierced and subdued all other sounds, even the beating of the ripples in his ears. Although no soldier, he had frequented camps enough to know the dread significance of that deliberate, drawling, aspirated chant; the lieutenant on shore was taking a part in the morning's work. How coldly and pitilessly—with what an even, calm intonation, presaging, and enforcing tranquility in the men—with what accurately measured intervals fell those cruel words:

"Attention, company! . . . Shoulder arms! . . . Ready! . . . Aim! . . . Fire!"

Farquhar dived—dived as deeply as he could. The water roared in his ears like the voice of Niagara, yet he heard the dulled thunder of the volley and, rising again toward the surface, met shining bits of metal, singularly flattened, oscillating slowly downward. Some of them touched him on the face and hands, then fell away,

continuing their descent. One lodged between his collar and neck; it was uncomfortably warm and he snatched it out.

As he rose to the surface, gasping for breath, he saw that he had been a long time under water; he was perceptibly farther down stream—nearer to safety. The soldiers had almost finished reloading; the metal ramrods flashed all at once in the sunshine as they were drawn from the barrels, turned in the air, and thrust into their sockets. The two sentinels fired again, independently and ineffectually.

The hunted man saw all this over his shoulder; he was now swimming vigorously with the current. His brain was as energetic as his arms and legs; he thought with the rapidity of lightning.

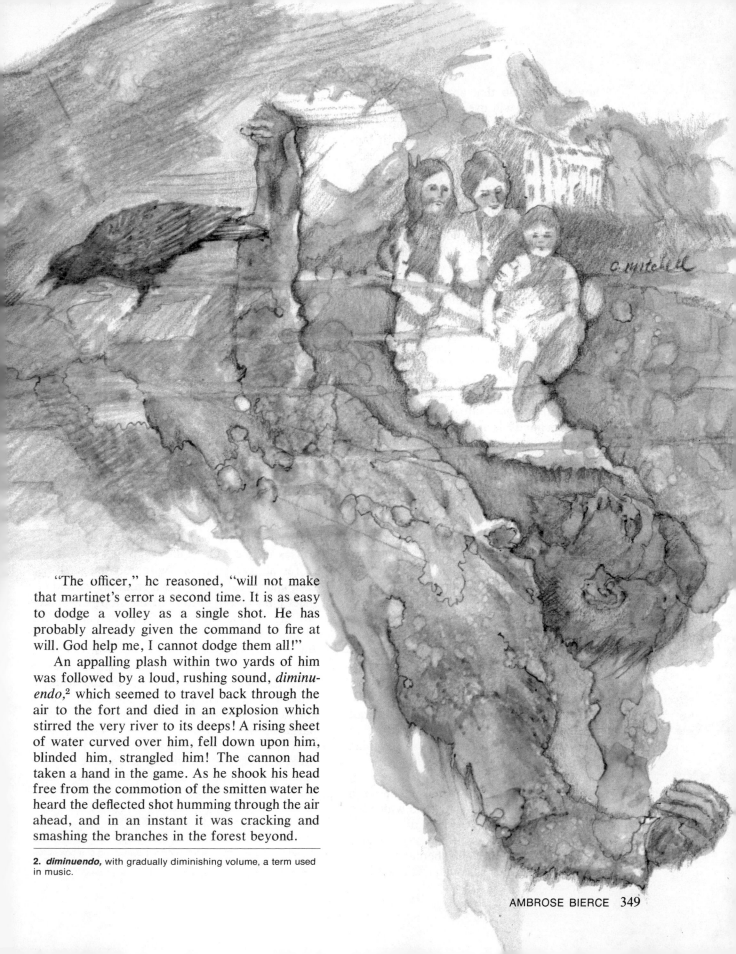

"The officer," he reasoned, "will not make that martinet's error a second time. It is as easy to dodge a volley as a single shot. He has probably already given the command to fire at will. God help me, I cannot dodge them all!"

An appalling plash within two yards of him was followed by a loud, rushing sound, *diminuendo*,[2] which seemed to travel back through the air to the fort and died in an explosion which stirred the very river to its deeps! A rising sheet of water curved over him, fell down upon him, blinded him, strangled him! The cannon had taken a hand in the game. As he shook his head free from the commotion of the smitten water he heard the deflected shot humming through the air ahead, and in an instant it was cracking and smashing the branches in the forest beyond.

---

2. *diminuendo*, with gradually diminishing volume, a term used in music.

"They will not do that again," he thought; "the next time they will use a charge of grape. I must keep my eye upon the gun; the smoke will apprise me—the report arrives too late; it lags behind the missile. That is a good gun."

Suddenly he felt himself whirled round and round—spinning like a top. The water, the banks, the forests, the now distant bridge, fort and men—all were commingled and blurred. Objects were represented by their colors only; circular horizontal streaks of color—that was all he saw. He had been caught in a vortex and was being whirled on with a velocity of advance and gyration that made him giddy and sick. In a few moments he was flung upon the gravel at the foot of the left bank of the stream—the southern bank—and behind a projecting point which concealed him from his enemies. The sudden arrest of his motion, the abrasion of one of his hands on the gravel, restored him, and he wept with delight. He dug his fingers into the sand, threw it over himself in handfuls and audibly blessed it. It looked like diamonds, rubies, emeralds; he could think of nothing beautiful which it did not resemble. The trees upon the bank were giant garden plants; he noted a definite order in their arrangement, inhaled the fragrance of their blooms. A strange, roseate light shone through the spaces among their trunks and the wind made in their branches the music of aeolian harps.[3] He had no wish to perfect his escape—was content to remain in that enchanting spot until retaken.

A whiz and rattle of grapeshot among the branches high above his head roused him from his dream. The baffled cannoneer had fired him a random farewell. He sprang to his feet, rushed up the sloping bank, and plunged into the forest.

All that day he traveled, laying his course by the rounding sun. The forest seemed interminable; nowhere did he discover a break in it, not even a woodman's road. He had not known that he lived in so wild a region. There was something uncanny in the revelation.

By nightfall he was fatigued, footsore, famishing. The thought of his wife and children urged him on. At last he found a road which led him in what he knew to be the right direction. It was as wide and straight as a city street, yet it seemed untraveled. No fields bordered it, no dwelling anywhere. Not so much as the barking of a dog suggested human habitation. The black bodies of the trees formed a straight wall on both sides, terminating on the horizon in a point, like a diagram in a lesson in perspective. Overhead, as he looked up through this rift in the wood, shone great golden stars looking unfamiliar and grouped in strange constellations. He was sure they were arranged in some order which had a secret and malign significance. The wood on either side was full of singular noises, among which—once, twice, and again—he distinctly heard whispers in an unknown tongue.

His neck was in pain and lifting his hand to it he found it horribly swollen. He knew that it had a circle of black where the rope had bruised it. His eyes felt congested; he could no longer close them. His tongue was swollen with thirst; he relieved its fever by thrusting it forward from between his teeth into the cold air. How softly the turf had carpeted the untraveled avenue—he could no longer feel the roadway beneath his feet!

Doubtless, despite his suffering, he had fallen asleep while walking, for now he sees another scene—perhaps he has merely recovered from a delirium. He stands at the gate of his own home. All is as he left it, and all bright and beautiful in the morning sunshine. He must have traveled the entire night. As he pushes open the gate and passes up the wide white walk, he sees a flutter of female garments; his wife, looking fresh and cool and sweet, steps down from the veranda to meet him. At the bottom of the steps she stands waiting, with a smile of ineffable joy, an attitude of matchless grace and dignity. Ah, how beautiful she is! He springs forward with extended arms. As he is about to clasp her he feels a stunning blow upon the back of the neck; a blinding white light blazes all about him with a sound like the shock of a cannon—then all is darkness and silence!

Peyton Farquhar was dead; his body, with a broken neck, swung gently from side to side beneath the timbers of the Owl Creek bridge.

□□

---

3. **aeolian harps,** musical instruments consisting of a box across which strings are stretched. They are placed at open windows where the wind can produce harmonic, sweet tones.

Discussion

Bierce, like Poe, wrote many tales of the uncanny and supernatural. In "An Occurrence at Owl Creek Bridge," he has reshaped an experience so that colors, sounds, and sensations are heightened, time is rearranged, and the dream life of the imagination is woven inextricably into physical events. In this imaginary realm, events are depicted as if the reader were seeing reality through a kaleidoscope.

1. (a) Cite paragraphs where sight and sound explode into sudden brilliance. **(b)** List the events of the story in straightforward chronological sequence. What effects are created by Bierce's rearrangement of time?

2. Discuss the problem of "real" reality in this story. What actually occurred? Did Peyton Farquhar escape or did he only imagine it; or did the Union officer only imagine that Peyton was hanged? Explain.

3. How does the title contribute to the ambiguity of the tale's conclusion? Explain.

4. Assuming that Peyton is hanged at the end of the tale, what hints does the author give the reader that this is only a desperate dream?

5. How does the tale illustrate our attachment to life?

Ambrose Bierce 1842 • 1914?

Raised on an Ohio farm, Bierce was the youngest of a large, poor, pious family. He was later reluctant to talk about his beginnings and is said to

have despised his relatives. At fifteen he left home and spent two years as a printer's devil (apprentice). There followed a year at the Kentucky Military Institute, the only schooling he would receive, and then the Civil War broke out. He enlisted as a drummer boy, fought bravely in some of the most difficult fighting of the war, and, by war's end had earned the honorary rank of major.

Living in San Francisco afterwards, Bierce began writing short satiric pieces for a news weekly, was given his own column, and soon was made editor of the paper. It was a period of fiery personal journalism for which Bierce's vitriolic wit was ideally suited. Bierce was married in 1871, and a few months later he and his wife sailed for England. He stayed there four years, working on the staff of *Fun* magazine. But his wife grew tired of England and returned to California. From there she announced the impending arrival of their third child and Bierce was soon sailing for San Francisco. For the

next ten years he wrote his famous "Prattler" column for the *Argonaut*. The column was bought in 1887 by William Randolph Hearst and placed on the editorial page of the Sunday *Examiner*.

By this time Bierce's merciless wit had made him the dictator of literary tastes for the West Coast. He was capable of championing the mediocre and attacking the genuine for personal reasons. Though his journalism showed remarkable talent, he lacked an underlying compassion necessary if one's satire is to be more than momentarily entertaining.

His fiction, however, seems to have won for itself a small but lasting place. He wrote haunting, climactic stories, often with strange psychological twists, a few of which have emerged with time as classics.

Bierce spent a number of his later years in Washington, D.C., exposing corrupt deals between politicians and industrialists for the Hearst newspapers. In 1913, at the age of seventy-one, he seemed perhaps weary of it all. He left for Mexico to cover the revolution there and disappeared from sight. Upon leaving he wrote a friend, "Goodbye, if you hear of my being stood up against a Mexican stone wall and shot to rags please know that I think it a pretty good way to depart this life. It beats old age, disease, or falling down the cellar stairs."

Stephen Crane

An Episode of War

The lieutenant's rubber blanket lay on the ground, and upon it he had poured the company's supply of coffee. Corporals and other representatives of the grimy and hot-throated men who lined the breastwork had come for each squad's portion.

The lieutenant was frowning and serious at this task of division. His lips pursed as he drew with his sword various crevices in the heap, until brown squares of coffee, astoundingly equal in size, appeared on the blanket. He was on the verge of a great triumph in mathematics, and the corporals were thronging forward, each to reap a little square, when suddenly the lieutenant cried out and looked quickly at a man near him as if he suspected it was a case of personal assault. The others cried out also when they saw blood upon the lieutenant's sleeve.

He had winced like a man stung, swayed dangerously, and then straightened. The sound of his hoarse breathing was plainly audible. He looked sadly, mystically, over the breastwork at the green face of a wood, where now were many little puffs of white smoke. During this moment the men about him gazed statuelike and silent, astonished and awed by this catastrophe which happened when catastrophes were not expected—when they had leisure to observe it.

As the lieutenant stared at the wood, they too swung their heads, so that for another instant all hands, still silent, contemplated the distant forest as if their minds were fixed upon the mystery of a bullet's journey.

The officer had, of course, been compelled to take his sword into his left hand. He did not hold it by the hilt. He gripped it at the middle of the blade, awkwardly. Turning his eyes from the hostile wood, he looked at the sword as he held it there, and seemed puzzled as to what to do with it, where to put it. In short, this weapon had of a sudden become a strange thing to him. He looked at it in a kind of stupefaction, as if he had been endowed with a trident, a scepter, or a spade.

Finally he tried to sheathe it. To sheathe a sword held by the left hand, at the middle of the blade, in a scabbard hung at the left hip, is a feat worthy of a sawdust ring.[1] This wounded officer engaged in a desperate struggle with the sword and the wobbling scabbard, and during the time of it he breathed like a wrestler.

But at this instant the men, the spectators, awoke from their stonelike poses and crowded forward sympathetically. The orderly-sergeant took the sword and tenderly placed it in the scabbard. At the time, he leaned nervously backward, and did not allow even his finger to brush the body of the lieutenant. A wound gives strange dignity to him who bears it. Well men shy from this new and terrible majesty. It is as if the wounded man's hand is upon the curtain which hangs before the revelations of all existence—the meaning of ants, potentates, wars, cities, sunshine, snow, a feather dropped from a bird's wing; and the power of it sheds radiance upon a bloody form, and makes the other men understand sometimes that they are little. His comrades look at him with large eyes thoughtfully. Moreover, they fear vaguely that the weight of a finger upon him might send him headlong, precipitate the tragedy, hurl him at once into the dim, gray unknown. And so the orderly-sergeant, while sheathing the sword, leaned nervously backward.

There were others who proffered assistance. One timidly presented his shoulder and asked the lieutenant if he cared to lean upon it, but the latter waved him away mournfully. He wore the

---

From the *London Gentleman* (December 1899).
1. **sawdust ring,** circus ring.

look of one who knows he is the victim of a terrible disease and understands his helplessness. He again stared over the breastwork at the forest, and then, turning, went slowly rearward. He held his right wrist tenderly in his left hand as if the wounded arm was made of very brittle glass.

And the men in silence stared at the wood, then at the departing lieutenant; then at the wood, then at the lieutenant.

As the wounded officer passed from the line of battle, he was enabled to see many things which as a participant in the fight were unknown to him. He saw a general on a black horse gazing over the lines of blue infantry at the green woods which veiled his problems. An aide galloped furiously, dragged his horse suddenly to a halt, saluted, and presented a paper. It was, for a wonder, precisely like a historical painting.

To the rear of the general and his staff a group, composed of a bugler, two or three orderlies, and the bearer of the corps standard, all upon maniacal horses, were working like slaves to hold their ground, preserve their respectful interval, while the shells boomed in the air about them, and caused their chargers to make furious quivering leaps.

A battery, a tumultuous and shining mass, was swirling toward the right. The wild thud of hoofs, the cries of the riders shouting blame and praise, menace and encouragement, and, last, the roar of the wheels, the slant of the glistening guns, brought the lieutenant to an intent pause. The battery swept in curves that stirred the heart; it made halts as dramatic as the crash of a wave on the rocks, and when it fled onward this aggregation of wheels, levers, motors had a beautiful unity, as if it were a missile. The sound of it was a war chorus that reached into the depths of man's emotion.

The lieutenant, still holding his arm as if it were of glass, stood watching this battery until all detail of it was lost, save the figures of the riders, which rose and fell and waved lashes over the black mass.

Later, he turned his eyes toward the battle, where the shooting sometimes crackled like bush fires, sometimes sputtered with exasperating irregularity, and sometimes reverberated like the thunder. He saw the smoke rolling upward and saw crowds of men who ran and cheered, or stood and blazed away at the inscrutable distance.

He came upon some stragglers, and they told him how to find the field hospital. They described its exact location. In fact, these men, no longer having part in the battle, knew more of it than others. They told the performance of every corps, every division, the opinion of every general. The lieutenant, carrying his wounded arm rearward, looked upon them with wonder.

At the roadside a brigade was making coffee and buzzing with talk like a girls' boarding school. Several officers came to him and inquired concerning things of which he knew nothing. One, seeing his arm, began to scold. "Why, man, that's no way to do. You want to fix that thing." He appropriated the lieutenant and the lieutenant's wound. He cut the sleeve and laid bare the arm, every nerve of which softly fluttered under his touch. He bound his handkerchief over the wound, scolding away in the meantime. His tone allowed one to think that he was in the habit of being wounded every day. The lieutenant hung his head, feeling, in this presence, that he did not know how to be correctly wounded.

The low white tents of the hospital were grouped around an old schoolhouse. There was here a singular commotion. In the foreground two ambulances interlocked wheels in the deep mud. The drivers were tossing the blame of it back and forth, gesticulating and berating, while from the ambulances, both crammed with wounded, there came an occasional groan. An interminable crowd of bandaged men were coming and going. Great numbers sat under the trees nursing heads or arms or legs. There was a dispute of some kind raging on the steps of the schoolhouse. Sitting with his back against a tree a man with a face as gray as a new army blanket was serenely smoking a corncob pipe. The lieutenant wished to rush forward and inform him that he was dying.

A busy surgeon was passing near the lieutenant. "Good morning," he said, with a friendly smile. Then he caught sight of the lieutenant's arm, and his face at once changed. "Well, let's have a look at it." He seemed possessed suddenly of a great contempt for the lieutenant. This wound evidently placed the latter on a very low

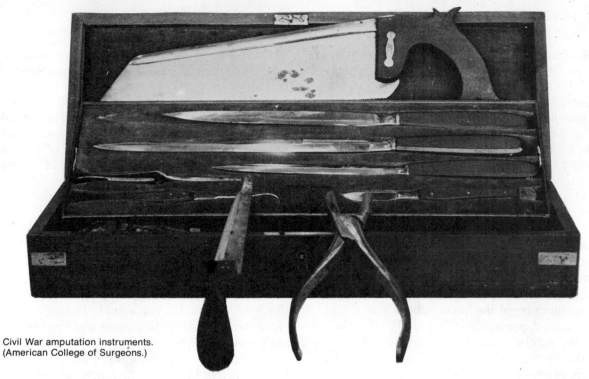

Civil War amputation instruments.
(American College of Surgeons.)

social plane. The doctor cried out impatiently: "What mutton-head had tied it up that way anyhow?" The lieutenant answered, "Oh, a man."

When the wound was disclosed the doctor fingered it disdainfully. "Humph," he said. "You come along with me and I'll 'tend to you." His voice contained the same scorn as if he were saying: "You will have to go to jail."

The lieutenant had been very meek, but now his face flushed, and he looked into the doctor's eyes. "I guess I won't have it amputated," he said.

"Nonsense, man! Nonsense! Nonsense!" cried the doctor. "Come along, now. I won't amputate it. Come along. Don't be a baby."

"Let go of me," said the lieutenant, holding back wrathfully, his glance fixed upon the door of the old schoolhouse, as sinister to him as the portals of death.

And this is the story of how the lieutenant lost his arm. When he reached home, his sisters, his mother, his wife, sobbed for a long time at the sight of the flat sleeve. "Oh, well," he said, standing shamefaced amid these tears, "I don't suppose it matters so much as all that." □□

Discussion

1. What devices does Crane use to bring his scenes to life?

2. Explain the **irony of situation** suggested **(a)** by the opening **vignette; (b)** by the lieutenant's initial response to his wound.

3. How does the lieutenant's being wounded change his men's attitude toward him? Explain their reaction.

4. **(a)** After the lieutenant is wounded, do the battle and its participants seem less or more vivid to him? Less or more "real" to him? Cite passages that support your opinion. **(b)** What **paradox** is there in the great knowledge of the battle displayed by the wounded soldiers? Explain how this paradox makes sense.

5. **(a)** What attitude does the lieutenant's final remark suggest? **(b)** What incidents indicate that he is a powerless spectator of his own life, both before and after being wounded?

6. Why is Crane's title more appropriate to the story's presentation of war than a title like "The Bloody Wound" or "A Victim of Battle"?

Reread the discussion of **realism** and **naturalism** in the Unit Background. What elements of each school of writing are displayed in the subject matter, theme, and techniques of this story? In what way is its view of life naturalistic? Explain your opinion in a brief composition, quoting examples from the story.

Use your Glossary to find the primary accented syllable in each italicized word below from "An Episode of War." Then, from the choices which follow each italicized word, select the word that rhymes with that accented syllable and write it on your paper. Be sure you know the definitions of the italicized words.

1. *potentate* (a) dough; (b) date; (c) den.

2. *maniacal* (a) cane; (b) ban; (c) by; (d) bull.

3. *tumultuous* (a) doom; (b) dew; (c) salt; (d) dull.

4. *reverberate* (a) key; (b) fir; (c) date.

5. *disdainful* (a) bliss; (b) main; (c) bull.

Stephen Crane 1871 • 1900

Crane was born into a family with printer's ink in their veins. Both his parents were writers and two of his brothers were reporters. He attended college for two semesters, spending more time on newspaper reporting and playing baseball than on his studies. The next five years he spent in New York. What little money he had came from occasional freelance reporting. His beat was the Bowery saloons and the slums around him.

He brought these grim experiences to life in his first book, *Maggie: A Girl of the Streets* (1893), the first American naturalist novel. Its story was so harsh and sordid that he was unable to find a publisher. Crane borrowed $700 and printed it himself, but he was able to sell only a few copies.

Two years later Crane published *The Red Badge of Courage,* a remarkably real war story which was his greatest achievement, especially considering that he had never experienced combat. Because of his renowned war novel, Crane was hired to cover the Cuban revolt against Spanish colonial rule. However, his ship sank off the coast of Florida. His ordeal in reaching shore in the ship's dinghy is the basis for his most famous short story, "The Open Boat."

Crane later covered the Greco-Turkish War and the Spanish-American War in Cuba. He died at twenty-eight, never having fully recovered from his ordeal when shipwrecked, which aggravated his tuberculosis.

notes and comments
Crane's Fictional Techniques

While naturalism best describes Crane's philosophy, impressionism and **symbolism** are the literary techniques that he most often used. In "An Episode of War" the wound suffered by the lieutenant is a symbol of his new vision or understanding of reality. The wound removes him from the struggle so that he can "see many things which as a participant in the fight were unknown to him."

Impressionism is a highly personal and subjective mode of writing, in that the author selects and organizes details strictly according to one character's point of view. "An Episode of War" is impressionistic because its events are conveyed to the reader through the eyes of the lieutenant who experiences various aspects of war as fixed and static vignettes. Reality seen subjectively seems unreal, something like "a historical painting," and the various participants seem "statuelike and silent."

Crane's use of impressionism and symbolism to express his grim naturalistic philosophy was a dramatic innovation that later influenced such noted novelists as Steinbeck and Hemingway (see Units 1 and 6).

Paul Laurence Dunbar

Sympathy

I know what the caged bird feels, alas!
When the sun is bright on the upland slopes;
When the wind stirs soft through the
      springing grass,
And the river flows like a stream of glass;
5 When the first bird sings and the first bud opes,
And the faint perfume from its chalice steals—
I know what the caged bird feels!

I know why the caged bird beats his wing
Till its blood is red on the cruel bars;
10 For he must fly back to his perch and cling
When he fain would be on the bough a-swing;
And a pain still throbs in the old, old scars
And they pulse again with a keener sting—
I know why he beats his wing!

15 I know why the caged bird sings, ah me,
When his wing is bruised and his bosom sore,—
When he beats his bars and he would be free;
It is not a carol of joy or glee,
But a prayer that he sends from his heart's
      deep core,
20 But a plea, that upward to Heaven he flings—
I know why the caged bird sings!

"Sympathy" and "We Wear the Mask" by Paul Laurence Dunbar. Reprinted by permission of Dodd, Mead & Company, Inc.
from THE COMPLETE POEMS OF PAUL LAURENCE DUNBAR.

We Wear the Mask

We wear the mask that grins and lies,
It hides our cheeks and shades our eyes,—
This debt we pay to human guile;
With torn and bleeding hearts we smile,
5 And mouth with myriad subtleties.

Why should the world be overwise,
In counting all our tears and sighs?
Nay, let them only see us, while
    We wear the mask.

10 We smile, but, O great Christ, our cries
To Thee from tortured souls arise.
We sing, but oh, the clay is vile
Beneath our feet, and long the mile;
But let the world dream otherwise,
15   We wear the mask.

Discussion

Sympathy

1. Discuss the possible **metaphorical** meanings of the cage, the bird, and the outdoors scene.

2. (a) Why does the caged bird beat his wings? (b) What contrast is drawn between the apparent feeling and the real feeling of his song?

3. Relate this **symbolic** statement to the poet's situation.

We Wear the Mask

1. (a) What does the "mask" symbolize? (b) Why is it necessary to its wearers? Who might they be?

2. Contrast the face shown to Christ and the face shown to the world.

3. What attitude toward the world is suggested in line 14?

Extension • Speaking

Dunbar is noted for highly skilled dialect poetry dealing with black folk material. His dialect poems can be found in *Lyrics of Lowly Life* or in his *Complete Poems*. Compare them in class with the literary poems above. Which do you prefer? Why?

Paul Laurence Dunbar
1872 • 1906

The son of former slaves who escaped by way of the Underground Railroad, Dunbar could not afford to go to college. After graduating from high school in Dayton, Ohio, he went to work as an elevator operator. He was holding this job when his first book of poetry, *Oak and Ivy,* was published in 1893. The book made little impression, but his second collection, *Majors and Minors* (1895), came to the attention of the noted novelist and editor, William Dean Howells. He persuaded Dunbar to combine the best poetry from both books into one volume. The result was *Lyrics of Lowly Life* (1896), which made Dunbar a national literary figure. Although his life was short, Dunbar published six collections of

poetry, four collections of short stories, and four novels. His *Complete Poems* was published in 1913 and heralded a new era in literature for black Americans.

Edwin Arlington Robinson

Don Quixote and Sancho Panza by Honoré Daumier (1808-1879). (The Metropolitan Museum of Art, Rogers Fund, 1927.)

Miniver Cheevy

Miniver Cheevy, child of scorn,
    Grew lean while he assailed the seasons;
He wept that he was ever born,
    And he had reasons.

5 Miniver loved the days of old
    When swords were bright and steeds
        were prancing;
The vision of a warrior bold
    Would set him dancing.

Miniver sighed for what was not,
10   And dreamed, and rested from his labors;
He dreamed of Thebes and Camelot,
    And Priam's neighbors.[1]

Miniver mourned the ripe renown
    That made so many a name so fragrant;
15 He mourned Romance, now on the town,[2]
    And Art, a vagrant.

Miniver loved the Medici,[3]
    Albeit he had never seen one;
He would have sinned incessantly
20   Could he have been one.

Miniver cursed the commonplace
    And eyed a khaki suit with loathing;
He missed the medieval grace
    Of iron clothing.

25 Miniver scorned the gold he sought,
    But sore annoyed was he without it;
Miniver thought, and thought, and thought,
    And thought about it.

Miniver Cheevy, born too late,
30   Scratched his head and kept on thinking;
Miniver coughed, and called it fate,
    And kept on drinking.

"Miniver Cheevy" from THE TOWN DOWN THE RIVER by Edwin Arlington Robinson is reprinted by permission of Charles Scribner's Sons. Copyright 1907 by Charles Scribner's Sons.
1. Thebes . . . neighbors. Thebes was the capital of ancient Egypt during its period of greatness. Camelot was the legendary site of King Arthur's palace. Priam was the last king of Troy; his neighbors were the Greeks, who conquered Troy in the Trojan War.
2. on the town, living on charity, a pauper.
3. the Medici (med′ə chē), the ruling family of Florence, Italy, during the fifteenth and sixteenth centuries, who were notable both for their generous patronage of art and for their lavish living and wicked lives.

Richard Cory

Whenever Richard Cory went downtown,
　We people on the pavement looked at him:
He was a gentleman from sole to crown,
　Clean-favored, and imperially slim.

5　And he was always quietly arrayed,
　And he was always human when he talked;
But still he fluttered pulses when he said,
　"Good morning," and he glittered when
　　he walked.

And he was rich—yes, richer than a king—
10　And admirably schooled in every grace:
In fine, we thought that he was everything
　To make us wish that we were in his place.

So on we worked, and waited for the light,
　And went without the meat, and cursed
　　the bread;
15　And Richard Cory, one calm summer night,
　Went home and put a bullet through his head.

Discussion

Miniver Cheevy

1. (a) What complaints does Miniver make about his own time? **(b)** Would he have been happy in the other times of which he dreams? Why or why not?

2. (a) What attitude does the speaker take toward Miniver in the last two stanzas? **(b)** Is there any ambivalence in Miniver's actions as described here?

3. What qualities does the name Miniver Cheevy suggest?

Richard Cory

1. (a) In what ways does Richard Cory stand out from other people? **(b)** What feelings do "we people" have toward him? Do they understand him? Explain.

2. (a) What possible motive might Cory have had for killing himself? **(b)** How is this motive implied in the poem?

Edwin Arlington Robinson
1869 • 1935

During the 1920s Robinson was generally regarded as America's greatest living poet. Three times during that decade he was awarded the Pulitzer Prize.

Robinson spent his youth in Gardiner, Maine. Financial difficulties following his father's death ended his schooling after two years at Harvard. He returned to Gardiner and devoted his time to writing poetry. When he moved to New York in 1897 he led a hermitlike existence, taking jobs only to enable him to live, and spending his greatest efforts on poetry. In 1916 *The Man Against the Sky* brought him sudden fame.

"Miniver Cheevy," "Richard Cory," and others of Robinson's best-known poems are part of the "Tilbury" portraits and grew out of his New England experiences. This Tilbury Town gallery is composed largely of "cheated dreamers" and "bewildered mediocrities," most of whom manage in one way or another to withdraw from hard reality. But Robinson's pessimism is always tempered by wit and imagination, often by flashes of wry humor.

Edgar Lee Masters

The following poems by Masters are taken from his Spoon River Anthology, *which first appeared as a series of poems in a St. Louis newspaper in 1914 and which became so popular that book publication followed the next year. The* Anthology *was set in the graveyard of Spoon River, an imaginary composite of several small towns in central Illinois. The speaker of each poem is a former resident of Spoon River, delivering from the grave an epitaph which gives a verdict on life, shaped by whether the dead speaker feels tranquil or embittered.*

Lucinda Matlock

I went to dances at Chandlerville,
And played snap-out at Winchester.
One time we changed partners,
Driving home in the moonlight of middle June,
5 And then I found Davis.
We were married and lived together for
      seventy years,
Enjoying, working, raising the twelve children,
Eight of whom we lost
Ere I had reached the age of sixty.
10 I spun, I wove, I kept the house, I
      nursed the sick,
I made the garden, and for holiday
Rambled over the fields where sang the larks,
And by Spoon River gathering many a shell,
And many a flower and medicinal weed—
15 Shouting to the wooded hills, singing to
      the green valleys.
At ninety-six I had lived enough, that is all,
And passed to a sweet repose.
What is this I hear of sorrow and weariness,
Anger, discontent, and drooping hopes?
20 Degenerate sons and daughters,
Life is too strong for you—
It takes life to love Life.

Richard Bone

When I first came to Spoon River
I did not know whether what they told me
Was true or false.
They would bring me the epitaph
5 And stand around the shop while I worked
And say "He was so kind," "He was wonderful,"
"She was the sweetest woman," "He was a
      consistent Christian."
And I chiseled for them whatever they wished,
All in ignorance of its truth.
10 But later, as I lived among the people here,
I knew how near to the life
Were the epitaphs that were ordered for them
      as they died.
But still I chiseled whatever they paid me
      to chisel
And made myself party to the false chronicles
15 Of the stones,
Even as the historian does who writes
Without knowing the truth,
Or because he is influenced to hide it.

Denley Karlson/Stock, Boston, Inc.

Mrs. Charles Bliss

Reverend Wiley advised me not to divorce him
For the sake of the children,
And Judge Somers advised him the same.
So we stuck to the end of the path.
5 But two of the children thought he was right,
And two of the children thought I was right.
And the two who sided with him blamed me,
And the two who sided with me blamed him,
And they grieved for the one they sided with.
10 And all were torn with the guilt of judging,
And tortured in soul because they could not admire
Equally him and me.
Now every gardener knows that plants
        grown in cellars
Or under stones are twisted and yellow and weak.
15 And no mother would let her baby suck
Diseased milk from her breast.
Yet preachers and judges advise the
        raising of souls
Where there is no sunlight, but only twilight,
No warmth, but only dampness and cold—
20 Preachers and judges!

Discussion

Lucinda Matlock

1. (a) How do the last five
lines in particular **characterize**
the speaker? (b) Has her life
been generally easy or hard?
Explain.

2. Do you think her children
are "degenerate" as she says,
or does this statement indicate
a certain heartless toughness in
her character? Defend your
view.

Richard Bone

1. What does Bone mean in
lines 10–12?

Mrs. Charles Bliss

1. (a) What metaphor most
powerfully describes the children's condition? What does it
imply about their future? (b)
Explain the **irony** in the speaker's married name.

2. How would you read the
last line aloud to emphasize
Mrs. Bliss's attitude toward
preachers and judges?

Edgar Lee Masters
1868 • 1950

As a young boy, Masters
began writing poems and stories, and during his brief so-
journ at Knox College and his
work in his father's law office,
this remained an important
interest. In 1891 he was admitted to the bar and became a
highly respected lawyer. With
the publication of *Spoon River
Anthology* in 1915 his fame as a
poet overshadowed his reputation as a lawyer. A few years
later he abandoned law to devote all his time to writing and
in 1924 published *The New
Spoon River*.

Since their publication, the
Spoon River epitaphs have
maintained their great popularity. Masters continued to write
poetry and biographies until his
death. Although his later works
were interesting and readable,
he never again achieved the
brilliance of the *Spoon River*
poems.

W. E. B. Du Bois

Of the Meaning of Progress

Once upon a time I taught school in the hills of Tennessee, where the broad dark vale of the Mississippi begins to roll and crumple to greet the Alleghanies. I was a Fisk student then, and all Fisk men thought that Tennessee—beyond the Veil[1]—was theirs alone, and in vacation time they sallied forth in lusty bands to meet the county school-commissioners. Young and happy, I too went, and I shall not soon forget that summer, seventeen years ago.

First, there was a Teachers' Institute at the county seat; and there distinguished guests of the superintendent taught the teachers fractions and spelling and other mysteries—white teachers in the morning, Negroes at night. A picnic now and then, and a supper, and the rough world was softened by laughter and song. I remember how—But I wander.

There came a day when all the teachers left the Institute and began the hunt for schools. I learn from hearsay (for my mother was mortally afraid of firearms) that the hunting of ducks and bears and men is wonderfully interesting, but I am sure that the man who has never hunted a country school has something to learn of the pleasures of the chase. I see now the white, hot roads lazily rise and fall and wind before me under the burning July sun; I feel the deep weariness of heart and limb as ten, eight, six miles stretch relentlessly ahead; I feel my heart sink heavily as I hear again and again, "Got a teacher? Yes." So I walked on and on—horses were too expensive—until I had wandered beyond railways, beyond stage lines, to a land of "varmints" and rattlesnakes, where the coming of a stranger was an event, and men lived and died in the shadow of one blue hill.

Sprinkled over hill and dale lay cabins and farmhouses, shut out from the world by the forests and the rolling hills toward the east. There I found at last a little school. Josie told me

of it; she was a thin, homely girl of twenty, with a dark brown face and thick, hard hair. I had crossed the stream at Watertown, and rested under the great willows; then I had gone to the little cabin in the lot where Josie was resting on her way to town. The gaunt farmer made me welcome, and Josie, hearing my errand, told me anxiously that they wanted a school over the hill; that but once since the war[2] had a teacher been there; that she herself longed to learn—and thus she ran on, talking fast and loud, with much earnestness and energy.

Next morning I crossed the tall round hill, lingered to look at the blue and yellow mountains stretching toward the Carolinas, then plunged into the wood, and came out at Josie's home. It was a dull frame cottage with four rooms, perched just below the brow of the hill, amid peach trees. The father was a quiet, simple soul, calmly ignorant, with no touch of vulgarity. The mother was different—strong, bustling, and energetic, with a quick, restless tongue, and an ambition to live "like folks." There was a crowd of children. Two boys had gone away. There remained two growing girls; a shy midget of eight; John, tall, awkward, and eighteen; Jim, younger, quicker, and better looking; and two babies of indefinite age. Then there was Josie herself. She seemed to be the center of the family: always busy at service, or at home, or berry-picking; a little nervous and inclined to scold, like her mother, yet faithful, too, like her father. She had about her a certain fineness, the shadow of an unconscious moral heroism that would willingly give all of life to make life broader, deeper, and

---

Du Bois (dü bois′).

From THE SOULS OF BLACK FOLK by W. E. Burghardt Du Bois, 1903.

1. *the Veil,* the barrier of racial segregation.
2. *the war,* the Civil War.

stream; the sun laughed and the water jingled, and we rode on. "Come in," said the commissioner—"come in. Have a seat. Yes, that certificate will do. Stay to dinner. What do you want a month?" "Oh," thought I, "this is lucky"; but even then fell the awful shadow of the Veil, for they ate first, then I—alone.

The schoolhouse was a log hut, where Colonel Wheeler used to shelter his corn. It sat in a lot behind a rail fence and thorn bushes, near the sweetest of springs. There was an entrance where a door once was, and within, a massive rickety fireplace; great chinks between the logs served as windows. Furniture was scarce. A pale blackboard crouched in the corner. My desk was made of three boards, reinforced at critical points, and my chair, borrowed from the landlady, had to be returned every night. Seats for the children—these puzzled me much. I was haunted by a New England vision of neat little desks and chairs, but, alas! the reality was rough plank benches without backs, and at times without legs. They had the one virtue of making naps dangerous—possibly fatal, for the floor was not to be trusted.

It was a hot morning late in July when the school opened. I trembled when I heard the patter of little feet down the dusty road, and saw the growing row of dark solemn faces and bright eager eyes facing me. First came Josie and her brothers and sisters. The longing to know, to be a student in the great school at Nashville, hovered like a star above this child-woman amid her work and worry, and she studied doggedly. There were the Dowells from their farm over toward Alexandria—Fanny, with her smooth black face and wondering eyes; Martha, brown and dull; the pretty girl-wife of a brother, and the younger brood.

There were the Burkes—two brown and yellow lads, and a tiny haughty-eyed girl. Fat Reuben's little chubby girl came, with golden face and old-gold hair, faithful and solemn. 'Thenie was on hand early—a jolly, ugly, good-hearted girl, who slyly dipped snuff and looked after her little bowlegged brother. When her mother could spare her, 'Tildy came—a midnight beauty, with starry eyes and tapering limbs; and her brother, correspondingly homely. And then the big boys—the hulking Lawrences; the lazy Neills,

fuller for her and hers. I saw much of this family afterwards, and grew to love them for their honest efforts to be decent and comfortable, and for their knowledge of their own ignorance. There was with them no affectation. The mother would scold the father for being so "easy"; Josie would roundly berate the boys for carelessness; and all knew that it was a hard thing to dig a living out of a rocky side-hill.

I secured the school. I remember the day I rode horseback out to the commissioner's house with a pleasant young white fellow who wanted the white school. The road ran down the bed of a

W. E. B. DU BOIS 363

unfathered sons of mother and daughter; Hickman, with a stoop in his shoulders, and the rest.

There they sat, nearly thirty of them, on the rough benches, their faces shading from a pale cream to a deep brown, the little feet bare and swinging, the eyes full of expectation, with here and there a twinkle of mischief, and the hands grasping Webster's blue-black spelling book. I loved my school, and the fine faith the children had in the wisdom of their teacher was truly marvelous. We read and spelled together, wrote a little, picked flowers, sang, and listened to stories of the world beyond the hill. At times the school would dwindle away, and I would start out. I would visit Mun Eddings, who lived in two very dirty rooms, and ask why little Lugene, whose flaming face seemed ever ablaze with the dark red hair uncombed, was absent all last week, or why I missed so often the inimitable rags of Mack and Ed. Then the father, who worked Colonel Wheeler's farm on shares,[3] would tell me how the crops needed the boys; and the thin, slovenly mother, whose face was pretty when washed, assured me that Lugene must mind the baby. "But we'll start them again next week." When the Lawrences stopped, I knew that the doubts of the old folks about book-learning had conquered again, and so, toiling up the hill, and getting as far into the cabin as possible, I put Cicero's "Pro Archia Poeta"[4] into the simplest English with local applications, and usually convinced them—for a week or so.

On Friday nights I often went home with some of the children—sometimes to Doc Burke's farm. He was a great, loud, thin Black, ever working, and trying to buy the seventy-five acres of hill and dale where he lived; but people said that he would surely fail, and the "white folks would get it all." His wife was a magnificent Amazon, with saffron face and shining hair, uncorseted and barefooted, and the children were strong and beautiful. They lived in a one-and-a-half-room cabin in the hollow of the farm, near the spring. The front room was full of great fat white beds, scrupulously neat; and there were bad chromos[5] on the walls, and a tired center-table. In the tiny back kitchen I was often invited to "take out and help" myself to fried chicken and wheat biscuit, "meat" and corn pone, string-beans and berries. At first I used to be a little

alarmed at the approach of bedtime in the one lone bedroom, but embarrassment was very deftly avoided. First, all the children nodded and slept, and were stowed away in one great pile of goose feathers; next, the mother and the father discreetly slipped away to the kitchen while I went to bed; then, blowing out the dim light, they retired in the dark. In the morning all were up and away before I thought of awaking. Across the road, where fat Reuben lived, they all went outdoors while the teacher retired, because they did not boast the luxury of a kitchen.

I liked to stay with the Dowells, for they had four rooms and plenty of good country fare. Uncle Bird had a small, rough farm, all woods and hills, miles from the big road; but he was full of tales—he preached now and then—and with his children, berries, horses, and wheat he was happy and prosperous. Often, to keep the peace, I must go where life was less lovely; for instance, 'Tildy's mother was incorrigibly dirty, Reuben's larder was limited seriously, and herds of untamed insects wandered over the Eddingses' beds. Best of all I loved to go to Josie's, and sit on the porch, eating peaches, while the mother bustled and talked: how Josie had bought the sewing machine; how Josie worked at service in winter, but that four dollars a month was "mighty little" wages; how Josie longed to go away to school, but that it "looked like" they never could get far enough ahead to let her; how the crops failed and the well was yet unfinished; and, finally, how "mean" some of the white folks were.

For two summers I lived in this little world; it was dull and humdrum. The girls looked at the hill in wistful longing, and the boys fretted and haunted Alexandria. Alexandria was "town"—a straggling, lazy village of houses, churches, and shops, and an aristocracy of Toms, Dicks, and Captains. Cuddled on the hill to the north was the village of the colored folks, who lived in three- or four-room unpainted cottages, some neat and homelike, and some dirty. The dwellings were

---

3. **on shares,** dividing the crop with the landlord, instead of paying rent.
4. **"Pro Archia Poeta"** (prō är′kē ä pō ā′tä), a Latin phrase meaning "on behalf of great poets." This speech by the Roman orator Cicero (sis′ə rō; 106–43 B.C.) supported the value of literature.
5. **chromos,** pictures printed in colors.

scattered rather aimlessly, but they centered about the twin temples of the hamlet, the Methodist, and the Hard-Shell Baptist churches. These, in turn, leaned gingerly on a sad-colored schoolhouse. Hither my little world wended its crooked way on Sunday to meet other worlds, and gossip, and wonder, and make the weekly sacrifice with frenzied priest at the altar of the "old-time religion." Then the soft melody and mighty cadences of Negro song fluttered and thundered.

I have called my tiny community a world, and so its isolation made it; and yet there was among us but a half-awakened common consciousness, sprung from common joy and grief, at burial, birth, or wedding; from a common hardship in poverty, poor land, and low wages; and, above all, from the sight of the Veil that hung between us and Opportunity. All this caused us to think some thoughts together; but these, when ripe for speech, were spoken in various languages. Those whose eyes twenty-five and more years before had seen "the glory of the coming of the Lord,"[6] saw in every present hindrance or help a dark fatalism bound to bring all things right in His own good time. The mass of those to whom slavery was a dim recollection of childhood found the world a puzzling thing: it asked little of them, and they answered with little, and yet it ridiculed their offering. Such a paradox they could not understand, and therefore sank into listless indifference, or shiftlessness, or reckless bravado. There were, however, some—such as Josie, Jim, and Ben—to whom War, Hell, and Slavery were but childhood tales, whose young appetites had been whetted to an edge by school and story and half-awakened thought. Ill could they be content, born without and beyond the World. And their weak wings beat against their barriers—barriers of caste, of youth, of life; at last, in dangerous moments, against everything that opposed even a whim.

The ten years that follow youth, the years when first the realization comes that life is leading somewhere—these were the years that passed after I left my little school. When they were past, I came by chance once more to the walls of Fisk University, to the halls of the chapel of melody. As I lingered there in the joy and pain of meeting old schoolfriends, there swept over me a sudden longing to pass again beyond the blue hill, and to see the homes and the school of other days, and to learn how life had gone with my schoolchildren; and I went.

Josie was dead, and the gray-haired mother said simply, "We've had a heap of trouble since you've been away." I had feared for Jim. With a cultured parentage and a social caste to uphold him, he might have made a venturesome merchant or a West Point cadet. But here he was, angry with life and reckless; and when Farmer Durham charged him with stealing wheat, the old man had to ride fast to escape the stones which the furious fool hurled after him. They told Jim to run away; but he would not run, and the constable came that afternoon. It grieved Josie, and great awkward John walked nine miles every day to see his little brother through the bars of Lebanon jail. At last the two came back together in the dark night. The mother cooked supper, and Josie emptied her purse, and the boys stole away. Josie grew thin and silent, yet worked the more. The hill became steep for the quiet old father, and with the boys away there was little to do in the valley. Josie helped them to sell the old farm, and they moved nearer town. Brother Dennis, the carpenter, built a new house with six rooms; Josie toiled a year in Nashville, and brought back ninety dollars to furnish the house and change it to a home.

When the spring came, and the birds twittered, and the stream ran proud and full, little sister Lizzie, bold and thoughtless, flushed with the passion of youth, bestowed herself on the tempter, and brought home a nameless child. Josie shivered and worked on, with the vision of schooldays all fled, with a face wan and tired—worked until, on a summer's day, some one married another; then Josie crept to her mother like a hurt child, and slept—and sleeps.

I paused to scent the breeze as I entered the valley. The Lawrences have gone—father and son forever—and the other son lazily digs in the earth to live. A new young widow rents out their cabin to fat Reuben. Reuben is a Baptist preacher now, but I fear as lazy as ever, though his

---

6. *"the glory . . . Lord,"* from the first line of the "Battle Hymn of the Republic."

cabin has three rooms; and little Ella has grown into a bouncing woman, and is ploughing corn on the hot hillside. There are babies a-plenty, and one half-witted girl. Across the valley is a house I did not know before, and there I found, rocking one baby and expecting another, one of my schoolgirls, a daughter of Uncle Bird Dowell. She looked somewhat worried with her new duties, but soon bristled into pride over her neat cabin and the tale of her thrifty husband, and the horse and cow, and the farm they were planning to buy.

My log schoolhouse was gone. In its place stood Progress; and Progress, I understand, is necessarily ugly. The crazy foundation stones still marked the former site of my poor little cabin, and not far away, on six weary boulders, perched a jaunty board house, perhaps twenty by thirty feet, with three windows and a door that locked. Some of the window glass was broken, and part of an old iron stove lay mournfully under the house. I peeped through the window half reverently, and found things that were more familiar. The blackboard had grown by about two feet, and the seats were still without backs. The county owns the lot now, I hear, and every year there is a session of school. As I sat by the spring and looked on the Old and the New I felt glad, very glad, and yet——

After two long drinks I started on. There was the great double log-house on the corner. I remembered the broken, blighted family that used to live there. The strong, hard face of the mother, with its wilderness of hair, rose before me. She had driven her husband away, and while I taught school a strange man lived there, big and jovial, and people talked. I felt sure that Ben and 'Tildy would come to naught from such a home. But this is an odd world; for Ben is a busy farmer in Smith County, "doing well, too," they say, and he had cared for little 'Tildy until last spring, when a lover married her. A hard life the lad had led, toiling for meat, and laughed at because he was homely and crooked. There was Sam Carlon, an impudent old skinflint, who had definite notions about "niggers," and hired Ben a summer and would not pay him. Then the hungry boy gathered his sacks together, and in broad daylight went into Carlon's corn; and when the hard-fisted farmer set upon him, the angry boy flew at him like a beast. Doc Burke saved a murder and a lynching that day.

The story reminded me again of the Burkes, and an impatience seized me to know who won in the battle, Doc or the seventy-five acres. For it is a hard thing to make a farm out of nothing, even in fifteen years. So I hurried on, thinking of the Burkes. They used to have a certain magnificent barbarism about them that I liked. They were never vulgar, never immoral, but rather rough and primitive, with an unconventionality that spent itself in loud guffaws, slaps on the back, and naps in the corner. I hurried by the cottage of the misborn Neill boys. It was empty, and they were grown into fat, lazy farmhands. I saw the home of the Hickmans, but Albert, with his stooping shoulders, had passed from the world. Then I came to the Burkes' gate and peered through; the inclosure looked rough and untrimmed, and yet there were the same fences around the old farm save to the left, where lay twenty-five other acres. And lo! the cabin in the hollow had climbed the hill and swollen to a half-finished six-room cottage.

The Burkes held a hundred acres, but they were still in debt. Indeed, the gaunt father who toiled night and day would scarcely be happy out of debt, being so used to it. Some day he must stop, for his massive frame is showing decline. The mother wore shoes, but the lionlike physique of other days was broken. The children had grown up. Rob, the image of his father, was loud and rough with laughter. Birdie, my school baby of six, had grown to a picture of maiden beauty, tall and tawny. "Edgar is gone," said the mother, with head half-bowed—"gone to work in Nashville; he and his father couldn't agree."

Little Doc, the boy born since the time of my school, took me horseback down the creek next morning toward Farmer Dowell's. The road and the stream were battling for mastery, and the stream had the better of it. We splashed and waded, and the merry boy, perched behind me, chattered and laughed. He showed me where Simon Thompson had bought a bit of ground and a home; but his daughter Lana, a plump, brown, slow girl, was not there. She had married a man and a farm twenty miles away. We wound on down the stream till we came to a gate that I did not recognize, but the boy insisted that it was

"Uncle Bird's." The farm was fat with the growing crop. In that little valley was a strange stillness as I rode up; for death and marriage had stolen youth and left age and childhood there. We sat and talked that night after the chores were done. Uncle Bird was grayer, and his eyes did not see so well, but he was still jovial. We talked of the acres bought—one hundred and twenty-five—of the new guest-chamber added, of Martha's marrying. Then we talked of death: Fanny and Fred were gone; a shadow hung over the other daughter, and when it lifted she was to go to Nashville to school. At last we spoke of the neighbors, and as night fell, Uncle Bird told me how, on a night like that, 'Thenie came wandering back to her home over yonder, to escape the blows of her husband. And next morning she died in the home that her little bowlegged brother, working and saving, had bought for their widowed mother.

My journey was done, and behind me lay hill and dale, and Life and Death. How shall man measure Progress there where the dark-faced Josie lies? How many heartfuls of sorrow shall balance a bushel of wheat? How hard a thing is life to the lowly, and yet how human and real! And all this life and love and strife and failure— is it the twilight of nightfall or the flush of some faint-dawning day?

Thus sadly musing, I rode to Nashville in the Jim Crow[7] car. □□

---

7. **Jim Crow car,** a segregated car for blacks only. Segregation laws were called Jim Crow laws.

Discussion

1. Du Bois says that "all Fisk men thought that Tennessee—beyond the Veil— was theirs alone." **(a)** What does this reveal about the attitudes of the young men? **(b)** How are these attitudes reflected in the young Du Bois? **(c)** At what points does he personally encounter "the Veil"?

2. What pleasures and hardships does Du Bois find in living and teaching in rural Tennessee?

3. **(a)** Describe Josie's character and ambitions. **(b)** What did slavery and the Civil War mean to her and the other youngsters? **(c)** What factors destroyed her dreams?

4. **(a)** What does "progress" mean to Du Bois? **(b)** In his view, what conditions are needed for progress? **(c)** From the examples he gives, does he seem optimistic or pessimistic about the possibilities of progress for rural blacks in the late nineteenth century?

5. Is Du Bois's philosophy mainly **naturalistic** or **realistic**? Explain.

W. E. B. Du Bois 1868 • 1963

The Souls of Black Folk (1903), from which the preceding essay is taken, was a landmark in American literature. In that book, Du Bois treated sociological questions of black identity and pride with the passion and symbolism of literary art.

Born in Massachusetts, Du Bois graduated from Fisk University in 1888 and in 1895 became the first black student to receive a Ph.D. degree from Harvard University. He then taught history and economics at Atlanta University. In 1909, he helped found the National Association for the Advancement of Colored People and edited its magazine, *The Crisis*, for twenty years before returning to Atlanta University.

Du Bois was regarded by many as one of the most incisive intellectuals in the United States. At the time of his death, he resided in Ghana and was working as editor-in-chief of the *Encyclopedia Africana.*

Edith Wharton

A Journey

As she lay in her berth, staring at the shadows overhead, the rush of the wheels was in her brain, driving her deeper and deeper into circles of wakeful lucidity. The sleeping car had sunk into its night silence. Through the wet window-pane she watched the sudden lights, the long stretches of hurrying blackness. Now and then she turned her head and looked through the opening in the hangings at her husband's curtains across the aisle. . . .

She wondered restlessly if he wanted any-thing and if she could hear him if he called. His voice had grown very weak within the last months and it irritated him when she did not hear. This irritability, this increasing childish petulance seemed to give expression to their imperceptible estrangement. Like two faces looking at one another through a sheet of glass they were close together, almost touching, but they could not hear or feel each other: the conductivity between them was broken. She, at least, had this sense of separation, and she fancied sometimes that she saw it reflected in the look with which he supplemented his failing words. Doubtless the fault was hers. She was too impenetrably healthy to be touched by the irrelevancies of disease. Her self-reproachful tender-ness was tinged with the sense of his irrationali-ty: she had a vague feeling that there was a purpose in his helpless tyrannies. The sudden-ness of the change had found her so unprepared. A year ago their pulses had beat to one robust measure; both had the same prodigal confidence in an exhaustless future. Now their energies no longer kept step: hers still bounded ahead of life, preempting unclaimed regions of hope and activ-ity, while his lagged behind, vainly struggling to overtake her.

When they married, she had such arrears of living to make up: her days had been as bare as the white-washed schoolroom where she forced innutritious facts upon reluctant children. His coming had broken in on the slumber of circum-stance, widening the present till it became the encloser of remotest chances. But imperceptibly the horizon narrowed. Life had a grudge against her: she was never to be allowed to spread her wings.

At first the doctors had said that six weeks of mild air would set him right; but when he came back this assurance was explained as having of course included a winter in a dry climate. They gave up their pretty house, storing the wedding presents and new furniture, and went to Colo-rado. She had hated it there from the first. Nobody knew her or cared about her; there was no one to wonder at the good match she had made, or to envy her the new dresses and the visiting cards which were still a surprise to her. And he kept growing worse. She felt herself beset with difficulties too evasive to be fought by so direct a temperament. She still loved him, of course; but he was gradually, undefinably ceas-ing to be himself. The man she had married had been strong, active, gently masterful: the male whose pleasure it is to clear a way through the material obstructions of life; but now it was she who was the protector, he who must be shielded from importunities and given his drops or his beef juice though the skies were falling. The routine of the sickroom bewildered her; this punctual administering of medicine seemed as idle as some uncomprehended religious mum-mery.

There were moments, indeed, when warm gushes of pity swept away her instinctive resent-ment of his condition, when she still found his old self in his eyes as they groped for each other

---

"A Journey" is reprinted by permission of Charles Scribner's Sons and A. Watkins, Inc. from THE GREATER INCLINATION by Edith Wharton.

through the dense medium of his weakness. But these moments had grown rare. Sometimes he frightened her: his sunken expressionless face seemed that of a stranger; his voice was weak and hoarse; his thin-lipped smile a mere muscular contraction. Her hand avoided his damp soft skin, which had lost the familiar roughness of health: she caught herself furtively watching him as she might have watched a strange animal. It frightened her to feel that this was the man she loved; there were hours when to tell him what she suffered seemed the one escape from her fears. But in general she judged herself more leniently, reflecting that she had perhaps been too long alone with him, and that she would feel differently when they were at home again, surrounded by her robust and buoyant family. How she had rejoiced when the doctors at last gave their consent to his going home! She knew, of course, what the decision meant; they both knew. It meant that he was to die; but they dressed the truth in hopeful euphemisms, and at times, in the joy of preparation, she really forgot the purpose of their journey, and slipped into an eager allusion to next year's plans.

At last the day of leaving came. She had a dreadful fear that they would never get away; that somehow at the last moment he would fail her; that the doctors held one of their accustomed treacheries in reserve; but nothing happened. They drove to the station, he was installed in a seat with a rug over his knees and a cushion at his back, and she hung out of the window waving unregretful farewells to the acquaintances she had really never liked till then.

The first twenty-four hours had passed off well. He revived a little and it amused him to look out of the window and to observe the humors of the car. The second day he began to grow weary and to chafe under the dispassionate stare of the freckled child with the lump of chewing gum. She had to explain to the child's mother that her husband was too ill to be disturbed: a statement received by that lady with a resentment visibly supported by the maternal sentiment of the whole car. . . .

That night he slept badly and the next morning his temperature frightened her: she was sure he was growing worse. The day passed slowly, punctuated by the small irritations of travel.

Watching his tired face, she traced in its contractions every rattle and jolt of the train, till her own body vibrated with sympathetic fatigue. She felt the others observing him too, and hovered restlessly between him and the line of interrogative eyes. The freckled child hung about him like a fly; offers of candy and picture books failed to dislodge her: she twisted one leg around the other and watched him imperturbably. The porter, as he passed, lingered with vague proffers of help, probably inspired by philanthropic passengers swelling with the sense that "something ought to be done"; and one nervous man in a skull cap was audibly concerned as to the possible effect on his wife's health.

The hours dragged on in a dreary inoccupation. Towards dusk she sat down beside him and he laid his hand on hers. The touch startled her. He seemed to be calling her from far off. She looked at him helplessly and his smile went through her like a physical pang.

"Are you very tired?" she asked.

"No, not very."

"We'll be there soon now."

"Yes, very soon."

"This time tomorrow—"

He nodded and they sat silent. When she had put him to bed and crawled into her own berth she tried to cheer herself with the thought that in less than twenty-four hours they would be in New York. Her people would all be at the station to meet her—she pictured their round unanxious faces pressing through the crowd. She only hoped they would not tell him too loudly that he was looking splendidly and would be all right in no time: the subtler sympathies developed by long contact with suffering were making her aware of a certain coarseness of texture in the family sensibilities.

Suddenly she thought she heard him call. She parted the curtains and listened. No, it was only a man snoring at the other end of the car. His snores had a greasy sound, as though they passed through tallow. She lay down and tried to sleep. . . . Had she not heard him move? She started up trembling. . . . The silence frightened her more than any sound. He might not be able to make her hear—he might be calling her now. . . . What made her think of such things? It was merely the familiar tendency of an overtired mind to fasten itself on the most intolerable chance within the range of its forebodings. . . . Putting her head out, she listened: but she could not distinguish his breathing from that of the other pairs of lungs about her. She longed to get up and look at him, but she knew the impulse was a mere vent for her restlessness, and the fear of disturbing him restrained her. . . . The regular movement of his curtain reassured her, she knew not why; she remembered that he had wished her a cheerful good night; and the sheer inability to endure her fears a moment longer made her put them from her with an effort of her whole sound-tired body. She turned on her side and slept.

She sat up stiffly, staring out at the dawn. The train was rushing through a region of bare hillocks huddled against a lifeless sky. It looked like the first day of creation. The air of the car was close, and she pushed up her window to let in the keen wind. Then she looked at her watch: it was seven o'clock, and soon the people about her would be stirring. She slipped into her clothes, smoothed her disheveled hair and crept to the dressing room. When she had washed her face and adjusted her dress she felt more hopeful. It was always a struggle for her not to be cheerful in the morning. Her cheeks burned deliciously under the coarse towel and the wet hair about her temples broke into strong upward tendrils. Every inch of her was full of life and elasticity. And in ten hours they would be at home!

She stepped to her husband's berth: it was time for him to take his early glass of milk. The window shade was down, and in the dusk of the curtained enclosure she could just see that he lay sideways, with his face away from her. She leaned over him and drew up the shade. As she did so she touched one of his hands. It felt cold. . . .

She bent closer, laying her hand on his arm and calling him by name. He did not move. She spoke again more loudly; she grasped his shoulder and gently shook it. He lay motionless. She caught hold of his hand again: it slipped from her limply, like a dead thing. A dead thing?

Her breath caught. She must see his face. She leaned forward, and hurriedly, shrinkingly, with a sickening reluctance of the flesh, laid her hands on his shoulders and turned him over. His head fell back; his face looked small and smooth; he gazed at her with steady eyes.

She remained motionless for a long time, holding him thus; and they looked at each other. Suddenly she shrank back: the longing to scream, to call out, to fly from him, had almost overpowered her. But a strong hand arrested her. Good God! If it were known that he was dead they would be put off the train at the next station—

In a terrifying flash of remembrance there arose before her a scene she had once witnessed in traveling, when a husband and wife, whose child had died in the train, had been thrust out at some chance station. She saw them standing on the platform with the child's body between them; she had never forgotten the dazed look with which they followed the receding train. And this was what would happen to her. Within the next hour she might find herself on the platform of some strange station, alone with her husband's body. . . . Anything but that! It was too horrible— She quivered like a creature at bay.

As she cowered there, she felt the train moving more slowly. It was coming then—they were approaching a station! She saw again the husband and wife standing on the lonely platform; and with a violent gesture she drew down the shade to hide her husband's face.

Feeling dizzy, she sank down on the edge of the berth, keeping away from his outstretched body, and pulling the curtains close, so that he and she were shut into a kind of sepulchral twilight. She tried to think. At all costs she must conceal the fact that he was dead. But how? Her mind refused to act: she could not plan, combine. She could think of no way but to sit there, clutching the curtains, all day long. . . .

She heard the porter making up her bed; people were beginning to move about the car; the dressing-room door was being opened and shut. She tried to rouse herself. At length with a supreme effort she rose to her feet, stepping into the aisle of the car and drawing the curtains tight behind her. She noticed that they still parted slightly with the motion of the car, and finding a pin in her dress she fastened them together. Now she was safe. She looked round and saw the porter. She fancied he was watching her.

"Ain't he awake yet?" he inquired.

"No," she faltered.

"I got his milk all ready when he wants it. You know you told me to have it for him by seven."

She nodded silently and crept into her seat.

At half-past eight the train reached Buffalo. By this time the other passengers were dressed and the berths had been folded back for the day. The porter, moving to and fro under his burden of sheets and pillows, glanced at her as he passed. At length he said: "Ain't he going to get up? You know we're ordered to make up the berths as early as we can."

She turned cold with fear. They were just entering the station.

"Oh, not yet," she stammered. "Not till he's had his milk. Won't you get it, please?"

"All right. Soon as we start again."

When the train moved on he reappeared with the milk. She took it from him and sat vaguely looking at it: her brain moved slowly from one idea to another, as though they were stepping-stones set far apart across a whirling flood. At length she became aware that the porter still hovered expectantly.

"Will I give it to him?" he suggested.

"Oh, no," she cried, rising. "He—he's asleep yet, I think—"

She waited till the porter had passed on; then she unpinned the curtains and slipped behind them. In the semiobscurity her husband's face stared up at her like a marble mask with agate eyes. The eyes were dreadful. She put out her hand and drew down the lids. Then she remembered the glass of milk in her other hand: what was she to do with it? She thought of raising the window and throwing it out; but to do so she would have to lean across his body and bring her face close to his. She decided to drink the milk.

She returned to her seat with the empty glass and after a while the porter came back to get it.

"When'll I fold up his bed?" he asked.

"Oh, not now—not yet; he's ill—he's very ill. Can't you let him stay as he is? The doctor wants him to lie down as much as possible."

He scratched his head. "Well, if he's *really* sick—"

He took the empty glass and walked away, explaining to the passengers that the party behind the curtains was too sick to get up just yet.

She found herself the center of sympathetic eyes. A motherly woman with an intimate smile sat down beside her.

"I'm real sorry to hear your husband's sick. I've had a remarkable amount of sickness in my family and maybe I could assist you. Can I take a look at him?"

"Oh, no—no, please! He mustn't be disturbed."

The lady accepted the rebuff indulgently.

"Well, it's just as you say, of course, but you don't look to me as if you'd had much experience in sickness and I'd have been glad to assist you. What do you generally do when your husband's taken this way?"

"I—I let him sleep."

"Too much sleep ain't any too healthful either. Don't you give him any medicine?"

"Y—yes."

"Don't you wake him to take it?"

"Yes."

"When does he take the next dose?"

"Not for—two hours—"

The lady looked disappointed. "Well, if I was you I'd try giving it oftener. That's what I do with my folks."

After that many faces seemed to press upon her. The passengers were on their way to the dining car, and she was conscious that as they passed down the aisle they glanced curiously at the closed curtains. One lantern-jawed man with prominent eyes stood still and tried to shoot his projecting glance through the division between the folds. The freckled child, returning from breakfast, waylaid the passers with a buttery clutch, saying in a loud whisper, "He's sick"; and once the conductor came by, asking for tickets. She shrank into her corner and looked out of the window at the flying trees and houses, meaningless hieroglyphs of an endlessly unrolled papyrus.

Now and then the train stopped, and the newcomers on entering the car stared in turn at the closed curtains. More and more people seemed to pass—their faces began to blend fantastically with the images surging in her brain. . . .

Later in the day a fat man detached himself from the mist of faces. He had a creased stomach and soft pale lips. As he pressed himself into the seat facing her she noticed that he was dressed in black broadcloth, with a soiled white tie.

"Husband's pretty bad this morning, is he?"

"Yes."

"Dear, dear! Now that's terribly distressing, ain't it?" An apostolic smile revealed his gold-filled teeth. "Of course you know there's no sech thing as sickness. Ain't that a lovely thought? Death itself is but a deloosion of our grosser senses. On'y lay yourself open to the influx of the sperrit, submit yourself passively to the action of the divine force, and disease and dissolution will cease to exist for you. If you could indooce your husband to read this little pamphlet—"

The faces about her again grew indistinct. She had a vague recollection of hearing the motherly lady and the parent of the freckled child ardently disputing the relative advantages of trying several medicines at once, or of taking each in turn; the motherly lady maintaining that the competitive system saved time; the other objecting that you couldn't tell which remedy had effected the cure; their voices went on and on, like bell buoys droning through a fog. . . . The porter came up now and then with questions that she did not understand, but somehow she must have answered since he went away again without repeating them; every two hours the motherly lady reminded her that her husband ought to have his drops; people left the car and others replaced them. . . .

Her head was spinning and she tried to steady herself by clutching at her thoughts as they swept by, but they slipped away from her like bushes on the side of a sheer precipice down which she seemed to be falling. Suddenly her mind grew clear again and she found herself vividly picturing what would happen when the train reached New York. She shuddered as it occurred to her that he would be quite cold and that someone might perceive he had been dead since morning.

She thought hurriedly: "If they see I am not surprised they will suspect something. They will ask questions, and if I tell them the truth they won't believe me—no one would believe me! It will be terrible"—and she kept repeating to herself—"I must pretend I don't know. I must pretend I don't know. When they open the curtains I must go up to him quite naturally—and then I must scream!" She had an idea that the scream would be very hard to do.

Gradually new thoughts crowded upon her, vivid and urgent: she tried to separate and restrain them, but they beset her clamorously, like her school children at the end of a hot day, when she was too tired to silence them. Her head grew confused, and she felt a sick fear of forgetting her part, of betraying herself by some unguarded word or look.

"I must pretend I don't know," she went on murmuring. The words had lost their significance, but she repeated them mechanically, as though they had been a magic formula, until suddenly she heard herself saying: "I can't remember, I can't remember!"

Her voice sounded very loud, and she looked about her in terror; but no one seemed to notice that she had spoken.

As she glanced down the car her eye caught the curtains of her husband's berth, and she began to examine the monotonous arabesques woven through their heavy folds. The pattern was intricate and difficult to trace; she gazed fixedly at the curtains and as she did so the thick stuff grew transparent and through it she saw her husband's face—his dead face. She struggled to avert her look, but her eyes refused to move and her head seemed to be held in a vice. At last, with an effort that left her weak and shaking, she turned away; but it was of no use; close in front of her, small and smooth, was her husband's face. It seemed to be suspended in the air between her and the false braids of the woman who sat in front of her. With an uncontrollable gesture she stretched out her hand to push the face away, and suddenly she felt the touch of his smooth skin. She repressed a cry and half started from her seat. The woman with the false braids looked around, and feeling that she must justify her movement in some way she rose and lifted her traveling bag from the opposite seat. She unlocked the bag and looked into it; but the first object her hand met was a small flask of her husband's, thrust there at the last moment, in the haste of departure. She locked the bag and closed her eyes . . . his face was there again, hanging between her eyeballs and lids like a waxen mask against a red curtain. . . .

She roused herself with a shiver. Had she fainted or slept? Hours seemed to have elapsed; but it was still broad day, and the people about her were sitting in the same attitudes as before.

A sudden sense of hunger made her aware that she had eaten nothing since morning. The thought of food filled her with disgust, but she dreaded a return of faintness, and remembering that she had some biscuits in her bag she took one out and ate it. The dry crumbs choked her, and she hastily swallowed a little brandy from her husband's flask. The burning sensation in her throat acted as a counter-irritant, momentarily relieving the dull ache of her nerves. Then she felt a gently-stealing warmth, as though a soft air fanned her, and the swarming fears relaxed their clutch, receding through the stillness that enclosed her, a stillness soothing as the spacious quietude of a summer day. She slept.

Through her sleep she felt the impetuous rush of the train. It seemed to be life itself that was sweeping her on with headlong inexorable force—sweeping her into darkness and terror, and the awe of unknown days.—Now all at once everything was still—not a sound, not a pulsation. . . . She was dead in her turn, and lay beside him with smooth upstaring face. How quiet it was!—and yet she heard feet coming, the feet of the men who were to carry them away. . . . She could feel too—she felt a sudden prolonged vibration, a series of hard shocks, and then another plunge into darkness: the darkness of death this time—a black whirlwind on which they were both spinning like leaves, in wild uncoiling spirals, with millions and millions of the dead. . . .

She sprang up in terror. Her sleep must have lasted a long time, for the winter day had paled and the lights had been lit. The car was in confusion, and as she regained her self-possession she saw that the passengers were gathering up their wraps and bags. The woman with the false braids had brought from the dressing room a sickly ivy plant in a bottle, and the Christian Scientist was reversing his cuffs. The porter passed down the aisle with his impartial brush. An impersonal figure with a gold-banded cap asked for her husband's ticket. A voice shouted "Baiggage *ex*press!" and she heard the clicking of metal as the passengers handed over their checks.

Presently her window was blocked by an expanse of sooty wall, and the train passed into the Harlem tunnel. The journey was over; in a few minutes she would see her family pushing their joyous way through the throng at the station. Her heart dilated. The worst terror was past. . . .

"We'd better get him up now, hadn't we?" asked the porter, touching her arm.

He had her husband's hat in his hand and was meditatively revolving it under his brush.

She looked at the hat and tried to speak; but suddenly the car grew dark. She flung up her arms, struggling to catch at something, and fell face downward, striking her head against the dead man's berth. ☐ ☐

Discussion

1. **(a)** How much time actually elapses in the story? **(b)** For what reasons does the time seem longer to the woman? To the reader?

2. The story contains very little action. What then is most of the narrative given to? How is this "realistic"?

3. **(a)** What is the woman's greatest fear throughout the story? Why? **(b)** What is her greatest wish? Why? **(c)** Does this attitude seem callous to you? **(d)** Is it psychologically believable?

4. **(a)** Having kept her composure throughout the entire journey, why does the woman finally collapse? **(b)** What actions of the porter set off her collapse? Why?

5. Explain some of the characteristics of **realism** that are present in the story.

Extension • Speaking

Wharton was one of the first women to receive acclaim as well as success as a writer. Discuss in class why it took so long for women to receive recognition as novelists and poets. What factors might have contributed to this situation? What social realities made Wharton's success possible while hindering the aspirations of other women who wrote? How has the status of the woman writer changed in the last hundred years? How has it not changed?

**Vocabulary • Dictionary

Wharton tells the reader that her husband is going to die, but people "dressed the truth in hopeful euphemisms" (370 a, 22). Use your Glossary to find the definition of *euphemism*.

Each of the following sentences contains one or more euphemistic words or phrases. On your paper rewrite each sentence so that it says in a direct, literal way what has been expressed euphemistically.

1. The protective deterrence strike by the bombers proved to be remarkably effective.

2. Refusal to agree with the correct opinions could mean detention in a physical persuasion center.

3. The mayor announced that the one responsible for the all-night power blackout had been convinced that the position of chief engineer was no longer suitable for his talents and interests.

Edith Wharton 1862 • 1937

Edith Newbold Jones was born into a New York family of wealth and distinction. She was educated by private tutors and spent much of her youth traveling between New York and Europe. In 1885 she married Edward Wharton, a wealthy banker.

Although her first writings were poems, she published her first book of fiction, *The Greater Inclination*, in 1899. These stories, among them "A Journey," foreshadowed the psychological realism and the **themes** of her later novels: *The House of Mirth* (1905), *Ethan Frome* (1911), and her greatest novel *The Age of Innocence* (1920), which received the Pulitzer Prize.

With deft satire, Wharton examined the society of middle-class and aristocratic New York, where an individual's worth was measured by genteel manners. Her tragic figures are victims of social pressure and convention.

While she criticized the foibles of her society, she bitterly resisted the values and manners of the new century. Wharton's last years were spent in Paris.

notes and comments

Psychological Realism

Where Stephen Crane wished to depict the individual pitted against indifferent nature, Wharton preferred to represent the equally desperate inner conflicts of a woman in a personally tragic, yet not unusual, situation. Wharton wrote that "The art of rendering life in fiction can never, in the last analysis, be anything . . . but the disengaging of crucial moments from the welter of experience." A crucial moment occurs when individual desire comes in conflict with a basic moral standard of society. This theme, found in "A Journey," is paralleled in *The House of Mirth,* which is a more fully drawn portrait of a lovely young woman trapped between her own principles and the demands of society.

Thus, the **realist** writers' usual subject matter is the minor catastrophes of the middle class, and their themes tend to focus on people's manners and customs. Wharton strove through her works to imitate the plotless actualities of real life. At realism's most developed stage, as in Wharton's work, the writer explores the psychology of the individual. Such intense study of a **protagonist's** innermost thoughts, anxieties, and dilemmas became a characteristic of twentieth-century fiction.

Unit Review Tests 5: Variations and Departures

CONTENT REVIEW

1. **(a)** Compare the different ways in which the stories by Bierce, Crane, and Wharton explore a "crucial moment" in each protagonist's life. **(b)** Give examples from these stories of philosophical similarities and differences between **realism** and **naturalism**.

2. Discuss how their experience as reporters is reflected in the writing of Whitman, Clemens, Bierce, and Crane.

3. **(a)** Compare the portraits of small-town life presented by Clemens and Freeman. **(b)** What new attitudes toward rural America are expressed by Masters and Du Bois? Are their views less or more critical than those of Clemens and Freeman? Explain.

4. Compare the views of nature held by Lanier, Whitman, Satanta, and Dickinson. Which authors' views reflect Transcendentalist beliefs? How? Whose attitude resembles modern environmentalist thinking? Explain.

5. Two great themes of this period were democracy and "rugged individualism." Discuss how each theme is reflected in various selections in this unit.

Unit 5, Test I
INTERPRETATION: NEW MATERIAL

One of the following poems was written by Emily Dickinson, and one by Walt Whitman. Read them and on your paper answer the questions about each.

She Rose to His Requirement
Emily Dickinson

She rose to his requirement, dropped
The playthings of her life
To take the honorable work
Of woman and of wife.

5 If aught she missed in her new day
Of amplitude, or awe,
Or first prospective, or the gold
In using wore away,

It lay unmentioned, as the sea
10 Develops pearl and weed,
But only to himself is known
The fathoms they abide.

Emily Dickinson. POEMS (1890–1896) edited by H. R. Warfel. (Gainesville, Florida: Scholars' Facsimilies and Reprints), 1967.

1. *Road-blood* forms an example of a slant rhyme. The pair of words in the poem that form a slant rhyme are **(a)** *life-wife;* **(b)** *sea-known;* **(c)** *weed-abide;* **(d)** none appears in this poem.

2. The rhyme scheme in stanza 1 is **(a)** a-b-c-b; **(b)** a-b-a-b; **(c)** a-b-c-d; **(d)** a-b-a-c.

3. In line 1, to whom does "his" refer? The woman's **(a)** father; **(b)** brother; **(c)** husband; **(d)** son.

4. In line 2, what is meant by her "playthings"? **(a)** immature personality characteristics; **(b)** toys; **(c)** flirtatious behavior; **(d)** personal interests.

5. In the first stanza the attitude of the poet toward the woman's new life is **(a)** pitying; **(b)** respectful; **(c)** mocking; **(d)** joyous.

6. In lines 7–8, the gold is an example of **(a)** a simile; **(b)** personification; **(c)** a symbol; **(d)** onomatopoeia.

7. The best paraphrase of the second stanza is **(a)** if she has an overwhelming respect for the talents of her husband; **(b)** if she has worked so hard at being a good wife that her beauty quickly faded; **(c)** if the opportunity to develop her talents and to follow her interests has been lost; **(d)** if she has been continually depressed at the humdrum quality of her marriage.

8. Assonance is demonstrated by which pair of words? **(a)** *amplitude-awe;* **(b)** *woman-wife;* **(c)** *new-day;* **(d)** *or-or.*

9. In line 9, "It" refers to **(a)** her regret for her unfulfilled potential; **(b)** her joy at married life; **(c)** her desire to escape marriage; **(d)** her depression.

10. Lines 9–10 contain **(a)** a metaphor; **(b)** a simile; **(c)** personification; **(d)** hyperbole.

11. In line 10 the "pearl and weed" literally refer to **(a)** the stifling marriage; **(b)** her hidden talents; **(c)** her growing insensitivity; **(d)** her religious conversion.

12. The best paraphrase of the third stanza is **(a)** her husband has used his superior position to stifle her interests and talents; **(b)** she is in the depths of a depression so serious that only her husband can help her; **(c)** she has pursued her interests and therefore destroyed her marriage; **(d)** though she has never been able to pursue her interests, her husband is aware of her undeveloped abilities.

Tom Stack/Tom Stack and Associates.

A Noiseless Patient Spider
Walt Whitman

A noiseless patient spider,
I mark'd where on a little promontory[1] it stood isolated,
Mark'd how to explore the vacant vast surrounding,
It launch'd forth filament,[2] filament, filament, out of itself,
5 Ever unreeling them, ever tirelessly speeding them.

And you O my soul where you stand,
Surrounded, detached, in measureless oceans of space,
Ceaselessly musing, venturing, throwing, seeking the spheres to
    connect them,
Till the bridge you will need be form'd, till the ductile[3]
    anchor hold,
10 Till the gossamer[4] thread you fling catch somewhere, O my soul.

1. *promontory* (prom′ən tôr′ē), a peninsula.

2. *filament* (fil′ə mənt) , a thin thread.

3. *ductile* (duk′təl), easily stretched.

4. *gossamer* (gos′ə mər), filmy, like a cobweb.

13. The phrase "vacant vast surrounding" in line 3 contains an example of **(a)** metaphor; **(b)** onomatopoeia; **(c)** allusion; **(d)** alliteration.

14. The effect of the repetition of "filament" is to **(a)** emphasize the symbolic qualities of the spider's thread; **(b)** create the impression of a never ending stream of thread; **(c)** create the impression that all has come to a stop; **(d)** create a light-hearted mood.

15. According to the poet, why is the spider spinning the web? **(a)** to connect itself with and explore its surroundings; **(b)** because nature has required that it must do this; **(c)** to catch insects and stay alive; **(d)** to create a thing of beauty.

16. In the second stanza the soul is **(a)** claustrophobic from being closely surrounded by other souls; **(b)** content; **(c)** surrounded by reflections of itself; **(d)** isolated from everyone around it.

17. In the second stanza the soul is compared to **(a)** a plan-et; **(b)** space; **(c)** the ocean; **(d)** a bridge.

18. What phrase contains an example of an apostrophe? **(a)** "A noiseless patient spider"; **(b)** "measureless oceans of space"; **(c)** "O my soul"; **(d)** "till the ductile anchor hold."

19. In line 9, the "bridge" and the "ductile anchor" represent the desire of the soul to **(a)** reach out to other people; **(b)** build and progress; **(c)** ramble on; **(d)** dominate other people.

20. Whitman's theme in this poem is that **(a)** life is meaningless, so live for today; **(b)** no one has ever really wanted to die; **(c)** though people are physically isolated, their souls can reach out toward each other; **(d)** spiders are valuable creatures in the chain of life.

Choose one of the following topics for a composition. Assume you are writing for your class unless the assignment indicates another audience.

1. Suppose that you are putting together a collection of poems by Walt Whitman and Emily Dickinson. Write a preface for that collection that will prepare the reader for the radical differences in subject matter, theme, style, and tone between the poems of these writers. Refer to specific poems and lines to support your ideas.

2. Edith Wharton, Ambrose Bierce, and Stephen Crane were all skillful at creating mood. Reread the following passages:

(a) "A Journey": 374a, 2, to 374b, 1;

(b) "An Occurrence at Owl Creek Bridge": 346b, 9;

(c) "An Episode of War": the first five paragraphs.

Chose two of the passages and compare and contrast their dominant moods. Refer to those words, images, details, and actions that help to create the moods.

3. Miniver Cheevy, Richard Cory, Richard Bone, and Mrs. Charles Bliss all have pessimistic or cynical views of life, which they feel are justified by their experiences. Choose one of these characters and write a letter to him or her, explaining whether you agree or disagree with that person's attitudes and actions, and giving reasons for your opinion.

4. "A Journey" describes the courage of a woman who must keep her wits about her in spite of the tremendous pressure she feels from knowing she will be thrown off the train if her husband's corpse is discovered.

Write an account of a true experience in which a person courageously resisted the pressures and ideas of the majority. You may describe an experience undergone by yourself, someone you know, or a well-known figure. In your conclusion, explain whether this experience was like or unlike that of the woman in "A Journey."

1915   **1920**   **1925**   **19**

- Amy Lowell: *Men, Women, and Ghosts*
- Sandburg: *Chicago Poems*
- Frost: *Mountain Interval*
- Susan Glaspell: *Trifles*
- Angelina Grimké: *Rachel*
  - Eliot: *Prufrock and Other Observations*
  - Puerto Ricans made U.S. citizens
  - U.S. enters World War I

Cather: *My Ántonia* ●

Sherwood Anderson: *Winesburg, Ohio* ●

Prohibition begins ●

Sinclair Lewis: *Main Street* ●

Women get the vote ●

League of Nations formed without U.S. support ●

- Louis Armstrong's first records ●
- Transcontinental air mail
- First radio programs
  - Eugene O'Neill: *The Emperor Jones*
    - Eliot: *The Waste Land*

Fitzgerald: *Tales of the Jazz Age* ●

Toomer: *Cane* ●

Cummings: *Tulips and Chimneys* ●

Millay: *The Harp-Weaver* ●

● Elmer Rice: *The Adding Machine*

Jeffers: *Tamar* ●

Immigration restricted ●

The New Yorker founded ●

- Fitzgerald: *The Great Gatsby*
  - Hughes: *The Weary Blues*
  - Hemingway: *The Sun Also Rises*
  - Pound: *Personae*

Lindbergh's solo transatlantic flight ●

- Johnson: *God's Trombones*
- Cather: *Death Comes for the Archbishop*

Faulkner: *The Sound and the Fury* ●

First American Nobel Prize, to Sinclair Lew

Imagist poetry movement   Magazine fiction flourishes   "The Jazz Age"   "Talking" movies

Harlem Renaissance

The Modern Temper 1915 to 1945

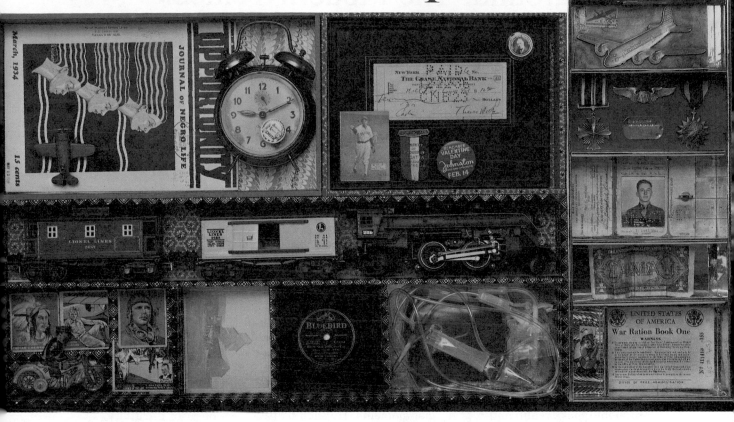

1935	1940	1945

O'Neill: *Mourning Becomes Electra* • Dos Passos: *U.S.A.* • Margaret Walker: *For My People*

• Teasdale: *Strange Victory* • Thornton Wilder: *Our Town*

• Prohibition ends • Lillian Hellman: *The Little Foxes*

• Hughes: *The Ways of White Folks* • Saroyan: *The Time of Your Life*

• Fitzgerald: *Tender is the Night* • Porter: *Pale Horse, Pale Rider*

Stevens: *Ideas of Order* • • Steinbeck: *The Grapes of Wrath*

Southern Review founded • Parker: *Here Lies* • Porter: *The Leaning Tower* •

Moore: *Selected Poems* • World War II begins •

Hughes: *Little Ham* • Hemingway: *For Whom the Bell Tolls* • Wright: *Black Boy* •

Clifford Odets: *Waiting for Lefty* • Wright: *Native Son* •

Eliot: *Murder in the Cathedral* • Dr. Charles Drew pioneers blood banking

Frost: *A Further Range* • Welty: *A Curtain of Green* •

Sandburg: *The People, Yes* • Atom bomb dropped •

Steinbeck: *Of Mice and Men* • Pearl Harbor attack: U.S. enters war •

Rodgers and Hammerstein: *Oklahoma!* •

The Great Depression   New Deal era   Wartime prosperity

Fascism spreads in Europe and Japan

Background: The Modern Temper 1915–1945

The period from 1915 to 1945 was one of the most eventful, colorful, exhilarating, tragic, prosperous, and poverty-stricken phases of the American experience. It was all these paradoxes because it was bracketed at either end by a devastating war that drastically changed people's lives. The happy-go-lucky twenties brought quick wealth and "flaming youth"—until the stock market crash of 1929. Then the Depression of the thirties brought poverty, social unrest, and despair.

The events of these decades were so dramatic, the times so strange and complex, that they might have overwhelmed artistic imagination. But the American writers of the time had the imaginative power to take on the challenge.

Seeing the cherished propriety and stability of Victorian times exploded by World War I, novelists, poets, and dramatists turned for inspiration to such earlier literary rebels as Walt Whitman, Emily Dickinson, Stephen Crane, and their European counterparts. Free verse, though still unacceptable

to most readers, became the rallying cry of young poets as diverse as Ezra Pound, Amy Lowell, and Carl Sandburg. Though popular commercial novels continued to be neatly plotted, authors like Sherwood Anderson, in his *Winesburg, Ohio* (1919), rearranged time sequences or concentrated on uneventful but emotionally crucial moments. By such techniques, novelists tried to get inside their characters' minds.

Another technique inspired by new psychological theories was stream-of-consciousness narration, which had already been used by Edith Wharton and Ambrose Bierce (Unit 5). This technique of reflecting a character's flow of thought is shown in Porter's "The Jilting of Granny Weatherall" (page 395).

In these decades, the audience for serious literature was expanded through vigorous effort. Poets like Carl Sandburg, Vachel Lindsay, and Robert Frost gave public readings which won many new readers. Prosperous magazines paid premium fees for short stories and serial novels and made stars

out of many writers, including F. Scott Fitzgerald. At the same time, the "little" movement, a rebellion against "big" publishing and Victorian conventionality, gave birth to dozens of "little magazines" like *Poetry* (1912), *The Fugitive* (1922), and *Opportunity* (1923). The many outlets for new talent and new ideas precipitated a burst of creativity.

Fitzgerald achieved celebrity with his first novel, *This Side of Paradise* (1920), whose protagonist lamented that he had "grown up to find all gods dead, all wars fought, all faiths in man shaken." The titles of Fitzgerald's collections of stories—*Flappers and Philosophers* (1920); *Tales of the Jazz Age* (1922)—suggest why he was regarded as the spokesman for reckless "flaming youth." In fact, his masterpiece, *The Great Gatsby* (1925), about the lure and corruption of great wealth, is now read as a good introduction to the mood that permeated the twenties.

Like so many American writers of the twenties, Fitzgerald went to Paris. There he met Ernest Hemingway, read in

Katherine Anne Porter

Ernest Hemingway

F. Scott Fitzgerald

manuscript Hemingway's *The Sun Also Rises*, and recommended it to his own publisher. Its publication in 1926 created a sensation. It portrayed a "lost generation" of Americans, wounded spiritually and physically by the war, wandering aimlessly around Europe seeking both the pleasures of the moment and meaning for their lives. The style—terse, direct, concealing much more emotion than it explicitly revealed— seemed exactly right for a war-weary, cynical generation. Hemingway's later works, such as *A Farewell to Arms* (1929), made him the most admired and imitated American novelist around the world.

Jean Toomer's *Cane* (1923) was one of the most radical literary experiments of the time. To explore varieties of black experience, Toomer wove together stories, poems, and dramatic sketches. These parts were unified by parallels between characters symbolizing various facets of the Southern black woman, and of the sophisticated black man of the Northern cities, who yearned to renew his identity with a vanishing rural past.

Like Toomer, William Faulkner was concerned with the effects of modern ways on the identity and traditions of Southerners, both black and white. To develop this theme, he chronicled his mythical county of Yoknapatawpha,

Mississippi, in many related novels, beginning with *The Sound and the Fury* (1929). His style contrasted sharply with the understated tautness of Hemingway's prose or with Toomer's clear, lyrical style. Faulkner conveyed the stream of consciousness of his characters through dense, complex, but poetic passages.

Other Southern writers who became prominent in the 1930s were Katherine Anne Porter, Eudora Welty, and Richard Wright. Although her later allegorical novel, *Ship of Fools* (1962), was highly successful, Porter's reputation rests mainly on her earlier short stories which, like "The Jilting of Granny Weatherall," are noted for psychological depth and technical complexity. Welty, who began publishing late in this period, set her work in her Mississippi birthplace. But she transcended the limits of local color fiction to portray the inward solitude of individuals and the power of love to unite them in human community.

Richard Wright's "The Man Who Saw the Flood" fuses Southern writing, black writing, and the social protest fiction of the 1930s. In *Native Son,* a naturalistic novel partly based on a murder case of 1938, Wright analyzed the dehumanizing forces of urban slums. Wright's masterwork is generally considered to be his autobiography, *Black Boy* (1945), which portrayed his own successful struggle to escape dehumanization.

The proletarian sympathies of many American writers in the 1930s are also reflected in

Dorothy Parker's "Soldiers of the Republic." Although Parker is perhaps better known as one of the witty social satirists of the Roaring Twenties, she was serious in describing Spain's citizen-soldiers defending their Republican government in a

Amy Lowell

Ezra Pound

Robert Frost

Langston Hughes

losing civil war against fascist rebels.

Perhaps the foremost protest novel of the Depression was John Steinbeck's *The Grapes of Wrath* (1939). It traced in accurate, moving detail the desperate exodus of an Oklahoma family from their ancestral farm, ruined by dust storms, to the migrant-worker camps of California, where they struggled to hold on to their family ties and self-respect.

In vigor and variety, the poetry of these decades was equal to the fiction. There was an underlying contrast, sometimes sparked into heated debate, between poets who, in general, regarded poetry as a pure art form, akin to painting or music, and poets who tended to emphasize poetry as a medium for social comment.

Ezra Pound was one of the founders of Imagism, a doctrine which stressed the precision and emotional impact of carefully selected images. (Imagism and its influence are more fully discussed on pages 442–443). Amy Lowell's "Patterns" (1915) is a striking example of Imagist poetry in its visual vividness, in its use of imagery to reveal rather than to describe feelings, and in its controlled understatement of emotion.

The poems by Sandburg and Hughes which follow "Patterns" are, in contrast, full of explicit social comment.

Whereas in "Patterns" and "The River-Merchant's Wife," the feelings expressed are those of an imaginary person, in "Chicago" and "Theme for English B," the poets are directly communicating their own emotions or ideas.

"Poetry," by Moore, to some extent supported the direct approach to poetic communication taken by Sandburg and Hughes, while "Ars Poetica," by MacLeish, summarized the principles of the Imagists and their successors.

Both the directness and the imagistic subtlety of modernist poetry are embraced in the poetry of Robert Frost. Frost had to go to England to get American recognition. It was there that Pound discovered and helped him get his first books published. In a career spanning seven decades, Frost gave voice to both the optimism and pessimism which were mingled in the modern temper.

Four highly gifted lyrical poets of this period were Cullen, Millay, Wylie, and Teasdale. Their works, like Frost's, often demonstrate the vitality of traditional forms in dealing with modern concepts of human relationships and the psychology of the inner being.

The psychological concerns of modern poets and novelists are strikingly amplified in T. S. Eliot's "The Love Song of J. Alfred Prufrock." Ezra Pound, as foreign editor of *Poetry* magazine, arranged for Eliot the publication of "Prufrock" in 1915. Pound also edited the manuscript of Eliot's "The Waste Land" (1922), a poem which influenced the themes and techniques of two generations of poets, and which to many critics remains a central statement of the social climate of the century. To other interpreters, the obsessive self-consciousness, world-weary sophistication, and complexities of irony in Eliot's verse are only one variety of modernism; but his work does represent the fullest development of the intellectual, socially detached poetry advocated by Pound.

By the 1930s, the experiments of the Imagists, the jazz poetry of Langston Hughes, the rolling, swinging rhythms of Carl Sandburg no longer seemed radical. Such trends were becoming a new tradition. Although Imagism had faded as a movement, its influence remained strong in the works of Wallace Stevens, Jean Toomer, Marianne Moore, and William Carlos Williams. Stevens wrote poems full of comic word play, but dealing seriously with the nature of imagination and reality. His works employed clear, simple images, but the complex meaning implied in these im-

ages emerges only with repeated, thoughtful reading.

Moore's work generally exemplified the precision and concreteness of imagery that she advocated in "Poetry" (page 440). Like Moore, Williams in "Spring and All" did not discuss ideas, but used imagery to shape a mood. His poetic rule was "no ideas but in things."

E. E. Cummings discovered even richer possibilities for free verse by discarding conventional punctuation and syntax, and by scattering lines in visual patterns to mirror his rhythms and images. Many of his poems also reflect the satirical mood that pervaded much poetry of the 1930s.

By then, many poets were preoccupied by the social ills of the Depression and the rise of fascism. Light verse mocking the excesses of modern social and psychological theories became very popular among magazine readers. Dorothy Parker, Ogden Nash, and Phyllis McGinley were especially cele-

brated for their puncturing of overblown fads and foibles.

The grimmer social concerns of many writers during the Depression often were voiced in the poems of Bontemps, McKay, Walker, and Jeffers. Unlike social poetry of the nineteenth century, these works attacked injustice not with rhetoric, but with concrete images symbolizing social maladies. Jeffers, a recluse in California, was concerned not so much with social decline as with a sense of cosmic decay, inspired by scientific theories about the ultimate death of the universe from heat loss.

T. S. Eliot, looking back in 1953, remarked: "In the nineteenth century, Poe and Whitman stand out as solitary international figures: in the last forty years, for the first time, there has been assembled a *body* of American poetry which has made its total impression in England and Europe." The same could be said of American fiction and drama in these decades, during which the world recognized that American literature had blossomed into full maturity.

Margaret Walker

Carl Sandburg

Sherwood Anderson

Brother Death

There were the two oak stumps, knee high to a not-too-tall man and cut quite squarely across. They became to the two children objects of wonder. They had seen the two trees cut but had run away just as the trees fell. They hadn't thought of the two stumps, to be left standing there; hadn't even looked at them. Afterwards Ted said to his sister Mary, speaking of the stumps: "I wonder if they bled, like legs, when a surgeon cuts a man's leg off." He had been hearing war stories. A man came to the farm one day to visit one of the farm-hands, a man who had been in the World War[1] and lost an arm. He stood in one of the barns talking. When Ted said that, Mary spoke up at once. She hadn't been lucky enough to be at the barn when the one-armed man was there talking, and was jealous. "Why not a woman or a girl's leg?" she said, but Ted said the idea was silly. "Women and girls don't get their legs and arms cut off," he declared. "Why not? I'd just like to know why not?" Mary kept saying.

It would have been something if they had stayed, that day the trees were cut. "We might have gone and touched the places," Ted said. He meant the stumps. Would they have been warm? Would they have bled? They did go and touch the places afterwards, but it was a cold day and the stumps were cold. Ted stuck to his point that only men's arms and legs were cut off, but Mary thought of automobile accidents. "You can't think just of wars. There might be an automobile accident," she declared, but Ted wouldn't be convinced.

They were both children, but something had made them both in an odd way old. Mary was fourteen and Ted eleven, but Ted wasn't strong and that rather evened things up. They were the children of a well-to-do Virginia farmer named John Grey in the Blue Ridge country in South-western Virginia. There was a wide valley called the "Rich Valley" with a railroad and a small river running through it and high mountains in sight, to the north and south. Ted had some kind of a heart disease, a lesion, something of the sort, the result of a severe attack of diphtheria when he was a child of eight. He was thin and not strong but curiously alive. The doctor said he might die at any moment, might just drop down dead. The fact had drawn him peculiarly close to his sister Mary. It had awakened a strong and determined maternalism in her.

The whole family, the neighbors on neighboring farms in the valley, and even the other children at the schoolhouse where they went to school recognized something as existing between the two children. "Look at them going along there," people said. "They do seem to have good times together, but they are so serious. For such young children they are too serious. Still, I suppose, under the circumstances, it's natural." Of course, everyone knew about Ted. It had done something to Mary. At fourteen she was both a child and a grown woman. The woman side of her kept popping out at unexpected moments.

She had sensed something concerning her brother Ted. It was because he was as he was, having that kind of a heart, a heart likely at any moment to stop beating, leaving him dead, cut down like a young tree. The others in the Grey family, that is to say, the older ones, the mother and father and an older brother, Don, who was eighteen now, recognized something as belonging to the two children, being, as it were, between them, but the recognition wasn't very definite.

1. *the World War,* World War I (1914–1918).

People in your own family are likely at any moment to do strange, sometimes hurtful things to you. You have to watch them. Ted and Mary had both found that out.

The brother Don was like the father, already at eighteen almost a grown man. He was that sort, the kind people speak of, saying: "He's a good man. He'll make a good solid dependable man." The father, when he was a young man, never drank, never went chasing the girls, was never wild. There had been enough wild young ones in the Rich Valley when he was a lad. Some of them had inherited big farms and had lost them, gambling, drinking, fooling with fast horses and chasing after the women. It had been almost a Virginia tradition, but John Grey was a land man. All the Greys were. There were other large cattle farms owned by Greys up and down the valley.

John Grey, everyone said, was a natural cattle man. He knew beef cattle, of the big so-called export type, how to pick and feed them to make beef. He knew how and where to get the right kind of young stock to turn into his fields. It was the blue-grass country. Big beef cattle went directly off the pastures to market. The Grey farm contained over twelve hundred acres, most of it in blue-grass.

The father was a land man, land hungry. He had begun, as a cattle farmer, with a small place, inherited from his father, some two hundred acres, lying next to what was then the big Aspinwahl place and, after he began, he never stopped getting more land. He kept cutting in on the Aspinwahls who were a rather horsey, fast lot. They thought of themselves as Virginia aristocrats, having, as they weren't so modest about pointing out, a family going back and back, family tradition, guests always being entertained, fast horses kept, money being bet on fast horses. John Grey getting their land, now twenty acres, then thirty, then fifty, until at last he got the old Aspinwahl house, with one of the Aspinwahl girls, not a young one, not one of the best-looking ones, as wife. The Aspinwahl place was down, by that time, to less than a hundred acres, but he went on, year after year, always being careful and shrewd, making every penny count, never wasting a cent, adding and adding to what was now the Grey place. The former Aspinwahl

house was a large old brick house with fireplaces in all the rooms and was very comfortable.

People wondered why Louise Aspinwahl had married John Grey, but when they were wondering they smiled. The Aspinwahl girls were all well educated, had all been away to college, but Louise wasn't so pretty. She got nicer after marriage, suddenly almost beautiful. The Aspinwahls were, as everyone knew, naturally sensitive, really first class but the men couldn't hang onto land and the Greys could. In all that section of Virginia, people gave John Grey credit for being what he was. They respected him. "He's on the level," they said, "as honest as a horse. He has cattle sense, that's it." He could run his big hand down over the flank of a steer and say, almost to the pound, what he would weigh on the scales or he could look at a calf or a yearling and say, "He'll do," and he would do. A steer is a steer. He isn't supposed to do anything but make beef.

There was Don, the oldest son of the Grey family. He was so evidently destined to be a Grey, to be another like his father. He had long been a star in the 4H Club of the Virginia county and, even as a lad of nine and ten, had won prizes at steer judging. At twelve he had produced, no one helping him, doing all the work himself, more bushels of corn on an acre of land than any other boy in the State.

It was all a little amazing, even a bit queer to Mary Grey, being as she was a girl peculiarly conscious, so old and young, so aware. There was Don, the older brother, big and strong of body, like the father, and there was the younger brother Ted. Ordinarily, in the ordinary course of life, she being what she was—female—it would have been quite natural and right for her to have given her young girl's admiration to Don but she didn't. For some reason, Don barely existed for her. He was outside, not in it, while for her Ted, the seemingly weak one of the family, was everything.

Still there Don was, so big of body, so quiet, so apparently sure of himself. The father had begun, as a young cattle man, with the two hundred acres, and now he had the twelve hundred. What would Don Grey do when he started? Already he knew, although he didn't say anything, that he wanted to start. He wanted to run things, be his own boss. His father had offered to send him away to college, to an agricultural college, but he wouldn't go. "No. I can learn more here," he said.

Already there was a contest, always kept under the surface, between the father and son. It concerned ways of doing things, decisions to be made. As yet the son always surrendered.

It is like that in a family, little isolated groups formed within the larger group, jealousies, concealed hatreds, silent battles secretly going on— among the Greys, Mary and Ted, Don and his father, the mother and the two younger children, Gladys, a girl child of six now, who adored her brother Don, and Harry, a boy child of two.

As for Mary and Ted, they lived within their own world, but their own world had not been established without a struggle. The point was that Ted, having the heart that might at any moment stop beating, was always being treated tenderly by the others. Only Mary understood that—how it infuriated and hurt him.

"No, Ted, I wouldn't do that."

"Now, Ted, do be careful."

Sometimes Ted went white and trembling with anger, Don, the father, the mother, all keeping at him like that. It didn't matter what he wanted to do, learn to drive one of the two family cars, climb a tree to find a bird's nest, run a race with Mary. Naturally, being on a farm, he wanted to try his hand at breaking a colt, beginning with him, getting a saddle on, having it out with him. "No, Ted. You can't." He had learned to swear, picking it up from the farm-hands and from the boys at the country school. "Hell!" he said to Mary. Only Mary understood how he felt, and she had not put the matter very definitely into words, not even to herself. It was one of the things that made her old when she was so young. It made her stand aside from the others of the family, aroused in her curious determination. "They shall not." She caught herself saying the words to herself. "They shall not."

"If he is to have but a few years of life, they shall not spoil what he is to have. Why should they make him die, over and over, day after day?" The thoughts in her mind did not become so definite. She had resentment against the others. She was like a soldier, standing guard over Ted.

The two children drew more and more away, into their own world and only once did what Mary felt come to the surface. That was with the mother.

It was on an early Summer day and Ted and Mary were playing in the rain. They were on a side porch of the house, where the water came pouring down from the eaves. At a corner of the porch there was a great stream, and first Ted and then Mary dashed through it, returning to the porch with clothes soaked and water running in streams from soaked hair. There was something joyous, the feel of the cold water on the body, under clothes, and they were shrieking with laughter when the mother came to the door. She looked at Ted. There was fear and anxiety in her voice. "Oh, Ted, you know you mustn't, you mustn't." Just that. All the rest implied. Nothing said to Mary. There it was. "Oh, Ted, you mustn't. You mustn't run hard, climb trees, ride horses. The least shock to you may do it." It was the old story again, and, of course, Ted understood. He went white and trembled. Why couldn't the rest understand that was a hundred times worse for him? On that day, without answering his mother, he ran off the porch and through the rain toward the barns. He wanted to go hide himself from everyone. Mary knew how he felt.

She got suddenly very old and very angry. The mother and daughter stood looking at each other, the woman nearing fifty and the child of fourteen. It was getting everything in the family reversed. Mary felt that but felt she had to do something. "You should have more sense, Mother," she said seriously. She also had gone white. Her lips trembled. "You mustn't do it any more. Don't you ever do it again."

"What, child?" There was astonishment and half anger in the mother's voice.

"Always making him think of it," Mary said. She wanted to cry but didn't.

The mother understood. There was a queer tense moment before Mary also walked off, toward the barns, in the rain. It wasn't all so clear. The mother wanted to fly at the child, perhaps shake her for daring to be so impudent. A child like that to decide things—to dare to reprove her mother. There was so much implied—even that Ted be allowed to die, quickly, suddenly, rather than that death, danger of sudden death, be brought again and again to his attention. There were values in life, implied by a child's words: "Life, what is it worth? Is death the most terrible thing?" The mother turned and went silently into the house while Mary, going to the barns, presently found Ted. He was in an empty horse stall, standing with his back to the wall, staring. There were no explanations. "Well," Ted said presently, and, "Come on, Ted," Mary replied. It was necessary to do something even perhaps more risky than playing in the rain. The rain was already passing. "Let's take off our shoes," Mary said. Going barefoot was one of the things forbidden Ted. They took their shoes off and, leaving them in the barn, went into an orchard. There was a small creek below the orchard, a creek that went down to the river and now it would be in flood. They went into it and once Mary got swept off her feet so that Ted had to pull her out. She spoke then. "I told Mother," she said, looking serious.

"What?" Ted said. "Gee, I guess maybe I saved you from drowning," he added.

"Sure you did," said Mary. "I told her to let you alone." She grew suddenly fierce. "They've all got to—they've got to let you alone," she said.

There was a bond. Ted did his share. He was imaginative and could think of plenty of risky things to do. Perhaps the mother spoke to the father and to Don, the older brother. There was a new inclination in the family to keep hands off the pair, and the fact seemed to give the two children new room in life. Something seemed to open out. There was a little inner world created, always, every day, being re-created, and in it there was a kind of new security. It seemed to the two children—they could not have put their feelings into words—that, being in their own created world, feeling a security there, they could suddenly look out at the outside world, and see, in a new way, what was going on out there in the world that belonged also to others.

It was a world to be thought about, looked at, a world of drama too, the drama of human relations, outside their own world, in a family, on a farm, in a farmhouse. . . . On a farm, calves and yearling steers arriving to be fattened, great heavy steers going off to market, colts being broken to work or to saddle, lambs born in the late Winter. The human side of life was more difficult, to a child often incomprehensible, but after the speech to the mother, on the porch of the house that day when it rained, it seemed to Mary almost as though she and Ted had set up a new family. Everything about the farm, the house and the barns got nicer. There was a new freedom. The two children walked along a country road, returning to the farm from school in the late afternoon. There were other children in the road but they managed to fall behind or they got ahead. There were plans made. "I'm going to be a nurse when I grow up," Mary said. She may have remembered dimly the woman nurse, from the county-seat town, who had come to stay in the house when Ted was so ill. Ted said that as soon as he could—it would be when he was younger yet than Don was now—he intended to leave and go out West . . . far out, he said. He wanted to be a cowboy or a bronco-buster or something, and that failing, he thought he would be a railroad engineer. The railroad that went down through the Rich Valley crossed a corner of the Grey farm, and, from the road in the afternoon, they could sometimes see trains, quite far away, the smoke rolling up. There was a faint rumbling noise, and on clear days they could see the flying piston rods of the engines.

As for the two stumps in the field near the house, they were what was left of two oak trees. The children had known the trees. They were cut one day in the early Fall.

There was a back porch to the Grey house—the house that had once been the seat of the Aspinwahl family—and from the porch steps a path led down to a stone spring house. A spring came out of the ground just there, and there was a tiny stream that went along the edge of a field, past two large barns and out across a meadow to a creek—called a "branch" in Virginia, and the two trees stood close together beyond the spring house and the fence.

They were lusty trees, their roots down in the rich, always damp soil, and one of them had a great limb that came down near the ground, so that Ted and Mary could climb into it and out another limb into its brother tree, and in the Fall, when other trees, at the front and side of the house, had shed their leaves, blood-red leaves

still clung to the two oaks. They were like dry blood on gray days, but on other days, when the sun came out, the trees flamed against the distant hills. The leaves clung, whispering and talking when the wind blew, so that the trees themselves seemed carrying on a conversation.

John Grey had decided he would have the trees cut. At first it was not a very definite decision. "I think I'll have them cut," he announced.

"But why?" his wife asked. The trees meant a good deal to her. They had been planted, just in that spot, by her grandfather, she said, having in mind just a certain effect. "You see how, in the Fall, when you stand on the back porch, they are so nice against the hills." She spoke of the trees, already quite large, having been brought from a distant woods. Her mother had often spoken of it. The man, her grandfather, had a special feeling for trees. "An Aspinwahl would do that," John Grey said. "There is enough yard, here about the house, and enough trees. They do not shade the house or the yard. An Aspinwahl would go to all that trouble for trees and then plant them where grass might be growing." He had suddenly determined, a half-formed determination in him suddenly hardening. He had perhaps heard too much of the Aspinwahls and their ways. The conversation regarding the trees took place at the table, at the noon hour, and Mary and Ted heard it all.

It began at the table and was carried on

afterwards out of doors, in the yard back of the house. The wife had followed her husband out. He always left the table suddenly and silently, getting quickly up and going out heavily, shutting doors with a bang as he went. "Don't, John," the wife said, standing on the porch and calling to her husband. It was a cold day but the sun was out and the trees were like great bonfires against gray distant fields and hills. The older son of the family, young Don, the one so physically like the father and apparently so like him in every other way, had come out of the house with the mother, followed by the two children, Ted and Mary, and at first Don said nothing, but, when the father did not answer the mother's protest but started toward the barn, he also spoke. What he said was obviously the determining thing, hardening the father.

To the two other children—they had walked a little aside and stood together watching and listening—there was something. There was their own child's world. "Let us alone and we'll let you alone." It wasn't as definite as that. Most of the definite thoughts about what happened in the yard that afternoon came to Mary Grey long afterwards, when she was a grown woman. At the moment there was merely a sudden sharpening of the feeling of isolation, a wall between herself and Ted and the others. The father, even then perhaps, seen in a new light, Don and the mother seen in a new light.

There was something, a driving destructive thing in life, in all relationships between people. All of this felt dimly that day—she always believed both by herself and Ted—but only thought out long afterwards, after Ted was dead. There was the farm her father had won from the Aspinwahls—greater persistence, greater shrewdness. In a family, little remarks dropped from time to time, an impression slowly built up. The father, John Grey, was a successful man. He had acquired. He owned. He was the commander, the one having the power to do his will. And the power had run out and covered, not only other human lives, impulses in others, wishes, hungers in others . . . he himself might not have, might not even understand . . . but it went far beyond that. It was, curiously, the power also of life and death. Did Mary Grey think such thoughts at that moment? . . . She couldn't have. . . . Still there was her own peculiar situation, her relationship with her brother Ted, who was to die.

Ownership that gave curious rights, dominances—fathers over children, men and women over lands, houses, factories in cities, fields. "I will have the trees in that orchard cut. They produce apples but not of the right sort. There is no money in apples of that sort any more."

"But, Sir . . . you see . . . look . . . the trees there against that hill, against the sky."

"Nonsense. Sentimentality."

Confusion.

It would have been such nonsense to think of the father of Mary Grey as a man without feeling. He had struggled hard all his life, perhaps, as a young man, gone without things wanted, deeply hungered for. Someone has to manage things in this life. Possessions mean power, the right to say "Do this" or "Do that." If you struggle long and hard for a thing it becomes infinitely sweet to you.

Was there a kind of hatred between the father and the older son of the Grey family? "You are one also who has this thing—the impulse to power, so like my own. Now you are young and I am growing old." Admiration mixed with fear. If you would retain power it will not do to admit fear.

The young Don was so curiously like the father. There were the same lines about the jaws, the same eyes. They were both heavy men. Already the young man walked like the father, slammed doors as did the father. There was the same curious lack of delicacy of thought and touch—the heaviness that plows through, gets things done. When John Grey had married Louise Aspinwahl he was already a mature man, on his way to success. Such men do not marry young and recklessly. Now he was nearly sixty and there was the son—so like himself, having the same kind of strength.

Both land lovers, possession lovers. "It is my farm, my house, my horses, cattle, sheep." Soon now, another ten years, fifteen at the most, and the father would be ready for death. "See, already my hand slips a little. All of this to go out of my grasp." He, John Grey, had not got all of these possessions so easily. It had taken much patience, much persistence. No one but himself would ever quite know. Five, ten, fifteen years of work and saving, getting the Aspinwahl farm piece by piece. "The fools!" They had liked to think of themselves as aristocrats, throwing the land away, now twenty acres, now thirty, now fifty.

Raising horses that could never plow an acre of land.

And they had robbed the land too, had never put anything back, doing nothing to enrich it, build it up. Such a one thinking: "I'm an Aspinwahl, a gentleman. I do not soil my hands at the plow."

"Fools who do not know the meaning of land owned, possessions, money—responsibility. It is they who are second-rate men."

He had got an Aspinwahl for a wife and, as it had turned out, she was the best, the smartest and in the end, the best-looking one of the lot.

And now there was his son, standing at the moment near the mother. They had both come down off the porch. It would be natural and right for this one—he being what he already was, what he would become—for him, in his turn, to come into possession, to take command.

There would be, of course, the rights of the other children. If you have the stuff in you (John Grey felt that his son Don had) there is a way to manage. You buy the others out, make arrangements. There was Ted—he wouldn't be alive—and Mary and the two younger children. "The better for you if you have to struggle."

All of this, the implication of the moment of sudden struggle between a father and son, coming slowly afterwards to the man's daughter, as yet little more than a child. Does the drama take place when the seed is put into the ground or afterwards when the plant has pushed out of the ground and the bud breaks open, or still later, when the fruit ripens? There were the Greys with their ability—slow, saving, able, determined, patient. Why had they superseded the Aspinwahls in the Rich Valley? Aspinwahl blood also in the two children, Mary and Ted.

There was an Aspinwahl man—called "Uncle Fred," a brother to Louise Grey—who came sometimes to the farm. He was a rather striking-looking, tall old man with a gray Vandyke beard and a mustache, somewhat shabbily dressed but always with an indefinable air of class. He came from the county-seat town, where he lived now with a daughter who had married a merchant, a polite courtly old man who always froze into a queer silence in the presence of the sister's husband.

The son Don was standing near the mother on the day in the Fall, and the two children, Mary and Ted, stood apart.

"Don't, John," Louise Grey said again. The father, who had started toward the barns, stopped.

"Well, I guess I will."

"No, you won't," said young Don, speaking suddenly. There was a queer fixed look in his eyes. It had flashed into life—something that was between the two men: "I possess" . . . "I will possess." The father wheeled and looked sharply at the son and then ignored him.

For a moment the mother continued pleading.

"But why, why?"

"They make too much shade. The grass does not grow."

"But there is so much grass, so many acres of grass."

John Grey was answering his wife, but now again he looked at his son. There were unspoken words flying back and forth.

"I possess. I am in command here. What do you mean by telling me that I won't?"

"Ha! So! You possess now but soon I will possess."

"I'll see you in hell first."

"You fool! Not yet! Not yet!"

None of the words, set down above, was spoken at the moment, and afterwards the daughter Mary never did remember the exact words that had passed between the two men. There was a sudden quick flash of determination in Don—even perhaps sudden determination to stand by the mother—even perhaps something else—a feeling in the young Don out of the Aspinwahl blood in him—for the moment tree love superseding grass love—grass that would fatten steers. . . .

Winner of 4H Club prizes, champion young corn-raiser, judge of steers, land lover, possession lover.

"You won't," Don said again.

"Won't what?"

"Won't cut those trees."

The father said nothing more at the moment but walked away from the little group toward the barns. The sun was still shining brightly. There was a sharp cold little wind. The two trees were like bonfires lighted against distant hills.

It was the noon hour and there were two men, both young, employees on the farm, who lived in a small tenant house beyond the barns. One of them, a man with a harelip, was married and the other, a rather handsome silent young man, boarded with him. They had just come from the midday meal and were going toward one of the barns. It was the beginning of the Fall corn-cutting time and they would be going together to a distant field to cut corn.

The father went to the barn and returned with the two men. They brought axes and a long cross-cut saw. "I want you to cut those two trees." There was something, a blind, even stupid determination in the man, John Grey. And at that moment his wife, the mother of his children . . . There was no way any of the children could ever know how many moments of the sort she had been through. She had married John Grey. He was her man.

"If you do, Father . . ." Don Grey said coldly.

"Do as I tell you! Cut those two trees!" This addressed to the two workmen. The one who had a harelip laughed. His laughter was like the bray of a donkey.

"Don't," said Louise Grey, but she was not addressing her husband this time. She stepped to her son and put a hand on his arm.

"Don't."

"Don't cross him. Don't cross my man." Could a child like Mary Grey comprehend? It takes time to understand things that happen in life. Life unfolds slowly to the mind. Mary was standing with Ted, whose young face was white and tense. Death at his elbow. At any moment. At any moment.

"I have been through this a hundred times. This is the way this man I married has succeeded. Nothing stops him. I married him; I have had my children by him.

"We women choose to submit.

"This is my affair, more than yours, Don, my son."

A woman hanging onto her things—the family, created about her.

The son not seeing things with her eyes. He shook off his mother's hand, lying on his arm. Louise Grey was younger than her husband, but, if he was now nearing sixty, she was drawing near fifty. At the moment she looked very delicate and fragile. There was something, at the moment, in her bearing . . . Was there, after all, something in blood, the Aspinwahl blood?

In a dim way perhaps, at the moment the child Mary did comprehend. Women and their men. For her then, at that time, there was but one male, the child Ted. Afterwards she remembered how he looked at that moment, the curiously serious old look on his young face. There was even, she thought later, a kind of contempt for both the father and brother, as though he might have been saying to himself—he couldn't really have been saying it—he was too young: *"We'll see. This is something. These foolish ones—my father and my brother. I myself haven't long to live. I'll see what I can, while I do live."*

The brother Don stepped over near to where his father stood.

"If you do, Father . . ." he said again.

"Well?"

"I'll walk off this farm and I'll never come back."

"All right. Go then."

The father began directing the two men who had begun cutting the trees, each man taking a tree. The young man with the harelip kept laughing, the laughter like the bray of a donkey. "Stop that," the father said sharply, and the sound ceased abruptly. The son Don walked away, going rather aimlessly toward the barn. He approached one of the barns and then stopped. The mother, white now, half ran into the house.

The son returned toward the house, passing the two younger children without looking at them, but did not enter. The father did not look at him. He went hesitatingly along a path at the front of the house and through a gate and into a road. The road ran for several miles down through the valley and then, turning, went over a mountain to the county-seat town.

As it happened, only Mary saw the son Don when he returned to the farm. There were three or four tense days. Perhaps, all the time, the mother and son had been secretly in touch. There

was a telephone in the house. The father stayed all day in the fields, and when he was in the house was silent.

Mary was in one of the barns on the day when Don came back and when the father and son met. It was an odd meeting.

The son came, Mary always afterwards thought, rather sheepishly. The father came out of a horse's stall. He had been throwing corn to work horses. Neither the father nor the son saw Mary. There was a car parked in the barn and she had crawled into the driver's seat, her hands on the steering wheel, pretending she was driving.

"Well," the father said. If he felt triumphant, he did not show his feeling.

"Well," said the son, "I have come back."

"Yes, I see," the father said. "They are cutting corn." He walked toward the barn door and then stopped. "It will be yours soon now," he said. "You can be boss then."

He said no more and both men went away, the father toward the distant fields and the son toward the house. Mary was afterwards quite sure that nothing more was ever said.

What had the father meant?

"When it is yours you can be the boss." It was too much for the child. Knowledge comes slowly. It meant:

"You will be in command, and for you, in your turn, it will be necessary to assert.

"Such men as we are cannot fool with delicate stuff. Some men are meant to command and others must obey. You can make them obey in your turn.

"There is a kind of death.

"Something in you must die before you can possess and command."

There was, so obviously, more than one kind of death. For Don Grey one kind and for the younger brother Ted, soon now perhaps, another.

Mary ran out of the barn that day, wanting eagerly to get out into the light, and afterwards, for a long time, she did not try to think her way through what had happened. She and her brother Ted did, however, afterwards, before he died, discuss quite often the two trees. They went on a cold day and put their fingers on the stumps, but the stumps were cold. Ted kept asserting that only men get their legs and arms cut off, and she protested. They continued doing things that had been forbidden Ted to do, but no one protested, and, a year or two later, when he died, he died during the night in his bed.

But while he lived, there was always, Mary afterwards thought, a curious sense of freedom, something that belonged to him that made it good, a great happiness, to be with him. It was, she finally thought, because having to die his kind of death, he never had to make the surrender his brother had made—to be sure of possessions, success, his time to command—would never have to face the more subtle and terrible death that had come to his older brother.

□□

Discussion

1. (a) What do the first five paragraphs reveal about Ted and Mary's personal traits? (b) About their relationship? (c) Why are they so fascinated by the tree stumps?

2. (a) Discuss the mother and father in the story as **foils** for each other. What are their differences, and what are the sources of their differences? (b) What other characters are foils to each other? Explain.

3. (a) Discuss the ways in which Anderson develops the reader's interest in the trees. (b) What various **symbolic** meanings do the trees take on in the story?

4. What various meanings can you discover for the title "Brother Death"? See, especially, the last three paragraphs of the story.

Extension • Writing

"There was something, a driving destructive thing in life, in all relationships between people." Thus begins a paragraph in the last half of "Brother Death." In a short essay, show how this sentence relates to the action of the story.

Sherwood Anderson
1876 • 1941

Anderson grew up in Clyde, Ohio, working at odd jobs ranging from errand boy to stable groom. His father, a wandering house painter and harness maker, never made much money but was a very entertaining storyteller and amateur actor. From him, and from a literary idol, Samuel Clemens, young Anderson learned to use the rhythms of the oral story, an ability that later enabled him to achieve in his writings a deceptively easy air of reminiscence and improvisation.

For a time he wrote advertising copy to support himself. Then in 1919 he published his first volume of short stories, *Winesburg, Ohio.* The book greatly extended the concept of **realism** in both the content and also the form of the American short story. Events in his stories often are not arranged in well-defined and completed patterns. Rather they seem to follow the natural rhythms of the lives of small-town Americans. With the additional publication of two other collections of short narratives, *The Triumph of the Egg* (1921) and *Horses and Men* (1923), Anderson became one of the important innovators in American literature.

Beginning in 1921 Anderson spent three restless years in part searching for a conducive atmosphere for his writing. After traveling in Europe, he lived for a time in New Orleans, where he met and encouraged William Faulkner. He finally settled in Marion, Virginia; bought the two town newspapers, one Republican and the other Democrat; and proceeded to act as managing editor for both of them. To the surprise of those who thought the move a momentary whim, Anderson lived there the rest of his life.

Katherine Anne Porter

The Jilting of Granny Weatherall

She flicked her wrist neatly out of Doctor Harry's pudgy careful fingers and pulled the sheet up to her chin. The brat ought to be in knee breeches. Doctoring around the country with spectacles on his nose! "Get along now, take your schoolbooks and go. There's nothing wrong with me."

Doctor Harry spread a warm paw like a cushion on her forehead where the forked green vein danced and made her eyelids twitch. "Now, now, be a good girl, and we'll have you up in no time."

"That's no way to speak to a woman nearly eighty years old just because she's down. I'd have you respect your elders, young man."

"Well, Missy, excuse me." Doctor Harry patted her cheek. "But I've got to warn you, haven't I? You're a marvel, but you must be careful or you're going to be good and sorry."

"Don't tell me what I'm going to be. I'm on my feet now, morally speaking. It's Cornelia. I had to go to bed to get rid of her."

Her bones felt loose, and floated around in her skin, and Doctor Harry floated like a balloon around the foot of the bed. He floated and pulled down his waistcoat and swung his glasses on a cord. "Well, stay where you are, it certainly can't hurt you."

"Get along and doctor your sick," said Granny Weatherall. "Leave a well woman alone. I'll call for you when I want you. . . . Where were you forty years ago when I pulled through milkleg and double pneumonia? You weren't even born. Don't let Cornelia lead you on," she shouted, because Doctor Harry appeared to float up to the ceiling and out. "I pay my own bills, and I don't throw my money away on nonsense!"

She meant to wave goodby, but it was too much trouble. Her eyes closed of themselves, it was like a dark curtain drawn around the bed. The pillow rose and floated under her, pleasant as a hammock in a light wind. She listened to the leaves rustling outside the window. No, somebody was swishing newspapers; no, Cornelia and Doctor Harry were whispering together. She leaped broad awake, thinking they whispered in her ear.

"She was never like this, *never* like this!" "Well, what can we expect?" "Yes, eighty years old. . . ."

Well, and what if she was? She still had ears. It was like Cornelia to whisper around doors. She always kept things secret in such a public way. She was always being tactful and kind. Cornelia was dutiful; that was the trouble with her. Dutiful and good: "So good and dutiful," said Granny, "that I'd like to spank her." She saw herself spanking Cornelia and making a fine job of it.

"What'd you say, Mother?"

Granny felt her face tying up in hard knots.

"Can't a body think, I'd like to know?"

"I thought you might want something."

"I do. I want a lot of things. First off, go away and don't whisper."

She lay and drowsed, hoping in her sleep that the children would keep out and let her rest a minute. It had been a long day. Not that she was tired. It was always pleasant to snatch a minute now and then. There was always so much to be done, let me see: tomorrow.

Tomorrow was far away and there was nothing to trouble about. Things were finished somehow when the time came; thank God there was always a little margin over for peace: then a person could spread out the plan of life and tuck in the edges orderly. It was good to have everything clean and folded away, with the hair brushes and tonic bottles sitting straight on the white embroidered linen: the day started without fuss and the pantry shelves laid out with rows of jelly glasses and brown jugs and white stone-china jars with blue whirligigs and words painted on them: coffee, tea, sugar, ginger, cinnamon, allspice: and the bronze clock with the lion on top nicely dusted off. The dust that lion could collect in twenty-four hours! The box in the attic with all those letters tied up, well, she'd have to go through that tomorrow. All those letters— George's letters and John's letters and her letters to them both—lying around for the children to find afterward made her uneasy. Yes, that would be tomorrow's business. No use to let them know how silly she had been once.

While she was rummaging around she found death in her mind and it felt clammy and unfamiliar. She had spent so much time preparing for death there was no need for bringing it up again. Let it take care of itself now. When she was sixty she had felt very old, finished, and went around making farewell trips to see her children and grandchildren, with a secret in her mind: This is the very last of your mother, children! Then she made her will and came down with a long fever. That was all just a notion like a lot of other things, but it was lucky too, for she had once and for all got over the idea of dying for a long time. Now she couldn't be worried. She hoped she had better sense now. Her father had lived to be one hundred and two years old and had drunk a noggin of strong hot toddy on his last birthday. He told the reporters it was his daily habit, and he owed his long life to that. He had made quite a scandal and was very pleased about it. She believed she'd just plague Cornelia a little.

"Cornelia! Cornelia!" No footsteps, but a sudden hand on her cheek. "Bless you, where have you been?"

"Here, Mother."

"Well, Cornelia, I want a noggin of hot toddy."

"Are you cold, darling?"

"I'm chilly, Cornelia. Lying in bed stops the circulation. I must have told you that a thousand times."

Well, she could just hear Cornelia telling her husband that Mother was getting a little childish and they'd have to humor her. The thing that most annoyed her was that Cornelia thought she was deaf, dumb, and blind. Little hasty glances and tiny gestures tossed around her and over her head saying, "Don't cross her, let her have her way, she's eighty years old," and she sitting there as if she lived in a thin glass cage. Sometimes Granny almost made up her mind to pack up and move back to her own house where nobody could remind her every minute that she was old. Wait, wait, Cornelia, till your own children whisper behind your back!

In her day she had kept a better house and had got more work done. She wasn't too old yet for Lydia to be driving eighty miles for advice when one of the children jumped the track, and Jimmy still dropped in and talked things over: "Now, Mammy, you've a good business head, I want to know what you think of this? . . ." Old. Cornelia couldn't change the furniture around without asking. Little things, little things! They had been so sweet when they were little. Granny wished the old days were back again with the children young and everything to be done over. It had been a hard pull, but not too much for her. When she thought of all the food she had cooked, and all the clothes she had cut and sewed, and all the gardens she had made—well, the children showed it. There they were, made out of her, and they couldn't get away from that. Sometimes she wanted to see John again and point to them and say, Well, I didn't do so badly, did I? But that would have to wait. That was for tomorrow. She

used to think of him as a man, but now all the children were older than their father, and he would be a child beside her if she saw him now. It seemed strange and there was something wrong in the idea. Why, he couldn't possibly recognize her. She had fenced in a hundred acres once, digging the postholes herself and clamping the wires with just a Negro boy to help. That changed a woman. John would be looking for a young woman with the peaked Spanish comb in her hair and the painted fan. Digging postholes changed a woman. Riding country roads in the winter when women had their babies was another thing: sitting up nights with sick horses and sick Negroes and sick children and hardly ever losing one. John, I hardly ever lost one of them! John would see that in a minute, that would be something he could understand, she wouldn't have to explain anything!

It made her feel like rolling up her sleeves and putting the whole place to rights again. No matter if Cornelia was determined to be everywhere at once, there were a great many things left undone on this place. She would start tomorrow and do them. It was good to be strong enough for everything, even if all you made melted and changed and slipped under your hands, so that by the time you finished you almost forgot what you were working for. What was it I set out to do? she asked herself intently, but she could not remember. A fog rose over the valley, she saw it marching across the creek swallowing the trees and moving up the hill like an army of ghosts. Soon it would be at the near edge of the orchard, and then it was time to go in and light the lamps. Come in, children, don't stay out in the night air.

Lighting the lamps had been beautiful. The children huddled up to her and breathed like little calves waiting at the bars in the twilight. Their eyes followed the match and watched the flame rise and settle in a blue curve, then they moved away from her. The lamp was lit, they didn't have to be scared and hang on to mother any more. Never, never, never more. God, for all my life I thank Thee. Without Thee, my God, I could never have done it. Hail, Mary, full of grace.[1]

I want you to pick all the fruit this year and see that nothing is wasted. There's always some-

---

1. *Hail, Mary, full of grace.* The opening line of a Catholic prayer.

one who can use it. Don't let good things rot for want of using. You waste life when you waste good food. Don't let things get lost. It's bitter to lose things. Now, don't let me get to thinking, not when I am tired and taking a little nap before supper. . . .

The pillow rose about her shoulders and pressed against her heart and the memory was being squeezed out of it: oh, push down the pillow, somebody: it would smother her if she tried to hold it. Such a fresh breeze blowing and such a green day with no threats in it. But he had not come, just the same. What does a woman do when she has put on the white veil and set out the white cake for a man and he doesn't come? She tried to remember. No, I swear he never harmed me but in that. He never harmed me but in that . . . and what if he did? There was the day, the day, but a whirl of dark smoke rose and covered it, crept up and over into the bright field where everything was planted so carefully in orderly rows. That was hell, she knew hell when she saw it. For sixty years she had prayed against remembering him and against losing her soul in the deep pit of hell, and now the two things were mingled in one and the thought of him was a smoky cloud from hell that moved and crept in her head when she had just got rid of Doctor Harry and was trying to rest a minute. Wounded vanity, Ellen, said a sharp voice in the top of her mind. Don't let your wounded vanity get the upper hand of you. Plenty of girls get jilted. You were jilted, weren't you? Then stand up to it. Her eyelids wavered and let in streamers of blue-gray light like tissue paper over her eyes. She must get up and pull the shades down or she'd never sleep. She was in bed again and the shades were not down. How could that happen? Better turn over, hide from the light, sleeping in the light gave you nightmares. "Mother, how do you feel now?" and a stinging wetness on her forehead. But I don't like having my face washed in cold water!

Hapsy? George? Lydia? Jimmy? No, Cornelia, and her features were swollen and full of little puddles. "They're coming, darling, they'll all be here soon." Go wash your face, child, you look funny.

Instead of obeying, Cornelia knelt down and put her head on the pillow. She seemed to be talking but there was no sound. "Well, are you tongue-tied? Whose birthday is it? Are you going to give a party?"

Cornelia's mouth moved urgently in strange shapes. "Don't do that, you bother me, daughter."

"Oh, no, Mother. Oh, no. . . ."

Nonsense. It was strange about children. They disputed your every word. "No what, Cornelia?"

"Here's Doctor Harry."

"I won't see that boy again. He just left five minutes ago."

"That was this morning, Mother. It's night now. Here's the nurse."

"This is Doctor Harry, Mrs. Weatherall. I never saw you look so young and happy!"

"Ah, I'll never be young again—but I'd be happy if they'd let me lie in peace and get rested."

She thought she spoke up loudly, but no one answered. A warm weight on her forehead, a warm bracelet on her wrist, and a breeze went on whispering, trying to tell her something. A shuffle of leaves in the everlasting hand of God, He blew on them and they danced and rattled. "Mother, don't mind, we're going to give you a little hypodermic." "Look here, daughter, how do ants get in this bed? I saw sugar ants yesterday." Did you send for Hapsy too?

It was Hapsy she really wanted. She had to go a long way back through a great many rooms to find Hapsy standing with a baby on her arm. She seemed to herself to be Hapsy also, and the baby on Hapsy's arm was Hapsy and himself and herself, all at once, and there was no surprise in the meeting. Then Hapsy melted from within and turned flimsy as gray gauze and the baby was a gauzy shadow, and Hapsy came up close and said, "I thought you'd never come," and looked at her very searchingly and said, "You haven't changed a bit!" They leaned forward to kiss, when Cornelia began whispering from a long way off, "Oh, is there anything you want to tell me? Is there anything I can do for you?"

Yes, she had changed her mind after sixty years and she would like to see George. I want you to find George. Find him and be sure to tell him I forgot him. I want him to know I had my husband just the same and my children and my house like any other woman. A good house too and a good husband that I loved and fine children out of him. Better than I hoped for even. Tell him I was given back everything he took away and more. Oh, no, oh, God, no, there was something else besides the house and the man and the children. Oh, surely they were not all? What was it? Something not given back. . . . Her breath crowded down under her ribs and grew into a monstrous frightening shape with cutting edges; it bored up into her head, and the agony was unbelievable: Yes, John, get the Doctor now, no more talk, my time has come.

When this one was born it should be the last. The last. It should have been born first, for it was the one she had truly wanted. Everything came in good time. Nothing left out, left over. She was strong, in three days she would be as well as ever. Better. A woman needed milk in her to have her full health.

"Mother, do you hear me?"

"I've been telling you—"

"Mother, Father Connolly's here."

"I went to Holy Communion only last week. Tell him I'm not so sinful as all that."

"Father just wants to speak to you."

He could speak as much as he pleased. It was like him to drop in and inquire about her soul as if it were a teething baby, and then stay on for a cup of tea and a round of cards and gossip. He always had a funny story of some sort, usually about an Irishman who made his little mistakes and confessed them, and the point lay in some absurd thing he would blurt out in the confessional showing his struggles between native piety and original sin. Granny felt easy about her soul. Cornelia, where are your manners? Give Father Connolly a chair. She had her secret comfortable understanding with a few favorite saints who cleared a straight road to God for her. All as surely signed and sealed as the papers for the new Forty Acres. Forever . . . heirs and assigns forever. Since the day the wedding cake was not cut, but thrown out and wasted. The whole bottom dropped out of the world, and there she was blind and sweating with nothing under her feet and the walls falling away. His hand had caught her under the breast, she had not fallen, there was the freshly polished floor with the green rug on it, just as before. He had cursed like a sailor's parrot and said, "I'll kill him for you."

Don't lay a hand on him, for my sake leave something to God. "Now, Ellen, you must believe what I tell you. . . ."

So there was nothing, nothing to worry about any more, except sometimes in the night one of the children screamed in a nightmare, and they both hustled out shaking and hunting for the matches and calling, "There, wait a minute, here we are!" John, get the doctor now, Hapsy's time has come. But there was Hapsy standing by the bed in a white cap. "Cornelia, tell Hapsy to take off her cap. I can't see her plain."

Her eyes opened very wide and the room stood out like a picture she had seen somewhere. Dark colors with the shadows rising toward the ceiling in long angles. The tall black dresser gleamed with nothing on it but John's picture, enlarged from a little one, with John's eyes very black when they should have been blue. You never saw him, so how do you know how he looked? But the man insisted the copy was perfect, it was very rich and handsome. For a picture, yes, but it's not my husband. The table by the bed had a linen cover and a candle and a crucifix. The light was blue from Cornelia's silk lampshades. No sort of light at all, just frippery. You had to live forty years with kerosene lamps to appreciate honest electricity. She felt very strong and she saw Doctor Harry with a rosy nimbus around him.

"You look like a saint, Doctor Harry, and I vow that's as near as you'll ever come to it."

"She's saying something."

"I heard you, Cornelia. What's all this carrying-on?"

"Father Connolly's saying—"

Cornelia's voice staggered and bumped like a cart in a bad road. It rounded corners and turned back again and arrived nowhere. Granny stepped up in the cart very lightly and reached for the reins, but a man sat beside her and she knew him by his hands, driving the cart. She did not look in his face, for she knew without seeing, but looked instead down the road where the trees leaned over and bowed to each other and a thousand birds were singing a Mass. She felt like singing too, but she put her hand in the bosom of her dress and pulled out a rosary, and Father Connolly murmured Latin in a very solemn voice and tickled her feet.[2] My God, will you stop that nonsense? I'm a married woman. What if he did run away and leave me to face the priest by myself? I found another a whole world better. I wouldn't have exchanged my husband for anybody except St. Michael himself, and you may tell him that for me with a thank you in the bargain.

Light flashed on her closed eyelids, and a deep roaring shook her. Cornelia, is that lightning? I hear thunder. There's going to be a storm. Close all the windows. Call the children in. . . . "Mother, here we are, all of us." "Is that you, Hapsy?" "Oh, no, I'm Lydia. We drove as fast as we could." Their faces drifted above her, drifted away. The rosary fell out of her hands and Lydia put it back. Jimmy tried to help, their hands

fumbled together, and Granny closed two fingers around Jimmy's thumb. Beads wouldn't do, it must be something alive. She was so amazed her thoughts ran round and round. So, my dear Lord, this is my death and I wasn't even thinking about it. My children have come to see me die. But I can't, it's not time. Oh, I always hated surprises. I wanted to give Cornelia the amethyst set—Cornelia, you're to have the amethyst set, but Hapsy's to wear it when she wants, and, Doctor

Harry, do shut up. Nobody sent for you. Oh, my dear Lord, do wait a minute. I meant to do something about the Forty Acres, Jimmy doesn't need it and Lydia will later on, with that worthless husband of hers. I meant to finish the altar cloth and send six bottles of wine to Sister Borgia for her dyspepsia. I want to send six bottles of wine to Sister Borgia, Father Connolly, now don't let me forget.

Cornelia's voice made short turns and tilted over and crashed. "Oh, Mother, oh, Mother, oh, Mother. . . ."

"I'm not going, Cornelia. I'm taken by surprise. I can't go."

You'll see Hapsy again. What about her? "I thought you'd never come." Granny made a long journey outward, looking for Hapsy. What if I don't find her? What then? Her heart sank down and down, there was no bottom to death, she couldn't come to the end of it. The blue light from Cornelia's lamp-shade drew into a tiny point in the center of her brain, it flickered and winked like an eye, quietly it fluttered and dwindled. Granny lay curled down within herself, amazed and watchful, staring at the point of light that was herself; her body was now only a deeper mass of shadow in an endless darkness and this darkness would curl around the light and swallow it up. God, give a sign!

For the second time there was no sign. Again no bridegroom and the priest in the house. She could not remember any other sorrow because this grief wiped them all away. Oh, no, there's nothing more cruel than this—I'll never forgive it. She stretched herself with a deep breath and blew out the light. ☐☐

---

2. **Father Connolly . . . feet.** The priest is administering the sacrament for the dying, which includes anointing the hands and feet.

Discussion

1. (a) Describe what actually happens in the sickroom while Granny is reliving the past. (b) How much time do these actual events cover? (c) How is the seemingly random order in which past events come into Granny's mind related to happenings in the sickroom? (d) To what situations in the past do Granny's thoughts keep returning? Why?

2. (a) Tell in detail the story

of the jilting mentioned in the title. **(b)** What significance do you find in Porter's choice of a surname for Granny? **(c)** How long ago did the jilting occur? **(d)** What is Granny's attitude toward it? **(e)** Why does the author reveal the facts about the jilting as she does instead of giving the information straightforwardly and then ending her story?

3. The **stream-of-consciousness** technique in this story suggests both the vagueness and confusion and also the moments of clarity that characterize Granny. Thus passages like ". . . Doctor Harry floated like a balloon around the foot of the bed" alternate with sharp images like " . . . white stone-china jars with blue whirligigs and words painted on them . . ." **(a)** Cite passages in which the manner of writing reflects Granny's state of mind. **(b)** Do most of the clearly visualized scenes relate to the present or the past? Explain why this is so.

Extension • Writing

1. One of the hardest things in the world to do is to observe your own mind at work or play. Try to catch your self off guard to see how your mind really moves from one idea or image to another. What set it in motion? What changed the direction? Write an account of spying on your own mind.

2. Taking examples from this story and Bierce's "An Occurrence at Owl Creek Bridge" (Unit 5), explain for your classmates the main elements of stream-of-consciousness writing. You should also deal with the differences between Porter and Bierce's use of this technique.

Katherine Anne Porter
1890 • 1980

In 1941 Porter was asked for a biographical sketch and responded in part as follows: "I was born at Indian Creek, Texas, brought up in Texas and Louisiana, and educated in small Southern convent schools. I was precocious, nervous, rebellious, unteachable, and made life very uncomfortable for myself and I suppose for those around me. As soon as I learned to form letters on paper, at about three years, I began to write stories, and this has been the basic and absorbing occupation, the intact line of my life which directs my actions, determines my point of view, and profoundly affects my character and personality, my social beliefs and economic status, and the kind of friendships I form. I did not choose this vocation, and if I had any say in the matter, I would not have chosen it. I made no attempt to publish anything until I was thirty, but I have written and destroyed manuscripts quite literally by the trunkful. I spent fifteen years wandering about, weighted horribly with masses of paper and little else. Yet for this vocation I was and am willing to live and die, and I consider very few other things of the slightest importance. . . ."

Porter's first published volume was *Flowering Judas and Other Stories,* which appeared in 1930. The stories, "The Jilting of Granny Weatherall" among them, were delicate and precise, sensitive and subtle. The years of preparation had paid off in a technical mastery of the art of writing which was impeccable. The important place Porter has won for herself among contemporary American writers is based on a remarkably small total output. A painstaking stylist, she produced only a few books in the more than forty years since *Flowering Judas* was first published. Her first and only novel, *Ship of Fools,* was begun in 1940 but did not reach completion until 1962. She called it the "hardest thing I ever did in my life."

In 1966 Porter won both the National Book Award and the Pulitzer Prize for *The Collected Stories of Katherine Anne Porter.*

William Faulkner

The Bear

He was ten. But it had already begun, long before that day when at last he wrote his age in two figures and he saw for the first time the camp where his father and Major de Spain and old General Compson and the others spent two weeks each November and two weeks again each June. He had already inherited then, without ever having seen it, the tremendous bear with one trap-ruined foot which, in an area almost a hundred miles deep, had earned for itself a name, a definite designation like a living man.

He had listened to it for years: the long legend of corncribs rifled, of shoats and grown pigs and even calves carried bodily into the woods and devoured, of traps and deadfalls overthrown and dogs mangled and slain, and shotgun and even rifle charges delivered at point-blank range and with no more effect than so many peas blown through a tube by a boy—a corridor of wreckage and destruction beginning back before he was born, through which sped, not fast but rather with the ruthless and irresistible deliberation of a locomotive, the shaggy tremendous shape.

It ran in his knowledge before ever he saw it. It looked and towered in his dreams before he even saw the unaxed woods where it left its crooked print, shaggy, huge, red-eyed, not malevolent but just big—too big for the dogs which tried to bay it, for the horses which tried to ride it down, for the men and the bullets they fired into it, too big for the very country which was its constricting scope. He seemed to see it entire with a child's complete divination before he ever laid eyes on either—the doomed wilderness whose edges were being constantly and punily gnawed at by men with axes and plows who feared it because it was wilderness, men myriad and nameless even to one another in the land where the old bear had earned a name, through which ran not even a mortal animal but an

Dr. E. R. Degginger.

anachronism, indomitable and invincible, out of an old dead time, a phantom, epitome and apotheosis of the old wild life at which the puny humans swarmed and hacked in a fury of abhorrence and fear, like pygmies about the ankles of a drowsing elephant: the old bear solitary, indomitable and alone, widowered, childless, and absolved of mortality—old Priam[1] reft of his old wife and having outlived all his sons.

Until he was ten, each November he would watch the wagon containing the dogs and the bedding and food and guns and his father and Tennie's Jim, the Negro, and Sam Fathers, the Indian, son of a slave woman and a Chickasaw chief, depart on the road to town, to Jefferson where Major de Spain and the others would join them. To the boy, at seven, eight, and nine, they were not going into the Big Bottom to hunt bear and deer, but to keep yearly rendezvous with the

1. **Priam** (prī´əm), the last king of Troy. His wife and sons were killed by the Greeks during the Trojan War.

bear which they did not even intend to kill. Two weeks later they would return, with no trophy, no head and skin. He had not expected it. He had not even been afraid it would be in the wagon. He believed that even after he was ten and his father would let him go too, for those two weeks in November, he would merely make another one, along with his father and Major de Spain and General Compson and the others, the dogs which feared to bay at it and the rifles and shotguns which failed even to bleed it, in the yearly pageant of the old bear's furious immortality.

Then he heard the dogs. It was in the second week of his first time in the camp. He stood with Sam Fathers against a big oak beside the faint crossing where they had stood each dawn for nine days now, hearing the dogs. He had heard them once before, one morning last week—a murmur, sourceless, echoing through the wet woods, swelling presently into separate voices which he could recognize and call by name. He had raised and cocked the gun as Sam told him and stood motionless again while the uproar, the invisible course, swept up and past and faded; it seemed to him that he could actually see the deer, the buck, blond, smoke-colored, elongated with speed, fleeing, vanishing, the woods, the gray solitude, still ringing even when the cries of the dogs had died away.

"Now let the hammers down," Sam said.

"You knew they were not coming here too," he said.

"Yes," Sam said. "I want you to learn how to do when you didn't shoot. It's after the chance for the bear or the deer has done already come and gone that men and dogs get killed."

"Anyway," he said, "it was just a deer."

Then on the tenth morning he heard the dogs again. And he readied the too-long, too-heavy gun as Sam had taught him, before Sam even spoke. But this time it was no deer, no ringing chorus of dogs running strong on a free scent, but a moiling yapping an octave too high, with something more than indecision and even abjectness in it, not even moving very fast, taking a long time to pass completely out of hearing, leaving them somewhere in the air that echo, thin, slightly hysterical, abject, almost grieving, with no sense of a fleeing, unseen, smoke-colored, grass-eating shape ahead of it, and Sam, who had taught him first of all to cock the gun and take position where he could see everywhere and then never move again, had himself moved up beside him; he could hear Sam breathing at his shoulder and he could see the arched curve of the old man's inhaling nostrils.

"Hah," Sam said. "Not even running. Walking."

"Old Ben!" the boy said. "But up here!" he cried. "Way up here!"

"He do it every year," Sam said. "Once. Maybe to see who in camp this time, if he can shoot or not. Whether we got the dog yet that can bay and hold him. He'll take them to the river, then he'll send them back home. We may as well go back, too; see how they look when they come back to camp."

When they reached the camp the hounds were already there, ten of them crouching back under the kitchen, the boy and Sam squatting to peer back into the obscurity where they huddled, quiet, the eyes luminous, glowing at them and vanishing, and no sound, only that effluvium of something more than dog, stronger than dog and not just animal, just beast, because still there had been nothing in front of that abject and almost painful yapping save the solitude, the wilderness, so that when the eleventh hound came in at noon and with all others watching—even old Uncle Ash, who called himself first a cook—Sam daubed the tattered ear and the raked shoulder with turpentine and axle grease, to the boy it was still no living creature, but the wilderness which, leaning for the moment down, had patted lightly once the hound's temerity.

"Just like a man," Sam said. "Just like folks. Put off as long as she could having to be brave, knowing all the time that sooner or later she would have to be brave to keep on living with herself, and knowing all the time beforehand what was going to happen to her when she done it."

That afternoon, himself on the one-eyed wagon mule which did not mind the smell of blood nor, as they told him, of bear, and with Sam on the other one, they rode for more than three hours through the rapid, shortening winter day. They followed no path, no trail even that he could see; almost at once they were in a country which he had never seen before. Then he knew why Sam had made him ride the mule which would not spook. The sound one stopped short and tried to whirl and bolt even as Sam got down, blowing its breath, jerking and wrenching at the rein, while Sam held it, coaxing it forward with his voice, since he could not risk tying it, drawing it forward while the boy got down from the marred one.

Then, standing beside Sam in the gloom of the dying afternoon, he looked down at the rotted over-turned log, gutted and scored with claw marks, and in the wet earth beside it, the print of the enormous warped two-toed foot. He knew now what he had smelled when he peered under the kitchen where the dogs huddled. He realized for the first time that the bear which had run in his listening and loomed in his dreams since before he could remember to the contrary, and which, therefore, must have existed in the listening and dreams of his father and Major de Spain and even old General Compson, too, before they began to remember in their turn, was a mortal animal, and that if they had departed for the camp each November without any actual hope of bringing its trophy back, it was not because it could not be slain, but because so far they had had no actual hope to.

"Tomorrow," he said.

"We'll try tomorrow," Sam said. "We ain't got the dog yet."

"We've got eleven. They ran him this morning."

"It won't need but one," Sam said. "He ain't here. Maybe he ain't nowhere. The only other way will be for him to run by accident over somebody that has a gun."

"That wouldn't be me," the boy said. "It will be Walter or Major or—"

"It might," Sam said. "You watch close in the morning. Because he's smart. That's how come he has lived this long. If he gets hemmed up and has to pick out somebody to run over, he will pick out you."

"How?" the boy said. "How will he know—" He ceased. "You mean he already knows me, that I ain't never been here before, ain't had time to find out yet whether I—" He ceased again, looking at Sam, the old man whose face revealed nothing until it smiled. He said humbly, not even amazed, "It was me he was watching. I don't reckon he did need to come but once."

The next morning they left the camp three hours before daylight. They rode this time because it was too far to walk, even the dogs in the wagon; again the first gray light found him in a place which he had never seen before, where Sam had placed him and told him to stay and then departed. With the gun which was too big for him, which did not even belong to him, but to Major de Spain, and which he had fired only once—at a stump on the first day, to learn the recoil and how to reload it—he stood against a gum tree beside a little bayou whose black still water crept without movement out of a canebrake and crossed a small clearing and into cane again, where, invisible, a bird—the big woodpecker called Lord-to-God by Negroes—clattered at a dead limb.

It was a stand like any other, dissimilar only in incidentals to the one where he had stood each morning for ten days; a territory new to him, yet no less familiar than that other which, after almost two weeks, he had come to believe he knew a little—the same solitude, the same loneliness through which human beings had merely passed without altering it, leaving no mark, no scar, which looked exactly as it must have looked when the first ancestor of Sam Fathers' Chickasaw predecessors crept into it and looked about, club or stone ax or bone arrow drawn and poised; different only because, squatting at the edge of the kitchen, he smelled the hounds huddled and cringing beneath it and saw the raked ear and shoulder of the one who, Sam said, had had to be brave once in order to live with herself, and saw yesterday in the earth beside the gutted log the print of the living foot.

He heard no dogs at all. He never did hear them. He only heard the drumming of the woodpecker stop short off and knew that the bear was looking at him. He never saw it. He did not know whether it was in front of him or behind him. He did not move, holding the useless gun, which he had not even had warning to cock and which even now he did not cock, tasting in his saliva that taint as of brass which he knew now because he had smelled it when he peered under the kitchen at the huddled dogs.

Then it was gone. As abruptly as it had

ceased, the woodpecker's dry, monotonous clatter set up again, and after a while he even believed he could hear the dogs—a murmur, scarce a sound even, which he had probably been hearing for some time before he even remarked it, drifting into hearing and then out again, dying away. They came nowhere near him. If it was a bear they ran, it was another bear. It was Sam himself who came out of the cane and crossed the bayou, followed by the injured bitch of yesterday. She was almost at heel, like a bird dog, making no sound. She came and crouched against his leg, trembling, staring off into the cane.

"I didn't see him," he said. "I didn't, Sam!"

"I know it," Sam said. "He done the looking. You didn't hear him neither, did you?"

"No," the boy said. "I—"

"He's smart," Sam said. "Too smart." He looked down at the hound, trembling faintly and steadily against the boy's knee. From the raked shoulder a few drops of fresh blood oozed and clung. "Too big. We ain't got the dog yet. But maybe someday. Maybe not next time. But someday."

So I must see him, he thought. *I must look at him.* Otherwise, it seemed to him that it would go on like this forever, as it had gone on with his father and Major de Spain, who was older than his father, and even with old General Compson, who had been old enough to be a brigade commander in 1865. Otherwise, it would go on so forever, next time and next time, after and after and after. It seemed to him that he could never see the two of them, himself and the bear, shadowy in the limbo from which time emerged, becoming time; the old bear absolved of mortality and himself partaking, sharing a little of it, enough of it. And he knew now what he had smelled in the huddled dogs and tasted in his saliva. He recognized fear. *So I will have to see him,* he thought, without dread or even hope. *I will have to look at him.*

It was in June of the next year. He was eleven. They were in camp again, celebrating Major de Spain's and General Compson's birthdays. Although the one had been born in September and the other in the depth of winter and in another decade, they had met for two weeks to fish and shoot squirrels and turkey and run coons and wildcats with the dogs at night. That is, he and Boon Hoggenback and the Negroes fished and shot squirrels and ran the coons and cats, because the proved hunters, not only Major de Spain and old General Compson, who spent those two weeks sitting in a rocking chair before a tremendous iron pot of Brunswick stew, stirring and tasting, with old Ash to quarrel with about how he was making it and Tennie's Jim to pour whiskey from the demijohn into the tin dipper from which he drank, but even the boy's father and Walter Ewell, who were still young enough, scorned such, other than shooting the wild gobblers with pistols for wagers on their marksmanship.

Or, that is, his father and the others believed he was hunting squirrels. Until the third day, he thought that Sam Fathers believed that too. Each morning he would leave the camp right after breakfast. He had his own gun now, a Christmas present. He went back to the tree beside the bayou where he had stood that morning. Using the compass which old General Compson had given him, he ranged from that point; he was teaching himself to be a better-than-fair woodsman without knowing he was doing it. On the second day he even found the gutted log where he had first seen the crooked print. It was almost completely crumbled now, healing with unbelievable speed, a passionate and almost visible relinquishment, back into the earth from which the tree had grown.

He ranged the summer woods now, green with gloom; if anything, actually dimmer than in November's gray dissolution, where, even at noon, the sun fell only in intermittent dappling upon the earth, which never completely dried out and which crawled with snakes—moccasins and water snakes and rattlers, themselves the color of the dappling gloom, so that he would not always see them until they moved, returning later and later, first day, second day, passing in the twilight of the third evening the little log pen enclosing the log stable where Sam was putting up the horses for the night.

"You ain't looked right yet," Sam said.

He stopped. For a moment he didn't answer. Then he said peacefully, in a peaceful rushing burst as when a boy's miniature dam in a little brook gives way, "All right. But how? I went to the bayou. I even found that log again. I—"

"I reckon that was all right. Likely he's been watching you. You never saw his foot?"

"I," the boy said—"I didn't—I never thought—"

"It's the gun," Sam said. He stood beside the fence, motionless—the old man, the Indian, in the battered faded overalls and the five-cent straw hat which in the Negro's race had been the badge of his enslavement and was now the regalia of his freedom. The camp—the clearing, the house, the barn and its tiny lot with which Major de Spain in his turn had scratched punily and evanescently at the wilderness—faded in the dusk, back into the immemorial darkness of the woods. *The gun,* the boy thought. *The gun.*

"Be scared," Sam said. "You can't help that. But don't be afraid. Ain't nothing in the woods going to hurt you unless you corner it, or it smells that you are afraid. A bear or a deer, too, has got to be scared of a coward the same as a brave man has got to be."

The gun, the boy thought.

"You will have to choose," Sam said.

He left the camp before daylight, long before Uncle Ash would wake in his quilts on the kitchen floor and start the fire for breakfast. He had only the compass and a stick for snakes. He could go almost a mile before he would begin to need the compass. He sat on a log, the invisible compass in his invisible hand, while the secret night sounds, fallen still at his movements, scurried again and then ceased for good, and the owls ceased and gave over to the waking of day birds, and he could see the compass. Then he went fast yet still quietly; he was becoming better and better as a woodsman, still without having yet realized it.

He jumped a doe and a fawn at sunrise, walked them out of the bed, close enough to see them—the crash of undergrowth, the white scut, the fawn scudding behind her faster than he had believed it could run. He was hunting right, upwind, as Sam had taught him; not that it mattered now. He had left the gun; of his own will and relinquishment he had accepted not a gambit, not a choice, but a condition in which not only the bear's heretofore inviolable anonymity but all the old rules and balances of hunter and

hunted had been abrogated. He would not even be afraid, not even in the moment when the fear would take him completely—blood, skin, bowels, bones, memory from the long time before it became his memory—all save that thin, clear, immortal lucidity which alone differed him from this bear and from all the other bear and deer he would ever kill in the humility and pride of his skill and endurance, to which Sam had spoken when he leaned in the twilight on the lot fence yesterday.

By noon he was far beyond the little bayou, farther into the new and alien country than he had ever been. He was traveling now not only by the old, heavy, biscuit-thick silver watch which had belonged to his grandfather. When he stopped at last, it was for the first time since he had risen from the log at dawn when he could see the compass. It was far enough. He had left the camp nine hours ago; nine hours from now, dark would have already been an hour old. But he didn't think that. He thought, *All right. Yes. But what?* and stood for a moment, alien and small in the green and topless solitude, answering his own question before it had formed and ceased. It was the watch, the compass, the stick—the three lifeless mechanicals with which for nine hours he had fended the wilderness off; he hung the watch and compass carefully on a bush and leaned the stick beside them and relinquished completely to it.

He had not been going very fast for the last two or three hours. He went no faster now, since distance would not matter even if he could have gone fast. And he was trying to keep a bearing on the tree where he had left the compass, trying to complete a circle which would bring him back to it or at least intersect itself, since direction would not matter now either. But the tree was not there, and he did as Sam had schooled him—made the next circle in the opposite direction, so that the two patterns would bisect somewhere, but crossing no print of his own feet, finding the tree at last, but in the wrong place—no bush, no compass, no watch—and the tree not even the tree, because there was a down log beside it and he did what Sam Fathers had told him was the next thing and the last.

As he sat down on the log he saw the crooked print—the warped, tremendous, two-toed indentation which, even as he watched it, filled with water. As he looked up, the wilderness coalesced, solidified—the glade, the tree he sought, the bush, the watch and the compass glinting where a ray of sunlight touched them. Then he saw the bear. It did not emerge, appear; it was just there, immobile, solid, fixed in the hot dappling of the green and windless noon, not as big as he had dreamed it, but as big as he had expected it, bigger, dimensionless against the dappled obscurity, looking at him where he sat quietly on the log and looked back at it.

Then it moved. It made no sound. It did not hurry. It crossed the glade, walking for an instant into the full glare of the sun; when it reached the other side it stopped again and looked back at him across one shoulder while his quiet breathing inhaled and exhaled three times.

Then it was gone. It didn't walk into the woods, the undergrowth. It faded, sank back into the wilderness as he had watched a fish, a huge old bass, sink and vanish into the dark depths of its pool without even any movement of its fins.

He thought, *It will be next fall.* But it was not next fall, nor the next nor the next. He was fourteen then. He had killed his buck, and Sam Fathers had marked his face with the hot blood, and in the next year he killed a bear. But even before that accolade he had become as competent in the woods as many grown men with the same experience; by his fourteenth year he was a better woodsman than most grown men with more. There was no territory within thirty miles of the camp that he did not know—bayou, ridge, brake, landmark, tree, and path. He could have led anyone to any point in it without deviation, and brought them out again. He knew the game trails that even Sam Fathers did not know; in his thirteenth year he found a buck's bedding place, and unbeknown to his father he borrowed Walter Ewell's rifle and lay in wait at dawn and killed the buck when it walked back to the bed, as Sam had told him how the old Chickasaw fathers did.

But not the old bear, although by now he knew its footprints better than he did his own, and not only the crooked one. He could see any one of the three sound ones and distinguish it from any other, and not only by its size. There were other bears within these thirty miles which left tracks almost as large, but this was more than

that. If Sam Fathers had been his mentor and the backyard rabbits and squirrels at home his kindergarten, then the wilderness the old bear ran was his college, the old male bear itself, so long unwifed and childless as to have become its own ungendered progenitor, was his alma mater. But he never saw it.

He could find the crooked print now almost whenever he liked, fifteen or ten or five miles, or sometimes nearer the camp than that. Twice while on stand during the three years he heard the dogs strike its trail by accident; on the second time they jumped it seemingly, the voices high, abject, almost human in hysteria, as on that first morning two years ago. But not the bear itself. He would remember that noon three years ago, the glade, himself and the bear fixed during that moment in the windless and dappled blaze, and it would seem to him that it had never happened, that he had dreamed that too. But it had happened. They had looked at each other, they had emerged from the wilderness old as earth, synchronized to the instant by something more than the blood that moved the flesh and bones which bore them, and touched, pledged something, affirmed something more lasting than the frail web of bones and flesh which any accident could obliterate.

Then he saw it again. Because of the very fact that he thought of nothing else, he had forgotten to look for it. He was still-hunting with Walter Ewell's rifle. He saw it cross the end of a long blowdown, a corridor where a tornado had swept, rushing through rather than over the tangle of trunks and branches as a locomotive would have, faster than he had ever believed it could move, almost as fast as a deer even, because a deer would have spent most of that time in the air, faster than he could bring the rifle sights with it. And now he knew what had been wrong during all the three years. He sat on a log, shaking and trembling as if he had never seen the woods before nor anything that ran them, wondering with incredulous amazement how he could have forgotten the very thing which Sam Fathers had told him and which the bear itself had proved the next day and had now returned after three years to reaffirm.

And now he knew what Sam Fathers had meant about the right dog, a dog in which size would mean less than nothing. So when he returned alone in April—school was out then, so that the sons of farmers could help with the land's planting, and at last his father had granted him permission, on his promise to be back in four days—he had the dog. It was his own, a mongrel of the sort called by Negroes a fyce, a ratter, itself not much bigger than a rat and possessing that bravery which had long since stopped being courage and had become foolhardiness.

It did not take four days. Alone again, he found the trail on the first morning. It was not a stalk; it was an ambush. He timed the meeting almost as if it were an appointment with a human being. Himself holding the fyce muffled in a feed sack and Sam Fathers with two of the hounds on a piece of a plowline rope, they lay downwind of the trail at dawn of the second morning. They were so close that the bear turned without even running, as if in surprised amazement at the shrill and frantic uproar of the released fyce, turning at bay against the trunk of a tree, on its hind feet; it seemed to the boy that it would never stop rising, taller and taller, and even the two hounds seemed to take a desperate and despairing courage from the fyce, following it as it went in.

Then he realized that the fyce was actually not going to stop. He flung, threw the gun away, and ran; when he overtook and grasped the frantically pinwheeling little dog, it seemed to him that he was directly under the bear.

He could smell it, strong and hot and rank. Sprawling, he looked up to where it loomed and towered over him like a cloudburst and colored like a thunderclap, quite familiar, peacefully and even lucidly familiar, until he remembered: This was the way he had used to dream about it. Then it was gone. He didn't see it go. He knelt, holding the frantic fyce with both hands, hearing the abashed wailing of the hounds drawing farther and farther away, until Sam came up. He carried the gun. He laid it down quietly beside the boy and stood looking down at him.

"You've done seed him twice now with a gun in your hands," he said. "This time you couldn't have missed him."

The boy rose. He still held the fyce. Even in his arms and clear of the ground, it yapped frantically, straining and surging after the fading uproar of the two hounds like a tangle of wire springs. He was panting a little, but he was neither shaking nor trembling now.

"Neither could you!" he said. "You had the gun! Neither did you!"

"And you didn't shoot," his father said. "How close were you?"

"I don't know, sir," he said. "There was a big wood tick inside his right hind leg. I saw that. But I didn't have the gun then."

"But you didn't shoot when you had the gun," his father said. "Why?"

But he didn't answer, and his father didn't wait for him to, rising and crossing the room, across the pelt of the bear which the boy had killed two years ago and the larger one which his father had killed before he was born, to the bookcase beneath the mounted head of the boy's first buck. It was the room which his father called the office, from which all the plantation business was transacted; in it for the fourteen years of his life he had heard the best of all talking. Major de Spain would be there and sometimes old General Compson, and Walter Ewell and Boon Hoggenback and Sam Fathers and Tennie's Jim, too, were hunters, knew the woods and what ran them.

He would hear it, not talking himself but listening—the wilderness, the big woods, bigger and older than any recorded document of white man fatuous enough to believe he had bought any fragment of it or Indian ruthless enough to pretend that any fragment of it had been his to convey. It was of the men, not white nor black nor red, but men, hunters with the will and hardihood to endure and the humility and skill to survive, and the dogs and the bear and deer juxtaposed and reliefed against it, ordered and compelled by and within the wilderness in the ancient and unremitting contest by the ancient and immitigable rules which voided all regrets and brooked no quarter, the voices quiet and weighty and deliberate for retrospection and recollection and exact remembering, while he squatted in the blazing firelight as Tennie's Jim squatted, who stirred only to put more wood on the fire and to pass the bottle from one glass to another. Because the bottle was always present, so that after a while it seemed to him that those fierce instants of heart and brain and courage and wiliness and speed were concentrated and distilled into that brown liquor which not women,

not boys and children, but only hunters drank, drinking not of the blood they had spilled but some condensation of the wild immortal spirit, drinking it moderately, humbly even, not with the pagan's base hope of acquiring the virtues of cunning and strength and speed, but in salute to them.

His father returned with the book and sat down again and opened it. "Listen," he said. He read the five stanzas aloud, his voice quiet and deliberate in the room where there was no fire now because it was already spring. Then he looked up. The boy watched him. "All right," his father said. "Listen." He read again, but only the second stanza this time, to the end of it, the last two lines, and closed the book and put it on the table beside him. "She cannot fade, though thou hast not thy bliss, for ever wilt thou love, and she be fair,"[2] he said.

"He's talking about a girl," the boy said.

"He had to talk about something," his father said. Then he said, "He was talking about truth. Truth doesn't change. Truth is one thing. It covers all things which touch the heart—honor and pride and pity and justice and courage and love. Do you see now?"

He didn't know. Somehow it was simpler than that. There was an old bear, fierce and ruthless, not merely just to stay alive, but with the fierce pride of liberty and freedom, proud enough of the liberty and freedom to see it threatened without fear or even alarm; nay, who at times even seemed deliberately to put that freedom and liberty in jeopardy in order to savor them, to remind his old strong bones and flesh to keep supple and quick to defend and preserve them. There was an old man, son of a Negro slave and an Indian king, inheritor on the one side of the long chronicle of a people who had learned humility through suffering, and pride through the endurance which survived the suffering and injustice, and on the other side, the chronicle of a people even longer in the land than the first, yet who no longer existed in the land at all save in the solitary brotherhood of an old Negro's alien blood and the wild and invincible spirit of an old bear. There was a boy who

---

2. **"She cannot . . . be fair,"** the last two lines of "Ode on a Grecian Urn," a poem by John Keats (1795–1821).

wished to learn humility and pride in order to become skillful and worthy in the woods, who suddenly found himself becoming so skillful so rapidly that he feared he would never become worthy because he had not learned humility and pride, although he had tried to, until one day and as suddenly he discovered that an old man who could not have defined either had led him, as though by the hand, to that point where an old bear and a little mongrel of a dog showed him that, by possessing one thing other, he would possess them both.

And a little dog, nameless and mongrel and many-fathered, grown, yet weighing less than six pounds, saying as if to itself, "I can't be dangerous, because there's nothing much smaller than I am; I can't be fierce, because they would call it just noise; I can't be humble, because I'm already too close to the ground to genuflect; I can't be proud, because I wouldn't be near enough to it for anyone to know who was casting the shadow, and I don't even know that I'm not going to heaven, because they have already decided that I don't possess an immortal soul. So all I can be is brave. But it's all right. I can be that, even if they still call it just noise."

That was all. It was simple, much simpler than somebody talking in a book about a youth and a girl he would never need to grieve over, because he could never approach any nearer her and would never have to get any farther away. He had heard about a bear, and finally got big enough to trail it, and he trailed it four years and at last met it with a gun in his hands and he didn't shoot. Because a little dog—But he could have shot long before the little dog covered the twenty yards to where the bear waited, and Sam Fathers could have shot at any time during that interminable minute while Old Ben stood on his hind feet over them. He stopped. His father was watching him gravely across the spring-rife twilight of the room; when he spoke, his words were as quiet as the twilight, too, not loud, because they did not need to be because they would last. "Courage, and honor, and pride," his father said, "and pity, and love of justice and of liberty. They all touch the heart, and what the heart holds to becomes truth, as far as we know the truth. Do you see now?"

Sam, and Old Ben, and Nip, he thought. And himself too. He had been all right too. His father had said so. "Yes, sir," he said. □□

Discussion

1. The four opening paragraphs, before the boy's first trip to the hunting camp, form the **exposition** of this story. (a) What has the boy already learned about the bear and the hunters' attitude toward it? (b) Describe the **mood** this exposition sets for the story.

2. (a) On the boy's first hunt, what lesson does Sam Fathers teach him? (b) Reread Sam Fathers's comment about the dog whose shoulder is raked by the bear (403,b,5). What does it

mean? (c) What does the boy discover from seeing the print of the bear's warped foot? (d) Why does Sam believe the bear can't be caught? (e) How does the boy discover on the next morning's hunt that the unseen bear is looking at him? (f) Describe his physical and emotional reactions to this experience.

3. When the boy is eleven he visits the swamp again. (a) How does he pass the time that the men think he spends squirrel hunting? (b) What choice concerning the gun does Sam

put to him? (c) What does he find it necessary to do before he finally sees the bear? (d) What is the significance of his quiet inhaling and exhaling three times when he sees the bear?

4. The boy is fourteen when he next meets Old Ben. (a) Give examples of his progress as a woodsman in the intervening years. (b) What does he remember after he has seen the bear "cross the end of a long blowdown"? (c) What does his dog do when they meet the bear? (d) What does he do?

5. (a) In the concluding conversation with his father, how does the boy explain his not shooting the bear? **(b)** What ideas does the boy get from this discussion? What point is the father making by the lines of poetry he emphasizes?

6. (a) By what means does Faulkner make the wilderness seem awesome? **(b)** What relationship does he imply people should feel toward the wilderness?

7. The **theme** of the story is a child's gradual growth to maturity. What lessons does the boy learn from **(a)** Sam Fathers? **(b)** the bear? **(c)** the boy's father?

8. Locate the various comments on the meaning of bravery. **(a)** What distinctions does Faulkner seem to draw between cowardice, foolhardiness, and true bravery? **(b)** How is his concept of true bravery related to the theme of maturity?

Extension • Writing

Write a short essay in which you explain how "humility" and "pride" may be justified, in the story or from your own experience, as compatible with each other.

Vocabulary • Dictionary

Use your Glossary to find the meaning of each word below from "The Bear." On your paper write the proper form of the word that correctly answers each question.

progenitor
coalesce
intermittent
anachronism
abrogate
abject
interminable
retrospection

1. If you saw a donkey and cart going down the middle of a modern expressway, what would you call this sight?

2. If a person has just lost her house, her car, and her job, what word describes her probable mood?

3. A company ends an agreement with one supplier in order to use another. What has happened to the first agreement?

4. Before the father's illness, the family was always bickering, but since then they have unified in order to solve their problems. Which word describes what they have done?

5. How would you describe rain showers that start and stop all day long?

6. If someone traced your family to its roots, what term would describe its earliest members?

7. If you go to a very dull film that seems never to end, what word best describes the experience?

William Faulkner 1897 • 1962

Faulkner came to writing partly by inheritance (his grandfather was an author); partly through his experiences with the Canadian Air Force in World War I; and partly by encouragement from Sherwood Anderson. After the war, he returned to his native Mississippi and enrolled briefly at the state university. Abandoning his studies, he worked at odd jobs while devoting much time to reading and writing poetry.

In 1924 his first book of poems, *The Marble Faun,* was published and in New Orleans he met Anderson, who convinced him to concentrate on writing fiction. With Anderson's aid, Faulkner's first novel, *Soldiers' Pay,* was published. After this novel about the war, Faulkner followed Anderson's advice to write from his first-hand knowledge of the South. In such great novels as *The Sound and the Fury* (1929), Faulkner began to create a microcosm of Southern society past and present.

Although his writing is not autobiographical, many of his characters and settings are drawn from his own life. For example, in the woods outside Oxford, Mississippi, there did live an enormous bear which no one was able to kill.

Faulkner was preoccupied with form and experimented with different means of bringing reality to his works. Because of his complex style, Faulkner's works were not widely read until he was awarded the 1949 Nobel Prize in literature.

Ernest Hemingway

In Another Country

In the fall the war[1] was always there, but we did not go to it any more. It was cold in the fall in Milan and the dark came very early. Then the electric lights came on, and it was pleasant along the streets looking in the windows. There was much game hanging outside the shops, and the snow powdered in the fur of the foxes and the wind blew their tails. The deer hung stiff and heavy and empty, and small birds blew in the wind and the wind turned their feathers. It was a cold fall and the wind came down from the mountains.

We were all at the hospital every afternoon, and there were different ways of walking across the town through the dusk to the hospital. Two of the ways were alongside canals, but they were long. Always, though, you crossed a bridge across a canal to enter the hospital. There was a choice of three bridges. On one of them a woman sold roasted chestnuts. It was warm, standing in front of her charcoal fire, and the chestnuts were warm afterward in your pocket. The hospital was very old and very beautiful, and you entered through a gate and walked across a courtyard and out a gate on the other side. There were usually funerals starting from the courtyard. Beyond the old hospital were the new brick pavilions, and there we met every afternoon and were all very polite and interested in what was the matter, and sat in the machines that were to make so much difference.

The doctor came up to the machine where I was sitting and said: "What did you like best to do before the war? Did you practice a sport?"

I said: "Yes, football."

"Good," he said. "You will be able to play football again better than ever."

My knee did not bend and the leg dropped straight from the knee to the ankle without a calf, and the machine was to bend the knee and make it move as in riding a tricycle. But it did not bend yet, and instead the machine lurched when it came to the bending part. The doctor said: "That will all pass. You are a fortunate young man. You will play football again like a champion."

In the next machine was a major who had a little hand like a baby's. He winked at me when the doctor examined his hand, which was between two leather straps that bounced up and down and flapped the stiff fingers, and said: "And will I too play football, captain-doctor?" He had been a very great fencer, and before the war the greatest fencer in Italy.

The doctor went to his office in the back room and brought a photograph which showed a hand that had been withered almost as small as the major's, before it had taken a machine course, and after was a little larger. The major held the photograph with his good hand and looked at it very carefully. "A wound?" he asked.

"An industrial accident," the doctor said.

"Very interesting, very interesting," the major said, and handed it back to the doctor.

"You have confidence?"

"No," said the major.

There were three boys who came each day who were about the same age I was. They were all three from Milan, and one of them was to be a lawyer, and one was to be a painter, and one had intended to be a soldier, and after we were finished with the machines, sometimes we walked back together to the Café Cova, which was next door to the Scala.[2] We walked the short way through the communist quarter because we were four together. The people hated us because we were officers, and from a wineshop some one called out, "A basso gli ufficiali!"[3] as we passed. Another boy who walked with us sometimes and

"In Another Country" is reprinted by permission of Charles Scribner's Sons and Jonathan Cape Ltd. from MEN WITHOUT WOMEN by Ernest Hemingway. (British Title: THE FIRST FORTY-NINE STORIES). Copyright 1927, Charles Scribner's Sons.

1. **the war,** World War I (1914–1919).
2. **the Scala,** La Scala, Milan's world-famous opera house.
3. **"A basso gli ufficiali!"** Down with the officers! [*Italian*]

made us five wore a black silk handkerchief across his face because he had no nose then and his face was to be rebuilt. He had gone out to the front from the military academy and been wounded within an hour after he had gone into the front line for the first time. They rebuilt his face, but he came from a very old family and they could never get the nose exactly right. He went to South America and worked in a bank. But this was a long time ago, and then we did not any of us know how it was going to be afterward. We only knew then that there was always the war, but that we were not going to it any more.

We all had the same medals, except the boy with the black silk bandage across his face, and he had not been at the front long enough to get any medals. The tall boy with a very pale face who was to be a lawyer had been a lieutenant of Arditi[4] and had three medals of the sort we each had only one of. He had lived a very long time with death and was a little detached. We were all a little detached, and there was nothing that held us together except that we met every afternoon at the hospital. Although, as we walked to the Cova through the tough part of town, walking in the dark, with light and singing coming out of the wineshops, and sometimes having to walk into the street when the men and women would crowd together on the sidewalk so that we would have had to jostle them to get by, we felt held together by there being something that had happened that they, the people who disliked us, did not understand.

We ourselves all understood the Cova, where it was rich and warm and not too brightly lighted, and noisy and smoky at certain hours, and there were always girls at the tables and the illustrated papers on a rack on the wall. The girls at the Cova were very patriotic, and I found that the most patriotic people in Italy were café girls— and I believe they are still patriotic.

The boys at first were very polite about my medals and asked me what I had done to get them. I showed them the papers, which were written in very beautiful language and full of *fratellanza* and *abnegazione,*[5] but which really said, with the adjective removed, that I had been given the medals because I was an American. After that their manner changed a little toward me, although I was their friend against outsiders.

I was a friend, but I was never really one of them after they had read the citations, because it had been different with them and they had done very different things to get their medals. I had been wounded, it was true; but we all knew that being wounded, after all, was really an accident. I was never ashamed of the ribbons, though, and sometimes after cocktail hour, I would imagine myself having done all the things they had done to get their medals; but walking home at night through the empty streets with the cold wind and all the shops closed, trying to keep near the street lights, I knew that I would never have done such things, and I was very much afraid to die, and often lay in bed at night by myself, afraid to die and wondering how I would be when I went back to the front again.

The three with the medals were like hunting hawks; and I was not a hawk, although I might seem a hawk to those who had never hunted; they, the three, knew better and so we drifted apart. But I stayed good friends with the boy who had been wounded his first day at the front, because he would never know now how he would have turned out; so he could never be accepted either, and I liked him because I thought perhaps he would not have turned out to be a hawk either.

The major, who had been the great fencer, did not believe in bravery, and spent much time while we sat in the machines correcting my grammar. He had complimented me on how I spoke Italian, and we talked together very easily. One day I had said that Italian seemed such an easy language to me that I could not take a great interest in it; everything was so easy to say. "Ah, yes," the major said. "Why, then, do you not take up the use of grammar?" So we took up the use of grammar, and soon Italian was such a difficult language that I was afraid to talk to him until I had the grammar straight in my mind.

The major came very regularly to the hospital. I do not think he ever missed a day, although I am sure he did not believe in the machines. There was a time when none of us believed in the machines, and one day the major said it was all

---

4. *Arditi,* a picked group of volunteers which served as storm troops of the Italian infantry.
5. *fratellanza* (frä tel län′zä) *and abnegazione* (äb′ nä gä tsyō′ne), brotherhood and self-denial. [*Italian*]

nonsense. The machines were new then and it was we who were to prove them. It was an idiotic idea, he said, "a theory, like another." I had not learned my grammar, and he said I was a stupid impossible disgrace, and he was a fool to have bothered with me. He was a small man and he sat straight up in his chair with his right hand thrust into the machine and looked straight ahead at the wall while the straps thumped up and down with his fingers in them.

"What will you do when the war is over if it is over?" he asked me. "Speak grammatically!"

"I will go to the States."

"Are you married?"

"No, but I hope to be."

"The more of a fool you are," he said. He seemed very angry. "A man must not marry."

"Why, Signor Maggiore?"[6]

"Don't call me 'Signor Maggiore.'"

"Why must not a man marry?"

"He cannot marry. He cannot marry," he said angrily. "If he is to lose everything, he should not place himself in a position to lose that. He should not place himself in a position to lose. He should find things he cannot lose."

He spoke very angrily and bitterly, and looked straight ahead while he talked.

"But why should he necessarily lose it?"

"He'll lose it," the major said. He was looking at the wall. Then he looked down at the machine and jerked his little hand out from between the straps and slapped it hard against his thigh. "He'll lose it," he almost shouted. "Don't argue with me!" Then he called to the attendant who ran the machines. "Come and turn this damned thing off."

He went back into the other room for the light treatment and the massage. Then I heard him ask the doctor if he might use his telephone and he shut the door. When he came back into the room, I was sitting in another machine. He was wearing his cape and had his cap on, and he came directly toward my machine and put his arm on my shoulder.

"I am so sorry," he said, and patted me on the shoulder with his good hand. "I would not be rude. My wife has just died. You must forgive me."

"Oh—" I said, feeling sick for him. "I am *so* sorry."

He stood there biting his lower lip. "It is very difficult," he said. "I cannot resign myself."

He looked straight past me and out through the window. Then he began to cry. "I am utterly unable to resign myself," he said, and choked. And then crying, his head up looking at nothing, carrying himself straight and soldierly, with tears on both his cheeks and biting his lips, he walked past the machines and out the door.

The doctor told me that the major's wife, who was very young and whom he had not married until he was definitely invalided out of the war, had died of pneumonia. She had been sick only a few days. No one expected her to die. The major did not come to the hospital for three days. Then he came at the usual hour, wearing a black band on the sleeve of his uniform. When he came back, there were large framed photographs around the wall, of all sorts of wounds before and after they had been cured by the machines. In front of the machine the major used were three photographs of hands like his that were completely restored. I do not know where the doctor got them. I always understood we were the first to use the machines. The photographs did not make much difference to the major because he only looked out of the window.

□□

---

6. **Signor Maggiore** (sē′nyôr mäj jô′re), Mr. Major. In Italy it is a sign of respect to prefix an officer's rank with *Signor*.

Discussion

1. A critic has pointed out that the opening paragraph offers a number of symbolic details which stand for the "'other countries' which the lonely characters portrayed in the story sense but do not enter." These countries are: "the country of battle from which (the characters') wounds have removed them; that of peace which (the characters) glimpse through lighted windows from darkened streets; the country of nature symbolized by the game; and the country, finally, of death connoted by the cold, the dark, and by the wind which blows from the mountains." How is the exclusion of the soldiers from these "countries" important in this story?

2. Not only are the soldiers, as a group, shut off from other groups; as individuals, they are separated from one another. **(a)** In what ways is the isolation of each man shown? **(b)** Have their war experiences had anything to do with their loneliness? Explain.

3. How does the major differ from the other invalids?

4. (a) Describe the **tone** of the major's comments about the machines and compare it with his tone in telling of his wife's death. **(b)** Which hurts him more—her death, or the crippling of his hand? **(c)** Relate his final situation to the theme of isolation in the story.

5. Cite examples of Hemingway's terse, understated **style** from this story.

Extension · Writing

Write a short essay comparing the picture of war presented in Hemingway's story with the picture in Crane's "An Episode of War" (Unit 5).

Ernest Hemingway 1899 · 1961

"In Another Country" is an excellent example of Hemingway's sparse, compressed literary style, which has influenced countless writers around the world. He once explained the style to an interviewer: "I always try to write on the principle of the iceberg. There is seven-eighths of it underwater for every part that shows. Anything you know, you can eliminate and it only strengthens your iceberg. It is the part that doesn't show. If a writer omits something because he does not know it then there is a hole in the story."

Hemingway grew up in Oak Park, Illinois, where he won a considerable reputation as a high-school football player and boxer. After graduation from high school, he worked as a newspaper reporter in Kansas City, where his skill as a sparring partner acquainted him with prizefighters and gunmen.

Before the United States entered World War I, he served in a French ambulance unit; later he was seriously wounded while fighting in the Italian infantry. After the war, Hemingway worked in Paris as a correspondent for American newspapers, and became identified with the "lost generation" of self-exiled American artists and writers. Among these was F.

Scott Fitzgerald, who helped Hemingway find a publisher for *In Our Time* (1924), his first volume of stories. Two years later *The Sun Also Rises,* his first successful novel, appeared.

As Hemingway's reputation grew, his fishing, boxing, hunting in Africa, and interest in bullfights made him a celebrity to millions who had never read his books. He also became a renowned war correspondent. What is possibly Hemingway's finest novel, *For Whom the Bell Tolls* (1940), grew out of his experiences in the Spanish Civil War. When America entered World War II, he spent two years on antisubmarine patrol duty in the Caribbean and then joined the American forces in Europe as a reporter.

Afterwards Hemingway lived on his estate in Cuba until the Castro revolution. In 1953 he published *The Old Man and the Sea,* which won the Pulitzer Prize. The following year he received the Nobel Prize for literature. He died from a gunshot wound while cleaning one of his weapons. Some friends believe he may have taken his own life. A last novel, *Islands in the Stream,* came out posthumously in 1970.

Richard Wright

The Man Who Saw the Flood

When the flood waters recede,
the poor folk along the river
start from scratch.

At last the flood waters had receded. A black father, a black mother, and a black child tramped through muddy fields, leading a tired cow by a thin bit of rope. They stopped on a hilltop and shifted the bundles on their shoulders. As far as they could see the ground was covered with flood silt. The little girl lifted a skinny finger and pointed to a mudcaked cabin.

"Look, Pa! Ain tha our home?"

The man, round-shouldered, clad in blue, ragged overalls, looked with bewildered eyes. Without moving a muscle, scarcely moving his lips, he said: "Yeah."

For five minutes they did not speak or move. The flood waters had been more than eight feet high here. Every tree, blade of grass, and stray stick had its flood mark; caky, yellow mud. It clung to the ground, cracking thinly here and there in spider web fashion. Over the stark fields came a gusty spring wind. The sky was high, blue, full of white clouds and sunshine. Over all hung a first-day strangeness.

"The henhouse is gone," sighed the woman.

"N the pigpen," sighed the man.

They spoke without bitterness.

"Ah reckon them chickens is all done drowned."

"Yeah."

"Miz Flora's house is gone, too," said the little girl.

They looked at a clump of trees where their neighbor's house had stood.

"Lawd!"

"Yuh reckon anybody knows where they is?"

"Hard t tell."

The man walked down the slope and stood uncertainly.

"There wuz a road erlong here somewheres," he said.

But there was no road now. Just a wide sweep of yellow, scalloped silt.

"Look, Tom!" called the woman. "Here's a piece of our gate!"

The gatepost was half buried in the ground. A rusty hinge stood stiff, like a lonely finger. Tom pried it loose and caught it firmly in his hand. There was nothing particular he wanted to do with it; he just stood holding it firmly. Finally he dropped it, looked up, and said:

"C mon. Les go down n see whut we kin do."

Because it sat in a slight depression, the ground about the cabin was soft and slimy.

"Gimme tha bag o lime, May," he said.

With his shoes sucking in mud, he went slowly around the cabin, spreading the white lime with thick fingers. When he reached the front again he had a little left; he shook the bag out on the porch. The fine grains of floating lime flickered in the sunlight.

"Tha oughta hep some," he said.

"Now, yuh be careful, Sal!" said May. "Don yuh go n fall down in all this mud, yuh hear?"

"Yessum."

The steps were gone. Tom lifted May and Sally to the porch. They stood a moment looking at the half-opened door. He had shut it when he left, but somehow it seemed natural that he should find it open. The planks in the porch floor were swollen and warped. The cabin had two colors; near the bottom it was a solid yellow, at the top it was the familiar gray. It looked weird, as though its ghost were standing beside it.

The cow lowed.

"Tie Pat t the pos on the en of the porch, May."

May tied the rope slowly, listlessly. When they attempted to open the front door, it would not budge. It was not until Tom placed his shoulder against it and gave it a stout shove that it scraped back jerkily. The front room was dark and silent. The damp smell of flood silt came fresh and sharp to their nostrils. Only one-half of the upper window was clear, and through it fell a rectangle of dingy light. The floors swam in ooze. Like a mute warning, a wavering flood mark went high around the walls of the room. A dresser sat cater-cornered, its drawers and sides bulging like a bloated corpse. The bed, with the mattress still on it, was like a giant casket forged of mud. Two smashed chairs lay in a corner, as though huddled together for protection.

"Les see the kitchen," said Tom.

The stovepipe was gone. But the stove stood in the same place.

"The stove's still good. We kin clean it."

"Yeah."

"But where's the table?"

"Lawd knows."

"It must've washed erway wid the rest of the stuff, Ah reckon."

They opened the back door and looked out. They missed the barn, the henhouse, and the pigpen.

"Tom, yuh bettah try tha ol pump n see ef eny watah's there."

The pump was stiff. Tom threw his weight on the handle and carried it up and down. No water came. He pumped on. There was a dry hollow cough. Then yellow water trickled. He caught his breath and kept pumping. The water flowed white.

"Thank Gawd! We's got some watah."

"Yuh bettah boil it fo yuh use it," he said.

"Yeah. Ah know."

"Look, Pa! Here's yo ax," called Sally.

Tom took the ax from her. "Yeah. Ah'll need this."

"N here's somethin else," called Sally, digging spoons out of the mud.

"Waal, Ahma git a bucket n start cleanin," said May. "Ain no use in waitin, cause we's gotta sleep on them floors tonight."

When she was filling the bucket from the pump, Tom called from around the cabin. "May, look! Ah done foun mah plow!" Proudly he dragged the silt-caked plow to the pump. "Ah'll wash it n it'll be awright."

"Ahm hongry," said Sally.

"Now, yuh jus wait! Yuh et this mawnin," said May. She turned to Tom. "Now, whutcha gonna do, Tom?"

He stood looking at the mud-filled fields.

"Yuh goin back t Burgess?"

"Ah reckon Ah have to."

"Whut else kin yuh do?"

"Nothin," he said. "Lawd, but Ah sho hate t start all over wid tha white man. Ah'd leave here ef Ah could. Ah owes im nigh eight hundred dollahs. N we needs a hoss, grub, seed, n a lot mo other things. Ef we keeps on like this tha white man'll own us body n soul."

"But, Tom, there ain nothin else t do," she said.

"Ef we try t run erway they'll put us in jail."

"It coulda been worse," she said.

Sally came running from the kitchen. "Pa!"

"Hunh?"

"There's a shelf in the kitchen the flood didn't git!"

"Where?"

"Right up over the stove."

"But, chile, ain nothin up there," said May.

"But there's somethin on it," said Sally.

"C mon. Les see."

High and dry, untouched by the flood-water, was a box of matches. And beside it a half-full sack of Bull Durham tobacco. He took a match from the box and scratched it on his overalls. It burned to his fingers before he dropped it.

"May!"

"Hunh?"

"Look! Here's ma bacco n some matches!"

She stared unbelievingly. "Lawd!" she breathed.

Tom rolled a cigarette clumsily.

May washed the stove, gathered some sticks, and after some difficulty, made a fire. The kitchen stove smoked, and their eyes smarted. May put water on to heat and went into the front room. It was getting dark. From the bundles they took a kerosene lamp and lit it. Outside Pat lowed longingly into the thickening gloam and tinkled her cowbell.

"Tha old cow's hongry," said May.

"Ah reckon Ah'll have t be gittin erlong t Burgess."

They stood on the front porch.

"Yuh bettah git on, Tom, fo it gits too dark."

"Yeah."

The wind had stopped blowing. In the east a cluster of stars hung.

"Yuh goin, Tom?"

"Ah reckon Ah have t."

"Ma, Ah'm hongry," said Sally.

"Wait erwhile, honey. Ma knows yuh's hongry."

Tom threw his cigarette away and sighed.

"Look! Here comes somebody!"

"Thas Mistah Burgess now!"

A mud-caked buggy rolled up. The shaggy horse was splattered all over. Burgess leaned his white face out of the buggy and spat.

"Well, I see you're back."

"Yessuh."

"How things look?"

"They don look so good, Mistah."

"What seems to be the trouble?"

"Waal. Ah ain got no hoss, no grub, nothin. The only thing Ah got is tha ol cow there . . ."

"You owe eight hundred dollahs down at the store, Tom."

"Yessuh, Ah know. But, Mistah Burgess, can't yuh knock somethin off tha, seein as how Ahm down n out now?"

"You ate that grub, and I got to pay for it, Tom."

"Yessuh, Ah know."

"It's going to be a little tough, Tom. But you got to go through with it. Two of the boys tried to run away this morning and dodge their debts, and I had to have the sheriff pick em up. I wasn't looking for no trouble out of you, Tom . . . The rest of the families are going back."

Leaning out of the buggy, Burgess waited. In the surrounding stillness the cowbell tinkled again. Tom stood with his back against a post.

"Yuh got t go on, Tom. We ain't got nothin here," said May.

Tom looked at Burgess.

"Mistah Burgess, Ah don wanna make no trouble. But this is jus *too* hard. Ahm worse off now than befo. Ah got to start from scratch."

"Get in the buggy and come with me. I'll stake you with grub. We can talk over how you can pay it back." Tom said nothing. He rested his back against the post and looked at the mud-filled fields.

"Well," asked Burgess. "You coming?" Tom said nothing. He got slowly to the ground and pulled himself into the buggy. May watched them drive off.

"Hurry back, Tom!"

"Awright."

"Ma, tell Pa t bring me some 'lasses," begged Sally.

"Oh, Tom!"

Tom's head came out of the side of the buggy.

"Hunh?"

"Bring some 'lasses!"

"Hunh?"

"Bring some 'lasses for Sal!"

"Awright!"

She watched the buggy disappear over the crest of the muddy hill. Then she sighed, caught Sally's hand, and turned back into the cabin.

□ □

Discussion

1. Compare the language of the black family with the language of Burgess at the end of the story. Discuss the ways in which Wright uses dialogue to bring his characters alive.

2. Explain the way in which Burgess keeps the black family in bondage.

3. By what signs does Tom show he is near rebellion toward the end of the story? Why doesn't he rebel?

4. (a) What is the effect of the story's conclusion with Tom promising to bring back molasses for Sally? Explain. **(b)** What does the molasses represent to Sally? To Tom?

5. Discuss the meanings of the title, "The Man Who Saw the Flood."

Extension • Writing

Go through the story with some care, noting the objects which the family seems most interested in finding. From these and other clues in the story, reconstruct the kind of life the family must have had before the flood and write an account of that life.

Richard Wright 1908 • 1960

Richard Wright was born on a plantation near Natchez, Mississippi. He grew up, by his own description, unruly and unwanted. Wright was five years old when his father deserted the family. Within another five years his mother had succumbed to complete paralysis and he was passed from relative to relative until at the age of fifteen Wright struck out on his own. He worked in Memphis, Tennessee, at various unskilled jobs and then during the Depression bummed all over the country, ending up in Chicago. There he became active in the labor movement and in 1936 joined the Communist Party.

Wright was working in a Memphis post office when his literary interests were awakened by reading the essays of H. L. Mencken. When he reached Chicago he was able to join a WPA Writer's Project and by 1938 had published *Uncle Tom's Children,* a collection of four stories, one of which had already won the annual *Story* magazine award.

He followed this with *Native Son* (1940), a best seller about a young black man executed for murder. This novel achieved a degree of recognition and popularity which black writers in the past had mainly received from black audiences. Wright's next important work was the autobiographical *Black Boy* (1945), a novel which confirmed Wright's position among America's leading writers. Wright had in the meantime broken with the Communist Party and would in a book-length essay, *The God That Failed* (1950), describe his disenchantment.

After World War II, Wright moved to France, living and writing in Paris, with visits to Africa, until his death at the age of fifty-two. "The Man Who Saw the Flood" is taken from *Eight Men,* published posthumously in 1961.

Eudora Welty

A Worn Path

It was December—a bright frozen day in the early morning. Far out in the country there was an old Negro woman with her head tied in a red rag, coming along a path through the pinewoods. Her name was Phoenix Jackson. She was very old and small and she walked slowly in the dark pine shadows, moving a little from side to side in her steps, with the balanced heaviness and lightness of a pendulum in a grandfather clock. She carried a thin, small cane made from an umbrella, and with this she kept tapping the frozen earth in front of her. This made a grave and persistent noise in the still air, that seemed meditative like the chirping of a solitary little bird.

She wore a dark striped dress reaching down to her shoe tops, and an equally long apron of bleached sugar sacks, with a full pocket: all neat and tidy, but every time she took a step she might have fallen over her shoelaces, which dragged from her unlaced shoes. She looked straight ahead. Her eyes were blue with age. Her skin had a pattern all its own of numberless branching wrinkles and as though a whole little tree stood in the middle of her forehead, but a golden color ran underneath, and the two knobs of her cheeks were illumined by a yellow burning under the dark. Under the red rag her hair came down on her neck in the frailest of ringlets, still black, and with an odor like copper.

Now and then there was a quivering in the thicket. Old Phoenix said, "Out of my way, all you foxes, owls, beetles, jack rabbits, coons and wild animals! . . . Keep out from under these feet, little bob-whites. . . . Keep the big wild hogs out of my path. Don't let none of those come running my direction. I got a long way." Under her small black-freckled hand her cane, limber as a buggy whip, would switch at the brush as if to rouse up any hiding things.

On she went. The woods were deep and still. The sun made the pine needles almost too bright

to look at, up where the wind rocked. The cones dropped as light as feathers. Down in the hollow was the mourning dove—it was not too late for him.

The path ran up a hill. "Seem like there is chains about my feet, time I get this far," she said, in the voice of argument old people keep to use with themselves. "Something always take a hold of me on this hill—pleads I should stay."

After she got to the top she turned and gave a full, severe look behind her where she had come.

"Up through pines," she said at length. "Now down through oaks."

Her eyes opened their widest, and she started down gently. But before she got to the bottom of the hill a bush caught her dress.

Her fingers were busy and intent, but her skirts were full and long, so that before she could pull them free in one place they were caught in another. It was not possible to allow the dress to tear. "I in the thorny bush," she said. "Thorns, you doing your appointed work. Never want to let folks pass, no sir. Old eyes thought you was a pretty little *green* bush."

Finally, trembling all over, she stood free, and after a moment dared to stoop for her cane.

"Sun so high!" she cried, leaning back and looking, while the thick tears went over her eyes. "The time getting all gone here."

At the foot of this hill was a place where a log was laid across the creek.

"Now comes the trial," said Phoenix.

Putting her right foot out, she mounted the log and shut her eyes. Lifting her skirt, leveling her cane fiercely before her, like a festival figure in some parade, she began to march across. Then she opened her eyes and she was safe on the other side.

"I wasn't as old as I thought," she said.

But she sat down to rest. She spread her skirts on the bank around her and folded her hands over her knees. Up above her was a tree in a pearly cloud of mistletoe. She did not dare to close her eyes, and when a little boy brought her a plate with a slice of marble cake on it she spoke to him. "That would be acceptable," she said. But when she went to take it there was just her own hand in the air.

So she left that tree, and had to go through a barbed-wire fence. There she had to creep and crawl, spreading her knees and stretching her fingers like a baby trying to climb the steps. But she talked loudly to herself: she could not let her dress be torn now, so late in the day, and she could not pay for having her arm or her leg sawed off if she got caught fast where she was.

At last she was safe through the fence and risen up out in the clearing. Big dead trees, like black men with one arm, were standing in the purple stalks of the withered cotton field. There sat a buzzard.

"Who you watching?"

In the furrow she made her way along.

"Glad this not the season for bulls," she said, looking sideways, "and the good Lord made his snakes to curl up and sleep in the winter. A pleasure I don't see no two-headed snake coming around that tree, where it come once. It took a while to get by him, back in the summer."

She passed through the old cotton and went into a field of dead corn. It whispered and shook and was taller than her head. "Through the maze now," she said, for there was no path.

Then there was something tall, black, and skinny there, moving before her.

At first she took it for a man. It could have

been a man dancing in the field. But she stood still and listened, and it did not make a sound. It was as silent as a ghost.

"Ghost," she said sharply, "who be you the ghost of? For I have heard of nary death close by."

But there was no answer—only the ragged dancing in the wind.

She shut her eyes, reached out her hand, and touched a sleeve. She found a coat and inside that an emptiness, cold as ice.

"You scarecrow," she said. Her face lighted. "I ought to be shut up for good," she said with laughter. "My senses is gone. I too old. I the oldest people I ever know. Dance, old scarecrow," she said, "while I dancing with you."

She kicked her foot over the furrow, and with mouth drawn down, shook her head once or twice in a little strutting way. Some husks blew down and whirled in streamers about her skirts.

Then she went on, parting her way from side to side with the cane, through the whispering field. At last she came to the end, to a wagon track where the silver grass blew between the red ruts. The quail were walking around like pullets, seeming all dainty and unseen.

"Walk pretty," she said. "This the easy place. This the easy going."

She followed the track, swaying through the quiet bare fields, through the little strings of trees silver in their dead leaves, past cabins silver from weather, with the doors and windows boarded shut, all like old women under a spell sitting there. "I walking in their sleep," she said, nodding her head vigorously.

In a ravine she went where a spring was silently flowing through a hollow log. Old Phoenix bent and drank. "Sweet-gum makes the water sweet," she said, and drank more. "Nobody know who made this well, for it was here when I was born."

The track crossed a swampy part where the moss hung as white as lace from every limb. "Sleep on, alligators, and blow your bubbles." Then the track went into the road.

Deep, deep the road went down between the high green-colored banks. Overhead the live-oaks met, and it was as dark as a cave.

A black dog with a lolling tongue came up out of the weeds by the ditch. She was meditating, and not ready, and when he came at her she only hit him a little with her cane. Over she went in the ditch, like a little puff of milkweed.

Down there, her senses drifted away. A dream visited her, and she reached her hand up, but nothing reached down and gave her a pull. So she lay there and presently went to talking. "Old woman," she said to herself, "that black dog come up out of the weeds to stall you off, and now there he sitting on his fine tail, smiling at you."

A white man finally came along and found her—a hunter, a young man, with his dog on a chain.

"Well, Granny!" he laughed. "What are you doing there?"

"Lying on my back like a June-bug waiting to be turned over, mister," she said, reaching up her hand.

He lifted her up, gave her a swing in the air, and set her down. "Anything broken, Granny?"

"No sir, them old dead weeds is springy enough," said Phoenix, when she had got her breath. "I thank you for your trouble."

"Where do you live, Granny?" he asked, while the two dogs were growling at each other.

"Away back yonder, sir, behind the ridge. You can't even see it from here."

"On your way home?"

"No sir, I going to town."

"Why, that's too far! That's as far as I walk when I come out myself, and I get something for my trouble." He patted the stuffed bag he carried, and there hung down a little closed claw. It was one of the bob-whites, with its beak hooked bitterly to show it was dead. "Now you go on home, Granny!"

"I bound to go to town, mister," said Phoenix. "The time come around."

He gave another laugh, filling the whole landscape. "I know you old colored people! Wouldn't miss going to town to see Santa Claus!"

But something held old Phoenix very still. The deep lines in her face went into a fierce and different radiation. Without warning, she had seen with her own eyes a flashing nickel fall out of the man's pocket onto the ground.

"How old are you, Granny?" he was saying.

"There is no telling, mister," she said, "no telling."

Then she gave a little cry and clapped her hands and said, "Git on away from here, dog! Look! Look at that dog!" She laughed as if in admiration. "He ain't scared of nobody. He a big black dog." She whispered, "Sic him!"

"Watch me get rid of that cur," said the man. "Sic him, Pete! Sic him!"

Phoenix heard the dogs fighting, and heard the man running and throwing sticks. She even heard a gunshot. But she was slowly bending forward by that time, further and further forward, the lids stretched down over her eyes, as if she were doing this in her sleep. Her chin was lowered almost to her knees. The yellow palm of her hand came out from the fold of her apron. Her fingers slid down and along the ground under the piece of money with the grace and care they would have in lifting an egg from under a setting hen. Then she slowly straightened up, she stood erect, and the nickel was in her apron pocket. A bird flew by. Her lips moved. "God watching me the whole time. I come to stealing."

The man came back, and his own dog panted about them. "Well, I scared him off that time," he said, and then he laughed and lifted his gun and pointed it at Phoenix.

She stood straight and faced him.

"Doesn't the gun scare you?" he said, still pointing it.

"No, sir, I seen plenty go off closer by, in my day, and for less than what I done," she said, holding utterly still.

He smiled, and shouldered the gun. "Well, Granny," he said, "you must be a hundred years old, and scared of nothing. I'd give you a dime if I had any money with me. But you take my advice and stay home, and nothing will happen to you."

"I bound to go on my way, mister," said Phoenix. She inclined her head in the red rag. Then they went in different directions, but she could hear the gun shooting again and again over the hill.

She walked on. The shadows hung from the oak trees to the road like curtains. Then she smelled wood-smoke, and smelled the river, and she saw a steeple and the cabins on their steep steps. Dozens of little black children whirled around her. There ahead was Natchez shining. Bells were ringing. She walked on.

In the paved city it was Christmas time. There were red and green electric lights strung and criss-crossed everywhere, and all turned on in the daytime. Old Phoenix would have been lost if she had not distrusted her eyesight and depended on her feet to know where to take her.

She paused quietly on the sidewalk where people were passing by. A lady came along in the crowd, carrying an armful of red-, green- and silver-wrapped presents; she gave off perfume like the red roses in hot summer, and Phoenix stopped her.

"Please, missy, will you lace up my shoe?" She held up her foot.

"What do you want, Grandma?"

"See my shoe," said Phoenix. "Do all right for out in the country, but wouldn't look right to go in a big building."

"Stand still then, Grandma," said the lady. She put her packages down on the sidewalk beside her and laced and tied both shoes tightly.

"Can't lace 'em with a cane," said Phoenix. "Thank you, missy. I doesn't mind asking a nice lady to tie up my shoe, when I gets out on the street."

Moving slowly and from side to side, she went into the big building, and into a tower of steps, where she walked up and around and around until her feet knew to stop.

She entered a door, and there she saw nailed up on the wall the document that had been stamped with the gold seal and framed in the gold frame, which matched the dream that was hung up in her head.

"Here I be," she said. There was a fixed and ceremonial stiffness over her body.

"A charity case, I suppose," said an attendant who sat at the desk before her.

But Phoenix only looked above her head. There was sweat on her face, the wrinkles in her skin shone like a bright net.

"Speak up, Grandma," the woman said. "What's your name? We must have your history, you know. Have you been here before? What seems to be the trouble with you?"

Old Phoenix only gave a twitch to her face as if a fly were bothering her.

"Are you deaf?" cried the attendant.

But then the nurse came in.

"Oh, that's just old Aunt Phoenix," she said.

"She doesn't come for herself—she has a little grandson. She makes these trips just as regular as clockwork. She lives away back off the Old Natchez Trace." She bent down. "Well, Aunt Phoenix, why don't you just take a seat? We won't keep you standing after your long trip." She pointed.

The old woman sat down, bolt upright in the chair.

"Now, how is the boy?" asked the nurse.

Old Phoenix did not speak.

"I said, how is the boy?"

But Phoenix only waited and stared straight ahead, her face very solemn and withdrawn into rigidity.

"Is his throat any better?" asked the nurse. "Aunt Phoenix, don't you hear me? Is your grandson's throat any better since the last time you came for the medicine?"

With her hands on her knees, the old woman waited, silent, erect and motionless, just as if she were in armor.

"You mustn't take up our time this way, Aunt Phoenix," the nurse said. "Tell us quickly about your grandson, and get it over. He isn't dead, is he?"

At last there came a flicker and then a flame of comprehension across her face, and she spoke.

"My grandson. It was my memory had left me. There I sat and forgot why I made my long trip."

"Forgot?" The nurse frowned. "After you came so far?"

Then Phoenix was like an old woman begging a dignified forgiveness for waking up frightened in the night. "I never did go to school, I was too old at the Surrender,"[1] she said in a soft voice. "I'm an old woman without an education. It was my memory fail me. My little grandson, he is just the same, and I forgot it in the coming."

"Throat never heals, does it?" said the nurse, speaking in a loud, sure voice to old Phoenix. By now she had a card with something written on it, a little list. "Yes. Swallowed lye. When was it?—January—two-three years ago—"

Phoenix spoke unasked now. "No, missy, he not dead, he just the same. Every little while his throat begin to close up again, and he not able to swallow. He not get his breath. He not able to

help himself. So the time come around, and I go on another trip for the soothing medicine."

"All right. The doctor said as long as you came to get it, you could have it," said the nurse. "But it's an obstinate case."

"My little grandson, he sit up there in the house all wrapped up, waiting by himself," Phoenix went on. "We is the only two left in the world. He suffer and it don't seem to put him back at all. He got a sweet look. He going to last. He wear a little patch quilt and peep out holding his mouth open like a little bird. I remembers so plain now. I not going to forget him again, no, the whole enduring time. I could tell him from all the others in creation."

"All right." The nurse was trying to hush her now. She brought her a bottle of medicine. "Charity," she said, making a check mark in a book.

Old Phoenix held the bottle close to her eyes, and then carefully put it into her pocket.

"I thank you," she said.

"It's Christmas time, Grandma," said the attendant. "Could I give you a few pennies out of my purse?"

"Five pennies is a nickel," said Phoenix stiffly.

"Here's a nickel," said the attendant.

Phoenix rose carefully and held out her hand. She received the nickel and then fished the other nickel out of her pocket and laid it beside the new one. She stared at her palm closely, with her head on one side.

Then she gave a tap with her cane on the floor.

"This is what come to me to do," she said. "I going to the store and buy my child a little windmill they sells, made out of paper. He going to find it hard to believe there such a thing in the world. I'll march myself back where he waiting, holding it straight up in this hand."

She lifted her free hand, gave a little nod, turned around, and walked out of the doctor's office. Then her slow step began on the stairs, going down. ☐☐

---

1. *the Surrender,* the surrender of the Confederate Army to the Union Army at Appomattox on April 9, 1865.

Discussion

1. As we accompany Phoenix Jackson on her solitary trek across the countryside and encounter with her the obstacles in her path and listen to her talking with the world, what kind of person do we discover her to be? In particular, consider the character traits she reveals in her encounter with the young hunter.

2. (a) How does the revelation of Phoenix Jackson's **motive** for her long walk affect your impression of her? **(b)** Why do you think Welty withholds this information until near the end of the story? **(c)** What does Phoenix's plan to buy her grandson a paper windmill suggest about their lives and their relationship?

3. What "worn paths"—both literal and **metaphorical**—do you find in this story?

4. (a) Reread the Background to Unit 5. What features of this story resemble **local color** fiction? **(b)** Besides the story's regional flavor, what deeper insights into human nature does it offer? How are the regional details useful in making these insights convincing to readers?

Extension • Writing

1. Imagine Phoenix Jackson's return journey from the town to her house, carrying the paper windmill. Suppose that she again encounters the hunter, who has by now missed the nickel that fell out of his pocket. Narrate this scene, with dialogue.

2. Write a final scene in which Phoenix Jackson enters her cabin and presents the paper windmill to her grandson.

Eudora Welty 1909 •

Welty was born in Jackson, Mississippi, and has spent most of her life in her native state. She attended the University of Wisconsin, then went to New York where she studied journalism at Columbia University, and wrote publicity, society news, and radio scripts. After returning to Mississippi, she settled down to a career of writing, with gardening, painting, and photography as hobbies.

Her first volume of short stories, *A Curtain of Green,* was published in 1941. The title story won the O. Henry Memorial Award for that year. Since then she has published several other volumes of short stories and a number of novels, including *Losing Battles* (1970) and *The Optimist's Daughter* (1972). She received the 1973 Pulitzer prize for *The Optimist's Daughter.* Although her stories are set in the South, her themes extend beyond geographical boundaries, dealing with the problems of adolescents, with loneliness and the failures of personal communication. Her style is a blend of shrewdness, sensitivity, and robust humor.

Welty lives quietly and alone in her home of forty years. She treasures her privacy and once commented, "Writing fiction is an interior affair. Novels and stories always will be put down little by little out of personal feeling and personal beliefs arrived at alone and at firsthand over a period of time as time is needed. To go outside and beat the drum is only to interrupt, interrupt . . . Fiction has, and must keep, a private address. For life is lived in a private placc; where it means anything is inside the mind and heart."

Dorothy Parker

Soldiers of the Republic

That Sunday afternoon we sat with the Swedish girl in the big cafe in Valencia.[1] We had vermouth in thick goblets, each with a cube of honeycombed gray ice in it. The waiter was so proud of that ice he could hardly bear to leave the glasses on the table, and thus part from it forever. He went to his duty—all over the room they were clapping their hands and hissing to draw his attention—but he looked back over his shoulder.

It was dark outside, the quick, new dark that leaps down without dusk on the day; but, because there were no lights in the streets, it seemed as set and as old as midnight. So you wondered that all the babies were still up. There

1. **Valencia** (vä len′sē ä). The Loyalist, or Republican, government of Spain moved to this city from Madrid in 1936, during the Spanish Civil War.

were babies everywhere in the café; babies serious without solemnity and interested in a tolerant way in their surroundings.

At the table next ours, there was a notably small one; maybe six months old. Its father, a little man in a big uniform that dragged his shoulders down, held it carefully on his knee. It was doing nothing whatever, yet he and his thin young wife, whose belly was already big again under her sleazy dress, sat watching it in a sort of ecstasy of admiration, while their coffee cooled in front of them. The baby was in Sunday white; its dress was patched so delicately that you would have thought the fabric whole had not the patches varied in their shades of whiteness. In its hair was a bow of new blue ribbon, tied with absolute balance of loops and ends. The ribbon was of no use; there was not enough hair to require restraint. The bow was sheerly an adornment, a calculated bit of dash.

"Oh, stop that!" I said to myself. "All right, so it's got a piece of blue ribbon on its hair. All right, so its mother went without eating so it could look pretty when its father came home on leave. All right, so it's her business, and none of yours. All right, so what have you got to cry about?"

The big, dim room was crowded and lively. That morning there had been a bombing from the air, the more horrible for broad daylight. But nobody in the café sat tense and strained, nobody desperately forced forgetfulness. They drank coffee or bottled lemonade, in the pleasant, earned ease of Sunday afternoon, chatting of small, gay matters, all talking at once, all hearing and answering.

There were many soldiers in the room, in what appeared to be the uniforms of twenty different armies until you saw that the variety lay in the differing ways the cloth had worn or faded. Only a few of them had been wounded; here and there you saw one stepping gingerly, leaning on a crutch or two canes, but so far on toward recovery that his face had color. There were many men, too, in civilian clothes—some of them soldiers home on leave, some of them governmental workers, some of them anybody's guess. There were plump, comfortable wives, active with paper fans, and old women as quiet as their grandchildren. There were many pretty girls and some beauties, of whom you did not remark, "There's a charming Spanish type," but said, "What a beautiful girl!" The women's clothes were not new, and their material was too humble ever to have warranted skillful cutting.

"It's funny," I said to the Swedish girl, "how when nobody in a place is best-dressed, you don't notice that everybody isn't."

"Please?" the Swedish girl said.

No one, save an occasional soldier, wore a hat. When we had first come to Valencia, I lived in a state of puzzled pain as to why everybody on the streets laughed at me. It was not because "West End Avenue" was writ across my face as if left there by a customs officer's chalked scrawl. They like Americans in Valencia, where they have seen good ones—the doctors who left their practices and came to help, the calm young nurses, the men of the International Brigade.[2] But when I walked forth, men and women courteously laid their hands across their splitting faces and little children, too innocent for dissembling, doubled with glee and pointed and cried, *"Ole!"* Then, pretty late, I made my discovery, and left my hat off; and there was laughter no longer. It was not one of those comic hats, either; it was just a hat.

The café filled to overflow, and I left our table to speak to a friend across the room. When I came back to the table, six soldiers were sitting there. They were crowded in, and I scraped past them to my chair. They looked tired and dusty and little, the way that the newly dead look little, and the first things you saw about them were the tendons in their necks. I felt like a prize sow.

They were all in conversation with the Swedish girl. She has Spanish, French, German, anything in Scandinavian, Italian, and English. When she has a moment for regret, she sighs that her Dutch is so rusty she can no longer speak it, only read it, and the same is true of her Rumanian.

They had told her, she told us, that they were at the end of forty-eight hours' leave from the trenches, and, for their holiday, they had all pooled their money for cigarettes, and something had gone wrong, and the cigarettes had never come through to them. I had a pack of American

---

2. International Brigade, volunteers from several countries who came to Spain to aid the Loyalist cause during the Spanish Civil War (1936–39).

cigarettes—in Spain rubies are as nothing to them—and I brought it out, and by nods and smiles and a sort of breast stroke, made it understood that I was offering it to those six men yearning for tobacco. When they saw what I meant, each one of them rose and shook my hand. Darling of me to share my cigarettes with the men on their way back to the trenches. Little Lady Bountiful. The prize sow.

Each one lit his cigarette with a contrivance of yellow rope that stank when afire and was also used, the Swedish girl translated, for igniting grenades. Each one received what he had ordered, a glass of coffee, and each one murmured appreciatively over the tiny cornucopia of coarse sugar that accompanied it. Then they talked.

They talked through the Swedish girl, but they did to us that thing we all do when we speak our own language to one who has no knowledge of it. They looked us square in the face, and spoke slowly, and pronounced their words with elaborate movements of their lips. Then, as their stories came, they poured them at us so vehemently, so emphatically that they were sure we must understand. They were so convinced we would understand that we were ashamed for not understanding.

But the Swedish girl told us. They were all farmers and farmers' sons, from a district so poor that you try not to remember there is that kind of poverty. Their village was next that one where the old men and the sick men and the women and children had gone, on a holiday, to the bullring; and the planes had come over and dropped bombs on the bullring, and the old men and the sick men and the women and the children were more than two hundred.

They had all, the six of them, been in the war for over a year, and most of that time they had been in the trenches. Four of them were married. One had one child, two had three children, one had five. They had not had word from their families since they had left for the front. There had been no communication; two of them had learned to write from men fighting next them in the trench, but they had not dared to write home. They belonged to a union, and union men, of course, are put to death if taken. The village where their families lived had been captured, and if your wife gets a letter from a union man, who knows but they'll shoot her for the connection?

They told about how they had not heard from their families for more than a year. They did not tell it gallantly or whimsically or stoically. They told it as if—Well, look. You have been in the trenches, fighting, for a year. You have heard nothing of your wife and your children. They do not know if you are dead or alive or blinded. You do not know where they are, or if they are. You must talk to somebody. That is the way they told about it.

One of them, some six months before, had heard of his wife and his three children—they had such beautiful eyes, he said—from a brother-in-law in France. They were all alive then, he was told, and had a bowl of beans a day. But his wife had not complained of the food, he heard. What had troubled her was that she had no thread to mend the children's ragged clothes. So that troubled him, too.

"She has no thread," he kept telling us. "My wife has no thread to mend with. No thread."

We sat there, and listened to what the Swedish girl told us they were saying. Suddenly one of them looked at the clock, and then there was excitement. They jumped up, as a man, and there were calls for the waiter and rapid talk with him, and each of them shook the hand of each of us. We went through more swimming motions to explain to them that they were to take the rest of the cigarettes—fourteen cigarettes for six soldiers to take to war—and then they shook our hands again. Then all of us said *"Salud!"*[3] as many times as could be for six of them and three of us, and then they filed out of the café, the six of them, tired and dusty and little, as men of a mighty horde are little.

Only the Swedish girl talked, after they had gone. The Swedish girl has been in Spain since the start of the war. She has nursed splintered men, and she has carried stretchers into the trenches and, heavier laden, back to the hospital. She has seen and heard too much to be knocked into silence.

Presently it was time to go, and the Swedish girl raised her hands above her head and clapped them twice together to summon the waiter. He came, but he only shook his head and his hand, and moved away.

The soldiers had paid for our drinks. ☐☐

---

3. *Salud!* Good health! [*Spanish*]

Discussion

1. What feelings does the **narrator** experience when looking at the six-month-old child with the bow in its hair?

2. The narrator mentions that when she had first come to Valencia everybody on the streets had laughed at her. Why were they laughing?

3. Twice the narrator calls herself a "prize sow." Why?

4. (a) What are the differences between the narrator and the Swedish girl? **(b)** Why might the narrator envy the Swedish girl?

5. Cite passages in which Parker uses **(a)** understatement; **(b)** the **vignette.**

6. (a) How does she suggest the horrors of civil war while describing a moment of tranquility? **(b)** Are the Spanish soldiers dehumanized by the war? Discuss the impression of them you get from the story.

7. What passage did you find the most moving? Why?

Extension • Writing

Have you ever been in a situation (in a poor neighborhood, a foreign country, a hospital ward) in which you felt guilty or embarrassed by your own comparative wealth or health? Describe the situation and your feelings in a brief composition.

Extension • Reading

Most libraries have a few books devoted to the humor of the Algonquin Round Table Wits, among whom Parker was prominent. Assign one or more students to bring to class a sampling of the impromptu humor of this remarkable group.

Dorothy Parker 1893 • 1967

Dorothy Parker is best known as a humorist in prose and poetry. Her acid wit is memorialized in such quips as her remark on hearing that the stodgy and expressionless Calvin Coolidge had died ("How could they tell?"); or in her self-assessment as a promising poet ("I was following in the exquisite footsteps of Miss Edna St. Vincent Millay, unhappily in my own horrible sneakers.")

Her first job was as a caption writer for *Vogue* magazine. There is no room for wordiness in a caption, so this experience may in part account for the precise wording and the conciseness of her prose and poetry. She later became drama critic for *Vanity Fair,* where her coworkers and closest friends were the soon-to-be famous humorist Robert Benchley and the playwright Robert Sherwood.

Parker, Benchley, and Sherwood were among the first of New York's literary set to begin taking lunch in a small dining room of the equally small Algonquin Hotel. The table talk was so clever and stimulating that the group attracted the sharpest wits of the theater and literature and became known as the Algonquin Round Table, sometimes called the Vicious Circle.

Beneath the sophistication and the slashing repartee always delivered in a sweet murmur ("A girl's best friend is her murmur," she is reported to have said), lay a troubled and unhappy woman. Two marriages ended in divorce. She always doubted the quality of even her best work and accused herself of frittering away her talent.

Despite Parker's low self-esteem, critics now recognize her as a major literary artist. Her two slim volumes of short stories contain some of the finest prose written during the 1920s and '30s.

Ezra Pound

The Garden

Like a skein of loose silk blown against a wall
She walks by the railing of a path in Kensington Gardens,[1]
And she is dying piece-meal of a sort of emotional anaemia.

And round about there is a rabble
5 Of the filthy, sturdy, unkillable infants of the very poor.
They shall inherit the earth.

In her is the end of breeding.
Her boredom is exquisite and excessive.
She would like some one to speak to her,
10 And is almost afraid that I will commit that indiscretion.

1. **Kensington** (ken′zing tən) **Gardens,** beautiful gardens in a palace near London.

Discussion

1. What impression of the lady's appearance is given by the **image** in the first line?

2. (a) What contrasts does the poem present between the lady and the "infants"? (b) Why are they more likely than she to "inherit the earth"?

3. (a) Explain the lady's reaction to the speaker as revealed in the last stanza. (b) Describe his attitude toward her.

The River-Merchant's Wife: A Letter

Discussion

1. The speaker of the poem never says, "I love you." In what ways is her love for her husband revealed?

2. What signs indicate the husband's love for her?

3. The two shortest sentences of the poem appear in line 25. **(a)** To what does "they" refer? **(b)** How do these sentences emphasize the depth of the speaker's grief?

Ezra Pound 1885 • 1972

Born in Idaho, Pound taught college in Indiana, but soon moved to Europe. By 1912, he had already published seven volumes of verse, had helped create Imagism, and was counseling and promoting other young poets like T. S. Eliot and Amy Lowell. The main qualities of Pound's work are: a sense of tradition fused with originality; precise imagery; command of verbal sound; and conciseness.

Pound was attracted to Mussolini's speeches and went to Italy where, in World War II, he made pro-Fascist broadcasts to Allied troops. In 1945 he was arrested by the Americans but was found mentally unfit to stand trial for treason. He was confined to a hospital in Washington, D.C. until 1958. After his release, he lived his last years in Italy.

While my hair was still cut straight across my forehead
I played about the front gate, pulling flowers.
You came by on bamboo stilts, playing horse,
You walked about my seat, playing with blue plums.
5 And we went on living in the village of Chōkan:
Two small people, without dislike or suspicion.

At fourteen I married My Lord you.
I never laughed, being bashful.
Lowering my head, I looked at the wall.
10 Called to, a thousand times, I never looked back.

At fifteen I stopped scowling,
I desired my dust to be mingled with yours
Forever and forever and forever.
Why should I climb the look out?

15 At sixteen you departed,
You went into far Ku-tō-en, by the river of swirling eddies.
And you have been gone five months.
The monkeys make sorrowful noise overhead.
You dragged your feet when you went out.
20 By the gate now, the moss is grown, the different mosses,
Too deep to clear them away!
The leaves fall early this autumn, in wind.
The paired butterflies are already yellow with August
Over the grass in the West garden;
25 They hurt me. I grow older.
If you are coming down through the narrows of the
    river Kiang,[1]
Please let me know beforehand,
And I will come out to meet you
              As far as Chō-fū-Sa.

            Based on a poem by Li T'ai Po[2]

1. *Kiang* (kē än′). The Yangtze (yän′sē′) Kiang River is China's longest.
2. *Li T'ai Po* (lē′tī′bō′; 701–762), one of China's greatest poets. His literary name was Li Po.

Amy Lowell

Robert Amft

Patterns

I walk down the garden-paths,
And all the daffodils
Are blowing, and the bright blue squills.
I walk down the patterned garden-paths
5 In my stiff, brocaded gown.
With my powdered hair and jeweled fan,
I too am a rare
Pattern. As I wander down
The garden-paths.
10 My dress is richly figured,
And the train
Makes a pink and silver stain
On the gravel, and the thrift
Of the borders.
15 Just a plate of current fashion,
Tripping by in high-heeled, ribboned shoes.
Not a softness anywhere about me,
Only whalebone and brocade.
And I sink on a seat in the shade
20 Of a lime-tree. For my passion

Discussion

1. (a) In what season of the year is this poem set? **(b)** How is this season appropriate to the narrative?

2. In what sense is the woman "a rare Pattern"?

3. In line 83, the speaker says, "We would have broke the pattern." What does she mean?

4. Near the end of the poem, why does the speaker refer to the war as a "pattern"?

Amy Lowell   1874 • 1925

Lowell was born into one of the wealthiest and most distinguished families of Massachusetts. Her grandfather had founded the cotton-manufacturing town of Lowell. Her grandfather's cousin was

Wars against the stiff brocade.
The daffodils and squills
Flutter in the breeze
As they please.
25 And I weep;
For the lime-tree is in blossom
And one small flower had dropped upon my bosom.

And the plashing of waterdrops
In the marble fountain
30 Comes down the garden-paths.
The dripping never stops.
Underneath my stiffened gown
Is the softness of a woman bathing in a marble basin,
A basin in the midst of hedges grown
35 So thick, she cannot see her lover hiding,
But she guesses he is near,
And the sliding of the water
Seems the stroking of a dear
Hand upon her.
40 What is Summer in a fine brocaded gown!
I should like to see it lying in a heap upon the ground.
All the pink and silver crumpled up on the ground.

I would be the pink and silver as I ran along the paths,
And he would stumble after,
45 Bewildered by my laughter.
I should see the sun flashing from his sword hilt and the buckles on his shoes.
I would choose
To lead him in a maze along the patterned paths,
A bright and laughing maze for my heavy-booted lover.
50 Till he caught me in the shade,
And the buttons of his waistcoat bruised my body as he clasped me
Aching, melting, unafraid.
With the shadows of the leaves and the sundrops,
And the plopping of the waterdrops,
55 All about us in the open afternoon—
I am very like to swoon
With the weight of this brocade,
For the sun sifts through the shade.
Underneath the fallen blossom
60 In my bosom,
Is a letter I have hid.
It was brought to me this morning by a rider from the Duke.[1]

---

1. *the Duke*, probably John Churchill, Duke of Marlborough (1650–1722), commander of the united English and Dutch armies during the War of the Spanish Succession (1701–1714). The initial campaign was fought in Belgium and adjoining countries.

"Madam, we regret to inform you that Lord Hartwell
Died in action Thursday se'nnight."[2]
65 As I read it in the white, morning sunlight,
The letters squirmed like snakes.
"Any answer, Madam," said my footman.
"No," I told him.
"See that the messenger takes some refreshment.
70 No, no answer."
And I walked into the garden,
Up and down the patterned paths,
In my stiff, correct brocade.
The blue and yellow flowers stood up proudly in the sun,
75 Each one.
I stood upright too,
Held rigid to the pattern
By the stiffness of my gown.
Up and down I walked,
80 Up and down.

In a month he would have been my husband.
In a month, here, underneath this lime,
We would have broke the pattern;
He for me, and I for him,
85 He as Colonel, I as Lady,
On this shady seat.
He had a whim
That sunlight carried blessing.
And I answered, "It shall be as you have said."
90 Now he is dead.

In Summer and in Winter I shall walk
Up and down
The patterned garden-paths
In my stiff, brocaded gown.
95 The squills and daffodils
Will give place to pillared roses, and to asters, and to snow.
I shall go
Up and down,
In my gown.
100 Gorgeously arrayed,
Boned and stayed.
And the softness of my body will be guarded from embrace
By each button, hook, and lace.
For the man who should loose me is dead,
105 Fighting with the Duke in Flanders,
In a pattern called a war.
Christ! What are patterns for?

the poet James Russell Lowell (see Unit 3). Her brothers were Percival Lowell, the astronomer, and Abbott Lawrence Lowell, for many years president of Harvard.

Not until she was twenty-eight years old did Amy Lowell decide seriously to become a poet, and then she studied for eight years before publishing a line. Her first volume of poetry, *A Dome of Many-Colored Glass* (1912), was conventional, and echoed the melodies of older poets. Soon after its publication, Lowell joined the Imagists, a group of English and American poets who believed in the use of free verse, in freedom to write about any subject, and, above all, in the use of the exact word to create strong and concrete images. Lowell's second volume of poetry, *Sword Blades and Poppy Seeds* (1914), brilliantly incorporated these beliefs; *Men, Women, and Ghosts* (1916), in which "Patterns" first appeared, showed that, in addition to being technically gifted, she was also a superb storyteller.

The "new poetry" of the Imagists was bitterly ridiculed. Lowell traveled across the country for ten years, reading and lecturing. Gradually scorn gave way to acceptance, and by the time she died her poetry held an honored place. She was posthumously awarded the Pulitzer Prize in 1926 for *What's O'Clock*.

---

2. se'nnight, an archaic word meaning a period of seven days and nights. Within the context of the poem it means that Lord Hartwell died a week ago Thursday.

Carl Sandburg

from Four Preludes
on Playthings of the Wind
"The past is a bucket of ashes."

Discussion

1. How is the subtitle appropriate to this poem?
2. What contrast does the poem develop? What details of the **imagery** illustrate this contrast?
3. Explain the **irony** of the actions of the crows.

It has happened before.
Strong men put up a city and got
       a nation together,
And paid singers to sing and women
5   to warble: We are the greatest city,
       the greatest nation,
       nothing like us ever was.

And while the singers sang
and the strong men listened
10 and paid the singers well
and felt good about it all,
       there were rats and lizards who listened
       . . . and the only listeners left now
       . . . are . . . the rats . . . and the lizards.

15 And there are black crows
crying, "Caw, caw,"
bringing mud and sticks
building a nest
over the words carved
20 on the doors where the panels were cedar
and the strips on the panels were gold
and the golden girls came singing:
       We are the greatest city,
       the greatest nation:
25   nothing like us ever was.

The only singers now are crows crying, "Caw, caw,"
And the sheets of rain whine in the wind and doorways.
And the only listeners now are . . . the rats . . . and the lizards.

"Four Preludes on Playthings of the Wind" from SMOKE AND STEEL by Carl Sandburg, copyright, 1920, by Harcourt Brace Jovanovich, Inc.; renewed, 1948, by Carl Sandburg. Reprinted by permission of the publishers.

Chicago

Hog Butcher for the World,
Tool Maker, Stacker of Wheat,
Player with Railroads and the Nation's Freight Handler;
Stormy, husky, brawling,
5   City of the Big Shoulders:

They tell me you are wicked and I believe them, for I have seen your painted women under the gas
    lamps luring the farm boys.
And they tell me you are crooked and I answer: Yes, it is true I have seen the gunman kill and go
    free to kill again.
And they tell me you are brutal and my reply is: On the faces of women and children I have seen
    the marks of wanton hunger.
And having answered so I turn once more to those who sneer at this my city, and I give them back
    the sneer and say to them:
10 Come and show me another city with lifted head singing so proud to be alive and coarse and strong
    and cunning.

Downtown Chicago, about 1910.
(Courtesy of The Chicago Historical Society.)

Flinging magnetic curses amid the toil of piling job on job, here is a tall bold slugger set vivid
     against the little soft cities;
Fierce as a dog with tongue lapping for action, cunning as a savage pitted against the wilderness,
     Bareheaded,
     Shoveling,
15   Wrecking,
     Planning,
     Building, breaking, rebuilding,
Under the smoke, dust all over his mouth, laughing with white teeth,
Under the terrible burden of destiny laughing as a young man laughs,
20 Laughing even as an ignorant fighter laughs who has never lost a battle,
Bragging and laughing that under his wrist is the pulse, and under his ribs the heart of the people,
     Laughing!
Laughing the stormy, husky, brawling laughter of Youth, half-naked, sweating, proud to be Hog
     Butcher, Tool Maker, Stacker of Wheat, Player with Railroads and Freight Handler to the
     Nation.

Discussion

1. (a) What impressions of the city does this poem emphasize? What images convey these impressions? (b) What is the **tone** of the poem?

2. When "Chicago" was first published before World War I, it created quite a sensation. (a) What qualities might have made the poem exciting at that time? (b) Are the poem's idea, tone, and statement equally appropriate today? Why or why not?

3. Compare the view of a big city in this poem with that presented in Sandburg's previous poem.

Carl Sandburg 1878 • 1967

The genius of Carl Sandburg is shown in several areas. He was a greatly admired poet. He wrote delightful stories for children. His multi-volumed biography of Lincoln placed him high among modern writers of biography. He received two Pulitzer Prizes, one for his *Complete Poems* (1951) and the other for *Abraham Lincoln: The War Years* (1939). He was a noted collector of folklore, and did much to popularize music of this type by singing folk songs and accompanying himself on the guitar.

Sandburg was born in Galesburg, Illinois, of Swedish immigrant parents. It was not until he was thirty-eight years old and had tried his hand at many different occupations that fame came to him with the publication of *Chicago Poems* (1916). Written in a free-verse style reminiscent of Walt Whitman, these poems, like those he wrote later, speak in the bold and often earthy idiom of the people. Sensitive to injustice and hypocrisy, fearful of the effects of industrialization on humanity, Sandburg found hope for the future in the common people.

Langston Hughes

Theme for English B

The instructor said,

    Go home and write
    a page tonight.
    And let that page come out of you—
5   *Then, it will be true.*

I wonder if it's that simple?
I am twenty-two, colored, born in
        Winston-Salem.
I went to school there, then Durham, then here
to this college on the hill above Harlem.
10 I am the only colored student in my class.
The steps from the hill lead down into Harlem,
through a park, then I cross St. Nicholas,
Eighth Avenue, Seventh, and I come to the Y,
the Harlem Branch Y, where I take the elevator
15 up to my room, sit down, and write this page:

It's not easy to know what is true for you or me
at twenty-two, my age. But I guess I'm what
I feel and see and hear, Harlem, I hear you:
hear you, hear me—we two—you, me,
        talk on this page.
20 (I hear New York, too.) Me—who?
Well, I like to eat, sleep, drink, and be in love.
I like to work, read, learn, and understand life.
I like a pipe for a Christmas present,
or records—Bessie, bop, or Bach.[1]
25 I guess being colored doesn't make me *not* like
the same things other folks like who are
        other races.
So will my page be colored that I write?

Being me, it will not be white.
But it will be
30 a part of you, instructor.
You are white—
yet a part of me, as I am a part of you.

That's American.
Sometimes perhaps you don't want to be
        a part of me.
35 Nor do I often want to be a part of you.
But we are, that's true!
As I learn from you,
I guess you learn from me—
although you're older—and white—
40 and somewhat more free.

This is my page for English B.

---

1. **Bessie, bop, or Bach.** Bessie Smith was one of the greatest blues singers of the early twentieth century. Bop is a form of jazz. Johann Sebastian Bach (1685–1750) is considered one of the most important composers of classical music.

Discussion

1. (a) How does the poem follow the instructor's directions to the letter? (b) In what way does it expand on the assignment?

2. Do you find this poem particularly direct and honest? Why or why not? Explain your response in terms of the language and imagery of the poem.

3. (a) How does the speaker feel his world differs from his instructor's? (b) In what ways does he feel they are the same?

Langston Hughes 1902 • 1967

Hughes was born in Joplin, Missouri, and began writing poetry as a student at Central High School in Cleveland, Ohio. After graduating, he worked his way on cargo ships to Africa and Europe.

In 1925 he was working as a busboy at a Washington hotel where the poet Vachel Lindsay stayed on one of his "vaude-ville" reading tours. Hughes left some of his poems beside Lindsay's dinner plate. Lindsay was so enthusiastic that he in-cluded some of them in a pub-lic reading and afterwards told newspaper reporters about his discovery of a talented young black poet. Hughes subsequent-ly became a leading figure in the Harlem Renaissance and, eventually, one of America's best-known poets.   By the time Hughes had graduated from Lincoln University in Pennsylvania in 1929, he was supporting himself with his writing. After the publication of his first book, *The Weary Blues*, in 1926, he began travel-ing across the country giving public readings of his poetry, which were well received. But he always returned to New York City, to his home in Har-lem, where he helped young writers who sought his advice.

In addition to poetry, Hughes wrote novels, dramas and musi-cals, newspaper columns, chil-dren's books, and a history of the N.A.A.C.P.

Marianne Moore

Poetry

I, too, dislike it: there are things that are important beyond all this fiddle.
  Reading it, however, with a perfect contempt for it, one discovers in
  it after all, a place for the genuine.
    Hands that can grasp, eyes
5   that can dilate, hair that can rise
      if it must, these things are important not because a

high-sounding interpretation can be put upon them but because they are
  useful. When they become so derivative as to become unintelligible,
  the same thing may be said for all of us, that we
10   do not admire what
    we cannot understand: the bat
      holding on upside down or in quest of something to

eat, elephants pushing, a wild horse taking a roll, a tireless wolf under
  a tree, the immovable critic twitching his skin like a horse that feels a flea, the base-
15 ball fan, the statistician—
    nor is it valid
      to discriminate against 'business documents and

school-books'; all these phenomena are important. One must make a distinction
  however: when dragged into prominence by half poets, the result is not poetry,
20 nor till the poets among us can be
    'literalists of
    the imagination'—above
      insolence and triviality and can present

for inspection, 'imaginary gardens with real toads in them,' shall we have
25 it. In the meantime, if you demand on the one hand,
    the raw material of poetry in
    all its rawness and
    that which is on the other hand
      genuine, you are interested in poetry.

Archibald MacLeish

Ars Poetica[1]

A poem should be palpable and mute
As a globed fruit

Dumb
As old medallions to the thumb

5 Silent as the sleeve-worn stone
Of casement ledges where the moss has grown—

A poem should be wordless
As the flight of birds

A poem should be motionless in time
10 As the moon climbs

Leaving, as the moon releases
Twig by twig the night-entangled trees,

Leaving, as the moon behind the winter leaves,
Memory by memory the mind—

15 A poem should be motionless in time
As the moon climbs

A poem should be equal to:
Not true

For all the history of grief
20 An empty doorway and a maple leaf

For love
The leaning grasses and two lights above the sea—

A poem should not mean
But be

---

1. **Ars Poetica** (ärz pō e′ti kä), the poetic art. [*Latin*]

Discussion

Poetry

1. (a) According to this poem, on what does the "usefulness" of poetry depend? **(b)** Need we always instantly like a poem for it to have a genuine effect upon us? Discuss.

2. (a) What is it that "half poets" do that makes poetry less effective? **(b)** In your opinion, are there any poems which you have recently read that demonstrate this? Explain.

3. (a) In what sense can modern poems be described as "imaginary gardens with real toads in them"? What comprises the "rawness" of modern poetry? **(b)** Choose one poem in this unit to illustrate your response.

(Moore's biography is on page 470.)

Ars Poetica

1. (a) To what is a poem compared in each of the first four **stanzas**? **(b)** How appropriate is each of the **similes** in conveying the abstract quality with which it is associated?

2. In what sense is the moon "motionless in time"?

3. The last couplet says, "A poem should not mean/But be." How is this thought demonstrated by the two preceding lines?

Archibald MacLeish 1892 •

In 1923 MacLeish gave up a thriving law practice to go to Paris, where he could discuss theory with writers and write his own poetry. Later he traveled in Mexico, following the route of Cortez. The result was the narrative poem *Conquistador*, which won the Pulitzer Prize in 1933.

In 1953 he was awarded both the National Book Award and a second Pulitzer Prize for his *Collected Poems 1917–1952*. And in 1959 he won a third Pulitzer Prize, this time for his verse play, *J.B.*

Robert Hayden: Poetry in the Modern Temper

Much that has occurred in contemporary American poetry can be seen as the culmination of tendencies originating in the nineteenth century with Walt Whitman, Emily Dickinson, and, to some extent, Stephen Crane. These poets are now generally considered to have been innovators, forerunners of modernism. And during the 1920s literary rebels eagerly claimed them as spiritual ancestors whose work had helped prepare the way for the New Poetry movement.

Known also as the Poetry Revival, the New Poetry Movement began in London as an international phenomenon before the First World War. Ezra Pound, the brilliant expatriate American poet, encouraged poets to break with the past in order to achieve greater freedom of expression. Pound's theories led to the concept of Imagism, which owed something to French Symbolism as well as to ancient Chinese, Japanese, and Greek poetry.

The Imagists, also including Amy Lowell, had some influence on Carl Sandburg, T. S. Eliot, Marianne Moore, and Wallace Stevens. Pound defined the principles of Imagism as precision of diction and image, freedom in the choice of subjects, and a controlled freedom of rhythm based on musical cadence and not on traditional meters—**free verse,** in other words.

The revolt against poetic conventions had started early in the twentieth century. Two great poets, Edwin Arlington Robinson and Robert Frost, had already produced fresh and original work by the end of the first decade. Ignored at first, they later emerged as luminaries of the Poetry Revival. But in 1912, Harriet Monroe published the first number of *Poetry: A Magazine of Verse* in Chicago. This magazine was of strategic importance, providing a medium for the work of poets here and abroad, disseminating the new poetic theories, and bringing them into focus and to the attention of the public.

The New Poetry movement, somewhat tentative during the war years, gained momentum in the 1920s. Now popularly referred to as the "Jazz Age," this was a period of drastic social change. Freudian psychology, the changing status of women, the development of science and technology—all suggested new possibilities for poetry. Religious skepticism, growing since the last century, and the moral disillusionment caused by the war were recurrent themes in the new poetry. The spiritual emptiness of an industrialized civilization, the sense of alienation and futility experienced by many were considered to be the themes of T. S. Eliot's "The Love Song of J. Alfred Prufrock" and "The Waste Land." These poems are thought by many critics to have captured the spirit of their age.

But if poets were critics of twentieth-century life, they were also explorers engaged in exciting voyages of personal discovery. Some looked for a genuine "American rhythm," seeking it in jazz and spirituals, in the poetry and song of the American Indian. Folk heroes and legendary figures were celebrated in ballads and other forms of narrative poetry.

The Harlem Renaissance, known also as the New Negro movement and the Negro Renaissance, was an important cultural manifestation of the mid-twenties. With Harlem as its center, the Renaissance was an upsurge of new racial attitudes and ideals on the part of Afro-Americans and an artistic and political awakening. The Harlem writers and artists were, like their white counterparts, in quest of new images, forms, techniques. They too were skeptical and disillusioned. What chiefly differentiated them, however, was their view of artistic endeavor as an extension of the struggle against oppression.

The Crisis and *Opportunity* magazines encouraged the Harlem writers by publishing their writing and awarding various prizes. Prominent young poets of the Renaissance were Langston Hughes, Claude McKay, Countee Cullen, Jean Toomer, and Arna Bontemps. James Weldon Johnson was a distinguished older poet associated with the New Negro movement and, together with its chief spokesman, Alain Locke, was honored as a mentor. Writing in both free and conventional verse, the Harlem poets expressed racial bitterness and racial pride more boldly than their predecessors had ever done. They affirmed their African heritage in poems often filled with exotic **imagery**, celebrating the "primitive" forces pulsing under the black man's veneer of civilization. This tendency to emphasize the primitive and exotic provoked the charge that the New Negroes replaced old **stereotypes** with new ones equally objectionable.

Jazz rhythms, images from big-city life (Harlem's in particular), and **themes** from history and folklore were found in the works of the Renaissance poets, several of whom were also novelists. Jean Toomer's *Cane* (1923) was a volume of poems, sketches, and stories garnered from his experiences in the South and from his impressions of Afro-American life in the North. Blues and jazz suggested **motifs** and verse patterns for Langston Hughes's first book, *The Weary Blues* (1926). In such novels as *Jonah's Gourd Vine* (1934), the anthropologist-novelist Zora Neale Hurston used the folkways of blacks in rural Florida to challenge the extreme materialism of the modern temper.

By the 1930s the ideals of the New Poetry had been accepted and no longer seemed radical or even controversial. Free verse was the preferred technique of many poets, and although Imagism as a distinct movement no longer existed, it was still a minor influence. Significant work in traditional forms continued, of course. Robert Frost pursued what he called his "lover's quarrel with the world" in verse forms that were conventional, though the poet's vision and **tone** were highly individual. Personal and metaphysical poetry employing meter and rhyme often achieved notable distinction through the artistry of Edna St. Vincent Millay, Countee Cullen, Paul Engle, and Elinor Wylie.

The twentieth century is often described as an era of rapid, almost breathless change. Fashions in the arts change not by the generation but by the decade, though, inevitably, much is carried over from one period to the next. Yet each decade has its own special focus. During the thirties, social consciousness and political awareness gave special impetus to American poetry.

A great deal of socially conscious verse has lost its patina, retaining only a certain period interest, if any. There are, however, some exceptions. Much of the poetry of Archibald MacLeish and Kenneth Fearing was written out of a deep concern over injustice and human exploitation, and has not entirely lost its vitality and relevance. Langston Hughes, Margaret Walker, Frank Marshall Davis, and Richard Wright wrote perceptively about the Afro-American condition. Carl Sandburg's *The People, Yes* (1936) was evidence of the continuing interest in the folk culture shared by a number of artists during the period.

Left-wing critics defined the role of the poet as that of propagandist, championing the oppressed victims of an unjust social order. The question whether a valid distinction between art and propaganda could really be made was hotly debated in these years. Notwithstanding his poems of protest, MacLeish could advocate, in "Ars Poetica," the concept of the "pure poem," detached from social purpose. This debate continued vigorously as the worldwide depression and the menace of fascism once more dragged the world toward global war.

Robert Frost

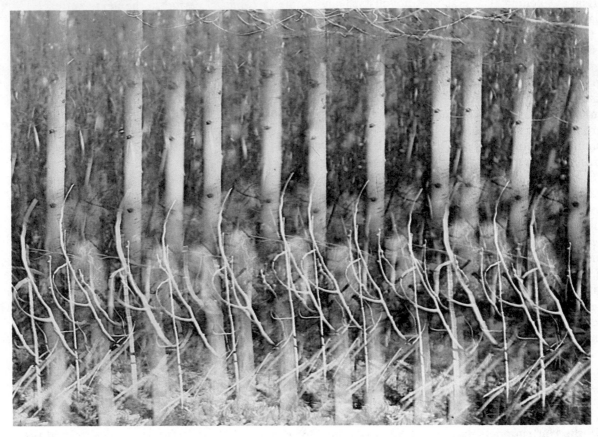

Robert Amft.

Birches

When I see birches bend to left and right
Across the lines of straighter darker trees,
I like to think some boy's been swinging them.
But swinging doesn't bend them down to stay
5 As ice storms do. Often you must have seen them
Loaded with ice a sunny winter morning
After a rain. They click upon themselves
As the breeze rises, and turn many-colored
As the stir cracks and crazes their enamel.

"Birches," "Out, Out—", "Stopping by Woods on a Snowy Evening," and "Mending Wall" are reprinted from THE POETRY OF ROBERT FROST edited by Edward Connery Lathem. Copyright 1916, 1923, 1930, 1939, © 1969 by Holt, Rinehart and Winston. Copyright 1944, 1951, © 1958 by Robert Frost. Copyright © 1967 by Lesley Frost Ballantine. Reprinted by permission of Holt, Rinehart and Winston, Publishers, the Estate of Robert Frost, and Jonathan Cape Ltd.

10 Soon the sun's warmth makes them shed crystal shells
   Shattering and avalanching on the snow crust—
   Such heaps of broken glass to sweep away
   You'd think the inner dome of heaven had fallen.
   They are dragged to the withered bracken by the load,
15 And they seem not to break; though once they are bowed
   So low for long, they never right themselves:
   You may see their trunks arching in the woods
   Years afterwards, trailing their leaves on the ground
   Like girls on hands and knees that throw their hair
20 Before them over their heads to dry in the sun.
   But I was going to say when Truth broke in
   With all her matter of fact about the ice storm,
   I should prefer to have some boy bend them
   As he went out and in to fetch the cows—
25 Some boy too far from town to learn baseball,
   Whose only play was what he found himself,
   Summer or winter, and could play alone.
   One by one he subdued his father's trees
   By riding them down over and over again
30 Until he took the stiffness out of them,
   And not one but hung limp, not one was left
   For him to conquer. He learned all there was
   To learn about not launching out too soon
   And so not carrying the tree away
35 Clear to the ground. He always kept his poise
   To the top branches, climbing carefully
   With the same pains you use to fill a cup
   Up to the brim, and even above the brim.
   Then he flung outward, feet first, with a swish,
40 Kicking his way down through the air to the ground.
   So was I once myself a swinger of birches.
   And so I dream of going back to be.
   It's when I'm weary of considerations,
   And life is too much like a pathless wood
45 Where your face burns and tickles with the cobwebs
   Broken across it, and one eye is weeping
   From a twig's having lashed across it open.
   I'd like to get away from earth awhile
   And then come back to it and begin over.
50 May no fate willfully misunderstand me
   And half grant what I wish and snatch me away
   Not to return. Earth's the right place for love:
   I don't know where it's likely to go better.
   I'd like to go by climbing a birch tree,
55 And climb black branches up a snow-white trunk
   Toward heaven, till the tree could bear no more,
   But dipped its top and set me down again.
   That would be good both going and coming back.
   One could do worse than be a swinger of birches.

Discussion

1. (a) What effect do ice storms have on birches? **(b)** What **images, metaphors,** and **similes** of sight and sound describe this effect? **(c)** In contrast, what effect does a boy's swinging on birches have?

2. (a) According to Frost, swinging on birches is a very precise art. Describe it in detail. **(b)** What metaphor is used in lines 37–38 to describe climbing to the top branches? **(c)** What does this metaphor imply about the satisfactions to be gained from reaching toward high goals?

3. (a) What is the poet's mood in lines 42–47? **(b)** Because of this mood, what does the poet sometimes feel like doing? **(c)** Why does he not wish to completely escape the earth?

4. (a) In the last third of the poem, what symbolic dimension does swinging on birches acquire? **(b)** In this entire poem, does Frost favor a realistic or idealistic attitude toward life? Defend your answer with specific references to the poem.

"Out, Out—"

The buzz saw snarled and rattled in the yard
And made dust and dropped stove-length sticks of wood,
Sweet-scented stuff when the breeze drew across it.
And from there those that lifted eyes could count
5 Five mountain ranges one behind the other
Under the sunset far into Vermont.
And the saw snarled and rattled, snarled and rattled,
As it ran light, or had to bear a load.
And nothing happened: day was all but done.
10 Call it a day, I wish they might have said
To please the boy by giving him the half hour
That a boy counts so much when saved from work.
His sister stood beside them in her apron
To tell them "Supper." At the word, the saw,
15 As if to prove saws knew what supper meant,
Leaped out at the boy's hand, or seemed to leap—
He must have given the hand. However it was,
Neither refused the meeting. But the hand!
The boy's first outcry was a rueful laugh,
20 As he swung toward them holding up the hand,
Half in appeal, but half as if to keep
The life from spilling. Then the boy saw all—
Since he was old enough to know, big boy
Doing man's work, though a child at heart—
25 He saw all spoiled. "Don't let him cut my hand off—
The doctor, when he comes. Don't let him, sister!"
So. But the hand was gone already.
The doctor put him in the dark of ether.
He lay and puffed his lips out with his breath.
30 And then—the watcher at his pulse took fright.
No one believed. They listened at his heart.
Little—less—nothing!—and that ended it.
No more to build on there. And they, since they
Were not the one dead, turned to their affairs.

Discussion

1. With which details throughout the poem is the buzz saw **personified**?

2. What do lines 10–12 imply about the nature of the boy's life?

3. Line 17 says, "He must have given the hand." (a) What is Frost implying about the accidental nature of the injury? (b) What do you think is the underlying motivation for the boy's action? Explain.

4. What does the boy do when he sees that his hand is injured?

5. Some may say that, based on lines 33–34, the others were indifferent to the boy. Others may claim that Frost is telling us that life must go on in spite of death. Which interpretation do you favor, and why?

6. Who do you think is most responsible for this "accident": the boy, the family, or fate, as represented by the saw? Explain.

Stopping by Woods on a Snowy Evening

Whose woods these are I think I know.
His house is in the village, though;
He will not see me stopping here
To watch his woods fill up with snow.

5 My little horse must think it queer
To stop without a farmhouse near
Between the woods and frozen lake
The darkest evening of the year.

He gives his harness bells a shake
10 To ask if there is some mistake.
The only other sound's the sweep
Of easy wind and downy flake.

The woods are lovely, dark, and deep,
But I have promises to keep,
15 And miles to go before I sleep,
And miles to go before I sleep.

Discussion

Stopping by Woods on a Snowy Evening

1. (a) Identify the **rhyme** scheme and **rhythm** pattern of the poem. (b) Find and list examples of **alliteration.** (c) How does each of the above devices unify the poem?

2. (a) What details of the surrounding woods does the observer note? (b) What quality about the woods does he find especially attractive?

3. (a) What is the effect of the repetition of the last two lines? (b) Some critics have commented that this poem is about death. Do you agree or disagree? Why?

Fire and Ice

Some say the world will end in fire,
Some say in ice.
From what I've tasted of desire
I hold with those who favor fire.
5 But if it had to perish twice,
I think I know enough of hate
To say that for destruction ice
Is also great
And would suffice.

Fire and Ice

1. (a) What two aspects of human nature are represented by fire and ice? (b) In what way is each of these aspects destructive when it becomes excessive? (c) Which does Frost see as being more destructive, and why?

2. Both "Fire and Ice" and "Out, Out—" are about grim subjects. Explain what the **tone** of each poem is by referring to specific passages.

Mending Wall

Something there is that doesn't love a wall,
That sends the frozen-ground-swell under it
And spills the upper boulders in the sun,
And makes gaps even two can pass abreast.
5 The work of hunters is another thing:
I have come after them and made repair
Where they have left not one stone on a stone,
But they would have the rabbit out of hiding,
To please the yelping dogs. The gaps I mean,
10 No one has seen them made or heard them made,
But at spring mending-time we find them there.
I let my neighbor know beyond the hill;
And on a day we meet to walk the line
And set the wall between us once again.
15 We keep the wall between us as we go.
To each the boulders that have fallen to each.
And some are loaves and some so nearly balls
We have to use a spell to make them balance:
"Stay where you are until our backs are turned!"
20 We wear our fingers rough with handling them.
Oh, just another kind of outdoor game,
One on a side. It comes to little more:
There where it is we do not need the wall:
He is all pine and I am apple orchard.
25 My apple trees will never get across
And eat the cones under his pines, I tell him.
He only says, "Good fences make good neighbors."
Spring is the mischief in me, and I wonder
If I could put a notion in his head:
30 "*Why* do they make good neighbors? Isn't it
Where there are cows? But here there are no cows.
Before I built a wall I'd ask to know
What I was walling in or walling out,
And to whom I was like to give offense.
35 Something there is that doesn't love a wall,
That wants it down." I could say "Elves" to him,
But it's not elves exactly, and I'd rather
He said it for himself. I see him there,
Bringing a stone grasped firmly by the top
40 In each hand, like an old-stone savage armed.
He moves in darkness as it seems to me,
Not of woods only and the shade of trees.
He will not go behind his father's saying,
And he likes having thought of it so well
45 He says again, "Good fences make good neighbors."

Discussion

1. (a) How does the speaker characterize his neighbor?
(b) How does each differ on the necessity of walls?
2. (a) What meanings does the word "wall" acquire beyond an actual physical wall?
(b) In what sense could you describe the neighbor as "walled in"?

Extension • Writing

The first line of "Mending Wall" states that "Something there is that doesn't love a wall." In the last line the neighbor says, "Good fences make good neighbors." Take one side or the other and write an essay defending your position.

Robert Frost 1874 • 1963

Though Robert Frost spent most of his life in New England, where nine generations of his ancestors had lived, he was a nationally known figure. And as a four-time winner of the Pulitzer Prize in Poetry, he did much to win acceptance for modern poetry.

Much of Frost's work seems to grow naturally from the changing seasons, the wooded mountains, and the rugged farms north of Boston. But in spite of the fact that he often used these New England settings, he is not primarily either a nature poet or a local colorist. Instead, his setting becomes a background for the unfolding of the drama of the human situation.

Like the New Englanders he writes about—and like most modern poets—Frost leaves much unsaid. His apparently simple poems often turn out to be rich in hidden meanings. A fine storyteller, he often gives only the facts of an episode and leaves it to the readers to relate the meaning of the episode to their own experience.

Part of Frost's popularity with the general reader has no doubt stemmed from the fact that his poetry looks and sounds "like poetry." Readers respond favorably to the familiar iambic pentameter lines and to other traditional verse forms that appear in his poetry. But careful reading reveals subtly changing rhythms, precise language, and the meticulous use of sound devices. Frost once said that art should "clean" life and "strip it to form." There is nothing superfluous in the poetry of Robert Frost.

Countee Cullen

Any Human to Another

The ills I sorrow at
Not me alone
Like an arrow,
Pierce to the marrow,
5 Through the fat
And past the bone.

Your grief and mine
Must intertwine
Like sea and river,
10 Be fused and mingle,
Diverse yet single,
Forever and forever.

Let no man be so proud
And confident,
15 To think he is allowed
A little tent

Pitched in a meadow
Of sun and shadow
All his little own.

20 Joy may be shy, unique,
Friendly to a few,
Sorrow never scorned to speak
To any who
Were false or true.

25 Your every grief
Like a blade
Shining and unsheathed
Must strike me down.
Of bitter aloes wreathed,
30 My sorrow must be laid
On your head like a crown.

If You Should Go

Love, leave me like the light,
  The gently passing day;
We would not know, but for the night,
  When it has slipped away.

5 Go quietly; a dream,
  When done, should leave no trace
That it has lived, except a gleam
  Across the dreamer's face.

Discussion

Any Human to Another

1. What various **images** does the poet use to convey the feeling of grief?

2. The ancient Greeks and Romans crowned victors with wreaths of laurel. From early times, grief has been symbolized by *aloes*, a bitter drug made from the leaves of a plant of the lily family. **(a)** Using this information, explain what Cullen is saying in the final stanza about the need to share grief. **(b)** How are the final three lines reminiscent of Christ's crucifixion?

If You Should Go

1. In the first stanza, what is love's leaving compared to?

2. **(a)** In the second stanza, what does the poet mean when he says that love should vanish like a dream? **(b)** With what emotion does he always want to associate his love?

Countee Cullen 1903 • 1946

An adopted son of a Methodist minister, Countee Cullen grew up in New York City. His major occupation, in addition to writing poetry, was teaching French.

In his lyrics he combines an understanding of human joys and sorrows with a thoughtful probing of the attitudes of blacks and whites toward one another. Cullen collected what he considered to be the best verse written by black poets and put them in an anthology which he titled *Caroling Dusk.*

Edna St. Vincent Millay

Discussion

1. (a) What human situation does this **sonnet** deal with?
(b) What is the speaker's attitude toward her experience?
(c) What **metaphor** conveys this attitude most powerfully?

2. What impression of the speaker's character does this sonnet create?

(Millay's biography is in Unit 1, page 42.)

Well, I Have Lost You

Well, I have lost you; and I lost you fairly;
In my own way, and with my full consent.
Say what you will, kings in a tumbrel rarely
Went to their deaths more proud than this one went.
5 Some nights of apprehension and hot weeping
I will confess; but that's permitted me;
Day dried my eyes; I was not one for keeping
Rubbed in a cage a wing that would be free.
If I had loved you less or played you slyly
10 I might have held you for a summer more,
But at the cost of words I value highly,
And no such summer as the one before.
Should I outlive this anguish—and men do—
I shall have only good to say of you.

"Well, I have lost you . . . ," from COLLECTED POEMS, Harper & Row. Copyright 1931, 1958 by Edna St. Vincent Millay and Norma Millay Ellis.

Nicholas Sapieha/Stock, Boston, Inc.

Elinor Wylie

Let No Charitable Hope

Now let no charitable hope
Confuse my mind with images
Of eagle and of antelope:
I am in nature none of these.

5 I was, being human, born alone;
I am, being woman, hard beset;
I live by squeezing from a stone
The little nourishment I get.

In masks outrageous and austere
10 The years go by in single file;
But none has merited my fear,
And none has quite escaped my smile.

Dr. E. R. Degginger.

Sara Teasdale

Day's Ending

(Tucson)

Aloof as aged kings,
Wearing like them the purple,
The mountains ring the mesa
Crowned with a dusky light;
5 Many a time I watched
That coming-on of darkness
Till stars burned through the heavens
Intolerably bright.

It was not long I lived there
10 But I became a woman
Under those vehement stars,
For it was there I heard
For the first time my spirit
Forging an iron rule for me,
15 As though with slow cold hammers
Beating out word by word:

"Only yourself can heal you,
Only yourself can lead you,
The road is heavy going
20 And ends where no man knows;
Take love when love is given,
But never think to find it
A sure escape from sorrow
Or a complete repose."

The Solitary

My heart has grown rich with the passing of years,
    I have less need now than when I was young
To share myself with every comer
    Or shape my thoughts into words with my tongue.

5 It is one to me that they come or go
    If I have myself and the drive of my will,
And strength to climb on a summer night
    And watch the stars swarm over the hill.

Let them think I love them more than I do,
10   Let them think I care, though I go alone;
If it lifts their pride, what is it to me
    Who am self-complete as a flower or a stone.

Discussion

Let No Charitable Hope

1. (a) What quality is usually associated with the eagle? With the antelope? (b) Why does the poet disavow both images?

2. In the second stanza, how does she characterize life? Quote specific phrases.

3. In the third stanza, what is the attitude of the poet toward the passing years?

Elinor Wylie 1885 • 1928

Born into a wealthy and cultured family, Elinor Wylie spent much of her childhood in Washington, D.C., where her father served as Assistant Attorney General under Theodore Roosevelt.

As an adult she made her home in New York City, where she became acquainted with most of the prominent writers of that time. Her poetry was delicate, finely wrought, and painstakingly intelligent.

Discussion

Day's Ending

1. How is the image of mountains surrounding a mesa related to the rest of the poem?

2. In your own words, what is the "iron rule" set forth in the last stanza?

3. What attitude toward life seems to be shared by Elinor Wylie and Sara Teasdale?

The Solitary

1. How does the speaker differ now from the time of her youth?

2. (a) On what is she still dependent? (b) What is her attitude toward other people's regard for her?

3. (a) Do you believe it is possible for a person to become as "self-complete as a flower or a stone"? Explain. (b) Do you agree with the philosophy stated in the poem? Why or why not?

Sara Teasdale 1884 • 1933

Sara Teasdale was truly the independent "solitary" she describes in her poems. After being raised and educated in St. Louis, she traveled to Europe and the Near East. Upon her return to America she settled in New York, where she lived in near-seclusion and wrote poetry despite frequent illness.

Her first book of poems, *Sonnets to Duse,* appeared in 1907. Other volumes followed, including *Rivers to the Sea* (1915), *Love Songs* (1917), which won her a special Pulitzer award, and the posthumously published *Strange Victory* (1933).

T. S. Eliot

The Love Song of J. Alfred Prufrock

S'io credesse che mia risposta fosse
A persona che mai tornasse al mondo,
Questa fiamma staria senza piu scosse.
Ma perciocche giammai di questo fondo
Non torno vivo alcun, s' i' odo il vero,
Senza tema d' infamia ti rispondo.[1]

Let us go then, you and I,
When the evening is spread out against the sky
Like a patient etherised upon a table;
Let us go, through certain half-deserted streets,
5 The muttering retreats
Of restless nights in one-night cheap hotels
And sawdust restaurants with oyster-shells:
Streets that follow like a tedious argument

---

1. **S'io credesse . . . ti rispondo.** "If I believed my answer were being made to one who could ever return to the world, this flame would gleam no more; but since, if what I hear is true, never from this abyss [hell] did living man return, I answer thee without fear of infamy." (Dante. *Inferno* XXVII, 61–66)

notes and comments

Prufrock's Fear of Love

Your appreciation of "The Love Song of J. Alfred Prufrock" may be enhanced if you are aware of the basic situation that T. S. Eliot is describing.

The poem is an interior **monologue**; that is, the **narrator**, Prufrock, is speaking to himself. Consequently, some parts of the poem seem disjointed because we are listening to Prufrock's flow of thoughts.

The story describes Prufrock's visit to a woman, his inability to declare his love for her, and his later agonized recollection of this experience. The "you and I" of the opening lines are considered by many critics to be the two parts of Prufrock's divided self; one part urges him to act, and the other holds him back.

On a first reading, it is more important to try to visualize the setting and the situation than to labor over the interpretation of individual lines. As Eliot himself recognized, appreciation may come before total comprehension of good poetry.

Of insidious intent
10 To lead you to an overwhelming question. . .
Oh, do not ask, "What is it?"
Let us go and make our visit.

In the room the women come and go
Talking of Michelangelo.

15 The yellow fog that rubs its back upon the window-panes,
The yellow smoke that rubs its muzzle on the window-panes
Licked its tongue into the corners of the evening,
Lingered upon the pools that stand in drains,
Let fall upon its back the soot that falls from chimneys,
20 Slipped by the terrace, made a sudden leap,
And seeing that it was a soft October night,
Curled once about the house, and fell asleep.

And indeed there will be time
For the yellow smoke that slides along the street,
25 Rubbing its back upon the window-panes;
There will be time, there will be time
To prepare a face to meet the faces that you meet;
There will be time to murder and create,
And time for all the works and days of hands
30 That lift and drop a question on your plate;
Time for you and time for me,
And time yet for a hundred indecisions,
And for a hundred visions and revisions,
Before the taking of a toast and tea.

35 In the room the women come and go
Talking of Michelangelo.

And indeed there will be time
To wonder, "Do I dare?" and, "Do I dare?"
Time to turn back and descend the stair,
40 With a bald spot in the middle of my hair—
[They will say: "How his hair is growing thin!"]
My morning coat, my collar mounting firmly to the chin,
My necktie rich and modest, but asserted by a simple pin—
[They will say: "But how his arms and legs are thin!"]
45 Do I dare
Disturb the universe?
In a minute there is time
For decisions and revisions which a minute will reverse.

For I have known them all already, known them all:—
50 Have known the evenings, morning, afternoons,
I have measured out my life with coffee spoons;
I know the voices dying with a dying fall

1. What **connotations** are suggested by the name "J. Alfred Prufrock"?

2. In lines 1–23, what are the dominant impressions of the environment that are formed by the speaker's **images**?

3. What do you think is the speaker's attitude toward the women who speak of Michelangelo (lines 13–14)?

4. In lines 23–34, what is the poet's attitude toward life and toward himself? Refer to specific phrases.

5. In lines 37–48, what is the speaker's attitude toward the passage of time?

6. What is the speaker objecting to in lines 55–58?

7. What frustrations and fantasies are implied in the references to arms and perfume in lines 63–69?

8. In the poem up to line 74, how would you characterize Prufrock's attitude toward (a) his environment? (b) himself? (c) life?

9. Of what particular failure is the speaker most fearful in lines 75–110?

10. In lines 111–119, what roles in life does Prufrock see as appropriate for himself?

11. (a) What do the mermaids represent in Prufrock's life? (b) Explain in your own words what has always happened to him in the end.

12. The following questions deal with the poem in its entirety. (a) What do you think is the "overwhelming question" that Prufrock ignores in lines 10–12? (b) In what way are the quoted lines at the start of the poem, in which Guido da Montefeltro suffers eternal torment, appropriate to the theme of Prufrock's song? (c) What primary feeling about life is the poet attempting to convey? (d) Does the poet allow Prufrock any escape from his torment? Explain. (e) In what way is the title of the poem ironic?

Beneath the music from a farther room.
   So how should I presume?

55 And I have known the eyes already, known them all—
The eyes that fix you in a formulated phrase,
And when I am formulated, sprawling on a pin,
When I am pinned and wriggling on the wall,
Then how should I begin
60 To spit out all the butt-ends of my days and ways?
   And how should I presume?

And I have known the arms already, known them all—
Arms that are braceleted and white and bare
[But in the lamplight, downed with light brown hair!]
65 Is it perfume from a dress
That makes me so digress?
Arms that lie along a table, or wrap about a shawl.
   And should I then presume?
   And how should I begin?
     · · · · ·

70 Shall I say, I have gone at dusk through narrow streets
And watched the smoke that rises from the pipes
Of lonely men in shirt-sleeves, leaning out of windows? . . .

I should have been a pair of ragged claws
Scuttling across the floors of silent seas.
     · · · · ·

75 And the afternoon, the evening, sleeps so peacefully!
Smoothed by long fingers,
Asleep . . . tired . . . or it malingers,
Stretched on the floor, here beside you and me.
Should I, after tea and cakes and ices,
80 Have the strength to force the moment to its crisis?
But though I have wept and fasted, wept and prayed,
Though I have seen my head [grown slightly bald] brought
     in upon a platter,
I am no prophet—and here's no great matter;
I have seen the moment of my greatness flicker,
85 And I have seen the eternal Footman hold my coat,
     and snicker,
And in short, I was afraid.

And would it have been worth it, after all,
After the cups, the marmalade, the tea,
Among the porcelain, among some talk of you and me,
90 Would it have been worth while,
To have bitten off the matter with a smile,
To have squeezed the universe into a ball
To roll it toward some overwhelming question,
To say: "I am Lazarus, come from the dead,

95 Come back to tell you all, I shall tell you all"—
　　If one, settling a pillow by her head,
　　　　Should say: "That is not what I meant at all.
　　　　That is not it, at all."

　　　　And would it have been worth it, after all,
100 Would it have been worth while,
　　After the sunsets and the dooryards and the sprinkled streets,
　　After the novels, after the teacups, after the skirts that
　　　　　trail along the floor—
　　And this, and so much more?—
　　It is impossible to say just what I mean!
105 But as if a magic lantern threw the nerves in patterns
　　　　　on a screen:
　　Would it have been worth while
　　If one, settling a pillow or throwing off a shawl,
　　And turning toward the window, should say:
　　　　"That is not it at all,
110 That is not what I meant, at all."
　　　　　　　　. . . . .

　　No! I am not Prince Hamlet,[2] nor was meant to be;
　　Am an attendant lord, one that will do
　　To swell a progress, start a scene or two,
　　Advise the prince; no doubt, an easy tool,
115 Deferential, glad to be of use,
　　Politic, cautious, and meticulous;
　　Full of high sentence, but a bit obtuse;
　　At times, indeed, almost ridiculous—
　　Almost, at times, the Fool.

120 　　I grow old . . . I grow old . . .
　　I shall wear the bottoms of my trousers rolled.

　　　　Shall I part my hair behind? Do I dare to eat a peach?
　　I shall wear white flannel trousers, and walk upon the beach.
　　I have heard the mermaids singing, each to each.

125 　　I do not think that they will sing to me.

　　　　I have seen them riding seaward on the waves
　　Combing the white hair of the waves blown back
　　When the wind blows the water white and black.

　　　　We have lingered in the chambers of the sea
130 By sea-girls wreathed with seaweed red and brown
　　Till human voices wake us, and we drown.

---

2. **Prince Hamlet,** the hero of William Shakespeare's play *Hamlet,* who set out to prove that his mother and uncle had murdered his father.

T. S. Eliot 1888 • 1965

T. S. Eliot was born in St. Louis and educated at Harvard University. In 1910 he began writing "The Love Song of J. Alfred Prufrock" and finished the poem the following year during a visit to Germany, but it wasn't published until 1915. After World War I broke out, Eliot went to England to work, was married, and became a British subject in 1926.

Through his poems and his discussions of technique, Eliot did much to win acceptance of "difficult" modern poetry. In describing Eliot's poetry, one critic has noted that he mixes "trivial and tawdry pictures with traditionally poetic subject-matter" to explore the state of humanity in the twentieth century. In recognition of his contribution to modern poetry, T. S. Eliot was awarded the Nobel Prize for literature in 1948.

James Weldon Johnson

The Creation

And God stepped out of space,
And he looked around and said:
I'm lonely—
I'll make me a world.

5 And as far as the eye of God could see
Darkness covered everything,
Blacker than a hundred midnights
Down in a cypress swamp.

Then God smiled,
10 And the light broke,
And the darkness rolled up on one side,
And the light stood shining on the other,
And God said: That's good!

Then God reached out and took the light
     in his hands,
15 And God rolled the light around in his hands
Until he made the sun;
And he set that sun a-blazing in the heavens.
And the light that was left from
     making the sun
God gathered it up in a shining ball
20 And flung it against the darkness,
Spangling the night with the moon and stars.
Then down between
The darkness and the light
He hurled the world;
25 And God said: That's good!

Then God himself stepped down—
And the sun was on his right hand,
And the moon was on his left;
The stars were clustered about his head,
30 And the earth was under his feet.
And God walked, and where he trod
His footsteps hollowed the valleys out
And bulged the mountains up.

Then he stopped and looked and saw
35 That the earth was hot and barren.
So God stepped over to the edge of the world

And he spat out the seven seas—
He batted his eyes, and the lightnings flashed—
He clapped his hands, and the thunders rolled—
40 And the waters above the earth came down,
The cooling waters came down.

Then the green grass sprouted,
And the little red flowers blossomed,
The pine tree pointed his finger to the sky,
45 And the oak spread out his arms,
The lakes cuddled down in the hollows
     of the ground,
And the rivers ran down to the sea;
And God smiled again,
And the rainbow appeared,
50 And curled itself around his shoulder.
Then God raised his arm and he waved his hand
Over the sea and over the land,
And he said: Bring forth! Bring forth!
And quicker than God could drop his hand,
55 Fishes and fowls
And beasts and birds
Swam the rivers and the seas,
Roamed the forests and the woods,
And split the air with their wings.
60 And God said: That's good!

Then God walked around,
And God looked around
On all that he had made.
He looked at his sun,
65 And he looked at his moon,
And he looked at his little stars;
He looked on his world
With all its living things,
And God said: I'm lonely still.

70 Then God sat down—
On the side of a hill where he could think;

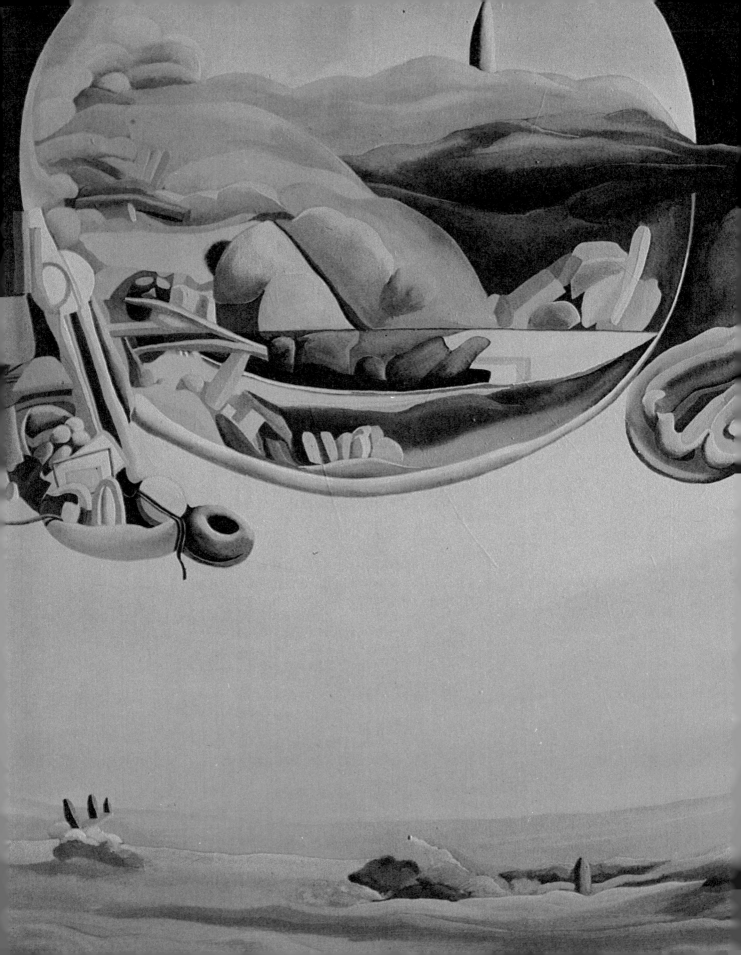

By a deep, wide river he sat down;
With his head in his hands,
God thought and thought,
75 Till he thought: I'll make me a man!

Up from the bed of the river
God scooped the clay;
And by the bank of the river
He kneeled him down;
80 And there the great God Almighty
Who lit the sun and fixed it in the sky,
Who flung the stars to the most far
    corner of the night,

Who rounded the earth in the middle
    of his hand;
This Great God
85 Like a mammy bending over her baby,
Kneeled down in the dust
Toiling over a lump of clay
Till he shaped it in his own image;

Then into it he blew the breath of life,
90 And man became a living soul.
Amen. Amen.

Discussion

1. "God made man in His own image, but man also makes God in his own image." **(a)** What does this statement mean? **(b)** Cite specific lines from "The Creation" that bear out the statement.

2. **(a)** The speaker of the poem is a preacher. Cite images that are used to bring God close to the everyday experience of the congregation. **(b)** Which lines in their rhythm and phraseology are most like Biblical language?

3. Describe the **tone** of the poem.

James Weldon Johnson
1871 • 1938

Although he will be longest remembered as a poet and essayist, James Weldon Johnson was successful in many fields. He taught school in his home town, Jacksonville, Florida, while studying law, and after being admitted to the Florida bar in 1897, he went to New York where he prospered as a writer of songs and light opera.

As Johnson became older, the flair for rhythm and the feeling for words that had made him a successful song writer found different channels. He edited books of Negro poetry and spirituals, and in 1927 he published *God's Trombones*, his finest poetic achievement.

From boyhood Johnson had been fascinated by the black preachers who translated Biblical events into simple, understandable stories. Believing that their congregations would find comfort in a God whose characteristics were human, the preachers pictured a gentle Father who experienced loneliness and worried over His children. In these poetic retellings, even the landscape of the Old Testament came to resemble the familiar rural South. It was such memories, along with

Johnson's own talent for rhythm and expression, that went into *God's Trombones*. The book is comprised of a series of seven Negro sermons in verse, in which the phraseology of the Bible is beautifully fused with the poetic eloquence of a preacher.

he Creation
y Zita Sodeika.

E. E. Cummings

pity this busy monster, manunkind

pity this busy monster, manunkind,

not. Progress is a comfortable disease:
your victim(death and life safely beyond)

plays with the bigness of his littleness
5 —electrons deify one razorblade
into a mountainrange; lenses extend

unwish through curving wherewhen till unwish
returns on its unself.
                        A world of made
10 is not a world of born—pity poor flesh

and trees,poor stars and stones,but never this
fine specimen of hypermagical

ultraomnipotence. We doctors know

a hopeless case if—listen:there's a hell
15 of a good universe next door;let's go

Discussion

1. (a) What is implied about humanity by the phrase "busy monster"? (b) What ambiguity is created by the placement of the word "not" at the beginning of the second line?

2. (a) Which **images** in the poem refer to the "world of made"? (b) Which refer to the "world of born"? (c) To which realm does humankind give its primary allegiance?

3. How do the words "hypermagical ultraomnipotence" further indicate the poet's attitude toward progress?

4. Do you feel that the playful ending is more effective than a serious indictment would be? Why or why not?

E. E. Cummings 1894 · 1962

Edward Estlin Cummings (or e. e. cummings, as he signed his poems) was reared according to a rather traditional New England pattern. During World War I, he served in the ambulance corps in France. After some time in Paris, he returned to America to live in Greenwich Village, New York.

Cummings experimented with the problem of representing sounds on paper. He broke compound words into parts and put explanatory words or phrases between the parts. He ran words together to increase the tempo, or separated them, putting one to a line to express slow movement. Through his experiments he created some of the most delightful lyrics in contemporary poetry.

Phyllis McGinley

Lament of the Normal Child

The school where I go is a modern school
  With numerous modern graces.
And there they cling to the modern rule
  Of "Cherish the Problem Cases!"
5 From nine to three
I develop Me.
  I dance when I'm feeling dancy,
Or everywhere lay on
With creaking crayon
10   The colors that suit my fancy.
But when the commoner tasks are done,
  Deserted, ignored, I stand.
For the rest have complexes, everyone;
  Or a hyperactive gland.
15 Oh, how can I ever be reconciled
  To my hatefully normal station?
Why couldn't I be a Problem Child
  Endowed with a small fixation?
Why wasn't I trained for a Problem Child
20   With an Interesting Fixation?

I dread the sound of the morning bell.
  The iron has entered my soul.
I'm a square little peg who fits too well
  In a square little normal hole.
25 For seven years
In Mortimer Sears
  Has the Oedipus angle flourished;
And Jessamine Gray,
She cheats at play
30   Because she is undernourished.
The teachers beam on Frederick Knipe
  With scientific gratitude,

For Fred, they claim, is a perfect type
  Of the Antisocial Attitude.
35 And Cuthbert Jones has his temper riled
  In a way professors mention.
But I am a Perfectly Normal Child,
  So I don't get any attention.
I'm nothing at all but a Normal Child,
40   So I don't get the least attention.

The others jeer as they pass my way.
  They titter without forbearance.
"He's Perfectly Normal," they shrilly say,
  "With Perfectly Normal parents."
45 I learn to read
With a normal speed.
  I answer when I'm commanded.
Infected antrums
Don't give me tantrums.
50   I don't even write left-handed.
I build with blocks when they give me blocks,
  When it's busy hour, I labor.
And I seldom delight in landing socks
  On the ear of my little neighbor.

55   I sit on the steps alone.
Why couldn't I be a Problem Child
  With a Case to call my own?
Why wasn't I born a Problem Child
  With a Complex of my own?

Discussion

1. What is the lament of the poem's speaker? Refer to specific passages in the poem.

2. What elements of **meter, rhyme,** and word choice suggest that this is a comic poem? Give examples.

3. What tendency of modern education is the poet satirizing? Explain.

Phyllis McGinley 1905 • 1978

Phyllis McGinley was born in Oregon and educated at the University of Utah and the University of California. She is widely known for her witty, sophisticated poems that appeared frequently in *The New Yorker*. In 1960 she was awarded the Pulitzer prize for *Times Three: Selected Verse from Three Decades*.

John Crowe Ransom

Janet Waking

Beautifully Janet slept
Till it was deeply morning. She woke then
And thought about her dainty-feathered hen,
To see how it had kept.

5 One kiss she gave her mother.
Only a small one gave she to her daddy
Who would have kissed each curl of his shining baby;
No kiss at all for her brother.

"Old Chucky, old Chucky!" she cried,
10 Running across the world upon the grass
To Chucky's house, and listening. But alas,
Her Chucky had died.

It was a transmogrifying bee
Came droning down on Chucky's old bald head
15 And sat and put the poison. It scarcely bled,
But how exceedingly

And purply did the knot
Swell with the venom and communicate
Its rigor! Now the poor comb stood up straight
20 But Chucky did not.

So there was Janet
Kneeling on the wet grass, crying her brown hen
(Translated far beyond the daughters of men)
To rise and walk upon it.

25 And weeping fast as she had breath
Janet implored us, "Wake her from her sleep!"
And would not be instructed in how deep
Was the forgetful kingdom of death.

Discussion

1. What **pun** is there on the word "wake" (as noun and verb)?

2. How do the speaker and Janet differ in their attitudes toward Chucky's death? Cite words or phrases supporting your opinion.

3. **(a)** In what sense does the experience "awaken" Janet from the innocence of childhood? **(b)** In what lines does it become apparent that she is resisting this process? **(c)** How do you explain this resistance?

John Crowe Ransom
1888 • 1974

Ransom was noted as a poet, literary critic, and teacher. While teaching at Vanderbilt University in Nashville, Tennessee, he and seven other Southern writers formed "The Fugitive Group" which supported the "new poetry" and published poems and critical essays in their periodical, *The Fugitive*. In 1937 Ransom went to Kenyon College, Ohio, where he founded the *Kenyon Review*.

His poems are notable for their gentle irony and lack of sentimentality. The scene is often a domestic one. Unlike some other modern poets such as Cummings, Ransom often worked within regular rhythms, rhyme schemes, and stanza forms. He published several volumes of poetry, including *Chills and Fever* (1924) and *Selected Poems* (1945 and 1963).

Jean Toomer

November Cotton Flower

Boll-weevil's coming, and the winter's cold,
Made cotton-stalks look rusty, seasons old,
And cotton, scarce as any southern snow,
Was vanishing; the branch, so pinched and slow,
5 Failed in its function as the autumn rake;
Drouth fighting soil had caused the soil to take
All water from the streams; dead birds were found
In wells a hundred feet below the ground—
Such was the season when the flower bloomed.
10 Old folks were startled, and it soon assumed
Significance. Superstition saw
Something it had never seen before:
Brown eyes that loved without a trace of fear,
Beauty so sudden for that time of year.

Beehive

Within this black hive to-night
There swarm a million bees;
Bees passing in and out the moon,
Bees escaping out the moon,
5 Bees returning through the moon,
Silver bees intently buzzing,
Silver honey dripping from the swarm of bees
Earth is a waxen cell of the world comb,
And I, a drone,
10 Lying on my back,
Lipping honey,
Getting drunk with silver honey,
Wish that I might fly out past the moon
And curl forever in some far-off farmyard flower.

Reprinted from CANE by Jean Toomer. By permission of Liveright Publishing Corporation. Copyright 1923 by Boni & Liveright. Copyright renewed 1951 by Jean Toomer.

Discussion

November Cotton Flower

1. In the first eight lines of this **sonnet**, what **mood** is created, and which images contribute to that mood?

2. **(a)** Why is the event described in the final six lines so startling? **(b)** What does the event **symbolize** in the lives of the people?

Beehive

1. **(a)** Who is the speaker, and what is he observing? **(b)** What does he wish he could do?

2. What human desire do you think Toomer is expressing through the image of the beehive? Explain.

Jean Toomer 1894 • 1967

Jean Toomer was born in Washington D. C. and went to the University of Wisconsin and City College of New York. He was for a time principal of a school in Georgia. In 1923 he published his one book, *Cane*, a mixture of poetry and poetic prose. The book was appreciated by a select few of the time, but has reached a wider audience since its reissue in 1967. Toomer's later career is wrapped in mystery, as he wrote much but published nothing.

Wallace Stevens

The Snow Man

One must have a mind of winter
To regard the frost and the boughs
Of the pine-trees crusted with snow;

And have been cold a long time
5 To behold the junipers shagged with ice,
The spruces rough in the distant glitter

Of the January sun; and not to think
Of any misery in the sound of the wind,
In the sound of a few leaves,

10 Which is the sound of the land
Full of the same wind
That is blowing in the same bare place

For the listener, who listens in the snow,
And, nothing himself, beholds
15 Nothing that is not there and the nothing that is.

notes and comments

Reading "The Snow Man"

"The Snow Man" speaks directly to those who have ever had the feeling that life itself is as cold and uncompromising as the deepest winter. Wallace Stevens professed no belief and admitted no desire that would prevent people from recognizing the true nature of reality as chaotic and everchanging.

He felt that in life nothing counts but the here and now, the concrete and factual. Over and over, his poems urge readers to drop the preconceptions that blind them to the beauties of the world and prevent them from experiencing its pains and pleasures. As a result of his philosophy, Stevens wrote poetry that is very concrete. He never comes right out and tells the reader what the poem is about, but rather implies his point through the way in which the images are presented.

Poetry was the way in which Stevens made sense out of existence. As you read, ask yourself how Stevens's philosophy is evident in the way in which he describes the cold and barren scene in "The Snow Man."

Discussion

1. In the first four stanzas, what aspects of the **setting** are emphasized? Cite specific words and phrases in your answer.

2. What should be the attitude of the observer in order to see the surroundings for what they are?

3. (a) Who is the "Snow Man" of the title? (b) Why is he given this name?

4. (a) What is the **paradox** that concludes the poem? (b) In your own words, explain what you think this line means.

Anecdote of the Jar

I placed a jar in Tennessee,
And round it was, upon a hill.
It made the slovenly wilderness
Surround that hill.

5 The wilderness rose up to it,
And sprawled around, no longer wild.
The jar was round upon the ground
And tall and of a port in air.

It took dominion everywhere.
10 The jar was gray and bare.
It did not give of bird or bush,
Like nothing else in Tennessee.

Discussion

1. How is the wilderness of Tennessee characterized? Refer to particular words and phrases.

2. The jar is "round" and "of a port in air," meaning that it has a stately importance. What effect does it have on the surroundings when placed on the ground?

3. Most critics interpret the jar as being a **symbol** of art and the imagination. If so, what does Stevens see as the function of art in relation to reality?

Wallace Stevens 1879 • 1955

"Poetry is a search for the inexplicable," wrote Wallace Stevens. His entire life was such a search. Born in Reading, Pennsylvania, he spent most of his long life as an executive of an insurance company in Hartford, Connecticut. But throughout his career in business, he wrote poetry.

He published his first vol-

ume, *Harmonium,* in 1923. His second volume, *Ideas of Order,* did not appear until 1935. *Notes Toward a Supreme Fiction,* a long philosophical poem on poetry and the imagination, appeared in 1942 and is perhaps his masterpiece.

Though Stevens's poetry is philosophical, he does not deal with ideas in an abstract manner, but rather represents them with concrete objects, settings, and characters. A recurring subject of his poetry is the role of the imagination in bringing order to a reality that is essentially chaotic. Stevens wrote in his book of essays, *The Necessary Angel* (1951): ". . . the imagination is the power that enables us to perceive the normal in the abnormal, the opposite of chaos in chaos."

Marianne Moore

The Steeple-Jack

Dürer[1] would have seen a reason for living
    in a town like this, with eight stranded whales
to look at; with the sweet sea air coming into your house
on a fine day, from water etched
5   with waves as formal as the scales
on a fish.

One by one in two's and three's, the seagulls keep
    flying back and forth over the town clock,
or sailing around the lighthouse without moving their wings—
10 rising steadily with a slight
      quiver of the body—or flock
mewing where

a sea the purple of the peacock's neck is
    paled to greenish azure as Dürer changed
15 the pine green of the Tyrol[2] to peacock blue and guinea
gray. You can see a twenty-five-
      pound lobster; and fish nets arranged
to dry. The

whirlwind fife-and-drum of the storm bends the salt
20   marsh grass, disturbs stars in the sky and the
star on the steeple; it is a privilege to see so
much confusion. Disguised by what
    might seem the opposite, the sea-
side flowers and

25 trees are favored by the fog so that you have
    the tropics at first hand: the trumpet vine,
foxglove, giant snapdragon, a salpiglossis that has
spots and stripes; morning-glories, gourds,
    or moon-vines trained on fishing twine
30 at the back door:

---

1. Dürer (dür′ər), Albrecht Dürer (1471–1528), a German artist.
2. Tyrol (tə rōl′), a section of Europe surrounded by the Alps.

Reading "The Steeple-Jack"

Like Ezra Pound and Amy Lowell, Marianne Moore belonged to the Imagist school of poets, meaning that she wrote poetry consisting of clear, sharp, "pure" images. Such poetry might be compared to the making of a collage, in which the relationship of the pictures to one another comprises the statement that the artist is making. Furthermore, there is a total absence of sentiment in Moore's poetry. For her, technique and observation are all.

Some knowledge of the organization of "The Steeple-Jack" may help you recognize the pattern of images in the poem. In stanzas 1–3, the objects and animals in the little fishing village are statically arranged as if they are in a painting.

This tranquillity is suddenly interrupted in stanzas 4–7 by a storm that brings confusion that is a "privilege" to see. During the storm, the climate is no longer suited to the plants cataloged in stanzas 5 and 6.

Finally, the poem shifts to the perspective of a college

student named Ambrose, who
is sitting on a hillside. From his
somewhat removed perspec-
tive, he recognizes both the romantic peace of stanzas 1–3
and the confusion of stanzas
4–7. Thus, any true picture of
things must include images
both of hope and of danger.

cattails, flags, blueberries and spiderwort,
    striped grass, lichens, sunflowers, asters, daisies—
yellow and crab-claw ragged sailors with green
        bracts[3]—toad-plant,
petunias, ferns; pink lilies, blue
35   ones, tigers; poppies; black sweet-peas.
The climate

---

3. bract (brakt), a small leaf that grows at the base of a flower.

is not right for the banyan, frangipani, or
     jack-fruit trees;[4] or for exotic serpent
life. Ring lizard and snakeskin for the foot, if you see fit;
40 but here they've cats, not cobras, to
     keep down the rats. The diffident
little newt

with white pin-dots on black horizontal spaced-
     out bands lives here; yet there is nothing that
45 ambition can buy or take away. The college student
named Ambrose sits on the hillside
     with his not-native books and hat
and sees boats

at sea progress white and rigid as if in
50   a groove. Liking an elegance of which
the source is not bravado, he knows by heart the antique
sugar-bowl shaped summerhouse of
     interlacing slats, and the pitch
of the church

55 spire, not true, from which a man in scarlet lets
     down a rope as a spider spins a thread;
he might be part of a novel, but on the sidewalk a
sign says C. J. Poole, Steeple-Jack,
     in black and white; and one in red
60 and white says

Danger. The church portico has four fluted
     columns, each a single piece of stone, made
modester by whitewash. This would be a fit haven for
waifs, children, animals, prisoners,
65   and presidents who have repaid
sin-driven

senators by not thinking about them. The
     place has a schoolhouse, a post-office in a
store, fish-houses, hen-houses, a three-masted schooner on
70 the stocks. The hero, the student,
     the steeple-jack, each in his way,
is at home.

It could not be dangerous to be living
     in a town like this, of simple people,
75 who have a steeple-jack placing danger signs by the church
while he is gilding the solid-
     pointed star, which on a steeple
stands for hope.

---

4. **banyan** (ban′yən), **frangipani** (fran′jə pan′ē), **or jack-fruit trees,** exotic trees of India.

Discussion

1. How are the **images** in stanzas 8–13 different from those in stanzas 4–7?

2. What specific images of danger and of hope are combined in stanzas 8–13?

3. What do the steeple-jack and his actions in the last stanza **symbolize**?

Marianne Moore 1887 • 1972

Marianne Moore was born just outside of St. Louis. Before turning to a full-time career as a writer, she taught at the U.S. Indian School in Carlisle, Pennsylvania, and then moved to New York where she worked as a private tutor, secretary, and assistant at the New York Public Library.

Moore's poetry is highly symbolic and frank. Most of her poems develop from her observation of animals. She has a strong visual sense that allows her to sees things clearly and truthfully.

Among the many prizes she won, her *Collected Works* (1952) was awarded all three of the major American prizes for poetry: the Pulitzer Prize, the National Book Award, and the Bollingen Prize. Her *Complete Poems* was published in 1967.

William Carlos Williams

1. (a) How does the description of spring given in this poem differ from conventional descriptions? **(b)** What aspects of the spring does the poem emphasize?

2. (a) What is the double referent of "they" in line 16? **(b)** What **metaphor** is developed throughout this stanza?

3. (a) How does the poet suggest that the beginning of life is not an easy process? **(b)** What kind of universe are the newborn entering?

William Carlos Williams
1883 • 1963

Although for many years Dr. Williams spent much of his time seeing patients and delivering babies in and around Rutherford, New Jersey, he found time to write more than thirty-seven volumes of prose and poetry. For Williams the everyday event had beauty, interest, and significance. His poetry deals with such common things as spring, plums, a wheelbarrow—things that one might see everyday yet never notice. His writing reflects the physician's experience of seeing people under all conditions of life—from when they are being born to the moment of their death. Such observation has given insight and substance to his poetry and stories. Two collections of his poetry are *Collected Later Poems* (1950) and *Collected Earlier Poems* (1951).

Spring and All

By the road to the contagious hospital
under the surge of the blue
mottled clouds driven from the
northeast—a cold wind. Beyond, the
5   waste of broad, muddy fields
brown with dried weeds, standing and fallen

patches of standing water
the scattering of tall trees

All along the road the reddish
10 purplish, forked, upstanding, twiggy
stuff of bushes and small trees
with dead, brown leaves under them
leafless vines—

Lifeless in appearance, sluggish
15 dazed spring approaches—

They enter the new world naked,
cold, uncertain of all
save that they enter. All about them
the cold, familiar wind—
20 Now the grass, tomorrow
the stiff curl of wild carrot leaf
One by one objects are defined—
It quickens: clarity, outline of leaf

But now the stark dignity of
25 entrance—Still, the profound change
has come upon them: rooted they
grip down and begin to awaken

Arna Bontemps

A Black Man Talks of Reaping

I have sown beside all waters in my day.
I planted deep, within my heart the fear
That wind or fowl would take the grain away.
I planted safe against this stark, lean year.

5 I scattered seed enough to plant the land
In rows from Canada to Mexico
But for my reaping only what the hand
Can hold at once is all that I can show.

Yet what I sowed and what the orchard yields
10 My brother's sons are gathering stalk and root,
Small wonder then my children glean in fields
They have not sown, and feed on bitter fruit.

Bontemps (bôn tän′).

"A Black Man Talks of Reaping" by Arna Bontemps from PER-SONALS. Reprinted by permission of Harold Ober Associates Incorporated. Copyright © 1963 by Arna Bontemps.

Discussion

1. **(a)** What fear is related in the first stanza? **(b)** How does this fear come true in the second stanza?

2. **(a)** Who are the "brother's sons" of line 10? **(b)** What are they reaping? **(c)** What is the reaction of the speaker's people?

3. What situation is **symbolized** by the sowing and reaping described in the poem?

Arna Bontemps 1902 • 1973

Born in Alexandria, Louisiana, Arna Bontemps graduated from Pacific Union College in 1923 and soon thereafter became associated with what has become known as the Harlem Renaissance. He won a number of prizes for his poetry in the 1920s, and soon turned to prose.

In the 1930s he studied at the University of Chicago and earned a degree in library science. He served as librarian at Fisk University for many years and was for a time a member of the faculty at the University of Illinois, Chicago Circle.

His anthologies of black literature and folklore are numerous and widely popular. He also wrote three novels, including *Black Thunder* (1936).

Claude McKay

If We Must Die

If we must die, let it not be like hogs
Hunted and penned in an inglorious spot,
While round us bark the mad and hungry dogs,
Making their mock at our accursed lot.
5 If we must die, O let us nobly die,
So that our precious blood may not be shed
In vain; then even the monsters we defy
Shall be constrained to honor us though dead!
O kinsmen! we must meet the common foe!
10 Though far outnumbered let us show us brave,
And for their thousand blows deal one deathblow!
What though before us lies the open grave?
Like men we'll face the murderous, cowardly pack,
Pressed to the wall, dying, but fighting back!

Discussion

1. (a) Against what threat is the poet rallying his people? (b) Why do you think he does not name the dangers explicitly?

2. (a) What emotions do you think this poem is intended to arouse? (b) Cite phrases or figures of speech that contribute to its emotional effect.

3. Compare the **tone** of this poem with that of "A Black Man Talks of Reaping." Which do you think is more effective as protest art? Why?

Claude McKay 1890 • 1948

McKay's first two collections of poems were published just after he turned twenty. Shortly after their publication, McKay came to the United States to study agriculture. But he soon discovered that he preferred writing and moved to New York, settled in Harlem and began publishing his poems in small literary magazines. In 1922 his most important collection of poetry, *Harlem Shadows*, was published. In it, he achieved poignant lyricism as well as effective protest.

Although McKay was primarily a poet, he was also a novelist and short-story writer. His writing is noted for his portrayals of black life, for his nostalgia for the tropics of his youth, and for his demands for unity among blacks in attacking social injustice.

Margaret Walker

Childhood

When I was a child I knew red miners
dressed raggedly and wearing carbide lamps.
I saw them come down red hills to their camps
dyed with red dust from old Ishkooda mines.
5 Night after night I met them on the roads,
or on the streets in town I caught their glance;
the swing of dinner buckets in their hands,
and grumbling undermining all their words.

I also lived in low cotton country
10 where moonlight hovered over ripe haystacks,
or stumps of trees, and croppers' rotting shacks
with famine, terror, flood, and plague near by;
where sentiment and hatred still held sway
and only bitter land was washed away.

Iowa Farmer

I talked to a farmer one day in Iowa.
We looked out far over acres of wheat.
He spoke with pride and yet not boastfully;
he had no need to fumble for his words.
5 He knew his land and there was love for home
within the soft serene eyes of his son.
His ugly house was clean against the storm;
there was no hunger deep within the heart
nor burning riveted within the bone,
10 but here they ate a satisfying bread.
Yet in the Middle West where wheat was plentiful;
where grain grew golden under sunny skies
and cattle fattened through the summer heat
I could remember more familiar sights.

"Iowa Farmer" and "Childhood" from FOR MY PEOPLE by Margaret Walker, published
by Yale University Press, 1942. Reprinted by permission of Margaret Walker Alexander.

Discussion

1. What aspects of the Iowa farmer's outlook on life does the speaker emphasize?

2. (a) How does "Childhood" (and the biographical sketch of the poet) explain the last line of "Iowa Farmer"? (b) What has the poet experienced that the farmer never has?

Margaret Walker 1915 •

Margaret Walker, the daughter of a Methodist minister, was born and raised in Birmingham, Alabama. She experienced a great deal of anguish living in the South and was confused by the prejudice against black people that she found there. When she left Birmingham to attend Northwestern University, she was surprised to find that life was little better for a black in the North than it was in the South. Her poetry is shaped by these experiences of prejudice in college and the memories of her personal anguish in the South.

In 1942 Walker gained sudden prominence when her first book, *For My People*, appeared as a result of her winning the Yale University Younger Poets Competition. The poems in this collection are divided into three groups: first there are the public poems in which she speaks directly for black people, then there are the folk ballads written in the black dialect, and finally there are the personal sonnets.

Robinson Jeffers

Shine, Perishing Republic

While this America settles in the mold of its vulgarity, heavily thickening to empire,
And protest, only a bubble in the molten mass, pops and sighs out, and the mass hardens,

I sadly smiling remember that the flower fades to make fruit, the fruit rots to make earth.
Out of the mother; and through the spring exultances, ripeness and decadence; and
      home to the mother.

5 You making haste haste on decay: not blameworthy; life is good, be it stubbornly long or suddenly
A mortal splendor: meteors are not needed less than mountains: shine, perishing republic.

But for my children, I would have them keep their distance from the thickening center; corruption
Never has been compulsory, when the cities lie at the monster's feet there are left the mountains.

And boys, be in nothing so moderate as in love of man, a clever servant, insufferable master.
10 There is the trap that catches noblest spirits, that caught—they say—God, when
      he walked on earth.

Discussion

1. (a) With what is America compared in lines 1–2?
(b) What other **metaphors** throughout the poem contribute to the impression of decay?

2. (a) Is the decay of the country viewed positively, neutrally, or negatively? (b) Does the poem place blame for this decay? Explain.

3. What is meant by the admonition: "be in nothing so moderate as in love of man"?

4. Would you say that this poem is less or more pessimistic than Cummings's "pity this busy monster manunkind" (page 462)? Explain.

Robinson Jeffers 1887 • 1962

Although John Robinson Jeffers was born in Pittsburgh and was educated in Europe, most of his life and poetry were shaped by California. His family moved there when he was sixteen, and when he married, he and his wife wandered to Carmel, California. Jeffers built a house, with his own hands, on the top of a hill, where they lived out their lives and where he did all his writing.

Jeffers's feeling that poetry must become realistic led to his writing narrative poems and drawing his subjects from contemporary life. His style is something between blank verse and free verse. In his poems, he often expresses his feeling that humans are of trifling importance, a species here today, gone tomorrow.

The Grand Council Fire
of American Indians

The Grand Council Fire has worked since 1923 to focus attention on the interests and problems of native Americans. In 1927, representatives of the organization asked the mayor of Chicago to help in achieving fairness in the teaching of American history. The date shows that concern with bias is not a new issue.

General Nelson Miles and his staff viewing a large Indian camp at Pine Ridge, South Dakota, in 1891, just after the Wounded Knee massacre in this area. (Library of Congress.)

Tell Your Children

You tell all white men "America First." We believe in that. We are the only ones, truly, that are one hundred percent. We therefore ask you while you are teaching school children about America First, teach them truth about the First Americans.

We do not know if school histories are pro-British, but we do know that they are unjust to the life of our people—the American Indian. They call all white victories, battles, and all Indian victories, massacres. The battle with Custer has been taught to school children as a fearful massacre on our part. We ask that this, as well as other incidents, be told fairly. If the Custer battle was a massacre, what was Wounded Knee?[1]

History books teach that Indians were murderers—is it murder to fight in self-defense? Indians killed white men because white men took their lands, ruined their hunting grounds, burned their forests, destroyed their buffalo. White men penned our people on reservations, then took away the reservations. White men who rise to protect their property are called patriots—Indians who do the same are called murderers.

Reprinted from I HAVE SPOKEN: AMERICAN HISTORY THROUGH THE VOICES OF INDIANS, © 1971 by Virginia Irving Armstrong, by permission of The Swallow Press, Inc., Chicago.
1. **Custer . . . Wounded Knee.** General George Custer and his force were killed by the Sioux at the Battle of the Little Big Horn in 1876. At Wounded Knee, South Dakota, in 1890, 200 Sioux were massacred by federal troops.

White men call Indians treacherous—but no mention is made of broken treaties on the part of the white man. . . .

White men called Indians thieves—and yet we lived in frail skin lodges and needed no locks or iron bars. White men call Indian savages. What is civilization? Its marks are a noble religion and philosophy, original arts, stirring music, rich story and legend. We had these. . . .

We sang songs that carried in their melodies all the sounds of nature—the running of waters, the sighing of winds, and the calls of the animals. Teach these to your children that they may come to love nature as we love it.

We had our statesmen—and their oratory has never been equalled. Teach the children some of these speeches of our people, remarkable for their brilliant oratory.

We played games—games that brought good health and sound bodies. Why not put these in your schools? We told stories. Why not teach school children more of the wholesome proverbs and legends of our people? Tell them how we loved all that was beautiful. That we killed game only for food, not for fun. Indians think white men who kill for fun are murderers.

Tell your children of the friendly acts of Indians to the white people who first settled here. Tell them of our leaders and heroes and their deeds. . . . Put in your history books the Indian's part in the World War. Tell how the Indian fought for a country of which he was not a citizen, for a flag to which he had no claim, and for a people that have treated him unjustly.

We ask this, Chief,[2] to keep sacred the memory of our people. ☐☐

---

2. **Chief.** "Big Bill" Thompson (1869–1944), mayor of Chicago, was being addressed.

Discussion

1. Oratory is the art of speaking in public eloquently or effectively. What is your opinion of the eloquence and rhetorical effectiveness of this speech? Explain.

2. (a) Name some examples of historical bias against native Americans given in the speech. **(b)** What positive aspects of native American societies are presented? **(c)** Compare this speech to earlier native American statements in Units 2, 4, and 5.

3. This plea for fair presentation of native American history was made in 1927. In what ways, if any, has the **stereotype** of native Americans in history books, fiction, and Western movies, changed of late? Give examples.

Extension • Speaking

Consult your school or public library for examples of Indian oratory. *I Have Spoken,* edited by Virginia Irving Armstrong, is just one of many readily available sources. Different students should select various speeches to practice and read aloud before the class. Analyze the emotional effect of the speeches themselves, and try to isolate techniques common to Indian oratory.

Extension • Writing

Choose any major event from the so-called "Indian Wars," such as the Battle of the Little Big Horn (1876) or the Ghost Dance movement (around 1890). Find several accounts of this event, including one by a native American, one from an old history book, and one from a current history book. For example, for the Little Big Horn battle, there are various accounts by both Sioux and white participants, as well as the many versions in history books. One Sioux eyewitness account is in *Black Elk Speaks* by John G. Neihardt. Compare these accounts, then write a summary of what you think actually happened. Afterwards, discuss in class the differences among the various published accounts and those written by yourself and other students.

Avis Carlson

The Wedding

Weddings are usually a time of confusion, but few achieve the wild muddlement of mine. Because it has become something of a legend among younger generations in two families, it should be described with whatever accuracy can now be summoned after all the tellings and retellings.

To begin, it was the occasion for no great joy in either family. The Carlson parents had barely met me, but were well aware that I was neither sturdy of body nor sedate of spirit, clearly a somewhat risky choice for their Scandinavian son. My parents approved of my young man but utterly lacked enthusiasm for my marrying *any one* before the ink had dried on my diploma. They had sacrificed to give me my "chance," and experience had instilled in them the conviction that a female college graduate can find better scope for her energies than marriage—a state, which in their experience meant, both soon *and* late, babies. Besides they argued truthfully, I was very young. A year or two of teaching would season me, indeed would earn me a right to marry. They themselves had waited years for the right time.

These were reasonable views. But I was crazy in love, I had already been separated from my love for a year, and there was a war[1] on. Whenever did parents win in that situation? By the time of my graduation, it was conceded in the family that there would be a summer wedding. After all these years I applaud them: once they had yielded to my determination, they did their best to put aside their disappointment and not to spoil my last summer at home. But I knew, how well I knew, they wished I had been willing to wait at least a year. From the knowledge came a sense of guilt and, from that, tension. If either they or I could have attempted communication, the gap might have been bridged. But none of us knew the right words or found the right moment.

The two months between commencement and wedding were probably the loneliest two months I would ever know.

By the first of June, graduation time, plans began to shape. By then we knew that Harry was not going to be drafted. In spite of his four years on a college football team, a never-repaired hernia classified him 4-F. But his younger brother, who had already assumed management of the farms, got by the Army doctors with flying colors. Some one would have to take over the wheat acreage which Woodrow Wilson was already beginning to say would be an important factor in Victory.

Later in the month more lines had appeared in the emerging picture. Howard would go into OTC[2] as soon as he had collected his Master's degree at Kansas University. He and Dessie would be married whenever they could fit it into his training program. Mabel was to be married when Merb finished OTC.

After all our double dating, it naturally seemed to Dessie and me that we couldn't possibly be married without each other's presence. But how was that to be possible when both grooms would be so up-to-their-ears in their patriotic duties that they might not be able to get off for even one wedding? And how could Mabel and all our other friends living near or in Winfield[3] be on hand? These were very solemn questions.

Dessie and Harry came to see me graduate. After much discussion we hit on the idea of a double wedding. It would be in Winfield,[3] and of

---

"The Wedding" from SMALL WORLD, LONG GONE by Avis D. Carlson. Copyright © 1977 by Chicago Review Press. Reprinted by permission of Porter, Gould & Dierks, Authors' Agents.

1. *war,* World War I, 1914–1918.
2. *OTC,* Officers' Training Corps.
3. *Winfield,* a town in southern Kansas.

all places in the Sigma-Delphian meeting room, which with extra chairs would accommodate nearly a hundred people. We would transport our families to Winfield for the big day. Lesser decisions followed rapidly. I would wear my graduation dress and Dessie would have a duplicate made. We lined up the wedding party, engaged the hall, decided to have two ministers, and asked Cleo Hamilton to play the wedding march and her fiance to sing—if, of course, he could get away from camp. Everything but the date was easily arranged.

The three of us studied a calendar. June was out—both bridegrooms were unavailable. July would be difficult because of wheat harvest and the uncertainty of a three-day pass at that stage of OTC, not to mention the fact that the brides' fathers would be furiously trying to get their corn "laid by." So it would have to be August. On account of the pass, it must be on a weekend. So we put a pencil down on the first Sunday in August, that year the fifth.

It was of course, a harebrained plan. Why both of the brides' mothers failed to put their feet down I cannot imagine, except that a new war addles lots of brains, not all of which are young.

But even as we studied the calendar a totally unplanned clock was ticking. Mother had come on for the graduation and was annoyed by a nasty little hack she had developed. It wasn't much, but it was persistent and it seemed to get more importunate with each passing day. By the time we had been home a week it was steady enough to confirm her worst suspicion. Small Brother had joined her in a busy warm-up for whooping cough. Another week and Hildred had entered the chorus; later, Idylene and, finally, Baby Sister.

I had never had it.

In those days pertussis serum[4] wasn't even a gleam in a researcher's eye. One got the disease and one wore it out or died in the process. The incubation period might take ten days; what our trusty old "doctor book" called the "catarrhal stage" lasted a week or more; the middle stage lasted a month to six weeks. Lying in bed those hot June and July nights in southern Kansas, I used to listen to a solo, or chorus, and shudder. How fearfully I checked off the incubation periods! But just as I would get safely through one,

another victim would begin to grow noisy and red-eyed. Even arithmetic as frail as mine could predict that the wedding ceremony might be rudely interrupted.

Add to all this apprehensiveness a more than usual share of the usual farm-woman summer work because three of the four of us were ailing; then add in the struggle to get together some kind of trousseau in a time when slips, petticoats, dresses, even panties were mostly made at home—and one gets a picture of my June and July. It is understandable that I did little worrying over a war in which the youth of Europe was being slaughtered and into which my classmates and friends were being propelled. There is a limit to what one person can worry about.

When, finally, at the end of July the last of the infectious periods were over, another peril menaced. I fell into what Grandmother D always indelicately called "the trots"—which everybody knows to be a very unhinging malady. Nowadays, probably my trouble would be labelled an allergy, perhaps to peaches, of which there was always a God's plenty on that farm in the last days of July. By whatever name, it was nothing new for me. Every midsummer I had to deal with it for a while.

But this was no usual time. Mother, bless her, recognized the gravity of my plight and had Hildred crank up the old Model T and take us to consult the doctor. He promptly ordered up a big round of castor oil. For the first time in my life I took the nasty stuff willingly, and swallowed it back down until at last my outraged stomach accepted it.

By Wednesday evening, August first, I was able to begin upon Mother's standard first-meal-after-washout: dry toast and potato water. Naturally, I was weak, but at such a time, if ever, spirit can dominate body.

The family was to drive to Winfield on Saturday. I had duties there that day. So on Friday afternoon I took the train to meet Dessie and help my aunt get ready a wedding breakfast for Carlsons and Dungans. I thought that everything that *could* happen had happened.

Saturday morning dawned hot and clear. By

---

4. **pertussis** (pèr tus′is) **serum,** a vaccine immunizing people against whooping cough.

ten o'clock a strong Kansas wind was searing a countryside that hadn't felt rain in a month. Later, I knew in retrospect that the day was more than hot and windy. It was what Father called a "weather-breeder."

At the time I was in no condition to notice weather. My aunt's household was frantic that Saturday morning. Hildred, who was famed in the family for angel food cakes, was to bring three of them for the breakfast. But a lot of other things were supposed to come before cake, in quantity to feed twenty-five people. The helpfulness of three children, aged nine, seven, and three can derail an ordinary social event. These kids had a WEDDING in their midst, and were naturally under every foot and ruffling every hair. Somebody, perhaps the bride herself, washed out her white silk hose and hung them out to dry. When they were brought in, the lady of the house stood in the middle of her kitchen and with her black eyes snapping besought heaven just to please let her know *who* could possibly be so ignorant as not to know that wet white silk turns yellow in the sun. Socialist or not, she could still get her Irish up.

It was quite a morning. I even managed to scorch the sheer white organdy in my dress, although luckily under an arm, so that if I remembered to keep my hand down, it wouldn't show.

But the first real temblor of the day did not come until about noon when a boy on a bicycle delivered a telegram.

The groom had been spending the summer on a wheat-and-cattle farm which he and a partner were buying from Carlson *fader*.[5] They jointly owned a two-passenger Model T, but in those days nobody put much confidence in Stuttering Liz as a mode of long-distance travel on roads which might be blanketed in six inches of dust or slashed with six inch ruts or, in case of rain, just plain impassable. So my groom had driven eleven miles into a little western county-seat town south of Dodge City and caught the train which once each day huffed and jerked eastward, picking up passengers and cream cans and stopping at every crossroad blessed with a grain elevator. Twelve hours later and one hundred seventy miles away, after a "layover" in one of the villages, the train would arrive in Winfield. At

some time during the long, jolting morning, it had dawned on my beloved that he would get into Winfield after the court house had closed. In 1917 such requisites as premarital blood tests and three-day waits were unheard of, but *no license, no wedding.* So at one of the villages he got off the train and wired me to get a license.

I was furious, to the point of good old Dungan-type explosion. Whoever heard of a bride getting the license? The county clerk would think I was having to drag the guy to the altar or maybe even that this was a new version of a shotgun wedding. In the whole two years of our relationship I had never been really angry with him. Now on the day before I was to marry him, I simply boiled. Why hadn't he bought that license, I raged. He must have driven past the courthouse every time he had been in town all summer. Was he ashamed to have his neighbors know what was afoot?

Eventually my aunt and uncle got me calmed down enough to perceive that I was only wasting energy—if I wanted to be married, I must go purchase the license. The uncle took me downtown, and his presence helped to make the transaction seem less indecently female.

All went well until the clerk asked me what the *G* in my Darling's name stood for. I said I thought it was "Gustavus." The official explained paternally that a marriage license is a legal document and it had to be right. Now it had happened that every time I had asked said darling about that *G,* he had smirked and claimed that his name was Harry Gustavus Adolphus Carlson. So I really didn't know for sure. The upshot was that the amused official offered to keep the courthouse open until after the train was in.

At six Uncle met the train and conveyed the groom to the courthouse. It was lucky for me that I had cooled off considerably. Very lucky, indeed, for when it was the groom's turn to be asked what *my* middle initial stood for, he had to say that he didn't know. The understandably irritated official, who had waited late as a favor, suggested testily that somebody really should introduce these two young people! A telephone call brought the information that there wasn't

---

5. *fader* (fä′dėr), Harry Carlson's father. [*Swedish*]

any middle name—I had simply an initial because everyone else seemed to have one and I wasn't going to be shorted. With sure foreknowledge that I would be twitted all the rest of my life, I eased out the last of my wrath and helped to get a big family-reunion meal ready for the table.

A 1920 telephone.

By this time we were expecting families to appear at any minute. My family had planned to start at midmorning. Even with time out for a picnic lunch along the way they should have covered the fifty miles by midafternoon. The Carlsons were leaving in early morning and should, we calculated, have done their two hundred miles by six o'clock.

Because fear of road accidents had not yet become imbedded in the human nervous system, I cannot remember worrying about the delay except in terms of the rehearsal Dessie and I had planned for the evening. Being very modern young women we were not to have ourselves "given away," but we did plan that a brother of each groom and a sister of each bride would be in the ceremony. One of the ministers had warned us that it would be well to have a small rehearsal Saturday evening. Therefore, it was important that the families get into town in time for bridesmaid and best man to remove dust and perspiration, eat and get to the rehearsal. At some time in the evening Hildred would also need time to ice her cakes and press the lovely soft-green dress she would wear on the morrow.

About seven the bridal pair went down to Orra's home, leaving directions that when Hildred and Frank appeared they were to follow. Dessie and Howard were already there. Amid many giggles and a few fairly serious thoughts as to what the words in the back of the hymnal meant, we went over the responses together. When the missing attendants still had not appeared, we all went out to the backyard for tennis. But because it was an August evening in Kansas and we were more excited than we really knew, tennis could not last long.

About the time we were back in the living room, my father appeared at the front door, something obviously very wrong. His movements were stiff and his voice unnatural. There had been an accident, he got out. Ten miles out of Winfield. The young children and the wedding guest were unhurt at my aunt's home. The rest of the family were in St. Mary's Hospital.

On the way to the hospital we learned, little by little, what had happened. The roadmakers of that time had a fad of grading the dirt roads up to a sharp peak in the middle, so as to get better drainage. Because a stiff south wind had blown all the dust over onto the west-bound side of the road and because no oncoming traffic was in sight, Hildred had pulled over into the dustless lane. At a sudden, imperious honk behind her she had swung the wheel too fast and too far. The car had rolled over, then half over again, and landed upside down in the ditch. A crowd of local people and passersby soon gathered. Hildred was screaming wildly, Idylene completely out. (Later Mother told me that Father himself had been so dazed that he simply went off and sat down, leaving her to cope.)

When the men had turned the car back over, they found its engine still running. Somebody had driven it with the unhurt passengers to my aunt's home. The only vehicle in the vicinity that could transport an unconscious girl and her mother to a hospital was a *hearse!*

When we got to the hospital we found Hildred sitting up in bed still hysterically trying to control the car and wailing that she had killed one sister and spoiled the other's wedding. Idylene was unconscious with what the staff doctors said was a serious concussion. Characteristically, Mother had held up until they were all in the hospital with nurses and doctors in charge. Now she too was out. Both she and Father had cracked ribs, and numerous contusions were beginning to show on all four of the injured.

It was quite a stroll the bridal pair had down that hospital corridor.

About ten the resident said that Idylene was showing signs of improvement and Aunt Ida, ever ready to take charge, told me to go to her home and get some sleep—she and Harry would stay in the hospital. The decision turned out to be about the worst which could have been made, for she would have been infinitely better able than I to cope with what happened the rest of the night.

Shortly after I got to the house, Grandfather managed to get the curtains in his room on fire. Still the incessant reader, he had been sitting as usual at his desk with the gas lamp nearby. In order not to miss any stray breeze in the hot sticky night, he had picked up the window curtains and draped them over the lamp arm. He had done this scores of times. It never happened before and it never happened afterwards, but that night it did. When Uncle and I heard his agonized shout we ran in and helped put out the flames, but not before they had consumed the papers on the desk and a good part of the skin on Grandfather's hand.

Hardly had that emergency passed than the neighbor-guest who had been unhurt and apparently calm, went into delayed hysteria over her near-disaster. All the rest of that long night she wept over it, agonizing over her selfishness in leaving husband and child forlorn while she set off to have a good time, wailing over the thought that she might never get back to them, moaning that the car was going over, OVER.

It was my first experience with pure hysteria and I hadn't the foggiest notion of what to do. I tried comforting, I tried cajoling. I even tried to exert some authority. But she continued to carry on, *all night!*

And just to add a final touch to the doings of that desperate night, when some impulse sent me into the room where Small Sister was sleeping, I found her lying in an open second story window whose screen latch was loose. One good childish flop and she would have crashed to the concrete walk beside the house.

About five o'clock, just as daylight began seeping in, the hospital watchers came home with word that Idylene was definitely better and that my parents said they would be able to come to the ceremony if we decided to go ahead.

But before any decisions, I pleaded that something had to be done for our guest. Aunt Ida put her head into the door for an instant before making for the telephone. Feeling very green and foolish, I presently watched a doctor take out a needle and give the poor woman peace.

By this time it was beginning to rain, a light, gentle rain that grew slowly more purposeful—the kind of rain that Kansans ordinarily welcome as a gift straight from the hands of God. Now it only added further difficulty to an occasion already gone hopelessly awry.

In the end we decided to proceed. We really hadn't a great deal of choice. There was no way to notify all the numerous people who would soon be dressing for the wedding. Howard and Dessie would be married, with or without us, in order to make their midmorning train. And besides, after all this calamity, who would ever have the nerve to plan another wedding?

By the time the guest was asleep and the decision made, the *day* was upon us. A cousin was drafted to take Hildred's place, even to wearing the green dress and hat. My uncle went to the hospital to get my parents. Aunt Ida sailed full steam into the sadly delayed preparations for a wedding breakfast. The red-headed children were anywhere and everywhere, always at the most inopportune moment.

After a time Father and Mother arrived, walking very stiffly and still somewhat groggy from their sedatives, and because of the cracked ribs unable to get hand to head. Who helped them dress? The bride. Who scrubbed and decked forth small brother and sister? The bride.

Meantime, though he didn't tell me about it until later, the groom had entered a hell of his own. He was not by nature a worrisome person but he hadn't been asleep all night, and bridegrooms are notoriously given to agitation. Perhaps the rain was also a factor. At any rate by this time the devastating thought had occurred to him that lightning does occasionally strike twice.

What if the missing Carlson family were also in some hospital! He was already in a first-class stew when he opened the box in which his suit had come from the cleaners. (He had decided not to buy a new suit but simply to have his good blue cleaned.) As he lifted out the contents he lost all remnants of his Scandinavian cool. The trousers were not his and they not only didn't match the coat, they were a good three sizes too big. It was Sunday, no shops were open. And the fatal hour was closing in on him. Frantic telephone calls located a pair that might do—navy blues belonging to the teen-aged son of the minister who was to marry us. There was a run through the rain to get them. The trousers turned out to be practically as tight as the skin God had bestowed, but the groom couldn't be choosy. So he had to go through the ceremony in mortal terror of splitting out his borrowed raiment.

Meantime, I had finished dressing my parents and the children, and time was closing in on me too. As I gathered up my trousseau underwear and yellowed silk stockings, a vast wave of self-pity hit me. A girl's wedding day was supposed to be the biggest, the happiest day of her life, wasn't it? Sitting on the edge of the bathtub, I felt my throat tighten and my stomach convulse. In another instant, experience warned, the flood would loosen. Luckily, my vanity overcame my self-pity. All that had happened was bad enough—was I going to add to it by getting my eyes swollen and my nose blocked? For the first time in my life, and almost the last time, I drew a cold bath and went into it with a fortifying gasp.

The Carlsons still had not arrived. In his panic over their absence, the groom added to his woes by forgetting the license and ring and had to go pelting back through the rain after them.

At last we all were in the hall, only twenty minutes late. Father and Mother were seated rigidly in the front row with the two youngsters. The White-Pope contingent were on the other side of the aisle—not a single fluster had marred *their* wedding preparations. Did they live so much better than we, I wondered dismally.

Upwards of a hundred people settled themselves and the musicians went to their work. Then, just as a tenor voice began what was then a newish song, "I Love You Truly," and Harry

was considering what friend he could nab at the very last moment to serve as best man, the Carlsons came puffing up the long series of steps that led to the main college building. After the ceremony we would learn that the rain had begun in western Kansas just as they were leaving home and had moved along with them at just about a Model T pace.

In 1917 there were not more than a few miles of paving or even gravel on that whole two hundred miles. Afraid to stop for fear they'd mire down, they slipped and sloshed, slogged and lurched through a tormenting day and night. No one in that family had slept either! (The brunt of the ordeal was borne by a brother's wife who was six weeks pregnant and had to spend a week in the hospital after she returned home.)

Frank was shoved into line and handed the ring and with only a word of whispered directions from the ministers, we were ready. Somebody signalled the pianist to begin the *Lohengrin*[6] and the procession began to move.

At that instant a curious thing happened to me. A blessed calm descended. All the mishaps and all the apprehensions faded, leaving only the nearest to quiet joy I have ever experienced. For me, it was a beautiful wedding. For the groom, however, the relief of his family's arrival still left his painfully tight pants as a subject for worry.

But even for me the moment of joy was fleeting. Ahead of us lay a trip to the hospital, where Idylene tried and failed to recognize us, and we tried and probably failed to convince Hildred that she had not spoiled the wedding.

Then followed the breakfast. There was little joy in *it*. The place being Kansas and all participants Methodist, there was, of course, no champagne. But nothing that comes from a bottle could have livened up that group of half-dead people. The food, to quote my aunt, had had to be "slapped together" and the table "set any old way." (The cakes never got iced.) Two of the important members of the party were absent and one of those present was so nauseous from her prolonged car trip that she could barely look at the food. The sedated guest dragged herself numbly to the table. Dungans and Carlsons in

---

6. *Lohengrin* (lō′ən grin), an opera by the German composer Richard Wagner, first performed in 1850.

their fatigue struggled to make a good impression on each other. If ever there was a wedding that was not *celebrated* ours was it.

Any soothsayer, knowing all the events preceding the wedding and beholding the two families' first introduction to each other, would have pronounced the marriage to be ill-omened, if not positively doomed.

In fact, however, it turned out to have great survival value. I still had to learn how to think "we"—first in terms of two persons, then of a family, then two small cities, then three large cities, and finally the human species. My father would die in a few months. The war and wheat-culture would engulf us, then the Depression, then another war, and still more wars, and change so vast and all encompassing that *nobody* could even imagine it. But under all the hammerings of life we would both continue to live—and grow.

Having come of age on the tranquil side of 1917, we would deal somehow with the turbulent side of that watershed year. □□

Discussion

1. Avis Carlson says that the two months between her graduation from college and her wedding were "the loneliest two months I would ever know." Why was this so?

2. List the problems and obstacles that made Avis Carlson's wedding such a frantic affair.

Vocabulary • Dictionary

The author speaks of 1917 as a "watershed year." Check your dictionary for the various meanings of "watershed." Which meaning does the author intend? How does that meaning apply to 1917 in terms of American history? In terms of the author's life?

Avis D. Carlson 1896 •

Avis Carlson's hectic wedding day was only one chapter in an active life that has seen her become one of the most prominent members of her community. Since she and her husband moved to St. Louis in 1943, she has been president of the St. Louis League of Women Voters, was a member of the city's Human Rights Commission, served on the Citizen's Committee on Public Housing and Social Services, and helped institute academic classes for people living in public housing.

At the same time that Carlson was involved in these public activities, she was also frequently contributing poems, articles, and short stories to *Harper's* magazine. "The Wedding" is taken from her autobiography, *Small World . . . Long Gone,* published in 1975. She has since written another book, *In the Fullness of Time: The Pleasures and Inconveniences of Growing Old* (1977).

Frances Lester Warner

To Horse

"A duck," we used to read in the primer at school, "a duck is a long low animal covered with feathers." Similarly, a horse is a long high animal, covered with confusion. This applies to the horse as we find him in the patriotic Parade, where a brass band precedes him, an unaccustomed rider surmounts him, and a drum corps brings up his rear.

In our own Welcome Home Parade, after the boys returned from France, the Legion[1] decided to double the number of its mounted effectives: all the overseas officers should ride. All the overseas officers were instantly on their feet. Their protests were loud and heated. A horse, they said, was something that they personally had never bestridden. They offered to ride anything else. They would fly down the avenue in Spads, or do the falling leaf[2] over the arch of triumph. They would ride tanks or motorcycles or army trucks. But a horse was a thing of independent locomotion, not to be trifled with. It was not the idea of getting killed that they objected to, it was the looks of the thing. By "the thing," they meant not the horse, but the rider. In spite of the veto of the officers, the motion was carried by acclamation. . . .

When Geoffrey came home and said that he was to ride a horse in the procession, our mother, who had been a good horsewoman in her girlhood, took him aside and gave him a few quiet tips. Some horses, she said, had been trained to obey certain signals, and some to obey the exact opposite. For instance, some would go faster if you reined them in, and some would slow down. Some waited for light touches from their master's hand or foot, and others for their master's voice. You had to study your horse as an individual.

Geoffrey said that he was glad to hear any little inside gossip of this sort, and made his way alone to the place appointed, skillfully dodging friends. We gathered that if he had to have an interview with a horse, he preferred to have it with nobody looking on.

The fence behind the garage was fringed with horses securely tied, and the top of the fence was fringed with a row of small boys, waiting. . . .

"Which of these horses," said he to the gang on the fence top, "would you take?"

"This one!" said an eager spokesman. "He didn't move a muscle since they hitched 'im."

This recommendation decided the matter instantly. Repose of manner is an estimable trait in the horse. . . .

In mounting, does one first untie one's horse and then get on, or may one, as in a steam launch, get seated first and then cast off the painter.[3] Geoffrey could not help recalling a page from *Pickwick Papers*,[4] where Mr. Winkle is climbing up the side of a tall horse at the Inn, and the 'ostler's boy whispers, "Blowed if the gen'l'man wasn't for getting up the wrong side." Well, what governs the right and wrong side of a horse? Douglas Fairbanks[5] habitually avoids the dilemma by mounting from above—from the roof of a

From LIFE'S MINOR COLLISIONS by Frances Lester Warner and Gertrude Warner. Copyright 1949 by Frances Warner Hersey. Reprinted by permission of Houghton Mifflin Company.

1. *Legion,* the American Legion, founded in 1919 for veterans of World War I.
2. *Spads . . . leaf.* A Spad was a single-seat biplane fighter in World War I. The falling leaf is a stunt in which the pilot makes the plane flutter down in a zigzag.
3. *painter,* rope holding a ship fast to the shore.
4. *Pickwick Papers,* a novel by Charles Dickens, published in 1836–37.
5. *Douglas Fairbanks,* an American actor who became famous in adventure films of the silent era.

Mexican monastery, for instance, or the fire escape of an apartment house. From these points he lands, perpendicularly. With this ideal in mind, Geoffrey stepped on from the fence, clamped his legs against the sides of the horse, and walked him out into the street.

When I say that he walked him out into the street, I use the English language as I have seen it used in books, but I think that it was an experienced rider who first used the idiom. Geoffrey says that he did not feel, at any time that afternoon, any sensation of walking his horse, or of doing anything else decisive with him. He walked, to be sure, dipping his head and rearing it, like a mechanical swan. But on a horse you miss the sensation of direct control that you have with a machine. With a machine, you press something, and if a positive reaction does not follow, you get out and fix something else. Not so with the horse. When you get upon him you cut yourself off from all accurately calculable connection with the world. He is, in the last analysis, an independent personality. His feet are on the ground, and yours are not. . . .

Far ahead of him, he saw the khaki backs of two of his friends who were also walking their horses. One by one they ambled up to the green and took places in the ranks. Geoffrey discovered that his horse would stand well if allowed to droop his long neck and close his eyes. Judged as a military figure, however, he was a disgrace to the army. If you drew up the reins to brace his head, he thought it a signal to start, and you had to take it all back, hastily. With the relaxed rein he collapsed again, his square head bent in silent prayer.

With the approach of the band, however, all this changed. He reared tentatively. Geoffrey discouraged that. Then he curled his body in an unlovely manner—an indescribable gesture, a sort of sidelong squirm in semicircular formation. His rider straightened him out with a fatherly slap on the flank.

It was time to start. The band led off. Joy to the world, thought the horse, the band is gone. The rest of the cavalry moved forward in docile files, but not he. If that band was going away, he would be the last person to pursue it. Instead of going forward, he backed. He backed and backed. There is no emergency brake on a horse.

He would have backed to the end of the procession, through the Knights of Columbus, the Red Cross, the Elks, the Masons, the D.A.R., the Fire Department, and the Salvation Army, if it had not been for the drum corps that led the infantry. The drum corps behind him was as terrifying as the band in front. To avoid the drum corps, he had to spend part of his time going away from it. Thus his progress was a little on the principle of the pendulum. He backed from the band until he had to flee before the drums.

The ranks of men were demoralized by needless mirth. Army life dulls the sensibilities to the spectacle of suffering. They could do nothing to help, except to make a clear passage for Geoffrey as he alternately backed from the brasses and escaped from the drums. Vibrating in this way, he could only discourse to his horse with words of feigned affection, and pray for the panic to pass off. With a cranky automobile, now, one could have parked down a side street, and later joined the procession, all trouble repaired. But there was nothing organic the matter with this horse. Geoffrey could not have parked him in any case, because it would have been no more possible to turn him toward the cheering crowds on the pavement than to make him follow the band. The crowds on the street, in fact, began to regard these actions as a sort of interesting and decorative maneuver, so regular was the advance and retirement—something in the line of a cotillion.[6] And then the band stopped playing for a little. Instantly the horse took his place in the ranks, marched serenely, arched his slim neck, glanced about. All was as it should be.

Geoffrey's place was just behind the marshal, supposedly to act as his aide. During all this absence from his post of duty, the marshal had not noticed his defection or turned around at all. Now he did so, hastily.

"Just slip back, will you," he said, "and tell Monroe not to forget the orders at the reviewing stand."

Geoffrey opened his mouth to explain his disqualifications as courier, but at that moment the band struck up, and his charger backed

---

6. *cotillion* (kə til′yən), a dance with complex steps and frequent changing of partners.

precipitately. The marshal, seeing this prompt obedience to his request, faced front, and Geoffrey was left steadily receding, no time to explain—and the drum corps was taking a vacation. There was, therefore, no reason for the horse ever to stop backing, unless he should back around the world until he heard the band behind him again. As he backed through the ranks of infantry, Geoffrey shouted the marshal's message to the officer of the day. He had to talk fast—ships that pass in the night. But the message was delivered, and he could put his whole mind on his horse.

He tried all the signals for forward locomotion that he could devise. Mother had told him that some horses wait for light touches from their master's hand or foot. Geoffrey touched his animal here and there, back of the ear—at the base of the brain. He even kicked a trifle. He jerked the reins in Morse Code and Continental, to the tune of S O S. The horse understood no codes.

They were now in the ranks of the Knights of Columbus, and the marching boys were making room for them with shouts of sympathetic glee.

Must they back through the Red Cross, where all the girls in town were marching, and into the Daughters of the Revolution float where our mother sat with a group of ladies around the spinning wheel? Geoffrey remembered that the Red Cross had a band, if it would only play. It struck up just in time. The horse instantly became a fugitive in the right direction. On they sped, the reviewing stand almost in sight. The drum corps had not begun to play. Could they reach the cavalry before it was too late? Geoffrey hated to pass the reviewing stand in the guise of a deserter, yet here he was cantering among the Odd Fellows, undoubtedly A.W.O.L.[7]

But Heaven was kind. The drums waited. Through their ranks dashed Geoffrey at full speed, and into the midst of his companions. The reviewing stand was very near. At a signal, all bands and all drums struck up together. The horse, in stable equilibrium at last, daring not to

---

7. **A.W.O.L.,** absent without leave, especially from a military post.

run forward or to run backward, or to bolt to either side, fell into step and marched. Deafening cheers, flying handkerchiefs; Geoffrey and his horse stole past, held in the ranks by a delicate balance of four-cornered fear. If you fear something behind you and something in front of you, and things on both sides of you, and if your fear of all points of the compass is precisely equal, you move with the movements of the globe. Geoffrey's horse moved that way past the stand.

People took their pictures. Our father, beaming down from the galaxy on the stand, was pleased. Later he told Geoffrey how well he sat his horse.

But that evening Geoffrey had a talk with his mother, as man to man. He told her that, if these Victory Parades were going to be held often, he should vote for compulsory military training for the horse. He told her the various things his horse had done, how he went to and fro, going to when urged fro, and going fro when urged not to.

"Probably he had been trained to obey the opposite signals," said our mother. "You must study your horse as an individual."

That horse was an individual. Geoffrey studied him as such. He is quite willing to believe that he had been trained to obey the opposite signals. But Geoffrey says that he still cannot stifle one last question in his mind:—signals opposite to what? □□

Discussion

1. **(a)** How did the officers react to the news that they were to ride horses in the Welcome Home Parade? **(b)** Does their reaction suggest anything about the town or region in which the action takes place? Explain.

2. For what reason does Geoffrey select the particular horse he ends up with?

3. How did the progress of Geoffrey's horse approximate "the principle of the pendulum"?

4. In what respects does the author compare riding a horse to operating an automobile?

Extension • Speaking

Discuss how Frances Warner achieves her humorous effects. Note in particular her choices of **figurative language** to describe the horse and its movements.

Frances Lester Warner
1888 •

Frances Lester Warner has a firmly established reputation as an essayist with a light and humorous touch. Besides being an English teacher at various schools and colleges, she was an assistant editor of the *Atlantic Monthly,* in which many of her essays were published. Perhaps her best known works were *Endicott and I* (1919), and *Surprising the Family* (1926).

Much of the material and many of the characters in Warner's essays were taken from her own experiences. She portrayed real people—often members of her own family—in everyday situations, both frenzied and tranquil, which are quickly recognizable to most American families. Whether dealing with happy or sad events in the lives of her characters, her essays are illuminated with wisdom, compassion, and a lively sense of the comic.

John Dos Passos

Tin Lizzie

"Mr. Ford *the automobileer*" the featurewriter wrote in 1900.

"*Mr. Ford the automobileer began by giving his steed three or four sharp jerks with the lever at the righthand side of the seat; that is, he pulled the lever up and down sharply in order, as he said, to mix air with gasoline and drive the charge into the exploding cylinder. . . . Mr. Ford slipped a small electric switch handle and there followed a puff, puff, puff. . . . The puffing of the machine assumed a higher key. She was flying along about eight miles an hour. The ruts in the road were deep, but the machine certainly went with a dreamlike smoothness. There was none of the bumping common even to a streetcar. . . . By this time the boulevard had been reached, and the automobileer, letting a lever fall a little, let her out. Whiz! She picked up speed with infinite rapidity. As she ran on there was a clattering behind, the new noise of the automobile.*"

For twenty years or more,

ever since he'd left his father's farm when he was sixteen to get a job in a Detroit machineshop, Henry Ford had been nuts about machinery. First it was watches, then he designed a steamtractor, then he built a horseless carriage with an engine adapted from the Otto gasengine[1] he'd read about in *The World of Science*, then a mechanical buggy with a onecylinder fourcycle motor, that would run forward but not back;

at last, in ninetyeight, he felt he was far enough along to risk throwing up his job with the Detroit Edison Company, where he'd worked his way up from night fireman to chief engineer, to put all his time into working on a new gasoline engine,

(in the late eighties he'd met Edison at a meeting of electriclight employees in Atlantic City. He'd gone up to Edison after Edison had delivered an address and asked him if he thought gasoline was practical as a motor fuel. Edison had said yes. If Edison said it, it was true. Edison was the great admiration of Henry Ford's life);

and in driving his mechanical buggy, sitting there at the lever jauntily dressed in a tightbuttoned jacket and a high collar and a derby hat, back and forth over the level illpaved streets of Detroit,

scaring the big brewery horses and the skinny trotting horses and the sleekrumped pacers with the motor's loud explosions,

looking for men scatterbrained enough to invest money in a factory for building automobiles.

He was the eldest son of an Irish immigrant who during the Civil War had married the daughter of a prosperous Pennsylvania Dutch farmer and settled down to farming near Dearborn in Wayne County, Michigan;

Dos Passos (dôs pa′sôs)

From "Tin Lizzie" in *U.S.A.* by John Dos Passos, published by Harcourt Brace Jovanovich, Inc., 1937. Reprinted by permission of Elizabeth H. Dos Passos.

1. *Otto gasengine.* Nikolaus Otto (1832–1891), was a German technician who developed an early internal combustion engine.

like plenty of other Americans, young Henry grew up hating the endless sogging through the mud about the chores, the hauling and pitching manure, the kerosene lamps to clean, the irk and sweat and solitude of the farm.

He was a slender, active youngster, a good skater, clever with his hands; what he liked was to tend the machinery and let the others do the heavy work. His mother had told him not to drink, smoke, gamble or go into debt, and he never did.

When he was in his early twenties his father tried to get him back from Detroit, where he was working as mechanic and repairman for the Drydock Engine Company that built engines for steamboats, by giving him forty acres of land.

Young Henry built himself an uptodate square white dwellinghouse with a false mansard roof and married and settled down on the farm,

but he let the hired men do the farming;

he bought himself a buzzsaw and rented a stationary engine and cut the timber off the woodlots.

He was a thrify young man who never drank

or smoked or gambled or coveted his neighbor's wife, but he couldn't stand living on the farm.

He moved to Detroit, and in the brick barn behind his house tinkered for years in his spare time with a mechanical buggy that would be light enough to run over the clayey wagonroads of Wayne County, Michigan.

By 1900 he had a practicable car to promote.

He was forty years old before the Ford Motor Company was started and production began to move.

Speed was the first thing the early automobile manufacturers went after. Races advertised the makes of cars.

Henry Ford himself hung up several records at the track at Grosse Pointe and on the ice on Lake St. Clair. In his 999 he did the mile in thirtynine and fourfifths seconds.

But it had always been his custom to hire others to do the heavy work. The speed he was busy with was speed in production, the records records in efficient output. He hired Barney Oldfield, a stunt bicyclerider from Salt Lake City, to do the racing for him.

Henry Ford had ideas about other things than the designing of motors, carburetors, magnetos, jigs and fixtures, punches and dies; he had ideas about sales,

that the big money was in economical quantity production, quick turnover, cheap interchangeable easilyreplaced standardized parts;

it wasn't until 1909, after years of arguing with his partners, that Ford put out the first Model T.

Henry Ford was right.

That season he sold more than ten thousand tin lizzies, ten years later he was selling almost a million a year.

In these years the Taylor Plan[2] was stirring up plantmanagers and manufacturers all over the country. Efficiency was the word. The same ingenuity that sent into improving the performance of a machine could go into improving the performance of the workmen producing the machine.

In 1913 they established the assemblyline at Ford's. That season the profits were something like twentyfive million dollars, but they had trouble in keeping the men on the job, machinists didn't seem to like it at Ford's.

Henry Ford had ideas about other things than production.

He was the largest automobile manufacturer in the world; he paid high wages; maybe if the steady workers thought they were getting a cut (a very small cut) in the profits, it would give trained men an inducement to stick to their jobs,

wellpaid workers might save enough money to buy a tin lizzie; the first day Ford's announced that cleancut properlymarried American workers who wanted jobs had a chance to make five bucks a day (of course it turned out that there were strings to it; always there were strings to it)

such an enormous crowd waited outside the Highland Park plant

all through the zero January night

that there was a riot when the gates were opened; cops broke heads, jobhunters threw bricks; property, Henry Ford's own property, was destroyed. The company dicks had to turn on the firehose to beat back the crowd.

The American Plan; automotive prosperity seeping down from above; it turned out there were strings to it.

But that five dollars a day

paid to good, clean American workmen

who didn't drink or smoke cigarettes or read or think,

and who didn't commit adultery

and whose wives didn't take in boarders.

made America once more the Yukon[3] of the sweated workers of the world;

made all the tin lizzies and the automotive age, and incidentally,

made Henry Ford the automobileer, the admirer of Edison, the birdlover,

the great American of his time.

In 1918 he had borrowed on notes to buy out his minority stockholders for the picayune sum of seventy-five million dollars.

In February, 1920, he needed cash to pay off some of these notes that were coming due. A banker is supposed to have called on him and offered him every facility if the bankers representative could be made a member of the board of directors. Henry Ford handed the banker his hat,

and went about raising the money in his own way:

he shipped every car and part he had in his plant to his dealers and demanded immediate cash payment. Let the other fellow do the borrowing had always been a cardinal principle. He shut down production and canceled all orders from the supplyfirms. Many dealers were ruined, many supplyfirms failed, but when he reopened his plant,

he owned it absolutely,

the way a man owns an unmortgaged farm with the taxes paid up.

In 1922 there started the Ford boom for President (high wages, waterpower, industry scattered to the small towns) that was skillfully pricked behind the scenes

by another crackerbarrel philosopher,

Calvin Coolidge;

---

2. **Taylor Plan.** Frederick Taylor (1856–1915) developed efficiency techniques that led to the establishment of the assembly line in industry.
3. **Yukon** (yü′kon), Alaskan territory that had a gold rush in 1898.

but in 1922 Henry Ford sold one million three hundred and thirtytwo thousand two hundred and nine tin lizzies; he was the richest man in the world.

Good roads had followed the narrow ruts made in the mud by the Model T. The great automotive boom was on. At Ford's production was improving all the time; less waste, more spotters, strawbosses, stoolpigeons (fifteen minutes for lunch, three minutes to go to the toilet, the Taylorized speedup everywhere, reach under, adjust washer, screw down bolt, shove in cotterpin, reachunder adjustwasher, screwdown bolt, reachunderadjustscrewdownreachunderadjust until every ounce of life was sucked off into production and at night the workmen went home grey shaking husks).

Ford owned every detail of the process from the ore in the hills until the car rolled off the end of the assemblyline under its own power, the plants were rationalized to the last tenthousandth of an inch as measured by the Johansen scale;

in 1926 the production cycle was reduced to eightyone hours from the ore in the mine to the finished salable car proceeding under its own power,

but the Model T was obsolete.

New Era prosperity and the American Plan
  (there were strings to it, always there were strings to it)
  had killed Tin Lizzie.

Ford's was just one of many automobile plants.

When the stockmarket bubble burst,[4]

Mr. Ford the crackerbarrel philosopher said jubilantly,

"I told you so.

Serves you right for gambling and getting in debt.

The country is sound."

But when the country on cracked shoes, in frayed trousers, belts tightened over hollow bellies,

  idle hands cracked and chapped with the cold of that coldest March day of 1932,

  started marching from Detroit to Dearborn, asking for work and the American Plan, all they could think of at Ford's was machineguns.

The country was sound, but they mowed the marchers down.

They shot four of them dead.

Henry Ford as an old man
is a passionate antiquarian,
  (lives besieged on his father's farm embedded in an estate of thousands of millionaire acres, protected by an army of servicemen, secretaries, secret agents, dicks under orders of an English exprizefighter,
  always afraid of the feet in broken shoes on the roads, afraid the gangs will kidnap his grandchildren,
  that a crank will shoot him,
  that Change and the idle hands out of work will break through the gates and the high fences;
  protected by a private army against
  the new America of starved children and hollow bellies and cracked shoes stamping on souplines,
  that has swallowed up the old thrifty farmlands
  of Wayne County, Michigan,
  as if they had never been).
Henry Ford as an old man
is a passionate antiquarian.

He rebuilt his father's farmhouse and put it back exactly in the state he remembered it in as a boy. He built a village of museums for buggies, sleighs, coaches, old plows, waterwheels, obsolete models of motorcars. He scoured the country for fiddlers to play old-fashioned squaredances.

Even old taverns he bought and put back into their original shape, as well as Thomas Edison's early laboratories.

When he bought the Wayside Inn near Sudbury, Massachusetts, he had the new highway where the newmodel cars roared and slithered and hissed oilily past (*the new noise of the automobile*),
  moved away from the door,
  put back the old bad road,
  so that everything might be
  the way it used to be,
  in the days of horses and buggies. □□

---

4. *stockmarket bubble burst.* Through the twenties stock market prices rose higher and higher, until they began a sudden plunge in October and November of 1929. The Great Depression resulted.

Discussion

1. In *The Big Money,* of which "Tin Lizzie" is an excerpt, Dos Passos tells the life stories of ten representative Americans. What aspects of Henry Ford and his career make him "representative" of America?

2. (a) What qualities of Ford does Dos Passos respect? **(b)** What facets of the man and his work does the author criticize? At what point in the **biography** does the critical **tone** begin to assert itself?

3. (a) What contrast does Dos Passos draw between Ford's social views and his ideas on engineering and business? Which acts of Ford best illustrate this contrast? **(b)** Can you reconcile Ford's differing attitudes, or do you think they were inconsistent? Explain.

4. List the unconventional features of Dos Passos's **style.** What effects does he achieve with these devices? Compare his style with that of E. E. Cummings in the poem on page 462.

Vocabulary
Structure and Dictionary

The three words in each group below have the same root. Write the word which correctly completes each sentence after the letter for the sentence in which that word fits.

1. Warner, "To Horse"
serene
serenade
serenity

(a) In order to study effectively one needs _____.

(b) According to custom, Spanish men would sometimes sing a _____ to their sweethearts.

(c) Last night the sky was _____, but this morning it was filled with threatening clouds.

2. Carlson, "The Wedding"
sedate
sedation
sedative

(a) Reading is more effective than any _____ in putting me to sleep.

(b) We tried to see Aunt Lily at the hospital, but she was under _____, and the nurse would not let us in.

(c) He is very _____ and would rather read than play football.

3. Dos Passos, "Tin Lizzie"
antique
antiquated
antiquarian

(a) Most museums have an _____ section for the collection of very old items.

(b) Once the Model-T was developed, the horse and buggy became _____.

(c) We are trying to sell our couch, which is made from handcarved wood, to an _____ dealer.

John Dos Passos 1896 • 1970

After graduating from Harvard, Dos Passos went to Spain to study architecture but soon entered World War I, first with the French ambulance service, later with the U.S. medical corps. After the conflict he traveled as a newspaper correspondent to Spain, Mexico, New York, and the Near East. He increasingly devoted time to his writing and, after a number of less important novels, in 1925 he published *Manhattan Transfer,* which depicted the complex life of contemporary New York City. With this success and such later works as the *U.S.A.* trilogy, Dos Passos influenced a whole generation of young writers.

Dos Passos in his youth was an advocate of the political left. He actively supported labor unions and in 1927 was twice arrested for demonstrating against the Sacco-Vanzetti trial. Over the years he grew disillusioned with the abuses of bureaucracy and his thinking gradually changed to that of a conservative.

6: The Modern Temper

CONTENT REVIEW

1. In "Theme for English B," Langston Hughes poses the problem of communication between two people of differing backgrounds or experience. Considering Hughes's poem and the following works, discuss the degree to which understanding is or is not achieved by the characters involved in these selections:

"In Another Country"; "Soldiers of the Republic"; "The Garden"; "Mending Wall"; "Iowa Farmer"; and "Tell Your Children."

2. It has often been emphasized that modern poetry tends to be gloomy in outlook. Consider the following poems and indicate whether you would describe them as **(a)** tending toward pessimism, **(b)** tending toward optimism, or **(c)** combining both attitudes. Explain the reasons for your classification.

"The Love Song of J. Alfred Prufrock"; "Spring and All"; "The Solitary"; "Chicago"; "Out, Out—"; "The Creation"; "Let No Charitable Hope"; "November Cotton Flower"; and "Shine, Perishing Republic."

3. What do "The Wedding" by Avis Carlson and "To Horse" by Frances Warner indicate about the general American attitude to World War I? What different attitudes are implicit in the war stories "Soldiers of the Republic" and "In Another Country"?

4. Compare the various aspects of courage presented in the following works: "The Jilting of Granny Weatherall"; "The Bear"; "The Man Who Saw the Flood"; "Soldiers of the Republic"; "Patterns"; and "Day's Ending."

Unit 6, Test I
INTERPRETATION: NEW MATERIAL

The Long Way Out
F. Scott Fitzgerald

Read the story below, then answer the questions that follow it by writing on your paper beside the number of each question the letter of the best answer to it.

We were talking about some of the older castles in Touraine and we touched upon the iron cage in which Louis XI imprisoned Cardinal Balue for six years, then upon oubliettes[1] and such horrors. I had seen several of the latter, simply dry wells thirty or forty feet deep where a man was thrown to wait for nothing; since I have such a tendency to claustrophobia that a Pullman berth is a certain nightmare, they had made a lasting impression. So it was rather a relief when a doctor told this story—that is, it was a relief when he began it, for it seemed to have nothing to do with the tortures long ago.

---

1. **oubliettes** (ü′blē ets′), secret dungeons with openings only at the top.

There was a young woman named Mrs. King who was very happy with her husband. They were well-to-do and deeply in love, but at the birth of her second child she went into a long coma and emerged with a clear case of schizophrenia[2] or "split personality." Her delusion,[3] which had something to do with the Declaration of Independence, had little bearing on the case and as she regained her health it began to disappear. At the end of ten months she was a convalescent[4] patient scarcely marked by what had happened to her and very eager to go back into the world.

She was only twenty-one, rather girlish in an appealing way and a favorite with the staff of the sanitarium. When she became well enough so that she could take an experimental trip with her husband there was a general interest in the venture. One nurse had gone into Philadelphia with her to get a dress, another knew the story of her rather romantic courtship in Mexico and everyone had seen her two babies on visits to the hospital. The trip was to Virginia Beach for five days.

It was a joy to watch her make ready, dressing and packing meticulously[5] and living in the gay trivialities of hair waves and such things. She was ready half an hour before the time of departure and she paid some visits on the floor in her powder-blue gown and her hat that looked like one minute after an April shower. Her frail lovely face, with just that touch of startled sadness that often lingers after an illness, was alight with anticipation.

"We'll just do nothing," she said. "That's my ambition. To get up when I want to for three straight mornings and stay up late for three straight nights. To buy a bathing suit by myself and order a meal."

When the time approached Mrs. King decided to wait downstairs instead of in her room and as she passed along the corridors, with an orderly carrying her suitcase, she waved to the other patients, sorry that they too were not going on a gorgeous holiday. The superintendent wished her well, two nurses found excuses to linger and share her infectious joy.

"What a beautiful tan you'll get, Mrs. King."

"Be sure and send a postcard."

About the time she left her room her husband's car was hit by a truck on his way from the city—he was hurt internally and was not expected to live more than a few hours. The information was received at the hospital in a glassed-in office adjoining the hall where Mrs. King waited. The operator, seeing Mrs. King and knowing that the glass was not sound proof, asked the head nurse to come immediately. The head nurse hurried aghast to a doctor and he decided what to do. So long as the husband was still alive it was best to tell her nothing, but of course she must know that he was not coming today.

Mrs. King was greatly disappointed.

"I suppose it's silly to feel that way," she said. "After all these months what's one more day? He said he'd come tomorrow didn't he?"

2. *schizophrenia* (skit′sə frē′nē ə), a psychotic deterioration of personality.

3. *delusion*, a false belief.

4. *convalescent* (kon′və les′ənt), recovering from an illness.

5. *meticulously* (mə tik′yə ləs′ li), very carefully.

The nurse was having a difficult time but she managed to pass it off until the patient was back in her room. Then they assigned a very experienced and phlegmatic[6] nurse to keep Mrs. King away from other patients and from newspapers. By the next day the matter would be decided one way or another.

But her husband lingered on and they continued to prevaricate.[7] A little before noon next day one of the nurses was passing along the corridor when she met Mrs. King, dressed as she had been the day before but this time carrying her own suitcase.

"I'm going to meet my husband," she explained. "He couldn't come yesterday but he's coming today at the same time."

The nurse walked along with her. Mrs. King had the freedom of the building and it was difficult to simply steer her back to her room, and the nurse did not want to tell a story that would contradict what the authorities were telling her. When they reached the front hall she signaled to the operator, who fortunately understood. Mrs. King gave herself a last inspection in the mirror and said:

"I'd like to have a dozen hats just like this to remind me to be this happy always."

When the head nurse came in frowning a minute later she demanded:

"Don't tell me George is delayed?"

"I'm afraid he is. There is nothing much to do but be patient."

Mrs. King laughed ruefully. "I wanted him to see my costume when it was absolutely new."

"Why, there isn't a wrinkle in it."

"I guess it'll last till tomorrow. I oughtn't to be blue about waiting one more day when I'm so utterly happy."

"Certainly not."

That night her husband died and at a conference of doctors next morning there was some discussion about what to do—it was a risk to tell her and a risk to keep it from her. It was decided finally to say that Mr. King had been called away and thus destroy her hope of an immediate meeting; when she was reconciled to this they could tell her the truth.

As the doctors came out of the conference one of them stopped and pointed. Down the corridor toward the outer hall walked Mrs. King carrying her suitcase.

Dr. Pirie, who had been in special charge of Mrs. King, caught his breath.

"This is awful," he said. "I think perhaps I'd better tell her now. There's no use saying he's away when she usually hears from him twice a week, and if we say he's sick she'll want to go to him. Anybody else like the job?"

One of the doctors in the conference went on a fortnight's vacation that afternoon. On the day of his return in the same corridor at the same hour, he stopped at the sight of a little procession coming toward him—an orderly carrying a suitcase, a

nurse and Mrs. King dressed in the powder-blue suit and wearing the spring hat.

"Good morning, Doctor," she said. "I'm going to meet my husband and we're going to Virginia Beach. I'm going to the hall because I don't want to keep him waiting."

He looked into her face, clear and happy as a child's. The nurse signaled to him that it was as ordered, so he merely bowed and spoke of the pleasant weather.

"It's a beautiful day," said Mrs. King, "but of course even if it was raining it would be a beautiful day for me."

The doctor looked after her, puzzled and annoyed—why are they letting this go on, he thought. What possible good can it do?

Meeting Dr. Pirie, he put the question to him.

"We tried to tell her," Dr. Pirie said. "She laughed and said we were trying to see whether she's still sick. You could use the word unthinkable in an exact sense here—his death is unthinkable to her."

"But you can't just go on like this."

"Theoretically no," said Dr. Pirie. "A few days ago when she packed up as usual the nurse tried to keep her from going. From out in the hall I could see her face, see her begin to go to pieces—for the first time, mind you. Her muscles were tense and her eyes glazed and her voice was thick and shrill when she very politely called the nurse a liar. It was touch and go there for a minute whether we had a tractable[8] patient or a restraint case—and I stepped in and told the nurse to take her down to the reception room."

He broke off as the procession that had just passed appeared again, headed back to the ward. Mrs. King stopped and spoke to Dr. Pirie.

"My husband's been delayed," she said. "Of course I'm disappointed but they tell me he's coming tomorrow and after waiting so long one more day doesn't seem to matter. Don't you agree with me, Doctor?"

"I certainly do, Mrs. King."

She took off her hat.

"I've got to put aside these clothes—I want them to be as fresh tomorrow as they are today." She looked closely at the hat. "There's a speck of dust on it, but I think I can get it off. Perhaps he won't notice."

"I'm sure he won't."

"Really I don't mind waiting another day. It'll be this time tomorrow before I know it, won't it?"

When she had gone along the younger doctor said:

"There are still the two children."

"I don't think the children are going to matter. When she 'went under,' she tied up this trip with the idea of getting well. If we took it away she'd have to go to the bottom and start over."

"Could she?"

"There's no prognosis,"[9] said Dr. Pirie. "I was simply explaining why she was allowed to go to the hall this morning."

"But there's tomorrow morning and the next morning."

"There's always the chance," said Dr. Pirie, "that some day he will be there."

The doctor ended his story here, rather abruptly. When we pressed him to tell what happened he protested that the rest was anticlimax—that all sympathy eventually wears out and that finally the staff of the sanitarium had simply affected the fact.

"But does she still go to meet her husband?"

"Oh yes, it's always the same—but the other patients, except new ones, hardly look up when she passes along the hall. The nurses manage to substitute a new hat every year or so but she still wears the same suit. She's always a little disappointed but she makes the best of it, very sweetly too. It's not an unhappy life as far as we know, and in some funny way it seems to set an example of tranquillity to the other patients. For God's sake, let's talk about something else—let's go back to oubliettes."

1. The first paragraph is related to the rest of the story because it (a) introduces the setting of the story; (b) tells who the main character is; (c) introduces the theme of suffering; (d) introduces the theme of claustrophobia.

2. The reader's sympathy for Mrs. King is engaged through

all of the following details *except* that (a) she is young and in love; (b) the people on the sanitarium staff like her; (c) her face seems sad and fragile; (d) her delusion had something to do with the Declaration of Independence.

3. How does the doctor who tells the story report the husband's accident? (a) melodramatically; (b) matter-of-factly; (c) ironically; (d) with a tragic tone.

4. The suitcase, new dress, and hat symbolize (a) hope; (b) impermanence; (c) vanity; (d) emptiness.

5. The complication in the story is (a) the information that Mrs. King had been in the hospital for ten months; (b) the plans for the vacation to Virginia Beach; (c) Mrs. King's appearance in the same blue dress as the day before; (d) the husband's accident.

6. The reader can infer that Mrs. King is kept away from the other patients because (a) her schizophrenic behavior might affect them badly; (b) she needs to rest from the excitement of the day; (c) they might make fun of her; (d) they might tell her about her husband's accident.

7. How do the doctors justify allowing Mrs. King to continue to believe that she is going on a vacation? (a) If she ceases to believe this, she may relapse into schizophrenia; (b) this belief makes her easier to handle; (c) she will eventually realize the truth herself; (d) she is beyond hope anyway.

8. At the end of the story the doctor implies that Mrs. King has been in her condition for (a) six months; (b) several years; (c) a few weeks; (d) a year.

9. At the end of the story, when the doctor suggests that his listeners return to the subject of oubliettes, he is demonstrating that he (a) is unmoved by Mrs. King's plight; (b) enjoys talking about methods of torture; (c) is bored with the conversation; (d) is unnerved by the tragedy of Mrs. King's life.

10. The narrator who introduces the story is (a) an unnamed participant in the conversation; (b) a doctor; (c) a nurse; (d) an omniscient narrator who plays no part in the story.

Unit 6, Test II
COMPOSITION

Choose one of the following topics for writing. Unless otherwise indicated, assume you are writing for your class.

1. Some of the poets in this unit rely on the traditional use of rhyme, rhythm, stanza form, imagery, and language. Others use more experimental techniques.

Choose one traditionalist and one experimenter, and compare their styles of poetry. Also discuss how the style of each is appropriate to the themes that each is expressing.

2. Some of the writers of this period rejected the traditional romantic view of love. Others accepted and even praised that view. As a newspaper feature writer, you are to write an article about the attitudes toward love and romance reflected in literature from 1915 to 1945.

Selections you might consider in developing your ideas are "The Wedding," "The Love Song of J. Alfred Prufrock," "If You Should Go," "Well, I Have Lost You," and "The Solitary."

3. Some social observers have stated that heroism is not possible in the twentieth century. Others argue that there are still heroes, but they are heroic for qualities far different from those of the Deerslayers of the nineteenth century.

Compare a work in Unit 6 which takes an antiheroic stance with one which suggests heroism is still possible. After your comparison, write a conclusion in which you discuss how twentieth-century attitudes toward heroism differ from those of the nineteenth century.

4. Both "To Horse" and "The Wedding" are examples of a genre that was popular in the 1930s: the casual essay. In this kind of writing, the author uses a conversational tone in relating anecdotes that reveal the personality of someone familiar to the author.

Write a casual essay about a person you know well for a general magazine like *Reader's Digest.* Through ancedotes, the essay should reveal important characteristics of that person. Remember to use a personal tone, and to make sure that every incident contributes to the development of a unifying idea or impression.

Tennessee Williams: The Glass Menagerie

Unit 7: A Modern Drama

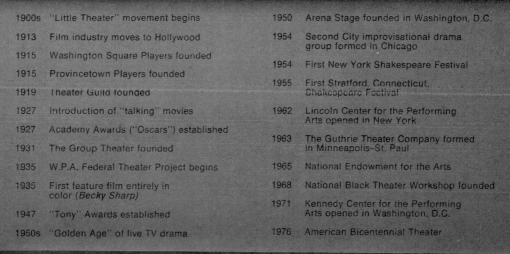

1900s	"Little Theater" movement begins	1950	Arena Stage founded in Washington, D.C.
1913	Film industry moves to Hollywood	1954	Second City improvisational drama group formed in Chicago
1915	Washington Square Players founded	1954	First New York Shakespeare Festival
1915	Provincetown Players founded	1955	First Stratford, Connecticut, Shakespeare Festival
1919	Theater Guild founded		
1927	Introduction of "talking" movies	1962	Lincoln Center for the Performing Arts opened in New York
1927	Academy Awards ("Oscars") established	1963	The Guthrie Theater Company formed in Minneapolis–St. Paul
1931	The Group Theater founded		
1935	W.P.A. Federal Theater Project begins	1965	National Endowment for the Arts
1935	First feature film entirely in color (*Becky Sharp*)	1968	National Black Theater Workshop founded
1947	"Tony" Awards established	1971	Kennedy Center for the Performing Arts opened in Washington, D.C.
1950s	"Golden Age" of live TV drama	1976	American Bicentennial Theater

Background: American Theater in the Twentieth Century

American drama has flourished in the twentieth century because our playwrights have employed the full possibilities of the modern stage in exploring human experience. Nowhere is this seen better than in the plays of Eugene O'Neill. *The Iceman Cometh* (1946) features characters destroyed by their own inability to face life without illusions. In *Long Day's Journey into Night* (1956), O'Neill used autobiographical materials to make a powerful statement about the compulsion of some people to destroy themselves.

The growing maturity of American drama is also reflected in the plays of Lillian Hellman. *The Little Foxes* (1939) slowly reveals the scheming of a Southern family consumed by its own material and emotional selfishness.

Two new forces in American theater emerged after World War II—Arthur Miller and Tennessee Williams. Miller's *The Crucible* (1953) has become an enduring analysis of the demands of conscience. In *Death of a Salesman* (1949), he portrays an ordinary man, Willy Loman, who achieves tragic stature in his ruinous pursuit of the American dream.

Williams often portrays characters who retreat from reality to an imaginary world. In *The Glass Menagerie* (1945) he used set and lighting in innovative ways to add poignancy to his account of a family that lives on illusion. Williams's other major plays, *A Streetcar Named Desire* (1947) and *Cat on a Hot Tin Roof* (1955), also deal with emotionally crippled characters who cannot face reality.

The leader of recent American experimenters in the theater has been Edward Albee, whose plays often attack the replacement of "real values" with artificial ones in American society. *The Sandbox* (1960), *The American Dream* (1961), and *Who's Afraid of Virginia Woolf?* (1962) all employ rather grim humor to develop this theme.

With the work of Langston Hughes and other noted playwrights, black drama came of age in the 1930s. From the 1950s on, such dramatists as James Baldwin, Lorraine Hansberry, Imamu Amiri Baraka (LeRoi Jones), and Ed Bullins developed a vigorously experimental theater inspired by black culture. Hansberry's *A Raisin in the Sun* (1959), which transcends racial concerns to address the universal quest for human dignity, became the first great popular success by a black playwright. The upsurgence of black drama characterizes an era in which young American playwrights are exploring many new directions.

From the time of the ancient Greeks to our own era, dramatists have been intrigued by conflicts between parents and children caused by the differences in outlook and aspirations from one generation to another. The play you are about to read explores such a conflict. In reading this play, try to imagine facial expressions, tones of voice, and other mannerisms that the actors must use to express conflicting emotions. Watch for personality clashes between characters.

For an interesting glimpse into the origin of the play, let us listen to its author.

Tennessee Williams:
Why It Is Called *The Glass Menagerie*

When my family first moved to St. Louis from the South, we were forced to live in a congested apartment neighborhood. It was a shocking change, for my sister and myself were accustomed to spacious yards, porches, and big shade trees. The apartment we lived in was about as cheerful as an Arctic winter. There were outside windows only in the front room and kitchen. The rooms between had windows that opened upon a narrow areaway that was virtually sunless and which we grimly named "Death Valley" for a reason which is amusing only in retrospect.

There were a great many alley cats in the neighborhood which were constantly fighting the dogs. Every now and then some unwary young cat would allow itself to be pursued into this areaway which had only one opening. The end of the cul-de-sac was directly beneath my sister's bedroom window and it was here that the cats would have to turn around to face their pursuers in mortal combat. My sister would be awakened in the night by the struggle and in the morning the hideously mangled victim would be lying under her window. Sight of the areaway had become so odious to her, for this reason, that she kept the shade constantly drawn so that the interior of her bedroom had a perpetual twilight atmosphere. Something had to be done to relieve this gloom. So my sister and I painted all her furniture white; she put white curtains at the window and on the shelves around the room she collected a large assortment of little glass articles, of which she was particularly fond. Eventually, the room took on a light and delicate appearance, in spite of the lack of outside illumination, and it became the only room in the house that I found pleasant to enter.

When I left home a number of years later, it was this room that I recalled most vividly and poignantly when looking back on our home life in St. Louis. Particularly the little glass ornaments on the shelves. They were mostly little glass animals.

By poetic association they came to represent, in my memory, all the softest emotions that belong to recollection of things past. They stood for all the small and tender things that relieve the austere pattern of life and make it endurable to the sensitive. The areaway where the cats were torn to pieces was one thing—my sister's white curtains and tiny menagerie of glass were another. Somewhere between them was the world that we lived in.

The Glass Menagerie

Tennessee Williams

THE GLASS MENAGERIE was produced by Eddie Dowling and Louis J. Singer at the Playhouse Theatre, New York City, on March 31, 1945, with the following cast:

All photographs accompanying the text are from the 1975 production of *The Glass Menagerie* at the Circle in the Square Theatre, New York City. Photographs by Inge Morath/Magnum Photos, Inc.

THE MOTHER	Laurette Taylor
HER SON	Eddie Dowling
HER DAUGHTER	Julie Haydon
THE GENTLEMAN CALLER	Anthony Ross

SCENE

An alley in St. Louis.

PART I: Preparation for a Gentleman Caller.
PART II: The Gentleman Calls.
TIME: Now and the Past.

Setting designed and lighted by
JO MIELZINER.
Original Music composed by PAUL BOWLES.
Staged by MR. DOWLING and MARGO JONES.

Act One SCENE 1

The Wingfield apartment is in the rear of the building, one of those vast hive-like conglomerations of cellular living-units that flower as warty growths in overcrowded urban centers of lower middle-class population and are symptomatic of the impulse of this largest and fundamentally enslaved section of American society to avoid fluidity and differentiation and to exist and function as one interfused mass of automatism. The apartment faces an alley and is entered by a fire-escape, a structure whose name is a touch of accidental poetic truth, for all of these huge buildings are always burning with the slow and implacable fires of human desperation. The fire-escape is included in the set—that is, the landing of it and steps descending from it. (Note that the stage L. *alley may be entirely omitted, since it is never used except for* TOM *'s first entrance, which can take place stage* R.) *The scene is memory and is therefore nonrealistic. Memory takes a lot of poetic license. It omits some details, others are exaggerated, according to the emotional value of the articles it touches, for memory is seated predominantly in the heart. The interior is therefore rather dim and poetic.* (CUE #1. *As soon as the house lights dim, dance-hall music heard on-stage* R. *Old popular music of, say 1915-1920 period. This continues until* TOM *is at fire-escape landing, having lighted cigarette, and begins speaking.)*

AT RISE: *At the rise of the house curtain, the audience is faced with the dark, grim rear wall of the Wingfield tenement. (The stage set proper is screened out by a gauze curtain, which suggests the front part, outside, of the building.) This building, which runs parallel to the footlights, is flanked on both sides by dark, narrow alleys which run into murky canyons of tangled clotheslines, garbage cans and the sinister lattice-work of neighboring fire-escapes. (The alleys are actually in darkness, and the objects just mentioned are not visible.) It is up and down these side alleys that exterior entrances and exits are made, during the play. At the end of* TOM *'s opening commentary, the dark tenement wall slowly reveals (by means of a transparency) the interior of the ground-floor Wingfield apartment. (Gauze curtain, which suggests front part of building, rises on the interior set.) Downstage is the living-room, which also serves as a sleeping room for* LAURA, *the day-bed unfolding to make her bed. Just above this is a small stool or table on which is a telephone. Up-stage,* C., *and divided by a wide arch or second proscenium with transparent faded portieres (or second curtain, "second curtain" is actually the inner gauze curtain between the living-room and the dining-room, which is up-stage of it), is the dining-room. In an old-fashioned whatnot in the living-room are seen scores of transparent glass animals. A blown-up photograph of the father hangs on the wall of the living-room, facing the audience, to the* L. *of the archway. It is the face of a very handsome young man in a doughboy's First World War cap. He is gallantly smiling, ineluctably smiling, as if to say, "I will be smiling forever." (Note that all that is essential in connection with dance-hall is that the window be shown lighting lower part of alley. It is not necessary to show any considerable part of dance-hall.) The audience hears and sees the opening scene in the dining-room through both the transparent fourth wall (this is the gauze curtain which suggests outside of building) of the*

*building and the transparent gauze portieres of
the dining-room arch. It is during this revealing
scene that the fourth wall slowly ascends, out of
sight. This transparent exterior wall is not
brought down again until the very end of the play,
during* TOM*'s final speech. The narrator is an
undisguised convention of the play. He takes
whatever license with dramatic convention as is
convenient to his purposes.*

TOM *enters, dressed as a merchant sailor, from
alley, stage* L. *(i.e., stage* R. *if* L. *alley is omitted),
and strolls across the front of the stage to the
fire-escape. (*TOM *may lean against grillwork of
this as he lights cigarette.) There he stops and
lights a cigarette. He addresses the audience.*

TOM. I have tricks in my pocket—I have things
up my sleeve—but I am the opposite of the
stage magician. He gives you illusion that has
the appearance of truth. I give you truth in the
pleasant disguise of illusion. I take you back to
an alley in St. Louis. The time that quaint
period when the huge middle class of America
was matriculating from a school for the blind.
Their eyes had failed them, or they had failed
their eyes, and so they were having their
fingers pressed forcibly down on the fiery
Braille alphabet of a dissolving economy.—In
Spain there was revolution.—Here there was
only shouting and confusion and labor distur-
bances, sometimes violent, in otherwise peaceful cities such as Cleveland—Chicago—
Detroit. . . . That is the social background
of this play. . . . The play is memory. (MUSIC
CUE #2.) Being a memory play, it is dimly
lighted, it is sentimental, it is not realistic.—

In memory everything seems to happen to
music.—That explains the fiddle in the wings.
I am the narrator of the play, and also a
character in it. The other characters in the
play are my mother, Amanda, my sister,
Laura, and a gentleman caller who appears in
the final scenes. He is the most realistic character in the play, being an emissary from a
world that we were somehow set apart
from.—But having a poet's weakness for symbols, I am using this character as a symbol—as
the long-delayed but always expected something that we live for.—There is a fifth character who doesn't appear other than in a photograph hanging on the wall. When you see the
picture of this grinning gentleman, please remember this is our father who left us a long
time ago. He was a telephone man who fell in
love with long distance—so he gave up his
job with the telephone company and skipped
the light fantastic out of town. . . . The last we
heard of him was a picture postcard from the
Pacific coast of Mexico, containing a message
of two words—"Hello—Good-bye!" and no
address.

*(*LIGHTS UP IN DINING-ROOM. TOM *exits* R. *He
goes off downstage, takes off his sailor overcoat
and skull-fitting knitted cap and remains off-
stage by dining-room* R. *door for his entrance
cue.* AMANDA*'s voice becomes audible through
the portieres—i.e., gauze curtains separating
dining-room and living-room.* AMANDA *and*
LAURA *are seated at a drop-leaf table.* AMANDA
is sitting in C. *chair and* LAURA *in* L. *chair.
Eating is indicated by gestures without food or
utensils.* AMANDA *faces the audience. The interior of the dining-room has lit up softly and
through the scrim—gauze curtains—we see*
AMANDA *and* LAURA *seated at the table in the
upstage area.)*

AMANDA. You know, Laura, I had the funniest
experience in church last Sunday. The church
was crowded except for one pew way down
front and in that was just one little woman. I
smiled very sweetly at her and said, "Excuse
me, would you mind if I shared this pew?" "I
certainly would," she said, "this space is rented." Do you know that is the first time that I
ever knew that the Lord rented space.
(Dining-room gauze curtains open automati-

cally.) These Northern Episcopalians! I can understand the Southern Episcopalians, but these Northern ones, no. *(TOM enters dining-room R., slips over to table and sits in chair R.)* Honey, don't push your food with your fingers. If you have to push your food with something, the thing to use is a crust of bread. You must chew your food. Animals have secretions in their stomachs which enable them to digest their food without mastication, but human beings must chew their food before they swallow it down, and chew, chew. Oh, eat leisurely. Eat leisurely. A well-cooked meal has many delicate flavors that have to be held in the mouth for appreciation, not just gulped down. Oh, chew, chew—chew! *(At this point the scrim curtain—if the director decides to use it—the one suggesting exterior wall, rises here and does not come down again until just before the end of the play.)* Don't you want to give your salivary glands a chance to function?

TOM. Mother, I haven't enjoyed one bite of my dinner because of your constant directions on how to eat it. It's you that makes me hurry through my meals with your hawk-like attention to every bite I take. It's disgusting—all this discussion of animal's secretion—salivary glands—mastication! *(Comes down to armchair in living-room R., lights cigarette.)*

AMANDA. Temperament like a Metropolitan star! You're not excused from this table.

TOM. I'm getting a cigarette.

AMANDA. You smoke too much.

LAURA *(Rising).* Mother, I'll bring in the coffee.

AMANDA. No, no, no, no. You sit down. I'm going to be the colored boy today and you're going to be the lady.

LAURA. I'm already up.

AMANDA. Resume your seat. Resume your seat. You keep yourself fresh and pretty for the gentlemen callers. *(LAURA sits.)*

LAURA. I'm not expecting any gentlemen callers.

AMANDA *(Who has been gathering dishes from table and loading them on tray).* Well, the nice thing about them is they come when they're least expected. Why, I remember one Sunday afternoon in Blue Mountain when your mother was a girl. . .

(Goes out for coffee, U. R.)

TOM. I know what's coming now! *(LAURA rises.)*

LAURA. Yes. But let her tell it. *(Crosses to L. of day-bed, sits.)*

TOM. Again?

LAURA. She loves to tell it.

AMANDA *(Entering from R. in dining-room and coming down into living-room with tray and coffee).* I remember one Sunday afternoon in Blue Mountain when your mother was a girl she received—seventeen—gentlemen callers! *(AMANDA crosses to TOM at armchair R., gives him coffee, and crosses C. LAURA comes to her, takes cup, resumes her place on L. of day-bed. AMANDA puts tray on small table R. of day-bed, sits R. on day-bed. Inner curtain closes, light dims out.)* Why sometimes there weren't chairs enough to accommodate them all and we had to send the colored boy over to the parish house to fetch the folding chairs.

TOM. How did you entertain all those gentlemen callers? *(TOM finally sits in armchair R.)*

AMANDA. I happened to understand the art of conversation!

TOM. I bet you could talk!

AMANDA. Well, I could. All the girls in my day could, I tell you.

TOM. Yes?

AMANDA. They knew how to entertain their gentlemen callers. It wasn't enough for a girl to be possessed of a pretty face and a graceful figure—although I wasn't slighted in either respect. She also needed to have a nimble wit and a tongue to meet all occasions.

TOM. What did you talk about?

AMANDA. Why, we'd talk about things of importance going on in the world! Never anything common or coarse or vulgar. My callers were gentlemen—all! Some of the most prominent men on the Mississippi Delta—planters and sons of planters! There was young Champ Laughlin. (MUSIC CUE #3.) He later became Vice-President of the Delta Planters' Bank. And Hadley Stevenson; he was drowned in Moon Lake.—My goodness, he certainly left his widow well provided for—a hundred and fifty thousand dollars in government bonds. And the Cutrere Brothers—Wesley and Bates. Bates was one of my own bright particular beaus! But he got in a quarrel with that wild Wainwright boy and they shot it out on the floor of Moon Lake Casino. Bates was shot through the stomach. He died in the ambulance on his way to Memphis. He certainly left his widow well provided for, too—eight or ten thousand acres, no less. He never loved that woman; she just caught him on the rebound. My picture was found on him the night he died. Oh and that boy, that boy that every girl in the Delta was setting her cap for! That beautiful (MUSIC FADES OUT) brilliant young Fitzhugh boy from Greene County!

TOM. What did he leave his widow?

AMANDA. He never married! What's the matter with you—you talk as though all my old admirers had turned up their toes to the daisies!

TOM. Isn't this the first you've mentioned that still survives?

AMANDA. He made an awful lot of money. He went North to Wall Street and made a fortune. He had the Midas touch—everything that boy touched just turned to gold! (*Gets up.*) And I could have been Mrs. J. Duncan Fitzhugh—mind you! (*Crosses L. C.*) But—what did I do?—I just went out of my way and picked your father! (*Looks at picture on L. wall. Goes to small table R. of day-bed for tray.*)

LAURA (*Rises from day-bed*). Mother, let me clear the table.

AMANDA (*Crossing L. for LAURA's cup, then crossing R. for TOM's*). No, dear, you go in front and study your typewriter chart. Or practice your shorthand a little. Stay fresh and pretty! It's almost time for our gentlemen callers to start arriving. How many do you suppose we're going to entertain this afternoon? (*TOM opens curtains between dining-room and living-room for her. These close behind her, and she exits into kitchen R. TOM stands U. C. in living-room.*)

LAURA (*To AMANDA, off-stage*). I don't believe we're going to receive any, Mother.

AMANDA (*Off-stage*). Not any? Not one? Why, you must be joking! Not one gentleman caller? What's the matter? Has there been a flood or a tornado?

LAURA (*Crossing to typing table*). It isn't a flood. It's not a tornado, Mother. I'm just not popular like you were in Blue Mountain. Mother's afraid that I'm going to be an old maid. (MUSIC CUE #4.) (*Lights dim out. TOM exits U. C. in blackout. LAURA crosses to menagerie R.*)

Act One SCENE 2

Scene is the same. Lights dim up on living-room.

LAURA *discovered by menagerie, polishing glass. Crosses to phonograph, plays record.[1] She times this business so as to put needle on record as* MUSIC CUE #4 *ends. Enter* AMANDA *down alley R. Rattles key in lock.* LAURA *crosses guiltily to typewriter and types. (Small typewriter table with typewriter on it is still on stage in living-room L.)* AMANDA *comes into room R. closing door. Crosses to armchair, putting hat, purse and gloves on it. Something has happened to* AMANDA. *It is written in her face: a look that is grim and hopeless and a little absurd. She has on one of those cheap or imitation velvety-looking cloth coats with imitation fur collar. Her hat is five or six years old, one of those dreadful cloche hats that were worn in the late twenties and she is clasping an enormous black patent-leather pocketbook with nickel clasps and initials. This is her fulldress outfit, the one she usually wears to the D.A.R.[2] She purses her lips, opens her eyes very wide, rolls them upward and shakes her head. Seeing her mother's expression,* LAURA *touches her lips with a nervous gesture.*

LAURA. Hello, Mother, I was just . . .

AMANDA. I know. You were just practicing your typing, I suppose. (*Behind chair R.*)

LAURA. Yes.

AMANDA. Deception, deception, deception!

LAURA (*Shakily*). How was the D.A.R. meeting, Mother?

AMANDA (*Crosses to LAURA*). D.A.R. meeting!

LAURA. Didn't you go to the D.A.R. meeting, Mother?

AMANDA (*Faintly, almost inaudibly*). No, I didn't go to any D.A.R. meeting. (*Then more forcibly.*) I didn't have the strength—I didn't have the courage. I just wanted to find a hole in the ground and crawl in it and stay there the rest of my entire life.

(*Tears type charts, throws them on floor.*)

LAURA (*Faintly*). Why did you do that, Mother?

AMANDA (*Sits on R. end of day-bed*). Why?

---

1. record. While "Dardanella" was used in the original production, any other worn and scratchy popular record of the 1920s may be substituted.
2. D.A.R., Daughters of the American Revolution, a society of women who can claim descent from Americans who fought in the Revolutionary War.

Why? How old are you, Laura?

LAURA. Mother, you know my age.

AMANDA. I was under the impression that you were an adult, but evidently I was very much mistaken.

(She stares at LAURA.)

LAURA. Please don't stare at me, Mother! *(AMANDA closes her eyes and lowers her head. Pause.)*

AMANDA. What are we going to do? What is going to become of us? What is the future? *(Pause.)*

LAURA. Has something happened, Mother? Mother, has something happened?

AMANDA. I'll be all right in a minute. I'm just bewildered—by life . . .

LAURA. Mother, I wish that you would tell me what's happened!

AMANDA. I went to the D.A.R. this afternoon, as you know; I was to be inducted as an officer. I stopped off at Rubicam's Business College to tell them about your cold and to ask how you were progressing down there.

LAURA. Oh. . .

AMANDA. Yes, oh—oh—oh. I went straight to your typing instructor and introduced myself as your mother. She didn't even know who you were. Wingfield, she said? We don't have any such scholar enrolled in this school. I assured her she did. I said my daughter Laura's been coming to classes since early January. "Well, I don't know," she said, "unless you mean that terribly shy little girl who dropped out of school after a few days' attendance?" "No," I said, "I don't mean that one. I mean my daughter, Laura, who's been coming here every single day for the past six weeks!" "Excuse me," she said. And she took down the attendance book and there was your name, unmistakable, printed, and all the dates you'd been absent. I still told her she was wrong. I still said, "No, there must have been some mistake! There must have been some mix-up in the records!" "No," she said, "I remember her perfectly now. She was so shy and her hands trembled so that her fingers couldn't touch the right keys! When we gave a speed-test—she just broke down completely—was sick at the stomach and had to be carried to the washroom! After that she never came back. We

telephoned the house every single day and never got any answer." *(Rises from day-bed, crosses R. C.)* That was while I was working all day long down at that department store, I suppose, demonstrating those—*(With hands indicates brassiere.)* Oh! I felt so weak I couldn't stand up! *(Sits in armchair.)* I had to sit down while they got me a glass of water! *(LAURA crosses up to phonograph.)* Fifty dollars' tuition. I don't care about the money so much, but all my hopes for any kind of future for you—gone up the spout, just gone up the spout like that. *(LAURA winds phonograph up.)* Oh, don't *do* that, Laura!—Don't play that victrola!

LAURA. Oh! *(Stops phonograph, crosses to typing table, sits.)*

AMANDA. What have you been doing every day when you've gone out of the house pretending that you were going to business college?

LAURA. I've just been going out walking.

AMANDA. That's not true!

LAURA. Yes, it is, Mother, I just went walking.

AMANDA. Walking? Walking? In winter? Deliberately courting pneumonia in that light coat? Where did you walk to, Laura?

LAURA. All sorts of places—mostly in the park.

AMANDA. Even after you'd started catching that cold?

LAURA. It was the lesser of two evils, Mother. I couldn't go back. I threw up on the floor!

AMANDA. From half-past seven till after five every day you mean to tell me you walked around in the park, because you wanted to make me think that you were still going to Rubicam's Business College?

LAURA. Oh, Mother, it wasn't as bad as it sounds. I went inside places to get warmed up.

AMANDA. Inside where?

LAURA. I went in the art museum and the bird-houses at the Zoo. I visited the penguins every day! Sometimes I did without lunch and went to the movies. Lately I've been spending most of my afternoons in the Jewelbox, that big glass house[3] where they raise the tropical flowers.

---

3. **big glass house,** the conservatory at the St. Louis zoo. Williams emphasizes the identification of Laura with the delicate flowers and the fragile, glass building.

AMANDA. You did all that to deceive me, just for deception! Why? Why? Why? Why?

LAURA. Mother, when you're disappointed, you get that awful suffering look on your face, like the picture of Jesus' mother in the Museum! *(Rises.)*

AMANDA. Hush!

LAURA *(Crosses R. to menagerie).* I couldn't face it. I couldn't. (MUSIC CUE #5.)

AMANDA *(Rising from day-bed).* So what are we going to do now, honey, the rest of our lives? Just sit down in this house and watch the parades go by? Amuse ourselves with the glass menagerie? Eternally play those worn-out records your father left us as a painful reminder of him? *(Slams phonograph lid.)* We can't have a business career. (END MUSIC CUE #5.) No, we can't do that—that just gives us indigestion. *(Around R. day-bed.)* What is there left for us now but dependency all our lives? I tell you, Laura, I know so well what happens to unmarried women who aren't prepared to occupy a position in life. *(Crosses L., sits on day-bed.)* I've seen such pitiful cases in the South— barely tolerated spinsters living on some brother's wife or a sister's husband—tucked away in some mousetrap of a room—encouraged by one in-law to go on and visit the next in-law— little birdlike women—without any nest— eating the crust of humility all their lives! Is that the future that we've mapped out for ourselves? I swear I don't see any other alternative. And I don't think that's a very pleasant alternative. Of course—some girls *do* marry. My goodness, Laura, haven't you ever liked some boy?

LAURA. Yes, Mother, I liked one once.

AMANDA. You did?

LAURA. I came across his picture a while ago.

AMANDA. He gave you his picture too? *(Rises from day-bed, crosses to chair R.)*

LAURA. No, it's in the year-book.

AMANDA *(Sits in armchair).* Oh—a high-school boy.

LAURA. Yes. His name was Jim. *(Kneeling on floor, gets year-book from under menagerie.)* Here he is in "The Pirates of Penzance."[4]

AMANDA *(Absently).* The what?

LAURA. The operetta the senior class put on. He had a wonderful voice. We sat across the aisle from each other Mondays, Wednesdays and Fridays in the auditorium. Here he is with a silver cup for debating! See his grin?

AMANDA. So he had a grin, too! *(Looks at picture of father on wall behind phonograph.[5] Hands year-book back.)*

LAURA. He used to call me—Blue Roses.

AMANDA. Blue Roses? What did he call you a silly name like that for?

LAURA *(Still kneeling).* When I had that attack of pleurosis—he asked me what was the matter when I came back. I said pleurosis—he thought that I said "Blue Roses." So that's what he always called me after that. Whenever he saw me, he'd holler, "Hello, Blue Roses!" I didn't care for the girl that he went out with. Emily Meisenbach. Oh, Emily was the best-dressed girl at Soldan. But she never struck me as being sincere . . . I read in a newspaper once that they were engaged. *(Puts year-book back on a shelf of glass menagerie.)* That's a long time ago—they're probably married by now.

AMANDA. That's all right, honey, that's all right. It doesn't matter. Little girls who aren't cut out for business careers sometimes end up married to very nice young men. And I'm just going to see that you do that, too!

LAURA. But, Mother—

AMANDA. What is it now?

LAURA. I'm—crippled!

AMANDA. Don't say that word! *(Rises, crosses to C. Turns to LAURA.)* How many times have I told you never to say that word! You're not crippled, you've just got a slight defect. *(LAURA rises.)* If you lived in the days when I was a girl and they had long graceful skirts sweeping the ground, it might have been considered an asset. When you've got a slight disadvantage like that, you've just got to cultivate something else to take its place. You have to cultivate charm—or vivacity—or *charm!* *(Spotlight on photograph. Then dim out.)* That's the only thing your father had plenty of—charm! (AMANDA *sits on day-bed.* LAURA *crosses to armchair and sits.)* (MUSIC CUE #6.) *(Blackout.)*

---

4. *"The Pirates of Penzance,"* an operetta by William S. Gilbert (1836–1911) and Sir Arthur Sullivan (1842–1900).

5. *picture . . . phonograph.* In the original production this photo was a life-sized head, spotlighted from time to time as indicated. The lighting is optional.

Act One SCENE 3

SCENE: *The same. Lights up again but only on* R. *alley and fire-escape landing, rest of the stage dark. (Typewriter table and typewriter have been taken offstage.) Enter* TOM, *again wearing merchant sailor overcoat and knitted cap, in alley* R. *As* MUSIC CUE #6 *ends,* TOM *begins to speak.*

TOM *(Leans against grill of fire-escape, smoking).* After the fiasco at Rubicam's Business College, the idea of getting a gentleman caller for my sister Laura began to play a more and more important part in my mother's calculations. It became an obsession. Like some archetype of the universal unconscious,[1] the image of the gentleman caller haunted our small apartment. An evening at home rarely passed without some allusion to this image, this spectre, this hope. . . . And even when he wasn't mentioned, his presence hung in my mother's preoccupied look and in my sister's frightened, apologetic manner. It hung like a sentence passed upon the Wingfields! But my mother was a woman of action as well as words. (MUSIC CUE #7.) She began to take logical steps in the planned direction. Late that winter and in the early spring—realizing that extra money would be needed to properly feather the nest and plume the bird—she began a vigorous campaign on the telephone, roping in subscribers to one of those magazines for matrons called "The Homemaker's Companion," the type of journal that features the serialized sublimations of ladies of letters who think in terms of delicate cup-like breasts, slim, tapering waists, rich creamy thighs, eyes like wood-smoke in autumn, fingers that soothe and caress like soft, soft strains of music. Bodies as powerful as Etruscan sculpture. *(He exits down* R. *into wings. Light in alley* R. *is blacked out, and a head-spot falls on* AMANDA, *at phone in living-room.* MUSIC CUE #7 *ends as* TOM *stops speaking.)*

AMANDA. Ida Scott? *(During this speech* TOM *enters dining-room* U. R. *unseen by audience, not wearing overcoat or hat. There is an unlighted reading lamp on table. Sits* C. *of dining-room table with writing materials.)* This is Amanda Wingfield. We missed you at the D.A.R. last Monday. Oh, first I want to know how's your sinus condition? You're just a Christian martyr. That's what you are. You're just a Christian martyr. Well, I was just going through my little red book, and I saw that your subscription to the "Companion" is about to expire just when that wonderful new serial by Bessie Mae Harper is starting. It's the first thing she's written since "Honeymoon for Three." Now, that was unusual, wasn't it? Why, Ida, this one is even lovelier. It's all about the horsey set on Long Island and a debutante is thrown from her horse while taking him over the jumps at the—regatta. Her spine—her spine is injured. That's what the horse did—he stepped on her. Now, there is only one surgeon in the entire world that can keep her from being completely paralyzed, and that's the man she's engaged to be married to and he's tall and he's blond and he's handsome. That's unusual, too, huh? Oh, he's not perfect. Of course he has a weakness. He has the most terrible weakness in the entire world. He just drinks too much. What? Oh, no, Honey, don't let them burn. You go take a look in the oven and I'll hold on . . . Why, that woman! Do you know what she did? She hung up on me. *(Dining-room and living-room lights dim in. Reading lamp lights up at same time.)*

LAURA. Oh, Mother, Mother, Tom's trying to write. *(Rises from armchair where she was left at curtain of previous scene, goes to curtain between dining-room and living-room, which is already open.)*

AMANDA. Oh! So he is. So he is. *(Crosses from phone, goes to dining-room and up to* TOM.)

TOM *(At table).* Now what are you up to?

AMANDA. I'm trying to save your eyesight. *(Business with lamp.)* You've only got one pair of eyes and you've got to take care of them. Oh, I know that Milton was blind, but that's not what made him a genius.

---

1. **archetype of the universal unconscious,** a key concept of the psychological theory of Carl G. Jung (1875–1961), eminent German psychologist. He believed everyone inherits unconscious memories of experiences that occur in all societies. According to Jung's theory, these "archetypes" give people their idea, for example, of what a parent should be, and they profoundly influence behavior. Tom satirically suggests that the image of a "gentleman caller" became an archetype dominating his mother's thinking.

TOM. Mother, will you please go away and let me finish my writing?

AMANDA *(Squares his shoulders).* Why can't you sit up straight? So your shoulders don't stick through like sparrows' wings?

TOM. Mother, please go busy yourself with something else. I'm trying to write.

AMANDA *(Business with* TOM*).* Now, I've seen a medical chart, and I know what that position does to your internal organs. You sit up and I'll show you. Your stomach presses against your lungs, and your lungs press against your heart, and that poor little heart gets discouraged because it hasn't got any room left to go on beating for you.

TOM. What in hell! . . . *(Inner curtains between living-room and dining-room close. Lights dim down in dining-room.* LAURA *crosses, stands* C. *of curtains in living-room listening to following scene[2] between* TOM *and* AMANDA.*)*

AMANDA. Don't you talk to me like that—

TOM. —am I supposed to do?

AMANDA. What's the matter with you? Have you gone out of your senses?

TOM. Yes, I have. You've driven me out of them.

AMANDA. What is the matter with you lately, you big—big—idiot?

TOM. Look, Mother—I haven't got a thing, not a single thing left in this house that I can call my own.

AMANDA. Lower your voice!

TOM. Yesterday you confiscated my books! You had the nerve to—

AMANDA. I did. I took that horrible novel back to the library—that awful book by that insane Mr. Lawrence.[3] I cannot control the output of a diseased mind or people who cater to them, but I won't allow such filth in my house. No, no, no, no, no!

TOM. House, house! Who pays the rent on the house, who makes a slave of himself to—!

AMANDA. Don't you dare talk to me like that! *(*LAURA *crosses* D. L. *to back of armchair.)*

TOM. No, *I* mustn't say anything! I've just got to keep quiet and let you do all the talking.

AMANDA. Let me tell you something!

TOM. I don't want to hear any more.

AMANDA. You will hear more—*(*LAURA *crosses to phonograph.)*

TOM *(Crossing through curtains between dining-room and living-room. Goes up stage of door* R. *where, in a dark spot, there is supposedly a closet).* Well, I'm not going to listen. I'm going out. *(Gets out coat.)*

AMANDA *(Coming through curtains into living-room, stands* C*).* You are going to listen to me, Tom Wingfield. I'm tired of your impudence.—And another thing—I'm right at the end of my patience!

TOM *(Putting overcoat on back of armchair and crossing back to* AMANDA*).* What do you think I'm at the end of, Mother? Aren't I supposed to have any patience to reach the end of? I know, I know. It seems unimportant to you, what I'm *doing*—what I'm trying to do—having a difference between them! You don't think that.

AMANDA. I think you're doing things that you're ashamed of, and that's why you act like this. *(*TOM *crosses to day-bed and sits.)* I don't believe that you go every night to the movies. Nobody goes to the movies night after night. Nobody in their right minds goes to the movies as often as you pretend to. People don't go to the movies at nearly midnight and movies don't let out at two A.M. Come in stumbling, muttering to yourself like a maniac. You get three hours' sleep and then go to work. Oh, I can picture the way you're doing down there. Moping, doping, because you're in no condition.

TOM. That's true—that's very, very true. I'm in no condition!

AMANDA. How dare you jeopardize your job? Jeopardize our security? How do you think we'd manage—? *(Sits armchair* R.*)*

TOM. Look, Mother, do you think I'm *crazy* about the *warehouse?* You think I'm in love with the Continental Shoemakers? You think I want to spend fifty-five years of my life down there in that—*celotex interior!* with *fluorescent tubes?!* Honest to God, I'd rather somebody picked up a crow-bar and battered out my brains—than go back mornings! But I *go!* Sure, every time you come in yelling that bloody

---

2. *following scene.* Tom and Amanda remain in the dining-room throughout their argument.
3. *Mr. Lawrence,* D. H. Lawrence (1885–1930), English novelist and poet. Some of his works aroused considerable protest on moral grounds. The artistic merit of much of his work, however, is unquestioned.

Rise and Shine! Rise and shine!! I think how lucky dead people are! But I get up. *(Rises from day-bed.)* I *go!* For sixty-five dollars a month I give up all that I dream of doing and being *ever!* And you say that is all I think of. Oh, God! Why, Mother, if self is all I ever thought of, Mother, *I'd* be where *he* is—GONE! *(Crosses to get overcoat on back of armchair.)* As far as the system of transportation reaches! (AMANDA *rises, crosses to him and grabs his arm.)* Please don't grab at me, Mother!

AMANDA *(Following him).* I'm not grabbing at you. I want to know where you're going now.

TOM *(Taking overcoat and starts crossing to door* R.*)* I'm going to the movies!

AMANDA *(Crosses* C*).* I don't believe that lie!

TOM *(Crosses back to* AMANDA*).* No? Well, you're right. For once in your life you're right. I'm not going to the movies. I'm going to opium dens! Yes, Mother, opium dens, dens of vice and criminals' hang-outs, Mother. I've joined the Hogan gang. I'm a hired assassin, I carry a tommy-gun in a violin case! I run a string of cathouses in the valley! They call me Killer, Killer Wingfield, I'm really leading a double life. By day I'm a simple, honest warehouse worker, but at night I'm a dynamic czar of the underworld. Why, I go to gambling casinos and spin away a fortune on the roulette table! I wear a patch over one eye and a false moustache, sometimes I wear green whiskers. On those occasions they call me—El Diablo![4] Oh, I could tell you things to make you sleepless! My enemies plan to dynamite this place some night! Some night they're going to blow us all sky-high. And will I be glad! Will I be happy! And so will you be. You'll go up—up—over Blue Mountain on a broomstick! With seventeen gentlemen callers. You ugly babbling old witch! *(He goes through a series of violent, clumsy movements, seizing his overcoat, lunging to* R. *door, pulling it fiercely open. The*

---

4. *El Diablo* (el di äb′lô), the devil. [*Spanish*]

women watch him, aghast. His arm catches in the sleeve of the coat as he struggles to pull it on. For a moment he is pinioned by the bulky garment. With an outraged groan he tears the coat off again, splitting the shoulder of it, and hurls it across the room. It strikes against the shelf of LAURA's *glass collection, there is a tinkle of shattering glass.* LAURA *cries out as if wounded.)*

LAURA. My glass!—menagerie . . . *(She covers her face and turns away.* MUSIC CUE #8 *though to end of scene.)*

AMANDA *(In an awful voice).* I'll never speak to you again as long as you live unless you apologize to me! *(*AMANDA *exits through living-room curtains.* TOM *is left with* LAURA. *He stares at her stupidly for a moment. Then he crosses to shelf holding glass menagerie. Drops awkwardly on his knees to collect fallen glass, glancing at* LAURA *as if he would speak, but couldn't. Blackout.* TOM, AMANDA *and* LAURA *exit in blackout.)*

Act One SCENE 4

The interior is dark. Faint light in alley R. *A deep-voiced bell in a church is tolling the hour of five as the scene commences.*

TOM *appears at the top of* R. *alley. After each solemn boom of the bell in the tower he shakes a little toy noisemaker or rattle as if to express the tiny spasm of man in contrast to the sustained power and dignity of the Almighty. This and the unsteadiness of his advance make it evident that he has been drinking. As he climbs the few steps to the fire-escape landing light steals up inside.* LAURA *appears in night-dress, entering living-room from* L. *door of dining-room, observing* TOM's *empty bed (day-bed) in the living-room.* TOM *fishes in his pockets for door-key, removing a motley assortment of articles in the search, including a perfect shower of movie-ticket stubs and an empty bottle. At last he finds the key, but just as he is about to insert it, it slips from his fingers. He strikes a match and crouches below the door.*

TOM *(Bitterly).* One crack—and it falls through! *(*LAURA *opens door* R.*)*[1]

LAURA. Tom! Tom, what are you doing?

TOM. Looking for a door-key.

LAURA. Where have you been all this time?

TOM. I have been to the movies.

LAURA. All this time at the movies?

TOM. There was a very long program. There was a Garbo picture and a Mickey Mouse and a travelogue and a newsreel and a preview of coming attractions. And there was an organ solo and a collection for the milk-fund—simultaneously—which ended up in a terrible fight between a fat lady and an usher!

LAURA *(Innocently).* Did you have to stay through everything?

TOM. Of course! And, oh, I forgot! There was a big stage show! The headliner on this stage show was Malvolio the Magician. He performed wonderful tricks, many of them, such as pouring water back and forth between pitchers. First it turned to wine and then it turned to beer and then it turned to whiskey. I know it was whiskey it finally turned into because he needed somebody to come up out of the audience to help him, and I came up—both shows! It was Kentucky Straight Bourbon. A very generous fellow, he gave souvenirs. *(He pulls from his back pocket a shimmering rainbow-colored scarf.)* He gave me this. This is his magic scarf. You can have it, Laura. You wave it over a canary cage and you get a bowl of gold-fish. You wave it over the gold-fish bowl and they fly away canaries. . . . But the wonderfullest trick of all was the coffin trick. We nailed him into a coffin and he got out of the coffin without removing one nail. *(They enter.)* There is a trick that would come in handy for me—get me out of this 2 by 4 situation! *(Flops onto day-bed and starts removing shoes.)*

LAURA. Tom—shhh!

TOM. What're you shushing me for?

LAURA. You'll wake up Mother.

TOM. Goody goody! Pay'er back for all those "Rise an' Shines." *(Lies down groaning.)* You know it don't take much intelligence to get yourself into a nailed-up coffin, Laura. But who in hell ever got himself out of one without

---

1. *Laura opens door* R. The next few speeches are spoken on fire-escape landing.

removing one nail? (*As if in answer, the father's grinning photograph lights up.* LAURA *exits up* L. *Lights fade except for blue glow in dining-room. Pause after lights fade, then clock chimes six times. This is followed by the alarm clock. Dim in fore-stage.*)

Act One SCENE 5

Scene is the same. Immediately following. The churchbell is heard striking six. At the sixth stroke the alarm clock goes off in AMANDA'*s room off* R. *of dining-room and after a few moments we hear her calling, "Rise and shine! Rise and shine!* LAURA, *go tell your brother to rise and shine!"*

TOM (*Sitting up slowly in day-bed*). I'll rise—but I won't shine. (*The light increases.*)

AMANDA (*Offstage*). Laura, tell your brother his coffee is ready. (LAURA, *fully dressed, a cape over her shoulders, slips into living-room.* TOM *is still in bed, covered with blanket, having taken off only shoes and coat.*)

LAURA. Tom!—It's nearly seven. Don't make Mother nervous. (*He stares at her stupidly. Beseechingly.*) Tom, speak to Mother this morning. Make up with her, apologize, speak to her!

TOM (*Putting on shoes*). She won't to me. It's her that started not speaking.

LAURA. If you just say you're sorry she'll start speaking.

TOM. Her not speaking—is that such a tragedy?

LAURA. Please—please!

AMANDA (*Calling offstage* R. *from kitchen*). Laura, are you going to do what I asked you to do, or do I have to get dressed and go out myself?

LAURA. Going, going—soon as I get on my coat! (*She rises and crosses to door* R.) Butter and what else?

(*To* AMANDA.)

AMANDA (*Offstage*). Just butter. Tell them to charge it.

LAURA. Mother, they make such faces when I do that.

AMANDA (*Offstage*). Sticks and stones can break our bones, but the expression on Mr. Garfinkel's face won't harm us! Tell your brother his coffee is getting cold.

LAURA (*At door* R.). Do what I asked you, will you, will you, Tom? (*He looks sullenly away.*)

AMANDA. Laura, go now or just don't go at all!

LAURA (*Rushing out* R.). Going—going! (*A second later she cries out. Falls on fire-escape landing.* TOM *springs up and crosses to door* R. AMANDA *rushes anxiously in from dining-room, puts dishes on dining-room table.* TOM *opens door* R.)

TOM. Laura?

LAURA. I'm all right. I slipped, but I'm all right. (*Goes up* R. *alley, out of sight.*)

AMANDA (*On fire-escape*). I tell you if anybody falls down and breaks a leg on those fire-escape steps, the landlord ought to be sued for every cent he——(*Sees* TOM.) Who are you? (*Leaves fire-escape landing, crosses to dining-room and returns with bowls, coffee cup, cream, etc. Puts them on small table* R. *of day-bed, crosses to armchair, sits. Counts 3.* MUSIC CUE #9. *As* TOM *reenters* R., *listlessly for his coffee, she turns her back to him, as she sits in armchair. The light on her face with its aged but childish features is cruelly sharp, satirical as a Daumier print.* TOM *glances sheepishly but sullenly at her averted figure and sits on day-bed next to the food. The coffee is scalding hot, he sips it and gasps and spits it back in the cup. At his gasp,* AMANDA *catches her breath and half turns. Then catches herself and turns away.* TOM *blows on his coffee, glancing sidewise at his mother. She clears her throat.* TOM *clears his. He starts to rise. Sinks back down again, scratches his head, clears his throat again.* AMANDA *coughs.* TOM *raises his cup in both hands to blow on it, his eyes staring over the rim of it at his mother for several moments. Then he slowly sets the cup down and awkwardly and hesitantly rises from day-bed.*)

TOM (*Hoarsely*). I'm sorry, Mother. I'm sorry for all those things I said. I didn't mean it. I apologize.

AMANDA (*Sobbingly*). My devotion has made me a witch and so I make myself hateful to my children!

TOM. No, you don't.

AMANDA. I worry so much, I don't sleep, it makes me nervous!

TOM (Gently). I understand that.

AMANDA. You know I've had to put up a solitary battle all these years. But you're my right hand bower! Now don't fail me. Don't fall down.

TOM (Gently). I try, Mother.

AMANDA (With great enthusiasm). That's all right! You just keep on trying and you're bound to succeed. Why, you're—you're just full of natural endowments! Both my children are—they're very precious children and I've got an awful lot to be thankful for; you just must promise me one thing.

(MUSIC CUE #9 stops.)

TOM. What is it, Mother?

AMANDA. Promise me you're never going to become a drunkard!

TOM. I promise, Mother. I won't ever become a drunkard!

AMANDA. That's what frightened me so, that you'd be drinking! Eat a bowl of Purina.

TOM. Just coffee, Mother.

AMANDA. Shredded Wheat Biscuit?

TOM. No, no, Mother, just coffee.

AMANDA. You can't put in a day's work on an empty stomach. You've got ten minutes—don't gulp! Drinking too-hot liquids makes cancer of the stomach. . . . Put cream in.

TOM. No, thank you.

AMANDA. To cool it.

TOM. No! No, thank you, I want it black.

AMANDA. I know, but it's not good for you. We have to do all that we can to build ourselves up. In these trying times we live in, all that we have to cling to is—each other . . . That's why it's so important to—Tom, I—I sent out your sister so I could discuss something with you. If you hadn't spoken I would have spoken to you. (Sits down.)

TOM (Gently). What is it, Mother, that you want to discuss?

AMANDA. Laura! (TOM puts his cup down slowly. MUSIC CUE #10.)

TOM. —Oh.—Laura . . .

AMANDA (Touching his sleeve). You know how Laura is. So quiet but—still water runs deep! She notices things and I think she—broods about them. (TOM looks up.) A few days ago I came in and she was crying.

TOM. What about?

AMANDA. You.

TOM. Me?

AMANDA. She has an idea that you're not happy here.

(MUSIC CUE #10 stops.)

TOM. What gave her that idea?

AMANDA. What gives her any idea? However, you do act strangely. (TOM slaps cup down on small table.) I—I'm not criticizing, understand that! I know your ambitions do not lie in the warehouse, that like everybody in the whole wide world—you've had to—make sacrifices, but—Tom—Tom—life's not easy, it calls for—Spartan endurance! There's so many things in my heart that I cannot describe to you! I've never told you but I—loved your father . . .

TOM (Gently). I know that, Mother.

AMANDA. And you—when I see you taking after his ways! Staying out late—and—well, you had been drinking the night you were in that—terrifying condition! Laura says that you hate the apartment and that you go out nights to get away from it! Is that true, Tom?

TOM. No. You say there's so much in your heart that you can't describe to me. That's true of me, too. There's so much in my heart that I can't describe to you! So let's respect each other's—

AMANDA. But why—why, Tom—are you always so restless? Where do you go to, nights?

TOM. I—go to the movies.

AMANDA. Why do you go to the movies so much, Tom?

TOM. I go to the movies because—I like adventure. Adventure is something I don't have much of at work, so I go to the movies.

AMANDA. But, Tom, you go to the movies entirely too much!

TOM. I like a lot of adventure. (AMANDA looks baffled, then hurt. As the familiar inquisition resumes he becomes hard and impatient again. AMANDA slips back into her querulous attitude toward him.)

AMANDA. Most young men find adventure in their careers.

TOM. Then most young men are not employed in a warehouse.

AMANDA. The world is full of young men employed in warehouses and offices and factories.

TOM. Do all of them find adventure in their careers?

AMANDA. They do or they do without it! Not everybody has a craze for adventure.

TOM. Man is by instinct a lover, a hunter, a fighter, and none of those instincts are given much play at the warehouse!

AMANDA. Man is by instinct! Don't quote instinct to me! Instinct is something that people have got away from! It belongs to animals! Christian adults don't want it!

TOM. What do Christian adults want, then, Mother?

AMANDA. Superior things! Things of the mind and the spirit! Only animals have to satisfy instincts! Surely your aims are somewhat higher than theirs! Than monkeys—pigs——

TOM. I reckon they're not.

AMANDA. You're joking. However, that isn't what I wanted to discuss.

TOM *(Rising).* I haven't much time.

AMANDA *(Pushing his shoulders).* Sit down.

TOM. You want me to punch in red at the warehouse, Mother?

AMANDA. You have five minutes. I want to talk about Laura.

TOM. All right! What about Laura?

AMANDA. We have to be making some plans and provisions for her. She's older than you, two years, and nothing has happened. She just drifts along doing nothing. It frightens me terribly how she just drifts along.

TOM. I guess she's the type that people call home girls.

AMANDA. There's no such type, and if there is, it's a pity! That is unless the home is hers, with a husband!

TOM. What?

AMANDA *(Crossing* D. R. *to armchair).* Oh, I can see the handwriting on the wall as plain as I see the nose in front of my face! It's terrifying! More and more you remind me of your father! He was out all *(Sits in armchair)* hours without explanation!—Then left! Good-bye! And me with the bag to hold. I saw that letter you got from the Merchant Marine. I know what you're dreaming of. I'm not standing here blindfolded. Very well, then. Then do it! But not till there's somebody to take your place.

TOM. What do you mean?

AMANDA. I mean that as soon as Laura has got somebody to take care of her, married, a home of her own, independent—why, then you'll be free to go wherever you please, *(Rises, crosses to* TOM*)* on land, on sea, whichever way the wind blows you! But until that time you've got to look out for your sister. *(Crosses* R. *behind armchair.)* I don't say me because I'm old and don't matter! I say for your sister because she's young and dependent. I put her in business college—a dismal failure! Frightened her so it made her sick at the stomach! I took her over to the Young People's League at the church. Another fiasco. She spoke to nobody, nobody spoke to her. *(Sits armchair.)* Now all she does is fool with those pieces of glass and play those worn-out records. What kind of a life is that for a girl to lead?

TOM. What can I do about it?

AMANDA. Overcome selfishness! Self, self, self is all that you ever think of! *(*TOM *springs up and crosses* R. *to get his coat and put it on. It is ugly and bulky. He pulls on a cap with earmuffs.)* Where is your muffler? Put your wool muffler on! *(He snatches it angrily from the hook and tosses it around his neck and pulls both ends tight.)* Tom! I haven't said what I had in mind to ask you.

TOM. I'm too late to——

AMANDA *(Catching his arm—very importunately. Then shyly).* Down at the warehouse, aren't there some—nice young men?

TOM. No!

AMANDA. There must be—some . . .

TOM. Mother——*(Gesture.)*

AMANDA. Find out one that's clean-living—doesn't drink and—ask him out for sister!

TOM. What?

AMANDA. For sister! To meet! Get acquainted!

TOM *(Stamping to door* R.*).* Oh, my go-osh!

AMANDA. Will you? *(He opens door. Imploringly.)* Will you? *(He starts out.)* Will you? Will you, dear? *(*TOM *exits up alley* R. AMANDA *is on fire-escape landing.)*

TOM *(Calling back).* Yes!

AMANDA (*Re-entering* R. *and crossing to phone.* MUSIC CUE #11). Ella Cartwright? Ella, this is Amanda Wingfield. First, first, how's that kidney trouble? Oh, it has? It has come back? Well, you're just a Christian martyr, you're just a Christian martyr. I was noticing in my little red book that your subscription to the "Companion" has run out just when that wonderful new serial by Bessie Mae Harper was starting. It's all about the horsey set on Long Island. Oh, you have? You have read it? Well, how do you think it turns out? Oh, no. Bessie Mae Harper never lets you down. Oh, of course, we have to have complications. You have to have complications—oh, you can't have a story without them—but Bessie Mae Harper always leaves you with such an uplift——What's the matter, Ella? You sound so mad. Oh, because it's seven o'clock in the morning. Oh, Ella, I forgot that you never got up until nine. I forgot that anybody in the world was allowed to sleep as late as that. I can't say any more than I'm sorry, can I? Oh, you will? You're going to take that subscription from me anyhow? Well, bless you, Ella, bless you, bless you, bless you. (MUSIC #11 *faces into* MUSIC CUE #11-A, *dance music, and continues into next scene. Dim out lights.* MUSIC CUE #11-A.)

Act One SCENE 6

SCENE: *The same.—Only* R. *alley lighted, with dim light.*

TOM (*Enters down* R. *and stands as before, leaning against grillwork, with cigarette, wearing merchant sailor coat and cap*). Across the alley was the Paradise Dance Hall. Evenings in spring they'd open all the doors and windows and the music would come outside. Sometimes they'd turn out all the lights except for a large glass sphere that hung from the ceiling. It would turn slowly about and filter the dusk with delicate rainbow colors. Then the orchestra would play a waltz or a tango, something that had a slow and sensuous rhythm. The young couples would come outside, to the relative privacy of the alley. You could see them kissing behind ashpits and telephone poles. This was the compensation for lives that passed like mine, without change or adventure. Changes and adventure, however, were imminent this year. They were waiting around the corner for all these dancing kids. Suspended in the mist over Berchtesgaden, caught in the folds of Chamberlain's umbrella.[1] In Spain there was Guernica![2] Here there was only hot swing music and liquor, dance halls, bars, and movies, and sex that hung in the gloom like a chandelier and flooded the world with brief, deceptive rainbows. . . . While these unsuspecting kids danced to "Dear One, The World Is Waiting for the Sunrise." All the world was really waiting for bombardments. (MUSIC #11-A *stops. Dim in dining-room: faint glow.* AMANDA *is seen in dining-room.*)

AMANDA. Tom, where are you?

TOM (*Standing as before*). I came out to smoke. (*Exit* R. *into the wings, where he again changes coats and leaves hat.*)

AMANDA (TOM *re-enters and stands on fire-escape landing, smoking. He opens door for* AMANDA, *who sits on hassock on landing*). Oh, you smoke too much. A pack a day at fifteen cents a pack. How much would that be in a month? Thirty times fifteen? It wouldn't be very much. Well, it would be enough to help towards a night-school course in accounting at the Washington U! Wouldn't that be lovely?

TOM. I'd rather smoke.

AMANDA. I know! That's the tragedy of you. This fire-escape landing is a poor excuse for the porch we used to have. What are you looking at?

TOM. The moon.

AMANDA. Is there a moon this evening?

TOM. It's rising over Garfinkel's Delicatessen.

---

1. *Berchtesgaden* (bĕrн′təs gä′dən) . . . *Chamberlain's umbrella.* Adolph Hitler, the German Chancellor, was visited at Berchtesgaden, his mountain retreat, by Britain's Prime Minister, Neville Chamberlain, in 1938. Chamberlain agreed to let Hitler annex part of Czechoslovakia in return for a pledge of peace by Hitler. Hitler's breaking of this pledge brought on World War II.
2. *Guernica* (ger nē′kä), a town in northern Spain, held by the democratic faction during the Spanish Civil War. It was bombed in 1937 by German airplanes supporting Fascist forces and thus became a symbol of the cruelty of the Fascist overthrow of the Spanish Republic.

AMANDA. Oh! So it is! Such a little silver slipper of a moon. Have you made a wish on it?

TOM. Um-mm.

AMANDA. What did you wish?

TOM. That's a secret.

AMANDA. All right, I won't tell you what I wished, either. I can keep a secret, too. I can be just as mysterious as you.

TOM. I bet I can guess what you wished.

AMANDA. Why, is my head transparent?

TOM. You're not a sphinx.

AMANDA. No, I don't have secrets. I'll tell you what I wished for on the moon. Success and happiness for my precious children. I wish for that whenever there's a moon, and when there isn't a moon, I wish for it, too.

TOM. I thought perhaps you wished for a gentleman caller.

AMANDA. Why do you say that?

TOM. Don't you remember asking me to fetch one?

AMANDA. I remember suggesting that it would be nice for your sister if you brought home some nice young man from the warehouse. I think that I've made that suggestion more than once.

TOM. Yes, you have made it repeatedly.

AMANDA. Well?

TOM. We are going to have one.

AMANDA. *What?*

TOM. A gentleman caller!

AMANDA. You mean you have asked some nice young man to come over? (*Rising from stool, facing* TOM.)

TOM. I've asked him to dinner.

AMANDA. You really did?

TOM. I did.

AMANDA. And did he—accept?

TOM. He did!

AMANDA. He did?

TOM. He did.

AMANDA. Well, isn't that lovely!

TOM. I thought that you would be pleased.

AMANDA. It's definite, then?

TOM. Oh, very definite.

AMANDA. How soon?

TOM. Pretty soon.

AMANDA. How soon?

TOM. Quite soon.

AMANDA. How soon?

TOM. Very, very soon.

AMANDA. Every time I want to know anything you start going on like that.

TOM. What do you want to know?

AMANDA. Go ahead and guess. Go ahead and guess.

TOM. All right, I'll guess. You want to know when the gentleman caller's coming—he's coming tomorrow.

AMANDA. Tomorrow? Oh, no, I can't do anything about tomorrow. I can't do anything about tomorrow.

TOM. Why not?

AMANDA. That doesn't give me any time.

TOM. Time for what?

AMANDA. Time for preparations. Oh, you should have phoned me the minute you asked him—the minute he accepted!

TOM. You don't have to make any fuss.

AMANDA. Of course I have to make a fuss! I can't have a man coming into a place that's all sloppy. It's got to be thrown together properly. I certainly have to do some fast thinking by tomorrow night, too.

TOM. I don't see why you have to think at all.

AMANDA. That's because you just don't know. (*Enter living-room, crosses to* C. *Dim in living-room.*) You just don't know, that's all. We can't have a gentleman caller coming into a pig-sty! Now, let's see. Oh, I've got those three pieces of wedding silver left. I'll polish that up. I wonder how that old lace tablecloth is holding up all these years? We can't wear anything. We haven't got it. We haven't got anything to wear. We haven't got it. (*Goes back to door* R.)

TOM. Mother! This boy is no one to make a fuss over.

AMANDA (*Crossing to* C.). I don't know how you can say that when this is the first gentleman caller your little sister's ever had! I think it's pathetic that that little girl has never had a single gentleman caller! Come on inside! Come on inside!

TOM. What for?

AMANDA. I want to ask you a few things.

TOM (*From doorway* R.). If you're going to make a fuss, I'll call the whole thing off. I'll call the boy up and tell him not to come.

AMANDA. No! You mustn't ever do that. People hate broken engagements. They have no place to go. Come on inside. Come on inside. Will you come inside when I ask you to come inside? Sit down. (TOM *comes into living-room.*)

TOM. Any particular place you want me to sit?

AMANDA. Oh! Sit anywhere. (TOM *sits armchair* R.) Look! What am I going to do about that? *(Looking at day-bed.)* Did you ever see anything look so sad? I know, I'll get a bright piece of cretonne. That won't cost much. And I made payments on a floor lamp. So I'll have that sent out! And I can put a bright cover on the chair. I wish I had time to paper the walls. What's his name?

TOM. His name is O'Connor.

AMANDA. O'Connor—he's Irish and tomorrow's Friday—that means fish. Well, that's all right, I'll make a salmon loaf and some mayonnaise dressing for it. Where did you meet him? *(Crosses to day-bed and sits.)*

TOM. At the warehouse, of course. Where else would I meet him?

AMANDA. Well, I don't know. Does he drink?

TOM. What made you ask me that?

AMANDA. Because your father did.

TOM. Now, don't get started on that!

AMANDA. He drinks, then.

TOM. No, not that I know of.

AMANDA. You have to find out. There's nothing I want less for my daughter than a man who drinks.

TOM. Aren't you being a little bit premature? After all, poor Mr. O'Connor hasn't even appeared on the scene yet.

AMANDA. But he will tomorrow. To meet your sister. And what do I know about his character? *(Rises and crosses to* TOM *who is still in armchair, smooths his hair.)*

TOM *(Submitting grimly).* Now what are you up to?

AMANDA. I always did hate that cowlick. I never could understand why it won't sit down by itself.

TOM. Mother, I want to tell you something and I mean it sincerely right straight from my heart. There's a lot of boys who meet girls which they don't marry!

AMANDA. You know you always had me worried because you could never stick to a subject. *(Crosses to day-bed.)* What I want to know is what's his position at the warehouse?

TOM. He's a shipping clerk.

AMANDA. Oh! Shipping clerk! Well, that's fairly important. That's where you'd be if you had more get-up. How much does he earn? *(Sits on day-bed.)*

TOM. I have no way of knowing that for sure. I judge his salary to be approximately eighty-five dollars a month.

AMANDA. Eighty-five dollars? Well, that's not princely.

TOM. It's twenty dollars more than I make.

AMANDA. I know that. Oh, how well I know that! How well I know that! Eighty-five dollars a month. No. It can't be done. A family man can never get by on eighty-five dollars a month.

TOM. Mother, Mr. O'Connor is not a family man.

AMANDA. Well, he might be some time in the future, mightn't he?

TOM. Oh, I see. . . . Plans and provisions.

AMANDA. You are the only young man that I know of who ignores the fact that the future becomes the present, the present the past, and the past turns into everlasting regret if you don't plan for it.

TOM. I will think that over and see what I can make of it!

AMANDA. Don't be supercilious with your mother! Tell me some more about this.—What do you call him? Mr. O'Connor, Mr. O'Connor. He must have another name besides Mr.——?

TOM. His full name is James D. O'Connor. The D. is for Delaney.

AMANDA. Delaney? Irish on both sides and he doesn't drink?

TOM *(Rises from armchair).* Shall I call him up and ask him? *(Starts toward phone.)*

AMANDA *(Crossing to phone).* No!

TOM. I'll call him up and tell him you want to know if he drinks. *(Picks up phone.)*

AMANDA *(Taking phone away from him).* No, you can't do that. You have to be discreet about that subject. When I was a girl in Blue Mountain if it was (TOM *sits on* R. *of day-bed*) suspected that a young man was drinking and any girl was receiving his attentions—if any girl *was* receiving his attentions, she'd go to the minister of his church and ask about his character—or her father, if her father was living, then it was his duty to go to the minister of his church and ask about his character, and that's how young girls in Blue Mountain were kept from making tragic mistakes. *(Picture dims in and out.)*[3]

TOM. How come you made such a tragic one?

AMANDA. Oh, I don't know how he did it, but that face fooled everybody. All he had to do was grin and the world was bewitched. *(Behind day-bed, crosses to armchair.)* I don't know of anything more tragic than a young girl just putting herself at the mercy of a handsome appearance, and I hope Mr. O'Connor is *not* too goodlooking.

TOM. As a matter of fact he isn't. His face is covered with freckles and he has a very large nose.

AMANDA. He's not right-down homely?

TOM. No. I wouldn't say right-down—homely—medium homely, I'd say.

AMANDA. Well, if a girl had any sense she'd look for character in a man anyhow.

TOM. That's what I've always said, Mother.

AMANDA. You've always said it—you've always said it! How could you've always said it when you never even thought about it?

TOM. Aw, don't be so suspicious of me.

AMANDA. I am. I'm suspicious of every word that comes out of your mouth, when you talk to me, but I want to know about this young man. Is he up and coming?

TOM. Yes. I really do think he goes in for self-improvement.

AMANDA. What makes you think it?

TOM. He goes to night school.

AMANDA. Well, what does he do there at night school?

TOM. He's studying radio engineering and public speaking.

AMANDA. Oh! Public speaking! Oh, that shows, that shows that he intends to be an executive some day—and radio engineering. Well, that's coming . . . huh?

TOM. I think it's here.

AMANDA. Well, those are all very illuminating facts. *(Crosses to back of armchair.)* Facts that every mother should know about any young man calling on her daughter, seriously or not.

TOM. Just one little warning, Mother. I didn't tell him anything about Laura. I didn't let on we had dark ulterior motives. I just said, "How about coming home to dinner some time?" and he said, "Fine," and that was the whole conversation.

AMANDA. I bet it was, too. I tell you, sometimes you can be as eloquent as an oyster. However, when he sees how pretty and sweet that child is, he's going to be, well, he's going to be very glad he was asked over here to have some dinner. *(Sits in armchair.)*

TOM. Mother, just one thing. You won't expect too much of Laura, will you?

AMANDA. I don't know what you mean. *(TOM crosses slowly to AMANDA. He stands for a moment, looking at her. Then—)*

TOM. Well, Laura seems all those things to you and me because she's ours and we love her. We don't even notice she's crippled any more.

AMANDA. Don't use that word.

TOM. Mother, you have to face the facts; she is, and that's not all.

AMANDA. What do you mean "that's not all"? *(TOM kneels by her chair.)*

TOM. Mother—you know that Laura is very different from other girls.

AMANDA. Yes, I do know that, and I think that difference is all in her favor, too.

TOM. Not quite all—in the eyes of others—strangers—she's terribly shy. She lives in a world of her own and those things make her seem a little peculiar to people outside the house.

AMANDA. Don't use that word peculiar.

TOM. You have to face the facts.—She is.

AMANDA. I don't know in what way she's peculiar. *(MUSIC CUE #12, till curtain. TOM pauses a moment for music, then—)*

TOM. Mother, Laura lives in a world of little glass animals. She plays old phonograph records—and—that's about all——*(TOM rises slowly, goes quietly out the door R., leaving it open, and exits slowly up the alley. AMANDA rises, goes on to fire-escape landing R., looks at moon.)*

AMANDA. Laura! Laura! *(LAURA answers from kitchen R.)*

LAURA. Yes, Mother.

---

3. *Picture dims in and out.* See note 5, page 511.

AMANDA. Let those dishes go and come in front! (LAURA *appears with dish towel. Gaily.*) Laura, come here and make a wish on the moon!

LAURA (*Entering from kitchen* R. *and comes down to fire-escape landing*). Moon—moon?

AMANDA. A little silver slipper of a moon. Look over your left shoulder, Laura, and make a wish! (LAURA *looks faintly puzzled as if called out of sleep.* AMANDA *seizes her shoulders and turns her at an angle on the fire-escape landing.*) Now! Now, darling, wish!

LAURA. What shall I wish for, Mother?

AMANDA (*Her voice trembling and her eyes suddenly filling with tears*). Happiness! And just a little bit of good fortune! (*The stage dims out.*)

CURTAIN
End of Act One

Discussion

Early in a play, a dramatist usually makes the characters introduce themselves. This process, known as *dramatic exposition,* shows characters in situations where they reveal enough of their past and their personalities to clarify their present situation and relationships.

Scene 1

1. (a) In what ways does the initial stage setting (music and lighting, as well as scenery) create the mood of a "memory play"? **(b)** Summarize what the stage notes and Tom's remarks tell about his family's past and present situation.
2. What differences in temperament do you notice between Tom as Narrator and Tom as Character?
3. Which incidents early in the play reveal tension in the family?
4. (a) What past events does Amanda often recall? **(b)** What emotional value do they have for her? **(c)** What clues are there that her past was not exactly as she remembers it?

Scene 2

1. What do you learn about Laura's personality and self-concept?
2. (a) What efforts has Amanda made to help Laura? **(b)** Why have her efforts failed? **(c)** In what ways may Amanda unintentionally be making Laura's problems worse?
3. What new plan does Amanda decide upon toward the end of this scene?

Scenes 3 and 4

1. (a) What are the underlying causes of tension between Amanda and Tom? **(b)** How does Tom show his desire for independence? **(c)** What impression of his character do scenes 3 and 4 give you?
2. What tones of voice should the three actors use at various points in these scenes? Read examples aloud.

Scene 5

1. How does Amanda go about implementing the plan she has formed?
2. (a) Why does Amanda attempt to sell magazines by telephone? **(b)** What character traits are shown by this call and the one opening scene 3?

Scene 6

1. (a) Point out how Tom teases his mother with his announcement of the impending visit. **(b)** A play's humor is much more obvious on stage than in a book. What might actors do to emphasize humorous moments in this scene?
2. (a) How does this scene advance the action? **(b)** What indication is there of the fate of Amanda's plan?

Act Two SCENE 7

SCENE: *The same.*

Inner curtains closed between dining-room and living-room. Interiors of both rooms are dark as at beginning of play. TOM *has on the same jacket and cap as at first. Same dance-hall music as* CUE #1, *fading as* TOM *begins.*

TOM (*Discovered leaning against grill on fire-escape landing, as before, and smoking*). And so the following evening I brought Jim home to dinner. I had known Jim slightly in high school. In high school, Jim was a hero. He had tremendous Irish good nature and vitality with the scrubbed and polished look of white chinaware. He seemed to move in a continual spotlight. He was a star in basketball, captain of the debating club, president of the senior class and the glee club, and he sang the male lead in the annual light opera. He was forever running or bounding, never just walking. He seemed always just at the point of defeating the law of gravity. He was shooting with such velocity through his adolescence that you would just logically expect him to arrive at nothing short of the White House by the time he was thirty. But Jim apparently ran into more interference after his graduation from high school because his speed had definitely slowed. And so, at this particular time in our lives he was holding a job that wasn't much better than mine. He was the only one at the warehouse with whom I was on friendly terms. I was valuable to Jim as someone who could remember his former glory, who had seen him win basketball games and the silver cup in debating. He knew of my secret practice of retiring to a cabinet of the washroom to work on poems whenever business was slack in the warehouse. He called me Shakespeare. And while the other boys in the warehouse regarded me with suspicious hostility, Jim took a humorous attitude toward me. Gradually his attitude began to affect the other boys and their hostility wore off. And so, after a time they began to smile at me too, as people smile at some oddly fashioned dog that trots across their path at some distance. I knew that Jim and Laura had known each other in high school because I had heard my sister Laura speak admiringly of Jim's voice. I didn't know if Jim would remember her or not. Because in high school Laura had been as unobtrusive as Jim had been astonishing. And, if he did remember Laura, it was not as my sister, for when I asked him home to dinner, he smiled and said, "You know, a funny thing, Shakespeare, I never thought of you as having folks!" Well, he was about to discover that I did . . . (MUSIC CUE #13. TOM *exits* R. *Interior living-room lights dim in.* AMANDA *is sitting on small table* R. *of day-bed sewing on hem on* LAURA's *dress.* LAURA *stands facing the door* R. AMANDA *has worked like a Turk in preparation for the gentleman caller. The results are astonishing. The new floor lamp with its rose-silk shade is in place,* R. *of living-room next to wall, a colored paper lantern conceals the broken light fixture in the ceiling, chintz covers are on chairs and sofa, a pair of new sofa pillows make their initial appearance.* LAURA *stands in the middle of room with lifted arms while* AMANDA *crouches before her, adjusting the hem of the new dress, devout and ritualistic. The dress is colored and designed by memory. The arrangement of* LAURA's *hair is changed; it is softer and more becoming. A fragile, unearthly prettiness has come out in* LAURA; *she is like a piece of translucent glass touched by light, given a momentary radiance, not actual, not lasting.* AMANDA, *still seated, is sewing* LAURA's *dress.* LAURA *is standing* R. *of* AMANDA.)

AMANDA. Why are you trembling so, Laura?

LAURA. Mother, you've made me so nervous!

AMANDA. Why, how have I made you nervous?

LAURA. By all this fuss! You make it seem so important.

AMANDA. I don't understand you at all, honey. Every time I try to do anything for you that's the least bit different you just seem to set yourself against it. Now take a look at yourself. (LAURA *starts for door* R.) No, wait! Wait just a minute—I forgot something. (*Picks two powder puffs from day-bed.*)

LAURA. What is it?

AMANDA. A couple of improvements. (*Business with powder puffs.*) When I was a girl we had round little lacy things like that and we called them "Gay Deceivers."

LAURA. I won't wear them!

AMANDA. Of course you'll wear them.

LAURA. Why should I?

AMANDA. Well, to tell you the truth, honey, you're just a little bit flat-chested.

LAURA. You make it seem like we were setting a trap.

AMANDA. We are. All pretty girls are a trap and men expect them to be traps. Now look at yourself in that glass. (LAURA *crosses* R. *Looks at mirror, invisible to audience, which is in darkness up* R. *of* R. *door.*) See? You look just like an angel on a postcard. Isn't that lovely? Now you just wait. I'm going to dress myself up. You're going to be astonished at your mother's appearance. (END OF MUSIC CUE. *End of* MUSIC CUE *leads into dance music,[1] which then leads in* MUSIC CUE #14, *a few lines below, at stage direction.* AMANDA *exits through curtains upstage off* L. *in dining-room.* LAURA *looks in mirror for a moment. Removes "Gay Deceivers," hides them under mattress of day-bed. Sits on small table* R. *of day-bed for a moment, goes out to fire-escape landing, listens to dance music, until* AMANDA's *entrance.* AMANDA, *off.*) I found an old dress in the trunk. But what do you know? I had to do a lot to it but it broke my heart when I had to let it out. Now, Laura, just look at your mother. Oh, no! Laura, come look at me now! (*Enters dining-room* L. *door. Comes down through living-room curtain to living-room* C. MUSIC CUE #14.)

LAURA (*Re-enters from fire-escape landing. Sits on* L. *arm of armchair*). Oh, Mother, how lovely! (AMANDA *wears a girlish frock. She carries a bunch of jonquils.*)

AMANDA (*Standing* C., *holding flowers*). It used to be. It used to be. It had a lot of flowers on it, but they got awful tired so I had to take them all off. I led the cotillion in this dress years ago. I won the cake-walk twice at Sunset Hill, and I wore it to the Governor's ball in Jackson. You should have seen your mother. You should have seen your mother how she just sashayed around (*Crossing around* L. *of day-bed back to* C.) the ballroom, just like that. I had it on the day I met your father. I had malaria fever, too. The change of climate from East Tennessee to the Delta—weakened my resistance. Not enough to be dangerous, just enough to make me restless and giddy. Oh, it was lovely. Invi-

tations poured in from all over. My mother said, "You can't go any place because you have a fever. You have to stay in bed." I said I wouldn't and I took quinine and kept on going and going. Dances every evening and long rides in the country in the afternoon and picnics. That country—that country—so lovely—so lovely in May, all lacy with dogwood and simply flooded with jonquils. My mother said, "You can't bring any more jonquils in this house." I said, "I will," and I kept on bringing them in anyhow. Whenever I saw them I said, "Wait a minute, I see jonquils," and I'd make my gentlemen callers get out of the carriage and help me gather some. To tell you the truth, Laura, it got to be a kind of a joke. "Look out," they'd say, "here comes that girl and we'll have to spend the afternoon picking jonquils." My mother said, "You can't bring any more jonquils in the house, there aren't any more vases to hold them." "That's quite all right," I said, "I can hold some myself." Malaria fever, your father and jonquils. (AMANDA *puts jonquils in* LAURA's *lap and goes out on to fire-escape landing.* MUSIC CUE #14 *stops. Thunder heard.*) I hope they get here before it starts to rain. I gave your brother a little extra change so he and Mr. O'Connor could take the service car home. (LAURA *puts flowers on armchair* R., *and crosses to door* R.)

LAURA. Mother!

AMANDA. What's the matter now? (*Re-entering room.*)

LAURA. What did you say his name was?

AMANDA. O'Connor. Why?

LAURA. What is his first name?

AMANDA (*Crosses to armchair* R.). I don't remember—Oh, yes, I do too—it was—Jim! (*Picks up flowers.*)

LAURA. Oh, Mother, not Jim O'Connor!

AMANDA. Yes, that was it, it was Jim! I've never known a Jim that wasn't nice. (*Crosses* L., *behind day-bed, puts flowers in vase.*)

LAURA. Are you sure his name was Jim O'Connor?

AMANDA. Why, sure I'm sure. Why?

---

1. *dance music.* Optional. Not on regular record of incidental music to the play.

LAURA. Is he the one that Tom used to know in high school?

AMANDA. He didn't say so. I think he just got to know him—(*Sits on day-bed.*) at the warehouse.

LAURA. There was a Jim O'Connor we both knew in high school. If that is the one that Tom is bringing home to dinner——Oh, Mother, you'd have to excuse me, I wouldn't come to the table!

AMANDA. What's this now? What sort of silly talk is this?

LAURA. You asked me once if I'd ever liked a boy. Don't you remember I showed you this boy's picture?

AMANDA. You mean the boy in the year-book?

LAURA. Yes, that boy.

AMANDA. Laura, Laura, were you in love with that boy?

LAURA (*Crosses to* R. *of armchair*). I don't know, Mother. All I know is that I couldn't sit at the table if it was him.

AMANDA (*Rises, crosses* L. *and works up* L. *of day-bed*). It won't be him! It isn't the least bit likely. But whether it is or not, you will come to the table—you will not be excused.

LAURA. I'll have to be, Mother.

AMANDA (*Behind day-bed*). I don't intend to humor your silliness, Laura, I've had too much from you and your brother, both. So just sit down and compose yourself till they come. Tom has forgotten his key, so you'll *have* to let them in when they arrive.

LAURA. Oh, Mother—*you* answer the door! (*Sits chair* R.)

AMANDA. How can I when I haven't even finished making the mayonnaise dressing for the salmon?

LAURA. Oh, Mother, please answer the door, don't make me do it! (*Thunder heard off-stage.*)

AMANDA. Honey, do be reasonable! What's all this fuss about—just one gentleman caller— that's all—just one! (*Exits through living-room curtains.* TOM *and* JIM *enter alley* R., *climb fire-escape steps to landing and wait outside of closed door. Hearing them approach,* LAURA *rises with a panicky gesture. She retreats to living-room curtains. The doorbell rings.* LAURA *catches her breath and touches her throat. More thunder heard off-stage.*)

AMANDA (*Off-stage*). Laura, sweetheart, the door!

LAURA. Mother, please, you go to the door! (*Starts for door* R., *then back.*)

AMANDA (*Off-stage, in a fierce whisper*). What is the matter with you, you silly thing? (*Enters through living-room curtains, and stands by day-bed.*)

LAURA. Please you answer it, please.

AMANDA. Why have you chosen this moment to lose your mind? You go to that door.

LAURA. I can't.

AMANDA. Why can't you?

LAURA. Because I'm sick. (*Crosses to* L. *end of day-bed and sits.*)

AMANDA. You're sick! Am I sick? You and your brother have me puzzled to death. You can never act like normal children. Will you give me one good reason why you should be afraid to open a door? You go to that door. Laura Wingfield, you march straight to that door!

LAURA (*Crosses to door* R.). Yes, Mother.

AMANDA (*Stopping* LAURA). I've got to put courage in you, honey, for living. (*Exits through living-room curtains, and exits* R. *into kitchen.* LAURA *opens door.* TOM *and* JIM *enter.* LAURA *remains hidden in hall behind door.*)

TOM. Laura—(LAURA *crosses* C.) this is Jim. Jim, this is my sister Laura.

JIM. I didn't know that Shakespeare had a sister! How are you, Laura?

LAURA (*Retreating stiff and trembling. Shakes hands*). How—how do you do?

JIM. Well, I'm okay! Your hand's *cold*, Laura! (TOM *puts hats on phone table.*)

LAURA. Yes, well—I've been playing the victrola. . . .

JIM. Must have been playing classical music on it. You ought to play a little hot swing music to warm you up. (LAURA *crosses to phonograph.* TOM *crosses up to* LAURA. LAURA *starts phonograph*[2]—*looks at* JIM. *Exits through living-room curtains and goes off* L.)

JIM. What's the matter?

TOM. Oh—Laura? Laura is—is terribly shy. (*Crosses and sits on day-bed.*)

---

2. **Laura starts phonograph.** A worn record of "Dardanella" or some other popular tune of 1920s.

JIM (*Crosses down* C.). Shy, huh? Do you know it's unusual to meet a shy girl nowadays? I don't believe you ever mentioned you had a sister?

TOM. Well, now you know I have one. You want a piece of the paper?

JIM (*Crosses to* TOM). Uh-huh.

TOM. Comics?

JIM. Comics? Sports! (*Takes paper. Crosses, sits chair* R.) I see that Dizzy Dean[3] is on his bad behavior.

TOM (*Starts to door* R. *Goes out*). Really?

JIM. Yeah. Where are *you* going? (*As* TOM *reaches steps* R. *of fire-escape landing.*)

TOM (*Calling from fire-escape landing*). Out on the terrace to smoke.

JIM (*Rises, leaving newspaper in armchair, goes over to turn off victrola. Crosses* R. *Exits to fire-escape landing*). You know, Shakespeare—I'm going to sell you a bill of goods!

TOM. What goods?

JIM. A course I'm taking.

TOM. What course?

JIM. A course in public speaking! You know you and me, we're not the warehouse type.

TOM. Thanks—that's good news. What has public speaking got to do with it?

JIM. It fits you for—executive positions!

TOM. Oh.

JIM. I tell you it's done a helluva lot for me.

TOM. In what respect?

JIM. In all respects. Ask yourself: what's the difference betweeen you and me and the guys in the office down front? Brains?—No!—Ability?—No! Then what? Primarily, it amounts to just one single thing——

TOM. What is that one thing?

JIM. Social poise! The ability to square up to somebody and hold your own on any social level!

AMANDA (*Off-stage*). Tom?

TOM. Yes, Mother?

AMANDA. Is that you and Mr. O'Connor?

TOM. Yes, Mother.

AMANDA. Make yourselves comfortable.

TOM. We will.

AMANDA. Ask Mr. O'Connor if he would like to wash his hands?

JIM. No, thanks, ma'am—I took care of that down at the warehouse. Tom?

TOM. Huh?

JIM. Mr. Mendoza was speaking to me about you.

TOM. Favorably?

JIM. What do you think?

TOM. Well——

JIM. You're going to be out of a job if you don't wake up.

TOM. I'm waking up——

JIM. Yeah, but you show no signs.

TOM. The signs are interior. I'm just about to make a change. I'm right at the point of committing myself to a future that doesn't include the warehouse or Mr. Mendoza, or even a night school course in public speaking.

JIM. Now what are you gassing about?

TOM. I'm tired of the movies.

JIM. The movies!

TOM. Yes, movies! Look at them. (*He waves his hands.*) All of those glamorous people—having adventures—hogging it all, gobbling the whole thing up! You know what happens? People go to the *movies* instead of *moving.* Hollywood characters are supposed to have all the adventures for everybody in America, while everybody in America sits in a dark room and watches them having it! Yes, until there's a war. That's when adventure becomes available to the masses! Everyone's dish, not only Gable's! Then the people in the dark room come out of the dark room to have some adventures themselves—goody—goody! It's our turn now to go to the South Sea Island—to make a safari—to be exotic, far off! . . . But I'm not patient. I don't want to wait till then. I'm tired of the movies and I'm about to move!

JIM (*Incredulously*). Move?

TOM. Yes.

JIM. When?

TOM. Soon!

JIM. Where? Where?

TOM. I'm starting to boil inside. I know I seem dreamy, but inside—well, I'm boiling! Whenever I pick up a shoe I shudder a little, thinking how short life is and what I am doing!—Whatever that means, I know it doesn't mean shoes—except as something to

---

3. *Dizzy Dean,* a famous baseball pitcher, noted for eccentricity.

wear on a traveler's feet! (*Gets card from inside coat pocket.*) Look!

JIM. What?

TOM. I'm a member.

JIM (*Reading*). The Union of Merchant Seamen.

TOM. I paid my dues this month, instead of the electric light bill.

JIM. You'll regret it when they turn off the lights.

TOM. I won't be here.

JIM. Yeah, but how about your mother?

TOM. I'm like my father. The bastard son of a bastard. See how he grins? And he's been absent going on sixteen years.

JIM. You're just talking, you drip. How does your mother feel about it?

TOM. Sh! Here comes Mother! Mother's not acquainted with my plans!

AMANDA (*Off-stage*). Tom!

TOM. Yes, Mother?

AMANDA (*Off-stage*). Where are you all?

TOM. On the terrace, Mother.

AMANDA (*Enters through living-room curtain and stands* C.). Why don't you come in? (*They start inside. She advances to them.* TOM *is distinctly shocked at her appearance. Even* JIM *blinks a little. He is making his first contact with girlish Southern vivacity and in spite of the night-school course in public speaking is somewhat thrown off the beam by the unexpected outlay of social charm. Certain responses are attempted by* JIM *but are swept aside by* AMANDA*'s gay laughter and chatter.* TOM *is embarrassed but after the first shock* JIM *reacts very warmly. Grins and chuckles, is altogether won over.* TOM *and* JIM *come in, leaving door open.*)

TOM. Mother, you look so pretty.

AMANDA. You know, that's the first compliment you ever paid me. I wish you'd look pleasant when you're about to say something pleasant, so I could expect it. Mr. O'Connor? (JIM *crosses to* AMANDA.)

JIM. How do you do?

AMANDA. Well, well, well, so this is Mr. O'Connor? Introduction's entirely unnecessary. I've heard so much about you from my boy. I finally said to him, "Tom, good gracious, why don't you bring this paragon to supper finally? I'd like to meet this nice young man at the warehouse! Instead of just hearing you sing his praises so much?" I don't know why my son is so stand-offish—that's not Southern behavior. Let's sit down. (TOM *closes door, crosses* U. R.*, stands.* JIM *and* AMANDA *sit on day-bed,* JIM, R., AMANDA L.) Let's sit down, and I think we could stand a little more air in here. Tom, leave the door open. I felt a nice fresh breeze a moment ago. Where has it gone to? Mmmm, so warm already! And not quite summer, even. We're going to burn up when summer really gets started. However, we're having—we're having a very light supper. I think light things are better fo'—for this time of year. The same as light clothes are. Light clothes and light food are what warm weather calls fo'. You know our blood get so thick during th' winter—it takes a while fo' us to adjust ourselves—when the season changes. . . . It's come so quick this year. I wasn't prepared. All of a sudden—Heavens! Already summer!—I ran to the trunk an'—pulled out this light dress—terribly old! Historical almost! But feels so good—so good and cool, why, y' know——

TOM. Mother, how about our supper?

AMANDA (*Rises, crosses* R. *to* TOM). Honey, you go ask sister if supper is ready! You know that sister is in full charge of supper. Tell her you hungry boys are waiting for it. (TOM *exits through curtains and off* L. AMANDA *turns to* JIM.) Have you met Laura?

JIM. Well, she came to the door.

AMANDA. She let you in?

JIM. Yes, ma'am.

AMANDA (*Crossing to armchair and sitting*). She's very pretty.

JIM. Oh, yes ma'am.

AMANDA. It's rare for a girl as sweet an' pretty as Laura to be domestic! But Laura is, thank heavens, not only pretty but also very domestic. I'm not at all. I never was a bit. I never could make a thing but angel-food cake. Well, in the South we had so many servants. Gone, gone, gone. All vestige of gracious living! Gone completely! I wasn't prepared for what the future brought me. All of my gentlemen callers were sons of planters and so of course I assumed that I would be married to one and raise my family on a large piece of land with plenty of servants. But man proposes—and

woman accepts the proposal!—To vary that old, old saying a little bit—I married no planter! I married a man who worked for the telephone company!—That gallantly smiling gentleman over there! *(Points to picture.)* A telephone man who—fell in love with long-distance!—Now he travels and I don't even know where!—But what am I going on for about my—tribulations? Tell me yours—I hope you don't have any! Tom?

TOM *(Re-enters through living-room curtains from off* L.*).* Yes, Mother.

AMANDA. What about that supper?

TOM. Why, supper is on the table. *(Inner curtains between living-room and dining-room open. Lights dim up in dining-room, dim out in living-room.)*

AMANDA. Oh, so it is. *(Rises, crosses up to table* C. *in dining-room and chair* C.*)* How lovely. Where is Laura?

TOM *(Going to chair* L. *and standing).* Laura is not feeling too well and thinks maybe she'd better not come to the table.

AMANDA. Laura!

LAURA *(Off-stage. Faintly).* Yes, Mother? *(*TOM *gestures re:* JIM.*)*

AMANDA. Mr. O'Connor. *(*JIM *crosses up* L. *to table and to chair* L. *and stands.)*

JIM. Thank you, ma'am.

AMANDA. Laura, we can't say grace till you come to the table.

LAURA *(Enters* U. L., *obviously quite faint, lips trembling, eyes wide and staring. Moves unsteadily toward dining-room table).* Oh, Mother, I'm so sorry. *(*TOM *catches her as she feels faint. He takes her to day-bed in living-room.)*

AMANDA *(As* LAURA *lies down).* Why, Laura, you are sick, darling! Laura—rest on the sofa. Well! *(To* JIM.) Standing over the hot stove made her ill!—I told her that it was just too warm this evening, but——*(To* TOM.) Is Laura all right now?

TOM. She's better, Mother. *(Sits chair* L. *in dining-room. Thunder off-stage.)*

AMANDA *(Returning to dining-room and sitting at table, as* JIM *does).* My goodness, I suppose we're going to have a little rain! Tom, you say grace.

TOM. What?

AMANDA. What do we generally do before we have something to eat? We say grace, don't we?

TOM. For these and all Thy mercies—God's Holy Name be praised. *(Lights dim out.* MUSIC CUE #15.)

Act Two SCENE 8

SCENE: *The same. A half-hour later. Dinner is coming to an end in dining-room.*

AMANDA, TOM *and* JIM *sitting at table as at end of last scene. Lights dim up in both rooms, and* MUSIC CUE #15 *ends.*

AMANDA *(Laughing, as* JIM *laughs too).* You know, Mr. O'Connor, I haven't had such a pleasant evening in a very long time.

JIM *(Rises).* Well, Mrs. Wingfield, let me give you a toast. Here's to the old South.

AMANDA. The old South. *(Blackout in both rooms.)*

JIM. Hey, Mr. Light Bulb!

AMANDA. Where was Moses when the lights went out? Do you know the answer to that one, Mr. O'Connor?

JIM. No, ma'am, what's the answer to that one?

AMANDA. Well, I heard one answer, but it wasn't very nice. I thought you might know another one.

JIM. No, ma'am.

AMANDA. It's lucky I put those candles on the table. I just put them on for ornamentation, but it's nice when they prove useful, too.

JIM. Yes, ma'am.

AMANDA. Now, if one of you gentlemen can provide me with a match we can have some illumination.

JIM *(Lighting candles. Dim in glow for candles).* I can, ma'am.

AMANDA. Thank you.

JIM *(Crosses back to* R. *of dining-room table).* Not at all, ma'am.

AMANDA. I guess it must be a burnt-out fuse. Mr. O'Connor, do you know anything about a burnt-out fuse?

JIM. I know a little about them, ma'am, but where's the fuse box?

AMANDA. Must you know that, too? Well it's in the kitchen. *(*JIM *exits* R. *into kitchen.)* Be careful. It's dark. Don't stumble over anything. *(Sound of crash off-stage.)* Oh, my goodness, wouldn't it be awful if we lost him! Are you all right, Mr. O'Connor?

JIM *(Off-stage).* Yes, ma'am, I'm all right.

AMANDA. You know, electricity is a very mysterious thing. The whole universe is mysterious to me. Wasn't it Benjamin Franklin who tied a key to a kite? I'd like to have seen that—he might have looked mighty silly. Some people say that science clears up all the mysteries for us. In my opinion they just keep on adding more. Haven't you found it yet?

JIM *(Re-enters* R.). Yes, ma'am. I found it all right, but them fuses look okay to me. *(Sits as before.)*

AMANDA. Tom.

TOM. Yes, Mother?

AMANDA. That light bill I gave you several days ago. The one I got the notice about?

TOM. Oh—yeah. You mean last month's bill?

AMANDA. You didn't neglect it by any chance?

TOM. Well, I——

AMANDA. You did! I might have known it!

JIM. Oh, maybe Shakespeare wrote a poem on that light bill, Mrs. Wingfield?

AMANDA. Maybe he did, too. I might have known better than to trust him with it! There's such a high price for negligence in this world today.

JIM. Maybe the poem will win a ten-dollar prize.

AMANDA. We'll just have to spend the rest of

the evening in the nineteenth century, before Mr. Edison found that Mazda lamp!

JIM. Candle-light is my favorite kind of light.

AMANDA. That shows you're romantic! But that's no excuse for Tom. However, I think it was very nice of them to let us finish our dinner before they plunged us into everlasting darkness. Tom, as a penalty for your carelessness you can help me with the dishes.

JIM (Rising. TOM rises). Can I be of some help, ma'am?

AMANDA (Rising). Oh, no, I couldn't allow that.

JIM. Well, I ought to be good for *something*.

AMANDA. What did I hear?

JIM. I just said, "I ought to be good for something."

AMANDA. That's what I thought you said. Well, Laura's all by her lonesome out front. Maybe you'd like to keep her company. I can give you this lovely old candelabrum for light. (JIM *takes candles*.) It used to be on the altar at the Church of the Heavenly Rest, but it was melted a little out of shape when the church burnt down. The church was struck by lightning one spring, and Gypsy Jones who was holding a revival meeting in the village, said that the church was struck by lightning because the Episcopalians had started to have card parties right in the church.

JIM. Is that so, ma'am?

AMANDA. I never say anything that isn't so.

JIM. I beg your pardon.

AMANDA (Pouring wine into glass—hands it to JIM). I'd like Laura to have a little dandelion wine. Do you think you can hold them both?

JIM. I can try, ma'am.

AMANDA (Exits U. R. into kitchen). Now, Tom, you get into your apron.

TOM. Yes, Mother. (Follows AMANDA. JIM looks around, puts wine-glass down, takes swig from wine decanter, replaces it with thud, takes wine-glass—enters living-room. Inner curtains close as dining-room dims out. LAURA sits up nervously as JIM enters. Her speech at first is low and breathless from the almost intolerable strain of being alone with a stranger. In her speeches in this scene, before JIM's warmth overcomes her paralyzing shyness, LAURA's voice is thin and breathless as though she has just run up a steep flight of stairs.)

JIM (Entering holding candelabra with lighted candles in one hand and glass of wine in other, and stands). How are you feeling now? Any better? (JIM's attitude is gently humorous. In playing this scene it should be stressed that while the incident is apparently unimportant, it is to LAURA the climax of her secret life.)

LAURA. Yes, thank you.

JIM (Gives her glass of wine). Oh, here, this is for you. It's a little dandelion wine.

LAURA. Thank you.

JIM (Crosses C.). Well, drink it—but don't get drunk. (He laughs heartily.) Say, where'll I put the candles?

LAURA. Oh, anywhere . . .

JIM. Oh, how about right here on the floor? You got any objections?

LAURA. No.

JIM. I'll spread a newspaper under it to catch the drippings. (Gets newspaper from armchair. Puts candelabra down on floor C.) I like to sit on the floor. (Sits on floor.) Mind if I do?

LAURA. Oh, no.

JIM. Would you give me a pillow?

LAURA. What?

JIM. A pillow!

LAURA. Oh . . . (Puts wine-glass on telephone table, hands him pillow, sits L. on day-bed.)

JIM. How about you? Don't you like to sit on the floor?

LAURA. Oh, yes.

JIM. Well, why don't you?

LAURA. I—will.

JIM. Take a pillow! (Throws pillow as she sits on floor.) I can't see you sitting way over there. (Sits on floor again.)

LAURA. I can—see you.

JIM. Yeah, but that's not fair. I'm right here in the limelight. (LAURA moves a little closer to him.) Good! Now I can see you! Are you comfortable?

LAURA. Yes. Thank you.

JIM. So am I. I'm comfortable as a cow! Say, would you care for a piece of chewing-gum? (Offers gum.)

LAURA. No, thank you.

JIM. I think that I will indulge. (Musingly unwraps it and holds it up.) Gee, think of the fortune made by the guy that invented the first piece of chewing gum! It's amazing, huh? Do you know that the Wrigley Building is one of the sights of Chicago?—I saw it summer before last at the Century of Progress.[1] Did you take in the Century of Progress?

LAURA. No, I didn't.

JIM. Well, it was a wonderful exposition, believe me. You know what impressed me most? The Hall of Science. Gives you an idea of what the future will be like in America. Oh, it's more wonderful than the present time is! Say, your brother tells me you're shy. Is that right, Laura?

LAURA. I—don't know.

JIM. I judge you to be an old-fashioned type of girl. Oh, I think that's a wonderful type to be. I hope you don't think I'm being too personal—do you?

LAURA. Mr. O'Connor?

JIM. Huh?

LAURA. I believe I *will* take a piece of gum, if you don't mind. *(JIM peels gum—gets on knees, hands it to LAURA. She breaks off a tiny piece. JIM looks at what remains, puts it in his mouth, and sits again.)* Mr. O'Connor, have you—kept up with your singing?

JIM. Singing? Me?

LAURA. Yes. I remember what a beautiful voice you had.

JIM. You heard me sing?

LAURA. Oh, yes! Very often. . . . I—don't suppose—you remember me—at all?

JIM *(Smiling doubtfully).* You know, as a matter of fact I did have an idea I'd seen you before. Do you know it seemed almost like I was about to remember your name. But the name I was about to remember—wasn't a name! So I stopped myself before I said it.

LAURA. Wasn't it—Blue Roses?

JIM *(Grinning).* Blue Roses! Oh, my gosh, yes—Blue Roses! You know, I didn't connect you with high school somehow or other. But that's where it was, it was high school. Gosh, I didn't even know you were Shakespeare's sister! Gee, I'm sorry.

LAURA. I didn't expect you to.—You barely knew me!

JIM. But, we did have a speaking acquaintance.

LAURA. Yes, we—spoke to each other.

JIM. Say, didn't we have a class in something together?

LAURA. Yes, we did.

JIM. What class was that?

LAURA. It was—singing—chorus!

JIM. Aw!

LAURA. I sat across the aisle from you in the auditorium Mondays, Wednesdays, and Fridays.

JIM. Oh, yeah! I remember now—you're the one who always came in late.

LAURA. Yes, it was so hard for me, getting upstairs. I had that brace on my leg then—it clumped so loud!

JIM. I never heard any clumping.

LAURA *(Wincing at recollection).* To me it sounded like—thunder!

JIM. I never even noticed.

LAURA. Everybody was seated before I came in. I had to walk in front of all those people. My seat was in the back row. I had to go clumping up the aisle with everyone watching!

JIM. Oh, gee, you shouldn't have been selfconscious.

LAURA. I know, but I was. It was always such a relief when the singing started.

JIM. I remember now. And I used to call you Blue Roses. How did I ever get started calling you a name like that?

LAURA. I was out of school a little while with pleurosis. When I came back you asked me what was the matter. I said I had pleurosis and you thought I said Blue Roses. So that's what you always called me after that!

JIM. I hope you didn't mind?

LAURA. Oh, no—I liked it. You see, I wasn't acquainted with many—people . . .

JIM. Yeah. I remember you sort of stuck by yourself.

LAURA. I never did have much luck at making friends.

JIM. Well, I don't see why you wouldn't.

LAURA. Well, I started out badly.

JIM. You mean being——?

LAURA. Well, yes, it—sort of—stood between me . . .

JIM. You shouldn't have let it!

LAURA. I know, but it did, and I——

---

1. **Century of Progress,** the world's fair held in Chicago in 1933–1934.

JIM. You mean you were shy with people!

LAURA. I tried not to be but never could——

JIM. Overcome it?

LAURA. No, I—never could!

JIM. Yeah. I guess being shy is something you have to work out of kind of gradually.

LAURA. Yes—I guess it——

JIM. Takes time!

LAURA. Yes . . .

JIM. Say, you know something, Laura? *(Rises to sit on day-bed* R.*)* People are not so dreadful when you know them. That's what you have to remember! And everybody has problems, not just you but practically everybody has problems. You think of yourself as being the only one who is disappointed. But just look around you and what do you see—a lot of people just as disappointed as you are. You take me, for instance. Boy, when I left high school I thought I'd be a lot further along at this time than I am now. Say, you remember that wonderful write-up I had in "The Torch"?

LAURA. Yes, I do! *(She gets year-book from under pillow* L. *of day-bed.)*

JIM. Said I was bound to succeed in anything I went into! Holy Jeez! "The Torch"! *(She opens book, shows it to him and sits next to him on day-bed.)*

LAURA. Here you are in "The Pirates of Penzance"!

JIM. "The Pirates"! "Oh, better far to live and die under the brave black flag I fly!" I sang the lead in that operetta.

LAURA. So beautifully!

JIM. Aw . . .

LAURA. Yes, yes—beautifully—beautifully!

JIM. You heard me then, huh?

LAURA. I heard you all three times!

JIM. No!

LAURA. Yes.

JIM. You mean all three performances?

LAURA. Yes!

JIM. What for?

LAURA. I—wanted to ask you to—autograph my program. *(Takes program from book.)*

JIM. Why didn't you ask me?

LAURA. You were always surrounded by your own friends so much that I never had a chance.

JIM. Aw, you should have just come right up and said, "Here is my——"

LAURA. Well, I—thought you might think I was——

JIM. Thought I might think you was—what?

LAURA. Oh——

JIM *(With reflective relish).* Oh! Yeah, I was beleaguered by females in those days.

LAURA. You were terribly popular!

JIM. Yeah . . .

LAURA. You had such a—friendly way——

JIM. Oh, I was spoiled in high school.

LAURA. Everybody liked you!

JIM. Including you?

LAURA. I—why, yes, I—I did, too. . . .

JIM. Give me that program, Laura. *(She does so, and he signs it.)* There you are—better later than never!

LAURA. My—what a—surprise!

JIM. My signature's not worth very much right now. But maybe some day—it will increase in value! You know, being disappointed is one thing and being discouraged is something else. Well, I may be disappointed but I am not discouraged. Say, you finished high school?

LAURA. I made bad grades in my final examinations.

JIM. You mean you dropped out?

LAURA *(Rises).* I didn't go back. *(Crosses* R. *to menagerie.* JIM *lights cigarette still sitting on day-bed.* LAURA *puts year-book under menagerie. Rises, picks up unicorn—small glass object—her back to* JIM. *When she touches unicorn,* MUSIC CUE #16-A.*)* How is Emily Meisenbach getting along?

JIM. That kraut-head!

LAURA. Why do you call her that?

JIM. Because that's what she was.

LAURA. You're not still—going with her?

JIM. Oh, I never even see her.

LAURA. It said in the Personal section that you were—engaged!

JIM. Uh-huh. I know, but I wasn't impressed by that—propaganda!

LAURA. It wasn't the truth?

JIM. It was only true in Emily's optimistic opinion!

LAURA. Oh . . . *(Turns* R. *of* JIM. JIM *lights a cigarette and leans indolently back on his elbows, smiling at* LAURA *with a warmth and charm which lights her inwardly with altar candles. She remains by the glass menagerie table and turns in her hands a piece of glass to cover her tumult.* CUT MUSIC CUE #16-A.*)*

JIM. What have you done since high school? Huh?

LAURA. What?

JIM. I said what have you done since high school?

LAURA. Nothing much.

JIM. You must have been doing something all this time.

LAURA. Yes.

JIM. Well, then, such as what?

LAURA. I took a business course at business college . . .

JIM. You did? How did that work out?

LAURA *(Turns back to* JIM*).* Well, not very—well. . . . I had to drop out, it gave me—indigestion. . . .

JIM *(Laughs gently).* What are you doing now?

LAURA. I don't do anything—much. . . . Oh, please don't think I sit around doing nothing! My glass collection takes a good deal of time. Glass is something you have to take good care of.

JIM. What did you say—about glass?

LAURA *(She clears her throat and turns away again, acutely shy).* Collection, I said—I have one.

JIM *(Puts out cigarette. Abruptly).* Say! You know what I judge to be the trouble with you? *(Rises from day-bed and crosses* R.*)* Inferiority complex! You know what that is? That's what they call it when a fellow low-rates himself! Oh, I understand it because I had it, too. Uh-huh! Only my case was not as aggravated as yours seems to be. I had it until I took up public speaking and developed my voice, and learned that I had an aptitude for science. Do you know that until that time I never thought of myself as being outstanding in any way whatsoever!

LAURA. Oh, my!

JIM. Now I've never made a regular study of it—*(Sits armchair* R.*)* mind you, but I have a friend who says I can analyze people better than doctors that make a profession of it. I don't claim that's necessarily true, but I can sure guess a person's psychology. Excuse me, Laura. *(Takes out gum.)* I always take it out

when the flavor is gone. I'll just wrap it in a piece of paper. *(Tears a piece of paper off the newspaper under candelabrum, wraps gum in it, crosses to day-bed, looks to see if* LAURA *is watching. She isn't. Crosses around day-bed.)* I know how it is when you get it stuck on a shoe. *(Throws gum under day-bed, crosses around* L. *of day-bed. Crosses* R. *to* LAURA.*)* Yep—that's what I judge to be your principal trouble. A lack of confidence in yourself as a person. Now I'm basing that fact on a number of your remarks and on certain observations I've made. For instance, that clumping you thought was so awful in high school. You say that you dreaded to go upstairs? You see what you did? You dropped out of school, you gave up an education all because of a little clump, which as far as I can see is practically non-existent! Oh, a little physical defect is all you have. It's hardly noticeable even! Magnified a thousand times by your imagination! You know what my strong advice to you is? You've got to think of yourself as *superior* in some way! *(Crosses* L. *to small table* R. *of day-bed. Sits.* LAURA *sits in armchair.)*

LAURA. In what way would I think?

JIM. Why, man alive, Laura! Look around you a little and what do you see? A world full of common people! All of 'em born and all of 'em going to die! Now, which of them has one-tenth of your strong points! Or mine! Or anybody else's for that matter? You see, everybody excels in some one thing. Well—some in many! You take me, for instance. My interest happens to lie in electrodynamics. I'm taking a course in radio engineering at night school, on top of a fairly responsible job at the warehouse. I'm taking that course *and* studying public speaking.

LAURA. Ohhhh. My!

JIM. Because I believe in the future of television! I want to be ready to go right up along with it. *(Rises, crosses* R.*)* I'm planning to get in on the ground floor. Oh, I've already made the right connections. All that remains now is for the industry itself to get under way—full steam! You know, *knowledge*—ZSZZppp! *Money*—Zzzzzzpp! *POWER!* Wham! That's the cycle democracy is built on! *(Pause.)* I guess you think I think a lot of myself!

LAURA. No—o-o-o, I don't.

JIM (Kneels at armchair R). Well, now how about you? Isn't there some one thing that you take more interest in than anything else?

LAURA. Oh—yes . . .

JIM. Well, then, such as what?

LAURA. Well, I do—as I said—have my—glass collection . . . (MUSIC CUE #16-A.)

JIM. Oh, you do. What kind of glass is it?

LAURA (Takes glass ornament off shelf). Little articles of it, ornaments mostly. Most of them are little animals made out of glass, the tiniest little animals in the world. Mother calls them the glass menagerie! Here's an example of one, if you'd like to see it! This is one of the oldest, it's nearly thirteen. (Hands it to JIM.) Oh, be careful—if you breathe, it breaks! (THE BELL SOLO SHOULD BEGIN HERE. This is last part of CUE #16-A and should play to end of record.)

JIM. I'd better not take it. I'm pretty clumsy with things.

LAURA. Go on, I trust you with him! (JIM takes horse.) There—you're holding him gently! Hold him over the light, he loves the light! (JIM holds horse up to light.) See how the light shines through him?

JIM. It sure does shine!

LAURA. I shouldn't be partial, but he is my favorite one.

JIM. Say, what kind of a thing is this one supposed to be?

LAURA. Haven't you noticed the single horn on his forehead?

JIM. Oh, a unicorn, huh?

LAURA. Mmmm-hmmmmm!

JIM. Unicorns, aren't they extinct in the modern world?

LAURA. I know!

JIM. Poor little fellow must feel kind of lonesome.

LAURA. Well, if he does he doesn't complain about it. He stays on a shelf with some horses that don't have horns and they all seem to get along nicely together.

JIM. They do. Say, where will I put him?

LAURA. Put him on the table. (JIM crosses to small table R. of day-bed, puts unicorn on it.) They all like a change of scenery once in a while!

JIM (C., facing upstage, stretching arms). They do. (MUSIC CUE #16-B: Dance Music.) Hey! Look how big my shadow is when I stretch.

LAURA (Crossing to L. of day-bed). Oh, oh, yes—it stretched across the ceiling!

JIM (Crosses to door R., exits, leaving door open, and stands on fire-escape landing. Sings to music. [Popular record of day for dance-hall.] When JIM opens door, music swells). It's stopped raining. Where does the music come from?

LAURA. From the Paradise Dance Hall across the alley.

JIM (Re-entering room, closing door R., crosses to LAURA). How about cutting the rug a little, Miss Wingfield? Or is your program filled up? Let me take a look at it. (Crosses back C. Music, in dance hall, goes into a waltz. Business here with imaginary dance-program card.) Oh, say! Every dance is taken! I'll just scratch some of them out. Ahhhh, a waltz! (Crosses to LAURA.)

LAURA. I—can't dance!

JIM. There you go with that inferiority stuff!

LAURA. I've never danced in my life!

JIM. Come on, try!

LAURA. Oh, but I'd step on you!

JIM. Well, I'm not made out of glass.

LAURA. How—how do we start?

JIM. You hold your arms out a little.

LAURA. Like this?

JIM. A little bit higher. (Takes LAURA in arms.) That's right. Now don't tighten up, that's the principal thing about it—just relax.

LAURA. It's hard not to.

JIM. Okay.

LAURA. I'm afraid you can't budge me.

JIM (Dances around L. of day-bed slowly). What do you bet I can't?

LAURA. Goodness, yes, you can!

JIM. Let yourself go, now, Laura, just let yourself go.

LAURA. I'm——

JIM. Come on!

LAURA. Trying!

JIM. Not so stiff now—easy does it!

LAURA. I know, but I'm——!

JIM. Come on! Loosen your backbone a little! (When they get to up-stage corner of day-bed—so that the audience will not see him lift

her—JIM*'s arm tightens around her waist and he swings her around* C. *with her feet off floor about 3 complete turns before they hit the small table* R. *of day-bed. Music swells as* JIM *lifts her.*) There we go! (JIM *knocks glass horse off table.* MUSIC FADES.)

LAURA. Oh, it doesn't matter——

JIM (*Picks horse up*). We knocked the little glass horse over.

LAURA. Yes.

JIM (*Hands unicorn to* LAURA). Is he broken?

LAURA. Now he's just like all the other horses.

JIM. You mean he lost his——?

LAURA. He's lost his horn. It doesn't matter. Maybe it's a blessing in disguise.

JIM. Gee, I bet you'll never forgive me. I bet that was your favorite piece of glass.

LAURA. Oh, I don't have favorites—(*Pause*) much. It's no tragedy. Glass breaks so easily. No matter how careful you are. The traffic jars the shelves and things fall off them.

JIM. Still I'm awfully sorry that I was the cause of it.

LAURA. I'll just imagine he had an operation. The horn was removed to make him feel less—freakish! (*Crosses* L., *sits on small table.*) Now he will feel more at home with the other horses, the ones who don't have horns. . . .

JIM (*Sits on arm of armchair* R., *faces* LAURA). I'm glad to see that you have a sense of humor. You know—you're—different than anybody else I know? (MUSIC CUE #17.) Do you mind me telling you that? I mean it. You make me feel sort of—I don't know how to say it! I'm usually pretty good at expressing things, but—this is something I don't know how to say! Did anybody ever tell you that you were pretty? (*Rises, crosses to* LAURA.) Well, you are! And in a different way from anyone else. And all the nicer because of the difference. Oh, boy, I wish that you were my sister. I'd teach you to have confidence in yourself. Being different is nothing to be ashamed of. Because other people aren't such wonderful people. They're a hundred times one thousand. You're one times one! They walk all over the earth. You just stay here. They're as common as—weeds, but—you, well you're—*Blue Roses!*

LAURA. But blue is—wrong for—roses . . .

JIM. It's right for you!—You're pretty!

LAURA. In what respect am I pretty?

JIM. In all respects—your eyes—your hair. Your hands are pretty! You think I'm saying this because I'm invited to dinner and have to be nice. Oh, I could do that! I could say lots of things without being sincere. But I'm talking to you sincerely. I happened to notice you had this inferiority complex that keeps you from feeling comfortable with people. Somebody ought to build your confidence up—way up! and make you proud instead of shy and turning away and—blushing—— *(JIM lifts LAURA up on small table on "way up.")* Somebody ought to—*(Lifts her down.)* somebody ought to kiss you, Laura! *(They kiss. JIM releases her and turns slowly away, crossing a little D. R. Then, quietly, to himself: As JIM turns away, MUSIC ENDS.)* Gee, I shouldn't have done that—that was way off the beam. *(Gives way D. R. Turns to LAURA. LAURA sits on small table.)* Would you care for a cigarette? You don't smoke, do you? How about a mint? Peppermint—Life-Saver? My pocket's a regular drug-store. . . . Laura, you know, if I had a sister like you, I'd do the same thing as Tom. I'd bring fellows home to meet you. Maybe I shouldn't be saying this. That may not have been the idea in having me over. But what if it was? There's nothing wrong with that.—The only trouble is that in my case—I'm not in a position to——I can't ask for your number and say I'll phone. I can't call up next week end—ask for a date. I thought I had better explain the situation in case you—misunderstood and I hurt your feelings . . .

LAURA *(Faintly)*. You—won't—call again?

JIM *(Crossing to R. of day-bed, and sitting)*. No, I can't. You see, I've—got strings on me. Laura, I've—been going steady! I go out all the time with a girl named Betty. Oh, she's a nice quiet home girl like you, and Catholic and Irish, and in a great many ways we—get along fine. I met her last summer on a moonlight boat trip up the river to Alton, on the *Majestic*. Well—right away from the start it was—love! Oh, boy, being in love has made a new man of me! The power of love is pretty tremendous! Love is something that—changes the whole world. It happened that Betty's aunt took sick and she got a wire and had to go to Centralia. So

naturally when Tom asked me to dinner—naturally I accepted the invitation, not knowing—I mean—not knowing. I wish that you would—say something. *(LAURA gives JIM unicorn.)* What are you doing that for? You mean you want me to have him? What for?

LAURA. A—souvenir. *(She crosses R. to menagerie. JIM rises.)*

AMANDA *(Off-stage)*. I'm coming, children. *(She enters into dining-room from kitchen R.)* I thought you'd like some liquid refreshment. *(Puts tray on small table. Lifts a glass.)* Mr. O'Connor, have you heard that song about lemonade? It's "Lemonade, lemonade, Made in the shade and stirred with a spade—And then it's good enough for any old maid!"

JIM. No, ma'am, I never heard it.

AMANDA. Why are you so serious, honey? *(To LAURA.)*

JIM. Well, we were having a serious conversation.

AMANDA. I don't understand modern young people. When I was a girl I was gay about everything.

JIM. You haven't changed a bit, Mrs. Wingfield.

AMANDA. I suppose it's the gaiety of the occasion that has rejuvenated me. Well, here's to the gaiety of the occasion! *(Spills lemonade on dress.)* Oooo! I baptized myself. *(Puts glass on small table R. of day-bed.)* I found some cherries in the kitchen, and I put one in each glass.

JIM. You shouldn't have gone to all that trouble, ma'am.

AMANDA. It was no trouble at all. Didn't you hear us cutting up in the kitchen? I was so outdone with Tom for not bringing you over sooner, but now you've found your way I want you to come all the time—not just once in a while—but all the time. Oh, I think I'll go back in that kitchen. *(Starts to exit U. C.)*

JIM. Oh, no, ma'am, please don't go, ma'am. As a matter of fact, I've got to be going.

AMANDA. Oh, Mr. O'Connor, it's only the shank of the evening! *(JIM and AMANDA stand U.C.)*

JIM. Well, you know how it is.

AMANDA. You mean you're a young working man and have to keep workingmen's hours?

JIM. Yes, ma'am.

AMANDA. Well, we'll let you off early this time,

but only on the condition that you stay later next time, much later——What's the best night for you? Saturday?

JIM. Well, as a matter of fact, I have a couple of time-clocks to punch, Mrs. Wingfield, one in the morning and another one at night!

AMANDA. Oh, isn't that nice, you're so ambitious! You work at night, too?

JIM. No, ma'am, not work but—Betty!

AMANDA *(Crosses* L. *below day-bed).* Betty? Who's Betty?

JIM. Oh, just a girl. The girl I go steady with!

AMANDA. You mean it's serious? *(Crosses* D. L.*)*

JIM. Oh, yes, ma'am. We're going to be married the second Sunday in June.

AMANDA *(Sits on day-bed).* Tom didn't say anything at all about your going to be married?

JIM. Well, the cat's not out of the bag at the warehouse yet. *(Picks up hat from telephone table.)* You know how they are. They call you Romeo and stuff like that.—It's been a wonderful evening, Mrs. Wingfield. I guess this is what they mean by Southern hospitality.

AMANDA. It was nothing. Nothing at all.

JIM. I hope it don't seem like I'm rushing off. But I promised Betty I'd pick her up at the Wabash depot an' by the time I get my jalopy down there her train'll be in. Some women are pretty upset if you keep them waiting.

AMANDA. Yes, I know all about the tyranny of women! Well, good-bye, Mr. O'Connor. *(*AMANDA *puts out hand.* JIM *takes it.)* I wish you happiness—and good fortune. You wish him that, too, don't you, Laura?

LAURA. Yes, I do, Mother.

JIM *(Crosses* L. *to* LAURA*).* Good-bye, Laura. I'll always treasure that souvenir. And don't you forget the good advice I gave you. So long, Shakespeare! *(Up* C.*)* Thanks, again, ladies.— Good night! *(He grins and ducks jauntily out* R.*)*

AMANDA *(Faintly).* Well, well, well. Things have a way of turning out so badly——*(*LAURA *crosses to phonograph, puts on record.)* I don't believe that I would play the victrola. Well, well—well, our gentleman caller was engaged to be married! Tom!

TOM *(Off).* Yes, Mother?

AMANDA. Come out here. I want to tell you something very funny.

TOM *(Entering through* R. *kitchen door to dining-room and into living-room, through curtains,* D. C.*).* Has the gentleman caller gotten away already?

AMANDA. The gentleman caller made a very early departure. That was a nice joke you played on us, too!

TOM. How do you mean?

AMANDA. You didn't mention that he was engaged to be married.

TOM. Jim? Engaged?

AMANDA. That's what he just informed us.

TOM. I'll be jiggered! I didn't know.

AMANDA. That seems very peculiar.

TOM. What's peculiar about it?

AMANDA. Didn't you tell me he was your best friend down at the warehouse?

TOM. He is, but how did I know?

AMANDA. It seems very peculiar you didn't know your best friend was engaged to be married!

TOM. The warehouse is the place where I work, not where I know things about people!

AMANDA. You don't know things anywhere! You live in a dream; you manufacture illusions! *(*TOM *starts for* R. *door.)* Where are you going? Where are you going? Where are you going?

TOM. I'm going to the movies.

AMANDA *(Rises, crosses up to* TOM*).* That's right, now that you've had us make such fools of ourselves. The effort, the preparations, all the expense! The new floor lamp, the rug, the clothes for Laura! All for what? To entertain some other girl's fiancé! Go to the movies, go! Don't think about us, a mother deserted, an unmarried sister who's crippled and has no job! Don't let anything interfere with your selfish pleasure! Just go, go, go—to the movies!

TOM. All right, I will, and the more you shout at me about my selfish pleasures, the quicker I'll go, and I won't go to the movies either. *(Gets hat from phone table, slams door* R., *and exits up alley* R.*)*

AMANDA *(Crosses up to fire-escape landing, yelling).* Go, then! Then go to the moon—you selfish dreamer! *(*MUSIC CUE #18. INTERIOR LIGHT *dims out. Re-enters living-room, slamming* R. *door.* TOM'*s closing speech is timed with the interior pantomime. The interior scene*

is played as though viewed through soundproof glass, behind outer scrim curtain. AMANDA, *standing, appears to be making a comforting speech to* LAURA *who is huddled on* R. *side of day-bed. Now that we cannot hear the mother's speech, her silliness is gone and she has dignity and tragic beauty.* LAURA's *hair hides her face until at the end of the speech she lifts it to smile at her mother.* AMANDA's *gestures are slow and graceful, almost dance-like, as she comforts her daughter.* TOM, *who has meantime put on, as before, the jacket and cap, enters down* R. *from off-stage, and again comes to fire-escape landing, stands as he speaks. Meantime lights are upon* AMANDA *and* LAURA, *but are dim.)*

TOM. I didn't go to the moon. I went much farther. For time is the longest distance between two places. . . . I left Saint Louis. I descended these steps of this fire-escape for the last time and followed, from then on, in my father's footsteps, attempting to find in motion what was lost in space. . . . I travelled around a great deal. The cities swept about me like dead leaves, leaves that were brightly colored but torn away from the branches. I would have stopped, but I was pursued by something. It always came upon me unawares, taking me altogether by surprise. Perhaps it was a familiar bit of music. Perhaps it was only a piece of transparent glass. . . . Perhaps I am walking along a street at night, in some strange city, before I have found companions, and I pass the lighted window of a shop where perfume is sold. The window is filled with pieces of colored glass, tiny transparent bottles in delicate colors, like bits of a shattered rainbow. Then all at once my sister touches my shoulder. I turn around and look into her eyes. . . . Oh, Laura, Laura, I tried to leave you behind me, but I am more faithful than I intended to be! I reach for a cigarette, I cross the street, I run into a movie or a bar. I buy a drink, I speak to the nearest stranger—anything that can blow your candles out! —for nowadays the world is lit by lightning! Blow out your candles, Laura . . . *(Laura blows out candles still burning in candelabrum and the whole interior is blacked out.)* And so—good-bye! *(Exits up alley* R. *Music continues to the end.)*

CURTAIN
(End of play.)

Discussion

Jim's visit brings on a climactic confrontation of all characters. To see why, consider what he represents to each of the other characters.

Scenes 7 and 8

1. Explain Laura's feelings and reactions when: (a) her mother tells her to let Jim in; (b) she starts to join Jim and the family at dinner; (c) Jim joins Laura in the parlor; (d) Jim dances with her and kisses her; (e) Jim explains that he is engaged.

2. By what means does Amanda try to charm the "gentleman caller"? Do you think she succeeds? Explain.

3. Describe Jim O'Connor's character, paying particular attention to: (a) Tom's comments on him; (b) Jim's behavior to Amanda, to Tom, and to Laura; (c) his view of himself; (d) his general outlook on people and life.

4. (a) Do you think Jim's self-confidence is genuine or a pose? Discuss. (b) In what ways does he try to build up Laura's confidence? (c) To what extent does he succeed?

5. (a) What is Amanda's reaction when her plan fails? **(b)** How does this affect your opinion of her?

6. Each of the characters, including Jim, has a private world in which to escape from unpleasant realities. **(a)** What situations does each character find unpleasant? **(b)** Describe the fantasy world in which each hides.

7. (a) Why has Laura's image haunted Tom since his leaving home? **(b)** What has he done about his fantasy?

Extension • Writing

Artists use symbols to reinforce meanings and to make the abstract more concrete. Choose four of these details and explain briefly the symbolic meaning of each:

1. Tom's movie-going.
2. The glass unicorn.
3. Jim's giant shadow.
4. Blue Roses.
5. The Paradise Dance Hall.
6. The candelabrum and its history.
7. Laura's being crippled.

Vocabulary
Context, Pronunciation, and Dictionary

Act One

Try to determine the meaning of each of the italicized words in the sentences below by using the context clues. If there are not enough clues, write *e*. Be sure you can pronounce and spell all the italicized words.

1. "Animals have secretions in their stomachs which enable them to digest their food without *mastication*, but human beings must chew their food before they swallow it down, and chew, chew." **(a)** gagging; **(b)** gaining weight; **(c)** chewing; **(d)** eating grass; **(e)** not enough clues.

2. TOM. Yesterday you *confiscated* my books! You had the nerve to—
AMANDA. I did. I took that horrible novel back to the library. . . . **(a)** removed; **(b)** burned; **(c)** hid; **(d)** tore up; **(e)** not enough clues.

3. "I didn't tell him anything about Laura. I didn't let on we had dark *ulterior* motives." **(a)** exterior; **(b)** generous; **(c)** good; **(d)** hidden; **(e)** not enough clues.

4. "Changes and adventure, however, were *imminent* this year. They were waiting around the corner for all these dancing kids." **(a)** important; **(b)** about to occur; **(c)** dangerous; **(d)** lucky; **(e)** not enough clues.

Act Two

With the help of your Glossary and the pronunciation key in the upper right hand corner of each Glossary page, answer the following questions.

A. AMANDA. "Tom, good gracious, why don't you bring this *paragon* [Jim] to supper finally . . .?
1. Does *paragon* rhyme with *marathon* or *telephone?*
2. Is Amanda favorable or unfavorable toward Jim?

B. AMANDA. Well, in the South we had so many servants. Gone, gone, gone. All *vestige* of gracious living!
1. On which syllable does the accent fall in *vestige?*
2. Which Glossary definition of *vestige* fits this context?

C. [STAGE DIRECTIONS.] Jim lights a cigarette and leans *indolently* back on his elbows, smiling at Laura with a warmth and charm which lights her inwardly with altar candles.
1. On which syllable does the accent fall in *indolently?*
2. In your own words, describe the manner in which Jim leans back.

D. AMANDA. You don't know things anywhere! You live in a dream; you manufacture *illusions!*
1. Write a word that rhymes with *illusion.*
2. What is Amanda saying about Tom in these lines?

Tennessee Williams 1914 •

Tom "Tennessee" Williams began writing as a child in Mississippi, trading sleep for poems and stories. At fourteen he was published in *Weird Tales* magazine; by twenty he was committed to drama. But first came years of college, odd jobs, and roaming. While working in a shoe factory, as Tom Wingfield does, Williams would sit up almost till dawn laboring over his manuscripts. The drab underside of Depression America would later inspire his dramas of lonely, rootless losers, "trapped by circumstance."

In 1943, when Williams was earning $17 weekly as a New York theater usher, MGM hired him as a screenwriter at $1000 a month. Six months later he was fired for writing the script which became *The Glass Menagerie,* the Broadway hit of 1945, which was soon acclaimed as a theater classic.

CONTENT REVIEW

1. The key word in *The Glass Menagerie* is *illusion*. In varying degrees, all four characters cherish escapist illusions. (a) Which character, despite some reliance on fantasy, basically accepts his or her lot in life? Is that character contented or merely resigned? Explain. (b) What does the play imply about illusions both as aids and as handicaps in coping with life?

2. Amanda believes her children will succeed since they are "just full of natural endowments." How are Laura and Tom each affected by their mother's unrealistic expectations of them? Do you find their responses believable? Discuss.

3. After Jim's departure, Williams notes in a stage direction that Amanda's "silliness is gone and she has dignity and tragic beauty." How do her final actions reveal this change of character?

4. At the outset, Tom says that the play's social background is "that quaint period when the huge middle class of America . . . were having their fingers pressed forcibly down on the fiery Braille alphabet of a dissolving economy." Are the the characters' lives or the play's general atmosphere influenced by the Depression or not? Discuss.

5. What might Tom mean when he remarks at the end of the play, "for nowadays the world is lit by lightning! Blow out your candles, Laura"?

Unit 7, Test I
INTERPRETATION: NEW MATERIAL

from The Little Foxes, Act I
Lillian Hellman

Characters

REGINA GIDDENS	A good-looking woman in her forties, she is the sister of Ben and Oscar Hubbard. Her husband is Horace Giddens, a wealthy banker now hospitalized in Baltimore.
ALEXANDRA GIDDENS	She is the seventeen-year-old daughter of the Giddens.
LEO HUBBARD	He is the twenty-year-old son of Oscar and Birdie.
BEN HUBBARD	Regina's older brother and a partner with Oscar in Hubbard Sons, Merchandise.

ADDIE	She is the black servant in the Giddens' house.
BIRDIE HUBBARD	She is Oscar's wife and comes from an old Southern aristocratic family.
OSCAR HUBBARD	Regina's other brother, he married Birdie when the Hubbard family took over Birdie's family's cotton estate.

The play is set in the living room of the Giddens house, located in a small town of the deep South. The playwright describes the room as being "good-looking, the furniture expensive; but it reflects no particular taste. Everything is of the best and that is all." It is the spring of 1900.

In the first part of Act I there is discussion of a business deal that Ben, Oscar, and Regina are anxious to complete. Mr. Marshall, a Northern industrialist, is going to help the Hubbards finance a cotton mill in the South. After celebrating the agreement, he is driven to the train station by Leo and Alexandra.

While they are gone, Oscar and Ben remind Regina that they have raised their shares of $75,000, but the money she has promised from Horace is still not paid. She suggests that Horace is holding out for a greater share of the profits, and she gets Ben and Oscar to agree to give her 40 percent, which will come out of Oscar's share. In exchange Regina agrees to think about having Alexandra marry Leo. Birdie overhears these marriage plans.

Read the selection. Then on your paper write the letter of the correct answer for each item.

REGINA *(calling)*. Alexandra? Are you back?

ALEXANDRA. Yes, Mama.

LEO *(comes into the room)*. Mr. Marshall got off safe and sound. Weren't those fine clothes he had? You can always spot clothes made in a good place. Looks like maybe they were done in England. Lots of men in the North send all the way to England for their stuff.

BEN *(to LEO)*. Were you careful driving the horses?

LEO. Oh, yes, sir. I was. *(ALEXANDRA has come in on BEN's question, hears the answer, looks angrily at LEO.)*

ALEXANDRA. It's a lovely night. You should have come, Aunt Birdie.

REGINA. Were you gracious to Mr. Marshall?

ALEXANDRA. I think so, Mama. I like him.

REGINA. Good. And now I have great news for you. You are going to Baltimore in the morning to bring your father home.

ALEXANDRA *(gasps, then delighted)*. Me? Papa said I should come? That must mean— *(Turns to ADDIE.)* Addie, he must be well. Think of it. He'll be back home again. We'll bring him home.

REGINA. You are going alone, Alexandra.

ADDIE *(ALEXANDRA has turned in surprise)*. Going alone? Going by herself? A child that age! Mr. Horace ain't going to like Zan traipsing up there by herself.

REGINA *(sharply).* Go upstairs and lay out Alexandra's things.

ADDIE. He'd expect me to be along—

REGINA. I'll be up in a few minutes to tell you what to pack. *(ADDIE slowly begins to climb the steps. To* ALEXANDRA.*)* I should think you'd like going alone. At your age it certainly would have delighted me. You're a strange girl, Alexandra. Addie has babied you so much.

ALEXANDRA. I only thought it would be more fun if Addie and I went together.

BIRDIE *(timidly).* Maybe I could go with her, Regina, I'd really like to.

REGINA. She is going alone. She is getting old enough to take some responsibilities.

OSCAR. She'd better learn now. She's almost old enough to get married. *(Jovially, to* LEO, *slapping him on shoulder.)* Eh, son?

LEO. Huh?

OSCAR *(annoyed with* LEO *for not understanding).* Old enough to get married, you're thinking, eh?

LEO. Oh, yes, sir. *(Feebly.)* Lots of girls get married at Zan's age. Look at Mary Prester and Johanna and—

REGINA. Well, she's not getting married tomorrow. But she is going to Baltimore tomorrow, so let's talk about that. *(To* ALEXANDRA.*)* You'll be glad to have Papa home again.

ALEXANDRA. I wanted to go before, Mama. You remember that. But you said *you* couldn't go, and that *I* couldn't go alone.

REGINA. I've changed my mind. *(Too casually.)* You're to tell Papa how much you missed him, and that he must come home now—for your sake. Tell him that you *need* him home.

ALEXANDRA. Need him home? I don't understand.

REGINA. There is nothing for you to understand. You are simply to say what I have told you.

BIRDIE *(rises).* He may be too sick. She couldn't do that—

ALEXANDRA. Yes. He may be too sick to travel. I couldn't make him think he had to come home for me, if he is too sick to—

REGINA *(looks at her, sharply, challengingly).* You *couldn't* do what I tell you to do, Alexandra?

ALEXANDRA *(quietly).* No. I couldn't. If I thought it would hurt him.

REGINA *(after a second's silence, smiles pleasantly).* But you are doing this for Papa's own good. *(Takes* ALEXANDRA*'s hand.)* You must let me be the judge of his condition. It's the best possible cure for him to come home and be taken care of here. He mustn't stay there any longer and listen to those alarmist doctors. You are doing this entirely for his sake. Tell your papa that I want him to come home, that I miss him very much.

ALEXANDRA *(slowly).* Yes, Mama.

REGINA *(to the others. Rises).* I must go and start getting Alexandra ready now. Why don't you all go home?

BEN *(rises)*. I'll attend to the railroad ticket. One of the boys will bring it over. Good night, everybody. Have a nice trip, Alexandra. The food on the train is very good. The celery is so crisp. Have a good time and act like a little lady. *(Exits.)*

REGINA. Good night, Ben. Good night, Oscar— *(Playfully.)* Don't be so glum, Oscar. It makes you look as if you had chronic indigestion.

BIRDIE. Good night, Regina.

REGINA. Good night, Birdie. *(Exits upstairs.)*

OSCAR *(starts for hall)*. Come along.

LEO *(to* ALEXANDRA*)*. Imagine your not wanting to go! What a little fool you are. Wish it were me. What I could do in a place like Baltimore!

ALEXANDRA *(angrily, looking away from him)*. Mind your business. I can guess the kind of things *you* could do.

LEO *(laughs)*. Oh, no, you couldn't. *(He exits.)*

REGINA *(culling from the top of the stairs)*. Come on, Alexandra.

BIRDIE *(quickly, softly)*. Zan.

ALEXANDRA. I don't understand about my going, Aunt Birdie. *(Shrugs.)* But anyway, Papa will be home again. *(Pats* BIRDIE's *arm.)* Don't worry about me. I can take care of myself. Really I can.

BIRDIE *(shakes her head, softly)*. That's not what I'm worried about. Zan—

ALEXANDRA *(comes close to her)*. What's the matter?

BIRDIE. It's about Leo—

ALEXANDRA *(whispering)*. He beat the horses. That's why we were late getting back. We had to wait until they cooled off. He always beats the horses as if—

BIRDIE *(whispering frantically, holding* ALEXANDRA's *hands)*. He's my son. My own son. But you are more to me—more to me than my own child. I love you more than anybody else—

ALEXANDRA. Don't worry about the horses. I'm sorry I told you.

BIRDIE *(her voice rising)*. *I am not worrying about the horses.* I am worrying about *you.* You are *not* going to marry Leo. I am not going to let them do that to you—

ALEXANDRA. Marry? To Leo? *(Laughs.)* I wouldn't marry, Aunt Birdie. I've never even thought about it—

BIRDIE. But they have thought about it. *(Wildly.)* Zan, I couldn't stand to think about such a thing. You and—

*(*OSCAR *has come into the doorway on* ALEXANDRA's *speech. He is standing quietly, listening.)*

ALEXANDRA *(laughs)*. But I'm not going to marry. And I'm certainly not going to marry Leo.

BIRDIE. Don't you understand? They'll make you. They'll make you—

ALEXANDRA *(takes* BIRDIE's *hands, quietly, firmly)*. That's foolish, Aunt Birdie. I'm grown now. Nobody can make me do anything.

BIRDIE. I just couldn't stand—

OSCAR *(sharply)*. Birdie. *(*BIRDIE *looks up, draws quickly away from* ALEXANDRA. *She stands rigid, frightened. Quietly.)* Birdie, get your hat and coat.

ADDIE *(calls from upstairs)*. Come on, baby. Your mama's waiting for you, and she ain't nobody to keep waiting.

ALEXANDRA. All right. *(Then softly, embracing* BIRDIE.*)* Good night, Aunt Birdie. *(As she passes* OSCAR.*)* Good night, Uncle Oscar. *(*BIRDIE *begins to move slowly toward the door as* ALEXANDRA *climbs the stairs.* ALEXANDRA *is almost out of view when* BIRDIE *reaches* OSCAR *in the doorway. As* BIRDIE *quickly attempts to pass him, he slaps her hard, across the face.* BIRDIE *cries out, puts her hand to her face. On the cry,* ALEXANDRA *turns, begins to run down the stairs.)* Aunt Birdie! What happened? What happened? I—

BIRDIE *(softly, without turning)*. Nothing, darling. Nothing happened. *(Quickly, as if anxious to keep* ALEXANDRA *from coming close.)* Now go to bed. *(*OSCAR *exits.)* Nothing happened I only—I only twisted my ankle. *(She goes out.* ALEXANDRA *stands on the stairs looking after her as if she were puzzled and frightened.)*

CURTAIN

1. By describing the living room as "good-looking, the furniture expensive; but it reflects no particular taste. Everything is of the best and that is all," the playwright reveals that (a) Regina is sophisticated; (b) Regina has poor taste; (c) Regina is more interested in the money that bought the furniture than in the total effect of the room; (d) the furniture, though of good quality, is somewhat old-fashioned and shabby in appearance.

2. When Leo and Alexandra return from driving Mr. Marshall to the train, Alexandra's look at Leo indicates that (a) he had insulted her on the drive back; (b) he did not drive carefully; (c) she loves Leo; (d) she is angry because he would not let her drive.

3. Through the things she says, we can infer that Regina is (a) weak-willed; (b) sympa-

thetic; (c) dreamy; (d) practical.

4. In line 28 on page 544, Regina is instructed to speak her lines "too casually." The implication of this stage direction is that Regina (a) doesn't care whether Horace comes home or not; (b) misses Horace more than she will admit; (c) doesn't want Alexandra to know Horace is dying; (d) doesn't want Alexandra to question her motives.

5. Throughout this scene Alexandra is (a) somewhat shy; (b) not completely convinced of her mother's sincerity; (c) lost in thought about the coming trip; (d) worried about traveling alone on a train.

6. In explaining why she and Leo were late, Alexandra refers to Leo and the horses. The implication here is that Leo is (a) cruel; (b) clever; (c) dishonest; (d) competitive.

7. How does Alexandra re-

spond to Birdie's mention of marriage to Leo? (a) She is overwhelmed because of her love for him; (b) she is surprised and cannot take it seriously; (c) she is thrown into a fit of depression; (d) she is angry.

8. Birdie's fear throughout this part of Act I is best revealed through (a) Alexandra's reactions to Birdie; (b) Oscar's actions toward Birdie; (c) the stage directions to Alexandra; (d) the stage directions to Birdie.

9. In line 41, page 545, the audience is aware that Oscar is standing in the doorway, but Birdie is not aware of him. This is an example of (a) climax; (b) connotation; (c) dramatic irony; (d) flashback.

10. The call from Addie at the top of the stairs to Alexandra below (a) helps to develop the conflict in the play; (b) is a dramatic device to leave Birdie

alone with Oscar; **(c)** helps to develop the character of Alexandra; **(d)** adds an important symbol to the play.

11. Oscar slaps Birdie because he **(a)** overheard what she said to Alexandra; **(b)** is sick; **(c)** was angry about her talking so much at dinner; **(d)** realizes that she is closer to Alexandra than he is.

12. The last stage direction of Act I, in which Alexandra stands as if she were "puzzled and frightened," implies that Alexandra **(a)** has figured out that Oscar slapped Birdie; **(b)** hopes Birdie will recover quickly from her twisted ankle; **(c)** is nervous about the coming train trip; **(d)** has started to take Birdie's fears more seriously.

13. The *central* conflict in this scene is between **(a)** Birdie and Regina; **(b)** Alexandra and Regina; **(c)** Birdie and Oscar; **(d)** Alexandra and Leo.

14. This scene establishes that these two families **(a)** value close personal relationships; **(b)** want to escape the past; **(c)** consist of schemers who try to manipulate each other; **(d)** are trying to overcome the generation gap.

15. The mood of this excerpt is best described as **(a)** tense; **(b)** light-hearted; **(c)** supernatural; **(d)** gloomy.

Unit 7, Test II
COMPOSITION

Choose one of the topics below for a composition.

1. Suppose *The Glass Menagerie* is going to be produced at your school this year. You want to make sure that the director interprets the play properly. Therefore, you need to explain in a memo what the climax is, so that he or she will direct the play toward that emotional peak. Your explanation should include reasons why this scene or part of this scene is the climax.

2. As you read the play, you probably noticed ways in which Tom and his mother Amanda were the same and ways in which they were different. Imagine that you are Tom, and a year after leaving home you write a letter to Amanda in which you express those similarities and differences to her. This comparison might include actions, personality, and values.

3. Imagine that you are Laura and have continued to think about your meeting with Jim. Write a letter to Tom in which you explain whether or not you have changed. You might deal with how you (Laura) feel about yourself, about your mother, and about

Tom before the scene with Jim. Then describe how your feelings changed after the encounter.

4. One of the major themes of this play is the nature of family relationships. Several other selections in *The United States in Literature* deal with the same theme. Pick one of the selections below. Compare the parent vs. child conflict in that selection to the one in *The Glass Menagerie*. This comparison is being written for those of your classmates who do not have a full understanding of both works.

You may choose from these selections:

"Brother Death" by Sherwood Anderson;

"The First Seven Years" by Bernard Malamud;

"The Leader of the People" by John Steinbeck.

1945 1950 1955 1960

- Williams: *The Glass Menagerie*
- Brooks: *A Street in Bronzeville*
- U.N. established
  - McCullers: *The Member of the Wedding*
  - Robert Penn Warren: *All the King's Men*
    - Shapiro: *Trial of a Poet*
    - Williams: *A Streetcar Named Desire*
      - Norman Mailer: *The Naked and the Dead*
        - Arthur Miller: *Death of a Salesman*
- Korean War •
- Hemingway: *The Old Man and the Sea* •
- Ralph Ellison: *Invisible Man* •
  - Roethke: *The Waking* •
  - Robert Anderson: *Tea and Sympathy* •
    - Miller: *The Crucible* •

- Welty: *The Ponder Heart* •
- Elizabeth Bishop: *Poems: North and South* •
- Paddy Chayefsky: *Marty* (on TV) •
  - O'Neill: *Long Day's Journey into Night* •
  - Jack Kerouac: *On the Road* •
- Leonard Bernstein: *West Side Story* •
  - MacLeish: *J.B.* •
  - Malamud: *The Magic Barrel* •
  - Hansberry: *A Raisin in the Sun* •

- Edward Albee: *The American Dream* •
- Jesús Colón: *A Puerto Rican in New York* •
- Jarrell: *Selected Poems* •
- Institute of Puerto Rican Culture founded
  - Baldwin: *Another Country* •
  - Porter: *Ship of Fools* •
  - Albee: *Who's Afraid of Virginia Woolf?* •
  - Nemerov: *The Next Room of the Dream*
  - Baldwin: *The Fire Next Time*
- Flannery O'Connor: *The Violent Bear It Away* •
- John Updike: *Rabbit, Run* •

Atomic Age begins Civil Rights movement grows

War novels Beat poetry movement

McCarthy era Space Age begins

New Frontiers 1945–

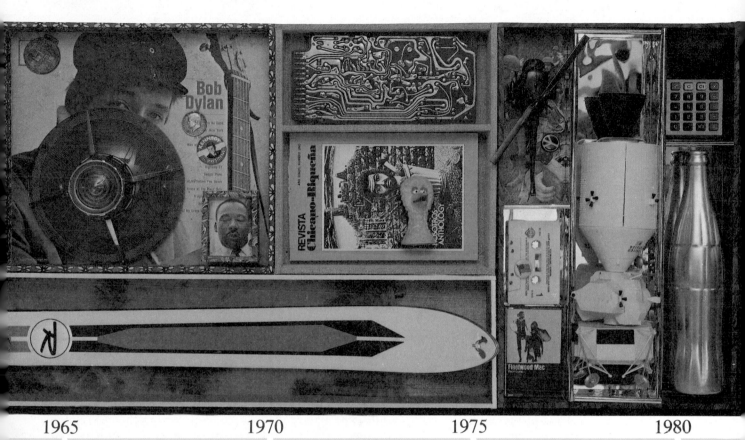

1965	1970	1975	1980

- Bellow: *Herzog*
  - *The Autobiography of Malcolm X*
    - Miller: *The Price*
    - Baraka: *Slave Ship*
    - Rodolfo Gonzales: *I Am Joaquín/Yo Soy Joaquín*
      - Robert Anderson: *I Never Sang for My Father*
      - Momaday: *House Made of Dawn*
      - Mailer: *The Armies of the Night*

- Vonnegut: *Breakfast of Champions*
- Watergate hearings

- Alex Haley: *Roots*
- Hellman: *Pentimento*
- Flor y Canto: *Anthology I*
  - Mars landings by Viking space probes
  - Robert Lowell: *Day by Day*

Puerto Rican Traveling Theatre founded •

Vonnegut: *Slaughter-House Five* •

First manned Moon landing •

Elizabeth Bishop: *The Complete Poems* •

Charles Gordone: *No Place to Be Somebody* •

James Dickey: *Deliverance* •

Simpson: *Adventures of the Letter I* •

Vietnam War protests

Ecology movement

Background: New Frontiers 1945–

World War II, climaxed by the first destruction of cities by atomic bombs, must be acknowledged as a definite starting point of new social, cultural, and literary developments. The war had ended the Depression and the postwar boom gave birth to an affluent society. Millions of Americans entered the middle class for the first time. Their children grew up taking prosperity for granted. The problems of the poor and minorities were largely ignored.

Yet, through this euphoric mood ran the anxieties created by the Cold War between East and West and the possibility of nuclear war. Totalitarianism had been crushed in Germany, Japan, and Italy. But dictatorships—old and new, capitalist and communist— flourished around the globe. Writers and intellectuals generally were preoccupied with the grimness of the recent past, the bleak prospects for the future, and soon with the challenge to intellectual freedom posed by Senator Joseph McCarthy's claims of Communist influence in American government, education, and the arts.

In such a social climate, many writers took refuge in despair and cynicism. William Faulkner, in his eloquent Nobel Prize Address of 1950 (page 82), warned against such easy escape from the challenges confronting the human spirit.

Yet in the late 1940s, the recent war was understandably a preoccupation of writers. There was a succession of war novels, such as Irwin Shaw's *The Young Lions*, Norman Mailer's *The Naked and the Dead*, and James Jones's *From Here to Eternity*. Karl Shapiro won the Pulitzer Prize in 1945 for *V-Letter and Other Poems*. Randall Jarrell also won acclaim for poetry focused on the feelings of young soldiers in combat.

At the same time, prewar literary trends continued. Gwendolyn Brooks's poems in *A Street in Bronzeville* (1945) called attention to the joys, sorrows, pride, and vitality of urban black life. In 1952, Ralph Ellison won the National Book Award for *Invisible Man*, a subtle and technically brilliant novel foreshadowing the ghetto riots of the 1960s.

William Faulkner, Katherine

Anne Porter, Eudora Welty and a host of talented newcomers continued the "Southern Renaissance." Among these authors were Carson McCullers, Flannery O'Connor, Robert Penn Warren, and later Truman Capote, William Styron, and Alice Walker. While much of their fiction, like Faulkner's, focused on tight-knit rural communities, most of these writers moved on to settings outside the South or to themes reflecting the effect on Southerners, both black and white, of new social patterns and ways of thinking.

Poetry was still dominated by the standards of Ezra Pound and T. S. Eliot: intellectual objectivity, stylistic complexity, and suppression of emotion or personal statement. Literature must be studied without reference to either the life of its authors or the time in which it was created.

Such intellectual detachment matched the mood of the mid–1950s, which was compounded of complacency, materialism, political apathy, and tension and suspicion engendered by Cold-War politics. Few writers were willing to commit themselves to any stand. A retreat into obscure, personal symbolism by many poets was met by a shrinking audience. Novelists such as Capote, Bellow, and John Cheever turned to social satire and comedy, reflecting, analyzing, and satirizing the "plastic" middle-class culture of status symbols. A typical best-selling novel of the decade was Sloan Wilson's *The Man in the Gray Flannel Suit* (1955), which depicted the destruction of a marriage by the "status game."

Robert Lowell

Carson McCullers

Gwendolyn Brooks

But a major change was already shaping. The civil rights movement, spurred by new leaders such as Martin Luther King and by the Supreme Court's school desegregation verdict of 1954, gained nationwide attention it had scarcely received in the five preceding decades. Sit-ins, boycotts, and, later, voter registration drives were mounted throughout the North and South. In *Go Tell It on the Mountain* (1953), James Baldwin chronicled the struggle of rural Southern blacks to ad-

just their spiritual values of life in the ghetto.

Borrowing much from black American culture—especially music, dance, and diction—the Beatniks became the first generation of middle-class youth to "drop out" of the "system." They foreshadowed the "hippie" counterculture of the 1960s and formed a new wave in literature. Jack Kerouac's novel *On the Road* (1957),

known as the "Beat Bible," was the prototype of many free-flowing narratives that recorded the roaming of young drop-outs in search of meanings for their lives beyond what they termed the middle-class "rat race." Although the Beats cultivated "cool"—an attitude of ironic detachment from social conventions and political concerns—their writing was personal, socially committed, and written in the language of the streets. The Beat poets and others like Denise Levertov, Robert Creeley, and William Stafford scorned poetic artificiality, writing straightforward verse that expressed emotion directly. The tone of early Beat poetry is suggested by the title of Ginsberg's best-known poem: "Howl."

Those Americans in flight from alienation and apathy and in search of ideals worthy of commitment found inspiration in President John Kennedy's inaugural speech of 1961: "Ask not what your country can do for you. Ask rather what you can do for your country." Young volunteers flocked to register black voters and to join the Peace Corps. Established writers like Gwendolyn Brooks, Robert Lowell, and James Baldwin became prominent champions of various causes; younger writers arose to voice the impulse for equality and pride among Chicanos, native Americans, Puerto Ricans, and other ethnic groups; the women's rights movement began to revive and won attention for such writers as Joyce Carol Oates and Maxine Kumin. The 1960s became a decade of challenges to traditional values and institutions.

Faith in peaceful reform was expressed by the Freedom March of 300,000 civil rights supporters in Washington in 1963. But in the same year, John Kennedy and Medgar

(1963). Truman Capote's *In Cold Blood* (1965), using fictional techniques to analyze a real murder case, gave birth to the "nonfiction novel" and to the "New Journalism." In this type of work, also called "advocacy journalism," writers abandoned the news reporter's traditional objectivity to participate in the events they were observing.

too close to the literary trends of the 1970s, to see them clearly, but some recent developments may be outlined.

The intellectual ferment of the 1960s popularized new concepts of reality that emphasized the influence of experience and state of mind on any observer's view of events. Such

Elizabeth Bishop

James Baldwin

Kurt Vonnegut, Jr.

Evers, a civil rights leader, were killed, the first victims of a long series of political assassinations. By 1965 American soldiers were being poured into Vietnam. The issues of the war and civil rights were tightly enmeshed. The optimism of the Kennedy years was shattered as clashes between protestors and police mounted into street violence in cities and on college campuses.

American literature both affected and was affected by this climate of rage. The tone of much writing became stridently rhetorical. A new type of militant cultural commentary emerged, notably with Baldwin's *The Fire Next Time*

The war novel was revived, notably by Joseph Heller's *Catch-22* (1961) and Kurt Vonnegut's *Slaughter-House Five* (1969). The theme of both books is that war is insane. For Heller, the only sane response is madcap, hilarious "insanity." For Vonnegut, the love and compassion of individuals for each other may somehow redeem the world from the madness that views mass bombing as "rational."

The tide of rebellion was ebbing when the United States withdrew its forces from Southeast Asia in 1975. We are

notions are reflected in the experimental fiction of writers like John Barth, Thomas Pynchon, and Ronald Arias. In their works, what is related is not a fixed series of events, but rather the view of those happenings as shaped, and often distorted, by the subjective consciousness or points of view of the characters.

A related trend may be termed "pop" fiction, in which reality consists largely of the trivia of popular culture. Such writing is in part an extension of the 1950s fiction satirizing the "plastic" society, especially of suburbia.

Science fiction, long associated with the lurid covers of pulp magazines, has risen to literary respectability partly because it appeals to readers faced with the bewildering pace of change. Though long on gimmickry and short on believable characterization, early science fiction was dealing with the themes of nuclear power, robots, and space travel long before most people were aware of these possibilities. Science fiction promises to remain a lively genre because it is entertaining and because scientists and futurologists are now using it as one means of probing such social problems as pollution and overpopulation.

Another aspect of the quest for stability is the reexamination of the American experience. This trend seems to have combined with the ethnic literature which developed so rapidly in the era of protest. But writers such as Lawson Fusao Inada, Gary Soto, Alex Haley, Judy Dothard Simmons, and Michael Arlen are now going beyond the political concerns of the 1960s to treat broad universal themes of human striving and of the importance of maintaining kinship with one's past. The tone of such works, as writers rediscover the variety of the American past, tends to be reflective, introspective, wondering, and not a little loving.

Indeed, as has been true since the foundation of what Walt Whitman called this "teeming nation of nations," the question of identity—personal, ethnic, national—remains the central theme of our literature. It is a vital literature, always open to experiment in content and form. It is a literature of search—perhaps with less patina than the literature of older nations. But such is the spirit of search and experiment, a spirit captured by Thomas Wolfe in his novel *You Can't Go Home Again:* "I believe that we are lost here in America, but I believe we shall be found. . . . I think that the true discovery of America is before us. I think the true fulfillment of our spirit, of our people, of our mighty and immortal land, is yet to come."

Thomas Wolfe. YOU CAN'T GO HOME AGAIN. (New York: Harper & Brothers), 1940.

Lawson Fusao Inada

Gary Soto

Victor Hernández Cruz

James Baldwin

from Notes of a Native Son

Autobiographical Notes

I was born in Harlem thirty-one years ago. I began plotting novels at about the time I learned to read. The story of my childhood is the usual bleak fantasy, and we can dismiss it with the restrained observation that I certainly would not consider living it again. In those days my mother was given to the exasperating and mysterious habit of having babies. As they were born, I took them over with one hand and held a book with the other. The children probably suffered, though they have since been kind enough to deny it, and in this way I read *Uncle Tom's Cabin* and *A Tale of Two Cities* over and over and over again; in this way, in fact, I read just about everything I could get my hands on—except the Bible, probably because it was the only book I was encouraged to read. I must also confess that I wrote—a great deal—and my first professional triumph, in any case, the first effort of mine to be seen in print, occurred at the age of twelve or thereabouts, when a short story I had written about the Spanish revolution won some sort of prize in an extremely short-lived church newspaper. I remember the story was censored by the lady editor, though I don't remember why, and I was outraged.

Also wrote plays, and songs, for one of which I received a letter of congratulations from Mayor La Guardia,[1] and poetry, about which the less said, the better. My mother was delighted by all these goings-on, but my father wasn't; he wanted me to be a preacher. When I was fourteen I became a preacher, and when I was seventeen I stopped. Very shortly thereafter I left home. For God knows how long I struggled with the world of commerce and industry—I guess they would say they struggled with *me*—and when I was about twenty-one I had enough done of a novel to get a Saxton Fellowship. When I was twenty-two the fellowship was over, the novel turned out to be unsalable, and I started waiting on tables in a Village restaurant and writing book reviews—mostly, as it turned out, about the Negro problem, concerning which the color of my skin made me automatically an expert. Did another book, in company with photographer Theodore Pelatowski, about the storefront churches in Harlem. This book met exactly the same fate as my first—fellowship, but no sale. (It was a Rosenwald Fellowship.) By the time I was twenty-four I had decided to stop reviewing books about the Negro problem—which, by this time, was only slightly less horrible in print than it was in life—and I packed my bags and went to France, where I finished, God knows how, *Go Tell It on the Mountain*.[2]

Any writer, I suppose, feels that the world into which he was born is nothing less than a conspiracy against the cultivation of his talent—which attitude certainly has a great deal to support it. On the other hand, it is only because the world looks on his talent with such a frightening indifference that the artist is compelled to make his talent important. So that any writer, looking back over even so short a span of time as I am here forced to assess, finds that the things which hurt him and the things which helped him cannot be divorced from each other; he could be helped in a certain way only because he was hurt in a certain way; and his help is simply to be

1. *Mayor La Guardia.* Fiorello La Guardia (1882–1947) was mayor of New York from 1934 to 1945.

2. *Go Tell It on the Mountain,* a novel published in 1953 dealing with black life in the United States. With it, Baldwin's reputation was established.

enabled to move from one conundrum to the next—one is tempted to say that he moves from one disaster to the next. When one begins looking for influences one finds them by the score. I haven't thought much about my own, not enough anyway; I hazard that the King James Bible, the rhetoric of the store-front church, something ironic and violent and perpetually understated in Negro speech—and something of Dickens' love for bravura—have something to do with me today; but I wouldn't stake my life on it. Likewise, innumerable people have helped me in many ways; but finally, I suppose, the most difficult (and most rewarding) thing in my life has been the fact that I was born a Negro and was forced, therefore, to effect some kind of truce with this reality. (Truce, by the way, is the best one can hope for.)

One of the difficulties about being a Negro writer (and this is not special pleading, since I don't mean to suggest that he has it worse than anybody else) is that the Negro problem is written about so widely. The bookshelves groan under the weight of information, and everyone therefore considers himself informed. And this information, furthermore, operates usually (generally, popularly) to reinforce traditional attitudes. Of traditional attitudes there are only two—For or Against—and I, personally, find it difficult to say which attitude has caused me the most pain. I am speaking as a writer; from a social point of view I am perfectly aware that the change from ill-will to good-will, however motivated, however imperfect, however expressed, is better than no change at all.

But it is part of the business of the writer—as I see it—to examine attitudes, to go beneath the surface, to tap the source. From this point of view the Negro problem is nearly inaccessible. It is not only written about so widely; it is written about so badly. It is quite possible to say that the price a Negro pays for becoming articulate is to find himself, at length, with nothing to be articulate about. ("You taught me language," says Caliban to Prospero,[3] "and my profit on't is I know how to curse.") Consider: the tremendous social activity that this problem generates imposes on whites and Negroes alike the necessity of looking forward, of working to bring about a better day. This is fine, it keeps the waters

---

3. *Caliban . . . Prospero.* In William Shakespeare's play, *The Tempest,* Caliban is a deformed slave of Prospero, the rightful Duke of Milan, who was deposed by his brother and the King of Naples.

troubled; it is all, indeed, that has made possible the Negro's progress. Nevertheless, social affairs are not generally speaking the writer's prime concern, whether they ought to be or not; it is absolutely necessary that he establish between himself and these affairs a distance which will allow, at least, for clarity, so that before he can look forward in any meaningful sense, he must first be allowed to take a long look back. In the context of the Negro problem neither whites nor blacks, for excellent reasons of their own, have the faintest desire to look back; but I think that the past is all that makes the present coherent, and further, that the past will remain horrible for exactly as long as we refuse to assess it honestly.

I know, in any case, that the most crucial time in my own development came when I was forced to recognize that I was a kind of bastard of the West; when I followed the line of my past I did not find myself in Europe but in Africa. And this meant that in some subtle way, in a really profound way, I brought to Shakespeare, Bach, Rembrandt, to the stones of Paris, to the cathedral at Chartres, and to the Empire State Building, a special attitude. These were not really my creations, they did not contain my history; I might search in them in vain forever for any reflection of myself. I was an interloper; this was not my heritage. At the same time I had no other heritage which I could possibly hope to use—I had certainly been unfitted for the jungle or the tribe. I would have to appropriate these white centuries, I would have to make them mine—I would have to accept my special attitude, my special place in this scheme—otherwise I would have no place in *any* scheme. What was the most difficult was the fact that I was forced to admit something I had always hidden from myself, which the American Negro has had to hide from himself as the price of his public progress; that I hated and feared white people. This did not mean that I loved black people; on the contrary, I despised them, possibly because they failed to produce Rembrandt. In effect, I hated and feared the world. And this meant, not only that I thus gave the world an altogether murderous power over me, but also that in such a self-destroying limbo I could never hope to write.

One writes out of one thing only—one's own experience. Everything depends on how relentlessly one forces from this experience the last drop, sweet or bitter, it can possibly give. This is the only real concern of the artist, to recreate out of the disorder of life that order which is art. The difficulty then, for me, of being a Negro writer was the fact that I was, in effect, prohibited from examining my own experience too closely by the tremendous demands and the very real dangers of my social situation.

I don't think the dilemma outlined above is uncommon. I do think, since writers work in the disastrously explicit medium of language, that it goes a little way towards explaining why, out of the enormous resources of Negro speech and life, and despite the example of Negro music, prose written by Negroes has been generally speaking so pallid and so harsh. I have not written about being a Negro at such length because I expect that to be my only subject, but only because it was the gate I had to unlock before I could hope to write about anything else. I don't think that the Negro problem in America can be even discussed coherently without bearing in mind its context; its context being the history, traditions, customs, the moral assumptions and preoccupations of the country; in short, the general social fabric. Appearances to the contrary, no one in America escapes its effects and everyone in America bears some responsibility for it. I believe this the more firmly because it is the overwhelming tendency to speak of this problem as though it were a thing apart. But in the work of Faulkner, in the general attitude and certain specific passages in Robert Penn Warren, and most significantly, in the advent of Ralph Ellison,[4] one sees the beginnings—at least—of a more genuinely penetrating search. Mr. Ellison, by the way, is the first Negro novelist I have ever read to utilize in language, and brilliantly, some of the ambiguity and irony of Negro life.

About my interests: I don't know if I have any, unless the morbid desire to own a sixteen-millimeter camera and make experimental movies can be so classified. Otherwise, I love to eat

---

4. Faulkner . . . Robert Penn Warren . . . Ralph Ellison. Relationships among black and white Americans are frequently a theme in the works of these three writers.

and drink—it's my melancholy conviction that I've scarcely ever had enough to eat (this is because it's *impossible* to eat enough if you're worried about the next meal)—and I love to argue with people who do not disagree with me too profoundly, and I love to laugh. I do *not* like bohemia, or bohemians, I do not like people whose principal aim is pleasure, and I do not like people who are *earnest* about anything. I don't like people who like me because I'm a Negro; neither do I like people who find in the same accident grounds for contempt. I love America more than any other country in the world, and, exactly for this reason, I insist on the right to criticize her perpetually. I think all theories are suspect, that the finest principles may have to be modified, or may even be pulverized by the demands of life, and that one must find, therefore, one's own moral center and move through the world hoping that this center will guide one aright. I consider that I have many responsibilities, but none greater than this: to last, as Hemingway[5] says, and get my work done.

I want to be an honest man and a good writer. □□

---

5. **Hemingway,** Ernest Hemingway (see page 415).

Discussion

1. Writers have remarked, time and again, that serious writing is the hardest work on earth. **(a)** What aspects of this **autobiography** bear out this observation? **(b)** From your own experience, would you agree or disagree? Why?

2. (a) What attitude does Baldwin take toward his early attempts at writing? **(b)** How is his attitude toward his role as a mature writer different? **(c)** What impression do you get of the man who wrote these statements?

3. What parts of this piece would you cite to emphasize its honesty and directness?

Extension • Writing

In the next-to-final paragraph, Baldwin writes a *credo*, or statement of his beliefs. Try writing your own credo, following Baldwin's concise and direct manner.

James Baldwin   1924 •

James Baldwin was born in New York City and raised in Harlem. The son of a clergyman, he spent three years while still in high school as a Baptist preacher before a major reexamination of his beliefs caused him to leave the church. After graduation he moved from one odd job to another. He wrote in his free time, but his first novel, completed at the age of twenty-two, was a failure. Two years later, seeking a more relaxed racial climate, Baldwin left for Europe. He lived for ten years in Paris and while there produced *Go Tell It on the Mountain* (1953), *Giovanni's Room* (1956), and *Notes of a Native Son* (1955), a collection of essays from which the preceding selection is taken. The success of these works quickly established Baldwin as one of America's finest new writers.

He has, since those years in France, lived in America, for a time in Istanbul, and now once again in Paris. He has branched out to write plays, the most notable being *Blues for Mr. Charlie* (1964). In 1962 he published what many consider his finest novel to date, *Another Country.* But despite the popularity of his fiction, it seems increasingly likely that he will be remembered first for the brilliance of his essays. *The Fire Next Time* (1963) is a widely recognized masterpiece.

Erma Bombeck

Teenage Diseases

Virgin Feet

The other day my son's guidance counselor asked, "What do you want your boy to be when he grows up?"

"A pedestrian," I said.

I know I'm a fool for hoping. My son has suffered from virgin feet since he was nine months old. Just after he took his first step, he slumped to the floor in a heap and mumbled, "No, na, knee, noo" (Meaning: Is that all there is to feet?).

Since then he has been wheeled about in buggies, strollers and wagons, supported in papoose back-packs, bicycle baskets, grocery carts and car seats, slung over hips and shoulders and transported on sleds, escalators, gocarts and automobiles.

In all that time he has never had his shoes half-soled. Never grown a corn. Never worn a hole in his socks. Never gotten wet feet and had his socks fade. Never tripped over a shoelace.

The other night he stood in front of me impatiently.

"What's the matter," I asked. "Is the Garbage Can Car Pool running late?"

"I am waiting for you to run me over to the school," he said.

"What for?"

"Practice."

"Practice for what?"

"Track. I am running the mile."

"How far is it to school?"

"About a mile."

"How long does it take you to run a mile?"

"About five minutes, forty seconds," he said proudly.

"Then run it. It would take me that long to find my car keys."

"RUN IT! You've got to be kidding. I can't run a mile to school, then run another mile cross-country."

"Why not?"

"It's dumb. It's like going on a Boy Scout hike and not riding in a truck."

"Look," I said, "we've got to have a talk about your virgin feet."

"What about them? They look great."

"They should," I snapped. "They're brand-new. They've been propped up on sofas and chairs and tables and covered with twenty-dollar shoes for the last seventeen years. Now I want you to start using them again."

"For what?"

"For walking. Think of it, boy. This could open up a whole new world if kids started to walk again. Imagine, walk-in movies, walk-in hamburger emporiums, walk-in banks, walk-in sit-ins."

"I can't do it," he whined.

"Of course you can. You simply stand up straight for balance, put your weight alternately on one foot and then the other and extend one foot at a time in front of you."

He stood up slowly and tried it. "It feels awful," he said. "Couldn't I get a motorcycle or a golf cart until I get the hang of it?"

"You'll never get well if you don't try," I said. "Today I want you to walk all the way to school and back."

Later that afternoon, he came limping back from track practice.

"What happened?" I asked.

"I tried walking," he said falling into a chair. "About halfway I got a piece of gravel in my shoe and I leaned down to take it out. A bicycle plowed into me, cut my knee and bruised my leg. I lost my shoe in a ditch and got a sprained ankle when I fell trying to find it. A car stopped to help and got sideswiped. I was lucky to get out alive.

No wonder there aren't any old pedestrians. If you ask me, feet will never catch on."

"Have I ever lied to you?" I said, putting my hand on his shoulder.

"Yes. The time you told me the tooth fairy liked to be paid yearly by check to keep her income-tax records straight."

"What about the time before that?" I persisted.

Convenient Hearing

The first time I observed my son with a case of Convenient Hearing, I thought he had been smoking old gym shoes.

I had called him six times to come to dinner. There was no response. Finally, I went directly to his room. He was sitting on the register in a fetal position. The record player was going full blast (Mr. Wonderful and the Electric Pimples). The television set was up to its aerial in decibels. He had a transistor cord in one ear and a telephone receiver in the other. He was teasing a yapping dog with a sock between his toes.

I pulled all the plugs, hung up the phone, silenced the dog and demanded, "Why didn't you answer me when I called?"

He looked up slowly, made a peace sign with his fingers and said, "You know I can't hear you with a war on."

What I had suspected was true. My son heard what he wanted to hear with maddening inconsistency or regard to an individual's sanity. He tuned on or tuned out when he felt like hearing.

There were many incongruities.

He could not hear the phone ring when he was leaning on it and you were in the shower.

If it was a girl calling for him, he heard it before it even rang.

He could not hear the dog scratch when he wanted in or out.

He could hear his buddies "lay a patch" twenty minutes away from the house.

He could not hear you ask him to take out the trash when your lips touched his ear.

He overheard your discussion of his report card when you talked in a whisper in the northeast corner of the garage.

He could not hear his alarm clock in the morning.

He could hear football plays whispered in a windstorm by a quarterback with a lisp and all of his teeth missing.

My neighbor Maxine was puzzled by our case of Convenient Hearing.

"How do you communicate?" she asked one day over coffee.

"We don't," I said. "My son has only spoken four words to me all year."

"What were they?"

"It was last April. I was separating some eggs for a cake. As I dumped the yolk from one shell to another, I miscalculated and the egg slid down the counter top, along the cupboard and onto my new kitchen carpet. My son was standing there watching. He looked at me and said, 'Way to go, Mom.'"

"That was it?"

"I was thrilled," I said. "I didn't think he even knew my name."

"I don't see how you can raise him when you don't talk," she sighed.

"There are ways," I said. "There's the old bumper-sticker-with-the-message trick. I hang homemade posters and stickers around his room reading 'HELP THE ECONOMY—TAKE A LEFT-

OVER TO LUNCH!' or 'STAMP OUT POLLUTION IN YOUR AREA—SEND YOUR GYM SHOES OUT OF STATE.' Of course, there's the ever-popular, 'DON'T LET YOUR MOLARS BE DROPOUTS: SEE YOUR DENTIST AT 1:30 THURSDAY.'"

"Oh good grief," she said, "does it work?"

"Most of the time. Of course, we have to get drastic on occasions and buy time on local rock stations to get through to him. This is how he found out we moved last April."

"I don't see how you have the patience to talk all the time to a boy who only listens at his own convenience."

"The beautiful thing about Convenient Hearing," I said, grinning, "is that it can be contagious. I can catch it too, you know. Like the other day, I was vacuuming the kitchen. The dryer buzzer was going off, the washer was pulsating, my favorite soap opera was on television and the disposer was grinding up chicken bones. My son came out and yelled, 'Hey Mom, you got two dollars?'

"I didn't move a muscle.

"'Mom, did you hear me?' he shouted. 'I need two dollars. Where's your purse?'

"Finally, he unplugged all my appliances and put his face in mine. 'Are you deaf?'

"I made the sign of the Women's Liberation fist and cross and said, 'You know I can't hear you while I'm being liberated.'" ☐☐

Discussion

1. Erma Bombeck's humor depends largely on exaggeration, but beneath the exaggeration there is always a grain of truth. **(a)** Do you know anyone who dislikes walking as much as the boy in this article? Describe that person. **(b)** Is it fair to label either "virgin feet" or "convenient hearing" *teenage* diseases? Explain.

Extension • Writing

Using Bombeck's **satirical** formula (humorous exaggeration, clever metaphors and similes), write an article about "Parental Diseases" that afflict offspring. For instance, are parents overprotective? Do they have a habit of starting discussions or arguments with "When I was your age . . ."? Do their tastes in music vary from yours?

Erma Bombeck 1927 •

Bombeck's humorous column, "At Wit's End," first appeared in a suburban weekly newspaper in Ohio, where she was born. It was discovered by a Dayton newspaper and has since 1965 been syndicated in over five hundred newspapers across the country. Bard of the Breakfast Nook, Guru of the Garbage Can, Bombeck finds laughter in fatness ("I've dieted continually for the past two decades and have lost a total of 758 pounds"), childhood disease ("We have measles. . . . It must be Christmas"), and domestic squabbles ("The hands that hold the car keys rule the world.")

Having come a long way since her first journalistic job as an obituary writer, Bombeck now is a popular lecturer and a frequent guest on television talk shows. Her books get

laughs with their titles alone: *Just Wait Till You Have Children of Your Own,* written with cartoonist Bil Keane; *I Lost Everything in the Post-Natal Depression*; and *The Grass Is Always Greener over the Septic Tank.*

Michael Arlen

Fresno, California

Fresno, California: *"Fresno"* is a Spanish word meaning "ash tree." There are still some ash trees here, scattered far out of town, but the Spanish influence, as they call it, is pretty well gone by now, unless you count the roadside Margarita places and Taco Pete's. The Armenian[1] presence is a little more visible, but not much. There are two Armenian churches. An Armenian bakery. Two or three Armenian restaurants. There used to be an Armenian community—"Armenian Town"—but it has largely disappeared, torn up to make way for the new expressway and the shopping center. There is a Basque presence, also an Italian presence, and a Japanese presence, but mainly a Wasp presence, for this is a California town, a microcity. "Fresno: Pop. 180,000," say the big green signs. What is going on here is agribusiness, which means the great earth factory of the San Joaquin Valley: untold acres of farmland, fruitland, vineland. Trees and vines and pastureland extending for miles between the invisible Pacific and the dimly visible Sierra: snowcapped blue mountains seen through a bluish haze. Over on the coast is Monterey—John Steinbeck's Cannery Row and Tortilla Flat.[2] Here was William Saroyan's[3] hot, flat valley filled with fruit and crops and poverty and life. "A man could walk four or five miles in any direction from the heart of our city and see our streets dwindle to land and weeds," Saroyan wrote in the nineteen-thirties. "In many places the land would be vineyard and orchard land, but in most places it would be desert land and the weeds would be the strong dry weeds of deserts . . . Our trees were not yet tall enough to make much shade, and we had planted a number of kinds of trees we ought not to have planted because they were of weak stuff and would never live a century, but we had made a pretty good beginning. Our cemeteries were few and the graves in them were few. We had buried no great men because we hadn't had time to produce any great men, we had been too busy trying to get water into the desert." I don't know what I expected it to be like now. I know not like that, because nothing is like that any more—certainly not in California. I think I expected to see Armenian faces at the airport or on the street. I think I expected to walk off the plane and see Armenians hanging around the car-rental counters, behind the car-rental counters. Armenians—for it was our town, wasn't it?

I stood one afternoon in a field on the outskirts of the city and looked at the fruit trees, which were bare in the March wind, and looked at the grapevines, which were also bare—brown tendrils close to the brown soil, stretching out to the horizon as far as the eye could see. The man who owned the field was an Armenian named Gadalian. He had thick, graying hair and a wide, leathery face and thick hands. He was about fifty years old, but an outdoor fifty—square shoulders and a large, tough belly. He was worrying about frost. "The frost is strange here," he said. "It comes in waves across the valley. In one place there may be frost, but on the farm across the road there may be no frost. Look at this." He held up a grapevine that had been bent or broken around another vine. "Nobody knows how to

Excerpts from pp. 41–54 reprinted with the permission of Farrar, Straus & Giroux, Inc. and Chatto & Windus from PASSAGE TO ARARAT by Michael J. Arlen, Copyright © 1975 by Michael J. Arlen. This selection appeared originally in *The New Yorker*. Quotes from stories by William Saroyan reprinted by permission of the author.

1. **Armenian,** (är mē′nē ən), an immigrant from Armenia, once a kingdom of Asia Minor, now divided between Russia, Turkey, and Iran.
2. **Monterey . . . Tortilla Flat.** *Cannery Row* and *Tortilla Flat* are the titles Steinbeck (see page 18) gave to books of short stories set in those poor neighborhoods of Monterey.
3. **William Saroyan's.** See his play on page 63.

work the vines any more," he said. It was a modest farm, about eighty acres. There was a comfortable small farmhouse on the edge of the property, just off the dirt road, with grapefruit trees in the front and a kennel for two or three large dogs in the back. We were standing next to a ramshackle old house or hut of dark redwood, weathered by rain and sun—a place for tools and empty boxes. "My father lived here," said Gadalian, pointing inside. "This is where we grew up. He was a good man, my father. He worked very hard."

My father committed no crime. The bare trees stretch out everywhere. Bare branches against the metallic gray sky. Plums. Peaches. Apples. Grapefruit. Grapes. Fertility. The bluish mountains swim in haze against the sky.

"Did you know the Armenians brought the melons to California?" said Gadalian. "The melon they call the Persian melon. The casaba melon, whose seeds come from Kasaba, in Turkey. Most of the melons in this valley were grown by Arakelian. They called old Arakelian the Melon King."

"Where is he?" I asked.

"He is dead, I think. Anyway, his sons have moved to Los Angeles."

"Are there many Armenians here?" I asked.

"There are some," he said. "There are not too many any more."

We stood beside stacks of empty raisin crates. Old boxes, weathered like the hut.

"Look at this one," said Gadalian, pointing to a box so old that its sides had started to split apart. "This one goes back to my father's time. Look at the way they made the corners."

"How is it your father came here?" I asked.

"I don't know," said Gadalian. Then, "I think he and my mother came from the old country around 1900, some time like that. For a while, they were in the East, around Worcester, Massachusetts. They worked in the shoe factories. There were a number of Armenians who worked in the shoe factories. Then they heard about California, where they could grow things."

"Was your father happy here?" I asked.

Gadalian seemed puzzled. "I don't know," he said. "It is hard to tell if a father is happy." Then, "He worked very hard. I remember that."

Little farms scattered around the great valley.

These were some of the names on the mailboxes: Pirogian, Kavanessian, Agajanian. A sign on an abandoned warehouse: "SIMOJIAN RAISINS, THE FINEST IN THE WORLD." I thought of Bud and his tropical fish in New York. I thought of my father,[4] who had journeyed to Hollywood a number of times in his career but never to Fresno. What was here in Fresno? What had been here?

I thought of the simple warmth of a Saroyan story: "Walking along Alvin Street he felt glad to be home again. Everything was fine, common and good, the smell of earth, cooking suppers, smoke, the rich summer air of the valley full of plant growth, grapes growing, peaches ripening, and the oleander bush swooning with sweetness, the same as ever . . . This valley, he thought, all this country between the mountains, is mine, home to me, the place I dream about, and everything is the same."

I thought, too, of what a friend of Gadalian's had said when I asked him where most of the Armenians in Fresno lived.

"Oh, now they can live anywhere," he said.

"What do you mean, anywhere?"

"There are no more restrictions," he said. "Before, it wasn't always so easy. Of course, you have to understand that a lot of the first Armenians here were country people. Farmers. Rough people." He smiled. He had enormous hands, fingers as thick as roots, palms caked with dirt. "They took away the restrictions at the end of the war," he said. And "This valley is my home. It's the place I dream about." Sometimes the dreams of people make one gasp.

And now William Saroyan himself, standing in the lobby of the Fresno Hilton. William Saroyan at sixty-six. The hair thick but graying. A burly man. Stocky. A fine mustache. Also large hands. A laugh. Good eyes, a good face.

"I was out in the country," I said.

"It's beautiful, isn't it? You should come back in the summer," said Saroyan. "Of course, it is terrible in the summer. You sweat all day long. But then everybody is busy."

We drove through side streets, past the sterile

---

4. *my father,* Michael Arlen, the elder (1895–1956), a romantic novelist and screenwriter.

glass office buildings of the new downtown, past the immense modern convention center. "Everything has changed," said Saroyan. "But of course it has changed. Look at that shopping center. Nobody comes to it. Do you see that street? I used to deliver papers up and down that street. It was a good job, too. The paper was called the Fresno *Republican*, and it was edited and published by Mr. Chester Rowell. Both are gone now, though there's a statue of the paper's founder in Courthouse Square."

We drove under a viaduct over which the new expressway was being built. The land ahead of us was mostly desolate from the bulldozers, but here and there a few small frame houses remained. "I'd show you where I grew up, but they tore that down, too," said Saroyan. "I hope for their sake more people use the new expressway than use the shopping center."

"There don't seem to be very many Armenians around," I said.

"There are still a few," said Saroyan. "Maybe ten thousand in the valley. But the town has grown, and the Armenians sold their land and moved to the cities."

"What about you?" I asked.

"I got tired of knocking around too much. One day, I decided to come back. Once you like a place, you always like it."

We drove away from the little streets and little houses, and out past the familiar landmarks of modern California: the endless strip of car lots and Mexican restaurants and bowling alleys and garden-supply stores and farm-hardware warehouses and motels with banquet and convention facilities.

I thought of a story of Saroyan's that I'd read long ago, which began, "I don't suppose you ever saw a two-hundred-and-fifty-pound Filipino." It's hard to forget a story that begins that way. I had read that story in school, when my favorite writers were Ernest Hemingway, Robert Benchley,[5] and William Saroyan: Hemingway because he was so sexy with those sleeping bags; Benchley because he was so funny; and Saroyan because nobody could write to a person (me) the way that William Saroyan wrote.

There was another story, which I'd read on the plane to California—a story called "Five Ripe Pears." It began like this: "If old man

Pollard is still alive I hope he reads this because I want him to know I am not a thief and never have been. Instead of making up a lie, which I could have done, I told the truth, and got a licking. I don't care about the licking because I got a lot of them in grammar school . . . The licking Mr. Pollard gave me I didn't deserve, and I hope he reads this because I am going to tell him why. I couldn't tell him that day because I didn't know how to explain what I knew . . . It was about spring pears." It was not an important story, but it was a lovely story—a story with a voice. It made one think with a kind of pleasure that J. D. Salinger must have heard that voice, and Richard Brautigan, and Jack Kerouac,[6] and all those writers of the personal sound, the flower-writers, the writers of our modern Era of Feeling.

"I'm glad you decided to find out about Armenians," said Saroyan. "They're a crazy people, you know. Or sometimes they seem that way. But they're a very simple people."

We drove on a while. Saroyan talked about his children—a daughter in New York, a son in San Francisco. Family talk. He asked me about my wife and children, about my sister, about my work. I felt something surprisingly paternal in his voice. It was a strange, deep feeling, as if we had known each other all along, when in fact I had met Saroyan only once before, briefly, a few years ago in New York, and had called him in Fresno only a week earlier to arrange our meeting.

We stopped to have dinner at a roadside restaurant, a roadside Armenian restaurant called Stanley's. A nice place, too, with bright lights and the ubiquitous Olde Steake House furniture and a photograph of Mt. Ararat[7] behind the cashier's desk.

"Sometime I hope you'll meet my Uncle Aram," said Saroyan. "He's eighty-two now, and a fine man. I've written a lot of stories about Aram. People would ask me, 'Are they true

---

5. *Ernest Hemingway, Robert Benchley.* See Hemingway's story and biography (page 412). Benchley (1889–1945) was a popular humorist.
6. *J. D. Salinger . . . Richard Brautigan . . . Jack Kerouac* (ker′ə wak), American writers popular in the 1950s and 1960s.
7. *Mt. Ararat,* the highest mountain and a national symbol of Armenia.

stories?' I'd always reply, 'Of course not. I am a writer. I make things up. I embellish.' But it's been hard to embellish Aram."

Saroyan began to tell some stories about his Uncle Aram in a loud, resonant voice. The waiter brought some Armenian bread and a bottle of wine, then shish kebab. Saroyan laughed as he spoke. I looked at him and thought, My father was sixty when he died; he would be seventy-nine now. I thought of my father's frailness, his thin elegance; it seemed like such a different presence.

"You know, your father was a fine man," Saroyan said, as if he were reading my mind.

"Did you think of him as an Armenian?" I asked.

"Of course I did," said Saroyan. "An Armenian can never not be an Armenian. But your father went about it differently. I think he had other things on his mind."

"What kind of things?"

"I don't know," said Saroyan. "The truth is, I didn't see him often. We were different. But we were also close. I can't quite explain it. I remember the first time I met him. It was just after the war. I heard he was in New York, and I was passing through, and so I telephoned. We met at some hotel—the Hampshire House, or maybe the Pierre. I remember how we embraced; that is what I remember. Another time, this was a few years later, we had dinner at that restaurant—did you ever go?—the Golden Horn, and afterward we went back to where I was living. I had an apartment that winter on Central Park West. We talked about writing and families, I remember. Your father was about to start another book; at least, that is what he said, although I guess he never finished it. But it was a close time. I remember him standing in the corridor and looking in on our children, who were sleeping. The children were very young and they kept stirring in their sleep, and your father kept saying 'Shhh,' the way fathers do."

I thought of that photograph in the Golden Horn. The two comrades, the two Armenian writers—both of them in fact then passing the peak of their fame, my father putting on a graceful front of having "retired," Saroyan both more and less fortunate in not being able to retire but, instead, turning out a stream of novels and plays that critics were beginning to say did not compare to the early work.

A waitress came over to Saroyan with a menu she wished him to autograph. Saroyan signed it with a flourish and then asked her to sign one for him.

"I will tell you," Saroyan said to me. "If you want to know about Armenians, then you must go to Armenia, or what remains of it. You must go to Erevan—in Soviet Armenia."

"Have you been there?" I asked.

"Yes, I've been there. I went there the first time I earned any money. This was in 1935, and it wasn't much money, either. I went to New York and took one of those beautiful ships they had then. The *Berengaria*. I went to Europe and then to Soviet Armenia. They didn't have much in Armenia in those days, but it was a trip I had to make. I went back once again, in 1960."

"What did you find out when you went there?" I asked.

"I found out that there was an Armenia," said Saroyan. "Of course, it isn't what it used to be, but it *is* there; it is something."

We went back to Saroyan's house: a small tract house on one of the new streets—a modest house, on a street lined with perhaps a hundred similar houses. Inside, there was an extraordinary jumble of objects: not so much a disorder as a plenitude of things—books, and cartons, and suitcases, and boxes of this and that. In a large room off the kitchen, a tiny portable typewriter stood in the middle of a table piled with books and paper and manuscript. "I've always worked, and so I work now," said Saroyan. "Besides, I have to live."

"What are you writing?" I asked.

"I mostly write plays now. Sometimes people want to produce them, sometimes they do not. But that is what I do. Besides, my writing is better than my painting." He pointed to innumerable bright-colored abstract designs that had been pinned or Scotch-taped to the walls. Then he bent down in front of a pile of dusty magazines and pulled one out. "Did you ever see this?" he said. It was a copy of an old English-language Armenian magazine. Saroyan opened it to a picture of my father; in fact, it was a reproduction of a photograph that had appeared on a cover of *Time* in 1927—now with a short note beside it on the "popular Anglo-Armenian novelist, formerly Dikran Kouyoumjian." Saroyan held the magazine open for a moment, and then put it down on the table. "It's a good photo of him, isn't it?" he said. "Such confidence."

"How is it that he never wrote anything serious about Armenians?" I asked.

"I think he wasn't that kind of writer," Saroyan said. "He liked to be entertaining. He made a couple of good jokes about Armenians, as I remember."

"Yes," I said. "But how is it that you wrote all the time about Armenians and he never did?"

"I don't know," said Saroyan. "Except that we all go on different journeys. Just like you. Now you come here. And soon, I think, you must go to Erevan."

We stood in the semidarkness of Saroyan's small house, surrounded by the clutter, the books, the magazines, the cartons, the jars of "treasures" that Saroyan had picked up on his travels or on the street. "I am a writer," Saroyan said. "It is something to be a writer. All my life, I have written. Also talked and drunk and gambled and everything else." He laughed. "They say that Armenians live to be very old. Did you know that? My grandmother Lucy Saroyan died at eighty-eight. My father's kid brother Mirhan died at eighty. Come on. Let's go and look at the graveyard."

It was now midnight, or a bit later. We got in the car and drove through the silent streets of Fresno. It was hard to tell in which direction we were going—out toward the country or in toward the downtown. Darkened houses flicked by in the night. "It is too bad you don't know Armenian," Saroyan said. "Although you will survive. But it is a marvelous language—marvelous sounds. Do you know their songs? I shall sing one for you."

Saroyan sang, rolling down the window of the car. Outside, it had begun to rain—one of those fine, sprinkling nighttime rains. Saroyan's voice filled the car, the countryside silent except for the sound of our tires on the wet road. "It is a song about love and injustice and about pomegranates getting ripe," said Saroyan. "In other words, about the important things in life."

The car stopped beside the road. "Come on," he said, getting out. The rain was pouring down more heavily, but the air was warm and had a kind of fragrance. "Now, over there is the Protestant graveyard," he said. "And somewhere down there are the Catholics. And right here are the Armenians." Saroyan was wearing an old hat, a kind of old newspaperman's hat—a hat from *The Time of Your Life*,[8] maybe. Now he began to run at a trot through the graveyard. We passed dim gravestones in the darkness. "Over there is Levon!" he called. "I think one of Lucy's sisters is here!" The grass was soft and slippery underfoot. Saroyan kept up a steady jog. "I think somewhere over there is Uncle Mirhan!" He stopped, breathing heavily. "You know, everybody seems the same in a graveyard—Protestant, Catholic, and Armenian. But still there is something different. I don't know what it is." He wiped his forehead, which was damp with rain and sweat. "Come on," he said. "It's wet here. It's time to go home."

Later on, when we said goodbye, Saroyan embraced me. I could feel his rough cheek scrape against mine. His rough, robust cheek. "Fathers and sons are always different," he said. "But they are also the same. Maybe you will find out about that, too. Anyway, I was truly fond of him and now I am fond of you, and that is something, is it not?" He clasped my hand, and put the newspaperman's hat back on his head, and tugged his jacket about him more closely, for a cold wind was blowing now, and stuffed his hands in his pockets, and turned back to the car, and got in and drove away across "the valley full of plant growth, grapes growing, peaches ripening, and the oleander bush swooning with sweetness," to the house with the cartons and suitcases and the small portable typewriter.

I watched him go, still feeling the roughness of his face against mine. □□

---

8. *The Time of Your Life*, a play by Saroyan about people at a waterfront bar who represent essential goodness and zest for life.

Discussion

1. What has happened to the Armenian community in Fresno? How does the author feel about this change?

2. What do you sense about the author's feelings for his father? Explain.

3. What impression of William Saroyan do you get from this article? What things about him stand out most clearly in the article?

4. What bond is formed between the young Arlen and Saroyan during the visit?

Extension • Writing

Investigate any ethnic group of your community whose traditions interest you. How did their ancestors come to settle in your part of the country? How long has the group lived there? In what ways have its members contributed to your community? To what extent have these people preserved their ancestral customs and traditions? To what extent have they blended in with other groups in your community? Write a composition covering the above questions.

Vocabulary • Dictionary

The following words are in the excerpt from *Notes of a Native Son* by James Baldwin or "Fresno, California" by Michael Arlen. Using the Glossary, find a word to match each of the meanings or etymological clues that follow the list of words. (Two words will not match any clue.) Be sure you can spell and pronounce all the words.

> conundrum
> rhetoric
> bravura
> ubiquitous
> embellish
> plenitude
> resonant

1. Means "being everywhere."

2. Comes partly from an Old French word meaning "handsome."

3. Comes from the Greek word for "orator."

4. Comes from a Latin word meaning "full."

5. Comes from the Italian word for "bravery."

Michael J. Arlen 1930 •

As is evident in "Fresno, California," Michael Arlen carries on a family literary tradition inherited from his father, who was a sophisticated writer of "popular entertainments." After attending Harvard University, the younger Arlen gained experience as a reporter and then became a staff writer for *The New Yorker*. He is still the television critic for that magazine, and his perceptive reviews say as much about American culture as they do about television.

Passage to Ararat, from which "Fresno, California" is taken, describes Arlen's travels in search of his Armenian heritage. His other books include *Exiles* and *Living Room War*, a collection of essays about the world as depicted on televison.

Alice Walker

In Search of Our Mothers' Gardens

When the poet Jean Toomer[1] walked through the South in the early twenties, he discovered a curious thing: Black women whose spirituality was so intense, so deep, so *unconscious,* that they were themselves unaware of the richness they held. They stumbled blindly through their lives: creatures so abused and mutilated in body, so dimmed and confused by pain, that they considered themselves unworthy even of hope. . . .

In the still heat of the Post–Reconstruction South,[2] this is how they seemed to Jean Toomer: exquisite butterflies trapped in an evil honey, toiling away their lives in an era, a century, that did not acknowledge them, except as "the *mule* of the world." They dreamed dreams that no one knew—not even themselves, in any coherent fashion—and saw visions no one could understand. They wandered or sat about the countryside crooning lullabies to ghosts, and drawing the mother of Christ in charcoal on courthouse walls. . . .

Our mothers and grandmothers, some of them: moving to music not yet written. And they waited.

They waited for a day when the unknown thing that was in them would be made known; but guessed, somehow in their darkness, that on the day of their revelation they would be long dead. Therefore to Toomer they walked, and even ran, in slow motion. For they were going nowhere immediate, and the future was not yet within their grasp. . . .

How was the creativity of the Black woman kept alive, year after year and century after century, when for most of the years Black people have been in America, it was a punishable crime for a Black person to read or write? And the freedom to paint, to sculpt, to expand the mind with action, did not exist. Consider, if you can bear to imagine it, what might have been the result if singing, too, had been forbidden by law.

Listen to the voices of Bessie Smith, Billie Holiday, Nina Simone, Roberta Flack, and Aretha Franklin,[3] among others, and imagine those voices muzzled for life. Then you may begin to comprehend the lives of our "crazy," "Sainted" mothers and grandmothers. The agony of the lives of women who might have been Poets, Novelists, Essayists, and Short Story Writers (over a period of centuries), who died with their real gifts stifled within them.

And, if this were the end of the story, we would have cause to cry out in my paraphrase of Okot p'Bitek's[4] great poem:

> O, my clanswomen
> Let us all cry together!
> Come,
> Let us mourn the death of our mother,
> The death of a Queen
> The ash that was produced
> By a great fire!
> O this homestead is utterly dead
> Close the gates
> With *lacari* thorns,[5]
> For our mother
> The creator of the Stool is lost!
> And all the young women
> Have perished in the wilderness!

Abridgement from "In Search of Our Mothers' Gardens" by Alice Walker. Reprinted by permission of the Julian Bach Literary Agency, Inc. Copyright © 1974 by Alice Walker. First appeared in *Ms. Magazine.*

1. **Jean Toomer.** See page 465.
2. **Post–Reconstruction South.** During Reconstruction (1865–1877), the South was governed by pro-Union blacks and whites, backed by federal troops. After this era, resentful former Confederate supporters regained power, and oppression of blacks resumed.
3. **Bessie Smith . . . Aretha Franklin,** famous jazz and blues singers. Smith and Holiday performed mainly in the 1920s and '30s, Simone in the 1950s and '60s, while Flack and Franklin became popular in the late 1960s.
4. **Okot p'Bitek's** (o′kot pə bə tek′), a poet, novelist, essayist, and anthropolgist (1931–) from Uganda in Africa.
5. ***lacari* thorns,** probably a kind of dense thorn bush used to block African village gates at night.

But this is not the end of the story, for all the young women—our mothers and grandmothers, *ourselves*—have not perished in the wilderness. And if we ask ourselves why, and search for and find the answer, we will know beyond all efforts to erase it from our minds, just exactly who, and of what, we Black American women are.

One example, perhaps the most pathetic, most misunderstood one, can provide a backdrop for our mothers' work: Phillis Wheatley,[6] a slave in the 1700s.

Virginia Woolf,[7] in her book, *A Room of One's Own,* wrote that in order for a woman to write fiction she must have two things, certainly: a room of her own (with key and lock) and enough money to support herself.

What then are we to make of Phillis Wheatley, a slave, who owned not even herself? This sickly, frail, Black girl who required a servant of her own at times—her health was so precarious—and who, had she been white, would have been easily considered the intellectual superior of all the women and most of the men in the society of her day. . . .

When we read the poetry of Phillis Wheatley—as when we read the novels of Nella Larsen or the oddly false-sounding autobiography of that freest of all Black women writers, Zora Hurston[8]—evidence of "contrary instincts" is everywhere. Her loyalties were completely divided, as was, without question, her mind.

But how could this be otherwise? Captured at seven, a slave of wealthy, doting whites who instilled in her the "savagery" of the Africa they "rescued" her from . . . one wonders if she was even able to remember her homeland as she had known it, or as it really was. . . .

In the last years of her brief life, burdened not only with the need to express her gift but also with a penniless, friendless "freedom" and several small children for whom she was forced to do strenuous work to feed, she lost her health, certainly. Suffering from malnutrition and neglect and who knows what mental agonies, Phillis Wheatley died.

So torn by "contrary instincts" was Black, kidnapped, enslaved Phillis that her description of "the Goddess"—as she poetically called the Liberty she did not have—is ironically, cruelly humorous. And, in fact, has held Phillis up to ridicule for more than a century. It is usually read prior to hanging Phillis's memory as that of a fool. She wrote:

> The Goddess comes, she moves divinely fair,
> Olive and laurel binds her *golden* hair:
> Wherever shines this native of the skies,
> Unnumber'd charms and recent graces rise.
>
> (Emphasis mine)

It is obvious that Phillis, the slave, combed the "Goddess's" hair every morning; prior, perhaps, to bringing in the milk, or fixing her mistress's lunch. She took her imagery from the one thing she saw elevated above all others.

With the benefit of hindsight we ask, "How could she?"

But at last, Phillis, we understand. No more snickering when your stiff, struggling, ambivalent lines are forced on us. We know now that you were not an idiot nor a traitor; only a sickly little Black girl, snatched from your home and country and made a slave; a woman who still struggled to sing the song that was your gift, although in a land of barbarians who praised you for your bewildered tongue. It is not so much what you sang, as that you kept alive, in so many of our ancestors, *the notion of song.* . . .

We must fearlessly pull out of ourselves and look at and identify with our lives the living creativity some of our great-grandmothers were not allowed to know. I stress *some* of them because it is well known that the majority of our great-grandmothers knew, even without "knowing" it, the reality of their spirituality, even if they didn't recognize it beyond what happened in the singing at church—and they never had any intention of giving it up.

How they did it: those millions of Black women who were not Phillis Wheatley, or Lucy Terry or Frances Harper or Zora Hurston or Nella Larsen or Bessie Smith—nor Elizabeth

6. **Phillis Wheatley.** See page 141.
7. **Virginia Woolf** (1882–1941), a British author noted for psychological studies of women in fiction and essays.
8. **Nella Larsen . . . Zora Hurston.** Larsen (1893–1963) was a novelist of the Harlem Renaissance (see page 442). Hurston (1901–1960), an anthropologist and writer, published several books in the 1930s and '40s.

Catlett, nor Katherine Dunham,[9] either—bring me to the title of this essay, "In Search of Our Mothers' Gardens," which is a personal account that is yet shared, in its theme and its meaning, by all of us. I found, while thinking about the far-reaching world of the creative Black woman, that often the truest answer to a question that really matters can be found very close. So I was not surprised when my own mother popped into my mind.

In the late 1920s my mother ran away from home to marry my father. Marriage, if not running away, was expected of seventeen-year-old girls. By the time she was twenty, she had two children and was pregnant with a third. Five children later, I was born. And this is how I came to know my mother: she seemed a large, soft, loving-eyed woman who was rarely impatient in our home. Her quick, violent temper was on view only a few times a year, when she battled with the white landlord who had the misfortune to suggest to her that her children did not need to go to school.

She made all the clothes we wore, even my brothers' overalls. She made all the towels and sheets we used. She spent the summers canning vegetables and fruits. She spent the winter evenings making quilts enough to cover all our beds.

During the "working" day, she labored beside—not behind—my father in the fields. Her day began before sunup, and did not end until late at night. There was never a moment for her to sit down, undisturbed, to unravel her own private thoughts; never a time free from interruption—by work or the noisy inquiries of her many children. And yet, it is to my mother—and all our mothers who were not famous—that I went in search of the secret of what has fed that muzzled and often mutilated, but vibrant, creative spirit that the Black woman has inherited, and that pops out in wild and unlikely places to this day.

But when, you will ask, did my overworked mother have time to know or care about feeding the creative spirit?

The answer is so simple that many of us have spent years discovering it. We have constantly looked high, when we should have looked high—and low.

For example: in the Smithsonian Institution in Washington, D.C., there hangs a quilt unlike any other in the world. In fanciful, inspired, and yet simple and identifiable figures, it portrays the story of the Crucifixion. It is considered rare, beyond price. Though it follows no known pattern of quilt-making, and though it is made of bits and pieces of worthless rags, it is obviously the

9. *Lucy Terry . . . Katherine Dunham,* examples of creative black women. Terry and Harper were poets, Catlett an educator and sculptor, and Dunham is a dancer and choreographer.

work of a person of powerful imagination and deep spiritual feeling. Below this quilt I saw a note that says it was made by "an anonymous Black woman in Alabama, a hundred years ago."

If we could locate this "anonymous" Black woman from Alabama, she would turn out to be one of our grandmothers—an artist who left her mark in the only materials she could afford, and in the only medium her position in society allowed her to use. . . .

And so our mothers and grandmothers have, more often than not anonymously, handed on the creative spark, the seed of the flower they themselves never hoped to see: or like a sealed letter they could not plainly read.

And so it is, certainly, with my own mother. Unlike "Ma" Rainey's[10] songs, which retained their creator's name even while blasting forth from Bessie Smith's mouth, no song or poem will bear my mother's name. Yet so many of the stories that I write, that we all write, are my mother's stories. Only recently did I fully realize this: that through years of listening to my mother's stories of her life, I have absorbed not only the stories themselves, but something of the manner in which she spoke, something of the urgency that involves the knowledge that her stories—like her life—must be recorded. It is probably for this reason that so much of what I have written is about characters whose counterparts in real life are so much older than I am.

But the telling of these stories, which came from my mother's lips as naturally as breathing, was not the only way my mother showed herself as an artist. For stories, too, were subject to being distracted, to dying without conclusion. Dinners must be started, and cotton must be gathered before the big rains. The artist that was and is my mother showed itself to me only after many years. This is what I finally noticed:

Like Mem, a character in *The Third Life of Grange Copeland*,[11] my mother adorned with flowers whatever shabby house we were forced to live in. And not just your typical straggly country stand of zinnias, either. She planted ambitious gardens—and still does—with over fifty different varieties of plants that bloom profusely from early March until late November. Before she left home for the fields, she watered her flowers, chopped up the grass, and laid out new beds. When she returned from the fields she might divide clumps of bulbs, dig a cold pit, uproot and replant roses, or prune branches from her taller bushes or trees—until night came and it was too dark to see.

Whatever she planted grew as if by magic, and her fame as a grower of flowers spread over three counties. Because of her creativity with her flowers, even my memories of poverty are seen through a screen of blooms—sunflowers, petunias, roses, dahlias, forsythia, spirea, delphiniums, verbena . . . and on and on.

And I remember people coming to my mother's yard to be given cuttings from her flowers; I hear again the praise showered on her because whatever rocky soil she landed on, she turned into a garden. A garden so brilliant with colors, so original in its design, so magnificent with life and creativity, that to this day people drive by our house in Georgia—perfect strangers and imperfect strangers—and ask to stand or walk among my mother's art.

I notice that it is only when my mother is working in her flowers that she is radiant, almost to the point of being invisible—except as Creator: hand and eye. She is involved in work her soul must have. Ordering the universe in the image of her personal conception of Beauty.

Her face, as she prepares the Art that is her gift, is a legacy of respect she leaves to me, for all that illuminates and cherishes life. She has handed down respect for the possibilities—and the will to grasp them.

For her, so hindered and intruded upon in so many ways, being an artist has still been a daily part of her life. This ability to hold on, even in very simple ways, is work Black women have done for a very long time.

This poem is not enough, but it is something, for the woman who literally covered the holes in our walls with sunflowers:

> They were women then
> My mama's generation
> Husky of voice—Stout of
> Step

10. *"Ma" Rainey's* (1886–1939). One of the earliest blues singers, she had a great influence on Bessie Smith.
11. *The Third Life of Grange Copeland,* Walker's first novel (1970). It is about a family of sharecroppers.

With fists as well as
Hands
How they battered down
Doors
And ironed
Starched white
Shirts
How they led
Armies
Headragged Generals
Across mined
Fields
Booby-trapped
Ditches
To discover books
Desks
A place for us
How they knew what we
Must know
Without knowing a page
Of it
Themselves.

Guided by my heritage of a love of beauty and a respect for strength—in search of my mother's garden, I found my own.

And perhaps in Africa over two hundred years ago, there was just such a mother; perhaps she painted vivid and daring decorations in oranges and yellows and greens on the walls of her hut; perhaps she sang—in a voice like Roberta Flack's—*sweetly* over the compounds of her village; perhaps she wove the most stunning mats or told the most ingenious stories of all the village storytellers. Perhaps she was herself a poet—though only her daughter's name is signed to the poems that we know.

Perhaps Phillis Wheatley's mother was also an artist.

Perhaps in more than Phillis Wheatley's biological life is her mother's signature made clear. □□

Discussion

1. According to Alice Walker, what was the one creative, artistic outlet available to black women in earlier generations?

2. (a) What does Phillis Wheatley represent for the author? **(b)** What is meant by Wheatley's "contrary instincts"? **(c)** Is Wheatley's greatest contribution her poetry or something else? Explain.

3. What do the "gardens" of the title **symbolize**?

4. By what means did Alice Walker's mother influence her daughter's literary **style** and subject matter?

Alice Walker 1944 •

One of eight children of hardworking farmers in Geor-

gia, Alice Walker sensed her own rare gift for language and vowed to develop it. She at-

tended Spelman College and Sarah Lawrence College, did social work, and then became a writer-in-residence and teacher of black studies at Jackson State College in Mississippi. Her second volume of poetry, *Revolutionary Petunias and Other Poems* (1973), was nominated for a National Book Award. In that year, she also published *In Love and Trouble: Stories of Black Women*, a collection of stories which received the Rosenthal Foundation Award from the National Institute of Arts and Letters. Her novel, *The Third Life of Grange Copeland* (1970), referred to in the foregoing selection, is dedicated to her husband and is also "for my mother, who made a way out of no way."

Louis Simpson

American Poetry

Whatever it is, it must have
A stomach that can digest
Rubber, coal, uranium, moons, poems.

Like the shark, it contains a shoe.
5 It must swim for miles through the desert
Uttering cries that are almost human.

Calvin C. Hernton

The Distant Drum

I am not a metaphor or symbol.
This you hear is not the wind in the trees,
Nor a cat being maimed in the street.
I am being maimed in the street.
5 It is I who weep, laugh, feel pain or joy,
Speak this because I exist.
This is my voice.
These words are my words,
My mouth speaks them,
10 My hand writes—
I am a poet.
It is my fist you hear
Beating against your ear.

Discussion

1. The "it" referred to in the first line is found in the title, "American Poetry." Why is it that American poetry must be able to digest "rubber, coal, uranium, moons, poems"?

2. (a) Why is American poetry like a shark? (b) Explain the meaning of swimming "for miles through the desert"; of cries "that are almost human."

Louis Simpson 1923 •

"American Poetry" is a good example of Louis Simpson's brand of surrealism. Born in Jamaica, Simpson completed graduate work at Columbia and entered a teaching career. He has taught in California and New York. His fourth volume of verse, *At the End of the Open Road* (1963), won the Pulitzer Prize. His critical work, *Three on the Tower* (1975), interweaves the lives and poetry of Ezra Pound, T. S. Eliot, and William Carlos Williams.

Discussion

1. How is "The Distant Drum" a sample of American poetry as defined in "American Poetry"?

2. Explain the meaning of the **metaphor** that appears in the last two lines: How can you hear a fist.

Calvin C. Hernton 1932 •

Hernton was born in Chattanooga, Tennessee, and attended Talladega College in Alabama, Fisk University, and Columbia University. He has taught college in the South and in London, where he lived for a time. His book, *Sex and Racism in America* (1965), has been widely read and discussed.

Denise Levertov

The Secret

Two girls discover
the secret of life
in a sudden line of
poetry.

5 I who don't know the
secret wrote
the line. They
told me

(through a third person)
10 they had found it
but not what it was,
not even

what line it was. No doubt
by now, more than a week
15 later, they have forgotten
the secret,

the line, the name of
the poem. I love them
for finding what
20 I can't find,

and for loving me
for the line I wrote,
and for forgetting it
so that

25 a thousand times, till death
finds them, they may
discover it again, in other
lines,

in other
30 happenings. And for
wanting to know it,
for

assuming there is
such a secret, yes,
35 for that
most of all.

Discussion

1. (a) What will the girls forget in a week? (b) Why do you think the poet loves the girls for "assuming there is/such a secret"? Explain.

2. What do you think is the "secret" of this poem?

Denise Levertov 1923 •

Denise Levertov was born in England, where she was educated privately. Her early poems were influenced by the romanticism that was popular in England at that time. During World War II she served as a nurse. At the end of the war she married an American and in 1948 came to this country to live.

In America Levertov came under the influence of William Carlos Williams, Ezra Pound, and H.D. The result is her concentration on the particulars of her own experience. Her poems are concrete, precise, intense, and shaped; they present compact perceptions of people, things, and feelings.

Carlos Cortez

This Is the Land

On the Sun-swept *llanos*[1]
Where imperceptible chants of long-dead tribesmen
And imperceptible hoof beats of long-dead buffalo
Are lost on the ears of the speeding motorist
5 And the barreling semi driver,

The Sun beats down upon the parched grass
And naked rock-croppings
Of the horizon-less eternity of flatlands,

Flatlands of the Dakota, the Arapaho, the Kansa, the Kiowa[2]
10 And the escaped ante-bellum[3] fugitive slave
And the sod-busting homesteader
And the farmed-out Okies and Arkies
Y los braceros y los alambres y los mojados,[4]

Where millenniums before *la Raza*
15 Rested on their long trek from the Bering Straits
To Anahuac, Tenochtitlan *y* Mayab[5]
Y dos mil generaciones después[6]
Are returning to their old tramping grounds,

Great endless sea of no water where a silent Jack Rabbit
20 Can be mistaken for a scrub tree
And where a scrub tree can be mistaken for a prairie dog
By the speeding motorist and barreling truck driver
Out in the distance-less infinity of unbroken sitting-duck sky
Where loneliness can be measured according to how much gas
25 Is left in the tank and how far it is to the next town

Cortez (kôr tes′).

1. *llanos* (yä′nôs), "plains." [*Spanish*]
2. **the Dakota, the Arapaho, the Kansa, the Kiowa,** tribes of the Great Plains.
3. *ante-bellum* (an′ti bel′əm), before the Civil War. [*Latin*]
4. *Y los braceros* (brä se′rôs) *y los alambres* (ä läm′bres) *y los mojados* (mô hä′dos), "and the farm-workers and the wire-cutters and the wetbacks." *Braceros* are legal immigrants from Mexico to the U.S.A. *Alambres* and *mojados* are derogatory terms for illegal border-crossers.
5. *la Raza* (lä rä′sä) . . . **Anahuac** (ə nä′wäk′), **Tenochtitlan** (te näch′tē tlän′) *y* **Mayab** (mī′yäb). *La Raza* ("the race") refers to all Latin peoples of the New World, the first of whom were Asian tribes which migrated into the Western Hemisphere through Alaska. Tenochtitlan (now Mexico City) was the capital of the Aztec Empire in the valley of Anahuac. Mayab was a center of the Mayan culture south of the Aztecs in Mexico.
6. *Y dos mil generaciones después* (ē dôs′ mēl′ he ne rä syô′nes des pwes′), "and two thousand generations after." [*Spanish*]

---

notes and comments

Bilingual Poetry

Every language expresses uniquely the culture from which it has grown. Each contains words, idioms, and expressions which have no true equivalent in other tongues. In "This Is the Land," the words "llanos" and "flatlands" both mean, roughly, *plains*. Yet their **connotations**, though difficult to define, differ markedly. To readers familiar with the Mexican culture of the Southwest in the 1800s, the Spanish word *llanos* might suggest the free life of the *llaneros* (yä ne′rôs) or horsemen of the plains. To readers of English, the word *flatlands* might evoke the overwhelming vastness of the desert landscape.

Bilingual poetry involves more than the occasional use of foreign phrases. It is the purposeful combination of words and images from two or more languages so that readers familiar with both of them can sense a range of emotional connotations broader than either language could provide alone. To a bilingual poet, neither language is "foreign." Such contemporary poets as Tino Villanueva (page 597) and Alurista frequently blend Spanish and English to represent the experiences of Latinos who live within two cultural traditions in the United States.

Bilingual poetry is not a new phenomenon. In a sense, such Medieval poets as Geoffrey Chaucer (?1340–1400) of England and Dante (1265–1321) of Italy were bilingual authors. Not only could they write with skill in either Latin or their native tongues, but also they used very early forms of, respectively, English and Italian, in which terms drawn from Latin and various European languages still appeared side-by-side.

Bilingual poetry requires that readers who do not know both of the languages used in a poem pay close attention to translations in footnotes in order to sense what the poet is trying to convey by juxtaposing two languages and cultures. This process is, however, simply another dimension of the interpretation involved in "translating" the symbols and metaphors of any poem.

Where Goodyear four-plies rolling over asphalt and concrete
Tamp down the Western Earth that was once tamped down
By herds of buffalo stretching from horizon to horizon
Only to be slaughtered *en masse* by the invader
30 To starve the original plainsmen into submission
When gatling guns, rotgut whiskey, and typhoid-infected blankets
Were not doing the job fast enough.

And now the invader's grandsons press their speedometers
To get away from all this endlessness
35 And the Sun makes its exit from the western edge of the sky
When the land becomes an ocean of flame
Burning away into a flat mighty cinder
That emerges with an ashy pale glow
When the pallid flapjack tortilla moon
40 Comes out to pinch-hit for the Sun

And the flapjack tortilla moon is momentarily eclipsed
By an airliner with its human cargo
Of dozing night-light reading passengers
To whom the Great Plains is something vaguely remembered
45 From grammar school geography books
As they idly contemplate Disneyland and North Beach[7]

And somewhere
A coyote
Howls.

---

7. **Disneyland and North Beach,** an amusement park near Los Angeles and a nightclub district of San Francisco.

Discussion

1. The speaker is musing on the history of the Great Plains. (a) What occurrences of the past does he allude to? (b) In lines 27–30, what process is he describing?

2. (a) What images from the present are in the poem? (b) How do they contrast with the images of the past?

3. (a) What **irony** is described in lines 41–46? (b) What statement do you think Cortez is making in the entire poem?

Carlos Cortez 1923 •

Carlos Cortez has noted that artists—painters, poets, musicians—"have remained in the historical memory far longer than rulers of their own times." The artist, he believes, "has a responsibility to the whole of society and must be always committed to building a better world."

Carlos Cortez was born in Milwaukee of Mexican and German parents, and lives in Chicago with his Greek wife and their "trilingual dog." He has made his living as a construction worker, factory worker, and bookseller. Before his marriage, he enjoyed "long periods of loafing." In addition to being a poet, he is a graphic artist and designer of posters. His poems and posters have turned up in many countries around the world.

Robert Amft.

Theodore Roethke

Night Journey

Now as the train bears west,
Its rhythm rocks the earth,
And from my Pullman berth
I stare into the night
5 While others take their rest.
Bridges of iron lace,
A suddenness of trees,
A lap of mountain mist
All cross my line of sight,
10 Then a bleak wasted place,
And a lake below my knees.
Full on my neck I feel
The straining at a curve;
My muscles move with steel,
15 I wake in every nerve.
I watch a beacon swing
From dark to blazing bright;
We thunder through ravines
And gullies washed with light.
20 Beyond the mountain pass
Mist deepens on the pane;
We rush into a rain
That rattles double glass.
Wheels shake the roadbed stone,
25 The pistons jerk and shove,
I stay up half the night
To see the land I love.

Roethke (ret′ ki).

Discussion

1. (a) What images of the land are presented in the poem? (b) How does the poet's love of the land become evident in his choice of imagery?

2. Explain how the poem recreates the sensation of traveling on a train at night with the use of (a) rhythm; (b) rhyme; (c) line length; (d) figurative language.

Theodore Roethke 1908 • 1963

Roethke grew up in Saginaw, Michigan. In his spare time he worked in his father's green-house, and his liking for plants and flowers appears now and again in his poetry. Roethke left Saginaw to attend the University of Michigan and later Harvard.

Roethke was highly praised by contemporary critics, some of whom considered him one of the three or four best poets writing in the United States at mid-century. An extremely skillful technician, he manipulates rhyme and rhythm so subtly that the reader often senses the meaning of a poem before he has grasped it intellectually. In 1954 Roethke won a Pulitzer Prize for his volume of poems, *The Waking.*

David Wagoner

Breaking Camp

Having spent a hard-earned sleep, you must break camp in the mountains
At the break of day, pulling up stakes and packing,
Scattering your ashes,
And burying everything human you can't carry. Lifting
5 Your world now on your shoulders, you should turn
To look back once
At a place as welcoming to a later dead-tired stranger
As it was to your eyes only the other evening,
As the place you've never seen
10 But must hope for now at the end of a day's rough journey:
You must head for another campsite, maybe no nearer
Wherever you're going
Than where you've already been, but deeply, starkly appealing
Like a lost home: with water, the wind lying down
15 On a stretch of level earth,
And the makings of a fire to flicker against the night
Which you, traveling light, can't bring along
But must always search for.

From COLLECTED POEMS 1956–1976 by David Wagoner, copyright © 1976 by Indiana University Press. Reprinted by permission of the publisher.

Discussion

1. What specific advice does the poet give the reader on how to break camp?

2. What do you think is the poet's attitude toward the outdoors? Cite specific words or phrases.

3. (a) With what words and phrases does the poet make it evident that he is drawing an **analogy** between camping and life? (b) What advice on getting through life do you think the poet is giving? Explain.

David Wagoner 1926 •

Wagoner's poetry, like the titles of his books, evokes the images of the outdoors and self-reliance. His work includes *Dry Sun, Dry Wind* (1953), *A Place to Stand* (1958), and *Staying Alive* (1966). He was born in Massillon, Ohio, and went to school at Penn State University and Indiana University.

Imamu Amiri Baraka

Preface to a Twenty Volume Suicide Note

Lately, I've become accustomed to the way
The ground opens up and envelops me
Each time I go out to walk the dog.
Or the broad edged silly music the wind
5 Makes when I run for a bus—

Things have come to that.

And now, each night I count the stars,
And each night I get the same number.
And when they will not come to be counted
10 I count the holes they leave.

Nobody sings anymore.

And then last night, I tiptoed up
To my daughter's room and heard her
Talking to someone, and when I opened
15 The door, there was no one there . . .
Only she on her knees,
Peeking into her own clasped hands.

Discussion

1. The first ten lines of the poem use exaggerated language (**hyperbole**) to make a point about the speaker's condition. **(a)** What is that condition? **(b)** What is the speaker's attitude toward his condition?

2. Do you think the speaker's discovery of his daughter "talking to someone" has made any difference? How?

Imamu Amiri Baraka
(LeRoi Jones) 1934 •

Although he considers himself primarily a poet, Baraka also writes essays, novels, short stories, plays, and jazz articles. He grew up in Newark, New Jersey, and received his degree from Howard University in Washington, D.C. It was while serving with the Strategic Air Command that he decided to become a writer.

Early in his career, Baraka was often identified as the angry young man of the ghetto. In 1967 he was arrested as a leader of the Newark ghetto riots. Since the riots, he has been leading task forces to rebuild the area and improve conditions in Newark. To some people his poetry seems homicidal, to others it seems caustic and biting, and to still others it seems delicate and gentle.

Gloria C. Oden

Speculation

Discussion

1. In your own words, tell why the poet is not concerned about being in the sun too long.

2. (a) Who or what do you think the poet is addressing in lines 32–37? **(b)** In your opinion, what does the poet mean when she says that she has been burned blue?

3. Explain how the title is related to the poem.

Gloria C. Oden   1923 •

Gloria Oden was born and raised in Yonkers, New York. Her poems have been published in numerous anthologies, and twice she has received awards for creative writing from the John Hay Whitney Foundation. In addition, a collection of her poems entitled *The Naked Frame: A Love Poem and Sonnets* attracted widespread attention when it was published in 1952. Oden has taught at the State University of New York, Long Island Center, and at the University of Maryland.

In my girlhood
Mother would call
"Rest in the shade!"
when exhausted from play
5 I would spread
on the grass
like a picnic.

"Move!" she would cry
and I did.
10 Out of reach
of the sun;
away from
its sulphurous eye
lest falling on me
15 it scorch me browner
than what by nature
I already was.

Summer sun was her enemy.
She made it mine.
20 But less concerned with
blackness as penalty,
continuously I fretted
the bonnets and parasols
of her untiring insistence.
25 Born burnt of God
what further need to be sun shy?
Still,
I was an obedient child, and
from the virulent roundings
30 of its patrol
learned to withhold myself.

Now I am grown to woman.
What would Mother say
seeing me focused here
35 in your red radiance
and eyes that burn me
blue?

May Miller

Gift from Kenya

Within the day a seventh time
I touch the pale wood antelope.
Forever squat on spindle legs
He tips his head to danger.
5 (But O to see the pronghorn herd
Run the ridge of a blunted hill
With the skyline copper-red.)
It is too late to hear the axe
Which, in the ruined cedar grove,
10 Shivered down like a death drum note
To fell the trees that would become
The multi-hundred antelopes.

Some fluid centuries ago
My ancient father knew the tree;
15 Then young and bending in a wind,
Played near the sapling

While the hours of morning whipped
Singing round his loins.
When dark came down and the vultures slept,
20 In the fragrance of dew-heavy bark
He watched determined stars in course.
As man, in a glittering night of power
He traced with others curving paths
Leading out from the sheltering boughs.

25 The cedar carved to figurine,
And to all its counterparts,
Is hunched upon the years to come.
The man and his way are old to me,
Old in the unborn who wait
30 To hold the ice-aged heritage
That has no end in single flesh
However wound in death.

Discussion

1. (a) What is the gift from Kenya? (b) As the poet touches the figurine, what action does she imagine in lines 8–12?

2. (a) Whom does the poet mean by "my ancient father"? (b) What was the state of the cedar at the time that she is thinking about? (c) In your own words, what did the "ancient father" do when he became a man?

3. (a) What does the figurine represent? (b) In the last stanza, what is the poet saying about the past and the passage of time?

May Miller

May Miller has taught theater and dramatics and collaborated on the book *Plays and Pageants from the Life of the Negro*. She was born in Washington, D. C., and graduated from Howard University. She has published four volumes of poetry: *Into the Clearing* (1959), *Poems* (1962), *The Clearing and Beyond* (1974), and *Dust of Uncertain Journey* (1975).

Constance Carrier

Merry-Go-Round

Out of the sterile eye he sees, or does not see,
the live ones galloping by in angular grace,
their manes and their tails blown back by the wind like banners,
their hoof-beats heavily hollow against the ground.

5 And now the music begins, the machinery starts,
and the wooden horse moves with it, his lifted forefoot
ignorant always of motion, of the feel of the ground,
the flare of his nostril a travesty on breath.

But he gains momentum, and the moving air
10 slides over his painted body as over live hide:
he is carried around the core of the music—around
and around and faster and faster, till surely
he must come into freedom at last, for almost the hoof
paws at the air, almost the carved mane breaks
15 the pattern to which hand shaped it, almost he leaps
to run with the others across the measureless meadow.

But the music stops, and the ancient crazy engine
slows to a grinding halt, and the moment is over,
and the others, the living ones, gone, and he only left tethered,
20 staring inscrutably, fiercely, speared on a rod,
his mane blown back by no wind, his forefoot lifted.

Discussion

1. In the first two stanzas, what impression of the horse do you form, and which words and phrases create that impression?

2. (a) What almost happens to the horse in stanza three? **(b)** Which images create a sense of life and of movement?

3. (a) What are the meaning and effect of the phrase "speared on a rod" (line 20)? **(b)** What happens in the last stanza?

Constance Carrier 1908 •

Constance Carrier published a book of poems, *The Middle Voice*, in 1955. She was born in New Britain, Connecticut, and graduated from Smith College and took an M. A. at Trinity College. She has been a high-school Latin teacher.

Maxine Kumin

Amanda Dreams She Has Died and Gone to the Elysian Fields

This morning Amanda
lies down during breakfast.
The hay is hip high.
The sun sleeps on her back
5 as it did on the spine
of the dinosaur
the fossil bat
the first fish with feet
she was once.
10 A breeze fans
the deerflies from lighting.
Only a gaggle of gnats
housekeeps in her ears.
A hay plume sticks out of her mouth.

15 I come calling with a carrot
from which I have taken
the first bite.
She startles
she considers rising
20 but retracts the pistons
of her legs and accepts
as loose-lipped as a camel.
We sit together.
In this time and place
25 we are heart and bone.
For an hour
we are incorruptible.

Eyes

At night Amanda's eyes
are rage red with toy worlds inside.
Head on they rummage the dark
of the paddock like twin cigars
5 but flicker at the edges with
the shyer tongues of the spirit lamp.

There's little enough for her to see:
my white shirt, the sleeves
rolled high, two flaps of stale bread
10 in my fish paws. I can't sleep.
I have come back from
the feed-bag-checkered restaurant
from the pale loose tears of my dearest friend
her blue eyes sinking into the highball glass
15 her eyeballs clinking on ice
and her mouth drawn down in the grand
comedy of anguish.

Today a sparrow has been put
in the hawk's hands and in the net
20 a monarch[1] crazes its wings on gauze.
A doe run down by the dogs
commonly dies of fright before
its jugular opens at the fang hole.
In my friend's eyes the famine victim
25 squats, holding an empty rice bowl.

O Amanda, burn out my dark.
Press the warm suede of your horseflesh
against my cold palm.
Take away all that is human.

Kumin (kü′min).
From HOUSE, BRIDGE, FOUNTAIN, GATE by Maxine Kumin.
Copyright © 1971, 1972, 1973, 1974, 1975 by Maxine Kumin.
Reprinted by permission of The Viking Press, Inc. and Curtis
Brown Ltd.
1. *monarch,* a large orange and black butterfly.

Discussion

1. The Elysian Fields were the place of Paradise in Greek mythology. Relate the title of the poem to the images of the first stanza.

2. What seems to be the relationship between the speaker of the poem and Amanda in the final five lines of "Amanda Dreams"?

3. (a) Whose eyes are indicated in the first stanza of "Eyes"? (b) In the second stanza? (c) What is the mood of the person described in the second stanza?

4. How does the list of tragedies in stanza 3 fit into this poem?

5. Why does the poem conclude with the speaker's plea to Amanda, "Take away all that is human"?

Maxine Kumin 1925 •

Kumin was born in Philadelphia and attended Radcliffe College. Since 1960 she has published many volumes of poetry, including some for children. Her book *Up Country: Poems of New England* won the Pulitzer Prize in 1973.

Lawson Fusao Inada

My Father and Myself Facing the Sun

We are both strong, dark, bright men,
though perhaps you might not notice,
finding two figures flat against the landscape
like the shadowed backs of mountains.

5 Which would not be far from wrong,
for though we both have on western clothes
and he is seated on a yellow spool
of emptied and forgotten telephone cable
and I recline on a green aluminum lounge,

10 we are both facing into the August sun
as august as Hiroshima[1] and the coming
    of autumn.

There are differences, however, if you care
to discover, coming close, respectfully.
You must discover the landscape as you go.

15 Come. It is in the eyes, the face, the way
we would greet you stumbling as you arrive.
He is much the smooth, grass-brown slopes
reaching knee-high around you as you walk;
I am the cracks of cliffs and gulleys,
20 pieces of secret deep in the back of the eye.

But he is still my father, and I his son.

After a while, there is time to go fishing,
both of us squatting on rocks in the dusk,
leaving peaks and treeline responsible for light.
25 There is a lake below, which both of us
acknowledge, by facing, forward, like the sun.

Ripples of fish, moon, luminous insects.
Frogs, owls, crickets at their sound.
Deer, raccoon, badger come down to drink.

30 At the water's edge, the children are fishing,
casting shadows from the enormous shoreline.
Everything functions in the function of summer.

And gradually, and not by chance, the action
stops, the children hush back among rocks
35 and also watch, with nothing to capture but dusk.

There are four of us, together among others.

And I am not at all certain what all this means,
if this mean anything, but feel with all my being
that I must write this down, if I write anything.

40 My father, his son, his grandsons, strong, serene.

Night, night, night, before the following morning.

Fusao Inada (fü sa′ô ē na′da).
"My Father and Myself Facing the Sun" by Lawson Fusao Inada from *Bridge, an Asian-American Perspective* (November 1976). Reprinted by permission of the author.
1. *Hiroshima* (hir′ō shē′mə), a Japanese city on which the U. S. dropped an atom bomb in August, 1945, which killed 92,000 people.

Lawson Fusao Inada 1938 •

Inada writes that he has been chiefly interested in helping create and discover an Asian-American culture. He was born in Fresno, California, and studied at Fresno State College, the University of Iowa, and the University of Oregon. He published *Before the War* in 1971.

Discussion

1. In the first three stanzas, how are the father and the son similar?

2. In lines 12–20, how do the images associated with the father differ from those the poet associates with himself?

3. In lines 33–35, why does the action they have been watching come to an end?

4. (a) What do you think is meant by "all this" in line 37? (b) What meaning do you see in the scene that the poet has described? Explain.

Richard Wilbur

The Writer

In her room at the prow of the house
Where light breaks, and the windows are tossed with linden,
My daughter is writing a story.

I pause in the stairwell, hearing
5 From her shut door a commotion of typewriter-keys
Like a chain hauled over a gunwale.

Young as she is, the stuff
Of her life is a great cargo, and some of it heavy:
I wish her a lucky passage.

10 But now it is she who pauses,
As if to reject my thought and its easy figure.
A stillness greatens, in which

The whole house seems to be thinking,
And then she is at it again with a bunched clamor
15 Of strokes, and again is silent.

I remember the dazed starling
Which was trapped in that very room, two years ago;
How we stole in, lifted a sash

And retreated, not to affright it;
20 And how for a helpless hour, through the crack of the door,
We watched the sleek, wild, dark

And iridescent creature
Batter against the brillance, drop like a glove
To the hard floor, or the desk-top,

25 And wait then, humped and bloody,
For the wits to try it again; and how our spirits
Rose when, suddenly sure,

It lifted off from a chair-back,
Beating a smooth course for the right window
30 And clearing the sill of the world.

It is always a matter, my darling,
Of life or death, as I had forgotten. I wish
What I wished you before, but harder.

Discussion

1. (a) What is the situation described in the first part of the poem? (b) With what **metaphor** in lines 7–9 does the poet describe his daughter's efforts?

2. (a) Describe in your own words the incident involving a "dazed starling." (b) How is this incident related to the situation of the first five stanzas?

3. Why do you think the poet's memory of the anecdote of the starling makes him wish even more for his daughter's success?

Richard Wilbur 1921 •

Richard Wilbur was born into a family that encouraged his early attempts to create poetry. In the summers while he was a student at Amherst College, he widened his knowledge of the United States by riding across the country on freight cars. His first volume of verse, *The Beautiful Changes*, appeared in 1947.

N. Scott Momaday

Crows in a Winter Composition

This morning the snow,
The soft distances
Beyond the trees
In which nothing appeared—
5 Nothing appeared—
The several silences,
Imposed one upon another,
Were unintelligible.

I was therefore ill at ease
10 When the crows came down,
Whirling down and calling,
Into the yard below
And stood in a mindless manner
On the gray, luminous crust,
15 Altogether definite, composed,
In the bright enmity of my regard,
In the hard nature of crows.

"Crows in a Winter Composition." From THE GOURD DANCER
by N. Scott Momaday. Copyright © 1976 by N. Scott Momaday.
Reprinted by permission of Harper & Row, Publishers, Inc.

"Snow by Morning" by May Swenson, which first appeared in
The New Yorker, is reprinted with the permission of the author
from TO MIX WITH TIME, copyright © 1963 by May Swenson
and Charles Scribner's Sons.

May Swenson

Snow by Morning

Some for everyone,
plenty,
and more coming—

fresh, dainty, airily arriving
5 everywhere at once,

transparent at first,
each faint slice—
slow, soundlessly tumbling;

then quickly, thickly, a gracious fleece
10 will spread like youth, like wheat,
over the city.

Each building will be a hill,
all sharps made round—

dark, worn, noisy narrows made still,
15 wide, flat, clean spaces;

streets will be fields,
cars be fumbling sheep;

a deep, bright harvest will be seeded
in a night.

20 By morning we'll be children
feeding on manna,
a new loaf on every doorsill.

Discussion

Crows in a Winter Composition

1. Why do you think the scene in stanza 1 is "unintelligible" to the poet?

2. How do the crows contrast with the scene in stanza 1?

(Momaday's biography is on page 606.)

Snow by Morning

1. How will the snow transform the urban scene into a country scene?

2. Compare and contrast the depiction of winter in this poem with that in "Crows in a Winter Composition."

May Swenson 1919 •

May Swenson was born in Logan, Utah, and went to Utah State University. Her books include *Another Animal* (1954) and *Half Sun Half Sleep* (1967). Her poems have appeared frequently in *The New Yorker.*

Pamela Alexander

Air

It holds us, gently,
together.
It presses out, against the eardrum.
It presses in. It curls
5 in the palms of our hands

but holds nothing
to itself. It steps over
the sock flung onto the chair, the blouse
on the floor. When we touch in it,
10 it moves aside—a modest medium

that solid things displace.
The children running down the street
punch through it, leaving
a cut-out shape of each position
15 floating behind them
for an instant.

It is made of round
spinning things, but
it will adjust to a rectangular space such as
20 a room.
It's the only company
the old man who stays in his underwear all day
has.
He comes onto the porch at noon
25 to get more.

People identify it by objects it surrounds.
It is then called "atmosphere."
What people see is
themselves: they approve or they don't,
30 they leave for good or they come back.
Air is innocent of such judgments, having
no personality to protect.

It has only
a simple habit:
35 it fills anything.
It occupies entire hotels
in the off season.

It is drawn to emptiness as to
a question it answers. Only a person
40 can puzzle it: the vacancy interior,
locked behind the eyes.

It stays whole, flows around
the wall, the knife.
We can change it
45 as much as ourselves, or another person:
very little.

"Air" by Pamela Alexander from THE ARDIS ANTHOLOGY OF NEW AMERICAN POETRY (Ardis, 1977). Reprinted by permission of the author.

Discussion

1. In what lines is air depicted as (a) gentle? (b) pervasive? (c) amiable?

2. (a) How is air different from people? (b) How is it similar?

3. Taking the entire poem into account, what statement do you think the poet is making about humanity?

Pamela Alexander

Pamela Alexander grew up in Natick, Massachusetts, and attended Bates College in Maine and the University of Iowa Writer's Workshop. Her poems have appeared in many magazines, including *Poetry* and *The Atlantic Monthly*.

Adrienne Rich

Bears

Wonderful bears that walked my room all night,
Where have you gone, your sleek and fairy fur,
Your eyes' veiled and imperious light?

Brown bears as rich as mocha or as musk,
5　White opalescent bears whose fur stood out
Electric in the deepening dusk,

And great black bears that seemed more blue
　　　than black,
More violet than blue against the dark—
Where are you now? Upon what track

10　Mutter your muffled paws that used to tread
So softly, surely, up the creakless stair
While I lay listening in bed?

When did I lose you? Whose have you become?
Why do I wait and wait and never hear
15　Your thick nocturnal pacing in my room?
My bears, who keeps you now, in pride and fear?

"Bears" by Adrienne Rich from THE DIAMOND CUTTERS AND OTHER POEMS (Harper & Row). Reprinted by permission; © 1954 The New Yorker Magazine, Inc.

Discussion

1. (a) What different kinds of bears does the poet remember? (b) What details about them does she refer to? (c) What feelings about the bears do these details convey?

2. (a) What did the bears represent in the poet's childhood? (b) Why do you think that she can no longer see or hear them?

Extension • Writing

Most children "see" things when they are falling asleep at night. Some see "monsters" when the lights are turned off; others imagine they are flying on a magic carpet. Try to remember one of your childhood fantasies, and write a composition describing it as vividly as you can. Did the fantasy make you afraid? Happy? Sad? Attempt to convey this feeling in your writing.

Adrienne Rich　1929 •

Adrienne Rich was born in Maryland and graduated from Radcliffe in 1951. She is the author of several volumes of poems, including *Diving into the Wreck,* which won the National Book Award for 1974. Her prose work, *Of Woman Born: Motherhood as Experience and Institution,* based in large part on her own life and experience, appeared in 1976.

Poetry—Personal and Public

The most influential poets and critics of the early twentieth century advocated a poetry that, in its ideal form, was impersonal and without ambition to make changes in the world. Archibald MacLeish provided the best-known formula for this "New Poetry" in "Ars Poetica," concluding: "A poem should not mean/But be." At its best, poetry that was written in accord with the new principles was aesthetically rewarding and classically compelling. But at its worst, it was dry, hard, allusive, intellectual poetry that neither involved nor moved the reader. By the time of World War II, in the 1940s, the New Poetry had lost its revolutionary momentum and had become an academically approved movement, producing a poetry that was predictable in form and subject.

But during the 1950s and 1960s, poets rediscovered the possibilities of making poems out of their personal lives. The personal was revived in part, no doubt, because poetry was threatened with annihilation in a mass culture in which individual identity was becoming a mere annoyance to the ever larger and more impersonal institutions of government, industry, education. And the meaning of poetry was renewed in part because of the growing realization that injustices not only existed but were often embedded in the very institutions created to protect and extend human rights.

Thus it was that poets rediscovered the personal voice with all its human inflections; and thus it was that this personal voice was raised at times in a cry of anguish and protest, grief and outrage.

The Beat poet Allen Ginsberg is credited by some critics with dragging poetry, screaming, out of the classrooms into the streets. Representing a general disillusionment with the Establishment in all its forms, the Beat movement reached its peak during the late 1950s. Poets like Ginsberg became the wandering minstrels of an urban culture, appearing in offbeat bookstores and bohemian clubs to read their poetry to enthusiastic crowds.

As the civil rights movement of the period grew stronger, oppressed groups of all kinds began to demand more and more from a too often complacent society. And the Vietnam War turned the 1960s into America's "long, dark night of the soul." Then it was that poets—especially young ones, but also many of an older generation—proclaimed a renewed public role for poetry, a poetry that not only meant, but also declaimed, and sometimes howled.

The new-found freedom of poetry to say what it wanted or needed to say was accompanied by new freedoms of language and form. The language of poetry became more relaxed, more conversational, more clearly the language of the streets than of the universities. At the same time poets tended to throw over the old forms and create their own. Robert Creeley said: "Form is never more than an extension of content." Denise Levertov refined this formula: "Form is never more than a *revelation* of content." Content—the meaning of a poem—was thus proclaimed a poem's main excuse for being.

Some poets used the new freedoms to write a kind of free-flowing poetry that is sometimes called "process poetry," in which the poem remains open to whatever thoughts or feelings the poet experiences in the process of creating the poem. The poem becomes a kind of ramble through a segment of life with the poet. "This Is the Land," by Carlos Cortez, has elements of this kind of poetry.

The new freedoms breathed new life into poetry. As the restrictive, academic formulas were overthrown, new poets appeared, writing a simple, clear poetry, sometimes understandable on a first reading or hearing. Audiences that had been baffled and bored by poems of the past discovered that poetry could delight and instruct, move and amuse, depress and inspire.

Diane Vreuls

Young Girls Who Play the Harp

YOUNG GIRLS
WHO PLAY
THE HARP
TURN INTO
WOMEN WHO
PLAY THE
HARP · WOMEN
WHO PLAY
THE HARP
TURN INTO

OLD WOMEN
WHO PLAY
THE HARP
OLD WOMEN
WHO PLAY
THE HARP
DO NOT
TURN INTO
ANGELS

Mari Evans

. . . and the old women gathered
(The Gospel Singers)

and the old women gathered
and sang His praises
standing
resolutely together
5 like supply sergeants who
have seen
everything
and are still
Regular Army: It
10 was fierce and
not melodic and
although we ran
the sound of it
stayed in our ears . . .

Discussion

1. One quality of poetry is surprise. What is the surprise in "Young Girls Who Play the Harp"?

2. What impression of the old women and their singing does Mari Evans create by comparing them to supply sergeants?

3. (a) In "The Gift," what do you think is meant by the reference to the rope in the last line? **(b)** Explain in what ways hope is an "ominous" gift.

Diane Vreuls

Diane Vreuls's writing includes poems (*Instructions*, 1971) and fiction (*Are We There Yet?* 1975). She was born in Chicago, took a degree from the University of Wisconsin, and has studied at Oxford University in England.

(No biographical information on Mari Evans is available. Momaday's biography is on page 606.)

N. Scott Momaday

The Gift

Older, more generous,
We give each other hope.
The gift is ominous:
Enough praise, enough rope.

Vreuls (vrüls).

"Young Girls Who Play the Harp" by Diane Vreuls from INSTRUCTIONS, 1971. Reprinted by permission of Russell and Volkening, Inc. as agents for the author. Copyright © 1971 by Diane Vreuls.

". . . and the old women gathered" by Mari Evans from I AM A BLACK WOMAN, published by William Morrow and Company, 1970, by permission of the author.

"The Gift." From THE GOURD DANCER by N. Scott Momaday. Copyright © 1976 by N. Scott Momaday. Reprinted by permission of Harper & Row, Publishers, Inc.

Elizabeth Bishop

One Art

The art of losing isn't hard to master;
so many things seem filled with the intent
to be lost that their loss is no disaster.

Lose something every day. Accept the fluster
5 of lost door keys, the hour badly spent.
The art of losing isn't hard to master.

Then practice losing farther, losing faster:
places, and names, and where it was you meant
to travel. None of these will bring disaster.

10 I lost my mother's watch. And look! my last, or
next-to-last, of three loved houses went.
The art of losing isn't hard to master.

I lost two cities, lovely ones. And, vaster,
some realms I owned, two rivers, a continent.
15 I miss them, but it wasn't a disaster.

—Even losing you (the joking voice, a gesture
I love) I shan't have lied. It's evident
the art of losing's not too hard to master
though it may look like (*Write* it!) like disaster.

"One Art" Reprinted with the permission of Farrar, Straus &
Giroux, Inc. and Chatto and Windus, Ltd. from GEOGRAPHY III
by Elizabeth Bishop, Copyright © 1976 by Elizabeth Bishop,
"One Art" appeared originally in *The New Yorker*.

Discussion

1. Through the first five stanzas, what losses does the poet refer to?

2. **(a)** What has she lost in the last stanza? **(b)** How do you think she really feels about this loss? Explain.

(Elizabeth Bishop's biography is on page 48.)

Morris Bishop

The Witch of East Seventy-Second Street

"I will put upon you the Telephone Curse," said the witch.
"The telephone will call when you are standing on a chair with a Chinese vase in either hand,
And when you answer, you will hear only the derisive popping of corks."
But I was armed so strong in honesty
5 Her threats passed by me like the idle wind.

"And I will put upon you the Curse of Dropping," said the witch.
"The dropping of tiny tacks, the dropping of food gobbets,
The escape of wet dishes from the eager-grasping hand,
The dropping of spectacles, stitches, final consonants, the abdomen."
10 I sneered, jeered, fleered; I flouted, scouted; I pooh-pooh-poohed.

"I will put upon you the Curse of Forgetting!" screamed the witch.
"Names, numbers, faces, old songs, old joy,
Words that once were magic, love, upward ways, the way home."
"No doubt the forgotten is well forgotten," said I.

15 "And I will put upon you the Curse of Remembering," bubbled the witch.
Terror struck my eyes, knees, heart;
And I took her charred contract
And signed in triplicate.

Discussion

1. What is the poet's attitude toward **(a)** the Telephone Curse? **(b)** the Curse of Dropping? **(c)** the Curse of Forgetting?

2. **(a)** What is his reaction to the Curse of Remembering? **(b)** Why do you think this particular curse causes him terror?

Morris Bishop 1893 • 1973

Morris Bishop spent his life teaching literature at Cornell University. He was born in Willard, New York, and studied as an undergraduate and as a graduate student at Cornell. Occasionally, as he found time for creative writing, he contributed poems to *The New Yorker.*

Howard Nemerov

To David, About His Education

The world is full of mostly invisible things,
And there is no way but putting the mind's eye,
Or its nose, in a book, to find them out,
Things like the square root of Everest
5 Or how many times Byron goes into Texas,
Or whether the law of the excluded middle
Applies west of the Rockies. For these
And the like reasons, you have to go to school
And study books and listen to what you are told,
10 And sometimes try to remember. Though I don't know
What you will do with the mean annual rainfall
On Plato's Republic, or the calorie content
Of the Diet of Worms,[1] such things are said to be
Good for you, and you will have to learn them
15 In order to become one of the grown-ups
Who sees invisible things neither steadily nor whole,
But keeps gravely the grand confusion of the world
Under his hat, which is where it belongs,
And teaches small children to do this in their turn.

Nemerov (nem′ə rov)
"To David, About His Education" from THE NEXT ROOM OF
THE DREAM by Howard Nemerov. Reprinted by permission of
the author.
1. *Plato's Republic . . . Diet of Worms* (vôrms). *The Republic* by
Plato is a book about just government, based on the teachings
of Socrates; both were philosophers of ancient Greece. In 1521,
a council at the German city of Worms declared Martin Luther,
the Protestant leader, a heretic against Roman Catholicism.

Discussion

1. In line 1 the poet speaks of a class of things that share the common characteristic of being "mostly invisible." Judging from the examples of this class of objects given in lines 4–7 and 11–13, what other characteristics do they have in common?

2. Why must "the grand confusion of the world" be kept under the hat of the adult person? What is the poet's attitude toward this necessity?

Howard Nemerov 1920 •

The prize-winning poet, novelist, and short-story writer, Howard Nemerov, was born and raised in New York City and was educated at Harvard.

Nemerov's writings are praised for their originality, wit, insight into the human condition, rhythm, imagery, and diction. The three main influences upon his writing are his childhood in the city, the violence he experienced during the war, and the world of nature. Many of his poems are analogies between elements in nature and characteristics of man. These analogies give his poetry a thoughtful quality rather than a felt lyric intensity. His *Collected Poems* were published in 1977 by the University of Chicago Press.

William Stafford

Judgments

"Judgments" from THE RESCUED YEAR by William Stafford.
Copyright © 1964 by William E. Stafford. Reprinted by permission of Harper & Row, Publishers, Inc.

I accuse—
   Ellen: you have become forty years old,
   and successful, tall, well-groomed,
   gracious, thoughtful, a secretary.
5   Ellen, I accuse.

George—
   You know how to help others;
   you manage a school. You never
   let fear or pride or faltering plans
10   break your control.
   George, I accuse.

I accuse—
   Tom: you have found a role;
   now you meet all kinds of people
15   and let them find the truth of your
   eminence; you need not push.
   Oh, Tom, I do accuse.

Remember—
   The gawky, hardly to survive students
20   we were: not one of us going to succeed,
   all of us abjectly aware of how cold,
   unmanageable the real world was?
   I remember. And that fear was true.
   And is true.

25 Last I accuse—
   Myself: my terrible poise, knowing
   even this, knowing that then we
   sprawled in the world
   and were ourselves part of it; now
30   we hold it firmly away with gracious
   gestures (like this of mine!) we've achieved.

I see it all too well—
   And I am accused, and I accuse.

Discussion

1. Judging only from the first three stanzas, what is the nature of the accusation the speaker makes against Ellen, George, and Tom?

2. The accusation is not completed until the fourth stanza. What precisely is it? Why does the speaker include himself?

William Stafford 1914 •

In commenting on his own poetry, Stafford has said, "My poetry seems to me direct and communicative, with some oddity and variety. It is usually not formal. It is much like talk, with some enhancement. Often my poetry is discursive and reminiscent, or at least is that way at one level; it delivers a sense of place and event; it has narrative impulses. Forms are not usually much evident, though tendencies and patterns are occasionally flirted with. . . . The voice I most consistently hear in my poetry is my mother's voice." William Stafford was raised in Kansas and received his education at the University of Kansas and the University of Iowa., During World War II he was a conscientious objector and is still active in pacifist organizations. He has taught at Manchester College in Indiana and San Jose State College in California, and is presently Professor of Literature at Lewis and Clark College in Portland, Oregon.

Tino Villanueva

Jugábamos[1]/We Played

en el barrio
—en las tardes de fuego
when the dusk prowls
    en la calle desierta
pues los jefes y jefas
    trabajan
    —*often late hours*
after school
    we play canicas. . . .
           Alurista[2]

The memories of childhood
have no order, and no end.
        Dylan Thomas[3]

we would play/we would jump/
we would play at everything.
ritual and recreation it was, in the patio of my barrio
in the just-awakening week: kneeling there
5 in sunnybronzed delight
when my kingdom was a pocketful of
golden marbles.
how in wide-eyed wonder i sought winning
two agates for my eyes/& so,
10 not knowing what it meant, i played for keeps.

we would play/we would put our lives on the line—

    my posse always got its man/
    i was the Chicano Lone Ranger/i was Tarzan
    of backyard pecan trees/time-tall trees blooming

Tino Villanueva (tē′nô vē′yä nwe′vä).
"Jugábamos/We Played." Copyright © 1975 by Tino Villanueva. From CHICANO
VOICES. Reprinted by permission.
1. *Jugábamos* (hü gä′ba môs).
2. *en el barrio . . . Alurista.* In these lines by the bilingual poet Alurista
(ä lü rēs′tä), the Spanish parts mean: "in the neighborhood/—in the afternoon of
fire/ . . . in the deserted street/while our fathers and mothers/are working/ . . . we
play marbles. . . .
3. *Dylan Thomas,* a Welsh poet (1914–1953).

15   with the color of adventure/trees that ripened
        with my age through rain-ruined days.

        running/gamboling i played oblivious to
        fine earth shifting in the cuffs of my fading jeans/
        crawling/leaping always reaching/
20   reaching/reaching even the delicacies of the indomitable
        void/
        running about the nooks and corners of my patio
        where grandma had tulips and carnations planted/
        running between the sun and its reverberant glare
25   in those afternoons of that fire.

        we would play/we would leap/
        we would play at everything.
        myth and sensation it was, when the tree-house wind blew
        in simultaneous weathers: it was a green wind
30   tasting of fig, of mint, of peaches at times—

            our garden's aromas.

        and in my Cracker-Jack-joy of late saturday afternoons
        my red wagon was full of dog/& my tricycle traveled
        one last time every turnpike of my yard.

35   now the fun running to soothe the dry sun on my tongue/
        now the tireless striding toward stilled water of
        buoyant ice cubes in a glass transparent dripping
        in the gripping of my mother's hand.

        we would play/we would run/
40   we would play at everything.
        shouting and emotion it was, in my chosen pastime:

            thirteen years out of the womb i was
            pubescent Walter Mitty fleet as Mickey Mantle
            at the Stadium:

45   *tok! . . . there's a long drive to center . . . Villanueva*
            is back/back/back/the ball is up against the wall . . .

            as i banged my back against our dilapidated
            picket fence. grandpa repaired it twelve times over.
            yes, i dreamed of spikes and baseball diamonds/
50   meantime
            barefooted i played in narrow dusty streets
            (a dust decreed by the City Council, i know now.)
            my buddies in bubble-gum smiles chose up sides/
            so batter up 'cause i'm a portsider like
55   Whitey Ford/i've the eagle eye of Ted Williams.

i tugged the bill of my sea-blue cap for luck/
had NY on it:

time out! let the dust settle/as it must/
traffic should slow down on gravel streets—

60 *especially Coca-Cola trucks.*

but the game goes on/dust mixing with perspiration.
inning after inning this game becomes a night game too/
this 100-watt bulb lights the narrow playing field.

such were the times of year-rounded yearnings
65 when at the end of light's flight i listened in
reflective boyhood silence.
then the day-done sun glistened, burned deeply,
disappearing into my eyes blinking: innocently
i blinked toward the towering twilight.

70 we would play/we would jump/
we would play at everything.

Marisha Chamberlain

No Respect for Authority

While Mom and Dad
sip their evening wine
in the low, white livingroom,
the giant teenagers
5 return from play rehearsal
with three friends.
Politely bowing and introducing,
trying to be graceful,
they fill up half the room,
10 even crowded together.
"Don't get up, Mr. and Mrs.
Chamberlain, all we want
is a drink of water."
For the next three hours,
15 the tap is constantly running.
Dad has an ear trained to the
pump in the basement.
In another while, two of them
stoop through the doorway
20 and proudly present the parents
with a nice bowl of popcorn.
Each popped kernel is the size
of a grapefruit and dripping
in butter. The bowl itself is
25 too big to fit on the coffee table,
the parents ask for
it to be placed on the floor,
decline the gallon tumblers
of cherry limeade.
30 The guests go out the back
door at eleven,
ripping the porch off the
outside wall as they step
out under the stars,
35 never looking back and not
meaning any harm.

Discussion

1. There is reference in the poem to, among other things, popcorn kernels the size of grapefruit and gallon tumblers of cherry limeade. What other exaggerations do you find in the poem, and what do they symbolically suggest?

2. Explain the title, "No Respect for Authority." Are the teenagers impolite?

Marisha Chamberlain   1952 •

Marisha Chamberlain has published poems in a number of magazines, including *Dacotah Territory* and *Rapport*. She was awarded an NEA (National Endowment for the Arts) Fellowship in 1976 to write poetry. She was born in Sarasota, Florida, and now lives in Minnesota, where she co-directs Poetry Out Loud.

Victor Hernández Cruz

The Latest Latin Dance Craze

Discussion

1. What elements of exaggeration do you see in this description of the "Latest Latin Dance Craze?"

2. Why does the poem end without giving the second step of the dance? What do you think the second step would be?

Victor Hernández Cruz 1949 •

Victor Hernández Cruz was born in Puerto Rico and came to New York City when he was four years old. His poetry has appeared in *Evergreen Review, Umbra,* and *For Now, Down Here.* In 1968 Random House published his first book of poems, *Snaps.*

First
You throw your head back twice
Jump out onto the floor like a
Kangaroo
5 Circle the floor once
Doing fast scissor work with your
Legs
Next
Dash towards the door
10 Walking in a double cha cha cha
Open the door and glide down
The stairs like a swan
Hit the street
Run at least ten blocks
15 Come back in through the same
Door
Doing a mambo-minuet
Being careful that you don't fall
And break your head on that one
20 You have just completed your first
Step.

Hernández Cruz (er nän′des crüs).

"The Latest Latin Dance Craze" by Victor Hernández Cruz from *Nuestro Magazine* (June 1977). © Victor Hernández Cruz 1976. Reprinted by permission of the author.

Gary Soto

History

Grandma lit the stove.
Morning sunlight
Lengthened in spears
Across the linoleum floor.
5 Wrapped in a shawl,
Her eyes small
With sleep,
She sliced *papas*,[1]
Pounded chiles
10 With a stone
Brought from Guadalajara.[2]
                 After
Grandpa left for work,
She hosed down
The walk her sons paved
15 And in the shade
Of a chinaberry,
Unearthed her
Secret cigar box
Of bright coins
20 And bills, counted them
In English,

Then in Spanish,
And buried them elsewhere.
Later, back
25 From the market,
Where no one saw her,
She pulled out
Pepper and beet, spines
Of asparagus
30 From her blouse,
Tiny chocolates
From under a paisley bandana,
And smiled.

That was the '50s,
35 And Grandma in her '50s,
A face streaked
From cutting grapes
And boxing plums.
I remember her insides
40 Were washed of tapeworm,
Her arms swelled into knobs
Of small growths—

Her second son
Dropped from a ladder
45 And was dust.
And yet I do not know
The sorrows
That sent her praying
In the dark of a closet,
50 The tear that fell
At night
When she touched
Loose skin
Of belly and breasts.
55 I do not know why
Her face shines
Or what goes beyond this shine,
Only the stories
That pulled her
60 From Taxco to San Joaquin,
Delano to Westside,[3]
The places
In which we all begin.

"History" from THE ELEMENTS OF SAN JOAQUIN by Gary Soto, published by the University of Pittsburgh Press, 1977. Reprinted by permission of the author.

1. **papas** (pä′päs), potatoes. [*Spanish*]
2. **Guadalajara** (gwä′dä lä hä′rä), a city in central Mexico.
3. **Taxco** (tä′skô) **to San Joaquin** (sän′ wä kēn′), **Delano to Westside.** Many Chicano families stem from migrants who left Mexican towns like Taxco to work on farms in such areas as the San Joaquin Valley of California. Migrant workers follow the harvest from Delano in the Valley's center to its west side.

Discussion

1. In the first half of the poem, Grandma is characterized by her routine activities of the day. Describe these activities and what they reveal about her.

2. In the second half of the poem there is more emphasis on Grandma's past. How does this information help explain the activities described in the first half of the poem?

Gary Soto 1952 •

Gary Soto was raised in Fresno, California. He has a master's degree in Fine Arts from the University of California at Irvine. In 1976 his first published collection of poetry, *The Elements of San Joaquin*, was given the U. S. Award of the International Poetry Forum. He lives in Berkeley, California.

Judy Dothard Simmons

Generations

1863, my great grandmother—
   cut eleven years from Cherokee cord
   reared to wait upon her half-relations
   a servant in the kitchen of her father—

5 drank of freedom from a rusty pail
   by the dirt-floored shanty where her mother,
   wife now to an African transplanted,
   conceived and bore the black half of our kin

   ate meal gruel with a scraped hog jowl that
10 man and woman earned in dawn-dusk labor
   planting, hoeing, picking for her father
   cyclicly creating cotton snow

   spurred the gathered pine knots' daylight burning
   lest the night be met without salute
15 rose and slept and rose from corn-husk pallets
   to feed the fire, starve the morning chill

   1953, my silent mother
   rode a slat-bed truck to dusty fields
   knelt on brown sky picking cotton clouds
20 brought home three dollars earned in
      dawn-dusk labor

I carried water, chopped dead pine
   grateful that the summer used no coal
   played, I guess, and had the supper waiting:
   atonement for her wheeze and swollen hands

25 in winter she taught school for croppers' wages
   breathed coarse smoke and soot from
      coal-stoked stoves
   soothed and scolded fifty first-grade children
   heard her rich contralto rasp, kept on

   1970, and I, the daughter—
30 cut these ninety years from Cherokee cord
   reared for twenty-six in proper manner
   fit, at last, to join my father's mainstream—

   live in corporate rooms with blanched relations
   find most still a crasser kind of father
35 hear them talk as through a one-way window
   the speech of self-reflection, stupid, blind

   feel the killing fury of four lifetimes
   explode through coal gas tunnels in my eyes
   but cap the pits with poems, so stay alive
40 to carry on tradition:
        we survive

Discussion

1. The poem appears to be divided into three chronological parts, 1863, 1953, 1970, with three individual portraits. Discuss the title of the poem, "Generations," as it relates to the poem's three-part structure.

2. The speaker apparently feels a "killing fury" when she meditates on her past generations—a fury that explodes "through coal gas tunnels in my eyes." But, she adds, she caps "the pits with poems." Explain and discuss.

Judy Dothard Simmons 1944 •

As indicated in her poem "Generations," Judy Simmons's ancestry is partly black, partly Cherokee. She graduated from the University of California at Sacramento in 1970. She is a pianist, a singer, and a songwriter as well as a poet. She has published her poetry in anthologies and recorded it on tape. Her book, *Judith's Blues*, was published in 1973.

Ellen Bryant Voigt

Claiming Kin

Insistent as a whistle, her voice up
the stairs pried open the blanket's
tight lid and piped me
down to the pressure cooker's steam and rattle.
5 In my mother's kitchen, the hot iron
spit on signal, the vacuum
cleaner whined and snuffled.
Bright face and a snazzy apron,
clicking her long spoons,
10 how she commandeered the razzle-dazzle!

In the front room I dabbed
the company chairs with a sullen rag
(Father's drawers—nothing
wasted). Pale lump blinking
15 at the light, I could hear her sing
in her shiny kingdom: the sound
drifted out like a bottled message.
It was the voice of a young girl,
who stopped to gather cool moss, forgetting
20 the errand, spilling the cornmeal,
and cried and cried in her bearish papa's ear.

At night, while I flopped
like a fish on grandma's spool bed,
up from her bed and my wheezing
25 father she rose to the holly,
flat-leaf and Virginia Creeper.
Soft ghost, plush as a pillow,
she wove and fruited against the black hours:
red berries and running cedar, green signatures
30 on the table, on the mantle.

Mother, this poem is from your middle
child who, like your private second self,
rising at night to wander the dark house,
grew in the shady places:
35 a green plant in a brass pot,
rootbound, without blossoms.

Discussion

1. Characteristics of the mother in "Claiming Kin" are described in a number of vivid comparisons and descriptions: her voice came upstairs and "pried open the blanket's/tight lid"; the sound of her singing "drifted out like a bottled message"; at night, "she wove and fruited against the black hours." Discuss the meaning and appropriateness of these comparisons and descriptions.

2. What is the self-image of the speaker of the poem in the closing lines? What is the relation to the mother? Discuss the connection of these lines to the title, "Claiming Kin."

Ellen Bryant Voigt

Ellen Bryant Voigt published her first book of poems, *Claiming Kin,* in 1976. Her poems have appeared in many magazines, including *The Nation, Sewanee Review,* and *Salt Creek Reader.* She teaches in Vermont at Goddard College.

Robert Lowell

Middle Age

Now the midwinter grind
is on me, New York
drills through my nerves,
as I walk
5 the chewed-up streets.

At forty-five,
what next, what next?
At every corner,
I meet my Father,
10 my age, still alive.

Father, forgive me
my injuries,
as I forgive
those I
15 have injured!

You never climbed
Mount Sion,[1] yet left
dinosaur
death-steps on the crust,
20 where I must walk.

Imamu Amiri Baraka

Each Morning

Each morning
I go down
to Gansevoort St.[1]
and stand on the docks.
5 I stare out
at the horizon
until it gets up
and comes to embrace
me. I
10 make believe
it is my father.
This is known
as genealogy.

---

1. **Mount Sion** (Zion), the site of the ancient Jewish Temple in Jerusalem, a symbol of spiritual aspirations.

Imamu Amiri Baraka (ē mä′mü ä mē′rē bä rä′kä).

1. **Gansevoort St.**, a street on the waterfront in New York City.

Discussion

Middle Age

1. The speaker notes that his father is "my age." What does this suggest about the speaker's experience of meeting his father?

2. Why must the speaker follow the path of "dinosaur/death steps" left by his father? What other path is there?

Robert Lowell 1917 • 1977

Lowell once said: "What I write almost always comes out of the pressure of some inner concern, temptation or obses-sive puzzle. . . . All my poems are written for catharsis; none can cure melancholia or arthri-tis."

Lowell's poetry was received enthusiastically from the start. In 1947 he received a Pulitzer Prize, in 1960 a National Book Award, and in 1962 the Bollin-gen Translation Prize. He is re-garded as one of the new poets of the mid-century who might influence the literature of his generation.

Lowell was raised in Boston and educated at Harvard and Kenyon College in Ohio. Dur-ing World War II he was drafted but filed as a conscien-tious objector and went to pris-on. He later served as the Con-sultant in Poetry to the Library of Congress.

Discussion

Each Morning

1. How is the word "geneal-ogy" used here? Literally? Hu-morously? What attitude does the speaker have toward family pedigrees? With what does he identify?

(Baraka's biography is on page 578.)

N. Scott Momaday

The Gourd Dancer *(Mammedaty 1880–1932)*

1. The Omen

Another season centers on this place.
Like memory the blood congeals in it;
Like memory the sun recedes in time
Into the hazy, southern distances.

5 A vagrant heat hangs on the dark river,
And shadows turn like smoke. An owl ascends
Among the branches, clattering, remote
Within its motion, intricate with age.

2. The Dream

Mammedaty saw to the building of this house.
10 Just there, by the arbor, he made a camp in the old way.
And in the evening when the hammers had fallen silent
and there were frogs and crickets in the black grass—
and a low, hectic wind upon the pale, slanting plane
of the moon's light—he settled deep down in his mind
15 to dream. He dreamed of dreaming, and of the summer
breaking upon his spirit, as drums break upon the
intervals of the dance, and of the gleaming gourds.

3. The Dance

Dancing,
He dreams, he dreams—
20 The long wind glances, moves
Forever as a music to the mind;
The gourds are flashes of the sun.
He takes the inward, mincing steps
That conjure old processions and returns.

25 Dancing,
His moccasins,
His sash and bandolier
Contain him in insignia;
His fan is powerful, concise
30 According to his agile hand,
And holds upon the deep, ancestral air.

Gourd dancers performing the Green Corn ritual of the Jemez Pueblo of New Mexico. (The Bettmann Archive.)

Discussion

1. What are the indications in "The Dance" (Part 3) that the Gourd Dance is a ritual of identity for the dancer?

2. Explain how the ceremony portrayed in "The Giveaway" (Part 4) is a ceremony of the passing from boyhood to manhood.

Navarre Scott Momaday 1934 •

N. Scott Momaday was born in Lawton, Oklahoma, the son of artists and educators. His father is the distinguished contemporary Kiowa painter and art teacher Alfred Morris Momaday. His mother, Natachee Scott Momaday, is a novelist and writer of juvenile fiction as well as an artist and teacher.

Momaday spent his childhood on a number of Indian

---

4. The Giveaway

Someone spoke his name, Mammedaty, in which
his essence was and is. It was a serious matter that his
name should be spoken there in the circle, among the
35 many people, and he was thoughtful, full of wonder,
and aware of himself and of his name. He walked
slowly to the summons, looking into the eyes of the man
who summoned him. For a moment they held each
other in close regard, and all about them there was
40 excitement and suspense.

Then a boy came suddenly into the circle, leading
a black horse. The boy ran, and the horse after him.
He brought the horse up short in front of Mammedaty,
and the horse wheeled and threw its head and cut
45 its eyes in the wild way. And it blew hard and quivered
in its hide so that light ran, rippling, upon its shoulders
and its flanks—and then it stood still and was calm.
Its mane and tail were fixed in braids and feathers, and
a bright red chief's blanket was draped in a roll over
50 its withers. The boy placed the reins in Mammedaty's
hands. And all of this was for Mammedaty, in his honor,
as even now it is in the telling, and will be, as long as
there are those who imagine him in his name.

reservations. He now lives in California where he teaches English and comparative literature at Stanford University in California.

Although his most recent publications have been fiction and prose, Momaday has said that he thinks of himself primarily as a poet. It was in poetry that he was awarded a Stanford University Creative Writing Fellowship in 1959. In 1968 a publishing house suggested he submit some poetry; instead he sent them a novel, *House Made of Dawn*. It won the 1969 Pulitzer Prize.

---

notes and comments

The Gourd Dance Ceremony

In *The Names* (1976), Scott Momaday wrote about his ancestors, including his grandfather Mammedaty, who is the subject of "The Gourd Dancer." Momaday was born after his grandfather's death, but in his boyhood he visited the house that Mammedaty had built in 1913 on the "north side of Rainy Mountain Creek." There Momaday had the imaginative "recollection" recounted in the poem, the ritual or ceremony of naming in which, as a boy, Mammedaty participated as the gourd dancer and received the gift of the horse. In the ceremony of naming, the boy's "essence" is affirmed in his name, Mammedaty. In Part I, "The Omen," the poet reconstructs his boyhood visit to his grandfather's house ("this place"), and the mystical experience of remembering his grandfather's past. Part 2, "The Dream," portrays the grandfather waiting for his house of marriage to be constructed and dreaming of the time of his boyhood dance. Part 3, "The Dance," presents the young Mammedaty's gourd dance. And Part 4, "The Giveaway," completes the "nominal ceremony" in which Mammedaty's name is pronounced and the horse is presented.

Taos Pueblo (tribal authorship)

I Have Killed the Deer

I have killed the deer
I have crushed the grasshopper
And the plants he feeds upon
    I have cut through the heart
5   Of trees growing old and straight.
I have taken fish from water
And birds from the sky.
In my life I have needed death
So that my life can be.
10 When I die I must give life
To what has nourished me.
The earth receives my body
And gives it to the plants
And to the caterpillars
15 To the birds
And to the coyotes
Each in its own time so that
The circle of Life is never broken.

N. Scott Momaday

The Stalker

Sampt'e drew the string back and back until he felt
the bow wobble in his hand, and he let the arrow go.
It shot across the long light of the morning and struck
the black face of a stone in the meadow; it glanced
5 then away towards the west, limping along in the air;
and then it settled down in the grass and lay still.
Sampt'e approached; he looked at it with wonder and was
wary; honestly he believed that the arrow might take flight
again; so much of his life did he give into it.

Discussion

1. What details in the prayer "I Have Killed the Deer" show that the last line is true?

2. In what way has the stalker given so much of his life into his arrow?

Taos Pueblo

Taos Pueblo is an ancient village near Taos, New Mexico. The Pueblo Indians believe in collective authorship of their prayers and chants.

James Masao Mitsui

The Morning My Father Died,
April 7, 1963

The youngest son, I left the family inside and stood
alone in the unplanted garden by a cherry tree
we had grown ourselves, next to a trash barrel
smoldering what we couldn't give away or move
5 to Seattle. Looking over the rusty edge I could see
colors of volcano. Feathers of ash floated
up to a sky that was changing. I stared at the sound
of meadowlarks below the water tank
on the pumice-colored hill where the sun would come.
10 I couldn't stop smelling sagebrush, the creosote
bottoms of posts, the dew that was like a thunderstorm
had passed an hour before. Thoughts were trees
under a lake; that moment was sunflower, killdeer
and cheatgrass. Volunteer wheat grew strong
15 on the far side of our place along the old highway.
Undeberg's rooster gave the day its sharper edge,
the top of the sun. Turning to go back inside,
twenty years of Big Bend Country
took off like sparrows from a startled fence.

Discussion

1. (a) What do you think were the poet's feelings when his father died? (b) How are these feelings revealed in his description of the sights, smells, and sounds of the unplanted garden?

2. What does the poet mean in lines 18–19 when he compares twenty years to sparrows taking off from a fence?

James Masao Mitsui 1940 •

James Mitsui's first book of poetry, *Journal of the Sun*, received the Pacific Northwest Bookseller's Award for 1974. On the basis of that volume, he was awarded a grant from the National Endowment for the Arts in 1976 and 1977.

A native of Washington state, Mitsui received his master's degree from the University of Washington and currently teaches high-school English. His second volume of poetry is entitled *Crossing the Phantom River*.

Karl Shapiro

Auto Wreck

Its quick soft silver bell beating, beating,
And down the dark one ruby flare
Pulsing out red light like an artery,
The ambulance at top speed floating down
5 Past beacons and illuminated clocks
Wings in a heavy curve, dips down,
And brakes speed, entering the crowd.
The doors leap open, emptying light;
Stretchers are laid out, the mangled lifted
10 And stowed into the little hospital.
Then the bell, breaking the hush, tolls once,
And the ambulance with its terrible cargo
Rocking, slightly rocking, moves away,
As the doors, an afterthought, are closed.

15 We are deranged, walking among the cops
Who sweep glass and are large and composed.
One is still making notes under the light.
One with a bucket douches ponds of blood
Into the street and gutter.
20 One hangs lanterns on the wrecks that cling,
Empty husks of locusts, to iron poles.

Our throats were tight as tourniquets,
Our feet were bound with splints, but now
Like convalescents intimate and gauche,
25 We speak through sickly smiles and warn
With the stubborn saw of common sense,
The grim joke and the banal resolution.
The traffic moves around with care,
But we remain, touching a wound
30 That opens to our richest horror.

Already old, the question Who shall die?
Becomes unspoken Who is innocent?
For death in war is done by hands;
Suicide has cause and stillbirth, logic.
35 But this invites the occult mind,
Cancels our physics with a sneer,
And spatters all we knew of denouement
Across the expedient and wicked stones.

1. Find a passage in the poem that strikes you as particularly vivid and analyze the elements of language in it that contribute to the effect: the **imagery,** the rhythm or sound repetitions, the **metaphors** or **similes,** the words with particularly rich connotative meaning.

2. Explain the metaphor presented in the last two lines of stanza 3.

3. Relate the fourth paragraph of Karl Shapiro's letter to the last stanza of the poem. How is death by accident different from death in war or by suicide or in stillbirth?

notes and comments

From the Author

"Auto Wreck" seems to be my most popular poem. I don't mind really.

Its genesis is partly imaginary, partly composite, partly based on observation, like most poems. Notice that there are no sounds of pain or anguish in the poem. The people are silent, as in a silent film. Even the ambulance bell has a soft almost beautiful music. The accident is at night and the "arterial" light of the ambulance comes and goes through the darkness. And everything is somewhat in slow motion.

The bystander (the Poet) is dissociated from the scene and merely wonders at its meaning and its horror. I watched the police wash the blood down the gutters and sweep away the broken glass, and the rest. I had a particular accident in mind, and the poem was written after witnessing a particularly bad one one midnight in Baltimore, but I drew upon similar scenes such as everyone has experienced from time to time.

The questions asked towards the end of the poem have a certain grisly banality, the very kind of question that loved ones would ask. *Why? Why?* For, given another second there would be no accident.

Incidentally, the first line is a deliberate wrenching of an iambic pentameter line, with two reversed feet at the end, "beating, beating". I think the device works well, considering the subject.

I hope these remarks will help.

Born in Baltimore in 1913, Karl Shapiro grew up wanting to write poetry. So strong was his interest that he neglected his studies at the University of Virginia to work on his verses. His second volume of verse, V-Letter and Other Poems, *poems of World War II, was awarded the Pulitzer Prize in 1945. In 1946 he was appointed Consultant in Poetry to the Library of Congress.*

Shapiro has also won fame as critic and editor. From 1950 to 1956 he was editor of Poetry *and from 1956 to 1966 he was editor of* The Prairie Schooner. *He has taught at the Chicago Circle Campus of the University of Illinois and at the Davis campus of the University of California.*

Randall Jarrell

Losses

It was not dying: everybody died.
It was not dying: we had died before
In the routine crashes—and our fields
Called up the papers, wrote home to our folks,
5 And the rates rose, all because of us.
We died on the wrong page of the almanac,
Scattered on mountains fifty miles away;
Diving on haystacks, fighting with a friend,
We blazed up on the lines we never saw.
10 We died like aunts or pets or foreigners.
(When we left high school nothing else had died
For us to figure we had died like.)

In our new planes, with our new crews, we bombed
The ranges by the desert or the shore,
15 Fired at towed targets, waited for our scores—
And turned into replacements and woke up
One morning, over England, operational.
It wasn't different: but if we died
It was not an accident but a mistake
20 (But an easy one for anyone to make).
We read our mail and counted up our missions—
In bombers named for girls, we burned
The cities we had learned about in school—
Till our lives wore out; our bodies lay among
25 The people we had killed and never seen.
When we lasted long enough they gave us medals;
When we died they said, "Our casualties were low."

They said, "Here are the maps"; we burned the cities.

It was not dying—no, not ever dying;
30 But the night I died I dreamed that I was dead,
And the cities said to me: "Why are you dying?
We are satisfied, if you are; but why did I die?"

Discussion

1. (a) Who are the "we" of the poem? (b) What were their specific actions in the war?

2. (a) What do you think is the attitude of the poet toward war? (b) Which specific images help to convey this attitude?

3. What do you think is the answer to the cities' question in line 32: "Why did I die"? Explain.

Randall Jarrell 1914 • 1965

Randall Jarrell was born and raised in Tennessee. After college and graduate studies, he began teaching and writing poetry. In 1942 he entered the Army Air Corps. The poetry that grew out of the war years was stark and almost violent. *Little Friend, Little Friend* (1945) and *Losses* (1948) brought Jarrell recognition and influence.

In 1946 Jarrell returned to teaching and also acted as literary editor to *The Nation*. From 1956 to 1958 Jarrell left teaching to serve as Poetry Consultant to the Library of Congress, and in 1961 he won the National Book Award for *The Woman at the Washington Zoo*, a volume of poetry and translations.

Robert Hayden

Homage to the Empress of the Blues

Because there was a man somewhere in a candystripe silk shirt,
gracile and dangerous as a jaguar and because a woman moaned
for him in sixty-watt gloom and mourned him Faithless Love
Twotiming Love Oh Love Oh Careless Aggravating Love,

5 She came out on the stage in yards of pearls, emerging like
a favorite scenic view, flashed her golden smile and sang.

Because grey laths began somewhere to show from underneath
torn hurdygurdy lithographs of dollfaced heaven;
and because there were those who feared alarming fists of snow
10 on the door and those who feared the riot-squad of statistics,

She came out on the stage in ostrich feathers, beaded satin,
and shone that smile on us and sang.

"Homage to the Empress of the Blues" and "Unidentified Flying Object." Reprinted from ANGLE OF ASCENT, New and Selected Poems, by Robert Hayden.
By permission of Liveright Publishing Corporation. Copyright © 1975, 1972, 1970,
1966, by Robert Hayden.

Discussion

1. What loves, disillusions, and fears are described in the first and third stanzas?

2. **(a)** What details of the blues singer does the poet include? **(b)** What overall impression do you get from these details?

3. What need does the blues singer fulfill that causes the poet to pay her homage?

Unidentified Flying Object

It's true Mattie Lee
has clean disappeared.
And shouldn't we notify
the sheriff? No use, Will
5 insists, no earthly use.

He was sleeping one off
under the trees that night,
he claims, and woke up when
the space-ship
10 landed—a silvery dome

with gassy-green and red-
hot-looking lights like eyes
that stared blinked stared.
Says he hid himself
15 in the bushes and watched,

shaking. Pretty soon
a hatch slides open, a ramp
glides forward like
a glowing tongue poked out.
20 And who or what is it

silently present there?
Same as if Will's
trying to peer through webs
and bars of gauzy glare
25 screening, distorting a shape

he sees yet cannot see.
But crazier than that
was when Mattie Lee
came running from her house
30 toward the thing.

She's wearing her sunflower hat
and the dress the lady she cooked
for gave her, and it's like
she's late for work the way
35 she scurries up the ramp.

And it seems to Will
that in its queer
shining, plain Mattie Lee's

transformed—is every teasing brown
40 he's ever wanted, never had.

He's fixing to shout, Come back,
Mattie Lee, come back;
but a heavy hand is over his mouth
when he hears her laugh
45 as she steps inside

without even a goodbye glance
around. The next Will knew,
the UFO rose in the air—
no blastoff roar, no flame,
50 he says—hung in the dark,

hovered, shimmered,
its eyes pulsing, then whirred
spiraling into the sky,
vanished as though
55 it had never been.

Will's tale anyhow.
All I'm certain of
is Mattie Lee's
nowhere to be found
60 and must have gone

off in a hurry. Left her doors
unlocked and the radio on
and a roast in the oven. Strange.
As for Will, he's a changed man,
65 not drinking nowadays and sad.

Mattie Lee's friends—
she's got no kinfolks, lived
alone—are worried, swear
Will was craving her
70 and she held herself too good

for him, being head of Mount
Nebo's usher board and such.
And some are hinting what I,
for one—well, never mind.
75 The talk is getting mean.

Discussion

1. Using whatever evidence you can find in the poem, characterize Will and Mattie Lee and their relationship.

2. In the last three lines of the poem, the speaker starts to pass on some rumors about Mattie Lee's disappearance. (a) What do you think the rumors are? (b) Why does the poem end abruptly this way?

from The Islands

I wake and see
the morning like a god
in peacock-flower mantle dancing

on opalescent waves—
5 and can believe my furies[1] have
abandoned for a time their long pursuit.

"The Islands" by Robert Hayden. Reprinted by permission.
1. *furies,* in ancient Greek and Roman myths, avenging spirits
that provoke madness in wrongdoers.

Discussion

1. **(a)** How does the poet feel
about the pictures he sees
when he awakens? **(b)** Which
words convey his feelings?

2. **(a)** Explain in your own
words the last two lines of the
poem. **(b)** What has caused the
speaker's "furies" to rest tem-
porarily?

Robert Hayden 1913 • 1980

Robert Earl Hayden had been
writing and publishing his poetry since 1940, but not until
1966 did he receive the attention his work merits. In that
year he was awarded the prize
for English language poetry at
the First World Festival of
Negro Arts at Dakar, Senegal.

In 1970 he received the Russell Loines Award, presented
by the National Institute of
Arts and Letters. In 1972 he
was a nominee for the National
Book Award in poetry.

Hayden was born in Detroit,
Michigan, and received his
higher education at Wayne
State University and the University of Michigan. Before accepting a position as a professor
of English at the University of
Michigan, he taught for more
than twenty years at Fisk University.

Among Hayden's publica-
tions are *A Ballad of Remembrance* (1962), *Selected Poems*
(1966), and *Words in the*
Mourning Time (1970). He
also edited *Kaleidoscope:
Poems by American Negro
Poets* (1967) and was co-editor
of *A Source Book of Afro-
American Literature.*

In 1975 Hayden was elected
to the National Academy of
American Poets, and since 1975
he was twice appointed Poetry
Consultant to the Library of
Congress.

Gwendolyn Brooks

To Be In Love

To be in love
Is to touch things with a lighter hand.

In yourself you stretch, you are well.

You look at things
5 Through his eyes.
    A Cardinal is red.
    A sky is blue.
Suddenly you know he knows too.
He is not there but
10 You know you are tasting together
The winter, or light spring weather.

His hand to take your hand is overmuch.
Too much to bear.

You cannot look in his eyes
15 Because your pulse must not say
What must not be said.

When he
Shuts a door—
Is not there—
20 Your arms are water.

And you are free
With a ghastly freedom.

You are the beautiful half
Of a golden hurt.
25 You remember and covet his mouth,
To touch, to whisper on.

Oh when to declare
Is certain Death!

Oh when to apprize
30 Is to mesmerize,

To see fall down, the Column of Gold,
Into the commonest ash.

Discussion

1. What specific effects of love are described in lines 1–11?

2. In what ways does love overwhelm the poet in lines 12–16?

3. (a) What memories and feelings does the poet describe in the last four stanzas? (b) What is meant by the gold column becoming ash in the last two lines of the poem?

Gwendolyn Brooks 1917 •

For all but one month of her life Gwendolyn Brooks has lived on the South Side of Chicago. After graduation from Wilson Junior College in Chicago, she did editorial work on a magazine and secretarial work. While she was working she took a writing course, submitted one of her poems to *Poetry* magazine, and had it accepted.

Her first volume of poetry, *A Street in Bronzeville* (1945), led to both an American Academy of Arts and Letters award and a Guggenheim Fellowship. Her second book of poems, *Annie Allen*, won the Pulitzer Prize for poetry in 1950. In 1968, the same year *In the Mecca* was published, she was named successor to the late Carl Sandburg as Poet Laureate of Illinois. In 1971 a group of new black poets, in recognition of her influence, support, and encouragement, published a collection of their works entitled *To Gwen with Love*.

Carson McCullers

The Haunted Boy

Hugh looked for his mother at the corner, but she was not in the yard. Sometimes she would be out fooling with the border of spring flowers— the candytuft, the sweet William, the lobelias (she had taught him the names)—but today the green front lawn with the borders of many-colored flowers was empty under the frail sunshine of the mid-April afternoon. Hugh raced up the sidewalk, and John followed him. They finished the front steps with two bounds, and the door slammed after them.

"Mamma!" Hugh called.

It was then, in the unanswering silence as they stood in the empty, wax-floored hall, that Hugh felt there was something wrong. There was no fire in the grate of the sitting room, and since he was used to the flicker of firelight during the

"The Haunted Boy" from THE COLLECTED SHORT STORIES AND THE NOVEL THE BALLAD OF THE SAD CAFÉ by Carson McCullers. Copyright 1936, 1955 by Carson McCullers. Reprinted by permission of the publisher, Houghton Mifflin Company and Floria Lasky as the Executor of the Estate of Carson McCullers.

cold months, the room on this first warm day seemed strangely naked and cheerless. Hugh shivered. He was glad John was there. The sun shone on a red piece in the flowered rug. Red-bright, red-dark, red-dead—Hugh sickened with a sudden chill remembrance of "the other time." The red darkened to a dizzy black.

"What's the matter, Brown?" John asked. "You look so white."

Hugh shook himself and put his hand to his forehead. "Nothing. Let's go back to the kitchen."

"I can't stay but just a minute," John said. "I'm obligated to sell those tickets. I have to eat and run."

The kitchen, with the fresh checked towels and clean pans, was now the best room in the house. And on the enameled table there was a lemon pie that she had made. Assured by the everyday kitchen and the pie, Hugh stepped back into the hall and raised his face again to call upstairs.

"Mother! Oh, Mamma!"

Again there was no answer.

"My mother made this pie," he said. Quickly, he found a knife and cut into the pie—to dispel the gathering sense of dread.

"Think you ought to cut it, Brown?"

"Sure thing, Laney."

They called each other by their last names this spring, unless they happened to forget. To Hugh it seemed sporty and grown and somehow grand. Hugh liked John better than any other boy at school. John was two years older than Hugh, and compared to him the other boys seemed like a silly crowd of punks. John was the best student in the sophomore class, brainy but not the least bit a teacher's pet, and he was the best athlete too. Hugh was a freshman and didn't have so many friends that first year of high school—he had somehow cut himself off, because he was so afraid.

"Mamma always has me something nice for after school." Hugh put a big piece of pie on a saucer for John—for Laney.

"This pie is certainly super."

"The crust is made of crunched-up graham crackers instead of regular pie dough," Hugh said, "because pie dough is a lot of trouble. We think this graham-cracker pastry is just as good.

Naturally, my mother can make regular pie dough if she wants to."

Hugh could not keep still; he walked up and down the kitchen, eating the pie wedge he carried on the palm of his hand. His brown hair was mussed with nervous rakings, and his gentle gold-brown eyes were haunted with pained perplexity. John, who remained seated at the table, sensed Hugh's uneasiness and wrapped one gangling leg around the other.

"I'm really obligated to sell those Glee Club tickets."

"Don't go. You have the whole afternoon." He was afraid of the empty house. He needed John, he needed someone; most of all he needed to hear his mother's voice and know she was in the house with him. "Maybe Mamma is taking a bath," he said. "I'll holler again."

The answer to his third call too was silence.

"I guess your mother must have gone to the movie or gone shopping or something."

"No," Hugh said. "She would have left a note. She always does when she's gone when I come home from school."

"We haven't looked for a note," John said. "Maybe she left it under the door mat or somewhere in the living room."

Hugh was inconsolable. "No. She would have left it right under this pie. She knows I always run first to the kitchen."

"Maybe she had a phone call or thought of something she suddenly wanted to do."

"She *might* have," he said. "I remember she said to Daddy that one of these days she was going to buy herself some new clothes." This flash of hope did not survive its expression. He pushed his hair back and started from the room. "I guess I'd better go upstairs. I ought to go upstairs while you are here."

He stood with his arm around the newel post; the smell of varnished stairs, the sight of the closed white bathroom door at the top revived again "the other time." He clung to the newel post, and his feet would not move to climb the stairs. The red turned again to whirling, sick dark. Hugh sat down. *Stick your head between your legs,* he ordered, remembering Scout first aid.

"Hugh," John called. "Hugh!"

The dizziness clearing, Hugh accepted a fresh

chagrin—Laney was calling him by his ordinary first name; he thought he was a sissy about his mother, unworthy of being called by his last name in the grand, sporty way they used before. The dizziness cleared when he returned to the kitchen.

"Brown," said John, and the chagrin disappeared. "Does this establishment have anything pertaining to a cow? A white, fluid liquid. In French they call it *lait*. Here we call it plain old milk."

The stupidity of shock lightened. "Oh, Laney, I am a dope! Please excuse me. I clean forgot." Hugh fetched the milk from the refrigerator and found two glasses. "I didn't think. My mind was on something else."

"I know," John said. After a moment he asked in a calm voice, looking steadily at Hugh's eyes: "Why are you so worried about your mother? Is she sick, Hugh?"

Hugh knew now that the first name was not a slight; it was because John was talking too serious to be sporty. He liked John better than any friend he had ever had. He felt more natural sitting across the kitchen table from John, somehow safer. As he looked into John's gray, peaceful eyes, the balm of affection soothed the dread.

John asked again, still steadily: "Hugh, is your mother sick?"

Hugh could have answered no other boy. He had talked with no one about his mother, except his father, and even those intimacies had been rare, oblique. They could approach the subject only when they were occupied with something else, doing carpentry work or the two times they hunted in the woods together—or when they were cooking supper or washing dishes.

"She's not exactly sick," he said, "but Daddy and I have been worried about her. At least, we used to be worried for a while."

John asked: "Is it a kind of heart trouble?"

Hugh's voice was strained. "Did you hear about that fight I had with that slob Clem Roberts? I scraped his slob face on the gravel walk and nearly killed him sure enough. He's still got scars or at least he did have a bandage on for two days. I had to stay in school every afternoon for a week. But I nearly killed him. I would have if Mr. Paxton hadn't come along and dragged me off."

"I heard about it."

"You know why I wanted to kill him?"

For a moment John's eyes flickered away.

Hugh tensed himself; his raw boy hands clutched the table edge; he took a deep, hoarse breath. "That slob was telling everybody that my mother was in Milledgeville. He was spreading it around that my mother was crazy."

"The dirty . . . ."

Hugh said in a clear, defeated voice, "My mother *was* in Milledgeville. But that doesn't mean that she was crazy," he added quickly. "In that big State hospital, there are buildings for people who are crazy, and there are other buildings, for people who are just sick. Mamma was sick for a while. Daddy and me discussed it and decided that the hospital in Milledgeville was the place where there were the best doctors and she would get the best care. But she was the furtherest from crazy than anybody in the world. You know Mamma, John." He said again, "I ought to go upstairs."

John said: "I have always thought that your mother is one of the nicest ladies in this town."

"You see, Mamma had a peculiar thing happen, and afterward she was blue."

Confession, the first deep-rooted words, opened the festered secrecy of the boy's heart, and he continued more rapidly, urgent and finding unforeseen relief.

"Last year my mother thought she was going to have a little baby. She talked it over with Daddy and me," he said proudly. "We wanted a girl. I was going to choose the name. We were so tickled. I hunted up all my old toys—my electric train and the tracks . . . I was going to name her Crystal—how does the name strike you for a girl? It reminds me of something bright and dainty."

"Was the little baby born dead?"

Even with John, Hugh's ears turned hot; his cold hands touched them. "No, it was what they call a tumor. That's what happened to my mother. They had to operate at the hospital here." He was embarrassed and his voice was very low. "Then she had something called change of life." The words were terrible to Hugh. "And afterward she was blue. Daddy said it was a shock to her nervous system. It's something that happens to ladies; she was just blue and run-down."

Although there was no red, no red in the kitchen anywhere, Hugh was approaching "the other time."

"One day, she just sort of gave up—one day last fall." Hugh's eyes were wide open and glaring: again he climbed the stairs and opened the bathroom door—he put his hand to his eyes to shut out the memory. "She tried to—hurt herself. I found her when I came in from school."

John reached out and carefully stroked Hugh's sweatered arm.

"Don't worry. A lot of people have to go to hospitals because they are run-down and blue. Could happen to anybody."

"We had to put her in the hospital—the best hospital." The recollection of those long, long months was stained with a dull loneliness, as cruel in its lasting unappeasement as "the other time"—how long had it lasted? In the hospital Mamma could walk around and she always had on shoes.

John said carefully: "This pie is certainly super."

"My mother is a super cook. She cooks things like meat pie and salmon loaf—as well as steaks and hot dogs."

"I hate to eat and run," John said.

Hugh was so frightened of being left alone that he felt the alarm in his own loud heart.

"Don't go," he urged. "Let's talk for a little while."

"Talk about what?"

Hugh could not tell him. Not even John Laney. He could tell no one of the empty house and the horror of the time before. "Do you ever cry?" he asked John. "I don't."

"I do sometimes," John admitted.

"I wish I had known you better when Mother was away. Daddy and me used to go hunting nearly every Saturday. We *lived* on quail and dove. I bet you would have liked that." He added in a lower tone, "On Sunday we went to the hospital."

John said: "It's a kind of a delicate proposition selling those tickets. A lot of people don't enjoy the High School Glee Club operettas. Unless they know someone in it personally, they'd rather stay home with a good TV show. A lot of people buy tickets on the basis of being public-spirited."

"We're going to get a television set real soon."

"I couldn't exist without television," John said.

Hugh's voice was apologetic. "Daddy wants to clean up the hospital bills first because as everybody knows sickness is a very expensive proposition. Then we'll get TV."

John lifted his milk glass. "Skoal," he said. "That's a Swedish word you say before you drink. A good-luck word."

"You know so many foreign words and languages."

"Not so many," John said truthfully. "Just 'kaput' and 'adios' and 'skoal' and stuff we learn in French class. That's not much."

"That's *beaucoup,*" said Hugh, and he felt witty and pleased with himself.

Suddenly the stored tension burst into physical activity. Hugh grabbed the basketball out on the porch and rushed into the back yard. He dribbled the ball several times and aimed at the goal his father had put up on his last birthday. When he missed he bounced the ball to John, who had come after him. It was good to be outdoors and the relief of natural play brought Hugh the first line of a poem. "My heart is like a basketball." Usually when a poem came to him he would lie sprawled on the living room floor, studying to hunt rhymes, his tongue working on the side of his mouth. His mother would call him Shelley-Poe when she stepped over him, and sometimes she would put her foot lightly on his behind. His mother always liked his poems; today the second line came quickly, like magic. He said it out loud to John: " 'My heart is like a basketball, bouncing with glee down the hall.' How do you like that for the start of a poem?"

"Sounds kind of crazy to me," John said. Then he corrected himself hastily. "I mean it sounds—odd. Odd, I meant."

Hugh realized why John had changed the word, and the elation of play and poems left him instantly. He caught the ball and stood with it cradled in his arms. The afternoon was golden and the wisteria vine on the porch was in full, unshattered bloom. The wisteria was like lavender waterfalls. The fresh breeze smelled of sun-warmed flowers. The sunlit sky was blue and cloudless. It was the first warm day of spring.

"I have to shove off," John said.

"No!" Hugh's voice was desperate. "Don't you want another piece of pie? I never heard of anybody eating just one piece of pie."

He steered John into the house and this time he called only out of habit because he always called on coming in. "Mother!" He was cold after the bright, sunny outdoors. He was cold not only because of the weather but because he was so scared.

"My mother has been home a month and every afternoon she's always here when I come home from school. Always, always."

They stood in the kitchen looking at the lemon pie. And to Hugh the cut pie looked somehow—odd. As they stood motionless in the kitchen the silence was creepy and odd too.

"Doesn't this house seem quiet to you?"

"It's because you don't have television. We put on our TV at seven o'clock and it stays on all day and night until we go to bed. Whether anybody's in the living room or not. There're plays and skits and gags going on continually."

"We have a radio, of course, and a vic."

"But that's not the company of a good TV. You won't know when your mother is in the house or not when you get TV."

Hugh didn't answer. Their footsteps sounded hollow in the hall. He felt sick as he stood on the first step with his arm around the newel post. "If you could just come upstairs for a minute—"

John's voice was suddenly impatient and loud. "How many times have I told you I'm obligated to sell those tickets. You have to be public-spirited about things like Glee Clubs."

"Just for a second—I have something important to show you upstairs."

John did not ask what it was and Hugh sought desperately to name something important enough to get John upstairs. He said finally: "I'm assembling a hi-fi machine. You have to know a lot about electronics—my father is helping me."

But even when he spoke he knew John did not for a second believe the lie. Who would buy a hi-fi when they didn't have television? He hated John, as you hate people you have to need so badly. He had to say something more and he straightened his shoulders.

"I just want you to know how much I value your friendship. During these past months I had somehow cut myself off from people."

"That's O.K., Brown. You oughtn't to be so sensitive because your mother was—where she was."

John had his hand on the door and Hugh was trembling. "I thought if you could come up for just a minute—"

John looked at him with anxious, puzzled eyes. Then he asked slowly: "Is there something you are scared of upstairs?"

Hugh wanted to tell him everything. But he could not tell what his mother had done that September afternoon. It was too terrible and—odd. It was like something a *patient* would do, and not like his mother at all. Although his eyes were wild with terror and his body trembled he said: "I'm not scared."

"Well, so long. I'm sorry I have to go—but to be obligated is to be obligated."

John closed the front door, and he was alone in the empty house. Nothing could save him now. Even if a whole crowd of boys were listening to TV in the living room, laughing at funny gags and jokes, it would still not help him. He had to go upstairs and find her. He sought courage from the last thing John had said, and repeated the words aloud: "To be obligated is to be obligated." But the words did not give him any of John's thoughtlessness and courage; they were creepy and strange in the silence.

He turned slowly to go upstairs. His heart was not like a basketball but like a fast, jazz drum, beating faster and faster as he climbed the stairs. His feet dragged as though he waded through knee-deep water and he held on to the banisters. The house looked odd, crazy. As he looked down at the ground-floor table with the vase of fresh spring flowers that too looked somehow peculiar. There was a mirror on the second floor and his own face startled him, so crazy did it seem to him. The initial of his high school sweater was backward and wrong in the reflection and his mouth was open like an asylum idiot. He shut his mouth and he looked better. Still the objects he saw—the table downstairs, the sofa upstairs—looked somehow cracked or jarred because of the dread in him, although they were the familiar things of everyday. He fastened his eyes on the closed door at the right of the stairs and the fast, jazz drum beat faster.

He opened the bathroom door and for a

moment the dread that had haunted him all that afternoon made him see again the room as he had seen it "the other time." His mother lay on the floor and there was blood everywhere. His mother lay there dead and there was blood everywhere, on her slashed wrist, and a pool of blood had trickled to the bathtub and lay dammed there. Hugh touched the doorframe and steadied himself. Then the room settled and he realized this was not "the other time." The April sunlight brightened the clean white tiles. There was only bathroom brightness and the sunny window. He went to the bedroom and saw the empty bed with the rose-colored spread. The lady things were on the dresser. The room was as it always looked and nothing had happened . . . nothing had happened and he flung himself on the quilted rose bed and cried from relief and a strained, bleak tiredness that had lasted so long. The sobs jerked his whole body and quieted his jazz, fast heart.

Hugh had not cried all those months. He had not cried at "the other time," when he found his mother alone in that empty house with blood everywhere. He had not cried but he made a Scout mistake. He had first lifted his mother's heavy, bloody body before he tried to bandage her. He had not cried when he called his father. He had not cried those few days when they were deciding what to do. He hadn't even cried when the doctor suggested Milledgeville, or when he and his father took her to the hospital in the car—although his father cried on the way home. He had not cried at the meals they made—steak every night for a whole month so that they felt steak was running out of their eyes, their ears; then they had switched to hot dogs, and ate them until hot dogs ran out of their ears, their eyes. They got in ruts of food and were messy about the kitchen, so that it was never nice except the Saturday the cleaning woman came. He did not cry those lonesome afternoons after he had the fight with Clem Roberts and felt the other boys were thinking queer things of his mother. He stayed at home in the messy kitchen, eating fig newtons or chocolate bars. Or he went to see a neighbor's television—Miss Richards, an old maid who saw old-maid shows. He had not cried when his father drank too much so that it took his appetite and Hugh had to eat alone. He had not even cried on those long, waiting Sundays when they went to Milledgeville and he twice saw a lady on a porch without any shoes on and talking to herself. A lady who was a patient and who struck at him with a horror he could not name. He did not cry when at first his mother would say: *Don't punish me by making me stay here. Let me go home.* He had not cried at the terrible words that haunted him—"change of life"—"crazy"—"Milledgeville"—he could not cry all during those long months strained with dullness and want and dread.

He still sobbed on the rose bedspread which was soft and cool against his wet cheeks. He was sobbing so loud that he did not hear the front door open, did not even hear his mother call or the footsteps on the stairs. He still sobbed when his mother touched him and burrowed his face hard in the spread. He even stiffened his legs and kicked his feet.

"Why, Loveyboy," his mother said, calling him a long-ago child name. "What's happened?"

He sobbed even louder, although his mother tried to turn his face to her. He wanted her to worry. He did not turn around until she had finally left the bed, and then he looked at her. She had on a different dress—blue silk it looked like in the pale spring light.

"Darling, what's happened?"

The terror of the afternoon was over, but he could not tell it to his mother. He could not tell her what he had feared, or explain the horror of things that were never there at all—but had once been there.

"Why did you do it?"

"The first warm day I just suddenly decided to buy myself some new clothes."

But he was not talking about clothes; he was thinking about "the other time" and the grudge that had started when he saw the blood and horror and felt *why did she do this to me.* He thought of the grudge against the mother he loved the most in the world. All those last, sad months the anger had bounced against the love with guilt between.

"I bought two dresses and two petticoats. How do you like them?"

"I hate them!" Hugh said angrily. "Your slip is showing."

She turned around twice and the petticoat

showed terribly. "It's supposed to show, goofy. It's the style."

"I still don't like it."

"I ate a sandwich at the tearoom with two cups of cocoa and then went to Mendel's. There were so many pretty things I couldn't seem to get away. I bought these two dresses and look, Hugh! The shoes!"

His mother went to the bed and switched on the light so he could see. The shoes were flat-heeled and *blue*—with diamond sparkles on the toes. He did not know how to criticize. "They look more like evening shoes than things you wear on the street."

"I have never owned any colored shoes before. I couldn't resist them."

His mother sort of danced over toward the window, making the petticoat twirl under the new dress. Hugh had stopped crying now, but he was still angry.

"I don't like it because it makes you look like you're trying to seem young, and I bet you are forty years old."

His mother stopped dancing and stood still at the window. Her face was suddenly quiet and sad. "I'll be forty-three years old in June."

He had hurt her and suddenly the anger vanished and there was only love. "Mamma, I shouldn't have said that."

"I realized when I was shopping that I hadn't been in a store for more than a year. Imagine!"

Hugh could not stand the sad quietness and the mother he loved so much. He could not stand his love or his mother's prettiness. He wiped the tears on the sleeve of his sweater and got up from the bed. "I have never seen you so pretty, or a dress and slip so pretty." He crouched down before his mother and touched the bright shoes. "The shoes are really super."

"I thought the minute I laid eyes on them that you would like them." She pulled Hugh up and kissed him on the cheek. "Now I've got lipstick on you."

Hugh quoted a witty remark he had heard before as he scrubbed off the lipstick. "It only shows I'm popular."

"Hugh, why were you crying when I came in? Did something at school upset you?"

"It was only that when I came in and found you gone and no note or anything—"

"I forgot all about a note."

"And all afternoon I felt—John Laney came in but he had to go sell Glee Club tickets. All afternoon I felt—"

"What? What was the matter?"

But he could not tell the mother he loved about the terror and the cause. He said at last: "All afternoon I felt—odd."

Afterward when his father came home he called Hugh to come out into the back yard with him. His father had a worried look—as though he spied a valuable tool Hugh had left outside. But there was no tool and the basketball was put back in its place on the back porch.

"Son," his father said, "there's something I want to tell you."

"Yes, sir?"

"Your mother said that you had been crying this afternoon." His father did not wait for him to explain. "I just want us to have a close understanding with each other. Is there anything about school—or girls—or something that puzzles you? Why were you crying?"

Hugh looked back at the afternoon and already it was far away, distant as a peculiar view seen at the wrong end of a telescope.

"I don't know," he said. "I guess maybe I was somehow nervous."

His father put his arm around his shoulder. "Nobody can be nervous before they are sixteen years old. You have a long way to go."

"I know."

"I have never seen your mother look so well. She looks so gay and pretty, better than she's looked in years. Don't you realize that?"

"The slip—the petticoat is supposed to show. It's a new style."

"Soon it will be summer," his father said. "And we'll go on picnics—the three of us." The words brought an instant vision of glare on the yellow creek and the summer-leaved, adventurous woods. His father added: "I came out here to tell you something else."

"Yes, sir?"

"I just want you to know that I realize how fine you were all that bad time. How fine, how damn fine."

His father was using a swear word as if he were talking to a grown man. His father was not a person to hand out compliments—always he was strict with report cards and tools left around. His father never praised him or used grown words or anything. Hugh felt his face grow hot and he touched it with his cold hands.

"I just wanted to tell you that, Son." He shook Hugh by the shoulder. "You'll be taller than your old man in a year or so." Quickly his father went into the house, leaving Hugh to the sweet and unaccustomed aftermath of praise.

Hugh stood in the darkening yard after the sunset colors faded in the west and the wisteria was dark purple. The kitchen light was on and he saw his mother fixing dinner. He knew that something was finished; the terror was far from him now, also the anger that had bounced with love, the dread and guilt. Although he felt he would never cry again—or at least not until he was sixteen—in the brightness of his tears glistened the safe, lighted kitchen, now that he was no longer a haunted boy, now that he was glad somehow, and not afraid. □□

Discussion

1. In what sense is Hugh a "haunted boy"?

2. (a) What pretexts does Hugh use to keep John around? **(b)** Why doesn't Hugh tell John that he is afraid and that he needs his help?

3. What is the effect on Hugh of his mother's arrival and of her conversation about her shopping expedition and purchases?

4. The story concludes with the father having a private talk with Hugh. **(a)** What is the effect of this talk on Hugh? **(b)** How is the conversation significant as a conclusion to the story?

Extension • Writing

1. Write an account of the fight that Hugh had with that "slob Clem Roberts."

2. Study the **techniques** Mc-Cullers used to build suspense, especially in the early part of the story. Then try writing the first few paragraphs of a suspense story. It is important to set a **mood** of tension and to give hints that **foreshadow** the events to come. But do not disclose these developments directly. You will be able to tell if you have created suspense when you read your story introduction to the class. If you have succeeded, your audience will want to go on and write the rest of the story.

Carson Smith McCullers
1917 • 1967

Born in Columbus, Georgia, Carson McCullers was sixteen when she finished high school and began writing. She also had hopes of becoming a concert pianist, and two years later she left for New York expecting to attend classes at both Columbia University and the Juilliard School of Music. But on her second day in the city she lost all her tuition money on the subway. She took a series of part-time jobs and tried to attend classes at night, but her heart wasn't in it. She was fired from her jobs, did little studying, and spent her time walking around the waterfront and dreaming of voyages to other lands. But she continued to write, and the following year two of her stories were published. With renewed determination she spent two years writing in North Carolina, and by the time she was twenty-two could boast a successful major novel, *The Heart Is a Lonely Hunter* (1940).

Her total life's output was small, with many years between publications, but her works were consistently valuable, unique, and compassionate. *The Ballad of the Sad Café* (1951) is considered her finest effort.

Kurt Vonnegut, Jr.

The Hyannis Port Story

The farthest way from home I ever sold a storm window was in Hyannis Port, Massachusetts, practically in the front yard of President Kennedy's summer home. My field of operation is usually within about twenty-five miles of my home, which is in North Crawford, New Hampshire.

The Hyannis Port thing happened because somebody misunderstood something I said, and thought I was an ardent Goldwater Republican.[1] Actually, I hadn't made up my mind one way or the other about Goldwater.

What happened was this: The program chairman of the North Crawford Lions Club was a Goldwater man, and he had this college boy named Robert Taft Rumfoord come talk to a meeting one day about the Democratic mess in Washington and Hyannis Port. The boy was national president of some kind of student organization that was trying to get the country back to what he called First Principles. One of the First Principles, I remember, was getting rid of the income tax. You should have heard the applause.

I got a funny feeling that the boy didn't care much more about politics than I did. He had circles under his eyes, and he looked as though he'd just as soon be somewhere else. He would say strong things, but they came out sounding like music on a kazoo. The only time he got really interesting was when he told about being in sailboat races and golf and tennis matches with different Kennedys and their friends. He said that there was a lot of propaganda around about what a fine golfer Bobby Kennedy was, whereas Bobby actually couldn't golf for sour apples. He said Pierre Salinger[2] was one of the worst golfers in the world, and didn't care for sailing or tennis at all.

Robert Taft Rumfoord's parents were there to hear him. They had come all the way from Hyannis Port. They were both very proud of him—or at least the father was. The father had on white flannel trousers and white shoes, even though there was snow on the ground, and a double-breasted blue coat with brass buttons. The boy introduced him as *Commodore* William Rumfoord. The Commodore was a short man with very shaggy eyebrows and pale blue eyes. He looked like a gruff, friendly teddybear, and so did his son. I found out later, from a Secret Service man, that the Kennedys sometimes called the Rumfoords *"the Pooh People,"* on account of they were so much like the bear in the children's book *Winnie the Pooh.*

The Commodore's wife wasn't a Pooh person, though. She was thin and quick, and maybe two inches taller than the Commodore. Bears have a way of looking as though they're pretty much satisfied with everything. The Commodore's lady didn't have that look. I could tell she was jumpy about a lot of things.

After the boy was through pouring fire and brimstone on the Kennedys, with his father applauding everything he said, Hay Boyden, the building mover stood up. He was a Kennedy Democrat, and he said some terrible things to the boy. The only one I remember is the first thing he said: "Son, if you keep blowing off steam like this during your Boy Scout days, you aren't going to have an ounce of pressure left when

Vonnegut (von′nə gət).

"The Hyannis Port Story" excerpted from the book WELCOME TO THE MONKEY HOUSE by Kurt Vonnegut, Jr. Copyright © 1950, 1951, 1953, 1954, 1955, 1956, 1958, 1960, 1961, 1962, 1964, 1966, 1968 by Kurt Vonnegut, Jr. Reprinted by permission of DELACORTE PRESS/SEYMOUR LAWRENCE, Jonathan Cape Ltd., and Donald C. Farber.

1. *Goldwater Republican,* a supporter of the conservative Senator Barry Goldwater, the Republican nominee for President in 1964.
2. *Bobby Kennedy. . . . Pierre Salinger.* In John Kennedy's Presidency, his brother Robert was Attorney General and Salinger was Press Secretary.

you're old enough to vote." It got worse from there on.

The boy didn't get mad. He just got embarrassed, and answered back with some more kazoo music. It was the Commodore who really cared. He turned the color of tomato juice. He stood up and he argued back, did it pretty well, even though his wife was pulling at the bottom of his brass-buttoned coat the whole time. She was trying to get him to stop raising such an uproar, but the Commodore loved the uproar.

The meeting broke up with practically everybody embarrassed, and I went over to Hay Boyden to talk to him about something that didn't have anything to do with Kennedy *or* Goldwater. It was about a bathtub enclosure I had sold him. He had insisted on installing it himself, saving himself about seven dollars and a half. Only it leaked, and his dining-room ceiling fell down, and Hay claimed that was the fault of the merchandise and not the installation. Hay had some poison left in his system from his argument with the boy, so he used it up on me. I answered him back with the truth, and walked away from him, and Commodore Rumfoord grabbed my hand and shook it. He thought I'd been defending his boy and Barry Goldwater.

"What business you in?" he asked me.

I told him, and, the next thing I knew, I had an order for storm windows all around on a four-story house in Hyannis Port.

The Commodore called that big old house a cottage.

"You're a Commodore in the Navy?" I asked him.

"No," he said. "My father, however, was Secretary of the Navy under William Howard Taft. That's my full name: Commodore William Howard Taft Rumfoord."

"You're in the Coast Guard?" I said.

"You mean the *Kennedy Private Fleet?*" he said.

"Pardon me?" I said.

"That's what they ought to call the Coast Guard these days," he said. "Its sole mission seems to be to protect Kennedys while they water-ski behind high-powered stinkpots."

"You're *not* in the Coast Guard?" I said. I couldn't imagine what was left.

"I was Commodore of the Hyannis Port Yacht Club in nineteen-forty-six," he said.

He didn't smile, and neither did I, and neither did his wife, whose name was Clarice. But Clarice *did* give a little sigh that sounded like the whistle on a freight train far, far away on a wet morning.

I didn't know what the trouble was at the time, but Clarice was sighing because the Commodore hadn't held any job of any description since 1946. Since then, he'd made a full-time career of raging about whoever was President of the United States, including Eisenhower.

Especially Eisenhower.

So I went down to Hyannis Port in my truck to measure the Commodore's windows late in June. His driveway was on Irving Avenue. So was the Kennedys' driveway. And President Kennedy and I hit Cape Cod on the very same day.

Traffic to Hyannis Port was backed up through three villages. There were license plates from every state in the Republic. The line was moving about four miles an hour. I was passed by several groups of fifty-mile hikers.[3] My radiator came to a boil four times.

I was feeling pretty sorry for myself, because I was just an ordinary citizen, and had to get stuck in lines like that. But then I recognized the man in the limousine up ahead of me. It was Adlai Stevenson.[4] He wasn't moving any faster than I was, and his radiator was boiling, too.

One place there, we got stuck so long that Mr. Stevenson and I got out and walked around a little. I took the opportunity to ask him how the United Nations were getting along. He told me they were getting along about as well as could be expected. That wasn't anything I didn't already know.

When I finally got to Hyannis Port, I found out Irving Avenue was blocked off by police and Secret Service men. Adlai Stevenson got to go down it, but I didn't. The police made me get back into line with the tourists, who were being

---

3. *fifty-mile hikers.* In 1963 a fad of long-distance hiking was inspired by President Kennedy's interest in physical fitness.
4. *Adlai Stevenson* (1900–1965), U.S. ambassador to the United Nations, appointed by Kennedy.

shunted down a street one block over from Irving Avenue.

The next thing I knew, I was in Hyannis, going past the *Presidential Motor Inn,* the *First Family Waffle Shop,* the *PT-109 Cocktail Lounge,* and a miniature golf course called the *New Frontier.*

I went into the waffle shop, and I called up the Rumfoords to find out how an ordinary storm-window salesman was supposed to get down Irving Avenue without dying in a hail of lead. It was the butler I talked to. He took down my license number, and found out how tall I was and what color my eyes were and all. He said he would tell the Secret Service, and they would let me by next time.

It was late in the afternoon, and I'd missed lunch, so I decided to have a waffle. All the different kinds of waffles were named after Kennedys and their friends and relatives. A waffle with strawberries and cream was a *Jackie.* A waffle with a scoop of ice cream was a *Caroline.* They even had a waffle named *Arthur Schlesinger, Jr.*[5]

I had a thing called a *Teddy*—and a cup of *Joe.*

I got through next time, went right down Irving Avenue behind the Defense Minister of Pakistan. Except for us, that street was as quiet as a stretch of the Sahara Desert.

There wasn't anything to see at all on the President's side, except for a new, peeled-cedar fence about eight feet high and two hundred feet long, with a gate in it. The Rumfoord cottage faced the gate from across the street. It was the biggest house, and one of the oldest, in the village. It was stucco. It had towers and balconies, and a veranda that ran around all four sides.

On a second-floor balcony was a huge portrait of Barry Goldwater. It had bicycle reflectors in the pupils of its eyes. Those eyes stared right through the Kennedy gate. There were floodlights all around it, so I could tell it was lit up at night. And the floodlights were rigged with blinkers.

A man who sells storm windows can never be really sure about what class he belongs to, especially if he installs the windows, too. So I was prepared to keep out from underfoot, and go about my business, measuring the windows. But

the Commodore welcomed me like a guest of great importance. He invited me to cocktails and dinner, and to spend the night. He said I could start measuring the next day.

So we had martinis out on the veranda. Only we didn't sit on the most pleasant side, which looked out on the Yacht Club dock and the harbor. We sat on the side that looked out on all the poor tourists being shunted off toward Hyannis. The Commodore liked to talk about all those fools out there.

"Look at them!" he said. "They wanted glamor, and now they realize they're not going to get it. They actually expected to be invited to play touch football with Eunice and Frank Sinatra[6] and the Secretary of Health and Welfare. Glamor is what they voted for, and look at 'em now. They don't even get to look at a Kennedy chimney up above the trees. All the glamor they'll get out of this administration is an over-priced waffle named *Caroline.*"

A helicopter went over, very low, and it landed somewhere inside the Kennedy fence. Clarice said she wondered who it was.

"Pope John the Sixth," said the Commodore.

---

5. *Jackie . . . Arthur Schlesinger, Jr.* The foods are named after people close to Kennedy, such as his wife, Jacqueline, his daughter, Caroline, and Schlesinger, a historian and advisor to Kennedy.
6. *Eunice and Frank Sinatra.* Eunice Shriver, Kennedy's sister, and Sinatra, the popular singer, had campaigned for Kennedy. The Kennedy family enjoyed playing touch football on the grounds of the White House.

The butler, whose name was John, came out with a big bowl. I thought it was peanuts or popcorn, but it turned out to be Goldwater buttons. The Commodore had John take the bowl out to the street, and offer buttons to the people in cars. A lot of people took them. Those people were disappointed. They were sore.

Some fifty-mile hikers, who'd actually hiked sixty-seven miles, all the way from Boston, asked if they could please lie down on the Rumfoord lawn for a while. They were burned up, too. They thought it was the duty of the President, or at least the Attorney General, to thank them for walking so far. The Commodore said they could not only lie down, but he would give them lemonade, if they would put on Goldwater buttons. They were glad to.

"Commodore," I said, "where's that nice boy of yours, the one who talked to us up in New Hampshire."

"The one who talked to you is the only one I've got," he said.

"He certainly poured it on," I said.

"Chip off the old block," he said.

Clarice gave that faraway freight-whistle sigh of hers again.

"The boy went swimming just before you got here," said the Commodore. "He should be back at any time, unless he's been decapitated by a member of the Irish Mafia[7] on water skis."

We went around to the water side of the veranda to see if we could catch sight of young Robert Taft Rumfoord in swimming. There was a Coast Guard cutter out there, shooing tourists in motorboats away from the Kennedy beach. There was a sightseeing boat crammed with people gawking in our direction. The barker on the boat had a very loud loudspeaker, and we could hear practically everything he said.

"*The white boat there is* Honey Fitz, *the President's personal yacht,*" said the barker. "*Next to it is the* Marlin, *which belongs to the President's father, Joseph C. Kennedy, former Ambassador to the Court of St. James.*"[8]

"The President's stinkpot, and the President's father's stinkpot," said the Commodore. He called all motorboats stinkpots. "This is a harbor that should be devoted exclusively to sail."

There was a chart of the harbor on the veranda wall. I studied it, and found a *Rumfoord*

Point, a *Rumfoord Rock,* and a *Rumfoord Shoal.* The Commodore told me his family had been in Hyannis Port since 1884.

"There doesn't seem to be anything named after the Kennedys," I said.

"Why *should* there be?" he said. "They only got here day before yesterday."

"Day before yesterday?" I said.

And he asked me, "What would *you* call nineteen-twenty-one?"

"*No, sir,*" the barker said to one of the passengers, "*that is* not *the President's house. Everybody asks that. That great big ugly stucco house, folks, that's the Rumfoord Cottage. I agree with you, it's too big to be called* cottage, *but you know how rich people are.*"

"Demoralized and bankrupt by confiscatory taxation," said the Commodore. "You know," he said, "it isn't as though Kennedy was the first President we ever had in Hyannis Port. Taft, Harding, Coolidge, and Hoover were all guests of my father in this very house. Kennedy is simply the first President who's seen fit to turn the place into an eastern enclave of *Disneyland.*"

"*No, mam,*" said the barker, "*I don't know where the Rumfoords get their money, but they don't have to work at all, I know that. They just sit on that porch there, and drink martinis, and let the old mazooma roll in.*"

The Commodore blew up. He said he was going to sue the owners of the sightseeing boat for a blue million. His wife tried to calm him down, but he made me come into his study with him while he called up his lawyers.

"You're a witness," he said.

But his telephone rang before he could call his lawyers. The person who was calling him was a Secret Service Agent named Raymond Boyle. I found out later that Boyle was known around the Kennedy household as the *Rumfoord Specialist* or the *Ambassador to Rumfoordiana.* Whenever anything came up that had to do with the Rumfoords, Boyle had to handle it.

The Commodore told me to go upstairs and listen in on the extension in the hall. "This will

---

7. **Irish Mafia,** a joint nickname for Kennedy's closest political advisors, who were mostly Irish Americans.
8. **Court of St. James,** the British court, where Joseph P. Kennedy (the barker gives the wrong middle initial) was U.S. ambassador, 1937–1940.

give you an idea of how arrogant civil servants have become these days," he said.

So I went upstairs.

"The Secret Service is one of the least secret services I've ever come in contact with," the Commodore was saying when I picked up the phone. "I've seen drum and bugle corps that were less obtrusive. Did I ever tell you about the time Calvin Coolidge, who was also a President, as it happened, went fishing for scup with my father and me off the end of the Yacht Club dock?"

"Yessir, you have, many times," said Boyle. "It's a good story, and I want to hear it again sometime. But right now I'm calling about your son."

The Commodore went right ahead with the story anyway. "President Coolidge," he said, "insisted on baiting his own hook, and the combined Atlantic and Pacific Fleets were not anchored offshore, and the sky was not black with airplanes, and brigades of Secret Service Agents were not trampling the neighbors' flowerbeds to purée."

"Sir—" said Boyle patiently, "your son Robert was apprehended in the act of boarding the President's father's boat, the *Marlin*."

"Back in the days of Coolidge, there *were* no stinkpots like that in this village, dribbling petroleum products, belching fumes, killing the fish, turning the beaches a gummy black."

"Commodore Rumfoord, sir," said Boyle, "did you hear what I just said about your son?"

"Of course," said the Commodore. "You said Robert, a member of the Hyannis Port Yacht Club, was caught touching a vessel belonging to another member of the club. This may seem a very terrible crime to a landlubber like yourself; but it has long been a custom of the sea, Mr. Boyle, that a swimmer, momentarily fatigued, may, upon coming to a vessel not his own, grasp that vessel and rest, without fear of being fired upon by the Coast Guard, or of having his fingers smashed by members of the Secret Service, or, as I prefer to call them, the *Kennedy Palace Dragoons*."

"There has been no shooting, and no smashing, sir," said Boyle. "There has also been no evidence of swimmer's fatigue. Your Robert went up the anchor line of the *Marlin* like a

chimpanzee. He *swarmed* up that rope, Commodore. I believe that's the proper nautical term. And I remind you, as I tried to remind him, that persons moving, uninvited, unannounced, with such speed and purposefulness within the vicinity of a President are, as a matter of time-honored policy, to be turned back at all costs—to be turned back, if need be, *violently*."

"Was it a Kennedy who gave the order that the boarder be repelled?" the Commodore wanted to know.

"There was no Kennedy on board, sir."

"The stinkpot was unoccupied?"

"Adlai Stevenson and Walter Reuther[9] and one of my men were on board, sir," said Boyle. "They were all below, until they heard Robert's feet hit the deck."

"Stevenson and Reuther?" said the Commodore. "That's the last time I let my son go swimming without a dagger in his teeth. I hope he was opening the seacocks[10] when beaten insensible by truncheons."

"Very funny, sir," said Boyle, his voice developing a slight cutting edge.

"You're sure it was my Robert?" said the Commodore.

"Who else but your Robert wears a Goldwater button on his swimming trunks?" asked Boyle.

"You object to his political views?" the Commodore demanded.

"I mention the button as a means of identification. Your son's politics do not interest the Secret Service. For your information, I spent seven years protecting the life of a Republican, and three protecting the life of a Democrat," said Boyle.

"For your information, Mr. Boyle," said the Commodore, "Dwight David Eisenhower was *not* a Republican."

"Whatever he was, I protected him," said Boyle. "He may have been a Zoroastrian, for all I know. And whatever the next President is going to be, I'll protect him, too. I also protect the lives of persons like your son from the consequences of excessive informality where the Presidential presence is concerned." Now Boyle's voice real-

---

9. *Walter Reuther* (rü/thər), American labor leader (1907–1970).
10. *seacocks*, underwater valves in a ship's hull.

ly started to cut. It sounded like a band saw working on galvanized tin. "I tell you, officially and absolutely unsmilingly now, your son is to cease and desist from using Kennedy boats as love nests."

That got through to the Commodore, bothered him. "Love nests?" he said.

"Your Robert has been meeting a girl on boats all over the harbor," said Boyle. "He arranged to meet her today on the *Marlin*. He was sure it would be vacant. Adlai Stevenson and Walter Reuther were a shock."

The Commodore was quiet for a few seconds, and then he said, "Mr. Boyle, I resent your implications. If I ever hear of your implying such a thing about my son to anyone else, you had better put your pistol and shoulder holster in your wife's name, because I'll sue you for everything you've got. My Robert has never gone with a girl he wasn't proud to introduce to his mother and me, and he never will."

"You're going to meet this one any minute now," said Boyle. "Robert is on his way home with her."

The Commodore wasn't tough at all now. He was uneasy and humble when he said, "Would you mind telling me her name?"

"Kennedy, sir," said Boyle, "*Sheila* Kennedy, fresh over from Ireland, a fourth cousin of the President of the United States."

Robert Taft Rumfoord came in with the girl right after that, and announced they were engaged to be married.

Supper that night in the Rumfoord cottage was sad and beautiful and happy and strange. There were Robert and his girl, and me, and the Commodore and his lady.

That girl was so intelligent, so warm, and so beautiful that she broke my heart every time I looked at her. That was why supper was so peculiar. The girl was so desirable, and the love between her and Robert was so sweet and clean, that nobody could think of anything but silly little things to say. We mainly ate in silence.

The Commodore brought up the subject of politics just once. He said to Robert, "Well— uh—will you still be making speeches around the country, or—uh——"

"I think I'll get out of politics entirely for a while," said Robert.

The Commodore said something that none of us could understand, because the words sort of choked him.

"Sir?" said Robert.

"I said," said the Commodore, " 'I would think you would.' "

I looked at the Commodore's lady, at Clarice. All the lines had gone out of her face. She looked young and beautiful, too. She was completely relaxed for the first time in who-knows-how-many years.

One of the things I said that supper was was *sad*. The sad part was how empty and quiet it left the Commodore.

The two lovers went for a moonlight sail. The Commodore and his lady and I had brandy on the veranda, on the water side. The sun was down. The tourist traffic had petered out. The fifty-mile hikers who had asked to rest on the lawn that afternoon were still all there, sound asleep, except for one boy who played a guitar. He played it slowly. Sometimes it seemed like a minute between the time he would pluck a string and the time he would pluck one again.

John, the butler, came out and asked the Commodore if it was time to turn on Senator Goldwater's floodlights yet.

"I think we'll just leave him off tonight, John," said the Commodore.

"Yes, sir," said John.

"I'm still *for* him, John," said the Commodore. "Don't anybody misunderstand me. I just think we ought to give him a rest tonight."

"Yes, sir," said John, and he left.

It was dark on the veranda, so I couldn't see the Commodore's face very well. The darkness, and the brandy, and the slow guitar let him start telling the truth about himself without feeling much pain.

"Let's give the Senator from Arizona a rest," he said. "Everybody knows who *he* is. The question is: Who am I?"

"A lovable man," said Clarice in the dark.

"With Goldwater's floodlights turned off, and with my son engaged to marry a Kennedy, what am I but what the man on the sightseeing boat said I was: A man who sits on this porch, drinking martinis, and letting the old mazooma roll in."

"You're an intelligent, charming, well-educated man, and you're still quite young," said Clarice.

"I've got to find some kind of work," he said.

"We'll both be so much happier," she said. "I would love you, no matter what. But I can tell you now, darling—it's awfully hard for a woman to *admire* a man who actually doesn't do anything."

We were dazzled by the headlights of two cars coming out of the Kennedys' driveway. The cars stopped right in front of the Rumfoord Cottage. Whoever was in them seemed to be giving the place a good looking-over.

The Commodore went to that side of the veranda, to find out what was going on. And I heard the voice of the President of the United States coming from the car in front.

"Commodore Rumfoord," said the President, "may I ask what is wrong with your Goldwater sign?"

"Nothing, Mr. President," said the Commodore respectfully.

"Then why isn't it on?" asked the President.

"I just didn't feel like turning it on tonight, sir," said the Commodore.

"I have Mr. Khrushchev's[11] son-in-law with me," said the President. "He would very much enjoy seeing it."

"Yes, sir," said the Commodore. He was right by the switch. He turned it on. The whole neighborhood was bathed in flashing light.

"Thank you," said the President. "And *leave* it on, would you please?"

"Sir?" said the Commodore.

The cars started to pull away slowly. "That way," said the President, "I can find my way home." □□

---

11. *Mr. Khrushchev* (krüsh chôf′ or krüsh′chef; 1894–1971), Premier of the Soviet Union (1958–1964), who came into conflict with Kennedy in 1962 over the Cuban missile crisis.

Discussion

1. Characterize Commodore William Rumfoord. What details of his dress and appearance reveal the kind of person he is?

2. What does the author achieve by having the story told from the **point of view** of a storm-window salesman and installer?

3. What appears to be the *underlying* reason for Rumfoord's attacks on the Kennedys?

4. Commodore Rumfoord is a changed person once he meets his son's fiancée. How and why does he change?

Extension • Writing

Imagine that the storm-window salesman is invited to the wedding of Robert Taft Rumfoord and Sheila Kennedy at the Kennedy mansion in Hyannis Port. Describe the scene from the point of view of the salesman. Focus especially on the interaction of the senior Rumfoord with the President.

Kurt Vonnegut, Jr. 1922 •

Kurt Vonnegut is one of today's most popular writers. His stories, novels, and plays have the uncommon ability to appeal equally to young and old. He mixes "black comedy" with science fiction in many of his stories and novels.

Slaughterhouse-Five, for instance, combines humor and horror as Vonnegut depicts the World War II fire-bombing of Dresden by Allied bombers. The author himself was a prisoner of the Germans in Dresden when the attack occurred. At the end of that novel, love and compassion reestablish a degree of harmony.

Born in Indianapolis, Vonnegut studied biochemistry and anthropology before being drafted. He returned to college after the war but never graduated. After holding various jobs, he turned to full-time writing in the 1950s. His first novel was *Player Piano* (1952), which was not widely read until after his later successes, *The Sirens of Titan* (1959) and *Cat's Cradle* (1963). Vonnegut has taught creative writing at the University of Iowa and Harvard University.

Eugenia Collier

Marigolds

When I think of the home town of my youth, all that I seem to remember is dust—the brown, crumbly dust of late summer—arid, sterile dust that gets into the eyes and makes them water, gets into the throat and between the toes of bare brown feet. I don't know why I should remember only the dust. Surely there must have been lush green lawns and paved streets under leafy shade trees somewhere in town; but memory is an abstract painting—it does not present things as they are, but rather as they *feel*. And so, when I think of that time and that place, I remember only the dry September of the dirt roads and grassless yards of the shanty-town where I lived. And one other thing I remember, another incongruency of memory—a brilliant splash of sunny yellow against the dust—Miss Lottie's marigolds.

Whenever the memory of those marigolds flashes across my mind, a strange nostalgia comes with it and remains long after the picture has faded. I feel again the chaotic emotions of adolescence, illusive as smoke, yet as real as the potted geranium before me now. Joy and rage and wild animal gladness and shame become tangled together in the multi-colored skein of fourteen-going-on-fifteen as I recall that devastating moment when I was suddenly more woman than child, years ago in Miss Lottie's yard. I think of those marigolds at the strangest times; I remember them vividly now as I desperately pass away the time waiting for you, who will not come.

I suppose that futile waiting was the sorrow-ful background music of our impoverished little community when I was young. The Depression that gripped the nation was no new thing to us, for the black workers of rural Maryland had always been depressed. I don't know what it was that we were waiting for; certainly not for the prosperity that was "just around the corner," for those were white folks' words, which we never believed. Nor did we wait for hard work and thrift to pay off in shining success as the American Dream promised, for we knew better than that, too. Perhaps we waited for a miracle, amorphous in concept but necessary if one were to have the grit to rise before dawn each day and labor in the white man's vineyard until after dark, or to wander about in the September dust offering one's sweat in return for some meager share of bread. But God was chary with miracles in those days, and so we waited—and waited.

We children, of course, were only vaguely aware of the extent of our poverty. Having no radios, few newspapers, and no magazines, we were somewhat unaware of the world outside our community. Nowadays we would be called "culturally deprived" and people would write books and hold conferences about us. In those days everybody we knew was just as hungry and ill-clad as we were. Poverty was the cage in which we all were trapped, and our hatred of it was still the vague, undirected restlessness of the zoo-bred flamingo who knows that nature created him to fly free.

As I think of those days I feel most poignantly the tag-end of summer, the bright dry times when we began to have a sense of shortening days and the imminence of the cold.

By the time I was fourteen my brother Joey and I were the only children left at our house, the older ones having left home for early marriage or the lure of the city, and the two babies having been sent to relatives who might care for them better than we. Joey was three years younger than I, and a boy, and therefore vastly inferior. Each morning our mother and father trudged wearily down the dirt road and around the bend, she to her domestic job, he to his daily unsuccessful quest for work. After our few chores around the tumble-down shanty, Joey and I were free to run wild in the sun with other children similarly situated.

For the most part, those days are ill-defined in my memory, running together, combining like a fresh water-color painting left out in the rain. I remember squatting in the road drawing a picture in the dust, a picture which Joey gleefully erased with one sweep of his dirty foot. I remember fishing for minnows in a muddy creek and watching sadly as they eluded my cupped hands, while Joey laughed uproariously. And I remember, that year, a strange restlessness of body and of spirit, a feeling that something old and familiar was ending, and something unknown and therefore terrifying was beginning.

One day returns to me with special clarity for some reason, perhaps because it was the beginning of the experience that in some inexplicable way marked the end of innocence. I was loafing under the great oak tree in our yard, deep in some reverie which I have now forgotten except that it involved some secret, secret thoughts of one of the Harris boys across the yard. Joey and a bunch of kids were bored now with the old tire suspended from an oak limb which had kept them entertained for awhile.

"Hey, Lizabeth," Joey yelled. He never talked when he could yell. "Hey, Lizabeth, let's us go somewhere."

I came reluctantly from my private world. "Where at, Joey?"

The truth was that we were becoming tired of the formlessness of our summer days. The idleness whose prospect had seemed so beautiful during the busy days of spring now had degenerated to an almost desperate effort to fill up the empty midday hours.

"Let's go see can we find us some locusts on the hill," someone suggested.

Joey was scornful. "Ain't no more locusts there. Y'all got 'em all while they was still green."

The argument that followed was brief and not really worth the effort. Hunting locust trees wasn't fun any more by now.

"Tell you what," said Joey finally, his eyes sparkling. "Let's us go over to Miss Lottie's."

The idea caught on at once, for annoying Miss Lottie was always fun. I was still child enough to scamper along with the group over rickety fences and through bushes that tore our already raggedy clothes, back to where Miss Lottie lived. I think now that we must have made a tragicomic spectacle, five or six kids of different ages, each of us clad in only one garment—the girls in faded dresses that were too long or too short, the boys in patchy pants, their sweaty brown chests gleaming in the hot sun. A little cloud of dust followed our thin legs and bare feet as we tramped over the barren land.

When Miss Lottie's house came into view we stopped, ostensibly to plan our strategy, but actually to reinforce our courage. Miss Lottie's house was the most ramshackle of all our ramshackle homes. The sun and rain had long since faded its rickety frame siding from white to a sullen gray. The boards themselves seemed to remain upright not from being nailed together but rather from leaning together like a house that a child might have constructed from cards. A brisk wind might have blown it down, and the fact that it was still standing implied a kind of enchantment that was stronger than the elements. There it stood, and as far as I know is standing yet—a gray rotting thing with no porch, no shutters, no steps, set on a cramped lot with no grass, not even any weeds—a monument to decay.

In front of the house in a squeaky rocking chair sat Miss Lottie's son, John Burke, completing the impression of decay. John Burke was what was known as "queer-headed." Black and ageless, he sat, rocking day in and day out in a mindless stupor, lulled by the monotonous squeak-squawk of the chair. A battered hat atop his shaggy head shaded him from the sun. Usually John Burke was totally unaware of everything outside his quiet dream world. But if you disturbed him, if you intruded upon his fantasies, he would become enraged, strike out at you, and curse at you in some strange enchanted language which only he could understand. We children made a game of thinking of ways to disturb John Burke and then to elude his violent retribution.

But our real fun and our real fear lay in Miss Lottie herself. Miss Lottie seemed to be at least a hundred years old. Her big frame still held traces of the tall, powerful woman she must have been in youth, although it was now bent and drawn. Her smooth skin was a dark reddish-brown, and her face had Indian-like features and the stern stoicism that one associates with Indian faces. Miss Lottie didn't like intruders either, especially children. She never left her yard, and nobody ever visited her. We never knew how she managed those necessities which depend on human interaction—how she ate, for example, or even whether she ate. When we were tiny children, we thought Miss Lottie was a witch and we made up tales, that we half believed ourselves, about her exploits. We were far too sophisticated now, of course, to believe the witch nonsense. But old fears have a way of clinging like cobwebs, and so when we sighted the tumble-down shack, we had to stop to reinforce our nerves.

"Look, there she is," I whispered, forgetting that Miss Lottie could not possibly have heard me from that distance. "She's fooling with them crazy flowers."

"Yeh, look at 'er."

Miss Lottie's marigolds were perhaps the strangest part of the picture. Certainly they did not fit in with the crumbling decay of the rest of her yard. Beyond the dusty brown yard, in front of the sorry gray house, rose suddenly and shockingly a dazzling strip of bright blossoms, clumped together in enormous mounds, warm and passionate and sun-golden. The old black witch-woman worked on them all summer, every summer, down on her creaky knees, weeding and cultivating and arranging, while the house crum-bled and John Burke rocked. For some perverse reason, we children hated those marigolds. They interfered with the perfect ugliness of the place; they were too beautiful; they said too much that we could not understand; they did not make sense. There was something in the vigor with which the old woman destroyed the weeds that intimidated us. It should have been a comical sight—the old woman with the man's hat on her cropped white head, leaning over the bright mounds, her big backside in the air—but it wasn't comical, it was something we could not name. We had to annoy her by whizzing a pebble into her flowers or by yelling a dirty word, then dancing away from her rage, reveling in our youth and mocking her age. Actually, I think it was the flowers we wanted to destroy, but nobody had the nerve to try it, not even Joey, who was usually fool enough to try anything.

"Y'all git some stones," commanded Joey now, and was met with instant giggling obedience as everyone except me began to gather pebbles from the dusty ground. "Come on, Lizabeth."

I just stood there peering through the bushes, torn between wanting to join the fun and feeling that it was all a bit silly.

"You scared, Lizabeth?"

I cursed and spat on the ground—my favorite gesture of phony bravado. "Y'all children get the stones, I'll show you how to use 'em."

I said before that we children were not consciously aware of how thick were the bars of our cage. I wonder now, though, whether we were not more aware of it than I thought. Perhaps we had some dim notion of what we were, and how little chance we had of being anything else. Otherwise, why would we have been so preoccupied with destruction? Anyway, the pebbles were collected quickly, and everybody looked at me to begin the fun.

"Come on, y'all."

We crept to the edge of the bushes that bordered the narrow road in front of Miss Lottie's place. She was working placidly, kneeling over the flowers, her dark hand plunged into the golden mound. Suddenly zing—an expertly aimed stone cut the head off one of the blossoms.

"Who out there?" Miss Lottie's backside came down and her head came up as her sharp eyes searched the bushes.

"You better git!"

We had crouched down out of sight in the bushes, where we stifled the giggles that insisted on coming. Miss Lottie gazed warily across the road for a moment, then cautiously returned to her weeding. *Zing*—Joey sent a pebble into the blooms, and another marigold was beheaded.

Miss Lottie was enraged now. She began struggling to her feet, leaning on a rickety cane and shouting. "Y'all git! Go on home!" Then the rest of the kids let loose with their pebbles, storming the flowers and laughing wildly and senselessly at Miss Lottie's impotent rage. She shook her stick at us and started shakily toward the road crying, "John Burke! John Burke, come help!"

Then I lost my head entirely, mad with the power of inciting such rage, and ran out of the bushes in the storm of pebbles, straight toward Miss Lottie chanting madly, "Old witch, fell in a ditch, picked up a penny and thought she was rich!" The children screamed with delight, dropped their pebbles and joined the crazy dance, swarming around Miss Lottie like bees and chanting, "Old lady witch!" while she screamed curses at us. The madness lasted only a moment, for John Burke, startled at last, lurched out of his chair, and we dashed for the bushes just as Miss Lottie's cane went whizzing at my head.

I did not join the merriment when the kids gathered again under the oak in our bare yard. Suddenly I was ashamed, and I did not like being ashamed. The child in me sulked and said it was all in fun, but the woman in me flinched at the thought of the malicious attack that I had led. The mood lasted all afternoon. When we ate the beans and rice that was supper that night, I did not notice my father's silence, for he was always silent these days, nor did I notice my mother's absence, for she always worked until well into evening. Joey and I had a particularly bitter argument after supper; his exuberance got on my nerves. Finally I stretched out upon the pallet in the room we shared and fell into a fitful doze.

When I awoke, somewhere in the middle of the night, my mother had returned, and I vaguely listened to the conversation that was audible through the thin walls that separated our rooms. At first I heard no words, only voices. My mother's voice was like a cool, dark room in summer—peaceful, soothing, quiet. I loved to listen to it; it made things seem all right somehow. But my father's voice cut through hers, shattering the peace.

"Twenty-two years, Maybelle, twenty-two years," he was saying, "and I got nothing for you, nothing, nothing."

"It's all right, honey, you'll get something. Everybody out of work now, you know that."

"It ain't right. Ain't no man ought to eat his woman's food year in and year out, and see his children running wild. Ain't nothing right about that."

"Honey, you took good care of us when you had it. Ain't nobody got nothing nowadays."

"I ain't talking about nobody else, I'm talking about *me*. God knows I try." My mother said something I could not hear, and my father cried out louder, "What must a man do, tell me that?"

"Look, we ain't starving. I git paid every week, and Mrs. Ellis is real nice about giving me things. She gonna let me have Mr. Ellis's old coat for you this winter——"

"Damn Mr. Ellis's coat! And damn his money! You think I want white folks' leavings? Damn. Maybelle"—and suddenly he sobbed, loudly and painfully, and cried helplessly and hopelessly in the dark night. I had never heard a man cry before. I did not know men ever cried. I covered my ears with my hands but could not cut off the sound of my father's harsh, painful, despairing sobs. My father was a strong man who could whisk a child upon his shoulders and go singing through the house. My father whittled toys for us and laughed so loud that the great oak seemed to laugh with him, and taught us how to fish and hunt rabbits. How could it be that my father was crying? But the sobs went on, unstifled, finally quieting until I could hear my mother's voice, deep and rich, humming softly as she used to hum to a frightened child.

The world had lost its boundary lines. My mother, who was small and soft, was now the strength of the family; my father, who was the rock on which the family had been built, was sobbing like the tiniest child. Everything was suddenly out of tune, like a broken accordion.

Where did I fit into this crazy picture? I do not now remember my thoughts, only a feeling of great bewilderment and fear.

Long after the sobbing and the humming had stopped, I lay on the pallet, still as stone with my hands over my ears, wishing that I too could cry and be comforted. The night was silent now except for the sound of the crickets and of Joey's soft breathing. But the room was too crowded with fear to allow me to sleep, and finally, feeling the terrible aloneness of 4 A.M., I decided to awaken Joey.

"Ouch! What's the matter with you? What you want?" he demanded disagreeably when I had pinched and slapped him awake.

"Come on, wake up."

"What for? Go 'way."

I was lost for a reasonable reply. I could not say, "I'm scared and I don't want to be alone," so I merely said, "I'm going out. If you want to come, come on."

The promise of adventure awoke him. "Going out now? Where at, Lizabeth? What you going to do?"

I was pulling my dress over my head. Until now I had not thought of going out. "Just come on," I replied tersely.

I was out the window and halfway down the road before Joey caught up with me.

"Wait, Lizabeth, where you going?"

I was running as if the Furies[1] were after me, as perhaps they were—running silently and furiously until I came to where I had half-known I was headed: to Miss Lottie's yard.

The half-dawn light was more eerie than complete darkness, and in it the old house was like the ruin that my world had become—foul and crumbling, a grotesque caricature. It looked haunted, but I was not afraid because I was haunted too.

"Lizabeth, you lost your mind?" panted Joey.

I had indeed lost my mind, for all the smoldering emotions of that summer swelled in me and burst—the great need for my mother who was never there, the hopelessness of our poverty and degradation, the bewilderment of being neither child nor woman and yet both at once, the fear unleashed by my father's tears. And these feelings combined in one great impulse toward destruction.

"Lizabeth!"

I leaped furiously into the mounds of marigolds and pulled madly, trampling and pulling and destroying the perfect yellow blooms. The fresh smell of early morning and of dew-soaked marigolds spurred me on as I went tearing and mangling and sobbing while Joey tugged my dress or my waist crying, "Lizabeth, stop, please stop!"

And then I was sitting in the ruined little garden among the uprooted and ruined flowers, crying and crying, and it was too late to undo what I had done. Joey was sitting beside me, silent and frightened, not knowing what to say. Then, "Lizabeth, look."

I opened my swollen eyes and saw in front of me a pair of large calloused feet; my gaze lifted to the swollen legs, the age-distorted body clad in a tight cotton night dress, and then the shadowed Indian face surrounded by stubby white hair. And there was no rage in the face now, now that the garden was destroyed and there was nothing any longer to be protected.

"M-miss Lottie!" I scrambled to my feet and just stood there and stared at her, and that was the moment when childhood faded and womanhood began. That violent, crazy act was the last act of childhood. For as I gazed at the immobile face with the sad, weary eyes, I gazed upon a kind of reality which is hidden to childhood. The witch was no longer a witch but only a broken old woman who had dared to create beauty in the midst of ugliness and sterility. She had been born in squalor and lived in it all her life. Now at the end of that life she had nothing except a falling-down hut, a wrecked body, and John Burke, the mindless son of her passion. Whatever verve there was left in her, whatever was of love and beauty and joy that had not been squeezed out by life, had been there in the marigolds she had so tenderly cared for.

Of course I could not express the things that I knew about Miss Lottie as I stood there awkward and ashamed. The years have put words to the things I knew in that moment, and as I look back upon it, I know that the moment marked the end of innocence. Innocence involves an unsee-

---

1. *Furies*, avenging spirits in Greek and Roman myth.

ing acceptance of things at face value, an ignorance of the area below the surface. In that humiliating moment I looked beyond myself and into the depths of another person. This was the beginning of compassion, and one cannot have both compassion and innocence.

The years have taken me worlds away from that time and that place, from the dust and squalor of our lives and from the bright thing that I destroyed in a blind childish striking out. Miss Lottie died long ago and many years have passed since I last saw her hut, completely barren at last, for despite my wild contrition she never planted marigolds again. Yet, there are times when the image of those passionate yellow mounds returns with a painful poignancy. For one does not have to be ignorant and poor to find that his life is barren as the dusty yards of our town. And I too have planted marigolds. □□

Discussion

1. (a) Describe the **setting** of the story. (b) How are the **narrator's** recollections "like an abstract painting" rather than being purely realistic?

2. What triggered Lizabeth's second assault on the marigolds?

3. Why was Miss Lottie not so enraged by the second attack as she was by the first one?

4. (a) At what stage of life is the narrator when the main events of the story take place? (b) Why is the incident involving the marigolds so important to her even in her later life?

Extension • Speaking

Often we read newspaper accounts about "trashing"—apparently senseless destruction of public or personal property. Does this story give any insight into possible reasons why people might riot and destroy beautiful things purely for the sake of destruction? Discuss.

Extension • Writing

Write a composition about childhood mischief you engaged in. Could it always be excused as "all in fun"? Or did it involve cruelty, meanness, or destruction of property. Looking back, do you feel differently about your actions than you felt when you first performed them?

Eugenia Collier 1928 •

Eugenia Collier has stated that the source of her creativity is her blackness. Nowhere is this more evident than in "Marigolds," which in 1969 won the Gwendolyn Brooks Award for Fiction presented by *Negro Digest.*

After a traditional education at Howard University, Collier worked as a caseworker for a public welfare department. During this time she came to a new awareness of the importance of her heritage and began to write poems and stories for *Black World, Negro Digest*, and

the *New York Times.* In addition, she has contributed to many anthologies portraying life in black America.

Besides her stories, Collier has written several critical articles and currently teaches English at the Community College of Baltimore.

Ronald Arias

El Mago

Luisa's father called him *el curandero*.[1] Sally's mother called him an unfortunate. The girls simply called him El Mago.[2]

There was no odor of age about him, though he was older than the girls could imagine, only the smell of papered hairless skin, it seemed. He was squat, fat and had nicotine stains on one hand. Luisa remembered he had a harsh brittle cough; years later she thought his chest was like an empty milk carton filled with tiny bone particles.

This Sunday, like many Sundays before, the two girls sat fidgeting in their blue corduroy jumpers and plain white blouses, just behind the nuns, listening to words about Christ and God and the Virgin and so many saints they would never keep count, sat watching a fly rub together what looked like its hands, watching the sleepy altar boy with his shoelaces untied, sat playing silent games with their fingers and feet, folding and unfolding catechism pamphlets, waiting, finally tiring, and waiting some more. They had gone to Mass by themselves. Their parents, who were at home asleep, would attend later in the day.

Luisa and Sally had been best friends since third grade, and often told strangers they were twins, even though Luisa was darker and smaller, Sally being rounder and the "*huera*."[3] The first thing El Mago told them was that they weren't twins. He said it in a friendly way, not trying to hurt, and told them it was good to play sisters.

El Mago, whose clients called him Don Noriega,[4] lived alone in a shabby-looking wooden house halfway up a steep hill overlooking the old streetcar line to Glendale. The community knew him since two generations back when he arrived from an obscure town in northern Durango.[5] A hypnotist, a soothsayer and doctor of sorts, he rarely left his house, receiving payment usually in the form of food or small gifts. Around the sides of his house and in back he grew all the herbs, spices and exotic plants he needed for his cures. His living—or reception—room was lavishly decorated with thick Moroccan rugs, plaster sphinxes, pictures and figurines from pre-Columbian cultures,[6] soft plushy chairs and odd-shaped lamps. On one side was a water-filled glass tank with tiny, slender fish from the Amazon. On the other side were two cages of birds from New Guinea and the rain forests of Panama. An adjoining room was lined, and divided, with filled bookcases.

Luisa and Sally met him the time they accompanied Sally's grandmother on a visit about her migraines and pains in her vesiculas.[7] Don Noriega, instead of immediately attending to business, devoted a few minutes to the girls. He overcame their shyness by giving them each a piece of *biznaga* candy, and then in a raspy voice told them not to worry about breaking things in the house. He insisted they explore whatever attracted their curiosity. When Luisa, the more awkward of the two girls, tipped over a metal stand with zodiac charts on it, Don Noriega helped her replace the stand. Gently and with a wink, he said all things can be repaired. It's the

Arias (ä′ryäs).

"El Mago" by Ronald Arias from EL GRITO (Spring 1970). Reprinted by permission of the author.

1. *el curandero* (el kü rän de′rô), "the curer," a healer who uses herbs and other folk remedies. [*Spanish*]
2. *El Mago* (el mä′gô), "the magician." [*Spanish*]
3. "*huera*" (we′rä), "the fair one." [*Spanish*]
4. *Don Noriega* (dôn nô rye′gä). In Spanish, *don* is a respectful title for a man.
5. *Durango* (dü rän′gô), a state of northern Mexico.
6. *pre–Columbian cultures,* Native-American cultures before the arrival of Columbus.
7. *vesiculas* (və sik′yə las), gall bladders. [*Spanish*]

damage here, and he pointed over his heart, that cannot be fixed. Then he sat down to chat with the old woman, and the girls were left to their own.

After standing fascinated before the tank of colored fish, the girls moved on to another room which was dimly lighted, cluttered with boxes and books, and saturated with a strange incense. Sally's grandmother could be heard laughing in the other room. The girls began poking around, running their fingers across dusty surfaces, looking into corners. With an innocent curiosity they held the tiny statues of half-men and animals which they had taken timidly from the shelves.

It wasn't long before Sally shrieked and came running out with a terrified look on her face.

"Mama! *Un hombre muerto, muerto de a tiro!*"[8] she screamed.

Puzzled, the old woman looked to Don Noriega for an explanation. He sat back in his deep chair, and after an unhurried draw on his cigarette, told Sally and her grandmother that it was a fake mummy of a boy, not even a man. He gingerly explained what a mummy was and why people long ago used to preserve bodies. It was a reminder, he said, for the dead must leave something behind to remind the living of those once known and loved.

But the old woman, with Sally still trembling in her arms, was set on leaving. Don Noriega went into the other room to tell Luisa she would have to go too, and that they were waiting for her. He found her standing beside a desk tinkering with the beads on the taut wires of a small boxlike instrument. In a corner, on the other side of the room, was the opened mummy case propped up against the wall. Don Noriega told Luisa she would have to go, but that she could come another day. He promised to play music for her on the little instrument.

She raised her eyes. "Why do you have so many funny-looking things?" she asked.

Don Noriega looked down at her wonder-filled face. Luisa could see the thin lines deepen at the corners of his mouth, his eyes become friendlier. "If you like these things," he said, "why do you ask?"

At the door the old woman was still comforting Sally, who now eyed Don Noriega the way she might watch some unpredictable ogre. Luisa,

biting her lips in thought, waved goodbye to him from the sidewalk.

When the story of the mummy was told, the girls' parents forbad them ever to visit Don Noriega again.

For months afterward Luisa was torn between wanting to see him and not wanting to disobey her parents. The girls had to pass by Don Noriega's street every Sunday after Mass, but Luisa never told Sally about her private wish. Walking along the weeded-over streetcar tracks, Sally would invariably poke fun at "that crazy old *mago* who slept with mummies and who was seen at night flying around with one of his birds." Luisa always kept silent, not knowing what to say about such things.

As usual, this Sunday the girls left the church eager for daylight and make-believe games along the pass through the hills on their way home. But more than that, today Luisa had firmly made up her mind. She would visit Don Noriega. When they approached the street on which he lived she would simply say goodbye to Sally and leave. Unconsciously she somehow felt that seeing him was worth the risk of a strapping from her father's belt.

"Luisa! You'll get in trouble," Sally warned. "What d'you want to see that old guy for?"

"Nothing will happen if you don't tell," Luisa replied calmly.

"Aren't you scared?"

Luisa looked down at the gravel between the track ties, her mind pulsing with excitement. "No," she said, trying to sound casual. "He even asked me to come back."

"Oh, Luisa, I wouldn't do that," Sally said, clutching her hands together.

"Go ahead and tell," Luisa challenged. "I won't get mad." She started up the hill. "Go on, Sally. Don't wait for me."

Sally stood watching her friend climb the long sidewalk and turn at Don Noriega's house.

The place was cluttered with scattered and charred boards, cans, pieces of cloth, blackened books, metal, chairs and sofas exuding tufts of

---

8. **"Mama! Un hombre muerto, muerto de a tiro!"** (mä/mä/ ún ôm/bre mwer/tô, mwer/tô de a tē/rô). "Mother! A dead man, killed by a shot!" [Spanish]

wool, bottles and jars with dried dead plants. The front door was boarded closed, as were the broken windows to each side. Luisa looked like a waif standing in front of a ruined dream. She felt limp and bewildered, not yet sensing the numbness of death within the paint-peeled walls.

She stepped around a marble lamp base and picked her way along the side of the house to the rear. There was no back door, only a blackened doorway. She knocked softly, almost unheard, on the frame. Into the quiet she called hello. The darkness in there was still. After a moment, a wheezing brittle voice, filled with entreaty, came from within. Luisa hesitated, then stepped in. She was careful not to trip, though she bumped into strange objects at every turn, going from room to room, cautiously looking into every corner and closet. A painting fell down, a plaster statue tipped over. She fought to control her fear. In the front room, behind the door to the street, she saw the water-filled fish tank. The little creatures were still there, floating on the surface. Luisa pursed her lips. With her forefinger she pushed one of the slivers and it slipped past the others, bumping into the side of the tank.

In the silence she heard a cough. The floorboards creaked as she stepped through the room where the mummy was, now resting on the floor. She went into the hallway, which was pierced with soft light through holes between the skeletal roof timbers. There, in the first room to the left, sat Don Noriega. He was on the edge of a metal cot which had no mattress. Luisa stood in the doorway, unable to speak but trying to smile.

"*Siéntate, niña,*"[9] he said and patted the space next to him on the cot. He had been waiting for her, Luisa thought, and would play that strange instrument. Afterward she would kiss him just above his whiskery eyebrows, saying, or not saying, thank you. He would ask her how things had been with her, and she would say fine. She would be as friendly and bright as possible. Maybe she could cheer him and make him forget about the house.

Now she moved toward the cot and sat down. A quiet music came from the delicate box beside her on the cot. The sunlight filtered in, and the notes from the strings seemed to dance and slip and twine themselves around the pale white rays in short bursts of joy, in what Don Noriega, she

thought, might have felt had he played. She sat for a long while listening to the music.

But there was another voice, a human one, calling her faintly. I have to go now, she whispered, sitting straight all of a sudden, her small amber eyes losing that vision of awe. For a moment she could not move. Something held her back, something weighed in her chest and throat, and Luisa began to cry. The blurred image before her placed the small box lightly in her open hands.

In the hallway Luisa groped toward the back porch. The smell of incense and spices was strong. The hot autumn wind blew through the house like a warm voice wiping dry her moist skin.

Sally was out front, hands on hips, calling Luisa. Luisa came from around back, stepping over the mess on the ground and holding a black

---

9. "*Siéntate, niña*" (syen′tä te′ nē′nyä). "Sit down, girl." [Spanish]

piece of wood in her hands, two metal strings dangling.

"What's that?" Sally demanded impatiently.

Luisa seemed surprised. "What's what?"

"That thing, what you got in your hand."

"Oh this . . ." and she held it up for Sally to inspect. "A present."

"A what?"

"A present I picked up."

"Oh." Sally moved her eyes to the house. "Looks like his place burned down. What d'you find inside?"

"Just this," Luisa said, gazing blankly at the house.

"What d'you want that for?"

Luisa pulled a wire loose and after a pause seemed to speak to herself. "Nothing, I guess. It's no good any more," and knelt down to place it on the ground, remembering that after all it was not her heart she was laying down, as Don Noriega might say. It was only a thing, a piece of charred wood.

"Come on!" Sally whined. "Place gives me the creeps." □□

Discussion

1. What qualities of Don Noriega and his home endear him to Luisa?

2. What might the charred music box **symbolize**? Is it really a gift from Don Noriega or merely something Luisa picked up and took with her? Explain.

3. In Arias's stories, what "actually happens" is often less important than the different versions of "reality" that unfold in each character's mind. (a) In the final scene at Don Noriega's house, compare what Luisa observes with what Sally observes. For instance, to which girl is Don Noriega alive and to which is he dead? Explain. (b) What is the significance of Sally's remark that concludes the story? (c) Considering the two girls' contrasting attitudes toward the old man, explain their differing experiences at the ruined house.

(d) To you, what is the true "reality" of the final episode? Explain.

Extension • Reading

Many novels and stories center on the relationship between young people and an old person or persons whom other people consider crazy or at least eccentric. Sometimes the younger people are profoundly affected by these relationships, and sometimes they are not affected at all. Compare "El Mago" and "Marigolds" with other similar stories you know or could find in your library. For instance, you might consider Elizabeth Enright's story, following this one; "A Visit of Charity" by Eudora Welty; "Mice and Birds and Boy" by Elizabeth Taylor; or *To Kill a Mockingbird* by Harper Lee. Your teacher may be able to suggest other titles.

Ron Arias 1941 •

Ron Arias advises writers to look to their ethnic roots for inspiration. Certainly he has done this in his own writing by drawing on both his Mexican and American cultural heritages.

After writing several short stories for the magazines *Caracol* and *Revista Chicano-Riqueña*, Arias published his first novel, *The Road to Tamazunchale*, in 1975. Because of the masterful way in which the book combined fantasy with realistic elements, it was nominated for a National Book Award. Arias was also winner of the 1974–75 Chicano Literary Contest of the University of California's Irvine campus.

He currently teaches English at Crofton Hills College in California.

Elizabeth Enright

When the Bough Breaks

Miss Pruitt Clovelly lived with her mother in the yellow house on the corner of Pine and Van Buren streets; the one that had been boarded up for so many years before they moved in. It was a narrow alert-looking house with tall gables which were trimmed with wooden rickrack, and all the upstairs windows had pointed tops like church windows. It stood in a perpetual green revery all summer long, for the maples were close-pressed around it, and the grass grew as high as the porch steps. Vines spread their fingers across the shutters and held them closed. When Miss Pruitt and her mother moved in they did remarkably little to the place; they pruned the vines and shrubs, of course, or at least Ben Dwyer did it for them, and he cut a path from the front gate to the front steps, but that was about all. They seemed to like to have a tall lake of grass around the house, and when you passed that corner in summertime the crickets were louder than anywhere else, and on June nights the fireflies floated and glimmered there like the lights of a fairy regatta.

Lorna Reckettson and her mother and sisters had watched from their house across the street when Mrs. Clovelly and her daughter moved in, though everyone except Lorna pretended to be doing something else; and everyone except Lorna thought it strange that old Mrs. Clovelly and Ben Dwyer and the truckmen did all the heavy lifting, while Miss Pruitt, who looked able-bodied enough in a middle-aged way, just sat on the porch railing and directed, or left the whole project to take care of itself and wandered through the high grass picking twigs of mock orange.

"She may have heart trouble," Mrs. Reckettson murmured to Stella. "Heart conditions often look healthy, you know," and she went back to pretending to tie up the tree peonies.

Lorna pretended nothing. She was seven and a half and at that age it was still all right to stare.

She stood on the gate and swung it slowly, grindingly, to and fro, and stared at the couch being warped through the doorway like a ship into port, and at the upright piano, and the chairs and the pictures with gold frames. A large pier glass leaning against a maple gave back her image to her: a fat girl swinging forward on a gate with sunshine behind her.

"Maybe she's just getting over an illness," said Stella. "Maybe she has to guard her strength."

"Maybe she's just bone lazy," said Josephine, who was fourteen and did not like people.

Something was strange about Miss Pruitt Clovelly, certainly, and about her mother, too. They seemed to have no wish for society, no wish for entertainment. Every day or so one of them would go down the street to the stores, carrying a market basket: sometimes it was Miss Pruitt, walking with her tranquil, unhurried pace, and sometimes it was Mrs. Clovelly, head bent forward and feet scuffing hastily as if the wind were at her back; but these were the only occasions on which they left the house. Why they had moved to that town and where they had come from no one knew for many years.

Mrs. Clovelly was a little old parched thing with all different kinds of wrinkles, and a high witch voice. When people called she seemed always half-abstracted, more apt to watch her daughter than the guests. And on the front porch as she guided them out she murmured, "Pru is delicate, you know. She's always, from a little girl, been very delicate."

"Doesn't look delicate to *me*," the callers remarked to each other as they walked along the

street. "Why, I'd say she was the picture of health, wouldn't you?"

The queer thing was that not one of the calls was ever returned; and in that town no other hint was needed: the Clovellys were studiously left to their solitude. Except for the children, about the only people who entered the house at all were Ben Dwyer, who worked for the ladies, and Dr. Oliver Purcell, and whether the latter came in a professional or social capacity was never known for certain. But the children! They were welcome there at all times, as Lorna soon found out.

One day as she was swinging on the gate watching Mrs. Clovelly prune the hydrangea bush she saw Miss Pruitt come out on the porch with a plate in her hand which she put down on the front steps. Then she stood up and looked across the street at Lorna and called the word "FUDGE!"

Lorna swung and stared, her mouth blank.

"Little girl, I've just made a plate of fudge!" Miss Pruitt insisted. "Come on over and help me cut it when it cools, and then we can sample it."

Lorna stepped down from the gate.

Don't ever accept candy from strangers, warned the stern memory of her mother's voice; Lorna listened to it for a moment, appraised it, and pushed it back into the cupboard where many such admonitions were laid away.

She walked to the curbstone, and listening to another admonition, looked once to the left, once to the right, though nothing was in sight but a faraway horse and wagon, and took the plunge across the empty street.

"Good morning, dear," said Mrs. Clovelly, looking up from the hydrangea bush and smiling her crumpled smile, and Miss Pruitt said, "Hello, honey. Come on up here and sit in the hammock while the fudge cools."

Lorna walked up the porch steps which had an empty sound like wooden boxes, never taking her eyes from Miss Pruitt's face. She went over to the hammock and sank her bottom in it, still never taking her eyes away from Miss Pruitt's face. Miss Pruitt smiled at her and rocked her chair back and forth, and took some pink knitting out of a pinned towel. The plate of fudge on the front steps gave off a faint, rare fragrance of chocolate.

"I have a dog home," Lorna suddenly decided to say. "His name is Sport and he's fourteen years old. Old as my sister Josephine."

After that Lorna spent a lot of her time at Miss Pru's house. In the beginning her mother was inclined to disapprove, but in the end she consented tacitly, saying only: "What in mercy's name do you want to hang around *there* for all the time? I declare it's more than I can understand when you've got your own lovely yard with a swing and a playhouse and all!"

How could Lorna explain that her own lovely yard was tame territory to her; every stone in it as familiar as a family face, while at Miss Pru's there was a feeling of wilderness and wonder as one pressed through the feathery grass of the yard, tall as lion grass on the African plain; or climbed the warped branches of the quince bush at the back of the house, or swung around and around on the arms of the whirligig clothes drier, or hid in the dark, rich-smelling corners of the woodshed. Every child in the neighborhood could be located in the Clovelly place at some time during the day; they sat on the front steps blowing sedum leaves into frogs' tongues, or rocked and sailed, two or three together in the string hammock; they were rooted out of the shrubbery and the back porch by the loud calling of relatives at mealtime, and in the long twilight their voices could be heard shrill and high, in bursts of acrimony or excitement, as they played hide-and-seek, or still-pond-no-more-moving. There were cookies in the Clovelly kitchen always, big oatmeal cookies, and brownies and cinnamon wheels. Often there was a dish of fudge or a special kind of jaw-locking vinegar candy.

But stronger, more magnetic, than any of these interests and enticements was the quality of Miss Pru herself. Mrs. Clovelly was all right, nobody minded her, but Miss Pru was special. For one thing, the most important thing, she was happy all the time. That may not sound like anything, but consider it. Happy *all* the time. Most people are happy now and then, but their state is something which is temporary and foredoomed, something to be appreciated rather frantically; a condition bright and evanescent. There are other people who know how to maintain a passive contentment for months at a time; but Miss Pruitt was not like these. She was happy in a tranced durable way as though she knew a secret, a wonderful personal secret that never lost its value.

On summer days she sat on the front porch rocking and sewing, rocking and sewing, with that shut-away, faraway, impervious smile on her lips. "See-cret. See-cret. I know a see-cret," croaked the rocking chair interminably. And in the wintertime you could see her in the kitchen window, rocking and sewing, rocking and sewing, with a shawl across her shoulders and smiling that same smile all to herself.

"I think she's a little— Well, a little— *you* know," Lorna's mother said to her father across the supper table, and gave him an adult glance, with her mouth turned down at the corners.

"Harmless, I hope?" said her father.

"Oh, *harmless*! Heavens yes."

What could the thought of harm have to do with Miss Pru, Lorna wondered. Miss Pruitt was good as gold and her kindness was as easy to take as the summer air itself. It was as though from some central love she had a lot of spare love spilled over; for children at least, and for animals. There were always kittens in that house, and through the winter the cardinals and chickadees found their breakfast on the broad porch railing.

Lorna did not inquire into her mother's comment. She had learned early in life that to protect her loves she must keep them secret, and especially from grownups, from whom there was often apt to be a bald, mirthful, merciless response to a child's confessions of attachment.

So when her mother asked questions she became vague and absent-minded.

"What's Miss Pruitt like, Lorna?"

"Oh I do' know. She's all right I guess. Can I have some bread and sugar?"

"No. What's the house like upstairs?"

"It's—well, it's just plain bedrooms and things. And a bathroom. Can I have some bread and sugar?"

"No. Are there any pictures on the walls?"

"I guess so. Some brownish ones. Can't I just have a little teeny slice with sugar on it?"

"Oh for pitysakes. No. Oh, all right. I don't care."

So Miss Pruitt was protected and she was worth protecting. When Lorna and the others

came to her on rainy or dreary days in the unspeakable boredom of childhood she never failed them.

"Miss Pru, what can we *doo*-oo?"

"Do, honey? Well, let's see. How'd you like it if I made us a cake and you-all could lick the bowl?"

Or she might suggest making clothespin dolls. That was fun once in a while and it was the kind of thing you always forget about between times: drawing the little ink faces on the top of the clothespin and making the clothes from scraps in Miss Pru's piece bag. Little skirts and trousers cut out of silk and crumpled satin, and tiny capes, never coats, for clothespin dolls were armless.

Or she might say, "Why, I tell you what, you can dress up in some of our long skirts and pretend like you're grown-up ladies at a ball. I'll play the piano for you to dance."

The piano was old and it sounded as if there were knives and forks inside it, but Miss Pru got music out of it anyway. She played the "Valse Bleue," Bartlett's "Dream," and "When the Swallows Homeward Fly." She could play for hours on end, but she would never, never dance with them.

"No, honey," she would say, smiling that slow, blissful smile of hers. "I mustn't dance with you. I mustn't tire myself out."

She was very careful of herself, Miss Pru; never lifting anything heavy, never hurrying, always holding onto the railing when she went up the stairs or down. She moved quietly, as if she tiptoed through a world asleep, and she spoke quietly, too, in a very smooth even voice. Sometimes when the children staggered onto the porch worn out with play, red-cheeked, moist-browed and quarreling, she would say, "Come on, you-all, sit down somewhere or other and I'll tell you a story." And then in that peaceful, uneventful voice she spun them long tales about princesses and villains and narrow escapes and virtue's inevitable reward. Sometimes she drew upon her own memory and gave them detailed accounts of childhood exploits with her long-ago chum Anne-Ethel Pritchett.

"Once, when Mama bought the piano, Anne-Ethel and I made a little house out of the piano box. A great big wooden box, it was——"

"The same piano as you have *now*, Miss Pru?"

"The very one. Anne-Ethel's father cut a window in the side of the piano box for us, and he leaned a couple of old doors against the front, so it was a regular little house. We kept our dolls and our doll dishes in it, and sometimes when it rained we'd take our supper out there and eat it; and the rain on the roof—oh, that sound of rain on the roof——" Miss Pru laid her sewing in her lap, leaned back in her chair with her eyes closed as if that remembered sound of raindrops made her almost too happy for endurance.

She and Anne-Ethel had had lots of dolls but Miss Pru had had the most. Lorna knew the names of all of them: Lillian, Heliotrope, Ethel (named for Anne-Ethel), Shirley, Rebecca and Rowena, Roger, Grover Cleveland, and all the others. Billy Boy had been the favorite one, a big baby doll with a soft rag body.

"Honey, I've still got that dolly packed away in a trunk somewhere. I loved him like he was alive. Oh, like he was alive! The paint's all worn off his poor little nose and one of his arms is broken, but I declare I love him still."

Miss Pru's smile of reminiscence forced upon Lorna a faint feeling of guilt. She had never felt tenderness for her dolls; in the end they had all suffered at her hands. Their glue-smelling wigs had been ripped from their heads and their round glass eyeballs plucked out of their empty skulls. Scalped and blind they lay in the cupboard, their limbs dangling from tendons of loose elastic.

"Mine are all girl dolls; all dumb and all pretty," said Lorna. "*Were*," she added with satisfaction. "Miss Pru, is that a doll's dress you're making now?"

Miss Pru held up the tiny thing. "No. That's for a baby I know of, honey. A real live baby."

Miss Pruitt knew a lot of babies, it seemed. She was always knitting pink things or blue things, or stitching the tucks on small yokes. She liked to sew and did it almost without noticing it. When she wasn't sewing or knitting she was in the kitchen baking, or out in the garden taking casual care of her flowers. Flowers grew for her in return for very little, and even they seemed more interesting than other people's flowers. In the two cleared beds beside the porch bloomed pink freckled rubrum lilies and triple-crowned

spider plants. In spring there were blue and purple columbines there, and bleeding hearts like strings of lockets; in the fall came crowds of white-stemmed autumn crocuses. Inside the house there were flowers too: round, velvety calceolarias pressed against the windowpane, and a begonia with glittering blood-red flowers.

Sometimes, in the winter, Lorna took her homework to the Clovellys' house. She liked to do it there at the kitchen table with the big coal range rustling and breathing like another person, a huge strong quiet person in the room. The catsup bottle and the pickle jar and a tumbler with a flower in it surveyed her work dispassionately. Old Mrs. Clovelly creaked and scurried about the house, and Miss Pru sat sewing beside the kitchen window never speaking or interrupting. Sometimes she sighed, a full soft sound which seemed the final expression of contentment, as impersonal and involuntary in its peacefulness as the breath of wind on a summer day.

To have her there was wonderful; a comfort. For any other purpose she was nearly useless. "Honey, I can't add two and two," she said complacently, when Lorna applied to her for help. "When it comes to arithmetic I'm just as *helpless . . .*" Her spelling was almost as bad, though not quite, and geography, for her, did not exist. "The things I know about are things I can touch and look at, real things," said Miss Pru. "Real things like cats and children and cooking and making things. Playing a piano, too. That's kind of real. But silly old commas and periods and long division, why those are just a waste of time and good eyesight. Nobody needs them except the old bookkeepers and the old storekeepers and the men in banks."

Lorna agreed with this, and her own sighs were rebellious, but not for long. Presently the peacefulness enveloped her again. Her pencil scratched and paused, the eraser rubbed brusquely, and then the pencil scratched on again. Being in this place made Lorna feel good, it made her feel smooth and loving. At home Stella and Josephine lived in a state of peevish civil war, her mother was constantly being overtaken by her temper, and as a result of these things her father lived nine-tenths below the surface like an iceberg. But here all was placid, untorn, unhurried. Now and then Mrs. Clovelly came in and looked at her daughter, felt of her forehead, and asked questions: "Did you have your glass of milk, Pru? Don't you want to lay down for a while?"

"Yes, I suppose I *ought* to have a little rest," Miss Pru might say, standing up slowly and stretching, and the cat that fell out of her lap stretched too, paw by paw. Lorna closed her book reluctantly; it was time to go home.

The winter that Lorna was twelve years old Mrs. Clovelly died. She died abruptly, with no notice, as if she were in a hurry to let go. The neighbors forgot their grievances and did all they could to help. After all, though living people may be dull, eccentric, irritating, once they die they attain a terrible, immense dignity. They must be placated: Who knows what they have become? It is then that we cluster about the bereaved with our kindnesses, trying in vain to improve a memory of ourselves which is now completed. Miss Pruitt's house was suddenly full of grown-up people, tiptoeing through the rooms, whispering in the hallway, arranging flowers, and making cups of tea in the kitchen.

"And she just *let* us," said Lorna's mother the day after the funeral. "I don't mind helping people, never did. When people are in trouble I can't do too much for them, I'm funny that way. I'll just give everything I've got to help them, just wear myself out, but I must say! The way that woman sat back and watched us do *every*thing. Well, honestly! And half the time she was smiling, too, she hardly shed a tear. I wonder if she's got a heart at all!"

Mother doesn't understand anything, Lorna thought; I wish I had a mother like Miss Pru; and after school for those next days she helped her friend pack away old Mrs. Clovelly's old clothes, folding them, and sprinkling them with black pepper to keep out the moths, and wrapping them in newspaper. They ought to see her now, Lorna thought resentfully, watching Miss Pruitt's silent tears drop onto the printed paper where they made dark spreading stars of damp.

"She was a good mother," was all she said.

"You would have been a good mother, too," Lorna told her on impulse.

And suddenly Miss Pruitt smiled again.

That year and the next one went by like the years before. Except for the absence of Mrs. Clovelly everything was the same; but the year she was fourteen the world began to change for Lorna. Both her sisters got married, for one thing, and she went to high school for the first time and fell in love with the sophomore football captain who did not fall in love with her. She then fell in love with the senior football captain who did not know she was on the earth. At the same time she fell in love with the boy at the Idlewild Drug Store soda counter and he seemed to like her, too, since he called her "fish face." The rest of the time she was engaged in deadly combat with Latin declensions and algebra, and in the afternoons she made extra money by wheeling babies on their mothers' bridge afternoons, or sitting with them in the evenings. Nowadays when she went to see Miss Pru she was always in a hurry, gasping and red-cheeked in her haste; and Miss Pru herself was not quite the same, either: Lorna was a little hurt that now and then she mislaid her name, fumbling first with names like Pearl or Barbara or Maureen, before she came to Lorna. Nowadays, too, there was a whole new group of children playing about the place, kid sisters, kid brothers of her own contemporaries; and though she herself no longer used Miss Pruitt's home as headquarters she resented the small new babbling rabble that did, and passed among them without looking at them.

She had regular babies to take care of: little Millicent Quintz, Linda Lesser, and Gary Alan Gellhouse. Gary Alan was her favorite because he never cried and because she had helped look after him from the time he was newborn, with a little red face like a clenched fist, till now when he was a large pale silent baby with a sort of impervious acceptance of life. After school closed in June Lorna planned to take him calling on Miss Pru, but somehow she never got around to it. . . . She seemed to do nothing but wheel Gary Alan along the deep summer streets, along miles of streets, hardly seeing where she was going she was so intent upon her own vision of the future: the mirage of beautiful faces, and successes; of words spoken, and deeds done.

In September she stopped in to see Miss Pruitt one day after school. Something was different, though. There was now an impression of *haste* about Miss Pru. She was not settled down with her sewing, nor was she moving with her ample leisure about the house. She had a hand-kerchief bound around her head; a broom and dustpan leaned in the doorway, and all the time Lorna was there she kept rising from her chair to straighten the curtains, or adjust the ornaments on the parlor mantel. For the first time in that house Lorna had the feeling that she had not only caused, but was herself, an interruption.

She had never looked at Miss Pru in any way but the same one. Almost daily for seven years she had seen her, if only to wave as she went by; she had been a familiar factor in her life, reliable in her changelessness, always kind. Yet now, as if a searching light penetrated the shadowed house, Lorna saw that her old friend had changed. The face which for so many years had been calm and rosy was now clay-colored, hag-gard, and its expression of great happiness shone oddly from it. The happiness seemed out of place, as if an inner source of strength had become too powerful, too dominating, and was now able to destroy what it had sustained so long.

She talked a lot, too; and that was not like her: rapid, restless talk about the children, the summer just gone by, the weight of housework; reminiscences of the past in which Lorna shared, and still earlier ones in which she did not, except that she had heard them all before. At last she interrupted.

"Miss Pru, you shouldn't be doing all this housecleaning. You're working too hard."

"I'm in a hurry, honey. I want everything ready, every single thing."

"Ready for what?" Lorna felt strange, a little scared. "Miss Pru, are you feeling all right? You look kind of—tired."

But the bright queer look of joy intensified.

"It's all right, honey. You'll understand some day. All women understand some day."

Understand what? Lorna wondered, and for an instant she was overwhelmed by a sense of the woman's life ahead of her: a long, long vista of alternating mystery and revelation, mystery and revelation, forever and ever until the ulti-mate mystery. And after that the ultimate revela-tion?

She was worried about her friend, and now and then in the midst of her school activities, in the midst of fantasies concerning herself and her heroes, in the midst of eating, and wheeling babies, and arguing with her mother, she was suddenly caught by a memory of Miss Pruitt's worn joyful face.

"You," she said to Gary Alan, thumping him into his carriage one autumn day. "You're going to go calling this afternoon. Try and stay dry for once."

Gary Alan gazed remotely at nothing with his tranced brown eyes. He summoned a sound from within himself, a voice sound, wordless, uneven, but filled with an inflection of assertion. The sound pleased him and he summoned forth an-other. As Lorna pushed the carriage along the street these noises gained in authority, became loud crowings of power.

"Okay, Sinatra," Lorna said, scuffling her feet through the drifts of maple leaves.

Miss Pruitt was not on her porch, though the day was mild and golden. In the cleared beds beside the steps the autumn crocuses bloomed on pale stems; Lorna went up the steps and turned the winding doorbell handle with a rusty tingle of sound. Then she opened the door and called "Miss Prue-oo!" before she saw Dr. Pur-cell's black bag on the hall table.

She heard his footsteps on the carpetless upstairs floor and his head looked over the banisters.

"Oh, Lorna Reckettson. Thank the Lord you came. Get my office on the phone, please, and tell Miss Findlay to pack a bag right away. She'll have to spend the night here."

"Is Miss Pru—is anything the matter?"

"Yes, plenty. I just happened to drop in and I found her in a heap on the kitchen floor. Don't know how long she'd—but make that call now, like a good girl, and then bring my bag up here and give me a hand."

Miss Pruitt's telephone grew out of a box on the wall and wore its two round gongs like a pair of spectacles. Lorna wound the little handle at the side and took down the receiver with a damp hand.

When she went upstairs Dr. Purcell was bending over the bed. "See if you can find a shawl or a blanket to put over her," he said, without turning.

Lorna pulled open the drawers of the marble-topped old huge bureau and shut them again, one by one. She opened the two chests in the room, one cedar, and one wicker, and shut them again. She opened the door of the wardrobe and looked at the shelves, quite certain, now, of what she would see there.

In every one of the drawers, in every chest, and on every shelf in the wardrobe were orderly piles of tiny dresses: pink, blue, white. There were small folded shawls with fringed edges and nests of moth balls in the centers of them. There were little flannel jackets, and robes trimmed with feather stitching; shirts, socks, petticoats, bonnets, hoods, and hundreds upon hundreds of bird's-eye squares, hand-hemmed. Diapers, dresses, booties for a regiment of infants; perfect to the tiniest embroidered bud, the finest tucked yoke.

Lorna closed the wardrobe door and looked over her shoulder at Dr. Purcell. He had turned and was now looking at her, too, above his eyeglasses. He sighed regretfully.

"I didn't realize——" he said. "I'm sorry, Lorna, I just wasn't thinking that naturally that's what you'd have to find out about if you went looking among her things. . . . Now, of course, you've discovered her secret, haven't you? But try to remember, try to realize, that this was her only aberration. Believing it kept her happy for twenty-seven years, probably a world's record, and it did no one any harm. *You* liked her."

Lorna was thinking of the smiling face, the tranquil, unhurried steps, the hand always holding onto the stair rail. . . .

"Come here, Lorna. Bring some of those baby blankets, anything to keep her warm."

Lorna did not want to obey. Superimposed on all that was well loved and familiar was something new and strange, and she was afraid of Miss Pru, now, afraid to look at her.

"Please get the blankets, Lorna," said Dr. Purcell sternly. "And then come here and help me. Hold her head up while I try to get her to take this."

And after all, it was all right. At sight of Miss Pru the unfamiliar frightening thing dissolved into nothing: all that was left was her old friend lying on the bed, diminished, dying, but still good, still lovable. She looked shrunken and blue and her breath came hard, but as Lorna bent over

her she looked up, a struggling, triumphant, urgent look. A whisper rustled from her.

"What?" Lorna bent closer.

"The baby. The baby."

Above Miss Pruitt's head Lorna saw that Dr. Purcell looked helpless, almost scared; and then she heard her voice, her own calm voice, saying the words: "A fine boy." As if she were a nurse of years' experience.

Miss Pru searched for her voice again. "Let-me-see."

"Now look what you've done," said Dr. Purcell, the words coming out on a great despairing sigh. But Lorna was inspired. I know what I'm doing, she thought, running down the stairs, and out into the fresh evening air.

Gary Alan was heavy when she lifted him out of the buggy, and wet everywhere; he was an inert lump in her arms, smelling of wool and rubber and good health. As she carried him up the stairs she could feel his nose brush against her cheek as he turned his head to look at this new place.

Dr. Purcell, a man aghast, stared as Lorna took the baby to the bed and sat him against the pillow beside Miss Pruitt where he lay passively, with most of one hand in his mouth, drooling around each side of it.

"There," said Lorna, repeating the splendid words. "A fine boy!" She never knew why instinct assured her that Miss Pruitt's wandering intellect would protect her from wonder at having produced a baby seven months old, but this was the case. On the top of Gary Alan's head, under the frail nap of hair, the fontanel[1] stirred with its tiny life-beat. Miss Pruitt laid her finger there to feel it moving.

"His coloring . . ." she whispered. "The Clovelly coloring . . ."

Lorna looked across the bed at Dr. Purcell with a feeling of triumph and competence and saw in his face a sort of irritated awe.

"Just why you knew you could get away with it," he said. "Just *how* you knew . . ." Then he glanced at Miss Pruitt and laid his fingers on her wrist. "She's tired now, Lorna, take the baby

---

1. **fontanel** (fŏn′tə nel′), "the soft spot" or gap in the skull of an infant.

away." He bent close to his patient, and spoke gently. "You must sleep now. Go to sleep."

"Yes—doctor." Weak tears of joy trembled in Miss Pruitt's eyes.

"But tomorrow morning," Lorna said, when Dr. Purcell followed her from the room, "I have to go to school and then she'll find out."

"No she won't, Lorna. For her there's not likely to be any tomorrow." He hesitated. "Go home now and thank God that you know how to tell a lie at the proper time."

Lorna stuffed Gary Alan into his carriage again and wheeled him back along Van Buren Street. She was not yet ready to grieve, and as she walked she felt within herself a great strengthening of pride and hope and promise. The air was still and smelled of autumn; a big clear star stood in the deepening sky. Gary Alan resumed his voice sounds, but this time on a quieter, more thoughtful level; he was getting sleepy. ☐☐

Discussion

1. There are numerous **fore-shadowing** clues in this story. Glance back through the story and cite early passages that suggest the nature of Miss Pruitt's delusion.

2. At one point Miss Pru became hurried and "mislaid (Lorna's) name, fumbling first with names like Pearl or Barbara or Maureen, before she came to Lorna." Why did she have this difficulty?

3. Lorna's final deception of Miss Pru and Dr. Purcell's acceptance of Lorna's lie raise serious moral problems which are central to interpreting the story. **(a)** Do you think that Lorna was wrong in telling Miss Pru she had given birth to "a fine boy"? Why, or why not? **(b)** Did Lorna have any right to use Gary Alan as an instrument of such a deception? **(c)** How do you think Gary Alan's mother might react if she learned of this episode?

(d) If Miss Pru had survived, what problems might have arisen? **(e)** Would you blame Dr. Purcell for never having tried to cure Miss Pru of her delusion? Explain your answers.

4. It is essential to remember that in fiction an author does not always approve of the actions of characters. What seems to be the author's attitude toward Lorna's lie and the doctor's acceptance of it?

Elizabeth Enright 1909 • 1968

In a sense, Elizabeth Enright entered her writing career through a back door. Originally a magazine illustrator, she decided to start writing stories to accompany illustrations she had drawn. After a time she concentrated entirely on writing.

Besides publishing stories in magazines like *The New Yorker*, Enright wrote many books for children. In fact, her *Thimble Summer* won the John Newbery Medal in 1939. Her

adult short stories were also highly regarded and appeared in several volumes of *Prize Stories: The O. Henry Awards* and *Best American Short Stories*. As in "When the Bough Breaks," Enright drew on the experiences of childhood for much of her material.

Donald Barthelme

In the diaries of the famous Swiss abstract painter, Paul Klee (klā; 1879–1940), Donald Barthelme discovered the germ of a story. During World War I Klee served in the German air corps. Between his duties of painting and transporting airplanes, Klee squeezed in brief leaves with his wife, Lily, and visits to art museums in the towns he passed through. What follows is Barthelme's version of the artist's confrontation with military officialdom.

Engineer-Private Paul Klee Misplaces an Aircraft Between Milbertshofen and Cambrai, March 1916

Paul Klee said:

"Now I have been transferred to the Air Corps. A kindly sergeant effected the transfer. He thought I would have a better future here, more chances for promotion. First I was assigned to aircraft repair, together with several other workers. We presented ourselves as not just painters but artist-painters. This caused some shaking of heads. We varnished wooden fuselages, correcting old numbers and adding new ones with the help of templates. Then I was pulled off the painting detail and assigned to transport. I escort aircraft that are being sent to various bases in Germany and also (I understand) in occupied territory. It is not a bad life. I spend my nights racketing across Bavaria[1] (or some such) and my days in switching yards. There is always bread and wurst and beer in the station restaurants. When I reach a notable town I try to see the notable paintings there, if time allows. There are always unexpected delays, reroutings, backtrackings. Then the return to the base. I see Lily fairly often. We meet in hotel rooms and that is exciting. I have never yet lost an aircraft or failed to deliver one to its proper destination. The war seems interminable. Walden has sold six of my drawings."

The Secret Police said:

"We have secrets. We have many secrets. We desire all secrets. We do not have your secrets and that is what we are after, your secrets. Our first secret is where we are. No one knows. Our second secret is how many of us there are. No one knows. Omnipresence is our goal. We do not even need real omnipresence. The theory of omnipresence is enough. With omnipresence, hand-in-hand as it were, goes omniscience. And with omniscience and omnipresence, hand-in-hand-in-hand as it were, goes omnipotence. We are a three-sided waltz. However our mood is melancholy. There is a secret sigh that we sigh, secretly. We yearn to be known, acknowledged, admired even. What is the good of omnipotence if nobody knows? However that is a secret, that sorrow. Now we are everywhere. One place we are is here watching Engineer-Private Klee, who is escorting three valuable aircraft, B.F.W. 3054/16-17-18, with spare parts, by rail from Milbertshofen to Cambrai.[2] Do you wish to know what Engineer-Private Klee is doing at this very moment, in the baggage car? He is reading a book of Chinese short stories. He has removed his boots. His feet rest twenty-six centimeters from the baggage-car stove."

---

1. *Bavaria* (bə ver′ē ə), a southern state of West Germany.
2. *Milbertshofen* (mil′bèrts höf′ən) *to Cambrai* (kän brā′). Milbertshofen is near Munich, the capital of Bavaria. Cambrai is a town in northern France.

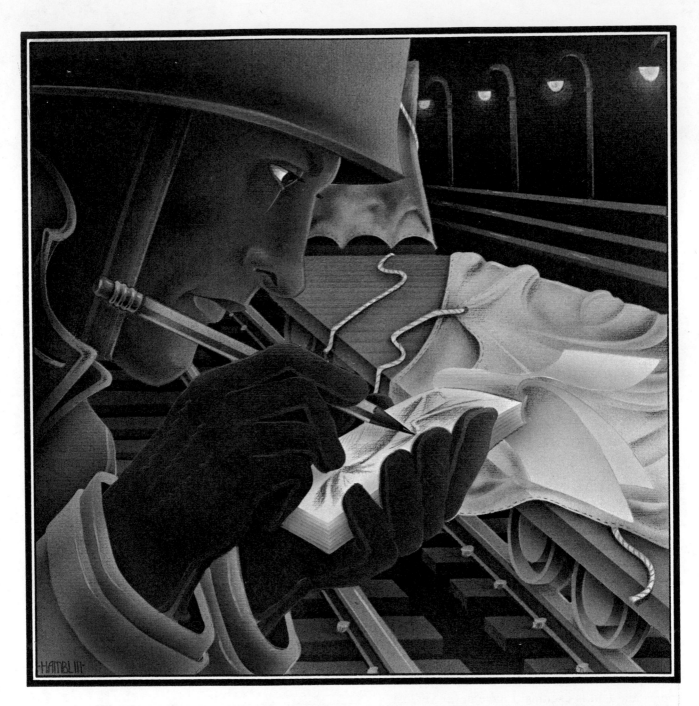

Paul Klee said:

"These Chinese short stories are slight and lovely. I have no way of knowing if the translation is adequate or otherwise. Lily will meet me in our rented room on Sunday, if I return in time. Our destination is Fighter Squadron Five. I have not had anything to eat since morning. The fine chunk of bacon given me along with my expense money when we left the base has been eaten. This morning a Red Cross lady with a squint gave me some very good coffee, however. Now we are entering Hohenbudberg."[3]

---

3. Hohenbudberg (hō ən bŭd′bėrg), apparently, from Klee's diary, a village in northwest Germany, near France.

The Secret Police said:

"Engineer-Private Klee has taken himself into the station restaurant. He is enjoying a hearty lunch. We shall join him there."

Paul Klee said:

"Now I emerge from the station restaurant and walk along the line of cars to the flatcar on which my aircraft (I think of them as *my* aircraft) are carried. To my surprise and dismay, I notice that one of them is missing. There had been three, tied down on the flatcar and covered with canvas. Now I see with my trained painter's eye that instead of three canvas-covered shapes on the flatcar there are only two. Where the third aircraft had been there is only a puddle of canvas and loose rope. I look around quickly to see if anyone else has marked the disappearance of the third aircraft."

The Secret Police said:

"We had marked it. Our trained policemen's eyes had marked the fact that where three aircraft had been before, tied down on the flatcar and covered with canvas, now there were only two. Unfortunately we had been in the station restaurant, lunching, at the moment of removal, therefore we could not attest as to where it had gone or who had removed it. There is something we do not know. This is irritating in the extreme. We closely observe Engineer-Private Klee to determine what action he will take in the emergency. We observe that he is withdrawing from his tunic a notebook and pencil. We observe that he begins, very properly in our opinion, to note down in his notebook all the particulars of the affair."

Paul Klee said:

"The shape of the collapsed canvas, under which the aircraft had rested, together with the loose ropes—the canvas forming hills and valleys, seductive folds, the ropes the very essence of looseness, lapsing—it is irresistible. I sketch for ten or fifteen minutes, wondering the while if I might not be in trouble, because of the missing aircraft. When I arrive at Fighter Squadron Five with less than the number of aircraft listed on the manifest, might not some officious person become angry? Shout at me? I have finished sketching. Now I will ask various trainmen and station personnel if they have seen anyone carrying away the aircraft. If they answer in the

negative, I will become extremely frustrated. I will begin to kick the flatcar."

The Secret Police said:

"Frustrated, he begins to kick the flatcar."

Paul Klee said:

"I am looking up in the sky, to see if my aircraft is there. There are in the sky aircraft of several types, but none of the type I am searching for."

The Secret Police said:

"Engineer-Private Klee is searching the sky—an eminently sound procedure, in our opinion. We, the Secret Police, also sweep the Hohenbudberg sky, with our eyes. But find nothing. We are debating with ourselves as to whether we ought to enter the station restaurant and begin drafting our preliminary report, for forwarding to higher headquarters. The knotty point, in terms of the preliminary report, is that we do not have the answer to the question 'Where is the aircraft?' The damage potential to the theory of omniscience, as well as potential to our careers, dictates that this point be omitted from the preliminary report. But if this point is omitted, might not some officious person at the Central Bureau for Secrecy note the omission? Become angry? Shout at us? Omissiveness is not rewarded at the Central Bureau. We decide to observe further the actions of Engineer-Private Klee, for the time being."

Paul Klee said:

"I who have never lost an aircraft have lost an aircraft. The aircraft is signed out to me. The cost of the aircraft, if it is not found, will be deducted from my pay, meager enough already. Even if Walden sells a hundred, a thousand drawings, I will not have enough money to pay for this cursed aircraft. Can I, in the time the train remains in the Hohenbudberg yards, construct a new aircraft or even the simulacrum[4] of an aircraft, with no materials to work with or indeed any special knowledge of aircraft construction? The situation is ludicrous. I will therefore apply Reason. Reason dictates the solution. I will diddle the manifest. With my painter's skill which is after all not so different from a forger's, I will change the manifest[5] to reflect conveyance

---

4. *simulacrum* (sim′yə lā′krəm), a faint likeness.
5. *manifest,* a list of items in a shipment.

of *two* aircraft, B.F.W. 3054/16 and 17, to Fighter Squadron Five. The extra canvas and ropes I will conceal in an empty boxcar—this one, which according to its stickers is headed for Essigny-le-Petit.[6] Now I will walk around town and see if I can find a chocolate shop. I crave chocolate."

The Secret Police said:

"Now we observe Engineer-Private Klee concealing the canvas and ropes which covered the former aircraft into an empty boxcar bound for Essigny-le-Petit. We have previously observed him diddling the manifest with his painter's skill which resembles not a little that of the forger. We applaud these actions of Engineer-Private Klee. The contradiction confronting us in the matter of the preliminary report is thus resolved in highly satisfactory fashion. We are proud of Engineer-Private Klee and of the resolute and manly fashion in which he has dealt with the crisis. We predict he will go far. We would like to embrace him as a comrade and brother but unfortunately we are not embraceable. We are secret, we exist in the shadows, the pleasure of the comradely/brotherly embrace is one of the pleasures we are denied, in our dismal service."

Paul Klee said:

"We arrive at Cambrai. The planes are unloaded, six men for each plane. The work goes quickly. No one questions my altered manifest. The weather is clearing. After lunch I will leave to begin the return journey. My release slip and travel orders are ready, but the lieutenant must come and sign them. I wait contentedly in the warm orderly room. The drawing I did of the collapsed canvas and ropes is really very good. I eat a piece of chocolate. I am sorry about the lost aircraft but not overmuch. The war is temporary. But drawings and chocolate go on forever."

□□

---

6. **Essigny-le-Petit** (es sē nyē′ lə pə tē′), a district or street of St. Quentin in northern France.

Discussion

1. What is absurd about Klee's being assigned to aircraft repair and transport?

2. (a) What sorts of things do the Secret Police know? **(b)** What "secrets" of Paul Klee do they fail to get? **(c)** What conclusions can be drawn about the Secret Police organization from what its officials say and from how they phrase their reports?

3. What humorous elements do you see in this story?

4. (a) How does Klee use his artistic skills to solve his problem? **(b)** Describe his attitude toward military life. **(c)** How do you interpret Klee's final comment about war, drawings, and chocolate? Do you agree with him or not? Explain.

5. Which do you think is the *main* target of Barthelme's satire: **(a)** secret agents? **(b)** war? **(c)** bureaucratic red tape? Discuss.

Extension • Speaking

Report to the class about two other satirical or absurd treatments of war in fiction and film. For instance, you might select Joseph Heller's *Catch 22* or Kurt Vonnegut's *Slaughterhouse-Five*, both of which have been adapted to film. Do you think absurdist satire is an effective way to protest war? Why, or why not?

Donald Barthelme 1931 •

Within four years of publishing his first collection of short stories in 1964, Barthelme was being described as "probably the most perversely gifted writer in the U.S." Born in Philadelphia, he was raised and educated in Houston, Texas. He has since worked as a newspaper reporter, university public relations official, magazine editor, and curator of a modern art gallery. As well as his frequent collections of experimental short stories, he has also published the novels *Snow White* (1967) and *The Dead Father* (1975). In 1972 his children's book *The Slightly Irregular Fire Engine or the Hithering Thithering Djinn* received the National Book Award for children's literature.

Bienvenido N. Santos

Scent of Apples

When I arrived in Kalamazoo, it was October and the war was still on. Gold and silver stars[1] hung on pennants above silent windows of white and brick-red cottages. In a backyard an old man burned leaves and twigs while a gray-haired woman sat on the porch, her red hands quiet on her lap, watching the smoke rising above the elms, both of them thinking the same thought, perhaps, about a tall, grinning boy with blue eyes and flying hair who went out to war; where could he be now this month when leaves were turning into gold and the fragrance of gathered apples was in the wind?

It was a cold night when I left my room at the hotel for a usual speaking engagement. I walked but a little way. A heavy wind coming up from Lake Michigan was icy on the face. It felt like winter straying early in the northern woodlands. Under the lampposts the leaves shone like bronze. And they rolled the pavements like the ghost feet of a thousand autumns long dead, long before the boys left for faraway lands without great icy winds and promise of winter early in the air, lands without apple trees, *the singing and the gold!*

It was the same night I met Celestino Fabia, "just a Filipino farmer," as he called himself, who had a farm about thirty miles east of Kalamazoo.

"You came all that way on a night like this just to hear me talk?" I asked.

"I've seen no Filipino for so many years now," he answered quickly. "So when I saw your name in the papers where it says you come from the islands and that you're going to talk, I come right away."

Earlier that night I had addressed a college crowd, mostly women. It appeared that they wanted me to talk about my country; they wanted me to tell them things about it because my country had become a lost country. Everywhere in the land the enemy stalked.[2] Over it a great silence hung; and their boys were there, unheard from, or they were on their way to some little-known island in the Pacific, young boys all, hardly men, thinking of harvest moons and smell of forest fire.

It was not hard talking about our own people. I knew them well and I loved them. And they seemed so far away during those terrible years that I must have spoken of them with a little fervor, a little nostalgia.

In the open forum that followed, the audience wanted to know whether there was much difference between our women and the American women. I tried to answer the question as best I could, saying, among other things, that I did not know much about American women except that they looked friendly, but differences or similarities in inner qualities such as naturally belonged to the heart or to the mind, I could only speak about with vagueness.

While I was trying to explain away the fact that it was not easy to make comparisons, a man rose from the rear of the hall, wanting to say something. In the distance, he looked slight and old and very brown. Even before he spoke, I knew that he was, like me, a Filipino.

"I'm a Filipino," he began, loud and clear, in a voice that seemed used to wide open spaces. "I'm just a Filipino farmer out in the country." He waved his hand towards the door. "I left the Philippines more than twenty years ago and have never been back. Never will, perhaps. I want to

---

Bienvenido Santos (byen′ve nē′dô sän′tōs).

"Scent of Apples" from YOU LOVELY PEOPLE by Bienvenido N. Santos. Reprinted by permission of the author.

1. Gold and silver stars. In World War II pennants hung in house windows showed by stars how many family members were in the military. A gold star indicated someone killed in action.

2. the enemy stalked, a reference to the Japanese, who occupied the Philippines in World War II.

BIENVENIDO N. SANTOS **657**

find out, sir, are our Filipino women the same like they were twenty years ago?"

As he sat down, the hall filled with voices, hushed and intrigued. I weighed my answer carefully. I did not want to tell a lie, yet I did not want to say anything that would seem platitudinous, insincere. But more important than these considerations, it seemed to me that moment as I looked towards my countryman, I must give him an answer that would not make him so unhappy. Surely, all these years, he must have held on to certain ideals, certain beliefs, even illusions peculiar to the exile.

"First," I said as the voices gradually died down and every eye seemed upon me. "First, tell me what our women were like twenty years ago."

The man stood to answer. "Yes," he said, "you're too young. . . . Twenty years ago our women were nice, they were modest, they wore their hair long, they dressed proper and went for no monkey business. They were natural, they went to church regular, and they were faithful." He had spoken slowly, and now, in what seemed like an afterthought, added, "It's the men who ain't."

Now I knew what I was going to say.

"Well," I began, "it will interest you to know that our women have changed—but definitely! The change, however, has been on the outside only. Inside, here," pointing to the heart, "they are the same as they were twenty years ago, God-fearing, faithful, modest, and *nice*."

The man was visibly moved. "I'm very happy sir," he said, in the manner of one who, having stakes on the land, had found no cause to regret one's sentimental investment.

After this, everything that was said and done in that hall that night seemed like an anticlimax; and later, as we walked outside, he gave me his name and told me of his farm thirty miles east of the city.

We had stopped at the main entrance of the hotel lobby. We had not talked very much on the way. As a matter of fact, we were never alone. Kindly American friends talked to us, asked us questions, said good night. So now I asked him whether he cared to step into the lobby with me and talk shop.

"No, thank you," he said, "you are tired. And I don't want to stay out too late."

"Yes, you live very far."

"I got a car," he said; "besides. . . ."

Now he smiled, he truly smiled. All night I had been watching his face, and I wondered when he was going to smile.

"Will you do me a favor, please," he continued, smiling almost sweetly. "I want you to have dinner with my family out in the country. I'd call for you tomorrow afternoon, then drive you back. Will that be all right?"

"Of course," I said. "I'd love to meet your family." I was leaving Kalamazoo for Muncie, Indiana, in two days. There was plenty of time.

"You will make my wife very happy," he said.

"You flatter me."

"Honest. She'll be very happy. Ruth is a country girl and hasn't met many Filipinos. I mean Filipinos younger than I, cleaner-looking. We're just poor farmer folks, you know, and we don't get to town very often. Roger, that's my boy, he goes to school in town. A bus takes him early in the morning and he's back in the afternoon. He's a nice boy."

"I bet he is. I've seen the children of some of the boys by their American wives, and the boys are tall, taller than the father, and very good-looking."

"Roger, he'd be tall. You'll like him."

Then he said goodbye, and I waved to him as he disappeared in the darkness.

The next day he came, at about three in the afternoon. There was a mild, ineffectual sun shining; and it was not too cold. He was wearing an old brown tweed jacket and worsted trousers to match. His shoes were polished, and although the green of his tie seemed faded, a colored shirt hardly accentuated it. He looked younger than he appeared the night before, now that he was clean-shaven and seemed ready to go to a party. He was grinning as we met.

"Oh, Ruth can't believe it. She can't believe it," he kept repeating as he led me to his car—a nondescript thing in faded black that had known better days and many hands. "I says to her, I'm bringing you a first-class Filipino, and she says, aw, go away, quit kidding, there's no such thing as first-class Filipino. But Roger, that's my boy, he believed me immediately. What's he like, daddy, he asks. Oh, you will see, I says, he's first-class. Like you, daddy? No, no, I laugh at him, your daddy ain't first-class. Aw, but you are, daddy, he says. So you can see what a nice boy he is, so innocent. Then Ruth starts griping about the house, but the house is a mess, she says. True it's a mess, it's always a mess, but you don't mind, do you? We're poor folks, you know."

The trip seemed interminable. We passed through narrow lanes and disappeared into thickets, and came out on barren land overgrown with weeds in places. All around were dead leaves and dry earth. In the distance were apple trees.

"Aren't those apple trees?" I asked, wanting to be sure.

"Yes, those are apple trees," he replied. "Do you like apples? I got lots of 'em. I got an apple orchard. I'll show you."

All the beauty of the afternoon seemed in the distance, on the hills, in the dull soft sky.

"Those trees are beautiful on the hills," I said.

"Autumn's a lovely season. The trees are getting ready to die, and they show their color, proud-like."

"No such thing in our own country," I said.

That remark seemed unkind, I realized later. It touched him off on a long deserted tangent, but ever there, perhaps. How many times did the lonely mind take unpleasant detours away from the familiar winding lanes towards home for fear of this, the remembered hurt, the long-lost youth, the grim shadows of the years; how many times indeed, only the exile knows.

It was a rugged road we were traveling, and the car made so much noise that I could not hear everything he said, but I understood him. He was telling his story for the first time in many years. He was remembering his own youth. He was thinking of home. In these odd moments there seemed no cause for fear, no cause at all, no pain. That would come later. In the night perhaps. Or lonely on the farm under the apple trees.

In this old Visayan[3] town, the streets are narrow and dirty and strewn with coral shells. You have been there? You could not have missed our house; it was the biggest in town, one of the oldest; ours was a big family. The house stood right on the edge of the street. A door opened heavily and you enter a dark hall leading to the stairs. There is the smell of chickens roosting on the low-topped walls; there is the familiar sound they make, and you grope your way up a massive staircase, the banisters smooth upon the trembling hand. Such nights, they are no better than the days; windows are closed against the sun; they close heavily.

Mother sits in her corner looking very white and sick. This was her world, her domain. In all these years I cannot remember the sound of her voice. Father was different. He moved about. He shouted. He ranted. He lived in the past and talked of honor as though it were the only thing.

I was born in that house. I grew up there into a pampered brat. I was mean. One day I broke their hearts. I saw Mother cry wordlessly as Father heaped his curses upon me and drove me out of the house, the gate closing heavily after me. And my brothers and sisters took up my father's hate for me and multiplied it numberless times in their own broken hearts. I was no good.

But sometimes, you know, I miss that house, the roosting chickens on the low-topped walls. I miss my brothers and sisters. Mother sitting in her chair, looking like a pale ghost in a corner of the room. I would remember the great live posts, massive tree trunks from the forests. Leafy plants grow on the sides, buds pointing downwards, wilted and died before they could become flowers. As they fell on the floor, Father bent to pick them and throw them out into the coral streets. His hands were strong; I have kissed those hands . . . many times, many times. . . .

Finally, we rounded a deep curve and suddenly came upon a shanty, all but ready to crumble in a heap on the ground; its plastered walls were rotting away, the floor was hardly a foot from the ground. I thought of the cottages of the poor colored folk in the South, the hovels of the poor everywhere in the land. This one stood all by itself as though by common consent all the folk that used to live here had decided to stay

---

3. **Visayan** (və sīʹən). The Visayan islands are in the middle of the Philippine archipelago.

away, despising it, ashamed of it. Even the lovely season could not color it with beauty.

A dog barked loudly as we approached. A fat blond woman stood at the door with a little boy by her side. Roger seemed newly scrubbed. He hardly took his eyes off me. Ruth had a clean apron around her shapeless waist. Now, as she shook my hands in sincere delight, I noticed shamefacedly (that I should notice) how rough her hands, how coarse and red with labor, how ugly! She was no longer young and her smile was pathetic.

As we stepped inside and the door closed behind us, immediately I was aware of the familiar scent of apples. The room was bare except for a few ancient pieces of secondhand furniture. In the middle of the room stood a stove to keep the family warm in winter. The walls were bare. Over the dining table hung a lamp yet unlighted.

Ruth got busy with the drinks. She kept coming in and out of a rear room that must have been the kitchen, and soon the table was heavy with food, fried chicken legs and rice, and green peas and corn on the ear. Even as we ate, Ruth kept standing and going to the kitchen for more food. Roger ate like a little gentleman.

"Isn't he nice looking?" his father asked.

"You are a handsome boy, Roger," I said.

The boy smiled at me. "You look like daddy," he said.

Afterwards I noticed an old picture leaning on the top of a dresser and stood to pick it up. It was yellow and soiled with many fingerings. The faded figure of a woman in Philippine dress could yet be distinguished, although the face had become a blur.

"Your . . ." I began.

"I don't know who she is," Fabia hastened to say. "I picked that picture many years ago in a room on La Salle Street in Chicago. I have often wondered who she is."

"The face wasn't a blur in the beginning?"

"Oh, no. It was a young face and good."

Ruth came with a plate full of apples.

"Ah," I cried, picking out a ripe one, "I've been thinking where all the scent of apples came from. The room is full of it."

"I'll show you," said Fabia.

He showed me a back room, not very big. It was half-full of apples.

"Every day," he explained, "I take some of them to town to sell to the groceries. Prices have been low. I've been losing on the trips."

"These apples will spoil," I said.

"We'll feed them to the pigs."

Then he showed me around the farm. It was twilight now, and the apple trees stood bare against a glowing western sky. In apple-blossom time it must be lovely here, I thought. But what about winter time?

One day, according to Fabia, a few years ago, before Roger was born, he had an attack of acute appendicitis. It was deep winter. The snow lay heavy everywhere. Ruth was pregnant and none too well herself. At first she did not know what to do. She bundled him in warm clothing and put him on a cot near the stove. She shoveled the snow from their front door and practically carried the suffering man on her shoulders, dragging him through the newly made path towards the road, where they waited for the U.S. Mail car to pass. Meanwhile snowflakes poured all over them, and she kept rubbing the man's arms and legs as she herself nearly froze to death.

"Go back to the house, Ruth!" her husband cried, "you'll freeze to death."

But she clung to him wordlessly. Even as she massaged his arms and legs, her tears rolled down her cheeks. "I won't leave you, I won't leave you," she repeated.

Finally the U.S. Mail car arrived. The mailman, who knew them well, helped them board the car, and without stopping on his usual route, took the sick man and his wife direct to the nearest hospital.

Ruth stayed in the hospital with Fabia. She slept in a corridor outside the patients' ward and in the daytime helped in scrubbing the floor and washing the dishes and cleaning the men's things. They didn't have enough money, and Ruth was willing to work like a slave.

"Ruth's a nice girl," said Fabia. "Like our own Filipino women."

Before nightfall, he took me back to the hotel. Ruth and Roger stood at the door holding hands and smiling at me. From inside the room of the shanty, a low light flickered. I had a last glimpse of the apple trees in the orchard under the darkened sky as Fabia backed up the car. And soon we were on our way back to town. The dog had started barking. We could hear it for some time, until finally we could not hear it any more, and all was darkness around us, except where the headlamps revealed a stretch of road leading somewhere.

Fabia did not talk this time. I didn't seem to have anything to say myself. But when finally we came to the hotel and I got down, Fabia said, "Well, I guess I won't be seeing you again."

It was dimly lighted in front of the hotel and I could hardly see Fabia's face. Without getting off the car, he moved to where I had sat, and I saw him extend his hand. I gripped it.

"Tell Ruth and Roger," I said, "I love them."

He dropped my hand quickly. "They'll be waiting for me now," he said.

"Look," I said, not knowing why I said it, "one of these days, very soon, I hope, I'll be going home. I could go to your town."

No," he said softly, sounding very much defeated but brave. "Thanks a lot. But you see, nobody would remember me now."

Then he started the car, and as it moved away, he waved his hand.

"Goodbye," I said, waving back into the darkness. And suddenly the night was cold like winter straying early in these northern woodlands.

I hurried inside. There was a train the next morning that left for Muncie, Indiana, at a quarter after eight. □□

Discussion

1. **(a)** What indicates the strength of Fabia's desire to hear the **narrator's** lecture? **(b)** What is he so anxious to find out? **(c)** Why is the narrator so careful in answering Fabia's question?

2. **(a)** What do Fabia's memories in the long italicized passage reveal? **(b)** What feelings in him are suggested by his keeping the old picture on his dresser?

3. Compare Fabia's view of himself with his son's attitude toward him.

4. **(a)** What are the differences between Fabia and the narrator? **(b)** What common ground between them enables them to understand each other's feelings?

Extension • Writing

Interview someone you know who was born and reared in another country. Which of his or her recollections of the homeland are pleasant and which are unpleasant? What foods, customs, or other characteristics of that homeland does he or she miss? Write up the person's reminiscences. You might use Fabia's italicized recollection on page 659 as a model.

Vocabulary
Pronunciation and Dictionary

Use your Glossary to answer on your paper the questions about the pronunciation of each italicized word below. Be sure you know the definition and spelling of each word.

1. Does the accented syllable in *exotic* rhyme with *legs, cot,* or *lick?* (Arias, "El Mago")

2. Does the last syllable of *oblique* rhyme with *reek* or *sick*? (McCullers, "The Haunted Boy")

3. Does the first *u* in *platitudinous* sound like the vowel in *do* or in *cud*? (Santos, "Scent of Apples")

4. Divide *accentuate* into syllables and mark the accented syllable. (Santos, "Scent of Apples")

Bienvenido N. Santos 1911 •

One of the foremost authors from the Philippines, Santos has focused most of his writing on the Filipino experience in the United States. Among his works are *The Volcano* (a novel), *You Lovely People* (short stories), and *The Wounded Stag* (poems). He has received the Philippine Republic Cultural Heritage Award in Literature and fellowships from the Rockefeller and Guggenheim Foundations.

Santos has moved freely between the Philippines and this country, studying and teaching at various American universities. He is now Distinguished Writer in Residence at Wichita State University.

Abelardo Díaz Alfaro

Puerto Rico is a meeting ground for Spanish- and Anglo-American traditions. See what results when Santa Claus runs into the festival of The Three Wise Men, celebrated on January 6.

"Santa Clo" Comes to La Cuchilla

A piece of red bunting on a bamboo pole marked the location of Peyo Mercé's[1] one-room schoolhouse. A partition down the middle divided the tiny school into two classrooms; over one of them a new teacher—Mister Johnny Rosas[2] —now presided.

Because of a lamentable incident in which Peyo Mercé had made the superintendent appear in an unfavorable light, the latter thought it wise to appoint a second teacher to the district of La Cuchilla[3] so he could instruct Peyo in the newest educational methods and bring the lamp of progress to illuminate that unenlightened district.

He called the young teacher to his office. Johnny Rosas, a recent graduate, had spent a short time in the United States. Solemnly the superintendent said to him:

"Listen, Johnny; I'm going to send you to the district of La Cuchilla so you can take them the most up-to-date techniques you learned in your Education courses. That Peyo doesn't know a thing about it; he's forty years behind the times in the subject. Try to change their ways, and above all you must teach a great deal of English . . . a lot of English."

One day Peyo Mercé saw the fledgling teacher coming up the hill toward the school on an old horse. He even felt a little sorry for him, and said to himself: "Life is probably cutting furrows in him already, just as a plough does in the earth." And he told some farm children to take the harness off the horse and put it out to pasture.

Peyo knew that life was going to be very hard for the young man. Out in the country living conditions are bad, and meals are poor: rice, beans, codfish, and plenty of water. The roads are almost impassable, and always full of pud-dles. Baths had to be taken in mountain streams, and the only drinking water was rain water. Peyo Mercé had to make his lesson plans by the flickering light of an oil lamp.

One day Johnny Rosas said to Peyo, "This district is very backward; we have to make it over. It is imperative to bring in new things, replace what is traditional. Remember what the superintendent said: 'Down with tradition.' We have to teach a great deal of English, and copy the customs of the Americans."

And Peyo, not very enthusiastic, managed to squeeze out these words:

"True, English is good, and we need it. But good Heavens! We don't even know how to speak Spanish well! And hungry children turn into dull-witted little animals. Once the fox said to the snails: 'You have to learn how to walk before you can run.' "

But Johnny didn't understand what Peyo meant.

The tobacco region took on a somewhat livelier mood: the Christmas holidays were approaching. Peyo had already observed with affection that some of his pupils were fashioning rustic guitars out of cedar wood. These fiestas always brought him happy memories of times gone by, and he seemed to hear the Christmas carol that goes:

Abelardo Díaz Alfaro (ä be lär′dô dē′äs äl fä′rô).

" 'Santa Clo' Comes to La Cuchilla" from TERRAZO by Abelardo Díaz Alfaro. Reprinted by permission.

1. *Peyo Mercé's* (pā′yô mer se′).
2. *Rosas* (rô′säs).
3. *La Cuchilla* (lä kü chē′yä), a mountainous rural district in Puerto Rico.

The door of this house is open wide:
It shows a gentleman lives inside.

Johnny Rosas ended Peyo's pleasant reverie with these words:

"This year Santa Claus will make his debut in La Cuchilla. All that business about the gifts of the Three Wise Men on January the sixth is growing old-fashioned; it's no longer done to any extent in San Juan.[4] That belongs to the past. I'll invite the superintendent, Mister Rogelio Escalera,[5] to the party; he'll like that a lot."

Peyo scratched his head and said quietly, "I'm just a country fellow who's never left these hills, so the story of the Three Wise Men is right here in my heart. We country folk are sensitive to the things in the atmosphere around us, just as we can smell codfish cooking."

Johnny, by means of class projects, set to work preparing the atmosphere for what he called the "gala première" of Santa Claus in La Cuchilla. He showed his pupils a picture of Santa Claus riding in a sleigh pulled by reindeer. And Peyo, who had stopped for a moment at the threshold of the door between the two classrooms, saw in his mind's eye another picture: an old farmer pulled along on a palm-leaf sledge by goats.

Mister Rosas asked the farm children, "Who is this important person?"

And Benito[6] answered, "Mister, that is the Old Year, painted red."

Johnny was amazed at the ignorance of those children, and at the same time angry at Peyo Mercé's negligence.

Christmas came, and the parents were invited. Peyo held a typical little fiesta in his room. Some farm children sang Puerto Rican songs and Christmas carols to the accompaniment of rustic guitars. And to conclude the performance the Three Wise Men appeared, while an old singer named Simón[7] improvised verses like this:

They come and go from far and near;
We country folk just stay right here.

Peyo handed out traditional rice sweets and candies, and the children exchanged little presents. Then he told his children to file into the room of Mister Johnny Rosas, who had a sur-

prise for them and had even invited the superintendent, Mister Rogelio Escalera.

In the middle of the classroom stood an artificial Christmas tree. Red streamers were stretched from one bookcase to another, and from the walls hung little wreaths with green leaves and red berries. In frosted white letters was a sign that said in English, "Merry Christmas." Artificial snow was sprinkled over the whole display.

The spectators looked in amazement at all this, which they had never seen before. Mister Rogelio Escalera was greatly pleased.

Some of the children went up on an improvised platform and arranged themselves so that they spelled out "Santa Claus." One told about the life of Father Christmas, and a children's chorus sang "Jingle Bells" in English as they shook some tiny bells. The parents looked at one another in astonishment.

Mister Rosas went outside a moment. Superintendent Escalera spoke to the parents and children. He congratulated the district upon such a lovely Christmas party, and upon having such a progressive teacher as Mister Rosas. And then Mister Escalera asked the audience to be very quiet, because soon they were going to meet a strange and mysterious person.

A tiny chorus immediately burst into song:

Santa's coming in his sleigh,
Riding slowly all the way.
Clip, clop! Clip, clop!

Suddenly there appeared at the classroom door the figure of Santa Claus, carrying a pack over his shoulder. His deep voice boomed out in English: "Here is Santa! Merry Christmas to you all!"

A scream of terror shook the classroom. Some farmers threw themselves out the windows; the smallest children began to cry, and clung to their mothers' skirts as they fled in wild

---

4. **San Juan** (sän hwän′), the largest city and capital of Puerto Rico.
5. **Rogelio Escalera** (rō he′lyō es kä le′rä). *Escalera* in Spanish means "staircase."
6. **Benito** (be nē′tô).
7. **Simón** (sē môn′).

disorder. Everyone looked for a way to escape. Mister Rosas ran after them to explain that he was the one who had dressed up so strangely. But this only increased the screaming and made the panic worse. An old woman crossed herself and said:

"Heaven help us! It's the Devil himself talking American!"

The superintendent made useless efforts to calm the people and shouted:

"Don't run away! Don't act like a bunch of Puerto Rican hillbillies! Santa Claus is human, and a good man!"

In the distance the shouts of the fleeing people could be heard. Mister Escalera, observing that Peyo Mercé had been standing there unconcerned, vented all his anger upon him, and shouted at the top of his voice:

"It's your fault, Peyo Mercé, that such stupidity should exist here in the middle of the twentieth century!"

Peyo Mercé answered, without changing his expression:

"Mister Escalera, it is not my fault that Santa Claus is not listed among the Puerto Rican saints." □□

Discussion

1. This story involves a conflict between two theories of education—the traditional approach of Peyo Mercé and the progressive method favored by the superintendent. On which side does the author seem to be? Cite passages early in the story where the author's **tone** and **diction** indicate his attitude.

2. (a) Describe Peyo Mercé's attitude toward the new teacher, Johnny Rosas. **(b)** What is Peyo Mercé's opinion of the superintendent's accusation that he, Peyo, and his teaching are "backward"?

3. (a) Why is Peyo's portion of the Christmas festivity so much more successful than the second half? **(b)** Explain the reasons for the fear and astonishment of the spectators.

Abelardo Díaz Alfaro
1920 •

Abelardo Díaz Alfaro came to know the customs and problems of the Puerto Rican farmer well as a young social worker in the rural areas. He drew on these experiences for his first book, *Terrazo,* a series of sketches that won first prize from the Institute of Puerto Rican Literature in 1947. " 'Santo Clo' Comes to La Cuchilla" is from this collection.

Díaz Alfaro has claimed that the Spanish culture of Puerto Rico is in danger of extinction because of growing Americanization. In the past, compromises between the teaching of Spanish and of English in schools often meant that students learned both languages inadequately. Recently, however, the situation has improved because Spanish is used for most instruction while English is studied as a separate subject.

Díaz Alfaro has helped to preserve the Hispanic influence on the island by producing a radio series about the problems of the Puerto Rican farmer. He is also a frequent contributor to Puerto Rican magazines.

Isaac Asimov

The Singing Bell

Louis Peyton never discussed publicly the methods by which he had bested the police of Earth in a dozen duels of wits and bluff, with the psychoprobe always waiting and always foiled. He would have been foolish to do so, of course, but in his more complacent moments, he fondled the notion of leaving a testament to be opened only after his death, one in which his unbroken success could clearly be seen to be due to ability and not to luck.

In such a testament he would say, "No false pattern can be created to cover a crime without bearing upon it some trace of its creator. It is better, then, to seek in events some pattern that already exists and then adjust your actions to it."

It was with that principle in mind that Peyton planned the murder of Albert Cornwell.

Cornwell, that small-time retailer of stolen things, first approached Peyton at the latter's usual table-for-one at Grinnell's. Cornwell's blue suit seemed to have a special shine, his lined face a special grin, and his faded mustache a special bristle.

"Mr. Peyton," he said, greeting his future murderer with no fourth-dimensional qualm, "it is so nice to see you. I'd almost given up, sir, almost given up."

Peyton, who disliked being approached over his newspaper and dessert at Grinnell's, said, "If you have business with me, Cornwell, you know where you can reach me." Peyton was past forty and his hair was past its earlier blackness, but his back was rigid, his bearing youthful, his eyes dark, and his voice could cut the more sharply for long practice.

"Not for this, Mr. Peyton," said Cornwell, "not for this. I know of a cache, sir, a cache of . . . you know, sir." The forefinger of his right hand moved gently, as though it were a clapper striking invisible substance, and his left hand momentarily cupped his ear.

Peyton turned a page of the paper, still somewhat damp from its tele-dispenser, folded it flat and said, "Singing Bells?"

"Oh, hush, Mr. Peyton," said Cornwell in whispered agony.

Peyton said, "Come with me."

They walked through the park. It was another Peyton axiom that to be reasonably secret there was nothing like a low-voiced discussion out of doors.

Cornwell whispered, "A cache of Singing Bells; an accumulated cache of Singing Bells. Unpolished, but such beauties, Mr. Peyton."

"Have you seen them?"

"No, sir, but I have spoken with one who has. He had proofs enough to convince me. There is enough there to enable you and me to retire in affluence. In absolute affluence, sir."

"Who was this other man?"

A look of cunning lit Cornwell's face like a smoking torch, obscuring more than it showed and lending it a repulsive oiliness. "The man was a lunar grubstaker who had a method for locating the Bells in the crater sides. I don't know his method; he never told me that. But he has gathered dozens, hidden them on the Moon, and come to Earth to arrange the disposing of them."

"He died, I suppose?"

"Yes. A most shocking accident, Mr. Peyton. A fall from a height. Very sad. Of course, his activities on the Moon were quite illegal. The Dominion is very strict about unauthorized Bell-mining. So perhaps it was a judgment upon him after all . . . In any case, I have his map."

Peyton said, a look of calm indifference on his face, "I don't want any of the details of your little transaction. What I want to know is why you've come to me."

Cornwell said, "Well, now, there's enough for both of us, Mr. Peyton, and we can both do our bit. For my part, I know where the cache is located and I can get a spaceship. You . . ."

"Yes?"

"You can pilot a spaceship, and you have such excellent contacts for disposing of the Bells. It is a very fair division of labor, Mr. Peyton. Wouldn't you say so, now?"

Peyton considered the pattern of his life—the pattern that already existed—and matters seemed to fit.

He said, "We will leave for the Moon on August the tenth."

Cornwell stopped walking and said, "Mr. Peyton! It's only April now."

Peyton maintained an even gait and Cornwell had to hurry to catch up. "Do you hear me, Mr. Peyton?"

Peyton said, "August the tenth. I will get in touch with you at the proper time, tell you where to bring your ship. Make no attempt to see me personally till then. Good-bye, Cornwell."

Cornwell said, "Fifty-fifty?"

"Quite," said Peyton. "Good-bye."

Peyton continued his walk alone and considered the pattern of his life again. At the age of twenty-seven, he had bought a tract of land in the Rockies on which some past owner had built a house designed as refuge against the threatened atomic wars of two centuries back, the ones that had never come to pass after all. The house remained, however, a monument to a frightened drive for self-sufficiency.

It was of steel and concrete in as isolated a spot as could well be found on Earth, set high above sea level and protected on nearly all sides by mountain peaks that reached higher still. It had its self-contained power unit, its water supply fed by mountain streams, its freezers in which ten sides of beef could hang comfortably, its cellar outfitted like a fortress with an arsenal of weapons designed to stave off hungry, panicked hordes that never came. It had its air-conditioning unit that could scrub and scrub the air until anything *but* radioactivity (alas for human frailty) could be scrubbed out of it.

In that house of survival, Peyton passed the month of August every subsequent year of his perennially bachelor life. He took out the communicators, the television, the newspaper teledispenser. He built a force-field fence about his property and left a short-distance signal mechanism to the house from the point where the fence crossed the one trail winding through the mountains.

For one month each year, he could be thoroughly alone. No one saw him, no one could reach him. In absolute solitude, he could have the only vacation he valued after eleven months of contact with a humanity for which he could feel only a cold contempt.

Even the police—and Peyton smiled—knew of his rigid regard for August. He had once jumped bail and risked the psychoprobe rather than forgo his August.

Peyton considered another aphorism for possible inclusion in his testament: There is nothing so conducive to an appearance of innocence as the triumphant lack of an alibi.

On July 30, as on July 30 of every year, Louis Peyton took the 9:15 A.M. non-grav stratojet at New York and arrived in Denver at 12:30 P.M. There he lunched and took the 1:45 P.M. semi-grav bus to Hump's Point, from which Sam Leibman took him by ancient ground-car—full grav!—up the trail to the boundaries of his property. Sam Leibman gravely accepted the ten-dollar tip that he always received, touched his hat as he had done on July 30 for fifteen years.

On July 31, as on July 31 of every year, Louis Peyton returned to Hump's Point in his non-grav aeroflitter and placed an order through the Hump's Point general store for such supplies as he needed for the coming month. There was nothing unusual about the order. It was virtually the duplicate of previous such orders.

MacIntyre, manager of the store, checked gravely over the list, put it through to Central

Warehouse, Mountain District, in Denver, and the whole of it came pushing over the mass-transference beam within the hour. Peyton loaded the supplies onto his aeroflitter with MacIntyre's help, left his usual ten-dollar tip and returned to his house.

On August 1, at 12:01 A.M., the force field that surrounded his property was set to full power and Peyton was isolated.

And now the pattern changed. Deliberately he had left himself eight days. In that time he slowly and meticulously destroyed just enough of his supplies to account for all of August. He used the dusting chambers which served the house as a garbage-disposal unit. They were of an advanced model capable of reducing all matter up to and including metals and silicates to an impalpable and undetectable molecular dust. The excess energy formed in the process was carried away by the mountain stream that ran through his property. It ran five degrees warmer than normal for a week.

On August 9 his aeroflitter carried him to a spot in Wyoming where Albert Cornwell and a spaceship waited. The spaceship, itself, was a weak point, of course, since there were men who had sold it, men who had transported it and helped prepare it for flight. All those men, however, led only as far as Cornwell, and Cornwell, Peyton thought—with the trace of a smile on his cold lips—would be a dead end. A very dead end.

On August 10 the spaceship, with Peyton at the controls and Cornwell—and his map—as passenger, left the surface of Earth. Its non-grav field was excellent. At full power, the ship's weight was reduced to less than an ounce. The micropiles fed energy efficiently and noiselessly, and without flame or sound the ship rose through the atmosphere, shrank to a point, and was gone.

It was very unlikely that there would be witnesses to the flight, or that in these weak, piping times of peace there would be a radar watch as in days of yore. In point of fact, there was none.

Two days in space; now two weeks on the Moon. Almost instinctively Peyton had allowed for those two weeks from the first. He was under no illusions as to the value of homemade maps by non-cartographers. Useful they might be to the designer himself, who had the help of memory. To a stranger, they could be nothing more than a cryptogram.[1]

Cornwell showed Peyton the map for the first time only after takeoff. He smiled obsequiously. "After all, sir, this was my only trump."

"Have you checked this against the lunar charts?"

"I would scarcely know how, Mr. Peyton. I depend upon you."

Peyton stared at him coldly as he returned the map. The one certain thing upon it was Tycho Crater, the site of the buried Luna City.

In one respect, at least, astronomy was on their side. Tycho was on the daylight side of the Moon at the moment. It meant that patrol ships were less likely to be out, they themselves less likely to be observed.

Peyton brought the ship down in a riskily quick non-grav landing within the safe, cold darkness of the inner shadow of a crater. The sun was past zenith and the shadow would grow no shorter.

Cornwell drew a long face. "Dear, dear, Mr. Peyton. We can scarcely go prospecting in the lunar day."

"The lunar day doesn't last forever," said Peyton shortly. "There are about a hundred hours of sun left. We can use that time for acclimating ourselves and for working out the map."

The answer came quickly, but it was plural. Peyton studied the lunar charts over and over, taking meticulous measurements, and trying to find the pattern of craters shown on the homemade scrawl that was the key to—what?

Finally Peyton said, "The crater we want could be any one of three: GC-3, GC-5, or MT-10."

"What do we do, Mr. Peyton?" asked Cornwell anxiously.

"We try them all," said Peyton, "beginning with the nearest."

The terminator[2] passed and they were in the night shadow. After that, they spent increasing periods on the lunar surface, getting used to the eternal silence and blackness, the harsh points of the stars and the crack of light that was the Earth peeping over the rim of the crater above. They left hollow, featureless footprints in the dry dust

that did not stir or change. Peyton noted them first when they climbed out of the crater into the full light of the gibbous[3] Earth. That was on the eighth day after their arrival on the moon.

The lunar cold put a limit to how long they could remain outside their ship at any one time. Each day, however, they managed for longer. By the eleventh day after arrival they had eliminated GC-5 as the container of the Singing Bells.

By the fifteenth day, Peyton's cold spirit had grown warm with desperation. It would have to be GC-3. MT-10 was too far away. They would not have time to reach it and explore it and still allow for a return to Earth by August 31.

On that same fifteenth day, however, despair was laid to rest forever when they discovered the Bells.

They were not beautiful. They were merely irregular masses of gray rock, as large as a double fist, vacuum-filled and feather-light in the moon's gravity. There were two dozen of them and each one, after proper polishing, could be sold for a hundred thousand dollars at least.

Carefully, in double handfuls, they carried the Bells to the ship, bedded them in excelsior, and returned for more. Three times they made the trip both ways over ground that would have worn them out on Earth but which, under the Moon's lilliputian[4] gravity, was scarcely a barrier.

Cornwell passed the last of the Bells up to Peyton, who placed them carefully within the outer lock.

"Keep them clear, Mr. Peyton," he said, his radioed voice sounding harshly in the other's ear. "I'm coming up."

He crouched for the slow high leap against lunar gravity, looked up, and froze in panic. His face, clearly visible through the hard carved lusilite of his helmet, froze in a last grimace of terror. "No, Mr. Peyton. Don't—"

Peyton's fist tightened on the grip of the blaster he held. It fired. There was an unbearably brilliant flash and Cornwell was a dead fragment

---

1. *cryptogram* (krip′tə gram), writing in code.
2. *terminator*, the borderline between the day and night sides of a planet or moon.
3. *gibbous* (gib′əs), shining between half-full and full.
4. *lilliputian* (li′li pü′shən), very small. The Lilliputians were tiny people in the novel *Gulliver's Travels* by Jonathan Swift (1667–1745).

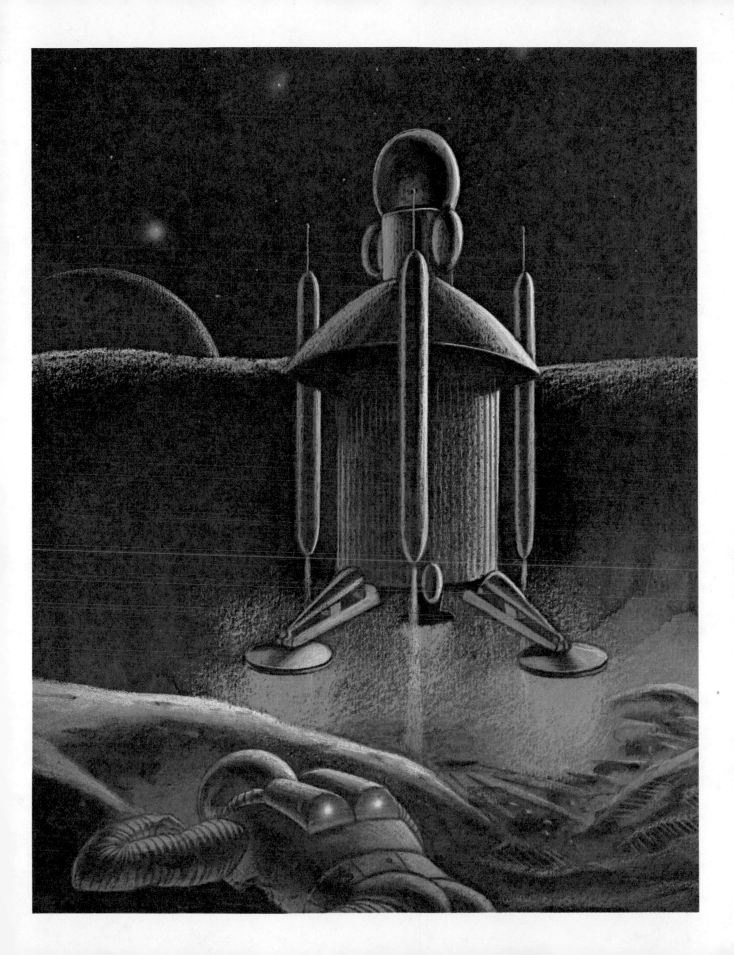

of a man, sprawled amid remnants of a spacesuit and flecked with freezing blood.

Peyton paused to stare somberly at the dead man, but only for a second. Then he transferred the last of the Bells to their prepared containers, removed his suit, activated first the non-grav field, then the micropiles, and, potentially a million or two richer than he had been two weeks earlier, set off on the return trip to Earth.

On the twenty-ninth of August, Peyton's ship descended silently, stern bottomward, to the spot in Wyoming from which it had taken off on August 10. The care with which Peyton had chosen the spot was not wasted. His aeroflitter was still there, drawn within the protection of an enclosing wrinkle of the rocky, tortuous countryside.

He moved the Singing Bells once again, in their containers, into the deepest recess of the wrinkle, covering them, loosely and sparsely, with earth. He returned to the ship once more to set the controls and make last adjustments. He climbed out again and two minutes later the ship's automatics took over.

Silently hurrying, the ship bounded upward and up, veering to westward somewhat as the Earth rotated beneath it. Peyton watched, shading his narrow eyes, and at the extreme edge of vision there was a tiny gleam of light and a dot of cloud against the blue sky.

Peyton's mouth twitched into a smile. He had judged well. With the cadmium safety-rods bent back into uselessness, the micropiles had plunged past the unit-sustaining safety level and the ship had vanished in the heat of the nuclear explosion that had followed.

Twenty minutes later, he was back on his property. He was tired and his muscles ached under Earth's gravity. He slept well.

Twelve hours later, in the earliest dawn, the police came.

The man who opened the door placed his crossed hands over his paunch and ducked his smiling head two or three times in greeting. The man who entered, H. Seton Davenport of the Terrestrial Bureau of Investigation, looked about uncomfortably.

The room he had entered was large and in semidarkness except for the brilliant viewing lamp focused over a combination armchair-desk. Rows of book-films covered the walls. A suspension of Galactic charts occupied one corner of the room and a Galactic Lens gleamed softly on a stand in another corner.

"You are Dr. Wendell Urth?" asked Davenport, in a tone that suggested he found it hard to believe. Davenport was a stocky man with black hair, a thin and prominent nose, and a star-shaped scar on one cheek which marked permanently the place where a neuronic whip had once struck him at too close a range.

"I am," said Dr. Urth in a thin, tenor voice. "And you are Inspector Davenport."

The Inspector presented his credentials and said, "The University recommended you to me as an extraterrologist."

"So you said when you called me half an hour ago," said Urth agreeably. His features were thick, his nose was a snubby button, and over his somewhat protuberant eyes there were thick glasses.

"I shall get to the point, Dr. Urth. I presume you have visited the Moon . . ."

Dr. Urth, who had brought out a bottle of ruddy liquid and two glasses, just a little the worse for dust, from behind a straggling pile of book-films, said with sudden brusqueness, "I have never visited the Moon, Inspector. I never intend to! Space travel is foolishness. I don't believe in it." Then, in softer tones, "Sit down, sir, sit down. Have a drink."

Inspector Davenport did as he was told and said, "But you're an. . . ."

"Extraterrologist. Yes. I'm interested in other worlds, but it doesn't mean I have to go there. I don't have to be a time traveler to qualify as a historian, do I?" He sat down, and a broad smile impressed itself upon his round face once more as he said, "Now tell me what's on your mind."

"I have come," said the Inspector, frowning, "to consult you in a case of murder."

"Murder? What have I to do with murder?"

"This murder, Dr. Urth, was on the Moon."

"Astonishing."

"It's more than astonishing. It's unprecedented, Dr. Urth. In the fifty years since the Lunar Dominion has been established, ships have blown up and spacesuits have sprung leaks. Men have boiled to death on sun-side, frozen on dark-side, and suffocated on both sides. There have even been deaths by falls, which, considering lunar gravity, is quite a trick. But in all that time, not one man has been killed on the Moon as the result of another man's deliberate act of violence—till now."

Dr. Urth said, "How was it done?"

"A blaster. The authorities were on the scene within the hour through a fortunate set of circumstances. A patrol ship observed a flash of light against the Moon's surface. You know how far a flash can be seen against the night-side. The pilot notified Luna City and landed. In the process of circling back, he swears that he just managed to see by Earthlight what looked like a ship taking off. Upon landing, he discovered a blasted corpse and footprints."

"The flash of light," said Dr. Urth, "you suppose to be the firing blaster."

"That's certain. The corpse was fresh. Interior portions of the body had not yet frozen. The footprints belonged to two people. Careful measurements showed that the depressions fell into two groups of somewhat different diameters, indicating differently sized spaceboots. In the main, they led to craters GC-3 and GC-5, a pair of—"

"I am acquainted with the official code for naming lunar craters," said Dr. Urth pleasantly.

"Umm. In any case, GC-3 contained footprints that led to a rift in the crater wall, within which scraps of hardened pumice were found. X-ray diffraction patterns showed—"

"Singing Bells," put in the extraterrologist in great excitement. "Don't tell me this murder of yours involves Singing Bells!"

"What if it does?" demanded Davenport blankly.

"I have one. A University expedition uncovered it and presented it to me in return for— Come, Inspector, I must show it to you."

Dr. Urth jumped up and pattered across the room, beckoning the other to follow as he did. Davenport, annoyed, followed.

They entered a second room, larger than the first, dimmer, considerably more cluttered. Davenport stared with astonishment at the heterogeneous mass of material that was jumbled together in no pretense at order.

He made out a small lump of "blue glaze" from Mars, the sort of thing some romantics considered to be an artifact of long-extinct Martians, a small meteorite, a model of an early spaceship, a sealed bottle of nothing scrawlingly labeled "Venusian atmosphere."

Dr. Urth said happily, "I've made a museum of my whole house. It's one of the advantages of being a bachelor. Of course, I haven't quite got things organized. Someday, when I have a spare week or so. . . ."

For a moment he looked about, puzzled; then, remembering, he pushed aside a chart showing the evolutionary scheme of development of the marine invertebrates that were the highest life forms on Barnard's Planet and said, "Here it is. It's flawed, I'm afraid."

The Bell hung suspended from a slender wire, soldered delicately onto it. That it was flawed was obvious. It had a constriction line running halfway about it that made it seem like two small globes, firmly but imperfectly squashed together. Despite that, it had been lovingly polished to a dull luster, softly gray, velvety smooth, and faintly pock-marked in a way that laboratories, in their futile efforts to prepare synthetic Bells, had found impossible to duplicate.

Dr. Urth said, "I experimented a good deal before I found a decent stroker. A flawed Bell is temperamental. But bone works. I have one here"—and he held up something that looked like a short thick spoon made of a gray-white substance—"which I had made out of the femur of an ox. Listen."

With surprising delicacy, his pudgy fingers maneuvered the Bell, feeling for one best spot. He adjusted it, steadying it daintily. Then, letting the Bell swing free, he brought down the thick end of the bone spoon and stroked the Bell softly.

It was as though a million harps had sounded a mile away. It swelled and faded and returned. It came from no particular direction. It sounded inside the head, incredibly sweet and pathetic and tremulous all at once.

It died away lingeringly and both men were silent for a full minute.

Dr. Urth said, "Not bad, eh?" and with a flick of his hand set the Bell to swinging on its wire.

Davenport stirred restlessly. "Careful! Don't break it." The fragility of a good Singing Bell was proverbial.

Dr. Urth said, "Geologists say the Bells are only pressure-hardened pumice, enclosing a vacuum in which small beads of rock rattle freely. That's what they *say*. But if that's all it is, why can't we reproduce one? Now a flawless Bell would make this one sound like a child's harmonica."

"Exactly," said Davenport, "and there aren't a dozen people on Earth who own a flawless one, and there are a hundred people and institutions who would buy one at any price, no questions asked. A supply of Bells would be worth murder."

The extraterrologist turned to Davenport and pushed his spectacles back on his inconsequential nose with a stubby forefinger. "I haven't forgotten your murder case. Please go on."

"That can be done in a sentence. I know the identity of the murderer."

They had returned to the chairs in the library and Dr. Urth clasped his hands over his ample abdomen. "Indeed? Then surely you have no problem, Inspector."

"Knowing and proving are not the same, Dr. Urth. Unfortunately he has no alibi."

"You mean, unfortunately he *has*, don't you?"

"I mean what I say. If he had an alibi, I could crack it somehow, because it would be a false one. If there were witnesses who claimed they had seen him on Earth at the time of the murder, their stories could be broken down. If he had documentary proof, it could be exposed as a forgery or some sort of trickery. Unfortunately he has none of it."

"What does he have?"

Carefully Inspector Davenport described the Peyton estate in Colorado. He concluded, "He has spent every August there in the strictest isolation. Even the T.B.I. would have to testify to that. Any jury would have to presume that he was on his estate this August as well, unless we could present definite proof that he was on the Moon."

"What makes you think he *was* on the Moon? Perhaps he is innocent."

"No!" Davenport was almost violent. "For

fifteen years I've been trying to collect sufficient evidence against him and I've never succeeded. But I can *smell* a Peyton crime now. I tell you that no one but Peyton, no one on Earth, would have the impudence or, for that matter, the practical business contacts to attempt disposal of smuggled Singing Bells. He is known to be an expert space pilot. He is known to have had contact with the murdered man, though admittedly not for some months. Unfortunately none of that is proof."

Dr. Urth said, "Wouldn't it be simple to use the psychoprobe, now that its use has been legalized?"

Davenport scowled, and the scar on his cheek turned livid. "Have you read the Konski-Hiakawa law, Dr. Urth?"

"No."

"I think no one has. The right to mental privacy, the government says, is fundamental. All right, but what follows? The man who is psychoprobed and proves innocent of the crime for which he was psychoprobed is entitled to as much compensation as he can persuade the courts to give him. In a recent case a bank cashier was awarded twenty-five thousand dollars for having been psychoprobed on inaccurate suspicion of theft. It seems that the circumstantial evidence which seemed to point to theft actually pointed to a small spot of adultery. His claim that he lost his job, was threatened by the husband in question and put in bodily fear, and finally was held up to ridicule and contumely because a news-strip man had learned the results of the probe held good in court."

"I can see the man's point."

"So can we all. That's the trouble. One more item to remember: Any man who has been psychoprobed once for any reason can never be psychoprobed again for any reason. No one man, the law says, shall be placed in mental jeopardy twice in his lifetime."

"Inconvenient."

"Exactly. In the two years since the psychoprobe has been legitimized, I couldn't count the number of crooks and chiselers who've tried to get themselves psychoprobed for purse-snatching so that they could play the rackets safely afterward. So you see the Department will not allow Peyton to be psychoprobed until they have firm evidence of his guilt. Not legal evidence, maybe, but evidence that is strong enough to convince my boss. The worst of it, Dr. Urth, is that if we come into court without a psychoprobe record, we can't win. In a case as serious as murder, not to have used the psychoprobe is proof enough to the dumbest juror that the prosecution isn't sure of its ground."

"Now what do you want of me?"

"Proof that he was on the Moon sometime in August. It's got to be done quickly. I can't hold him on suspicion much longer. And if news of the murder gets out, the world press will blow up like an asteroid striking Jupiter's atmosphere. A glamorous crime, you know—first murder on the Moon."

"Exactly when was the murder committed?" asked Urth, in a sudden transition to brisk cross-examination.

"August twenty-seventh."

"And the arrest was made when?"

"Yesterday, August thirtieth."

"Then if Peyton were the murderer, he would have had time to return to Earth."

"Barely. Just barely." Davenport's lips thinned. "If I had been a day sooner—If I had found his place empty—"

"And how long do you suppose the two, the murdered man and the murderer, were on the Moon altogether?"

"Judging by the ground covered by the footprints, a number of days. A week, at the minimum."

"Has the ship they used been located?"

"No, and it probably never will. About ten hours ago, the University of Denver reported a rise in background radioactivity beginning day before yesterday at 6 P.M. and persisting for a number of hours. It's an easy thing, Dr. Urth, to set a ship's controls so as to allow it to blast off without crew and blow up, fifty miles high, in a micropile short."

"If I had been Peyton," said Dr. Urth thoughtfully, "I would have killed the man on board ship and blown up corpse and ship together."

"You don't know Peyton," said Davenport grimly. "He enjoys his victories over the law. He values them. Leaving the corpse on the Moon is his challenge to us."

"I see." Dr. Urth patted his stomach with a rotary motion and said, "Well, there is a chance."

"That you'll be able to prove he was on the Moon?"

"That I'll be able to give you my opinion."

"Now?"

"The sooner the better. If, of course, I get a chance to interview Mr. Peyton."

"That can be arranged. I have a non-grav jet waiting. We can be in Washington in twenty minutes."

But a look of the deepest alarm passed over the plump extraterrologist's face. He rose to his feet and pattered away from the T.B.I. agent toward the duskiest corner of the cluttered room.

"No!"

"What's wrong, Dr. Urth?"

"I won't use a non-grav jet. I don't believe in them."

Davenport stared confusedly at Dr. Urth. He stammered, "Would you prefer a monorail?"

Dr. Urth snapped, "I mistrust all forms of transportation. I don't believe in them. Except walking. I don't mind walking." He was suddenly eager. "Couldn't you bring Mr. Peyton to this city, somewhere within walking distance? To City Hall, perhaps? I've often walked to City Hall."

Davenport looked helplessly about the room. He looked at the myriad volumes of lore about the light-years. He could see through the open door into the room beyond, with its tokens of the worlds beyond the sky. And he looked at Dr. Urth, pale at the thought of non-grav jet, and shrugged his shoulders.

"I'll bring Peyton here. Right to this room. Will that satisfy you?"

Dr. Urth puffed out his breath in a deep sigh. "Quite."

"I hope you can deliver, Dr. Urth."

"I will do my best, Mr. Davenport."

Louis Peyton stared with distaste at his surroundings and with contempt at the fat man who bobbed his head in greeting. He glanced at the seat offered him and brushed it with his hand before sitting down. Davenport took a seat next to him, with his blaster holster in clear view.

The fat man was smiling as he sat down and

patted his round abdomen as though he had just finished a good meal and were intent on letting the world know about it.

He said, "Good evening, Mr. Peyton. I am Dr. Wendell Urth, extraterrologist."

Peyton looked at him again, "And what do you want with me?"

"I want to know if you were on the Moon at any time in the month of August."

"I was not."

"Yet no man saw you on Earth between the days of August first and August thirtieth."

"I lived my normal life in August. I am never seen during that month. Let him tell you." And he jerked his head in the direction of Davenport.

Dr. Urth chuckled. "How nice if we could test this matter. If there were only some physical manner in which we could differentiate Moon from Earth. If, for instance, we could analyze the dust in your hair and say, 'Aha, Moon rock.' Unfortunately we can't. Moon rock is much the same as Earth rock. Even if it weren't, there wouldn't be any in your hair unless you stepped onto the lunar surface without a spacesuit, which is unlikely."

Peyton remained impassive.

Dr. Urth went on, smiling benevolently, and lifting a hand to steady the glasses perched precariously on the bulb of his nose. "A man traveling in space or on the Moon breathes Earth air, eats Earth food. He carries Earth environment next to his skin whether he's in his ship or in his spacesuit. We are looking for a man who spent two days in space going to the Moon, at least a week on the Moon, and two days coming back from the Moon. In all that time he carried Earth next to his skin, which makes it difficult."

"I'd suggest," said Peyton, "that you can make it less difficult by releasing me and looking for the real murderer."

"It may come to that," said Dr. Urth. "Have you ever seen anything like this?" His hand pushed its pudgy way to the ground beside his chair and came up with a gray sphere that sent back subdued highlights.

Peyton smiled. "It looks like a Singing Bell to me."

"It *is* a Singing Bell. The murder was committed for the sake of Singing Bells. What do you think of this one?"

"I think it is badly flawed."

"Ah, but inspect it," said Dr. Urth, and with a quick motion of his hand, he tossed it through six feet of air to Peyton.

Davenport cried out and half-rose from his chair. Peyton brought up his arms with an effort, but so quickly that he managed to catch the Bell.

Peyton said, "You fool. Don't throw it around that way."

"You respect Singing Bells, do you?"

"Too much to break one. That's no crime, at least." Peyton stroked the Bell gently, then lifted it to his ear and shook it slowly, listening to the soft clicks of the Lunoliths, those small pumice particles, as they rattled in vacuum.

Then, holding the Bell up by the length of steel wire still attached to it, he ran a thumbnail over its surface with an expert, curving motion. It twanged! The note was very mellow, very flutelike, holding with a slight *vibrato* that faded lingeringly and conjured up pictures of a summer twilight.

For a short moment, all three men were lost in the sound.

And then Dr. Urth said, "Throw it back, Mr. Peyton. Toss it here!" and held out his hand in peremptory gesture.

Automatically Louis Peyton tossed the Bell. It traveled its short arc one-third of the way to Dr. Urth's waiting hand, curved downward and shattered with a heartbroken, sighing discord on the floor.

Davenport and Peyton stared at the gray slivers with equal wordlessness and Dr. Urth's calm voice went almost unheard as he said, "When the criminal's cache of crude Bells is located, I'll ask that a flawless one, properly polished, be given to me, as replacement and fee."

"A fee? For what?" demanded Davenport irritably.

"Surely the matter is now obvious. Despite my little speech of a moment ago, there is one piece of Earth's environment that no space traveler carries with him and that is *Earth's surface gravity*. The fact that Mr. Peyton could so egregiously misjudge the toss of an object he obviously valued so highly could mean only that his muscles are not yet readjusted to the pull of Earthly gravity. It is my professional opinion,

Mr. Davenport, that your prisoner has, in the last few days, been away from Earth. He has either been in space or on some planetary object considerably smaller in size than the Earth—as, for example, the Moon."

Davenport rose triumphantly to his feet. "Let me have your opinion in writing," he said, hand on blaster, "and that will be good enough to get me permission to use a psychoprobe."

Louis Peyton, dazed and unresisting, had only the numb realization that any testament he could now leave would have to include the fact of ultimate failure. ☐☐

Discussion

1. (a) Describe the main character traits of both Lewis Peyton and Dr. Urth. Cite passages in which they reveal these traits. (b) Do these characters seem to you to be "real" individuals or **stereotypes**? Explain.

2. (a) What technical advances are described that establish the time as the future? (b) Name some features of the story that seem contemporary rather than futuristic.

3. (a) Explain Inspector Davenport's statement that the problem is that Peyton does *not* have an alibi. (b) Why is the Inspector unwilling to use the psychoprobe on Peyton?

4. (a) What character trait of Peyton's leads to his defeat? (b) How is he finally trapped? Explain Dr. Urth's reasoning.

5. A reader of this story demonstrated that people threw objects of identical size but different weights nearly the same distance. Asimov replied that a person unconsciously judges an object's weight before throwing it, but that moving between different gravity fields, as Peyton did, might confuse someone's judgment of weight. Do you think Dr. Urth's argument is disproved or not? Consider reports of astronauts' reactions after returning from low gravity.

Extension • Speaking

Read some famous detective or spy stories. Half of the class might report on the peculiarities of the villains, such as Sherlock Holmes's archenemy, Dr. Moriarty, or James Bond's foes, Dr. No and Ernst Stavro Blofeld. The other half of the class should report on an eccentric detective like Dr. Urth. Some renowned fictional sleuths are Dorothy Sayers's Lord Peter Wimsey, Rex Stout's Nero Wolfe, and Agatha Christie's Miss Marple and Hercule Poirot.

Isaac Asimov 1920 •

Asimov was born in Russia and was brought to the United States when he was three. Having taught himself to read by age five, he began reading everything he could get his hands on. He entered Columbia University at fifteen and eventually received a doctorate in enzyme chemistry.

In 1977 Asimov calculated that he had produced 188 books and over 1000 magazine and newspaper articles. He publishes about twelve books and forty articles a year. The breadth of his interests is shown by his commentaries on Shakespeare, Milton, Byron, and the Bible, as well as by writings in more than twenty different scientific fields.

Among Asimov's outstanding contributions to science fiction are the three *Foundation* novels, the *I, Robot* series, and the novel *The Gods Themselves*, which in 1972 won both a Hugo and a Nebula, science fiction's highest awards. Asimov invented the science-fiction mystery. His armchair detective Dr. Wendell Urth, an eccentric like Sherlock Holmes, has been said to resemble in some ways the author himself.

8: New Frontiers

CONTENT REVIEW

1. To what extent are personal **themes** really characteristic of recent American literature? In what ways are writers trying to get readers closely involved with their subjects? Choose one selection from each **genre** in Unit 8 and discuss the personal elements of theme and **tone** in those works. You might consider, for example, the self-analysis of Baldwin's *Notes of a Native Son*, the sense of closeness with readers in Levertov's "The Secret," or the way that Vonnegut's **narrator** in "The Hyannis Port Story" seems to be "talking out" his yarn.

2. One recent development in poetry might be called the "process poem"—a poem that freely follows the **mood** of an experience as the poet recreates it. In what ways might the following poems fit this description: "This Is the Land" by Cortez? "Night Journey" by Roethke? "My Father and Myself Facing the Sun" by Inada? "Jugábamos/We Played" by Villanueva? For fuller discussion of "process poetry," see page 589.

3. Discuss the various ways in which many poets have departed from the doctrine set forth in "Ars Poetica" by MacLeish: "A poem must not mean/ but be" (page 441). Some of the poems you might consider are: Wagoner's "Breaking Camp," Miller's "Gift from Kenya," Wilbur's "The Writer," Soto's "History," and Shapiro's "Auto Wreck."

4. Nearly all humor involves some degree of **satire**, but the tone of such satire may range from almost affectionate teasing to harsh mockery. What personality types, attitudes, or institutions are satirized in "The Hyannis Port Story," "Engineer-Private Paul Klee. . . ," "Teenage Diseases," and " 'Santa Clo' Comes to La Cuchilla"? What writing techniques—for example, **irony**, exaggeration, caricature—are used in each work to make the targets of satire seem ridiculous? How would you describe the tone of each selection?

5. Cite some works—stories, poems, and factual prose—which focus on the importance of tradition, as does Momaday's "The Gourd Dancer." Choose one selection of each genre to discuss in class and compare the views of the past presented in these works. In what ways do they suggest the value of maintaining links with one's personal and/or ancestral past?

6. Describe the relationships between young and old or parent and child in "El Mago," "In Search of Our Mothers' Gardens," "Preface to a Twenty-Volume Suicide Note," "The Writer," "Marigolds," and "When the Bough Breaks." Choose three of these works and discuss the value of the experience described to either the older or the younger person involved.

The test for this unit requires that you read two selections.
The subject of the first selection is a state of mind with which
most people are familiar, loneliness.

The second selection contains observations about the world of
nature.

On your paper write the letter of the best answer for each
number.

Song

Adrienne Rich

You're wondering if I'm lonely:
OK then, yes, I'm lonely
as a plane rides lonely and level
on its radio beam, aiming
5 across the Rockies
for the blue-strung aisle
of an airfield on the ocean

You want to ask, am I lonely?
Well, of course, lonely
10 as a woman driving across country
day after day, leaving behind
mile after mile
little towns she might have stopped
and lived and died in, lonely

15 If I'm lonely
it must be the loneliness
of waking first, of breathing

Jonathan Rawle/Stock, Boston, Inc.

dawn's first cold breath on the city
of being the one awake
20 in a house wrapped in sleep

If I'm lonely
it's with the rowboat ice-fast on the shore
in the last red light of the year
that knows what it is, that knows it's neither
25 ice nor mud nor winter light
but wood, with a gift for burning

1. The phrase "I'm lonely/as a plane rides lonely" contains an example of (a) a metaphor; (b) a simile; (c) hyperbole; (d) personification.

2. The poet's tone when she says "OK then, yes, I'm lonely" is best described as (a) horrified; (b) angry; (c) resigned; (d) contented.

3. Line 3 contains an example of (a) alliteration; (b) assonance; (c) rhyme; (d) onomatopoeia.

4. Lines 6–7 contain a pun on which word? (a) *isle;* (b) *blew;* (c) *four;* (d) *stunned.*

5. The repetition of "day" and "mile" in the second stanza creates the impression of (a) excitement; (b) mystery; (c) boredom; (d) distance.

6. In the third stanza the dawn is compared to (a) a cocoon; (b) a house; (c) the city; (d) a person.

7. In stanza four, which object is personified? (a) the red light; (b) the rowboat; (c) mud; (d) ice.

8. Which image appears in both of the last two stanzas? (a) cold; (b) sleep; (c) heat; (d) dawn.

9. What is the best paraphrase of the last stanza? (a) Loneliness has driven me to despair; (b) though I appear to be stuck in one place, I have actually continued to develop; (c) though I appear to be lonely, I have actually merged with those around me; (d) I am aware of my identity and have the potential for self-fulfillment.

10. In each stanza the poet uses one central image to describe herself. In order, these images are (a) a radio beam, a little town, a city, wood; (b) an airfield, a little town, a house, winter; (c) a plane, a woman driving, a person waking up, a rowboat; (d) the ocean, miles, cold breaths, a red light.

11. Which technique helps draw this poem together? (a) the use of rhyme; (b) the repetition of certain words and phrases; (c) the use of the same alliterative sounds in the first line of each stanza; (d) the mention of the same color in all four stanzas.

12. The poet's purpose is to (a) analyze the causes of and solutions for loneliness; (b) depress the reader; (c) criticize society for allowing people to be lonely; (d) define loneliness and express her love of it through concrete images.

from Pilgrim at Tinker Creek

Annie Dillard

Once, when I was ten or eleven years old, my friend Judy brought in a Polyphemus moth[1] cocoon. It was January; there were doily snowflakes taped to the schoolroom panes. The teacher kept the cocoon in her desk all morning and brought it out when we were getting restless before recess. In a book we found what the adult moth would look like; it would be beautiful. With a wingspread of up to six inches, the Polyphemus is one of the few huge American silk moths, much larger than, say, a giant or tiger swallowtail butterfly. The moth's enormous wings are velveted in a rich, warm brown, and edged in bands of blue and pink delicate as a watercolor wash. A startling "eyespot," immense, and deep blue melding[2] to an almost translucent yellow, luxuriates in the center of each hind wing. The effect is one of a masculine splendor foreign to the butterflies, a fragility unfurled to strength. The Polyphemus moth in the picture looked like a mighty wraith,[3] a beating essence[4] of the hardwood forest, alien-skinned and brown, with spread, blind eyes. This was the giant moth packed in the faded cocoon. We closed the book and turned to the cocoon. It was an oak leaf sewn into a plump oval bundle; Judy had found it loose in a pile of frozen leaves.

We passed the cocoon around; it was heavy. As we held it in our hands, the creature within warmed and squirmed. We were delighted, and wrapped it tighter in our fists. The pupa[5] began to jerk violently, in heart-stopping knocks. Who's there? I can still feel those thumps, urgent through a muffling of spun silk and leaf, urgent through the swaddling of many years, against the curve of my palm. We kept passing it around. When it came to me again it was hot as a bun; it jumped half out of my hand. The teacher intervened. She put it, still heaving and banging, in the ubiquitous[6] Mason jar.

It was coming. There was no stopping it now, January or not. One end of the cocoon dampened and gradually frayed in a furious battle. The whole cocoon twisted and slapped around in the bottom of the jar. The teacher fades, the classmates fade, I fade: I don't remember anything but that thing's struggle to be a moth or die trying. It emerged at last, a sodden crumple. It was a male; his long antennae were thickly plumed, as wide as his fat abdomen. His body was very thick, over an inch long, and deeply furred. A gray, furlike plush covered his head; a long, tan furlike hair hung from his wide thorax[7] over his brown-furred, segmented abdomen. His multijointed legs, pale and powerful, were shaggy as a bear's. He stood still, but he breathed.

He couldn't spread his wings. There was no room. The chemi-

1. *Polyphemus* (pol′ə fē′məs) *moth,* a large moth usually having a buff or pink color.

2. *melding,* merging.

3. *wraith* (rāth), a specter or ghost

4. *essence,* a necessary part.

5. *pupa* (pyü′pə), the stage between larva and adult.

6. *ubiquitous* (yü bik′wə təs), located everywhere.

7. *thorax,* the part of the body between the head and the abdomen.

cal that coated his wings like varnish, stiffening them permanently, dried, and hardened his wings as they were. He was a monster in a Mason jar. Those huge wings stuck on his back in a torture of random pleats and folds, wrinkled as a dirty tissue, rigid as leather. They made a single nightmare clump still wracked with useless, frantic convulsions.

The next thing I remember, it was recess. The school was in Shadyside, a busy residential part of Pittsburgh. Everyone was playing dodgeball in the fenced playground or racing around the concrete schoolyard by the swings. Next to the playground a long delivery drive sloped downhill to the sidewalk and street. Someone—it must have been the teacher—had let the moth out. I was standing in the driveway, alone, stock-still, but shivering. Someone had given the Polyphemus moth his freedom, and he was walking away.

He heaved himself down the asphalt driveway by infinite degrees, unwavering. His hideous crumpled wings lay glued and rucked[8] on his back, perfectly still now, like a collapsed tent. The bell rang twice; I had to go. The moth was receding down the driveway, dragging on. I went; I ran inside. The Polyphemus moth is still crawling down the driveway, crawling down the driveway hunched, crawling down the driveway on six furred feet, forever.

8. *rucked,* wrinkled.

13. The two impressions of the moth created by the details in the first paragraph are **(a)** dullness and femininity; **(b)** strength and delicacy; **(c)** beauty and impracticality; **(d)** strength and fearsomeness.

14. Which phrase contains a metaphor? **(a)** "delicate as a watercolor wash"; **(b)** "moth in the picture looked like a mighty wraith"; **(c)** "wings are velveted in a rich, warm brown"; **(d)** "with a wingspread of up to six inches."

15. Which detail in the second paragraph does *not* help to create the impression of the stirring of invisible life? **(a)** "creature within warmed and squirmed"; **(b)** "heart-stopping knocks"; **(c)** "hot as a bun"; **(d)** "it was heavy."

16. When the author says in the third paragraph that "The teacher fades, the classmates fade, I fade," she is implying that **(a)** the cocoon's struggle is more vivid to her than the surroundings are; **(b)** she faints; **(c)** she is slipping from reality into a world of illusion; **(d)** everyone leaves her alone because they see how fascinated she is.

17. Which word best describes the appearance of the moth in paragraph four? **(a)** proud; **(b)** untamed; **(c)** grotesque; **(d)** ferocious.

18. The author's own emotional reaction to the sight of the moth is implied in which phrase from paragraph five? **(a)** "it was recess"; **(b)** "Someone . . . had let the moth out"; **(c)** "I was standing in the driveway, . . . shivering"; **(d)** "he was walking away."

19. The meaning of the last sentence of the selection is that **(a)** the moth went so slowly that it is probably still walking down that same driveway; **(b)** the driveway to the school was very long; **(c)** the scene repeats itself over and over throughout nature; **(d)** the author has never been able to erase the memory of the moth's difficult progress down the driveway.

20. The author's attitude toward the moth is one of **(a)** apathy; **(b)** interest; **(c)** pity; **(d)** awe.

21. Do you think that the author blames her teacher for putting the moth into a Mason jar and crippling it? Write a paragraph supporting your answer.

Choose one of the following topics for a composition.

1. The passage from innocence to experience that is associated with maturing is treated in several of the stories in this unit.

Suppose you are the main character in one of these stories. Write to another character in that story and analyze how the experience you went through has matured you. What were you like before the experience? After? How do you define maturity?

2. Varieties of the American ethnic experience are reflected in several of the selections in this unit, including "from *Notes of a Native Son*," "In Search of Our Mothers' Gardens," "Fresno, California," "El Mago," "Marigolds," and "Scent of Apples." As the narrator of a television documentary, you must give an introduction that examines what it means to be a member of an ethnic group in the United States. Base your observations on two or three of the selections mentioned above.

What characteristics of ethnic life are presented in each selection? What are the unique problems of ethnic people in America? What are the sources of pride?

Feel free to refer to your own experiences as well as to those presented in the selections.

3. In "Night Journey" and several other poems in Unit 8, the land, or an outdoor setting, is important in developing the theme. Suppose you are writing an article for an ecology or conservation magazine, in which you are to compare the various ways in which contemporary poets use natural settings. As specific examples for your article, choose three nature poems from this unit, each by a different poet.

In writing about each poem, ask yourself which characteristics of the setting are emphasized? What is the relationship between the poet and this setting? To what symbolic or metaphorical use does the poet put this environment? What similarities and differences in treatment of setting exist among the three poems?

4. Because these selections were written after World War II, they deal with a United States with which you have had direct experience. Choose that selection, either prose or poetry, which seems to you to be the most accurate reflection of the world in which you have grown up. Then choose the selection that gives the least accurate picture.

Suppose that you are the author of the selection that gives the most accurate picture. Write a letter to the author you have judged least accurate, in which you explain, as respectfully and persuasively as possible, why you think your story or poem creates a more authentic picture of contemporary American life. In your letter refer to specifics in both selections.

5. Write a personal essay in which you explore the attitudes toward death of three poets from this unit. What is the central event of each poem? What mood is associated with death? What tone? Which symbols and images are central to the poem? What is the poet's philosophy about death? By comparing the poems, what conclusions can be drawn about twentieth-century attitudes toward death?

The poems from which you may choose are "Losses," "The Morning My Father Died," "Middle Age," "I Have Killed the Deer," and "Auto Wreck."

Definitions of Literary Terms

Words in SMALL CAPITAL LETTERS indicate other entries in the *Definitions of Literary Terms.* Numbers after a title or example refer to pages in the text where the selections referred to can be found.

allegory (al′ə gôr′ē), a NARRATIVE, either in verse or prose, in which characters, action, and sometimes SETTING represent abstract concepts apart from the literal meaning of a story. The underlying meaning usually has moral, social, religious, or political significance, and the characters are often PERSONIFICATIONS of abstract ideas such as charity, hope, greed, and so on. Though more clearly based in reality than such classic English allegories as John Bunyan's *Pilgrim's Progress,* "My Kinsman, Major Molineux," page 261, is sometimes viewed as an allegory (or as having an allegorical level of meaning) as are some other works by Hawthorne.

alliteration (ə lit′ə rā′shən), the repetition of consonant sounds at the beginnings of words or within words, particularly in accented syllables. It can be used to reinforce meaning, unify thought, or to create a musical effect.

> *S*inuous *s*outhward and *s*inuous northward
>   the *s*himmering band
> of the *s*and-beach *f*astens the *f*ringe of
>   the marsh to the *f*olds of the land.
>   Lanier, "The Marshes of Glynn"

allusion (ə lü′zhən), a brief reference to a person, event, or place, real or fictitious, or to a work of art. The title of Longfellow's poem "Mezzo Cammin," page 176, is an allusion to the first line of Dante's *Divine Comedy;* in T. S. Eliot's "The Love Song of J. Alfred Prufrock," page 457, lines 94–95, there is a biblical allusion to Lazarus, the brother of Mary and Martha, whom Jesus raised from the dead.

analogy (ə nal′ə jē), a literal comparison made between two items, situations, or ideas that are somewhat alike but unlike in most respects. Frequently an unfamiliar or complex object or idea will be compared to a familiar or simpler one in order to explain the first. In "Upon What Base?" page 120, there is an analogy between earthly craftsmen and the creator of the universe.

anapest (an′ə pest), a three-syllable metrical FOOT consisting of two unaccented syllables followed by an accented syllable, as in the word *buccanéer.* In the following line, the feet are divided by slashes, and since there are four feet, the line can be described as anapestic TETRAMETER.

> For the moon / never beams, / without bring /
>
>   ing me dreams . . .
>   Poe, "Annabel Lee," page 212

anastrophe (ə nas′trə fē), inversion of the usual order of the parts of a sentence, primarily for emphasis or to achieve a certain rhythm or rhyme. "Wrecked is the ship of pearl" is a reversal or inversion of the normal order of subject-verb-object (complement), "The ship of pearl is wrecked."

antagonist (an tag′ə nist), a character in a story or play who opposes the chief character or PROTAGONIST. In "The Devil and Tom Walker," page 156, the devil is the antagonist.

aphorism (af′ə riz′əm) (See MAXIM.)

apostrophe (ə pos′trə fē), a figure of speech in which an absent person, an abstract concept, or an inanimate object is directly addressed. "Helen, thy beauty is to me . . ." is an example of the first ("To Helen," page 213); "Build thee more stately mansions, O my soul . . ." is an example of the second ("The Chambered Nautilus," page 178); and "O Shenandoah, I long to hear you" (page 314) an example of the third.

assonance (as′n əns), the repetition of similar vowel sounds followed by different consonant sounds in stressed syllables or words. It is used instead of RHYME. *Fade* and *stayed* are examples of rhyme; *fade* and *pale,* examples of assonance. In "Upon what base was fixed the lathe . . ." the words *base* and *lathe* are assonant. ("Upon What Base?" page 120.)

atmosphere, the MOOD of a literary work. An author establishes atmosphere partly through description of SETTING and partly by the objects chosen to be described. For example, in the first three paragraphs of "An Occurrence at Owl Creek Bridge," page 344, Bierce creates an atmosphere of foreboding.

autobiography (See BIOGRAPHY.)

ballad, a NARRATIVE of unknown authorship passed on in the oral tradition. It often makes use of repetition and DIALOGUE. "El Corrido de Gregorio Cortez," page 316, is a ballad. A ballad whose author is known is called a literary ballad.

ballad stanza, a STANZA usually consisting of four alternating lines of IAMBIC TETRAMETER and TRIMETER and rhyming the second and fourth line.

> Ay, tear her tattered ensign down!
> Long has it waved on high,
> And many an eye has danced to see
> That banner in the sky . . .
> Holmes, "Old Ironsides"

biography, any account of a person's life. (See "Tin Lizzie," page 489.) Autobiography is the story of all or part of a person's life written by the person who lived it. (See "To Be Young, Gifted and Black," page 77.)

blank verse, unrhymed IAMBIC (~/) PENTAMETER, a line of five feet. (See the first four lines of "Birches," page 444.)

burlesque (See SATIRE.)

cacophony (kə kof′ə nē), a succession of harsh, discordant sounds in either poetry or prose, used to achieve a specific effect. Note the harsh, somewhat explosive sounds in these lines:

> In a clamorous appealing to the mercy of the fire,
> In a mad expostulation with the deaf and frantic fire . . .
> Poe, "The Bells"

(See also EUPHONY.)

caesura (si zhùr′ə, si zyùr′ə), a pause in a line of verse, usually dictated by the sense of the line and often greater than a normal pause. For purposes of study, the mark indicating a caesura is two short vertical lines (‖). A caesura can be indicated by punctuation, the grammatical construction of a sentence, or the placement of lines on a page. It is used to add variety to regular meter and therefore to add emphasis to certain words.

> And from its station in the hall
> An ancient timepiece says to all,—
> "Forever— ‖ never!
> Never— ‖ forever!"
> Longfellow,
> "The Old Clock on the Stairs"

characterization, the method an author uses to acquaint a reader with his or her characters. A character's physical traits and personality may be described, as in the first two paragraphs of "A Worn Path," page 420; a character's speech and behavior may be presented, as in "The Man Who Saw the Flood," page 416; or the thoughts and feelings of a character or the reactions of other characters to an individual may be shown, as in "The Jilting of Granny Weatherall," page 395. Any or all of these methods may be used in the same story or novel.

cliché (kli shā′), an expression or phrase that is so overused as to become trite and meaningless: *cool* as a cucumber, wrack and ruin, tried and true are examples. Sinclair Lewis, Ring Lardner, and James Thurber have been successful in satirizing certain character types by having them speak in clichés.

climax, the decisive point in a story or play when the problem must be resolved in one way or another. In "The Oyster and the Pearl," page 63, the immediate problem to be resolved is whether or not to open the oyster to see if it has a pearl. The climax occurs when the jeweler arrives to open the oyster, and the problem is resolved by the writer's purchase of the unopened oyster. This is the climax. Not every story or play has this kind of dramatic climax. Sometimes a character may simply resolve a problem in his or her mind. At times there is no resolution of the plot; the climax then comes when a character realizes that a resolution is impossible. (See also PLOT.)

comedy, a play written primarily to amuse the audience. In addition to arousing laughter, comic writing often appeals to the intellect. Thus the comic mode has often been used to "instruct" the audience about the follies of certain social conventions and human foibles, as is done to some extent in "The Oyster and the Pearl," page 63. When so used, the comedy becomes SATIRE.

conflict, the struggle between two opposing forces. The four basic kinds of conflict are: (1) a person against another person ("The Cask of Amontillado," page 199); (2) a person against nature ("The Bear," page 402); (3) a person against society ("A Journey," page 368); and (4) two elements within a person struggling for mastery ("The Haunted Boy," page 618). More than one kind of conflict can be and often is present in a work. As Robert Penn Warren put it, "no conflict, no story." (See also PLOT.)

connotation, the emotional associations surrounding a word or phrase, as opposed to its literal meaning or DENOTATION. Some connotations are fairly universal, others quite personal. The author of "My Mother Pieced Quilts," page 7, has built her poem around the many personal connotations that *mother* and *quilt* have for her.

consonance (kon′sə nəns), the repetition of consonant sounds that are preceded by different vowel sounds.

> The autumn-time has come;
> On woods that dream of bloom . . .
> Whittier, "My Triumph"

Consonance is an effective device for reinforcing mood and meaning. In the lines above, the *m* sounds contribute to the drowsy, end-of-summer feeling.

couplet, a pair of rhyming lines with identical meter.

> Thou blossom bright with autumn dew,
> And colored with the heaven's own blue,
> That openest when the quiet light
> Succeeds the keen and frosty night.
> Bryant, "To the Fringed Gentian"

(See also the last two lines of "Well, I Have Lost You," page 451.)

dactyl (dak′tl), a three-syllable metrical FOOT, consisting of one accented syllable followed by two unaccented syllables, as in the word *mérrīlȳ*. In the following line, the feet are divided by slashes. The first five feet are dactylic, and the last is a SPONDEE.

> Méanwhīle hăd / spréad īn thĕ / víllāgĕ
>
> thĕ / tídĭngs ŏf / íll, ănd ŏn / áll sídes . . .
>
> Longfellow, *Evangeline*

denotation, the strict, literal meaning of a word. (See CONNOTATION.)

denouement (dā′nü män′), the resolution of the PLOT. The word is derived from a French word meaning literally "the untying." In "When the Bough Breaks," page 644, the denouement concerns the explanation of Miss Clovelly's "aberration." In a mystery story, such as "The Singing Bell," page 665, it is the explanation or summation of clues, motives, red herrings, and any loose ends not explained earlier. The CLIMAX and the denouement may come very close together, or, in a novel, several chapters may intervene.

dialogue, the conversation between two or more people in a literary work. Dialogue can serve many purposes, among them: (1) CHARACTERIZATION, both of those speaking and of those spoken about, as in "The Hyannis Port Story," page 627; (2) the creation of MOOD or ATMOSPHERE, as in "The Portrait," page 74; (3) the advancement of the PLOT, as in "The Cask of Amontillado," page 199; and (4) the development of a THEME, as in "The Leader of the People," page 9.

diction, the author's choice of words or phrases in a literary work. This choice involves both the connotative and denotative meaning of a word as well as levels of usage. In "The Devil and Tom Walker," page 156, Irving refers to Mrs. Tom Walker as "a tall termagant," a choice of words that reveals something about Irving as well as about Walker's wife, whom another writer might have chosen to describe as a common scold.

dramatic convention, any of several devices which the audience accepts as a substitution for reality in a dramatic work. For instance, the audience accepts that an interval between acts is a substitute for a passage of time greater than the interval, that a bare stage may be a meadow, that a balcony is attached to a house instead of an invisible scaffold, that an audible dialogue is really supposed to be whispered, or that dawn approaches with a rosy spotlight.

dramatic irony (See IRONY.)

dramatic monologue (mon′l ôg), a LYRIC poem in which the speaker, usually at a critical moment in life, addresses someone whose replies are not recorded. Sometimes the one addressed seems to be present, sometimes not. See "Well, I Have Lost You," page 451, and "The Love Song of J. Alfred Prufrock," page 454. A dramatic monologue differs from a SOLILOQUY in that a soliloquy usually occurs in a

drama and is a speech delivered when a speaker is alone on stage.

elegy, a solemn, reflective poem, usually about death, written in a formal style. "When Lilacs Last in the Dooryard Bloom'd" is Walt Whitman's elegy written on the death of Abraham Lincoln.

end rhyme, the rhyming of words at the ends of lines of poetry as in "Richard Cory," page 359. (See also INTERNAL RHYME.)

end-stopped line, a line of poetry that contains a complete thought, thus necessitating the use of a semicolon or period at the end.

> The ship, becalmed, at length stands still;
> The steed must rest beneath the hill;
> Thoreau, "Though All the Fates"

(See also RUN-ON LINE.)

epigram, any short, witty verse or saying, often ending with a wry twist.

> Let us all be happy and live within our means,
> even if we have to borrow the money to do it
> with.
>
> Artemus Ward

(Compare with MAXIM and PROVERB.)

essay, a prose composition that presents a personal point of view. An essay may present a viewpoint through formal analysis and argument, as in "Fear" by Millay, page 38, or it may be informal in style, as in "The Calculating Machine" by White, page 23.

euphony (yü′fə nē), a combination of pleasing sounds in poetry or prose.

> Then came the laborers home from the field,
>   and serenely the sun sank
> Down to his rest, and twilight prevailed.
>
> Longfellow, *Evangeline*

(See also CACOPHONY for a comparison.)

exposition, the beginning of a work of fiction, particularly a play, in which the author sets the ATMOSPHERE and TONE, explains the SETTING, introduces the characters, and provides the reader with any other information needed in order to understand the PLOT.

extended metaphor, a figure of speech that is used throughout an entire work or a great part of it. It is common in poetry but is often used in prose as well. The spiritual "Swing Low, Sweet Chariot," page 193, contains an extended metaphor, with *home* representing "heaven" throughout and the chariot representing the means by which the believer will be transported to heaven.

fable, a brief tale, in which the characters are often animals, told to point out a MORAL truth. (See Emerson's "Fable," page 224.)

fantasy, a work that takes place in an unreal world and that often concerns incredible characters. Science fiction, a kind of fantasy, tends to deal chiefly with events that take place in the future or on other planets and employs physical and scientific principles not yet discovered or proven but distinctly possible. Washington Irving was the first American author to write fantasy, with such stories as "Rip Van Winkle" and "The Legend of Sleepy Hollow," and this tradition continues today in the works of Ray Bradbury, Ursula Le Guin, and others.

farce, a type of COMEDY that depends on outlandish situations rather than on witty DIALOGUE, PLOT, or CHARACTER. Many comic silent films were farces since, by necessity, the humor had to be exaggerated and chiefly visual.

figurative language, language used in a nonliteral way to express a suitable relationship between essentially unlike things. When Twain compares the jaw of a bulldog to the "fo'castle of a steamboat" or says that a frog whirled in the air "like a doughnut," he is using a figure of speech or figurative language. The more common figures of speech are SIMILE, METAPHOR, PERSONIFICATION, HYPERBOLE, and SYNECDOCHE.

flashback, interruption of the narrative to show an episode that happened before that particular point in the story. In "Brother Death," there is a flashback which begins "It was on an early Summer day, . . ." page 388.

foil, a character whose traits are the opposite of those of another character and who thus points up the strengths or weaknesses of another character. The two brothers in "Brother Death," page 386, Ted and Don, are opposites in their views of life and death, as are the two men who cut down the tree.

folklore, the customs, proverbs, legends, superstitions, songs, and tales of a people or nation. Literature often borrows elements from folklore. For instance, the belief that the devil can assume human form and the old legend (common to the folklore of many countries) of someone who strikes a bargain with the devil were incorporated into "The Devil and Tom Walker" by Washington Irving, page 156.

foot, in verse, a group of syllables usually consisting of one accented syllable and all unaccented syllables associated with it. (A foot may occasionally, for variety, have two accented syllables. See SPONDEE.) In the following lines the feet are divided by slashes:

> Ăt mí d / nǐght, ĭn / thĕ mónth / ŏf Júne,
>
> Ĭ stánd / bĕnéath / thĕ mýs / tǐc móon.
>
> Poe, "The Sleeper"

It is probable that this use of the word *foot* refers to the movement of the foot in beating time. The most common line lengths are five feet (PENTAMETER), four feet (TETRAMETER), and three feet (TRIMETER). The quoted lines above are IAMBIC TETRAMETER. (See also RHYTHM.)

foreshadowing, a hint given to the reader of what is to come. In "The First Seven Years," page 49, the reader knows, even if Feld does not, that when Sobel breaks the last and runs out, this foreshadows the revelation of his love for Miriam.

free verse, a type of poetry that differs from conventional verse forms in being "free" from a fixed pattern of METER and RHYME, but uses RHYTHM and other poetic devices. Walt Whitman, pages 304–313, was the first recognized poet to use free verse extensively.

genre (zhän′rə), a form or type of literary work. For example, the novel, the short story, and the poem are all genres. The term is a very loose one, however, so that subheadings under these would themselves also be called genres, for instance, the MYTH and the epic.

gothic novel, type of novel which aims at evoking terror through a gloomy SETTING and sensational, sometimes supernatural action. The English writer Horace Walpole is credited with writing the first gothic novel, *The Castle of Otranto* (1764). The term *Gothic* referred at first to a style of architecture developed in Western Europe during the Middle Ages. Since the setting of Walpole's novel is a medieval castle, the term was extended to apply to this type of writing. *Gothic* can also describe a story such as Poe's "The Fall of the House of Usher." The term is also used to describe a type of present-day novel which, though it may not have a medieval setting, takes place in a terrifying and mysterious place and often involves a love story as well.

hexameter (hek sam′ə tər), a verse line of six feet.

> Yé whŏ bĕ / liéve ĭn ǎf / féctiŏn thǎt / hópes,
>
> ǎnd ĕn / dúres ǎnd ĭs / pátiĕnt . . .
>
> Longfellow, *Evangeline*

The first five feet of the line are DACTYLIC; the last foot is a SPONDEE (spondaic). Hexameter is not very common in American poetry.

hyperbole (hī pər′bə lē), a figure of speech involving great exaggeration. The effect may be satiric, sentimental, or comic. American folklore abounds with hyperbole, such as the story about the man who was so stingy that he stood on one foot at a time to avoid wearing out his shoes. "The Latest Latin Dance Craze," page 601, makes use of hyperbole.

iamb (ī′amb), a two-syllable metrical FOOT consisting of one unaccented syllable followed by one accented syllable, as in the word *dĕcíde*.

imagery, the sensory details that provide vividness in a literary work and tend to arouse emotions or feelings in a reader which abstract language does not. The paragraph below illustrates the use of details that appeal to the senses, in this case sight, hearing, and possibly, taste:

> When he came to the well, he flung himself face downward and peered into its darkness. There were furtive silver glintings some feet from the surface. He

grabbed one of the canteens and, unfastening its cap, swung it down by the cord. The water flowed slowly in with an indolent gurgle.

Stephen Crane, "A Mystery of Heroism"

inference, a reasonable conclusion about the behavior of a character or the meaning of an event drawn from the limited information presented by the author.

internal rhyme, rhyming words within lines which also may or may not rhyme at the end: "I spy a fly upon the rye."

inversion (See ANASTROPHE.)

irony, the term used to describe a contrast between what appears to be and what really is. In *verbal irony,* the actual meaning of a statement is different from (often the opposite of) what the statement literally says. *Understatement,* in which a fact is expressed less emphatically than it could be, is a form of verbal irony, usually used for humorous effect. Twain's remark that "[James Fenimore] Cooper's art has some defects" is an example of understatement and thus is verbal irony. *Irony of situation* refers to an occurrence that is contrary to what is expected or intended, as in "Miniver Cheevy," page 358. *Dramatic irony* refers to a situation in which events or facts not known to a character on stage or in a fictional work are known to another character and the audience or reader. In "The Cask of Amontillado," page 199, Fortunato is unaware of the narrator's plans for him, although the narrator of course knows and the reader suspects.

legend, a traditional anonymous story which may have some basis in fact. There are many legends about Johnny Appleseed, for example, who was a real person named John Chapman, but about whom relatively little is actually known. Both Betsy Ross and George Washington figure in legends. Places, too, sometimes prompt legends—cliffs from which unhappy lovers are said to have leaped, for instance. (See also MYTH.)

literary ballad (See BALLAD.)

local color, detailed representation in fiction of SETTING, dialect, dress, climate, manners, customs, etc., of a particular area. The term is not used as much today as it was in the 1880s when writers such as Bret Harte, Sarah Orne Jewett, and Kate Chopin limited themselves chiefly to writing about a particular region such as the West or New England or the South.

lyric, a poem, usually short, that expresses some basic emotion or state of mind. It usually creates a single impression and is highly personal. It may be rhymed or unrhymed. "To Be in Love," page 617, fulfills the qualifications of a lyric.

main idea (See THEME.)

maxim, a brief saying embodying a moral, such as "Diligence is the mother of good luck" [Franklin]. It is sometimes also called an aphorism.

metaphor, a figure of speech involving an implied comparison. In "The Jilting of Granny Weatherall," page 396, Porter makes a comparison between the plan of life and a sheet or comforter: ". . . then a person could spread out the plan of life and tuck in the edges orderly." (See also SIMILE and FIGURATIVE LANGUAGE.)

meter, the pattern of stressed and unstressed syllables in poetry. (See RHYTHM and FOOT.)

metonomy (mə ton/ə mē), a figure of speech in which a term is substituted for another with which it is closely associated, as when the term "city hall" is used to refer to a mayor or "the bench" is used to refer to persons who sit as judges.

monologue (mon/l ôg), an extended speech given by one speaker. Sometimes a distinction is made between a SOLILOQUY and a monologue, with the term *soliloquy* describing the extended speech of a character on stage who is in effect talking to him or herself and expressing inner thoughts aloud. These musings are supposed to be known only to the audience and not to other characters. The term *monologue* is usually used to express any rather long speech given by one person—a character in a story or a real person.

mood, the overall ATMOSPHERE of a work. The mood of "An Occurrence at Owl Creek Bridge," page 344, might be said to be eerie while the mood of "The Celebrated Jumping Frog of Calaveras County," page 319, could be described as light-hearted. (See TONE for a comparison.)

moral, the lesson taught in a work such as a FABLE. A moral, such as "let sleeping dogs lie," directs that the reader should act in a certain way.

motif (mō tēf/), a character, incident, or idea that recurs in various works or in various parts of the same work. In the poem "Patterns," page 432, the motif is patterns—the patterns of a garden, a dress, a fan, paths, and of life itself.

motivation, the portrayal of circumstances and aspects of personality that make a character's actions and reactions plausible or believable. In "A New England Nun," page 336, Louisa Ellis's decision not to marry Joe seems plausible because of the author's description of events and Louisa's thoughts about her future.

myth, a traditional tale of unknown authorship involving gods and goddesses or other supernatural beings. A myth often attempts to explain some aspect of nature. There are, for instance, myths about the creation of the world, the seasons, and animals in nearly every culture of the world.

narrative, a story or account of an event or a series of events. It may be told either in poetry or prose; it may be either fictional or true. Sarah Kemble Knight's account, page 121, is a narrative, as is "April 2005: Usher II," page 25.

narrator, the teller of a story. The teller may be a character in the story, as in "The Cask of Amontillado"; the author himself, as in "Escape: A Slave Narrative," page 183; or an anonymous voice outside the story, as in "A Worn Path," page 420. A narrator's attitude toward his or her subject is capable of much variation; it can range from one of apparent indifference to one of extreme conviction and feeling. When a narrator appears to have some bias regarding his or her subject, as in "The Portrait," page 74, or "Soldiers of the Republic," page 426, it becomes especially important to determine whether the narrator and the author are to be regarded as the same person. (See also PERSONA and POINT OF VIEW.)

naturalism, writing that depicts events as rigidly determined by the forces of heredity and environment. Stephen Crane has been called a naturalist because his writing tends to expound the philosophy that the world can be understood by examining cause-and-effect relationships and that all events are determined by antecedent causes.

ode, a long LYRIC poem, formal in style and complex in form, often written in commemoration or celebration of a special occasion. Few odes are composed today except for the purpose of expressing IRONY or SATIRE.

omniscient point of view (See POINT OF VIEW.)

onomatopoeia (on′ə mat′ə pē′ə), use of a word or words whose sounds imitate the sound of the thing spoken about. Words such as *hiss, mumble, caw,* and *mew* are onomatopoetic words. In the example below, the author has tried to convey the sound of rustling leaves.

> The tree-tops faintly rustle beneath the
> breeze's flight,
> A soft and soothing sound, yet it whispers
> of the night . . .
> Bryant, "Waiting by the Gate"

parable, a brief fictional work which concretely illustrates an abstract idea or teaches some lesson or truth. It differs from a FABLE in that the characters in it are generally people rather than animals; it differs from an ALLEGORY in that its characters do not necessarily represent abstract qualities. "The Last Flower," page 84, is a parable.

paradox, a statement, often metaphorical, that seems to be self-contradictory but which has valid meaning. "In death there is life" is a paradox.

parody (See SATIRE.)

pentameter (pen tam′ə tər), a metrical line of five feet. (See also FOOT.)

> O star / of morn / ing and / of lib / erty!
> O bring / er of / the light, / whose splen / dor
> shines
> Above / the dark / ness of / the Ap / pennines,
> Forerun / ner of / the day / that is / to be!
> Longfellow, *Divina Commedia*

persona (pər sō′nə), the mask or voice which a writer assumes in a particular work. *Persona* is derived from a Latin word meaning "mask." Eliot is of course the author of "The Love Song of J. Alfred Prufrock," page 454, but the persona is Prufrock, through whom Eliot speaks. In "The Devil and Tom Walker," page 156, Irving has assumed a voice or persona, gently ironic, somewhat indulgent, in telling the story.

personification (pər son′ə fə kā′shən), the representation of abstractions, ideas, animals, or inanimate objects as human beings by endowing them with human qualities. Death is personified in Dickinson's "Because I Could Not Stop for Death," page 334. (See FIGURATIVE LANGUAGE.)

plot, in the simplest sense, a series of happenings in a literary work; but the word is often used to refer to the action as it is organized around a CONFLICT and builds through complication to a CLIMAX followed by a DENOUEMENT or resolution.

point of view, the relationship assumed between the teller of a story and the characters in it. The teller, or NARRATOR, may be a character, in which case the story is told from the *first-person* point of view, as in "In Another Country," page 412. A writer who describes, in the third person, both the thoughts and actions of one or all of the characters is said to use the *omniscient* (om nish′ənt) point of view. "The First Seven Years," page 49, is told from the omniscient point of view. A writer who confines himself, in the third person, to describing thoughts and actions of a single character is sometimes said to use the *limited omniscient* point of view. (See "The Jilting of Granny Weatherall," page 395.) An author who describes only what can be seen, like a newspaper reporter, is said to use the *dramatic* point of view. The narrator may then be a minor character in the story who plays the roles of eyewitness and confidant.

prologue, section of a work preceding the main plot, serving as an introduction.

propaganda, writing that directly advocates a certain doctrine as the solution to some social or political problem. Writing that tends to support views opposite to one's own is most frequently termed propaganda, but the term should legitimately be applied to the advocation of any doctrine. Thomas Paine was writing propaganda in *The American Crisis,* page 147, as was Millay in "Fear," page 38.

prose poem, a piece of writing set down as prose but having the rhythms, language, and imaginative quality usually associated with poetry. "Young Girls Who Play the Harp," page 590, is a prose poem.

protagonist (prō tag′ə nist), the leading character in a literary work.

proverb, a brief, traditional saying that makes an observation on character or conduct or contains some bit of popular wisdom such as "Red sky at morning, sailors take warning," or "A watched pot never boils," or "Cold hands, warm heart." (Compare MAXIM and EPIGRAM.)

pun, simultaneous use of two or more different senses of the same word, or different words with the same sound. Puns are used for expressive or humorous effect, as in the following epitaph:

> No knot for me,
> No knot I sought.
> No child to mourn;
> Forget me not.

quatrain (kwot′rān), verse STANZA of four lines, as in the epitaph above.

realism, a way of representing life as it seems to the common reader. The material selected tends to represent, with almost photographic precision and detail, ordinary people in everyday experiences and settings. Much of the work of Mark Twain and Edith Wharton has realistic aspects, as does the writing of Sherwood Anderson, Eudora Welty, and the novelists William Dean Howells, Henry James, and Ernest Hemingway.

refrain, the repetition of one or more lines in each STANZA of a poem. "Go Down, Moses," page 194, has a refrain.

rhyme, exact repetition of sounds in at least the final accented syllable of two or more words. (See also INTERNAL RHYME, END RHYME, and SLANT RHYME.)

rhyme scheme, any pattern of rhyme in a STANZA. For purposes of study, the pattern is labeled as shown below, with the first rhyme labeled *a,* as are all the words rhyming with it; the second rhyme labeled *b,* the third rhyme labeled *c,* and so on.

> And what is so rare as a day in June?   *a*
> Then, if ever, come perfect days;   *b*
> Then Heaven tries earth if it be in tune,   *a*
> And over it softly her· warm ear lays: *b*
> Whether we look, or whether we listen,   *c*
> We hear life murmur, or see it glisten . . . *c*
> Lowell, *The Vision of Sir Launfal*

rhythm, the arrangement of stressed and unstressed syllables in speech or writing. Rhythm, or METER, may be regular, taDUM, taDUM, taDUM, or it may vary within a line or work. The four most common meters are IAMB or *iambus* (‿ /), TROCHEE (/ ‿), ANAPEST (‿ ‿ /), and DACTYL (/ ‿ ‿).

rising action, the building of tension between opposing characters or forces toward a CLIMAX. In "An Episode of War," page 352, the climax falls so near the end that nearly the whole story constitutes the rising action.

romanticism, unlike REALISM, romanticism tends to portray the uncommon. The material selected tends to deal with extraordinary people in unusual experiences. In romantic literature there is often a stress on the past (as in the writings of James Fenimore Cooper) and an emphasis on nature (as in the works of William Cullen Bryant).

run-on line, a line in which the thought continues beyond the end of the poetic line. There should be no pause after *might* in the stanza below, the unbroken rhythm making a run-on line.

> Oh, dumb be passion's stormy rage,
> When he who might
> Have lighted up and led his age,
> Falls back in night.
> Whittier, "Ichabod"

(See also END-STOPPED LINE.)

sarcasm, the use of language to hurt, wound, or ridicule. It is less subtle in TONE than IRONY. There are several sarcastic lines in "Teenage Diseases," page 558, but the overall tone is satiric. (Compare with IRONY and SATIRE.)

satire, the TECHNIQUE that employs wit to ridicule a subject, usually some social institution or human foible, with the intention to inspire reform. SARCASM and IRONY are often used in writing satire. *Burlesque* and *parody* are closely related to satire. *Burlesque* is a literary or dramatic composition that treats a serious subject ridiculously or a trivial subject as if it were important. Either way, exaggeration is used. *Parody* is humorous imitation of serious writing. "Muck-a-Muck," page 169, is a parody of the writing of Cooper.

scansion (skan′shən), the marking off of lines of poetry into feet. (See also RHYTHM and FOOT.)

science fiction (See FANTASY.)

setting, the time (both time of day or season and period in history) and place in which the action of a NARRATIVE occurs. The setting may be suggested through dialogue and action, or it may be described by the NARRATOR or one of the characters. Setting contributes strongly to the MOOD or atmosphere and plausibility of a work. The detailed, precise description of the swamp in "The Devil and Tom Walker," for example, convinces us that if the devil is ever going to appear in the flesh, he will do so in this fiendish setting.

simile (sim′ə lē), a figure of speech involving a comparison using *like* or *as.*

> ". . . like mourning weeds, dark festoons of
> sea-grass slimily swept to and fro over
> the name, with every hearselike roll of the
> hull."
>
> Melville, "Benito Cereno"

In the above example the similarity between the festoons of sea-grass and mourning clothes (weeds) is based, at least partly, on the dark color of both. The death image is reinforced by the "hearse*like* roll of the hull." (See METAPHOR for comparison.)

slant rhyme, rhyme in which the vowel sounds are not quite identical, as in the first and third lines below.

> By the rude bridge that arched the flood,
> Their flag to April's breeze unfurled,
> Here once the embattled farmers stood
> And fired the shot heard round the world.
> Emerson, "Concord Hymn"

soliloquy (sə lil′ə kwē), a DRAMATIC CONVENTION which allows a character to speak his or her thoughts aloud. If someone else is on stage, a soliloquy becomes an *aside*. (Compare with MONOLOGUE.)

sonnet, a LYRIC poem with a traditional form of fourteen IAMBIC PENTAMETER lines and one of several fixed RHYME schemes. (See "Well, I Have Lost You," page 451.)

spondee (spon′dē), a metrical FOOT of two accented syllables (//). It serves occasionally as a substitute foot to vary the meter, as in the first foot below.

> Tóm, Tóm, / thĕ pí / pĕr's són . . .

stanza, a group of lines which are set off and form a division in a poem.

stereotype, a conventional character, plot, or setting, which thus possesses little or no individuality. Although it is true that there are no new plots, there are some situations, characters, and settings that are frequently predictable, usually because of the author's treatment. Examples of such stereotypes include "the dead body in the library," "the wandering, lone hero," or "the poet starving in a garret."

stream of consciousness, the recording or re-creation of a character's flow of thought without any attempt at explanation, as in "The Jilting of Granny Weatherall," page 395.

style, the distinctive handling of language by an author. It involves the specific choices made with regard to DICTION, FIGURATIVE LANGUAGE, etc. For a comparison of two very different styles, see John Dos Passos, page 489, and James Baldwin, page 554.

subject, the topic about which an author is writing. (See THEME for a comparison.)

symbolism, the use in literature of objects or events to represent something other than themselves, frequently abstract ideas or concepts. In "The Chambered Nautilus," page 178, the shell symbolizes the body and the animal in the shell, the soul.

synecdoche (si nek′də kē), a type of FIGURATIVE LANGUAGE in which the whole is used for the part or the part used for the whole. In "the dying year," the whole is used to stand for a part, "autumn"; the use of "Wall Street" to refer to the money market or financial affairs of the entire U.S. is an example of the second—using a part to stand for the whole (or the special to stand for the general).

tall tale, a humorous, simple NARRATIVE which recounts extraordinary, impossible happenings. A distinctly American GENRE, it originated on the American frontier when "yarn-spinners" passed on the legendary feats of such folk heroes as Paul Bunyan and Babe the Blue Ox, Mike Fink (the Mississippi Riverman), and John Henry. The tall tale found its way into the American literary tradition after the Civil War and its form is preserved in "The Celebrated Jumping Frog of Calaveras County," page 319.

technique, the craftsmanship used by an author to give a work form and meaning. Also, a specific literary device, such as SYMBOLISM or SATIRE, may be referred to as a technique.

tercet (tėr′sit), a stanza of three rhyming lines.

> Maiden! with the meek, brown eyes,
> In whose orbs a shadow lies
> Like the dusk in evening skies!
> Longfellow, "Maidenhood"

tetrameter (te tram′ə tər), a metrical line of four feet.

> One au / tumn night, / in Sud / bury town,
> Across / the mead / ows bare / and brown.
> Longfellow, *Tales of a Wayside Inn*

theme, the main idea or underlying meaning of a literary work. A theme may be directly stated but more often is implied. In "Upon the Burning of Our House," page 118, the topic or subject is described in the title, but the theme is the poet's reconciliation of her loss with the belief that true treasures are heavenly ones. Not all works have a theme.

tone, the author's attitude toward his or her subject matter. Cabeza de Vaca's tone, page 107, is sometimes matter-of-fact, sometimes wondering. Satanta's tone, page 328, is firm and forthright.

topic, the subject about which an author writes. (See THEME.)

tragedy, dramatic or narrative writing in which the main character suffers disaster after a serious and significant struggle but faces his or her downfall in such a way as to attain heroic stature.

trimeter (trim′ə tər), metrical line of three feet.

> "Oft to / his fro / zen lair
> Tracked I / the gris / ly bear . . ."
> Longfellow, "The Skeleton in Armor"

triplet (See TERCET.)

trochee (trō′kē), metrical foot made up of one accented syllable followed by an unaccented syllable, as in the word *púmpkĭn*. In the following lines the feet are divided by slashes, and since there are four feet, the line can be described as trochaic TETRAMETER.

> Lúrĭd / séemed thĕ / ský ă / bóve hǐm,
> Lúrĭd / séemed thĕ / earth bĕ / néath hǐm.
> Longfellow, *The Song of Hiawatha*

verbal irony (See IRONY.)

verse, in its most general sense, a synonym for *poetry*. Verse also may be used to refer to poetry carefully composed as to RHYTHM and RHYME scheme, but of inferior literary value.

vignette (vi nyet′), a brief narrative or description written with precision and grace, and intended to give a vivid impression of a personality or scene. "Wouter Van Twiller," page 154, is a vignette.

voice (See PERSONA.)

Glossary

The pronunciation of each word is shown just after the word, in this way: **ab bre vi ate** (ə brē′vē āt). The letters and signs used are pronounced as in the words below. The mark ′ is placed after a syllable with primary or heavy accent, as in the example above. The mark ′ after a syllable shows a secondary or lighter accent, as in **ab bre vi a tion** (ə brē′vē ā′shən).

Some words, taken from foreign languages, are spoken with sounds that do not otherwise occur in English. Symbols for these sounds are given in the key as "foreign sounds."

Full pronunciation key

a	hat, cap	j	jam, enjoy	u	cup, butter
ā	age, face	k	kind, seek	u̇	full, put
ä	father, far	l	land, coal	ü	rule, move
		m	me, am		
b	bad, rob	n	no, in	v	very, save
ch	child, much	ng	long, bring	w	will, woman
d	did, red			y	young, yet
		o	hot, rock	z	zero, breeze
e	let, best	ō	open, go	zh	measure, seizure
ē	equal, be	ô	order, all		
ėr	term, learn	oi	oil, voice	ə	represents:
		ou	house, out		a in about
f	fat, if				e in taken
g	go, bag	p	paper, cup		i in pencil
h	he, how	r	run, try		o in lemon
		s	say, yes		u in circus
i	it, pin	sh	she, rush		
ī	ice, five	t	tell, it		
		th	thin, both		
		ᴛʜ	then, smooth		

foreign sounds

ʏ as in French *du.*
Pronounce (ē) with the lips rounded as for (ü).

à as in French *ami.*
Pronounce (ä) with the lips spread and held tense.

œ as in French *peu.*
Pronounce (ā) with the lips rounded as for (ō).

ɴ as in French *bon.*
The ɴ is not pronounced, but shows that the vowel before it is nasal.

ʜ as in German *ach.*
Pronounce (k) without closing the breath passage.

Grammatical key

adj.	adjective	*prep.*	preposition
adv.	adverb	*pron.*	pronoun
conj.	conjunction	*v.*	verb
interj.	interjection	*v.i.*	intransitive verb
n.	noun	*v.t.*	transitive verb
sing.	singular	*pl.*	plural

FROM *Thorndike-Barnhart Advanced Dictionary*, Second Edition. Copyright © 1974 by Scott, Foresman and Company. Reprinted by permission.

a bash (ə bash′), *v.t.* embarrass and confuse; make uneasy and somewhat ashamed. [< Old French *esbaïss-*, a form of *esbaïr* astonish] —**a bash′ment**, *n.*

a bate (ə bāt′), *v.i.*, **a bat ed**, **a bat ing.** become less in force or intensity; diminish. [< Old French *abatre* beat down < *a-* to + *batre* to beat] —**a bat′a ble**, *adj.* —**a bat′er**, *n.*

ab di cate (ab′də kāt), *v.t.*, **-cat ed**, **-cat ing.** give up or relinquish (office, power, or authority) formally; renounce; resign. [< Latin *abdicatum* renounced < *ab-* away + *dicare* proclaim] —**ab′di ca′tion**, *n.* —**ab′di ca′tor**, *n.*

ab er rant (ab er′ənt), *adj.* deviating from what is regular, normal, or right. —*n.* person who deviates from normal behavior.

ab er ra tion (ab′ə rā′shən), *n.* **1** a deviating from the right path or usual course of action. **2** an abnormal structure or development. **3** a temporary mental disorder. [< Latin *aberrationem* < *ab-* away + *errare* wander]

a bet (ə bet′), *v.t.*, **a bet ted**, **a bet ting.** encourage by aid or approval in doing something wrong. [< Old French *abeter* arouse < *a-* to + *beter* to bait]

ab hor (ab hôr′), *v.t.*, **-horred**, **-hor ring.** regard with horror or disgust; hate completely; detest; loathe. [< Latin *abhorrere* < *ab-* from + *horrere* to shudder, shrink] —**ab hor′rer**, *n.*

a bide (ə bīd′), *v.i.*, **a bode** or **a bid ed**, **a bid ing.** **1** stay; remain. **2** continue to live (in a place); dwell; reside. [Old English *abidan* stay on, and *onbīdan* wait for] —**a bid′er**, *n.*

ab ject (ab′jekt, ab jekt′), *adj.* **1** so low or degraded as to be hopeless; wretched; miserable. **2** slavish: *abject submission.* [< Latin *abjectum* cast down < *ab-* down + *jacere* to throw] —**ab ject′ly**, *adv.* —**ab ject′ness**, *n.*

-able, *suffix forming adjectives from verbs and nouns.* **1** that can be ____ed: *Enjoyable = that can be enjoyed.* **2** giving ____; suitable for ____: *Comfortable = giving comfort.* **3** inclined to ____: *Peaceable = inclined to peace.* **4** deserving to be ____ed: *Lovable = deserving to be loved.* **5** liable to be ____: *Breakable = liable to be broken.*

ab o li tion (ab′ə lish′ən), *n.* **1** an abolishing. **2** a being abolished; abrogation. **3** the abolishing of slavery.

a bom i na ble (ə bom′ə nə bəl), *adj.* arousing disgust and hatred; detestable; loathsome. —**a bom′i na bly**, *adv.*

a bo rig i ne (ab′ə rij′ə nē), *n.* an original inhabitant of a country or area, especially as distinguished from European or other colonists. [< Latin < *ab origine* from the beginning]

ab ro gate (ab′rə gāt), *v.t.*, **-gat ed**, **-gat ing.** **1** abolish or annul by an authoritative act; repeal; cancel. **2** do away with. [< Latin *abrogatum* repealed < *ab-* away + *rogare* propose (a law)]

ab scond (ab skond′), *v.i.* go away hurriedly and secretly, especially to avoid punishment; go off and hide. [< Latin *abscondere* < *abs-* away + *condere* store up]

ab solve (ab solv′, ab zolv′), *v.t.*, **-solved**, **-solv ing.** **1** pronounce or set (a person) free from sin, guilt, blame, or their penalties or consequences. **2** set free (*from* a promise, obligation, or duty); release. [< Latin *absolvere* < *ab-* from + *solvere* loosen]

ab stract (ab strakt′), *v.t.* take away secret-ly, slyly, or dishonestly. [Latin *abstractum* drawn away < *abs-* away + *trahere* draw]

ab stract ed (ab strak′tid), *adj.* absent-minded; preoccupied.

ac cen tu ate (ak sen′chü āt), *v.t.*, **-at ed**, **-at ing.** call special attention to; emphasize.

ac ces si ble (ak ses′ə bəl), *adj.* **1** easy to reach, enter, or use; convenient or attainable. **2** that can be entered or reached; approachable. **3** capable of being influenced; susceptible *(to).*

ac cli mate (ə klī′mit, ak′lə māt), *v.t.*, *v.i.*, **-mat ed**, **-mat ing.** accustom or become accustomed to a new climate, surroundings, or conditions. —**ac cli ma tion** (ak′lə mā′shən), *n.*

ac cliv i ty (ə kliv′ə tē), *n., pl.* **-ties.** an upward slope of ground; ascent. [< Latin *acclivitatem* < *acclivis* ascending < *ad-* toward + *clivus* a slope]

ac com plice (ə kom′plis), *n.* person who knowingly aids another in committing a crime or other wrong act. [< earlier *a complice* < confederate < Middle French *complice* < Late Latin *complicem* < Latin *complicare* fold together]

ac cost (ə kôst′, ə kost′), *v.t.* approach and speak to first; address. [< Middle French *accoster* < Latin *ad-* to + *costa* side, rib]

ac ri mo ny (ak′rə mō′nē), *n.* biting sharpness of temper; bitterness of language or manner; acerbity. [< Latin *acrimonia* < *acer, acris* sharp]

ad her ent (ad hir′ənt), *n.* a faithful supporter or follower.

a dieu (ə dü′, ə dyü′), *interj., n., pl.* **a dieus** or **a dieux** (ə düz′, ə dyüz′). good-by. [< Middle French <*à Dieu* to God]

ad mon ish (ad mon′ish), *v.t.* **1** advise against something; warn. **2** scold gently; reprove. **3** recall to a duty overlooked or forgotten; remind. —**ad′mo ni′tion**, *n.*

ad ver si ty (ad vėr′sə tē), *n., pl.* **-ties.** condition of being in unfavorable circumstances, especially unfavorable financial circumstances; misfortune; distress.

af fec ta tion (af′ek tā′shən), *n.* behavior that is not natural, but assumed to impress others; pretense.

af fin i ty (ə fin′ə tē), *n., pl.* **-ties.** **1** a natural attraction to a person or liking for a thing. **2** relation; connection. [< Latin *affinitatem* relation < *affinis* related, bordering on < *ad-* on + *finis* border]

ag ate (ag′it), *n.* a variety of quartz with variously colored stripes, clouded colors, or mosslike formations. [< Old French *agathe* < Latin *achates* < Greek *achatēs*]

ag gre ga tion (ag′rə gā′shən), *n.* **1** the collecting of separate things into one mass or whole. **2** the group or mass collected.

a ghast (ə gast′), *adj.* struck with surprise or horror; filled with shocked amazement. [past participle of obsolete *agast* terrify < Old English *on-* on + *gæstan* frighten. Related to GHOST.]

-al¹, *suffix forming adjectives from nouns.* of; like; having the nature of: *Ornamental = having the nature of ornament.* Also, **-ial.**

-al², *suffix forming nouns from verbs.* act of ____ing: *Refusal = act of refusing.*

a lac ri ty (ə lak′rə tē), *n.* **1** brisk and eager action; liveliness. **2** cheerful willingness. [< Latin *alacritatem* < *alacer* brisk]

al be it (ôl bē′it), *conj.* even though; even if; although. [Middle English *al be it* although it be]

al bur num (al bėr′nəm), *n.* sapwood. [< Latin < *albus* white]

---

hat, āge, fär; let, ēqual, tėrm;
it, īce; hot, ōpen, ôrder;
oil, out; cup, pùt, rüle;
ch, child; ng, long; sh, she;
th, thin; ₮H, then; zh, measure;

ə represents *a* in about, *e* in taken,
i in pencil, *o* in lemon, *u* in circus.

< = from, derived from, taken from.

---

al i bi (al′ə bī), *n.* **1** the plea or fact that a person accused of an offense was somewhere else when the offense was committed. **2** U.S. INFORMAL. an excuse. [< Latin, elsewhere]

al lay (ə lā′), *v.t.*, **-layed, -lay ing.** **1** put at rest; quiet; *My fears were allayed by the news that my family was safe.* **2** relieve (pain, trouble, thirst, etc.); alleviate. [Old English *ālecgan* < *ā-* away, off + *lecgan* to lay] —**al lay′er**, *n.*

al lude (ə lüd′), *v.i.*, **-lud ed, -lud ing.** refer indirectly *(to);* mention slightly in passing. [< Latin *alludere* < *ad-* + *ludere* to play]

al lure ment (ə lur′mənt), *n.* **1** charm; fascination. **2** thing that allures; temptation; attraction.

al oe (al′ō), *n.* **1** plant of the lily family growing chiefly in the warm, dry parts of southern Africa. **2 aloes**, *pl. in form, sing. in use.* a bitter drug made from the dried juice of this plant's leaves, used as a laxative or tonic.

am ber (am′bər), *adj.* yellow or yellowish-brown. [< Old French *ambre* < Arabic *'anbar* ambergris]

am bi ent (am′bē ənt), *adj.* all around; surrounding; encompassing. [< Latin *ambientem* < *ambi-* around + *ire* go]

am bi gu i ty (am′bə gyü′ə tē), *n., pl.* **-ties.** **1** possibility of being understood in two or more ways. **2** lack of clarity; vagueness; uncertainty.

am biv a lent (am biv′ə lənt), *adj.* acting in opposite ways; having or showing conflicting feelings. —**am biv′a lent ly**, *adv.*

am e thyst (am′ə thist), *n.* a purple or violet variety of quartz, used for jewelry.

a mor phous (ə môr′fəs), *adj.* **1** having no definite form; shapeless; formless. **2** of no particular type or pattern; not classifiable; anomalous. [< Greek *amorphos* < *a-* without + *morphē* shape]

-an, *suffix forming adjectives and nouns, especially from proper nouns.* **1** of or having to do with ____: *Mohammedan = of or having to do with Mohammed.* **2** of or having to do with ____ or its people: *Asian = of or having to do with Asia or its people.* **3** person who knows much about or is skilled in ____: *Magician = person skilled in magic.* Also, **-ian, -ean.**

a nach ro nism (ə nak′rə niz′əm), *n.* anything out of keeping with a specified time, especially something proper to a former age but not to the present. [< Greek *anachronismos* < *ana-* back + *chronos* time]

an ar chist (an′ər kist), *n.* **1** person who seeks to bring about the destruction of government and law; advocate of anarchism. **2** person who promotes disorder and stirs up revolt. —*adj.* anarchistic.

-ance, *suffix forming nouns chiefly from verbs.* **1** act or fact of ____ing: *Avoidance =*

act or fact of avoiding. **2** quality or state of being ____ed: *Annoyance = quality or state of being annoyed.* **3** thing that ____s: *Conveyance = thing that conveys.* **4** what is ____ed: *Contrivance = what is contrived.* **5** quality or state of being ____ant: *Importance = quality or state of being important.*

a ne mi a (ə nē′mē ə), *n.* **1** condition resulting from an insufficiency of hemoglobin or red blood cells or by a loss of blood, characterized by weakness, pallor, palpitation of the heart, and a tendency to fatigue. **2** lack of vigor or strength; weakness. Also, **anaemia.** [< Greek *anaimia* < *an-* not + *haima* blood]

an gu lar (ang′gyə lər), *adj.* **1** having an angle or angles; having corners; pointed. **2** somewhat thin and bony; not plump. **3** stiff and awkward.

anti-, *prefix.* **1** against ____; opposed to ____: *Antiaircraft = against aircraft.* **2** not ____; the opposite of ____: *Antisocial = the opposite of social.* **3** rival ____: *Antipope = rival pope.* **4** reducing or counteracting ____: *Antifriction = reducing or counteracting friction.* **5** preventing, curing, or alleviating ____: *Antiscorbutic = preventing or curing scurvy.*

an ti cli max (an′ti klī′maks), *n.* **1** an abrupt descent from the important to the trivial or unimportant. **2** descent (in importance, interest, etc.) contrasting sharply with a previous rise or high point.

an ti her o (an′ti hir′ō), *n., pl.* **-her oes.** a main character in a novel, play, etc., who has none of the qualities normally expected of a hero.

an tip a thy (an tip′ə thē), *n., pl.* **-thies.** a strong or fixed dislike; feeling against; aversion. [< Greek *antipatheia* < *anti-* against + *pathos* feeling]

an tip o des (an tip′ə dēz′), *n.pl.* **1** two opposites or contraries. **2** *pl.* or *sing. in use.* the direct opposite. [< Greek, with feet opposite < *anti-* + *pous, podos* foot]

an ti quar y (an′tə kwer′ē), *n., pl.* **-quar ies.** student or collector of relics from ancient times. —**an′ti quar′i an,** *n.*

an ti quat ed (an′tə kwā′tid), *adj.* **1** old-fashioned; out-of-date. **2** too old for work or service.

an trum (an′trəm), *n., pl.* **-tra** (-trə). cavity, especially one in a bone, often applied to the sinus in the maxilla.

aph o rism (af′ə riz′əm), *n.* a short sentence expressing a general truth or some practical wisdom; maxim. [< Greek *aphorismos* definition < *apo-* off + *horos* boundary]

ap os tol ic or **Ap os tol ic** (ap′ə stol′ik), *adj.* **1** of or having to do with an apostle or apostles. **2** of the Apostles, their beliefs, teachings, time, or nature.

a poth e o sis (ə poth′ē ō′sis, ap′ə thē′ə-sis), *n., pl.* **-ses** (-sēz′). **1** a glorified ideal. **2** the raising of a human being to the rank of a god; deification. [< Greek *apotheōsis* < *apo-* + *theos* god]

ap pease (ə pēz′), *v.t.,* **-peased, -peas ing. 1** put an end to by satisfying (an appetite or desire). **2** make calm or quiet; pacify. [< Old French *apaisier* < *a-* to + *pais* peace] —**ap peas′er,** *n.* —**ap peas′ing ly,** *adv.*

ap pease ment (ə pēz′mənt), *n.* an appeasing or a being appeased; pacification; satisfaction.

ap pel la tion (ap′ə lā′shən), *n.* **1** name or title describing or identifying someone. In

"John the Baptist," the appellation of *John* is *the Baptist.* **2** act of calling by a name.

ap praise (ə prāz′), *v.t.,* **-praised, -prais ing.** estimate the value of; fix a price for; value. [< Middle French *aprisier* < Latin *appretiare* < *ad-* to + *pretium* price] —**ap prais′ing ly,** *adv.*

ap pre hen sion (ap′ri hen′shən), *n.* expectation of misfortune; dread of impending danger; fear.

ap prise (ə prīz′), *v.t.,* **-prised, -pris ing.** give notice to; let know; inform; notify; advise. [< French *appris,* past participle of *apprendre* learn < Latin *apprehendere*]

ap prize (ə prīz′), *v.t.,* **-prized, -priz ing.** apprise.

ap pro ba tion (ap′rə bā′shən), *n.* favorable opinion; approval. [< Latin *approbationem*]

ap pro pri a tion (ə prō′prē ā′shən), *n.* sum of money or other thing appropriated.

ap pur te nance (ə pèrt′n əns), *n.* addition to something more important; added thing; accessory. [< Anglo-French *apurtenance*]

ar a besque (ar′ə besk′), *n.* an elaborate and fanciful design of flowers, leaves, geometrical figures, etc. [< French < Italian *arabesco* < *Arabo* Arab]

ar bi trar y (är′bə trer′ē), *adj.* **1** based on one's own wishes, notions, or will; not going by rule or law. **2** using or abusing unlimited power; tyrannical; despotic. —**ar′bi trar′i ly,** *adv.* —**ar′bi trar′i ness,** *n.*

ar che type (är′kə tīp), *n.* an original model or pattern from which copies are made, or out of which later forms develop; prototype. [< Greek *archetypon* < *archein* begin + *typos* type]

ar dent (ärd′nt), *adj.* **1** glowing with passion; passionate; impassioned: *ardent love.* **2** eager; keen. **3** burning; fiery; hot: *an ardent fever.* **4** glowing. [< Latin *ardentem* burning] —**ar′dent ly,** *adv.*

ar du ous (är′jü əs), *adj.* hard to do; requiring much effort; difficult. [< Latin *arduus* steep] —**ar′du ous ly,** *adv.* —**ar′du ous ness,** *n.*

ar is toc ra cy (ar′ə stok′rə sē), *n., pl.* **-cies.** government in which the nobility or any privileged upper class rules. [< Late Latin *aristocratia* < Greek *aristokratia* < *aristos* best + *kratos* rule]

ar is to crat ic (ə ris′tə krat′ik), *adj.* **1** of or connected with aristocrats: *the aristocratic class.* **2** in keeping with the character of an aristocrat; stylish or grand: *an aristocratic air.* **3** snobbish; exclusive. **4** favoring aristocrats or government by aristocrats. —**a ris′to crat′i cal ly,** *adv.*

ar o mat ic (är′ə mat′ik), *adj.* sweet-smelling; fragrant; spicy. —**ar′o mat′i cal ly,** *adv.*

ar ray (ə rā′), *v.t.* dress in fine clothes; adorn. [< Anglo-French *arayer* < Old French *a-* to + *rei* order]

ar rears (ə rirz′), *n.pl.* **1** unpaid debts. **2** unfinished work; things not done on time. [< Old French *arere* < Popular Latin *ad retro* to the rear]

ar ro gant (ar′ə gənt), *adj.* excessively proud and contemptuous of others. [< Latin *arrogantem* < *ad-* to + *rogare* ask] —**ar′ro gant ly,** *adv.*

ar ti fice (är′tə fis), *n.* **1** a clever device or trick. **2** trickery; craft. **3** skill or ingenuity. [< Latin *artificium* < *artem* art + *facere* make]

-ary, *suffix forming nouns and adjectives.* **1** place for ____: *Infirmary = place for the infirm.* **2** collection of ____: *Statuary =*

collection of statues. **3** person or thing that ____s: *Boundary = thing that bounds.* **4** of or having to do with ____: *Legendary = of legend.* **5** being; having the nature of ____: *Secondary = being second.* **6** characterized by ____: *Customary = characterized by custom.*

as cer tain (as′ər tan′), *v.t.* find out for certain by trial and research; make sure of; determine. [< Old French *ascertener* < *a-* to + *certain* certain]

as cribe (ə skrib′), *v.t.,* **-cribed, -crib ing. 1** think of as caused by or coming from; assign; attribute *(to).* **2** consider as belonging *(to).* [< Latin *ascribere* < *ad-* to + *scribere* write]

as pi rate (*v.* as′pə rāt′; *adj., n.* as′pər it), *v.,* **-rat ed, -rat ing,** *adj., n.* —*v.t.* **1** begin (a word or syllable) with a breathing or *h-* sound. *Hot* is aspirated; *honor* is not. **2** pronounce with such a sound. The *h* in *forehead* is usually not aspirated. —*adj.* pronounced with a breathing or *h-*sound. The *h* in *here* is aspirate. [< Latin *aspiratum* breathed toward < *ad-* + *spirare* breathe]

as pi ra tion (as′pə rā′shən), *n.* earnest desire; longing; ambition.

as sail (ə sāl′), *v.t.* attack with hostile words, arguments, or abuse. [< Old French *asalir* < Latin *ad-* at + *salire* to leap] —**as sail′a ble,** *adj.* —**as sail′er,** *n.*

as sess (ə ses′), *v.t.* examine critically and estimate the merit, significance, value, etc., of. [< Medieval Latin *assessare* fix a tax < Latin *assidere* sit by, attend < *ad-* by + *sedere* sit]

as sid u ous (ə sij′ü əs), *adj.* careful and attentive; diligent. [< Latin *assiduus* < *assidere* sit by] —**as sid′u ous ly,** *adv.*

a sun der (ə sun′dər), *adv.* in pieces; into separate parts. [Old English *on sundran*]

-ate, *suffix forming adjectives, verbs, and nouns.* **1** of or having to do with ____: *Collegiate = having to do with college.* **2** having or containing ____: *Compassionate = having compassion.* **3** having the form of ____; like ____: *Stellate = having the form of a star.* **4** become ____: *Maturate = become mature.* **5** cause to be ____: *Alienate = cause to be alien.* **6** produce ____: *Ulcerate = produce ulcers.*

a tone ment (ə tōn′mənt), *n.* a giving of satisfaction for a wrong, loss, or injury; amends. [< earlier *at onement* a being at one, that is, in accord]

au dac i ty (ô das′ə tē), *n.* **1** reckless daring; boldness. **2** rude boldness; impudence; presumption. [< Latin *audacia* < *audax* bold < *audere* to dare]

au di tor (ô′də tər), *n.* hearer; listener.

au re o la (ô rē′ə lə), *n.* aureole.

au re ole (ôr′ē ōl), *n.* ring of light surrounding the sun. [< Late Latin *aureola* golden < Latin *aurum* gold]

aus tere (ô stir′), *adj.* **1** stern in manner or appearance; harsh. **2** severe in self-discipline; strict in morals. **3** severely simple. [< Greek *austēros* < *auos* dry] —**aus tere′ly,** *adv.* —**aus tere′ness,** *n.*

au toc ra cy (ô tok′rə sē), *n., pl.* **-cies.** supreme power of government exerted by one person.

au to crat (ô′tə krat), *n.* **1** ruler who claims or exerts unrestricted power and uncontrolled authority over his subjects. **2** person who rules with undisputed sway or supremacy in any group or sphere. [< Greek *autokratēs* ruling by oneself < *auto-* + *kratos* strength]

au tom a tism (ô tom′ə tiz′əm), *n.* action

not controlled by the will; involuntary action; automatic action.

av ar ice (av′ər is), *n.* too great a desire for money or property; greed for wealth. [< Old French < Latin *avaritia* < *avarus* greedy]

a verse (ə vèrs′), *adj.* having a strong or fixed dislike; opposed or unwilling. [< Latin *aversum* turned away < *ab-* from + *vertere* to turn]

a vert (ə vèrt′), *v.t.* turn away or turn aside (the face, eyes, mind, etc.). [< Latin *avertere* < *ab-* from + *vertere* to turn]

ax i om (ak′sē əm), *n.* 1 statement taken to be true without proof; self-evident truth. 2 a well-established principle; rule or law. [< Latin *axioma* < Greek *axiōma* < *axios* worthy]

az ure (azh′ər), *n.* the clear blue color of the unclouded sky; sky blue. —*adj.* sky-blue. [< Old French *l'azur* the azure < Arabic *lāzuward* < Persian *lajward* lapis lazuli]

ba nal (bā′nl, bə nal′, ban′l), *adj.* not new or interesting; commonplace; trite. [< French] —**ba′nal ly,** *adv.*

ban do leer or **ban do lier** (ban′dl ir′), *n.* a broad belt worn over the shoulder and across the breast, often with loops for carrying cartridges or with small cases for bullets, gunpowder, etc. [< French *bandoulière* < Spanish *bandolera*]

bar ba rism (bär′bə riz′əm), *n.* 1 condition of uncivilized people: *People who have no form of writing live in barbarism.* 2 a barbarous act, custom, or trait.

bar bar ous (bär′bər əs), *adj.* 1 not civilized; savage. 2 savagely cruel; brutal. 3 rough and rude; coarse; unrefined. —**bar′bar ous ly,** *adv.* —**bar′bar ous ness,** *n.*

bark (bärk), *n.* 1 a three-masted ship, square-rigged on the first two masts and fore-and-aft-rigged on the other. 2 ARCHAIC. boat; ship. Also, **barque.** [< Middle French *barque* < Italian *barca* < Late Latin]

bel lig er ent (bə lij′ər ənt), *adj.* 1 waging or carrying on regular recognized war; actually engaged in hostilities; at war; fighting. 2 having to do with nations or persons at war. 3 fond of fighting; tending or inclined to war; warlike; pugnacious. [< Latin *belligerantem* < *bellum* war + *gerere* to wage] —**bel lig′er ent ly,** *adv.*

be nef i cent (bə nef′ə sənt), *adj.* 1 doing good; kind. 2 having good results. —**benef′i cent ly,** *adv.*

be reave (bi rēv′), *v.t.,* **-reaved** or **-reft, -reav ing.** leave desolate and alone. [Old English *berēafian* < *be-* away + *rēafian* rob]

be reft (bi reft′), *adj.* bereaved: *Bereft of hope and friends, the old man led a lonely life.* —*v.* a pt. and a pp. of **bereave.**

be stow (bi stō′), *v.t.* 1 give (something) as a gift; give; confer. 2 make use of; apply.

be to ken (bi tō′kən), *v.t.* be a sign or token of; indicate; show.

blanch (blanch), *v.t.* 1 make white or pale. 2 whiten or prevent from becoming green by excluding the light, as the stems or leaves of plants such as celery or lettuce. —*v.i.* turn white or pale: *blanch with fear.* [< Old French *blanchir* < *blanc* white]

blas phe my (blas′fə mē), *n., pl.* **-mies.** abuse or contempt for God or sacred things; profanity.

blight (blīt), *n.* 1 disease of plants that causes leaves, stems, fruits, and tissues to wither and die. 2 anything that withers hope

or causes destruction or ruin. 3 decay; deterioration.

blithe (blīŦH, blīth), *adj.* 1 happy and cheerful; gay; joyous. 2 heedless. [Old English *blithe*] —**blithe′ly,** *adv.* —**blithe′ness,** *n.*

bow er (bou′ər), *n.* 1 shelter of leafy branches. 2 summerhouse or arbor. [Old English *būr* dwelling]

brack en (brak′ən), *n.* 1 a large, coarse fern common on hillsides, in woods, etc. 2 thicket of these ferns. [Middle English *braken,* apparently < Scandinavian (Swedish) *bräken*]

brack ish (brak′ish), *adj.* 1 slightly salty. 2 distasteful. [< earlier *brack* brackish < Dutch *brak*] —**brack′ish ness,** *n.*

brass y (bras′ē), *adj.* INFORMAL. shameless; impudent.

bra va do (brə vä′dō), *n., pl.* **-does** or **-dos.** a show of courage or boldness without much real courage; defiant or blustering behavior. [< Spanish *bravada,* ultimately < *bravo*]

bra vur a (brə vyur′ə), *n.* 1 show of brilliant performance. 2 dash; spirit. [< Italian, bravery]

breast work (brest′werk′), *n.* a low, sometimes hastily built wall for defense.

bro cade (brō kād′), *n., v.,* **-cad ed, -cad ing.** —*n.* an expensive cloth woven with raised designs on it, used for clothing or upholstery. —*v.t.* weave or decorate with raised designs. [< Spanish *brocado*]

brusque (brusk), *adj.* abrupt in manner or speech; blunt. [< French < Italian *brusco* coarse] —**brusque′ness,** *n.*

bur go mas ter (bėr′gə mas′tər), *n.* mayor of a town in Austria, Belgium, Germany, or the Netherlands. [< Dutch *burgemeester* < *burg* borough + *meester* master]

bux om (buk′səm), *adj.* (of a woman) plump and good to look at; healthy and cheerful. [Middle English *buhsum* < Old English *būgan* to bend]

cache (kash), *n.* 1 a hiding place, especially of goods, treasure, food, etc. 2 the store of food or supplies hidden. [< French < *cacher* to hide]

cach in na tion (kak′ə nā′shən), *n.* loud or immoderate laughter. [< Latin *cachinnationem* < *cachinnare* laugh loudly]

ca dence (kād′ns), *n.* 1 fall of the voice. 2 a rising and falling sound; modulation. [< French < Italian *cadenza* < Latin *cadere* to fall]

cad mi um (kad′mē əm), *n.* a soft, bluish-white; ductile metallic element resembling tin, which occurs only in combination with other elements and is used in plating to prevent corrosion and in making alloys.

ca jole (kə jōl′), *v.t.,* **-joled, -jol ing.** persuade by pleasant words, flattery, or false promises; coax. [< French *cajoler*] —**cajol′er,** *n.*

cal ce o lar i a (kal′sē ə ler′ē ə), *n.* American plant with very striking flowers.

cal i co (kal′ə kō), *n., pl.* **-coes** or **-cos,** *adj.* —*n.* a cotton cloth that usually has colored patterns printed on one side. —*adj.* 1 made of calico: *a calico dress.* 2 spotted in colors.

cal lous (kal′əs), *adj.* unfeeling; insensitive: *Only a callous person can see suffering without trying to relieve it.* —**cal′lous ly,** *adv.* —**cal′lous ness,** *n.*

cam bric (kām′brik), *n.* a fine, thin linen or cotton cloth. [< *Cambrai,* city in France]

can o py (kan′ə pē), *n., pl.* **-pies,** *v.,* **-pied, -py ing.** —*n.* 1 a covering fixed over a bed,

hat, āge, fär; let, ēqual, tėrm;
it, īce; hot, ōpen, ôrder;
oil, out; cup, pùt, rüle;
ch, child; ng, long; sh, she;
th, thin; ŦH, then; zh, measure;

ə represents *a* in about, *e* in taken,
i in pencil, *o* in lemon, *u* in circus.

< = from, derived from, taken from.

throne, entrance, etc., or carried on poles over a person. 2 a rooflike covering; shelter or shade. —*v.t.* cover with a canopy. [< Old French *canape* < Medieval Latin *canapeum* < Greek *kōnōpion* a couch with curtains of mosquito netting < *kōnōps* gnat]

ca pa cious (kə pā′shəs), *adj.* able to hold much; large and roomy; spacious: *a capacious closet.* —**ca pa′cious ly,** *adv.* —**ca pa′cious ness,** *n.*

ca pit u late (kə pich′ə lāt), *v.i.,* **-lat ed, -lat ing.** surrender on certain terms or conditions. [< Medieval Latin *capitulatum* arranged under headings or chapters < Latin *capitulum* small head < *caput* head]

ca price (kə prēs′), *n.* 1 a sudden change of mind without reason; unreasonable notion or desire; whim. 2 tendency to change suddenly and without reason. [< French < Italian *capriccio,* literally, a shiver]

car bun cle (kär′bung kəl), *n.* a very painful, inflamed swelling under the skin caused by infection. [< Latin *carbunculus* < *carbonem* coal]

car i ca ture (kar′ə kə chùr, kar′ə kə chər), *n., v.,* **-tured, -tur ing.** 1 picture, cartoon, or description that exaggerates the peculiarities of a person or the defects of a thing. 2 imitation or rendering of something by ridiculous exaggeration of flaws in the original.

car nage (kär′nij), *n.* slaughter of a great number of people. [< Middle French < Italian *carnaggio,* ultimately < Latin *carnem* flesh]

car niv or ous (kär niv′ər əs), *adj.* 1 of or having to do with an order of mammals that feed chiefly on flesh. 2 using other animals as food; flesh-eating: *the strong carnivorous eagle.* [< Latin *carnivorus* < *carnem* flesh + *vorare* devour] —**car niv′or ous ly,** *adv.*

car tog ra pher (kär tog′rə fər), *n.* maker of maps or charts.

case ment (kās′mənt), *n.* 1 window or part of a window which opens on hinges like a door. 2 a casing; covering; frame.

cat a comb (kat′ə kōm), *n.* Usually, **catacombs,** *pl.* an underground gallery forming a burial place, especially a network of such galleries with recesses in which to place the dead. [< Late Latin *catacumbae,* plural]

cat a mount (kat′ə mount), *n.* wildcat, such as a puma or lynx. [short for *catamountain* cat of (the) mountain]

cat a ract (kat′ə rakt′), *n.* 1 a large, steep waterfall. 2 a violent rush or downpour of water; flood. [< Latin *cataracta* < Greek *kataraktēs* < *kata-* down + *arassein* to dash]

ca tas tro phe (kə tas′trə fē), *n.* outcome, especially of a literary work; ending. The catastrophe of a tragedy usually brings death or ruin to the leading character.

caulk (kôk), *v.t.* fill up (a seam, crack, or joint) so that it will not leak; make watertight. Sailors caulk wooden boats with oakum and tar. Also, **calk.** [< Old French *cauquer* press in, tread < Latin *calcare* < *calcem* heel] **—caulk′er,** *n.*

cau ter y (kôt′ə rē), *n.* a heated iron with which dead tissue is burned away.

ca vort (kə vôrt′), *v.* U.S. prance about; jump around.

ce les tial (sə les′chəl), *adj.* of or belonging to heaven as the place of God and the angels; heavenly; divine. [< Latin *caelestis* < *caelum* heaven]

cel i ba cy (sel′ə bə sē), *n.* unmarried state; single life.

cel lu lar (sel′yə lər), *adj.* 1 having to do with the cells. 2 cell-like.

cen sure (sen′shər), *n., v.,* **-sured, -sur ing.** —*n.* 1 expression of disapproval; unfavorable opinion; criticism. 2 penalty, as a public rebuke or suspension from office. —*v.t.* express disapproval of; find fault with; criticize. [< Latin *censura* < *censere* appraise]

cen tri fuge (sen′trə fyüj), *n.* machine for separating two substances varying in density, as cream from milk or bacteria from a fluid, by means of centrifugal force.

chafe (chāf), *v.,* **chafed, chaf ing.** —*v.t.* 1 rub so as to wear away, scrape, or make sore: *The stiff collar chafed my neck.* 2 rub to make warm: *She chafed her cold hands.* 3 make angry: *Their teasing chafed me.* —*v.i.* become angry: *I chafed under their teasing.* [< Old French *chaufer* to warm < Latin *calefacere* < *calere* be warm + *facere* make]

chal ice (chal′is), *n.* 1 cup or goblet. 2 cup that holds the wine used in the Communion service. 3 a cup-shaped blossom of a flower. [< Old French < Latin *calicem* cup]

char y (cher′ē, char′ē), *adj.,* **char i er, char i est.** 1 showing caution; careful; wary. 2 shy. 3 sparing; stingy. [Old English *cearig* sorrowful < *caru* care]

chas tise ment (cha stīz′mənt, chas′tiz ment), *n.* punishment.

chide (chīd), *v.,* **chid ed, chid, chid ing.** —*v.t.* find fault with; reproach or blame; scold. —*v.i.* find fault; speak in rebuke. [Old English *cīdan*]

chol er ic (kol′ər ik), *adj.* 1 having an irritable disposition; easily made angry. 2 enraged; angry; wrathful.

churl ish (chėr′lish), *adj.* rude or surly; bad-tempered.

cir cum nav i gate (sèr′kəm nav′ə gāt), *v.t.,* **-gat ed, -gat ing.** sail around. **—cir′ cum nav′i ga′tion,** *n.*

cir cum spect (sèr′kəm spekt), *adj.* watchful on all sides; cautious or prudent; careful.

ci ta tion (sī tā′shən), *n.* honorable mention for bravery in war.

ci vil i ty (sə vil′ə tē), *n., pl.* **-ties.** polite behavior; courtesy.

clam or ous (klam′ər əs), *adj.* loud and noisy; shouting.

clem en cy (klem′ən sē), *n., pl.* **-cies.** gentleness in the use of power or authority; mercy or leniency.

clois ter (kloi′stər), *n.* 1 place of religious retirement; convent or monastery. 2 a quiet place shut away from the world. —*v.t.* shut away in a quiet place.

clo ven (klō′vən), *adj.* split; divided.

cloy (kloi), *v.t., v.i.* 1 make or become weary by too much, too sweet, or too rich food. 2 make or become weary by too much of anything pleasant.

co a lesce (kō′ə les′), *v.i.,* **-lesced, -lesc ing.** 1 grow together. 2 unite into one body,

mass, party, etc.; combine. [< Latin *coalescere* < *co-* together + *alescere* grow]

col um bine (kol′əm bīn), *n.* any of a genus of plants of the same family as the buttercup, whose flowers have petals shaped like hollow spurs.

com bus ti ble (kəm bus′tə bəl), *adj.* capable of taking fire and burning; easily burned: *Gasoline is highly combustible.* —*n.* a combustible substance. **—com bus′ti bly,** *adv.* **—com bus′ti bil′i ty,** *n.*

come li ness (kum′lē nis), *n.* pleasant appearance; attractiveness.

com min gle (kə ming′gəl), *v.t., v.i.,* **-gled, -gling.** mingle with one another; blend.

com mun ion (kə myü′nyən), *n.* 1 act of sharing; a having in common. 2 exchange of thoughts and feelings; intimate talk; fellowship. 3 a close spiritual relationship.

com pas sion (kəm pash′ən), *n.* feeling for another's sorrow or hardship that leads to help; sympathy; pity. [< Latin *compassionem* < *compati* suffer with < *com-* with + *pati* suffer]

com pel (kəm pel′), *v.t.,* **-pelled, -pel ling.** 1 drive or urge with force; force. 2 cause or get by force. [< Latin *compellere* < *com-* + *pellere* to drive] **—com pel′ling ly,** *adv.*

com pla cent (kəm plā′snt), *adj.* pleased with oneself or what one has; self-satisfied: *The winner's complacent smile annoyed the loser.* [< Latin *complacentem,* < *com-* + *placere* please] **—com pla′cent ly,** *adv.*

com pli ance (kəm plī′əns), *n.* 1 a complying or doing as another wishes; yielding to a request or command. 2 tendency to yield to others. 3 **in compliance with,** complying with; according to.

com port (kəm pôrt′, kəm pōrt′), *v.t.* conduct (oneself) in a certain manner; behave: *Judges should comport themselves with dignity.* —*v.i.* agree; suit: *Bigotry does not comport with the position of judge.* [< Latin *comportare* < *com-* together + *portare* carry]

com po sure (kəm pō′zhər), *n.* calmness; quietness; self-control.

com pul sion (kəm pul′shən), *n.* 1 a compelling or a being compelled; use of force; force; coercion. 2 impulse that is hard to resist. [< Late Latin *compulsionem* < Latin *compellere.* See COMPEL.]

con ceiv a ble (kən sē′və bəl), *adj.* that can be conceived or thought of; imaginable. **—con ceiv′a bly,** *adv.*

con ceive (kən sēv′), *v.,* **-ceived, -ceiv ing.** —*v.t.* form in the mind; think up; have an idea or feeling; think; imagine. [< Old French *conceveir* < Latin *concipere* take in < *com-* + *capere* take] **—con ceiv′er,** *n.*

con cen tric (kən sen′trik), *adj.* having the same center; *concentric circles.*

con cil i ate (kən sil′ē āt), *v.t.,* **-at ed, -at ing.** 1 gain (good will, regard, favor, etc.) by friendly acts. 2 bring into harmony; reconcile. [< Latin *conciliatum* brought together, made friendly < *concilium*] **—con cil′i a to′ry,** *adj.*

con do lence (kən dō′ləns), *n.* expression of sympathy: *Their friends sent condolences.*

con duce (kən düs′, kən dyüs′), *v.i.,* **-duced, -duc ing.** be favorable; lead; contribute: *Darkness and quiet conduce to sleep.* [< Latin *conducere.* See CONDUCT.]

con du cive (kən dü′siv, kən dyü′siv), *adj.* favorable; helpful: *Exercise is conducive to health.* **—con du′cive ness,** *n.*

con duct (kən dukt′), *v.t.* 1 direct the course of; manage. 2 guide; lead. [< Latin *conductum* < *conducere* to lead together < *com-* together + *ducere* lead]

con duc tiv i ty (kon′duk tiv′ə tē), *n.* 1 power of conducting heat, electricity, etc. 2 mutual understanding.

con fis cate (kon′fə skāt), *v.t.,* **-cat ed, -cat ing.** 1 seize for the public treasury. 2 seize by authority; take and keep. [< Latin *confiscatum* laid away in a chest < *com-* + *fiscus* chest, public treasury] **—con fis′ca to′ry,** *adj.*

con fla gra tion (kon′flə grā′shən), *n.* a great and destructive fire. [< Latin *conflagrationem* < *conflagrare* burn up < *com-* up + *flagrare* burn]

con for ma tion (kon′fôr mā′shən), *n.* 1 form of a thing resulting from the arrangement of its parts; structure; shape. 2 a symmetrical arrangement of the parts of a thing. 3 a conforming; adaptation.

con geal (kən jēl′), *v.t., v.i.* 1 change from a liquid to a solid by freezing; freeze. 2 thicken; stiffen; coagulate. [< Old French *congeler* < Latin *congelare* < *com-* up + *gelare* to freeze] **—con geal′ment,** *n.*

con glom e ra tion (kən glom′ə rā′shən), *n.* a mixed-up mass of various things or persons; mixture.

con jure (kon′jər, kun′jər), *v.t.,* **-jured, -jur ing.** 1 compel (a spirit, devil, etc.) to appear or disappear by a set form of words. 2 cause to appear or happen as if by magic: *conjure up a whole meal in a jiffy.* 3 cause to appear in the mind: *conjure a vision.* [< Old French *conjurer* < Latin *conjurare* make a compact < *com-* together + *jurare* swear]

con nate (kon′āt), *adj.* existing from birth or origin.

con niv ance (kə nī′vəns), *n.* a conniving; pretended ignorance or secret encouragement of wrongdoing.

con nois seur (kon′ə sèr′), *n.* a critical judge of art or of matters of taste; expert: *a connoisseur of antique furniture.* [< Old French < *connoistre* know < Latin *cognoscere*] **—con′nois seur′ship,** *n.*

con san guin i ty (kon′sang gwin′ə tē), *n.* 1 relationship by descent from the same parent or ancestor; relationship by blood. 2 likeness or affinity.

con se crate (kon′sə krāt), *v.t.,* **-crat ed, -crat ing.** 1 set apart as sacred; make holy; sanctify. 2 make an object of veneration or cherished regard; hallow. [< Latin *consecratum* made sacred < *com-* + *sacer* sacred]

con sort (kən sôrt′), *v.i.* 1 keep company; associate. 2 agree; accord. [< Middle French < Latin *consortem* sharer < *com-* with + *sortem* lot]

con spic u ous (kən spik′yü əs), *adj.* 1 easily seen; clearly visible. 2 worthy of notice; remarkable. [< Latin *conspicuus* visible < *conspicere* look at < *com-* + *specere* look]

con spir a cy (kən spir′ə sē), *n., pl.* **-cies.** 1 act of conspiring; secret planning with others to do something unlawful or wrong, especially against a government, public personage, etc. 2 a plot or intrigue.

con spire (kən spīr′), *v.i.,* **-spired, -spir ing.** 1 plan secretly with others to do something unlawful or wrong; plot. 2 act together: *All things conspired to make her birthday a happy one.*

con ster na tion (kon′stər nā′shən), *n.* great dismay; paralyzing terror. [< Latin *consternationem* < *consternare* terrify]

con stit u ent (kən stich′ü ənt), *n.* voter.

con strain (kən strān′), *v.t.* 1 force; compel: *The principal was constrained to punish the rude child.* 2 confine; imprison.

3 repress; restrain. [< Old French *constreindre* < Latin *constringere* < *com-* together + *stringere* pull tightly] —**con strain′er**, *n.*

con strict (kən strikt′), *v.t.* draw together; contract; compress. [< Latin *constrictum* constricted < *com-* together + *stringere* pull tightly]

con ta gious (kən tā′jəs), *adj.* 1 spreading by direct or indirect contact; catching: *Scarlet fever is a contagious disease.* 2 causing contagious diseases.

con tempt (kən tempt′), *n.* 1 the feeling that a person, act, or thing is mean, low, or worthless; scorn; despising; disdain. 2 a being scorned; disgrace. [< Latin *contemptus* < *contemnere*]

con temp tu ous (kən temp′chü əs), *adj.* showing contempt; scornful: *a contemptuous look.* —**con temp′tu ous ly,** *adv.*

con tral to (kən tral′tō), *n.,* pl. **-tos,** *adj.* —*n.* the lowest female voice; alto. —*adj.* of or for a contralto. [< Italian < *contra-* counter to + *alto* high]

con tri tion (kən trish′ən), *n.* 1 sorrow for one's sins or guilt; being contrite; penitence. 2 deep regret.

con triv ance (kən trī′vəns), *n.* thing invented; mechanical device.

con trive (kən trīv′), *v.t.,* **-trived, -triv ing.** 1 plan with cleverness or skill; invent; design. 2 plan; scheme; plot: *contrive a robbery.* [< Old French *controver* < Late Latin *contropare* compare]

con tu me ly (kən tü′mə lē, kən tyü′mə lē; kon′tü mə lē, kon′tyə mə lē), *n.,* pl. **-lies.** 1 insolent contempt; insulting words or actions; humiliating treatment. 2 a humiliating insult. [< Latin *contumelia,* related to *contumacia* contumacy]

co nun drum (kə nun′drəm), *n.* 1 riddle whose answer involves a pun or play on words. EXAMPLE: "When is a door not a door?" *Answer:* "When it's ajar." 2 any puzzling problem. [origin unknown]

con vul sion (kən vul′shən), *n.* 1 Often, **convulsions,** *pl.* a violent, involuntary contracting and relaxing of the muscles; spasm; fit. 2 a fit of laughter. 3 a violent disturbance: *The country was undergoing a political convulsion.*

con vul sive (kən vul′siv), *adj.* 1 violently disturbing. 2 having convulsions. 3 producing convulsions. —**con vul′sive ly,** *adv.* —**con vul′sive ness,** *n.*

co pi ous (kō′pē əs), *adj.* 1 more than enough; plentiful; abundant: *a copious harvest.* 2 containing much matter. 3 containing many words. [< Latin *copiosus* < *copia* plenty < *co-* with + *ops* resources] —**co′pi ous ly,** *adv.* —**co′pi ous ness,** *n.*

co quette (kō ket′), *n.* woman who tries to attract men merely to please her vanity.

cor nice (kôr′nis), *n.* 1 an ornamental, horizontal molding along the top of a wall, pillar, building, etc. 2 a molding around the walls of a room just below the ceiling or over the top of a window. [< French *corniche* < Italian *cornice*]

cor nu co pi a (kôr′nə kō′pē ə), *n.* 1 a horn-shaped container represented as overflowing with fruits, vegetables, and flowers; horn of plenty. 2 a horn-shaped container or ornament. [< Late Latin, for Latin *cornu copiae* horn of plenty]

cor pu lent (kôr′pyə lənt), *adj.* large or bulky of body; fat. —**cor′pu lent ly,** *adv.*

cor set (kôr′sit), *n.* a woman's stiff, close-fitting undergarment, worn about the waist and hips to support or shape the body.

co til lion (kə til′yən), *n.* 1 a dance with complicated steps and much changing of partners, led by one couple. 2 an early French social dance for couples. 3 any large social dance. [< French *cotillon,* originally, petticoat]

coun te nance (koun′tə nəns), *n.,* *v.,* **-nanced, -nanc ing.** —*n.* 1 expression of the face: *an angry countenance.* 2 face; features: *a noble countenance.* 3 approval; encouragement. 4 calmness; composure: *lose countenance.* —*v.t.* approve or encourage; sanction. [< Old French *contenance* < Medieval Latin *continentia* demeanor < Latin, self-control < *continere*]

coun ter feit (koun′tər fit), *v.t.* 1 copy (money, handwriting, pictures, etc.) in order to deceive or defraud; forge. 2 pretend; dissemble. —*adj.* not genuine; sham. [< Old French *contrefait* imitated, past participle of *contrefaire* < *contre-* against + *faire* make] —**coun′ter feit′er,** *n.*

cov e nant (kuv′ə nənt), *n.* 1 a solemn agreement between two or more persons or groups to do or not to do a certain thing; compact. 2 a formal agreement that is legal; legal contract. 3 (in the Bible) the solemn promises of God to man; compact between God and man. [< Old French, present participle of *covenir* agree < Latin *convenire*]

crass (kras), *adj.* 1 gross or stupid. 2 thick; coarse. [< Latin *crassus* thick] —**crass′ly,** *adv.* —**crass′ness,** *n.*

crep i tate (krep′ə tāt), *v.i.,* **-tat ed, -tat ing.** crackle; rattle. [< Latin *crepitatum* crackled < *crepare* to crack] —**crep′i ta′tion,** *n.*

cro quet (krō kā′), *n.* an outdoor game played by driving wooden balls through wickets with mallets.

crypt (kript), *n.* an underground room or vault. The crypt beneath the main floor of a church was formerly often used as a burial place. [< Latin *crypta* < Greek *kryptē* vault < *kryptos* hidden]

cryp to gram (krip′tə gram), *n.* something written in secret code or cipher. [< Greek *kryptos* hidden + English *-gram*]

cudg el (kuj′əl), *n.* a short, thick stick used as a weapon; club. [Old English *cycgel*]

cu mu la tive (kyü′myə lə tiv, kyü′myə lā′tiv), *adj.* increasing or growing in amount, force, etc., by additions; accumulated. A cumulative dividend is one that must be added to future dividends if not paid when due. —**cu′mu la tive ly,** *adv.* —**cu′mu la tive ness,** *n.*

cu po la (kyü′pə lə), *n.* 1 a rounded roof; dome. 2 a small dome or tower on a roof. [< Italian < Late Latin *cupula,* diminutive of Latin *cupa* tub]

dam ask (dam′əsk), *n.* 1 a firm, shiny, reversible linen, silk, or cotton fabric with woven designs. 2 linen material of this type used especially for tablecloths and napkins. —*adj.* 1 made of damask. 2 rose-colored; pink. [< Greek *Damaskos* Damascus]

de bauch (di bôch′), *v.i.* indulge excessively in sensual pleasures, eating, drinking, etc. —**de bauch′ee,** *n.*

deb u tante or **dé bu tante** (deb′yə tänt, deb′yə tant, deb′yə tänt′), *n.* 1 a young woman during her first season in society. 2 woman making a debut. [< French *débutante*]

dec a dence (dek′ə dəns, di kād′ns), *n.* a

hat, āge, fär; let, ēqual, tėrm;
it, īce; hot, ōpen, ôrder;
oil, out; cup, pút, rüle;
ch, child; ng, long; sh, she;
th, thin; ᴛH, then; zh, measure;

ə represents *a* in about, *e* in taken,
i in pencil, *o* in lemon, *u* in circus.

< = from, derived from, taken from.

falling off; growing worse; decline; decay: *The decadence of morals was one of the causes of the fall of Rome.* [< Middle French *décadence* < Medieval Latin *decadentia* < Latin *de-* + *cadere* to fall]

de cap i tate (di kap′ə tāt), *v.t.,* **-tat ed, -tat ing.** cut off the head of; behead.

de clen sion (di klen′shən), *n.* in grammar: the giving of the different forms of nouns, pronouns, and adjectives according to their case, number, and gender, usually in a given order, so far as such variations occur in the language to which the words belong. [ultimately < Latin *declinationem* < *declinare*]

de co rum (di kôr′əm, di kōr′əm), *n.* proper behavior; good taste in conduct, speech, dress, etc. [< Latin, (that which is) seemly < *decor* seemliness]

def er ence (def′ər əns), *n.* 1 a yielding to the judgment, opinion, wishes, etc., of another. 2 great respect.

def e ren tial (def′ə ren′shəl), *adj.* showing deference; respectful. —**def′e ren′tial ly,** *adv.*

de fin i tive (di fin′ə tiv), *adj.* 1 that decides or settles a question; conclusive; final. 2 authoritative; completely reliable. 3 limiting; defining. —**de fin′i tive ly,** *adv.* —**de fin′i tive ness,** *n.*

de gen e rate (*v.* di jen′ə rāt′; *adj., n.* di jen′ər it), *v.,* **-rat ed, -rat ing,** *adj., n.* —*v.i.* grow worse; decline in physical, mental, or moral qualities. —*adj.* that has degenerated; showing a decline in physical, mental, or moral qualities. —*n.* person having a degenerate or unwholesome character. [< Latin *degeneratum* away from one's kind < *de-* away + *generem* race, kind] —**de gen′e rate ly,** *adv.* —**de gen′e rate ness,** *n.*

de grade (di grād′), *v.t.,* **-grad ed, -grad ing.** 1 reduce in rank, especially as a punishment. 2 bring into dishonor or contempt. 3 lower in character or quality; debase. [< Late Latin *degradare* < Latin *de-* down + *gradus* grade] —**deg′ra da′tion,** *n.*

de i fy (dē′ə fī), *v.t.,* **-fied, -fy ing.** 1 make a god of. 2 worship or regard as a god: *deify wealth.* [< Old French *deifier* < Late Latin *deificare* < Latin *deus* god + *facere* make]

del e gate (del′ə gāt), *v.t.* 1 appoint or send (a person) as a representative: *Each club delegated one member to attend the state meeting.* 2 give over to another so that he may act for one. [< Latin *delegatum* delegated < *de-* + *legare* send with a commission]

de lib e ra tion (di lib′ə rā′shən), *n.* 1 careful thought. 2 discussion of reasons for and against something; debate. 3 slowness and care.

de lin e ate (di lin′ē āt), *v.t.,* **-at ed, -at ing.** 1 trace the outline of. 2 draw; sketch. 3 describe in words; portray. [< Latin *delineatum* delineated < *de-* + *linea* line] —**de lin′e a′tor,** *n.*

de loo sion, delusion.

de lu sion (di lü′zhən), *n.* 1 a false belief or opinion. 2 a fixed belief maintained in spite of unquestionable evidence to the contrary. People with mental disorders often have delusions. [< Latin *delusionem* < *deludere*]

de mur (di mėr′), *v.,* **-murred, -mur ring,** *n.* —*v.i.* show disapproval or dislike; take exception; object. [< Old French *demurer* < Latin *demorari* < *de-* + *morari* to delay]

de noue ment or **dé noue ment** (dā′nü mäN′), *n.* 1 solution of a plot in a story, play, situation, etc. 2 outcome; end. [< French *dénouement* < *dénouer* untie]

de pos i to ry (di poz′ə tôr′ē, di poz′ə tōr′ē), *n., pl.* **-ries.** place where anything is stored for safekeeping; storehouse.

dep re cate (dep′rə kāt), *v.t.,* **-cat ed, -cat ing.** express strong disapproval of. [< Latin *deprecatum* pleaded in excuse, averted by prayer < *de-* + *precari* pray]

de pre ci a tion (di prē′shē ā′shən), *n.* reduction in the value of money.

dep ri va tion (dep′rə vā′shən), *n.* 1 act of depriving. 2 condition of being deprived; loss; privation.

de ride (di rīd′), *v.t.,* **-rid ed, -rid ing.** make fun of; laugh at in scorn. [< Latin *deridere* < *de-* + *ridere* to laugh]

de ri sive (di rī′siv), *adj.* that ridicules; mocking: *derisive laughter.*

de riv a tive (di riv′ə tiv), *adj.* coming from a source; not original; derived. —*n.* something derived. —**de riv′a tive ly,** *adv.*

der vish (dėr′vish), *n.* member of a Moslem mystical religious order that practices self-denial and devotion. Some dance and spin about violently. [< Turkish *derviş* < Persian *darvīsh*]

des ig na tion (dez′ig nā′shən), *n.* a descriptive title; name: *"Your Honor" is a designation given to a judge.*

des patch (dis pach′), *v., n.* dispatch.

de spoil (di spoil′), *v.t.* strip of possessions; rob; plunder. [< Latin *despoliare* < *de-* + *spolium* armor, booty]

des pot ic (des pot′ik), *adj.* of a despot; having unlimited power; tyrannical. —**des pot′i cal ly,** *adv.*

des pot ism (des′pə tiz′əm), *n.* 1 government by a despot. 2 tyranny or oppression.

des ti tu tion (des′tə tü′shən, des′tə tyü′shən), *n.* 1 destitute condition; extreme poverty. 2 a being without; lack.

det ri men tal (det′rə men′tl), *adj.* causing loss or damage; injurious; harmful. —**det′ri men′tal ly,** *adv.*

de vi ous (dē′vē əs), *adj.* 1 out of the direct way; winding; roundabout. 2 straying from the right course; not straightforward. [< Latin *devius* turning aside < *de-* out of + *via* way] —**de′vi ous ly,** *adv.* —**de′vi ous ness,** *n.*

de volve (di volv′), *v.i.,* **-volved, -volv ing.** be handed down to someone else; be transferred. [< Latin *devolvere* < *de-* down + *volvere* to roll]

di a dem (dī′ə dem), *n.* 1 a crown. 2 an ornamental band of cloth formerly worn as a crown. [< Latin *diadema* < Greek *diadēma* < *diadein* bind across < *dia-* + *dein* bind]

di as to le (dī as′tl ē), *n.* the normal, rhythmical dilation of the heart, especially that of the ventricles. During diastole the chambers of the heart fill up with blood.

dic tum (dik′təm), *n., pl.* **-tums** or **-ta.** 1 a formal comment; authoritative opinion. 2 maxim; saying. [< Latin, (thing) said < *dicere* say]

did dle (did′l), *v.t.,* **-dled, -dling.** INFORMAL. cheat; swindle.

dif fi dent (dif′ə dənt), *adj.* lacking in self-confidence; shy. [< Latin *diffidentem* < *dis-* + *fidere* to trust] —**dif′fi dent ly,** *adv.*

dif frac tion (di frak′shən), *n.* a spreading of light around an obstacle into a series of light and dark bands or into the colored bands of the spectrum.

dif fuse (di fyüz′), *v.i.,* **-fused, -fus ing.** 1 scatter widely; spread. 2 mix together by spreading into one another, as one gas with another or one liquid with another. [< Latin *diffusum* poured forth < *dis-* + *fundere* to pour]

di lap i dat ed (də lap′ə dā′tid), *adj.* fallen into ruin or disrepair; decayed through neglect. [< Latin *dilapidatum* scattered; ruined (as by hailstones) < *dis-* + *lapis* stone]

di late (dī lāt′, də lāt′), *v.i.,* **-lat ed, -lat ing.** become larger or wider.

diph ther i a (dif thir′ē ə, dip thir′ē ə), *n.* an acute, infectious disease of the throat, usually accompanied by a high fever and the formation of a membranous substance that hinders respiration.

dirge (dėrj), *n.* a funeral song or tune.

dis af fect ed (dis′ə fek′tid), *adj.* unfriendly, disloyal, or discontented.

dis cern (də zėrn′, də sėrn′), *v.t.* see clearly; distinguish or recognize. [< Latin *discernere* < *dis-* off + *cernere* to separate] —**dis cern′er,** *n.*

dis cern ing (də zėr′ning, də sėr′ning), *adj.* keen in seeing and understanding; with good judgment; shrewd. —**dis cern′ing ly,** *adv.*

dis con so late (dis kon′sə lit), *adj.* 1 without hope; forlorn; unhappy. 2 causing discomfort; cheerless. [< Medieval Latin *disconsolatus* < Latin *dis-* + *consolari* to console]

dis cord (dis′kôrd), *n.* disagreement of opinions and aims; dissension. [< Old French < *discorder* disagree < Latin *discordare* < *discordem* discordant < *dis-* apart + *cordem* heart]

dis creet (dis krēt′), *adj.* very careful and sensible in speech and action; having or showing good judgment; wisely cautious. [< Old French *discret* < Late Latin *discretus* discerning < Latin *discernere* discern]

dis dain (dis dān′), *v.t.* think unworthy of oneself or one's notice; regard or treat with contempt; scorn. [< Old French *desdeignier* < *des-* dis- + *deignier* deign] —**dis dain′ful,** *n.*

di shev eled or **di shev elled** (də shev′əld), *adj.* 1 not neat; rumpled; mussed; untidy. 2 hanging loosely or in disorder: *disheveled hair.*

dis pas sion ate (dis pash′ə nit), *adj.* free from emotion or prejudice; calm and impartial. —**dis pas′sion ate ly,** *adv.*

dis patch (dis pach′), *v.t.* 1 send off to some place or for some purpose: *The captain dispatched a boat to bring a doctor on board ship.* 2 get done promptly or speedily; settle; conclude. 3 kill. Also, **despatch.** [< Italian *dispacciare* or Spanish *despachar*]

dis po si tion (dis′pə zish′ən), *n.* 1 one's habitual ways of acting toward others or of thinking about things; nature: *a cheerful disposition.* 2 tendency; inclination.

dis rep u ta ble (dis rep′yə tə bəl), *adj.* 1 having a bad reputation. 2 not fit to be used or seen; in poor condition.

dis sem ble (di sem′bəl), *v.,* **-bled, -bling.** —*v.t.* 1 hide (one's real feelings, thoughts, plans, etc.); disguise. 2 pretend; feign. —*v.i.* conceal one's opinions, motives, etc. —**dis sem′bler,** *n.*

dis sev er (di sev′ər), *v.t.* cut into parts; sever; separate. —*v.i.* separate. —**dis sev′er ment,** *n.*

dis sim u late (di sim′yə lāt), *v.,* **-lat ed, -lat ing.** —*v.t.* disguise or hide under a pretense; dissemble. —*v.i.* hide the truth; dissemble. —**dis sim′u la′tion,** *n.* —**dis sim′u la′tor,** *n.*

dis si pate (dis′ə pāt), *v.,* **-pat ed, -pat ing.** —*v.t.* 1 spread in different directions; scatter. 2 cause to disappear; dispel. —*v.i.* scatter so as to disappear; disperse. [< Latin *dissipatum* scattered < *dis-* apart + *supare* to throw] —**dis′si pa′tion,** *n.*

dis so lu tion (dis′ə lü′shən), *n.* 1 a breaking up or ending of an association of any kind. 2 the breaking up of an assembly by ending its session. 3 ruin; destruction. 4 death.

dis tem per (dis tem′pər), *n.* 1 an infectious viral disease of dogs and other animals, accompanied by fever, a short, dry cough, and a loss of strength. 2 any sickness of the mind or body; disorder; disease. [< Late Latin *distemperare* mix improperly < Latin *dis-* + *temperare* to temper]

dis tend (dis tend′), *v.t., v.i.* stretch out by pressure from within; swell out; expand. [< Latin *distendere* < *dis-* apart + *tendere* to stretch]

dis tin guish (dis ting′gwish), *v.t.* see or hear clearly; make out plainly; discern. [< Latin *distinguere* < *dis-* between + *stinguere* to prick] —**dis tin′guish a ble,** *adj.*

di ur nal (dī ėr′nl), *adj.* 1 occurring every day; daily. 2 of or belonging to the daytime: *the diurnal temperature.* 3 active only in the daytime. [< Late Latin *diurnalis* < Latin *dies* day]

di vers (dī′vərz), *adj.* more than one; several different; various. [< Old French < Latin *diversum* turned aside, diverted]

div i na tion (div′ə nā′shən), *n.* 1 act of foreseeing the future or discovering what is hidden or obscure by supernatural or magical means. 2 augury; prophecy.

doc ile (dos′əl; British dō′sīl, dos′īl), *adj.* 1 easily managed or dealt with; obedient. 2 easily taught; willing to learn. [< Middle French < Latin *docilem* < *docere* teach] —**doc′ile ly,** *adv.*

do cil i ty (dō sil′ə tē), *n.* docile quality.

doi ly (doi′lē), *n., pl.* **-lies.** a small piece of linen, lace, paper, or plastic put under plates, bowls, vases, etc., on a table. [< *Doily,* name of an English dry-goods dealer of the 1700's]

do mes ti cate (də mes′tə kāt), *v.t.,* **-cat ed, -cat ing.** 1 make fond of home and family life. 2 cause to be or feel at home; naturalize.

dom i cile (dom′ə sīl, dom′ə səl), *n.* a dwelling place; house; home. [< Latin *domicilium* < *domus* house]

do min ion (də min′yən), *n.* 1 power or right of governing and controlling; rule; control. 2 territory under the control of one ruler or government. [< Medieval Latin, alteration of Latin *dominium* ownership < *dominum* lord, master]

dough boy (dō′boi′), *n.* U.S. INFORMAL. an infantryman in the United States Army during World War I.

dow a ger (dou′ə jər), *n.* 1 woman who holds some title or property from her dead husband. 2 INFORMAL. a dignified, elderly woman, usually of high social position. [< Old French *douagere* < *douage* dower < *douer* endow < Latin *dotare* < *dotem* dowry]

draft (draft), *n.* 1 a single act of drinking: *I emptied the glass at one draft.* 2 amount taken in a single drink; drink or dose.

dra goon (drə gün′), *n.* a mounted soldier trained to fight on foot or on horseback. [< French *dragon* dragon, pistol, (later) soldier]

dram (dram), *n.* 1 a small drink of intoxicating liquor. 2 a small amount of anything. Also, **drachm.** [< Old French *drame* < Latin *drachma*]

draught (draft), *n.*, *v.t.*, *adj.* draft.

dray (drā), *n.* a low, strong cart or wagon for carrying heavy loads. [Old English *dræge* dragnet < *dragan* to draw]

drom e dar y (drom′ə der′ē, drum′ə-der′ē), *n.*, *pl.* **-dar ies.** a swift camel with one hump and short hair, specially reared and trained for riding, found in parts of India, Arabia, and northern Africa; Arabian camel.

drone (drōn), *v.i.*, **droned, dron ing.** 1 make a deep, continuous humming sound: *Bees droned among the flowers.* 2 talk in a dull, monotonous voice.

du bi ous (dü′bē əs, dyü′bē əs), *adj.* 1 filled with or being in doubt. 2 feeling doubt; wavering or hesitating. 3 of questionable character; probably bad. [< Latin *dubiosus* < *dubius* doubtful] **—du′bi ous ly,** *adv.* **—du′bi ous ness,** *n.*

dul cet (dul′sit), *adj.* soothing, especially to the ear; sweet or pleasing. [< Latin *dulcis*]

dul ci mer (dul′sə mər), *n.* a musical instrument with metal strings, played by striking the strings with two hammers. [< Old French *doulcemer, doulcemele* < Latin *dulcis* sweet + *melos* song]

eb on (eb′ən), ARCHAIC. *n.*, *adj.* ebony.

eb on y (eb′ə nē), *n.*, *pl.* **-on ies,** *adj.* **—*n.*** a hard, durable, black wood, used for the black keys of a piano, for the backs and handles of brushes, for ornamental woodwork, etc. **—*adj.*** like ebony; black; dark. [< Greek *ebenos* ebony < Egyptian *hbnj*]

ec cen tric (ek sen′trik), *adj.* out of the ordinary; not usual; odd; peculiar.

ec sta sy (ek′stə sē), *n.*, *pl.* **-sies.** 1 condition of very great joy; thrilling or overwhelming delight. 2 any strong feeling that completely absorbs the mind; uncontrollable emotion. 3 trance. [< Greek *ekstasis* distraction, trance < *existanai* put out of place < *ex-* out + *histanai* to place]

ef face (ə fās′), *v.t.*, **-faced, -fac ing.** rub out; blot out; wipe out; obliterate. [< Middle French *effacer* < *es-* away + *face* face]

ef fi ca cy (ef′ə kə sē), *n.*, *pl.* **-cies.** power to produce the effect wanted; effectiveness. [< Latin *efficacia* < *efficere* accomplish < *ex-* + *facere* do, make]

ef flu vi um (i flü′vē əm), *n.*, *pl.* **-vi a** (-vē ə), **-vi ums.** vapor or odor, usually unpleasant. [< Latin, a flowing out]

ef fuse (i fyüz′), *v.t.*, **-fused, -fus ing.** pour out; spill; shed. [< Latin *effusum* poured out < *ex-* out + *fundere* pour]

e go tism (ē′gə tiz′əm, eg′ə tiz′əm), *n.* 1 habit of thinking, talking, or writing too much of oneself; conceit. 2 selfishness.

e gre gious (i grē′jəs), *adj.* 1 remarkably or extraordinarily bad; outrageous; flagrant: *an egregious blunder.* 2 remarkable; extraordinary. [< Latin *egregius* < *ex-* out + *gregem* herd, flock]

e jac u late (i jak′yə lāt), *v.t.*, *v.i.*, **-lat ed, -lat ing.** say suddenly and briefly; exclaim. [< Latin *ejaculatum* thrown out < *ex-* out + *jacere* to throw]

e las tic (i las′tik), *adj.* 1 not permanently or easily depressed; buoyant. 2 easily changed to suit conditions; flexible; adaptable: *an elastic conscience.*

e las tic i ty (i las′tis′ə tē, ē′las tis′ə tē), *n.* elastic quality.

el o cu tion (el′ə kyü′shən), *n.* 1 art of speaking or reading clearly and expressively in public, including the use of the voice, gestures, etc. 2 manner of speaking or reading in public; delivery. [< Latin *elocutionem* < *eloqui* speak out] **—el′o cu′tion ist,** *n.*

e lon gate (i lông′gāt, i long′gāt), *v.*, **-gat ed, -gat ing,** *adj.* **—*v.t.*, *v.i.** make or become longer; lengthen; extend; stretch. **—*adj.*** lengthened. [< Latin *elongatum* lengthened < *ex-* out + *longus* long]

el o quence (el′ə kwəns), *n.* 1 flow of speech that has grace and force. 2 power to win by speaking; the art of using language so as to stir the feelings.

e ma ci ate (i mā′shē āt), *v.t.*, **-at ed, -at ing.** make unnaturally thin; cause to lose flesh or waste away: *A long illness had emaciated the patient.* [< Latin *emaciatum* made lean < *ex-* + *macies* leanness]

e man ci pa tion (i man′sə pā′shən), *n.* a release from slavery or restraint.

em bed (em bed′), *v.t.*, **-bed ded, -bed ding.** fix or enclose in a surrounding mass; fasten firmly. Also, **imbed.**

em bel lish (em bel′ish), *v.t.* interesting by adding real or imaginary details. [< Old French *embelliss-,* a form of *embellir* embellish < *en-* in + *bel* handsome]

em bow er (em bou′ər), *v.t.* enclose in a shelter of leafy branches.

em bra sure (em brā′zhər), *n.* an opening in a wall for a gun.

em i nence (em′ə nəns), *n.* 1 rank or position above all or most others; high standing. 2 a high place; high point of land.

em i nent (em′ə nənt), *adj.* 1 above all or most others; outstanding; distinguished. 2 conspicuous; noteworthy. 3 high; lofty. 4 standing out above other things; prominent. [< Latin *eminentem* standing out, prominent < *ex-* out + *minere* jut] **—em′i nent ly,** *adv.*

em is sar y (em′ə ser′ē), *n.*, *pl.* **-sar ies.** 1 person sent on a mission or errand. 2 a secret agent; spy. [< Latin *emissarius* < *emittere*]

-ence, *suffix forming nouns chiefly from verbs.* 1 act or fact of ____ing: *Abhorrence = act or fact of abhorring.* 2 quality or condition of being ____ent: *Prudence = quality of being prudent.* Also, **-ency.**

en com pass (en kum′pəs), *v.t.* 1 surround completely; encircle. 2 include; contain.

en deav or (en dev′ər), *v.i.*, *v.t.* make an effort; try hard; attempt earnestly. **—*n.*** an earnest attempt; hard try; effort. [< *en-* + Old French *devoir* duty]

en dow ment (en dou′mənt), *n.* inborn ability, quality, or talent.

en fran chise (en fran′chīz), *v.t.*, **-chised, -chis ing.** give the rights of citizenship to, especially the right to vote. **—en fran′chise ment,** *n.*

en tice (en tīs′), *v.t.*, **-ticed, -tic ing.** attract by arousing hopes or desires; tempt. [< Old French *enticier* stir up, incite < *en-* in + Latin *titio* firebrand] **—en tice′ment,** *n.* **—en tic′ing ly,** *adv.*

en treat y (en trē′tē), *n.*, *pl.* **-treat ies.** an earnest request; prayer or appeal.

hat, āge, fär; let, ēqual, tèrm;
it, īce; hot, ōpen, ôrder;
oil, out; cup, pùt, rüle;
ch, child; ng, long; sh, she;
th, thin; ₮H, then; zh, measure;

ə represents *a* in about, *e* in taken, *i* in pencil, *o* in lemon, *u* in circus.

< = from, derived from, taken from.

e nu me rate (i nü′mə rāt′, i nyü′mə rāt′), *v.t.*, **-rat ed, -rat ing.** 1 name one by one; list. 2 find out the number of; count. [< Latin *enumeratum* counted < *ex-* out + *numerus* number] **—e nu′me ra′tion,** *n.* **—e nu′me ra′tor,** *n.*

e nun ci ate (i nun′sē āt), *v.*, **-at ed, -at ing.** **—*v.i.*** speak or pronounce words: *He enunciates very distinctly.* **—*v.t.*** speak or pronounce; articulate. [< Latin *enuntiatum* announced < *ex-* out + *nuntius* messenger]

ep ic (ep′ik), *n.* a long narrative poem that tells the adventures and achievements of one or more great heroes, written in a dignified, majestic style, and often giving expression to the ideals of a nation or race. The *Odyssey* and *Beowulf* are epics. [< Latin *epicus* < Greek *epilos* < *epos* story, word]

ep i logue or **ep i log** (ep′ə lôg, ep′ə log), *n.* a concluding section added to a novel, poem, etc., that rounds out or interprets the work. [< Greek *epilogos,* ultimately < *epi-* above + *legein* speak]

e pit o me (i pit′ə mē), *n.* person or thing that is typical or representative of something. [< Greek *epitomē* < *epitemnein* cut short < *epi-* + *temnein* to cut]

ep och (ep′ək, ē′pok), *n.* 1 period of time; era; age. 2 period of time in which striking things happened.

e rad i cate (i rad′ə kāt), *v.t.*, **-cat ed, -cat ing.** 1 get rid of entirely; destroy completely; eliminate. 2 pull out by the roots: *eradicate weeds.* [< Latin *eradicatum* rooted out < *ex-* out + *radicem* root] **—e rad′i ca′tion,** *n.*

es cu lent (es′kyə lənt), *adj.* suitable for food; edible. [< Latin *esculentus* < *esca* food]

es trange ment (e strānj′mənt), *n.* a turning away in feeling; becoming distant or unfriendly.

e ther (ē′thər), *n.* a colorless, volatile, flammable, sweet-smelling liquid, produced by the action of sulfuric acid on ethyl alcohol. Because its fumes cause unconsciousness when deeply inhaled, ether is used as an anesthetic. [< Latin *aether* < Greek *aithēr* upper air]

e the re al (i thir′ē əl), *adj.* 1 light; airy; delicate: *the ethereal beauty of a butterfly.* 2 not of the earth; heavenly. 3 of or having to do with the upper regions of space.

e ther ize (ē′thə rīz′), *v.t.*, **-ized, -iz ing.** make unconscious with ether fumes.

E trur i a (i trür′ē ə), *n.* ancient country in W central Italy.

E trus can (i trus′kən), *adj.* of or having to do with Etruria, its people, their language, art, or customs.

eu lo gy (yü′lə jē), *n.*, *pl.* **-gies.** 1 speech or writing in praise of a person or thing, especially a set oration in honor of a deceased person. 2 high praise. [< Greek *eulogia* < *eu-* well + *legein* speak]

eu phe mism (yü′fə miz′əm), *n.* 1 use of a mild or indirect expression instead of one that is harsh or unpleasantly direct. 2 word or expression used in this way. "Pass away" is a common euphemism for "die." [< Greek *euphēmismos* < *euphēmizein* speak with fair words < *eu-* good + *phēmē* speaking < *phanai* speak]

ev a nes cent (ev′ə nes′nt), *adj.* gradually disappearing; soon passing away; vanishing.

e vince (i vins′), *v.t.*, **e vinced, e vinc ing.** 1 show clearly; manifest. 2 show that one has (a certain quality, trait, etc.). [< Latin *evincere* < *ex-* out + *vincere* conquer]

ev i ta ble (ev′ə tə bəl), *adj.* avoidable.

ex cel si or (ek sel′sē ər), *n.* fine, curled shavings of soft wood used for packing dishes, glassware, and other breakable articles.

ex e cra tion (ek′sə krā′shən), *n.* 1 act of execrating. 2 a curse.

ex ec u tor (eg zek′yə tər), *n.* person named in a will to carry out the provisions of the will.

ex hil a ra tion (eg zil′ə rā′shən), *n.* a being or feeling exhilarated; high spirits; lively joy.

ex hort (eg zôrt′), *v.t.* urge strongly; advise or warn earnestly. [< Latin *exhortari* < *ex-* + *hortari* urge strongly] **—ex hort′er,** *n.*

ex ot ic (eg zot′ik), *adj.* 1 from a foreign country; not native. 2 fascinating or interesting because strange or different. [< Greek *exōtikos* < *exō* outside < *ex* out of] **—ex ot′i cal ly,** *adv.*

ex pe di ent (ek spē′dē ənt), *adj.* 1 helping to bring about a desired result; desirable or suitable under the circumstances; useful; advantageous. 2 giving or seeking personal advantage; based on self-interest. —*n.* means of bringing about a desired result. **—ex pe′di ent ly,** *adv.* **—ex pe′di en cy.**

ex pi ate (ek′spē āt), *v.t.*, **-at ed, -at ing.** pay the penalty of; make amends for a wrong, sin, etc.; atone for.

ex pli cate (ek′splə kāt), *v.t.*, **-cat ed, -cat ing.** make clear the meaning of (anything); explain. [< Latin *explicatum* unfolded < *ex-* out + *plicare* to fold] **—ex′pli ca tor,** *n.*

ex pli ca tion (ek′splə kā′shən), *n.* explanation.

ex plic it (ek splis′it), *adj.* 1 clearly expressed; distinctly stated; definite. 2 not reserved; frank; outspoken. [< Latin *explicitum* unfolded, explained < *ex-* out + *plicare* to fold] **—ex plic′it ly,** *adv.* **—ex plic′it ness,** *n.*

ex po si tion (ek′spə zish′ən), *n.* 1 a detailed explanation. 2 speech or writing explaining a process, thing, or idea. 3 part of a work of literature in which the theme is introduced. 4 where something is placed in relation to the sun.

ex qui site (ek′skwi zit, ek skwiz′it), *adj.* 1 very lovely; delicate. 2 sharp; intense. 3 of highest excellence; most admirable. [< Latin *exquisitus* sought out < *ex-* out + *quaerere* seek] **—ex′qui site ly,** *adv.*

extra-, *prefix.* outside ____; beyond ____: *Extraordinary = outside the ordinary.* [< Latin < *extra* outside]

ex tra ne ous (ek strā′nē əs), *adj.* 1 from outside; not belonging or proper to a thing; foreign. 2 not essential. [< Latin *extraneus* < *extra* outside]

ex u ber ant (eg zü′bər ənt), *adj.* 1 profuse in growth; luxuriant. 2 abounding in health and spirits; overflowing with good cheer. [< Latin *exuberantem* growing luxuriantly <

ex- thoroughly + *uber* fertile] **—ex u′ber ance,** *n.*

ex ude (eg züd′, ek syüd′), *v.*, **-ud ed, -ud ing.** —*v.i.* come out in drops; ooze. —*v.t.* 1 send out in drops. 2 give forth; emit. [< Latin *exsudare* < *ex-* out + *sudare* to sweat]

fab ri cate (fab′rə kāt), *v.t.*, **-cat ed, -cat ing.** 1 make (anything that requires skill); build or manufacture. 2 make up; invent (a story, lie, excuse, etc.). **—fab′ri ca tor,** *n.* **—fab′ri ca′tion,** *n.*

fa cade or **fa çade** (fə säd′), *n.* 1 the front part of a building. 2 any side of a building that faces a street or an open space. 3 outward appearance: *a façade of honesty.* [< French *façade*]

fa cil i tate (fə sil′ə tāt), *v.t.*, **-tat ed, -tat ing.** make easy; lessen the labor of; help bring about; assist; expedite. **—fa cil′i ta′tion,** *n.*

fac sim i le (fak sim′ə lē), *n.* an exact copy or likeness; perfect reproduction. [< Latin *fac* make! + *simile* similar, like]

fag ot (fag′ət), *n.* bundle of sticks or twigs tied together for fuel. [< Old French]

fain (fān), ARCHAIC. —*adv.* gladly; willingly. —*adj.* 1 willing, but not eager. 2 obliged. 3 glad. 4 eager. [Old English *fægen*]

fat u ous (fach′ü əs), *adj.* stupid but self-satisfied; foolish; silly. [< Latin *fatuus*] **—fat′u ous ly,** *adv.* **—fat′u ous ness,** *n.*

feign (fān), *v.t.* 1 put on a false appearance of; make believe; pretend. 2 make up to deceive; invent falsely. —*v.i.* make oneself appear; pretend (to be). [< Old French *feign-,* a form of *feindre* feign < Latin *fingere* to form] **—feign′er,** *n.*

fe lic i ty (fə lis′ə tē), *n., pl.* **-ties.** 1 great happiness; bliss. 2 good fortune; blessing. [< Latin *felicitatem* < *felicem* happy]

fer rule (fer′əl, fer′ül), *n.* a metal ring or cap put around the end of a cane, wooden handle, umbrella, etc., to strengthen it or to prevent splitting and wearing. Also, **ferule.**

fer ule (fer′əl, fer′ül), *n.* ferrule.

fer vid (fėr′vid), *adj.* 1 full of strong feeling; intensely emotional; ardent; spirited. 2 intensely hot.

fes ter (fes′tər), *v.i.* 1 form pus. 2 cause soreness or pain; rankle. 3 decay; rot. —*v.t.* cause to rankle: *Time festered the insult to his pride.* [< Old French *festre* < Latin *fistula* ulcer]

fet id (fet′id, fē′tid), *adj.* smelling very bad; stinking. [< Latin *foetidus* < *foetere* to stink]

fi as co (fē as′kō), *n., pl.* **-cos** or **-coes.** a complete or ridiculous failure; humiliating breakdown. [< Italian, literally, flask]

fig ur a tive (fig′yər ə tiv), *adj.* 1 using words out of their literal or ordinary meaning to add beauty or force. 2 representing by a likeness or symbol; symbolic.

fil let (fi lā′, fil′ā), *n.* slice of fish or meat without bones or fat; filet. —*v.t.* cut (fish or meat) into fillets. When a fish is filleted, the flesh is cut away from the skeleton. Also, **filet.**

fir ma ment (fėr′mə mənt), *n.* arch of the heavens; sky.

fix a tion (fik sā′shən), *n.* an abnormal attachment or prejudice.

fla grant (flā′grənt), *adj.* 1 glaringly offensive; notorious; outrageous; scandalous: *a flagrant crime.* 2 glaring: *a flagrant error.* [< Latin *flagrantem* burning, blazing]

flail (flāl), *n.* instrument for threshing grain

by hand, consisting of a wooden handle at the end of which a stouter and shorter pole or club is fastened so as to swing freely.

flam beau (flam′bō), *n., pl.* **-beaux** or **-beaus** (-bōz). 1 a flaming torch. 2 a large, decorated candlestick. [< French]

fluc tu ate (fluk′chü āt), *v.i.*, **-at ed, -at ing.** rise and fall; change continually; vary irregularly; waver; vacillate. [< Latin *fluctuatum* moving as a wave < *fluctus* wave < *flucere* to flow]

flu id (flü′id), *adj.* changing easily; not fixed, firm, or stable. [< Latin *fluidus* < *fluere* to flow] **—flu id′i ty,** *n.*

flu o res cent (flü′ə res′nt), *adj.* that gives off light by fluorescence. Fluorescent substances glow in the dark when exposed to X rays.

fon ta nel or **fon ta nelle** (fon′tə nel′), *n.* any of the soft spots, closed by membrane and later to be filled by bone, on the head of an infant or fetus.

fop (fop), *n.* a vain man who is very fond of fine clothes and has affected manners; dandy.

fop per y (fop′ər ē), *n., pl.* **-per ies.** behavior or dress of a fop.

for bear (fôr ber′, fôr bar′), *v.i.*, **-bore, -borne, -bear ing.** 1 hold back; keep from doing, saying, using, etc. 2 be patient; control oneself. [Old English *forberan*]

for bear ance (fôr ber′əns, fôr bar′əns), *n.* patience; self-control.

fore bod ing (fôr bō′ding, fōr bō′ding), *n.* 1 prediction; warning. 2 a feeling that something bad is going to happen; presentiment.

fore go (fôr gō′, fōr gō′), *v.t.*, **-went, -gone, -go ing.** forgo. **—fore go′er,** *n.*

for go (fôr gō′), *v.t.*, **-went, -gone, -go ing.** do without; give up. Also, **forego.**

for mi da ble (fôr′mə də bəl), *adj.* hard to overcome; hard to deal with; to be dreaded. [< Latin *formidabilis* < *formidare* to dread < *formido* terror, dread]

for mu late (fôr′myə lāt), *v.t.*, **-lat ed, -lat ing.** 1 state definitely or systematically. 2 express in a formula; reduce to a formula.

for ti tude (fôr′tə tüd, fôr′tə tyüd), *n.* courage in facing pain, danger, or trouble; firmness of spirit.

Free ma son (frē′mā′sn), *n.* member of a worldwide secret society (the Free and Accepted Masons), whose purpose is mutual aid and fellowship; Mason.

frol ic some (frol′ik səm), *adj.* full of fun; playful; merry.

frow zy (frou′zē), *adj.*, **-zi er, -zi est.** 1 dirty and untidy; slovenly. 2 smelling bad; musty. [origin uncertain]

fru gal i ty (frü gal′ə tē), *n., pl.* **-ties.** avoidance of waste; thrift.

fur row (fėr′ō), *v.t.* make wrinkles in; wrinkle: *The old man's face was furrowed with age.*

fur tive (fėr′tiv), *adj.* done quickly and with stealth to avoid being noticed; secret. [< Latin *furtivus* < *furtum* theft < *fur* thief] **—fur′tive ly,** *adv.* **—fur′tive ness,** *n.*

fu se lage (fyü′sə läzh, fyü′sə lij), *n.* body of an airplane, to which the wings, tail, etc., are fastened. The fuselage holds the passengers, crew, and cargo.

gain say (gān′sā′), *v.t.*, **-said, -say ing.** deny; contradict; dispute.

gal va nize (gal′və nīz), *v.t.*, **-nized, -niz ing.** cover (iron or steel) with a thin coating of zinc to prevent rust.

gam bol (gam′bəl), *v.i.* run and jump about in play; frolic.

gar goyle (gär′goil), *n.* spout for carrying off rainwater, ending in a grotesque figure of a head that projects from the gutter of a building.

gar net (gär′nit), *n.* a hard, glassy silicate mineral occurring in many varieties. A common, deep-red, transparent variety is used as a gem and as an abrasive.

gar ru lous (gar′ə ləs, gar′yə ləs), *adj.* 1 talking too much; talkative. 2 using too many words; wordy. [< Latin *garrulus* < *garrire* to chatter]

gauche (gōsh), *adj.* lacking grace or tact; awkward. [< French, literally, left]

geld (geld), *v.t.*, **geld ed** or **gelt** (gelt), **geld ing.** remove the testicles of (a horse or other animal); castrate.

geld ing (gel′ding), *n.* a gelded horse or other animal.

gem ma ry (je′mə rē), *n.* the science of gems.

gen der (jen′dər), *n.* 1 the grouping of nouns into certain classes, such as masculine, feminine, or neuter. 2 sex: *the female gender.* [< Old French *gendre* < Latin *generis* kind, sort, class]

ge ne al o gy (jē′nē al′ə jē, jē′nē ol′ə jē; jen′ē al′ə jē, jen′ē ol′ə jē), *n.*, *pl.* **-gies.** 1 account of the descent of a person or family from an ancestor or ancestors. 2 the making or investigation of accounts of descent. [< Greek *genealogia* < *genea* breed, generation + *-logos* treating of]

ges tic u la tion (je stik′yə lā′shən), *n.* 1 a making lively or excited gestures. 2 a lively or excited gesture.

gib bous (gib′əs), *adj.* (of a heavenly body) so illuminated as to be convex on both margins. A gibbous moon is more than half full but less than full.

gin ger ly (jin′jər lē), *adv.* with extreme care or caution.

gnarled (närld), *adj.* knotted; twisted. [variant of *knurled*]

gourd (gôrd, gōrd, gùrd), *n.* any of various fleshy fruits with hard rinds and many flat seeds. Gourds are often dried and hollowed out for use as cups, bottles, bowls, darning eggs, etc.

green horn (grēn′hôrn′), *n.* INFORMAL. 1 person without training or experience. 2 person easy to trick or cheat.

griev ance (grē′vəns), *n.* a real or imagined wrong; reason for being angry or annoyed; cause for complaint.

griev ous (grē′vəs), *adj.* 1 hard to bear; causing great pain or suffering; severe. 2 very evil or offensive; outrageous.

gro tesque (grō tesk′), *adj.* 1 odd or unnatural in shape, appearance, manner, etc.; fantastic. 2 ridiculous; absurd. [< French < Italian *grottesco*, literally, of caves, cavelike < *grotta*] —**gro tesque′ly**, *adv.* —**gro tesque′ness**, *n.*

guf faw (gu fô′), *n.* burst of loud, coarse laughter. —*v.i.* laugh loudly and coarsely.

gui don (gid′n, gī′don), *n.* flag, streamer, or pennant of a company, regiment, etc.

guile (gīl), *n.* crafty deceit; sly tricks; cunning.

gut tur al (gut′ər əl), *adj.* 1 of the throat. 2 formed in the throat; harsh: *The visitor from Germany spoke in a deep, guttural voice.* 3 formed between the back of the tongue and the soft palate. The *g* in *go* is a guttural sound.

gy ra tion (jī rā′shən), *n.* circular or spiral motion; whirling; rotation.

hag gard (hag′ərd), *adj.* looking worn from pain, fatigue, worry, hunger, etc.; careworn; gaunt. [perhaps < Old French *hagard*]

hag gle (hag′əl), *v.*, **-gled, -gling,** *n.* —*v.i.* dispute, especially about a price or the terms of a bargain. [< Scottish *hag* to chop < Scandinavian (Old Icelandic) *höggva*] —**hag′gler**, *n.*

hap haz ard (hap′haz′ərd), *adj.* not planned; random. —**hap′haz′ard ly**, *adv.* —**hap′haz′ard ness**, *n.*

har ass (har′əs, hə ras′), *v.t.* 1 trouble by repeated attacks; harry. 2 distress with annoying labor, care, misfortune, etc.; disturb; worry; torment. [< French *harasser* < Old French *harer* set a dog on < *hare* a shout to excite dogs to attack] —**har′ass ment**, *n.*

har le quin (här′lə kwən, här′lə kən), *n.* 1 Harlequin, character in comedy and pantomime, the lover of Columbine. He is usually masked and wears a costume of varied colors. 2 a mischievous person; buffoon.

har row (har′ō), *v.t.* 1 hurt; wound. 2 cause pain or torment to; distress. [Middle English *harwe*]

haugh ty (hô′tē), *adj.*, **-ti er, -ti est.** too proud and scornful of others. [Middle English *haute* < Middle French *haut* < Latin *altus* high]

heark en (här′kən), *v.i.* pay attention to what is said; listen attentively; listen.

het er o ge ne ous (het′ər ə jē′nē əs, het′-ər ə jē′nyəs), *adj.* 1 different in kind or nature; unlike; varied. 2 composed of unlike parts or elements; miscellaneous. [< Medieval Latin *heterogeneus*, ultimately < Greek *heteros* other + *genos* kind]

hir sute (hèr′süt), *adj.* hairy. [< Latin *hirsutus*] —**hir′sute ness**, *n.*

hith er to (hiŦH′ər tü′), *adv.* until now.

hoar y (hôr′ē, hōr′ē), *adj.*, **hoar i er, hoar i est.** 1 white or gray. 2 white or gray with age. 3 old; ancient. —**hoar′i ness**, *n.*

hom i ly (hom′ə lē), *n.*, *pl.* **-lies.** 1 sermon, usually on one part of the Bible. 2 serious moral talk or writing that warns, urges, or advises.

hos tler (os′lər, hos′lər), *n.* person who takes care of horses at an inn or stable. Also, **ostler.**

hov el (huv′əl, hov′əl), *n.* 1 house that is small, crude, and unpleasant to live in. 2 an open shed for sheltering cattle, tools, etc. [Middle English]

hur dy-gur dy (hèr′dē gèr′dē), *n.*, *pl.* **-dies.** hand organ or street piano.

hy a cinth (hī′ə sinth), *n.* 1 plant of the lily family that grows from a bulb and has a spike of small, fragrant, bell-shaped flowers. 2 its flower. [< Latin *hyacinthus* < Greek *hyakinthos* kind of flower or gem]

hy dran gea (hī drān′jə), *n.* shrubs with large, showy clusters of small white, pink, or blue flowers.

hy per ac tive (hī′pər ak′tiv), *adj.* overactive: *hyperactive children.*

hy poc ri sy (hi pok′rə sē), *n.*, *pl.* **-sies.** 1 a pretending to be very good or religious. 2 a pretending to be what one is not; pretense. [< Greek *hypokritēs* actor < *hypo-* under + *kritēs* a judge]

-ible, *suffix added to verbs to form adjectives.* that can be ____ed: *Reducible = that can be reduced.*

il lim it a ble (i lim′ə tə bəl), *adj.* without limit; boundless; infinite.

il lu mi nate (i lü′mə nāt), *v.t.*, **-nat ed,**

hat, āge, fär; let, ēqual, tèrm;
it, īce; hot, ōpen, ôrder;
oil, out; cup, pùt, rüle;
ch, child; ng, long; sh, she;
th, thin; ŦH, then; zh, measure;

ə represents *a* in about, *e* in taken,
i in pencil, *o* in lemon, *u* in circus.

< = from, derived from, taken from.

-nat ing. 1 make clear; explain. 2 enlighten; inform; instruct.

il lu sion (i lü′zhən), *n.* 1 appearance or feeling that misleads because it is not real; thing that deceives by giving a false idea. 2 a false impression or perception: *an optical illusion.* 3 a false notion or belief. [< Latin *illusionem* < *illudere* mock < *in-* at + *ludere* play]

il lu sive (i lü′siv), *adj.* illusory. —**il-lu′sive ly**, *adv.* —**il lu′sive ness**, *n.*

il lu sor y (i lü′sər ē), *adj.* due to an illusion; misleading; deceptive.

il lus tri ous (i lus′trē əs), *adj.* 1 very famous; great; outstanding. 2 bringing or conferring glory; glorious. [< Latin *illustris* lighted up, bright < *in-* in + *lustrum* lighting]

im bed (im bed′), *v.t.*, **-bed ded, -bed ding.** embed.

im bue (im byü′), *v.t.*, **-bued, -bu ing.** fill the mind of; inspire.

im mac u late (i mak′yə lit), *adj.* 1 without a spot or stain; absolutely clean. 2 without sin; pure.

im mi nent (im′ə nənt), *adj.* likely to happen soon; about to occur. [< Latin *imminen-tem* overhanging, threatening] —**im′mi-nence**, *n.*

im mit i ga ble (i mit′ə gə bəl), *adj.* that cannot be softened or mitigated.

im mo late (im′ə lāt), *v.t.*, **-lat ed, -lat ing.** 1 kill as a sacrifice. 2 offer in sacrifice; sacrifice.

im pair (im per′, im par′), *v.t.* make worse; damage; harm; weaken. [< Old French *em-peirer*, ultimately < Latin *in-* + *pejor* worse]

im pal pa ble (im pal′pə bəl), *adj.* that cannot be felt by touching; intangible.

im ped i ment (im ped′ə mənt), *n.* 1 hindrance; obstruction. 2 some physical defect, especially a defect in speech.

im pen e tra ble (im pen′ə trə bəl), *adj.* 1 that cannot be penetrated, pierced, or passed. 2 impossible to explain or understand; inscrutable. —**im pen′e tra bly**, *adv.*

im per cep ti ble (im′pər sep′tə bəl), *adj.* that cannot be perceived or felt; very slight, gradual, subtle, or indistinct.

im pe ri ous (im pir′ē əs), *adj.* 1 haughty or arrogant; domineering; overbearing. 2 not to be avoided; necessary; urgent.

im per ti nent (im pèr′tn ənt), *adj.* rudely bold; impudent; insolent. —**im per′-ti nence**, *n.*

im per turb a ble (im′pər tèr′bə bəl), *adj.* not easily excited or disturbed; calm. —**im′per turb′a bly**, *adv.*

im per vi ous (im pèr′vē əs), *adj.* 1 allowing no passage; impermeable. 2 not open to argument, suggestions, etc.

im pet u ous (im pech′ü əs), *adj.* 1 acting or done with sudden or rash energy; hasty. 2 rushing with force and violence.

im pla ca ble (im plā′kə bəl, im plak′ə bəl), *adj.* unable to be appeased; refusing to be reconciled; unyielding: *implacable enemies.*

im plore (im plôr′, im plōr′), *v.t.,* **-plored,** **-plor ing.** 1 beg or pray earnestly for. 2 beg (a person) to do something. [< Latin *implorare* < *in-* toward + *plorare* cry]

im por tu nate (im pôr′chə nit), *adj.* asking repeatedly; annoyingly persistent; urgent.

im por tune (im′pôr tün′, im′pôr tyün′, im pôr′chən), *v.t.,* **-tuned, -tun ing.** ask urgently or repeatedly; annoy with pressing demands. [< Latin *importunus* inconvenient]

im por tu ni ty (im′pôr tü′nə tē, im′pôr tyü′nə tē), *n., pl.* **-ties.** persistence in asking; act of demanding again and again.

im pose (im pōz′), *v.t.,* **-posed, -pos ing.** 1 force or thrust (oneself or one's company) on another or others; obtrude; presume. 2 **impose on** or **impose upon, a** take advantage of; use for selfish purposes. **b** deceive; cheat; trick. [< Middle French *imposer* < *in-* on + *poser* put, place] **—im pos′er,** *n.*

im po tent (im′pə tənt), *adj.* not having power; helpless.

im preg na ble (im preg′nə bəl), *adj.* able to resist attack; not yielding to force, persuasion, etc.

im preg nate (im preg′nāt), *v.t.,* **-nat ed, -nat ing.** 1 make pregnant. 2 spread through the whole of; fill; saturate: *Sea water is impregnated with salt.* [< Late Latin *impraegnatum* made pregnant < Latin *in-* + *praegnas* pregnant]

im pu dent (im′pyə dənt), *adj.* shamelessly bold; very rude and insolent. [< Latin *impudentem* < *in-* not + *pudere* be modest] **—im′pu dent ly,** *adv.* **—im′pu dence,** *n.*

im pu ni ty (im pyü′nə tē), *n.* freedom from punishment, injury, or other bad consequences.

in-¹, *prefix.* not; the opposite of; the absence of: *Inexpensive = not expensive. Inattention = the absence of attention.* Also **i-, il-, im-,** and **ir-.**

in-², *prefix.* in; into; on; upon: *Incase = (put) into a case. Intrust = (give) in trust.* Also **il-, im-, ir-.**

in-³, *prefix.* in; within; into; toward: *Indoors = within doors. Inland = toward land.*

in ac ces si ble (in′ək ses′ə bəl), *adj.* 1 hard to get at; hard to reach or enter. 2 difficult to solve.

in al ien a ble (in ā′lyə nə bəl, in ā′lē ə nə bəl), *adj.* that cannot be given or taken away; that cannot be transferred to another: *an inalienable right.* Also, **unalienable.**

in ar tic u late (in′är tik′yə lit), *adj.* 1 not uttered in distinct syllables or words: *an inarticulate mutter.* 2 unable to speak in words; dumb.

in ca pac i tate (in′kə pas′ə tāt), *v.t.,* **-tat ed, -tat ing.** deprive of ability, power, or fitness; disable.

in ces sant (in ses′nt), *adj.* never stopping; continued or repeated without interruption; continual. [< Late Latin *incessantem* < Latin *in-* not + *cessare* cease] **—in ces′sant ly,** *adv.*

in com mode (in′kə mōd′), *v.t.,* **-mod ed, -mod ing.** cause trouble, difficulty, etc., to; inconvenience. [< Latin *incommodare* < *in-* not + *commodus* convenient]

in con gru ence (in kong′grü əns), *n.* lack of agreement; incongruity.

in con gru ous (in kong′grü əs), *adj.* 1 out of keeping; not appropriate; out of place. 2 lacking in agreement or harmony; not consistent.

in con se quen tial (in′kon sə kwen′shəl), *adj.* unimportant; trifling.

in con tro vert i ble (in′kon trə vėr′tə bəl), *adj.* that cannot be disputed or denied; too clear or certain to be argued about; unquestionable.

in cor ri gi ble (in kôr′ə jə bəl, in kor′ə jə bəl), *adj.* 1 too firmly fixed in bad ways, an annoying habit, etc., to be reformed or changed. 2 so fixed that it cannot be changed or cured. **—in cor′ri gi bly,** *adv.*

in cred u lous (in krej′ə ləs), *adj.* 1 not ready to believe; doubting; skeptical. 2 showing a lack of belief. **—in cred′u lous ly,** *adv.*

in dec or ous (in dek′ər əs, in′di kôr′əs, in′di kōr′əs), *adj.* not in accordance with proper behavior; in poor taste; improper.

in dif fer ence (in dif′ər əns), *n.* 1 lack of interest or attention. 2 lack of importance.

in dig na tion (in′dig nā′shən), *n.* anger at something unworthy, unjust, unfair, or mean; anger mixed with scorn; righteous anger.

in dis cre tion (in′dis kresh′ən), *n.* lack of good judgment; unwiseness; imprudence.

in do lent (in′dl ənt), *adj.* disliking work; lazy; idle. **—in′do lent ly,** *adv.*

in dom i ta ble (in dom′ə tə bəl), *adj.* that cannot be conquered; unyielding.

in dulge (in dulj′), *v.,* **-dulged, -dulg ing.** **—v.i.** give in to one's pleasure; let oneself have, use, or do what one wants. **—v.t.** give in to; let oneself have, use, or do.

in dul gence (in dul′jəns), *n.* 1 act of indulging. 2 favor; privilege.

in e bri ate (in ē′brē it), *n.* a drunken person. **—adj.** intoxicated; drunk. [< Latin *inebriatum* made drunk < *in-* + *ebrius* drunk]

in e bri e ty (in′i brī′ə tē), *n.* drunkenness.

in ef fa ble (in ef′ə bəl), *adj.* not to be expressed in words; too great to be described in words.

in ef fec tu al (in′ə fek′chü əl), *adj.* without effect; useless.

in ert (in ėrt′), *adj.* 1 having no power to move or act; lifeless. 2 inactive; slow; sluggish. [< Latin *inertem* idle, unskilled < *in-* without + *artem* art, skill]

in es ti ma ble (in es′tə mə bəl), *adj.* 1 not capable of being estimated; incalculable. 2 too precious to be estimated; priceless; invaluable. **—in es′ti ma bly,** *adv.*

in ev i ta ble (in ev′ə tə bəl), *adj.* not to be avoided; sure to happen; certain to come: *Death is inevitable.* [< Latin *inevitabilis* < *in-* not + *evitare* avoid < *ex-* out + *vitare* shun]

in ex or a ble (in ek′sər ə bəl), *adj.* not influenced by pleading or entreaties; relentless; unyielding: *The forces of nature are inexorable.* [< Latin *inexorabilis* < *in-* not + *exorare* prevail upon, pray earnestly < *ex-* out + *orare* pray, entreat]

in ex pli ca ble (in′ik splik′ə bəl, in ek′splə kə bəl), *adj.* that cannot be explained, understood, or accounted for; mysterious. **—in′ex plic′a bly,** *adv.*

in fal li ble (in fal′ə bəl), *adj.* 1 free from error; that cannot be mistaken. 2 absolutely reliable; sure. **—in fal′li bly,** *adv.*

in fir mi ty (in fėr′mə tē), *n., pl.* **-ties.** 1 weakness; feebleness. 2 sickness; illness. 3 weakness, flaw, or defect in a person's character.

in flame (in flām′), *v.t.,* **-flamed, -flam ing.** make more violent; excite. [< Latin *inflammare* < *in-* in + *flamma* flame]

in flam ma tion (in′flə mā′shən), *n.* a being inflamed.

in flec tion (in flek′shən), *n.* a change in the tone or pitch of the voice: *We usually end questions with a rising inflection.*

in flux (in′fluks), *n.* a flowing in; steady flow. [< Late Latin *influxus* < Latin *influere* to flow in < *in-* in + *fluere* to flow]

in her ent (in hir′ənt, in her′ənt), *adj.* belonging to a person or thing as a permanent and essential quality or attribute; intrinsic.

in hos pi ta ble (in′ho spit′ə bəl, in hos′pi tə bəl), *adj.* not making visitors comfortable.

in im i ta ble (in im′ə tə bəl), *adj.* impossible to imitate or copy; matchless.

in iq ui ty (in ik′wə tē), *n., pl.* **-ties.** gross injustice or unrighteousness; wickedness; sin.

in noc u ous (i nok′yü əs), *adj.* not hurtful or injurious; harmless.

in or di nate (in ôrd′n it), *adj.* much too great; not kept within proper limits; excessive. [< Latin *inordinatus* not ordered, disarranged < *in-* not + *ordo* order]

in qui si tion (in′kwə zish′ən), *n.* 1 a thorough investigation; searching inquiry. 2 an official investigation; judicial inquiry. 3 **the Inquisition,** court appointed by the Roman Catholic Church in the 1200's to discover and suppress heresy. It was abolished in the 1800's. [< Latin *inquisitionem* < *inquirere*]

in scru ta ble (in skrü′tə bəl), *adj.* that cannot be understood; so mysterious or obscure that one cannot make out its meaning; incomprehensible. [< Late Latin *inscrutabilis* < Latin *in-* not + *scrutari* examine, ransack < *scruta* trash]

in sen si ble (in sen′sə bəl), *adj.* 1 not sensitive; not able to feel or notice. 2 not aware; unmoved; indifferent. 3 not able to feel anything; unconscious; senseless. **—in sen′si bly,** *adv.*

in sid i ous (in sid′ē əs), *adj.* 1 seeking to entrap or ensnare; wily or sly; crafty; tricky. 2 working secretly or subtly; developing without attracting attention. [< Latin *insidiosus* < *insidiae* ambush < *insidere* sit in < *in-* in + *sedere* sit]

in sig ni a (in sig′nē ə), *n., pl.* **-ni a** or **-ni as.** medal, badge, or other distinguishing mark of a position, honor, military rank, etc.

in sist ent (in sis′tənt), *adj.* 1 insisting. 2 compelling attention or notice; pressing; urgent: *an insistent knocking on the door.* **—in sist′ent ly,** *adv.*

in sol ence (in′sə ləns), *n.* bold rudeness; insulting behavior or speech.

in so lent (in′sə lənt), *adj.* boldly rude; intentionally disregarding the feelings of others; insulting. [< Latin *insolentem* < *in-* not + *solere* be accustomed]

in stan ta ne ous (in′stən tā′nē əs), *adj.* coming or done in an instant.

in stinct (in′stingkt), *n.* a natural tendency or ability; talent. [< Latin *instinctus* impulse < *instinguere* incite, impel]

in stinc tive (in stingk′tiv), *adj.* of or having to do with instinct. **—in stinc′tive ly,** *adv.*

in sur rec tion (in′sə rek′shən), *n.* a rising against established authority; revolt.

in teg ri ty (in teg′rə tē), *n.* 1 honesty or sincerity; uprightness. 2 wholeness; completeness.

inter-, *prefix.* 1 one with the other; together: *Intercommunicate = communicate with each other.* 2 between: *Interpose = put between.* 3 between or among a group: *International = between or among nations.*

in ter ject (in′tər jekt′), v.t. throw in between other things; insert abruptly. —**in′ter jec′tion al,** adj.

in ter lace (in′tər lās′), v., **-laced, -lac ing.** —v.t. arrange (threads, strips, or branches) so that they go over and under each other; weave together; intertwine. —v.i. cross each other over and under; mingle together in an intricate manner.

in ter lop er (in′tər lō′pər), n. person who thrusts himself in where he is not wanted or has no right; intruder.

in ter me di ate (in′tər mē′dē it), adj. being or occurring between; middle. [< Latin *intermedius* < *inter-* between + *medius* in the middle]

in ter mi na ble (in tėr′mə nə bəl), adj. 1 never stopping; unceasing; endless. 2 so long as to seem endless; very long and tiring.

in ter min gle (in′tər ming′gəl), v.t., v.i., **-gled, -gling.** mix together; mingle.

in ter mit tent (in′tər mit′nt), adj. stopping for a time and beginning again; pausing at intervals. —**in′ter mit′tent ly,** adv.

in ter ne cine (in′tər nē′sn, in′tər nē′sīn), adj. 1 destructive to both sides within a group. 2 deadly; destructive. [< Latin *internecinus* < *internecare* to kill, destroy < *inter-* between + *necare* kill]

in ter pose (in′tər pōz′), v.i., **-posed, -pos ing.** 1 come or be between other things. 2 interrupt. 3 interfere in order to help; intervene; intercede.

in ter rog a tive (in′tə rog′ə tiv), adj. asking a question; having the form or force of a question: *an interrogative look, an interrogative tone of voice.*

in ter twine (in′tər twīn′), v.t., v.i., **-twined, -twin ing.** twine, one with another; interlace.

in ter wo ven (in′tər wo′vən), adj. mixed together; blended.

in tim i date (in tim′ə dāt), v.t., **-dat ed, -dat ing.** 1 make afraid; frighten. 2 influence or force by fear.

in to na tion (in′tō nā′shən, in′tə nā′shən), n. the rise and fall in the tone of voice during speech.

intra-, prefix. within; inside; on the inside, as in *intramural, intrastate.*

in trin sic (in trin′sik), adj. 1 belonging to a thing by its very nature; essential; inherent. 2 originating or being inside the part on which it acts: *the intrinsic muscles of the larynx.* [< Late Latin *intrinsecus* internal < Latin, inwardly]

in var i a ble (in ver′ē ə bəl, in vār′ē ə bəl), adj. always the same; unchanging; unchangeable; constant. —**in var′i a ble ness,** n. —**in var′i a bly,** adv.

in ver te brate (in vėr′tə brit, in vėr′tə brāt), adj. without a backbone. —n. animal without a backbone. Worms and insects are invertebrates.

in vin ci ble (in vin′sə bəl), adj. unable to be conquered; impossible to overcome; unconquerable. [< Latin *invincibilis* < *in-* not + *vincere* conquer]

in vi o la ble (in vī′ə lə bəl), adj. that must not be violated or injured; sacred.

-ion, suffix forming nouns chiefly from verbs. 1 act of ____ing: *Attraction = act of attracting.* 2 condition of being ____ed: *Adoption = condition of being adopted.* 3 result of ____ing: *Abbreviation = result of abbreviating.* Also, **-tion, -ation.**

i ras ci ble (i ras′ə bəl), adj. 1 easily made angry; with a quick temper; irritable. 2 showing anger. [< Late Latin *irascibilis* < Latin *irasci* grow angry < *ira* anger]

ir i des cent (ir′ə des′nt), adj. displaying changing colors; changing color when moved or turned. [< Latin *iris, iridis* rainbow]

i ron ic (ī ron′ik), adj. ironical.

i ron i cal (ī ron′ə kəl), adj. 1 expressing one thing and meaning the opposite: *"Speedy" was the ironical name of our turtle.* 2 contrary to what would naturally be expected. 3 using or given to using irony. —**i ron′i cal ly,** adv.

ir re proach a ble (ir′i prō′chə bəl), adj. free from blame; faultless.

ir re sist i ble (ir′i zis′tə bəl), adj. that cannot be resisted; too great to be withstood; overwhelming.

ir res o lute (i rez′ə lüt), adj. not resolute; unable to make up one's mind; not sure of what one wants; hesitating. —**ir res′o lute ly,** adv. —**ir res′o lute ness,** n.

-ism, suffix forming nouns from other nouns and from adjectives and verbs. 1 act or practice of ____ing: *Baptism = act or practice of baptizing.* 2 quality or condition of being a ____: *Heroism = quality of being a hero.* 3 illustration or instance of being ____: *Witticism = instance of being witty.* 4 an unhealthy condition caused by ____: *Alcoholism = an unhealthy condition caused by alcohol.* 5 doctrine, theory, system, or practice of ____: *Darwinism = theory of Charles Darwin.*

-ist, suffix forming nouns chiefly from other nouns. 1 person who does or makes: *Tourist = a person who tours.* 2 an expert in an art or science: *Botanist = an expert in botany.* 3 person who plays a musical instrument: *Organist = person who plays the organ.* 4 person engaged in or working with: *Journalist = a person engaged in journalism.* 5 person who believes in: *Socialist = a person who believes in socialism.*

-ity, suffix forming nouns from adjectives. quality, condition, or fact of being ____: *Sincerity = quality or condition of being sincere.*

-ive, suffix forming adjectives from nouns. 1 of or having to do with, as in *interrogative, inductive.* 2 tending to; likely to, as in *active, appreciative.*

-ize, suffix forming verbs from adjectives and nouns. 1 make ____: *Legalize = make legal.* 2 become ____: *Crystallize = become crystal.* 3 engage in or use ____: *Criticize = engage in criticism.*

jas mine or **jas min** (jas′mən, jaz′mən), n. any of several plants bearing fragrant flowers.

ju di cial (jü dish′əl), adj. of or by judges; having to do with courts or the administration of justice. [< Latin *judicialis* < *judicium* judgment < *judicem* judge]

ju di ci ar y (jü dish′ē er′ē), n., pl. **-ar ies.** 1 branch of government that administers justice; system of courts of law of a country. 2 judges of a country, state, or city.

ju di cious (jü dish′əs), adj. having, using, or showing good judgment; wise; sensible. —**ju di′cious ly,** adv. —**ju di′cious ness,** n.

jug u lar (jug′yə lər, jü′gyə lər), n. jugular vein.

jugular vein, one of the two large veins in each side of the neck and head that return blood from the head and neck to the heart.

ju ni per (jü′nə pər), n. any of a genus of evergreen shrubs or trees of the same family as the cypress, with small berrylike cones.

hat, āge, fär; let, ēqual, tėrm;
it, īce; hot, ōpen, ôrder;
oil, out; cup, pút, rüle;
ch, child; ng, long; sh, she;
th, thin; ͞ŦH, then; zh, measure;

ə represents *a* in about, *e* in taken,
i in pencil, *o* in lemon, *u* in circus.

< = from, derived from, taken from.

jur is dic tion (jür′is dik′shən), n. 1 right, power, or authority to administer justice or exercise judicial functions. 2 authority; power; control. 3 extent of authority. [< Latin *jurisdictionem* < *jus, juris* law + *dicere* say]

kin dred (kin′drid), adj. 1 related in character or properties; like; similar. 2 related by birth or descent: *kindred tribes.* —n. 1 a person's family or relatives. 2 family relationship; kinship. 3 a being alike; resemblance. [Middle English *kynrede* < *kyn* family (Old English *cynn*) + *-rede,* Old English *rǣden* condition]

kins man (kinz′mən), n., pl. **-men.** a male relative.

lam en ta ble (lam′ən tə bəl), adj. ARCHAIC. sorrowful; mournful.

lau rel (lôr′əl, lor′əl), n. 1 a small evergreen tree of southern Europe, with smooth, shiny leaves; bay; sweet bay. 2 its leaves. 3 any tree or shrub of the same family as the laurel. 4 mountain laurel

lave (lāv), v., **laved, lav ing.** —v.t. 1 wash; bathe. 2 wash or flow against: *The stream laves its banks.*

le sion (lē′zhən), n. 1 an injury; hurt. 2 an abnormal change in the structure of an organ or body tissue, caused by disease or injury. [< Latin *laesionem* injury < *laedere* to strike]

lieu (lü), n. 1 place; stead. 2 **in lieu of,** in place of; instead of.

lig ne ous (lig′nē əs), adj. of or like wood; woody. [< Latin *ligneus* < *lignum* wood]

lim bo (lim′bō), n. 1 place for persons and things forgotten, cast aside, or out of date: *The belief that the earth is flat belongs to the limbo of outworn ideas.* 2 prison; jail; confinement.

lin den (lin′dən), n. 1 any of a genus of shade trees with heart-shaped leaves and clusters of small, fragrant, yellowish flowers. 2 the light, white wood of any of these trees.

lin e a ment (lin′ē ə mənt), n. part or feature, especially a part or feature of a face with attention to its outline.

lin tel (lin′tl), n. a horizontal beam or stone over a door, window, etc., to support the structure above it.

lit er al ist (lit′ər ə list), n. 1 person who adheres to the exact literal meaning. 2 person who represents or portrays without idealizing.

lith o graph (lith′ə graf), n. print made by lithography.

li thog ra phy (li thog′rə fē), n. art or process of printing from a smooth, flat stone or metal plate on which the picture, design, etc., is made with a greasy material that will hold printing ink, the rest of the surface being made ink-repellent with water.

lit i ga tion (lit′ə gā′shən), *n.* 1 a carrying on a lawsuit. 2 a going to law. 3 a lawsuit or legal proceeding.

li ti gious (lə tij′əs), *adj.* having the habit of going to law.

loam (lōm), *n.* rich, fertile earth in which much humus is mixed with clay and sand.

loam y (lō′mē), *adj.* of or like loam.

loath some (lōᵀH′səm), *adj.* making one feel sick; disgusting.

lu di crous (lü′də krəs), *adj.* causing derisive laughter; amusingly absurd; ridiculous. [< Latin *ludicrus* < *ludus* sport]

lu mi nar y (lü′mə ner′ē), *n., pl.* -nar ies, *adj.* —*n.* 1 a heavenly body that gives or reflects light. 2 a famous person. [< Late Latin *luminarium* < Latin *lumen* light]

lu mi nous (lü′mə nəs), *adj.* 1 shining by its own light. 2 full of light; shining; bright.

lur id (lur′id), *adj.* 1 lighted up with a red or fiery glare. 2 glaring in brightness or color.

lus trous (lus′trəs), *adj.* 1 having luster; shining; glossy: *lustrous satin.* 2 brilliant; splendid.

-ly¹, *suffix forming adverbs from adjectives.* 1 in a ____ manner: *Cheerfully = in a cheerful manner.* 2 in ____ ways or respects: *Financially = in financial respects.* 3 to a ____ degree or extent: *Greatly = to a great degree.*

-ly², *suffix forming adjectives from nouns.* 1 like a ____: *Ghostly = like a ghost.* 2 like that of a ____; characteristic of a ____: *Brotherly = like that of a brother.* 3 suited to a ____; fit or proper for a ____: *Womanly = suited to a woman.*

mag is tra cy (maj′ə strə sē), *n., pl.* -cies. district under a magistrate.

mag is trate (maj′ə strāt, maj′ə strit), *n.* 1 a government official who has power to apply the law and put it in force. 2 judge in a minor court. 3 A justice of the peace is a magistrate. [< Latin *magistratus,* ultimately < *magister* master < *magnus* great]

mag na nim i ty (mag′nə nim′ə tē), *n., pl.* -ties. nobility of soul or mind; generosity.

mag ni tude (mag′nə tüd, mag′nə tyüd), *n.* 1 greatness of size. 2 great importance, effect, or consequence. 3 size, whether great or small. 4 degree of brightness of a star. The brightest stars are of the first magnitude. [< Latin *magnitudo* < *magnus* large]

maize (māz), *n.* 1 corn; Indian corn. 2 the color of ripe corn; yellow. [< Spanish *maíz* < Arawak *mahiz*]

ma lev o lent (mə lev′ə lənt), *adj.* wishing evil to happen to others; showing ill will; spiteful. [< Latin *malevolentem* < *male* badly + *velle* to wish]

ma lin ger (mə ling′gər), *v.i.* pretend to be sick, injured, etc., in order to escape work or duty; shirk. [< French *malingre* sickly]

man dar in (man′dər ən), *n.* an official of any of nine ranks under the Chinese empire.

man gle (mang′gəl), *v.t.,* -gled, -gling. 1 cut or tear (the flesh) roughly; lacerate. 2 spoil; ruin.

ma ni a cal (mə nī′ə kəl), *adj.* insane; raving. —**ma ni′a cal ly,** *adv.*

man i fest (man′ə fest), *v.t.* 1 show plainly; reveal; display. 2 put beyond doubt; prove. —*n.* list of cargo of a ship or aircraft.

man i fes ta tion (man′ə fə stā′shən), *n.* a showing; making manifest; making plain.

man i fold (man′ə fōld), *adj.* 1 of many kinds; many and various: *manifold duties.* 2 having many parts or forms. 3 doing many things at the same time.

mar gue rite (mär′gə rēt′), *n.* any of various species of chrysanthemums with daisylike flowers, especially a species having flowers with white petals and a yellow center.

mar ti net (märt′n et′), *n.* person who upholds and enforces very strict discipline. [< J. *Martinet,* died 1672, French general and drillmaster]

ma son (mā′sn), *n.* 1 person whose work is building with stone or brick. 2 **Mason,** Freemason.

mas ti cate (mas′tə kāt), *v.t., v.i.,* -cat ed, -cat ing. grind (food) to a pulp with the teeth; chew. [< Late Latin *masticatum* chewed < Greek *mastichan* gnash the teeth] —**mas′ti ca′tion,** *n.* —**mas′ti ca′tor,** *n.*

ma ter i al (mə tir′ē əl), *adj.* caring too much for the things of this world and neglecting spiritual needs; worldly.

ma ter i al ist (mə tir′ē ə list), *n.* person who cares too much for the things of this world and neglects spiritual needs. —*adj.* materialistic.

ma ter nal (mə tėr′nl), *adj.* of or like a mother; motherly. [< Middle French *maternel* < Latin *maternus* < *mater* mother] —**ma ter′nal ly,** *adv.* —**ma ter′nal ism,** *n.*

ma tric u late (mə trik′yə lāt), *v.t., v.i.,* -lat ed, -lat ing. enroll, especially in a college or university, as a candidate for a degree.

me an der (mē an′dər), *v.i.* 1 follow a winding course. 2 wander aimlessly.

med i ta tive (med′ə tā′tiv), *adj.* fond of or given to meditating; thoughtful.

mel an chol y (mel′ən kol′ē), *n., pl.* -chol ies, *adj.* —*n.* 1 condition of sadness and low spirits; gloominess; dejection. 2 sober thoughtfulness; pensiveness. —*adj.* depressed in spirits; sad; gloomy. [< Greek *melancholia* < *melanos* black + *cholē* bile]

mel io rate (mē′lyə rāt′, mē′lē ə rāt′), *v.t., v.i.,* -rat ed, -rat ing. improve. [< Latin *melior* better] —**mel′io ra′tion,** *n.*

me men to (mə men′tō), *n., pl.* -tos or -toes. something serving as a reminder of what is past or gone; souvenir.

-ment, *suffix added to verbs to form nouns.* 1 act, process, or fact of ____ing: *Enjoyment = act of enjoying.* 2 condition of being ____ed: *Amazement = condition of being amazed.* 3 product or result of ____ing: *Pavement = product of paving.* 4 means of or instrument for ____ing: *Inducement = means of inducing.* [< French < Latin *-mentum* result of]

men tor (men′tər), *n.* a wise and trusted adviser.

mer ce nar y (mėr′sə ner′ē), *adj., n., pl.* -nar ies. —*adj.* working for money only; acting with money as the motive; hireling. —*n.* soldier serving for pay in a foreign army.

Mer cu ro chrome (mər kyür′ə krōm′), *n.* trademark for a red solution containing a compound of mercury, used externally as an antiseptic.

mes mer ize (mez′mə rīz′, mes′mə rīz′), *v.t., v.i.,* -ized, -iz ing. hypnotize. [< Franz A. *Mesmer,* 1734-1815, Austrian physician who made hypnotism popular]

met a mor phose (met′ə môr′fōz), *v.,* -phosed, -phos ing. —*v.t.* change in form, structure, or substance by or as if by witchcraft; transform. —*v.i.* undergo metamorphosis or metamorphism.

me thod i cal (mə thod′ə kəl), *adj.* done according to a method; systematic; orderly. —**me thod′i cal ly,** *adv.*

me tic u lous (mə tik′yə ləs), *adj.* extremely or excessively careful about small details. [< Latin *meticulosus* fearful, timid < *metus* fear] —**me tic′u lous ly,** *adv.*

met ro nome (met′rə nōm), *n.* device that can be adjusted to make loud ticking sounds at different speeds. Metronomes are used especially to mark time for persons practicing on musical instruments.

mi cro cosm (mī′krō koz′ əm), *n.* community, etc., regarded as an epitome of the world; a little world; universe in miniature. [< Late Greek *mikros kosmos* little world]

mi graine (mī′grān), *n.* a severe headache, usually recurrent, on one side of the head only, and accompanied by nausea.

mil len ni um (mə len′ē əm), *n., pl.* -len ni ums, -len ni a (-len′ē ə). 1 period of a thousand years. 2 a thousandth anniversary. [< New Latin < Latin *mille* thousand + *annus* year]

mince (mins), *v.,* minced, minc ing. —*v.t.* speak or do in an affectedly polite or elegant manner. —*v.i.* walk with short, affectedly dainty steps.

min ster (min′stər), *n.* 1 church of a monastery. 2 a large or important church; cathedral. [Old English *mynster* < Late Latin *monasterium*]

mis-, *prefix.* 1 bad: *Misgovernment = bad government.* 2 badly: *Misbehave = behave badly.* 3 wrong: *Mispronunciation = wrong pronunciation.* 4 wrongly: *Misapply = apply wrongly.*

mit i gate (mit′ə gāt), *v.t., v.i.,* -gat ed, -gat ing. make or become mild or milder; make or become less harsh; soften. [< Latin *mitigatum* made gentle < *mitis* gentle]

mo cha (mō′kə), *n.* a choice variety of coffee originally coming from Arabia.

moil (moil), *v.i.* work hard; drudge. —*n.* 1 hard work; drudgery. 2 confusion, turmoil, or trouble.

mon o syl la ble (mon′ə sil′ə bəl), *n.* word of one syllable. *Yes, no,* and *grand* are monosyllables.

mor bid (môr′bid), *adj.* 1 not wholesome; unhealthy. 2 caused by disease; characteristic of disease; diseased. 3 horrible; gruesome; grisly. [< Latin *morbidus* < *morbus* disease]

mo sa ic (mō zā′ik), *n.* 1 decoration made of small pieces of stone, glass, wood, etc., of different colors inlaid to form a picture or design. 2 such a picture or design. Mosaics are used in the floors, walls, or ceilings of some fine buildings. 3 art or process of making such a picture or design. 4 anything like a mosaic: *Her music is a mosaic of folk melodies.* —*adj.* formed by, having to do with, or resembling a mosaic. [< Medieval Latin *mosaicus, musaicus* of the Muses, artistic]

mot tle (mot′l), *v.t.,* -tled, -tling. mark with spots or streaks of different colors or shades.

mul ti plic i ty (mul′tə plis′ə tē), *n., pl.* -ties. 1 manifold variety; diversity. 2 a great many; great number.

mul ti tude (mul′tə tüd, mul′tə tyüd), *n.* a great many; crowd; host.

musk (musk), *n.* substance with a strong and lasting odor, used in making perfumes. Musk is found in a gland in the abdomen of the male musk deer.

mu tate (myü′tāt), *v.t., v.i.,* **-tat ed, -tat ing.** 1 change. 2 undergo or produce mutation.

myr i ad (mir′ē əd), *n.* a very great number. —*adj.* countless; innumerable. [< Greek *myriados* ten thousand, countless]

mys ti cal (mis′tə kəl), *adj.* 1 having some secret meaning; beyond human understanding; mysterious. 2 spiritually symbolic. 3 of or having to do with secret rites open only to the initiated.

neb u lous (neb′yə ləs), *adj.* 1 hazy; vague; confused. 2 cloudlike. 3 of or like a nebula or nebulae. —**neb′u lous ly,** *adv.*

neg li gence (neg′lə jəns), *n.* 1 lack of proper care or attention; neglect. 2 carelessness; indifference. [< Latin *negligentia* < *negligere* to disregard, neglect < *nec* not + *legere* pick up]

ne o clas si cism (nē′ō klas′ə siz′əm), *n.* movement in art, music, and literature to revive or restore classical principles or practices.

-ness, *suffix added to adjectives to form nouns.* 1 quality or condition of being ____: *Preparedness = condition of being prepared.* 2 ____ action; ____ behavior: *Carefulness = careful action; careful behavior.*

neu ron ic (nü ron′ik, nyü ron′ik), *adj.* of or having to do with a neuron.

new el (nü′əl, nyü′əl), *n.* the post at the top or bottom of a stairway that supports the railing.

ni ter (nī′tər), *n.* potassium nitrate, especially when it occurs naturally as a white salt in the soil and encrusted on rocks.

ni tre (nī′tər), *n.* niter.

noc tur nal (nok tėr′nl), *adj.* 1 of the night. 2 active in the night. [< Latin *nocturnus* of the night < *noctem* night]

non de script (non′də skript), *adj.* not easily classified; not of any one particular kind: *She had nondescript eyes, neither brown, blue, nor gray.* —*n.* a nondescript person or thing. [< *non-* + Latin *descriptum* (to be) described]

o blique (ə blēk′), *adj.* not straightforward; indirect: *She made an oblique reference to her illness, but did not mention it directly.*

o bliv i ous (ə bliv′ē əs), *adj.* not mindful; forgetful.

ob scene (əb sēn′), *adj.* offending modesty or decency; impure; filthy; vile. [< Latin *obscenus*] —**ob scene′ly,** *adv.*

ob se qui ous (əb sē′kwē əs), *adj.* polite or obedient from hope of gain or from fear; servile. [< Latin *obsequiosus* < *obsequium* dutiful service < *ob-* after + *sequi* follow]

ob sti na cy (ob′stə nə sē), *n., pl.* **-cies.** a being obstinate; stubbornness.

ob trude (əb trüd′), *v.i.,* **-trud ed, -trud ing.** come unasked and unwanted; force oneself; intrude. [< Latin *obtrudere* < *ob-* toward + *trudere* to thrust] —**ob tru′sive,** *adj.*

ob tuse (əb tüs′, əb tyüs′), *adj.* 1 slow in understanding; stupid. 2 not sensitive; dull. [< Latin *obtusum* blunted < *ob-* against + *tundere* to beat]

oc cult (ə kult′, ok′ult), *adj.* 1 beyond the bounds of ordinary knowledge; mysterious. 2 outside the laws of the natural world; magical. 3 not disclosed; secret; revealed only to the initiated. [< Latin *occultum* hidden < *ob-* up + *celare* to hide]

oc u lar (ok′yə lər), *adj.* 1 of or having to do with the eye. 2 received by actual sight; seen: *ocular proof.*

of fal (ô′fəl, of′əl), *n.* 1 the waste parts of an animal killed for food. 2 garbage; refuse. [< *off* + *fall*]

of fi cious (ə fish′əs), *adj.* too ready to offer services or advice; minding other people's business; meddlesome. [< Latin *officiosus* dutiful < *officium* service]

o le ag i nous (ō′lē aj′ə nəs), *adj.* having the nature or properties of oil; oily; greasy.

o le an der (ō′lē an′dər), *n.* a poisonous evergreen shrub of the same family as the dogbane, with fragrant red, pink, white, or purple flowers. [< Medieval Latin]

om nip o tence (om nip′ə təns), *n.* complete power; unlimited power.

om nip o tent (om nip′ə tənt), *adj.* 1 having all power; almighty. 2 having very great power or influence. —*n.* **the Omnipotent,** God. —**om nip′o tent ly,** *adv.*

om ni pres ence (om′nə prez′ns), *n.* presence everywhere at the same time: *God's omnipresence.*

om nis cience (om nish′əns), *n.* knowledge of everything; complete or infinite knowledge. [< Medieval Latin *omniscientia* < Latin *omnis* all + *scientia* knowledge]

om nis cient (om nish′ənt), *adj.* knowing everything; having complete or infinite knowledge. —**om nis′cient ly,** *adv.*

o pal (ō′pəl), *n.* a mineral somewhat like quartz, found in many varieties and colors, certain of which reflect light with peculiar rainbow play of colors and are valued as gems.

o pal es cent (ō′pə les′nt), *adj.* having a play of colors like that of an opal.

op pres sion (ə presh′ən), *n.* cruel or unjust treatment; tyranny; persecution; despotism.

-or, *suffix forming nouns from verbs.* person or thing that ____s: *Governor = person who governs. Accelerator = thing that accelerates.*

o rang-ou tang (ō rang′ü tang′), *n.* orangutan.

o rang u tan or **o rang-u tan** (ô rang′ü-tan′), *n.* a large anthropoid ape of the forests of Borneo and Sumatra, that has very long arms and long, reddish-brown hair. It lives mostly in trees and eats fruits and leaves.

or gan dy or **or gan die** (ôr′gən dē′), *n., pl.* **-dies.** a fine, thin, stiff, transparent muslin, used for dresses, curtains, etc.

-ory, *suffix forming adjectives and nouns.* 1 ____ing: *Contradictory = contradicting.* 2 of or having to do with ____ion; characterized by ____ion: *Illusory = of or having to do with illusion. Compulsory = characterized by compulsion.* 3 serving to ____: *Preparatory = serving to prepare.* 4 tending to ____; inclined to ____: *Conciliatory = inclined to conciliate.*

os cil late (os′l āt), *v.i.,* **-lat ed, -lat ing.** swing to and fro like a pendulum; move to and fro between two points. —**os′cil la′tion,** *n.*

os ten si ble (o sten′sə bəl), *adj.* according to appearances; declared as genuine; apparent; pretended; professed. [< Latin *ostensum* shown, ultimately < *ob-* toward + *tendere* to stretch] —**os ten′si bly,** *adv.*

os ten ta tion (os′ten tā′shən), *n.* a showing off; display intended to impress others. [< Latin *ostentationem,* ultimately < *ob-* toward + *tendere* to stretch]

ost ler (os′lər), *n.* hostler.

os tra cism (os′trə siz′əm), *n.* 1 banishment from one's native country. 2 a being shut out from society, favor, privileges, or

hat, āge, fär; let, ēqual, tėrm;
it, īce; hot, ōpen, ôrder;
oil, out; cup, pùt, rüle;
ch, child; ng, long; sh, she;
th, thin; ᴛʜ, then; zh, measure;

ə represents *a* in about, *e* in taken, *i* in pencil, *o* in lemon, *u* in circus.

< = from, derived from, taken from.

association with one's fellows. —**os′tra cize,** *v.*

ot to man (ot′ə mən), *n.* 1 a low, cushioned seat without back or arms. 2 a cushioned footstool. [< *Ottoman*]

-ous, *suffix forming adjectives from nouns.* 1 full of; having much; having: *Joyous = full of joy.* 2 characterized by: *Zealous = characterized by zeal.* 3 having the nature of: *Idolatrous = having the nature of an idolater.* 4 of or having to do with: *Monogamous = having to do with monogamy.* 5 like: *Thunderous = like thunder.*

pa laz zo (pä lät′sō), *n., pl.* **-zi** (-sē). palace, mansion, or large town house in Italy. [< Italian]

pall (pôl), *n.* 1 a heavy, dark cloth, often made of velvet, spread over a coffin, a hearse, or a tomb. 2 a dark, gloomy covering. [Old English *pæll* < Latin *pallium* cloak]

pal la di um (pə lā′dē əm), *n., pl.* **-di a** (-dē ə). anything regarded as an important safeguard. [< Latin < Greek *palladion,* diminutive of *Pallas*]

pal let (pal′it), *n.* bed of straw; small or poor bed. [< Old French *paillet* < *paille* straw < Latin *palea*]

pal lid (pal′id), *adj.* lacking normal color; wan; pale. [< Latin *pallidum*]

pan o ply (pan′ə plē), *n., pl.* **-plies.** 1 complete equipment or covering. 2 any splendid array. [< Greek *panoplia* < *pan-* + *hopla* arms]

par a gon (par′ə gon), *n.* model of excellence or perfection. [< Middle French, comparison < Italian *paragone* touchstone < Greek *parakonan* to whet < *para-* + *akonē* whetsone]

par a pet (par′ə pet, par′ə pit), *n.* a low wall or barrier at the edge of a balcony, roof, bridge, etc. [< Italian *parapetto* < *parare* defend + *petto* chest]

par ley (pär′lē), *v.i.* 1 discuss terms, especially with an enemy. 2 ARCHAIC. speak; talk. [< Old French *parlee,* past participle of *parler* speak < Late Latin *parabolare* < *parabola* speech, story]

par si mo ny (pär′sə mō′nē), *n.* extreme economy; stinginess. [< Latin *parsimonia* < *parcere* to spare]

passe men ter ie (pas men′trē), *n.* fancy edging for clothes.

pas tor al (pas′tər əl), *adj.* 1 of shepherds or country life. 2 simple or naturally beautiful like the country.

pa thos (pā′thos), *n.* 1 quality in speech, writing, music, events, or a scene that arouses a feeling of pity or sadness; power of evoking tender or melancholy emotion. 2 a pathetic expression or utterance. [< Greek, suffering, feeling < *path-,* stem of *paschein* suffer]

pa tri arch (pā′trē ärk), *n.* 1 father and ruler of a family or tribe. 2 person thought of as the father or founder of something. 3 a venerable old man, especially the elder of a village, community, etc. [< Latin *patriarcha* < Greek *patriarchēs* < *patria* family, clan + *archos* leader]

pee vish (pē′vish), *adj.* 1 feeling cross; fretful; complaining: *a peevish child.* 2 showing annoyance or irritation. [Middle English *pevysh*] —**pee′vish ly,** *adv.* —**pee′vish ness,** *n.*

pelf (pelf), *n.* money or riches, thought of as bad or degrading. [< Old French *pelfre* spoils]

pen i tent (pen′ə tənt), *adj.* sorry for sinning or doing wrong; repenting; repentant.

pen sive (pen′siv), *adj.* 1 thoughtful in a serious or sad way. 2 melancholy. [< Old French *pensif* < *penser* think < Latin *pensare* ponder < *pendere* weigh] —**pen′sive ly,** *adv.* —**pen′sive ness,** *n.*

pen ur y (pen′yər ē), *n.* great poverty; extreme want; destitution. [< Latin *penuria* want, need]

per cep ti ble (pər sep′tə bəl), *adj.* that can be perceived. —**per cep′ti bly,** *adv.*

per cus sion (pər kush′ən), *n.* 1 the striking of one body against another with force; stroke; blow. 2 the striking of a percussion cap or similar device to set off the charge in a firearm. [< Latin *percussionem* < *per-* thoroughly + *quatere* to strike, beat]

pe remp tor y (pə remp′tər ē, per′əmp tôr′ē, per′əmp tōr′ē), *adj.* 1 leaving no choice; decisive; final; absolute. 2 allowing no denial or refusal. [< Latin *peremptorius* that puts an end to, ultimately < *per-* to the end + *emere* to take]

per fi dy (pèr′fə dē), *n., pl.* **-dies.** a breaking faith; base treachery; being false to a trust. [< Latin *perfidia* < *perfidus* faithless < *per-* + *fides* faith]

per i o dic i ty (pir′ē ə dis′ə tē), *n., pl.* **-ties.** periodic character; tendency to happen at regular intervals.

per me ate (pèr′mē āt), *v.t.,* **-at ed, -at ing.** 1 spread through the whole of; pass through; pervade. 2 penetrate through pores or openings; soak through. [< Latin *permeatum* passed through < *per-* through + *meare* to pass] —**per′me a′tion,** *n.*

per se ver ance (pèr′sə vir′əns), *n.* a sticking to a purpose or an aim; a persevering; tenacity.

per tain (pər tān′), *v.i.* 1 belong or be connected as a part, possession, etc. 2 have to do with; be related; refer. [< Old French *partenir* < Latin *pertinere* reach through, connect < *per-* through + *tenere* to hold]

per ti nac i ty (pèrt′n as′ə tē), *n.* great persistence; holding firmly to a purpose, action, or opinion.

per tur ba tion (pèr′tər bā′shən), *n.* thing, act, or event that causes disturbance or agitation.

per vade (pər vād′), *v.t.,* **-vad ed, -vad ing.** go or spread throughout; be throughout. [< Latin *pervadere* < *per-* through + *vadere* go]

per verse (pər vèrs′), *adj.* 1 contrary and willful; obstinately opposing what is wanted, reasonable, or required. 2 morally bad; perverted; depraved. [< Latin *perversum* turned away, perverted] —**per verse′ly,** *adv.* —**per verse′ness,** *n.*

per vert (*v.* pər vèrt′), *v.t.* give a wrong meaning to; distort. [< Latin *pervertere* < *per-* to destruction + *vertere* to turn] —**per vert′ed ly,** *adv.* —**per vert′er,** *n.*

pet u lant (pech′ə lənt), *adj.* likely to have little fits of bad temper; irritable over trifles. —**pet′u lance,** *n.*

phi lan thro py (fə lan′thrə pē), *n., pl.* **-pies.** love of mankind shown by practical kindness and helpfulness to humanity. [< Greek *philanthrōpia* < *philos* loving + *anthrōpos* man]

phoe be (fē′bē), *n.* any of various small flycatchers having a grayish-brown back, a yellowish-white breast, and a low crest on the head.

phys i og no my (fiz′ē og′nə mē, fiz′ē-on′ə mē), *n., pl.* **-mies.** kind of features or type of face one has; one's face. [< Greek *physis* nature + *gnōmōn* judge < *gnōnai* recognize]

pic a yune (pik′ə yün′), *adj.* small; petty; mean; paltry. [< Creole *picaillon,* a coin worth 5 cents]

pin ion (pin′yən), *n.* wing. [< Middle French *pignon* < Popular Latin *pinnionem* < Latin *penna* feather and *pinna* wing]

pipe (pīp), *n.* 1 cask, varying in size, for wine, etc. 2 as much as such a cask holds, now usually reckoned as four barrels or 126 (wine) gallons.

pique (pēk), *v.t.,* **piqued, pi quing.** cause a feeling of anger in; wound the pride of. [< French < *piquer* to prick, sting]

pit e ous (pit′ē əs), *adj.* to be pitied; moving the heart; deserving pity.

pit tance (pit′ns), *n.* 1 a small allowance of money. 2 a small amount or share. [< Old French *pitance* portion of food allotted a monk, piety, pity, ultimately < Latin *pietatem* piety]

pla cate (plā′kāt, plak′āt), *v.t.,* **-cat ed, -cat ing.** soothe or satisfy the anger of; make peaceful; appease. [< Latin *placatum* soothed]

plain tive (plān′tiv), *adj.* expressive of sorrow; mournful; sad. [< Old French *plaintif* < *plaint* plaint]

plat i tude (plat′ə tüd, plat′ə tyüd), *n.* a dull or commonplace remark, especially one given out solemnly as if it were fresh and important. [< French < *plat* flat]

plat i tu di nous (plat′ə tüd′n əs, plat′ə-tyüd′n əs), *adj.* characterized by platitudes.

plau si ble (plô′zə bəl), *adj.* appearing true, reasonable, or fair. [< Latin *plausibilis* deserving applause, pleasing < *plaudere* applaud]

plen i tude (plen′ə tüd, plen′ə tyüd), *n.* fullness; completeness; abundance. [< Latin *plenitudo* < *plenus* full]

pleur i sy (plùr′ə sē), *n.* inflammation of the pleura, often marked by fever, chest pains, and difficulty in breathing.

pleur o sis (plür ō′sis), *n.* pleurisy.

plight (plīt), *v.t.* promise solemnly; pledge: *plight one's loyalty.* [Old English *plihtan* < *pliht,* originally, danger, risk]

poign ant (poi′nyənt), *adj.* 1 very painful; piercing. 2 stimulating to the mind, feelings, or passions; keen; intense. [< Old French, present participle of *poindre* to prick < Latin *pungere*] —**poign′ant ly,** *adv.*

pome gran ate (pom′gran′it, pom gran′it, pum′gran′it), *n.* a reddish-yellow fruit with a thick skin and many seeds, each enveloped in a juicy red pulp which has a pleasant, slightly sour taste.

por tal (pôr′tl, pōr′tl), *n.* door, gate, or entrance, usually an imposing one.

[< Medieval Latin *portale* < Latin *porta* gate]

por ti co (pôr′tə kō, pōr′tə kō), *n., pl.* **-coes** or **-cos.** roof supported by columns, forming a porch or a covered walk. [< Italian < Latin *porticus*]

post-, *prefix.* 1 after in time; later: *Postwar = after a war.* 2 after in space; behind: *Postnasal = behind the nasal cavity.*

pos ter i ty (po ster′ə tē), *n.* 1 generations of the future. 2 all of a person's descendants. [< Latin *posteritatem* < *posterus* coming after]

po ta tion (pō tā′shən), *n.* 1 act of drinking. 2 a drink, especially of alcoholic liquor. [< Latin *potationem* < *potare* to drink]

po ten tate (pōt′n tāt), *n.* 1 person having great power. 2 ruler; sovereign.

prat tle (prat′l), *v.,* **-tled, -tling,** —*v.i.* 1 talk as a child does; tell freely and carelessly. 2 talk or tell in a foolish way. [< *prate*] —**prat′tler,** *n.*

pre car i ous (pri ker′ē əs, pri kar′ē əs), *adj.* 1 not safe or secure; uncertain; dangerous; risky. 2 dependent on chance or circumstance. [< Latin *precarius* obtainable by prayer, uncertain < *precem* prayer] —**pre car′i ous ly,** *adv.* —**pre car′i ous ness,** *n.*

pre cept (prē′sept), *n.* rule of action or behavior; maxim. [< Latin *praeceptum* < *praecipere* instruct, anticipate < *prae-* pre- + *capere* to take]

pre cip i tate (pri sip′ə tāt), *v.t.,* **-tat ed, -tat ing.** 1 hasten the beginning of; bring about suddenly. 2 throw headlong; hurl. [< Latin *praecipitatum* thrown headlong < *praecipitem* headlong]

pre clude (pri klüd′), *v.t.,* **-clud ed, -clud ing.** shut out; make impossible; prevent. [< Latin *praecludere* < *prae-* pre- + *claudere* to shut]

pre con cep tion (prē′kən sep′shən), *n.* idea or opinion formed beforehand.

pre cur sor (pri kèr′sər, prē′kər sər), *n.* 1 forerunner. 2 predecessor. [< Latin *praecursor* < *praecurrere* run before < *prae-* pre- + *currere* run]

pred e ces sor (pred′ə ses′ər), *n.* 1 person holding a position or office before another. 2 ARCHAIC. ancestor; forefather. [< Late Latin *praedecessor* < Latin *prae-* pre- + *decedere* retire < *de-* from + *cedere* go]

pre di lec tion (prē′də lek′shən, pred′ə-lek′shən), *n.* a liking; preference. [< Medieval Latin *praedilectum* preferred < Latin *prae-* pre- + *diligere* choose]

pre dis pose (prē′dis pōz′), *v.t.,* **-posed, -pos ing.** give an inclination or tendency to; make liable or susceptible.

pre dom i nant (pri dom′ə nənt), *adj.* 1 having more power, authority, or influence than others; superior. 2 most noticeable; prevailing. —**pre dom′i nant ly,** *adv.*

pre empt or **pre-empt** (prē empt′), *v.t.* 1 secure before someone else can; acquire or take possession of beforehand. 2 settle on (land) with the right to buy it before others. —**pre emp′tor, pre-emp′tor,** *n.*

pre mo ni tion (prē′mə nish′ən, prem′ə-nish′ən), *n.* notification or warning of what is to come; forewarning. [< Latin *praemonitionem* < *praemonere* warn beforehand < *prae-* pre- + *monere* warn]

pres age (pres′ij; *also* pri sāj′ *for v.*), *n., v.,* **pre saged, pre sag ing.** —*n.* sign felt as a warning; omen. —*v.t.* 1 give warning of; predict. 2 have or give a presentiment or prophetic impression of. [< Latin *praesagium* < *prae-* pre- + *sagus* prophetic]

pre sen ti ment (pri zen′tə mənt), *n.* a feeling or impression that something, especially something evil, is about to happen; vague sense of approaching misfortune; foreboding.

pre sume (pri züm′), *v.i.,* **-sumed, -suming.** 1 take an unfair advantage. 2 act with improper boldness; take liberties. [< Latin *praesumere* take for granted < *prae-* pre- + *sumere* take] —**pre sum′er,** *n.* —**presum′ing ly,** *adv.*

pre sump tu ous (pri zump′chü əs), *adj.* acting without permission or right; too bold; forward. —**pre sump′tu ous ly,** *adv.* —**pre sump′tu ous ness,** *n.*

pre ten sion (pri ten′shən), *n.* 1 claim. 2 a doing things for show or to make a fine appearance; showy display.

pre ten tious (pri ten′shəs), *adj.* 1 making claims to excellence or importance. 2 doing things for show or to make a fine appearance; showy; ostentatious. —**pre ten′tious ly,** *adv.* —**pre ten′tious ness,** *n.*

pre ter nat ur al (prē′tər nach′ər əl), *adj.* 1 out of the ordinary course of nature; abnormal. 2 due to something above or beyond nature; supernatural. [< Latin *praeter* beyond + *natura* nature] —**pre′ter nat′ur al ly,** *adv.*

prev a lent (prev′ə lənt), *adj.* in general use; widespread; common.

prim (prim), *adj.,* **prim mer, prim mest.** stiffly precise, neat, proper, or formal.

pris mat ic (priz mat′ik), *adj.* varied in color; brilliant.

pro- *prefix.* 1 forward, as in *project.* 2 forth; out, as in *prolong, prolapse.* 3 on the side of; in favor of, as in *pro-British.* 4 in place of; acting as, as in *pronoun, proconsul.*

pro cure (prə kyūr′), *v.t.,* **-cured, -cur ing.** 1 obtain by care or effort; secure. 2 bring about; cause. [< Latin *procurare* manage < *pro-* before + *cura* care] —**pro cur′a ble,** *adj.* —**pro cure′ment,** *n.*

prod i gal (prod′ə gəl), *adj.* abundant; lavish: *God's prodigal mercies.* [< Latin *prodigus* wasteful < *prodigere* drive forth, squander < *prod-, pro-* forth + *agere* to drive]

pro di gious (prə dij′əs), *adj.* 1 very great; huge; vast. 2 wonderful; marvelous. [< Latin *prodigiosus* < *prodigium* prodigy, omen]

prof fer (prof′ər), *v.t.* offer for acceptance; present; tender. [< Anglo-French *proffrir* < Old French *pro-* forth + *offrir* to offer]

pro found (prə found′), *adj.* 1 very deep. 2 deeply felt; very great. 3 going far deeper than what is easily understood; having or showing great knowledge or understanding. [< Latin *profundus* < *pro-* before + *fundus* bottom] —**pro found′ly,** *adv.* —**pro found′ness,** *n.*

pro fuse (prə fyüs′), *adj.* very abundant: *profuse thanks.* [< Latin *profusum* poured forth + *pro-* forth + *fundere* pour] —**pro fuse′ly,** *adv.* —**pro fuse′ness,** *n.*

pro gen i tor (prō jen′ə tər), *n.* ancestor in the direct line; forefather.

pro mis cu ous (prə mis′kyü əs), *adj.* 1 mixed and in disorder. 2 making no distinctions; not discriminating. [< Latin *promiscuus* < *pro-* forth + *miscere* to mix] —**pro mis′cu ous ly,** *adv.* —**pro mis′cu ous ness,** *n.*

prong horn (prông′hôrn′, prong′hôrn′), *n., pl.* **-horns** or **-horn.** a ruminant mammal resembling an antelope, found on the plains of western North America.

prop a gan da (prop′ə gan′də), *n.* 1 systematic effort to spread opinions or beliefs; any plan or method for spreading opinions or beliefs. 2 opinions or beliefs thus spread. [< New Latin *(congregatio de) propaganda (fide)* (congregation for) propagating (the faith)]

pro pi ti ate (prə pish′ē āt), *v.t.,* **-at ed, -at ing.** prevent or reduce the anger of; win the favor of; appease or conciliate (one offended or likely to be). —**pro pi′ti a′tor,** *n.*

pro pi ti a to ry (prə pish′ē ə tôr′ē, prəpish′ē ə tōr′ē), *adj.* intended to propitiate; making propitiation; conciliatory: *a propitiatory offering.*

pro pi tious (prə pish′əs), *adj.* 1 holding well; favorable. 2 favorably inclined; gracious. [< Latin *propitius,* originally, falling forward < *pro-* forward + *petere* go toward]

prop o si tion (prop′ə zish′ən), *n.* 1 what is offered to be considered; proposal. 2 INFORMAL. a business enterprise; an undertaking: *a paying proposition.*

pro pound (prə pound′), *v.t.* put forward; propose. [earlier *propone* < Latin *proponere* < *pro-* forth + *ponere* put] —**propound′er,** *n.*

pro pri e ty (prə prī′ə tē), *n., pl.* **-ties.** 1 quality or condition of being proper; fitness. 2 proper behavior. [< Latin *proprietatem* appropriateness, property < *proprius* one's own, proper]

pros trate (pros′trāt), *adj.* 1 lying flat with face downward. 2 lying flat. [< Latin *prostratum* thrown down flat < *pro-* forth + *sternere* spread out]

pro to type (prō′tə tīp), *n.* the first or primary type of anything; the original or model.

pro tract (prō trakt′), *v.t.* 1 draw out; lengthen in time; prolong: *protract a visit.* 2 slide out; thrust out; extend. [< Latin *protractum* drawn out < *pro-* forward + *trahere* to draw]

pro tu ber ance (prō tü′bər əns, prōtyü′bər əns), *n.* part that sticks out; bulge; swelling.

pro tu ber ant (prō tü′bər ənt, prōtyü′bər ənt), *adj.* bulging out; sticking out; prominent. [< Late Latin *protuberantem* bulging < *pro-* forward + *tuber* lump] —**pro tu′ber ant ly,** *adv.*

pro ver bi al (prə vėr′bē əl), *adj.* well-known: *the proverbial loyalty of dogs.* —**pro ver′bi al ly,** *adv.*

prov i dence (prov′ə dəns), *n.* 1 God's care and help. 2 **Providence,** God. 3 instance of God's care and help. 4 a being provident; prudence.

prov i dent (prov′ə dənt), *adj.* 1 having or showing foresight; careful in providing for the future; prudent. 2 economical; frugal. —**prov′i dent ly,** *adv.*

pro vin cial (prə vin′shəl), *adj.* 1 having the manners, speech, dress, point of view, etc., of people living in a province. 2 lacking refinement or polish; narrow. —*n.* a provincial person. —**pro vin′cial ly,** *adv.*

pru dence (prüd′ns), *n.* wise thought before acting; good judgment.

pu ber ty (pyü′bər tē), *n.* age or condition of becoming first able to produce offspring; the physical beginning of manhood and womanhood. [< Latin *pubertatem* < *puber, pubes* adult]

pu bes cent (pyü bes′nt), *adj.* arriving or arrived at puberty.

pu er ile (pyü′ər əl), *adj.* youthful; juvenile. [< Latin *puerilis* < *puer* boy, child]

pule (pyül), *v.i.,* **puled, pul ing.** cry in a thin voice, as a sick child does; whimper; whine.

pul let (pul′it), *n.* a young hen, usually less

hat, āge, fär; let, ēqual, tėrm;
it, īce; hot, ōpen, ôrder;
oil, out; cup, put, rüle;
ch, child; ng, long; sh, she;
th, thin; ŦH, then; zh, measure;

ə represents *a* in about, *e* in taken,
i in pencil, *o* in lemon, *u* in circus.

< = from, derived from, taken from.

than a year old. [< Old French *poulet,* diminutive of *poule* hen]

pul ve rize (pul′və rīz′), *v.,* **-rized, -riz ing.** —*v.t.* 1 grind to powder or dust. 2 break to pieces; demolish. —*v.i.* become dust. [< Late Latin *pulverizare* < Latin *pulvis* dust] —**pul′ver i za′tion,** *n.* —**pul′ve riz′er,** *n.*

pum ice (pum′is), *n.* a light, porous, glassy lava used, especially when powdered, for cleaning, smoothing, and polishing. [< Latin *pumicem*]

pum mel (pum′əl), *v.t., v.i.,* **-meled, -meling** or **-melled, -mel ling.** strike or beat; beat with the fists. Also, **pommel.**

pun cheon (pun′chən), *n.* 1 a large cask for liquor, varying in size from 70 to 120 gallons. 2 amount that it holds, used as a unit of capacity. [< Old French *poinchon, poinçon, ponson*]

purge (pėrj), *v.,* **purged, purg ing.** —*v.t.* 1 wash away all that is not clean from; make clean. 2 clear of any undesired thing or person, such as air in a water pipe or opponents in a nation. —*v.i.* become clean. [< Old French *purgier* < Latin *purgare* cleanse < *purus* pure + *agere* to drive] —**purg′er,** *n.*

qua drille (kwə dril′), *n.* a square dance for four couples that usually has five parts or movements.

quer u lous (kwer′ə ləs, kwer′yə ləs), *adj.* complaining; fretful; peevish. [< Latin *querulus* < *queri* complain]

quince (kwins), *n.* 1 the hard, yellowish, acid, pear-shaped fruit of a small Asiatic tree of the rose family, used for preserves and jelly. 2 tree it grows on.

ra di ant (rā′dē ənt), *adj.* shining; bright; beaming.

rai ment (rā′mənt), *n.* clothing; garments. [short for *arraiment* < *array*]

ram i fi ca tion (ram′ə fə kā′shən), *n.* 1 a dividing or spreading out into branches or parts. 2 manner or result of branching; branch; part; subdivision.

ram shack le (ram′shak′əl), *adj.* loose and shaky; likely to come apart. [ultimately < *ransack*]

ran cor (rang′kər), *n.* bitter resentment or ill will; extreme hatred or spite. [< Late Latin, rankness < Latin *rancere* be rank]

ra pi er (rā′pē ər), *n.* a long and light sword used for thrusting. [< Middle French *rapière*]

rasp (rasp), *n.* a harsh, grating sound. [< Old French *rasper*]

rationalize

ra tion al ize (rash′ə nə līz), *v.t.,* **-ized, -iz ing.** find (often unconsciously) an explanation or excuse for. —**ra′tion al i za′tion,** *n.*

re-, *prefix.* **1** again; anew; once more: *Reappear = appear again.* **2** back: *Repay = pay back.* Also, sometimes before vowels, **red-.**

re ac tion ar y (rē ak′shə ner′ē), *adj.* having to do with or favoring a return to a previous, usually more conservative, state of affairs.

re buke (ri byük′), *n.* expression of disapproval; scolding. [< Anglo-French *rebuker* < Old French *rebuchier* < *re-* back + *buchier* to strike]

re cede (ri sēd′), *v.i.,* **-ced ed, -ced ing.** go backward; move backward. [< Latin *recedere* < *re-* back + *cedere* go]

rec om pense (rek′əm pens), *v.t.,* **-pensed, -pens ing.** make a fair return for (an action, anything lost, damage done, or hurt received). [< Late Latin *recompensare* < Latin *re-* back + *compensare* compensate]

re count (ri kount′), *v.t.* tell in detail; give an account of. [< Middle French *reconter* < *re-* + *conter* relate, count]

rec ti tude (rek′tə tüd, rek′tə tyüd), *n.* upright conduct or character; honesty; righteousness. [< Late Latin *rectitudo* < Latin *rectus* straight]

red o lent (red′l ənt), *adj.* **1** having a pleasant smell; fragrant; aromatic. **2** smelling strongly; giving off an odor. [< Latin *redolentem* emitting scent < *re-* back + *olere* to smell] —**red′o lent ly,** *adv.* —**red′o lence,** *n.*

re dress (*v.* ri dres′; *n.* rē′dres, ri dres′), *v.t.* set right; repair; remedy. —*n.* a setting right; reparation; relief. [< Middle French *redresser* < *re-* again + *dresser* straighten, arrange] —**re dress′er,** *n.*

re gat ta (ri gat′ə, ri gät′ə), *n.* a boat race or a series of boat races. [< Italian]

re ju ve nate (ri jü′və nāt), *v.t.,* **-nat ed, -nat ing.** make young or vigorous again; give youthful qualities to. [< *re-* + Latin *juvenis* young] —**re ju′ve na′tion,** *n.* —**re ju′ve na′tor,** *n.*

re lent less (ri lent′lis), *adj.* without pity; not relenting; unyielding. —**re lent′less ly,** *adv.* —**re lent′less ness,** *n.*

re lin quish (ri ling′kwish), *v.t.* **1** give up; let go; release. **2** abandon. [< Old French *relinquiss-,* a form of *relinquir* leave behind < Latin *relinquere* < *re-* + *linquere* to leave]

rem i nis cence (rem′ə nis′ns), *n.* a remembering; recalling past persons, events, etc. [< Latin *reminiscentia* < *reminisci* remember < *re-* again + *mens* mind]

re mon strance (ri mon′strəns), *n.* act of remonstrating; protest; complaint.

ren dez vous (rän′də vü), *n., pl.* **-vous** (-vüz). —*n.* an appointment or engagement to meet at a fixed place or time; meeting by agreement. [< Middle French < *rendez-vous* present yourself!]

re pent ance (ri pen′təns), *n.* sorrow for having done wrong; contrition.

re pine (ri pīn′), *v.i.,* **-pined, -pin ing.** be discontented; fret; complain.

rep re hen sion (rep′ri hen′shən), *n.* reproof, rebuke, or blame.

re proach (ri prōch′), *n.* blame or censure. —*v.t.* blame or censure; upbraid. [< Middle French *reproche* < *reprocher* < Popular Latin *repropiare* lay at the door of, ultimately < Latin *re-* again + *prope* near]

re prove (ri prüv′), *v.t.,* **-proved, -prov ing.** show disapproval of; find fault with; blame. [< Old French *reprover* < Late Latin *reprobare* < Latin *re-* + *probare* to test] —**re prov′er,** *n.* —**re prov′ing ly,** *adv.*

re pug nant (ri pug′nənt), *adj.* **1** disagreeable or offensive; distasteful; objectionable. **2** objecting; averse; opposed. [< Latin *repugnantem* resisting, opposing < *re-* back + *pugnare* to fight] —**re pug′nant ly,** *adv.*

re quite (ri kwīt′), *v.t.,* **-quit ed, -quit ing.** **1** pay back; make return for. **2** make return to; reward. **3** make retaliation for; avenge. [< *re-* + *quite,* variant of *quit*]

re sent ment (ri zent′mənt), *n.* the feeling that one has at being injured or insulted; indignation.

res o nant (rez′n ənt), *adj.* continuing to sound; resounding. [< Latin *resonantem* < *re-* back + *sonus* sound] —**res′o nant ly,** *adv.*

res tive (res′tiv), *adj.* **1** restless; uneasy. **2** hard to manage. **3** refusing to go ahead; balky. [< Old French *restif* motionless < *rester* remain] —**res′tive ly,** *adv.* —**res′tive ness,** *n.*

re stric tive (ri strik′tiv), *adj.* restricting; limiting. —**re stric′tive ly,** *adv.* —**re stric′tive ness,** *n.*

re tract (ri trakt′), *v.t.* draw back or in. [< Latin *retractum* drawn back < *re-* + *trahere* to draw] —**re tract′a ble,** *adj.*

ret ri bu tion (ret′rə byü′shən), *n.* a deserved punishment; return for evil done. [< Latin *retributionem,* ultimately < *re-* back + *tribuere* assign]

retro-, *prefix.* backward; back; behind, as in *retrocede.* [< Latin < *retro* back]

ret ro spec tion (ret′rə spek′shən), *n.* **1** act of looking back on things past. **2** survey of past events or experiences.

rev e la tion (rev′ə lā′shən), *n.* **1** act of making known. **2** the thing made known. [< Latin *revelationem* < *revelare* reveal]

re ver ber ant (ri vėr′bər ənt), *adj.* reverberating.

re ver be rate (ri vėr′bə rāt′), *v.i.,* **-rat ed, -rat ing.** **1** echo back. **2** be cast back; be reflected a number of times, as light or heat. [< Latin *reverberatum* beaten back < *re-* back + *verbera* blow] —**re ver′be ra′tion,** *n.*

rev er ence (rev′ər əns), *n.* a feeling of deep respect, mixed with wonder, awe, and love; veneration.

rev er ent (rev′ər ənt), *adj.* feeling reverence; showing reverence.

rev er ie (rev′ər ē), *n.* **1** dreamy thoughts; dreamy thinking of pleasant things. **2** condition of being lost in dreamy thoughts. Also, **revery.** [< French *rêverie* < *rêver* to dream]

rev er y (rev′ər ē), *n., pl.* **-er ies.** reverie.

re vile (ri vīl′), *v.,* **-viled, -vil ing.** —*v.t.* call bad names; abuse with words. —*v.i.* speak abusively. [< Old French *reviler* despise < *re-* again + *vil* vile]

rhet or ic (ret′ər ik), *n.* **1** art of using words effectively in speaking or writing. **2** mere display in language. [< Latin *rhetorica* < Greek *rhētorikē (technē)* (art) of an orator < *rhētōr* orator]

rheum (rüm), *n.* a watery discharge, such as mucus or tears.

right eous (rī′chəs), *adj.* **1** doing right; virtuous; behaving justly. **2** proper; just; right. [Old English *rihtwīs* < *riht* right + *wīs* way, manner] —**right′eous ness,** *n.*

ro guish (rō′gish), *adj.* **1** having to do with or like rogues; dishonest; rascally. **2** playfully mischievous. —**ro′guish ly,** *adv.* —**ro′guish ness,** *n.*

ro se ate (rō′zē it, rō′zē āt), *adj.* **1** rose-colored; rosy. **2** bright; cheerful; optimistic.

ru di ment (rü′də mənt), *n.* something in an early stage; undeveloped or imperfect form. [< Latin *rudimentum* < *rudis* rude, ignorant]

rue ful (rü′fəl), *adj.* **1** sorrowful; unhappy; mournful: *a rueful expression.* **2** causing sorrow or pity: *a rueful sight.* —**rue′ful ly,** *adv.* —**rue′ful ness,** *n.*

ru mi nate (rü′mə nāt), *v.,* **-nat ed, -nat ing.** —*v.i.* **1** chew the cud. **2** think or ponder; meditate; reflect. —*v.t.* **1** chew again (food which has been previously chewed and swallowed). **2** turn over in the mind; meditate on. —**ru′mi na′tor,** *n.*

Sab bath (sab′əth), *n.* **1** day of the week used for rest and worship. Sunday is the Sabbath for most Christians; Saturday is the Jewish Sabbath. **2 sabbath,** period of rest, quiet, etc. [< Latin *sabbatum* < Greek *sabbaton* < Hebrew *shabbāth* < *shābath* to rest]

sab bat i cal (sə bat′ə kəl), *n.* sabbatical leave or sabbatical year.

sabbatical leave, leave of absence for a year or half year given to teachers, commonly once in seven years, for rest, study, or travel.

sa chem (sā′chəm), *n.* (among some North American Indians) the chief of a tribe or confederation. [of Algonquian origin]

saf fron (saf′rən), *n.* **1** an autumn crocus with purple flowers having orange-yellow stigmas. **2** an orange yellow. —*adj.* orange-yellow. [< Old French *safran,* ultimately < Arabic *za'farān*]

sa ga cious (sə gā′shəs), *adj.* wise in a keen, practical way; shrewd. [< Latin *sagacem*]

sa gac i ty (sə gas′ə tē), *n.* keen, sound judgment; mental acuteness; shrewdness.

salivary gland, any of various glands that empty their secretions into the mouth. The salivary glands of human beings and certain other vertebrates are digestive glands that secrete saliva containing the digestive enzyme ptyalin, salts, mucus, etc.

sal ly (sal′ē), *v.i.,* **-lied, -ly ing.** **1** rush forth suddenly; go out. **2** set out briskly or boldly. [< Old French *saillie* a rushing forth < *saillir* to leap < Latin *salire*]

sanc ti fy (sangk′tə fī), *v.t.,* **-fied, -fy ing.** **1** make holy; make legitimate or binding by a religious sanction. **2** set apart as sacred; observe as holy. [< Latin *sanctificare* < *sanctus* holy + *facere* to make] —**sanc′ti fi′er,** *n.*

sanc ti ty (sangk′tə tē), *n., pl.* **-ties.** **1** holiness of life; saintliness; godliness. **2** holy character; sacredness.

sanc tu ar y (sangk′chü er′ē), *n., pl.* **-ar ies.** place of refuge or protection.

sar casm (sär′kaz′əm), *n.* **1** a sneering or cutting remark; ironical taunt. **2** act of making fun of a person to hurt his feelings; harsh or bitter irony. [< Greek *sarkasmos* < *sarkazein* to sneer, strip off flesh < *sarkos* flesh]

sav in or **sav ine** (sav′ən), *n.* a juniper shrub whose tops yield an oily drug used in medicine.

scab bard (skab′ərd), *n.* sheath or case for the blade of a sword, dagger, etc. [< Anglo-French *escaubers,* plural; of Germanic origin]

scar i fy (skar′ə fī), *v.t.,* **-fied, -fy ing.** make scratches or cuts in the surface of (the skin, etc.). [< Old French *scarifier* < Late Latin *scarificare* < Latin *scarifare* < Greek *skariphasthai* to scratch < *skariphos* stylus]

scep ter (sep′tər), *n.* the rod or staff carried by a ruler as a symbol of royal power or authority. Also, **sceptre.** [< Latin *sceptrum* < Greek *skēptron* staff]

scin til la tion (sin′tl ā′shən), *n.* 1 a sparkling; flashing. 2 a spark; flash.

sconce (skons), *n.* bracket projecting from a wall, used to hold a candle or other light. [< Medieval Latin *sconsa* < Latin *abscondere* abscond, hide]

scourge (skėrj), *n., v.,* **scourged, scourging.** —*n.* 1 a whip; lash. 2 any means of punishment. —*v.t.* whip; flog; punish severely. [< Old French *escorge,* ultimately < Latin *ex-* out + *corium* a hide] —**scourg′er,** *n.*

scru ple (skrü′pəl), *n.* 1 a feeling of doubt about what one ought to do. 2 a feeling of uneasiness that keeps a person from doing something. [< Latin *scrupulus* a feeling of uneasiness, originally diminutive of *scrupus* sharp stone, figuratively, uneasiness, anxiety]

scru ti nize (skrüt′n īz), *v.t.,* **-nized, -nizing.** examine closely; inspect carefully.

scull (skul), *n.* oar worked with a side twist over the stern of a boat to propel it.

scull er (skul′ər), *n.* person who sculls.

se date (si dāt′), *adj.* quiet; calm; serious. [< Latin *sedatum,* related to *sedere* sit] —**se date′ly,** *adv.* —**se date′ness,** *n.*

se da tion (si dā′shən), *n.* 1 treatment with sedatives. 2 the calm or relaxed state induced by such treatment.

sed a tive (sed′ə tiv), *n.* 1 medicine that lessens nervousness or excitement. 2 anything soothing or calming. —*adj.* 1 lessening pain or excitement. 2 soothing; calming.

sed en tar y (sed′n ter′ē), *adj.* used to sitting still much of the time. [< Latin *sedentarius,* ultimately < *sedere* sit] —**sed′en tar′i ly,** *adv.* —**sed′en tar′i ness,** *n.*

sedge (sej), *n.* any of a large family of monocotyledonous herbs growing chiefly in wet places, resembling grasses but having solid, three-sided stems and small, inconspicuous flowers usually in spikes or heads.

se dum (sē′dəm), *n.* any of a large genus of fleshy herbs and small shrubs, most of which have clusters of yellow, white, or pink flowers; stonecrop. [< Latin, houseleek]

sem blance (sem′bləns), *n.* 1 outward appearance. 2 likeness. [< Old French < *sembler* seem < Latin *similare* make similar < *similis* similar]

semi-, *prefix.* 1 half: *Semicircle = half circle.* 2 partly; incompletely: *Semicivilized = partly civilized.* 3 twice. Semi____ly means in each half of a ____, or twice in a ____: *Semiannually = every half year, or twice a year.*

se nil i ty (sə nil′ə tē), *n.* 1 old age. 2 the mental and physical deterioration often characteristic of old age.

sen si bil i ty (sen′sə bil′ə tē), *n., pl.* **-ties.** 1 ability to feel or perceive. 2 sensitiveness. 3 fineness of feeling. 4 Usually, **sensibilities,** *pl.* sensitive feelings.

sen su al (sen′shü əl), *adj.* 1 liking the pleasures of the senses. 2 indulging too much in the pleasures of the senses; lustful; lewd. [< Late Latin *sensualis* < Latin *sensus*] —**sen′su al ly,** *adv.*

sen su ous (sen′shü əs), *adj.* 1 of or derived from the senses; having an effect on the senses; perceived by the senses. 2 enjoying the pleasures of the senses. —**sen′su ous ly,** *adv.* —**sen′su ous ness,** *n.*

sen tence (sen′təns), *n.* 1 group of words

(or sometimes a single word) that is grammatically complete and expresses a statement, request, command, exclamation, etc. 2 a short, wise saying; proverb. [< Latin *sententia,* originally, feeling, opinion < *sentire* to feel]

sen ti ment (sen′tə mənt), *n.* 1 mixture of thought and feeling. Admiration, patriotism, and loyalty are sentiments. 2 feeling, especially refined or tender feeling. [< Late Latin *sentimentum* < Latin *sentire* to feel]

sen ti men tal (sen′tə men′tl), *adj.* 1 having or showing much tender feeling: *sentimental poetry.* 2 likely to act from feelings rather than from logical thinking. —**sen′ti men′tal ly,** *adv.*

sen ti men tal i ty (sen′tə men tal′ə tē), *n., pl.* **-ties.** tendency to be influenced by sentiment rather than reason.

sep ul cher (sep′əl kər), *n.* 1 place of burial; tomb; grave. 2 structure or recess in some old churches in which sacred relics were deposited. Also, **sepulchre.** [< Old French < Latin *sepulcrum* < *sepelire* bury]

se pul chral (sə pul′krəl), *adj.* 1 of sepulchers or tombs. 2 deep and gloomy; dismal; suggesting a tomb.

ser aph (ser′əf), *n., pl.* **-aphs** or **-a phim.** one of the highest order of angels. [< *seraphim,* plural, < Late Latin < Hebrew *sērāphīm*]

se raph ic (sə raf′ik), *adj.* like a seraph; angelic.

ser e nade (ser′ə nād′), *n.* music played or sung outdoors at night, especially by a lover under his sweetheart's window. [< French *sérénade* < Italian *serenata,* ultimately < Latin *serenus* serene]

se rene (sə rēn′), *adj.* 1 peaceful; calm. 2 not cloudy; clear; bright. —*n.* an expanse of clear sky or calm sea. [< Latin *serenus*] —**se rene′ly,** *adv.* —**se ren′i ty,** *n.*

ser vile (sėr′vəl), *adj.* like that of slaves; mean; base. [< Latin *servilis* < *servus* slave] —**ser′vile ly,** *adv.* —**ser′vile ness,** *n.*

sex an gu lar (seks ang′gyə lər), *adj.* having six sides.

sex ton (sek′stən), *n.* man who takes care of a church building. A sexton's duties sometimes include ringing the church bell, arranging burials, etc.

shal lop (shal′əp), *n.* a small, light, open boat with sail or oars. [< French *chaloupe* < Dutch *sloepe*]

shame faced (shām′fāst′), *adj.* 1 showing shame and embarrassment. 2 bashful; shy. —**shame′fac′ed ly,** *adv.* —**shame′fac′ed ness,** *n.*

sheathe (shēᵀʜ), *v.t.,* **sheathed, sheathing.** put (a sword, etc.) into a sheath.

shift less (shift′lis), *adj.* lazy; inefficient. —**shift′less ly,** *adv.* —**shift′less ness,** *n.*

shim mer (shim′ər), *v.i.* shine with a flickering light; gleam faintly. [Old English *scimerian*]

shish ke bab (shish′ kə bob′), dish of kabob roasted or broiled on skewers. [< Armenian *shish kabab*]

shroud (shroud), *n.* 1 cloth or garment in which a dead person is wrapped or dressed for burial. 2 something that covers, conceals, or veils. [Old English *scrūd*]

sib i lant (sib′ə lənt), *adj.* hissing. [< Latin *sibilantem*] —**sib′i la′tion,** *n.*

si dle (sī′dl), *v.i.,* **-dled, -dling.** move sideways slowly so as not to attract attention. [< *sideling,* variant of *sidelong*]

sil i cate (sil′ə kit, sil′ə kāt), *n.* compound containing silicon with oxygen and a metal.

hat, āge, fär; let, ēqual, tėrm;
it, īce; hot, ōpen, ôrder;
oil, out; cup, pùt, rüle;
ch, child; ng, long; sh, she;
th, thin; ᴛʜ, then; zh, measure;

ə represents *a* in about, *e* in taken,
i in pencil, *o* in lemon, *u* in circus.

< = from, derived from, taken from.

Mica, soapstone, asbestos, and feldspar are silicates.

sim u la crum (sim′yə lā′krəm), *n., pl.* **-cra** (-krə), **-crums.** 1 a faint, shadowy, or unreal likeness; mere semblance. 2 image. [< Latin < *simulare* simulate < *similis* like]

skein (skān), *n.* 1 a small, coiled bundle of yarn or thread. There are 120 yards in a skein of cotton yarn. 2 a confused tangle. [< Old French *escaigne*]

slea zy (slē′zē), *adj.,* **-zi er, -zi est.** flimsy and poor: *sleazy cloth.*

slough (slou *for 1;* slü *for 2),* *n.* 1 a soft, deep, muddy place. 2 a swampy place; marshy inlet; slew; slue.

slov en ly (sluv′ən lē), *adj.,* **-li er, -li est.** untidy, dirty, or careless in dress, appearance, habits, work, etc. —**slov′en li ness,** *n.*

smat ter (smat′ər), *n.* slight knowledge; smattering. [originally verb, to dabble, Middle English *smateren* to dirty]

smite (smīt), *v.t.,* **smote, smit ten** or **smit, smit ing.** 1 give a hard blow to (a person, etc.) with the hand, a stick, or the like; strike. 2 give or strike (a blow, stroke, etc.). [Old English *smītan*]

smol der (smōl′dər), *v.i.* 1 burn and smoke without flame. 2 exist or continue in a suppressed condition. 3 show suppressed feeling. Also, **smoulder.** [Middle English]

so bri quet (sō′brə kā), *n.* nickname. Also, **soubriquet.** [< French]

so lic i tude (sə lis′ə tüd, sə lis′ə tyüd), *n.* anxious care; anxiety; concern.

spec tro scope (spek′trə skōp), *n.* instrument for the production and examination of a spectrum of radiation from any source by the passage of rays through a prism or a grating.

spec u late (spek′yə lāt), *v.i.,* **-lat ed, -lat ing.** buy or sell when there is a large risk, with the hope of making a profit from future price changes. [< Latin *speculatum* observed, viewed < *specula* watchtower < *specere* to view]

spec u la tive (spek′yə lā′tiv, spek′yə lə tiv), *adj.* 1 carefully thoughtful; reflective. 2 theoretical rather than practical. —**spec′u la′tive ly,** *adv.* —**spec′u la′tive ness,** *n.*

sphinx (sfingks), *n.* 1 statue of a lion's body with the head of a man, ram, or hawk. 2 **Sphinx,** (in Greek myths) a monster with the head of a woman, the body of a lion, and wings. The Sphinx proposed a riddle to every passer-by and killed those unable to answer it. [< Greek]

spin dle (spin′dl), *n.* 1 any rod or pin that turns around, or on which something turns. Axles and shafts are spindles. 2 something shaped like a spindle. [Old English *spinel,* related to *spinnan* to spin]

spruce (sprüs), *adj.,* **spruc er, spruc est.** smart in appearance; neat; trim.

spurn (spėrn), *n.* 1 disdainful rejection; contemptuous treatment. 2 a kick.

squalor

squal or (skwol′ər), *n.* 1 misery and dirt; filth. 2 quality or condition of being morally squalid. [< Latin]

squeam ish (skwē′mish), *adj.* 1 too proper, modest, etc.; easily shocked; prudish. 2 too particular; too scrupulous. 3 slightly sick at one's stomach; nauseated. [< Anglo-French *escoymous*] —**squeam′ish ly,** *adv.* —**squeam′ish ness,** *n.*

squill (skwil), *n.* plant of the lily family, whose onionlike bulb is used in medicine. [< Latin *squilla* < Greek *skilla*]

staunch (stônch, stänch), *adj.* 1 strong or firm. 2 loyal; steadfast. [< Middle French *estanche* < *estanchier* to stop, hinder] —**staunch′ly,** *adv.* —**staunch′ness,** *n.*

stead fast (sted′fast′), *adj.* firmly fixed; not moving or changing: *a steadfast gaze.* [Old English *stedefæst* < *stede* place + *fæst* fast, firm] —**stead′fast′ly,** *adv.*

stent (stent), *n.* stint.

ste ril i ty (stə ril′ə tē), *n.* sterile condition or character; barrenness.

stig ma (stig′mə), *n., pl.* **-mas** or **-ma ta.** mark of disgrace; stain or reproach on one's reputation.

stint (stint), *n.* task assigned: *Washing the breakfast dishes was her daily stint.* [Old English *styntan* to blunt]

sto i cism (stō′ə siz′əm), *n.* patient endurance; indifference to pleasure and pain.

stra ta (strā′tə, strat′ə), *n.* a pl. of **stratum.**

stra tum (strā′təm, strat′əm), *n., pl.* **-ta** or **-tums.** layer of material, especially one of several parallel layers placed one upon another. [< Latin, something spread out < *sternere* to spread]

sub-, *prefix.* 1 under; below: *Subnormal = below normal.* 2 down; further; again: *Subdivide = divide again.* 3 near; nearly: *Subtropical = nearly tropical.* 4 lower; subordinate: *Subcommittee = a lower or subordinate committee.*

sub ter fuge (sub′tər fyüj), *n.* trick, excuse, or expedient used to escape something unpleasant. [< Late Latin *subterfugium,* ultimately < Latin *subter-* from under + *fugere* flee]

sub ter ra ne an (sub′tə rā′nē ən), *adj.* underground. [< Latin *subterraneus* < *sub-* under + *terra* earth]

suc cor (suk′ər), *n.* person or thing that helps or assists; help; aid. [< Old French *sucurs,* ultimately < Latin *succurrere* run to help < *sub-* up to + *currere* to run]

suf fer ance (suf′ər əns), *n.* 1 permission or consent given only by a failure to object or prevent. 2 power to bear or endure; patient endurance.

suf fice (sə fīs′), *v.,* **-ficed, -fic ing.** —*v.i.* be enough; be sufficient. —*v.t.* make content; satisfy. [< Latin *sufficere* < *sub-* near + *facere* to make]

sul fur ous (sul′fər əs, sul′fyər əs), *adj.* 1 of or having to do with sulfur. 2 of or like the fires of hell; hellish. Also, **sulphurous.**

sul len (sul′ən), *adj.* 1 silent because of bad humor or anger. 2 showing bad humor or anger. 3 dismal; dismal. [Middle English *soleine,* ultimately < Latin *solus* alone] —**sul′len ly,** *adv.* —**sul′len ness,** *n.*

sul phur ous (sul′fər əs), *adj.* sulfurous.

sump tu ous (sump′chü əs), *adj.* lavish and costly; magnificent; rich. [< Latin *sumptuosus* < *sumptus* expense < *sumere* spend]

—sump′tu ous ly, *adv.* —**sump′tu ous ness,** *n.*

sun dry (sun′drē), *adj.* several; various. [Old English *syndrig* separate < *sundor* apart]

super-, *prefix.* 1 over; above: *Superimpose = impose over or above.* 2 besides; further: *Superadd = add besides or further.* 3 in high proportion; to excess; exceedingly: *Superabundant = abundant to excess.* 4 surpassing: *Supernatural = surpassing the natural.* [< Latin *super* over, above]

su per cil i ous (sü′pər sil′ē əs), *adj.* haughty, proud, and contemptuous; disdainful; showing scorn or indifference because of a feeling of superiority. [< Latin *superciliosus* < *supercilium* eyebrow, pride < *super-* above + *-cilium* (< *celare* to cover, conceal)]

su per flu ous (sù pėr′flü əs), *adj.* 1 more than is needed. 2 needless; unnecessary. [< Latin *superfluus,* ultimately < *super-* over + *fluere* to flow]

su per im pose (sü′pər im pōz′), *v.t.,* **-posed, -pos ing.** put on top of something else.

su per sede (sü′pər sēd′), *v.t.,* **-sed ed, -sed ing.** 1 take the place of; cause to be set aside; displace. 2 succeed and supplant; replace. [< Latin *supersedere* be superior to, refrain from < *super-* above + *sedere* sit]

sup pli cate (sup′lə kāt), *v.i.,* **-cat ed, -cat ing.** pray humbly. [< Latin *supplicatum* bent down, suppliant < *sub-* down + *plicare* to bend] —**sup′pli cat′ing ly,** *adv.* —**sup′pli ca′tor,** *n.*

sup pli ca tion (sup′lə kā′shən), *n.* Usually, **supplications,** *pl.* a humble prayer addressed to God or a deity.

sur ly (sėr′lē), *adj.,* **-li er, -li est.** bad-tempered and unfriendly; rude; gruff. [Middle English *sirly,* perhaps < *sir* lord] —**sur′li ness,** *n.*

sur mise (*v.* sər mīz′; *n.* sər mīz′, sėr′mīz), *v.,* **-mised, -mis ing,** *n.* —*v.t., v.i.* infer or guess. —*n.* formation of an idea with little or no evidence; a guessing. [< Old French, accusation, ultimately < *sur-* upon + *mettre* to put]

sur mount (sər mount′), *v.t.* 1 rise above. 2 be above or on top of. [< Old French *surmonter* < *sur-* over + *monter* to mount] —**sur mount′a ble,** *adj.*

sur re al ism (sə rē′ə liz′əm), *n.* a modern movement in art and literature that tries to show what takes place in dreams and in the subconscious mind. Surrealism is characterized by unusual and unexpected arrangements and distortions of images. [< French *surréalisme*]

sus cep ti ble (sə sep′tə bəl), *adj.* 1 easily influenced by feelings or emotions; very sensitive. 2 **susceptible of,** a capable of receiving, undergoing, or being affected by. b sensitive to. 3 **susceptible to,** easily affected by; liable to; open to. [< Late Latin *susceptibilis,* ultimately < Latin *sub-* up + *capere* to take]

swathe (swāᴛʜ), *v.t.,* **swathed, swath ing.** 1 wrap up closely or fully. 2 bind, wrap, or bandage. [Old English *swathian*]

swoon (swün), *v.i.* faint. [ultimately < Old English *geswōgen* in a swoon]

syl van (sil′vən), *adj.* of, in, or having woods. [< Latin *sylvanus, silvanus* < *silva* forest]

syn od (sin′əd), *n.* assembly called together under authority to discuss and decide church affairs; a church council. [< Greek *synodos* assembly, meeting < *syn-* together + *hodos* a going]

sy ringe (sə rinj′, sir′inj), *n.* 1 a narrow tube fitted with a plunger or rubber bulb for drawing in a quantity of fluid and then forcing it out in a stream. 2 hypodermic syringe.

sys to le (sis′tl ē), *n.* the normal rhythmical contraction of the heart, especially that of the ventricles, when blood is pumped from the heart into the arteries. [< Greek *systolē* contraction < *syn-* together + *stellein* to put]

ta bor et or **ta bour et** (tab′ər it, tab′ə-ret′), *n.* 1 stool. 2 a small, low stand or table. 3 frame for embroidery.

tac it (tas′it), *adj.* implied or understood without being openly expressed; implicit. [< Latin *tacitum* < *tacere* be silent] —**tac′it ly,** *adv.* —**tac′it ness,** *n.*

tac i turn (tas′ə tėrn′), *adj.* speaking very little; not fond of talking. [< Latin *taciturnus* < *tacitum* unspoken, tacit]

tan gent (tan′jənt), *n.* 1 (in geometry) the part of a line tangent to a curve from the point of tangency to the horizontal axis. 2 **fly off at a tangent** or **go off at a tangent,** change suddenly from one course of action or thought to another. [< Latin *tangentem*]

tarn (tärn), *n.* a small lake or pool in the mountains. [< Scandinavian (Swedish) *tjärn* pool]

tem blor (tem blôr′), *n.* u.s. earthquake. [< Spanish < *temblar* to tremble]

te mer i ty (tə mer′ə tē), *n.* reckless boldness; rashness; foolhardiness. [< Latin *temeritatem* < *temere* heedlessly]

tem per a ment (tem′pər ə mənt), *n.* 1 a person's nature or disposition. 2 an easily irritated, sensitive nature. An artist, singer, or actress often has temperament.

tem per a men tal (tem′pər ə men′tl), *adj.* subject to moods and whims; easily irritated; sensitive: *a temperamental actor.* —**tem′per a men′tal ly,** *adv.*

tem per ance (tem′pər əns), *n.* 1 a being moderate in action, speech, habits, etc.; self-control. 2 a being moderate in the use of alcoholic drinks.

tem pes tu ous (tem pes′chü əs), *adj.* 1 stormy. 2 violent.

tem plate (tem′plit), *n.* 1 pattern, gauge, or mold of a thin, flat piece of wood or metal, used in shaping a piece of work. 2 any pattern or mold on which something is formed. [variant of *templet,* diminutive of *temple* (part of a loom)]

ten dril (ten′drəl), *n.* a threadlike part of a climbing plant that attaches itself to something and helps support the plant. [< Middle French *tendrillon*]

ten e ment (ten′ə mənt), *n.* 1 tenement house. 2 any house or building to live in; dwelling house. [< Old French, ultimately < Latin *tenere* to hold]

tenement house, building, especially in a poor section of a city, divided into sets of rooms occupied by separate families.

ten ta tive (ten′tə tiv), *adj.* 1 done as a trial or experiment; experimental. 2 hesitating. [< Medieval Latin *tentativus* < Latin *tentare* to try] —**ten′ta tive ly,** *adv.* —**ten′ta tive ness,** *n.*

ten ure (ten′yər), *n.* 1 a holding or possessing. 2 length of time of holding or possessing. [< Old French, ultimately < Latin *tenere* to hold]

ter ma gant (tėr′mə gənt), *n.* a violent, quarreling, scolding woman. [< *Termagant,* a fictitious Moslem deity in medieval plays]

ter mi na tion (tėr/mə nā/shən), *n.* an ending; end; conclusion.

thrall (thrôl), *n.* person in bondage; slave or serf. [< Scandinavian (Old Icelandic) *thrǽll*]

tip ple (tip/əl), *v.,* **-pled, -pling.** drink (alcoholic liquor) often or too much. —**tip/pler,** *n.*

tor por (tôr/pər), *n.* apathy; lethargy. [< Latin < *torpere* be numb]

trag i com e dy (traj/i kom/ə dē), *n., pl.* **-dies.** incident or situation in which serious and comic elements are blended.

tram mel (tram/əl), *v.t.,* **-meled, -mel ing** or **-melled, -mel ling.** 1 hinder; restrain. 2 catch in or as if in a trammel; entangle. [< Old French *tramail* < Late Latin *trimaculum* < Latin *tri-* three + *macula* mesh] —**tram/mel er, tram/mel ler,** *n.*

trance (trans), *n., v.,* **tranced, tranc ing.** —*n.* 1 a dazed or stunned condition. 2 a dreamy, absorbed condition that is like a trance. 3 a high emotion; rapture. —*v.t.* hold in a trance; enchant. [< Old French *transe* < *transir* pass away < Latin *transire* cross over < *trans-* across + *ire* go] —**trance/like/,** *adj.*

trans-, *prefix.* 1 across; over; through, as in *transcontinental, transmit.* 2 on the other side of; beyond, as in *transatlantic.* 3 to a different place, condition, etc., as in *transmigration, transform.* [< Latin *trans* across]

tran scend ent (tran sen/dənt), *adj.* 1 surpassing ordinary limits; excelling; superior; extraordinary. 2 above and independent of the physical universe. —**tran scend/ent ly,** *adv.*

trans gres sion (trans gresh/ən, tranz gresh/ən), *n.* breaking a law, command, etc.; sin.

tran sient (tran/shənt), *adj.* passing soon; fleeting; not lasting. [< Latin *transientem* going through < *trans-* + *ire* go] —**tran/sient ly,** *adv.*

trans lu cent (tran slü/snt, tranz lü/snt), *adj.* letting light through without being transparent. [< Latin *translucentem* < *trans-* through + *lucere* to shine] —**trans lu/cent ly,** *adv.* —**trans lu/cen cy,** *n.*

trans mog ri fy (tran smog/rə fī, tranz mog/rə fī), *v.t.,* **-fied, -fy ing.** change in form or appearance; transform in a surprising or grotesque manner. [< *trans-* + *mogrify* (origin unknown)] —**trans mog/ri fi ca/tion,** *n.*

trav erse (trav/ərs, trə vėrs/), *v.t.,* **-ersed, -ers ing.** 1 pass across, over, or through: *We traversed the desert.* 2 go to and fro over or along (a place, etc.); cross. [< Old French *traverser* < Late Latin *transversare* < Latin *transversum* transverse] —**trav/ers a ble,** *adj.* —**trav/ers er,** *n.*

trav es ty (trav/ə stē), *n., pl.* **-ties.** any treatment or imitation that makes a serious thing seem ridiculous. [< French *travesti* disguised, ultimately < Latin *trans-* over + *vestire* to dress]

trel lis (trel/is), *n.* frame of light strips of wood or metal crossing one another with open spaces in between. —*v.t.* 1 furnish with a trellis. 2 support or train (vines, etc.) on a trellis. [< Old French *trelis,* ultimately < Latin *trilix* triple-twilled < *tri-* three + *licium* thread]

trem u lous (trem/yə ləs), *adj.* 1 trembling; quivering. 2 timid; fearful. [< Latin *tremulus* < *tremere* to tremble]

tri dent (trīd/nt), *n.* a three-pronged spear. [< Latin *tridentem* < *tri-* three + *dentem* tooth]

troth (trôth, trōth), *n.* ARCHAIC. 1 faithfulness or fidelity; loyalty. 2 promise.

3 **plight one's troth,** promise to marry. [Old English *trēowth* < *trēow* faith]

trous seau (trü/sō, trü sō/), *n., pl.* **trousseaux** (trü/sōz, trü sōz/), **trous seaus.** a bride's outfit of clothes, linen, etc. [< French, originally, bundle]

trun cheon (trun/chən), *n.* a stick cut and shaped for use as a weapon; club. [< Old French *tronchon,* ultimately < Latin *truncus*]

tum brel or **tum bril** (tum/brəl), *n.* 1 any of various two-wheeled carts, especially one used on a farm for hauling and dumping manure. 2 cart that carried prisoners to be executed during the French Revolution. [< Old French *tomberel* cart < *tomber* to fall; of Germanic origin]

tu mult (tü/mult, tyü/mult), *n.* a violent disturbance of mind or feeling; confusion or excitement. [< Latin *tumultus*]

tu mul tu ous (tü mul/chü əs, tyü mul/chü-əs), *adj.* 1 characterized by tumult; very noisy or disorderly; violent. 2 greatly disturbed. 3 rough; stormy. —**tu mul/tu ous ly,** *adv.* —**tu mul/tu ous ness,** *n.*

u biq ui tous (yü bik/wə təs), *adj.* that is everywhere at the same time; present everywhere. —**u biq/ui tous ly,** *adv.* —**u biq/ui tous ness,** *n.*

ul ter i or (ul tir/ē ər), *adj.* beyond what is seen or expressed; hidden. [< Latin, comparative of root of *ultra* beyond] —**ul ter/i or ly,** *adv.*

un-[1], *prefix.* not _____; the opposite of _____: *Unequal = not equal; the opposite of equal. Unchanged = not changed. Unjust = not just.*

un-[2], *prefix.* do the opposite of _____; do what will reverse the act: *Unfasten = do the opposite of fasten. Uncover = do the opposite of cover.*

un al ter a ble (un ôl/tər ə bəl), *adj.* not changeable; permanent.

un be known (un/bi nōn/), *adj.* not known: *He arrived unbeknown to anyone.*

un be knownst (un/bi nōnst/), *adj.* unbeknown.

un du la tion (un/jə lā/shən, un/dyə-lā/shən), *n.* a wavelike motion.

un in tel li gi ble (un/in tel/ə jə bəl), *adj.* not able to be understood. —**un/in tel/li gi ble ness,** *n.* —**un/in tel/li gi bly,** *adv.*

un prec e dent ed (un pres/ə den/tid), *adj.* never done before; never known before.

un re mit ting (un/ri mit/ing), *adj.* never stopping; not slackening; maintained steadily.

un rul y (un rü/lē), *adj.* hard to rule or control; not manageable; disorderly.

un scru pu lous (un skrü/pyə ləs), *adj.* not careful about right or wrong; without principles or conscience. —**un scru/pu lous ly,** *adv.* —**un scru/pu lous ness,** *n.*

un seem ly (un sēm/lē), *adj.* not suitable; improper: *unseemly haste.* —*adv.* improperly; unsuitably.

un war rant a ble (un wôr/ən tə bəl, un-wor/ən tə bəl), *adj.* not justifiable or defensible; improper. —**un war/rant a bly,** *adv.*

u sur er (yü/zhər ər), *n.* person who lends money at an extremely high or unlawful rate of interest.

u sur pa tion (yü/zər pā/shən, yü/sər pā/-shən), *n.* the seizing and holding of the place or power of another by force or without right.

hat, āge, fär; let, ēqual, tėrm;
it, īce; hot, ōpen, ôrder;
oil, out; cup, půt, rüle;
ch, child; ng, long; sh, she;
th, thin; ₮H, then; zh, measure;

ə represents *a* in about, *e* in taken, *i* in pencil, *o* in lemon, *u* in circus.

< = from, derived from, taken from.

u sur y (yü/zhər ē), *n., pl.* **u sur ies.** the lending of money at an extremely high or unlawful rate of interest. [< Medieval Latin *usuria,* alteration of Latin *usura* use < *uti* to use]

u til i tar i an (yü til/ə ter/ē ən), *adj.* aiming at or designed for usefulness rather than beauty, style, etc.

vag a bond (vag/ə bond), *n.* 1 an idle wanderer; tramp; vagrant. 2 a disreputable person; rascal. [< Old French < Latin *vagabundus* < *vagari* wander < *vagus* rambling]

va gar y (və gėr/ē, vā/gər ē), *n., pl.* **-gar ies.** 1 an odd fancy; extravagant notion. 2 odd action; caprice; freak. [probably < Latin *vagari* wander < *vagus* rambling]

var i e gate (ver/ē ə gāt, ver/i gāt; var/ē ə-gāt, var/i gāt), *v.t.,* **-gat ed, -gat ing.** vary in appearance; mark, spot, or streak with different colors. [< Latin *variegatum* varied < *varius* various]

ve he mence (vē/ə məns), *n.* strong feeling; forcefulness; violence.

ve he ment (vē/ə mənt), *adj.* 1 having or showing strong feeling; caused by strong feeling; eager; passionate. 2 forceful; violent. [< Latin *vehementem* being carried away < *vehere* carry] —**ve/he ment ly,** *adv.*

ven er a ble (ven/ər ə bəl), *adj.* worthy of reverence; deserving respect because of age, character, or importance.

ven er ate (ven/ə rāt/), *v.t.,* **-rat ed, -rat ing.** regard with deep respect; revere. [< Latin *veneratum* revered < *Venus* Venus, originally, love] —**ven/e ra/tor,** *n.*

ven er y (ven/ər ē), *n.* practice or pursuit of sexual pleasure; gratification of sexual desire. [< Latin *Venus*]

ven om ous (ven/ə məs), *adj.* 1 poisonous. 2 spiteful; malicious. —**ven/om ous ly,** *adv.* —**ven/om ous ness,** *n.*

ven ture some (ven/chər səm), *adj.* inclined to take risks; rash; daring.

ve ran da or **ve ran dah** (və ran/də), *n.* a large porch or gallery along one or more sides of a house. [< Hindustani *varandā*]

ves tige (ves/tij), *n.* 1 a slight remnant; trace; mark. 2 (in biology) a part, organ, etc., that is no longer fully developed or useful but performed a definite function in an earlier stage of the existence of the same organism or in lower preceding organisms. [< French < Latin *vestigium* footprint]

vex (veks), *v.t.* 1 anger by trifles; annoy; provoke. 2 worry; trouble; harass. 3 disturb by commotion; agitate. [< Latin *vexare*]

vi brant (vī/brənt), *adj.* throbbing with vitality, enthusiasm, etc.

Vic tro la (vik trō/lə), *n.* trademark for a kind of phonograph.

vict ual (vit/l), *n.* **victuals,** *pl.* food or provisions. [< Latin *victualia,* plural of *vic-*

tualis of food < *victus* food, sustenance < *vivere* to live]

vig i lance (vij′ə ləns), *n.* watchfulness; alertness; caution.

vile (vīl), *adj.,* **vil er, vil est. 1** very bad: *vile weather.* **2** foul; disgusting; obnoxious. **3** poor; mean; lowly. [< Latin *vilis* cheap] —**vile′ly,** *adv.* —**vile′ness,** *n.*

vi per (vī′pər), *n.* **1** any of a family of poisonous Old World snakes. **2** a spiteful, treacherous person. [< Latin *vipera*]

vir tu o so (vèr′chü ō′sō), *n., pl.* **-sos, -si** (sē), *adj.* —*n.* **1** person skilled in the techniques of an art, especially in playing a musical instrument. **2** person who has a cultivated appreciation of artistic excellence; connoisseur. —*adj.* showing the artistic qualities and skills of a virtuoso. [< Italian, learned, virtuous]

vir u lence (vir′yə ləns, vir′ə ləns), *n.* **1** quality of being very poisonous or harmful; deadliness. **2** intense bitterness or spite; violent hostility.

vir u lent (vir′yə lənt, vir′ə lənt), *adj.* **1** very poisonous or harmful; deadly: *a virulent poison.* **2** intensely bitter or spiteful; violently hostile. [< Latin *virulentus* < *virus* poison]

vis age (viz′ij), *n.* **1** face. **2** appearance or aspect. [< Old French < *vis* face < Latin *visus* sight < *videre* to see]

vi vac i ty (vī vas′ə tē, vi vas′ə tē), *n., pl.* **-ties.** liveliness; sprightliness; animation; gaiety. [< Latin *vivacitatem* < *vivacis* lively < *vivere* to live]

viz., that is to say; namely [for Latin *videlicet*].

wag ger y (wag′ər ē), *n., pl.* **-ger ies.** act or habit of joking.

waif (wāf), *n.* person without home or friends, especially a homeless or neglected child. [< Anglo-French; probably < Scandinavian]

wan ton (won′tən), *adj.* **1** reckless, heartless, or malicious: *wanton cruelty.* **2** without reason or excuse. [Middle English *wantowen* < Old English *wan-* not, lacking + *togen* brought up] —**wan′ton ly,** *adv.* —**wan′ton ness,** *n.*

whirl i gig (hwèr′lē gig′), *n.* anything that whirls.

wick er work (wik′ər wèrk′), *n.* **1** twigs or branches woven together. **2** objects made of wicker.

wis ter i a (wi stir′ē ə), *n.* any of a genus of

vo cif e rate (vō sif′ə rāt′), *v.t., v.i.,* **-rated, -rat ing.** cry out loudly or noisily; shout; clamor. [< Latin *vociferatum* shouted out < *vocem* voice + *ferre* carry] — **vo cif′e ra′tion,** *n.* —**vo cif′e ra′tor,** *n.*

vor tex (vôr′teks), *n., pl.* **-tex es** or **-ti ces.** a whirling mass of water, etc., that sucks everything near it toward its center; whirlpool. [< Latin, variant of *vertex*]

vouch safe (vouch sāf′), *v.t.,* **-safed, -saf ing.** be willing to grant or give; deign (to do or give).

vul gar (vul′gər), *adj.* **1** showing a lack of good breeding, manners, taste, etc.; not refined; coarse; low. **2** of the common people. [< Latin *vulgaris* < *vulgus* common people] —**vul′gar ly,** *adv.* —**vul′gar ness,** *n.*

climbing shrubs of the pea family, with large, drooping clusters of showy purple, blue, or white flowers.

wist ful (wist′fəl), *adj.* longing; yearning. [< obsolete *wist* attentive (< *wistly* intently, of uncertain origin) + *-ful*]

with er (wiŦH′ər), *v.i., v.t.* lose or cause to lose freshness, vigor, etc.; dry up; shrivel. [Middle English *wideren,* variant of *wederen* to weather]

wit ti cism (wit′ə siz′əm), *n.* a witty remark.

wont (wunt, wōnt), *adj.* accustomed: *He was wont to read the paper at breakfast.* —*n.* custom; habit: *She rose early, as was her wont.* [originally past participle of Old English *wunian* be accustomed]

wor sted (wus′tid, wèr′stid), *n.* **1** a firmly twisted woolen thread or yarn. **2** cloth made from such thread or yarn. —*adj.* made of worsted. [< *Worsted* (now Worstead), village in England, where it was originally made]

wrought (rôt), *v.* ARCHAIC. a pt. and a pp. of **work.** —*adj.* **1** made. **2** formed with care; not rough or crude.

wrought-up (rôt′up′), *adj.* stirred up; excited.

zeph yr (zef′ər), *n.* any soft, gentle wind; mild breeze.

Zo ro as ter (zôr′ō as′tər, zōr′ō as′tər), *n.* Persian religious teacher who lived about 600 B.C. Also, **Zarathustra.**

Zo ro as tri an (zôr′ō as′trē ən, zōr′ō as′trē ən), *n.* person believing in the teachings of Zoroaster.

Time Line Notes

The two pages preceding each unit background are occupied by three-dimensional constructions composed of objects that suggest the theme or the historical period of the following unit. In Unit 1, "American Mosaic," and Unit 7, "A Modern Drama,"—units that are not primarily historical in character—the constructions are intended to reflect the theme, tone, aura, or emphasis of those respective units. In the chronological sections, Units 2 through 6 and Unit 8, the objects represent the developing life and culture of the United States in each period.

Below the chronological constructions are time lines, showing by relative position the interweaving of some of the important literary, cultural, economic, and political events of each period. The dots are used to indicate the years of those events which occurred or began at a specific date; e.g. the colonization of New Mexico, starting in 1598, or the founding of Jamestown in 1607. Below these dated events are events of uncertain date or long-term trends, which are presented without dots, such as

the formation of the Iroquois Confederation, which took several decades in the seventeenth and early eighteenth centuries. Also among these trends, some of the literary genres most characteristic of each period are noted, such as the explorers' narratives of the sixteenth and seventeenth centuries, or the journals and almanacs which, like *Poor Richard's Almanack,* were so popular throughout the eighteenth century.

Authors represented in *United States in Literature* are identified in the time lines by last names only, except for those who share the same surname and whose lives overlap in time (e.g. Amy and Robert Lowell). Full names are given for people not represented in this anthology, except for widely familiar figures, such as Thomas Edison.

The paragraphs that follow briefly discuss each construction.

Unit 1: American Mosaic
(pages 2–3)

Frost's poem, "It Bids Pretty Fair," was chosen as an epigraph to this unit because its cautious but positive affirmation suggests the broad range of tone and theme to be found in modern American literature. The selections in this unit provide an introductory sample of the rich variety which is found throughout the entire scope of American literature.

The two elements of the construction—pieces of a patchwork quilt and varieties of lighting—form a visual "American Mosaic" and also reflect the motif of lighting in Frost's poem. The types of lighting shown have all been associated with American society, from the candle molds of the earliest centuries (page 2, bottom left) to the decorative neon tube (page 2, center). Other lamps of interest are the fire fighter's lantern (page 2, top left); the nineteenth-century oil lamp (page 2, top center); the detachable head lamp from an early automobile (page 3, left of center); and an assortment of miner's lamps, including the primitive unshielded model which resembles a small coffeepot (page 3, lower left).

Unit 2: The New Land
(pages 98–99)

The objects on page 98 represent various aspects of early colonial times, beginning at extreme left with the peyote fan made of golden pheasant feathers and beadwork. Such fans are still used in the religious dances which originated among the desert people of the Southwest. The ornamental Venetian ceramic bead (page 98, top right) was a typical item used for trading for slaves in West Africa. Below this bead is a pair of matched powder horns for a flintlock rifle of the eighteenth century, the larger horn containing gunpowder, while the smaller held the fine-grained priming powder.

On page 99, at the left, can be seen a model of an eighteenth-century merchant ship in a bottle. The skull next to it is a scrimshaw carving by a Revolutionary soldier held captive on a British prison ship. The word *LIBERTY* can be seen on the forehead and suggests the unyielding spirit of these prisoners of war confined under terrible conditions which the poet Philip Freneau condemned in "The British Prison Ship." To the right of the skull is a Sioux man's medicine bag, used to contain sacred medicine objects which protected the wearer, and which re-

mained secret even to him. Just right of center on this page appear two pieces of genuine colonial currency. A close look at the colonial four-shilling note to the left reveals the slogan, "To Counterfeit is Death." The note to the right in that box is a two-dollar bill issued by Maryland's colonial Assembly in 1774. Below the skull are antique horse bits. To their right is a modern oak reproduction of a pogamoggan (pog'ə mog'ən) or ceremonial war club used by Eastern Woodlands tribes such as the Miami and the Ojibway. Such clubs were carved with great skill, usually from the root and trunk of a maple sapling, the ball being the root. Made from one solid piece of hardwood, the clubs possessed tremendous strength.

Unit 3: Literary Nationalism
(pages 150–151)

The focus of this construction is the westward expansion of the United States which, though begun in colonial times, became the central national concern of the first half of the nineteenth century. Many historians date the start of the great migrations beyond the Mississippi River from 1816.

The wooden carpenter's plane (page 150, far left) represents the independent craftsmen who were still the backbone of the economy, although the Industrial Revolution was just opening in New England. The iron plow blade to the

right of the plane was the tool that permitted farming the western prairies, where the sod was too thick to be broken by old wooden plows. Below the plow is a working replica of a .45-caliber Kentucky long rifle, mainstay of early pioneers both for hunting and defense. This model was a design of the skilled gunsmiths of Lancaster, Pennsylvania. The *S*-shaped tool beside the trigger guard was used for disassembling the rifle.

River steamboats (page 151, top right) were introduced on the Ohio and Mississippi Rivers in 1811. The toy iron stage-coach represents the beginnings of regular stage service. The slow, primitive, but roomy Conestoga wagon appears on the cup (page 150, bottom center) and on a pewter chocolate mold (page 151, right). These vehicles, new and old, were the main means of trade and transportation between the established towns of the East and New Mexico and the pioneer settlements of the Great Plains. At bottom right on page 151 appears a star badge of the Texas Rangers, founded in 1835 as a volunteer cavalry unit of Texans resisting the central government of Mexico. The Indian dance pipe at top center and the toy figures of a brave and a cowboy below it represent the two sides of the long struggle for possession of the Great Plains. The pipe is a small calumet used in the pipe dance to welcome white guests and then presented to them after the ceremony.

Another important development of this period was the effort, led by Noah Webster, to create American schoolbooks for American students to replace those imported from England or imitated from British models. This trend is represented by the child's alphabet scroll below the rifle.

Among domestic implements of this period were the turkey-bone case (above the stage coach), used by frontier women to hold sewing needles; and the decorative pewter chocolate molds, one in the shape of a Conestoga wagon, the other being a row of small Santa Claus figures (page 150, top center).

Unit 4: American Classic
(pages 218–219)

The construction for this crucial period of United States history, which includes the Civil War, indicates the rapid modernization of our society in these decades. On page 218, far left, there are three antique candle molds; next to those is a toy model of an early sewing machine; then on page 219, at left, is an early mechanical egg beater; and, near extreme right, a lithograph of an early steam locomotive.

Among the many handcrafted toys of this era was the large mechanical "China doll" (page 218, left), consisting of a painted porcelain head on a cloth-stuffed body. This doll says *"Maman"* and *"Papa"* in French and can move its arms and walk. Another elaborate

toy is the cast-iron artillery coin bank: When a penny is placed into the cannon and the lever at the rear of the cannon is cocked, the soldier's arm rises; as the lever is pressed, the soldier's arm drops and the penny is fired through a slot in the fort tower. This century-old toy is still in working condition, although the penny must be placed carefully for accurate aim.

Above the photograph of Lincoln are children's glass marbles and a Union Army officer's pistol holster. Below the photograph is a Confederate ten-dollar bill, hand-signed by Treasury officials, as each bill in those days had to be. The developing American schoolbook is typified at far bottom right by *THE NATIONAL FIRST READER or WORD-BUILDER* (A. S. Barnes & Co., 1873). Just above the book is a wrought-iron tack hammer used for nailing down carpets. To the right of the hammer are early photographs of this period in which Matthew Brady and other Civil War photographers began to win recognition for their new art form.

Unit 5: Variations and Departures
(pages 296–297)

The five decades following the Civil War saw the United States change from a prosperous agricultural nation, largely isolated from international politics, into one of the industrial giants and superpowers of the

world. The wooden hayfork, which is the centerpiece of this construction, represents the old agrarian way of life that began to break down in this era. This fork was actually used in Indiana until 1912. Around it are grouped various symbols of the new technology and the leisure society which began to grow from mass production.

At left, above the hayfork, are a toy steam engine and patent drawings for such inventions as Thomas Edison's light bulb and Elijah McCoy's automatic lubrication system for heavy industrial machinery. This device was the original "real McCoy." Many of America's most ingenious inventors lived in these years, changing the world with their new devices: Alexander Graham Bell with his telephone; Granville T. Woods with his electric railway system for cities; Wilbur and Orville Wright with their powered airplane. Near the top of page 297, left of center, is a toy steam tractor, indicating the beginnings of mechanized farming. To its right, lying on *The World Almanac* for 1909, is an Orville Wright trading card. In 1909, after much unpublicized development, the Wright brothers were beginning to demonstrate their improved aircraft around the United States and in Europe.

But technology had its lighter side. Near the far top left of page 296 can be seen a label for a patent medicine for animals, which is illustrated like the gaudy cover of a Western "dime novel." The most successful author of these thrillers was "Ned Buntline" ("Colonel"

E. Z. C. Judson), an Easterner who reputedly wrote over a thousand novels, and who also made "Buffalo Bill" Cody and Annie Oakley show-business stars. Flooding off the new Linotype machines and rotary presses of the late nineteenth century, these wildly inaccurate and cheaply printed novels provided entertainment for the rapidly growing numbers of newly literate Americans until movies arrived with the 1900s. At bottom right, page 297, is a wooden clockwork model of Gar Wood's *Miss America,* a sleek speedboat that set many world records in the early twentieth century and that represented the luxuries that were now coming within the reach, not only of millionaires, but of the country's increasingly prosperous professional middle class. A more widespread benefit of industrial prosperity was the mass-produced car, represented by the 1912 license plate above the boat.

Unit 6: The Modern Temper
(pages 380–381)

This construction is bracketed at far left by mementoes of World War I and by mementoes of World War II at far right. At left on page 380 are a helmet of a "doughboy" (American soldier of World War I), an artillery shell, and a bust of Woodrow Wilson, President of the United States during the war that was to "end all wars." Further to the right are various artifacts of the "Roaring Twenties," including the photograph of the chorus line from a revue such as the Ziegfeld Follies, popular in the 1920s; and the spats which a gentleman in evening dress once wore over his shoes. Below the spats is a model of a horsedrawn ice wagon of those days before refrigerators were common. Further below is a statuette of Will Rogers, the cowhand from Oklahoma, whose fancy rope-twirling and witticisms at the expense of politicians and other prominent figures made him the most popular humorist of the 1920s and 1930s.

Opportunity magazine (page 381, top left), published by the National Urban League, helped many writers of the Harlem Renaissance (see pages 382 and 442) to get their early works in print. The cover of this 1934 issue, like the painting on the talcum-powder tin beside Wilson's bust (page 380, center), shows the Art Deco style which dominated graphic arts and home decoration during much of this period.

In the 1930s, air travel was still regarded as risky and extravagant, and this decade saw the heyday of the railroads, represented by an electric model train. Trains carried most of the nation's freight, and to travel on the Broadway Limited, the Twentieth Century Limited, or the Santa Fe Super Chief was to travel in high style. In the box above the locomotive is a check signed by the writer Thomas Wolfe (1900–1938), whose novels— especially *Look Homeward, Angel* and *Of Time and the River*—made him one of the foremost authors of the 1930s. Beneath the rear car of the train are trading cards, including one of Amelia Earhart and one of Charles Lindbergh, famous aviation pioneers. Further to the right is a 78 RPM record of the famous Bluebird jazz label, this disc being a recording of Coleman Hawkins's version of the hit song "Body and Soul." Next to this is a modern plastic version of the blood-plasma collecting bottle. The process of separating red cells from blood plasma, which could be shipped and stored with little spoilage, was developed by Dr. Charles Drew, who also pioneered blood banking. Dr. Drew's new transfusion techniques and his organization of the Allied military blood-transfusion system saved the lives of countless soldiers in World War II.

At the top of the far right column on page 381 are a six-cent air-mail stamp and a printer's embossing plate showing a Douglas DC-4. This airliner, developed on the eve of World War II, was among the first generation of landplanes capable of regular nonstop transoceanic and transcontinental service. During the war, such planes were used to ferry troops and cargo across the Atlantic; then, after 1945, they became the backbone of the rapidly spreading network of airline routes in the United States. Below these items are an Army Air Corps pilot's wings, dog tags, and medals. The dollar bill beneath the pilot's identification booklet is wartime currency from Hawaii.

Unit 7: A Modern Drama
(pages 500–501)

The objects composing this construction represent not only traditional stagecraft, but also, as shown by the microphone and film reel, the modern extensions of drama into radio, movies, and television. The time line presents many of the highlights of twentieth-century dramatic history, on both stage and screen, in the United States.

The major new trends of the early decades of the century were the parallel growth of experimental drama through the "Little Theater" movement and of the film industry. The early works of such major playwrights as Eugene O'Neill and Clifford Odets were first brought to audiences by the Provincetown Players and The Group Theater respectively. Movies came of age in the 1930s when sound and color enlarged the possibilities of realistic screenplays, while the Academy Awards helped win recognition and respectability for the new art.

The Depression severely damaged all the performing arts, but the effects were partly staved off by the Federal Theater Project, which provided work for actors and directors during the hardest years and which helped develop the ca-

reers of Langston Hughes, Clifford Odets, and other later prominent dramatists.

The musical comedy, the most notable contribution of the United States to the theater arts, flourished throughout the Depression, perhaps because spectacular musicals on stage and screen offered relief from the grimness of the 1930s. The following decade saw the first performances of many classic, often revived musicals, including *Oklahoma!* and *South Pacific.* The popularity of musicals continued following their heyday in the 1940s and this American version of light opera became perhaps the most typical kind of production of the 1950s and early 1960s, with theater and movie audiences flocking to such new hits as *West Side Story* and *1776.*

By the early 1950s, Broadway, "little theaters," and movie theaters were all threatened by the rising popularity of television. Yet, in 1950 there began a new trend that was to prove the enduring strength of legitimate (stage) drama in the United States: the creation of many important regional theater companies outside New York. Of these, the Arena Stage in Washington was the first. Over the next two decades, major professional theaters, which had been traditionally centered on New York's Broadway, opened "Off-Broadway" in New York and all across the country in such cities as Minneapolis-St. Paul, Chicago, Atlanta, and Los Angeles. Annual festivals of Shakespearean and other drama began in New York, Stratford,

and, in the 1960s, in San Diego. The improvisational drama of such groups as Second City developed into the street theater of the 1960s.

As costs of theatrical production soared, local and federal agencies and private foundations stepped in to subsidize performing groups. Among the most notable achievements were the construction of Lincoln Center and Kennedy Center, and the development of ethnic and other experimental theater groups such as the National Black Theater Workshop. The National Endowment for the Arts has helped create lively experimental theater groups in all parts of the nation.

The revivals of major plays by the American Bicentennial Theater, performing on nationwide tours, demonstrated the vitality combined with rich tradition which American theater had attained by the 1970s. The movie industry has also successfully weathered the competition from television. Audiences today can choose from the richest variety of drama ever available in history.

Unit 8: New Frontiers
(pages 548–549)

Contemporary readers are familiar with almost all these items from the decades following World War II, such as the TV "rabbit-ears" antenna and the Barbie doll. The model of a green vinyl lounge chair shows a style of furniture considered the last word in modernity by many home decorators in the 1950s. The albums by Elvis Presley and Bob Dylan are among the earliest recorded by these pop-music stars of the 1950s and 1960s respectively. The growth of many ethnic publications in the 1960s is represented by a cover of *Revista Chicano-Riqueña* (page 548, center). This cover, with a painting by Gamaliel Ramirez, comes from a special issue, *The Nosotros Anthology,* containing the works of young poets and photographers from the Chicago area. To the right of this box, a "Huey" helicopter and a peace-movement button are juxtaposed to symbolize the political controversies of the Vietnam War years. Some of the latest developments in technology are suggested by the electronic printed circuit to the left of the helicopter, by the cassette below it, and by the Apollo spacecraft and pocket-size digital calculator at far right.

The editors would like to thank the following people and organizations for their help in providing materials for the Time Line constructions:

Acme Rentals, Inc., Chicago; the Library of the Garrett Theological Seminary, Evanston, Illinois; Professor Nicolás Kanellos, Co-Editor, *Revista Chicano-Riqueña,* Indiana University Northwest; Mr. Paul A. Kuffel; Mr. and Mrs. D. B. Moss; Mark Galleries, Chicago; the National Urban League, New York; Mr. Gamaliel Ramirez; and Mr. Charles Schultz of "Kings 3," Evanston, Illinois.

Index of Authors and Titles

Index of Extension Assignments

Index of Vocabulary Exercises